10,001
HINTS
&TIPS
for the HOME

10,001
HINTS
&TIPS
for the HOME

Cassandra Kent • Julian Cassell
& Peter Parham • Christine France
Pippa Greenwood

DK Publishing, Inc.

A DK PUBLISHING BOOK

Project Editor Jude Garlick
Project Art Editor Sarah Hall
US Editor Ray Rogers
Production Controller Alison Jones
DTP Designer Jason Little

Managing Editor Stephanie Jackson
Managing Art Editor Nigel Duffield

First American Edition, 1998
2 4 6 8 10 9 7 5 3

Published in the United States by
DK Publishing, Inc.
95 Madison Avenue
New York, New York 10016

Visit us on the World Wide Web at
http://www.dk.com

**Library of Congress
Cataloging-in-Publication Data**

10,001 hints and tips for the home /
by Cassandra Kent, Julian Cassell & Peter Parham,
Christine France, Pippa Greenwood
p.   cm.
Includes index.
ISBN 0-7894-3520-9
1. Home economics.
TX159.A15 1998   98–15603
640'.41– –dc21   CIP

Printed and bound by
Kyodo Printing Co., Singapore

CONTENTS

Using This Book   8
Running a Busy Household   10

ORGANIZING YOUR HOUSEHOLD 12

Utilizing Space   **14**
Planning Room by Room 15
Using Storage Space 22
Storing Special Items 27
Solving Storage 30

Running a Household   **32**
Organizing Personal Care 33
Caring for Children 36
Meeting Special Needs 41
Arranging Medical Care 43
Handling Crises 46
Planning Events 48
Transportation 50
Planning Pet Care 52

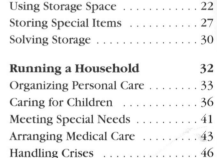

Cleaning the Home   **54**
General Cleaning 56
Floors 58
Walls and Ceilings 62
Furnishings 66
Bathrooms 68
Kitchens 70
Cleaning Checklist 75

Dealing with Stains   **76**
Tackling Stains 78
Food Stains 80
Spilled Beverages 83
Biological Stains 86
Pigment and Synthetic Stains 90
Household Product Stains 93
Wear-and-Tear Marks 96
Other Stains 99

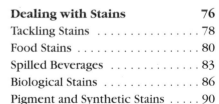

Laundering   **100**
Washing Clothes 102
Special Treatments 104
Drying Clothes 106
Ironing Clothes 108
Caring for Clothes 111
Caring for Shoes 113

Care and Repair   **114**
Wood 115
Metal 118
Glass and China 122
Ornamental Surfaces 125
Upholstery Fabrics 126
Items around the Home 128
Accessories 130

Maintaining A Home   **132**
Plumbing 133
Electricity and Fuel 137
Heating and Cooling 140
General Repairs 142
Home Security 144

Moving   **146**
Preparing to Move 147
Sorting and Packing 148
Moving Out 153
Moving In 155
Sharing a Home 157

Structuring Work   **158**
Setting up a Home Office 159
Managing Work Time 163
Communicating Effectively 166
Keeping Records 168

Ensuring Safety   **170**
Acting in Emergencies 172
Resuscitating Victims 174
Dealing with Major Injuries 176
Dealing with Other Injuries 179
Treating Common Ailments 185

DECORATING 188

Color and Style   **190**
Using Color 192
Color Scheming 196
Setting Styles 198
Reflecting Lifestyles 200

Painting Walls   **202**
Preparing to Paint 204
Improving Techniques 206
Creating Paint Effects 210
Finishing 218

Covering Walls   **220**
Choosing Wallpaper 222
Preparing to Wallpaper 224
Improving Techniques 226
Wallpapering Awkward Areas . . . 230
Adding Borders 233
Choosing Other Coverings 234
Finishing 236

Tiling Walls   **238**
Preparing to Tile 240
Planning a Tiling Strategy 242
Improving Techniques 243
Tiling Creatively 245
Finishing 249

Decorating Woodwork   **252**
Preparing to Paint 254
Painting Specific Areas 256
Enhancing Wood 258
Creating Paint Effects 259
Painting Furniture 263
Finishing 266

Covering Floors   **268**
Selecting Floor Types 269
Preparing Floors 271
Laying Wooden Floors 273
Carpeting Floors 276

Laying Utility Flooring 278
Laying Hard-tile Flooring 280
Painting Floors 282
Finishing 284

Window Treatments   **286**
Selecting Materials 288
Choosing Curtains 289
Choosing Blinds 292
Adding Trimmings 294
Decorating Glass 296

Finishing Touches   **298**
Lighting 299
Shelving 302
Wall Decorations 304
Soft Furnishings 306
Final Details 309

COOKING 312

Kitchen Equipment   **314**
Kitchen Improvements 315
Cooking Appliances 318
Cold Storage 321
Pots and Pans 324
Bakeware 326
Utensils 327
Small Appliances 332

Prepared Ingredients   **334**
Dry Storage 335
Pantry Staples 337
Sugars and Sweet Flavorings 342
Herbs, Spices, and Seasonings . . . 344

Convenience Foods 347

Fresh Ingredients   **348**
Vegetables, Fruits, and Herbs   350
Dairy Foods 354
Meat and Poultry 356
Fish and Shellfish 358
Baked Goods 360

Preparing Ingredients   **362**
Vegetables 363
Fruits and Nuts 366
Herbs and Spices 370
Dairy Foods 372
Meat and Poultry 374
Fish and Shellfish 376

Cooking Methods   **378**
Vegetables 379
Salads 382
Fruits 384
Eggs 386
Meat and Poultry 388
Fish and Shellfish 394
Soups, Stocks, and Sauces 398
Grains, Pasta, and Legumes 400
Desserts 402
Baking 406
Preserving 414
Freezing 418
Drinks 420

Entertaining   **422**
Table Settings and Decorations . . 424
Cocktail Parties 430
Buffets 432
Dinner Parties 434
Party Management 438
Children's Parties 440
Barbecues 442
Picnics 444
Impromptu Entertaining 446

GARDENING 448

Restoring Landscapes   **450**
Transforming Lawns 452
Restoring Borders 456
Renovating Patios 459
Transforming Paths and Steps . . . 464
Transforming Walls 466
Constructing Screens 469
Adding Height and Perspective . . 475

Plants and Planting   **478**
Planting Preparation 480
Choosing Plants 485
Planting Know-How 487
Planting Shrubs 488
Planting Perennials 490
Planting Annuals 494
Planting Bulbs 496
Moving Plants 498

Container Gardening   **502**
Container Know-how 504
Planting Up Containers 506
Pots and Barrels 510
Windowboxes 513
Hanging Baskets 515
Recycling Containers 518

Plant Care   **520**
Protecting Plants 522
Feeding Plants 524
Watering Plants 529
Weeding 534
Pruning Plants 540

Pests and Diseases   **544**
Preventing Problems 548
Controlling Animals 553
Using Pest Controls 555
Controlling Specific Problems . . . 558

Lawns   **562**
Creating a Lawn 564
Planting in a Lawn 566
Lawn Maintenance 568
Lawn Problems 570

Water Features   **572**
Introducing Water 573
Water Plants 575
Pond Maintenance 577
Pond Repair 579

Propagating Plants   **580**
Sowing Seeds Outdoors 582
Sowing Seeds Indoors 584
Thinning Seedlings 588
Layering Plants 590
Taking Cuttings 592
Division 595

General Maintenance   **598**
Wooden Structures 600
Concrete and Brickwork 604
Garden Furniture 609
Garden Tools 610
Greenhouses 612
Spring Tasks 614
Summer Tasks 616
Autumn Tasks 618
Winter Tasks 620

Useful Information   **622**
Glossary of Terms 630
Index 638
Acknowledgments 671

INTRODUCTION

ONE OF THE WAYS YOU CAN ENSURE the smooth, efficient, and successful running of your household is to organize effectively the various compartments of your life in and around the home so that you save time and money, maximize your efforts, and prevent problems of any kind from cropping up.

USING THIS BOOK

SORTING OUT THE BASICS

Organize routine, day-to-day tasks and you will have an efficient framework around which to arrange other household jobs and projects. Allocating space, and placing and storing items within it, is a good starting point. Consider the specific needs of those sharing your home, and plan for ordinary as well as extraordinary events in the domestic calendar. Most people move at one time or another, and those who work – many from home – need to organize this part of life, too. Finally, preventing accidents, dealing with emergencies, and administering first aid should be high priority in every household.

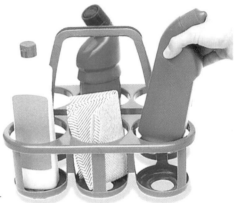

Assembling a cleaning kit
Take some of the tedium out of cleaning by keeping all your materials together and handy in a container you can carry easily.

PLANNING OTHER PROJECTS

Once daily household tasks are in hand, you can turn your attention to more creative jobs around the home. Decorating, cooking and entertaining, and gardening can all serve a recreational as well as a practical purpose. Whether renovating your home completely or giving one room a quick coat of paint, there are tips to take the stress out of decorating. Whether entertaining friends or feeding the family, hints on how to shop for, prepare, and serve food are invaluable. And, moving outside, advice on all aspects of nurturing a garden – from weeding to water features – will ensure success.

Painting perfectly
Improve your decorating methods to ensure a professional result.

SPECIAL FEATURES

All sections of the *10,001 Hints and Tips for the Home* contain a number of special features designed to ensure that the information they contain is readily accessible to the serious reader and casual browser alike. Features include quick-reference boxes for each chapter, highly illustrated equipment boxes, a variety of tip boxes, safety boxes, warning boxes, and checklists.

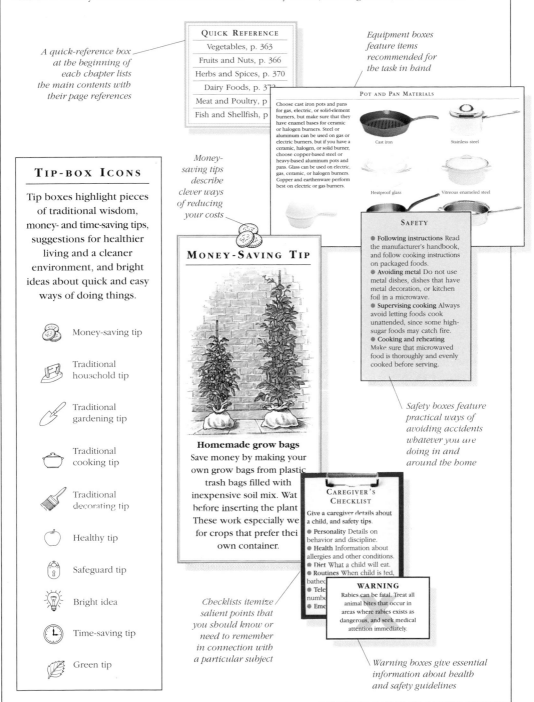

A quick-reference box at the beginning of each chapter lists the main contents with their page references

QUICK REFERENCE

Vegetables, p. 363

Fruits and Nuts, p. 366

Herbs and Spices, p. 370

Dairy Foods, p. 3?

Meat and Poultry, p

Fish and Shellfish, p

Equipment boxes feature items recommended for the task in hand

POT AND PAN MATERIALS

Choose cast iron pots and pans for gas, electric, or solid-element burners, but make sure that they have enamel bases for ceramic or halogen burners. Steel or aluminum can be used on gas or electric burners, but if you have a ceramic, halogen, or solid burner, choose copper-based steel or heavy-based aluminum pots and pans. Glass can be used on electric, gas, ceramic, or halogen burners. Copper and earthenware perform best on electric or gas burners.

Cast iron

Stainless steel

Heatproof glass

Vitreous enameled steel

TIP-BOX ICONS

Tip boxes highlight pieces of traditional wisdom, money- and time-saving tips, suggestions for healthier living and a cleaner environment, and bright ideas about quick and easy ways of doing things.

Money-saving tip

Traditional household tip

Traditional gardening tip

Traditional cooking tip

Traditional decorating tip

Healthy tip

Safeguard tip

Bright idea

Time-saving tip

Green tip

Money-saving tips describe clever ways of reducing your costs

MONEY-SAVING TIP

Homemade grow bags
Save money by making your own grow bags from plastic trash bags filled with inexpensive soil mix. Wat before inserting the plant These work especially we for crops that prefer thei own container.

SAFETY

● **Following instructions** Read the manufacturer's handbook, and follow cooking instructions on packaged foods.
● **Avoiding metal** Do not use metal dishes, dishes that have metal decoration, or kitchen foil in a microwave.
● **Supervising cooking** Always avoid letting foods cook unattended, since some high-sugar foods may catch fire.
● **Cooking and reheating** Make sure that microwaved food is thoroughly and evenly cooked before serving.

Safety boxes feature practical ways of avoiding accidents whatever you are doing in and around the home

CAREGIVER'S CHECKLIST

Give a caregiver details about a child, and safety tips.
● **Personality** Details on behavior and discipline.
● **Health** Information about allergies and other conditions.
● **Diet** What a child will eat.
● **Routines** When child is fed, bathed
● Tele
numbe
● Eme

WARNING
Rabies can be fatal. Treat all animal bites that occur in areas where rabies exists as dangerous, and seek medical attention immediately.

Checklists itemize salient points that you should know or need to remember in connection with a particular subject

Warning boxes give essential information about health and safety guidelines

MANAGING DOMESTIC ROUTINES

Many people lead hectic lives, juggling the demands of work and home with leisure activities and other commitments. Managing a busy household is like running an office: set aside regular periods for basic chores, then organize the rest of your time around other essential tasks. Use the same devices for making domestic life easier as at work: make lists, file information, use logs to plan specific jobs, make notes of job details, apportion time efficiently, put items away, and set up systems and routines. An organized approach will mean that you spend less time, money, and effort on ordinary jobs, leaving you more time and energy for the interesting aspects of life.

Organizing the family
Make and display an organizer so that everyone knows what they and other members of the household are doing each day and what they need to remember to take with them.

ORGANIZING OTHER ESSENTIAL TASKS

Most people move from time to time. Make this onerous task easy with careful planning, sorting, and packing beforehand, then sound organization on moving day. If you work, organize space, time, equipment, and specific tasks in order to maximize your efforts. Finally, make sure that you know how to administer basic first aid and that you have the right materials on hand to do so.

Getting rid of stains
It is extremely useful to know how to remove all manner of difficult stains from a variety of household items, such as furniture and floor coverings, as well as clothes.

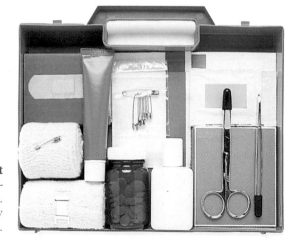

Making up a first-aid kit
Every household should have a well-stocked, comprehensive first-aid kit. Keep it in a cool, dark place that is easily accessible to adults but not to children.

DECORATING LIKE A PROFESSIONAL

A beautifully decorated home will provide you with a refuge from the hurly-burly of modern life and a haven for relaxation and recreation. Doing the decorating provides many people with a leisure activity, while others do it for economic reasons or as a creative outlet. Whatever the reason or the project, the same guidelines apply. Spend as much money as you can afford on decorating equipment and materials; experiment so that you make the right decisions about decor; prepare surfaces well before you start; consider environmentally friendly products; and finish off carefully and cleanly for a professional look.

Mixing colors
Experimenting with and mixing colors is part of the fun of creating paint effects when decorating your home.

Stir-frying food
Stir-frying is a method of cooking that enables you to seal food quickly, thus locking in all the goodness.

COOKING WITH CONFIDENCE

Fast living means fast food in the sense of time-saving tips and a wealth of helpful suggestions – both traditional and innovative – to make your cooking healthy, manageable, and enjoyable, whether it's a simple family supper or a special dinner with friends. Equip your kitchen well and choose a versatile variety of prepared and staple foods for your cupboard. In addition, buy the best, freshest ingredients and choose simple, healthy recipes for everyday meals as well as for entertaining. You will thus enjoy cooking your food as well as eating it.

GARDENING FOR PLEASURE

Whether you inherit a beautiful garden or create one yourself, it will need regular attention and care. This will include the pruning and propagation of plants, watering and weeding, keeping pests at bay, mowing and feeding lawns, and maintaining nonliving items such as paths and garden furniture. Handy hints and traditional wisdom will take the sweat out of gardening, encourage you to garden creatively, construct special garden features such as ponds or pergolas, and enjoy work or pleasure in your garden throughout the year.

Gardening creatively
Planting up a plastic pot that rests in the top of a tall, decorative container will save on soil mix.

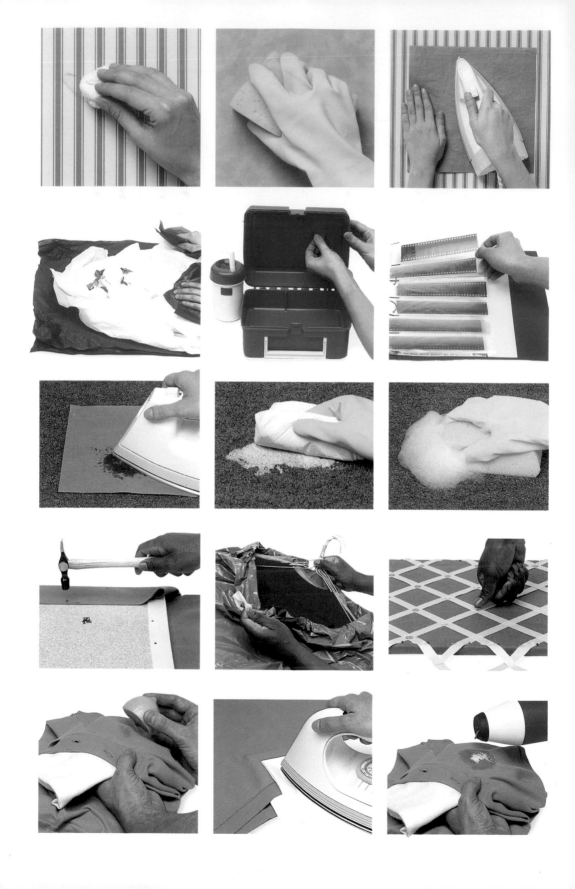

ORGANIZING YOUR
HOUSEHOLD

RUNNING A BUSY HOME

•

CLEANING EFFECTIVELY

•

MAKING REPAIRS

•

MOVING SMOOTHLY

•

WORKING WELL

•

KEEPING SAFE

UTILIZING SPACE

QUICK REFERENCE

Planning Room by
Room, p. 15

Using Storage
Space, p. 22

Storing Special
Items, p. 19

Solving
Storage, p. 30

*T*HERE ARE NO SET RULES *for organizing your own home. How you plan the layout of your home will depend on the space available, the number of people living there, their ages and states of health, and your own individual taste. Remember to allow enough space for people to move freely between different rooms or areas, and be sure that you organize all storage spaces efficiently to minimize clutter.*

MAKING THE MOST OF ROOMS IN A HOME

Make sure that the overall plan of your home includes enough space for everyone's possessions and activities. Before planning a layout for each room, consider the amount of available space and the locations of all windows, doors, outlets, and radiators. Organize the rooms so that any areas that are used for related purposes, such as a kitchen and a dining room, are close to each other.

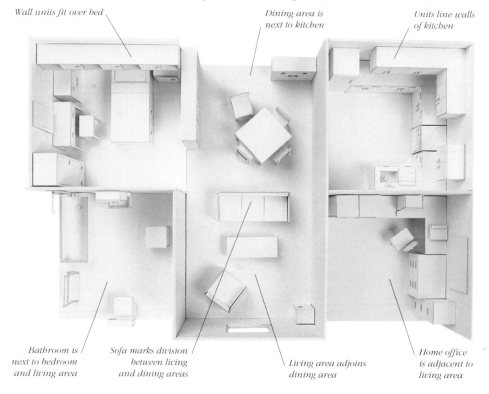

Wall units fit over bed

Dining area is next to kitchen

Units line walls of kitchen

Bathroom is next to bedroom and living area

Sofa marks division between living and dining areas

Living area adjoins dining area

Home office is adjacent to living area

PLANNING ROOM BY ROOM

Y̲OU CAN REARRANGE THE FURNITURE in your home at any time, either to organize storage space more efficiently or for a change of surroundings. Before starting, consider the structure and function of each room, and plan what to do.

MAKING THE MOST OF STRUCTURE

While you cannot easily change the design of your home, you should be able to make the most of the rooms as they are. Check that your home utilizes energy efficiently. Plan the use of the available space by considering different layouts for the furniture in each room.

MONEY-SAVING TIP

Insulating a carpet
For an economical alternative to rug pad, clean a hard floor, then put down a thick layer of newspaper, overlapping the sheets. Lay the carpet over the newspaper.

MAXIMIZING WARMTH

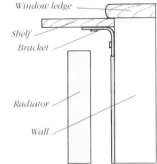

Window ledge
Shelf
Bracket
Radiator
Wall

Deflecting heat
Where a radiator is fitted under a window, fit a shelf between it and the window, directly beneath the ledge. This will deflect heat into the room so that it does not escape through the glass.

ADDING INSULATION
● **Blocking out drafts** Seal gaps around windows and doors to save heat. Make sure that rooms are well ventilated to prevent condensation.
● **Fitting double glazing** If you cannot afford to fit double glazing in every room, then concentrate on rooms that face away from the sun.
● **Insulating a roof** Install roof insulation to trap the heat that rises through the house.
● **Protecting a water tank** Install insulation around the water heater. Keep the insulation well away from the heating element or gas flame at the base of the heater.

MAKING A FURNITURE FLOOR PLAN

By making a floor plan, you can work out where to put furniture if you are reorganizing rooms. You can also make one to use if you move (see p. 152).

● Positioning furniture Use a floor plan to find the best place for each item of furniture. Bear in mind practical considerations. For example, do not put wooden or upholstered furniture in direct sunlight. The light may bleach wood and fade fabrics.
● Laying out a living room Place all the seating within reach of low tables. If you have audio equipment or a television in the room, make sure that all the seating allows easy access to it.

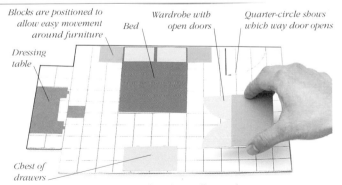

Blocks are positioned to allow easy movement around furniture
Dressing table
Chest of drawers
Bed
Wardrobe with open doors
Quarter-circle shows which way door opens

Constructing and using a furniture floor plan
On graph paper, make a plan for a room or a floor, using a scale such as 1:20. Mark the positions of windows, doors, outlets, and radiators. Cut thin cardboard shapes, to the same scale as your plan, to represent pieces of furniture. Label each one. Attach them to the plan with spray glue so that you can reposition them if you change your mind.

PLANNING A KITCHEN

Organize a kitchen for safety and ease of use. Decide on your preferred layout, and adjust this to fit in with the existing structure of your kitchen. If you plan to install a new kitchen, check safety and hygiene regulations with your local environmental health authority.

BASING A KITCHEN LAYOUT ON A TRIANGLE

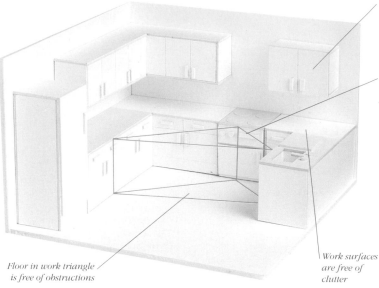

High-level units are shallow to allow easy access to back of work surface

Triangle shows clear paths between frequently used areas of kitchen

Floor in work triangle is free of obstructions

Work surfaces are free of clutter

Planning a layout
The stove, sink, and refrigerator, and the work surfaces next to them, are the most frequently used areas in a kitchen. The paths between these areas often form a triangle. For easy access, keep this triangle clear.

SAVING SPACE IN A KITCHEN

By using space effectively you can maximize storage and leave plenty of room for work. Keep everyday items together and within easy reach of the stove and work surfaces. Store as much as possible in the available space. Stack utensils, and hang items from a ceiling.

STACKING EQUIPMENT

● **Storing saucepans** Keep a set of saucepans on a narrow, vertical stacking rack.
● **Organizing dishes** Stack plates and saucers on plastic-coated racks with different-sized shelves. Stand the racks in any corners of work surfaces that cannot be used for food preparation.
● **Grouping bowls and pans** Store different-sized bowls and baking pans one inside the other to take up a minimum of space. Leave room around them so that you can remove and replace them easily.
● **Arranging cleaning items** Use stackable plastic baskets to hold small cleaning items.

HANGING POTS & PANS FROM A CEILING

Hooks are hung in mesh

Border of frame is 1¾ in (4.5 cm) wide

Mesh is attached to upper edge of frame

Saucepans are hung from holes in handles

Using a frame
Make a wooden frame 18 x 12 in (45 x 30 cm). Tack strong wire mesh across the frame. Suspend the frame from the ceiling with chains so that it is level and a little above head height. Hang butchers' hooks in the mesh to hold pots and pans.

ORGANIZING STORAGE IN A KITCHEN

Making the best use of storage spaces and using space-saving devices in a kitchen will allow you to keep work surfaces clear. You can buy specialized items that enable you to keep a lot of equipment in a particular place, or you can easily modify a kitchen area yourself.

UTILIZING DRAWERS

Adapting a drawer
To create an extra work surface, measure the depth of a cutting board, and attach wooden battens in a kitchen drawer at this depth. To use the surface, lay the board on the battens. You can keep items in the drawer while using it as a work surface.

UTILIZING WALL AREAS
● **Holding rolls** Hang paper towel holders on a wall to store materials on rolls such as paper towels and plastic wrap.

Fitting a microwave oven
Mount a microwave oven on a wall using strong metal brackets. Check that the oven is at an appropriate height for everyone who uses it. Use the work surface underneath for storing food jars.

KEEPING AREAS CLEAR
● **Reducing clutter** Use work surfaces to store only those items that you use constantly. Group the items together. For example, put wooden spoons and spatulas in a large jar.
● **Using wall space** Attach cup hooks to walls under shelves or high-level units. Hang lightweight items such as ladles and sieves from the hooks.
● **Using a peg board** Fix a peg board to a wall, then hang small items from the pegs.
● **Holding recipe books** Fold a piece of clear polyethylene in half, then attach the back and edges to a wall near a stove. Leave the top open to form a pocket. Put open recipe books in the pocket while you are using them to leave the work surface clear.

HIDING WASTE BASKETS

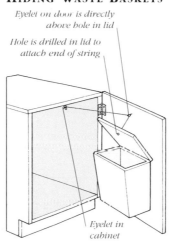

Eyelet on door is directly above hole in lid

Hole is drilled in lid to attach end of string

Eyelet in cabinet

Attaching a garbage can
Mount a plastic garbage can on brackets inside a cabinet door. Attach eyelets inside the cabinet and above the bin. Thread string through the eyelets and the lid. The lid will lift as the door opens.

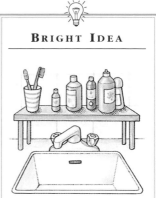

BRIGHT IDEA

Putting a shelf over a sink
Attach a small shelf over the sink to hold items such as dishwashing detergent and sponges. Make sure that the shelf is high enough to allow easy access to the faucets. Support the shelf on lengths of thick dowels.

FILLING CABINETS
● **Fitting shelves** You do not need to keep the shelving that is already fitted in a cabinet. If you need more storage surfaces, attach small brackets at different levels to hold adjustable shelving.
● **Adding hooks** Attach a batten along the back of a cabinet. Screw hooks into the batten to hold cups, measuring jugs, and similar small items.
● **Storing flat objects** Fit plywood boards vertically in cabinets to make narrow compartments. Use the spaces to store flat items such as baking trays and cooling racks within easy reach.
● **Utilizing doors** Attach favorite recipes and other useful information to the insides of cabinet doors for quick reference.

PLANNING A BATHROOM

Organize a bathroom so that it is safe and comfortable to use. If you do not wish to redo it completely, add inexpensive storage units and decorative features. Make several plans before beginning work to find the most effective way of using the space available.

MAKING THE MOST OF A BATHROOM

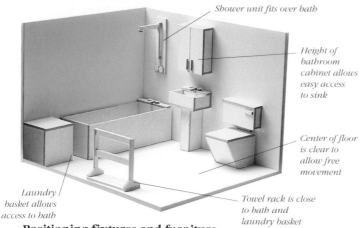

Shower unit fits over bath

Height of bathroom cabinet allows easy access to sink

Center of floor is clear to allow free movement

Laundry basket allows access to bath

Towel rack is close to bath and laundry basket

Positioning fixtures and furniture

Whatever the size of your bathroom, leave at least 3 ft (1 m) of clear space in front of the bath, sink, and toilet, so that you have easy access to them. Position furniture so that it will not restrict access to these fixtures. For example, use space at the end of a tub to keep a laundry basket out of the way of people using the bathroom.

ORGANIZING BASICS

Before you plan or reorganize a bathroom, take the following steps to ensure that it will be easy to clean and safe to use.

● **Plumbing** If pipes or water valves are hidden behind cabinet doors, clear space in front of them so that you can reach them in an emergency.
● **Surfacing** For areas around baths and basins, choose surfaces such as tiles, which are easy to clean and will not harbor bacteria.
● **Flooring** Install nonskid surfacing in a bath or shower and on the floor.
● **Electrical items** Ask a qualified electrician to check that any electrical outlets, such as an outlet for an electric razor, are well insulated.

SAVING SPACE IN A BATHROOM

Bathrooms are often small, so it is important to make the most of the space. Put shelves in empty areas such as the space above a door. Use odd-shaped areas, such as the space under a sink to give extra storage. Group toiletries so that they are within easy reach of users.

USING SINK AREAS

Storing under a sink

To create enclosed storage space, fix waterproof curtains around a sink. Attach the curtains to the sink with touch-and-close tape. Remove and clean the curtains every few weeks.

USING SMALL SPACES

● **Storing around a toilet** Use the space behind a toilet bowl to keep cleaning items.
● **Collecting bath toys** To prevent bath toys from cluttering a bathroom, store the toys in a plastic dish rack. Wash the toys and the dish rack once a week.
● **Installing a seat** Instead of putting a chair in a bathroom, install a pull-down seat on one wall to keep the floor clear.
● **Using another room** If a bathroom is very small, keep nonessential items in another room. For example, put a laundry basket in an empty corner of a bedroom.

STORING TOILETRIES

Filling a corner

If you have a corner of empty space beside a bath, put a small set of shelves there for holding toiletries. Position the shelves so that they will not restrict access to the bath faucets.

PLANNING A BEDROOM

Organize a bedroom so that it will look attractive and accommodate clothes and other personal objects neatly. Make sure that there is sufficient storage space for the occupier's needs, so that they can keep surfaces clear when they are using the bedroom.

FURNISHING A ROOM

● **Testing a new bed** Before buying a bed, the person who will use the bed should lie on it to see if it is the correct size and softness for them.
● **Adding cushions** Buy a triangular or armchair-shaped cushion to support your back while sitting up in bed.
● **Adapting a table** Cut down the legs of a small table to make a surface for food or hobbies when you are in bed.
● **Lighting a dressing table** Install small light bulbs around a dressing-table mirror. Choose bulbs that emit clear light.
● **Lighting a bed area** Position bedside lights so that they can be turned off from the bed.

CREATING HEADBOARDS

Hanging drapes
Screw two brass rings into the wall above a bed. Drape a long piece of lightweight, sheer fabric through the rings, leaving a swag between them. Hide the ends behind the pillows or mattress.

PROVIDING STORAGE

● **Choosing a bed** Increase storage space by buying a bed that is equipped with drawers in the base (see p. 22).

Keeping stuffed toys
To store stuffed toys, hang two hooks on adjoining walls at one corner of a room. Put a hook at the point at which the walls meet. Attach a triangular piece of netting. Put toys in the netting.

SAVING SPACE IN A BEDROOM

Arrange furniture and storage units so that you can make the best possible use of the available space. Use all potential storage areas, such as a gap under a bed or the top of an armoire. With careful planning, you can even make room for other activities such as exercise.

MONEY-SAVING TIP

Creating a bedside table
Place a sturdy wooden box by a bed, with the open end facing forward. Drape fabric over the box. You can then stand items on the box and store objects inside it.

ADDING BED SPACE

● **Keeping a cot** Stow a cot under a regular bed so that it will be easily accessible whenever you need it.
● **Using a mattress** Keep an old mattress to use as a spare bed. Vacuum clean it regularly, and examine it to check that the fabric has not worn out.
● **Converting a futon** Put a futon in your bedroom or living room. Keep it rolled up so that you can use it as a low-level couch when you do not need the bed space.
● **Using a sofabed** Keep a sofabed in a spare room or living room to accommodate guests. Leave space in front of it so that you can unfold it when you need to use it.

FILLING CLOSETS

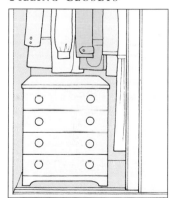

Installing drawers
Stand a small chest of drawers on the floor of a closet with built-in hardware. Hang short garments such as jackets above it. Check that the handles of the drawers do not obstruct the closet doors.

PLANNING LIVING AND DINING AREAS

These are the areas of the home that are used the most, so be sure that furniture and furnishings are sturdy and fairly dirt proof. If you are working on a tight budget, you can buy second-hand furniture and use the tips below to create an attractive effect for little expense.

CREATING DINING SPACE
● **Finding an area** If you do not have a dining room, convert part of a living room. You could also use a kitchen, a spare bedroom, or a large hall.
● **Making a table** To create a dining table quickly, use a wallpaper table or trestle that folds away when not in use, and cover it with a cloth.
● **Adding a tabletop** If you occasionally wish to enlarge a dining table but do not have an expanding table, have a thick piece of board cut to the shape and size that you need. Rest it on the tabletop. If you wish to store the board, cut it in half, and fit it with a hinge so that you can fold it flat.

PLACING SPEAKERS

Make neat pile to form stable column

Making a speaker stand
Stand speakers off the floor to protect them from damage and stop sound from being muffled. Place them on piles of unwanted telephone directories or books. Drape with attractive fabric.

SAVING SPACE IN LIVING AREAS

Make the most of living space by keeping it neat. The less clutter there is on display, the more attractive, relaxing, and safe the area will be. Allow enough storage space for items such as cassettes and magazines, and display only those objects that you really want to see.

ORGANIZING YOUR LIVING SPACE

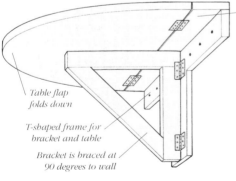

Lip of support allows room for bracket when table is folded

Table flap folds down

T-shaped frame for bracket and table

Bracket is braced at 90 degrees to wall

Fitting a folding table
If you have no space or money for a dining table, attach a wall-mounted folding table in an empty space, and put it up when you need it. Keep the area clear so that you can always use the table.

MAKING STORAGE SPACE

Storing drinks
Decorate an old filing cabinet by spraying with aerosol paint, and use it as a liquor cabinet. Use a lockable drawer to keep alcohol from children. Fill any other drawers with soft drinks.

CLEARING AWAY CLUTTER FROM LIVING AREAS
● **Tidying up** Clear your living areas each evening to prevent clutter from building up.
● **Storing chairs** If you eat in a living room, use stacking chairs. Put them against a wall when you do not need them.
● **Putting away toys** Keep a large, plastic laundry basket in an unobtrusive place for tidying children's toys quickly.
● **Using a magazine rack** Use a rack to store newspapers and magazines neatly.

PLANNING A HOBBY ROOM

It is best to reserve a special room or area for hobbies. This will keep leisure equipment from cluttering the rest of the home and allow enthusiasts to pursue their particular hobby uninterrupted, without having to clear away their equipment immediately after using it.

KEEPING EQUIPMENT FOR ACTIVITIES

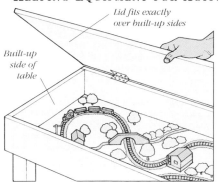

Lid fits exactly over built-up sides

Built-up side of table

Covering a train set
Conceal a train set or car track on a table by making sides and a lid for the table. Build high sides onto the edges of the table. Cut a large board to form the lid. Attach it to one long side with two or three hinges. Allow plenty of space for the lid to fold out of the way.

USING POWER TOOLS

Make sure that the circuits in your house can handle the demands of all the tools and equipment that you are using.

● **Power** Be sure that a hobby room has enough outlets for all your equipment. Never try to run more than two items off one power outlet.
● **Space** Check that there is plenty of space for air to circulate around the back of electrical machinery. This will prevent heat from building up to a dangerous level.
● **Electric cords** Straighten any loose cords by folding them into loops and slipping them into a cardboard tube.

ORGANIZING HOBBIES IN THE HOME

● **Straightening equipment**
Keep small objects in sturdy plastic vegetable racks. If the racks are used for several hobbies, label each section.

● **Promoting safety** For tasks such as welding, which create fumes and fire risks, make sure that there is good ventilation and show a "No Smoking" sign.

PLANNING CORRIDORS AND HALLWAYS

Areas between rooms can often be used for extra storage or living space, provided that you do not hinder access to rooms or create a fire hazard by blocking doors. For example, you could adapt a corner of a wide hallway to form an office area, or hang shelving in a corridor.

FILLING EMPTY AREAS

● **Ensuring safety** Hallways, corridors, and stairs are all essential fire escape routes. Keep these areas clear of obstructions at all times.
● **Hanging coats** Position coat racks or hooks so that they do not obstruct a door. For small children, hang a second row of coat hooks below the first, at a height within easy reach.
● **Adding hanging space** Keep a collapsible dress rack in a spare room or closet, and put it in a hallway to hold coats when you have a party.
● **Using temporary storage** Hang a shelf to hold items such as sports equipment, so that people can find the items easily when they need them.

USING STAIRWAYS

Creating a mini-office
Make an area for office work or homework by putting a desk in the space under a flight of stairs. Provide good lighting, preferably wall-mounted to save desk space, and a comfortable chair.

FILLING ODD CORNERS

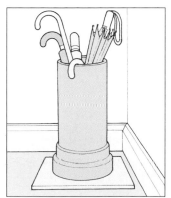

Holding umbrellas
Stand a length of earthenware pipe on a large ceramic tile or in a shallow, waterproof container to hold umbrellas and canes. Put the stand in an inconspicuous place near the front door.

21

USING STORAGE SPACE

C ABINETS, SHELVES, AND OTHER STORAGE UNITS can be adapted to suit any home. Position them so that you make the fullest use of existing storage spaces, and fit extra units in otherwise unused parts of the home for long-term storage.

ORGANIZING CABINETS

T ake care of cabinets and their contents. Do not overload shelves or stand heavy items on top of cabinets. Group the contents so that they will be easily accessible, and sort out the cabinet space from time to time to clear away any rubbish that has accumulated.

CHOOSING CABINETS

Cabinets can be built-in or they can be free-standing units. Each type of cabinet has different advantages.

● **Built-in cabinets** Design these cabinets to fit a space. You can also adapt the interiors for items such as audio or visual equipment.
● **Freestanding cupboards** It is quite easy to reposition these cupboards if changing the layout of a room, and you can take them with you when you move.

CONSIDERING SCALE

● **Planning a small kitchen** To make the most of kitchen space, use wall cabinets in place of floor cabinets, since wall cabinets are less deep and take up less space. Check that items and appliances will fit on the narrow counters and inside the cabinets.
● **Suiting your height** To check if a wall cabinet is positioned at the correct height for you, stand in front of it, and try to rest a hand flat on the upper shelf. If you cannot reach, lower the cabinet.

STRAIGHTENING LINEN

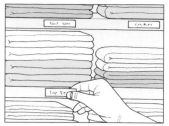

Organizing a linen cabinet
Sort linen into categories such as sheets and pillowcases. Label each shelf of a linen cabinet to show its contents. This will allow you to put the right type of linen in the right place every time.

POSITIONING CABINETS IN A BEDROOM

This plan shows how to use space in a bedroom for different types of cabinet. Whichever room you are planning, use the following tips to make the most of this storage space.

● **Ensuring free access** Leave sufficient space in front of cabinets so that you are able to open the doors fully.
● **Using awkward spaces** Place cupboards with sliding doors in areas without much clearance.
● **Filling recessed areas** Use a small cupboard in a recessed area such as a window bay.
● **Filling a fireplace** Stand a small, decorative cupboard in an old fireplace. Check that the chimney has been sealed. If not, brush out the fireplace regularly to remove soot deposits.

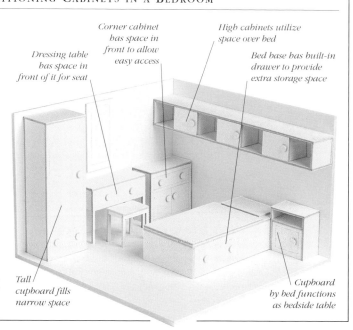

Dressing table has space in front of it for seat

Corner cabinet has space in front to allow easy access

High cabinets utilize space over bed

Bed base has built-in drawer to provide extra storage space

Tall cupboard fills narrow space

Cupboard by bed functions as bedside table

ORGANIZING CLOSET SPACE

You can fit a great deal in a closet if you make use of horizontal as well as vertical space. Before hanging or stacking items, group them by length or width, and separate those to be folded or kept in boxes. Put garments in the same place every time to keep the space neat.

ARRANGING SPACE IN CLOSETS

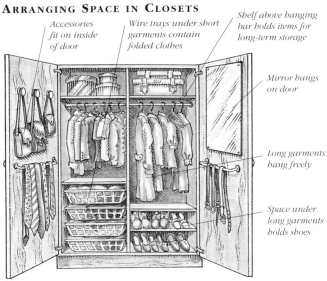

Accessories fit on inside of door

Wire trays under short garments contain folded clothes

Shelf above hanging bar holds items for long-term storage

Mirror hangs on door

Long garments hang freely

Space under long garments holds shoes

Arranging clothes and accessories
To keep your closet neat, do not overload hanging bars or shelves. Leave enough room to remove and replace clothes and accessories easily. Make use of all the space, including the insides of doors. If you hang items on a door, do not overload it, since you could put stress on the hinges. Use doors to hang lightweight objects such as ties and costume jewelry, and use one hook for each item.

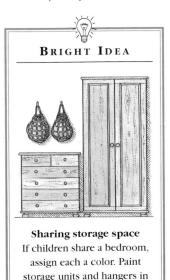

💡 **BRIGHT IDEA**

Sharing storage space
If children share a bedroom, assign each a color. Paint storage units and hangers in these colors to show where each child's items are kept.

CREATING CLOSETS

Making use of a niche
Attach a rail across a niche so that you can hang up clothes. Leave enough room between the rail and the back wall to use hangers. If there is no space for doors, hang a roller blind at the front of the niche instead.

PROTECTING ITEMS
● **Covering delicate garments** Make or buy cotton covers to protect expensive clothes or fragile garments in a closet. Alternatively, save the plastic bags from a dry cleaner, and use these to cover garments.

Attach photograph onto box

Storing shoes efficiently
Keep little-used shoes in boxes on a closet floor or shelf. Take a photograph of each pair, and attach the picture to the relevant box so that you can find the shoes instantly.

SAVING SPACE
● **Compacting clothes** On closet shelves, store noncreasing clothes such as thin sweaters by rolling them rather than folding them.
● **Utilizing doors** Attach a towel bar to the inside of a closet door. Slip shower curtain hooks onto the bar, and hang belts and ties from them.
● **Attaching a mirror** In place of a freestanding mirror, attach a mirror to a closet door. Choose a door with its back to the light, so that light falls on you and not on the mirror.
● **Using in a spare room** Fill a closet in a spare room with seldom-worn clothes. Empty the closet whenever it is needed for guests' use.

MAKING USE OF SHELVES

Shelves can enhance the look of a room as well as provide storage space. They can be made from different materials for a variety of uses, such as wood for holding books and household equipment, and glass for displaying ornaments, photographs, and small plants.

FILLING SHELVES

● **Filling shelves safely** Be careful not to overload a shelf, because it may sag. If you plan to build shelves, add more supports than you think you will need. If adding objects to a shelf, make sure that the span is adequately supported to bear the extra load.

● **Organizing objects** Keep objects near where they are most likely to be used. Do not put frequently used items on shelves that are too high to reach comfortably.

● **Storing small objects** Create shelves within shelves to store small items. For example, put a spice rack at the back of a shelf, or use a wooden cutlery holder placed on its side.

● **Keeping shelves neat** Label the fronts of shelves so that people can put objects back in the correct places after use.

USING OPEN SHELVES IN A LARGE ROOM

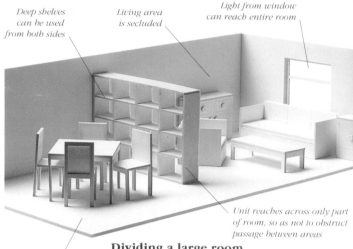

Deep shelves can be used from both sides

Living area is secluded

Light from window can reach entire room

Unit reaches across only part of room, so as not to obstruct passage between areas

Dining area is small and intimate

Dividing a large room

Use open shelves to divide a large room for different functions. For example, place open shelves between a living area and a dining area to form a practical screen. Make the shelves deep enough that both sides of the unit can be used for storage or displaying objects.

CREATING INSTANT SHELVES

You can construct simple shelves quickly and easily using only bricks and wooden boards, without the need for any special tools or equipment. It is best to choose attractive bricks that are in good condition, and sturdy wooden boards that are at least ⅝ in (15 mm) thick. Build one or two more shelves than you think you will need. As you work, make sure that each level is steady and properly supported.

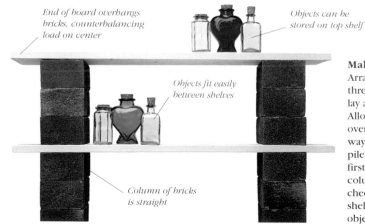

End of board overhangs bricks, counterbalancing load on center

Objects can be stored on top shelf

Objects fit easily between shelves

Column of bricks is straight

Making basic shelves

Arrange bricks in columns, each three or four bricks high, and lay a board across the bricks. Allow the ends of each shelf to overhang the bricks by a little way for stability. To add shelves, pile more bricks on top of the first shelf, following the original columns. When adding bricks, check that the height of each shelf will accommodate the objects that you intend to display.

MAKING USE OF DRAWERS

Drawers provide many different types of storage space, and can be large or small, deep or shallow, to suit particular items. It is possible to divide space inside drawers so that you can see the contents at a glance, and keep small items neat and easily accessible.

PLANNING USE OF SPACE

● **Fitting drawers into spaces**
When shopping for a chest of drawers, take with you the dimensions of the space where you wish to stand it so that you can check that it will fit before buying.

● **Positioning a set of drawers**
Allow enough room for an adult to kneel in front of a chest of drawers when a drawer is fully open.

● **Choosing units** If possible, select units with drawers of varying depths. Store items such as underwear in shallow drawers, and larger items such as sweaters in deep drawers.

● **Storing items flat** For large objects that must be kept flat, such as artwork or fabrics, use a flat file, available from art shops. Flat files have wide, shallow drawers designed to hold such items.

● **Using deep spaces** Consider installing deep, sturdy drawers for large objects such as board games or photograph albums.

KEEPING DRAWERS NEAT

Making drawer dividers
To organize items such as socks in a drawer, use a divider from a bottle box. Cut the divider to the size of the drawer, and push it in. Place small items in the spaces.

USING DRAWERS SAFELY

Do not overfill drawers. Every few months, clean out the drawers to remove accumulated dust and dirt. At the same time, examine each of the drawers for any signs of damage.

● **Filling drawer space** Leave at least 1 in (2.5 cm) between the top edge of a drawer and the top of the contents. This will keep the objects inside from spilling over and jamming the drawer.

● **Packing sharp objects** Wrap blades and sharp edges before storing items. Otherwise, bare metal points and blades could blunt one another, and could cut anyone using the drawer.

● **Limiting weight of contents**
Never keep a very heavy object in a drawer. Even if the object fits in the space, its weight may put excessive strain on the bottom of the drawer.

● **Waxing runners** Rub a piece of soap, or the end of a wax candle, along drawer runners occasionally. This will enable the drawers to slide smoothly and keep them from sticking.

● **Making safety stops** If an old set of drawers has rails that separate the drawers, nail a line of corks into the underside of each rail. The corks will catch the back edge of each drawer so that it cannot be pulled out.

ORGANIZING CONTENTS

● **Labeling for clarity** It is often useful to label the front of each drawer with details of what is in it. It may be helpful to children if you label their drawers with lists of the clothes that they contain. Make separate labels for items such as socks, T-shirts, and sweaters.

● **Preserving clothes** Arrange clothes in drawers so that the most delicate are at the top and durable garments are at the bottom. For example, keep blouses on top of T-shirts. This will prevent clothes from becoming overly creased.

● **Arranging implements** Lay long, thin objects such as ladles so that they all face the same way. This will keep them from becoming jumbled.

● **Keeping tiny objects** Put a miniature set of drawers on a shelf, desk, or table, to hold objects such as jewelry or sewing items that might get lost in a larger drawer.

KEEPING DRAWERS CLEAN

● **Maintaining interiors** Line drawers with wallpaper scraps so that they will be quick and easy to keep clean. Replace the lining paper as soon as this becomes necessary.

● **Cleaning up spills** To stop spills in a drawer from congealing, wipe out instantly

Place bottles behind elastic

Grouping small bottles
Using drawing pins, attach elastic to the left and right sides of a drawer. Tuck bottles inside the elastic. They will not fall over and will be easy to remove.

MAKING USE OF OTHER SPACES

Many parts of your home have potential as storage space; don't limit yourself to built-in units and shelves. Consider using the spaces above doors and windows, the backs of doors, unused walls, and any nooks and crannies that could hold a small shelf or cabinet.

USING SMALL SPACES
● **Decorating windows**
Small empty spaces can fulfill decorative as well as practical functions. For example, you could put glass shelves across a window with no view. Display glass ornaments on them; the objects will catch the light coming through the window.

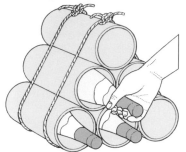

Improvising a wine rack
Make a wine rack from plastic drain pipe 5-6 in (12-15 cm) in diameter. Cut the pipe into 12-in (30-cm) lengths. Glue these together in groups of six, and secure the groups with rope.

STORING UNDER BEDS
● **Creating storage units** Keep spare bedding, unused clothes, and children's toys in sturdy cardboard or plastic boxes. Before storing clothes and bedding, line the boxes with plain white paper. Tuck lavender sachets into fabrics to protect them from moths.

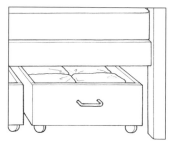

Making mobile boxes
Keep large, shallow boxes under high beds for extra storage. To make the boxes mobile, screw castors to the undersides, at each corner. Attach a handle or loop of rope to the front of each box.

UTILIZING GAPS
● **Filling a niche** If there is a gap between kitchen cabinets, slide a clothes rack into it to hold dish towels. Alternatively, if the space is high enough, use it to store brooms and mops or keep an ironing board.
● **Hanging shelves above doors** If there is a reasonable space between a ceiling and the top of a door, install a narrow, well-supported shelf to hold ornaments or small objects.
● **Using empty wall spaces** Put narrow shelves in the space between a door or window and a side wall. If a door opens onto the wall where you will put the shelves, make sure that they will not obstruct the door.
● **Using a child's room** Store rarely used items in high cabinets or on top shelves in a child's room. Check that the child cannot reach the area, so that he or she is not likely to pull items down and get hurt.

STORING ITEMS IN GARAGES AND SHEDS

Be careful that you do not allow a garage or shed to become disorganized. It is only too easy to use the space as a dumping ground for objects instead of clearing them away immediately.

● **Arranging storage** Group items such as tools together so that you can find them easily.
● **Adding space** Hang secondhand kitchen cabinets on the walls. Put locks on cabinets used to store harmful substances.
● **Adding a work surface** Mount a fold-down table on one wall for repair work and other tasks.
● **Using electricity** If you plan to use the space as a workshop, install plenty of outlets.

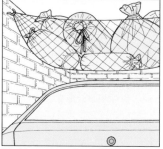

Making use of a ceiling
Hang a net across the ceiling of a garage to hold large, light items. If the garage door slides upward to open, ensure that the net does not obstruct the mechanism. Do not overload the net; otherwise, it may sag onto the roof of your car.

Hanging long tools on a wall
Cut a length of wood. Drill a line of holes along it, holding the drill at an angle, then put dowel pegs in the holes so that the pegs point upward. Attach the wood to a wall. Hang tools on pegs with bristles or tines facing the wall.

STORING SPECIAL ITEMS

T HINK CAREFULLY about how you organize space for bulky or valuable items. Keep large objects where they will not get in the way of daily life, unless they are in regular use. Put valuables well out of sight of potential burglars.

ORGANIZING VIDEOTAPES AND MUSIC

P rotect videotapes, cassettes, compact discs, and vinyl records from possible damage. Store them in a safe place near the equipment on which you play them, and keep the area tidy to prevent losses or damage. Set out collections logically, so that you can find items easily.

SORTING VIDEOTAPES
● **Labeling tapes** Label each tape with its contents and the date of recording.
● **Filing tapes** Institute a videotape filing system, with categories such as "Movies" and "Television Programs".
● **Dealing with old tapes** Review your video collection regularly, and erase or discard tapes that you do not want.
● **Collecting clean tapes** Label clean tapes ready for writing on after making a recording.

STORING COMPACT DISCS

Cut along lines with a fretsaw

Making a storage rack
Drill two lines of equally spaced holes down a length of plastic gutter. Attach the gutter to a stiff board. Mark lines to join pairs of holes, then cut to form slots.

PROTECTING ITEMS
● **Avoiding damage** Keep vinyl records and compact discs out of direct heat, which may warp them. Store tapes away from sources of magnetism such as the back of a television. Always put them back in their cases when not playing them.
● **Listing for insurance** Note the title of each item and whether it is a compact disc, cassette, vinyl record, or videotape. Keep the list safely in case you need it for insurance purposes.

STORING BULKY OBJECTS

P ositioning bulky items demands ingenuity and some lateral thinking. Work out which items must be accessible and which can be put away neatly in less reachable places. Be careful to position large or heavy objects safely so that you do not hurt yourself when moving them.

USING WALL SPACE

Stowing a bicycle
Hang a bicycle by its crossbar on a pair of brackets. Shape the tops of the brackets to make stoppers so that the bicycle does not slide off. Pad the brackets so that they do not scratch the bicycle.

KEEPING LEISURE ITEMS
● **Tidying sports equipment** Put durable items such as footballs and hockey sticks into a large plastic laundry basket. Store the basket in a corner near an outside door.
● **Putting away sleeping bags** If sleeping bags do not have covers, roll them tightly, and tie them with fabric tape so that they occupy the minimum of space in a box or closet. Alternatively, use them with blankets as ordinary bedding.
● **Storing picnic items** Hang a cooler out of the way on a strong hanging-plant hook. Store plates, cutlery, and other picnic equipment inside it.

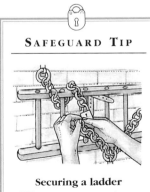

SAFEGUARD TIP

Securing a ladder
When you are not using a ladder, keep it out of the way by attaching it to a wall with securely fastened chains and padlocks. This will also stop burglars from taking it.

ORGANIZING PHOTOGRAPHS AND FILM

Photographs are precious mementoes. Store them in a cool, dry place to protect them from damage. Keep any that have particular value in a fireproof box or safe, or leave copies in the bank. Group photographs in boxes or albums to keep them neat and accessible.

SORTING PHOTOGRAPHS
● **Labeling prints** If prints or packages do not already have a date, write the month and year on the back of each print, along with the location.

Dividers are visible above prints

Arranging prints neatly
Store prints in shoeboxes instead of putting them in an album. To find photographs quickly, create a filing system using index cards as dividers. Label the cards to show the contents of each section.

KEEPING NEGATIVES
● **Avoiding marks** Handle negatives carefully, touching only the edges. Do not leave fingerprints on them because this will result in poor reprints.

Filing negatives neatly
To store negatives flat, keep them in their plastic sleeves. Punch holes in the sleeves, taking care to avoid the negatives, and file in a ring binder. Label each sleeve to indicate the contents.

DEALING WITH FILM
● **Keeping undeveloped film** Heat damages film, so keep rolls in a refrigerator. Place them in a covered rack in the door, well away from food.
● **Storing exposed film** Put undeveloped rolls back in their original containers, and keep in a cool, dark place. Put negatives in the package in which they were returned.
● **Developing film** Have film developed as soon as possible after using up a roll. If film is left for a long time, the images may deteriorate.
● **Taking films on vacation** In hot weather, wrap your camera and film in a plastic bag, and keep in a cooler to protect them from dust and heat.

STORING JEWELRY

Keep valuable items of jewelry separate so that they do not scratch one another. Put these pieces and items of sentimental value in a safe at home or in a safe-deposit box at a bank. Have jewelry valued for insurance, and tell the insurers if you sell or buy any pieces.

BRIGHT IDEA

Jewelry is laid flat

Disk is cut to fit can

Keeping jewelry safe
Open a food can at the base, empty it, and wash it. Fill it with jewelry wrapped in cotton, then plug the base with a disk of cork. Hide the can in a food cabinet.

KEEPING SMALL ITEMS
● **Tidying rings** Make a ring post for holding inexpensive rings. Cut a piece of dowel 3 in (7.5 cm) long, and attach one end to a wood or cork base. Slip rings onto the post.
● **Grouping earrings** To store earrings for pierced ears, stick them into a pincushion.
● **Hanging clip-on earrings** Pin a ribbon inside a drawer with thumb tacks. Hang clip-on earrings on the ribbon.
● **Collecting items** Use a small tray or box to hold accessories that you wear every day. Make a habit of putting these accessories into the tray at night so that you will be sure to find them in the morning.

STORING NECKLACES
● **Arranging necklaces** Keep inexpensive necklaces in a long box or poster tube, or loop them onto a coat hanger, and hang them in a closet.

Long necklace folded in half before hanging

Hanging up a necklace
Attach a cup hook to the inside of an armoire door. Store an inexpensive necklace or bracelet by hanging it on the cup hook.

ORGANIZING BOOKS AND PAPERS

The writer John Milton said "a good book is the precious lifeblood of a master spirit." Well-kept books give years of pleasure. Mark your place with a bookmark instead of folding the corners of pages. When you lend a book, note its title and the name of the borrower.

TRADITIONAL TIP

Preventing mildew
Sprinkle a little oil of cloves on wooden bookshelves to stop mildew from developing. Rub the oil into the shelves thoroughly so that it does not soak into the books.

PLANNING STORAGE
● **Setting up a system** Group your books into categories. For example, arrange them alphabetically by the authors' surnames, or by subject matter.
● **Allowing room** Leave at least 1 in (2.5 cm) between the tops of the books and the base of the shelf above so that you can remove books easily. Allow at least 1 in (2.5 cm) of shelf width for every book.
● **Arranging sheet music** Use a magazine rack to hold small quantities of sheet music. Sort large collections alphabetically, and allocate a shelf for them.

PRESERVING BOOKS
● **Minimizing humidity** Keep books in dry places. Combat humidity by putting a small moisture absorber near places that attract condensation, such as double-glazed windows.
● **Caring for covers** Protect paperbacks with plastic jacket covers. Wipe leather bindings with leather cleaner.
● **Keeping down dirt** Remove books regularly, and dust them and the bookshelves.
● **Making dust shields** Tack 2-in (5-cm) wide leather strips to the fronts of shelves to keep dust off the books beneath.

STORING TOOLS

Garden and household tools are expensive, so take care of them to prolong their useful lives. Keep implements with blades in a safe place, out of reach of children, and with the blades sheathed in thick cloth or bubble wrap. See page 31 for making a blade protector.

KEEPING IMPLEMENTS
● **Hanging tools** Protect tools from damage by hanging them up. Keep them on hooks or on a metal or wooden rack. If a tool has no hole by which to hang it, drill a hole in the handle, thread string through it, and tie to form a loop.
● **Storing small items** Use plastic storage boxes to keep garden items such as trowels, and household implements such as wrenches and drill bits.
● **Maintaining implements** Clean all tools after you have used them. Wash dirty garden tools under an outside faucet, then dry them carefully.
● **Storing for a season** At the end of the gardening season, clean all tools thoroughly. Oil metal parts to prevent rusting, and protect unpainted wood by rubbing it with linseed oil.

STORING LARGE ITEMS
● **Storing a wheelbarrow** Prop a barrow up against a wall. Put a brick in front of the wheel, and fix the handles to the wall with bungee cords.

Keeping a hose
Punch four holes in the base of an old enamel basin, and screw it onto a large board. Screw the board to one wall of a garage or shed, then wrap the hose around the basin to keep it neat.

CLEARING A WORKSHOP
● **Utilizing work surfaces** Keep work surfaces clean and clear so that they are ready for use. Use shelves, or spaces under work surfaces, for storage.

Making a tool board
Wrap tools in plastic wrap, and lay on a board. Attach nails where the tools are to hang. Spray the tools and board with paint, and let dry. Unwrap the tools, then hang them in the marked places.

Solving Storage

Whe**HEN PLANNING STORAGE**, first assess which items must be near at hand and which are used only rarely. Lay out storage areas so that you can easily find everyday items, and utilize less accessible places for seldom-used objects.

Organizing Long-term Storage

For long-term storage, select areas out of the way of daily activities. Utilize all available spaces including rarely used containers such as luggage. For example, use suitcases for storing clothes; leave the clothes on a bed when you are away and using the suitcases.

Putting Away Clothes

Preserving delicate items
Fold white tissue paper carefully around delicate white clothes to protect the fabric from dirt, then wrap blue tissue paper over the white to block out light and keep the fabric from turning yellow.

Packing Other Items

● **Keeping blankets** Wrap woolen blankets in several sheets of newspaper. Seal the open edges of the paper with packing tape. This will protect the blankets from moths.
● **Protecting hats** Store hats in hat boxes, which can be kept in any dry place.
● **Keeping leather bags** Clean the outsides and insides of leather bags. Fill with tissue paper so that they keep their shape and do not crease. Put bags in a cardboard box, and store in a cool, dry place to protect the leather from mold.

TRADITIONAL TIP

Deterring moths
Cloth sachets of lavender will keep moths away from stored clothes and bedding. Hang the sachets in closets, and tuck them in stored fabrics.

Storing Rarely Used Items

You can use secluded or even hard-to-reach places, such as a loft or a high shelf, for storing things that you seldom need. To remind yourself where you have put an item, note its location on a sheet of paper, and file the paper with a home maintenance log if you have one.

Packing Fragile Items

Dividers separate glasses

Wrapping glasses
Pad the insides of glasses with bubble wrap, then wrap the outsides in more bubble wrap. Store the glasses in a wooden wine box that contains dividers for holding bottles securely.

Keeping Decorations

Wire lies flat on shape

Storing festive lights
Take a rectangular piece of stiff cardboard, and cut a large notch in each of the short sides to form an "H" shape. Wind the lights carefully around the center of the cardboard shape.

Storing for a Season

● **Packing clothes** Designate an area for clothes that you do not need for part of each year. For example, one space could hold sweaters in summer and thin clothes in winter. Wash the clothes, and make any repairs, before packing them.
● **Keeping leisure equipment** Some items used for a limited season, such as surfboards and skis, are bulky. Hang them in a shed or little-used part of the house. If you do not often use such items, consider renting them when necessary.

STORING FREQUENTLY USED ITEMS

Ideally, store frequently used items as close as possible to the places where you use them. If they are needed in several different areas, put them in portable containers, and carry them with you. Position the items in places that are easy to reach – preferably at about waist height.

KEEPING ESSENTIALS

The following is a list of items that you are likely to need every day. Keep them where you can find them instantly.

- Toiletries (see p. 34).
- Spectacles, if used.
- Medication, if needed.
- Outdoor wear.
- Clothes, shoes, and accessories for next day (see p. 33).
- Basic cooking equipment.
- Everyday foods.
- Cleaning fluids and rags.
- Towels.
- Keys for house and car.
- Equipment and papers for work.
- Equipment and books that children need to take to school with them.
- Sports equipment.
- Remote controls for audio equipment, television, and video cassette recorder.

GETTING READY

● **Preparing for the next day** Every evening, take out clothes, papers, and other objects that you will need for the next day. Put them in a place where you will see them easily the next morning.

● **Using lists** Each evening, make a list of objects that you need to find and errands for you to do the following day.

● **Checking personal items** Every time you use toiletries or cosmetics, ensure that they will be ready for use the next time. For example, renew used-up bars of soap, change blunt blades on razors, and sharpen blunt eye pencils.

● **Putting out breakfast items** Set the breakfast table with dishes and cutlery the night before, and put out containers of nonperishable items such as cereals and preserves.

STORING SUPPLIES

● **Setting out items** Decide which areas must be cleaned daily, such as the bathroom and the kitchen. Make up a set of cleaning supplies to be kept in each of these areas.

Making a carrier
Collect all the cleaning fluids, detergents, and rags that you will need to clean a particular room. Keep these items together in a sturdy container that you can carry around while you work, such as a bottle carrier.

STORING HOUSEHOLD OBJECTS SAFELY

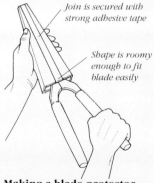

Join is secured with strong adhesive tape

Shape is roomy enough to fit blade easily

Making a blade protector
Trace the shape of a tool's blade onto cardboard. Turn the tool over; trace again. Cut around both shapes, allowing enough room to form sides for the protector. Bend the cardboard to fit the tool, then tape.

Keep fragile or dangerous items in places where people will not disturb them accidentally. Take care to put these objects out of reach of small children.

● **Protecting tools from damp** Keep tools in a cool, dry place. Never put them in a damp cellar or utility room or in a small kitchen, because the humidity could cause them to rust.

● **Locking items away** Fit locks to cabinets containing medicines or cleaning products to stop children from gaining access to them.

● **Positioning fragile objects** Keep breakable items out of reach of children. Make sure that these objects are not displayed where people are likely to brush against them or knock them over.

● **Protecting blades** Hang tools and kitchen implements with their blades pointing downward so that people will not injure themselves on the sharp edges.

● **Shielding points** Push corks onto the points of sharp items such as knives and skewers to stop the points from becoming blunt or injuring people.

● **Storing metal objects** Wrap sharp objects in cloth, or keep them on a magnetic rack. Do not store them in a drawer because they will become blunt through contact with other items.

● **Storing cleaning equipment** If you have small children, store cleaning fluids in high cabinets that children cannot reach. Use floor-level cabinets for buckets, dishpans, and rags.

RUNNING A HOUSEHOLD

QUICK REFERENCE
Personal Care, p. 33
Caring for Children, p. 36
Meeting Special Needs, p. 41
Arranging Medical Care, p. 43
Handling Crises, p. 46
Planning Events, p. 48
Transportation, p. 50
Planning Pet Care, p. 52

ORGANIZING YOUR HOME LIFE can be a complex operation, whether you have children to care for, hold down a demanding career, or have special physical needs. If you set up systems that run smoothly, you should find yourself with some free time to enjoy. Break down complex tasks into a number of simple jobs so that you can handle them easily, or delegate them to other members of your household. Plan carefully for major family events, and find out how to prepare yourself for any possible crises that may arise.

MAKING AND USING A HOUSEHOLD ORGANIZER

Make and display an organizer like the one below so that everyone in your household knows what they and the rest of the household will be doing each day. Use it not only for logging activities but also for listing any equipment needed for them, such as swimming gear or library books.

● **Using an organizer** Plan each week's activities in advance, and refer to the chart so that you do not forget details. Encourage the household to make a habit of updating the chart each evening.

Cut along lines drawn on photograph

Spread glue on underside of picture

1 Take a photograph of each member of your household. On each photograph, draw a square around the person's face, and – following the lines – cut out the face. Make sure that the trimmed photographs are all the same size.

2 On a piece of cardboard, draw a column for activities, then one for each photograph. Draw a row for each activity. Leave the first column empty, and glue the photographs to the tops of the other columns.

Symbols indicate regular activities

Members of household

Wipe chart clean with soft cloth every day

3 In the first column, draw a symbol for each activity. Cover the chart with clear adhesive plastic, and display it in a prominent place such as the kitchen wall. To fill it in, use a pen with ink that can be wiped off. Check the activities for each person on a particular day, and add any other details required.

ORGANIZING PERSONAL CARE

GOOD GROOMING IS AN IMPORTANT ELEMENT of personal organization. If you take the time to arrange your closet so that it is easy to present yourself neatly, you will feel confident and will make a good impression on other people.

PUTTING TOGETHER A CLOSET

Group clothes so you can find them easily. Keep frequently worn garments in the most accessible places. Do not hang clothes that need to be cleaned or mended. Instead, put them in a prominent place, and make time to deal with them as soon as possible.

GROUPING BELONGINGS

● **Grouping by use** Group casual clothes, dressy clothes, sports gear, and formal wear.
● **Matching accessories** Hang scarves on the same hangers as outfits. Group shoes, bags, belts, and gloves so that you can match them to outfits.
● **Matching jewelry** Make labels listing items of jewelry to wear with each outfit, and attach the labels to the hangers holding the relevant clothes. Use code words for valuable jewelry so that it cannot easily be identified by burglars.
● **Keeping outdoor wear** Hang coats by an outside door, rather than in a closet, so that they are easily accessible.

GROUPING BY COLOR

Coordinating clothes
Arrange clothes of each type (such as daywear or sportswear) into similar or complementary colors, so that you can select coordinated outfits quickly and easily from your closet.

CHOOSING CLOTHES

Check that your closet contains a selection of basic garments that you can mix and match to form outfits. Include the following items.

● Underwear for at least 2 weeks.
● 6 sets of sleepwear.
● 3 dressy skirts and/or pairs of pants.
● 5 dressy shirts or blouses.
● 5 casual shirts.
● 2 jackets.
● 2 sweaters.
● 3 pairs of dress shoes.
● 2 pairs of casual shoes.
● 1 dressy overcoat.
● 1 casual overcoat.
● Accessories.

TIMESAVING TIP

Assembling an outfit
The evening before an important occasion, assemble a complete outfit, including accessories, on a hanger. Hang it in a prominent place, and put the shoes underneath.

BUYING CLOTHING

● **Choosing colors** If you find a garment that fits and suits you, buy it in several colors.
● **Selecting underwear** Choose underwear that is not too tight or too loose. Avoid patterned items that may show under pants or pale colors.
● **Embellishing garments** If you are on a limited budget, buy inexpensive clothes, and dress them up by changing the buttons or adding decorations.
● **Buying for others** Record the measurements of all your family members in a diary. Before buying a garment for someone, refer to the figures to check the size.

KEEPING OLD CLOTHES

Rejuvenating coat sleeves
If the sleeves of a coat are short or frayed at the ends, but the rest still fits and is in good condition, sew a trim onto the cuffs to extend or dress up the sleeves. Attach the trim so that it extends beyond the end of each sleeve.

PLANNING PERSONAL GROOMING

It is important to set aside time every day to keep yourself clean and neat. Create a daily care routine that you can carry out quickly even when you are busy in the morning or tired in the evening. Keep your toiletries within easy reach in the bathroom or bedroom.

ESSENTIAL TOILETRIES

You need only a basic selection of toiletries. The items shown here should be sufficient. Choose brands that suit your skin and do not irritate it.

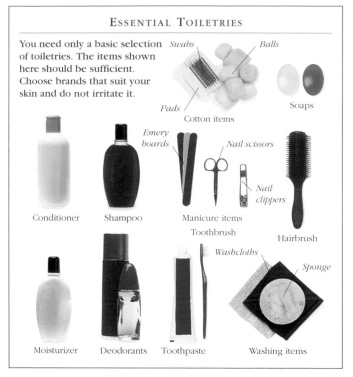

Swabs

Balls

Pads

Cotton items

Soaps

Conditioner

Shampoo

Emery boards

Nail scissors

Nail clippers

Manicure items

Hairbrush

Toothbrush

Washcloths

Sponge

Moisturizer

Deodorants

Toothpaste

Washing items

ARRANGING DAILY CARE
- **Keeping a portable kit** Make up a small toiletries kit to keep in your briefcase or handbag. Include basic items such as tissues, contact lens cleaners, toothbrush and toothpaste, and moisturizer.
- **Creating conditioner** If you have dry hair, beat one egg, and rub it into your hair. Leave for a few minutes, then rinse off with cold water.
- **Improvising dry shampoo** If you have no time to wash your hair, shake some talcum powder into your hand, and rub it into your scalp. Brush out the powder thoroughly.
- **Applying moisturizer** Use just enough to coat your skin. Excess moisturizer will not sink in and will not benefit you.
- **Refreshing your face** After cleaning, splash warm water on your face to refresh the skin.

USING LIPSTICK
- **Cleaning after use** Wipe lipstick with a tissue after every use to clean the surface and remove bacteria. Do this even if you use a lip brush.

Coat bristles of lip brush lightly with lipstick

Using up old lipstick
Make the best use of lipstick by removing the last traces with a lip brush. If the lipstick does not come away easily, stand the open lipstick container in a little hot water for a few minutes.

CARING FOR EQUIPMENT
- **Maintaining hairbrushes** Pull loose hair out of hairbrush bristles with a comb.
- **Preserving soap** Store soap in a dish that lets it drain, so that it will not become mushy.
- **Cleaning washcloths** Rinse washcloths after every use to prevent soap deposits from building up on them. Launder the washcloths once a week.
- **Storing scents** Keep perfume bottles in a dark place. If scent is exposed to light, it will discolor and deteriorate.
- **Cleaning equipment** Wash hairbrushes, combs, and makeup applicators once a week in a gentle shampoo.
- **Storing nail polish** Store nail polish in a refrigerator to keep it runny for use.

MONEY-SAVING TIP

Making moisturizer
Mix 1 tbsp each of vegetable oil, coconut oil, and olive oil with 2 tbsp crushed strawberries. Put the mixture into a clean, screw-topped jar, and store it in a refrigerator to keep it fresh. Use the moisturizer within 10 days.

Taking Time for Relaxation

Allow some time every week for pampering yourself. Listen to music, read, or take a long bath. Ask other people in your household not to disturb you. For deep relaxation, try one of the methods listed in the chart below. Seek expert advice before trying these techniques.

RELAXATION METHODS

METHOD	TECHNIQUE	BENEFITS
Yoga	Uses sequences of movements and breathing techniques.	Gently stretches and tones muscles, and reduces anxiety.
Meditation	Involves focusing on a specific word or image for about 10 minutes.	Improves thought processes and reduces stress level.
Progressive relaxation	Involves tensing, then relaxing, each part of the body in turn.	Reduces mental and physical tension. If practiced in bed, aids restful sleep.
Aromatherapy	Uses natural oils diluted in a base oil in a bath, or applied by massage.	Lessens stress. Used with expert advice, it can ease physical problems.
Massage	Involves relaxing muscles with types of touching and stroking.	Relieves stiff or tense muscles and comforts the mind.

MASSAGING TO REDUCE TENSION

● **Preparing for a massage** When you massage yourself or someone else, use a warm, quiet, softly lit room. Lie on a firm, padded surface such as a pile of blankets on the floor.

● **Using oil** To make your hands glide over the skin, use aromatherapy oil or a light cooking oil. Pour a tiny amount into one hand. Rub your hands to warm the oil before use.

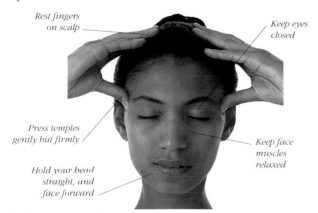

Rest fingers on scalp

Keep eyes closed

Press temples gently but firmly

Hold your head straight, and face forward

Keep face muscles relaxed

Giving yourself a relaxing facial massage

To begin the massage, put your hands over your face, hold for a moment, then stroke outward once. Using both hands, stroke the backs of your fingers up each cheek, from your mouth to your ear, 10 times. Stroke your forehead with your fingers, from your nose to your hairline, 10 times. Massage your temples by rubbing in small circles with your thumbs. To finish the massage, warm your eyelids with your palms, then put your hands over your face and stroke.

CALMING YOUR MIND

● **Getting exercise** Release tension in your body through activities such as swimming or walking. Exercise will improve the blood supply to your brain, helping you to clear your mind and lift your mood. It will also encourage restful sleep.

● **Breathing deeply** Sit or lie in a comfortable position. Take a deep breath, hold it for a few seconds, then breathe out. Let your abdomen as well as your chest move with your breath. Repeat for up to five minutes.

● **Using your thoughts** Sit or lie comfortably, then visualize a peaceful scene such as a sunlit beach. Imagine that you are there, sensing the light and warmth. Feel your body relax as your mind forms the image.

● **Listening to music** Play your favorite calming music. Wear headphones so that you can concentrate on the sound.

● **Popping bubble wrap** Dispel tension instantly by popping the bubbles in bubble wrap.

CARING FOR CHILDREN

W HETHER YOU TAKE CARE OF YOUR CHILDREN YOURSELF or pay someone to do it, you will have to adapt your lifestyle so that the children's needs come first. Advance planning will help you make the most of your resources.

ESSENTIAL EQUIPMENT FOR A NEWBORN BABY

The choice of baby equipment and clothes is considerable and can be bewildering. The items shown here make up the basic kit that you will need to care for a newborn baby.

● **Assembling equipment** If you cannot afford to buy everything at once, buy essentials such as clothes, diapers, and a bed before the baby arrives, and gradually buy the rest later.
● **Ensuring safety** Make sure that you choose equipment and clothes that are flame retardant.
● **Finding dual-purpose items** Look for items that will suit the baby as it grows. For example, choose a carriage that can be converted later into a stroller.
● **Sharing with others** Babies grow quickly, so their clothes may last only a few weeks. Buy secondhand garments from a consignment shop or thrift store, and in return pass on anything that your baby has outgrown.

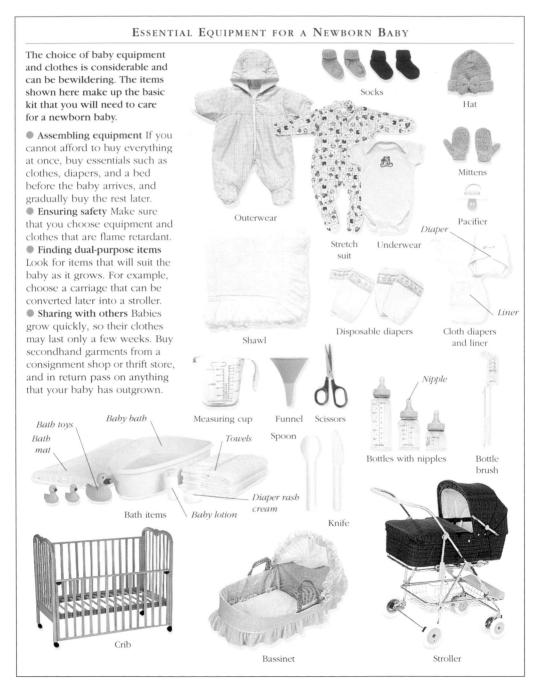

Socks

Hat

Mittens

Outerwear

Pacifier

Diaper

Stretch suit

Underwear

Liner

Shawl

Disposable diapers

Cloth diapers and liner

Nipple

Measuring cup

Funnel

Scissors

Spoon

Bottles with nipples

Bottle brush

Bath toys

Baby bath

Bath mat

Towels

Bath items

Baby lotion

Diaper rash cream

Knife

Crib

Bassinet

Stroller

ORGANIZING TIME WITH A BABY

Your child will be a baby for only a short time, so enjoy the experience – baby care need not consist solely of feeding, giving baths, and changing diapers. Babies like company, so spend time with yours, especially if you plan to start work outside the home after a few months.

SETTING UP A ROUTINE

● **Organizing daily activities** Establish a routine for feeding, diaper changing, sleep, and cuddling. This will minimize stress for you and the baby.

● **Checking body heat** Babies cannot regulate their body temperatures. Feel the back of the neck to make sure that a baby is not overly hot or cold.

● **Helping a baby to sleep** Do not let anyone overexcite a baby just before bedtime. An unsettled baby will not go to sleep – and neither will you.

● **Finding time to sleep** Fit your rest around your baby's sleep pattern, even if he or she tends to sleep during the day and be active at night. Use a baby monitor (see p. 38) to alert you if the baby wakes up.

BATHING A BABY

● **Timing baths** Young babies need a full bath only every two or three days. Set aside sufficient time to allow for play as well as washing.

Drying a baby easily
Before you start bathing a baby, tuck a towel into the waistband of your clothes. Once you have finished, lift the baby onto your lap, and wrap the towel around it.

ORGANIZING FEEDINGS

● **Preparing equipment** When bottle-feeding, sterilize bottles before use if your doctor recommends it. If not, clean bottles and all equipment thoroughly in hot soapy water.

● **Making feedings in batches** Prepare a whole day's formula at once, and store it in a refrigerator. Warm formula in a pot or cup of hot water, not in a microwave oven. Check that the feeding is the correct temperature by squeezing a few drops from a bottle onto the back of your hand.

● **Introducing solid food** When you cook for adults, save plainly cooked vegetables to feed to a baby. Purée and freeze in meal-sized portions. Reheat as needed.

CATERING FOR CHILDREN'S NEEDS

As children grow, it is important to make sure that they feel safe in their environment, while gradually making them aware of any potential dangers – first in the home and then outdoors. Supply as much stimulation as they need, without encouraging overexcitement.

STIMULATING A BABY

Decorating a portable crib
Tuck colorful cards and pictures around the inside of a crib to give a baby something to look at. A new baby is not likely to pull them out. If the baby grabs at the cards, remove them.

CARING FOR A TODDLER

● **Choosing clothes** Learning how to dress is a necessary skill that can also be fun for toddlers. Select clothes with simple fastenings such as touch-and-close tape, or large, colorful buttons.

● **Teaching through daily life** Let your child come with you while you do routine tasks around the house. Use the time to teach the child about his or her environment.

● **Coping with tantrums** The best way to deal with a small child having a tantrum is to leave the room. Tell the child why you are going, and return when the tantrum is over.

STARTING SCHOOL

Marking possessions
Label every object that a child takes to school, including cup and lunchbox. If a child cannot read, use blank labels in a bright color so that the child will be able to identify the objects easily.

KEEPING CHILDREN SAFE INDOORS

The family home can be a dangerous place for children, but with a little forethought you can prevent many accidents. Note the possible hazards in each room. Move harmful objects out of reach of children, and put gates across areas such as the top of a stairway.

CHILDPROOF SAFETY EQUIPMENT

In most cases, you can make areas safe just by rearranging the objects in them. However, to protect small children, you will need safety items as well, such as the pieces shown on the right.

● **Using safety gates** Install gates at the tops and bottoms of stairs. Make sure that the bars are vertical so that a child cannot climb them. Check that the gates have childproof locks.

● **Making a stovetop safe** Install a stove guard so that children cannot touch hot surfaces. Use the back burners whenever possible, and turn pan handles away from the front of the stove.

● **Testing a baby monitor** Check all parts regularly to see that they are working properly.

● **Fitting a door stop** Attach a stop to the top of a door so that a child cannot reach the stop.

Reins

Harness

Anchor straps

Harness and reins

Step for toilet

Toilet seat

Combined toilet seat and step

Safety gate

Receiver

Transmitter

Stove guard

Door stop

Baby monitor

BRIGHT IDEA

Using a box as a step
Keep an upturned box for a child to use as a step to reach a sink or toilet. Check that the box will bear the child's weight. Always supervise small children in the bathroom.

PREVENTING ACCIDENTS

● **Making a floor safe** Remove any loose rugs. Sand wooden flooring to remove splinters. Fit durable surfaces such as vinyl in areas used by children.

● **Preventing burns** Put guards in front of fireplaces and heaters. Make sure that a child cannot knock the guards over.

● **Fitting safe wires** Use coiled wires on electrical appliances. These wires take up little space, and should not dangle within reach of children.

● **Storing harmful items** Store items such as cleaning fluids and medicines in cabinets that a child cannot reach. When using the items, keep them away from the child.

● **Using stairs safely** When carrying a child up or down stairs, hold on to a banister.

CREATING A SAFE HOME

● **Securing doors** Install locks or high-up bolts to the doors of potentially hazardous rooms such as the kitchen. Keep the rooms locked when not in use.

Fit ball snugly on corner

Covering table corners
To protect each corner of a low table, make a dent in a ping-pong ball, then glue it to the wood. The balls will make the corners visible, and will act as shields if a child falls against the table.

KEEPING CHILDREN SAFE OUTDOORS

Most children enjoy playing outdoors and going on trips, but it can be difficult to keep them safe, since the hazards are less predictable than those in the home. Accompany your children whenever they leave the home, until they have learned the safety rules.

TAKING PRECAUTIONS

By following these simple pointers, you can help keep a child safe if he or she becomes separated from you.

● **Using telephones** Before going out, always check that your child knows emergency numbers, including your own, and has enough money for telephone calls.

● **Checking the surroundings** Teach children to spot street names or store names, so that they can tell the emergency services where they are if you do become separated.

● **Walking around** Teach a child to call the emergency services if they are lost.

● **Calling for help** Teach children to carry a loud whistle and to blow it if they are lost, in trouble, or being bothered by a stranger.

PREVENTING PROBLEMS

● **Arranging rides** If your child is at someone else's house, carry the telephone number of the house so that you can telephone immediately if you will not be able to pick up the child at the expected time.

● **Accepting rides** Teach a child never to accept a ride from a stranger, or to take a ride with someone they know, unless you have told the child about this in advance.

● **Using a code word** Agree on a special code word with your child so that, if you need another adult to pick them up, the child will know that the person has been sent by you.

● **Protecting teenagers** When teenage children go out, ask them to leave an address and contact telephone number.

USING TRANSPORTATION

● **Taking a child in a car** Always put a baby or child in the back seat of a car, and never in the front passenger seat of a car fitted with airbags. If a bag inflates, it could seriously harm the child's skull.

● **Using a car seat** Follow the manufacturer's instructions when securing a car seat to a back seat. Always keep the child strapped in. This will prevent the child from being thrown out of the seat if you have to brake suddenly.

● **Choosing a stroller** When buying a stroller, choose a type that has a high, padded seat, which will protect a child's head as well as its body. Test the brakes to make sure that they are effective.

MAKING PLAY SAFE

● **Adapting a garden** Remove or fence off any toxic plants in your garden. Do not let a child near any area that has been sprayed with chemicals.

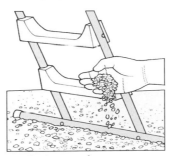

Surfacing a play area
If you have a swing or jungle gym in your garden, dig a shallow pit beneath it, and fill the pit with wood chips or fine sand. This will prevent children from being hurt if they slip or fall off.

TEACHING SAFETY

● **Crossing streets safely** When you cross streets with a child, teach them to choose crossing places away from curves or parked cars. Tell them to look both ways and to wait until the road is clear before crossing.

Making children visible
Select a bright- or pale-colored coat for a child. Stick or sew reflective shapes onto it. Be sure that the child wears it in poor light conditions, so that he or she is always visible to traffic.

SAFEGUARD TIP

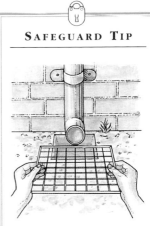

Covering a drain
If you have an open drain outside your home, attach an old oven tray or cooling rack over the hole so that children cannot drop objects into it or trap their feet inside it.

SETTING UP A CHILD-CARE ROUTINE

There are many types of caregivers, such as live-in helpers, home daycare providers, day centers, and baby-sitters for occasional help. Take time to choose the right caregiver for your child – the most important thing is that you and your child are happy.

EMPLOYING A LIVE-IN CAREGIVER

Set aside a few days for meeting candidates. Once you have made a choice, make a formal agreement with the caregiver.

● **Checking legal rights** To set fair pay and conditions, check caregivers' employment rights.
● **Agreeing hours** Discuss the hours that a caregiver will work, and which days she or he can have off. Make arrangements for weekends and holidays.

● **Defining duties** Write a list of child-care and household duties that you would like a caregiver to do. In return, ask what she or he is prepared or qualified to do. (For example, do not expect a nanny to do housework that is not directly linked to child care.)
● **Discussing money** Decide on payment and who will deal with insurance and tax. Tell a caregiver if she or he is to pay costs such as part of telephone bills.

● **Insuring your car** If a caregiver needs to use your car, include her on your insurance policy.
● **Allowing visitors** Say whether a caregiver may entertain guests. Tell the person if you object to visitors staying overnight.
● **Having a trial** Set a trial period of employment at the end of which you will both review the situation. Agree how much notice each side will give before ending the arrangement.

BEGINNING CARE

● **Testing a child's reaction** When you introduce a new caregiver to a child, leave the child with her or him for a short time. When you return, see if the child is happy.
● **Briefing a child** Tell a child to do what a caregiver asks unless this is something very unusual or unpleasant.
● **Following up** After the first day of care, ask the child what the caregiver did. You can then decide if the caregiver is suitable for the child.

CAREGIVER'S CHECKLIST

Give a caregiver details about a child, and safety tips.

● **Personality** Details on behavior and discipline.
● **Health** Information about allergies and other conditions.
● **Diet** What a child will eat.
● **Routines** When child is fed, bathed, and put to bed.
● **Telephone** Contact numbers for parents.
● **Emergencies** What to do.

USING DAYCARE

● **Looking for daycare** Ask friends with children the same age as yours whom they would recommend. Their advice is likely to be up-to-date and accurate.
● **Assessing daycare** Visit a daycare center or provider during the day to see how the facility is run. Ask about the ratio of staff to children.
● **Agreeing on care** Ask how children are fed and cared for, in case the daycare provider's views conflict with yours.
● **Discussing activities** Ask a home daycare provider if there are special activities for children, such as painting or visiting parks.
● **Dealing with illness** Make arrangements for looking after your child if the child is ill. A daycare provider will not usually care for sick children, and a child who feels unwell should not leave home.
● **Arranging informal care** If you employ a friend or a relative as a daycare provider, discuss payment, hours, and duties, as you would with a professional caregiver.

USING A BABY-SITTER

● **Employing a young person** Do not use anyone under the age of 14, because they may not be able to handle a crisis.
● **Giving advice** Advise a baby-sitter on how to cope if a child is ill or badly behaved.
● **Showing around** Show a baby-sitter where to find the first-aid kit and necessary items such as diapers.

BRIEFING A BABY-SITTER

Looking after a baby
When leaving a baby with a baby-sitter, check that the person knows how to handle the baby. For example, when they pick up a baby, ensure that they support its head and body securely.

MEETING SPECIAL NEEDS

I F YOU HAVE a condition such as arthritis or a physical disability, or if you care for someone in this situation, ask a doctor to suggest equipment to help with physical tasks In addition, find ways in which home life can be adapted.

EQUIPMENT FOR A PERSON WITH SPECIAL PHYSICAL NEEDS

The devices shown in this box are designed to aid tasks such as putting on socks, handling objects easily, or lifting items off the floor without bending down. Ask your doctor how to obtain such items to help with everyday life.

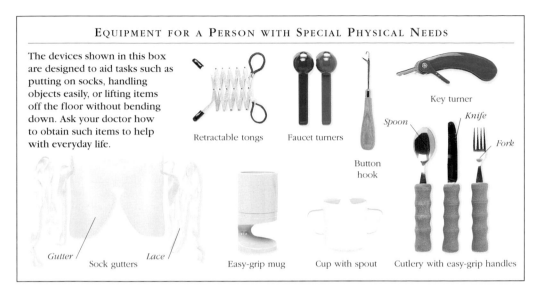

Retractable tongs

Faucet turners

Key turner

Button hook

Spoon

Knife

Fork

Gutter

Lace

Sock gutters

Easy-grip mug

Cup with spout

Cutlery with easy-grip handles

PRESERVING INDEPENDENCE

There are several ways to cope with physical problems such as reduced mobility, vision, or memory. Try the tips given below to make common tasks easier, or to adapt household routines. Even a few of these steps can increase one's ability to manage everyday life.

OPENING CONTAINERS

Opening a jar
If a jar has a screw-top lid, put two or three thick rubber bands around the body and lid so that it will be easy to grip when you open it. Alternatively, put on rubber gloves before opening it.

TAKING EXERCISE

Keeping hands supple
To prevent stiffness in your hands, squeeze a large binder clip several times with each hand. Keep your fingers away from the open end of the clip. Do this exercise once or twice a day.

MANAGING DAILY LIFE
● **Choosing bedding** Select a comforter and a fitted sheet for ease of use. Check that you can open and close the snaps on the comforter cover.
● **Prompting memory** Attach large labels to drawers and cabinets with a list of their contents to give an instant reminder when necessary.
● **Marking faucets** Paint hot water faucets with red nail polish to make them visible.
● **Buying an electric kettle** If buying a kettle, choose a cordless type for safety.
● **Monitoring heat** Keep easy-to-read thermometers in rooms that you use daily. The rooms should be at least 70°F (21°C).

MODIFYING A HOME

If you are elderly or have a disability, you may be able to have your home adapted so that you can lead an independent life. You can equip your home with special aids such as a chairlift for a staircase, and you can also make inexpensive items for use every day.

ADAPTING OBJECTS
● **Typing recipes** The measures in most recipes are intended to make dishes for several people. Reduce the quantities to suit one or two, then have the recipes typed in large type. Store them in a ring binder.
● **Lengthening a shoe horn** Attach a bamboo cane securely to a standard shoe horn, so that you can use it without bending to reach your feet.
● **Adapting implements** Cut up an old bicycle inner tube, and slide lengths of it over the handles of tools or kitchen implements. Glue the lengths in place to make easy-grip surfaces for the handles.
● **Improvising a duster** If you have stiff hands, use a sock as a duster. Slip the sock over your hand, spray it with polish, and stroke surfaces clean.

SAFEGUARD TIP

Modifying a stairway
Install a second stair rail on the wall opposite an existing banister, so that those using the stairs can steady themselves with both hands. Make the existing rail safe.

CREATING USEFUL ITEMS
● **Making a knee protector** Stick several layers of bubble wrap to a piece of board. This makes a comfortable surface to kneel on for gardening.

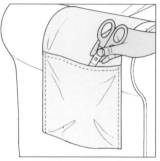

Sewing a chair pouch
Cut a length of narrow canvas. Fold up one end, and stitch along the outside edges. Sew curtain weights to the other end. Drape over the arm of a chair, and use the pocket to keep small items.

CHOOSING EQUIPMENT
● **Aiding mobility** Install grip bars to walls around a bath and a toilet, and in frequently used areas. Hold the handles to steady yourself while using the bathroom or walking around.
● **Buying kitchen appliances** Check that you can operate the controls of kitchen appliances. Choose types that have lights to show when they are on.
● **Using an electric blanket** Select a UL-listed blanket. Do not leave electric blankets on for long periods, and avoid the blankets during pregnancy.
● **Using alarms** Install an alarm linked to a neighbor's house or a care center. Alternatively, wear a personal alarm on a pendant so that you can attract instant help from passers-by.

ADAPTING ROOMS
● **Altering layout** If you find it difficult to climb stairs but cannot afford a chairlift, and you have a toilet on the ground floor, turn a downstairs room into a bedroom. Use top-floor rooms for long-term storage.
● **Choosing new lighting** If you need to put in lights that are brighter than those that you already have, consider using halogen spotlights to brighten dim corners of rooms.
● **Working in a kitchen** Use an office chair on casters so that you can sit at a comfortable height while preparing food, and move around without standing up. Never stand or kneel on a chair with casters.
● **Showering in comfort** Place a sturdy plastic stool on a rubber suction mat to provide seating in a shower.

ENSURING SAFETY
● **Making floors safe** Check that floor surfaces have no uneven or broken patches. Avoid using loose rugs, or add nonskid backing.

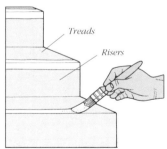

Treads

Risers

Making steps visible
Paint a white or luminous strip along the edges of uncarpeted steps, using good-quality outdoor paint so that the markings will last. Paint the treads (flat parts) and the risers (vertical parts).

ARRANGING MEDICAL CARE

BEFORE YOU DECIDE ON A DOCTOR, find out who practices at the doctor's office and what the appointment system is. Discuss any preferences that you have, such as seeing a doctor of the same sex or a specialist in pediatric care.

SEEING A DOCTOR

Unless it is an emergency, make doctor's appointments at least one week in advance, when the office is likely to have a range of times to offer you. Remember that there may be a delay before you are able to see the doctor, so take something to occupy yourself.

PLANNING A VISIT

Make a list of points you need to raise with your doctor.

- **Symptoms** Pain. Changes in temperature, bodily functions, eating and drinking habits, appearance, or energy levels. Stress or depression.
- **Reactions and feelings** Allergies, reactions to any medicines taken.
- **Requests** Prescription to be renewed or sick note needed.

UTILIZING TIME

- **Giving information** Record medical facts about yourself and your family in a diary. The doctor may ask about family medical history when treating illnesses, so take these notes with you for instant reference.
- **Dressing for comfort** If you are likely to undergo a physical examination or have your blood pressure taken, wear clothing that you can easily adjust or remove.

TALKING TO A DOCTOR

- **Describing symptoms** Use plain language, rather than medical jargon. Mention all symptoms, not just those that you believe are relevant.
- **Letting children talk** Let a child describe his symptoms before you add details.
- **Concluding an appointment** Be sure that you understand the doctor's recommendations on treatment. Ask for extra information if available.

ORGANIZING HOME MEDICINES

Keep a basic medical kit in a safe place so that you can treat minor wounds and ailments yourself. Check the kit regularly, and replace items before they are completely used up. Return any expired or unused medicines to a pharmacy to ensure safe disposal.

STOCKING MEDICAMENTS

- **Pain relief** Always keep painkillers (acetaminophen or aspirin); they will also lower a raised temperature. In addition, include a nonsteroidal anti-inflammatory drug (NSAID) such as ibuprofen. For children, keep acetaminophen syrup; never give them aspirin, except on medical advice.
- **Soothing creams** Keep an antihistamine cream for stings and bites, an antiseptic cream for cuts and scrapes, and an emollient cream for dry skin.
- **Stomach settlers** Stock antacid pills or liquid for indigestion. Keep oral rehydration formula to give to children who have diarrhoea and vomiting.

MAINTAINING SAFETY

- **Keeping dressings sterile** Keep all bandages, dressings, and eye pads in their original wrappers. They should be sterile when applied.
- **Removing hazards** Make sure that sharp scissors or glass thermometers cannot fall from shelves, causing injury.
- **Protecting children** Always buy products with "child-proof" tops in case children get into the medicine cabinet.
- **Sharing medicines** Never take medicine that have been prescribed for someone else, even if your symptoms appear similar. Always complete a course of treatment that has been prescribed for you.

REMEMBERING MEDICINES

- **Using a system** If you find it difficult to remember to take medicines, employ a system to help draw attention to them.

Put pills for each dose together

Labels show days and time

Sorting a week's doses
Put doses of pills in film canisters, which keep out air and light. Label the lids to show day and time to be taken. Keep out of reach of children.

MAKING A FAMILY HEALTH LOG

Organize all the health information for each family member to make a log for quick reference. Update each person's data regularly. Keep the log in a ring binder, together with other important medical information such as vaccination certificates and test results.

INFORMATION TO INCLUDE IN A FAMILY HEALTH LOG			
TYPE OF INFORMATION	DETAILS TO RECORD	DATES AND TIMES TO REMEMBER	TREATMENTS TO FOLLOW
Personal details	● **Physical data** Note each person's sex, birth date, height, and weight. ● **Blood group** Make a note of the blood group. ● **Allergies** List any food, drug, or object causing allergies, and the resulting symptoms.	● **Eye and hearing tests** Record the dates of the next appointments. ● **Medications** Note the dates for renewing any repeat prescriptions. ● **Children's data** Note the dates of checkups on children's development.	● **Medications** Record name and dosage of any regular medications. ● **Eyesight** Note the details of prescriptions for glasses or contact lenses. ● **Allergies** Note any preventative action to take for allergies.
Medical appointments	● **Symptoms** Make a list of any symptoms that you need to discuss with a doctor (see p. 43). ● **Causes** Make a note of external factors that may influence symptoms, such as poor air quality.	● **Appointments** Note the dates of forthcoming medical appointments. ● **Inoculations** Record the dates and types of inoculations for children. ● **Results** Note when any test results are due.	● **Medication** Note the dosage of recommended medications, and any other relevant details. ● **Routines** Note any changes suggested by a doctor, such as changes in diet or exercise habits.
Hospital visits	● **Information** Record the name and contact number of the hospital. ● **Reference** If a hospital assigns a reference number to a patient, write down this number.	● **Operations** Note the dates of operations, and specify what was done. ● **Emergencies** Record the dates and purposes of any emergency visits to the hospital.	● **Treatment** Record the details of treatment given at the hospital. ● **Time in the hospital** If a hospital stay is necessary, note the duration of the stay.
Illnesses or injuries	● **Details** Write down the symptoms of illness or the signs of injury. Note the date when the problem first appeared. ● **Causes** Record the cause of an illness or injury, if known.	● **Tests** Note the nature of any tests carried out, and the dates when the results are due. ● **Return visits** Write down the dates of any additional appointments for treatment.	● **Action** Ask medical staff for guidelines on coping with the illness or injury at home. ● **Side effects** Record the details of any benefits or side effects resulting from the treatment.
Dental checkups	● **Information** List the details of any problems to discuss with a dentist. ● **Children's teeth** Note when baby teeth and adult teeth emerge in children. Keep records of any problems.	● **Appointments** Note the next appointments with a dentist or a dental hygienist. ● **Major events** Note the dates of any operations, or when dentures are due to be replaced.	● **Routines** Note any suggestions given by a dentist or hygienist, such as changes in daily care. ● **Treatments** Give the details of treatments such as operations or the fitting of braces.

VISITING A HOSPITAL

Try to prepare for a hospital stay so that you will have all the necessary supplies with you. If you are to visit someone else who is in the hospital, check the preferred visiting times before you go, and take items to make the person's stay pleasant, as well as necessities.

PREPARING TO STAY

● **Obtaining extra supplies** If it is allowed, arrange for foods, such as fruits, to be brought to you every few days by family or friends.

Stocking a freezer
You may well feel too fatigued to cook when you return from the hospital, so cook, label, and freeze meals in single portions before you go. Defrost and reheat them as required.

SUPPLIES TO PACK FOR A HOSPITAL STAY

You are unlikely to have much storage space in the hospital, so pack only necessary items. However, days in the hospital can seem long and tedious, so include items to keep you occupied during your stay, such as a personal stereo and some music, a variety of reading matter, or materials for writing letters.

● **Taking medication** If you are on regular medication, take it with you and hand it to hospital staff for them to administer.

Earphones

Personal stereo   Medication   Moisturizer

Underwear

Slippers   Pajamas   Book

CARING FOR A CHILD

● **Providing news** Ask family and friends to record cassettes telling a sick child what is going on at home and at school. This will reassure the child that he or she is not forgotten.
● **Taking reminders of home** Place photographs of family, pets, and friends on a child's bedside table, and put a favorite cuddly toy in the bed.
● **Bringing extra meals** If a child is not eating hospital food, ask whether you may bring a few meals from home to encourage the child to eat.
● **Planning the trip home** Plan nice things for a sick child to do after returning home. However, do not discuss with a child when he or she might return until you know for sure, to avoid disappointment.

ORGANIZING GIFTS

Pack items in gift bag

Packing treats for a child
Fill a small bag with items such as a toy, a sketch pad, crayons, and pieces of fruit. Label the items with each day of a child's hospital stay. Tell the child to take out only one item each day.

VISITING A PATIENT

● **Arranging a visit** Call a patient's family before visiting to find out how the patient feels. Some people prefer to have no visitors for a few days after treatment because they become tired easily.
● **Considering other visitors** If you are one of several visitors, try to coordinate your arrival and departure times so that you are not all there at once, and keep visits short.
● **Comforting a patient** Do not feel obliged to be cheerful all the time. Simply sitting quietly with a patient may be enough to be comforting.
● **Taking children** Young children can easily become bored when visiting the hospital or waiting. Take quiet activities to occupy them.

HANDLING CRISES

B Y KNOWING WHAT TO DO in a particular crisis, you can limit damage and find suitable professional help. Find out in advance how to deal with problems, since it can be difficult to think clearly in the midst of a tense situation.

HANDLING CRISIS SITUATIONS

CRISIS	ACTION	PREVENTION
Assault/ rape	● **Contact police** Inform the police immediately. Do not wash yourself or change your clothes – your appearance may provide vital evidence. ● **Seek medical help** Have any injuries treated that day or the next morning. Ask someone to take you for treatment – you may be too shocked to go by yourself. ● **Make notes** Write down everything that you can remember about an attack. ● **Ask for support** Call a relative or friend for practical help and moral support. ● **Maintain confidence** Make yourself go out in public as soon as you can so that you will not lose your confidence.	● **Secure your car** Lock your car when you are inside it. Roll up windows before you stop at traffic lights. ● **Dress comfortably** If you are a woman, cover revealing clothing. Wear flat shoes so that you can walk comfortably. ● **Look confident** Check your route beforehand. Walk briskly. Be calmly aware of what is going on around you. ● **Shake off followers** If you suspect that someone is following you, walk away, cross the street, or go into a store. ● **Plan in advance** Find your keys before you reach your house, so that you do not have to linger on the doorstep.
Theft/ mugging	● **Avoid violence** If a mugger becomes violent, hand over your money or purse immediately. If you resist and struggle with the person, you may be injured. ● **Contact police** Find a police officer as soon as possible. Ask police for a report on the crime for insurance purposes. ● **Contact your bank** Cancel any credit or debit cards, and let the bank know if your checkbook has been stolen. ● **Make notes** Try to write down as much as you can remember about the attacker's appearance. Note where you were attacked; the mugger may target other people in the same area.	● **Dress sensibly** Wear comfortable clothes, and dress in a way that will not attract attention to yourself. Avoid wearing a lot of jewelry or any other expensive items, such as a gold wristwatch. ● **Organize cash** If you will be visiting an area where muggers are known to operate, carry some loose cash in an inexpensive purse or wallet. If you are attacked, hand this over. ● **Protect valuables** If you are on vacation and have to carry valuable items such as a passport or travelers' checks, conceal these items in a money belt or inside a hidden pocket.
Burglary	● **Repel burglars** If burglars are still in your home, make a noise to scare them away. Do not confront them. ● **Contact police** Contact the police immediately. Do not disturb the scene of the crime until the police have finished examining it. Ask them to write a report for you to send to your insurers. ● **Contact your insurers** Telephone immediately. If nobody is there, leave a message stating the time of the burglary. ● **Change locks** If entry has been forced or you suspect that the burglar may have a key, change the locks immediately.	● **Replace locks** Change the locks as soon as you move into a new home, or if your keys are stolen. ● **Lock up securely** Lock windows and doors whenever you go out. If you feel vulnerable, lock outside doors even when you are in the house. ● **Make your home look occupied** Before going away, put timers on light switches in heavily used rooms. If you go out for a short time, leave a radio or television on. ● **Hide valuables** Situate expensive or valued items so that opportunist burglars cannot see them through windows.

HANDLING PERSONAL TRAUMAS

TRAUMA	ACTION	PROBLEM PREVENTION
Loss of work	● **Finding another job** Reassess your abilities and experience, update your resume, and turn your search for new employment into a project. ● **Filling time** Plan your time on a day-to-day and week-by-week basis. Set yourself tasks – even reading a newspaper. ● **Retraining** Learn a new skill that will complement your previous profession or is something you have always wanted to do, such as speaking a foreign language. ● **Sorting finances** Talk to your bank and other financial institutions if you anticipate difficulties in making payments. ● **Working in the interim** Consider alternative kinds of work, or voluntary work, on a temporary basis.	● **Keeping active** Make sure that you take regular exercise, maintain your appearance to boost your confidence, and have regular changes of scene. ● **Feeling positive** Learn how to cope with negative feelings about your abilities and self-worth. ● **Adjusting to others** If you are spending a lot more time with family members, allow each other space and time for readjustment to new roles. ● **Realizing ambitions** Look upon the turn of events as an opportunity to learn new skills and take up new interests. ● **Treating yourself** Buy yourself a small treat, especially if you are feeling low, even if it is just a bunch of flowers.
Relationship breakdown	● **Making practical arrangements** If you are unable to stay in your home, find a temporary sanctuary while you sort out the problem. If you have financial or other difficulties, seek qualified advice. ● **Reassuring children** However young the children involved are, keep them informed, answer their questions honestly, and stress the positive aspects of the family that will not change. ● **Considering counseling** Seek the help of professionals if you need advice about your legal rights and obligations, if you want marriage counseling or conciliatory arbitration, and if you need personal counseling or therapy.	● **Expressing feelings** Expect a range of emotions – whether you instigated the separation or you are the rejected partner – including shock, anger, guilt, and grief. Do not suppress them. ● **Making decisions** Do not be rushed into making important decisions about your future while you are very upset. ● **Gaining perspective** Try to balance distorted thoughts about the world being full of couples or your ex-partner's unparalleled virtues with positive, more realistic appraisals. ● **Keeping busy** Distract yourself by keeping fit, going out with friends, or thinking up a new project.
Bereavement	● **Reporting a death** Call out a doctor to confirm the death of someone at home. ● **Organizing papers** Obtain a death certificate from the person's doctor, register the death with the local registrar, and, if you have no instructions about the deceased's will, contact his or her bank or lawyer for any information. ● **Informing family and friends** Use the deceased's address book to make sure that everyone is informed of the death. ● **Planning a funeral** Make any arrangements that the deceased has requested. Alternatively, organize a ceremony that you think would be appropriate. Arrange a wake or simple gathering for mourners after the funeral.	● **Seeing the body** Ask to view the body of the deceased if you believe that this will help you to accept the death. ● **Expressing grief** Acknowledge your emotions, and allow yourself to express them. Take your time over grieving. ● **Talking to family and friends** Discuss your loss and reminisce with people who knew the deceased. ● **Looking after yourself** Do not neglect yourself physically, and ask friends for help if you feel lonely or unable to cope. ● **Accepting change** When you are ready, acknowledge the changes to your circumstances by instigating other changes yourself – such as taking up a new hobby or doing a course.

PLANNING EVENTS

ORGANIZE FAMILY CELEBRATIONS METICULOUSLY so that they run smoothly, with no crises or sudden changes of plan. Carry out all of the necessary tasks as far in advance as possible, so that you can relax and enjoy the occasion.

ORGANIZING A WEDDING

Allow plenty of time for planning so that you can be sure to have the arrangements that you would like. Halls, caterers, and florists are usually booked up a long time in advance, so you may need to make arrangements with them up to a year before the wedding date.

COORDINATING PLANS

● **Organizing tasks** Write out a countdown list that states the nature and time of each task to be done, so that all of the arrangements are made at the right time. Check off tasks as you complete them.
● **Choosing guests** Make a provisional guest list with your partner. Allow roughly equal numbers of guests for each of your families.
● **Ordering clothes** If you are having clothes made, allow sufficient time for fittings.
● **Preparing maps** Draw simple maps showing how to reach the wedding venues. Include a map with each invitation.

THINGS TO REMEMBER

Whatever your wedding plans, be sure to include the following main elements.

● Participants.
● Marriage certificate.
● Official.
● Guests.
● Presents.
● Ceremony site.
● Reception site.
● Catering, music, flowers.
● Accommodations for wedding couple and guests.
● Honeymoon: insurance, travel, and accommodations.
● Clothing, hair styling, makeup.
● Transportation.
● Photography.

ARRANGING A CEREMONY

● **Planning a religious service** Reserve the church or temple and official well in advance. If there are other weddings on that day, contact the families involved to ask if you can share flowers and decorations.
● **Choosing a site** You can have a religious ceremony in places other than a church or synagogue. For example, you may wish to use a historic house or a garden.
● **Planning a secular service** You can use an official form of ceremony or write a service yourself. Arrange to have an official witness or a registrar present to certify the marriage.

WORKING OUT EXPENSES

● **Planning a budget** Find out the cost of every element in advance, down to minor items such as stationery. Choose a range of options for each, and compare prices and quality.
● **Controlling food costs** If you intend to use a caterer, take care to keep track of the costs. Ask the caterer for a written estimate specifying what is included in the price.
● **Trimming costs** If you have a limited budget, look for ways in which to reduce costs. For example, ask family or friends to help with preparing food, grow your own plants for displays, or design and print stationery on a computer.

TRADITIONAL TIP

Making a gift for guests
Prepare small cloth bags of Jordan almonds or potpourri as "favors" for the guests at a wedding. Give out the favors after the wedding meal.

PLANNING A RECEPTION

● **Choosing a site** Try to choose a reception place that is not far from the ceremony site, so that guests will not have to travel a long way.
● **Selecting food** Decide how formal the reception will be, so that you know whether to plan finger food, a buffet, or a full service with waiters.
● **Ordering drinks** Ask for more than you think you need. Suppliers will often take back any unopened bottles.
● **Listing presents** Ask a friend or relative to mark the name of the giver on the label of each wedding present so that you will be able to write thank-you letters after the wedding.

COUNTING DOWN THE DAYS TO A WEDDING

As soon as you have fixed a wedding date, start to book major elements such as the place for the ceremony, and notify anyone whom you would like to assist with the wedding. The chart below gives numbers of days before a wedding and suggests arrangements to make at these times.

180

- **Documents** Arrange marriage license.
- **Attendants** Select and notify people.
- **Guests** Draw up list.
- **Ceremony** Choose place, service, and official.
- **Reception** Reserve place/entertainment.
- **Catering** Reserve chefs and serving staff.
- **Transportation** Make arrangements for all participants.
- **Clothing** Order clothes and order rings.
- **Wedding night** Book hotel.
- **Honeymoon** Book hotel and travel.
- **Stationery** Order wedding invitations.

90

- **Guests** Send invitations.
- **Presents** Register for presents at stores.
- **Catering** Plan menu with caterers. Order drinks and wedding cake.
- **Clothing** Advise guests to order formal dress.
- **Flowers** Ask florists for quotations for displays.
- **Honeymoon** Make any further arrangements.

30

- **Guests** Call if they have not replied to invitations.
- **Accommodation** Book hotel rooms for guests.
- **Bride** Book hairdresser and makeup stylist.
- **Reservations** Reconfirm details with any places with whom you have made reservations.

14

- **Clothing** Arrange fittings for wedding outfits. See that all participants have required accessories.
- **Reception** For a formal meal, draw up a seating plan.

7

- **Ceremony** Reserve rehearsal time with people involved in ceremony.
- **Presents** Organize collection of presents on the wedding day.

1

- **Car rental** Confirm collection times for next day.
- **Evening** Have a light supper. Go to bed early.

ARRANGING FAMILY CELEBRATIONS

While family events such as anniversaries do not usually require as much work as a wedding, it is still important to organize them efficiently. Make a plan, and organize helpers. Provide foods and entertainment to suit all of the guests, bearing in mind different age groups.

ORGANIZING AN EVENT

- **Planning a formal event** For a formal occasion such as a baptism, make a detailed plan including guests to be invited, site, food, and other details.
- **Involving children** If a child is to be the center of a formal event, explain to him or her what the occasion entails. Involve the child's siblings as well – give them duties to do on the day, and put aside small presents for them so that they do not feel left out.
- **Celebrating achievements** Plan ahead so that if a child gets good grades or wins a sports event, you can surprise him or her by having a simple celebration.

CREATING A THEME

Spread twigs so that you can see color

Choosing a color

For a special anniversary, choose decorations in an appropriate color. For a golden wedding anniversary, spray bare twigs gold and arrange them in a vase to make an attractive display.

MAKING PREPARATIONS

If you are organizing an intimate family occasion, it is best to create a relaxed atmosphere where everyone can easily mingle and enjoy themselves, rather than making complex plans.

- **Guests** If you are holding a family event at home, do not invite so many people that your home will be uncomfortably crowded.
- **Food** When doing your own cooking, make some dishes beforehand and freeze them. Buy some ready-made dishes as well, so that you do not need to spend a lot of time in the kitchen.

TRANSPORTATION

FAMILY VEHICLES CAN RANGE FROM VALUABLE CARS to inexpensive, secondhand bicycles. Whatever types of vehicle you own, keep them in good condition and protect them from theft so that they will have long working lives.

USING VEHICLES

Take care of motor vehicles so that they will be safe and reliable. Have them serviced regularly. Read the owner's manuals to learn how to maintain them correctly. When a vehicle runs well, make a note of its performance so that you can learn to spot any problems.

MAINTAINING CARS

● **Correcting problems** As soon as you notice a problem, arrange to have it repaired. Do not ignore it, even if the problem seems minor.

● **Building up a tool set** When buying tools, start with only those items that you will need for basic car maintenance. Buy additional tools only if you are sure that you will use them regularly.

● **Cleaning interiors** If you or any regular passengers suffer from car sickness, spray the interior of your car with anti-static spray after cleaning. This will stop the accumulation of static electricity, which can make some people feel ill.

MAKING REGULAR CHECKS ON CARS	
INSPECTING A CAR	PREPARING TO DRIVE
Make the following checks to be sure that your car is in good condition and safe to drive.	Immediately before driving a car, always carry out the following safety checks.
● **Brakes** Test the brakes. Add brake fluid if necessary. ● **Glass** See that all mirrors and windows are clean. ● **Lights** See that lights work. Replace blown-out bulbs. ● **Tires** Check that tread is not damaged or overly worn. ● **Oil** Check the oil level, and add more if necessary. ● **Radiator** Check the water level. Add more if necessary. ● **Battery** Check the fluid level. Add distilled water if necessary.	● **Doors** Check that all doors are securely closed. ● **Driver's seat** Check that you are comfortable. Make sure that you can see all around and that you can reach controls. ● **Mirrors** Make sure that rearview and sideview mirrors are all correctly adjusted. ● **Gas** Check that you have enough gas for the trip. ● **Seat belts** Make sure that you and any passengers are wearing seat belts.

LOADING MOTORCYCLES

Load is balanced over rear wheel so that weight is supported

Saddle space is clear for rider

Bag on tank is clear of handlebars

Panniers are compact to minimize wind resistance

Load is clear of exhaust pipe

Tires are well inflated to cope with extra load

Carrying luggage safely on a motorcycle
Load luggage onto a motorcycle so that it does not interfere with the flow of air around you while you are in motion. The load should be no wider than the rider and should not overbalance the rear of the motorcycle. Check that the luggage does not hamper the wheels.

CHECKING MOTORCYCLES

● **Checking mechanical brakes** Look at the brake cables to see if they have stretched. If so, have them adjusted.

● **Checking hydraulic brakes** Examine the brakes to be sure that they are not leaking fluid.

● **Inspecting wheels** Regularly check the nuts and bolts on wheels to make sure that they are sufficiently tight.

● **Examining treads** Follow the tread pattern all around each tire to be sure that the pattern is complete. If parts of it have worn away, replace the tire.

● **Maintaining an engine** Have the engine serviced regularly so that it works efficiently.

MAINTAINING BICYCLES

Bicycles are a convenient, environmentally friendly form of transportation. Bicycles need much less care than cars or motorcycles, but you must maintain them properly to keep them in peak running condition. Be sure to lock your bicycle whenever you are not using it.

CHECKING BICYCLES FOR SAFETY

● **Testing brakes** As you ride, suddenly apply and release both brakes. They should grip the wheels instantly, allowing no further movement.

● **Checking a saddle** If you remove the saddle, check it once you have replaced it to make sure that it is tight. You should not be able to move it.

Saddle is straight and secure

Brake cables are securely fixed to frame

Brake blocks are aligned with wheel rim

Tire treads are in good condition

Chain is taut

Spokes are straight

Wheels are straight

Examining a bicycle

See that a bicycle frame is aligned and undamaged. Check that the wheels are true, and that the spokes are straight. If the bicycle has mudguards, make sure that they fit correctly. Look for any cracks in the tires, then check the inner tubes to see that they are in good condition. Make sure that the chain links are lubricated.

SAFEGUARD TIP

Marking a bicycle frame
Scratch the number and zip code of your home on one or two hidden areas like the frame under the saddle and the back wheel rim. Photograph the identification, and note the parts of the bicycle shown.

LOCKING BICYCLES

● **Locking wheels** If you use a lock on a chain, thread the chain through both wheels as well as around the frame to make it difficult to remove. Alternatively, equip your bicycle with two locks to secure both wheels from theft.

● **Removing parts** If your bicycle is fitted with quick-release mechanisms for removing the saddle and front wheel, practice using them to avoid having any difficulty at your destination.

● **Removing accessories** When you leave a bicycle unattended, remove any valuable accessories such as lights or panniers.

● **Decorating a frame** Paint colorful designs on a bicycle frame, or cover it with strongly adhesive colored stickers or tape. This will make the bicycle a less attractive target for thieves.

ESSENTIAL BICYCLE MAINTENANCE EQUIPMENT

The equipment shown below is necessary for general cleaning tasks and simple repairs. Refer to a bicycle manual to see if you will need any specialized tools for carrying out repairs.

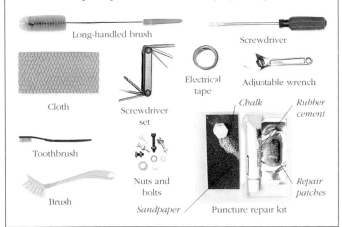

Long-handled brush

Screwdriver

Cloth

Electrical tape

Adjustable wrench

Screwdriver set

Chalk

Rubber cement

Toothbrush

Nuts and bolts

Repair patches

Brush

Sandpaper

Puncture repair kit

PLANNING PET CARE

Pets make excellent companions for single people. They are also good for children, who can learn useful life skills through caring for them. Whatever animal you choose, make sure that you can give it the attention that it needs.

KEEPING CATS AND DOGS

Cats are independent animals, requiring little more than regular feeding and a litter box. However, they do need human attention if they are to be happy. Dogs need regular exercise and can become miserable if left alone, so do not have one if you are out all day.

ADAPTING YOUR HOME

Push cinnamon sticks firmly into soil

Discouraging digging
If a potted plant is within reach of a cat or dog, put cinnamon sticks or strips of lemon peel into the soil. Animals dislike the smell, so they will be unlikely to dig up the soil or chew the plants.

ORGANIZING CARE

● **Selecting carers** Before you buy an animal, agree who in the household will look after it. If you share tasks, draw up a roster so that people take turns in caring for a pet.
● **Setting rules** Take special care of a new animal so that it feels secure in its new home. Do not be overly indulgent or encourage bad habits.
● **Planning a diet** Ask a pet's breeder or previous owner for guidelines on diet. Introduce any new foods gradually, so you do not upset the animal.

CALMING PETS

Soothing a restless puppy
If a new puppy cries at night, wrap a ticking clock in a soft towel, and put it in the puppy's bed. The quiet, regular noise is like the mother's heartbeat and will comfort the animal.

TAKING CARE OF RODENTS

Rodents, such as rabbits, hamsters, and mice, are easy to keep. However, these animals are often nervous, so handle them with care – otherwise they may bite. Some can be let out to play for a time, but watch them to make sure that they do not escape.

※ **BRIGHT IDEA**

Providing toys
Use large marbles and plastic spools as sturdy, inexpensive toys for small rodents such as guinea pigs, hamsters, and gerbils.

KEEPING MICE

Small bowl half-filled with vinegar

Neutralizing odors
Mice always smell, even if their cage is regularly cleaned. To absorb odors, put a bowl of vinegar by a cage with mice in it. Change the vinegar regularly.

CARING FOR RODENTS

● **Placing a hutch or cage** Put an outdoor cage in a place that is free from drafts and safe from predators. If a rodent lives indoors, try not to keep it in a bedroom because rodents may be noisy at night.
● **Providing company** Before buying a rodent, find out whether the species prefers to live alone or with others. For example, hamsters are solitary, but rabbits need company.
● **Handling a rodent safely** Do not hold a rodent a long way off the ground, because it could be killed if it falls.

CARING FOR FISH, REPTILES, AND AMPHIBIANS

Fish, reptiles, and amphibians are fascinating pets. They are not as friendly as mammals but can be rewarding to observe. Monitor their health and environment to avoid problems. If you have children, check that your pets are not likely to pass on diseases such as salmonella.

KEEPING REPTILES

Very few pet reptiles are dangerous, but they all need special care. When buying a reptile, ask the breeder or shop for instructions on care.

● **Handling** If a reptile bites, wear rubber gloves when handling it. The animal will dislike the taste of the gloves, so they should not bite you.
● **Keeping groups** If you plan to keep several species of reptile together, check that none of them is likely to kill or injure other types.
● **Feeding** Be sure that you are able to feed the reptiles properly. For example, you may have to kill rodents or frogs for some snakes.

LOOKING AFTER FISH

● **Draining a tank** Fill a hose with water. Put one end in the tank, and the other in a bucket below it. The water will flow out of the tank by itself.

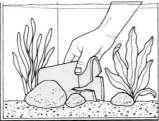

Decorating a tank
Fill a tank with features that will interest fish. Add natural objects such as water plants and a few large stones, and include some broken terra-cotta pots for the fish to hide in and explore.

USING A TERRARIUM

● **Choosing a tank** Make sure that the tank has a secure lid. Snakes, especially, are very good at escaping from tanks.
● **Creating an environment** Provide the right surroundings for an animal's lifestyle and habits. For example, provide a water area for bathing, sand for burrowing, or branches for tree-climbing animals.
● **Regulating temperature** Use a thermometer in a terrarium so that you can monitor the temperature. To give heat for basking, shine a desk lamp on to the terrarium.
● **Lining the floor** Choose shredded paper or cedar chips. They are easy to clean and do not harbor parasites.

CHOOSING AND KEEPING BIRDS

Birds are intelligent, sociable creatures. They need company and attention as well as practical care. Keep them in pairs or groups if possible. Make sure that birds have room to move around their cage. Give them toys, and talk to them – even if they do not talk back.

BUYING BIRDS

● **Checking origin** Before you buy a bird, find out its country of origin and whether the species is bred in captivity. You can then avoid buying a bird that may have been illegally captured in the wild.
● **Determining life expectancy** Find out how long a bird is likely to live. Small birds may survive only a few years, but some parrot species may live as long as a human being.
● **Choosing a bird that will talk** If you wish to train a bird to talk, buy a young one about six weeks old. Keep the bird on its own, but give it a lot of attention so that it will listen to you and learn words easily.

KEEPING BIRDS

● **Checking air quality** Birds can suffer from breathing problems if exposed to dirty air. Never smoke cigarettes near them. Keep them away from strong smells such as burning fat or fresh paint.
● **Avoiding disease** Species imported from tropical areas may carry psittacosis (parrot fever), a disease that is fatal to humans. To avoid infection, wash your hands after handling a bird or cleaning a cage.
● **Positioning a cage** Place a bird cage on a sturdy stand, high enough for you to reach easily when you stand beside it. Position the cage away from direct light and drafts.

TRADITIONAL TIP

Prompting a bird to sing
If you want a bird to sing, position a small mirror in its cage so that the bird can see itself. It will think it is looking at another bird and will sing to its reflection.

CLEANING THE HOME

QUICK REFERENCE
General Cleaning, p. 56
Floors, p. 58
Walls & Ceilings, p. 62
Furnishings, p. 66
Bathrooms, p. 68
Kitchens, p. 70
Cleaning Checklist, p. 75

CLEANING DOES NOT HAVE TO BE hard work if you follow a few basic rules. Invest in the right equipment, and take care of it. Dusting is the key to a clean home, so keep that task on your regular agenda. Sensible use of the vacuum cleaner and all its attachments makes light work of many chores, not just cleaning carpets. There is no need to be obsessive; a home need not be squeaky clean to look good.

HOUSE-CLEANING EQUIPMENT

These are the essential items you will need for keeping your home clean. Buy a plastic storage box with a handle, which you can use for carrying equipment around. If your home has lots of stairs, consider investing in two sets of cleaning tools to avoid carrying them. Clean all equipment after use.

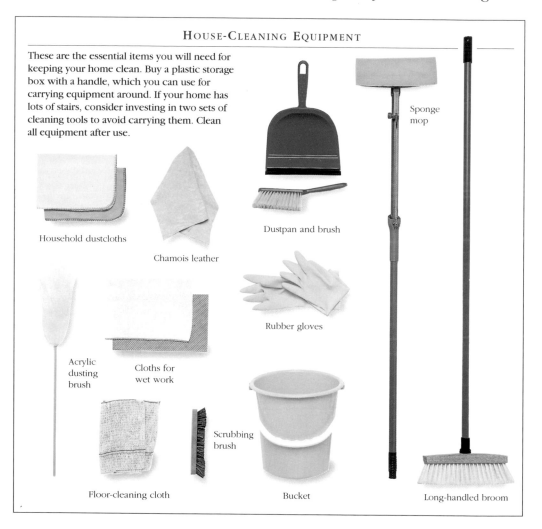

Household dustcloths

Chamois leather

Dustpan and brush

Sponge mop

Rubber gloves

Acrylic dusting brush

Cloths for wet work

Scrubbing brush

Floor-cleaning cloth

Bucket

Long-handled broom

HOUSE-CLEANING MATERIALS

Nowadays, there is a product to clean almost everything in your home. Although manufacturers would like you to believe that their products are essential, all you need are some key items. A cleaning kit that contains dishwashing liquid, nonabrasive and abrasive household detergent, detergent with enzymes, furniture polish, and metal polish will maintain all the surfaces in your home.

Household bleach

Cream cleaner

Spray cleaner

Furniture polish

Ammonia

EXTRA ITEMS
● **For specific marks** Ammonia, household bleach, rubbing alcohol, laundry borax, washing soda, and turpentine are useful for cleaning particular surfaces, and for removing difficult stains. Keep them away from children.
● **From the kitchen** Salt, lemon juice, glycerin, white vinegar, and baking soda can be used as gentle, environmentally friendly household cleaners.
● **Specialized cleaners** Buy TSP for washing down very dirty walls. Keep a supply of leather food for feeding and protecting leather furniture.

Denatured alcohol (dyed)

Denatured alcohol

Liquid cleaner

Turpentine

Dishwashing liquid

MAKING RECORDS
● **A cleaning file** Make a record of how you cleaned special items, and what you used, to avoid trial and error the next time. Keep this file in a home log book.

Laundry borax

Floor and wall cleaner

Detergent with enzymes

Washing soda

Metal polish

Baking soda

Salt

Lemon juice

Glycerin

White vinegar

CLEANING AND SAFETY

● **Keep children safe** Keep your cleaning kit locked away in a closet. Do not leave children alone with cleaning products if you are interrupted by the telephone or the doorbell.
● **Label items clearly** If you buy products in bulk and decant them, make sure you label the new container clearly with its contents.

● **Protect your skin** Wear rubber gloves if you are using strong household cleaners. Avoid contact with skin, eyes, and clothes when using bleach or ammonia.
● **Beware of fumes** Open windows in the rooms you are cleaning (if possible) to provide ventilation. Avoid open flames, as they may cause chemicals to ignite.

● **Do not mix cleaners** Some chemicals react adversely when mixed. If a cleaning product has not worked on a surface, rinse it off before using another cleaner.
● **Watch your step** If you are cleaning hard-to-reach places, always stand on a ladder or stepstool. Standing on a chair or table is dangerous, and could cause an accident.

GENERAL CLEANING

LITTLE AND OFTEN is the best way to keep your home clean. If you leave things for weeks, you will find yourself with a major chore on your hands. Clean living rooms once a week; sinks and kitchen surfaces should be cleaned daily.

MAINTAINING EQUIPMENT

Keep your equipment in good condition; otherwise, you will have to spend extra time getting it back into shape. Always clean equipment before you put it away, and store items properly. Wash cleaning rags regularly, and discard any that are too dirty to reuse.

STORING CLEANING EQUIPMENT

Tie bag with string

Place used pads in soapy water

Pad cut in half

Household broom
Wash brooms in soapy water from time to time. Store upside down to prevent the bristles from bending – you can make a rack using two thread spools.

Sponge mops
Rinse floor mops thoroughly after use (they should not need any extra washing). Store the heads in plastic bags so that they do not dry out and warp.

Steel-wool pads
Keep steel-wool pads in soapy water to stop them from rusting, or wrap them in aluminum foil. Save money by cutting them in half so that they go twice as far.

CLOTHS AND SPONGES
● **Cleaning and storage** Shake dustcloths well in the yard or out of a window after you have used them. Soak slimy sponges in vinegar and water. Store dustcloths and polishing cloths in plastic bags.

CHAMOIS LEATHERS
● **General care** Chamois leathers are expensive, but will last for years if well cared for. Wash in warm, soapy water, and rinse thoroughly. Let dry away from direct heat to preserve the skin's natural oils.

SMALL BRUSHES
● **Using toothbrushes** Old toothbrushes are perfect tools for cleaning intricate metalwork, grouting, around taps, and awkward spaces. Save as many as you can, and keep them in your cleaning kit.

VACUUM CLEANERS

Use your vacuum cleaner for as many tasks as possible. The range of attachments can be used to clean curtains, furniture, and upholstery, as well as floors. Check the brushes and rollers before you start vacuuming – the machine will not work well if it is clogged up. A range of vacuum cleaners is available for carrying out different tasks. Handheld vacuum cleaners are ideal for cars and for cleaning up spills.

● **Upright vacuum cleaners** These are best for covering large areas of floor, but they cannot always get under furniture or into awkward corners.
● **Cylinder vacuum cleaners** These are good for cleaning awkward areas, such as stairs and under low furniture, but can be cumbersome to use.
● **Wet-and-dry vacuum cleaners** These suck up water as well as doing routine cleaning.

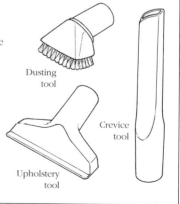

Dusting tool

Crevice tool

Upholstery tool

METHODS AND ROUTINES

Establish and maintain a cleaning routine so that all areas of your home receive regular attention and the work does not pile up. Use these tips to get around rooms efficiently and make your home appear tidy – even when you know it is not as clean as it could be.

CLEANING METHODS

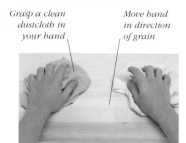

Grasp a clean dustcloth in your hand

Move hand in direction of grain

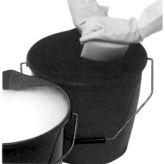

Two-handed dusting
Using two dustcloths – one in each hand – will help you clean the surfaces in a room in half the time and with half the effort.

Two-bucket method
Wash floors and walls using two buckets: fill one with cleaning solution, and the other with water for rinsing the sponge or mop.

MAKING A TIMESAVING DUSTCLOTH

Let dustcloth soak up kerosene and vinegar

Wear gloves to protect your hands

1 To create a dustcloth that leaves a shine, soak a dustcloth in oil with a few drops of lemon oil added.

2 Remove the dustcloth when it is fully saturated and squeeze dry. Store it in a screwtop jar. Buff to finish.

ROOMS	CLEANING FREQUENCY
BATHROOMS AND KITCHENS	Clean these rooms daily to maintain good hygiene.
BEDROOMS	Air beds each morning, as we lose 1 cup (250 ml) of moisture every night. Clean rooms weekly.
LIVING ROOMS	Clean once a week. Vacuum floors twice a week if necessary.
OTHER AREAS	Vacuum halls twice a week. Clean little-used rooms monthly.

TIMESAVING TIP

Cleaning in a hurry
If visitors are coming and you are unprepared, make do with cleaning the hallway, tidying obvious clutter, and throwing away dead flowers. Straighten cushions, chairs, and rugs to create the impression of order. Spray room freshener and dim the lighting or use candlelight.

CLEANING ROUTINES
● **Daily cleaning** Kitchens and bathrooms should be cleaned daily (see p. 68–69).
● **Regular cleaning** Bedrooms and living rooms should be cleaned weekly. Begin by ventilating the room and tidying up. Starting at one side of a door, dust all items and surfaces, working around the whole room. Always dust higher surfaces first, since some dust may fall onto lower surfaces. Finally, vacuum or sweep the floor.
● **Occasional cleaning** Every few months, give all rooms a thorough going over. Take down curtains for cleaning, shampoo upholstery and carpets, and clean walls and windows. Tidy up closets, and dispose of any items that you no longer use.

FLOORS

Dirt is transmitted to floors from outdoors, so lay a doormat inside all exterior doors to remove dirt from shoes. If you keep floors clean by sweeping or vacuuming regularly, you will cut down on heavy-duty cleaning.

CLEANING HARD FLOORS

Hard floors that are dusty look dirtier than unvacuumed carpets. Sweep, vacuum, or mop them regularly – particularly hallway, kitchen, and bathroom floors. Wooden floors need polishing; marble, vinyl, and tile floors require heavy-duty cleaning from time to time.

SWEEPING FLOORS

Removing dust
Sweep or vacuum hard floors every few days, paying special attention to corners, where dirt collects and builds up.

MOPPING FLOORS

Effective mopping
Damp mop all sealed floors weekly, using the two-bucket method. Do not use soap when mopping slate or stone floors.

SCRUBBING FLOORS

Heavy-duty washing
Scrub stone, concrete, and tile floors with floor cleaner and a scrub brush occasionally to get rid of accumulated dirt.

POLISHING FLOORS

Give floors a good shine, and your home will look well cared for. Use the right type of polish for your floor, and remember that polish builds up and will need to be removed from time to time. Use floor cleaner, ammonia, or commercial wax remover to remove polish.

TYPES OF POLISH

SOLID PASTE POLISHES
These solvent-based polishes are suitable for vinyl, wood, and cork. Application is difficult and must be done by hand, but the shine lasts a long time.

LIQUID SOLVENT POLISHES
These are also suitable for vinyl, wood, and cork. They are easier to use than solid paste polish, but they are not as long lasting.

WATER-BASED EMULSION POLISHES
These usually contain silicone. They can be used on all floors except linoleum, unsealed wood, and cork. They are easy to apply and long lasting.

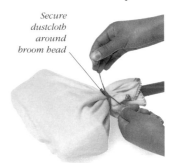

Secure dustcloth around broom head

Improvising a polisher
Tie a dustcloth around a soft broom, and use this instead of an electric polisher to apply and buff wax polish. Always clean floors thoroughly before you apply polish for the first time.

TYPES OF FLOORING

Some floors take a lot of heavy wear, and different types of surface need varying amounts of attention. Sweep hard floors daily if necessary, and clean them according to their type. Do not let dirt build up so that cleaning a floor becomes a hands-and-knees job.

TYPE	TREATMENT
VINYL An easy-care floor covering that lasts well if cared for correctly.	● Sweep regularly. When dirty, wash vinyl with a solution of household detergent and warm water. Rinse with clear water. Twice a year remove the vinyl gloss coating with a proprietary stripper. When dry, coat the vinyl with the manufacturer's recommended floor dressing. ● Remove stubborn marks with emulsion polish.
LINOLEUM A tough flooring, but take care not to overwet, because this can cause damage.	● Wipe linoleum floors with a mop dampened in a weak solution of water and household detergent. Use a water-based polish – which will not leave a watermark – on kitchen and bathroom floors, and a wax polish on floors elsewhere in the home. ● Remove scuff marks by rubbing with fine-grade steel wool dipped in turpentine.
WOOD Treatment depends on whether or not the wood is sealed.	● Sweep or dry mop unsealed floors regularly to remove dust and dirt. Clean sealed wooden floors with a mop dampened and wrung out. To give the floor a shine, polish with wax or emulsion polish. ● Use a damp cloth to remove sticky marks on unsealed floors. Remove wax polish from sealed wooden floors with a cloth and turpentine.
CORK Needs regular sweeping. Make sure you do not overwet cork while mopping or it will crack.	● Mop regularly with a solution of warm water and household detergent, and apply wax polish occasionally. Try to avoid a buildup of polish around the edges of the room as this eventually results in a sticky deposit that attracts dirt. ● When laying cork tiles, ensure that the edges are sealed to stop water seeping in from the sides.
CERAMIC TILES This surface is as hard as nails, so anything dropped on it will break. Be careful.	● Clean with a solution of dishwashing liquid applied with a sponge mop or a cloth, then wipe over with a chamois leather. Mop up spills immediately – wet floors are dangerously slippery. ● Do not polish ceramic tiles, since this will make them slippery. Clean grouting with a soft-bristled brush dipped in a strong solution of detergent.
QUARRY TILES Pretty, but porous unless sealed. Rub faded tiles with steel wool and turpentine, then apply colored solid paste polish.	● Glazed quarry tiles need mopping regularly with water and a little general-purpose cleaner. Scrub unglazed quarry tiles with this solution to remove dirt. Rinse thoroughly. Polish with liquid or solid paste polish, preferably nonskid. ● Treat newly laid tiles with linseed oil. Do not wash them for at least two weeks afterward.

SPECIAL FLOOR TREATMENTS

Avoid scuffing or scratching hard floors, because these marks can be difficult to remove. Polish the rockers on rocking chairs to prevent them from scratching floors, and slip small mats underneath furniture when moving heavy pieces across a room.

REMOVING STAINS FROM WOODEN FLOORS

● **Ink stains** Treat ink stains by dabbing them with household bleach, applied on a cotton swab. Blot quickly with paper towels, and repeat if necessary.

● **Candle wax** Harden spilled candle wax with an ice cube, then ease off the wax with a blunt knife. Rub in a little liquid floor polish, then buff well, using a soft cloth.

REMOVING SCRATCHES FROM WOODEN FLOORS

Rub scratch gently

1 Rub the scratch with fine steel wool. Be careful not to spread the rubbed area any farther than necessary. Wear gloves when using steel wool.

2 Mix a little brown shoe polish with floor wax, and apply the mixture to the area. Rub in well, so that it blends with the rest of the floor.

TRADITIONAL TIP

Keeping dust down
Sprinkle damp tea leaves on wood floors to help collect dust when sweeping. Damp tea leaves will also control dust when you are cleaning ashes out of fireplaces. (This is particularly useful for people who have dust allergies.)

REPAIRING FLOORS

● **Vinyl and cork** Remove burn marks by rubbing with fine sandpaper. If a burn is very noticeable, cut out the damaged part with a craft knife and insert a new piece.
● **Linoleum** These floors tend to crack with age. Cover any cracks with clear packing tape, then apply a coat of clear polyurethane varnish.
● **Tiled floors** Repair holes in tiles with wall or wood filler. Apply the filler slightly higher than the floor, and sand down when dry. Apply color (shoe polish or artist's oils), then finish with clear floor sealant.
● **Wooden floors** Where a wet basement is causing rising dampness, a fairly easy solution is to lift the flooring and paint the concrete subfloor with a special waterproof coating.

QUARRY TILES

● **Restoring color** If color has faded, remove any old polish with steel wool and turpentine. Wash, rinse, and apply pigmented wax polish when dry. Buff well to make sure that the polish is not picked up on shoes.

Treating white patches
These are caused by lime in the subfloor and will disappear eventually. Hasten the processs by washing with a solution of 4 tbsp (60 ml) vinegar to 5 quarts (5 liters) water. Do not rinse.

VINYL AND LINOLEUM

● **Removing paint** Remove fresh latex by rubbing with a damp cloth. Rub fresh oil-based paint stains with steel wool dipped in solid paste polish. Saturate dried paint stains with boiled linseed oil. Let stand, then wipe off.

Wear gloves when using strong chemicals

Dealing with scuff marks
Remove scuff marks on vinyl floors with turpentine applied on a cloth. A pencil eraser may also do the trick, or try rubbing the mark with a cloth dipped in water-based polish.

FLOOR COVERINGS

Carpets and rugs are among the most expensive items of room decoration, so take care of them to make them last. Always follow care instructions given by the carpet manufacturer to ensure that your carpet stays in good condition for as long as possible.

CLEANING CARPETS

● **Vacuuming** Vacuum regularly to remove dust and dirt, and keep the pile in good condition. Ideally, go over each area eight times – but fewer will do if you are in a hurry. Take advantage of all the attachments to clean around the edges of each room and under low furniture.

● **Shampooing** Apply carpet shampoo by hand to dirty patches. If the whole carpet is dirty, shampoo it using a machine, or call a professional cleaner. Shampoo wall-to-wall carpets in place – they may shrink if you take them up and wet them, and you will have to pay for relaying the carpet.

GREEN TIP

Dry shampoo
To freshen your carpet cheaply and ecologically, liberally sprinkle baking soda all over it. Leave for 15 minutes, then vacuum thoroughly. Not only will your carpet be clean, you will have discouraged pests and neutralized odors.

FURNITURE MARKS ON CARPETS

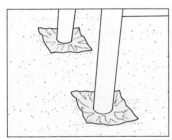

Damp carpets
If you need to replace furniture before a recently shampooed carpet is fully dry, place squares of foil beneath the furniture legs to prevent the furniture from marking the carpet.

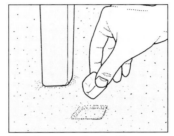

Raising crushed pile
To raise indentations in carpets caused by the weight of heavy furniture, place an ice cube in the dent, and let the ice cube melt. Let the area dry naturally, then vacuum.

RUGS AND MATS

● **Cleaning** Take rugs outside and beat with a carpet beater or an old tennis racket. Vacuum natural floor coverings (rush, sisal, coconut matting); when dirty, scrub with salty water, rinse, then let dry away from direct heat.

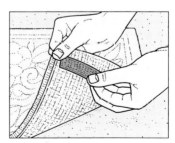

Creeping rugs
Prevent rugs from sliding around on hard floor surfaces by sticking pieces of heavy-duty double-sided tape around the edges. Use pieces of touch-and-close tape to prevent rugs from creeping on carpet.

HOUSEHOLD PESTS AND SMELLS

Carpets and rugs are susceptible to pests such as carpet beetles, and they also pick up and hold smells from cigarette smoke, frying food, and pets.

● **Carpet beetles** A telltale sign of carpet beetles is their shed skins, usually around carpet edges. These pests are difficult to eradicate because they get into well-hidden places. Kill as many as you can by sprinkling laundry borax around the carpet edges, and also over the padding before a new carpet is laid.

● **Cigarette smoke** The smell of smoke lingers in carpets and upholstery. Put a bowl of water in a discreet place if you are expecting smoking visitors. Lighting candles also helps. Cover the bottoms of ashtrays with baking soda to prevent butts from smoldering.
● **Vinegar air freshener** A small container of vinegar left in any room of the house keeps the room smelling fresh, even if the house is closed for a while. Add vinegar to the water in humidifiers occasionally – it will keep the air fresher.

WALLS AND CEILINGS

UNLESS YOU LIVE IN A heavily polluted area or have a houseful of smokers, you do not need to clean your walls and ceilings more than once a year. Do not tackle more than a room at a time – this task is physically demanding.

WALL COVERINGS

Dust nonwashable wallpaper regularly to prevent dirt from building up. Never use water because it will loosen the paper from the wall. Sponge washable wall coverings with a dishwashing liquid solution, working from bottom to top. Rinse clean with warm water.

CLEANING NONWASHABLE WALLPAPER

Removing marks
Rub marks with a scrunched up piece of crustless white bread, or an eraser. Rub gently to avoid damaging the wall covering – it may take several attempts before the marks begin to disappear.

Removing grease marks
Apply a warm (not hot) iron over brown paper to absorb grease marks. Repeat using clean parts of the brown paper until all the grease is absorbed, then apply an aerosol grease solvent.

CLEANING VINYL

Washing walls down
Wash vinyl wall coverings occasionally, using a detergent solution applied on a sponge. Start from the bottom and work your way up, and rub gently so as not to damage the surface.

PATCHING WALLPAPER

1 Badly marked wallpaper may need to be patched rather than cleaned. Tear a matching piece, pulling away from you as you tear to create an uneven edge (which will show up less obviously than a cut edge).

2 Stick the new patch into position with wallpaper paste, making sure that the pattern matches. If you are patching old wallpaper, leave the new piece in the sun to fade for a few days before patching.

SPECIALTY WALL COVERINGS

● **Grasscloth** Clean carefully, since the grasses can come loose very easily. Simply dusting is sufficient – use a soft-brush vacuum-cleaner attachment on low suction. Be careful not to place furniture against grasscloth; it may rub the grasses loose and leave unsightly marks.
● **Burlap paper** Dust regularly, using a vacuum-cleaner attachment. Dyes in burlap paper tend to run, so do not wet. Remove marks by rubbing with a piece of crustless white bread.

PAINTED SURFACES

Painted walls and ceilings can be kept in good condition for a long time with regular cleaning. But marks such as heavy tobacco stains can be difficult to eradicate. If this is a problem, redecorating may be a better solution than trying to scrub off the stains.

CEILINGS
● **Cleaning** Do not wash ceilings – a fresh coat of paint is more effective. Dust with the improvised duster shown below, a long-handled brush, or the upholstery attachment on your vacuum cleaner.

WALLS, DOORS, & TRIMMINGS
● **Cleaning walls** Use a warm solution of dishwashing liquid to clean walls. Do not stop in the middle of cleaning – you will create a tidemark that is difficult to remove. Wash one wall at a time completely.

● **Very dirty walls** Clean with a solution of TSP (follow the manufacturer's instructions for strength of dilution) before using other cleaners.
● **Doors and baseboards** Wash with a solution of dishwashing liquid (not detergent, which can affect paint color). Rinse with clear water, and pat dry.

MARKS ON WALLS
● **Tackling stains** Most marks come off painted walls, but treat them gently to avoid damaging the paintwork. Rub fingerprints and pencil marks gently with an eraser. Wash food stains off with undiluted nonabrasive household cleaner. Where furniture has bumped into a wall and left a mark, try rubbing it out with an eraser first, then apply household cleaner as above.

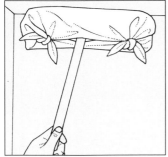

Making a ceiling duster
Tie a clean dustcloth loosely around a broom head, and use to dust ceilings thoroughly from time to time. Remember to give the broom a shake at intervals.

Wall-washing method
Always start at the bottom of a wall and work upward. This may sound like extra work, but it is easier to wipe dirty trickles off a clean surface than off a dirty one.

OTHER WALL TYPES

Ceramic tiles often show dirt in the grouting between the tiles. Wood-paneled walls need frequent dusting (you can use your vacuum cleaner for this) and polishing once a year. Marks on bare brickwork are difficult to remove, so dust these walls frequently.

CERAMIC TILE WALLS

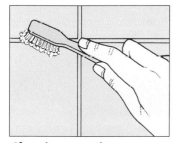

Cleaning grouting
Use an old, clean toothbrush dipped in a bleach solution to clean grouting between tiles. If the grout is filthy, it may be easier to apply new grouting.

WOOD PANELING

Removing polish
When the polish on wooden walls builds up, remove it using fine steel wool and turpentine. Rub gently but firmly, following the direction of the grain.

BRICKWORK

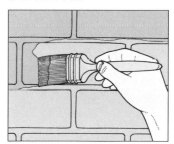

Sealing brick walls
Apply a sealer to bare brickwork so that the brickwork will just require dusting and damp wiping. Use a soft paintbrush, and make sure the wall is clean.

WINDOWS

Dirty windows spoil the look of a home. Clean the outsides as often as necessary, depending on the area in which you live, and wash the insides two or three times a year. Do not forget to dust windows when you clean each room. Use a soft acrylic brush.

WASHING WINDOWS

Homemade cleaner
Make your own solution for washing windows by adding vinegar to water in a plant-spray bottle. Vinegar cuts grease, and brings out the good shine.

WIPING WINDOWS

Using newspaper
Wipe newly washed windows clean with crumpled newspaper. This is a cheap alternative to a chamois leather, and the ink will give the glass an extra shine.

TIMESAVING TIP

Protecting curtains
To avoid removing curtains when cleaning windows, loop them over a hanger.

KEEPING WINDOWS SMEAR-FREE

● **Window-washing weather** Wash windows on cloudy days, when they are damp and every fingerprint and mark shows up. Sunny days are less ideal for window washing, since the windows dry too quickly, leaving smeary marks.

● **Smear finder** When cleaning the outside and inside of a window, use horizontal strokes on one side and vertical strokes on the other. This way you can easily tell which side of the window still has the odd smear left.

CLEANING MIRRORS

When cleaning mirrors, avoid using water, which can trickle down behind the glass and damage the silvering. Instead, use a commercial glass cleaner, then buff the mirror well.

ELECTRIC FIXTURES

Clean plastic wall outlets and light switches by wiping them with denatured alcohol on a clean cloth. Metal fixtures need the appropriate metal polish. Lightbulbs should be dusted and cleaned regularly – dirty bulbs can reduce lighting efficiency by up to 50 percent.

CLEANING FIXTURES

● **Using templates** To avoid getting cleaner or polish on walls when cleaning fixtures, make a template that fits around the fixture, and hold it in place during cleaning.

WARNING
Turn off electricity before cleaning electrical fixtures. Do not clean lightbulbs while they are in their sockets.

TREATING LIGHTBULBS WITH CARE

● **Lightbulbs** Before removing a lightbulb for cleaning, switch off the electricity. If the light has been on, wait for the bulb to cool down. Dry it thoroughly before replacing. Never use water on a bulb that is still in its socket.

● **Scented bulbs** Wipe a little vanilla extract on the tops of lightbulbs with a soft cloth. When you turn on the lights, the scent will be released.

Swivel bulb in cloth

Cleaning lightbulbs
Hold lightbulbs by the base and carefully wipe over with a wrung-out damp cloth.

RADIATORS AND HEATERS

Clean radiators once a week in winter and less often when not in use. Wipe with a dishwashing liquid solution, and clean behind them with a vacuum-cleaner attachment or a radiator brush. Wipe heaters with a dishwashing liquid solution.

AVOIDING PROBLEMS
● **Heating and air vents** These attract dust, so make sure that you catch them before they become clogged up. A bottle brush is the best way to remove grime as it builds up.
● **Protecting flooring** Place a drop cloth under radiators during cleaning so dust and liquid do not fall on the floor.
● **Marks above radiators** Rising hot air creates marks on walls above radiators. Installing shelves above radiators will help prevent this and will also direct heat into the room.

CLEANING BEHIND RADIATORS

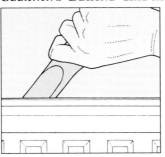

Vacuum cleaning
Use the crevice tool of your vacuum cleaner to either suck or blow accumulated dust from behind radiators.

Improvised brush
Cover a broom handle with a sponge, then an old sock. Use to clean behind radiators; change the sock when it gets dirty.

FIREPLACES

An open fire is very cheerful, but fireplaces will grow dirty with a buildup of soot unless you act before the soot becomes ingrained. (See page 98 for treatment of soot marks.) Clean the fire surround thoroughly as soon as the fireplace season is over.

CLEANING CHIMNEYS
● **Wood burning chimneys** Have chimneys that are used to burn wood swept twice as year, as residue resin from the wood may catch fire.

METAL PARTS
● **Polishing** To clean the metal on fireplaces, use blacking or a commercial cleaner.

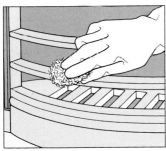

Applying blacking
Wearing gloves, apply blacking on a piece of steel wool. Polish the blacking with a soft cloth.

CLEARING GRATES
● **Removing ashes** Remove coal ashes weekly, but leave wood ashes in the grate – they will act as a good base for your fire all winter.

CLEANING SURROUNDS
● **Brick** Scrub well with a hard scrub brush and clean water. Sponge burn marks with vinegar, and rinse.
● **Ceramic tile** Wash with a solution of dishwashing liquid or household detergent, and rinse. Use a nonabrasive household cleaner on soot marks (see also p. 98).
● **Marble** Sponge with a soap flake solution, then rinse and dry with an old towel. If polished, use a product specially designed for marble. Products are also available for repairing damaged marble; see page 125 for treating stains.

DISPOSING OF ASHES
● **Hot embers** Always use a metal container when carrying ashes to the garbage bin, as any undetected hot embers will burn through plastic.

TRADITIONAL TIP

Making a scented fire
Throw pieces of dried citrus peel onto a fire to scent a room pleasantly. Pinecones have the same effect.

FURNISHINGS

THE UBIQUITOUS VACUUM cleaner and its attachments are useful for keeping most furniture, upholstery, and window coverings free from dust. Always remove stains when they occur; save the deep cleaning for an annual event.

WOODEN FURNITURE

Wooden furniture can last for years, even centuries. Dust wood frequently, always working along the direction of the grain. Be careful not to get unsealed wood wet; water will cause swelling. See pages 115–117 for special treatments for wooden furniture.

DUSTING WOOD

Carved wood
Dust with a synthetic fluffy duster. Rub the duster first to increase static collection. A soft paintbrush also works well.

EVERYDAY PIECES

● **Basic care** Clean wooden furniture with a detergent solution applied on a damp cloth. Rinse and buff to a shine. Occasionally, use an aerosol or pump polish.
● **Teak furniture** Modern teak furniture only needs dusting. Polish these items with teak oil or cream, used sparingly, once or twice a year.
● **Painted wood** Wipe with a solution of dishwashing liquid (unless fragile), then rinse with clear water, and dry. Use undiluted dishwashing liquid to remove marks.

VALUABLE PIECES

● **Antique furniture** Keep away from direct heat and sunlight, which cause damage. Dust regularly. Remove sticky marks with a little vinegar and water. Use a beeswax polish on antique furniture once or twice a year (see p. 115).
● **French-polished wood** Buff in the direction of the grain, using a soft dustcloth. Occasionally, use a wax polish and rub in well. Use a little turpentine to remove sticky marks and fingerprints. If the French polish is damaged, call a professional.

OTHER HARD FURNITURE

Wicker and cane furniture require regular dusting with a brush or vacuum-cleaner attachment. Marble and metal furniture need a little more care. Plastic furniture is easy to keep clean – just wipe with detergent solution occasionally, then rinse with clear water.

MARBLE FURNITURE

● **General care** Marble just needs dusting with a cloth or soft brush. Occasionally, wipe with soapy water, and rinse before buffing the surface. Do not use polish on white marble. See page 125 for removing stains on marble.

WICKER FURNITURE

● **Cleaning** Use a vacuum cleaner on blow to push out dust. Scrub wicker furniture occasionally with a nail brush dipped in dishwashing liquid solution. Rinse, and dry.

CANE FURNITURE

Apply salty water with a sponge

Thorough cleaning
Scrub cane furniture from time to time with a soap flake solution. Rinse with salty water to keep the cane stiff.

METAL FURNITURE

Removing rust
Use a stiff wire brush to remove rust on metal furniture. Coat metal furniture that is kept outdoors with rustproof paint.

UPHOLSTERY

Dust upholstered furniture with the dusting tool attachment of the vacuum cleaner. Feel down the backs and sides of chairs and sofas to retrieve items such as coins before using the crevice tool to remove dust. To remove stains on upholstery, see pages 76–99.

REGULAR CARE

● **Slipcovers** Remove covers when dirty, and wash them according to fabric. While the covers are still damp, put them back on the furniture, and press with a cool iron. Glazed chintz covers can be washed, but the glaze may be removed.
● **Upholstery** Clean this yourself using upholstery shampoo (always follow the manufacturer's instructions), or call in a professional firm. When removing marks, be careful not to overwet.

REMOVING LINT

Using adhesive tape
To remove lint and pet hair from upholstery, wind adhesive tape around your fingers (sticky side out) and brush it over the fabric.

LEATHER AND VINYL

● **Leather care** Dust leather frequently. Apply hide food occasionally. Rub it in well so it does not stain clothes.
● **Dirty leather** Wipe with a damp cloth wrung out in a soap flake solution (take care not to overwet). Do not rinse. Allow to dry naturally, then polish as usual.
● **Vinyl upholstery** Dust and wipe with a damp cloth regularly. Use a soap flake solution to clean dirty vinyl.

CURTAINS AND BLINDS

These are an important part of the effect of a room. Expensive curtains and blinds should be dry cleaned by a professional: an expert will measure them before taking them down and ensure that they are returned fitting as well as they did originally.

CURTAINS

● **Washing** Always have lined curtains professionally dry cleaned, even if they are washable – the different fabrics may shrink at varying rates if you wash them yourself. Wash large curtains in your bathtub, since they are too heavy for a machine and could cause damage.

General care
Dust curtains frequently, using the upholstery attachment of your vacuum cleaner. Stand on a stepstool to reach the top.

BLINDS

● **Roller blinds** Vacuum with the upholstery attachment or dusting tool. If the blinds are spongeable, wipe them with a solution of dishwashing liquid, then rinse with a damp cloth. An application of aerosol blind stiffener will help keep them clean. (It is best to apply this outdoors.)

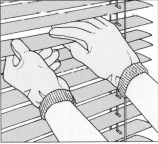

Venetian blinds
Dust by running hands encased in cotton gloves along the slats. Wash blinds in the bathtub (keep the roller mechanism dry).

ROUCHED BLINDS

● **Balloon shades** Vacuum folds regularly. Unfold shades occasionally, and wash or dry clean according to the fabric.

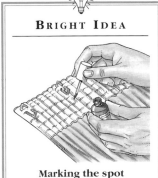

BRIGHT IDEA

Marking the spot
When removing curtain hooks, mark their spaces with nail polish. This way you will not have to spend time guessing the correct spacing when replacing the hooks.

BATHROOMS

T HESE ROOMS NEED daily cleaning. Encourage members of your household to clean sinks and bathtubs after they have used them. Dirty bathrooms are unattractive and unsanitary. They are also more difficult to clean if left dirty.

BATHROOM-CLEANING KIT

Store your bathroom-cleaning kit in the bathroom ready for everyone to use after they have finished. Rinse sponges, cloths, and toilet brushes after each use. If bathroom sponges become slimy from a buildup of soap, soak them in white vinegar and water, and wash them in the washing machine. Flush toilet cleaner away before using the toilet; otherwise, splashes might damage the skin.

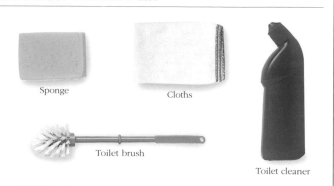

Sponge

Cloths

Toilet brush

Toilet cleaner

BATHS, SHOWERS, AND SINKS

D ishwashing liquid is fine for cleaning baths, showers, and sinks; you do not need special cleaners. Wipe around immediately after use to keep these areas clean. Prevent condensation in bathrooms by running cold water into baths before running the hot water.

ACRYLIC BATHS

Removing scratches
Rub with metal polish. For deep scratches, rub with ultrafine wet-and-dry sandpaper, then finish off with metal polish.

BATHROOM SINKS
● **Drains** Pay special attention to sink drain holes and overflows. Clean with a bottle brush, and pour a little bleach down them once a week.

OTHER BATH TYPES
● **Enamel and porcelain** Clean with a nonabrasive cleaner – harsh abrasives will dull the bath's surface. Rub stubborn marks with turpentine. Rinse with a solution of hot water and dishwashing liquid.
● **Fiberglass** Treat carefully, as the color is in the surface coating only. Use dishwashing liquid – avoid abrasives, metal polish, and harsh cleaners.

SHOWERS
● **Shower doors** Remove hard-water deposits by wiping with white vinegar. Leave for 30 minutes, then rinse.
● **Shower curtains** These tend to develop mildew, which can be removed by soaking in a bleach solution, rinsing, and hand or machine washing. Remove soap buildup by soaking in warm water with a little fabric softener.

STAINS ON BATHS AND SINKS

● **Blue-green marks** These are caused by the minerals in water from dripping faucets. Use a vitreous enamel cleaner to clean enameled surfaces.
● **Rust marks** Remove using a commercial bath-stain remover that contains scale remover.

● **Hard-water marks** Use a vitreous enamel cleaner on enameled surfaces, and cream cleaner on acrylic surfaces.
● **Tidemarks** Rub bad marks on enamel and acrylic with turpentine, then rinse with a dishwashing liquid solution.

FIXTURES

Clean faucets regularly so that dirt does not build up. For chrome faucets, remove greasy marks with dishwashing liquid, and serious marks with metal polish; restore dulled old chrome with special chrome cleaner for cars. Clean rubber plugs with turpentine.

CLEANING BATHROOM FAUCETS EFFECTIVELY

● **Removing scale** Where scale builds up on chrome faucets, rub with half a lemon until the scale disappears. Rinse thoroughly, then buff dry.

● **Gold-plated faucets** Wipe with a barely damp cloth after each use. Do not rub. Never use metal polish, because it will damage the finish.

SHOWERHEADS

● **Cleaning** Unscrew showerheads from time to time and rinse out hard-water scale. Rub deposits with white vinegar.

Descaling faucets
Tie a plastic bag or a yogurt cup containing vinegar or descaler over the faucet. Leave until the scale is dissolved, then rinse.

Cleaning faucet bases
Use an old, clean toothbrush dipped in cream cleaner to get rid of the deposit and grime that builds up behind faucets.

Submerge shower-head completely

Clogged showerhead
Soak in a bowl of warm, undiluted vinegar or descaler. Use a toothbrush or darning needle to clean blocked holes.

TOILETS

Brush toilets thoroughly each day. Wipe the seat, tank, and outside of the bowl once a week, and clean the bowl with a commercial toilet cleaner. Do not regularly use bleach to clean a toilet; if left for any length of time it may cause crazing or cracking in the glaze.

HEAVY-DUTY CLEANING

● **Dirty toilets** Use a toilet brush with a rag tied firmly over the head to push the water out of the bowl. Bale out the last bit, then clean the bowl thoroughly with bleach. Flush immediately.

● **Damaged surfaces** Treat hard-water deposits with a paste of laundry borax and white vinegar. Leave for a few hours, then rinse. Cracked and crazed bowls harbor germs and should be replaced.

OTHER BATHROOM TIPS

Slip soap into a sponge

● **Leftover soap** To use up ends of soap, cut a slit in a sponge, and place the soap pieces into it. This creates a delightful soapy sponge for the bath.
● **Bath plugs** If rubber plugs are difficult to remove, slip a curtain ring onto the top – the plug will pull out easily.

TRADITIONAL TIP

Removing smells
A clever method of getting rid of bathroom odors is to strike a match or light a candle. The flame burns away noxious gases.

KITCHENS

Like Bathrooms, kitchens need daily cleaning, since dirty food-preparation surfaces or equipment can cause food poisoning. Keep pets away from surfaces where food is prepared – or work strictly on cutting boards.

KITCHEN-CLEANING EQUIPMENT

Keep these items by your kitchen sink. Do not use dirty kitchen-cleaning equipment. Wash steel wool and scouring pads after each use, and get rid of cleaning cloths when they become worn or dirty. A dishwashing brush is more effective than a sponge, and it can be useful for getting into corners of pans and dishes.

Steel-wool pads

Dishwashing brush

Scouring pads

Cleaning cloth

Dishwashing liquid

SINKS AND SURFACES

Keep sinks and surfaces in the kitchen squeaky clean for sanitary reasons. Clean laminate countertops with a damp cloth dipped in baking soda or cream cleaner. Avoid harsh abrasives and any household cleaners containing bleaches, which can be poisonous.

PORCELAIN SINKS
● **Easy clean** Fill your sink with hot water and a few drops of household bleach. Wearing a rubber glove, reach in and adjust the drain so that the water drains out very slowly, giving everything a good cleaning. Rinse well.

STAINLESS STEEL SINKS
● **Restoring shine** Clean sinks daily with dishwashing liquid. Use denatured alcohol or white vinegar to remove water spots. Give the sink a good shine by rubbing with soda water or using stainless-steel polish. Rinse thoroughly.

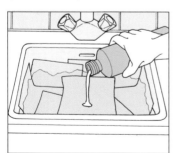

Making sinks sparkle
Place a layer of paper towels around the bowl of the sink, and saturate with diluted household bleach. Leave for five minutes, then remove towels (wearing gloves). Rinse well before use.

Removing lime scale
Lime scale tends to build up around drains in hard water areas. Cut a lemon in half and rub the deposit vigorously with the cut surface. Alternatively, use a commercial scale remover.

KITCHEN SURFACES

● **Kitchen cabinets** Empty cabinets several times a year, discarding anything that is no longer fresh. Wash interiors with a mild solution of detergent, then rinse. Wipe the base of each item before replacing in the cabinet.
● **Wooden kitchen tables** Scrub unsealed wooden tables that are used for meals or food preparation regularly to keep grease and germs at bay. Sealed wooden tables just need frequent wiping.

STOVES

Wipe stove exteriors from time to time with a damp cloth. Clean off spills with dishwashing liquid or household cleaner. If you are cooking food that may bubble over in the oven, place the dish on a baking tray; the tray is easier to clean than the oven floor.

CLEANING OVENS
● **Basic care** Keep ovens clean by wiping them out – while still warm – with a damp cloth dipped in baking soda. Use abrasive household detergent to remove stains on ovenproof glass, but wait until the glass is completely cold.
● **Dirty ovens** Clean with a commercial oven cleaner (this does not apply to self-cleaning ovens). Clean up any spills on oven floors to prevent them from becoming encrusted.

CLEANING MICROWAVES
● **Basic cleaning** Wipe out after each use. If the cavity smells, microwave a bowl of water with a little added lemon juice on High for one minute, then wipe out.

HOBS
● **Cleaning** Wipe hobs after cooking. Where food has burned around burners, cover with a cloth wrung out in dishwashing liquid solution. Leave for a couple of hours before wiping clean.

Preventing burns
Pouring salt onto food spills that occur during cooking will prevent the spills from burning; this works inside ovens as well.

REMOVABLE PARTS
● **Shelves and grills** Oven shelves can be cleaned in the dishwasher. Or, place dirty shelves and grills in the tub, and soak in a solution of enzymatic detergent and hot water. Use old towels to protect the tub surface.
● **Grill pans** Wash after each use; otherwise, the buildup of fat may become a fire hazard.

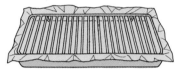

Lining grill pans
Place foil inside grill pans so that you can simply discard the foil when it becomes dirty, rather than having to wash the pan.

REFRIGERATORS AND FREEZERS

Use baking soda and warm water to wipe the insides of refrigerators and freezers – soap or dishwashing liquid will leave a smell and can taint food. If you need to defrost your freezer, store food in coolers, or ask friendly neighbors to borrow space in their freezers.

CLEANING & DEFROSTING

An old towel on refrigerator floor will soak up liquid from cleaning or defrosting

If defrosting freezer, place baking pan on floor to catch drips

Use a hair dryer to speed up defrosting – keep it away from plastic

Cleaning refrigerators
Once every few months, remove all the food, switch off the refrigerator, and wipe down all the surfaces. Defrost the freezer at the same time if necessary.

REFRIGERATOR SMELLS

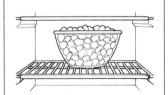

● **Deodorizing refrigerators** Leave a bowl filled with cat litter or charcoal to absorb smells in refrigerators that are going to be switched off.
● **Persistent smells** Wipe all nonmetal parts of the refrigerator with a solution of 2 tbs (30 g) baking soda in 1 quart (1 liter) of water to remove persistent smells.

WASHING DISHES

Do it right away! That is the golden rule if you wash your dishes by hand (people with dishwashers have a little more leeway). If you cannot wash dishes at once, remember to soak everything you can. Change dishwater as soon as it starts to look dirty or greasy.

GENERAL TIPS

● **Smells on hands** Immersing hands that smell from food preparation in hot water will set the smell. Prevent this by rubbing vinegar over hands before doing the dishes.

● **Stained china** Remove tea and coffee stains on cups and cigarette burns on china by rubbing with a damp cloth and baking soda.

DISHWASHING SEQUENCE

● **Glassware** Wash first. Rinse glasses used for milk or alcohol in cold water before washing. Place a rubber splash guard on your tap to reduce the risk of glasses being chipped.

● **Cutlery** Wash after glassware. Do not leave items with wood, bone, china, or plastic handles in water for any length of time.

● **Crockery** Wash after cutlery. Scrape or rinse off all food debris. Do not use hot water on egg-, milk-, or starch-based foods, or they will set.

● **Pots and pans** Wash last. Let soak while washing other items. Use the methods described opposite to clean discolored or burned pots and pans.

WASHING GLASSWARE AND CHINA BY HAND

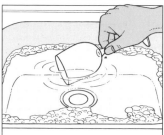

Preventing cracks
To ensure that glasses do not crack when you place them in hot water, slip them in sideways instead of bottom first. Always be sure to check the water temperature *before* you put on rubber gloves.

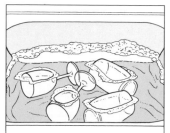

Crystal and fine china
Place a towel on the bottom of the sink to act as a cushion when washing crystal and fine china. Alternatively, use a plastic bin to prevent items from bumping against the hard surface of the sink.

GREEN TIP

Cutting through grease
Add a little vinegar to the rinse water. It cuts through grease and leaves dishes sparkling clean.

DISHWASHERS

These are the ultimate kitchen tools. Always use the recommended type and amount of detergent – too much detergent makes too many suds and prevents the machine from cleaning properly. Check the dishwasher's inlet and outlet hoses periodically for blockages.

BASIC CARE

● **Cleaning** Wipe dishwasher exteriors regularly, and clean the inside with household detergent. Run the dishwasher empty occasionally, using a special interior cleaner.

● **Choosing cycles** Try out all the cycles on a dishwasher; a shorter cycle may clean just as well as a longer one.

WASHING ITEMS

● **Not dishwasher safe** Wash valuable glassware, china and glassware decorated with a metal strip, delicate china, and antique china by hand – never wash them in a dishwasher.

● **Cutlery** Never put stainless steel with silver or silver-plated cutlery – the silver may become pitted or stained.

DEALING WITH PROBLEMS

● **Dishes not clean** If food specks remain on dishes after washing, you may have overloaded the dishwasher, not used enough detergent, or used the wrong cycle.

● **Cloudy glasses** This is the result of hard-water deposits. Use more detergent and – if suitable – rinse aid and salt.

POTS AND PANS

Soaking pots and pans after use makes them easier to clean. Some nonstick surfaces just need to be wiped over with paper towels. To remove persistent smells from a pan, fill the pan with water and 2 tbsp (30 ml) of white vinegar, and bring this mixture to a boil.

ALUMINUM

Use apple skins only

Removing discoloration
Boil natural acid – try an onion, lemon juice, rhubarb, or apple peel – in discolored aluminum pans. Do not soak aluminum (or stainless steel) pans for long or leave food in them because they will discolor and pit.

COPPER

Dip lemon in salt to make it mildly abrasive

Removing tarnish
Rub the exteriors of copper pots with the cut side of half a lemon dipped in salt to remove tarnish. Or fill a spray bottle with vinegar and 3 tbsp (45 g) salt, and spray onto the copper. Let sit, then rub clean.

CAST IRON
● **Cleaning** Dry cast iron thoroughly after washing to prevent rusting. Rub a little oil around the inside to keep it seasoned. Clean the outside with commercial oven cleaner.

BURNED POTS AND PANS
● **Soaking burns** Fill a badly burned pan with a solution of enzymatic detergent. Leave for a couple of hours, then bring to the boil and remove as much deposit as possible. This treatment may need to be repeated several times before the burn disappears.
● **Thick burns** Allow the burn to dry, pick off as much of the deposit as possible, then use the treatment above.

EQUIPMENT AND APPLIANCES

Take care of your kitchen equipment, and it will last for years. Do not put pots, pans, or other pieces of equipment away with any specks of food still adhering to them. Wash and dry wooden items immediately after use. Always disconnect appliances before cleaning.

HARD-TO-CLEAN ITEMS

Scrub with dish-washing liquid

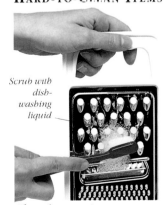

Cleaning graters
Get debris out of graters and sieves with an old toothbrush. Boil a few old toothbrushes to sterilize them, and keep them in your kitchen-cleaning kit.

SMALL APPLIANCES
● **Blenders** Rinse the jar as soon as you have used it. Pour in a little dishwashing liquid and warm water, and blend thoroughly to clean. Repeat with water to rinse.
● **Food processors** These usually have several parts, some of which can be washed in a dishwasher. Check the manufacturer's instructions; some plastic parts should be washed only on the top rack.
● **Coffeemakers** Keep the internal parts clean by running undiluted vinegar through them, as if making coffee. Run clean water through the cycle twice afterward to rinse away any remaining vinegar.

WOODEN ITEMS

Rub with cut lemon

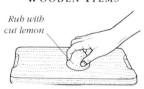

● **Cutting boards** After cutting foods such as fish or garlic, remove smells by rubbing cutting boards with half a lemon.
● **Rolling pins** Sprinkle with salt, and rub with your hand to loosen particles of pastry. Then wash, rinse, and dry.
● **Wooden bread bins** To stop mildew from developing, wipe bread bins with white vinegar on a cloth. Dry open.

KITCHEN WASTE

Keeping your kitchen free from waste is important for health as well as for aesthetics. If garbage is left around, particularly in hot weather, odors are produced, creating new problems. To discard fat, freeze it in an old can, then throw the can out.

DISPOSAL UNITS

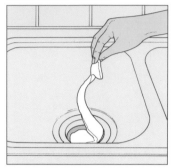

Cleaning and care
Stop electric waste-disposal units from becoming smelly by grinding citrus peels in them. Clear food debris by pouring a bucket of hot water with a handful of washing soda down them from time to time.

RECYCLING WASTE
● **Plastic containers** Keep plastic margarine and cottage cheese containers – they can be used for freezing food, and come in handy around the house when mixing glue or cleaning paintbrushes.
● **Plastic bags** After shopping, save and reuse plastic grocery bags as garbage can liners.

Clean foil with a damp cloth

Reusing kitchen foil
Recycle kitchen foil, which is rarely worn out after just one use. Wipe with a damp cloth, or – if it is very dirty – soak it in a hot solution of dishwashing liquid. When clean, rinse, and smooth out with a cloth.

SINK DRAINS
● **Weekly cleaning** Put a capful of washing soda down the drain once a week, and follow it with a potful of boiling water. This keeps the sink clean and removes blockages that have built up.
● **Grease and fat** If you pour fat down the sink by accident, follow it immediately with a potful of boiling water. Repeat the treatment until it clears. You can pour used fat down an outdoor drain, but follow it with some washing soda and boiling water.
● **Sink plugs** If your rubber plug tends to come out during washing up, roughen the plug edges with steel wool.

SCENTED KITCHEN

Cinnamon stick

● **Baking scent** Cook brown sugar and cinnamon on very low heat on a pan on the stove – this will make your kitchen smell as if you have been baking all day.
● **Simmering cloves** To create a delicious smell around the house and increase humidity, simmer some cloves in water.

DEALING WITH PESTS AND SMELLS

ANT DETERRENTS

● **Ant-free cabinets** Hang sprigs of dried pennyroyal, rue, or tansy in kitchen cabinets to keep ants away from your foods and dishes.
● **Keeping ants out** If you know where ants are coming in, sprinkle dried mint, chili powder, or laundry borax across their trail. Plant mint near windows and doors.

● **Ants' nests** Mix one part laundry borax with one part confectioners' sugar. Scatter the mixture over a piece of wood near the site of the nest. The ants will be attracted by the sweet sugar and will then be poisoned by the laundry borax.

OTHER PESTS
● **Cockroaches** Leave a mixture of equal parts of flour, cocoa powder, and laundry borax; or a mixture of equal parts of baking soda and confectioner's sugar in shallow dishes. Keep away from children and pets.

FOOD SMELLS
● **Burned food** Boil a few slices of lemon in a saucepan to clear the air of burned food smells.
● **Fried food** Place a small bowl of white vinegar next to the stove whenever you are frying foods. This helps prevent unpleasant fat smells.

CLEANING CHECKLIST

T HIS CHART CONTAINS brief guidelines for cleaning the different surfaces found in the home. For more detailed instructions on caring for various household items and surfaces, and undertaking minor repairs, see pages 114–131.

SURFACE	BASIC CLEANING METHOD	SPECIAL NOTES
TILES	Wipe with household detergent, and rinse to remove residual traces. Clean dirty grout with a household bleach solution.	Remove soap splashes with a solution of one part white vinegar to four parts water. Rinse.
BRICK	Scrub with a solution of dishwashing liquid, taking care not to overwet since bricks are porous. Rinse and dry.	Sponge burn marks with vinegar, and rinse. See p. 98 for removing soot marks from brick.
CONCRETE	Dissolve a cup of washing soda in a bucket of warm water, and wash. Sweep concrete floors regularly.	To remove stains, scrape off any deposit, scrub with sugar soap crystals, then rinse.
LEATHER	Wipe with a damp cloth rubbed on a bar of glycerin soap. Apply a thin coat of hide food occasionally.	See p. 67 and 126 for cleaning and caring for leather furniture.
GLASS	Use a window-cleaning product on glass surfaces. Do not get it on carpets; it will stain.	Try to avoid touching glass, as it shows fingerprints. Use vinegar to remove greasy marks on glass.
MARBLE	Sponge with a soap flake solution, and rinse. Use specialized products for any further treatments needed.	See p. 66 for caring for marble furniture, and p. 125 for removing unsightly stains on marble.
SLATE	Clean with a dishwashing liquid solution. Rinse with a damp cloth, then buff to a shine.	Use marble polish on smooth slate. Scrub textured slate with a brush and dishwashing liquid solution.
PLASTIC	Wipe over with dishwashing liquid. Use an aerosol cleaner to protect plastic from dust.	Soak smelly plastic containers overnight in a baking soda and warm water solution.
STAINLESS STEEL	Wash and dry immediately after use. Polish occasionally. See p. 70 and 120 for additional care advice.	Tends to discolor and pit, so immerse it in water for as short a time as possible.
SILVER	Polish regularly. If stored, keep items in tarnishproof paper or bags. See also p. 118–119.	Never mix silver and stainless steel in a dishwasher's cutlery basket. Egg will stain silver cutlery.
WOOD	Dust, sweep, and mop regularly, and polish only occasionally. Do not wet unsealed wood.	See p. 58–60 for wooden floors, p. 66 for wooden furniture, and p. 115–117 for caring for wood.

DEALING WITH STAINS

QUICK REFERENCE

Tackling Stains, p. 78

Food Stains, p. 80

Spilled Beverages, p. 83

Biological Stains, p. 86

Pigment Stains, p. 90

Product Stains, p. 93

Wear and Tear, p. 96

Other Stains, p. 99

*T*HE SECRET OF REMOVING STAINS *is to treat them at once – or as soon as possible after they occur. Stains that are left to soak in and dry are more difficult to remove and may, in some cases, be impossible to get out. Keep a kit with stain-removal equipment, cleaners, and solvents handy, so you can act quickly when accidents happen. Here you will find essential information on stain-removal equipment and methods, as well as specific treatments for the most common stains.*

STAIN-REMOVAL EQUIPMENT

These are the items that you will need for your stain-removal kit. Together with the cleaners and solvents on the opposite page, they will enable you to tackle stains effectively. Keep your kit in a separate box, and replace items as necessary.

● **To absorb grease** Use brown or blotting paper, together with an iron, to remove grease.
● **To blot stains** Use anything that is disposable, such as paper towels. Never use anything that is dyed.
● **To apply solvents** Use cotton balls or a white rag. Never use colored cloth, which may transfer dye to stained items.
● **To dilute stains** Use a sponge to apply clean water to stains, or use a soda syphon, which will flush stains out of carpets.
● **To scrape up deposits** Use an old spoon or a metal ruler to lift off stain deposits.
● **For protective covering** Rubber gloves protect your hands when you use harsh cleaners or toxic solvents. Always wear gloves when using ammonia and bleach.

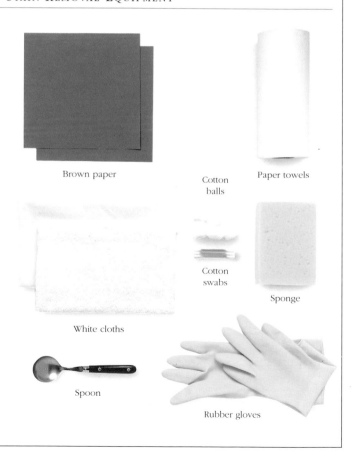

Brown paper

Cotton balls

Paper towels

Cotton swabs

Sponge

White cloths

Spoon

Rubber gloves

CLEANERS AND SOLVENTS

The cleaners and solvents shown here will remove most household stains. Keep the items that you use most in your stain-removal kit. Ammonia, denatured alcohol, laundry borax, hydrogen peroxide, turpentine, and acetone are toxic. Lemon, eucalyptus oil, glycerin, and vinegar are all natural stain remedies. Carpet shampoo, biological detergent with enzymes, and talcum powder are helpful for treating stains on carpets, clothes, and furniture, respectively.

Denatured alcohol (dyed in some areas)

Denatured alcohol

Carpet shampoo

Ammonia

DILUTION FORMULAS

● **Ammonia** Add 1 tsp (5 ml) to 2 cups (500 ml) of cold water.
● **Laundry borax** Add 1 tbsp (15 g) to 2 cups (500 ml) of warm water.
● **Hydrogen peroxide** Dilute one part to six parts cold water.
● **Glycerin** Dilute with equal parts warm water.

Laundry borax

Detergent with enzymes

Talcum powder

Lemon

Eucalyptus oil

Hydrogen peroxide

Glycerin

Turpentine

Dishwashing liquid

Acetone

White vinegar

COMMERCIAL CLEANERS

Specialized laundry products (for example, prewash sticks and sprays), commercial stain removers, and stain solvents are ideal for removing marks on fabric and carpets. You can also buy grease solvents for grease and oil marks, and commercial upholstery- and carpet-spotting kits, which contain small bottles of different chemicals that you mix together to treat stains.

Prewash stick

Foam stain remover

Aerosol stain remover

Prewash spray

Stain solvents

TACKLING STAINS

Treat stains at once, but test the method on a hidden part of the item first. To avoid spreading a stain, dab at it instead of rubbing it, and always work from the outside to the center. Never use hot water, which will set stains.

TYPES OF STAIN

Stains can be divided into two main types: built-up stains and absorbed stains. Some substances, such as blood and egg, produce a stain that is a combination of the two. Always treat these "combination stains" as built-up stains first, then treat them for absorption.

BUILT-UP STAINS

Removing deposits
Built-up stains are made by thick substances that need to be scraped off before treatment. Scoop them up quickly so that they do not penetrate far.

ABSORBED STAINS

Blotting liquid
Thin liquids will sink quickly into a surface. Blot the area with paper towels or a white cloth immediately. Launder or sponge to remove the rest of the stain.

OTHER STAINS

● **Mystery stains** If you do not know the cause of a stain, proceed with caution. Soak washable items, then launder them according to fabric. Sponge nonwashables with clear warm water. If staining persists, apply a hydrogen peroxide solution (see p. 77).
● **Dried stains** To loosen dried stains, use a glycerin solution (see p. 77). Sponge off this initial treatment before using another chemical that may react with the glycerin.

DIFFERENT SURFACES

Stains should be treated not only according to type, but also according to the surface on which they fall. The three methods below outline the basic treatments that can be used for stains on carpets, stains on nonwashable fabrics or upholstery, and stains on clothes.

CARPETS

Apply shampoo on a sponge

Shampooing carpets
After removing any deposit, treat the remaining mark with a solution of carpet shampoo. If this leaves a startlingly clean spot, you will need to shampoo the entire carpet using either a manual or an electric machine.

UPHOLSTERY

Absorbing stains
Scrape up any deposit, and blot the stain well. Apply talcum powder, and leave until it appears discolored, having absorbed the stain. Wipe away with a cloth. Apply more talcum powder if the mark persists.

CLOTHES

Dab mark, rather than rubbing it

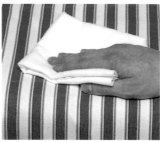

Dabbing away stains
Treat stains on washable clothes as soon as they occur, and always before you launder the item. Use lukewarm or cold water and a cloth to dab the mark. Alternatively, soak the garment if recommended.

STAINS ON WASHABLE FABRICS

L aundering a stained garment can set the stain, making it very difficult to remove. Always treat stains before laundering, using one of the three methods below. Observe the guidelines for different fabrics, and invest in any laundry aids you think might be useful.

GENERAL TREATMENT

Rinsing off stains
Rinse stains in cold or lukewarm water as soon as possible after they occur. Alternatively, sponge with clear water until the stain fades. Never use hot water on stains; it will cause them to set.

PROTEIN STAINS

Soaking items
Stains made from substances such as milk and blood respond best to soaking in enzymatic detergent. Do not soak items longer than recommended; always immerse the whole item.

PERSISTENT STAINS

Applying a solvent
If stains persist after rinsing or soaking, use a stain or grease solvent before laundering. Place a white cloth under the stain to avoid transferring the stain to another layer, then dab.

LAUNDRY AIDS

● **Detergents** These come in varying strengths, and many contain additives to remove stains. Some stains require extra treatment with one of the substances below

● **Detergent with enzymes** This works well on stains that contain proteins, such as egg yolk, blood, and sweat. It is often a constituent of ordinary detergents, but is best used separately for stain removal.

● **Bleach** This has a whitening effect, so it should be used with care on colors. Avoid contact with your skin and clothes. (See also p. 102.)

● **Laundry borax** This old-fashioned laundry aid is an excellent stain remover. Dilute for sponging or soaking (see p. 77), or sprinkle directly onto stains (see p. 85).

● **Other aids** Stain solvents and prewash sticks and sprays help remove marks on clothes (see p. 77). Ink stains are best treated by soap flakes.

FABRICS	TREATMENT NOTES
COLORS	Treat stains with care to avoid producing bleached patches. Soak the whole item when using a bleaching treatment such as laundry borax.
WHITES	Natural fabrics can usually be bleached. Synthetics and mixtures can yellow with this treatment and may respond better to the correct detergent.
NATURAL FABRICS	Because these can be washed at high temperatures, rinsing or presoaking items before laundering is usually enough to remove most stains.
SYNTHETIC FABRICS	These are easily damaged by some chemicals, so test any treatment on a hidden part before tackling the stain.
DELICATES	These fabrics should always be treated cautiously. Avoid using strong chemical treatments on delicate fabrics.

FOOD STAINS

OST FOOD STAINS can be removed using the basic methods shown on pages 78–79, provided you act quickly. The worst culprits are those featured here – stains from greasy foods, egg, and foods containing strong colorings.

OIL, FAT, AND GREASE STAINS

Grease stains are straightforward to remove from fabric, but they may cause more of a problem on carpets and furniture. Ties and scarves are susceptible to grease spots; use fabric-protection spray on nonwashable items when they are new or newly dry cleaned.

ON CARPETS

1 Place a piece of brown paper over the grease mark. Apply the tip of a warm iron until the grease is absorbed into the brown paper.

2 Apply a solution of carpet shampoo to the remaining mark, using a sponge. Rub into the carpet gently but firmly for a few minutes.

3 Wipe off the foam with a clean sponge or cloth. Inspect the mark; if it remains or reappears later, repeat the treatment from the beginning.

ON FURNITURE

Cover stain with talcum powder

Brush off talcum powder with dry, fluffy cloth

1 Sprinkle talcum powder thickly over the grease mark. Let stand until the grease begins to be absorbed.

2 After 10 minutes, brush off the talcum powder. If the mark still appears to be greasy, repeat the treatment.

ON CLOTHES

● **General treatment** Blot excess grease, using paper towels. Dab gently, taking care not to spread the stain. For nondelicate fabrics, which can be washed at reasonably high temperatures, laundering will remove residual marks.

● **Delicate fabrics** Dab delicate fabrics with a little eucalyptus oil, then either hand wash them, or machine wash at a low temperature. If the fabric is to be dry cleaned only, sponge the eucalyptus oil off with clear, warm water.

GREASE ON SHOES

Repair adhesive

● **Leather shoes** Apply a little bicycle puncture repair adhesive to grease spots. Leave overnight, then peel off. Use shoe polish or hide food to finish up. Well-cleaned leather shoes will resist grease – just wipe over with a paper towel.

● **Suede shoes** Blot well, then rub with a block suede cleaner. Treat bad stains with a pad of white cotton dampened with lighter fluid. Check first on a test area to make sure that the color is not adversely affected.

OTHER GREASY STAINS

Foods such as avocado, peanut butter, and those listed below contain oil or fat, and may leave behind a grease patch. Tackle the grease stain before dealing with any remaining color. Substances such as car oil, ointments, and lotions should also be treated as grease.

MAYONNAISE
● **On washable fabrics** Sponge with warm water, then soak in a solution of enzymatic detergent before laundering.
● **On nonwashable fabrics** Wipe with a damp cloth, then use an aerosol grease solvent.

ICE CREAM
● **On washable fabrics** Wipe with a damp cloth, then soak in a detergent solution.
● **On nonwashable fabrics** Blot, then wipe with a damp cloth wrung out in warm water. Use a grease solvent.

GRAVY
● **On washable fabrics** Soak overnight in tepid water, then launder according to the fabric. Soak dried marks in enzymatic detergent if the fabric permits.
● **On nonwashable fabrics** Use an aerosol stain remover.

Mayonnaise on carpets
Scrape up as much as possible, then blot. Use a general stain remover for light marks, and the carpet treatment opposite to remove heavier stains.

Ice cream on carpets
Scrape up the deposit, and wipe the area with a damp cloth. Clean with a solution of carpet shampoo. Use a stain remover or grease solvent if marks remain.

Gravy on carpets
Scoop up what you can with a spoon, or blot the area dry with paper towels. Treat with a liquid stain remover followed by an application of carpet shampoo.

EGG STAINS

Egg is a tricky stain. The merest drop of hot water causes it to set and form a crusty deposit that is much harder to remove than a fresh stain. If you cannot treat an egg stain immediately, cover it with a damp cloth to keep it moist and prevent it from setting.

ON FURNITURE

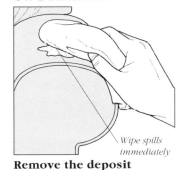
Wipe spills immediately

Remove the deposit
Use a damp white cloth to remove the spilled egg. If only egg white has been spilled, sponge the stain with cold, salty water. For yolk alone, dab repeatedly with lather from dishwashing liquid solution.

ON CARPETS
● **Basic treatment** Scrape up the deposit, then use a liquid stain remover to tackle what remains. If a mark is still visible when dry, apply a carpet-shampoo solution.

ON CLOTHES
● **Washable fabric** Sponge with cold, salty water. Rinse off when the stain has disappeared. Soak in an enzymatic detergent solution if necessary (and appropriate).
● **Nonwashable fabric** Sponge with salt water, then sponge off with clear water, and blot dry. Use an aerosol stain remover on remaining marks.

TRADITIONAL TIP

Stains on cutlery
Egg, especially boiled egg, stains silver cutlery black. Wipe fresh egg off cutlery after use. Rub black stains with salt.

COLORED FOOD STAINS

Color is the last thing you treat when dealing with a food stain. Get rid of the deposit first, then treat any grease element. Finally, tackle the color, which may require several attempts. Specific treatments for well-known "difficult" food stains appear below.

FOOD TYPE	ON WASHABLE FABRICS	ON OTHER SURFACES
TOMATO SAUCE Treat tomato sauce and other thick bottled sauces in the same way. 	Hold fresh stains under cold running water, and rub between your fingers. Apply a prewash treatment, then launder according to fabric.	On carpets, remove deposit, and sponge with warm water. Blot dry, apply carpet shampoo, and wipe off. When dry, use a spray stain remover. Follow these steps for nonwashable fabrics, omitting the shampoo.
MUSTARD Mustard powder can be brushed off. Prepared mustard produces a stain that is difficult to remove. 	Rub fresh stains between your fingers in a mild detergent solution, then sponge with an ammonia solution (see p. 77). Soften dried stains at first with a glycerin solution (see p. 77), and let stand for at least an hour.	Sponge carpets and furniture with a mild detergent solution, then an ammonia solution (see p. 77). Avoid overwetting, and finish by sponging with clean water. Stubborn stains require professional cleaning.
JAM AND PRESERVES These leave sticky residues that should be scooped up and wiped with a damp cloth. 	Laundering should remove stains. Soak dried marks for half an hour in a laundry borax solution (see p. 77).	Sponge furniture with a warm dishwashing liquid solution. Sprinkle laundry borax on the mark, and sponge off after 15 minutes. On carpets, use carpet shampoo, then denatured alcohol (try on a test area first).
CURRY AND TURMERIC These are two of the worst stains. Do not get them on wall coverings, where the only solution is a patch. 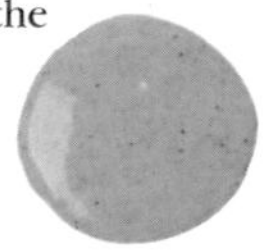	Rinse stains in tepid water. Rub in a glycerin solution (see p. 77), leave for half an hour, and rinse. Launder in enzymatic detergent, if suitable. Use a hydrogen peroxide solution (see p. 77) on persistent stains.	Sponge carpets and furniture with a laundry borax solution (see p. 77). If this does not work on furniture, have the covers dry cleaned (if possible). A laundry prewash stick may also be effective on carpets.
BEETS This stain is difficult to remove because the color is deep and persistent. 	Rinse under cold, running water until as much color as possible has come out. Soak colored fabrics in a laundry borax solution (see p. 77). For whites, use the treatment for dried tea stains shown on p. 85.	Do not attempt to remove stains on nonwashable fabrics or furniture yourself. Have both slipcovers and upholstery professionally cleaned.
CHOCOLATE Dropped pieces of chocolate are a problem once they get warm or if someone sits on them. 	Allow to set, then scrape the dry deposit with a blunt knife. Soak, then launder in enzymatic detergent if suitable; otherwise launder as usual. For persistent stains, use the treatment for dried tea stains shown on p. 85.	Allow to set, then scrape up with a blunt knife. Apply a lather of carpet shampoo (for both furniture and carpets), rubbing in gently. Wipe off with a damp cloth, and use a liquid stain remover when dry.

SPILLED BEVERAGES

Start by blotting stains caused by spilled drinks, then go on to more intensive measures. Always use white cloth, tissues, or paper towels. Never use colored paper towels, which may bleed dye into the stain and worsen it.

RED WINE STAINS

Red wine is one of the most common carpet stains. Salt is effective for preventing stains on table linen from spreading, but on carpets it creates a permanent damp patch that attracts dirt to the area. Use the three-step treatment below or pour white wine over the area.

ON CARPETS

1 Blot the spill immediately, then sponge repeatedly with warm water. If you have a soda syphon, use it to flush the stain – the soda water plus the spraying action will lift the stain effectively.

2 Blot dry, then apply the foam from carpet shampoo on a sponge, working it in well. Sponge again with clear water, and repeat the treatment as often as necessary until clear.

3 Cover any remaining stain with a glycerin solution (see p. 77), and leave for up to an hour. Sponge off with clear water, and blot well. Apply a little denatured alcohol on a sponge to reduce old stains. Use the tip at right for a quick rescue when you cannot treat stains properly.

QUICK ACTION

Pour white wine onto red wine spill immediately

Pour some white wine over a red wine spill as soon as it occurs. Blot both liquids well, sponge with clear, warm water, then pat the area dry.

DRIED STAINS ON FURNITURE

1 Apply a glycerin solution (see p. 77) to loosen the stain. Leave the solution on for at least 30 minutes.

2 Sponge off with a weak, warm solution of dish-washing liquid. Wipe with a cloth wrung out in clear water.

FRESH STAINS ON FURNITURE

1 Blot, sponge with warm water, and blot again. Repeat if necessary. Cover persistent marks with talcum powder while still damp.

2 Brush the talcum powder off after a few minutes, using a soft brush or cloth. Continue the treatment until the mark disappears.

ON CLOTHES

● **General treatment** Rinse fresh wine stains in warm water. If the stain persists, soak the garment in a laundry borax solution (see p. 77) or a heavy-duty detergent, then launder according to fabric type.

● **Delicate fabrics** Bleach stains on white wool or silk with a hydrogen peroxide solution (see p. 77). Rinse, then hand wash.

ON TABLE LINEN

● **Fresh stains** Bleach white cotton and linen items. Soak colored items in a heavy-duty detergent solution, then launder as usual. Alternatively, use the treatment for dried tea stains shown on page 85.

BEER AND ALCOHOL STAINS

Beer and alcohol stains are fairly easy to remove from most surfaces (unless they are brightly colored or sticky liqueur stains). Old beer and alcohol stains are another matter, however, and require more drastic treatment if they are to come out satisfactorily.

ON CLOTHES
● **Beer and alcohol** Rinse or soak in tepid water, then launder according to fabric type. On whites, use a hydrogen peroxide solution (see p. 77) to bleach any remaining marks. On colors, sponge with a white vinegar solution – 2 tbsp (30 ml) vinegar to 2 cups (500 ml) of water – until stains disappear.

ON FURNITURE
● **Beer** Blot thoroughly, then sponge with a cloth wrung out in clean, warm water. Treat remaining marks with a spray-on stain remover.
● **Spirits** Sponge with clean, warm water until all traces of stickiness are removed, then use an upholstery-spotting kit. Have delicate fabrics that might watermark professionally dry cleaned.

ON CARPETS
● **Beer stains** Sponge with clean, warm water, or flush with a soda syphon, then blot. If marks remain, use a solution of carpet shampoo.
● **Alcohol stains** Treat as above, acting quickly to prevent color from soaking in. If colored marks remain, sponge with denatured alcohol on a damp cloth.

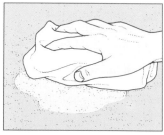

Old beer stains
Gently wipe old beer stains on carpets with denatured alcohol until the mark begins to fade.

LIQUEUR STAINS

These tend to be stickier than other spilled alcohol drinks. If any stains from highly colored liqueurs remain after treatment, use a stain remover or denatured alcohol on the mark, testing first on an inconspicuous area.

● **Carpets** Flush stain with a soda syphon to dissipate stickiness, and blot the residue with paper towels. Apply carpet shampoo.
● **Upholstery** Sponge with warm water until all traces of stickiness are gone. Take care not to overwet. Apply carpet shampoo; use an upholstery-spotting kit on any remaining marks. Professionally dry clean any slipcovers that might watermark.
● **Clothes** Rinse the mark in warm water, then wash or dry clean the item as usual.

FRUIT JUICE STAINS

Fruit juices cause problem stains because of the color residue they leave – especially dark-colored fruits such as red berries and black grapes. If they are allowed to dry they can be difficult to remove and – unless treated carefully – will leave a permanent mark.

FRESH STAINS
● **Clothes** Rinse under cold running water until as much of the mark as possible is removed. Treat any remaining color with denatured alcohol or a stain remover.
● **Carpets** Blot with paper towels. Rub the area with a laundry prewash stick, and let stand for a few minutes. Rinse off, blot, and shampoo. Treat any remaining color with denatured alcohol.
● **Furniture** Sponge with cold water, and blot dry. Use a liquid stain remover.

DRIED STAINS

Loosen stain with glycerin solution

Treating old stains
Hold a clean cloth under the stain and apply a glycerin solution (see p. 77) with a second cloth. Leave for one hour, rinse, then treat as for fresh stains (see left).

GREEN TIP

Nature's stain remover
Rub the cut side of half a lemon on fresh fruit juice stains. Lemon juice is a natural bleaching agent.

TEA, COFFEE, AND COCOA STAINS

These stains tend to be a combination of the coloring of the drink and grease from any added milk. Blot the whole stain initially, then attack the grease, and finally use a method that will get rid of the color of the stain. Dried tea stains on fabric require special treatment.

ON FABRIC

● **Fresh tea stains** Rinse stains on clothes in lukewarm water, then soak in a laundry borax solution (see p. 77). Rinse stains on blankets at once in warm water, then launder. Rinse table linen immediately under cold water, then soak and launder, preferably in a detergent with enzymes.

● **Coffee and cocoa** Rinse in warm water. Soak in a warm enzymatic detergent solution (if suitable), or in a laundry borax solution (see p. 77).

DRIED TEA STAINS

If treating linen or cotton, water should be boiling

1 Drape the stained item over a bowl or basin. Sprinkle with laundry borax until the whole stain is thickly covered.

2 Pour a potful of hot water around the stain, working toward the center. Repeat treatment if necessary.

ISOLATING A STAIN

Tie off area with string

On a comforter or pillow, push the filling down and tie off the stained area, then wash it. This way you do not have to wash the entire item.

ON CARPETS

● **Coffee with milk and cocoa** Sponge with tepid water, or flush with a soda syphon. Apply a little carpet shampoo, and – when dry – use a liquid stain remover (but not on foam-backed carpets).

● **Black coffee** Sponge the stain repeatedly with tepid water, or flush it several times with a soda syphon, then blot.

● **Tea** Blot with paper towels, then sponge with tepid water, or apply a squirt from a soda syphon. Use a little carpet shampoo, and use an aerosol stain remover when dry.

ON FURNITURE

● **Coffee with milk and cocoa** Blot the stain with paper towels, then sprinkle with enzymatic detergent. Wipe off with a damp sponge.

● **Black coffee** Blot, sponge, and, if necessary, shampoo. Lubricate dried stains with a glycerin solution (see p. 77). Rinse, and blot well. Use a spray stain remover on any remaining marks.

● **Tea** Sponge off with a laundry borax solution (see p. 77), then wipe with a damp cloth. When dry, apply a spray stain remover.

MILK STAINS

If milk is not treated immediately after it is spilled on carpet, it will dry and leave a smell that is virtually impossible to remove. Move fast with the treatment, or you could find yourself having to replace an expensive item because of the permanent smell.

ON CLOTHES

● **Fresh stains** Rinse in tepid water, then launder as usual. Use a liquid stain remover if a grease mark persists.

● **Dried stains** Soak the item in enzymatic detergent if the fabric is suitable.

ON FURNITURE

● **General treatment** Sponge with tepid water (but do not overwet padded upholstery). Blot dry with paper towels, tissues, or a white cloth. Treat any remaining marks with a spray stain remover.

ON CARPETS

● **Fresh stains** Sponge with clear, warm water, then apply a spray cleaner.

● **Dried stains** If a stain is allowed to dry, the smell may return after cleaning. Use a professional carpet cleaner.

BIOLOGICAL STAINS

Treat biological stains immediately, since they can be difficult to remove if they are allowed to set. Also, they invariably carry unpleasant smells, which tend to linger if the stain is not cleaned up as quickly as possible.

BLOODSTAINS

Blood is a combination stain that soaks into surfaces and leaves a deposit on the top. The deposit is not as thick as some biological stains and therefore cannot be scraped off, but it should be wiped off with a clean cloth immediately. After that, treat the colored stain.

ON CLOTHES

Add a generous handful of salt

Fill bucket with cold water

1 Add a handful of salt to a bucket of cold water. Soak the stained item of clothing for 15 minutes, making sure it is completely immersed.

2 Soak the item in enzymatic detergent next (if suitable), then launder as usual.

ON MATTRESSES

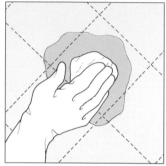

1 Follow the three steps in the box below. Next, apply a thick paste made up of baking soda and water to any stains that remain.

2 Let the paste dry, then brush it off with a dry cloth. Repeat if necessary.

ON CARPETS

● **General treatment** Sponge the area with cold water, and blot dry. Repeat until the stain disappears. If this does not work, use a carpet-spotting kit, followed by an application of carpet shampoo.

DRIED BLOODSTAINS

● **On clothes** Soak in a hydrogen peroxide solution (see p. 77) with ½ tsp (2.5 ml) added ammonia. (Do not use on nylon.)
● **On carpets** Use a glycerin solution (see p. 77), then treat as for fresh stains.
● **On untreated wood** Bleach stains with diluted household bleach, then stain the wood to its original shade.

REMOVING STAINS FROM MATTRESSES

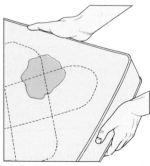

1 Turn the mattress on its side (this may take two people). Prop it up to prevent the stain and treatment from soaking in.

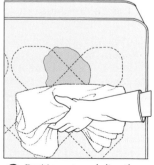

2 Position a towel directly beneath the stain. Always wear rubber gloves when treating biological stains.

3 Sponge the mark, repeating until it disappears. Hold the towel in place beneath the stain so that nothing trickles down.

URINE STAINS

Urine leaves an unpleasant stain that can result in a permanent mark and smell if it is not treated properly immediately. However, correct treatment is usually successful, so if this is a recurring problem in your household, keep the remedy on hand.

ON LEATHER SHOES
● **Fresh stains** Wipe polished shoes with a cloth wrung out in warm water. When dry, buff shoes well, then polish.

● **Dried stains** Wipe with a damp cloth to bring salts to the surface. Apply a product designed to remove salt stains.

ON SUEDE SHOES

Removing marks
Wipe gently with a damp cloth. Brush the damp area with a suede brush. On dry marks, use a shoe salt stain remover. Brush with a suede brush between applications.

Wipe with a cloth wrung out in warm water

GREEN TIP

Neutralize urine smells
Using a plant-spray bottle, squirt a weak white vinegar solution onto pet stains on carpets to help remove the smell. Rinse with clean water.

ON CARPETS
● **Fresh stains** Use a carpet cleaner containing deodorant. Alternatively, sponge with cold water, pat dry, then rinse with a little antiseptic added to a bowl of cold water.
● **Dried stains** Treat as for fresh stains to remove the smell and the mark. Raise any faded color by sponging with a mild ammonia solution.

ON CLOTHES
● **Colored fabrics** Rinse in cold water, then launder according to fabric type.
● **Pale fabrics** Bleach dried urine stains with a hydrogen peroxide solution (see p. 77), to which a few drops of ammonia have been added. Alternatively, soak the item in enzymatic detergent, or use a commercial stain remover.

DRYING MATTRESSES

Clean urine off mattresses using the method opposite. Stand the mattress on its side, then prop it leaning slightly forward so liquid does not soak in more. Speed dry with a hair dryer on a cool setting.

VOMIT STAINS

With vomit, it is vital to get rid of all the deposit before tackling the underlying stain. Wearing rubber gloves, use the bowl of a spoon to lift off as much as possible, and use a metal ruler to scrape up the final traces. Be careful not to spread the stain.

ON CARPETS
● **Removing stains** Sponge with laundry borax solution (see p. 77), then with clear, warm water that includes a few drops of antiseptic. If any discoloration remains, work in the lather from some carpet shampoo with a sponge, or use an aerosol foam cleanser.
● **Removing smells** If the smell persists, continue rinsing with clear water and antiseptic until it disappears.

ON FURNITURE
● **Upholstery** Sponge the area with warm water containing a little ammonia, then pat dry. Or, use an upholstery cleaner that contains a deodorizer. Clean expensive or delicate items professionally.
● **Mattresses** Remove stains by following the method shown opposite. Sponge with a warm solution of dishwashing liquid. Sponge off with warm water that contains a little antiseptic.

ON CLOTHES
● **Removing stains** Rinse the area under cold running water until the mark begins to fade, rubbing the fabric gently between your hands to help the process. Soak, then launder in enzymatic detergent if the fabric is suitable. Alternatively, launder the garment as usual according to fabric type.
● **Removing smells** If the smell persists after laundering, launder the item again.

MUD STAINS

The key to removing any mud stain is to let it dry completely before tackling it. Do not be tempted to apply any treatment whatsoever until the deposit has become hard and you can brush it off easily. After that, you can work on the stain that has been left behind.

ON CARPETS
● **Persistent marks** Use either a carpet-spotting kit or a little denatured alcohol to remove traces of color that remain after removing the deposit.

ON FURNITURE
● **Basic treatment** Remove the deposit, then sponge the area with a weak, warm solution of dishwashing liquid or mild detergent. Wipe, then pat dry.

ON CLOTHES
● **Coats and jackets** Remove dry mud with a soft brush. Apply a commercial dry-cleaning product to any stains that do not brush off.

REMOVING DRIED MUD DEPOSITS

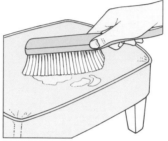

Brush mud off with a dry cloth

Vacuuming carpets
Let the mud dry (this usually takes one or two hours), then vacuum up the deposit. If necessary, use a stiff brush to loosen the dried mud first.

Brushing furniture
Use a soft brush to remove mud deposits on furniture without damaging the upholstery. Remove any remaining traces with a vacuum cleaner.

Wiping clothes
Brush dried mud off clothes with a dry cloth or a soft clothes brush. Launder to remove the remaining marks. Use denatured alcohol on persistent mud stains.

GRASS STAINS

Grass stains are inevitable if your household includes sports players or small children. They are very tricky to remove. As a rule, soak white cottons in bleach; a commercial stain remover help remove stains from other fabrics. Nonwashable fabrics should be dry cleaned.

ON WASHABLE FABRICS
● **Light stains** Provided the fabric is suitable, these stains should respond to a soak followed by laundering in enzymatic detergent. If marks remain, follow the treatment for nonwashable fabrics.
● **Heavy stains** Rub the stain with a heavy-duty hand cleaner – the kind used after serious do-it-yourself jobs. Apply a little denatured alcohol or a commercial stain remover to the area (test first), then rinse in cool, clean water before washing the garment according to fabric type.

ON CARPETS AND SHOES
● **Carpets** Pour a small amount of household detergent onto the stain, rub in, and let stand for a few hours. Scrub with a small brush. Wring out a clean cloth in clear water and wipe away the remains of the detergent.
● **Canvas shoes** Scrub grass stains with a nail brush dipped in a solution of dishwashing liquid and warm water. Wash the shoes in the washing machine, or on the top rack of the dishwasher (making sure all grit is removed first). Allow the shoes to dry naturally.

TRADITIONAL TIP

Treating old stains
Use egg white and glycerine in equal parts to loosen old grass stains on whites, then treat as for fresh stains.

OTHER BIOLOGICAL STAINS

Combat these stains on clothes by soaking in detergent with enzymes (if the fabric permits). Buy some disposable plastic gloves, or use a plastic bag over your hand when dealing with unpleasant deposits. Discard the bag or gloves after you have used them.

STAIN	SURFACE	TREATMENT
POLLEN STAINS	● These stains occur mainly on clothes and wall coverings, and can be very difficult to remove. Wear an apron when picking or arranging flowers, and keep floral arrangements well away from papered walls.	● Normal laundering will remove light stains on clothes. Failing this, dab lightly with denatured alcohol, then sponge off with warm water. ● Rub stains on wallpaper with a ball of white, crustless bread or an eraser. If this treatment fails, the wallpaper may need patching (see p. 62).
FLYSPECKS	● These tend to occur on lampshades, furnishings, and windows. Treat fabric lampshades with care.	● Wipe plastic lampshades with a dishwashing liquid solution. Use a spray stain remover on fabric lampshades, or apply a warm detergent solution with a soft toothbrush. ● Use denatured alcohol on windows, and a commercial stain remover on upholstery.
PERSPIRATION STAINS	● This appears as a yellowish or discolored patch in the armpit area of clothes.	● Sponge washable fabrics with an ammonia solution (see p. 77), then rinse. Where dye has run, sponge with 1 tbsp (15 ml) white vinegar diluted in 1 cup (250 ml) water.
PET STAINS	● These are urine, vomit, and fecal stains that occur mainly on carpets and furniture.	● See p. 87 for treating urine and vomit stains and for getting rid of unpleasant smells. See below for treating feces.
FECAL STAINS	● Always scrape up the deposit from carpets, furniture, and clothes with the bowl of a spoon immediately, taking care not to spread the stain.	● Sponge stains on carpets and furniture with a solution of warm water and a few drops of ammonia. Soak clothes in enzymatic detergent if suitable.
BIRD DROPPINGS	● Clothes drying on a wash line may sometimes become soiled by bird droppings.	● Remove the deposit, and relaunder washable fabrics. A bleach or hydrogen peroxide solution (see p. 77) may work on white and pale garments.
TOBACCO STAINS	● Nicotine can stain smokers' hands and fingernails with a yellowish tinge.	● Rub a pad soaked in a weak bleach solution over the stained areas. Use smoker's toothpaste on fingernails.

PIGMENT AND SYNTHETIC STAINS

THE VARIOUS PAINTS, PENS, and crayons used around most homes produce marks that can be difficult to eradicate, especially since it is not always clear which dyes they contain, and therefore what will remove them.

PAINT STAINS

Every household will suffer at one time or another from spilled paint stains, especially when homes are undergoing redecoration. Unfortunately, paint stains are often left until the end of the day. Dried paint stains can be removed satisfactorily, but you must be careful.

ARTIST'S PAINTS
● **Fresh stains on clothes** Blot water-based paint stains with paper towels, then wash under a tap with soap and water. Launder as usual. Dab at oil-based paints with turpentine, holding a white pad beneath the stain. Sponge off, then launder as usual.

LATEX PAINTS
● **Fresh stains on fabric** Blot immediately, sponge with cold water, then launder.
● **Dried stains on fabric** Recently dried stains should respond to a commercial stain remover. Apply denatured alcohol to older stains (testing first), then launder as usual.

OIL-BASED PAINTS
● **On clothes** Dab with turpentine, then sponge with cold water. You may need to repeat this several times. Do not launder until all the paint is gone – if you do, you will set the stain. Bad stains and acetate and viscose fabrics need professional treatment.

Use a pad of absorbent white cloth

Dried stains on clothes
Hold a pad under the stain. Dab at the mark with a stain remover or denatured alcohol. For oil-based paints, use a paint solvent (available from art shops).

Sponge carpet with clear water

Spills on carpet
Using a sponge and cold water, dab at the stain, taking care not to spread it. Work from the outside inward. When clear, apply carpet shampoo.

Oil-based paint on carpet
Blot fresh spills with paper towels, then treat the area with carpet shampoo. For old stains, try using a commercial solvent, or snip off the top of the pile.

DYE STAINS

Dried dye never comes out, so mop up spills immediately. Use a dry cloth to wipe spills on hard surfaces – water will dilute and spread the mark. Wear protective clothing, and cover surrounding areas when using dye. Lemon juice will help remove dye from skin.

ON CARPETS
● **Basic treatment** Add a few drops of household ammonia to some denatured alcohol in a small container. Apply on a white pad, repeating several times if necessary, then apply carpet shampoo.

ON CLOTHES
● **Colorfast fabrics** Soak in an enzymatic detergent solution, then launder the item as usual.
● **Noncolorfast fabrics** Sponge with, or soak in, a hydrogen peroxide solution (see p. 77) for 15 minutes.

OTHER DYE STAINS
● **Laundry color run** If you accidentally include an item that runs in a load of wash, relaunder the whole load (but not the offending item!) using a commercial color-run remover instead of detergent.

BALLPOINT PEN INK MARKS

These are particularly difficult stains to remove. For bad stains, it may be worth contacting the manufacturer for a remedy for the type of ink used, since the company may sell its own solvent. Dried ballpoint pen ink is especially difficult to get out, so act quickly.

ON FABRIC

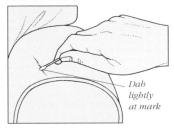

Dab lightly at mark

Blotting the stain
Press paper towels against the stain to absorb as much of it as possible. Then apply denatured alcohol using a cotton swab.

ON WALL COVERINGS

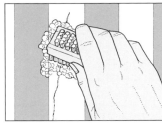

Treating immediately
Scrub vinyl wall coverings immediately with soap and water. Ordinary wall coverings may need patching (see p. 62).

ON OTHER SURFACES

● **Suede** Rub the stain with a fine emery cloth, emery board, or a commercial suede-cleaning block. Seek professional advice before cleaning valuable items.
● **Vinyl surfaces** Treat marks on vinyl immediately by gently rubbing the area with a nail brush and soapy water. If the ink is allowed to remain on the vinyl surface, it will merge into the plasticizer and leave a permanent mark.

FOUNTAIN PEN INK MARKS

Most fountain pen ink is washable, and it is worth making sure that the brand you use definitely is. Always screw on the cap of your pen firmly, especially when carrying it around with you. If you use ink from a bottle, rather than a cartridge, keep the top screwed on.

ON CARPETS

1 First dilute the stain by sponging repeatedly with clean water, or squirting with a soda syphon. Blot the area well with paper towels.

2 Make a hot, thick solution of soap flakes, and apply liberally on a white fabric pad. Let sit for 15 minutes.

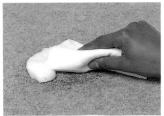

3 Wipe off the solution. If the mark persists, repeat Step 2 until it disappears.

ON SKIN

● **Removing marks** Scrub with a nail brush dipped in vinegar and salt. Or rub marks with the inside of a banana skin.

DRIED STAINS ON CLOTHES

1 If a fountain pen ink stain remains after you have washed a garment, rub the mark with half a lemon, or squeeze lemon juice onto it.

2 Press the stained area between two pieces of white cotton cloth. Repeat as necessary, then rinse. Launder according to the fabric.

TRADITIONAL TIP

Natural ink removers
Traditional wisdom recommends treating ink-stains with milk or tomato. Cover the stains with a little milk, or rub with the cut side of half a tomato. Rinse both treatments out well.

FELT-TIP PEN MARKS

Homes with small children are particularly susceptible to felt-tip pen marks on walls and furniture. Felt-tip pens also often leak into pockets of suit jackets – never attempt to tackle this yourself, but take the jacket to a dry cleaner and explain what the problem is.

ON FABRIC
● **Small marks** Press a paper towel on marks on clothes or furniture to remove as much ink as possible. Dab with denatured alcohol on a cotton swab, then launder using soap flakes, not detergent. (Soap is more effective than detergent on all types of ink.)
● **Large marks** Use a spray stain remover, repeating applications as necessary. Alternatively, buy a specific commercial stain remover.

ON WALL COVERINGS
● **Vinyl** Apply a nonabrasive household cleaner to marks, or use denatured alcohol.
● **Wallpaper** The best solution is to cover marks with a new patch of wallpaper (see p. 62).

ON OTHER SURFACES
● **Carpets and furniture** Blot stains with cotton swabs and paper towels, then dab with denatured alcohol.

Stains on vinyl
Wipe marks on vinyl surfaces such as toys with a white cloth wrapped around one finger and moistened with dishwashing liquid. Rinse with clear water.

OTHER PIGMENTS

● **Correction fluid** Let dry, brush off, then launder.
● **Crayon** Use a nonabrasive household cleaner for marks on vinyl. Painted walls may need to be repainted, and ordinary wall coverings may require patching (see p. 62).
● **Pencil** Use an eraser on walls and furniture. Sponge marks off clothes, then launder according to fabric.

STICKY SUBSTANCES

Chewing gum and colored plastic putty can be difficult to remove, especially from fluffy fabrics and carpets where rough removal can leave a bare patch. Freezing is the trick for removing chewing-gum stains; use a liquid stain remover on any marks that are left behind.

PLASTIC PUTTY
● **On clothes** Plastic putty does not freeze, so pick off as much as you can with your fingernails. Next, hold a folded white pad underneath the mark, and – using another white cloth – apply liquid stain remover until the deposit is dissolved. Rinse, then launder as usual.
● **On carpets** Pick off the deposit with your fingernails. Remove any residue with liquid lighter fluid (test on a hidden area, since lighter fuel may damage synthetic fibers). Do not overwet or allow the lighter fluid to reach the carpet backing.

CHEWING GUM ON CARPET

1 Hold a plastic bag filled with ice cubes over the chewing gum to harden it.

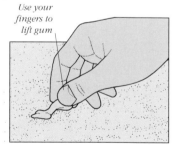

Use your fingers to lift gum

2 Pick off the hardened deposit, taking care not to remove the carpet pile.

CHEWING GUM ON CLOTHES
1 Place the stained garment in a plastic bag in the freezer for an hour, so that the chewing gum hardens.

2 Remove the item from the freezer. Bend the fabric across the stain to crack the gum. Pick off the pieces.

HOUSEHOLD PRODUCT STAINS

CLEANERS, MEDICINES, AND ADHESIVES are household substances that can cause difficult stains, particularly on carpets. Stains from cosmetics and candle wax are common in some homes. Tar and creosote stains require careful treatment.

POLISH STAINS

Try to avoid either spilling liquid household cleaners or getting polishes onto surfaces that are not intended for their use. Put caps on firmly when cleaners are not in use. Always store household cleaners in an upright position, away from children and direct sunlight.

SHOE POLISH
● On carpets Scrape off the deposit with a metal ruler. Apply turpentine or a liquid stain remover to dissolve any traces. Rinse with clear water, then use denatured alcohol to remove any remaining color. Apply carpet shampoo.
● On fabrics Washable fabrics will respond to either a stain remover or a little ammonia added to the rinse water when washing. Treat nonwashable fabrics as for carpet.

METAL POLISH
● On clothes Clean off any deposits with paper towels. Use a liquid stain remover, then launder as usual.

On carpets
Spoon and blot up as much polish as you can. Dampen the area with turpentine, and allow to dry. Brush off the dried deposit with a brush or cloth, then apply carpet shampoo.

● On furniture Sponge with warm water, let dry, and brush well. Apply a spray stain remover to lift marks.

Use a stiff-bristled brush

MEDICINE STAINS

These cause sticky, colored stains that should be treated quickly so that they do not set into a solid deposit. Ask your pharmacist what is in a particular medicine if you cannot get the stain out. Iodine is one of the worst offenders when it comes to medicine stains.

OINTMENTS

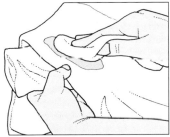

Spills on clothes
Ointments leave behind an oily residue. Scrape off the deposit, then treat the area with a grease solvent. If any color remains, apply denatured alcohol on a cotton pad (test first). Hold a pad beneath the stain to prevent any color transferring through.

LIQUID MEDICINE
● On clothes Laundering should remove most medicine stains from clothes. If any color remains, apply a little denatured alcohol. Hold a pad beneath the stain as you apply the denatured alcohol, testing this treatment on a hidden part of the item first.
● On carpets and upholstery Scrape up the deposit, then wipe the area with a damp cloth. Apply carpet shampoo.
● Preventing stains Keep a roll of paper towels nearby when giving liquid medicine. Use a bib made from a dish towel when giving medicine to small children.

IODINE STAINS
● On carpets To remove stains, use a solution of photographic hyposulfite (this is a chemical used in photography development, which you can purchase at camera stores). Dilute ½ tsp (2.5 ml) to 1 cup (250 ml) warm water. When clear, apply carpet shampoo.
● On washable fabrics Launder clothes by hand in soap flakes and water, with a few drops of ammonia. Wear rubber gloves.
● On nonwashable fabrics Have items professionally cleaned, or use a commercial tea-and-coffee stain remover.

COSMETICS STAINS

Cosmetics get spilled on and around the vanity, they come off on clothes and bedding, and they frequently leak inside handbags. Unfortunately, no all-purpose stain-removal technique exists for cosmetics stains. You must treat each item individually.

NAIL POLISH

Apply nail polish remover on cotton balls

On fabric
Hold a white absorbent pad beneath the stain, and dab with non-oily nail polish remover.

MASCARA
● **On clothes** Use a spray or liquid stain remover to remove mascara stains. If any marks remain after treatment, sponge, allow to dry, then apply a solution of one part ammonia to three parts cold water. Rinse, and launder.

● **On carpets** Blot up as much as possible with paper tissues. Apply non-oily nail polish remover on a cotton ball, testing at the edge of the carpet first, since the backing can be damaged if the solvent soaks through. Treat any remaining traces of color with denatured alcohol applied on a white pad of paper tissue. Finally, apply carpet shampoo.
● **On furniture** Blot well, then apply non-oily nail polish remover, testing carefully first.

LIPSTICK
● **On clothes** Sponge with denatured alcohol, then dishwashing liquid. Launder.
● **On walls** Rub marks gently with a damp cloth wrung out of a warm detergent solution. Use household cleaner on stubborn lipstick marks.

BRIGHT IDEA

Preventing spills
Make sure cosmetic bottles do not spill in luggage when traveling by taping the lids shut, or applying nail polish to the edges of the caps.

FOUNDATION CREAM
● **On clothes** Wipe off the excess cream, then soak in an ammonia solution (see p. 77). Launder according to fabric.

SCENT, SPRAY, AND LOTION STAINS

Sprays and scents tend to be cocktails of chemicals, usually containing some alcohol. They need to be treated with care in case they react with the chemicals used for removal. Creamy lotions usually contain oil or grease and should be treated accordingly.

PERFUME
● **On washable fabrics** Rinse out immediately, then launder the item. Apply a glycerin solution (see p. 77) to dried stains. Leave for an hour, then launder. Alternatively, rub with a laundry prewash stick.
● **On nonwashable fabrics** Apply a glycerin solution (see p. 77) as soon as possible. Let sit for one hour before wiping with a damp cloth. Take care not to wet any padding on furniture. Expensive items should be cleaned professionally.

DEODORANT
● **All surfaces** Blot, then sponge the area with warm water. Repeat if necessary. Use a commercial stain remover on remaining marks.

LOTION
● **Cleansing lotions** Blot with tissues, then treat the area with a grease solvent. Launder clothes; use carpet shampoo on carpets and upholstery.
● **Toning lotions** Squirt the area with soda water, or sponge with warm water. Allow to dry naturally.

HAIR SPRAY

On mirrors
Hair spray leaves a sticky deposit on mirrors, producing a blurred effect. Wipe off with a little denatured alcohol on a cloth.

CANDLE WAX STAINS

These are almost unavoidable if you enjoy candlelight. The wax is easy to remove, but colored candles may leave dye stains, which need to be treated after the wax has been removed. Wax does not set completely hard, so does not require immediate treatment.

ON CARPETS

Scoop up wax while it is soft

1 Scrape up as much of the wax deposit as you can with a spoon. If the wax is hard, use your fingernails.

Place iron on a warm setting

2 Place brown paper over the remaining wax. Iron with a warm iron until the wax melts into the paper.

ON OTHER SURFACES
- **Clothes** Use the treatment for carpets, left. Treat any residual color marks with denatured alcohol (testing first). Hold an absorbent white pad under the stain as you apply the denatured alcohol.
- **Furniture and wallpaper** Use the treatment for carpets, left, without lifting any wax first. Use denatured alcohol to remove color on furniture, and an aerosol stain remover for marks on wallpaper.
- **Wood** See page 60.

ADHESIVE MARKS

Adhesives stick to you as well as to whatever is being glued. Scrape up fresh spills immediately, then use the appropriate solvent. Dried stains are extremely difficult to remove. If you are doing a lot of gluing, buy the appropriate solvent when buying the adhesive.

FRESH ADHESIVE
- **Appropriate solvents** Use non-oily nail polish remover on clear adhesive. Remove contact adhesive with a manufacturer's solvent. Use a stain remover on airplane glue, liquid grease solvent on latex adhesive, and lighter fluid on epoxy.
- **On hard surfaces** Use denatured alcohol. Allow latex adhesives to set, then roll off with your finger.
- **On skin** Use lemon juice.

DRIED ADHESIVE

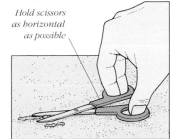
Hold scissors as horizontal as possible

On carpets
The best way to remove dried adhesive is to trim the top of the pile with a pair of scissors.

Apply solvent on cotton

On hard surfaces
To remove label residue marks, rub with lighter fluid, denatured alcohol, or cellulose thinners.

CREOSOTE AND TAR STAINS

These substances are best left outside, but they often creep in on shoes, swimwear, and beach towels – not to mention clothes. Because stains from creosote and tar are difficult to remove, take great care not to let them transfer onto any more surfaces.

- **On carpets** Blot gently, then apply a glycerin solution (see p. 77), and leave for one hour. Rinse with clear water, then use a carpet-spotting kit.
- **On clothes** Place an absorbent white cloth or tissue pad on top of the stain. Apply eucalyptus oil from below the stain with a cotton ball.
- **On shoes** Use lighter fluid, but test for affected color.
- **On furniture** Expensive furnishings should be dry cleaned professionally.

WEAR-AND-TEAR MARKS

WEAR AND TEAR IS INEVITABLE around the home. However, some problems, such as mildew, need to be controlled; otherwise, they may require professional treatment and can cause permanent damage to household items.

MILDEW PATCHES

Mildew tends to occur in damp parts of the home and should, if possible, be caught in the early stages. It appears as an unsightly growth of spores, which makes surfaces look as if they are covered in small dirty patches. Left unchecked, mildew develops a deposit.

ON CLOTHES

● **Whites** Bleach mildew with a hydrogen peroxide solution (see p. 77); do not use this treatment on nylon. Soak natural fabrics in a household bleach solution (see p. 102).
● **Colors** Dampen, then rub with a bar of hard soap. Let dry in the sun before laundering. Repeated washing will get rid of any remaining marks, and a specialized stain remover can be used on white and colorfast fabrics.

ON LACE

Cover mildew with soap

Using household soap
Rub the lace with soap so that a film develops. Leave in the sun for several hours, then rinse.

ON SHOWER CURTAINS

Removing marks
Sponge curtains with either a detergent solution, or a weak bleach solution (wear gloves).

ON WALLS

● **General treatment** Wash the whole wall (even areas where mildew does not show) with a mild detergent solution. Wipe the wall with a solution of commercial bactericide (a paint pad is good for this).

ON FURNITURE

● **Removing marks** Remove mildew spores as described below. If marks remain, have slip covers dry cleaned. Apply a hydrogen peroxide solution (see p. 77) to upholstery, then rinse thoroughly.

ON LEATHER

● **General treatment** Leather shoes, furniture, bags, and luggage all attract mildew in storage. Remove using the treatment below, then apply a coat of hide food or shoe polish. Rub in and buff well.

Tackling corners
Sponge carefully into corners of rooms. Be extra careful near windows in bathrooms and kitchens, where condensation could form pools that encourage mildew growth to develop.

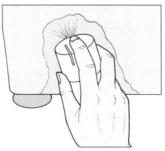

Killing mildew spores
Brush off as many of the spores as possible, then spray the item with a commercial solution designed to kill the spores. Do this outdoors so that the spores do not transfer to other items.

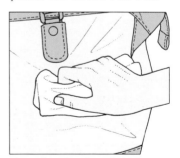

Treating leather bags
Sponge mildew with 1 tbsp (5 ml) disinfectant diluted in 2 cups (500 ml) of warm water. Alternatively, apply an antispetic mouthwash on a cotton pad. Wipe dry, and buff well.

WATER MARKS

Water marking is caused by minerals in water, and often occurs after an area of a garment has been sponged. To prevent water marks from forming after removing a stain, sprinkle the damp area with talcum powder, cover with a dry cloth, then iron dry.

ON HIDES AND WOOD
● **On leather** Wipe off rain spots on shoes and handbags before they dry with a clean cloth. Allow to dry naturally. If salt marks appear or water marks persist, redampen the area with a sponge or cloth, then dry by rubbing with a soft, absorbent cloth.
● **On suede** Allow rain spots to dry, then brush with a soft-bristled brush, or use a suede-cleaning pad or stick.
● **On wood** See page 116.

ON FABRIC

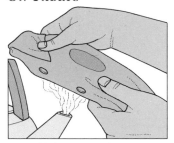

Rub toward center of mark

1 Hold the marked area over the steam from a boiling kettle. Take care not to burn your hands or the fabric.

2 Remove from the steam. Rub the area with a cloth over your finger. Start at the edge and work inward.

SCORCH MARKS

Scorch marks are usually the result of an accident with an iron left on clothing for too long, or cigarette and other tobacco burns. For severe burns on carpet, you may need to trim the top of the carpet pile, or to replace the burned area with a scrap (see below).

ON FABRIC
● **Washable fabrics** Rub the mark under cold running water, using another piece of the fabric rather than your fingers. Soak in a laundry borax solution (see p. 77), rubbing gently until clear.
● **Nonwashable fabrics** Apply a glycerin solution (see p. 77). Leave for two hours, then sponge with warm water.

ON CARPETS

Cigarette burns
Rub burns with fine sandpaper, using gentle circular motions until the mark disappears.

TREATING SEVERE SCORCH MARKS

1 Place a new piece of carpet over the burned area, and cut both layers together.

2 Insert the new patch into the space. Stick it down with double-sided tape.

TRADITIONAL TIP

Natural alternatives
To treat light scorch marks on carpets, boil together 1 cup (250 ml) white vinegar, ½ cup (50 g) unscented talcum powder, and two coarsely chopped onions. Let the mixture cool, then spread over the stain. Let dry and then brush off. To remove small burns on polished wood, rub the area gently with very fine steel wool, then rub in a small amount of linseed oil. Leave for 24 hours, then polish well.

RUST MARKS

Rust (iron mold) may seem like a difficult mark to remove, but in fact it does not require any drastic treatment. Lemon juice is useful as a gentle treatment for rust stains. If you do not have any fresh lemons on hand, lemon juice from a bottle works just as well.

ON CLOTHES

Cover mark thickly with salt

1 Hold a white, absorbent pad under the rust stain, and apply lemon juice from the cut half of a lemon.

2 Cover the lemon juice with salt, and let dry for an hour (if possible, in the sun). Rinse off, then launder.

OTHER SURFACES

● **On carpets** Remove rust marks with a commercial rust remover, following the instructions carefully.

● **On nonwashable fabrics** Use a commercial rust remover, then wipe with a damp cloth. A little lemon juice may help (be careful not to overwet the area).

● **On baths** Use a commercial cleaner that contains a rust remover. See page 68 for treating other bath stains.

SOOT MARKS

These are a common problem in homes that have open fires. Treat brick and stone fire surrounds as below; see page 65 for cleaning other fire-surround surfaces. Soot marks should wash out of clothes easily – but use a spray stain remover on any persistent stains.

LIGHT MARKS

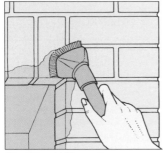

Dusting off soot
Keep soot marks at bay by cleaning your fireplace surround regularly, either with a vacuum-cleaner attachment or a brush.

ON CARPETS

● **Basic treatment** Vacuum well, or shake the carpet or rug. Do not brush the area because this will spread the mark. If this is not effective, apply unscented talcum powder, then vacuum. Have any large stains on carpets professionally dry cleaned.

SOOT STAINS

Scrubbing marks
If soot marks cannot be brushed or vacuumed away, scrub them vigorously with clean water, using a stiff scrub brush.

ON STONEWORK

● **Stubborn marks** Use a weak solution of dishwashing liquid on stubborn soot marks on stonework, then scrub the whole area with clear water. Treat heavy soot marking with a concentrated solution of household bleach, then rinse the area thoroughly.

PERSISTENT STAINS

Using acidic cleaners
Apply white vinegar on a sponge or brush to tough stains. Rinse well. If marks persist, treat with spirit of salts (see below).

WARNING
Spirit of salts is a solution of hydrochloric acid in water, and is poisonous and highly corrosive. Wear rubber gloves and protective goggles when handling this substance.

OTHER STAINS

M OST STAINS CAN BE REMOVED using the methods described previously. If you are faced with a mysterious stain, follow the treatment for the most similar substance, testing carefully first. Refer to page 34 for removing mystery stains.

STAIN	TREATMENT	STAIN	TREATMENT
BABY FORMULA	Treat as for milk, p. 85. Do not allow the stain to set.	HAIR OIL	On wooden headboards, rub with turpentine.
CARBON PAPER	Dab stain with denatured alcohol.	HEAT MARKS	See scorch marks, p. 97, and marks on wood, p. 116.
CHUTNEY	Treat as for jams and preserves, p. 82.	MOLASSES	Treat as for jams and preserves, p. 82.
COAL	Brush off marks. Launder clothes in warm water.	NEWSPRINT	Apply denatured alcohol on a cloth, then rinse well.
COLA DRINKS	Blot spill, then treat as for fruit juice, p. 84.	SHELLAC	Act quickly. Dab with denatured alcohol.
COPIER TONER POWDER	Brush off deposit, then wash item in warm water.	SORBET	Remove deposit, then treat as for fruit juice, p. 84.
CREAM	Treat as for oil, fat, and grease, p. 80.	SOUP	Rinse or blot spill, then treat as for grease, p. 80.
DUPLICATING INK	Dab marks with undiluted dishwashing liquid.	SOY SAUCE	Treat as for tomato sauce, p. 82. Do not allow to set.
EMBROIDERY TRANSFER	Dab with denatured alcohol, then launder.	TOMATO	Blot, rinse, then treat as for tomato sauce, p. 82.
FRUIT	Rinse stain, then treat as for fruit juice, p. 84.	YOGURT	Scoop up deposit, then treat as for milk, p. 85.

STAINS ON DIFFICULT SURFACES

ON WOOD
● **Unvarnished wood** Stains on unvarnished wood are almost impossible to remove. Bleach what you can, then wash the area with detergent solution. Seal the surface with varnish to prevent future marks.
● **Varnished wood** See page 116 for treating marks on furniture; see pages 59–60 for special treatments for wooden floors.

ON SKIN AND HAIR
● **Paint stains** Use turpentine to remove oil-based paint from skin and hair; or try vegetable oil on skin. Protect your hair with a cap when painting.
● **Inkstains** Scrub ink marks on the skin with a nail brush dipped in vinegar and salt.
● **Other stains** Use pure lemon juice to remove dye stains and adhesive marks on skin.

ON OTHER SURFACES
● **Paper** Remove grease spots by laying a piece of blotting paper over the mark and ironing with a warm iron.
● **Glass** Use white vinegar to remove grease marks on glass.
● **Leather and suede** See page 91 for removing ink stains; see page 97 for treating water marks; and page 126 for care and minor repairs to leather and suede.

LAUNDERING

QUICK REFERENCE

Washing Clothes, p. 102

Special Treatments, p. 104

Drying Clothes, p. 106

Ironing Clothes, p. 108

Caring for Clothes, p. 110

Caring for Shoes, p. 113

PROLONG THE LIFE *of your clothes and your household linens by ensuring that they do not become heavily soiled before washing. Take advantage of the variable programming of washing machines to clean fabrics at the right temperature and spin speed. Do not forget about the launderette – it is the best bet for washing heavy items such as pillows, which could damage your machine at home.*

DETERGENTS AND LAUNDRY AIDS

In addition to liquid or powder detergents for machine washing, use the following aids to keep clothes looking their best.

● **Fabric softener** Use a commercial fabric softener, or add 2 tbsp (30 ml) white vinegar to the final rinse.
● **Starch** This keeps cotton shirts and table linen crisp and clean (see p. 107).
● **Bleach** For use on whites. Always dilute household bleach. Lemon juice is a natural alternative to bleach.
● **Detergent with enzymes** Use to treat built-up protein stains.
● **Soap flakes and hand-washing detergent** Use to hand-wash baby and delicate items.
● **Borax** This removes stains. Commercial prewash sprays or sticks are also useful.

Fabric softener

Liquid detergent

Spray starch

Bleach

Powder detergent

Detergent with enzymes

Soap flakes

Borax

INTERNATIONAL FABRIC CARE SYMBOLS

The symbols on care labels fall into five categories. An "X" through a symbol means that a specific treatment should be avoided. Some detergent packages feature a complete list of the symbols.

Washing symbol

Bleaching symbol

Ironing symbol

Dry-cleaning symbol

Drying symbol

FABRIC CARE

Certain fabrics need more careful treatment than simply machine washing. Check the care label – if it says hand wash or dry clean, follow these instructions. Use a dry cleaner for tailored clothing, items with special finishes, and anything made of more than one fabric.

FABRIC	WASHING	DRYING AND IRONING
ACETATES Temperamental fabrics. Never use enzymatic detergent.	Machine or hand wash at a low temperature. Do not wring or fast spin in a washing machine.	Do not tumble dry. Allow acetate items to dry naturally, and iron while still damp.
ACRYLIC Needs frequent washing since it can smell of perspiration.	Usually machine washable, but check the care label. Wash items at a low temperature.	Pull into shape after washing, and remove excess water (see p. 104). Dry flat or line dry.
BROCADE Take care not to flatten the raised pile when washing.	Hand wash at cool temperature or dry clean, according to the care label. Do not wring.	Iron on the wrong side with the pile over a towel (see ironing embroidery, p. 109).
CASHMERE Expensive, so it merits the specialized care that it needs.	Hand wash in cool water in well-dissolved soap flakes. Rinse well. Do not wring.	Dry, and shape or "block" while drying. Iron inside out while damp with a cool iron.
CORDUROY Tough in wear but needs care in washing to avoid crushing pile.	Always wash inside out. Hand or machine wash, according to the care label instructions.	Iron inside out while evenly damp, then smooth the pile with a soft cloth.
COTTON When mixed with other fibers, wash as for the most delicate.	Machine wash cotton at a high temperature, always keeping whites separate from colors.	Tumble or line dry. Do not allow items to dry completely, as they will be difficult to iron.
DENIM A strong fabric, but prone to shrinking, fading, and streaking.	Wash separately until you are sure there is no color run (see p. 103). Wash items inside out.	Tumble dry or line dry. Iron denim items while still very damp, using a hot iron.
LACE An extremely delicate fabric. Wash and dry carefully.	Treat stains before hand washing in a mild detergent. Never use bleach – it causes yellowing.	Dry flat on a white towel away from direct sunlight. Iron, if you must, over a white towel.
LEATHER AND SUEDE Sometimes washable, but check the care label.	Protect items with a leather spray after hand washing so that marks do not build up.	Rub suede with another piece of suede or a suede brush to keep the nap looking good.
LINEN A tough fabric that withstands the highest temperatures.	Machine wash according to the label. Test colored linen items for colorfastness (see p. 104).	Iron while still very damp. Starch will prevent some creasing (but not on bed linen).
SILK A delicate fabric that requires special care to prevent damage.	Hand wash in warm water. Some silk items can be machine washed on the delicate cycle.	Line dry naturally, and iron while damp. Use a pressing cloth to protect the fabric.
WOOL Wash and dry carefully, since items easily lose their shape.	Some woolens can be machine washed, others must be done by hand. Check the care label.	Wool can be dried flat, line dried, or dried on a sweater rack. Do not tumble dry.

WASHING CLOTHES

A LWAYS READ THE CARE LABEL before washing clothes, to establish which method of cleaning is most suitable for the item. Soak heavily soiled clothes before washing. Treat stains as soon as they occur, then launder.

SOAKING CLOTHES

A good soak before washing loosens the dirt from clothes. Enzymatic detergent is best for protein-based stains. Soak clothes in the machine or in a bucket, immersing them completely. Be sure that enzymatic detergent is fully dissolved before you soak clothes.

DARK COLORS

● **Black garments** When these develop a "bloom" and do not look black any longer, it is because of a buildup of soap. Either soak the item in warm water with a little white vinegar, or add water softener (instead of detergent) to the machine's regular wash.

● **Color runs** Always wash dark colors separately until you are sure that the dye does not run (see washing colors, opposite). If dye from dark clothes runs onto pale fabrics in the wash, you can use a commercial dye-run remover to remove color from the lighter items.

DENIM ITEMS

Preserving color
To prevent a new pair of jeans from fading when washed, soak them in 4 tbsp (60 ml) of vinegar mixed with 5 quarts (5 liters) of water for about 30 minutes.

BRIGHT COLORS

Push items under water with a wooden spoon

Preventing fading
Preserve the brightness of colored clothes by soaking them in a bucket of cold water with a handful of salt added before washing them for the first time.

WHITENING DISCOLORED CLOTHES

Submerge socks with a wooden spoon

White cotton socks
Return white socks to pristine condition by boiling them in a saucepan with a few added slices of lemon. The lemon is a natural bleach. Dishwasher detergent also whitens socks – just add a little to the regular washload.

● **Cotton or linen** Soak items for 15 minutes in a solution of 1 tbsp (15 ml) household bleach to 10 quarts (10 liters) cold water. Rinse thoroughly before washing as usual.
● **Wool** Soak discolored wool overnight in one part hydrogen peroxide to eight parts cold water. Rinse, and wash according to care label.
● **Nylon** Soak nylon items in 6 tbsp (90 ml) of dishwasher detergent and 3 tbsp (45 ml) of household bleach to 5 quarts (5 liters) very hot water. Allow the mixture to cool to room temperature, then soak the nylon items in it for at least 30 minutes.

USING BLEACH

Always dilute bleach before you use it – straight bleach will "burn" holes in fabric. Follow the manufacturer's instructions for dilution. If in doubt, add a "glug" of bleach to a bucketful of cold water to make a standard bleach solution.

MACHINE WASHING

Sort clothes into matching loads, based on care label instructions. If you need to wash mixed fabrics together to make up a full load, set to the lowest recommended temperature. Do not be tempted to use more detergent than instructed – it will not get clothes any cleaner.

WASHING SYMBOLS

The washtub symbol contains details of the temperature and type of cycle to be used.

The figure indicates the maximum water temperature (here in Celsius).

Broken bars beneath the tub recommend using a gentle cycle.

The hand in the tub means that the item should always be hand washed.

WASHING COLORS

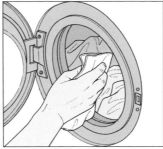

Checking for color run
Place an old, white handkerchief with colored garments to pick up any color run. When it stays white, all the excess dye has run out, and the colored items can be washed with white ones.

MACHINE BASICS

● **Cleaning machines** From time to time, clean your washing machine by running it empty on a hot cycle with 1 cup (250 ml) white vinegar in the detergent compartment, or added during the cycle. This cleans detergent deposits that may have built up.

● **Detergent quantities** Using too little detergent results in clothes remaining dirty; if you use too much, it will not rinse out of clothes completely.

● **Washing times** Whites may yellow if washed for too long at too high a temperature, and natural fibers may shrink.

SORTING CLOTHES

Close zippers and fasten buttons on garments before you machine wash them; otherwise they get battered, and they may not close when the wash cycle is finished. To avoid ending up with gray whites, do not mix whites and strong colors in the same load.

PREPARING CLOTHES FOR THE WASH

● **Checking pockets** Be sure to go through pockets before you put items in the wash – tissues disintegrate, pens leak, and money can be damaged.

Pin socks at tops

Keeping socks in pairs
Use safety pins to keep pairs of socks together in the wash, so that individual socks do not get lost. Leave the safety pins in while the socks dry (either in the dryer or on a clothesline).

Place items in pillowcase, then fasten at top

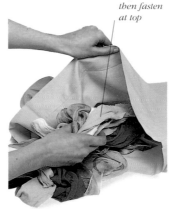

Protecting delicates
Place small or delicate items such as pantyhose and scarves in a pillowcase to machine wash. This will prevent them from snagging and from becoming tangled up with other garments.

MONEY-SAVING TIP

A stitch in time . . .
Mend holes and tears in clothes before you machine wash them. The machine's agitating action makes the damage worse, and you may have to replace items or have them professionally repaired. Fixing loose buttons before you launder an item ensures that the buttons will not get lost in the wash.

SPECIAL TREATMENTS

S ET ASIDE TIME EACH WEEK to deal with delicate and unusual items that cannot be washed in the machine. Treat household linen with care to prolong the life of individual items. Air bedding regularly to keep it in good condition.

HAND WASHING

H and wash wool, delicate fabrics, and colors that continue to run. Use warm water for hand washing, and if you use soap flakes, make sure that they are thoroughly dissolved. Do not skimp on rinsing: washing machines rinse several times, and so must you.

COLORFAST TEST

Using a steam iron
If you suspect that an item is not colorfast, steam iron an area between two layers of white fabric. If dye transfers onto the white, the item is not colorfast.

DELICATE FABRICS
● **Lace** Make a paper template of delicate lace items before you hand wash them. If they lose their shape, you can use the template to reshape the items correctly as they dry.
● **Silk** Add two lumps of sugar to the rinse water to give silk body; add a little lanolin to protect and restore silk.

RINSING TRICKS
● **Removing soap** Add 1 tbsp (15 ml) of white vinegar to the final rinse to remove soap.
● **Preventing freezing** Add a handful of salt to the final rinse to prevent clothes from freezing on the line in winter.

TIMESAVING TIP

Getting rid of suds
If you have too many suds after hand washing, sprinkle them with talcum powder to make them disperse. This saves having to let water out and add more fresh water.

DRY CLEANING

This is essential for fabrics that cannot take water. Use a professional dry cleaner for expensive items; cheaper garments can be cleaned in a coin-operated machine. The following tips will help minimize dry cleaning.

● **Outdoor clothes** Clean dirt from outdoor clothes as soon as you get home. Use an aerosol dry cleaner on coat and jacket collars and cuffs, which tend to get dirty faster than the main fabric.
● **Airing out clothes** Air non-washable items before putting away. Never wear items two days in a row.

WOOLEN CLOTHES

Drying woolens
Woolens can be distorted by machine spinning. After hand washing, roll them gently in a clean towel to remove excess water, then dry flat, shaping by hand on a dry towel (see p. 107).

Heat from hair dryer shrinks fibers on cuff

Reshaping stretched cuffs
Dip sweater cuffs in hot water, then dry them with a hair dryer on a hot setting. For a more permanent solution, stitch two or three rows of knitted elastic loosely around the cuffs.

BEDDING AND LINEN

Towels and bed linen get dirty quickly and require frequent laundering. Wash pillows and comforters only when it is necessary. When making beds, reverse pillows often to reduce wear on one side, and turn sheets from top to bottom – they will last twice as long.

WASHING PILLOWS

● **Hand washing** Wash pillows in the tub, using a soap flake solution. Knead vigorously, and rinse several times.

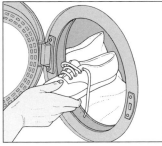

Drying pillows
Wet pillows are very heavy and may damage domestic machines. Remove all excess water before tumble drying, and add a clean tennis shoe to balance the load.

WASHING COMFORTERS

● **Dry cleaning** Comforters are too heavy to wash in home machines, and too large to be hand washed easily. Take them to a launderette or to a professional cleaner.

CARING FOR BATHROOM AND KITCHEN TOWELS

● **General care** Wash towels frequently, using hot water, to get rid of the skin debris that collects in the pile.

Vinegar removes soap residue

Soapy washcloths
Soak tired face cloths in 1 tbsp (15 ml) vinegar or lemon juice and 2 cups (500 ml) water before machine washing. This will remove all traces of soap.

● **Removing the "bloom"** Use a water-softening powder to remove any soap buildup and restore fading colors.

● **Eliminating germs** Wash and iron dish towels at the highest possible temperature to eliminate as many bacteria or germs as possible.

● **Drying outside** If you dry washed towels on a line in the open air, use fabric softener to prevent the pile from becoming roughened by wind.

● **Avoiding fading** Do not dry dark towels in bright sunlight since this will cause fading.

● **Lessening wear** Use towels in rotation to limit the wear that will occur if they are washed and re-used promptly.

STORING AND CARING FOR SHEETS

● **Laundering** Wash sheets according to the care labels Mixed-fiber sheets do not need ironing – simply fold them when dry. Natural-fiber sheets look better if ironed.

● **Storing** After laundering, place white linen or cotton sheets at the bottom of the pile in the linen closet. Regular rotation and use will prevent sheets from yellowing.

REMOVING DIRTY MARKS

Remove marks from clothes before washing, since laundering may cause stains to set. Use prewash sprays or sticks, soak items in enzymatic detergent if the fabric is suitable, or use the relevant stain-removal technique recommended on pages 76–99.

● **Collars and cuffs** Follow the method shown right to remove dirt from around collars and cuffs; alternatively, apply shampoo to these areas before washing. Using liquid or spray starch will keep collars and cuffs clean between washes.

Rub mark with soap

Scrub the soap well

1 Rub a piece of damp soap or a prewash stick along the mark or stain. Make sure that the mark is well covered.

2 Use a wet toothbrush to work the soap into a lather. Rinse the area in warm water, then launder the item.

DRYING CLOTHES

I F YOU DRY CLOTHES PROPERLY, you can cut down considerably on ironing. After line or tumble drying, fold clothes or put them on hangers. When hanging items on the line, try to keep seams and creases in the right places.

LINE DRYING

Hang clothes to dry outdoors whenever the weather permits – this will save electricity, and is gentler on clothes than tumble drying. Sunlight makes white clothes whiter. If you are short of outdoor space, hang two lines parallel to each other, and drape items across them.

DRYING SYMBOLS
The four variants to the square symbol indicate which drying method should be used.

○	Tumble dry (any dots in the circle indicate settings).
⫴	Drip dry items on a line.
⌄	Hang dry items after removing excess water.
—	Dry items flat after removing excess water.

TIGHTS AND SOCKS
● **Reducing snags** Clip clothespins to the feet of socks and or tights. This prevents them from blowing around and tangling or snagging.

Drying socks
To save space on lines, hang pairs of socks on a hanger. This will also enable you to remove the socks quickly if it rains.

PREVENTING PROBLEMS
● **Fading** Turn colored T-shirts inside out, and hang them in the shade so that they do not fade in the sunlight.

Cleaning washing lines
Dirt collects on washing lines and may transfer to fabric. To clean lines, run a damp sponge or a split cork along the length of the line from time to time.

DRYING TRICKS
● **Belts** To dry belts without creating a clothespin mark, loop around the washing line and fasten the belt buckle.
● **Pleated skirts** After washing, hang on the line from the waistband. Clip clothespins at the bottom of each pleat so that the pleats dry in place.

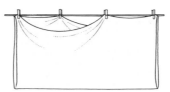

Quick-drying sheets
Pin the sheet at both ends first, then pin each side one-third of the way along. This "bag" shape allows air to circulate easily.

DRYING SWEATER

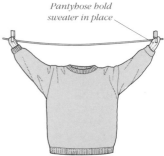

Pantyhose hold sweater in place

Preventing stretching
Sweaters will not stretch on a clothesline if you string an old pair of hose through the arms, and pin the pantyhose – rather than the sweater – to the line.

MONEY-SAVING TIP

Handy helpers
Use ordinary clothespins around the house to clip things together. They reseal food packages and hold notes and telephone messages together as effectively as gadgets sold for the purpose.

TUMBLE DRYING

Dryers work best when the drum is only half full – clothes will dry most quickly if they can move around freely. Do not let tumble-dried items become bone dry – if you do, you will find that they are difficult to iron. Clean the dryer filter after each use.

USING DRYERS

● **Avoiding creases** Certain items require little ironing if tumble dried – in particular, clothes made from polyester and cotton mixtures. Remove items as soon as the dryer stops, and fold or hang them.
● **Fabric-softener sheets** Use these in the dryer to keep items from creasing – particularly items that you do not wish to iron, such as sheets. Use half a sheet – it is as effective as a whole one.
● **Spin drying** You can use a no-heat setting to spin dry hand-washed items. Put woolens in pillowcases to prevent stretching.

USING FABRIC SOFTENER

Making your own softener

For an alternative to commercial fabric-softener sheets, soak a washcloth in a solution of fabric-softener liquid and water for a few minutes. Squeeze out excess liquid, then put the wash-cloth in with the clothes being dried in the dryer.

FLAT DRYING

Dry towel

Clothes made from delicate fabrics should always be dried flat. Roll them in a towel to remove excess moisture, then pat them into shape and let dry on a towel (as shown above). Do not expose colored items to direct sunlight while drying them, since this may cause fading.

AIRING AND STARCHING

Large items are best aired along parallel washing lines, which will not only take the weight but allow air to reach the entire area of fabric. Air items such as pillows and blankets on the clothesline. To improvise an airing rack indoors, use the method shown below.

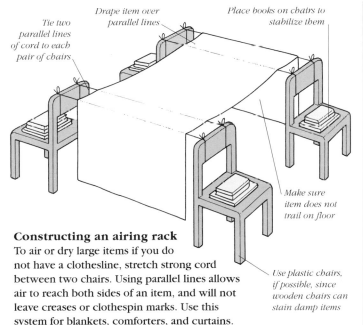

Tie two parallel lines of cord to each pair of chairs

Drape item over parallel lines

Place books on chairs to stabilize them

Make sure item does not trail on floor

Use plastic chairs, if possible, since wooden chairs can stain damp items

Constructing an airing rack

To air or dry large items if you do not have a clothesline, stretch strong cord between two chairs. Using parallel lines allows air to reach both sides of an item, and will not leave creases or clothespin marks. Use this system for blankets, comforters, and curtains.

USING STARCH

Apply starch to right side of fabric

Starching clothes and bed linen makes fabric crisp and helps reduce soiling. Rinsing kitchen towels used for drying dishes in a weak starch solution will prevent lint from coming off on glasses. Always apply starch to the right side of fabric, once the item is dry and just before it is ironed. Spray starch is easier to use than starch dip, but it does not last as long.

IRONING CLOTHES

ALWAYS IRON FABRICS that need the coolest setting first, and work up to the hottest setting. Iron as many items as possible at once, since irons use a lot of electricity heating up. Ironing is easiest if clothes are slightly damp.

IRONING BASICS

Use long, smooth strokes when ironing, and iron clothes until they are dry. Freshly ironed clothes crease easily, so hang them carefully afterward – do not simply drape them over chairs (especially not over wooden ones, which can transfer color onto clothes).

IRONING SYMBOLS

There are four ironing symbols: hot, warm, cool, and do not iron.

 Hot iron: 410°F (210°C).

 Warm iron: 320°F (160°C).

 Cool iron: 248°F (120°C).

 Do not iron.

EQUIPMENT
● **Iron safety** Check the cord frequently to make sure you have not accidentally burned it with the iron and destroyed the protective coating.
● **Steam irons** Empty steam irons after each use to prevent them from becoming clogged. Descale using a commercial descaler or white vinegar.
● **Ironing boards** Choose an ironing board that can be adjusted to your height, since ironing at the wrong height can cause backache. Starch your ironing-board cover so that it stays clean and crisp.

GREEN TIP

Energy-efficient ironing
Place aluminum foil under ironing-board covers to reflect heat onto garments.

SIMPLE IRONING TECHNIQUES
● **Fastenings** Iron around zippers and buttons, since metal zippers could damage the iron, and nylon zippers and buttons could melt.

● **Seams and hems** To avoid creating a line over seams and hems, iron the garment inside out, and stop just short of the seam or hemline.

CLEANING IRONS

Protecting delicates
Iron delicate fabrics over a clean cloth or tissue paper to avoid damaging the fabric. Make sure the garment is evenly damp.

Ironing collars
Always iron collars on both sides, wrong side first. Iron inward from the point to avoid pushing any creases to the tip.

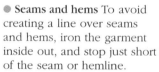

Unplug your iron before you clean it. Unless your iron is nonstick, clean the base (the sole plate) with toothpaste, applied on a soft cloth. Rub persistent marks gently with fine-grade steel wool. Clean nonstick sole plates with a sponge dipped in a detergent and warm water solution, or use denatured alcohol.

SPECIAL ITEMS

Some fabrics need special attention when ironing. Acetates, triacetates, and some polyesters should be ironed on the wrong side when evenly damp. Iron acrylics from the back when dry. Always iron corduroy and crêpe on the wrong side, covered with a damp cloth.

HOUSEHOLD LINEN

● **Timesaving technique** Fold large items such as sheets and tablecloths double, and iron one side. Fold in half again and iron the other two sides. This also works for smaller items such as tea towels, napkins, and handkerchiefs.

● **Large items** Stop sheets and other large items from trailing on the floor by putting the ironed half over a chair back. Cover wooden chairs with a towel to prevent stain from transferring from the wood.

PLEATED SKIRTS

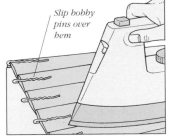

Slip bobby pins over hem

Hold pleats in place
Use bobby pins to keep pleats firmly in place. Press all but the hem, then remove the bobby pins and press the rest.

HEAVY FABRICS

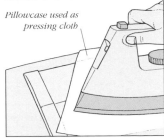

Pillowcase used as pressing cloth

Preventing shininess
Iron heavy fabrics such as wool and viscose rayon over a damp pressing cloth to prevent the fabric from becoming shiny.

IRONING SMALL AND UNUSUAL ITEMS

● **Trimmings** If items have trimmings that need a cooler setting than the main fabric, iron these first, before ironing the rest of the garment.

● **Hair ribbons** To "iron" in a hurry, grasp both ends and pull the ribbon back and forth against a tea kettle that has just been used to boil water.

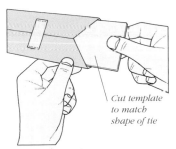

Cut template to match shape of tie

Creaseless ties
Slip a cardboard template into ties before ironing, so that the impression of the seam does not show through on the front.

Place embroidery face down

Ironing embroidery
Lay the piece of embroidery face down on a towel, and iron the reverse side. This way you will not flatten the embroidery.

DAMPENING ITEMS

Items that are too dry are difficult to iron. Use a plant-spray bottle to dampen dry clothes. Alternatively, put all the clothes into the tumble dryer together with a wet towel, and run the dryer on a no-heat setting. If you cannot finish a load of ironing, keep it damp by putting it in the freezer in a plastic bag.

ALTERNATIVES TO IRONING

● **Tumble-dry clothes** Take synthetic fabrics (cotton and polyester mixtures) out of the dryer as soon as the drying cycle is finished. Hang the items on coat hangers while they are still hot; creases will drop out as the items cool.

● **Drip-dry clothes** Straighten collars, seams, and pleats while still damp to ensure that they dry straight.

● **Velvet and silk** Hang silk and velvet items in a steamy bathroom to dry – the steam will make creases drop out.

● **Pressing without an iron** If you must press something but have no iron, put the item under your mattress overnight. The weight of your body will give it a thorough pressing. Dampen creases on pants with a wet towel first.

CARING FOR CLOTHES

CLOTHES NEED ATTENTION if they are to remain in good condition. Hang them properly after you take them off. Brush, remove stains, and make any repairs before wearing again. Never wear clothes or shoes two days in a row.

SOLVING PROBLEMS

Loose buttons, stuck zippers, and runs in pantyhose are common clothes problems. If a zipper is stuck remember to pull the zipper down, ease out the material, and start again. For back zippers that are difficult to reach, thread string through the tab, and pull.

BUTTONS

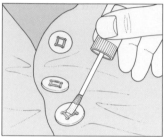

Long-lasting buttons
Buttons will not come off easily if you dab the threads of the buttons on new garments with clear nail polish. Sew children's buttons on with dental floss.

ZIPPERS

Fixing sticking zippers
Rub an ordinary pencil over a sticking zipper – the graphite will help it slide smoothly. Always ease a sticking zip gently; never force it.

CARING FOR HOSE

To prolong the life of pantyhose, wet them when new, and place them in a plastic bag in the freezer for a few hours. To stop holes from running, apply clear nail polish as a barrier.

MINOR REPAIRS

Prevention is always better than cure, so do not rush into wearing new garments when a simple treatment might keep them looking better longer. As clothes suffer wear and tear, mend holes and remove stains as they occur – and always before washing a garment.

RING MARKS

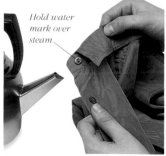

Hold water mark over steam

Steaming off marks
Sponging a small area of a garment often leaves behind a ring mark. Hold the stained area in the steam of a boiling kettle until the mark disappears.

SHINY PATCHES

Sponging with ammonia
Areas that get a lot of wear, such as knees and elbows, often become shiny. Sponge with 1 tbsp (15 ml) ammonia diluted in 1 cup (250 ml) of water.

RECYCLING ITEMS

Use old socks for dusting and for cleaning behind radiators (see page 21). Old pantyhose can be used to tie plants to stakes. Sew old shoulder pads inside the knees of old jeans for comfortable gardening.

MAINTAINING CLOTHES

Storing and hanging clothes properly is essential to keep them looking good. After wearing clothes, hang them to air before putting them in a closet. Remove lint from clothes with a piece of adhesive tape wrapped around your hand, or with a damp sponge.

CREASELESS CLOTHES

● **Drawer storage** Fold clothes across their width when storing in drawers. Creases will drop out more quickly than if folded lengthwise.

SCARVES

Roll scarf on flat surface

Tube should be at least as wide as scarf

Storing in drawers
Roll silk scarves around the paper tubes from aluminum foil or plastic wrap. This will prevent the scarves from creasing when they are stored.

ADAPTING HANGERS

Wind rubber bands around hanger

Nonslip hangers
Prevent clothes from slipping off wire hangers by winding two or three rubber bands around the ends of the hangers.

SPACE SAVERS FOR CLOSETS

● **Hanging items** Slip shower curtain hooks on the rod in your closet and hang belts and bags from them. Hang a string bag to hold socks.

LONG DRESSES

Hanging out
Prevent a long evening dress from trailing by sewing loops at waist level inside the dress. Turn the bodice inside out, and hang the loops from a hanger.

Cut away from yourself when using craft knife

Making a skirt hanger
Cut V-shaped notches near the ends of a wooden hanger to hold skirt loops securely. Use a sturdy craft knife to cut the notches.

CARING FOR SKINS AND FURS

● **Suede** Pick up threads and lint on suede bags and shoes by rubbing the suede with a piece of velvet fabric. This also works for dark clothes.

● **Odds and ends** Plastic shoe containers with pockets can be hung in a closet and then used for storing socks and other small items.

BRIGHT IDEA

Storing skirts
If you do not have any room in your closet to hang skirts, roll them around plastic bags or tissue paper to prevent creasing, then store them in a drawer.

ACCESSORIES

If you must get rid of good-quality accessories (they may come back in fashion!) donate them to charity.

● **Hats and bags** Paint straw hats and bags with a coat of clear varnish to prevent the straw from splitting.
● **Gloves** Marks on light gloves can often be removed by rubbing with a pencil eraser. Wash gloves in special glove shampoo and put them on your hands while they dry – this restores the shape.
● **Buttons** When throwing out garments, snip off the buttons. Keep sets of buttons in small plastic bags so you know how many you have.

● **Fur care** When wearing furs, always wear a scarf to prevent makeup from rubbing off onto the collar. Do not spray on perfume when wearing fur.

STORAGE

Do not allow clothes in your closets to become crowded – if they do, they will not air properly and will become creased.

Make space in closets by storing out-of-season clothes elsewhere. Alternatively, use a free-standing clothing rack kept in a spare room.

DAMP CLOSETS
● **Cure for dampness** Fill a coffee can with charcoal briquets. Punch holes in the lid, and put in the closet.

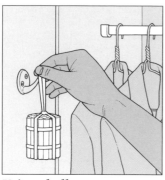

Using chalk
Tie 12 pieces of ordinary chalk together, and hang them inside a damp closet. The chalk will absorb moisture from the air.

STORING BED LINEN
● **Avoiding yellowing** Establish a separate closet for linen items – linen may yellow if stored on open shelving.

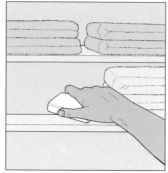

Scented linen closets
Store unwrapped soap in linen closets - the soap scents the linen and, at the same time, hardens to become long lasting.

VACATION PACKING

When packing for vacations, put makeup and toiletry bottles, however tightly closed, into plastic bags with twist ties. Mix the family's clothes in different suitcases – if one is lost, no one has to do entirely without extra clothes.

● **Saving space** Use small items such as underwear and socks to fill shoes, which should, in their turn, be packed in plastic bags.
● **Planning ahead** Pack two large plastic bags for the trip home – one for dirty laundry, the other for damp items.
● **Suitcase storage** When you return home, put a couple of sugar cubes in your empty suitcase to absorb odors.

MOTHPROOFING

Moths breed in dust and dirt, so clean and air items before you store them. Clean closets and cabinets out annually. Do not line drawers with prepasted wallpaper, since this may attracts moths. See page 96 for tackling mildew, which also affects items in storage.

NATURAL MOTH DETERRENTS

Citrus peel and cloves
Scatter dried citrus peel among clothes and shoes in closets and drawers. Put whole cloves in the pockets of coats before storing them for the summer, and into plastic bags for woolen sweaters.

Tie top of muslin bag with ribbon

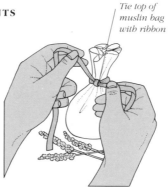

Lavender sachets
Make your own lavender bags by tying a handful of lavender into a square of muslin. Place the bags in drawers and chests. They help keep moths away and also scent clothes and linen.

BED LINEN
● **Heat cure** If you suspect moth eggs are in your bed linen, hang the items in bright sunlight for a few hours or put them in your dryer on the appropriate cycle.
● **Moth-proofing mixture** For washing a blanket for storage, mix 3 tbsp (45 ml) eucalyptus oil, 1 cup (225 ml) denatured alcohol, and 1 cup (225 g) soap flakes in a jar, and shake well. Add 1 tbsp (15 ml) of this mixture to 1 gallon (4.5 liters) of warm water, and soak the blanket, agitating until it is clean. Do not rinse. Spin dry without heat, then hang out in fresh air.

CARING FOR SHOES

S HOES ARE A VITAL AND EXPENSIVE PART of any wardrobe. Keep shoes clean, inspect them regularly, and repair them at the first sign of damage. Air shoes after wearing and use shoe trees to help shoes maintain their shape.

CLEANING SHOES

W ell-cleaned leather shoes resist scuffs. Apply polish, leave overnight, then buff in the morning. White canvas shoes benefit from being starched. Nail a metal bottle cap to the back of your shoe brush, and use this for removing dirt and mud from heels and soles.

PATENT LEATHER

Buff with a soft cloth

Raising a shine
Rub patent leather shoes with petroleum jelly – this shines the shoes and prevents them from sticking together. Buff well.

SUEDE

Ensure that shoe is dry

Use a clean eraser

Erasing marks
Use an eraser to remove mud and surface soil, and to raise crushed pile on suede shoes. Use a stain remover on grease.

CANVAS

Rub in shampoo until it creates a foam

Using carpet shampoo
Clean dirty canvas shoes with a toothbrush dipped in carpet shampoo. Treat new canvas shoes with fabric protector.

MAINTAINING SHOES

C oat new leather soles with castor oil or linseed oil to preserve them. Store your shoes and boots away from direct sunlight (rubber boots, in particular, may deteriorate if care is not taken). Touch up scuff marks on shoes with a felt-tip pen or a wax crayon.

USING NEWSPAPER

Stuff wet shoes and boots with newspaper to speed the drying process. Stretch tight shoes by stuffing them with wet, crumpled newspaper and letting them stand overnight. Stuffing rolls of newspaper into boots will help them to keep their shape.

COMMON PROBLEMS
● **Muddy shoes** Let the shoes dry thoroughly, then scrape off the mud with a blunt knife or a piece of wood. Sponge any marks with a damp cloth, and stuff with newspaper or shoe trees to keep the shoes in shape. Polish when dry.
● **Polish substitute** If you run out of shoe polish, try using a similarly colored furniture polish instead. Buff well.
● **Heel preserver** Paint the heels of new and newly repaired shoes with clear nail varnish – this prevents scuffing the finish and will keep cork heels from being damaged.

GREEN TIP

Shoe deodorant
Sprinkle baking soda liberally into smelly shoes. Let stand overnight, then shake out the baking soda before wearing.

CARE & REPAIR

QUICK REFERENCE
Wood, p. 115
Metal, p. 118
Glass and China, p. 122
Ornamental Surfaces, p. 125
Upholstery Fabrics, p. 126
Around the Home, p. 128
Accessories, p. 130

*S*OME OF THE OBJECTS *and surfaces in your home require more attention than a regular cleaning routine provides. Make it a rule always to mend items as soon as you can – letting things go just makes it harder to do repairs. During regular cleaning, watch out for problems that call for prompt remedial action. Keep a kit of the repair equipment and professional cleaners you are likely to use so you can swing into action at any time.*

CARE AND REPAIR EQUIPMENT

In addition to your cleaning kit (see p. 54-55), it is a good idea to assemble a kit of items that you might need for professional cleaning and repairs. A selection of adhesives, sandpaper, and brushes is useful, as are different types of solvent and polish.

● **Brushes and steel wool** Use clean, soft paintbrushes, old toothbrushes that have been sterilized, and steel wool to apply and remove substances.
● **Sandpaper** Keep a supply of different grades that can be used for a variety of tasks.
● **Adhesives** Use the correct adhesive for the material that you are mending. Adhesives are difficult to remove, so keep the appropriate solvent on hand during use. See page 95 for removing adhesive marks.
● **Solvents** Keep ammonia and denatured alcohol for cleaning. Store out of the reach of children. Always wear gloves when handling ammonia and open the bottle away from you.
● **Oil and polish** Linseed oil is a useful treatment for wood that also conditions leather. Metal polish will clean various metals and remove scratches from glass and acrylic surfaces.

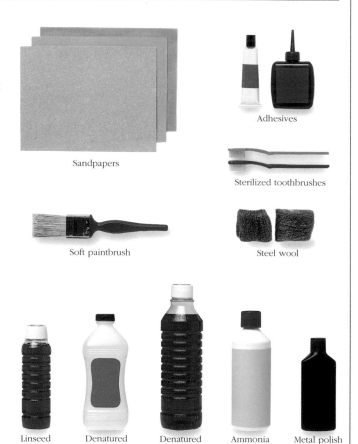

Sandpapers

Adhesives

Sterilized toothbrushes

Soft paintbrush

Steel wool

Linseed oil

Denatured alcohol

Denatured alcohol (dyed)

Ammonia

Metal polish

WOOD

MOST HOMES CONTAIN WOODEN surfaces, furniture, and objects, finished in a variety of ways. Although tough, wood is easily damaged. Polish protects wood, but will build up after time. Antique wood needs special care.

CARING FOR WOOD

Different types of wood vary in terms of hardness and color, but all can be damaged by dry air and exposure to sunlight. Position wooden furniture away from direct sunlight. Humidify rooms with houseplants and by concealing bowls of water nearby.

TEAK

Wear gloves when handling steel wool

Applying teak oil
Once or twice a year, rub teak furniture with a small amount of teak oil or cream, applied with fine steel wool. Buff well with a soft cloth. Dust regularly.

OAK

Apply polish with a soft brush

Making homemade polish
Polish oak with a mixture of 2 cups (600 ml) beer, a small lump of melted beeswax, and 2 tsp (10 g) of sugar. Buff well with chamois leather when dry.

CONDITIONING WOOD
- **Mahogany** To remove the bloom from mahogany, mix 1 tbsp (15 ml) each of linseed oil and turpentine in 4 cups (1.2 liters) of water, and wipe. Rub well, and polish.
- **Ebony** To revive dull ebony, apply petroleum jelly, let sit for half an hour, and rub off.
- **Other woods** Pine, beech, elm, and walnut need dusting regularly. Polish occasionally with wax polish that matches the color of the wood. To keep oak in good condition, wipe occasionally with warm vinegar. Dry before polishing.

MAKING BEESWAX POLISH

Polish antique furniture with natural beeswax polish; silicone polish gives antiques an unnatural sheen and is difficult to remove. Use the recipe below to make your own beeswax polish. Store it in a wide-necked jar so that you can dip a cloth into it. If the polish becomes hard, stand the jar in warm water.

Use coarse part of grater

1 Coarsely grate 2 oz (50 g) of natural beeswax. If the beeswax is too hard to grate, warm it in a microwave on Low for several seconds.

Pour turpentine onto beeswax

2 Place the grated beeswax in a screw-top jar. Add 5 fl oz (150 ml) of turpentine (do not use turpentine substitute), then place the lid loosely on the jar.

Water should be hot, not boiling

Cover jar loosely

3 Stand the jar in a bowl, and pour hot water in the bowl to melt the beeswax. Shake the jar gently so that the mixture forms a paste. Let cool.

REMOVING MARKS FROM WOOD

Wood is easily damaged by heat and scratching. Avoid placing hot objects directly onto wood – always use a trivet. Wipe up spills quickly. Check that ornaments do not have bases that could scratch a surface. If necessary, stick felt pads to their bases.

MARK	NOTES	TREATMENT
ALCOHOL STAINS	Alcohol damages polished wooden surfaces and leaves white marks. Spills should be blotted or wiped immediately; apply treatment as soon as you can.	Rub the area vigorously with your usual polish. If this does not work, rub along the grain of the wood with cream metal polish on a soft cloth.
MINOR BURNS	Minor burns on solid wood can usually be repaired. On veneered surfaces, you may need to cut out the damage and insert a new piece of veneer.	Rub with metal polish. If the wood is rough, scrape and sand the surface. Place wet blotting paper over the mark, and cover with plastic wrap. Leave overnight.
SERIOUS BURNS	These need more drastic treatment than light burns. Do not attempt to repair expensive pieces yourself; they require professional attention.	Scrape out the burned wood with a sharp knife. Fill with matching wood filler. When dry, sand, then paint the area to match the color of the grain with artist's paints.
HEAT MARKS	If hot dishes are placed on wooden surfaces they can cause white marks to appear. Use trivets to protect wood from hot dishes and saucepans.	Rub cream metal cleaner along the grain. Alternatively, apply a paste of vegetable oil and salt. Leave for a couple of hours, then apply polish.
DENTS	Treat as soon as possible. Dented veneer may split, in which case you will have to cut out the damaged piece and replace it with a new one.	Fill the hollow with warm water, and let it stand to swell the wood. Alternatively, cover with damp blotting paper, and apply a warm iron to the dent.
SCRATCHES	These must be filled. You can buy scratch-disguising sticks in a variety of shades to match different woods. Alternatively, use the treatment at right.	Rub with beeswax polish and a little linseed oil. Rub over the scratch, and buff well. Alternatively, use a colored wax crayon or suitable color of paste shoe polish.
WATER MARKS	Water marks wood and causes unvarnished wood to swell. Mop up as soon as possible, and allow the surface to dry before applying any treatment.	Rub with cream metal polish along the grain of the wood, or mix a little cigarette ash with petroleum jelly and rub it over the marked area.
GREASE MARKS	Spilled grease will leave a permanent dark patch on wood unless treated quickly. Remove excess grease at once, using paper towels or a dish towel.	Use straight vinegar to dissolve the grease, then wipe over the surface with a cloth wrung out with a solution of equal parts vinegar and warm water.

WOODEN FURNITURE

Modern furniture is not always solid wood, but may consist of particleboard or plywood covered with veneer. Minor repairs, such as fixing sticking drawers and wobbly legs, are relatively easy and do not take much time. Major repairs require expert attention.

SPECIAL TREATMENTS

● **Reviving dull polish** Use a mixture of 2 tbsp (30 ml) each of turpentine, white vinegar, and denatured alcohol, and 1 tbsp (15 ml) of linseed oil. Shake, and apply on a cloth.

● **Surplus polish** Use vinegar and water to remove a polish buildup. Rub off at once. This also removes finger marks.

● **Stuck paper** Moisten paper that is stuck to wood with baby oil. Let stand for a few minutes, then roll paper off.

● **Cane chairs** If the seat of a cane chair is sagging, saturate the seat with very hot water, then let it dry in the sun.

STABILIZING TABLES

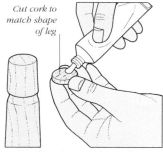

Cut cork to match shape of leg

Lengthening a short leg
If a table is wobbly because one leg is shorter than the others, cut a piece of cork to the right depth and width. Attach the piece to the bottom of the leg with woodwork adhesive.

RELEASING DRAWERS

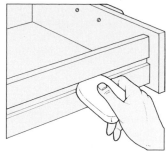

Greasing the runners
If a drawer does not slide in and out smoothly, rub the runners with soap or candle wax. If the drawer still sticks badly, rub the runners with fine sandpaper, and reapply the soap or candle wax.

WOODEN OBJECTS

Most homes contain a variety of wooden objects, such as ornaments, kitchen utensils, and musical instruments. These items need regular attention to prevent the wood from drying out and cracking. Keep wood out of direct sunlight, which may cause fading.

CARING FOR KITCHEN UTENSILS

● **New utensils** Soak new wooden utensils in cider vinegar overnight to prevent them from picking up food smells. Dry on paper towels.

● **Old tableware** Restore stained tableware by rubbing along the grain with fine steel wool (wear gloves to protect your hands). Apply a little vegetable oil, and rub in well.

OTHER OBJECTS

● **Boxes** Give ornamental wooden boxes a sheen and scent by rubbing them with lemon-balm leaves. Sanding wooden boxes lightly will bring back their natural scent.

Salad bowls
Rub new wooden salad bowls with a little olive oil on a soft cloth. Do not clean with soap. Instead, rinse in warm water, and reapply olive oil when dry.

Cover whole board

Cutting boards
Seal splits in a cutting board (caused by the wood drying out) by covering it with a damp cloth for several hours. This will make the wood fibers swell.

Pour in a handful of dry rice

Musical instruments
Remove dust inside stringed instruments, such as guitars and violins, by pouring raw rice through the center. Shake gently, then pour the rice out.

METAL

METAL ITEMS MUST BE CLEANED regularly, or they will tarnish and, on some metals, verdigris may appear. This is much harder to remove than a layer of dirt. If you do not have time to clean thoroughly, there are ways to restore shine.

CLEANING SILVER

Silver tarnishes easily so must be cleaned frequently. There are a number of different methods to choose from, some more suitable for particular types of silver than others. You may need more than one product, depending on the sizes of your silver objects.

SILVER-CLEANING EQUIPMENT

Keep silver polish or cloths impregnated with cleaning fluid for polishing large silver items. A silver dip is useful for cleaning jewelry. Use soft toothbrushes to clean embossed items, and dusters for buffing polish. If you use your silver only rarely, store it in a tarnish-proof bag, or wrap items in acid-free tissue paper – both of these will keep tarnish from developing in storage. Silver keeps best if it is used.

Tarnish-proof bag   Dust cloths Impregnated
                                        cloths

Silver polish Silver dip   Acid-free   Soft toothbrushes
                                   tissue paper

APPLYING BASIC CLEANING TECHNIQUES

● **General care** Wash your silver regularly in hot water and dishwashing liquid, and you will not have to polish it very often. Dust and wash ornaments once a week.

Scrub blackened areas gently but firmly for several minutes

Cleaning embossed silver
Use a soft toothbrush to apply silver polish to embossed silver. Alternatively, apply polish on a cotton swab, or on an orange stick wrapped with cotton.

● **Dos and don'ts** Clean silver near an open window to stop fumes from collecting. Do not rub hallmarks too hard – you will wear them away and reduce the value of the piece.

Gloves prevent fingerprints

Handling clean silver
After you have cleaned silver, wrap it in acid-free tissue paper or place in a tarnish-proof bag if you plan to store it. Wear gloves to avoid leaving finger marks.

KEEPING SILVER CLEAN

● **Preventing tarnish** Do not store silver items in plastic bags or plastic wrap. These trap condensation, which will encourage tarnishing.

● **Alternative cleaners** To remove bad tarnish from silver objects, first dissolve a handful of washing soda in hot water in an aluminum pan. Place the objects in the solution, and remove them as soon as the tarnish disappears. Rinse, and polish. Alternatively, use a paste made from salt and lemon juice. Brighten silver quickly with a drop of turpentine on a soft cloth.

● **Homemade cleaning cloths** Make your own impregnated cloths by saturating cotton squares in a solution of two parts ammonia, one part silver polish, and 10 parts cold water. Let cloths drip dry.

PROTECTING SILVER OBJECTS

Polish silver at the first hint of tarnish. Buy a tarnish-proof bag with compartments for each piece of sliver – or make your own from baize. Avoid overcleaning antique silver – its charm lies in its slightly aged look; there is no need to make it look brand new.

SILVER TABLEWARE

● **Salt shakers** Do not put salt directly into a silver shaker – use a glass liner. Remove the salt after each use.

● **Coffeepots** Remove stains from silver coffeepot interiors by rubbing them with a piece of fine steel wool dipped in white vinegar and salt.

● **Teapots** To clean tea-stained interiors, fill teapots with boiling water, and add a handful of washing soda. Soak overnight, then rinse.

● **Candlesticks** Remove wax by pouring hot water over the candlestick. Melt wax on the base with a hair dryer.

STORAGE

Sugar lumps absorb dampness

Preventing mustiness

Place a couple of white sugar lumps inside a silver coffee pot between uses to prevent a stale smell. Store with the lid off.

TRADITIONAL TIP

Avoiding tarnishing

Salt, egg yolk, broccoli, and fish are all notorious enemies of silver – they cause it to tarnish. Wash silverware immediately after it has been in contact with any of these foods. Then rinse and dry the silver thoroughly.

CLEANING SMALL ITEMS

Nail polish will prevent allergic reaction

Silver earrings

Paint clear nail polish on the posts of earrings to stop tarnish from causing car infections.

Use toothpaste as a mild abrasive

Napkin rings

To clean intricate engravings on silver napkin rings, rub in a little toothpaste with a soft cloth.

SILVERPLATED ITEMS

● **Cleaning** Treat silverplated items as if they were solid silver – but with more care, since the coating can come off. Do not polish silver gilt; you may rub it off. Just dust every now and again.

● **Restoring silverplate** Dip worn silverplate in a special solution that applies a silver coating to it. This will wear off with polishing and must be reapplied. Do not use the solution on valuable pieces.

CARING FOR SILVER CUTLERY

Cover all the silver with water

Always wash silver cutlery as soon as possible after it has been used – this prevents food from causing tarnish stains. To clean a lot of silver cutlery quickly, put strips of aluminum foil in a large bowl, and place the silver cutlery on top. Cover the cutlery with boiling water, then add 3 tbsp (45 ml) of baking soda, and soak for 10 minutes.

● **Dishwashing silver** Never wash silver and stainless-steel pieces of cutlery together in a dishwasher, since the silver may be damaged by the steel.

● **Decorative handles** Whiten bone handles with a paste of lemon juice and soapstone, applied and left for an hour. Do not immerse bone or mother-of-pearl handles in water, since they may be damaged.

CHROME AND STAINLESS STEEL

It is important not to use abrasive cleaners on chrome, since the plating can be damaged easily. To treat corrosion, use a special chrome cleaner. Although stainless steel is easy to care for, it can become stained by deposits from hard water, grease splashes, and silver cleaner.

CHROME
● **Minor marks** Remove these by wiping over with a little dishwashing liquid and water.
● **Shining faucets** For a quick shine, rub a handful of plain flour on faucets, then polish with a soft cloth. See page 69 for cleaning bathroom taps.

STAINLESS STEEL
● **General care** Dry stainless steel thoroughly after washing, to prevent a buildup of white film. Do not soak stainless steel – it may become pitted. To shine stainless steel, use a commercial cleaner, or one of the methods below.

See page 69 for cleaning bathroom taps.

Cleaning chrome
Gently clean chrome with white vinegar. Remove stubborn marks with a solution of baking soda and warm water. Rinse.

Buff flour well with a clean, soft cloth

Shining stainless steel
Give stainless-steel pans a good shine by rubbing with flour. Remove heat marks with a scouring pad and lemon juice.

CARING FOR KNIVES

Plunge knife blade in soil

● **Removing smells** If strong fish or garlic smells cling to a knife blade, plunge it into soil. Wash well before use.
● **Keeping knives sharp** Store knives in a wooden knife block, or on a magnetic rack. If you store them with other utensils, the blades will become blunt – and you may cut yourself when reaching into drawers. Alternatively, keep knives in plastic sleeves or in fabric rolls (available at restaurant-supply stores).

IRON AND PEWTER

Cast iron must always be dried thoroughly after being washed; otherwise, it will rust. Season it well with cooking oil before use. Pewter should have a soft glow rather than a shine. Wash it in soapy water, and buff well. Remove grease marks with denatured alcohol.

CAST IRON

Rub in oil with paper towel

Caring for cast iron
After washing and drying cast-iron pans, rub with vegetable oil. If the pans are rusty, rub them with 1 tbsp (15 ml) citric acid and 2 cups (600 ml) water.

PEWTER

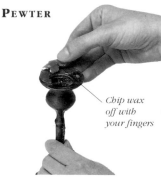

Chip wax off with your fingers

Removing wax
To remove wax from pewter candlesticks, place them in the freezer, and the wax will chip off. Use a hair dryer on low to melt away any remaining traces.

TRADITIONAL TIP

Cleaning pewter
Rub pewter objects with cabbage leaves, or immerse them in leftover water that has been used to boil eggs.

BRASS AND COPPER

Use the same methods to clean brass and copper. Apply a thin layer of lacquer to the surface of these metals to reduce the need for polishing. Use a cardboard template when cleaning brass and copper details on furniture, so that no metal polish spills onto the wood.

CLEANING BRASS AND COPPER

● **Removing tarnish** Use a paste of salt and lemon juice, or rub items with half a cut lemon dipped in salt. Rinse.

● **Copper pans** Have copper pans relined when the interior starts to show signs of wear. Copper reacts with food acids.

Solution of salt and ammonia

Removing verdigris

If brass or copper turns green, rub with a solution of ammonia and salt. Always wear gloves when using ammonia.

Cleaning ashtrays

After washing a brass or copper ashtray, spray a little wax polish on the inside. In future, you will be able to wipe it out easily.

CARING FOR BRONZE

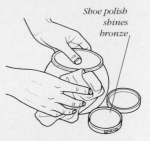

Shoe polish shines bronze

● **Shining bronze** Wipe bronze objects with a little shoe polish or vegetable oil to maintain a sheen.
● **Cleaning** Dust bronze with a soft cloth. Clean intricate areas with a cotton swab. Apply turpentine to remove any marks, then polish.

OTHER METALS

Precious metals, such as gold and platinum, are most commonly found in the home in the form of jewelry. Protect gold jewelry by storing it separately. Gold leaf is sometimes used on picture frames; it needs to be handled with care to prevent it from coming off.

CARING FOR GOLD

● **Gold chains** Wash in a bowl of soapy water. Use a soft toothbrush to get inside links. Drip dry on a towel; then rub with chamois leather.

Storing gold jewelry

Wrap clean gold jewelry in chamois leather to maintain brightness. Wash gold jewelry occasionally in soapy water.

LARGE GOLD ITEMS

● **Cleaning** Clean large gold objects such as goblets and plates with an impregnated cloth for silver cleaning. Buff with a chamois leather.

Apply paint with a soft paintbrush

Replacing gold leaf

If a modern gilt frame becomes damaged, use gilt paint, available from art suppliers, to touch up marks. (Gilt paint is poisonous.)

CLEANING METAL

● **Platinum** Clean platinum by immersing it for a few minutes in a jewelry dip. Use a soft toothbrush for intricate areas. Rinse and dry it thoroughly.
● **Lead** Scrub with turpentine. Place very dirty objects for approximately five minutes in a solution of one part white vinegar to nine parts water, with a little baking soda added. Rinse in distilled water.
● **Ormolu** Clean by making a solution of 2 tsp (10 ml) ammonia in a cup of warm water. Apply the solution to the object with a cotton swab. Rinse with clear water on a cotton ball, and dry with a soft cloth. Do not use metal polish on ormolu.

GLASS AND CHINA

GLASS AND CHINA LOOK BEST when sparkling clean. Items that you do not use often should be washed from time to time, or dust will build up and produce a grimy finish. Wipe regularly with a soapy cloth, then a damp one.

CRYSTAL AND GLASSWARE

Wash delicate glasses by hand – using a plastic bowl to prevent breakage – and dry carefully. Never put cut glass or fine crystal in a dishwasher; the strong detergents used will eventually cause a white bloom known as etching, which is impossible to remove.

CLEANING CRYSTAL AND GLASSWARE

Stemmed glasses
When drying stemmed glasses, hold the dish towel steady, and twist the glass around inside it. If you do it the other way around, you may snap the stem.

Making glass shine
Put some lemon peels in the rinse water used for glassware. Lemon cuts grease, and the acid released gives a clear shine and brilliance to the washed glasses.

TRADITIONAL TIP

Polishing glasses
Make a thin paste from baking powder and water, and rub it onto glass. Rinse well, and dry with a soft cloth to create a bright shine. This polish also works well on car windshields.

CARING FOR GLASS

● **Preventing heat damage** Do not expose glassware to high temperatures, or to extreme changes in temperature – the glassware may break. Gilt and silver decorations on glassware will come off if items are washed or soaked in hot water for too long.
● **Storing glasses** Store wine glasses upright. If you store them upside down, they will develop a musty smell and the rims may be damaged.
● **Removing smells** If bottles or jars smell strongly, wash them, then steep in a solution of 1 tsp (5 g) dry mustard to 4 cups (1 liter) warm water overnight. Rinse well.

SOLVING PROBLEMS WITH GLASSWARE

Inner tumbler is filled with ice cubes

Pour hot water into bowl

Unsticking glasses
If one glass becomes stuck in another, stand both in a bowl. Put ice cubes in the top tumbler to make it contract. Pour hot water into the bowl – this will make the outer tumbler expand and release its grip on the inner one.

Hold glass steady

Rub with sandpaper

Removing chips
There is no need to throw away glasses that get chipped. Rub the chip with a piece of extra-fine sandpaper until it is smooth. Then rub the surrounding area of the rim to smooth it and make the repair less obvious.

SPECIAL GLASS ITEMS

Glass items around the home will attract dust and look dull unless they are cleaned regularly. Do not let dirt build up, or cleaning will become a chore. If you have to carry glassware to another room for cleaning, put it in a wastepaper basket filled with newspaper.

CLEANING AND CARING FOR MIRRORS

Polishing mirrors
Create a sparkling finish on a mirror by applying a few drops of denatured alcohol. Do not allow any liquid to seep under the sides of the frame and behind the glass. Buff with a soft, dry, lint-free cloth.

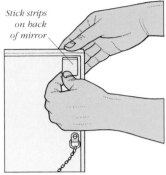

Stick strips on back of mirror

Hanging heavy mirrors
Large mirrors can often damage the wallpaper or paint on the wall they hang from. Prevent this by attaching strips of foam rubber or pieces of cork to the back corners of mirrors, using adhesive or double-sided tape.

DECANTERS AND VASES
● **Cleaning** Put a handful of salt and 2 tsp (10 ml) of white vinegar in dull decanters and vases. Shake vigorously, then rinse. Alternatively, use a solution of white vinegar and water, and a little coarse sand. Shake well, then rinse.
● **Stains in crystal vases** To remove stains and grime deposits, fill a vase with water and 2 tbsp (30 ml) ammonia. Leave for several hours, then wash and rinse. Always wear gloves when using ammonia.
● **Stains in decanters** Use a solution of household bleach to remove port stains from decanters. Be sure to rinse thoroughly – until all trace and smell of bleach has gone.
● **Storing decanters** Place a small silica packet (available from florists) in decanters to absorb any moisture and prevent mustiness.

WATCHES
● **Caring for watches** Get a professional to clean the insides of a watch. Always remove a watch off before putting your hands in water to prevent damage to the works.

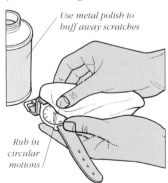

Use metal polish to buff away scratches

Rub in circular motions

Treating scratches
Remove scratches from watch crystals by rubbing firmly for 10 minutes with a piece of cloth wrapped around your finger and dipped in thick metal polish. Polish the face afterward.

CHANDELIERS

● **Regular dusting** Use a long-handled, fluffy brush to regularly dust a chandelier. This will reduce the need for frequent thorough cleaning.
● **Cleaning** Turn off the electricity at the fuse box, and cover each bulb with a plastic bag. Cover the ground below to catch drips. Standing on a ladder, wipe all glass parts with a solution of dishwashing liquid. Spray cleaners are available for glass beads. Unscrew and clean each bulb. Use a metal polish on the metal parts. If you have to dismantle the chandelier, make a diagram, so that you can put it together again.

SPECTACLES
● **Loose screws** If the screws of your eyeglasses tend to come out easily, dab the ends of the screws (while they are properly screwed in) with clear nail varnish.

Dip spectacles in soapy water

Cleaning eyeglasses
Wash eyeglasses regularly in a dishwashing liquid solution. Rub with undiluted dishwashing liquid to prevent eyeglasses from clouding over; or polish with eau de cologne.

CHINA AND DISHES

Take good care of your china and dishes; otherwise, you could end up with a set of mismatched, chipped items for which you cannot obtain matching replacements. If you break a piece from a set, replace it as soon as possible – some designs go out of production.

CHINA PLATES
● **Storing fine china** When stacking clean china plates, place a paper plate on top of each one – this prevents the base of a plate from damaging the decorated surface of the one sitting below it.

CASSEROLE DISHES
● **Preventing damage** Before using an unglazed casserole dish, season the outside by rubbing it with a cut onion or garlic cloves. This will give it added strength to withstand high temperatures.

CLEANING INTERIORS OF TEAPOTS

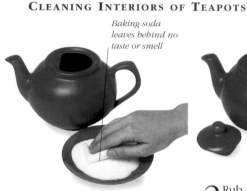

Baking soda leaves behind no taste or smell

1 Clean a china teapot by dipping a damp cloth into baking soda. (Roll up the cloth to clean the spout.)

Rub all stained areas firmly until clean

2 Rub the inside of the teapot with the cloth, then rinse it well. Store it with the lid off. An old glove thumb will protect the spout.

CHINA VASES

Sand will scour interior of vase

● **Cleaning** Pour a handful of sand or salt into dingy vases. Fill with a dishwashing-liquid solution, or pour in a little straight vinegar, and shake well. Let the mixture soak overnight, then rinse.
● **Deep vases** If a china vase is too deep for cut flowers, simply place some crumpled paper towels or newsprint in the bottom of the vase.

REPAIRING BROKEN CHINA

You can repair minor damage to china yourself, but valuable pieces are best repaired by an expert. Keep all broken pieces in a plastic bag until they can be reassembled. Do not eat or drink from chipped dishes, since the chipped parts may harbor germs.

REPAIRING CHINA
● **Using adhesive** Before you spread glue on broken china, wipe the edges with a piece of lint-free material (do not use cotton, which will leave lint). Try not to get fingerprints on the broken edges. Use epoxy for making repairs – this will allow you to expose the piece to low heat after the repair.
● **Improvised clamps** When gluing small pieces of china, use modeling clay or clothespins to hold the pieces.

MENDING A BROKEN HANDLE

Sand holds mug in position while you work

1 Place the mug in a box of sand, handle side up, to hold it in place. Apply adhesive to the broken edges of the handle and to the mug.

Check seam for extra adhesive

2 Glue the handle in position. Wipe away any extra adhesive around the seam. Leave the mug in the sand until the glue is dry.

ORNAMENTAL SURFACES

ORNAMENTAL SURFACES NEED MORE CARE than common substances such as wood, metal, and plastic. You cannot always use a basic household cleaner. Surfaces such as marble, alabaster, onyx, and jade each require a special treatment.

STONE SURFACES

Stone can be used for many surfaces, not just walls and floors. Special stone surfaces are often porous, so should not be wetted. They may also stain easily, so it is important to treat spills and marks quickly. Be careful when carrying stone items – they may be very heavy.

CARING FOR STONE

● **Marble** This is a porous stone, so treat stains at once. For wine, tea, or coffee stains, rub with a solution of one part hydrogen peroxide to four parts water. Wipe off at once, and repeat if necessary. For other stains, see right.

● **Alabaster** This is highly porous. Clean it with a little white spirit or turpentine. Remember not to put water in alabaster vases – they leak.

● **Jade** You can wash jade, but you must dry it at once with paper towels. Never use abrasive cleaners.

REMOVING STAINS FROM MARBLE

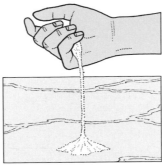

Sour milk will keep salt damp

1 Cover stains on marble surfaces with salt. If the stain is not serious, brush off and reapply the salt as the stain is soaked up.

2 If the stain persists, pour sour milk over the salt, and leave it for several days. Then wipe it off with a damp, wrung-out cloth.

BONE AND HORN

In general, bone, horn, and antique ivory should be wiped gently, not washed. Do not immerse bone knife handles when doing dishes. Keep bone and horn out of strong sunlight and away from high heat. Rinse horn goblets immediately after use, and dry them thoroughly.

CARING FOR BONE

● **Hairbrushes** Clean tortoiseshell hairbrushes with furniture cream, and ivory hairbrushes with turpentine. When washing brushes, rinse the bristles without wetting the backs, and dry with the bristles face down.

● **Bone handles** Wipe bone handles clean with denatured alcohol. Lay discolored handles in sunlight, or rub them with a paste of equal parts hydrogen peroxide and whiting (available from hardware stores).

CARING FOR IVORY

Cleaning piano keys
Use toothpaste on a damp cloth to clean piano keys. Rub gently so as not to damage them. Rinse with milk, and buff well.

CARING FOR PIANOS

● **Plastic keys** Dust regularly and wipe occasionally with a solution of warm water and vinegar on chamois leather.

● **Ivory keys** Leave the piano open on sunny days so that the keys will be bleached and not turn yellow. See left for cleaning. Keys that are badly discolored must be scraped and polished by a professional cleaner.

● **Casework** Use a vacuum cleaner to blow dust away from the inside casework.

UPHOLSTERY FABRICS

THE BEST WAY TO CARE FOR CURTAINS and upholstery is to vacuum them frequently. Do not let fabrics get grimy before they are cleaned. Wash or dry clean them as necessary. Regular cleaning makes these items last longer.

UPHOLSTERED FURNITURE

Upholstery is subject to much wear and tear and needs care, but simple techniques can make furniture look new. A few mothballs dropped down the backs of sofas prevents musty smells and keeps moths away. See pages 76–99 for removing stains on upholstery.

RENOVATIONS
● **Covering seats** Disguise worn-out chairs and sofas by covering them with large sheets of fabric. Alternatively, make replacement slipcovers, or dye existing ones.
● **Patching** Patch holes and worn areas as soon as they occur. First expose the new fabric to sunlight, so that it fades to match the old fabric.
● **Tapestry furniture** To revive dull colors and remove dust, rub damp salt into tapestry. Leave for half an hour, then dust off with a soft brush.

REPAIRS TO UPHOLSTERED FURNITURE

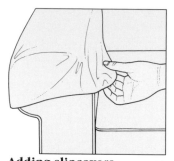

Adding slipcovers
Arms are the first part of a chair to show signs of wear. Make a slip-cover to place over a worn area to protect it from further damage.

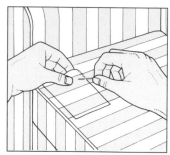

Applying a patch
To patch upholstery, cut a piece of matching fabric, and fold or tack the edges under. Sew the patch in place with tiny stitches.

LEATHER FURNITURE

Keep leather furniture out of direct sunlight; otherwise, it may dry out and crack. Use hide food once or twice a year to ensure that the leather remains supple. Rub it in well so that it does not come off on clothes. Dust or vacuum regularly, and clean with saddle soap.

REMOVING STAINS

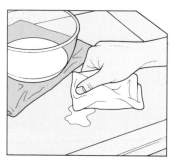

Ballpoint ink
Treat ballpoint ink with milk applied on a soft cloth. Wipe up other ink spills immediately, then sponge the area with tepid water or a little turpentine.

CARING FOR LEATHER
● **Treating leather** Keep leather upholstery looking new by wiping clean, then rubbing well with a soft cloth dipped in beaten egg white. Polish with a clean cloth.
● **Checking for washability** To see if leather is washable, drip a tiny amount of water onto an inconspicuous area. If the water remains as droplets on the surface, then the leather is washable. If the water is absorbed, the leather must not be washed – dust regularly, and wipe over with a barely damp cloth instead.

GREEN TIP

Natural leather polish
Boil 1¼ cups (300 ml) of linseed oil. Let cool and add 1¼ cups (300 ml) vinegar. Apply on a cloth, then buff.

CURTAINS AND HOUSEHOLD LINEN

Take care of your bed linen and curtains to prolong their useful life. If you move, curtains can be altered for your new home.

Bed linen can be repaired or recycled when it shows signs of wear. See page 112 for moth-proofing household linen in storage.

SOLVING CURTAIN PROBLEMS

● **Rings and rods** Boil rusty curtain rings in vinegar to make them bright again. Rub soap on old curtain rods to make them run smoothly.

● **Sheer curtains** To stop sheer curtains from being snagged when you are replacing them on rods, slip a finger cut from an old glove over the rod end.

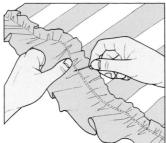

Lengthening curtains
Attach a ruffled edge to the bottom in a matching or similar fabric to lengthen a curtain. Use a fabric of the same weight.

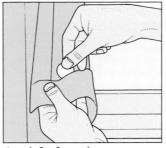

Straight hanging
To keep light curtains hanging properly, place coins inside the hem. Distribute the coins evenly, and stitch them in place.

BEDDING AND LINEN

Use all your linen in rotation, rather than saving some for guests. If linen is stored too long, it deteriorates along the folds and attracts moths. See page 105 for laundering linen.

● **Comforters** Shake daily spread the filling evenly. Comforters will last longer if aired regularly outdoors.
● **Electric blankets** Remove the wires before washing. Return blankets to the manufacturer for servicing about every three years.
● **Dish towels** These wear out all over. When worn, double them and sew the edges together to make them last for another few months.

LAMPSHADES

Clean lampshades regularly, or they will be difficult, if not impossible, to clean. In most people's homes lampshades are in full view, so they need frequent dusting with a vacuum cleaner or feather duster. Always unplug lamps before cleaning them.

CLEANING TIPS
● **Parchment shades** Dust gently, and remove marks with an eraser.
● **Plastic and glass shades** Wash in a dishwashing liquid solution, then rinse and dry.
● **Silk shades** Have silk shades cleaned professionally before dirt starts to show.
● **Straw shades** Vacuum raffia and straw shades frequently, since they tend to trap dust.
● **Vellum shades** Mix together one part soap flakes, one part warm water, and two parts denatured alcohol. Wipe the lampshade with this solution. Rinse with a cloth dipped in denatured alcohol, and apply a little wax furniture polish.

PAPER SHADES

Wipe dirt from creases

Regular dusting
Use a dustcloth to clean paper shades, and pay special attention to any creases. Do not use water, since it will cause distortion. Paper shades can be relatively cheap – consider replacing shades that become very dirty.

FABRIC SHADES

Vacuum cleaning
Use the upholstery tool on your vacuum cleaner to clean a fabric lampshade. Do not wash the shade – the fabric could shrink, and the metal frame may rust. If the shade is very dirty, have it professionally cleaned.

ITEMS AROUND THE HOME

THE MODERN HOME is full of items that need frequent cleaning and maintenance to keep them functioning properly and looking good. Electronic equipment, books, candlesticks, and pictures all need regular care.

ELECTRONIC EQUIPMENT

Dust is the enemy of electronic equipment, so items should be kept covered or protected when not in use. Situate equipment where it is least likely to sustain damage, and do not attempt any repairs unless you are certain that you know what you are doing.

CLEANING TIPS
● **Telephones** Use denatured alcohol to clean off marks. Clean the ear- and mouth-pieces with antiseptic fluid, applied on a cotton ball.
● **Portable radios** Dust these often. Clean occasionally with denatured alcohol applied on a cotton ball.
● **Cameras** Leave cleaning to a professional. Store cameras in their cases between uses.
● **Compact discs** Clean discs and players with special kits available from record stores.
● **Other equipment** See page 70 for caring for kitchen appliances. See page 108 for cleaning and caring for irons.

TELEVISIONS

Cleaning a television
Keep dust from settling on a television screen by spraying it with an antistatic product. Clean weekly with denatured alcohol or a window-cleaning product and buff with a paper towel.

TIMESAVING TIP

Protecting a telephone
Place a plastic bag near the telephone when you are engaged in messy tasks such as pastry making or painting. Slip the bag over your hand to answer the telephone.

CARING FOR VIDEO CASSETTE RECORDERS

Prevent dust from getting into your VCR by keeping the cover on. If the room is damp, keep silica packets (available from florists) on top of the VCR. Keep away from children and pets.

● **Cleaning VCRs** Clean VCRs occasionally, using a cleaning tape to ensure good-quality pictures on playback.
● **Storing videos** Store video-tapes in cardboard or plastic cases. Number each case and keep a log of what you have recorded. Keep a supply of labels for relabeling tapes when you record over them.

COMPUTERS

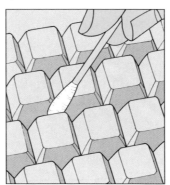

Cleaning computers
Dust between the keys of your computer with a cotton swab. Clean the key tops with denatured alcohol on a cotton swab. Dust the screen and spray with an antistatic product.

OFFICE EQUIPMENT
● **Safety** Before cleaning any electrical equipment, make sure it is unplugged.
● **Computer care** Make sure computers are situated out of direct sunlight, which can cause overheating. Sunlight also makes it difficult for the user to see the computer screen clearly.
● **Answering machines** Dust regularly with a feather duster, particularly inside the machine. You can use an aerosol cleaner, but make sure that the machine is dry before you replace the cassette.
● **Fax machines** Keep these dusted, and occasionally wipe them with denatured alcohol.

DECORATIVE OBJECTS AND BOOKS

The objects in your home are what gives it a distinctive character. Keep pictures and books clean and in good repair. Hang pictures with plexiglass away from open fires; do not smoke near them. Keep watercolor paintings away from direct sunlight to prevent fading.

PICTURE CARE
● **Cleaning picture glass** Apply denatured alcohol or vinegar on a tissue, then wipe off with a dry tissue. Do not use water, since it may seep around the edges and cause damage.
● **Drying damp prints** Place damp prints or drawings between several pieces of blotting paper under an even weight (a piece of board and a few books are ideal). Change the blotting paper as you find it necessary.

MISCELLANEOUS ITEMS
● **Clocks** Clean clock faces with denatured alcohol. Cover a valuable small clock with a plastic bag when doing your regular house cleaning.
● **Umbrella stands** Cut a piece of thick foam to put in the base of your umbrella stand to catch excess drips.

PICTURE FRAMES
● **Cleaning** Rub furniture polish into wooden frames. Wipe plastic frames with a dishwashing liquid solution.

Cleaning frames
Warm a turpentine bottle in hot water, and rub the warm liquid over the frame. Then clean it with 3 tbsp (45 ml) vinegar in 2¼ cups (600 ml) cold water. Dry and polish with a soft cloth.

HANGING PICTURES

● **Marking the spot** When you have chosen the spot for your picture, cover it with a cross of masking tape. This will prevent the plaster from cracking when you hammer in the nail and picture hook.
● **Preventing slips** If a picture keeps slipping to one side, twist tape around the center of the picture wire to give it a better grip on the hook.

CARING FOR BOOKS

● **Storing books** If you have doors on your bookshelves, leave them open from time to time to let the books air and to prevent mildewing. Do not pack books tightly on shelves; keep similar-sized books together. Beware of storing books above a radiator, which may cause the bindings to crack.
● **Preventing mildew** Oil of lavender, eucalyptus, or cloves, sprinkled onto bookshelves, will prevent mildew from developing.
● **Removing mildew** Cover mildew patches on books with cornstarch for a few days before brushing off.
● **Grease stains** See page 99 for treating grease on paper.

CANDLES
● **Securing a candle** Dip the candle end in hot water before placing it in a tight holder. For a loose holder, wrap the candle end in tape.

Wipe candles with denatured alcohol

Caring for candles
Wipe decorative candles that become dirty with denatured alcohol. Place new candles in the freezer for a few hours to help them burn longer.

CLEANING BOOKS
● **Dusting** Once a year, remove books from shelves and dust the tops of the leaves with a fluffy acrylic duster. Keep the books firmly shut.

Leather-bound books
Clean leather-bound books once a year with a mixture of lanolin and neat's-foot-oil (available in leather stores). Neutral shoe cream is a passable substitute.

ACCESSORIES

M OST PEOPLE HAVE VARIOUS ITEMS that they treasure, even if they are not particularly valuable. Keep them clean, and repair them if necessary. Insure valuable objects and take photographs of them in case they are stolen.

CARING FOR JEWELRY

C ostume jewelry needs minimal care, but valuable pieces should be cleaned often. Do not wear rings with stones during cleaning, since you could cause damage to the settings. See pages 118–119 for cleaning silver, and page 77 for cleaning gold and platinum.

PREVENTING DAMAGE
● **Checking jewelry** Check jewelry each time you wear it for any damaged links and faulty clasps. Have rings checked by a jeweler a few times a year for loose stones.
● **Chains** Fasten chains when you are not wearing them to prevent knotting. Do not wear gold chains when you go swimming – the chlorine in pools makes gold brittle.

COSTUME JEWELRY
● **Cleaning** Cover costume jewelry with baking powder, then brush off gently with a soft toothbrush.

CLEANING VALUABLE JEWELRY

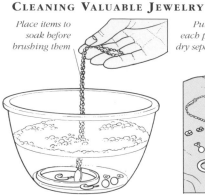

Place items to soak before brushing them

Put down each piece to dry separately

1 Soak jewelry in a solution of dishwashing liquid in a bowl for a few minutes – do not use a sink. Brush items gently with a toothbrush.

2 Rinse the jewelry and lay it on a dish towel. Dry it with a hair dryer on a low setting. Check the water for stones before you discard it.

BRIGHT IDEA

Ring holder
Keep a large safety pin near your kitchen sink at all times, and use it to attach rings to your clothes when you wash dishes. This will prevent rings from getting damaged or being misplaced.

PRECIOUS STONES

Amber

● **Fragile stones** Amber, coral, and jet are fragile stones. Wash using the method above. Do not use chemicals on them.

Ruby

● **Hard stones** Clean rubies, diamonds, and other hard stones as above, or use a special jewelry solution.

Emerald

● **Emeralds** These are soft and chip easily, allowing water into cracks. It is best to have them cleaned by a professional jeweler.

Jade

● **Jade** This should be washed, then dried immediately. Use a soft cloth – any abrasive surface or grit will scratch it.

Opal

● **Opals and turquoise** These are porous stones, so they should not be washed. Shine them with a chamois leather. Brush settings with a toothbrush.

Pearl

● **Pearls** The best way to keep these stones clean is to wear them. If you wear yours only infrequently, rub them gently with a chamois leather occasionally.

JEWELRY REPAIR AND STORAGE

Have a safety chain added to valuable brooches to back up the clasp. Wrap gold items in tissue and store in separate boxes to avoid scratching them. If a gold or silver ring is causing skin discoloration, coat it with clear nail polish – it will not damage the metal.

MAKING MINOR REPAIRS TO JEWELRY

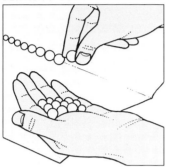

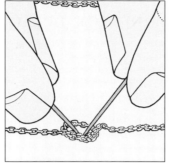

Restringing a necklace
Place the beads in the correct order along a crease in a piece of paper. Restring using fishing line - it is extremely strong.

Untangling chains
Lay a knotted chain on a piece of wax paper, and put a drop of baby oil on the knot. Untangle with a pair of needles.

STORING PIECES OF JEWELRY

● **Necklaces** Prevent necklaces from tangling by hanging them from cup hooks screwed into a wooden clothes hanger.

● **Costume jewelry** Use egg cartons to store jewelry – the bottom for small items, the lid for necklaces and bracelets.

GETTING RINGS OFF

● **Using soap** Loosen a stuck ring by wetting your hands and rubbing soap lather above and below the ring until the ring slides off.
● **Using ice** If a ring is stuck because your finger has swollen in hot weather, put your hand in a bowl of ice water. Soak your hand until the ring can be slipped off.

MISCELLANEOUS ITEMS

Objects such as combs, fountain pens, and handbags need regular attention to keep them in good condition. Clean canvas bags with household detergent, then rinse well. Rub leather bags with neutral shoe polish. See page 123 for cleaning watches and eyeglasses.

PERSONAL ITEMS

● **Handbags** To prevent metal handbag frames and clasps from tarnishing, paint them with two coats of clear nail polish before use. If a handbag handle breaks, replace it with chandelier chain from a hardware store.
● **Combs** Wash combs in cold water with a few drops of ammonia or 2 tsp (10 g) baking soda. See page 125 for cleaning brushes.
● **Stuffed toys** To clean non-washable stuffed toys, shake in a plastic bag that contains baking soda. Brush well, preferably outdoors.

PLAYING CARDS

Rub mark gently with piece of white bread

Cleaning off marks
Rub playing cards with crustless white bread to remove dirt and grease. Dust with talcum powder occasionally to keep them free from grease and grime.

FOUNTAIN PENS

Cleaning a fountain pen
Occasionally, take fountain pens apart and soak the pieces in vinegar. Let stand for an hour, then rinse them in warm water, and let dry on a paper towel.

MAINTAINING A HOME

QUICK REFERENCE
Plumbing, p. 133
Electricity & Fuel, p. 137
Heating & Cooling, p. 140
General Repairs, p. 142
Home Security, p. 144

KEEPING YOUR HOME in good repair means that all fixtures and equipment work properly and that long-term problems are avoided. Good repair maintains the value of your home if you own it, and helps safeguard your deposit if you rent it. Treat any problems as soon as you spot them, with sweat equity or by calling in professional help.

A WELL-MAINTAINED HOME

Take time to look at your home with an outsider's eye. It is only too easy to accept that a faucet drips or a lightbulb needs replacing and to live with the problem. Failure to put things right immediately can cause inconvenience – and sometimes even danger.

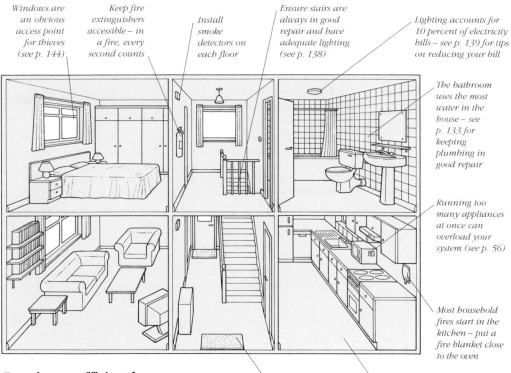

Windows are an obvious access point for thieves (see p. 144)

Keep fire extinguishers accessible – in a fire, every second counts

Install smoke detectors on each floor

Ensure stairs are always in good repair and have adequate lighting (see p. 138)

Lighting accounts for 10 percent of electricity bills – see p. 139 for tips on reducing your bill

The bathroom uses the most water in the house – see p. 133 for keeping plumbing in good repair

Running too many appliances at once can overload your system (see p. 56)

Most household fires start in the kitchen – put a fire blanket close to the oven

Place floor mats inside exterior doors to keep floors clean

Keep floors well insulated, and use a smooth, easy-to-clean surface in kitchens – see p. 142 for floor repairs

Running an efficient home

This costs extra time and money, but forestalls disasters such as burglaries, fires, and floods. Install smoke alarms, fire extinguishers, and burglar alarms, and place secure locks on doors and windows. Always make repairs immediately.

PLUMBING

D RIPS AND LEAKS MAY SEEM like minor irritations but can, if left unrepaired, cause flooding and damage. Leaks are also dangerous near electrical wiring. Call in a plumber if you cannot handle these problems yourself.

BASIC PLUMBING KIT

Be prepared for plumbing problems by keeping a tool kit for routine maintenance and emergencies. Buy the best tools you can afford, since they will be easier to use than cheap ones and will last longer. Make sure you know how to use them safely and effectively. Store your tools where you can easily find them in an emergency.

Mole wrench

Resin

Insulating tape

Sink plunger

Adjustable wrench

DRIPPING FAUCETS

D rips are extremely wasteful – particularly if they come from a hot-water tap. Drips also create a buildup of lime on sinks or tubs.

A dripping faucet may just need a new washer, it may need to be replaced, or may indicate a major problem, such as a cracked pipe.

REPLACING WASHERS

1 Turn off the water supply feeding the faucet. Use an adjustable wrench to unscrew the faucet cover, inserting a soft cloth between the faucet and the wrench to avoid scratching the finish.

2 Unscrew the large nut inside with an open-ended wrench. Remove the valve mechanism, lift out the old washer, and replace it. Reassemble the faucet.

PLUMBING BASICS

● **Water supply** Make sure you know where to turn off the water in your home. Turn it off and on from time to time so that you can easily shut it off in an emergency.
● **Timing jobs** It is always best to start plumbing jobs early in the morning. That way, if you have to make a trip to the hardware store for any missing parts, it will be open.
● **Buying washers** When buying a replacement washer, get several spares at once. Store where you can find them easily, for example, near the main shutoff valve.

STEMMING LEAKING FAUCET HANDLES

● **Old faucets** Leaking handles indicate that the gland, which prevents water coming past the spindle when the faucet is on, needs replacing.

● **Modern faucets** These have O-ring seals instead of glands. To buy a new O-ring, you need to know the name of the manufacturer of the faucet.

BRIGHT IDEA

Silencing drips
Tie a piece of string to the spout of a dripping faucet. The water will flow noiselessly down the string and into the sink.

DRIPPING PIPES

Burst and dripping pipes can cause floods that will ruin furnishings and even bring down ceilings. Therefore, you must act quickly when you find that there is damage to a pipe. Before attempting any repairs, turn off the water. You may have to call in a plumber.

TEMPORARY REPAIRS

● **Copper pipes** Enclose the cracked pipe in a piece of garden hose split along its length. Secure with hose clips.

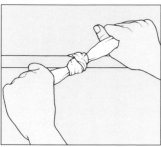

Lead and plastic pipes
Squeeze petroleum jelly into the crack. Wrap a rag or waterproof tape around the pipe until you can get it fixed properly.

> ### WARNING
> If a pipe is leaking near electrical fixtures or outlets, turn off the power immediately.

PERMANENT REPAIRS

1 Rub the pipe with abrasive paper so that epoxy adhesive will stick to it. Smear the adhesive over the crack.

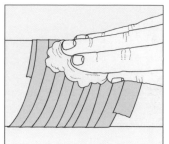

2 Bind fiberglass tape or plumber's waterproof tape around the damaged area at least twice. Smear more resin over the newly taped surface.

3 Let the adhesive to set hard before you turn on the water. Leave all the taps on until water comes through to prevent airlocks forming in the pipes (see below).

WHAT TO DO WHEN A PIPE BURSTS

1 Turn off the main water supply and open all the taps to drain the system.

2 Turn off the water heater to prevent the metal of the pipes from overheating and cracking.

3 If water is running through light fixtures, switch off the lights, and take the appropriate fuse out of the main fuse box.

4 Try to find the source of the leak. Bind the crack with a rag or waterproof tape. Keep a bucket under it, and call a plumber.

5 Meanwhile, if ceiling plaster is bulging, move furniture and carpets away, and place a bucket under the area. Pierce the bulge to let the accumulated water out. This will limit the damage to one area.

NOISY PIPES

Most pipe noises are caused by pipes vibrating against one another because they are not supported properly. If the pipes are not secure, put foam rubber between them and the walls, or secure them to a strip of wood. If this fails, you may have an airlock.

CAUSES OF NOISE

● **Airlocks** Air may get into pipes if a lot of water is suddenly drawn off the system. Try tapping along the pipes with a mallet wrapped in cloth to move the air.
● **Other causes** The main storage tank may need a larger ball float. You could also try installing a special equilibrium ball valve in place of a standard one. This will move less under water pressure, so will be quieter.

CURING AN AIRLOCK IN A PIPE

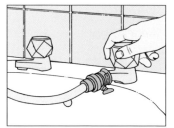

1 Turn all taps on full to run water through the pipes. If this fails, connect a piece of garden hose between a main tap and the problem faucet.

2 Turn on the problem tap, then the clear one. The pressure of the water should push the air out of the pipe and back into the tank.

3 Turn off the taps when the noise in the pipe stops. Remove the hose from the main tap, and drain it before disconnecting the other end. Reduce the pressure of the main water supply to prevent the airlock from recurring.

FROZEN PIPES

Frozen pipes should be thawed out as soon as possible to prevent them from cracking. Thaw U-bends under a sink by wrapping them in rags wrung out in hot water. You can thaw frozen outdoor pipes by pouring boiling water around the area of the pipe that is frozen.

THAWING A FROZEN INDOOR PIPE

1 Turn off the water. Turn on taps fed from the frozen pipe to let the water out. Feel all the way along the pipe to locate the frozen area.

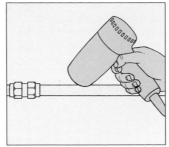

2 Hold a hair dryer on a warm setting close to the frozen part of the pipe. Do not put it too near plastic pipes, or they may melt.

PREVENTING FREEZES

● **Keeping cold air out** Keep bath and basin plugs in place to prevent waste pipes and drains from freezing.

● **Keeping water moving** For pipes that tend to freeze regularly, leave water faucets dripping overnight during cold spells in the winter.

● **Traditional cure** Put a handful of table salt down drains last thing at night to prevent pipes from freezing.

● **Insulating pipes** Insulate pipes using foam secured in place with duct tape.

BLOCKED DRAINS AND SINKS

Sinks and drains often become blocked because grease, food scraps, or other solid waste has been poured down them. Keep drains open with a mixture of salt, baking soda, and cream of tartar. Do not use lye decloggers – it will combine with fat to form a hard plug.

REMOVING BLOCKAGES FROM PIPES

● **Sinks and baths** Bale out water in a blocked sink into a bucket. Pour a cupful of washing soda followed by boiling water down the drain. Repeat if necessary.

● **Outside drains** Use the treatment for indoor drains to remove blockages outdoors. For serious blockages outdoors, you may have to use a snake or call a plumber.

SMELLY DRAINS

● **Keeping drains fresh** Flush baking soda down a drain with hot water to stop odors.

Using a plunger
If the treatment above fails, use a plunger. Smear the rim with petroleum jelly, place it over the plughole, and run water until the cup is covered. Pump the handle in an up-and-down movement.

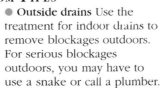
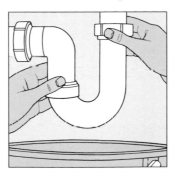

U-bend blockages
If the blockage is in the U-bend, it will not respond to a plunger. Place a bucket underneath the bend, and unscrew the U-bend. Carefully poke a piece of wire up the pipe until you free it.

TIMESAVING TIP

Unscrewing U-bends
Before replacing a U-bend, smear petroleum jelly around the threads of the screw. Next time you need to undo it, it will come off easily.

TOILETS AND APPLIANCES

Blocked toilets usually occur if something unsuitable has been flushed. You will know a toilet is blocked if water rises to the rim and drains slowly. Overflowing from toilet tanks and appliances such as dishwashers can cause major flooding if not fixed immediately.

UNBLOCKING TOILETS

1 If your toilet is blocked, stop flushing and let the water drain away as close to its usual level as possible.

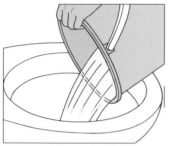

2 Throw a bucket of water into the bowl, all at once. If the blockage remains, push a toilet plunger to the bottom of the bowl, and pump up and down vigorously.

OVERFLOWING TANKS

● **Causes** Overflows may be caused by a damaged ball float, the float arm being at the wrong angle, or a worn washer in the inlet valve.

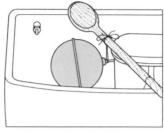

Stopping an overflow
If a toilet tank is overflowing, raise the ball float arm. Tie it to a wooden spoon to hold it in a raised position until you can get a new float arm installed.

OVERFLOWING APPLIANCES

● **Soap problems** Some washing machines and dishwashers may overflow if you use the wrong detergent, or too much. Turn the dial until the machine begins to empty. Run a rinse cycle with the machine empty before rinsing clothes or dishes to get rid of the excess soap.
● **Machine problems** If the detergent is not a problem, check that the filter and soap compartment have been put in properly. If you cannot locate the cause, unplug the machine, empty it, and call a repair person. Turn off electricity if the water is near switches or outlets.

SAVING WATER

Simple measures around the home will help you conserve water and save money on your household bills. Bathing uses more than 25 percent of all household water, so shower instead if possible. Never leave the bathroom faucet running while you brush your teeth.

KITCHEN

● **Washing dishes** Dishwashers are only economical if you have a full load of dishes. Wash small loads by hand.

Leftover water
Use water left in cups and kettles to water your indoor plants. Dishwater can be used to water outdoor plants if you do not use harsh detergents.

LAUNDRY

● **Washing machines** When buying a new washing machine, remember front-loading machines use less water than top-loading ones. Save water by washing full loads only (unless your machine has a half-load or short-cycle option).

OUTDOORS

● **Car washing** Use a bucket to wash your car, and use a hose only for rinsing. Leaving the hose running idly wastes hundreds of gallons of water.
● **Cleaning driveways** Sweep driveways and sidewalks clean with a stiff broom instead of hosing them down.

BATHROOM

● **Wasted water** Dripping taps waste hundreds of gallons of water each year. Drips from hot-water taps waste energy as well as water.

Food coloring stains water

Test for leaks
Your toilet tank may be leaking water. To test for leaks, drip food coloring in the tank. If the dye appears in the toilet bowl, call a plumber to fix the seal.

ELECTRICITY AND FUEL

E LECTRICITY CAN KILL, so it is vital to treat it with respect. Before working on anything electrical, turn off the power and remove the fuse that protects the circuit on which you are working. Check that the circuit is dead.

BASIC ELECTRICAL EQUIPMENT

Keep your electrical repair tools together in a box, so that in the event of a power outage you will know where to find everything. A flashlight is vital in such cases, so keep one especially for emergencies and check regularly that its batteries are still working. Make sure that you know how to use the repair tools safely and correctly.

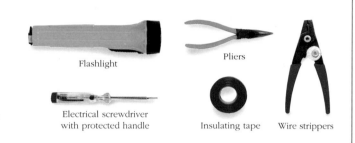

Flashlight

Pliers

Electrical screwdriver
with protected handle

Insulating tape   Wire strippers

SAFETY WITH ELECTRICITY

C heck all plugs and cords regularly for damage. Fix loose connections right away; otherwise, they may become dangerous. Never run cords under carpets, since they may become worn and the wires may be exposed. Do not hammer nails into walls near sockets.

BASIC SAFETY
● **Dry hands** Do not touch electrical equipment with wet hands, feet, or cloths. Water conducts electricity, and you may get a shock.
● **Avoid overloading** Do not use an adapter to plug in more appliances than a circuit can safely accommodate. You could overload the system.

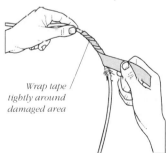

Wrap tape tightly around damaged area

Repairing cords
If a cord has become worn, wrap it tightly in insulating tape to make it safe. Replace it with a new cord as soon as possible.

APPLIANCES
● **Grounding** Ensure all metal appliances are grounded to prevent electric shocks,.
● **Plugs** Always unplug small appliances like irons and hair dryers immediately after each use. If you make this a habit, you will never have to worry "Did I turn off the coffee maker?" when you go out.

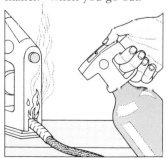

Electrical fires
Use a special fire extinguisher on electrical fires. Never use water – it will cause a short circuit and electrical shocks.

DANGER SIGNALS

Call an expert in to deal with electrical wiring problems, for example, if the wiring looks dangerous, or if an appliance is not working and you cannot discern the cause. Be aware of the warning signs of electrical problems given below, and familiarize yourself with the emergency treatment for electrical shock given on pages 173 and 177.

● A "fishy" or burning smell This can indicate that an appliance plug is overheating and starting to melt. Switch off the appliance and remove the plug from the outlet.
● Warm plugs If a plug feels warm, switch it off, and take it out of the wall. Turn off the power at the circuit breaker. Check the wiring in the plug and outlet. A problem with either, if left may cause a house fire.

LIGHTS AND APPLIANCES

Good lighting is essential in the home. Turn off lights in empty rooms, and put timer switches on lights in halls and outside so that they come on when the house is empty. Keep appliances in good repair – faulty items can cause fires, power failure, or electrical shock.

LIGHT CARE
● **Correct bulbs** Always use the recommended wattage bulb for each lamp. Clean lamps regularly.

Keep bulbs clean
Dust can reduce the light given out by a bulb by as much as 50 percent. Use a feather duster to clean ceiling bulbs and light fixtures. See also page 64.

LIGHTING YOUR HOME
● **Lighting plans** Take time to make a lighting plan before you decorate a home. Use the right wattage bulb for each area – dim lighting may suit eating areas, while kitchen, bathroom, and reading areas require bright lighting.
● **Light switches** Put luminous paint or stickers on all light switches so that you can find them easily in the dark.
● **Lighting and safety** In a home with small children, use childproof safety outlets and outlet covers. Use a night-light for children afraid of the dark. Illuminate hazards such as outdoor steps at night with low-level lights.

POWER FAILURE

If you suddenly lose electricity, it may mean that a fuse needs replacing, or that there is a widespread blackout. If you have advance warning of a power outage, turn refrigerator controls to maximum, and put candles and matches where you can find them easily.

CIRCUIT FAILURE
1 If several appliances or lights in one area fail at once, a circuit fuse in the fuse box has probably blown. Switch off everything on that particular circuit.

2 Replace the blown fuse. If the fuses are not labeled, look for scorch marks. Check for and repair broken wires.

3 Check for and repair any visible damage to plugs and cords used on the circuit.

4 Switch on appliances and lights one at a time. If the fuse blows again, the circuit may be overloaded or an appliance may be faulty.

BLACKOUTS
● **When power returns** Reset electric clocks and timer switches. Do not open the freezer for at least six hours.

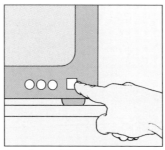

During a blackout
Turn off all your appliances and lights – apart from one bulb, and the refrigerator and freezer. A power surge when electricity is restored could blow a fuse.

BRIGHT IDEA

Emergency candles
Keep a pair of candles in the refrigerator or freezer at all times, so that you are sure to find them in a power failure.

OTHER FUEL SOURCES

Fuels such as gas and coal can be hazardous and should be treated with caution. If you smell gas or burning, investigate immediately. A gas leak could lead to an explosion, while an uncontrolled fire in a fireplace can burn down a building. Both can be fatal.

EMERGENCY ACTION FOR GAS LEAKS

1 If there is a strong smell of gas, extinguish cigarettes, candles, and gas stoves. Switch off any machines that might produce sparks, such as a vacuum cleaner. Leave lights either on or off.

2 Cut off the supply of gas to the house by turning off the valve beside the gas meter. In most cases, turn the handle of the valve until it is at a right angle to the pipe.

3 Open as many windows as possible to let in fresh air to dissipate the gas fumes. Evacuate the whole building, and warn neighbors. Take anyone unconscious outside for treatment (see p. 174).

4 Call the gas company's emergency number and report the problem. Never enter a room to investigate the smell of gas – the fumes may quickly overpower you.

OPEN FIRES

● **Safety** If an open fire gets out of control, pour water on it to put it out. If the chimney is on fire, call the fire department. Have chimneys swept regularly to prevent soot from building up.
● **Slow fires** Quicken a smoky fire by holding an open newspaper across the fireplace. Leave a 1–2 in (3–4 cm) gap at the bottom for air to reach the fire.

SAVING FUEL

Using fuel economically can save quite a bit of money. Even simple ideas, such as turning down the thermostat on the hot-water tank, can save fuel. Major tasks, such as insulating the attic or lagging your pipes, will make a considerable difference in the long run.

KETTLES

Use a mug as a measure

Boiling water
Do not overfill a tea kettle – boil only as much water as you require for the immediate need, using a mug or cup to measure the right amount. Turn off the heat on the stove as soon as the water comes to the boil.

ELECTRONICS

● **Televisions** Unplug the television if it has an "instant on" feature to cut down on the amount of energy it uses.
● **Choosing appliances** Buy energy-efficient appliances, and choose the best you can afford – they will last longest.

IN THE KITCHEN

● **Appliances** Buy energy-saving small appliances such as electric frying pans, slow cookers, and deep fryers. They use considerably less energy than ovens and stoves.
● **Ovens** When using a standard oven, make sure you benefit from its capacity. Rather than baking a single pizza, for example, cook several items at once.
● **Stoves** Keeping stoves clean will maximize reflective heat.
● **Microwave ovens** Use a microwave whenever possible. It uses far less energy than standard ovens.
● **Freezers** Open the freezer as infrequently as possible. Every time you let cold air out, the freezer works harder to regain its temperature.
● **Pots and pans** Make sure saucepan lids fit tightly. Use pots the same size or slightly larger than cooking elements.

MONEY-SAVING TIP

Paying for energy
Keep a money jar by main light switches, and fine family members each time a light is left on in an empty room.

LIGHTING

● **Reflecting light** Place lamps in corners of rooms to reflect light. Pale walls in a room will require less lighting than those with dark walls.

HEATING AND COOLING

INSULATING YOUR HOME WILL HELP to keep it warm in winter and cool in summer, and will also save you money on your heating and cooling bills. The initial expenditure on insulation could easily be recouped in just a couple of years.

A COOL HOME

A WARM HOME

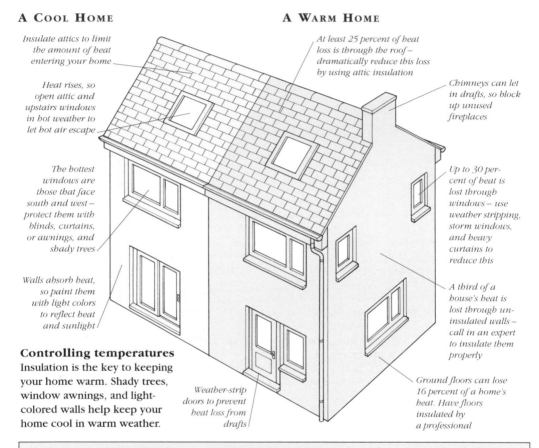

Insulate attics to limit the amount of heat entering your home

Heat rises, so open attic and upstairs windows in hot weather to let hot air escape

The hottest windows are those that face south and west – protect them with blinds, curtains, or awnings, and shady trees

Walls absorb heat, so paint them with light colors to reflect heat and sunlight

At least 25 percent of heat loss is through the roof – dramatically reduce this loss by using attic insulation

Chimneys can let in drafts, so block up unused fireplaces

Up to 30 per-cent of heat is lost through windows – use weather stripping, storm windows, and heavy curtains to reduce this

A third of a house's heat is lost through un-insulated walls – call in an expert to insulate them properly

Ground floors can lose 16 percent of a home's heat. Have floors insulated by a professional

Weather-strip doors to prevent heat loss from drafts

Controlling temperatures
Insulation is the key to keeping your home warm. Shady trees, window awnings, and light-colored walls help keep your home cool in warm weather.

REDUCING COOLING AND HEATING BILLS

COOLING BILLS

● **Windows** Install awnings over sunny windows to shade them, or plant trees and climbing plants to provide shade.
● **Fans** Install an attic fan to pull heat out of the house. A low-speed ceiling fan in the kitchen will be more efficient than a high-speed one.
● **Air conditioners** Put air conditioners on the shadier side of the house, or put up awnings over them. Make sure you clean air filters regularly.

HEATING BILLS

● **Thermostats** Turn down your central heating and hot water thermostats by a couple of degrees to save 10 percent off your electricity bills.
● **Insulating** The heat-saving benefits of insulating hot-water pipes and cylinders will be obvious almost immediately.
● **Storm windows** Storm windows are expensive to install, but will eventually pay for themselves in savings on your heating bill.

● **Floor insulation** Fill in cracks in floorboards, and insulate floors with carpets. Call an expert to insulate under the floor – it will be worth the cost in the long run.
● **Attic insulation** A quarter of a home's heat is lost through the roof. Prevent this by insulating the attic with fiberglass or other insulation.
● **Weather stripping** Buy adhesive insulation strips for drafty doors and windows.

KEEPING WARM

The cost of keeping warm in winter does not need to be high. Wear more or warmer clothes. Keep doors to heated rooms closed, and close off unused rooms so that you do not have to heat them through the winter. Block off unused chimneys at the top.

RADIATORS
● **Heat channel** Install a shelf directly above a radiator so that heat flows into the room rather than rising away.

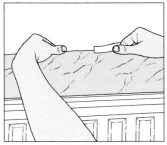

Heat reflector
Make radiators more efficient by taping aluminum foil to cardboard behind them, shiny side in. Foil will reflect heat into the room, not through the walls.

DRAFTS
● **Draft finder** Close doors and windows, and walk around with a candle. Where it flickers, you have a draft.

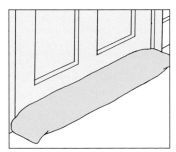

Draft protector
Stuff an old jacket sleeve with padding, and sew it up to make a draft protector for a door. Use a bright color so that no one will one trip over it.

DOUBLE GLAZING
● **Temporary measures** Use sheets of plexiglass or heavy plastic as "double glazing", secured with strong tape.

Using plastic sheeting
Clear plastic sheeting, stuck to windows with tape, provides instant "double glazing." Shrink it to fit with a hair dryer, and peel it off in the summer.

KEEPING COOL

Insulating your home properly will help keep it cool in summer and warm in winter. Wear loose clothing around the house in hot weather, and avoid using the oven in the heat of the day. Open attic or top-floor windows, and try to circulate air with cross-ventilation.

NATURAL SOLUTIONS
● **Avoid artifical light** Light-bulbs give off more heat than you might imagine. Use natural daylight as long as possible, and do not switch lights on until it is essential.
● **Landscaping for shade** Plant trees outside to shade your home. Deciduous trees will provide shade in summer and allow light in when their branches are bare in winter.

REDUCING HUMIDITY
● **Showering** Steam can dramatically increase the level of humidity in your home. When showering, open the windows to let as much moisture escape as possible.

KEEPING HEAT OUT
● **Draw curtains** Draw blinds and curtains during the hottest part of the day to shade rooms from the rays of the sun.

Reflect solar heat
Staple or tape aluminum foil inside the roof space to reflect the sun's heat outward. Heat passing into the house will be reduced by at least 20 percent.

GREEN TIP

Reduce humidity
Keep lids on saucepans to reduce the humidity caused by steam. You will also use less energy to cook foods and so save money. Close internal kitchen doors while cooking to keep other rooms cool.

GENERAL REPAIRS

Y OU CAN SAVE A LOT OF MONEY by doing simple repairs around the home yourself. Minor problems with floors, doors, windows, and stairs can be fixed without much expense. More complex jobs may require a professional.

FLOORS

C reaks and gaps in wooden floorboards cause irritation and drafts, but can be easily fixed. Concrete floors may sometimes be uneven, so bumps should be chipped away with a chisel and club hammer. Lift damaged vinyl tiles with a hot iron over aluminum foil.

WOODEN FLOORS
● **Square-edged boards** If a board is cracked or split, find the joists by locating the nails at each end. Drill close to the joists and cut out the board with a saw. Replace with a new piece of wood.
● **Tongue-and-groove boards** Saw out a damaged tongue-and-groove board along the edge. It cannot be replaced, so substitute it with an ordinary floorboard, supported at each end by a block of wood screwed to each joist.

QUICK INSULATION

Using homemade filler
Fill spaces between floorboards with papier-mâché made from newspaper and wallpaper paste. Sand smooth when dry.

SQUEAKY FLOORS

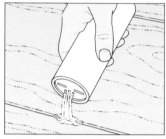

Using talcum powder
To silence squeaks, shake talcum powder between floorboards. Attach loose boards to the joists with long nails at an angle.

DOORS

T o prevent a door from slamming, install a spring-door closer or use a doorstop. Stop a door from rattling by moving the lock catch, or put a draft protector inside the frame. Lift a sagging door by tightening or moving the hinges. Repair rotten parts of wood quickly.

STICKING DOORS

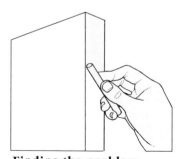

Finding the problem
Rub chalk down the edge of the door, then close it. The chalk will leave a mark on the frame at the contact point. Plane the area. If sliding doors stick, apply floor polish to the tracks.

STICKING HINGES

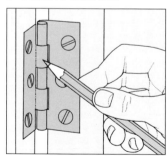

Lubricating a hinge
Treat a sticking hinge by rubbing pencil lead along the spine. Alternatively, smear a little light oil along the hinge with a cloth, working the hinge back and forth until it moves freely.

BRIGHT IDEA

Oiling sticking locks
To loosen a sticking lock, put a little oil on the key. Put the key in the lock, and give it a few turns to loosen the lock.

STAIRS

The best way to deal with creaking stairs is from below. If you cannot get underneath, take up any carpet and firmly screw the front of the tread to the top of the riser. Make sure that stairs are well lit and that any carpeting is securely laid so that no one can trip over it.

THREE WAYS TO REPAIR CREAKING STAIRS

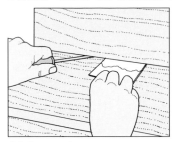

Gluing a riser
Push a screwdriver between the tread and the riser and insert a piece of cardboard covered with wood glue. Leave it there. Repeat until the squeak is gone.

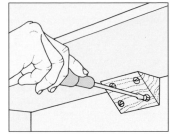

Adding a wood block
A persistent squeak may need tackling from under the stairs. Glue a triangular block of wood into the corner of the tread and riser. Secure it with screws.

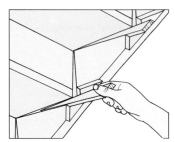

Replacing wedges
With old stairs, you may have to replace the stair wedges to fix a squeak. Clean off the old glue, reapply, then hammer the new wedges back into place.

WINDOWS

If a window has broken and you cannot repair it at once, board it up with chipboard. Always wear heavy gloves when dealing with glass. Cover small cracks temporarily with heavy plastic and masking tape. Be sure window panes are sealed properly.

REMOVING PANES
● Handling broken glass Wear thick gardening gloves when handling broken glass, and use goggles if you have to break any glass. Dispose of broken glass in newspaper.

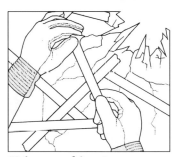

Using masking tape
Carefully crisscross pieces of masking tape over a broken windowpane. Cover the glass with a heavy cloth, then tap gently with a hammer to break away the pieces from the window without splintering.

REPLACING PANES
1 Buy a pane of glass that is ¹⁄₁₆ in (1.5 mm) smaller than the window opening on all sides. Chip out any old putty. Clean out the recess, and paint it with primer.

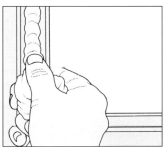

2 Lay a bed of fresh putty in the rabbet in the window frame. Press the new piece of glass into position around the edges – not in the center, where it could break. Insert glazing brads or clips to keep the pane of glass in place.

WINDOW PROBLEMS

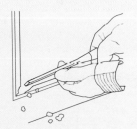

● Damaged putty As putty hardens, it may crack and fall out. Chip it out with a chisel, and replace all the putty – not just the damaged section.
● Sticking windows A build-up of paint may cause a wooden window to stick. Strip paint off the edge, and plane it to fit the frame. Repaint the wood.
● Condensation Install secondary double glazing to prevent condensation on metal window frames.

HOME SECURITY

Making your home more secure will help deter burglars. Install security locks on doors and windows, a good-quality burglar alarm, and outdoor lights. Join the local neighborhood crime watch if one exists in your area.

VULNERABLE AREAS OF THE HOME

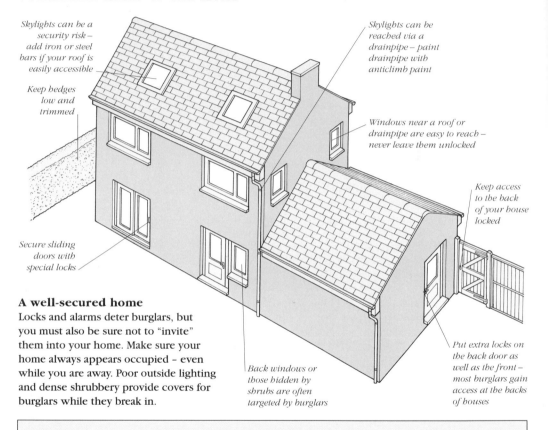

Skylights can be a security risk – add iron or steel bars if your roof is easily accessible

Keep hedges low and trimmed

Skylights can be reached via a drainpipe – paint drainpipe with anticlimb paint

Windows near a roof or drainpipe are easy to reach – never leave them unlocked

Keep access to the back of your house locked

Secure sliding doors with special locks

Back windows or those hidden by shrubs are often targeted by burglars

Put extra locks on the back door as well as the front – most burglars gain access at the backs of houses

A well-secured home

Locks and alarms deter burglars, but you must also be sure not to "invite" them into your home. Make sure your home always appears occupied – even while you are away. Poor outside lighting and dense shrubbery provide covers for burglars while they break in.

MAKING YOUR HOME MORE SECURE

● **Alarms** Install a house alarm system, and make sure it is clearly visible in order to deter any casual intruders.

● **Doors** Use good-quality, solid wood exterior doors. Flimsy doors can easily be kicked in. Put secure locks on exterior doors, and a chain or peephole so that you can inspect visitors.

● **Windows** Put locks on every window, especially windows close to drainpipes, ground-floor windows, and French windows. Lock them each time you go out.

● **Rear entrances** Make the back of your home as inaccessible as possible. Most burglars break in at the backs of houses.

● **Garage** Secure the door leading from the garage to the house, as well as the garage doors. A burglar could work unseen in the garage.

● **Hedges** Keep hedges trimmed as low as possible so that anyone trying to break in can be easily seen. Prickly hedges and shrubs will also act as a deterrent to intruders.

● **Cars** Always lock your car when you leave it, even if you are coming right back. Burglars can use tools they find in cars to break into the house.

● **Sheds** Lock sheds so that your tools cannot be used to break into the house. Put shed door hinges on the inside so that they cannot be removed by burglars to take the door off.

● **Ladders** Keep ladders locked up so that burglers cannot use them to break into the house through the upper floors.

INSIDE YOUR HOME

Locks, bolts, and alarms are only as good as the fabric of the home they are protecting. Make it more difficult for thieves to get in by having good-quality doors and windows that are always kept locked. Always change the locks when you move into a new house.

SECURING DOORS AND WINDOWS

● **Internal doors** Do not lock internal doors. Burglars will think you are hiding valuables and may break them down.

● **Exterior doors** Put special bolts into the hinge sides of exterior doors to make them harder to break through.

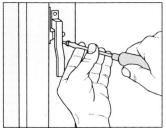

Casement windows
Sink a long screw into a casement window beside the handle to prevent it from being opened. Put permanent locks on windows as soon as possible.

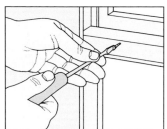

Sash windows
Install locks on sash windows, or put a long wood screw through the meeting rails. Do not permanently screw down windows, in case of a fire.

BRIGHT IDEA

Placing spare keys
Leave unlabeled spare keys with a reliable neighbor. Never leave keys under flowerpots or inside the mailbox – a thief will be familiar with these ploys.

DRAWING CURTAINS

● **Daytime** Open curtains during the day. Drawn curtains enable burglars to work unseen.
● **Evening** Draw your curtains when you have lights on, so that no one can see valuables.

POSSESSIONS

● **Marking** Print your name and zipcode on all valuables.
● **Photographing** Take a picture of all your valuables so you can identify them if they are stolen and recovered.

IN A BURGLARY

● **Confronting a burglar** If you interrupt burglars, do not provoke them. Cooperate if necessary, then call the police as soon as you can without endangering yourself.

HOME SECURITY EQUIPMENT

A home security system need not be elaborate, but it must be effective. Ensure that everyone in the household is able to use any locks or an alarm, and always puts them into operation when leaving the building, even if it is only for a short time.

● **Fitting locks** Before you fit a lock, check that the door or window and its frame are structurally sound. The lock will not deter burglars if they can easily destroy the surround.

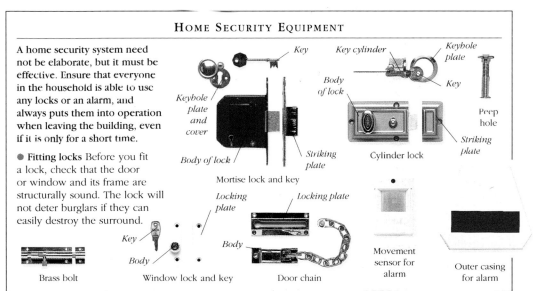

Key

Key cylinder

Keyhole plate

Keyhole plate

Body of lock

Key

Keyhole plate and cover

Peep hole

Body of lock

Striking plate

Striking plate

Mortise lock and key

Cylinder lock

Locking plate

Locking plate

Key

Body

Body

Movement sensor for alarm

Outer casing for alarm

Brass bolt

Window lock and key

Door chain

MOVING

QUICK REFERENCE

Preparing to Move, p. 147

Sorting and
Packing, p. 148

Moving Out,
p. 153

Moving In, p. 155

Sharing a Home, p. 157

MOVING INTO A NEW HOME can be a daunting prospect. Once you have chosen a new house or apartment, plan every stage of the move so that you will have sufficient time to finish the preparations. Be sure to allow enough money to cover movers, cleaning, and buying new possessions. If you are buying a home, have the structure checked properly by professionals.

MAKING PREPARATIONS IN THE DAYS BEFORE A MOVE

Once you have finalized your plans to move, allow several weeks to make preparations so that you will not be swamped with work as the moving day approaches. The countdown chart below gives specific numbers of days before a moving day, and suggests arrangements to make at these times.

35

- **Making inventory** Write an inventory to show every item that you intend to move.
- **Inspecting new home** Ask service people to show you locations of water shutoffs, meters, the water tank, and water heaters.
- **Checking appliances** Find out if any appliances will be left in your new home.

30

- **Making floor plans** Measure rooms in your new home. Make floor plans to show where your furniture will go.
- **Ordering furnishings** Order furnishings to be delivered to your new home.
- **Storing** If you need to put any items into storage, contact a storage firm.

21

- **Insuring items** Arrange to have all your possessions insured during the move.
- **Packing** Start to pack up little-used rooms, unless a moving company will be doing the packing for you.
- **Emptying a freezer** Begin to use up or dispose of existing freezer contents.

14

- **Changing address** Notify organizations and personal contacts of your new address.
- **Hiring moving company** If using a moving company, book a date and time.
- **Caring for pets** Arrange to leave pets in kennels, or with friends, during the move.
- **Servicing appliances** Arrange to have any appliances in your new home serviced.

7

- **Organizing child care** Arrange to have small children elsewhere during the move.
- **Briefing a moving company** Send a copy of your inventory to the moving company. Brief them on items that need special care.
- **Laundering** Start to launder clothes and bedding so that they are ready to pack.

4

- **Packing** Start to pack up living areas, unless a moving company will be doing the packing for you. Leave your curtains in place to ensure privacy.
- **Packing appliances** Find the instruction manuals for any appliances so that you can see how to pack them properly.

2

- **Checking moving times** Confirm all details with the moving company or with anyone else who will be helping you.
- **Confirming plans** Confirm that your new home will be ready for the move.
- **Packing appliances** Pack up all small appliances except for essential items.

1

- **Packing essential items** Pack a box of food and household supplies to keep on hand during the move (see p. 153).
- **Moving houseplants** Water plants well. Pack in boxes for moving (see p. 151).
- **Cleaning appliances** Empty and clean the refrigerator and freezer.
- **Moving pets** Take pets to kennels.

PREPARING TO MOVE

MAKE LISTS OF PREPARATIONS TO CARRY OUT in your existing home before a move, and of people to inform of a move. Make these lists several weeks in advance. If you need family or friends to help, ask them well in advance.

MAKING ARRANGEMENTS

Organize necessary tasks such as repairs and movers well before the moving day. Reconfirm your arrangements a couple of days before you move, in case there are any last-minute changes of plan. Notify family, friends, and official bodies of your change of address.

PLANNING AHEAD

● **Selecting a day** Arrange to move in the middle of a week when the roads will be quiet, rather than on a weekend or on a public holiday.

● **Planning repair work** If there are major repairs to be done in your new home, try to arrange it so that the work happens before you move in.

● **Having meters read** Arrange to have the gas and electricity meters read at both homes on the day of the move.

● **Servicing vehicles** If you will be moving a long way, arrange to have your car serviced well before the day of the move.

WHOM TO NOTIFY BEFORE A MOVE	
FINANCIAL INSTITUTIONS	**UTILITY COMPANIES**
Contact at least two weeks before a move. ● Banks and financial groups. ● Social Security. ● Insurance companies.	Arrange services for your new home two weeks in advance. ● Gas and electricity suppliers. ● Water supplier. ● Telephone companies.
LOCAL GROUPS	**PERSONAL CONTACTS**
Notify schools immediately. Contact other groups at least two weeks in advance. ● Schools. ● Local tax office. ● Postal service	Tell family and friends, and any other personal contacts, at least one week in advance. ● Doctor and dentist. ● Employer. ● Family and friends.

ORGANIZING YOURSELF AND OTHERS

Whether you use a moving company or ask friends to help you, make all the necessary arrangements well before a move. Make sure that anyone driving a moving van has directions for finding your new home. Confirm the plans a couple of days beforehand.

MOVING ITEMS YOURSELF

Move all fragile and valuable objects yourself. If you are using a car, do not leave it unattended during the move.

● **Jewelry** Lock it into the glove compartment of a car.

● **Audio equipment** Fit boxes securely into a car trunk.

● **Money** Carry small supplies of cash in a purse or fanny pack and in your pockets.

● **Documents** Carry important papers in a bag or a briefcase.

USING MOVERS

● **Selecting a mover** Ask several movers for estimates. Check what size truck they use, and what their insurance covers.

● **Assessing costs** A moving van may send an estimator to assess the cost of a move. Show the estimator everything to be moved so that he or she can work out a fair price.

● **Checking travel plans** If the moving vans are to make an overnight stop, ask where they will park, and insist that someone guard each one.

MANAGING HELPERS

● **Taking out insurance** Arrange extra insurance in case any of your helpers injures themselves during a move.

● **Organizing a team** Enlist at least two strong people to cope with large items, and two more to handle boxes.

● **Protecting possessions** Draw up a list of people to travel with moving vans and people to stay in each home. By doing this you will make sure that your belongings will never be left unattended.

SORTING AND PACKING

Afew weeks before a move, make a plan for packing the contents of each room, and collect packing materials. As you pack, dispose of clutter, and label boxes so that you can put them in the appropriate rooms in your new home.

LISTING AND INSURING POSSESSIONS

Before starting to pack, make an inventory of your possessions, including any appliances or fixtures that you will take with you. Keep this list for reference. When you pack up each room, use it to note which items have been packed and which have been thrown or given away.

MAKING AN INVENTORY
● **Working in pairs** Ask someone to help you make an inventory. Have one person calling out the names of items while the other logs them.
● **Recording reference** Make a note of the names and model numbers of appliances.
● **Listing sets of items** For items in groups, such as cutlery or dishes, note how many are in the group and if there are any missing.
● **Keeping an inventory** Put a completed inventory in an accessible place so that you can refer to it during a move.

INSURING OBJECTS
● **Insuring possessions** Check that your insurance policy covers your possessions while they are in transit, especially during overnight stops.
● **Making visual records** Take photographs of all valuable objects in case you need them for an insurance claim.
● **Recording damage** If an item is damaged before you pack it, photograph the damaged part. If the item suffers more damage during the move, you will have proof of what was done in transit and what had already been done.

TIMESAVING TIP

Recording an inventory
Walk around each room with a handheld tape recorder, and record the name of every object in the room. Make a copy of the tape for reference.

CLEANING ITEMS BEFORE A MOVE

Moving is a dusty business, so clean only very dirty objects before you pack them. Remove accumulated dirt from appliances such as a stove or vacuum cleaner. Clean your old home to make it pleasant and welcoming for the next occupants when they move in.

LEAVING ITEMS UNCLEANED

Do not clean the following items before moving, since they are likely to gather dust during the move.

● Dishes.
● Glassware.
● Cutlery.
● Mirrors.
● Pictures.
● Books.
● Pots and pans.
● Vases.
● Ornaments.
● Wooden furniture.

REMOVING DIRT

Wiping kitchen appliances
Clean appliances with a solution of 4 tbsp dishwashing liquid in 1 gallon (4.5 liters) of very hot water. Wipe areas such as door seals with a dry cloth.

REMOVING DUST

Cleaning a lampshade
Dust a fabric lampshade by using heavy-duty adhesive tape. Wrap a loop of tape around your hand sticky side out, then dab the shade with the tape to pick up the dust.

PACKING MATERIALS AND CONTAINERS

You can buy or rent packaging or crates for moving. For economy, reuse packaging materials or household items such as garbage bags.

● **Collecting packaging** Save old newspapers, boxes, bubble wrap, and cardboard, and ask your friends and neighbors to do the same. These materials are a fire risk, so store them away from sources of heat.

● **Saving containers** Keep any used containers or packages that might be useful on moving day. Even unlikely objects such as cosmetics packaging can be used to protect small items.

● **Asking in local stores** Ask staff in local stores to save used packaging for you. In particular, look for objects such as shoe boxes, shredded paper, and tissue paper. Collect materials promptly so that they do not clutter up the store.

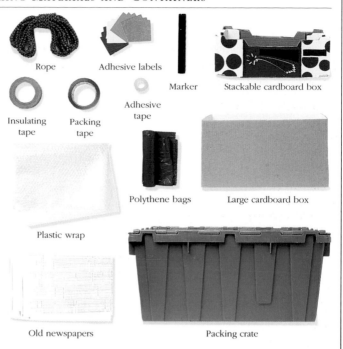

Rope

Adhesive labels

Marker

Stackable cardboard box

Insulating tape

Packing tape

Adhesive tape

Polythene bags

Large cardboard box

Plastic wrap

Old newspapers

Packing crate

PACKING FRAGILE AND VALUABLE ITEMS

Allow plenty of time for packing fragile or valuable items such as china and audio equipment. Pad the objects so that they do not move around in their containers. If possible, carry the objects with you when you move, rather than putting them in a moving van.

PACKING FRAGILE ITEMS

● **Protecting computers** If possible, transport a computer in its original packaging. Packaging for computers is often made to measure, and will hold items securely during a move. If you have not kept the packaging, ask a store for similar material.

● **Packing very small items** To protect delicate items such as small glass ornaments, wrap them in rolls of cotton before covering them with newspaper.

● **Padding fragile items** Wrap fragile items in newspaper, then cover in bubble wrap. Put the items in a sturdy box, and pad them well around the sides to make sure that they are held securely in place.

WRAPPING VALUABLES

● **Packing jewelry** Wrap pieces of jewelry in rolls of cotton to protect them.

Protecting ornaments
Wrap ornaments in cleaning cloths, then pack them into plastic food containers with lids. Tuck extra padding around the items to hold them securely.

PACKING DISHES

● **Using mugs** Put a wrapped item such as a glass inside a mug to protect both items.

Bubble wrap is laid on each plate

Padding plates
Cut circles of bubble wrap the same size as your plates. Sandwich bubble wrap between the plates as you stack them so that they do not chip one another.

149

PACKING FURNITURE

Before packing furniture, prepare it so that it will be easy to carry and safe from damage. If possible, dismantle it or remove parts such as drawers. Shield corners and surfaces. Secure any loose parts with masking tape, which can be peeled off without damaging most surfaces.

PACKING STORAGE UNITS

● **Preparing armoires** Secure armoire doors with masking tape so that the doors will not swing open when moved.

Wrapping a drawer
Leave drawers full. Slide them into plastic bags, and fasten the bags tightly around them to keep the contents clean. Label the bags to show the contents.

PACKING TABLES

● **Securing legs** To pack loose table legs, wrap the legs in newspaper, then tape them to the underside of the tabletop.

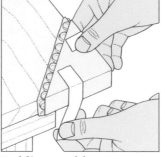

Padding a table corner
To shield the corners of a table, wrap in bubble wrap, then cover with corners cut from cardboard boxes. Secure with tape, avoiding surfaces that could be marked.

PACKING OTHER ITEMS

● **Stowing bookcases** Remove any loose shelves from a bookcase. Stack the shelves in the bottom of the case, or tape them to the back.

● **Wrapping mirrors** Put a mirror in several plastic bags, or wrap it in plastic sheeting. If the mirror shatters during the move, the shards of glass will not escape.

● **Using cupboard space** Fill space in empty cupboards with soft, bulky objects such as bedding, sleeping bags, and table linen.

● **Protecting appliances** Put sheets of cardboard around an appliance such as a stove so that its surface will not be damaged if it knocks against other objects during a move.

PACKING CLOTHES

When you pack clothes before moving, the main priorities are to keep them clean and make sure that none are lost. Put garments in plastic bags or suitcases, or keep them in their armoire or drawers. If you need extra packaging, use clothes to wrap other items.

PREPARING CLOTHES

● **Cleaning garments** Dry clean or launder dirty clothes before packing. However, do not iron them, in case they are creased during the move.

● **Keeping items in an armoire** You can transport clothes in their armoire if this will not make it too heavy to be lifted. Cover the clothes with plastic bags to keep them clean. Lock the armoire doors, or tape them shut.

● **Preparing shoes** Put shoe trees inside shoes, or stuff the shoes with newspaper, so that they will keep their shape. Put each pair of shoes in a plastic bag to keep the outsides clean.

WRAPPING & PACKING

● **Rolling up clothes** Roll up garments such as T-shirts so that they will take up as little space as possible.

Securing items on hangers
Group hangers holding clothes, and join the tops with tape. Pull plastic bags up over the clothes to keep them together.

BRIGHT IDEA

Packing in underwear
Wrap bedroom ornaments in underwear to protect them and keep them clean. Put them in containers and keep with other bedroom items so that they will be in the correct place when you unpack.

PACKING AND MOVING AWKWARD ITEMS

Some items may be difficult to pack because they are an awkward shape, are large and bulky, or because they have sharp surfaces that could make them dangerous to handle. Gather enough materials to pack the objects safely and to secure them inside moving vans.

PACKING HOUSEPLANTS

Stretch plastic over stakes

Stakes are higher than tallest plant

Stake is pushed into soil

Grouping plants
Stand plants on a layer of newspaper in a sturdy box. The cutaway box in this picture shows how to position plants. Push a thin, wooden stake into each pot. Stretch clear plastic sheeting over the top, and tape it to the box to seal in warmth and moisture for the plants.

PACKING RUGS

● **Rolling up rugs** To stop the top of a rug from being dirtied by the underside, use a drop cloth. Lay the cloth on top of the rug, then roll up the rug.

PREPARING EQUIPMENT

● **Packing a turntable** To protect the needle of a turntable, pad it with a piece of foam. Secure the arm to the base by attaching it with masking tape at 2-in (5-cm) intervals along the arm.
● **Packing up a computer** To keep loose parts of a computer such as a mouse and wires together, put these parts in a padded paper bag. Stick the bag to the top of the monitor or the body of the computer.
● **Carrying electrical items** Allow plenty of space in a car to fit delicate electrical items such as televisions or audio equipment. Secure these items inside the car so that they will not move around while you are driving.

WRAPPING PAINT CANS

● **Sealing safely** Paint may be flammable, so dispose of it if possible. If you do store cans, seal can lids with tape, then tie the cans in several plastic bags.

PACKING HEAVY ITEMS

● **Moving books** Do not fill boxes with books; they will be too heavy to lift. Half-fill each box with books, and put lighter objects on top.
● **Improvising rollers** As you pack, put aside wheeled items such as skateboards or roller skates. You can then use these items to help move heavy boxes or pieces of furniture.
● **Moving large items** To move a large object easily, lay it on a piece of plastic sheeting and attach the sheeting to the sides of the object. You can slide it across a floor without harming the object or the floor.
● **Shifting furniture** To move a heavy chair or sofa, turn it onto its back or side, and slide it across the floor.

PACKING TOOLS

Split length of garden hose

Safeguarding a saw blade
Cut a piece of garden hose lengthwise. Slide it over the teeth of a saw to prevent damage to objects or people.

● **Packing a lawn mower** Wrap newspaper around exposed lawn mower blades. Cover the body with plastic bags. Wrap old blankets around the machine, then add more bags to protect the blankets.

MOVING LARGE ITEMS

● **Using a roof rack** Buy or borrow a roof rack and bungee cords for transporting large items such as bicycles.

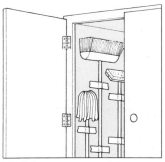

Packing mops and brooms
Secure objects such as mops and brooms inside an armoire with strong adhesive tape. Attach the handles at each end and in the middle to hold them firmly.

EMPTYING YOUR OLD HOME

Once you have completed the bulk of your packing, make a plan for emptying each room. Work out an order for loading items into vehicles. Make a note of supplies for use on the moving day, and of items that you will need once you have moved into your new home.

FINISHING PACKING
● **Buying labels** Buy packages of adhesive labels for your possessions, and for the doors of rooms in your new home.

Piece is cut to fit box exactly

Using leftover materials
If you have any leftover boxes, cut them into pieces, and use the pieces to reinforce other boxes. Put pieces in the base and around the inside of a box.

COLLECTING OBJECTS
● **Grouping boxes** Put packed boxes in a room that you do not use daily. Position them so that they will not obstruct access. Keep them out of sight of potential burglars.
● **Collecting essentials** Pack boxes of household equipment for use in your new home. Discard worn-out or nearly empty items. Put aside a few items for use during the move.
● **Gathering stray items** Search down the backs of chairs and sofas, and underneath pieces of furniture, to find any stray items such as socks or coins.
● **Finding keys** Collect and label door and window keys to give to the new occupants.

PREPARING FOR LOADING
● **Dealing with furniture** To save effort, leave furniture in place until you are ready to load it into a moving van.
● **Gathering equipment** Collect ropes and bungee cords for securing items inside vehicles, as well as coverings to protect floors in your new home.
● **Collecting work wear** Keep old clothes, strong gloves, and sturdy shoes for helpers to wear on the day of the move.
● **Using covers** Keep a few pieces of plastic sheeting handy to cover objects in case it rains on the moving day.
● **Leaving objects behind** Put labels on any items that are to remain in your old home.

USING A LABELING SYSTEM

To enable you to organize your new home quickly, plan in advance where you will put your possessions. Make a floor plan for the rooms, and work out a labeling system to show which containers and pieces of furniture are to go into each room of your home.

LABELING OBJECTS
● **Keeping labels visible** Attach labels where they will be clearly seen on objects at all times. For example, put them on the fronts of furniture, or the tops and sides of boxes.
● **Tying on labels** Use tie-on labels for any objects that might be damaged by an adhesive label, such as pieces of antique furniture.
● **Protecting labels** Cover labels on your belongings with clear adhesive tape so that they will not become wet if it rains on the day of the move.
● **Keeping spare supplies** Put aside several extra labels of each color for the day of the move, in case you need to add or replace labels on any items.

COLOR CODING ROOM CONTENTS

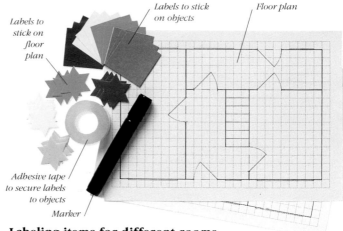

Labels to stick on floor plan

Labels to stick on objects

Floor plan

Adhesive tape to secure labels to objects

Marker

Labeling items for different rooms
Draw a floor plan of your new home (see p. 15). Write the name of each room on the plan. Stick labels of different colors to the rooms, and attach labels of the relevant colors to items that will go in the rooms. Keep the plan handy for reference on the day of the move.

MOVING OUT

O N THE DAY OF A MOVE, have a good breakfast to give you energy for work. Brief helpers on moving items and loading vehicles. Ensure that children or pets accompanying you will be safe and well cared for during the day.

LOADING A VEHICLE

N ever overload a vehicle; otherwise, you may damage the chassis. Make several trips or use several vehicles if you have a lot to move.

If you rent a vehicle, check the maximum load that it will carry. Carry essential items with you in a car so that they are easily accessible.

ARRANGING CONTENTS

● **Loading heavy items** Put heavy items around the edges of a vehicle. Space them out to spread their weight evenly.

● **Adding boxes** Fit boxes securely in the spaces between heavy items. Put padding, such as old blankets, around boxes so that they will not move.

● **Checking visibility** When loading a car, check at regular intervals to see that the load does not block the view in the rearview mirror. Leave a clear space so that you can use the mirror and drive safely.

SECURING LARGE ITEMS

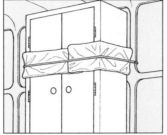

Fixing an item to a vehicle
Hold a large item to the inside of a vehicle with bungee cord or rope. Lay the cord or rope over an old blanket so that it does not scrape the surfaces of the item.

LOADING EFFICIENTLY

Make sure that you can move heavy objects smoothly, so that you do not damage the objects or cause anyone to be injured.

Lifting safely
Rent the best equipment to help move heavy items safely.

ITEMS TO KEEP ON HAND ON MOVING DAY

HOUSEHOLD ITEMS AND FOOD

● Toilet paper.
● Cleaning items.
● Lubricating oil.
● Basic tools such as an adjustable wrench.
● Packing tape.
● Safety pins.
● Vacuum flask.
● Flashlights.
● Batteries.
● Lightbulbs.

● Saucepan.
● Can opener.
● Picnic items.
● Moist wipes.
● Kitchen knives.
● Paper towels.
● Tea and coffee.
● Food for quick meals.

CLOTHES, LINENS, AND TOILETRIES

● One change of clothes per person.
● Towels.
● One set of bedding per person.
● Moisturizer.
● Soap.

● Shampoo.
● Hairbrush.
● Deodorant.
● Toothbrushes and toothpaste.
● Home medical kit for first aid (see p. 164).

SUPERVISING CHILDREN DURING A MOVE

Small children may obstruct workers or may be injured during a move, so it is best to ask a relative or friend to take care of children until the new home is ready for them. If you must have children with you, keep them safe and make them feel involved in the event.

CARING FOR CHILDREN

● **Traveling between homes** If you have to make several trips between homes, always check where the children are before you go, so that no child will be left alone in an empty house.
● **Making a long trip** Stop at intervals so that everyone can stretch their legs, go to the bathroom, and perhaps have something to eat. Do not leave your vehicle unattended.
● **Preparing a quiet room** Clear a space in a room away from moving work, so that children can watch television or keep themselves occupied with quiet activities.

INVOLVING CHILDREN IN A MOVE

Even very young children can be given useful tasks to do, and may enjoy feeling that they are part of the activities. However, they will become tired sooner than adults, so allow time and space for them to rest.

● **Preparing children** Tell the children how exciting it will be to move, so that they view the move positively.
● **Organizing bedrooms** Move furniture into children's bedrooms as soon as possible. Encourage the children to unpack their own belongings.

● **Delegating tasks** Ask older children to start jobs such as cleaning cabinets, unpacking items such as dishes and cutlery, and washing items before putting them away. Make sure that the children will not be in the way of movers.
● **Guarding pets** If you have brought pets with you, ask a child to put them in a quiet room and stay with them so that they do not escape.
● **Taking breaks** Whenever the movers take a break, ask the children to come and share refreshments and company.

TAKING CARE OF PETS

Once you have brought pets to your new home, make them feel settled as soon as you can. Give them food and water, and take them for a run or provide fresh litter for them. Keep pets well away from the movers so that they will not be disturbed by the commotion.

TRANSPORTING FISH

● **Taking water** Before packing a tank, put some of the tank water into thermoses. Use it to keep the fish at the correct temperature during the move.

Secure foam rubber with insulating tape

Moving tropical fish
To maintain tropical fish at the correct temperature, insulate a sturdy box with foam rubber. Put the fish into a plastic bag with water from the tank. Seal the bag, and place it in the box.

MOVING CATS & DOGS

● **Using kennels** Consider putting cats and dogs into kennels until your new home is organized, to keep them from being upset by a move.
● **Taking refreshments** When transporting a cat or dog with you, carry food and water, bowls, and a litter box (for cats). Take rest stops so that the animal can have a little fresh air or exercise.
● **Moving in** On arriving at your new home, shut a cat or dog in a room with food, water, and a litter box if needed. Put a "do not disturb" sign on the door to prevent further agitation of the animal.
● **Keeping indoors** Confine pets to your home or garden for a few days to let them settle into their new territory.

MOVING OTHER PETS

● **Traveling with rodents** Ask your vet if you may borrow a special pet carrier for rodents. Secure the carrier in a car using a seatbelt, and make sure someone sits beside it to look after the animals.

Using a hutch
If you do not have a pet carrier, adapt a hutch for travel. Attach a flap of old carpet over the front to keep out drafts. Cut some more carpet to fit the floor so that the pet will not slip around.

MOVING IN

ONCE YOU HAVE BROUGHT ALL YOUR POSSESSIONS to your new home, make some initial checks before unpacking. By working systematically, you can soon make your home habitable and pinpoint any existing or potential problems.

ORGANIZING A NEW HOME

Before you start to unpack, check the power supplies and structure of the property to make sure that there are no problems. If the previous occupants promised to leave you appliances or fixtures, check that these are in place. See that all areas are clean and safe.

MAKING A CHECKLIST

Check the following items to test the efficiency of all household items and systems.

- Door and window locks.
- Windows.
- Electricity.
- Boiler and radiators.
- Stove.
- Water valves and faucets.
- Drains.
- Telephone.
- Kitchen appliances.

FINDING PROBLEM AREAS

- **Assessing rooms** Look around the bare rooms. Make a note of problems such as scuffed walls or damp areas so that you can treat them before you settle into the property.
- **Testing floors** Walk across any bare floorboards to find out if they creak or sag. Avoid placing items on these areas, and repair before carpeting.
- **Checking insulation** Make a note of areas where insulation could be improved, such as gaps around a window or door.

MAKING A HOME SAFE

- **Masking danger spots** Cover unsafe areas, such as weak flooring or exposed wires, to make them safe until you can have them properly repaired.
- **Blocking windows** Place furniture in front of windows where children could fall out. When possible, replace the furniture with window guards.
- **Inspecting a garden** Check the garden for any poisonous plants. Do not let children or pets out until you have moved or destroyed such plants.

CHECKING SYSTEMS

- **Testing hot water** Run the hot tap of a bath for a few minutes, then run the shower. Check that the water is hot and the water pressure is adequate.
- **Assessing water quality** Turn on the faucets to see if the water is clear. If it is colored, leave the water running for a few minutes. If the water does not clear, call a plumber or contact the water company.
- **Looking for leaks** To check for leaks in water pipes, turn faucets up full force.
- **Testing electric circuits** Carry a small lamp, and plug it into all the sockets in each room to see if the outlets are working.
- **Trying a stove** Boil a small pan of water on each burner in turn to make sure that they all work. Turn on the oven and broiler to see if they work.

PREPARING ROOMS

- **Airing rooms** If your new home has been empty for longer than a few days, the air may be stale. Open the windows for a while, then close them, and turn on the heat if necessary. This will also give you an opportunity to check that the radiators work.
- **Cleaning quickly** Make sure that surfaces are clean before positioning furniture on them. Dust baseboards, vacuum the carpets, and wash the kitchen and bathroom floors.
- **Hanging curtains** Use a damp cloth to wipe curtain rods and clean windows before you hang curtains.
- **Airing furnishings** If pillows, cushions, or mattresses have been transported in plastic covers, unwrap them, and let them air well before use.

SAFEGUARD TIP

Repairing a leaking faucet
If the body of a faucet leaks, the packing inside may be worn. To replace it, remove the faucet handle and the topmost nut on the spindle. If the packing is string, scrape it out. Coat a new length of string with petroleum jelly, and wind it into the space. Push it in with a screwdriver.

UNLOADING POSSESSIONS SAFELY

Using your room plan (see p. 152), place each object in the desired position in the correct room before unloading the next. To keep people and possessions safe, make sure that you and your helpers do not risk injury, and never leave a moving van unattended.

ANTICIPATING ACCIDENTS
● **Shielding hands** Provide strong gloves for helpers to prevent cuts and blisters. Supply hand cream so that people can keep their hands from becoming dry.
● **Moving furniture upstairs** To move a large piece of furniture upstairs, first lay it on its back on the stairs. Have one or two people pushing it from below, and another person above the object to steady it.
● **Taking breaks** Make sure that everyone takes regular breaks for rest, and provide refreshments to help people maintain energy levels.

ORGANIZING VEHICLES
● **Reserving parking** Talk to your new neighbors before a move. Ask them to keep the road in front of your home clear for moving vans.
● **Parking safely** Before you unload a vehicle, have it parked as close as possible to the entrance of your home. Besides minimizing the distance for carrying objects, this will enable you to watch the vehicle from a window.
● **Standing guard** Ask a helper to stay with an open vehicle at all times, either unloading objects from the interior or standing guard beside it.

PLANNING A SYSTEM FOR UNLOADING

Prepare rooms before starting work. Unload items in a logical order to save yourself work once the move is over.

● **Preparing floors** Cover floors with newspapers to protect them from damage while you are unloading.
● **Labeling rooms** Label each door as shown on your floor plan. Display the plan by the front door for reference.
● **Moving possessions** Unload large pieces of furniture first, so that you can position them correctly at the outset.

UNPACKING POSSESSIONS

At first, unpack only furniture and items that you need immediately. Leave objects such as books, ornaments, and linens until you have finished organizing furniture and storage areas. Take time to decide where to put these items so that you can store them in a suitable way.

UNPACKING EFFICIENTLY
● **Cleaning spaces** Clean storage spaces before filling them. Dust and wash shelves and the insides of cabinets. Allow washed areas to dry completely before use.
● **Checking objects** As you unpack, check items for damage, and perform any necessary cleaning.
● **Dusting books** Brush books with a clean feather duster to remove any dust before putting them on bookshelves.
● **Washing ornaments** Wash ornaments carefully in a bowl of warm, soapy water, and dry them thoroughly using a clean dish towel.
● **Unpacking kitchen items** As you unpack equipment in a kitchen, position it nearest to the areas where it will be used.

RECYCLING MATERIALS
● **Saving plastic bags** Once you have unpacked items from plastic bags, fold the bags and keep them in a cabinet for reuse in garbage cans.

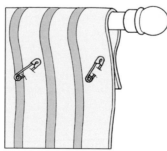

Improvising a curtain
If you have used any blankets for wrapping items, take them off the items and fasten them over a curtain rod with safety pins. This will give you some privacy until you can unpack your curtains.

MONEY-SAVING TIP

Using up packaging
If you have used newspapers as packing material during a move, save the newspapers and use them to buff windows after washing. Make sure that the windows are damp when you buff them; otherwise, the newspaper may scratch the glass.

SHARING A HOME

RENTING OUT SPACE IN YOUR HOME IS A GOOD WAY TO MAKE MONEY if you are on a tight budget. Besides sharing costs, a roommate or tenant also provides company. Choose people with care to ensure that they will be friendly and reliable.

FINDING A ROOMMATE OR TENANT

Roommates are equal partners in the home with you, sharing expenses on an equally divided basis, while tenants pay rent and a pre-agreed proportion of the bills to you. Whichever arrangement you choose, put it in writing and give a copy to all parties.

CHOOSING A ROOMMATE OR TENANT

Interview anyone who appears suitable. Discuss practical matters before the person moves in.

● **Advertising effectively** Before placing an advertisement in a magazine or newspaper, read a few issues to form an idea of the intended readership. This will enable you to judge if you are likely to attract a suitable person through that publication.

● **Interviewing candidates** Ask whether the person smokes. Find out if they have a steady partner or a busy social life. Ask for character references.
● **Giving notice** State the period of notice required if anyone wishes to end the arrangement.
● **Getting legal advice** Employ a lawyer to look at any agreement you draw up to make sure that nobody is at a disadvantage.

SETTING HOUSE RULES
● **Accommodating visitors** Find out in advance whether a roommate or tenant intends to have a guest staying for a long time. Arrange for visitors to contribute to the rent if they stay longer than a few days.
● **Drawing up a bath list** If you share a bathroom, draw up a list for showering to avoid disagreements at busy times. Give priority to those who go out first in the morning.

ESTABLISHING A HOUSEHOLD SYSTEM

Life in shared homes will run smoothly if everyone in the household agrees on how to allocate space and divide household chores. If you are new to a shared home, work out practical matters as soon as you have moved in so that you develop good habits from the start.

ALLOCATING SPACE

Sharing shelves
If shelves and cabinet space are shared, group each person's belongings in lids from large, sturdy cardboard boxes. Write each person's name clearly on the front edge of each lid.

DIVIDING TASKS
● **Organizing meals** Decide whether everyone will cook separately or for each other. If you all cook for yourselves, draw up a rotation list for using the stove. If you eat together, take turns cooking.
● **Cleaning common areas** Plan a schedule for cleaning shared areas, such as the kitchen.
● **Tidying quickly** Ask people to wipe the bath and sink after every use, and to wipe kitchen surfaces when they have finished cooking.
● **Washing dishes** Ask everyone in the household to do their own dishes. If you have shared a meal, nominate someone to wash up.

SHARING EXPENSES
● **Keeping a kitty** Have a kitty for buying household items. Agree an amount for each person to pay in every week.
● **Keeping an expenses file** Keep copies of bills in a file for reference. Put receipts for household goods with the bills so that you can monitor the costs for budgeting purposes.
● **Paying bills** Divide energy bills equally between all members of the household.
● **Logging telephone use** Log telephone calls in a book. Note the name, date, time, and duration. List the area code to help in working out the cost. Check telephone bills against the entries in the book.

STRUCTURING WORK

QUICK REFERENCE

Setting Up a Home
Office, p. 159

Managing Work
Time, p. 163

Communicating
Effectively, p. 166

Keeping
Records, p. 168

WHETHER YOU WORK *in an office or in your home, make sure that you function as efficiently as possible. Assess all aspects of your work, from the environment to the tasks that you do, to determine whether they suit you and meet the demands of the job. Take time to plan schedules for your work, and organize your office so that equipment and information are accessible.*

PLANNING A HOME OFFICE

If possible, set up a home office in a room away from the main living areas. Otherwise, use a quiet part of a living room or dining area, or adapt an empty space such as the area underneath a staircase (see p. 21). If you plan to work in an area that is also used by others in the household, set aside a place to store office items once you have finished work. Make sure that you have ample lighting for your needs, and install extra outlets if necessary. Make a floor plan to decide where to position furniture. Allow at least 39 in (1 meter) clearance around each large item. Organize your desk area, shelving, and cabinets so that you do not have to move far in order to find information.

● **Arranging an office** Position equipment so that vital items, such as a telephone, are within easy reach. At the same time, make sure that there is enough space on the desktop for work.

● **Siting outlets** Ask an electrician to install outlets near all electrical items so that you will not have to trail cords across a floor.

● **Securing cords** If you have to lay cords across a floor, secure them to the floor with insulating tape so that people will not trip over them.

● **Using daylight bulbs** Make sure that the work area is lit properly. If possible, fit lighting with daylight bulbs, which will minimize strain on your eyes.

● **Minimizing clutter** Keep the floor area and desktop free of clutter. If your work area is tidy you will be able to find items easily and will always have clear space for work.

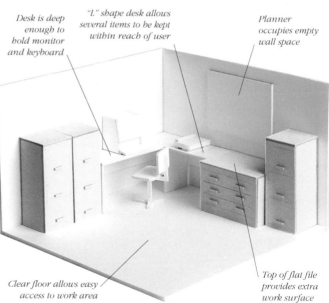

Desk is deep enough to hold monitor and keyboard

"L" shape desk allows several items to be kept within reach of user

Planner occupies empty wall space

Clear floor allows easy access to work area

Top of flat file provides extra work surface

Deciding on an office layout
When you lay out an office, consider how often you will need each piece of equipment. Keep essential objects within reach of your desk, and use areas away from your desk to store items that you seldom need.

SETTING UP A HOME OFFICE

L IST THE TASKS THAT YOU WILL BE DOING in your home office, and the equipment that you will need to do them. Determine the amount of space that you will need for your office, and work out a budget for equipping it.

ORGANIZING AN OFFICE LAYOUT

P lan a layout so that the items you use most often are within easy reach of your desk. Store seldom-used objects out of the way on high shelves, or in another room. In addition to planning space for equipment and files, allow room for you to lay out papers while you work.

USING SPACE CLEVERLY

● **Utilizing corners** If you have a small work area, fit a triangular desk in a corner.
● **Laying out stationery** Keep out only as much stationery as you will need for a few days. Store the rest out of the way.
● **Mounting items on walls** If you have limited space for work surfaces, mount items such as a telephone and a desk lamp on a wall.
● **Using a cart** Keep a cart to hold items that you use every day. Push the cart underneath your desk when you have finished work.

USING SHELF SPACE

● **Installing shelves** When you fit shelves, allow more shelf space than you think you will need so that you have room to store extra items in the future.
● **Using furniture** Use the tops of cabinets as shelving for lightweight objects. Make sure that you do not overload these surfaces.
● **Storing books** Put reference books on a shelf by your desk so that you can reach them without leaving your chair.
● **Storing files** Put filing trays on deep shelves to keep your work surface clear.

CREATING STORAGE

Improvising filing trays
Clean a set of unused, stackable vegetable racks, and use them instead of a filing tray to hold papers. Stand the racks on an accessible work surface or shelf.

DISPLAYING DATA

● **Using wall space** Display visual information such as planners and notices on a wall in front of your desk, where you can see the information without turning around.
● **Making bulletin boards** To make an inexpensive bulletin board, collect several dozen corks, cut them in half lengthwise, and glue the pieces onto a wooden board.
● **Using spaces under shelves** If you have shelves just above your desk, fit a panel of cork or bulletin board between the lowest shelf and the top of your desk so that you can make use of the wall space.

MAKING AN OFFICE MEMO BOARD

1 Pad a piece of wooden cork board with a sheet of foam. Cut a piece of scrap fabric to cover the board, leaving a 2-in (5-cm) edge of fabric all around the edge. Lay the foam-covered board on top of the material, and nail the excess material to the back.

2 Lay thin ribbons on top of the fabric in a crisscross pattern. Fasten the crossing points to the board with drawing pins, and pin the ends of ribbon to the back of the board. Mount the memo board on a wall, and tuck cards and notes under the ribbons.

EQUIPPING AN OFFICE

You do not always need to buy new office equipment. Secondhand objects are often much cheaper than new ones, and may be hardly worn. Consider improvising some items, particularly for storage and filing, in order to save money when outfitting a work area.

CHOOSING EQUIPMENT

Select the following items to equip your work area. These items should enable you to carry out all usual office tasks.

- Desk.
- Comfortable chair(s).
- Computer or typewriter.
- Telephone.
- Answering machine.
- Fax machine.
- Calculator.
- Files.
- Address book.
- Diary.
- Bulletin board.
- Clock.
- Paper and envelopes.
- Pens and pencils.
- Postage stamps.
- Paper clips and adhesives.

STORING STATIONERY

- **Collecting mail items** Keep a supply of stamps, new or recycled envelopes, air mail labels, and forms for couriers.

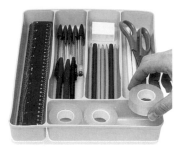

Keeping small items tidy
Put a cutlery divider in a drawer, and keep small items such as pens, rulers, and adhesive tape in it. Every couple of months, remove the divider, and dust it.

MONEY-SAVING TIP

Making a pencil holder
Cut the neck off a plastic bottle. Attach the base to a board, together with a can and an aerosol can lid. Decorate the holder with paint, then keep small items in it.

MAINTAINING SUPPLIES OF OFFICE STATIONERY

- **Buying in bulk** To save money, buy stationery in bulk. Form a group with other people working from home so that you can place joint orders.

- **Checking stock** Make a list of stationery items. Before you have used up supplies of an item, cross it off the list. Replenish the stock regularly.

RECYCLING PAPER

- **Minimizing waste** Take waste paper to a recycling center, or give it to a firm that recycles its paper. Keep old envelopes in a box for reuse.

CLEANING AND MAINTAINING EQUIPMENT

Every few weeks, set aside time for cleaning office equipment. Done correctly, this regular cleaning will prolong the lifespan of the equipment. Check to see if any item is faulty, and arrange for problems to be repaired.

- **Keeping a computer dust-free** Wipe the screen every day with an antistatic cloth. Cover the keyboard and screen when you have finished using a computer. Buy a specially made plastic cover, or make your own from a piece of lint-free cloth.
- **Storing cleaning items** Keep cleaning materials in a labeled box out of reach of children.

- **Cleaning a telephone** Wipe the mouth and earpiece with disinfectant. Use a soft brush to dust the keypad or dial.
- **Cleaning a typewriter** Rub the characters on a keyboard using a toothbrush.
- **Using chemicals safely** Before you start to use chemicals, such as cleaning fluid for computers, open a window so that you will not suffer ill effects from any fumes.
- **Dusting a mouse pad** Keep a mouse pad clean so that the mouse can move over it easily. To remove dirt off a fabric-covered pad, wrap adhesive tape around your fingers, sticky side out, and rub it lightly over the pad.

Work bristles between keys

Dusting a keyboard
Use a soft brush, such as a large cosmetic brush, to remove dust from the crevices in a keyboard. Check that the brush is clean, then rub the bristles on your hand to create static electricity, which will attract the dust.

KEEPING VALUABLE ITEMS SAFE

Take care of valuable office equipment and confidential data to protect them from loss or damage. Take precautions such as turning off electrical items and locking the office when you finish work. Protect sensitive information so that it cannot be misused by anyone else.

MAKING SAFEGUARDS IN AN OFFICE	
OBJECT	METHODS OF KEEPING ITEMS SECURE
Computer	● **Maintaining wires and plugs** Check cords, connectors, and plugs regularly to be sure that they are not loose or damaged. When using the computer, do not rest your chair leg on a cord. ● **Tidying cords** To keep trailing cords out of the way, anchor them to a wall or thread them all through a length of plastic drainpipe laid along a wall. ● **Hiding a laptop computer** Store a portable computer in a lockable drawer until you need to use it. Keep the power cable and any accessories in the drawer with the computer. ● **Recording identification** Make a note of the model names and identification numbers for each part of your computer, including such accessories as speakers.
Filing cabinet	● **Maintaining a cabinet** Check rarely used drawers in a filing cabinet to make sure that they open and shut smoothly. If you have to tug at the drawers, you may pull the cabinet over. ● **Preventing accidents** Never overload drawers or stand heavy items on top of a filing cabinet. Shut drawers as soon as you have finished with them. ● **Making a cabinet secure** Lock a filing cabinet whenever you are out of the office. Store the keys in a safe place, such as a lockable box. Keep spare keys in another place. Keep a note of the storage places. ● **Protecting files** If you have confidential papers, devise code names for the files so that other people cannot easily find them.
Telephone and fax	● **Installing a line for business** If possible, have a dedicated line for work. Put a lock on the work telephone so that nobody can use it when you are not there. ● **Encoding contact names** If you enter often-used numbers into a telephone, write each contact's initials, rather than their name, on the handset. This will ensure that they cannot be identified by anyone using your telephone. ● **Sending a fax** When sending a fax with private information, such as bank account details, remove the document from the machine immediately and file it in a safe place to be sure that it is not read by someone else. ● **Using a portable telephone** Put a portable telephone away in the same place each time you have finished using it so that you will be unlikely to mislay it.
Documents and money	● **Keeping certificates safe** Deposit stock certificates and other important documents in a safe-deposit box at the bank. If you wish to keep these documents in your home, store them in a wall or floor safe. ● **Handling cash** If you need to give money to strangers, have it ready before they arrive. Do not let callers see where you keep your cash supply. ● **Storing petty cash** Put money in a lockable box. Hide the cash box, or screw it to the floor or the inside of a drawer. Keep a record of petty cash used, for tax purposes and for your reference. ● **Identifying credit cards** Make a photocopy of each card, and file the copies in a safe place. You can then quote the numbers to the bank or credit card company if the cards are stolen.

WORKING IN COMFORT

You will work most efficiently when you are comfortable. Plan your work area to suit your physical needs. Take regular breaks to exercise your muscles and relax the eyes. Remember to rest your mind as well, perhaps by taking a stroll or talking to a friend.

AVOIDING REPETITIVE STRAIN INJURY

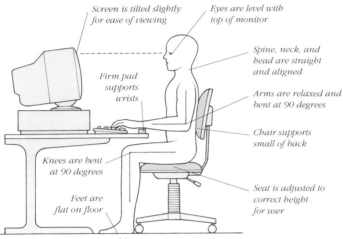

Screen is tilted slightly for ease of viewing

Eyes are level with top of monitor

Firm pad supports wrists

Spine, neck, and head are straight and aligned

Arms are relaxed and bent at 90 degrees

Chair supports small of back

Knees are bent at 90 degrees

Feet are flat on floor

Seat is adjusted to correct height for user

Positioning yourself to use a computer
Repetitive strain injury (RSI) is pain or muscle damage that occurs when you repeatedly overuse your shoulders, arms, or hands. If you use a computer regularly, adjust your computer, desk, and chair so that you can work comfortably. Make sure that your back, feet, and wrists are well supported. When you use the keyboard, regularly flex and relax your hands so that they do not become stiff and painful.

IMPROVING CONDITIONS

● **Lighting work areas** Prevent headaches and eyestrain by fitting overhead lighting that is bright and does not flicker.
● **Using a desk lamp** Angle a desk lamp so that it lights your work without dazzling you. If you use a lamp near a computer screen, make sure that the light does not reflect off the screen into your eyes.
● **Regulating temperature** Use equipment such as a portable heater or an electric fan to maintain the air around you at a comfortable temperature.
● **Adding plants** Plants release oxygen, which improves air quality. They also emit water vapor, which restores the moisture to dry air. If you wish to upgrade the air in which you work, position a few potted plants around your work area.

REDUCING WORK-RELATED STRESS

Excessive stress can reduce your efficiency and make you ill. Take action as soon as you start to feel overtired or unhappy. Do not allow stress to persist for a long time.

● **Relaxing eyes** From time to time, look up from your work and focus your eyes on objects at different distances.
● **Relieving face muscles** Frowning can create mental as well as physical tension, so try the following exercise to relieve this stress. Tense all of your face muscles, hold for a moment, and then relax the muscles. Repeat several times.
● **Staying active** To keep your energy levels high, do some form of exercise at least two or three times a week.

● **Having lunch** Make time to eat lunch in a relaxed manner. This will stop your blood sugar level from dropping and prevent indigestion.
● **Playing music** If you are not doing written work, relax by listening to music while you work. The music can block out background noise as well as give you pleasure.
● **Scheduling leisure time** Try not to let work extend beyond office hours. Keep in regular contact with your family and friends, so that you do not become lonely.
● **Boosting morale** Write a list of all your achievements, including minor ones. Refer to the list whenever you feel depressed or uncertain to boost your confidence.

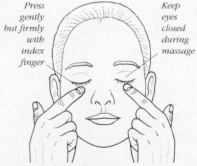

Press gently but firmly with index finger

Keep eyes closed during massage

Relaxing tired eyes
Using your index fingers, rub small circles just above the centers of your eyebrows, changing direction every 10 circles. Pinch the bridge of your nose several times, then rub small circles on the centers of your cheekbones. Finish by stroking large circles around your eye sockets, working outward from the bridge of your nose.

MANAGING WORK TIME

P LAN ALL OF YOUR WORK IN ADVANCE, allowing sufficient time to complete each
task on schedule. If you make a habit of dealing with work punctually, you
will minimize stress and give others confidence in your reliability.

WORKING EFFECTIVELY

A ssign each task a level of importance or
urgency, and schedule a specific time limit.
Be realistic about how much you can achieve, allowing more time than you think you will
need. Discipline yourself to do difficult jobs at
the scheduled time instead of putting them off.

SCHEDULING TASKS

● **Making a task list** At the end
of each day, list tasks to do
the next day, with the most
important at the top. Cross off
each task as you finish it. Put
any unfinished tasks at the top
of a list for the following day.
● **Planning ahead** When you
write a task list, check your
diary entries for the next
few days to ensure that you
include tasks recorded there.
● **Breaking down tasks** If a
project is lengthy or complex,
divide it into small tasks, each
with its own deadline.

MAKING USE OF TIME

● **Filling spare minutes** Make a
list of small jobs such as filing,
making telephone calls, or
straightening your desk. If you
have a little free time, carry out
two or three of these tasks.
● **Working during travel** If
you have to travel a long way
to attend a meeting, take
some work to do on the trip.
When traveling by train or
airplane, catch up on reading
or make notes. If you travel
by car, take a pocket tape
recorder and record plans
or answer letters.

CLASSIFYING JOBS

Drawing a chart
Divide a page into quarters.
Title the columns "Urgent"
and "Routine," and the rows,
"Simple" and "Complex." Note
tasks in the relevant areas to
help you to plan a schedule.

ORGANIZING YOURSELF AND OTHERS

T o keep to your work schedule, you need
to make it easy to accomplish tasks. Arrange
your work to suit you so that you will maintain your motivation. If you work with other people,
make appointments ahead of time, and brief
others carefully before delegating jobs to them.

THINGS TO REMEMBER

Note down any arrangements
that you make with other
people, or any discussions
that you have. Keep these
notes for future reference.

● **Appointments** As soon as
you make an appointment
with someone, write it in
your diary. Confirm the time
and place the day before.
● **Discussions** If you discuss
an important or contentious
subject face to face or on
the telephone, write a letter
to the other person to
confirm what was said.

MAKING WORK EASY

● **Selecting times** Do your most
demanding work when you
are most alert. For example, if
you are at your peak in the
morning, schedule demanding
jobs for that time, and use the
afternoon for routine tasks.
● **Setting financial goals** If you
are concerned about money,
set financial targets that will
be easy to achieve, rather than
overstretching yourself.
● **Planning rewards** Schedule
rewards for completing tasks
on time. For example, have a
mid-morning coffee break, or
a swim at the end of a day.

LIAISING WITH OTHERS

● **Briefing someone else** When
you ask someone to perform a
task, give them a date or time
by which you want the work.
● **Scheduling a meeting** Give
others a choice of times for a
meeting so that they can opt
for the most convenient time.
● **Preparing an agenda** List the
subjects for discussion in a
meeting, and set a specific
time for each. Send the agenda
to everyone who is to attend.
● **Saving time** Meetings are not
always necessary. If you simply
need to pass on information,
send a letter or a fax instead.

163

ALLOCATING WORK TIME

To calculate the best use of your time, first define how you already spend your working hours. Make a pie chart of your working week so that you can see which activities take up the most time. You can then decide whether or not to alter the way in which you divide your time.

MAKING A PIE CHART OF YOUR WORKING WEEK

ACTIVITY	NUMBER OF HOURS SPENT															HOURS SPENT	FRACTION OF TIME	DEGREES ON CHART
	1	2	3	4	5	6	7	8	9	10	11	12	13	14	15			
Meetings	✓	✓	✓	✓	✓	✓	✓	✓	✓	✓	✓	✓	✓	✓	✓	15	$\frac{1}{4}$	90
Travel	✓	✓	✓	✓	✓	✓	✓	✓	✓	✓	✓	✓	✓	✓	✓	15	$\frac{1}{4}$	90
Administration	✓	✓	✓	✓	✓	✓	✓	✓	✓	✓						10	$\frac{1}{6}$	60
Practical tasks	✓	✓	✓	✓	✓	✓	✓	✓	✓	✓						10	$\frac{1}{6}$	60
Correspondence	✓	✓	✓	✓	✓											5	$\frac{1}{12}$	30
Lunch breaks	✓	✓	✓	✓	✓											5	$\frac{1}{12}$	30

1 Make a chart to collect data for a pie chart. Draw rows to represent activities, then label the rows and use different colors to indicate each activity. Draw columns to represent numbers of hours. Over the course of a week, add check marks to rows to show the number of hours taken up by each activity. Include the time taken for commuting and other work-related travel, and for breaks.

2 Divide the total work time by the hours for each activity. Write the answers as fractions of the total time. To calculate the proportions for each activity on a pie chart, multiply 360 (the number of degrees in a circle) by each fraction.

TIMESAVING TIP

Preprinting labels
Have batches of labels preprinted so that you do not have to spend time writing or typing them individually. Set up templates on a computer for labels and forms, or type out master forms that you can photocopy as needed.

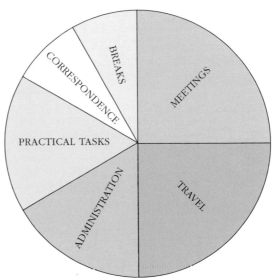

3 On a fresh sheet of paper, draw a large circle for the pie chart. Using a protractor, divide the circle into sectors of the correct size for each activity. Color in the sectors, using the same colors as on the original chart, and label them. You will then be able to see at a glance each activity as a proportion of your total work time.

MAKING A WORK LOG

At the end of each day, make a list of things to do the next day. Write down what each task involves, and by when the task must be finished. Organize the information into a chart, to make a work log. The chart below gives examples of information to include in a log.

USING LOGS
● **Reusing work logs** Make a template for a log, and mount it on a sheet of cardboard. Cover with clear adhesive film. Fill in the log with water-based ink so that you can clean it.

PRIORITIZING TASKS
● **Highlighting tasks** Mark the most important tasks for each day with a large asterisk, or mark them in highlighter pen. You can then prioritize your work easily during the day.

COMPARING GOALS
● **Grouping information** If you keep a year planner on your wall, display your work log beside it so that you can regularly compare your long-term and short-term goals.

INFORMATION TO INCLUDE IN A WORK LOG			
ACTIVITY	TIME AND PLACE	PEOPLE TO INVOLVE	ACTION TO TAKE
Meetings	● **Time** Note day, time, and duration. ● **Location** Include address and contact numbers if necessary. ● **Travel** Note time needed (if applicable).	● **Attending** Name people who are to attend. ● **Briefing** List people who need to receive agendas or briefing. Note people who are to be informed of outcome.	● **Agenda** List all subjects on agenda. ● **Reference** Note any extra information to be circulated. ● **Goal** Record intended goal of meeting.
Practical tasks	● **Time** Record day, time, and expected duration for each task. ● **Travel** Note time needed (if applicable). ● **Deadline** Give date for completion.	● **Recipient** Note person to receive finished work. ● **Assistants** Give names of any assistants. ● **Suppliers** Give names of people to supply materials or information.	● **Outline** Write down each part of a task. ● **Equipment** List tools, materials, and reference information. ● **Priority** Note urgency or importance of task.
Correspondence	● **Duration** Note time to allow for dealing with correspondence. ● **Deadline** Write down latest time by which to contact each correspondent.	● **Recipient** Record name, address, e-mail address, and contact numbers of recipient. ● **Copies** List people to receive copies of correspondence.	● **Contents** List main points of each subject to be discussed in correspondence. ● **Information** Note any extra information to give to correspondent.
Tasks to be delegated	● **Briefing** Note when to brief person to do task. ● **Duration** Write down time allowed for task. ● **Deadline** Give date for completion.	● **Name** Write down who is to perform task. ● **Number** Record location and contact numbers of person performing task.	● **Instructions** List tasks for person to do. ● **Information** Give names of sources that person can use for extra information.
Engagements outside work	● **Time** Note day, time, and expected duration. ● **Location** Record location of activity. ● **Travel** Note time needed (if applicable).	● **Companions** List names and contact numbers of anyone else involved. ● **Other contacts** Note whom to tell in case of delay or cancellation.	● **Nature** Write down brief description of engagement. ● **Equipment** List any special items needed, e.g., sports equipment.

COMMUNICATING EFFECTIVELY

P̲UT POINTS ACROSS in simple, direct statements to enable others to understand your ideas. Before communicating with anyone, decide exactly what you wish to express. After an important discussion, confirm the details in writing.

PLANNING TELEPHONE USE

T̲o make the best use of the telephone, plan calls in advance. Allow time each day for telephoning, and let regular callers know when you will be available to talk with them. Take notes while you are talking. Keep records of important telephone calls related to your work.

TAKING MESSAGES

When taking a message for someone else, record all of the following information.

● **Name** Note the full name, in case the recipient of the message knows other people with the same first name.
● **Telephone number** Take the number, even if the recipient of the message knows it.
● **Time** Record the time when the call was taken.
● **Message** Write down the content of a message after you have noted the relevant names and numbers.

MAKING CALLS
● **Planning a call** Write out points to discuss before you call someone. Keep the notes in front of you for reference while you are talking.
● **Speaking pleasantly** Try to sound pleasant without being false. Imagine that the person is in front of you and smiling at you. Smile back, and your voice will reflect your mood.
● **Staying on hold** If you are put on hold when you call someone, wait for only one minute. If the other person has not answered by then, leave a message or try later.

FOLLOWING UP
● **Recording details** As soon as you have finished an important call, note the date and time of the call, and summarize the points that were discussed.
● **Confirming information** After discussing an important matter with someone, write a letter to that person to confirm any decisions that you made.
● **Leaving a message** If you have to leave a message for someone, specify a time by which that person should respond. Note this time in your calendar, and call again if the person has still not answered.

ORGANIZING CORRESPONDENCE

D̲eal with business correspondence regularly so that it does not pile up. Allow adequate time in your schedule, and ensure that you are not disturbed during that time. File letters and faxes, with photocopies of your replies, as soon as you have dealt with them.

PLANNING STRUCTURE
● **Making a draft** On a sheet of scrap paper, note the points to be covered in a letter. With each main point, note any related minor points. Write a rough draft of the letter, and make any last changes on this before writing the final version.
● **Arranging information** Set out the main points of a letter or fax in brief paragraphs so that the recipient can read the information quickly. Allow one paragraph for each major point, and one sentence for each idea within a paragraph.

LAYING OUT TEXT
● **Giving a heading** Begin a fax or letter by giving a heading to the text. Write the heading in capital letters, or underline it. This will enable a reader to see at a glance what the document will be about.
● **Highlighting facts** Give each paragraph a number or a heading. Place this above the paragraph, and underline it or print it in bold type.
● **Listing points** When writing a list of items in the text of a letter, mark each one with a bullet (●) to give it emphasis.

WRITING LETTERS OF COMPLAINT

Be direct and accurate. Say only what is necessary, and try not to become emotional.

● **Defining a goal** First, decide what you wish to achieve by writing, such as receiving compensation or a refund.
● **Keeping it simple** Keep to the point. Support your message with facts, not with vague or emotional language.
● **Including evidence** Always send photocopies rather than original documents.

SETTING OUT INFORMATION IN DOCUMENTS	
DOCUMENT	**HOW TO CONVEY ESSENTIAL INFORMATION**
Résumé 	Keep your résumé brief. If possible, fit it onto one side of a single page of letter paper. Put your name and address clearly at the top. Use one paragraph for each stage of your career. ● **Arranging facts** Mention the most important parts of your work history first. If you are working, start with your current job, and work backward. If you have just left school or college, list your academic achievements first, starting with the most recent. ● **Highlighting skills** Mention any practical skills that may be useful for a job, such as the ability to drive or to speak a foreign language fluently. ● **Listing interests** Describe leisure activities so that they appear relevant to the job. For example, if you belong to a sports team, you could emphasize teamworking skills. ● **Checking for errors** Because you are aiming to make a good impression on a stranger, it is vital that your résumé is error-free. Read it carefully, and use a dictionary to check the spellings and meanings of words. ● **Adding a cover letter** Enclose a short cover letter with a résumé. State the job for which you are applying, and how you heard about it. Explain briefly why you are interested in the job, and why you may be suited to it.
Letter 	Make your points briefly, because the recipient of the letter may have only a few minutes to look at it. Give your address, contact numbers, and e-mail address so that people can contact you. Put the recipient's address in a prominent place on the page. ● **Saving time** Write a letter only if you are sure that this is necessary. For a brief message, consider sending a fax or making a telephone call. ● **Defining structure** Give each letter a beginning, middle, and end. Begin by saying why you are writing. Give the main points in the body of the letter. Finish by summing up your message or inviting the other person to reply. ● **Quoting a reference number** If you are replying to a letter, quote the date and reference number of that letter in your first paragraph. ● **Adding enclosures** If you have enclosed extra information, mention each enclosure in the paragraph for the relevant point so that the reader can refer to it instantly. ● **Giving your title** If you prefer to be addressed by a particular title, such as Ms. or Dr., include this when you give your name at the end of a letter. ● **Reading aloud** Read a letter aloud once you have finished writing it. If the text sounds good, and you can read it smoothly, it should be easy for the other person to follow.
Invoice 	Include your name and address, and that of the recipient. Give the date and any reference number for the work. Briefly describe the work, and note the amount to be paid. Sign the invoice. ● **Planning format** Set up a master form on a computer, or type it. Keep some preprinted forms ready for use. ● **Defining costs** If an invoice is for several pieces of work, give the cost for each item, and write the total amount beneath these figures. ● **Listing extra costs** When including costs such as tax or postage, give both the price of the work and the total figure including these extra costs. ● **Using reference numbers** Devise a system for numbering your invoices so that you can identify them easily for personal reference or tax purposes. ● **Giving a reply date** Write on your invoice the date by which you will expect payment (usually 30 days). Even if this has no legal force, it will be useful for future reference. ● **Sending an invoice** Mail or fax an invoice as soon as you have finished the work, or include it with the last installment of the work. ● **Noting dates of payments** Keep photocopies of all the invoices that you send out, and write on each of them the date when you are paid.

KEEPING RECORDS

K EEP CAREFUL RECORDS for both business purposes and personal reference. Whether you store records on paper or by electronic means, organize the information clearly and neatly, and in such a way that you can easily refer to it.

SETTING UP A FILING SYSTEM

A rrange information into general categories. If necessary, subdivide the information in each category. For example, subdivide a banking file by each account that you have. Enter all information in chronological order, with the most recent items at the front of a file.

LABELING & GROUPING
● **Identifying contents** Label files clearly with a general subject and the different categories within the subject.
● **Color-coding files** Use a different-colored file for each subject, so that you can identify files at a glance.
● **Labeling shelves** If you keep magazines or pamphlets that do not show their titles on their spines, group the items by title, and label the shelves underneath each title.

MONEYSAVING TIP

Making filing boxes
Clean out a couple of large detergent boxes. Cut off the tops, and slice a diagonal piece from the upper corners of each. Cover each box with adhesive plastic, and label to indicate the contents.

MAKING A CONTAINER FOR HANGING FILES

Dowel is slightly longer than box

Slot is 1 in (2.5 cm) deep

1 Find a wooden box that will hold hanging files. Mark the width of a file on the front and back of the box, near the top edges. Drill holes at the marks, and cut these into slots. Fit lengths of dowel into them.

2 Place the files in the box so that they hang from the dowels. Leave the box open for easy access, or add a cover to protect the files. Label the front of the box clearly to indicate the contents.

ORGANIZING DATA
● **Grouping data for vehicles** Keep a file for each vehicle. At the front, insert a sheet of paper giving the make, age, registration number, and date of purchase. Include all tax and insurance documents, and receipts for repairs.
● **Keeping data for pets** Keep a photograph of each pet, and record its breed, identification marks, and distinctive physical features. Include insurance documents, veterinary data, and any breed certificates.
● **Labeling floppy disks** Attach an adhesive label to each disk. Note the general category of information on the disk and, if there is room, the name of each file or folder.

FILING ON A COMPUTER
● **Cleaning a hard drive** Check your hard drive regularly, and remove any files and software programs that you do not use. This will free up memory for recent or important data.
● **Tidying folders** Delete all unnecessary documents. If you wish to keep copies, print them out and file them with the rest of your papers.
● **Recording file names** If you use coded names for files, keep a list of the codes and real names in a safe place.
● **Storing letters** Do not keep copies of letters on your hard disk. For maximum space on the computer, photocopy the printed letter once you have signed it, and file the copy.

KEEPING IMPORTANT DATA

Protect information such as financial records, legal documents, and confidential business data. Organize files and information carefully so that you have easy access to all of the material. Keep the most sensitive information in a secure place such as a coded file, a safe, or a bank.

STORING ON PAPER

● **Storing receipts** Keep files to hold receipts for valuable items. Set up one file for office equipment, and make another for household objects. You can then refer to the receipts if you need to value an object or prove your ownership. File any guarantees together with the relevant receipts.

● **Keeping hard copies** File a hard copy of every important document on your computer, in case the machine breaks down or is stolen and you cannot retrieve the documents.

● **Using an address book** List people in an address book or card index using only their initials and surnames. This will protect people's privacy if the information is lost or stolen.

USING FLOPPY DISKS

● **Keeping copies of files** Store copies of essential files on floppy disks. Put the disks in a lockable box. Keep the box in a secure place, away from heat and magnetic sources that could damage the disks.

Keeping business cards
Collect business cards in a small photograph album for quick and easy reference. Either file them alphabetically by surname or company name, or categorize them by profession.

ORGANIZING FINANCE

● **Monitoring your budget** Keep up-to-date files of your recent spending and allocate space for planning ahead.

● **Keeping receipts** Save receipts for credit cards and carbons for deposit slips so that you can check them against bank statements.

● **Studying statements** When a bank statement arrives, check each entry against your credit card receipts, checkbook, and carbons for deposit slips. Notify the bank immediately if you find any errors.

● **Saving money** Open separate savings accounts for different purposes. For example, have one for emergencies and one for treats such as vacations.

● **Managing financial matters** Take a bookkeeping course to learn how to organize your accounts and deal with taxes.

KEEPING DATA SECURE

● **Storing vital facts** Make a list of data such as the numbers and expiration dates of your credit cards and the numbers of your bank accounts and insurance policies. File the list in a secure place.

● **Encoding data** To keep information safe from other people, encode it in a way that you will easily understand.

● **Storing copies** Keep two copies of essential documents in separate safe places. This way, you will always have a backup if the original, or one of the copies, is lost.

● **Depositing with a lawyer** Leave important information, such as the location of your will and the combination of a safe, with your lawyer.

ENSURING MAXIMUM SECURITY

Keep valuable business and legal documents in a highly secure place such as a safe or a bank. Keep a list of any items that you store in such places.

● **Choosing a personal safe** If you wish to have easy access to documents or objects, install a safe in your home or office. Choose a safe that is not small enough to be stolen easily, and attach it securely into a wall or floor.

● **Storing in a bank** Use a safe-deposit box in a bank if you need documents or objects to be well guarded and safe from fire. Your access to them will be limited to the bank's working hours, so check these in advance. You should take identification, such as a passport, with you.

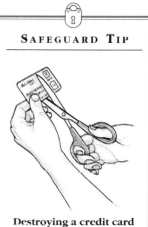

SAFEGUARD TIP

Destroying a credit card
When you receive a replacement credit card, cut the old one into small pieces immediately. Throw the pieces into different garbage cans to make sure that the card cannot be reconstructed. Always sign a new credit card as soon as you receive it.

ENSURING SAFETY

QUICK REFERENCE
Emergencies, p. 172
Resuscitation, p. 174
Major Injuries, p. 176
Other Injuries, p. 179
Common Ailments, p. 185

Making your home safe should be a top priority, especially if there are small children, or elderly or disabled people living there. Try to look at your home as a stranger would to spot possible danger areas. Bear in mind that learning first-aid techniques from a book, although useful, is not a substitute for the practical training of a first-aid course.

HOME MEDICAL KIT

Keep all first-aid items together in a substantial box that is easily accessible for adults but is out of reach of small children. Make sure that all adults know where it is. Store a medical kit in a cool, preferably dark place to help preserve the quality of the contents. Replace items as you use them, and dispose of any that are no longer in good condition or return them to the pharmacy. A basic first-aid kit for the home should include all of the items shown here.

● **Dressings** Your kit should contain two sterile pads, one sterile dressing with bandage, two sterile eye pads with bandages, and gauze swabs. Keep a selection of adhesive bandages for minor wounds.
● **Bandages** Include a variety of bandages of different sizes.
● **Fastenings and tools** Keep hypoallergenic tape or safety pins for securing dressings, tweezers for removing splinters, and blunt scissors for cutting dressings and bandages.
● **Creams and lotions** Keep antihistamine cream for insect bites and stings, and calamine lotion for sunburn.
● **Gloves** Keep disposable gloves for treating victims other than family members.

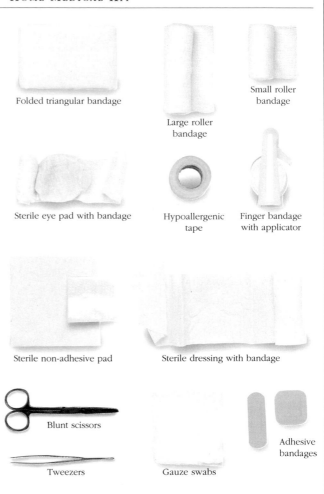

Folded triangular bandage

Large roller bandage

Small roller bandage

Sterile eye pad with bandage

Hypoallergenic tape

Finger bandage with applicator

Sterile non-adhesive pad

Sterile dressing with bandage

Blunt scissors

Adhesive bandages

Tweezers

Gauze swabs

SAFETY IN THE HOME

Simple precautions can prevent accidents and even save lives. The kitchen is the most dangerous room in the home, followed by the bathroom. Always mop up spills that could cause people to slip, especially on tiled floors. Put a safety rail on the bath-tub if necessary.

KITCHEN SAFETY

Cabinets and drawers fitted with safety catches

Pan handles face inward

Preventing accidents

Turn pan handles away from the stove edge, and keep children away from hot oven doors. Fit safety catches on cabinets, and store matches out of reach. Teach children about safety.

GENERAL SAFETY

● **Glass doors** Replace ordinary glass panels fitted into doors with safety or laminated glass, which does not splinter when broken.
● **Fireguards** Always use a fireguard when you leave an open fire unattended. This also applies to flame-effect fires, which get very hot.
● **Rugs** Fix any loose rugs or mats into position with antislip pads or tape.
● **Lighting** Ensure hazardous areas of the house, such as stairways and landings, are well lit at all times.
● **Irons** Always switch off an electric iron if you have to answer the door or telephone.
● **Adaptors** Unused plug outlets should be covered with plastic safety covers.

FIRE PRECAUTIONS

● **Smoke alarms** Fit a smoke alarm on each floor of your home. Check them regularly.
● **Fire blankets** Store a fire blanket in the kitchen.
● **Ashtrays** Keep ashtrays for smoldering cigarettes and cigars and their stubs.
● **Hinges** Fit self-closing hinges to doors in a home with a high fire risk.
● **Fire drills** Conduct regular family fire drills so that everyone knows the escape routes. Make sure that children know not to return to a burning building, even for family pets (see p. 172).
● **Furniture** Avoid buying old furniture that is stuffed with polyurethane foam. This can burst into flames in a fire and release poisonous fumes.

CALLING EMERGENCY SERVICES

Make a list of important telephone numbers, and keep the master in your home log book and a copy near each telephone. Stick the copies where they will not be moved, for example inside cabinet doors. Add written instructions to the list in case the caller panics.

EMERGENCY NUMBERS

Keep the telephone numbers of the following services and people on your list:

● Emergency services (fire, police, and ambulance).
● Doctor and dentist (include the office-hours).
● The nearest hospital with emergency services.
● Immediate family members (include workplace numbers).
● 24-hour pharmacy.
● Emergency numbers for electricity, gas, and water companies.
● Taxi service.
● Veterinarian.

MAKING THE CALL

● **Relevant information** When making an emergency call, you will need to give your telephone number, the exact location, the severity of the emergency, the age, sex, and condition of anyone involved, and details of any hazards, such as a gas leak.
● **Teaching children** Drill your children in the basics of calling the emergency services so that if you are injured they will know what to do.
● **Fires** If your house is on fire, call the emergency services from a neighbor's house or a public telephone.

STAYING IN CONTROL

Keeping calm

In an emergency, it is important to stay calm so that you think clearly. When calling emergency services, try to answer questions and give details precisely. Allow the dispatcher to hang up first.

ACTING IN EMERGENCIES

K NOWING WHAT TO DO IN AN EMERGENCY can contribute greatly to preventing and limiting casualties and damage to property. See pages 134 and 137 for what to do in the event of flooding in the home or a gas leak respectively.

ACTING IN CASE OF FIRE

F ire is frightening and can spread quickly. If you cannot put out a small fire yourself, the most important thing to do is to evacuate the building. If you live in an apartment building, sound the fire alarm, then save yourself and your family. Do not let anyone panic.

COPING WITH SMALL FIRES

● **Chimney fires** If an open fire is out of control, dowse it with water. If the chimney is alight, call the fire department. Pull furniture and carpets away from the fireplace.

● **Electrical fires** Do not use water on electrical fires. If an appliance such as a television or computer is on fire, turn off the electricity at the circuit breaker, and smother the flames with a blanket or coat.

● **Kitchen fires** If a skillet catches fire, immediately turn off the stove or jet. Cover the pan with a fire blanket, a damp kitchen cloth, or a large saucepan lid.

● **Controlling small fires** Close all doors and windows in order to contain a small fire within a room. Air fuels a fire.

PROTECTING YOURSELF IN A BURNING BUILDING

Open window and call for help

Close door firmly to keep fire out

Block door to keep smoke out

Escaping a fire

If you are unable to get out of a burning building, shut yourself as far away from the fire as possible. Block the door with rolled or folded fabric, damp if possible. Open a window and call for help. Do not jump out of the window unless it is the only way of saving your life.

WARNING
When evacuating a building, carry any babies and toddlers out with you. Never, for any reason, return to a burning building. Alert the emergency services if you know that someone is trapped.

DEALING WITH CLOTHES ON FIRE

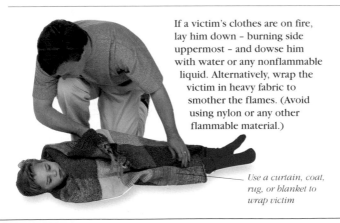

If a victim's clothes are on fire, lay him down – burning side uppermost – and dowse him with water or any nonflammable liquid. Alternatively, wrap the victim in heavy fabric to smother the flames. (Avoid using nylon or any other flammable material.)

Use a curtain, coat, rug, or blanket to wrap victim

ACTIONS TO AVOID

● **Feeding flames** Do not allow the victim to panic and rush outside, since movement or breeze will fan the flames.

● **Spreading burns** Roll the victim on the ground only if you have no alternative. Burns may spread to other areas.

TREATING YOURSELF

● **Extinguishing flames** Try not to panic and wrap yourself in heavy fabric. Then lie down.

ELECTRICAL INJURIES

Many electrical injuries in the home result from faulty switches, frayed cords, and defective appliances. Handling safe appliances with wet hands, or when standing on a wet floor, can greatly increase the risk of shock. See page 137 for Safety with Electricity.

BREAKING THE CONTACT

1 If someone has been injured by electricity, first break the current by switching off the supply at the circuit breaker or meter. If this is difficult, pull the cable free from the outlet.

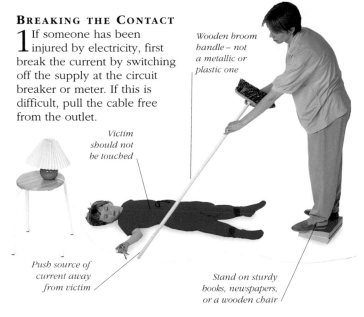

Wooden broom handle – not a metallic or plastic one

Victim should not be touched

Push source of current away from victim

Stand on sturdy books, newspapers, or a wooden chair

2 If you cannot cut the power, stand on insulating material and use a wooden broom handle to disconnect the current from the victim.

3 Wrap a dry towel around the victim's feet, and drag him away from the appliance. As a last resort, pull on his loose clothes (if they are dry).

4 Check for breathing and pulse if the victim is unconscious. Resuscitate if necessary (see p. 174). If the victim seems unharmed, make him rest, and call a doctor. Treat for shock and burns if necessary (see p. 176).

DROWNING

Reduce the risks of drowning by encouraging all members of the household to learn to swim as well as possible. Remember that a small child can drown in as little as 1 in (2.5 cm) of water. Watch children constantly if they are playing near or in water.

RESCUING A VICTIM FROM DROWNING

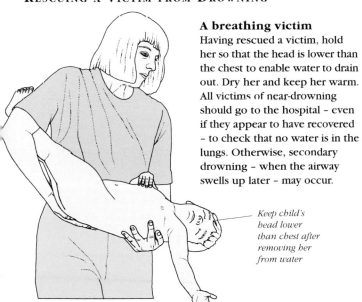

A breathing victim
Having rescued a victim, hold her so that the head is lower than the chest to enable water to drain out. Dry her and keep her warm. All victims of near-drowning should go to the hospital - even if they appear to have recovered - to check that no water is in the lungs. Otherwise, secondary drowning - when the airway swells up later - may occur.

Keep child's head lower than chest after removing her from water

A NONBREATHING VICTIM
● Administering CPR If a victim is unconscious after being rescued from drowning, check her breathing and pulse. Begin CPR (cardiopulmonary resuscitation – see p. 174) if she is not breathing. You may find CPR difficult to administer, however, if the victim's lungs are full of water.

PREVENTING PROBLEMS
● Hypothermia If a victim of drowning has spent some time in the water, she may suffer from hypothermia – a potentially fatal reduction in body temperature. Remove all her wet clothes as quickly as possible, dry her thoroughly, and keep her warm and quiet.

RESUSCITATING VICTIMS

WHEN TREATING AN UNCONSCIOUS VICTIM, the priority is to check whether the lungs and heart are working. Open the airway, then check for breathing and a pulse. If you suspect back or neck injury, do not move the victim.

A, B, C OF RESUSCITATION

These letters stand for Airway, Breathing, and Circulation – three areas that you must immediately assess in an unconscious victim.

If an unconscious victim is breathing and has a pulse, place him or her in the recovery position (see below) and call an ambulance.

ASSESSING THE CONDITION OF A VICTIM

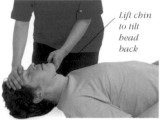

Lift chin to tilt head back

Look and listen for breathing

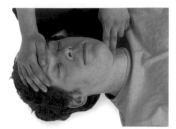

Opening the AIRWAY
Open the victim's mouth, and carefully remove anything inside it that could obstruct the airway. Open the airway by placing one hand on the victim's forehead and two fingers of the other hand under the victim's chin, tilting his head back slightly.

Checking BREATHING
Keeping the airway open, place your cheek beside the victim's mouth and nose for five seconds, and listen and feel for any breath being exhaled. At the same time, carefully look along the victim's chest to see if there is any sign of movement of the lungs.

Checking CIRCULATION
Place a finger at the side of the windpipe for five seconds. If there is a pulse but no breathing, begin rescue breathing (see opposite). If there is no pulse or breathing, call an ambulunce, then start cardiopulmonary resuscitation (see opposite).

THE RECOVERY POSITION

The recovery position shown below is the safest position for a victim who is unconscious, because the tongue cannot block the throat and liquids can drain from the mouth. This greatly reduces the risk of the victim inhaling vomit or stopping breathing.

PLACING A VICTIM IN THE RECOVERY POSITION

1 Bend the victim's near arm at a right angle to the body. Place the back of her far hand to her near cheek. With her near leg straight, bend the other leg so that the knee is at a right angle.

2 Holding the victim's hand against her cheek, pull the thigh of the bent leg toward you, and roll her onto her side. Working from this position, you should even be able to roll someone heavy.

3 Guide the victim's head as you turn her. Tilt her head back, and pull the jaw forward to open the airway. Continue to check the A, B, C of resuscitation (see above) until an ambulance arrives.

The Recovery Position

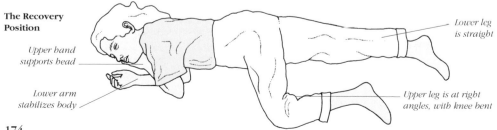

Upper hand supports head

Lower arm stabilizes body

Lower leg is straight

Upper leg is at right angles, with knee bent

RESCUE BREATHING

If an unconscious victim is not breathing, you will need to blow air into his or her lungs. Give 10 breaths per minute, and check for a pulse after every 10 breaths. Continue for as long as you can – until the victim starts to breathe again, or until help arrives.

ADMINISTERING RESCUE BREATHING

Cover victim's mouth completely, so that no air escapes

Look to see that chest is deflating

1 Lay the victim on his back. Remove obstructions from his mouth. Place your hand on his forehead, tilt his head back, and pinch his nose while placing two fingers under his chin.

2 Place your mouth over the victim's mouth, sealing it firmly. Blow in for two seconds; the chest will rise. Let the chest fall for four seconds, inhaling fresh air as it does so. Repeat 10 times per minute.

3 Repeat Step 2 until the victim is breathing unaided or professional help arrives. Stop every 10 breaths and check for a pulse. Start cardiopulmonary resuscitation if the victim's pulse stops.

CARDIOPULMONARY RESUSCITATION

Cardiopulmonary resuscitation (CPR) is a combination of rescue breathing and chest compressions. If there is no breathing or pulse, administer two breaths, followed by 15 chest compressions. Continue doing this – aiming for 100 compressions a minute – until help arrives.

ADMINISTERING CHEST COMPRESSIONS

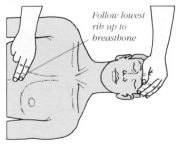

Follow lowest rib up to breastbone

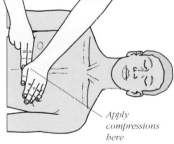

Apply compressions here

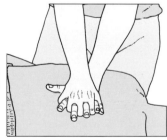

1 Lay the victim on a firm surface. To locate the area for applying compressions, feel for the victim's lowest rib with your first and middle fingers. Slide your fingers upward until your middle finger reaches where the rib meets the breastbone – there may be a slight hollow here.

2 Your first finger should now be lying on the victim's breastbone. Slide the heel of your other hand down the breastbone until it is next to the point where your first finger is resting. The heel of your hand is now sitting in the exact area to which the compressions will be applied.

3 Place the other hand on top of the first, and interlock your fingers. Keeping your arms straight, press down 2 in (5 cm) and release. After 15 chest compressions, administer two breaths, and repeat the two steps until help arrives. Check the victim's pulse and breathing regularly.

DEALING WITH MAJOR INJURIES

EVEN IF YOU KNOW THAT A VICTIM is going to receive medical treatment, you can keep him or her comfortable, reduce the risk of shock, and prevent any injuries from getting worse while waiting. Prompt, efficient action may save life.

BLEEDING

It is important to stop all bleeding as quickly as possible. Remove any clothing from around the wound, and wash away blood and dirt. Apply pressure to control the bleeding. You should wear a pair of disposable gloves if you are dealing with a stranger.

TREATING BLEEDING WOUNDS EFFECTIVELY

Raise wound above level of heart

Lay victim down so that wound can be easily elevated

3 Leave the pad in place, and cover the wound with a sterile dressing. Bandage this into place, keeping the wound above heart level. The bandage should be firm but should not cut off the blood supply. If blood starts to seep through the dressing, place another pad on top.

1 Make a pad from a folded piece of clean cloth and hold it over the wound, pressing firmly. Raise the wound above the level of the victim's heart to reduce the rate of bleeding. Do not try to remove anything that is embedded in the wound.

2 Lay the victim down, taking care to keep the wound above the level of the heart all the time. Keep him as flat as possible, using only a thin pad under the head for comfort. Continue to apply firm pressure to the wound for at least 10 minutes.

4 When the bleeding seems under control, keep the injured part elevated, and take the victim to the hospital. If there is an object embedded in the wound, place rolls of gauze around the wound – this will keep the bandage from pressing on the object.

RECOGNIZING AND TREATING SHOCK

Shock occurs when not enough oxygen circulates around the body. This may be as a result of failure of the circulatory system, as in the case of heart attack, or loss of fluid through bleeding, burns, vomiting, or diarrhea. The body responds to the problem by diverting blood to essential organs, and the victim's skin may become gray and clammy, and the pulse may begin to race. To treat a victim for shock, keep her still, and raise her legs about 12 in (30 cm) to increase the amount of blood returning to the heart. Loosen any tight clothing, and keep her warm.

Call an ambulance and be prepared to resuscitate (see p. 174). Do not give any food or drink.

Raise legs to improve circulation

Elevate any wounded limb to minimize loss of blood

CUTS AND SCRAPES

Minor cuts and abrasions can be treated without medical help, unless there is a foreign body or a risk of infection.

1 Wash dirt out of a cut or scrape gently, using soap and water on a gauze pad. Avoid fluffy cloths, since they may stick to the wound.

2 Press firmly on the wound with a clean gauze pad to stop the flow of bleeding.

3 Apply an antiseptic cream, then cover the wound with a dressing that is large enough to cover the entire area.

BURNS AND SCALDS

Cool burns and scalds at once to prevent further tissue damage and reduce pain. If a fire is the cause of the victim's injury, make sure that both you and she are safe before attempting treatment. See also rescuing from fire (p. 172) and from electric shock (p. 173).

TREATING MAJOR BURNS & SCALDS EFFECTIVELY

1 Remove the victim from the source of the burn. Pour cold water onto the burn for at least 10 minutes.

2 Carefully remove clothing and jewelry from the burn area, cutting around any cloth sticking to the wound.

3 Continue to cool the burn if necessary, by immersing it in cold water or any other cool liquid, such as milk.

4 Cover the burn with a clean dressing. If the burn is large, use a clean sheet or pillowcase. Do not apply any fats or creams.

5 Get medical attention as quickly as possible. Treat the victim for shock if necessary (see opposite). Do not offer her food or drink. Continue to reassure her.

Cool burn with cold water

Do not remove clothing until burn has been cooled

Avoid touching burn

TREATING MINOR BURNS

● **Treating** Cool the burn for at least 10 minutes, as above. Remove any jewelry and clothing from around the burn before the area starts to swell.
● **Dressing** Cover minor burns with any clean, nonfluffy material. Avoid applying adhesive dressings since they can damage skin near the burn when they are removed.

CHEMICAL BURNS

● **Detection** These can be caused by toxic household substances. They are less obvious than heat burns, and may take time to develop.

Removing chemicals
Hold the burned area under cool, running water for at least 10 minutes and wash away all traces of the chemical. Wear rubber gloves to prevent the chemical from splashing on to you. Treat the affected area as for major burns (see above).

ELECTRICAL BURNS

● **Causes** Electrical burns are caused by lightning, or high- or low-voltage current. In the home, low-voltage current can cause scorching to the skin.

Treating the injury
Make sure the current is off (see p. 167). Administer CPR or treat for shock if necessary. Hold the burn under cool, running water for at least 10 minutes. Cover with a sterile dressing. Seek medical help, since electrical current can cause internal injury.

BURNS TO THE AIRWAY

Administering water
Burns to the mouth or throat – caused by inhaling hot fumes for example – are dangerous, since they sometimes cause the airway to swell. Loosen clothing around the victim's neck, and give him sips of cold water. Reassure him and go to the hospital at once.

POISONING

Household chemicals can be poisonous if ingested, as can certain plants and drugs. Seek medical attention as soon as possible. Try to identify the type of poison involved. Keep a sample of the substance ingested, any vomit, or containers or pill bottles found nearby.

DEALING WITH POISONING BY HOUSEHOLD CHEMICALS

Read contents of bottle to identify poison

1 If you suspect that a caustic substance might have burned the mouth and throat, wipe any residue off the victim's mouth and lower face. Wash the area gently with cold water.

2 Give the victim frequent sips of cold water or milk to reduce burning on the lips and in the mouth. Take care at all times not to contaminate yourself, and remove any contaminated clothing.

3 Give relevant information off the chemical container when seeking qualified advice. Take the container with you to the hospital to facilitate treatment. See below if the victim is unconscious.

DEALING WITH DRUG POISONING

Tell emergency services what drug has been taken, and how much

Keep a conscious victim close to you until help arrives

1 If the victim is conscious, try to find out which drug has been taken, how much, and when it was ingested. If he has vomited, keep a sample for the doctor, and also keep the bottle in which the drugs were kept for identification.

2 Take the victim to the hospital, talking to him calmly to keep him conscious. Take the drug bottle with you. Be prepared to treat for shock (see p. 176). See below for the appropriate action if the victim is unconscious.

WARNING
Do not induce vomiting since this will bring back the poisonous chemical which may cause further damage.

IF THE VICTIM IS UNCONSCIOUS

BREATHING AND PULSE PRESENT

1 If breathing and pulse are present, place the victim in the recovery position (see p. 174) to keep the airway open, and call an ambulance.

2 Treat any related injuries such as chemical burns (see p. 177) if necessary.

NO BREATHING, BUT PULSE PRESENT

1 Give 10 breaths of rescue breathing (see p. 175). Call an ambulance, and repeat.

2 Continue to give rescue breathing to the victim until an ambulance arrives. Check the pulse every minute (after every 10 breaths).

NO BREATHING, NO PULSE

1 Tell someone to call an ambulance. Administer 15 chest compressions, followed by two breaths of rescue breathing (see p. 175).

2 Continue administering CPR until the heartbeat and breathing resume as normal.

DEALING WITH OTHER INJURIES

ACCIDENTS CAN HAPPEN AT ANY TIME AND IN ANY PLACE, even if every reasonable safety precaution has been taken. Children are at risk because they have less of a sense of danger than adults, who must be prepared for anything.

ANIMAL BITES

All animals, including humans, have germs in their mouths, and bites can not only break the skin but can also cause infection.

Always treat animal bites immediately – start by cleaning the wound thoroughly. Take every precaution to avoid being bitten yourself.

TETANUS & RABIES
● **Tetanus** This produces toxins in the nervous system and is a serious illness. It can be caused by organisms in the soil getting into cuts and bites. Immunization against tetanus is part of a childhood immunization schedule. Adults need boosters every 10 years.
● **Rabies** This is a potentially fatal disease that is spread by infected animals. If you are bitten or licked on broken skin where rabies is a danger, seek medical help, even if the animal does not look infected.

TREATING MINOR ANIMAL BITES

Hold wound under water

1 Wash a minor bite wound in soap and water. Then hold it under a running tap for at least five minutes to rinse away any dirt and reduce the risk of germs.

2 Pat the wound dry with a clean gauze pad or tissues. Do not apply an ointment or tincture. Cover with an adhesive bandage or sterile dressing. The wound should be checked by a doctor in case there is any infection.

> **WARNING**
> Rabies can be fatal. Treat all animal bites that occur in areas where rabies exists as dangerous, and seek medical attention immediately.

TREATING A BITE THAT IS BLEEDING

1 Wash the wound in soap and water. Hold it under a running tap for five minutes to remove as much dirt and as many germs as possible.

2 Press a clean dressing or pad firmly on the wound. Raise the affected part above the level of the heart. If the bleeding is severe, follow the procedure for dealing with major wounds (see p. 170).

3 When the bleeding stops, cover the wound with a sterile dressing or with a pad bandaged firmly in place. Take the victim to the hospital. Do not assume that the wound will heal on its own since it may have been infected by germs from the animal.

Cover wound with dressing and bandage

Victim should remain calm as you work

SNAKE BITES

Wash bite wound

Indications of a snake bite include a pair of puncture marks, severe pain, redness and swelling around the wound, vomiting, and breathing difficulties. Seek medical help immediately.

● **Treating a snake bite** Wash the wound with soap and water. Bandage it firmly, holding it below the level of the heart. Keep the casualty calm. Do not cut the wound or try to suck out the venom.

INSECT STINGS

For some people, insect stings can be dangerous and require immediate medical attention or treatment for anaphylactic shock (see below). For other people, the treatments described below are sufficient. Treat stings immediately. Do not let the victim panic.

INSECT STINGS

1 If the sting is still present, carefully remove it with a pair of tweezers, grasping the sting as near to the skin as possible. Take care not to snap it off while extracting it. Do not squeeze the poison sac at the top of the sting.

2 Apply a cold compress to the area to reduce pain and swelling. Use a cloth wrung out in cold water, or a bag of frozen peas or ice cubes, wrapped in a cloth. Leave the compress on the wound for 10 minutes.

MOUTH & THROAT

1 If a casualty has been stung in the mouth or throat, reduce the swelling by giving him or her an ice cube or an ice pop to suck, or by offering some very cold water to drink.

2 Take the victim to a doctor. Call an ambulance if the victim's breathing becomes difficult because of swelling. If the victim loses consciousness, treat immediately for anaphylactic shock (see below).

TICK BITES

● **Treatment** Ticks attach themselves to the skin to feed on blood, and can transmit infection. Grasp a tick with a pair of tweezers, taking care not to leave any part of the tick in the skin. Keep the tick to show a doctor in case the victim begins to feel sick.

HIVES

● **Description** This is a rash of red-edged lumps that both itch and hurt. Hives may be caused by exposure to many allergy-inducing substances, including cold, dust, pets, and a wide variety of foods.

Treating hives
The pain and itching of nettle rash can be relieved by applying a cold compress or calamine lotion. Leave on for 10 minutes. Reapply until the itching and pain have ceased. If the rash is extensive, call a doctor.

RECOGNIZING ANAPHYLACTIC SHOCK

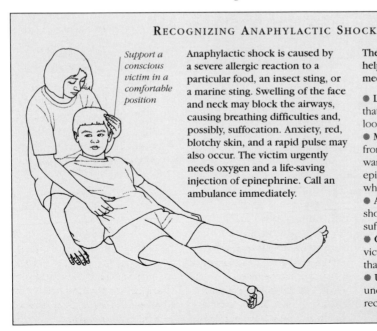

Support a conscious victim in a comfortable position

Anaphylactic shock is caused by a severe allergic reaction to a particular food, an insect sting, or a marine sting. Swelling of the face and neck may block the airways, causing breathing difficulties and, possibly, suffocation. Anxiety, red, blotchy skin, and a rapid pulse may also occur. The victim urgently needs oxygen and a life-saving injection of epinephrine. Call an ambulance immediately.

The following measures will help minimize shock until medical help arrives.

● **Loosen clothing** Make sure that any tight clothing is loosened to aid breathing.
● **Medication** A known sufferer from this condition may carry a warning bracelet or card, and epinephrine for self-injection, in which case assist him.
● **Avoiding panic** Anaphylactic shock can cause panic in the sufferer. Try to keep him calm.
● **Conscious victim** Help the victim to sit up in a position that he finds comfortable.
● **Unconsciousness** Place an unconscious victim in the recovery position (see p. 174).

BRUISES AND SWELLING

Bruising is caused by ruptured blood vessels beneath the surface of the skin, causing blood to leak into surrounding tissue. Severe bruising may indicate deep injury, such as a fracture. Swelling should be examined carefully, since it also may indicate serious injury.

TREATING BRUISES

1 Sit the victim down, with the injured limb supported. Elevate the injured area on a cushion in order to rest it.

2 Apply a cold compress to the injury. Hold the compress against the injury for 30 minutes to reduce the swelling.

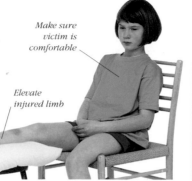

Make sure victim is comfortable

Elevate injured limb

MAKING & APPLYING A COLD COMPRESS

● **Making a cold compress**
Wring out a clean cloth in cold water, or wrap it around ice cubes. Keep it on the swelling for about 30 minutes, recooling it every five minutes.

TIME-SAVING TIP

Instant compress
If you need a cold compress in a hurry, use a package of frozen peas. Wrap it in a thin towel and lay over the injury. The peas should not be eaten, but the package may be used again as an ice pack.

BONE AND MUSCLE INJURIES

Treat all bone and muscle injuries as serious until you have discovered the extent of the damage. Look for bruises and swelling, and if you think there may be a fracture, take or send the victim to hospital for an X ray. Prevent movements that may aggravate the problem.

COMMON BONE AND MUSCLE INJURIES

● **Sprain** Elevate the injured area, and apply a cold compress. Wrap with cotton and bandage firmly. Take or send the victim to the hospital as soon as possible.
● **Dislocated shoulder** This occurs when the head of the arm comes out of the shoulder-joint socket. Support the arm in a sling with the hand across the chest. Get the victim to the hospital as soon as possible. Do not give the victim any food or drink.
● **Broken collarbone** Put the arm on the damaged side in a sling. The victim should go to the hospital.

IMMOBILIZING BONE INJURIES

Keep injured limb immobile

Support injured limb

Make a sling with triangular bandage

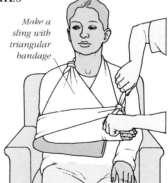

Supporting limbs
Bone injuries need to be supported. For an arm, seat the victim and ask her to support her arm across her chest. For a leg, lay the victim down. Support the leg – above and below the injury, not on it – in your hands.

Securing limbs
Keep the injured part supported by securing it properly. Support an injured arm in a sling, then bandage it to the chest, and take the victim to the hospital. Secure the damaged leg to the uninjured one. Call an ambulance.

CHOKING

A blocked airway can be frightening for the person who is choking and those around him or her. Action must be quick; otherwise, the victim may suffocate. Choking is usually caused by eating too fast, or by young children putting small objects in their mouths.

RECOGNIZING & AVOIDING CHOKING

● **Symptoms** The victim may have difficulty speaking and breathing, and the skin may be blue. The victim may clutch the throat or neck.

● **Prevention** Encourage family members to chew their food thoroughly. Make sure children do not put foreign objects in their mouths.

TREATING CHOKING IN CONSCIOUS ADULTS

1 If the victim is coughing forcefully, encourage him or her to cough the object up. Call an ambulance.

2 If the victim cannot speak, cough forcefully, or breathe, the airway is blocked completely. Stand behind him, and place your arms around his abdomen just above the navel. Center your fist, thumb side in, cover with the other hand, and thrust inward and upward several times (the Heimlich maneuver).

3 Continue to administer abdominal thrusts until you dislodge the object. (If this fails and the victim becomes unconscious, follow the treatment below.)

4 Once the object has been dislodged, encourage the victim to sit down. Help him calm down.

CHOKING IN INFANTS

The treatment for infants differs from the treatment for adults and children. The following steps are a quick outline; if your household includes an infant, a first-aid course is recommended.

1 Determine if the airway is completely blocked. The infant's face may turn blue, and he may make strange noises or no sound at all.

2 Lay the infant face down along your forearm, with the head low. Give five sharp blows to his back.

3 Turn the infant face up. Place two fingers on the breastbone just below the nipple line, and give five sharp downward thrusts.

4 If you can see an object in his mouth, remove it.

5 For unconscious infants, try to give breaths. Call 911. Repeat back blows and chest thrusts until the airway is cleared or help arrives.

TREATING CHOKING IN UNCONSCIOUS ADULTS

1 If choking has caused loss of consciousness, call for help as you lay the victim on his back. Give two breaths of rescue breathing. If chest does not rise, retilt head and try the two breaths again.

2 If the victim's chest still does not rise, straddle his body and place the heel of one hand against the middle of the abdomen above the navel. Give up to five abdominal thrusts. Lift tongue and sweep out the mouth if you can see an object.

3 Retilt the head and give rescue breathing. Continue these steps until breath goes in, breathing resumes, or professional help arrives. Once breathing resumes, place the victim in the recovery position (see p. 174). Get the victim to the hospital.

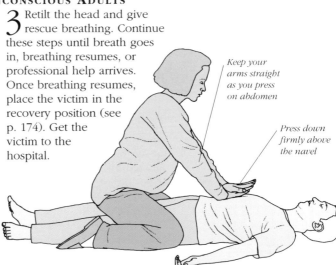

Keep your arms straight as you press on abdomen

Press down firmly above the navel

FOREIGN BODIES

Foreign bodies in the eyes, ears, nose, or throat are unpleasant, can be frightening, and may be dangerous. Use the appropriate technique below to deal with the obstruction, taking care not to cause harm to the victim. Get medical help as soon as possible.

IN THE EYE

1 Hold the eyelids apart with two fingers and get the victim to look up, down, left, then right. Carefully pour clean water into the inner corner of the eye to try to wash out the object.

2 If the object does not wash out, lift it out with a moist swab. Do not touch anything sticking to or embedded in the eye nor anything over the colored part of the eye; take the victim to a doctor.

IN THE EAR

● **Looking for objects** With a flashlight, try to see what is in the ear. If it is embedded, do not remove it – you may damage the eardrum. An adult or older child may know what the object is. Keep the victim calm, and take him or her to the hospital.

INSECT IN THE EAR

1 Place the victim in a chair with the affected ear upward. Flood the ear with tepid water so that the insect floats out. Use a towel to catch any overflow.

2 If the insect does not come out, or if it is a wasp inside the ear, keep the victim calm, and take him or her to the hospital. Never put anything in the ear to remove a foreign body.

IN THE NOSE

● **Recognition and treatment** An object inside the nose may cause difficult breathing, or a bloody discharge, or swelling. Encourage the victim to breathe through his mouth, keep him calm, and take him to the hospital. Do not attempt to remove the object even if you can see it.

SWALLOWED OBJECTS

● **Identification** Ask the victim what has been swallowed. If it is small and smooth, it will work through the body, but still get medical advice. Large items must be removed by a doctor.

WARNING
Do not allow the victim to eat or drink since an anesthetic may be needed. Take the victim to the hospital.

SPLINTERS AND BLISTERS

Splinters and burst blisters may cause infection if they are not treated properly. Remove splinters as soon as possible, but do not try to treat deeply embedded objects. Seat the victim while removing splinters, so that the affected area remains steady.

REMOVING SPLINTERS

Hold ends of tweezers over flame

Pull splinter out in direction it went in

1 Wash your hands, then clean the area around the splinter with soap and warm water. Sterilize a pair of tweezers by passing them through a flame. Alternatively, boil them in water for about 10 minutes. Let them cool before you use them.

2 Grasp the splinter with the pair of tweezers, as close to the skin as possible. Draw the splinter out at the angle at which it went in. Squeeze the wound so that it bleeds a little to flush out any dirt. Wash the area again, pat dry, and cover with an adhesive bandage.

TREATING BLISTERS

A blister is, in effect, a sterile dressing protecting an area of damaged skin. Do not puncture it.

● **Covering blisters** If a blister bursts accidentally, apply an adhesive dressing that extends well beyond the blister so that it is not damaged by the adhesive.
● **Burn blisters** Burns often cause fluid to collect under the skin. Never disturb it. See page 177 for treating burns.

NOSEBLEEDS

Nosebleeds often occur unexpectedly, and can be frightening if the blood flow is copious. Use a towel to clean up and protect the victim's clothes. Frequent and substantial nosebleeds may indicate a serious problem, and the nose should be checked by a doctor.

TREATING NOSEBLEEDS

1 Seat the victim with the head tilted forwards. Tell her to breathe through her mouth. Meanwhile, pinch the fleshy part of the nose so that the nostrils stay tightly together for 10 minutes.

Tilt victim's head forward

Pinch nostrils together

Lean victim over bowl to catch any fluid

2 Holding the head tilted over a bowl, encourage the victim to spit out excess fluid. Pinch the nostrils for 10 more minutes. Repeat if necessary, but if the bleeding lasts for more than 30 minutes, take her to the hospital.

3 Once the bleeding has stopped, clean around the nose and mouth with a damp towel or cotton wool and tepid water. Instruct her not to blow her nose, since this may cause the nosebleed to start again.

> ### WARNING
> If there is a watery discharge from the nose after a head injury, or if the nosebleed lasts for over 30 minutes, take the victim to the hospital.

BLEEDING MOUTH OR EAR

Cuts to the tongue, lips, or lining of the mouth may bleed profusely and cause alarm. A permanent tooth can and should be replanted in its socket – but a child's milk tooth cannot be replanted. Bleeding from inside an ear usually follows a rupture of the eardrum.

MOUTH WOUNDS

Victim should lean over bowl

Removing blood
Lean the victim over a bowl to collect the blood. Press the mouth wound with a gauze pad, and pinch it between your thumb and forefinger for about 10 minutes. Do not wash out the victim's mouth – this may disturb a blood clot.

TOOTH LOSS

Saving teeth
As long as the tooth is not a child's milk tooth, you can replant it in its socket. Alternatively, store the tooth in milk, and place a pad over the socket, making sure it is higher than surrounding teeth so that the victim can bite on it. Take him to a dentist at once.

EAR INJURIES
● **Ear wounds** Place a gauze pad over the wound. Press on the wound for about 10 minutes. When the bleeding stops, cover the wound with a sterile dressing lightly held in place with a bandage. Then take the victim to a doctor.
● **Bleeding from inside the ear** Seat the victim in a semi-upright position with the head turned towards the injury so that blood drains away. Bandage an absorbent pad over the ear; do not plug the ear. Take the victim to a doctor.
● **Danger signs** If bleeding from inside an ear follows a head injury, and the blood is watery, fluid may be leaking from around the brain. Take the victim to the hospital.

TREATING COMMON AILMENTS

COLDS AND FEVERS MAY not seem like serious complaints because they occur fairly frequently. However, they can have dangerous consequences if not treated correctly, especially for vulnerable people such as the elderly.

FEVER AND COLDS

The misery of the common cold is familiar to almost everyone – chills and nasal congestion being among the symptoms. A very high temperature may indicate a more serious infection. If a fever develops, you should try to bring it down as quickly as possible.

DEALING WITH FEBRILE CONVULSIONS

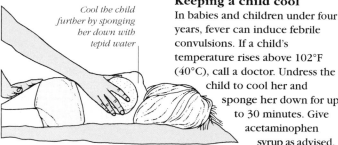

Cool the child further by sponging her down with tepid water

Keeping a child cool
In babies and children under four years, fever can induce febrile convulsions. If a child's temperature rises above 102°F (40°C), call a doctor. Undress the child to cool her and sponge her down for up to 30 minutes. Give acetaminophen syrup as advised.

TREATING FEVER IN ADULTS & CHILDREN

1 Take the temperature of the victim. It should be approximately 98.6°F (37°C); anything higher than 100°F (38°C) indicates a fever. Make the person comfortable, preferably by letting him or her rest in bed in a cool room.

2 Give the person plenty of water or diluted fruit juice to drink to prevent dehydration. An adult may take two acetaminophen pills; a child may be given acetaminophen syrup. Sponge with water if the fever is high or use a fan.

RELIEVING THE SYMPTOMS OF COLDS

● **Avoiding overheating** Be careful not to become overheated by wearing too many clothes or putting too many blankets on the bed. This will increase your general level of discomfort.
● **Improving breathing** Clear a congested nose by inhaling a few drops of eucalyptus oil sprinkled on a handkerchief. Another method is to hold your head over a bowl of hot water and inhale the steam. For greater effect, place a towel over your head and the bowl. Fresh air may also help clear breathing.

● **Easing a sore throat** If you have a sore throat, gargle with warm water in which you have dissolved some salt. The salt will help to retard the development of any bacterial infection, while the warmth will soothe the soreness.
● **Drinking frequently** Drink plenty of water or diluted fruit juice, especially if your cold is accompanied by a raised temperature, in order to avoid dehydration and soothe a dry mouth and throat. A child with a sore throat will often suck an ice pop even if he or she refuses drinks.

IDENTIFYING MENINGITIS

This is an inflammation of the tissues surrounding the brain. Prompt action is required since it is potentially a very serious condition.

● **Recognizing the signs** Symptoms of meningitis include a dislike of strong light, fever, vomiting, stiffness and pain in the neck, and a sporadic distribution of red or purple spots which are distinguished by the fact that they do not fade when pressure is applied to them. A loss of consciousness may also occur.
● **Taking action** If you suspect that a person may have meningitis, take him to the hospital immediately.

GREEN TIP

Natural soothers
Infuse honey, cloves, and lemon in hot water as a natural remedy for coughs and sore throats. Sucking a whole clove will quiet tickles in the throat.

STOMACHACHE

Pain in the stomach can be the result of relatively trivial indigestion, or it can indicate a damaged intestine – particularly if the pain fluctuates in intensity, and is accompanied by vomiting – or inflammation of the appendix, particularly in older children.

TREATING STOMACHACHES

1 Make sure that the person is comfortable in a bed or on a sofa, propped up on pillows. Leave a bowl nearby in case she wants to vomit.

2 Give her a covered hot-water bottle, or wrap one in a towel, to hold against her stomach. Do not give her medication or anything to eat.

3 If this fails to alleviate the pain after 30 minutes, or if the pain is severe, call a doctor. Severe pain could indicate a serious condition.

WARNING
Do not wait more than 30 minutes before calling a doctor if the pain continues. It could indicate appendicitis.

APPENDICITIS
● **Symptoms** Appendicitis tends to affect older children, particularly teenagers. The symptoms include pains in the middle of the abdomen, moving to the right lower abdomen, loss of appetite, raised temperature, nausea, vomiting, and diarrhea.
● **Medical help** Do not give food or drink to a person with symptoms of appendicitis. Call a doctor at once.

VOMITING

Adults can usually cope with their own vomiting, but children need assistance and care. Vomiting can cause them to panic, so reassurance is important. If diarrhea occurs with the vomiting, call a doctor since this may indicate a serious illness or cause dehydration.

ASSISTING A CHILD WHO IS VOMITING

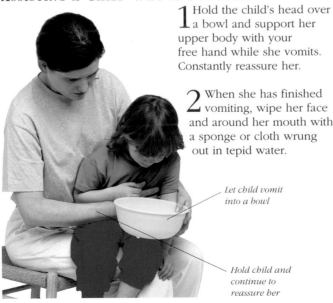

Let child vomit into a bowl

Hold child and continue to reassure her

1 Hold the child's head over a bowl and support her upper body with your free hand while she vomits. Constantly reassure her.

2 When she has finished vomiting, wipe her face and around her mouth with a sponge or cloth wrung out in tepid water.

3 Give her plenty of water to drink. This will replace lost fluid and remove any unpleasant taste. Encourage her to sip it slowly.

4 Encourage the child to rest on a sofa or in bed. If the vomiting persists, call a doctor. Do not give her milk to drink, since this may make the vomiting worse.

WARNING
A baby or small child can become dehydrated when vomiting. Administer sips of cooled, boiled water. Do not give formula or cow's milk, but continue to breastfeed.

EARACHE AND TOOTHACHE

Earaches may be caused by an infection, a cold, a boil in the ear canal, a foreign body in the ear, or pressure changes. Toothaches may be the result of a cavity, an abscess, or a mouth infection. Children may need a lot of attention while their ears are painful.

TREATING TOOTHACHE

1 Give the person the recommended dose of acetaminophen pills or syrup to ease the pain and make him or her more comfortable. If the pain persists, make an appointment with a dentist.

2 Lay the person down, or support the head with pillows. Place a covered, warm hot-water bottle under the affected cheek. You could give an adult a small measure of liquor to hold in the mouth – this helps alleviate pain.

TREATING EARACHE

1 Encourage the person to lie down, or make him as comfortable as possible if he is seated. Give the correct dose of acetaminophen pills or syrup to ease the pain and discomfort in the ear.

2 Cover a hot-water bottle, and give it to the person to lean the painful ear against. Advise the person to see a doctor. If you are worried about the person's condition, or if the earache does not subside, call a doctor.

WARNING

When treating a toothache, if the jaw is affected or swollen, consult a dentist. When treating an earache, call a doctor if there is discharge, fever, or hearing loss.

TRADITIONAL TIP

Temporary filling
If you need a tooth filled but cannot get to a dentist immediately, soak a small piece of cotton in oil of cloves. Pack it into the cavity to relieve the discomfort.

TREATING A PRESSURE-CHANGE EARACHE

Clearing the ears
Blocked ears may occur on flights during takeoff and landing, or when traveling through tunnels. Tell a victim to make the ears "pop" by closing the mouth, pinching the nostrils, and blowing out hard through the nose. Yawning or sucking hard candy will also help. Help a baby swallow by feeding it.

Victim should pinch her nose and blow out

HICCUPS

Hiccups are contractions of the diaphragm against a partially closed windpipe. They can be distressing if they persist. They usually go away on their own, but a few techniques may help. Consult a doctor if the hiccups last for more than a few hours.

HELPING HICCUPS TO GO AWAY

● **Drinking water** To cure hiccups, try drinking water from the wrong side of a cup. This awkward task will take your mind off the hiccups, which should then stop.
● **Holding breath** Try holding your breath for as long as possible. Repeat until the hiccups have stopped and then you can breathe normally.

● **Relaxing** It is best to stand or sit quietly while trying to cure hiccups – moving around may only make the hiccups worse.

Breathing expired air
Hold a paper bag over the mouth and nose and rebreathe your expired air for one minute. Never use a plastic bag.

DECORATING

COLOR SCHEMING

•

PAINTING & PAPERING

•

TILING SURFACES

•

PAINTING WOOD

•

CHOOSING FLOOR COVERINGS

•

ADDING OTHER DECORATION

COLOR & STYLE

QUICK REFERENCE

Using Color, p. 192

Color Scheming, p. 196

Setting Styles, p. 198

Reflecting
Lifestyles, p. 200

ONE OF THE JOYS of decorating is that it provides an opportunity to experiment with color and decorative styles while giving you a means of expressing your personal taste and preferences. Creating your own color combinations and choosing styles does, however, need thought and consideration of other factors before you make final decisions.

UNDERSTANDING COLOR

It is not necessary to understand the physics behind the derivation of color in order to appreciate why you like particular colors or to determine a color scheme when decorating. Rather, you need a working knowledge of how different colors are related and affect each other.

APPLYING COLORS

● **Defining aims** Decide whether or not you want to achieve a certain result with your color choice in a room, and the sort of mood you want to create. Select a main color with these needs in mind – restful colors in a bedroom, for example, or warm, inviting hues in a living area.

● **Evoking emotions** Colors produce different emotional responses in people. If you want to make a statement or attract attention, use a strong, hot color. Choose warm colors to be welcoming and comforting. Select strong, cold colors for a calming rather than a stimulating effect. Cool colors are invigorating but soothing at the same time.

● **Combining colors** Base your scheme around one main color. Then consider whether other colors should form a range of consecutive hues, be clashing or contrasting complementary colors, or be combined to create a more complex scheme altogether.

LEARNING THE LANGUAGE OF COLOR

All colors in the spectrum are derived from the three primary colors – red, yellow, and blue. Secondary colors are created by mixing two primaries: yellow and blue to make green, for example. All other colors are known as tertiary colors and are formed from a variety of combinations of primaries and secondaries. Shades and tones are produced by lightening or darkening colors with the addition of black or white.

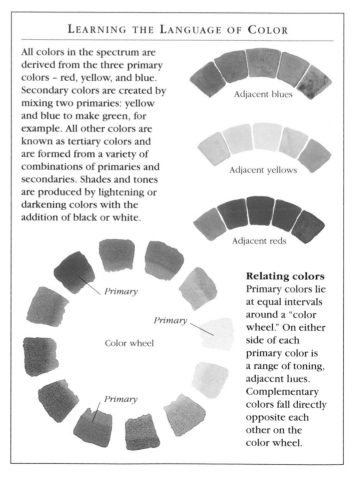

Adjacent blues

Adjacent yellows

Adjacent reds

Primary

Primary

Color wheel

Primary

Relating colors
Primary colors lie at equal intervals around a "color wheel." On either side of each primary color is a range of toning, adjacent hues. Complementary colors fall directly opposite each other on the color wheel.

COMBINING COLORS

Some people have an instinctive feel for how colors can be combined successfully within an extensive scheme. But you can soon learn whether colors contrast with or complement each other. Either alternative can provide the basis of a highly successful color scheme.

CONTRASTING SHADES

Juxtaposing light and dark
Using particularly light colors alongside much darker shades can provide good definition between the various surfaces in a room. Here, the light lemon of the alcove and the pale woodwork create a neat finish against dark blue walls.

COMBINING OPPOSITES

Using complementary colors
Red and green work well together because they are complementary colors – that is, they sit directly opposite each other on the color wheel. The color scheme that is featured here also includes the use of yellow, a contrasting color.

USING ADJACENT COLORS

Striking a balance with related colors
Contrasting colors emphasize features, but if they are adjacent hues they also unite a room. The red walls and window link this scheme, despite a great difference in wall colors. The vibrant yellow on the baseboard contrasts with the pale yellow wall while relating to it.

CHOOSING COLORS
● **Following instincts** Choose basic colors within a scheme according to your preferences. Once you have chosen these basics, you can make slight variations in shade to suit particular requirements.
● **Harmonizing a finish** Choose colors of the same intensity within a scheme to create a restful feel within a room. The greater the difference in intensity, the more colors will tend to stand out. You may wish to highlight a feature in a room using this effect.
● **Mixing complementaries** Combine a large area of one color with its complementary color, which will have the effect of softening the original shade. You can also use this method to take the edge off vibrant hues so that they lie more comfortably together.

USING COLOR

Colors have certain properties that can evoke particular feelings in a room. You may choose a color scheme simply to change the character of your room or to create a certain atmosphere by means of that color's characteristics.

TRANSFORMING ROOMS WITH COLOR

When starting the decoration of a room from scratch, examine the function of the room and who is going to be using it.

● **Catering for occupants** If a room is for communal use, cater for general taste rather than individual needs. Even a personal room such as a bedroom will require very different decor, in both practical and aesthetic terms, depending on whom it is designed for.

● **Considering function** Select your colors according to whether a room will be used for rest and relaxation, for fun and recreation, or for work.

Playing with greens
In a bedroom intended for use by a child, bear in mind that its functions will include both rest and recreation. You will have the scope to use different colors to enliven the atmosphere and add interest for the room's occupant.

Relaxing in warm pinks
You can transform a room almost completely just by changing its color. Use a uniform color scheme in an adult's bedroom, for example, to ensure that features do not leap out and to maintain a restful atmosphere.

SUBTLE OR BOLD

Subtlety and boldness are generally equated with conservatism and daring, respectively. This is because it is considered far more risky to use bright, vibrant colors than paler hues, since brighter colors tend to have a greater initial impact and effect than more subtle variations.

STAYING PALE

Limiting the difference
Maintain a narrow margin of difference between the colors in a scheme to produce a calming feel. The paler these colors, the more subtle the scheme and the greater the effect will be.

BEING BOLD

Going to extremes
Use bold, vibrant colors to give a dynamic feel to a room. A bright, cheerful atmosphere can also be relaxing, and subtle lighting can create a feeling of sumptuousness and calm.

MIXING & MATCHING

● **Highlighting features** Choose subtle colors for walls, woodwork, and floors to allow you to use bold colors and patterns for soft furnishings in order to draw attention to these items.

● **Framing walls** Use bold colors on woodwork and more subtle variations on walls, which will have the effect of "framing" the walls. Enhance this effect with a bold ceiling color. The walls will then set off pictures well.

● **Using white** Include white, which is perhaps the most subtle color of all, to show off other colors successfully.

WARM OR COOL

Colors have definite warming or cooling properties that can be used to great effect in all areas of the home. Combining several warm or cool colors, or using both warm and cool together, can produce a range of different atmospheres and moods to suit your needs.

WARMING UP & COOLING DOWN

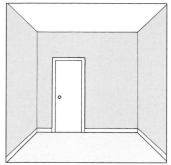

Bringing in warmth
The warming effect of these colors is enhanced by the fact that they appear to bring the walls nearer and reduce space in the room. Choose colors like these for coziness and intimacy.

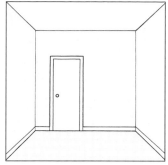

Creating space
Typical cool colors tend to have a receding effect on walls, which gives a greater feeling of space in a room. Use this to create an open, airy atmosphere, as well as creating a cool effect.

ADJUSTING EFFECTS
● **Emanating warmth** Oranges, reds, pinks, and warm yellows create a cozy atmosphere. Choose warm colors such as these for a room that receives little or no direct sunlight.
● **Freshening up** Select a cool, refreshing color scheme with blues and greens for areas such as narrow corridors that need opening up, or for sunny rooms that may overheat.
● **Varying intensity** The extent to which a color has a warming or cooling influence depends on its intensity and its shade. Use dark colors carefully, since these tend to have the most marked effect.

CREATING A WARM GLOW

Nurturing warmth and comfort
Create a feeling of coziness and reassurance by basing an entire color scheme on warm hues. In this room, the rich, red wall color is accentuated by similar tones in the furnishings. Even the orange undertones in the natural wooden floor contribute to the room's warm and welcoming atmosphere.

KEEPING COOL

Adopting a fresh approach
Choose a color scheme such as the all-over blues in this kitchen to provide a fresh, revitalizing feeling. In a room that is used mostly in the mornings, and which receives plenty of natural sunlight, there is probably no need to introduce warm colors to enliven the atmosphere.

LIGHT OR DARK

The use of a light or dark color does, of course, create a correspondingly light or dark atmosphere in a room. However, different shades of the same color also have additional characteristics, and can be used individually to dramatic effect in the overall color scheme.

MAKING LIGHT WORK

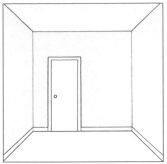

Enlarging a room
Light colors on large surfaces create a feeling of space. Use them to make a small room seem larger, or on selective surfaces such as ceilings to give an impression of greater height.

STAYING IN THE DARK

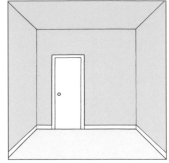

Enclosing a room
Dark colors tend to draw surfaces toward the viewer, therefore reducing the feeling of space. Use them to "lower" high ceilings or add coziness and intimacy to a large room.

MODIFYING CHOICES
● **Playing safe** Use light, pastel shades if you are unsure of your decorating skills. Even if you are inexperienced, you should be able to mix and match them with relative ease.
● **Covering blemishes** Dark colors, especially used on woodwork, will camouflage unevenness or blemishes better than lighter shades. Use dark colors to maximize the quality of the finish.
● **Extending life** Dark colors are better at concealing dirt and coping with general wear and tear. Choose darker shades, therefore, to prolong the life of a decorative scheme.

USING PALE COLORS EFFECTIVELY

Keeping a room light and airy
Use pale colors to produce a very light and airy feel, as in this living room, where it is further enhanced by the use of both natural and artificial light. Maintain the continuity of these creamy tones throughout all the decorations in the room to achieve a unified, harmonious atmosphere.

USING DARK COLORS EFFECTIVELY

Creating warmth and coziness
Combine relatively pale colors on the walls with contrasting darker shades for the rest of the decoration in a room. This will produce a slightly enclosed, yet at the same time very comfortable, impression. Create an extra touch of opulence by making the dark colors rich and warm.

BLENDING AND TONING

Blending and toning can often be the most difficult concept to grasp when choosing colors. You need to decide which features of a room should be accentuated and which should be blended in with the general decor in order to produce a sympathetic color scheme.

MAINTAINING A BLEND

● **Setting the tone** Choose colors to suit a room's function and the impact you wish to make. Use subtle tones in areas of rest, more intense hues in activity rooms.
● **Creating mood** Select a shade that is appropriate for a room's mood. Slightly tinting a color one way or another can make all the difference.
● **Reducing impact** Use colors to make unsightly features less noticeable. Paint a radiator the same color as the walls, for example.

COLOR COORDINATING

Blending together
Choose a main wall color so that it blends in with the color of another significant feature in the room. In the example shown here, the natural wood finish of the fireplace and the furniture tones effectively with the pale ochre walls and smaller items such as paintings and ornaments to create a harmonious and relaxed feel in the room.

EXTENDING COLOR

Extending the same colors and designs from one surface to another is a further way of using color to balance a decorative scheme. This link can be made between all surfaces in a room including the flooring and furnishings, as well as the smaller decorative details.

LOCATING COLOR IN LESS OBVIOUS PLACES

Maintaining a theme between features
Link features or rooms together by sharing a theme, for example by extending a pattern from one decorative feature to another. Here, the bands of tricolored squares running above the kitchen work surface and above the baseboard have also been applied to the painted frame. Use constituent colors separately on other selected surfaces to echo and maintain the theme between features or rooms.

FOLLOWING GUIDELINES

● **Including ornaments** As well as using similar colors on all the major surfaces in a room, extend your color scheme to your ornaments and collections on display to match the components of your decorative plan further.
● **Incorporating textures** The textured aspect of a decorative plan can also be linked in with a color scheme. For example, reflect the different shades and tones produced by a natural flooring, such as sea-grass, in wicker baskets and other accessories in the room.
● **Scheming simply** The best effects are often created by means of a few simple color statements. Avoid including too many colors, since this tends to produce a very cluttered feel that will be too busy for most rooms.

COLOR SCHEMING

CHOOSING A COLOR SCHEME is exciting, but it can also be a little daunting. You may find it easy to select a main color but more difficult to finalize the smaller details, although these can often make or break the finished effect.

FINDING INSPIRATION

Inspiration comes naturally and easily to some people, but most of us need a little help in developing our artistic flair, or even in defining our own personal preferences. Try to identify a few key areas to help you before you start to make decisions about decorating.

LOOKING AROUND YOU

When selecting colors, you may find that inspiration is close at hand, so look around you before searching farther afield.

● **Existing decorations** Examine why your existing decorative scheme does not suit you, and to what extent the color scheme needs to be changed.
● **Magazines** Flick quickly through magazines to see which pages and images attract you and which colors they feature.
● **Paintings** Use paintings and prints that you have bought in the past as reminders of what appeals to you visually.

Looking at photographs
Browse through a photograph album, identifying favorite vacation pictures. Make a note of those colors that appeal to you in landscape photographs to give you an indication of your color preferences.

SEEKING HELP
● **Observing friends' homes** Although inspiration is an individual experience, you can learn a lot by looking at the color schemes in friends' homes. Try combining ideas from several sources.
● **Consulting professionals** If you visit a decorating outlet, ask their experts for advice on color scheming. This service is often free, and you may find it extremely useful.
● **Visiting showrooms** Most large outlets build showrooms to display entire rooms. Here you may observe the work of interior designers.

TRADITIONAL TIP

Using color charts
Many manufacturers now provide more than simple color swatches to aid your choice of colors. They will also advise on period color styles and how to combine colors to create an authentic look. Many of their materials have traditional finishes.

STARTING OUT
● **Trying technology** There are many computer programs available to help with home design and decoration. You can try out a range of different color schemes on screen before making any decisions or doing any work.
● **Considering lighting** You need to be aware of the lighting in a room, since this will affect colors. Study both natural light conditions and artificial lighting before selecting a color scheme.
● **Choosing accessories** Pick out the decorative accessories for a room before completing the color scheme if there is an object you particularly like or find inspiring.

USING SWATCHES

Painting lining paper
Make a reasonably sized color swatch by painting a piece of lining paper. Stick this on a wall temporarily so that you can observe a color as the light changes throughout the day.

BUILDING UP A COMPLETE DECORATING PLAN

Choosing the decoration of a room from scratch can provide an exciting challenge and thus be very rewarding on completion. From the starting point of your chosen color or several colors, follow through to every last detail of decorative materials, furnishings, and ornamentation in the room.

Choose fabrics for upholstery and window treatments that highlight one – or combine several – of the colors in your decorative plan

Select bowls and other ceramic ornaments so that they reflect the colors you have chosen

Pick out combinations of colors – in this case blue and pale terracotta – from vacation photographs that you particularly like

Look through books on painting or photography for ideas on using and combining color and tone

Use carpet samples to select appropriate shades to coordinate with the colors of other decorative materials and to complete your chosen color scheme

Make a much-loved ceramic pot the anchor point for color scheming, or buy a new item specifically for that purpose

Try out paint on a wall using samples – which are available in small quantities – before making a final decision about colors

SETTING STYLES

WHEN MAKING A DECORATIVE PLAN, you need to decide whether to follow an established style or create your own look. A combination of both is possible, with many permutations allowing you to be as creative as you wish.

FORMING IDEAS

As with color scheming, look for additional inspiration from various external sources when choosing a decorative style. Balance a number of different ideas carefully to achieve a result that you will be happy with and which will also be appreciated by other people.

DECIDING ON STYLE
● **Verifying age** If you wish to give your home a period look, do some thorough research into the requisite colors and styles before beginning work.
● **Watching movies** Watch movies and television programs as a source of inspiration and reference. In their need for authenticity, producers – especially of period dramas – need to pay attention to precise details.
● **Keeping existing style** If you are happy with an existing style, you may need simply to update or renew it. Do not feel obliged to change a look each time you redecorate.

KEEPING WITHIN BUDGET
● **Decorating lavishly** Consider the costs of reproducing a particular style. Extravagant drapes may be needed for a period look, for example. You will then need to cut back on other expenditure, such as that for decorative accessories.
● **Making structural changes** Costs rise if major structural work is carried out. Decide whether or not the benefits of the work will justify the additional expense incurred.
● **Choosing paint** Paint is less expensive than wallpaper or other materials. Adapt a style to include painted surfaces for a less costly option.

DOING RESEARCH

Source material for planning your style can be found in a number of different locations. All of these may inspire you and help you to form your ideas before making decisions.

● Exhibitions.
● Libraries.
● Magazines.
● Illustrated books.
● Craft fairs.
● Lifestyle and home-decorating programs.
● Theaters.
● Trade shows.
● Art galleries.
● Museums.
● Places of historical interest.

BRIGHT IDEA

Viewing period homes
Seek inspiration for original styles from period homes. Visit a few, particularly locally, to get a feel for the character of the region, and note inspiring elements.

USING COLLECTIONS

Use a personal collection as a basis for a theme, extending its appeal and making it a significant part of a room's decoration.

● **Using furniture** Some people collect furniture that reflects a particular historical period or influence. Use this theme as a basis for other decorations by matching colors and designs to complement the pieces.
● **Using pictures** Decorate a room so that your pictures will be enhanced by their surroundings. Large paintings can usually cope with lavish wall coverings, whereas smaller prints need a subtler backdrop that will not compete with them.

Stenciling a design
Copy an image from an item that is displayed in the room – part of a collection, for example – by tracing over it. Use this to create a stencil design which, as well as adding decorative appeal to the wall, will also complement the item or collection.

CONSIDERING OTHER FACTORS

In setting a style, there are a number of supplementary considerations that you need to take into account in order to achieve an authentic effect. These factors may not be obvious but can help in making the practical decisions that will shape the final plan.

BEING LAVISH
● **Using the right fabric** Lavish, sumptuous styles rely heavily on soft furnishings. To create this sort of feel, emphasize elaborate window treatments, extravagant furnishings, and the impression of swaths of material and cushions as well as soft, luxurious carpeting.

THINKING AHEAD
● **Considering your stay** If you will not be in a home for long, plan for short-term needs and avoid extravagant decor that you will need to leave behind.
● **Increasing value** Make sure that your home is decorated well. It will be far easier to sell – and fetch a higher price – when the time comes.
● **Dealing with trends** Decorative styles change as quickly as other fashions. To play safe, choose a fairly neutral plan and reflect fashion only in accessories.

CREATING FORMALITY
● **Being ordered** Formal styles can range from opulence to minimalism. However, designs for wallpaper or fabric should be precise and obvious to give an impression of regimented order. For example, choose striped designs for a neat, tidy, and ordered appearance.

MINIMIZING CHANGES
● **Following a design** Massive overhauls are not necessary to inject the idea of a style into a decorative plan. Select fabrics carefully for immediate effect. Gingham designs, for example, give a country-cottage feel, even if used relatively sparingly in a room.

CONSIDERING BUILDING STYLES

A particular decorative plan will work better in some surroundings than in others.

● **Reflecting reality** Consider authenticity. For example, a country-kitchen look is most convincing in a rural setting.
● **Maintaining a theme** When decorating part of your home, think about the impact on other areas and whether you will extend the style to them later. If a finish reflects a particular era, changing it may mean replacing other decorative features, too.

Reflecting architecture
Certain types of building are best suited to particular styles of decor. A look that works well in a Mediterranean villa may be out of place in a townhouse or a rustic, wooden home.

TRANSFORMING A SPACE INTO A LIVING AREA

Starting from scratch
For a major room facelift, or the creation of a living area in previously unused space, clear the room as much as possible. Here, a cold, uninviting room (above) has become welcoming and comfortable (right), and good use has been made of inherent features such as its unusual shape and natural light.

REFLECTING LIFESTYLES

WHEN MAKING DECISIONS ABOUT DECORATING, consider your lifestyle as well as your feelings about how living environments should appear. You may be constrained by architectural features, but there are many ways to adapt them.

SELECTING A STYLE

All decorators are, in effect, presented with a blank canvas on which to work. When planning your creation, you will need to strike a balance between a look you like and the functions a room will serve. First resolve basic requirements, then make adjustments to style.

LIVING IN AN URBAN ENVIRONMENT

Maximizing space
Space may well be at a premium if you live in a city dwelling. Consider an open-plan layout to help create a feeling of greater space or simply to make the most of the space that you have available. Light colors are more likely than dark shades to make a room feel spacious, especially if it has high ceilings. Think very carefully about the layout of and furnishings for an open-plan home. It can be challenging enough to coordinate the decoration of a small area, let alone take a creative overview of a large room that must serve multiple purposes. So take your time when making choices.

DESIGNING A COUNTRY KITCHEN

REFLECTING A REGIONAL STYLE

Recalling the simple life
Choose a country look for a kitchen to reflect a theme of uncomplicated living and promote comfort and relaxation in one of the busiest areas of the home. Reinforce this atmosphere by using a lot of wood, both painted and unpainted.

Adding an ethnic flavor
You can develop a theme with just a few details or create a complete replica of a regional style – be it local or from far afield. This Hispanic theme is simply produced with a little basic knowledge about the appropriate colors and designs.

SELECTING A MODERN OR A TRADITIONAL APPROACH

Being thoroughly modern

Modern decorative plans are often characterized as much by their selection of furniture, such as these striking chairs, as by their color scheme and choice of fabrics. A modern style is innovative, so you can give yourself scope to experiment and produce a style that reflects your own ideas.

Upholding tradition

Many people feel comfortable with traditional decorative themes, like the classic look of this room. Tried and tested over the years, such styles are to a certain extent guaranteed to give a satisfying result. You can choose from a wide range of options and are likely to find a selection to suit your taste.

CREATING A HOME IN ONE ROOM

Planning a room layout carefully

When one room is to be used for a number of purposes, design the decor largely according to practical concerns. Here, split-level accommodation creates space by suspending the sleeping area above ground level. The choice of a few ornate accessories, such as the mirror and the pillar support of the raised area, adds interest.

MAKING YOUR MARK

● **Adding to a look** There is no need to complete your decorative plan as soon as the main decorating job is completed. Collect and add accessories and ornaments over time until you feel you have achieved a total look.

● **Creating a focus** The most successful decorative plans result from well-chosen focal points that draw attention to detail. Fireplaces, furniture, and pictures all fall into this category. However, do not clutter up a room and reduce the impact of such features. Minimalist decorative plans draw attention to focal points.

● **Adapting a style** Take an established style and adapt it to suit you. This can be great fun and will add a touch of individuality. For example, include an extravagant material in a Shaker-style kitchen to contrast with the simple, utilitarian designs.

Painting Walls

QUICK REFERENCE

Preparing to Paint, p. 204

Improving Techniques, p. 206

Creating Paint Effects, p. 210

Finishing, p. 218

WALLS AND CEILINGS are usually the largest surface areas that you will paint in a home. As a result, wall color and texture form the backdrop for other decoration in a room. It is therefore important to prepare surfaces thoroughly and to use the correct technique for the finish required to ensure both the quality and long life of the decoration.

SELECTING MATERIALS

There is a vast and ever-increasing variety of painting materials in the marketplace; they broadly fit into a number of general categories. Water-based paints tend to dominate the wall-finish market because they are quick-drying and easy to use over large surface areas.

PAINT TYPES AND THEIR CHARACTERISTICS			
TYPE	FINISH	USES	COVERAGE
Flat latex	Water-based, dull matte; easy to work with and low-odor, therefore user-friendly.	All walls and ceilings; particularly suitable for new plaster since it allows it to dry out thoroughly.	650 sq ft/gal (16 m²/l)
Vinyl flat latex	Water-based, wipeable matte; more hard-wearing than ordinary flat latex.	All walls and low-wear areas; matte properties help to conceal many surface imperfections.	650 sq ft/gal (16 m²/l)
Vinyl gloss latex	Water-based, high sheen; very practical since wipeable and even washable.	All walls and ceilings; particularly suitable for kitchens and bathrooms since easy to clean.	620 sq ft/gal (15 m²/l)
Store-brand flat latex	Water- or oil-based, flat latex; several brands available with slight finish variations.	All walls and ceilings; ideal for achieving a traditional, flat paint finish.	650 sq ft/gal (16 m²/l)
Semigloss	Oil-based, medium sheen; some are low-odor and therefore more user-friendly than others.	All walls and ceilings, but particularly suitable for high-wear areas.	650 sq ft/gal (16 m²/l)
Quick-drying semigloss	Water-based acrylic, medium sheen; some are impregnated with fungicides.	All walls and ceilings; hard-wearing, low-odor, and quick-drying properties.	620 sq ft/gal (15 m²/l)
Textured	Water-based, thick matte; can be left plain or painted, and can have pattern superimposed.	All walls and ceilings; hard-wearing and covers poor surfaces and cracks well.	200 sq ft/gal (5 m²/l)

BASIC PAINTING EQUIPMENT

Having the most suitable tools for painting projects is important. There are several basic tools that should form part of every home decorator's painting kit, which may then be added to for tasks with more specific requirements. Buying good-quality equipment will reap benefits in the form of better, longer-lasting results.

● **Creating paint effects** If you intend to use paint effects, you will require some additional equipment as well as certain different materials (see p. 211).
● **Testing equipment** Before buying any painting equipment – but especially large, costly pieces – test them for sturdiness, and make sure that they have an adequate guarantee.

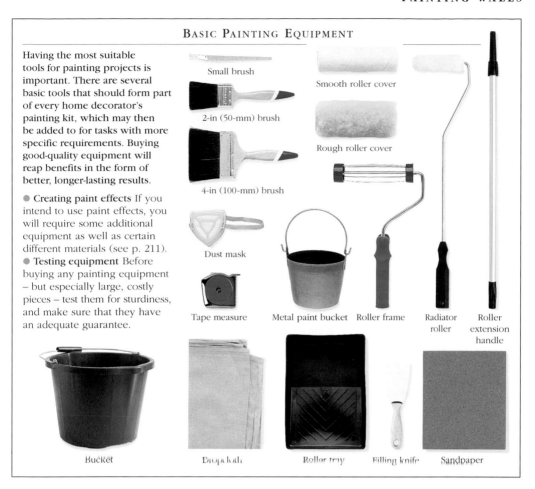

Small brush

Smooth roller cover

2-in (50-mm) brush

Rough roller cover

4-in (100-mm) brush

Dust mask

Tape measure   Metal paint bucket   Roller frame   Radiator roller   Roller extension handle

Bucket   Drop cloth   Roller tray   Filling knife   Sandpaper

MEASURING

Accuracy when estimating the amount of paint you require for decorating will save you money and result in less waste. Once the appropriate areas have been measured, use the chart opposite as a guide to rates of coverage in your calculations of paint quantities. These rates have been worked out assuming walls have average porosity.

● **Walls** Calculate the surface areas of walls simply by multiplying the height of a room from the ceiling to the top of the baseboard (or to the floor) by the entire length of the baseboard (or, alternatively, the perimeter of the floor).

● **Ceilings** To calculate the surface area of a ceiling, use the dimensions of the floor.
● **Doors and windows** Do not subtract the areas of doors or windows from your calculations. This means you will have enough paint left over for any touching up that may be necessary at a later date.
● **Extras** Make sure that you allow a little extra paint for items such as molding, wall or window recesses, pillars, covered beams, and alcoves.
● **Coverage** Most walls will require two coats of paint. Usually, the second coat will need only 80 percent of the paint required for the first coat.

SAFETY

Consider the following safety recommendations before you begin a painting project.

● **Preventing injury** Ensure that you store materials and tools away from children and pets. Many products contain chemicals that can cause irritation to the body.
● **Following instructions** Read all manufacturers' guidelines with regard to proper use of materials and equipment before using them.
● **Climbing safely** Inspect all ladders and stepladders carefully to make sure they are safe to use and show no serious signs of wear.

PREPARING TO PAINT

THE FIRST STAGE OF THE DECORATING PROCESS is important to the production of a top-quality finish, but it is often perceived as the most tedious. Taking time to prepare a wall thoroughly before painting will ensure a good result.

GETTING SURFACES READY

Protecting surfaces that are not to be painted is as important as preparing those that are. It is advisable to remove all furniture from a room to protect it from damage, to increase your working area, and to make it easier to identify those areas of wall needing most attention.

CLEARING & COVERING
● **Protecting furniture** If it is not possible to move all the furniture out of a room, stack large items in the center of the room and fit smaller pieces around them. Drape a plastic sheet over the furniture to keep dust off. Secure around the bottom with masking tape.
● **Covering floors** Cover floors with dropcloths or old household sheets. Use a double thickness of the latter since they are less impermeable.
● **Stopping movement** Secure dropcloths in position by baseboards with masking tape to prevent them from creeping.

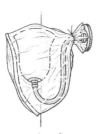
FILLING WALLS
● **Mixing filler** Mix filler to a firm, pastelike consistency. If too wet, it will shrink too much in a hole when it dries; if too dry, it will be difficult to work and dry too quickly.
● **Storing prepared filler** If you prepare too much filler, store the surplus, covered with plastic wrap, for later use.
● **Filling large gaps** Use newspaper to pack corner cracks and provide a base for filler. Deep holes will need a second fill before sanding.
● **Overfilling** Fill any holes slightly above the wall surface to allow for shrinkage.

COVERING LARGE AREAS

Using a caulking blade
If a wall has numerous scrapes and holes, use a caulking blade to spread filler across the whole or a large part of the damaged area. The broad blade surface will cover the area efficiently.

REPAIRING CORNERS

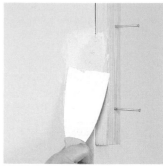

Using a support
To repair an external corner, nail a wood strip flush with one edge, then fill against it. Once the filler dries, remove the strip. Repeat on the other edge, and lightly sand.

MAKING ALTERATIONS
● **Putting up coving** Strip old wallpaper before attaching new coving to walls. Put coving in position before doing any further painting preparation.
● **Replacing woodwork** If you want to replace moldings or baseboards, do so before you paint the walls in order to avoid the possibility of them being damaged after they have been painted.
● **Organizing professionals** Hire qualified tradespeople to carry out any major electrical or plumbing alterations that are necessary before you start painting. Arrange for them to return once you have finished the decorating in order to attach any fixtures for you.

PREPARING WALLS

A smooth wall surface is essential, since paint highlights rather than hides imperfections. Sand excess filler and other rough areas back to a flat finish that is smooth to the touch. Prime with an appropriate sealer to stabilize the surface and make it ready to accept paint.

SANDING & SEALING
● **Sanding large areas** Use an electric sander for preparing large expanses of wall. Renting one for a day is not expensive.
● **Maximizing use** Once coarse sandpaper has become worn, you can use it for fine sanding before throwing it away.
● **Sealing new plaster** Dilute ten parts of flat latex with one part water for use as an excellent primer on new plaster. Choose white latex since it is the least expensive.
● **Sealing dusty walls** Mix one part PVA glue with five parts water to make an excellent sealer. It will have strong bonding properties and be ideal for use on powdery walls.

MAKING SANDING EASIER
● **Saving time** Before sanding, remove lumps of plaster or filler with a scraper. Only a light sanding will then be needed for total smoothness.

Fold sandpaper around wood

Using a sanding block
Wrap a piece of sandpaper tightly around a wood scrap to provide a firm base as you sand a wall. Rotate the sandpaper around the block as it wears.

CLEANING

Clean a ceiling thoroughly before you start painting it.

● **Reaching a ceiling** Rather than climbing a ladder with a bucket of water, use a squeegee mop to reach up.
● **Using detergent** Use a mild detergent for cleaning, then rinse with clean, warm water.

PREPARING PAINT

Paint will produce the finish that you require only if it is prepared correctly before you use it. Problems such as poor color matching, shadows, and a poor finish are usually not the fault of the paint manufacturer: more often they are the result of poor preparation by the user.

MIXING PAINT
Stir with slat

Maintaining color
You may require several cans of paint when decorating a large room. Pour all of them into one large bucket and mix to conceal color differences. Use a bucket with an airtight lid for storage.

REMOVING LUMPS
Pour paint into paint bucket through sieve

Sieving paint
However well it is stored, paint may form a skin in the can or acquire lumps and foreign bodies. Use a household sieve when decanting paint into a paint bucket to separate out these impurities.

STIRRING & DECANTING
● **Protecting paint** Before opening a can of paint, always use a soft brush to remove dust and dirt from the rim of the lid. Impurities may otherwise fall into the paint as you ease off the lid.
● **Hand stirring** Stir paint in several different directions rather than in a one-directional movement. Use a slight lifting motion as you stir to ensure an even color throughout and the dispersal of paint up from the base of the can.
● **Lining paint buckets** Use foil to line a paint bucket before decanting paint into it. Once the job is finished, the foil can be thrown away and there is no need to clean the bucket.

IMPROVING TECHNIQUES

IF YOUR PAINTING TECHNIQUES ARE GOOD, you will achieve the desired finish efficiently and accurately. You can cover large areas quickly with modern equipment. Never rush, and remember that speed will come with practice.

IMPROVING THE BASICS

Even if you have a preference for a particular technique, it is worth experimenting with alternative methods. You may be surprised to find that a technique that you had previously considered to be difficult is, in fact, easier than you thought and well within your capabilities.

FOLLOWING BASIC RULES
● **Smoothing walls** Rub down walls lightly between coats with fine-grade sandpaper.
● **Lighting efficiently** Paint with an indirect rather than a main light source illuminating your work. You will then be able to see more clearly where you have painted, especially on the second or third coat.
● **Keeping edges wet** Keep the edge wet as you paint along a wall, since differing drying times on the same surface may cause shading variations. Complete one wall at a time.
● **Covering well** Apply two coats if you are making a slight color change, but three if you are replacing dark with light.

LOADING PAINT
● **Filling trays and buckets** Fill a tray up to the bottom edge of its ribbed slope, and a paint bucket up to one-third full.

Distributing evenly
Run a roller head over the ribbed area of a paint tray to remove excess paint. This will also ensure that the paint is evenly distributed over the roller head.

TRADITIONAL TIP

Dampening brushes
Dampen paintbrushes before use to make them easier to work with. Wash your brushes regularly during painting to prevent the bristles from clogging up. Dampen rollers and pads, too.

SELECTING BRUSHES

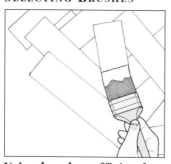

Using brushes efficiently
Choose a 4-in (100-mm) brush for painting walls. Using a smaller one will take too long, while a larger one will cause your wrist to tire. Apply random strokes in all directions, and do not overbrush. Lay off as with a roller.

ROLLING WALLS

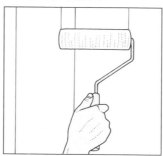

Covering evenly
Apply paint on a roller in vertical, slightly overlapping strips. One load should cover 1 sq yd (1 m²). Without reloading, lightly run the roller over the area to lay off the paint, removing excess and producing an even coverage.

USING PAINT PADS

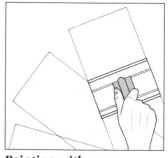

Painting with ease
Using a paint pad requires a minimal amount of technical ability. Prevent a buildup of paint by spreading it in all directions, but make sure that all areas within the range of the pad are sufficiently covered.

PAINTING AROUND EDGES

Painting around the edges of a wall is known as cutting in, and it requires great precision. Good defining lines between different surfaces will add professionalism to your decorating. Usually a brush is used, although corner rollers and miniature pads are available.

DEALING WITH EDGES

● **Overlapping** Cut in a little way onto molding and baseboards if they are to be painted. Then you will need to paint only one straight line – when you paint the woodwork.

● **Masking** If you are painting walls but not woodwork, apply a strip of masking tape along adjacent wooden edges. Do this also if you intend to apply a natural wood finish.

● **Painting around switches** Use a small brush to cut in around switches. Clean off oversplashes when they are dry with the edge of a filling knife or a window scraper.

● **Painting inaccessible areas** It is hard to paint between pipes and behind radiators. Use a long-handled radiator roller, or make a tool by taping a sawed-off paintbrush at a right angle to the end of a dowel.

PAINTING A WELL-DEFINED EDGE

● **Choosing brushes** Use a 2-in (50-mm) brush to paint in a corner. This will be small enough to maneuver, but will cover a reasonably sized area with a single loading of paint.

● **Hiding unevenness** Where the edge of the ceiling is undulating, cut in slightly below the wall–ceiling junction to produce a new line that is clearly defined and straight.

CUTTING IN AT A WALL–CEILING JUNCTION

1 Apply a strip of paint along the top of a wall between 1 and 2 in (2.5 and 5 cm) below the ceiling. Do not brush this trail out, and apply a thicker covering of paint than you would if you were painting the open wall.

2 With the brush now mostly unloaded of paint, spread the paint trail upward right into the wall–ceiling junction. Using the outermost bristles, bead the paint accurately into the corner, making a clean, straight line at the junction.

ADAPTING TECHNIQUES FOR PAINTING CEILINGS

Slight modifications in painting techniques are required when painting ceilings because of the difficulty in reaching them. You will need a sturdy stepladder. When decorating a whole room, make sure that you paint the ceiling first, thus preventing overspray onto walls that have already been decorated.

● **Increasing your height** If you find stepladders cumbersome, and you have low ceilings, you may be able to paint a ceiling merely by standing on an upturned wooden crate.

● **Dealing with light fixtures** Unscrew ceiling roses rather than attempting to paint around them. Make sure that the electricity is turned off first.

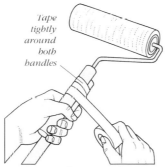

Tape tightly around both handles

Staying on the ground
Reduce the amount of work you have to do up a ladder when painting a ceiling by using an extension pole with a roller or paint pad. If you do not want to buy an extension pole, improvise by taping a roller or paint pad to one end of a broom handle.

● **Overlapping walls** If walls are to be painted, overlap ceiling paint 2 in (5 cm) onto the wall. You will find it is easier to cut in the wall color at the wall–ceiling junction than vice versa.

● **Protecting from overspray** If you are not using a drip guard, protect yourself from spray by wearing a long-sleeved shirt and a cap, or use nondrip paint.

● **Making a drip guard** Cut a dishwashing-liquid bottle in half vertically. Attach one half to a roller cage by screwing the cage's retaining screws through holes at ends of the bottle. When you roll, any paint spray will be caught by the guard. You may need to modify the design and method of attachment for different brands of roller.

USING EQUIPMENT

Technological developments continually bring new painting equipment and tools into the marketplace and improve existing decorating methods. Paint sprayers, for example, are more suitable for use in the home than they used to be and are readily available for purchase or rent.

EMBRACING TECHNOLOGY

● **Reducing effort** Use battery-powered rollers and brushes to eliminate the need for reloading. Paint is pumped through a tube onto the roller or brush head, thus speeding up the painting process and making it easier.

● **Improving coverage** Use commercial one-coat paints to reduce significantly the time it takes to decorate a room. These paints are ideal for partial redecoration and for freshening up a room quickly.

● **Buying multipurpose tools** These days manufacturers produce ladders, for example, with far more than their traditional purpose in mind. Combination ladders have several uses – as trestles and working platforms as well as conventional stepladders.

CHOOSING TO PAINT WITH A SPRAYER

● **Spraying with ease** Hand-held, airless spray guns are light and relatively easy to use. Practice on a piece of newspaper. Clean the nozzle regularly for an even coating.

● **Following guidelines** Apply several even, thin coats for a flat, even finish: thick coats make paint more likely to run. Spraying can be messy, so mask off bordering surfaces.

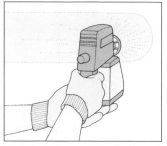

Maintaining a steady hand
With one hand in control of the trigger, use the other to steady the sprayer. Keep the nozzle about 12 in (30 cm) from the wall. Wear lightweight gloves to protect your hands from overspray.

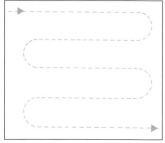

Covering a wall
Spray in a continuous motion, backward and forward across a wall and from top to bottom. Spray a little beyond each wall edge. Keep spraying until the wall is completely covered.

SAFETY

As with any equipment, read manufacturer's instructions carefully when using a paint sprayer. There are particularly important safety points to remember in this case.

● **Wearing protective clothing** Wear a mask and goggles when using a paint sprayer. Never inhale the fine mist of paint or get it into your eyes.

● **Protecting hands** Never put your hands in front of a sprayer's nozzle. The paint wis expelled at high pressure and could cause injury.

● **Disconnecting power** Always disconnect a paint sprayer from the power supply before you remove the nozzle – in order to clear blockages, for example.

CHOOSING PAINTING TOOLS

TOOLS	CHARACTERISTICS AND SUITABILITY
Brush	Brushes are multipurpose and come in many shapes and sizes. They are ideal for cutting in and painting intricate details, and can be used on open wall surfaces, but will be slower than other tools.
Roller	Rollers are ideal for wide, open surfaces, being by far the quickest tools for covering walls efficiently. The size of them varies, but rollers are too big for cutting in. The texture of rollers also varies.
Sprayer	Sprayers are ideal where little masking is required and for painting broad wall surfaces and inaccessible areas, such as behind pipes. Using a sprayer can be a messy business, so protect adjacent surfaces.
Pad	Pads are suitable for large surfaces, and small pads are available for cutting in. They cause less mess than rollers. Use them where extensive masking would otherwise be necessary, such as in kitchens.

EMPHASIZING TEXTURE

Greater depth and texture can be produced by applying specialty coatings and paints to wall surfaces. These finishes look effective and are almost as easy to apply as more conventional paints. Their thick formulation means that they literally add another dimension to your painting.

MAKING PATTERNS

Using tools
Use a small grout spreader to create a design. Work in areas of about 1 sq yd (1 m²), or the paint will dry before you have made the pattern. A semicircular shape is easy to reproduce if you want to keep the design relatively simple.

DEALING WITH CORNERS

Cutting in
Use a small stippling brush to apply paint in corners, since a textured roller will not reach right in. Dab lightly with a well-loaded brush to achieve the rough finish produced by a textured roller on an open wall.

LEAVING WALLS LOOKING NATURAL

Many wall surfaces provide a textured or natural look in their own right. This requires minimal additional finishing.

● Natural stone Seal natural stone with diluted PVA glue (one part PVA to five parts water). This will provide a finish, while the bonding properties of the PVA-based sealer will reduce dust.
● Brick Use commercial watersealants to give bricks a low-sheen finish that is attractive and functional.
● Bare plaster A well-plastered room can itself be pleasing. Seal with two or three coats of water-based matte varnish.

APPLYING SPECIALTY COATINGS TO CEILINGS

Specialty coatings designed with ceilings in mind can provide effective finishes. They are ideal for areas that are prone to cracking, or for uneven ceilings that need to look more uniform. As with textured paint, you can create a wide variety of patterns with tools designed specifically for the task, or, by improvising with different implements, you can create your own individual look.

● Getting help Try to find someone to help you with the application of a textured coating to a ceiling, since it is a difficult job to do on your own. One of you can apply the coating, while the other follows behind creating the pattern.
● Cleaning as you go Keep a bucket of clean water at hand as you texture a ceiling. Rinse your tools regularly in the water to prevent them from becoming clogged up with the coating.
● Finishing edges Frame a finished ceiling by dragging a 1-in (25-mm) brush through the textured coating all the way around the perimeter. This will create a precise, well-defined edge to enhance the finish.

Removing drip tips
Once a textured coating is dry, gently brush the ceiling with a household broom to remove any excess coating. Otherwise, when you paint the ceiling, rollers will catch on the drip tips, hampering an even paint distribution.

Creating effects
Use a crumpled plastic bag to create a textured effect. Turn the bag regularly so that you use a clean area to make the imprint. Wear surgical gloves to prevent your hands from becoming caked, and keep some bags at hand.

CREATING PAINT EFFECTS

YOU CAN CREATE A WIDE RANGE OF EFFECTS by using paints and glazes. Use paint for designing patterns and deceiving the eye with color and perspective. Use glazes for their semitransparent quality to produce depth and translucence.

CONSIDERING OPTIONS

Simple paint effects can have just as much impact as those involving more complex techniques. If you are a beginner, choose a simple effect that uses colored emulsions. You can mix colored glazes, and attempt more extravagant finishes, as you gain experience.

CHOOSING EFFECTS
● **Selecting methods** There are two main methods of creating paint effects. Either a tool is dipped into paint or glaze and then applied to a wall, or a glaze is applied to a wall with a brush and a tool is pressed into the glaze. The former is an "on" technique; the latter is "off." Even if you use the same glaze and the same tool, a different finish will be achieved depending on which method you employ.
● **Applying a base coat** Always apply a base coat. Light shades are best, since you can then build up color: semigloss or latex are ideal.

PREPARING TO PAINT
● **Roughing it** Examine walls carefully. Rough, textured walls are ideal for sponging, which disguises defects, while smooth, completely flat walls will show stippling off to its best.
● **Assessing suitability** Choose ragging and bagging rather than rag rolling on a wall that has pipework or switches. Rag rolling needs a constant motion without frequent interruptions. Joins are difficult to disguise.
● **Getting ready** Make sure that all materials and tools are ready for use, since once you start a wall you should finish it without interruption. If you do not, some areas will dry before others and the joins will show.

TYPES OF PAINT EFFECT

Whichever paint effect you choose, make sure that you have all tools and materials at hand.

Try to maintain consistent hand movements from one wall to another for an even overall finish.

Sponging on
Sponging (see p. 212) is probably the easiest paint effect to create. Latex paints or glazes can be used. Natural sea sponges are the ideal tools to work with, although synthetic sponges can be substituted.

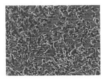

Sponging off
A mixed glaze should be used for this effect (see p. 212). A sea sponge must be used since substitutes tend to smudge the finish. This is a natural progression from sponging on in terms of difficulty.

Ragging
Ragging (see p. 213) involves a similar technique to that of sponging, except a crumpled, lint-free cloth is used instead of a sponge. A mixed glaze should be used for the best results.

Bagging
Bagging (see p. 213) involves the same technique as ragging, except a plastic bag is used instead of a rag. This creates a more sharply defined texture compared to the fabric alternatives used in ragging.

Rag rolling
Rag rolling (see p. 213) involves rolling a twisted rag down a wall to create a repeating pattern. It is best to rag roll off, since uniformity and consistency are difficult to achieve when applying on.

Stippling
A stippled effect (see p. 212) is created by pressing the bristle tips of a stippling brush into a wet glaze. The technique is only suitable with glazes, and continuity is important to prevent joins or overlaps.

ADDITIONAL PAINTING EQUIPMENT

Building up a paint-effect tool kit can be expensive, so do it gradually. Buy equipment as you need it, rather than purchasing everything that you think you may need in the future, only to find that you use few items.

● **Improvising** You can use tools other than special-effect equipment for paint techniques. Experiment with different objects – ordinary household items as well as decorating tools – to create unique effects.

Large decorating brush

Varnishing brush

Lint-free cloth

Stippling brush

Masking tape

Stenciling brush

Natural sponge

Craft knife

Plastic bag

Cutting mat

COLORWASHING

Colorwashing is probably the oldest paint technique. Use a large paint brush to apply a highly diluted glaze to wall surfaces. This will produce a translucent finish through which the base coat shows, creating depth and texture.

● **Stabilizing a wash** A wash should have the consistency of highly diluted paint. To prevent it from running off the walls, add a small amount of PVA glue to the mix to help it adhere to the wall.
● **Adding depth** Apply several coats, and vary color slightly to create a wonderful feeling of depth. Warm colors will give a glow to any room.
● **Choosing walls** Apply a wash to a rough surface to create texture. The color will clear from the peaks but build up in the troughs, creating a great textured finish.

MAKING GLAZES

A glaze is the medium for creating paint effects. It is distinguished by its ability to hold patterned impressions and by its long drying time that allows you to create effects. Glazes have traditionally been oil based, but modern acrylics are popular and are often premixed.

COLORING GLAZES

Mix colors before adding to glaze

Mixing acrylic colors

Use an artist's brush to mix acrylic colors. Mix the color first on a surface such as a paint-can lid, and make sure it is the right shade. Decant the basic glaze into an old jelly jar, and add the acrylic color to it.

CALCULATING QUANTITIES

● **Diluting color** For a good acrylic-based glaze, five to ten percent of the mixture should be color and the rest glaze. Add the color to the glaze and mix thoroughly. A clean jelly jar is ideal for mixing small quantities of color in this way, since you can screw the lid on tightly before shaking the colors to mix them well.
● **Estimating amounts** Glazes go much farther than standard paints. Dilute acrylic glazes with a small amount of water to increase the coverage of the glaze. Estimate how much you will need by halving the amount of standard paint you would require to cover the same-sized area of wall.

TRADITIONAL TIP

Mixing a traditional glaze

Mix six parts of turpentine with three parts of boiled linseed oil and one part of white, oil-based undercoat or semigloss. Tint the glaze using artist's oil paints.

SPONGING

Whether sponging whole walls or selected areas, such as beneath a chair rail, this effect transforms the look of a flat wall surface. A single layer of sponging produces a subtle, airy pattern, while multiple layers produce a busier, bolder effect that has greater depth.

SPONGING SUCCESSFULLY
● **Removing excess** When sponging on, decant the glaze onto an old plate or rimmed paint-can lid. Dip the face of a damp sponge into the glaze, and remove excess by drawing the sponge across the rim; otherwise, the first impression will be thick and blotchy. If you do apply too much, reapply some base color.
● **Rotating the hand** Rotate the hand into a slightly different position after each impression to keep the pattern random.
● **Sponging corners** Tape a small piece of sponge onto the end of a pencil to enable you to reach into corners.

USING COLOR EFFECTIVELY

Sponging dark onto light
Use a light base coat and gradually apply darker shades on top to produce a highly distinctive pattern. The color of the final coat applied will always be the most dominant.

Sponging light onto dark
Use a dark base coat and apply progressively lighter shades on top for a translucent effect. You will see a larger color range since the light colors will not obliterate preceding coats.

STIPPLING

Stippling is a subtle paint effect using a brush to create the impression of a textured surface that may range from a light, velvety appearance to a coarser finish, depending on the size and compactness of the bristles. This is a time-consuming technique, but it is very satisfying.

CHOOSING BRUSHES
● **Using specialty brushes** If you can afford one, buy a stippling brush, which is ideal for stippling since it consists of a thick wad of bristles.

Finding an alternative
For a less costly alternative to a stippling brush, trim the bristles of a wallpaper-hanging brush with sharp scissors. Make a flat pad of bristles so that all the ends will be in contact with the wall.

STIPPLING EFFECTIVELY
● **Working in sections** Apply glaze in areas of about 1 sq yd (1 m²), using a large paint brush. Cover as evenly as you can, then dab the stippling brush lightly on the wet glaze.
● **Creating uniformity** Work from left to right and top to bottom. Do not overlap stipples, because they will appear as more heavily shaded areas.
● **Preventing clogging** After each area has been stippled, wipe the head of the brush with a lint-free cloth to remove excess glaze. A buildup of glaze will create a patchy effect over the wall.
● **Adding depth** Use a slightly darker glaze in the corners of a wall than toward the center to create a feeling of depth.

TIME-SAVING TIP

Glazing with a roller
Use a fine mohair roller to apply glaze to a wall. This is much quicker than using a brush and therefore allows more time for creating an effect. Do not overload the roller, or the glaze might run.

RAGGING

Ragging is similar to sponging, except that a crumpled lint-free cloth is used rather than a sponge. Ragging "off" (see p. 210) is easier and more effective than ragging "on." With the latter, cloths become clogged up with glaze, producing a rather gummy, patchy finish.

CREATING THE EFFECT

Building up pattern
Using a damp, scrunched-up rag, apply light pressure on the glaze. Change your grip frequently to produce a random pattern. Return to missed areas before the glaze dries. Rinse the cloth regularly.

SHIELDING SURFACES

Avoiding smudges
Hold a strip of cardboard against the adjacent wall to prevent the edge of the rag from smudging color onto it. Move the cardboard down as you paint. Wipe it regularly to avoid a glaze buildup.

BAGGING

Use the same technique as for ragging, but substitute a plastic bag for the lint-free cloth.

● **Choosing bags** You will need a ready supply of bags at hand so that you can throw one away and pick up a new one as you need to.
● **Experimenting** Different types of plastic create different effects: do not be afraid to experiment.
● **Softening edges** Bagging creates an angular effect. For a more understated look, gently brush the bagged surface. Use a softening or wallpaper-hanging brush.

RAG ROLLING

Rag rolling requires a more ordered technique than simple ragging, because the effect created is one-directional: it mimics falling material. It is ideal for areas such as those beneath chair rails and in wall panels, since it is difficult to execute uniformly over large areas.

ROLLING SUCCESSFULLY

● **Choosing rags** Make sure that your rags are all cut to the same size and made from the same material. The pieces should not include seams.
● **Applying glaze** Apply the glaze in strips from top to bottom of the area to be ragged. Make each strip slightly wider than the rolls.
● **Dealing with corners** You need both hands to roll a rag down the wall, making it impossible to shield adjacent walls. Make sure that you mask the nearest 6 in (15 cm) of the adjacent wall with newspaper and masking tape.
● **Combining techniques** Stipple the glaze before rag rolling to create a softer, more material-like effect.

PREPARING RAGS

● **Having supplies at hand** Roll up a number of rags before you begin to create this paint effect, and keep them close at hand once you have started.

Keep rag rolls together in paint tray

Making lengths consistent
Tie off the ends of the rags so that the central portions are of a consistent size. Keep them in a paint tray to prevent them from picking up dust, which would then be transferred to the walls.

IMPROVING TECHNIQUE

Maintaining uniformity
Start rag rolling in one of the top corners of the area to be covered to establish a straight edge all the way down. Overlap each length of rolling slightly, to make a continuous pattern.

CREATING STRIPES

Stripes are commonly associated with formality and a sense of order within a room. Creating your own stripes gives you lots of scope to design highly original patterns and use color effectively. Choose imaginatively when it comes to equipment and methods of application.

USING A CHALK LINE

Ensuring that lines are straight is very important in decorating. Use this traditional technique to mark out lines in readiness for painting stripes.

● **Snapping a line** Measure and mark off the widths of the stripes along the top of the wall. At each mark, tap in a 1-in (2.5-cm) nail up to about half its length, having checked that there are no pipes or wires beneath the surface. Hook a chalk line over the nail, and pull taut to the floor, making sure that it is vertical. Gently pull the chalk line away, and snap it against the wall to create a chalk impression. Remove the nail, and repeat the process at the next mark.

MARKING OUT STRIPES

● **Chalking lines** Buy powdered chalk (contrasting with the wall color) to fill a chalk-line reservoir, or rub a stick of chalk along a piece of string.

Masking off areas

Run masking tape down the chalk guidelines before painting. Secure firmly the edge adjacent to the area to be painted; leave the other edge loose for easy removal. Use a soft brush to dust away the chalk before painting.

STRIPING FREEHAND

● **Rolling stripes** Masking guidelines can be a long job: save time by settling for a less exact finish. Use a masked roller – preferably a foam one.

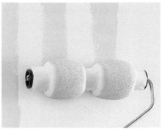

Using a masked roller

Wrap two pieces of 1-in (2.5-cm) masking tape tightly around a 7-in (17.5-cm) roller. Load with paint and roll the wall, creating the striped effect. Use the right-hand stripe as a guideline to align the roller for the next run.

ROLLING PATTERNS

● **Varying stripes** Extend the technique of creating stripes using a roller to include all kinds of patterns within the stripes. Create different designs by modifying the roller itself.

Cut-out areas do not pick up paint

Using a patterned roller

Use a craft knife to cut diamond shapes, for example, out of a foam roller sleeve before use. Apply paint from a tray in the usual way: the diamond-shaped holes will not pick up paint, creating a pattern on the wall.

MAKING A CHECKERED PATTERN

Combine horizontal and vertical stripes to produce a pattern of checks similar to that of gingham. The color that you use for the horizontal stripes should be lighter than that used for the verticals. This will create a third color at the crossover points.

1 Use a long level to keep the stripes vertical. Move the level down the wall each time you reload the roller. Work from right to left so that you do not smudge the stripes that have already been painted.

2 Allow the vertical stripes to dry thoroughly. Use the level horizontally to paint the top layer of stripes. Work from the top downward. The stripes may have uneven edges, but this adds to the material effect.

STENCILING

This technique allows you to reproduce a design or pattern accurately over a surface as many times as you like. Stencils can be made up of a single sheet or a number of superimposed layers. The latter option creates depth and allows you to use different colors.

USING STENCILS

● **Loading brushes** Cover the ends of the bristles evenly, but with only a minimal amount of paint. Remove excess on paper before applying to the wall. Too thick a coverage of paint will make it seep under the edges of the stencil.

● **Holding in place** Keep a stencil in position on a wall with masking tape. Low-tack tape will not pull the base coat off when the stencil is moved.

● **Mixing color** Stencils offer an excellent opportunity to mix and vary colors. Create subtle differences in shade from one area to another to produce a mellow, aged effect.

● **Keeping stencils clean** Wash acetate stencils regularly in warm water to keep their edges clean and free of paint.

CREATING DEPTH

● **Using shading** To lend a three-dimensional effect to a stenciled image, vary the degree of color shading across it.

Shading around edges
Make the color intensity greater around the edges of a design. To add more depth, shade one of the edges slightly more, creating an impression of shadow and hence directional sunlight.

CHOOSING AN IMAGE

● **Getting ideas** Use books and magazines as inspiration. Make sure that the image you choose has a distinct outline and clear detail within it.

TRACING & CUTTING A STENCIL

Cutting mat

1 If you make an acetate stencil, you will not need to trace an image first. Secure acetate over an image with masking tape, and trace outline and detail with a wax crayon.

2 Cut the stencil carefully so that it has smooth lines. You will use one stencil to create many images, so make a good job of it. Use a cutting mat if you are cutting a lot of stencils.

PLACING DESIGNS

● **Stenciling a border** Use a level and a soft pencil to draw a continuous line all around the walls about 12 in (30 cm) from the ceiling, having measured the correct drop at several points around the room. Sit the bottom edge of the stencil on this line, and follow the line around with the stencil, thus creating an attractive border. Do not forget to rub out the pencil line carefully with an eraser once you have finished.

● **Grouping images** Follow through a theme by grouping images together. Animals are a popular subject for this treatment. Three leaping dolphins in a bathroom, for example, or a collection of farmyard animals in a kitchen can look very effective.

SELECTING TOOLS

● **Cutting stencils** Use a craft knife, ideally with a narrow handle for easy maneuvering. Cut stencil edges at a slight angle to limit paint seepage.

FINDING ALTERNATIVES TO A BRUSH

Experiment with other implements for stenciling instead of a stenciling brush to produce a range of effects.

● **Sponging** Use a natural sea sponge to create a highly textured stenciled effect.

● **Crayoning** Try special stenciling crayons or traditional crayons. Ensure that the end of the crayon is very rounded, and use it in a circular motion.

● **Spraying** If you are using aerosol paints, which are ideal for stenciling, mask all around the stencil with newspaper to prevent overspray beyond the image.

● **Improvising** Cut down the bristles of an old paintbrush to make a stenciling brush.

PRINTING

Printing offers an alternative to stenciling in transferring a painted image on to a wall. It need not be an exact science, and you can use a variety of tools. Stamping and blocking are the techniques: an image stands above a stamp; with a block it takes up the whole surface area.

CHOOSING EQUIPMENT

● **Stamping** Buy stamps or make your own by cutting a design into a small piece of linoleum. Glue a wooden block to the back of the linoleum to act as a handle. Load paint onto the face of the stamp with a rigid mini-roller.
● **Blocking** Use household objects such as sponges or potato halves to make a block. These sorts of "tools" are readily available to you and achieve a very good texture.
● **Increasing depth** Vary texture by stamping or blocking onto a piece of paper before applying the tool to the wall, to reduce the density of paint.

USING STAMPS

Rolling onto a wall
Place the bottom edge of a stamp on the wall, and roll it onto the wall until the top edge makes contact. Hold for a second, then lift off carefully. This motion will ensure a crisp, clean impression.

CHOOSING BLOCKS

Making a block
Transfer a shape onto a household sponge, and cut it out with sharp scissors. Place the sponge fully onto the wall and agitate it slightly without changing its position. Reload frequently.

CREATING MURALS

Producing a mural is not as daunting as you may think; it is simply another method of transferring a drawn or copied image onto a wall. Some artistic ability is helpful but not essential, since – in its simplest form – this technique is no different from painting by numbers.

USING AN IMAGE OF YOUR OWN CHOICE

● **Selecting an image** Choose a subject that suits the nature of the room in which it is to appear, and that is not too detailed and difficult to copy.

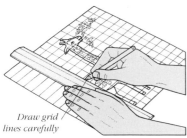

Draw grid lines carefully

1 Secure some tracing paper over an image. Measure out and draw an accurate grid so that it covers the picture. A grid made up of 1 in by 1 in (2.5 cm by 2.5 cm) squares is a standard workable size.

2 Scale up the grid onto the wall using chalk or a soft pencil. Using the first grid as a guide, fill in the corresponding squares on the wall. Erase the chalk dust or pencil lines when you have finished.

SAVING TIME

● **Projecting a design** Use a slide or overhead projector to transfer a design directly onto a wall. Adjust the size by moving the projector closer to or farther away from the wall.
● **Painting quickly** Have a selection of different-sized brushes at hand, so that you will have the right size for the area you are painting.
● **Painting with a steady hand** Hold one end of a 18-in (45-cm) length of dowel with your nonpainting hand, and place the other end against the wall (pad the dowel to prevent it from scratching the paintwork). Rest the forearm of your painting arm on the central section of the dowel to maintain a steady hand.

DECEIVING THE EYE

Paint can be used to create all sorts of different illusions on a flat surface. These illusions vary greatly in complexity, and many of them require a lot of time and care to execute. Simple applications, however, can often prove just as effective as more extravagant ideas.

CREATING THE IMPRESSION OF STONE BLOCKS

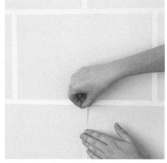  

1 Paint the whole wall with a light base color. Mark out block shapes with strips of ½-in (1-cm) masking tape. The masked areas will be the mortar lines in the finished effect.

2 Sponge on two coats that are darker than the mortar color. Apply the second before the first has dried, so that the colors merge. Apply lots of paint for texture. Allow to dry.

3 Remove the masking tape to reveal the mortar. For a weathered effect, mix burnt umber with a little yellow ochre, and paint some cracks with a fine-tipped artist's brush.

PAINTING INTERIOR SURFACES TO LOOK LIKE EXTERNAL WALLS

● **Increasing texture** Use coarse-grained, exterior masonry paint for the base coat to add texture and create effective mortar. You can add sand to interior latex for a similar effect.

● **Varying color and texture** Choose paint colors according to the type of surface you wish to mimic. Apply using a fibrous sea sponge to achieve a more finely textured finish.

● **Being authentic** Increase realism by enhancing the outlines of shapes with a soft pencil. Darkening the edges will add depth. Do this before removing the masking tape.

INCLUDING *TROMPE L'OEIL* IMAGERY IN YOUR DECORATING

Technically, painting stonework is *trompe l'oeil*, but the term is more commonly associated with the reproduction of specific objects on a wall. Such images appear three-dimensional and therefore seem lifelike.

● **Keeping it simple** If you are a beginner, do not be too bold. Recreating a life-sized kitchen cabinet, for example, would test the most experienced decorator. Small items such as picture frames are a good start.

● **Mixing real with false** This will often produce the most realistic *trompe l'oeil*. For example, paint in a decorative cord between a vertical row of hanging plates or pictures.

Painting flat surfaces
Producing an illusion of depth on a flat surface is not easy. Paying attention to small details, however, will add considerably to the realism of the effect. Paint an illusory cabinet in the same style as the real furniture in the room.

Using an alcove
Alcoves provide an opportunity to paint faux shelves. The depth of the recess adds yet another dimension to the effect. Hang real items alongside imaginary ones, which will help to bring the whole picture to life.

FINISHING

THERE ARE A NUMBER OF FINAL TOUCHES that can enhance the finish of any painting project and smooth the way for future work. Once you have finished, make sure that you clean equipment thoroughly and store it it well.

PREVENTING AND CORRECTING MISTAKES

It is almost inevitable that you will have some problems with your painted surfaces – most resulting from inadequate preparation or poor technique. Many can be corrected with only a little amount of extra work, which is well worth doing to avoid spoiling the overall finish.

DRYING PROPERLY
● **Avoiding patches** Not allowing paint to dry out fully before recoating may produce a shadowed or patchy finish. In such a case, leave for 24 hours, and apply another coat.
● **Speeding up drying** In a cold or damp room, reduce drying time by heating the room or opening windows. Otherwise, paint may wrinkle or discolor.

REMOVING OVERSPILL
● **Cleaning fixtures** If paint gets onto electrical fixtures, remove it carefully when dry using a scraper or filling knife.
● **Dealing with woodwork** Wall paint on woodwork need not be a problem if the woodwork is to be painted. Sand back pronounced drips or areas of roller spray.

DEALING WITH CRACKS
● **Settlement cracking** The appearance of cracks in wall surfaces soon after painting usually indicates movement of the building. This is common in new houses as settlement occurs. Redecorate affected areas when movement ceases.
● **Prolonged cracking** Persistent movement because of climate, the age of the building, or the installation of heating can be more of a problem. Consider using flexible commercial paints and fillers, or lining the walls to cover hairline cracks.

RECTIFYING PAINT FAULTS

There are various common paint faults that can haunt decorators. Most can be solved with relative ease, and few necessitate a fresh start. Use a fine-grade sandpaper when repairing a top coat.

Poor coverage
This is the simplest of mistakes, resulting from not enough paint or too few coats being applied. Recoat the area, being sure to load equipment correctly and spread the paint using the appropriate technique.

Brush marks
Brush marks may remain visible on the painted surface once they are dry. Small areas may be acceptable on the grounds that they create a traditional feel, but larger areas should be sanded and recoated.

Roller trails
Roller trails are caused by not laying off the paint during application and allowing too much paint to gather at the roller edges. Carefully sand back the affected area, and touch up carefully with a brush.

Flaking paint
Paint is likely to flake if it has been applied to an unsealed, dusty wall. Sand the affected area back until the flakes have been removed, stabilize the surface with a commercial sealer, then recoat with paint.

Assorted stains
There are a number of miscellaneous stains, resulting from rust spots for example, that may show through a top coat. Cover the area with an oil-based undercoat or primer, allow to dry, and repaint with top coat.

Drip marks
Drip marks on a painted surface occur when paint has been applied too thickly and therefore begins to sag or run down before it dries. Sand back the affected area, then touch up with top coat using a small brush.

CLEANING AND STORING EQUIPMENT

Keeping equipment clean ensures that it will be in good working order the next time you want to use it, and that it will not deteriorate more quickly than it should. Efficient and ordered storage makes it easy to find items and work out your requirements for future projects.

CARING AFTER USE

● **Conserving water** Most wall paints are water-based, so you can wash brushes and other painting equipment under a running tap. Remove excess paint on newspaper first, thus reducing the amount of water required for cleaning, and limiting the amount of paint entering the water supply.

● **Washing brushes** Massage a small amount of household detergent into the bristles of brushes to speed up cleaning. This will also make the bristles softer and more flexible when you need to use them again.

● **Preventing rust** After cleaning metal items such as roller cages and paint trays, make sure that you dry them thoroughly with a soft cloth; otherwise, they may rust.

● **Recycling paint cans** Wash out paint cans thoroughly when you have finished with the paint, and use for storing a variety of household items.

CLEANING THOROUGHLY

● **Using a scourer** If you do not clean a paintbrush well after you have finished using it, paint will accumulate at the base of the bristles and on the ferrule, and the brush's life will be reduced considerably.

Ferrule

Scouring a ferrule
Clean off dried-on or stubborn paint from ferrules and brush handles using a kitchen scourer. You can also use a scourer on the bristles but only lengthwise; otherwise, the bristles will splay out and lose their shape.

DISPOSING OF PAINT

● **Protecting the environment** Never dispose of decorating materials down sinks or drains. Pour all paint leftovers into one can, secure the lid tightly, and dispose of it with the rest of the household waste.

BRIGHT IDEA

Labeling paint cans
Always label cans after decorating, noting which room of the house they were used in, and on what date. Use self-adhesive labels or strips of masking tape.

STORING BRUSHES

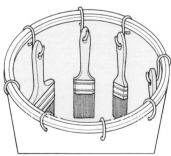

Hanging brushes
Hang brushes from hooks around the inside of a can or bucket. (Dry any damp bristles first with a hairdryer; otherwise, they will stick together.) Stored in this way, bristles will be protected from the risk of being crushed.

STORING MATERIALS

● **Keeping paint** Store paints inside the house if possible. They can be adversely affected by temperature fluctuations. Hold lids on firmly and shake cans to produce an airlock to prevent a skin from forming.

● **Storing glazes** Write the recipe for a glaze on the side of the jar in case you want to mix more at a later date.

● **Caring for stencils** Store stencils between pieces of cardboard and somewhere flat, such as in a book. Stencils can be reused only if they sit flat.

● **Storing dropcloths** Launder dropcloths before storing so that they do not spread dust.

REMOVING PAINT

However carefully you place dropcloths over a floor and fasten them down with masking tape before you start decorating, some paint splashes may find their way on to the carpet. Deal with them promptly and effectively.

● **Using a craft knife** Allow the paint to dry completely, then scrape across the surface with a craft knife. Hold the blade at right angles to the floor to avoid cutting into the carpet. The paint will gradually crumble, and you can then remove it with a vacuum cleaner.

COVERING WALLS

QUICK REFERENCE

Choosing Wallpaper, p. 222

Preparing to Paper, p. 224

Improving Techniques, p. 226

Papering Awkward
Areas, p. 230

Adding Borders, p. 233

Other Wall Coverings, p. 234

Finishing, p. 236

THE MOST COMMON ALTERNATIVE to painting walls is wallpapering. More innovative decorators may alternatively like to use fabric in a similar way to wallpaper. For a solid, traditional finish, various types of wooden paneling, which may be painted or left natural, can be used. The many wall-covering options make it easy to select a finish to suit your practical and economic needs, as well as satisfying your personal preferences.

SELECTING WALLPAPERING MATERIALS

Wallpapers are manufactured in a number of finishes. Prices vary greatly, and the most expensive wallpapers are not necessarily easy to hang, however aesthetically pleasing they are. There is a wide choice of inexpensive wallpapers, and they are usually easy to hang.

WALLPAPER TYPES AND THEIR CHARACTERISTICS

TYPE	FINISH	USES
Lining	Undecorated, smooth, off-white or buff-colored paper. Available in different grades of thickness.	Ideal base for painting and wallpapering; suitable for all areas of the home. Disguises blemishes well.
Woodchip	Undecorated, rough-textured, off-white or buff-colored wallpaper. Coarseness of wallpaper varies.	Excellent for covering walls and ceilings that are in poor condition; suitable for all areas of the home.
Embossed	Thick-textured wallpaper with relief-imprinted patterns. Produces a three-dimensional finish.	Wide choice of patterns available; suitable for any room. Heavyweight wallpaper, so difficult to use on ceilings.
Standard decorated	Flat wallpaper with a motif or pattern that has been machine-printed onto the surface of the wallpaper.	Highly decorative and excellent for use in bedrooms, but not suitable for high-wear areas of the home.
Flocked	Fibrous-material finish attached to backing paper. Synthetic-fiber makeup.	Creates a rich, sumptuous feel, so ideal for formal sitting or dining rooms.
Vinyl	Vinyl is a flat, decorative wallpaper with a clear, protective vinyl coating. Blown vinyl is embossed, with a protective vinyl layer, and is attached to backing paper. Heavy-duty vinyl is a thick, decorative paper with a protective vinyl coating.	Vinyl's wipeable surface makes it suitable in all rooms. Blown vinyl is more durable than standard embossed paper and hides blemishes well. Heavy-duty vinyl is ideal for kitchens and bathrooms since it can often be scrubbed.

BASIC WALLPAPERING EQUIPMENT

You will need more equipment for papering walls than for painting. Many tools, however, are required for both so, once those items are in your toolkit, they can be used for either job.

● **Prioritizing quality** Buy the best-quality tools that you can afford. This is particularly important for the items that are used most and those that come into direct contact with the wallpaper, such as wallpaper-hanging and pasting brushes, seam roller, scissors, and a craft knife. The latter two items are vital for making accurate cuts and, therefore, achieving the best possible finish.

● **Choosing brushes** Select a pasting brush that will cover a surface evenly and efficiently, and a wallpaper-hanging brush with long, flexible bristles.

● **Considering safety** Follow the same safety precautions with regard to wallpapering materials and equipment as for painting (see p. 203).

Goggles

Wallpaper-hanging brush

Pasting brush

Rubber gloves

Pasting table

Pencil

Phillips-head screwdriver

Screwdriver

Wallpaper-hanging scissors

Seam roller

Filling knife

Ruler

Level

Bucket

Chalk line

Steam stripper

Wallpaper scraper

Stepladder

Sponge

Craft knife

Measuring cup

Tape measure

CHOOSING WALLPAPER

THE SHAPE AND USAGE OF A ROOM, the style of your home, and any effect that you wish to achieve are factors to bear in mind when choosing wallpaper, but whether you like a wallpaper will have most influence on your choice.

CONSIDERING EFFECTS

If you want to achieve a specific effect in a room, the decisions that you make about pattern and design can be as important as your choice of color. A desire to create the illusion of space, for example, may influence you as much as a wallpaper's other decorative qualities.

CONSIDERING OPTIONS
● **Hiding defects** Choose a textured or heavily patterned wallpaper to detract from uneven walls. A busy pattern will disguise a problem best.
● **Creating order** Use bold, geometric designs if you want to create a sense of order and formality within a room.
● **Using two wallpapers** If a room has a natural dividing line, such as a chair rail, use two different wallpapers, therby creating a feeling of height, for example.
● **Considering other colors** Bear in mind the colors of walls and woodwork when choosing wallpaper. It should be complemented by nearby colors to maximize its effect.

COORDINATING DECOR
● **Creating a total look** Buy a complete range of decorative materials so that fabrics, wallpaper, and paint match.

Matching accessories
Use matching wallpaper and fabric to create a coordinated look. Tie in other accessories by picking out different tones of the colors used in the wallpaper.

CREATING HEIGHT

Using stripes
Vertical stripes make a room look taller and are ideal if ceilings are low. Here, a room divider covered in striped wallpaper contributes to the illusion of height.

CHOOSING LARGE PATTERNS

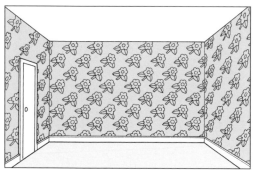

Reducing the size of large room
A large pattern can dominate the decoration in a room, since it will seem to bring the walls toward a viewer, reducing the feeling of space. In a small room a large pattern can be overpowering, but in a big room it can help to create a cozy feel.

CHOOSING SMALL PATTERNS

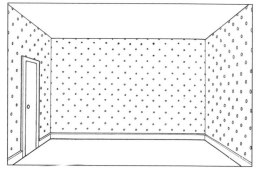

Creating a feeling of space
A small pattern has the effect of making a room appear larger, as long as the background color of the wallpaper is pale. The less dense the pattern, the greater the effect. A dense pattern, even if it is small-scale, creates a busy feel within a room.

PLANNING THE WALLPAPERING

It is highly important to figure out how much wallpaper is required for a room and to determine the order in which the room will be wallpapered. Measure walls accurately so that there will be no waste, and think very carefully about where in the room to start wallpapering.

MEASURING THE DIMENSIONS OF A ROOM

● **Measuring total surface area** Measure each wall as a separate entity. Add together wall areas, plus the ceiling area (obtained by measuring the floor), to give the total surface area.

● **Including repeats** To account for trimming and waste of large-patterned wallpaper, add the size of the pattern repeat to the room height. This will guarantee enough wallpaper.

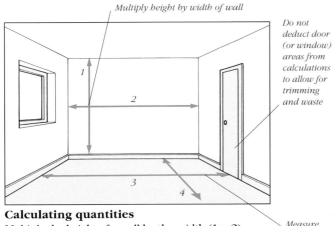

Multiply height by width of wall

Do not deduct door (or window) areas from calculations to allow for trimming and waste

Measure floor area instead of ceiling

Calculating quantities

Multiply the height of a wall by the width (1 x 2) to calculate the surface area. Measure the height in several places, since it may vary. To obtain a ceiling measurement, measure the floor (3 x 4). Divide the total surface area by the area of a roll of wallpaper to give the number of rolls required for the room.

CALCULATING ACCURATELY

● **Including lining** If you want to line the walls of a room before wallpapering them, remember to include lining paper in your calculations of material requirements. Lining paper has no pattern repeat, so the surface area alone is all you need for the calculation.

● **Doing a quick count** In a room that is already papered, count how many hangs were used before. This is a quick way to measure the number of rolls of wallpaper that you will need. In rooms of average height, small-patterned paper gives four hangs per roll, while large-patterned paper gives three. Most wallpapers conform to a standard roll length.

● **Wallpapering ceilings** Wallpaper a ceiling in the direction of its longest length. This will keep the number of lengths required to a minimum as well as reducing trimming and the waste of wallpaper.

STARTING & FINISHING IN THE CORRECT PLACE

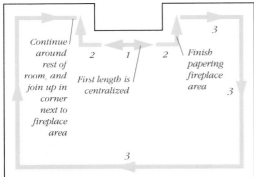

Continue around rest of room, and join up in corner next to fireplace area

First length is centralized

Finish papering fireplace area

Centralizing the first hang

If using a large-patterned wallpaper in a room with a focal point such as a fireplace area (1), start by centralizing the pattern on the focal point (see p. 229). Finish the focal point (2) before continuing to wallpaper around the rest of the room (3).

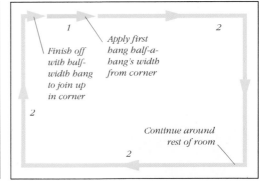

Finish off with half-width hang to join up in corner

Apply first hang half-a-hang's width from corner

Continue around rest of room

Wallpapering straightforward rooms

In rooms where no centralizing is required, start wallpapering near the corner that is least visible when entering or sitting in the room (1). Make sure that the first hang needs no complicated trimming and is a good point from which to continue (2).

PREPARING TO WALLPAPER

Acertain amount of preparation is necessary prior to wallpapering, depending on the finish you want and whether or not the walls have been papered before. Wallpaper faults are not always easy to put right, so prepare surfaces well.

STRIPPING WALLS

Strip all old wallpaper before hanging a new wallcovering. Some manufacturers suggest that you remove only the top layer of vinyl wallpapers and use the backing layer as a lining. This is only possible, however, if that backing layer is stuck firmly enough.

STRIPPING EASILY
● **Stripping dry** Remove any loose wallpaper before soaking to reduce the amount of mess caused by water and wet paper. Where seams have lifted, you can get a good hold. Vinyl top layers usually pull away easily.
● **Soaking walls** Use hot water to soak wallpaper. Apply the water with a large pasting brush. Allow it to penetrate for a few minutes before removing the wallpaper with a scraper.
● **Protecting floors** Stripping is messy, so you need to protect the floor. As well as dropcloths, put rolls of newspaper at the bases of walls to soak up water runoff.

SCORING WALLS

Making your own scorer
Adapt an old roller head by inserting long screws at regular intervals so they protrude out the other side. Run the roller over the wallpaper to pierce it and allow water to reach the paste.

TRADITIONAL TIP

Using vinegar
Add a small amount of vinegar to hot water to make a potent stripping agent. The vinegar will react with wallpaper paste, loosening it.

SAFETY

When using a stripper, wear goggles to protect your eyes, and keep out of the way of the hot steam. You may wish to protect your hands with gloves.

● **Following instructions** Read manufacturers' guidelines carefully before using a steam stripper, since they may differ from one machine to another.
● **Leaving unattended** Turn a stripper off when not in use.
● **Stripping ceilings** Beware of hot water droplets that can collect on the edge of the pad and drip onto you.
● **Keeping cords dry** Ensure that no water comes into contact with electrical cords.

USING A STEAM STRIPPER

Steam stripping is by far the most effective way of removing wallpaper from walls. Renting a steam stripper is not expensive, but consider buying one if you intend to strip a lot of wallpaper throughout a house.

● **Filling a stripper** Fill a steam stripper with hot water, not cold, to reduce the boiling time required. The equipment will then be ready to use sooner.
● **Checking water levels** Make sure that a steam stripper always has plenty of water in it. If you allow the stripper to boil dry, you may damage the element, which will necessitate some expensive repairs.

Stripping effectively
With one hand holding the stripper pad in position against the wall, use the other hand to scrape off the wallpaper where the pad has just been. Soaking times will vary, depending on the type of wallpaper.

PREPARING WALLS

Whether walls have just been stripped or are being wallpapered for the first time, good preparation is vitally important. Filling and sanding are essential. Some wallpapers may disguise wall imperfections, but a good surface is necessary for paper and paste adhesion.

DOING THE BASICS

● **Providing a key** Sand glossy walls or those with a silky-smooth finish to provide a key for wallpaper adhesion. This will also speed up drying: paste will dry into the wall and out through the paper.

● **Sealing dust** Seal dusty surfaces with a coat of size or a PVA glue solution (five parts water, one part PVA). This will help wallpaper to stick but allow you to move it easily.

● **Covering texture** If you cannot remove a highly textured coating with a steam stripper, apply a stabilizing coat of diluted PVA (five parts water, one part PVA), then coat the surface thinly with plaster.

HIDING IMPERFECTIONS

● **Masking stains** To prevent stains from bleeding through and discoloring wallpaper, spray the affected area with a commercial stain-blocking agent, or apply an oil-based primer before wallpapering.

● **Removing protrusions** Take old nails and screws out of the wall with a claw hammer, or drive them in and fill. Make sure they are well beneath the surface to prevent staining.

● **Covering dark backgrounds** When applying light-colored wallpaper to a previously dark or patchy wall, apply a coat of light latex paint to prevent the dark color from showing through and even out patches.

TIME-SAVING TIP

Filling and sizing
Fill any small holes. Before the filler dries, cover the area with a PVA glue solution (five parts water, one part PVA). Carefully smooth it with a brush to eliminate the need for sanding.

PREPARING AND PAPERING CEILINGS

As with most decorating jobs, it is best to start at the top and work down. Ceilings should be tackled first after all standard preparation has been carried out.

● **Filling edges** Ensure that the wall–ceiling junction is precisely filled and sanded, since this edge will provide the guideline for wallpapering on both the ceiling and the walls.

● **Testing ceilings** Old latex-painted ceilings may be unstable. The weight of wallpaper may pull the paint off, causing the wallpaper to sag. Apply a small test patch of wallpaper to the ceiling, and leave it overnight. If it is still firmly stuck in the morning, continue wallpapering.

● **Playing safe** If you are unsure about the stability of a ceiling, strip off the old paint with a scraper before proceeding any further. Then prepare the surface and seal as usual.

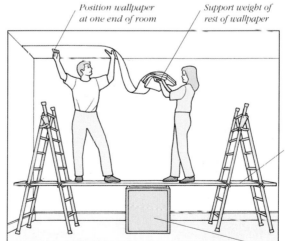

Position wallpaper at one end of room

Support weight of rest of wallpaper

Board supported at end across open stepladder

Board made sturdy by support of box in middle

Working safely and easily
Build a sturdy work platform by suspending a board between two stepladders. Support the board with a wooden box. Adjust the height of the platform so that the ceiling is about 6 in (15 cm) above your head – close enough to allow you to move the wallpaper easily without being cramped. To reduce the risk of tearing, ask a friend to help you to hold a length of wallpaper while you apply.it.

IMPROVING TECHNIQUES

THERE IS ONLY ONE TECHNIQUE for applying wallpaper to a wall – with a paper-hanging brush and-various trimming tools. The secret of success lies in the preparation of the surface and in your ability to wallpaper around obstacles.

MEASURING AND CUTTING

Accurate measuring will ensure that there is minimal wastage in what is inevitably a wasteful technique. Before unwrapping and cutting wallpaper, check that all the rolls have the same batch number, thereby avoiding the possibility of color variations between rolls.

STARTING OUT
● **Making equipment ready**
Make sure that scissors are sharp and that the surface of the pasting table is clean before you start work.
● **Measuring walls** Measure the exact distance between the ceiling and the top of the baseboard. Add the size of the pattern repeat, plus 4 in (10 cm) to allow for trimming.
● **Stacking hangs** Most hangs will be of a standard length within a room. Cut a number of these lengths to start with, so that you have them on hand when you need them.

WORKING WITH PAPER
● **Trimming by hand** Some expensive wallpapers may not have perfectly straight edges. Trim them with sharp scissors before application.
● **Dealing with length** Most of the lengths you cut will be longer than the pasting board itself, so allow the wallpaper to concertina back on itself, taking care not to crease it.
● **Cutting** When you have marked off measurements on the wallpaper, use a ruler to draw a guideline. Cut across this line. You may soon be able to cut a straight line by eye.

MEASURING EASILY

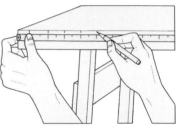

Marking a pasting table
Turn the edge of a pasting table into a ruler by marking off increments accurately and at appropriate intervals along the table's length. Measure lengths of wallpaper against this instead of using a ruler every time.

LINING WALLS

To improve wallpaper finish, it is worth lining the walls first: many manufacturers recommend it. The same techniques for wallpaper apply to lining paper, with a few minor adjustments.

● **Leveling** Lining paper does not need to be exactly vertical, since it is not seen. Treat each wall as a self-contained unit.
● **Sizing** Size lined surfaces once they are dry using a diluted paste solution mixed according to the manufacturer's guidelines. Sizing will allow you to move paper easily when positioning it.
● **Sealing edges** Seal trimmed edges with flexible filler to prevent them from lifting and to give a good edge against which you can trim wallpaper.

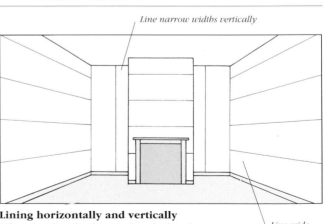

Line narrow widths vertically

Line wide surfaces horizontally

Lining horizontally and vertically
When deciding the direction in which to hang lining paper, be guided by the fewest number of hangs needed. The fewer the hangs, the less cutting and trimming. Horizontal lining around a fireplace area makes trimming and rounding the corners easier.

PASTING

Wallpaper requires adhesive to attach it to a wall. You can either mix wallpaper paste yourself or buy it premixed and apply it to the wallpaper. Some wallpapers are prepasted – water activates a coating on the back – while others require that you apply paste to the wall.

MIXING PASTE
● **Stirring well** Stir paste for longer than suggested by the manufacturer to ensure that there are no lumps. A wooden dowel makes an ideal stirrer. Also stir the paste from time to time during wallpapering.

PASTING PAPER
● **Keeping paper flat** To prevent wallpaper from curling, weight each end before you start. Cover evenly with paste. Fold it into a loose, crease-free concertina as you move along from one end to the other.

KEEPING PAPER CLEAN
● **Protecting from paste** Paste each length in the same position – flush with the edge of the pasting table – to avoid getting paste on the right side. Wipe the table with clean, warm water between lengths.

DEALING WITH PREPASTED WALLPAPER

Rolling up wallpaper
Prepasted wallpaper needs soaking to activate the paste. Loosely roll up a cut length with the pattern on the inside so that the water will come into contact with all the pasted surface easily, thus activating the paste.

Folding soaked paper
Let soaked wallpaper unroll on a pasting table. Fold each end back on itself into the middle of the length so that the pattern is on the outside. This will prevent the pasted side from drying out before you apply it to the wall.

MONEY-SAVING TIP

Using a kitchen table
Spread a plastic sheet over a kitchen table, and use it as a pasting table instead of buying one. Make sure that the sheet is held taut by taping it securely at each corner to the table legs.

HANDLING DAMP PAPER
● **Protecting wallpaper** As you transfer wallpaper from the container in which it is being soaked to a pasting table, the patterned side of the wallpaper may rub on the side of the table and be damaged. Soften the edges of the table by covering them with two or three layers of masking tape.
● **Anchoring edges** Have a small jar of premixed paste handy as you prepare to hang a length of wallpaper. The edges of prepasted wallpaper sometimes dry out too quickly, and you may need to apply a little more paste before you hang them.

STORING WALLPAPER WHILE IT SOAKS

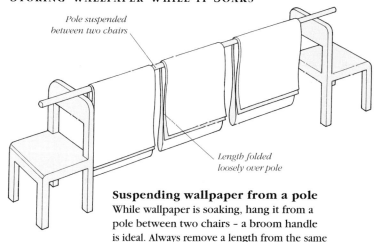

Pole suspended between two chairs

Length folded loosely over pole

Suspending wallpaper from a pole
While wallpaper is soaking, hang it from a pole between two chairs – a broom handle is ideal. Always remove a length from the same end then move the others along, so that you take the one that has soaked longest.

HANGING WALLPAPER

However much preparation you do, a good hanging technique is vital to give a quality finish to your wallpapered walls. It is important to master the basic method of application so that when you come across obstacles, you will have a sound technique on which to build.

STARTING ACCURATELY

Finding the vertical
Use a level as a straightedge to draw a pencil guideline at your chosen starting point on the wall. Extend this line by carefully moving the level down the wall to make sure of an accurate and continuous guide.

ADDRESSING A WALL

Preventing tears
Wallpaper that has been folded while soaking is more likely to tear, so support its weight with one hand as you unroll it. Make the first contact about 6 in (15 cm) below the ceiling, and follow guidelines down the wall.

HANGING SUCCESSFULLY

● **Allowing for expansion** When measuring out where lengths will hang, bear in mind that wallpaper expands from its dry measurement once it is pasted. Make an allowance of up to ¼ in (0.5 cm).

● **Smoothing wallpaper** Brush from the center of a length out toward and over the edges, and from top to bottom. This removes air bubbles.

● **Using embossed wallpaper** Do not apply too much pressure; otherwise, the raised pattern will be flattened.

● **Applying vinyl** Take care not to stretch vinyl wallpaper while smoothing it. This can distort its edges and make it difficult to join to the next hang.

TRIMMING WALLPAPER

Making a precise dividing line between wallpaper and the adjacent surfaces is important for the production of a neat and well-defined finished product. Sharp scissors and craft knives and a steady, accurate cutting technique are required to achieve this aim.

MONEY-SAVING TIP

Use an indelible felt-tip pen

Labeling craft-knife blades
Mark a dot on one end of a new craft-knife blade. Always use the marked end first, so that when you need to change the blade around you will be sure that the other end has not been used.

HIDING UNEVEN LINES

Smoothing lines
Where the wall–ceiling junction is not a straight edge, overlap the wallpaper slightly onto the ceiling, make a crease line with a pair of scissors, then trim. This will create a straighter line.

FIXING OVERTRIMMING

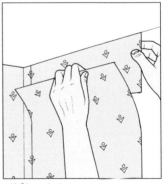

Hiding joins
If you have trimmed too much wallpaper, insert a small sliver at the top behind the main length. Overlap the main length onto the sliver. The overlap will not be seen from the floor.

JOINING WALLPAPER

Joining wallpaper accurately is as important as trimming well. You need to make neat, matching joins between lengths with no overlaps or gaps between hangs. Most wallpaper should meet exactly – in what is called a butt join – to produce a smooth, perfectly matching finish.

MAKING PERFECT SEAMS

- **Underbrushing** Brush only enough to remove air bubbles and secure wallpaper firmly to the wall. Overbrushing tends to polish seams, which will shine once wallpaper is dry.
- **Using a seam roller** Run a seam roller lightly up and down a join to secure the wallpaper and make a join that is almost invisible. Do not use a seam roller on embossed wallpapers, since it will flatten the relief.
- **Repasting seams** Wallpaper edges are the first areas to lift, so stick them down well. After a few lengths have been hung, return to the first hangs and repaste any lifting edges using a small brush. Smooth with a damp sponge.

CENTRALIZING A WALLPAPER PATTERN

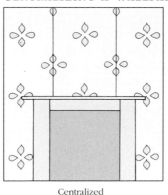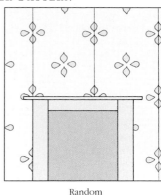

Centralized   Random

Using a feature within the room

Wallpaper with a medium- to large-sized pattern should always be centered on a focal point in a room (above left). This creates a well-balanced feel that sets off the rest of the decoration. Leaving where the pattern falls to chance might result in an off-center look (above right), which would draw attention to the focal point for the wrong reason. Start wallpapering from the focal point (see p. 223).

KEEPING WALLPAPER CLEAN

Wallpaper is a delicate, and often expensive, decorating material, and you should look after it carefully so that the surface does not become spoiled. Always keep a supply of clean water on hand for any cleaning requirements throughout the entire decorating project.

SEGREGATING TOOLS

Color coordinating

Keep different-colored buckets and sponges for different tasks. This will prevent items used for cleaning the pasting table, which soon become dirty, from being confused with those for wallpaper.

REMOVING EXCESS PASTE

- **Cleaning adjacent surfaces** After wallpaper lengths have been trimmed, remove excess paste from the paper surface. Also, clean the ceiling and baseboards before any paste dries and dulls the surface.
- **Cutting new lengths** However often you wash down a pasting table, it may become tacky. To prevent wallpaper from becoming sticky while being cut, cover the table first with a sheet of lining paper.
- **Disposing of rubbish** As soon as each length is hung, immediately place scraps in a trash bag. This will reduce the risk of paste being spread throughout the working area.

KEEPING YOUR WORK STATION CLEAN

It is advisable to keep surfaces and wallpapering equipment as clean as possible at all times to ensure the best results.

- **Removing excess paste** Scrape partly dried paste off a pasting table using the blade of a scraper, especially around the edge of the table.
- **Replacing water** Fill the cleaning bucket with a fresh supply of water after about ten lengths have been pasted.
- **Drying equipment** Keep scissors and craft-knife blades dry at all times by wiping with lint-free cloth.

WALLPAPERING AWKWARD AREAS

WITHIN ANY ROOM you may well have to modify your basic wallpapering technique in order to deal with nonstraightforward areas. Once learned, however, these adaptations will become part of your wallpapering repertoire.

AROUND WINDOWS AND DOORS

Windows and doors are commonplace obstacles in most rooms of the house, and you need to learn the correct procedure for negotiating them. Stick to a systematic approach that can be adapted depending on the design and size of each door and window.

COPING WITH OPENINGS

● **Keeping moisture out** Window recesses may be affected by condensation in damp climates. To prevent wallpaper from lifting, run a bead of clear silicone around the frame–paper junction to secure the wallpaper firmly.

● **Overlapping** Small overlaps may be unavoidable around a window. Try to position overlapping seams so that curtains will conceal them.

● **Preventing accidents** Lock a door when wallpapering above it to prevent it from opening while you are on a ladder. If the door does not lock, pin a warning note to the other side, or put an obstacle there.

WALLPAPERING ACCORDING TO PLAN

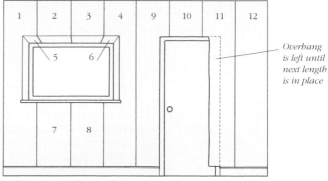

Overhang is left until next length is in place

Following a logical sequence
Wallpaper a wall that includes windows and doors in a certain order (1-12) to maintain the vertical as you wallpaper around them. Hang 12 before you trim 11 to ensure that 12 is vertical. If you trimmed 11 first, and followed that line, 12 might not be completely vertical.

WALLPAPERING ARCHWAYS

Overlaps are inevitable in archways, since wallpaper cannot stretch in different directions around a corner. This need not be a problem as long as overlaps are made correctly.

● **Choosing wallpaper** When joining wallpapers between rooms, use the one with the smallest design in the archway to minimize the pattern break.

● **Avoiding wallpapering** Wallpaper to the edge of an archway, but paint the inside the same color as the ceiling in the adjacent room. This will link the archway with that room and avoid wallpapering.

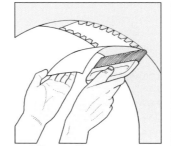

Molding wallpaper
Make small, right angled cuts in the wallpaper. It will then fold easily into an archway. You will cover the cuts with the length of wallpaper that you apply to the inside of the archway.

WALLPAPERING AROUND FIXTURES

Consider carefully whether or not you will want to move fixtures and pictures around once you have decorated.

● **Removing picture hooks** Remove all hooks before you decorate. You may decide once you have finished that you would like to reposition pictures or mirrors.

● **Marking shelving** If shelves or other fixtures are to stay in the same position, take them down and reinsert the screws. They will poke through when you wallpaper, revealing themselves for refitting.

AROUND CORNERS

Occasionally, wallpaper will bend around corners easily. When corners are not square or even, however, you will need to adjust your wallpapering technique when continuing the paper onto the adjacent wall. Check again that the hang is vertical as you start a new wall.

WALLPAPERING SUCCESSFULLY AROUND UNEVEN EXTERNAL CORNERS

1 Extend a length of wallpaper around an external corner. Hang the next length so that it overlaps the previous one by 2–4 in (5–10 cm). Cut through the center of the overlap.

2 Carefully peel back the edges of the overlap, and remove the two strips of excess wallpaper. Support the wallpaper with one hand to avoid any possibility of tearing.

3 Smooth the seam with a wallpaper-hanging brush to form a perfect butt join. Before the paste dries, remove any excess from around the join with a damp sponge.

WALLPAPERING SUCCESSFULLY AROUND UNEVEN INTERNAL CORNERS

● **Joining in corners** Wallpaper around an internal corner, and trim 1 in (2.5 cm) beyond. Place the next length on the second wall over the strip.

● **Cornering easily** To fit paper around an internal corner, cut two small slits at both the top and bottom of the length at the ceiling and baseboard.

● **Preventing lifting** To ensure that wallpaper will not lift, run border adhesive along the overlap with a small brush. This is essential with vinyl papers.

WALLPAPERING STAIRWELLS

Wallpapering a stairwell involves handling long lengths, angled trimming, and rounding corners.

● **Sharing the job** It is easier for two people than one to handle long lengths of wallpaper. One can position the top of a length while the other supports it.

● **Measuring hangs** Measuring is difficult because the bottom edge of each hang is angled. Start at the bottom of the stairs, and work up. This will make angled cutting easier to perform.

● **Pasting and soaking** Paste only one length at a time. Keep soaking times consistent so that all lengths expand equally and patterns will match up exactly.

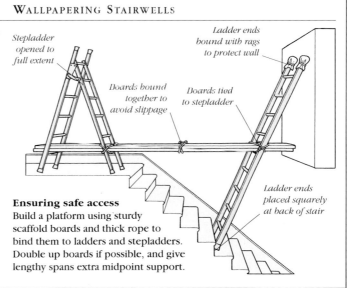

Ensuring safe access
Build a platform using sturdy scaffold boards and thick rope to bind them to ladders and stepladders. Double up boards if possible, and give lengthy spans extra midpoint support.

AROUND ELECTRICAL FIXTURES

Electrical fixtures are like any other obstacles you might come across when wallpapering; they need not present a problem as long as you follow the correct procedures. Take care to observe the necessary safety precautions when wallpapering around electrical fixtures.

ELECTRICITY PREP

● **Doing electrical work** If you have a room rewired, ask the electrician not to install socket plates and wall fixtures until the wallpapering is finished. Use portable lights from another room temporarily.

● **Coping with wall lights** Plan wallpapering so that seams will occur behind the center of a light fixture. You will then need only to loosen the fixture, and slip the wallpaper behind.

WARNING!

Before wallpapering around electrical fixtures, turn off the power. Wallpaper paste is a good conductor, so do not get it near exposed wires.

WALLPAPERING AROUND AN ELECTRICAL SWITCH

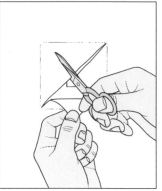

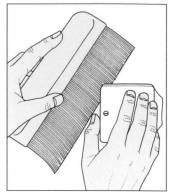

1 Paper loosely over a switch. Make a pencil mark just in from each corner impression in the wallpaper. Cut from the center out to each mark. Trim the resulting triangular flaps to leave a square hole.

2 Loosen the switch screws. Ease the plate away from the wall and in front of the wallpaper. Using a wallpaper-hanging brush, smooth the paper behind the plate. Replace screws and wipe the plate clean.

AROUND PIPES AND RADIATORS

Pipes and radiators are awkward obstacles around which to wallpaper. They have no straight edges to trim against, and it may be necessary to wallpaper the wall behind them. These obstacles can be overcome with a few adjustments to general wallpapering technique.

COPING WITH RADIATORS

Papering behind a radiator
If a radiator is bracketed to the wall, allow wallpaper to fall over it. Cut slits in line with the brackets. Using a radiator roller, feed the wallpaper behind, guiding it around the brackets.

AVOIDING PROBLEMS

● **Starting with pipes** Start your wallpapering behind a pipe so that the joining seam will be hidden by it. By doing this, you will also eliminate the need for complicated trimming around the pipe brackets.

● **Keeping pipes clean** Remove wallpaper paste from bare metal pipes immediately, since it can cause corrosion, which in turn results in the unsightly staining of the pipes.

● **Removing obstacles** Hire a professional plumber to remove radiators and cap off the pipes before you start to wallpaper. This is a quick, inexpensive job that will make wallpapering much easier.

BRIGHT IDEA

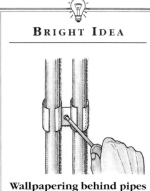

Wallpapering behind pipes
Unscrew and remove pipe brackets, and feed wallpaper behind the pipes. Replace the brackets while you can locate the screw holes easily through the wet wallpaper.

ADDING BORDERS

Borders are an important wallpapering accessory: they complement or highlight features of the wallpaper. Many borders are designed for use with a particular wallpaper, but they can also be used against a plain-colored wall.

ATTACHING BORDERS

Apply a border once the rest of the wall decoration has been completed. Whether the border is narrow or broad, textured or plain, the application method is the same. Attach a border very carefully in order to enhance the appearance of the already decorated wall.

POSITIONING BORDERS

● **Planning position** You can hang borders at ceiling, chair-rail, picture-rail, or baseboard level. Consider uneven wall–ceiling junctions, split-level ceilings, and the location of switches and other obstacles when making your decision.

● **Keeping level** If placing a border on wallpaper, follow a horizontal line in the pattern. If this is impossible, draw a guideline using a level.

● **Pasting up** Use a small brush to apply adhesive to a border. Place it on the wall right away. The adhesive dries quickly, so do not soak it unless the instructions say so.

DIVIDING WALLS

Using a border
Use a wallpaper border instead of a wooden or plaster chair rail to divide up an expanse of wall. This will be decorative without installation requirements and cost.

CHOOSING APPROPRIATELY

Coordinating details
Choose a border with an image that suits the room as well as matching the decor. In a child's bedroom, for example, pick a simple, brightly colored motif.

FRAMING WITH BORDERS

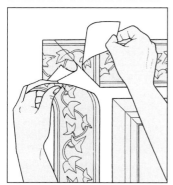

Mitering a corner
Allow one length of border to overlap the other with the pattern corresponding. Cut diagonally through both with a craft knife. Remove excess flaps, and smooth the remaining pieces into place.

APPLYING BORDERS

● **Cornering** Apply one length of border so that it overlaps onto the adjacent wall by ⅛ in (0.5 cm). Overlap the next length onto it so that the pattern matches at the join. Crease down the corner junction with a pair of scissors, and pull back the paper. Cut accurately down the crease guideline. Smooth the border back into place, producing a matching join in the corner with an invisible overlap.

● **Hanging quickly** Use a damp sponge rather than a wallpaper-hanging brush to position a border and remove any excess border adhesive quickly before it dries.

MONEY-SAVING TIP

Making your own border
Trim an old, leftover roll of wallpaper to create your own border. Wallpaper with a striped pattern is ideal, since it provides a ready-made guideline along which to cut.

CHOOSING OTHER WALL COVERINGS

THERE ARE MANY OPTIONS other than wallpaper for wall decoration. They include highly textured papers, different types of fabric, and the use of wood, wood paneling, and plaster if you prefer a heavy decorative finish.

WALL HANGINGS

In its most traditional form, a wall hanging consists of decorative fabric that is hung on a wall in a similar way to pictures and paintings. However, wall-hanging options do not stop there, since there are other ways of attaching decorative materials to a flat wall surface.

CHOOSING TEXTURED WALL COVERINGS

Some wall coverings attach to a wall like wallpaper but have a genuine fabric texture. Many less traditional wall coverings are commercial products with specific hanging systems.

● **Selecting fabrics for texture** Choose silk if you want to produce a very sumptuous finish. Burlap and grasscloth are much coarser in texture and create a rustic, earthy feel.

● **Choosing unusual textures** Modern ranges of wall coverings include some unusual options. You might like to create the impression on your wall of rough-hewn rock or fine mineral particles like sand or stones.

Silk

Burlap

Grasscloth

Stone effect

HANGING UNUSUAL ITEMS

Using a garden trellis
Mount a simple, painted garden trellis above or beneath a chair rail for an unusual decoration. A trellis is light, so you can attach it with any wood glue.

HANGING RUGS & CARPETS SUCCESSFULLY

● **Hanging flush** To attach a rug to a wall, screw a length of carpet gripper rod to the wall where the top of the rug will be placed. Press the rug firmly on to the rod's teeth.

● **Using curtain poles** If a rug or carpet has a looped fringe, thread the loops along a curtain pole. Attach this to the wall with the appropriate brackets supplied with it.

Featuring rugs
Rugs and other wall hangings come in all shapes and sizes, so you should be able to find ones to fit in with your decorative ideas. Choose unusual shapes, and place them in less obvious positions, such as above a window to create a point of special interest.

ATTACHING FABRICS

● **Using battens** Screw in battens, or thin strips of wood, at ceiling and baseboard level. Use a staple gun to attach a piece of fabric to the battens. Staple the material along the top batten, then stretch it to the bottom batten, and staple it to that. For more texture, pleat the fabric as you staple.

● **Covering staples** Hide the staple heads attaching material by placing a strip of fabric over the battens, using fabric glue.

● **Cleaning easily** Attach lightweight fabric using touch-and-close tape. The fabric can then be taken down easily from the wall and washed.

WOOD PANELING

Walls can be covered completely or in part with wood paneling to create a substantial decorative impact. Paint them or leave them natural, depending on your preference. You will need one or two woodworking tools and a few basic carpentry skills to panel successfully.

PANELING CLEVERLY

● **Allowing access** Cut access pieces into wood paneling in order to reach pipework and to house electrical sockets.
● **Covering edges** Neaten cuts and joins in paneling at ceiling level by attaching lengths of decorative wooden molding, using panel nails.
● **Faking wood panels** To create the effect of wood panels on a wall, cut four equal-sized lengths of molding or architrave, mitering the ends to make the corners of the panels. Position each piece on the wall, using all-purpose adhesive. A number of such panels beneath a chair rail, for example, creates a realistic effect – especially if the panels are grained (see p. 259).

BUILDING A FRAMEWORK

● **Using battens** Attach panels to a framework of 2-in by 1-in (5-cm by 2.5-cm) battens placed horizontally on the wall, about 12 in (30 cm) apart.

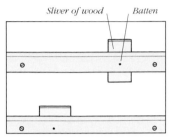
Sliver of wood   *Batten*

Infilling gaps
If a wall is not completely flat, pack out gaps behind the battens of the framework so that they are flush with the wall. Wedge slivers of wood behind the battens before tightening them.

ATTACHING PANELING

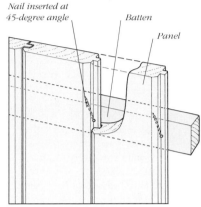
Nail inserted at 45-degree angle   *Batten*
Panel

Hiding nails
When installing tongue-and-groove paneling, insert a nail through the tongue of one length into the batten behind it. The groove of the adjacent panel will hide it when put in place.

DECORATIVE MOLDINGS

Decorative moldings create an impression of detail and are generally used to add a finishing touch to walls. Moldings can be made of wood, plaster, or polystyrene and are produced in a wide range of designs. Standard coving is still the most popular choice.

REPAIRING COVING

Applying filler successfully
It can be difficult to apply filler to ornate coving that has been damaged or has cracked. Use your finger to put the filler in place, then mold it into shape and smooth it with a damp brush.

INSTALLING COVING
● **Starting with the finish** Although coving is in effect a finishing, it should be applied before the decorating process begins. Fill and paint it before the walls are decorated.
● **Attaching** Use nails and adhesive to attach coving, since it needs support while the adhesive dries. Manufacturers suggest that nails can then be removed, but they are best left, filled, and painted over.
● **Smoothing** It is difficult to sand molding adhesive when dry, so remove rough areas and smooth joints while wet. After each piece has been applied, smooth with a damp sponge.

CHOOSING POLYSTYRENE COVING

Although less solid and realistic in appearance than plaster, polystyrene coving is much less expensive than its plaster equivalents.

● **Flexible** Because it is more flexible, polystyrene coving is easier to position, more suitable for uneven wall–ceiling junctions, and less likely to suffer from cracks.
● **Easy to use** Polystyrene is lightweight and easy to work with. To give it a more solid look, apply several coats of paint to fill the small holes that characterize its makeup.

FINISHING

I T IS IMPORTANT TO TAKE TIME to complete your wallpapering properly so that the finish looks as good as it possibly can and will last a long time. Make future decorating projects easier by looking after your equipment very carefully.

CORRECTING MISTAKES

S ome problems may develop after you have finished wallpapering. Most of these will be fairly minor and easily corrected, although they will need attention. Problems arising from serious deficiencies in technique may need more extensive work in order to correct them.

REMOVING STAINS

● **Dealing with damp patches**
Damp patches that persist after wallpaper has dried out may indicate a structural problem. Strip the paper off and line the whole area with commercial moisture-resistant foil before wallpapering again.
● **Using detergent** Remove miscellaneous stains and marks with a mild household detergent solution, dabbed on and wiped off with a sponge. Rub extremely gently.

IMPROVING MATCHING

● **Distracting the eye** Use a picture or wall hanging to detract from a mismatch. Always rectify or conceal any that occur at eye level.
● **Repapering** Apply another layer of paper to cover a bad pattern mismatch but only in small-scale, localized areas.

EVENING OFF EDGES

● **Sticking down** In bathrooms and kitchens, paper can lift at tiled edges because of excess moisture and poor adhesion. Run a thin band of grout or sealant over the paper at the tile–paper junction. Use masking tape to ensure a straight line.
● **Painting** If paper is poorly trimmed and overlaps onto wood, it will look bad and may lift. If necessary, paint over any overlapping paper using the woodwork paint.

RECTIFYING WALLPAPERING FAULTS

There are several fairly common wallpapering faults that may well affect only small areas yet can spoil your decorating if they are not corrected. However good your technique, faults can occur, but most can be solved using a few relatively simple methods.

Gaping seams
Use a felt-tip pen that matches the background color of the wallpaper to color in seams that have not been joined properly, or which have opened slightly as the wallpaper dried. Remove excess color by dabbing with a clean, damp sponge.

Shiny seams
Wiping down shiny or stained seams with a mild detergent solution should make them less conspicuous. To prevent shine when wallpapering in the future, remove any excess wallpaper paste from seams before it dries, and do not oversmooth seams.

Lifting edges
Stick back lifting edges with overlap adhesive or neat PVA. Use a brush to apply the adhesive along the entire length of the area that is lifting. Wipe away excess adhesive that spills out from beneath the edge with a clean, damp sponge.

Paper tears
Apply a small amount of PVA to the surface, then ease the torn piece of wallpaper back into position using a clean, damp sponge. As long as you maneuver the wallpaper carefully back into place, the repair will be almost invisible.

Bubbling
Most bubbles should disappear of their own accord as the wallpaper dries out. If they do not, pierce them with a sharp craft knife and stick the area back down with neat PVA. Apply it very carefully using a small artist's brush.

CLEANING AND MAINTAINING EQUIPMENT

After all types of decorating work – and wallpapering is no exception – make sure that you clean your equipment well, so that it will be in good working order in the future. Many tools are costly to replace, and it is all too easy to ruin them through needless neglect.

CLEANING SURFACES
● **Using soap** Wash down a pasting table with mild detergent after use; otherwise, any paste residue might be reactivated by water the next time the table is used.

CARING FOR BRUSHES
● **Softening bristles** Clean wallpapering brushes with a mild shampoo, then rinse them thoroughly. This will ensure that they remain soft until the next time they are used.

STORING LEVELS
● **Hanging up** Most levels have a hook on one end for hanging up after use. They are delicate and should be kept out of harm's way. Clean any paste off them first.

PROTECTING SCISSORS

Oiling a hinge
Use a lint-free cloth to apply oil to the hinging mechanism once scissors have been washed and dried. Do not use too much oil, or it may stain the paper next time.

MAINTAINING WALLPAPERED WALLS

There are several different ways to maintain and thus prolong the life of wall coverings.

● **Following recommendations** Check the label to see if you can wipe or scrub wallpaper.
● **Protecting paper** Apply a protective coat of acrylic matte varnish. Do a test patch in case the varnish reacts with the paper.
● **Caring for fabrics** Use a soft vacuum-cleaner attachment to remove dust from fabric-based, textured wall coverings.

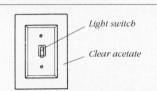

Light switch
Clear acetate

Making cleaning easy
Fit a rectangular-shaped piece of acetate (with a central area the size of the switch cut out of it) around an electrical switch. The wallpaper will still be visible, but you will be able to keep this frequently soiled area clean.

USING LEFTOVERS

Applying a wall covering tends to be a rather wasteful business, so try to use up some of the leftover pieces. Wallpaper pieces can be used for a variety of different purposes. Always keep some in case you have to make patch repairs to a wallpapered surface in future.

USING UP WALLPAPER
● **Wrapping gifts** Cut up scraps of patterned wallpaper for wrapping presents.
● **Enhancing decoration** Cover the panels of cupboard doors with wallpaper to add an extra decorative dimension to your papering. This will help to coordinate the decorative plan as well as enhancing a plain piece of furniture.
● **Using pattern** Patterns that include distinctive motifs can be cut up and the motifs put to use for a variety of other decorative purposes, such as découpage (see p. 265) or making a stencil (see p. 215).

MAXIMIZING USE
● **Recycling blades** Craft-knife blades are still relatively sharp even after they have been used for trimming wallpaper. Since only the tip of the blade will have been used, you can continue to use the blade for other purposes such as cutting carpet prior to laying it.
● **Keeping paste** If there is a chance that you may do more wallpapering shortly after your current project, do not throw away leftover wallpaper paste. It can be kept for several weeks, or even a few months, as long as you can transfer it to an airtight container.

MONEY-SAVING TIP

Lining a drawer
Trim wallpaper scraps to use as drawer liners. Iron and spray-starch each length so that it will sit flat inside a drawer. Secure in place with pins or tacks if necessary.

TILING WALLS

QUICK REFERENCE

Preparing to Tile, p. 240

Planning a Tiling
Strategy, p. 242

Improving Techniques,
p. 243

Tiling Creatively, p. 245

Finishing, p. 249

A*S WELL AS BEING highly decorative, tiles are a practical material for use in home decoration. They provide a durable surface that is long lasting and easy to clean. Many home decorators are reluctant to face tiling challenges and defer to experts. But cutting equipment, tile adhesives, and grout are more user-friendly than they used to be, so tiling is not as difficult as you might think.*

SETTING A STYLE

With an emphasis on the decorative aspect of tiles comes the opportunity to influence the style, design, and layout of a tiled area. Choosing a style and even creating your own tile designs are easy as long as you take a few basics into account before you start out.

BUDGETING WISELY
● **Planning** Tiles vary widely in price, so always bear your budget in mind. Less expensive tiles need not mean a less attractive finish.

APPRAISING YOUR SKILLS
● **Being realistic** Tile within your capabilities. If you are a first-time tiler, choose a simple project to start with. Proficiency will come with experience.

SAMPLING TILES
● **Borrowing tiles** If you find it difficult to visualize how tiles will look in your home, borrow samples from a supplier to take home and try out "dry."

ARRANGING WALL TILES

When you are choosing a design for the layout of an area to be tiled, you may find yourself limited by the size of the area. Bear in mind its practical purpose, and take the following stylistic points into account.

● **Choosing a basic style** The first aspect to consider when arranging wall tiles is whether to follow a traditional style of tiling, or choose from the range of modern styles, or adopt a more individualistic approach.
● **Thinking about color** When deciding which kind of design to create, consider the color of the tiles. Think in terms of the decoration of the whole room as well as color combinations within the tiled area itself.

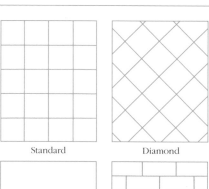

Standard   Diamond   Inset border

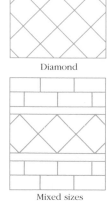

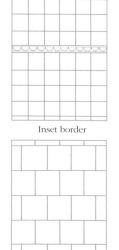

Edged border   Mixed sizes   Off-center or brick-bond

CHOOSING TILES

Size and shape are as important as color when you are choosing tiles. However much you like a particular tile, you must consider where it is going to be used. It is not advisable, for example, to choose a complicated design or large tiles if the area to be tiled is small.

TYPES OF TILE

Most wall tiles are machine-made and have a tough ceramic finish. Some are made from natural materials such as marble. Then there are handmade and hand-painted tiles. The huge choice of tiles should enable you to find some to match your decor.

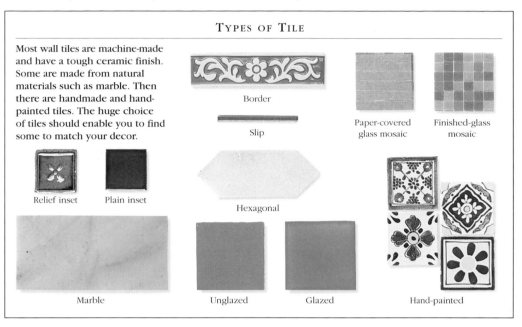

Border

Slip

Paper-covered glass mosaic

Finished-glass mosaic

Relief inset   Plain inset

Hexagonal

Marble   Unglazed   Glazed   Hand-painted

COORDINATING TILES WITH DECOR

Tiles have little impact unless they are well coordinated with the rest of the decor in a room. Extravagant tile designs require the rest of the decoration to be complementary, while a less complex design allows other decorative features to make a greater statement.

CONSIDERING OPTIONS
● **Choosing colors** Stick to plain, neutral colors for your tiles if you are concerned about changing styles and fashions. Remember that you will find it much easier to redecorate around neutral-colored tiles than around bold colors and designs that make a strong statement.
● **Using picture tiles** The most common way of adding more interest to a plain tiled surface is to include some picture tiles. However, be cautious in your choice: too many picture tiles can make a design look overdone, detracting from the rest of the tiled surface and from the room as a whole.

INTRODUCING THEMES
● **Adding interest** Incorporate a few themed tiles into a plain tiled design to transform the appearance of a tiled surface.

Using relief tiles
Include relief tiles in a tiled area to add another dimension. Here, frogs leaping along a tiled back-splash tie in with the theme of running water in a bathroom.

COORDINATING COLOR

Using color boldly
Use a tiled area to make a bold color statement. Paint a piece of furniture so that it picks up one of the colors in the tiles, thus coordinating the decor.

PREPARING TO TILE

Tiled areas tend to be redecorated infrequently because tiles are expensive and more of a permanent fixture than other wall coverings. You are likely to live with them for a while, so prepare well and do a thorough job.

BASIC TILING EQUIPMENT

A toolkit for tiling will include a few more specialized tools than are required for most other decorating jobs. However, some general tools are, in effect, multi-purpose and lend themselves to a number of different tasks.

● **Choosing a tile cutter** By far the most important piece of equipment you will buy for tiling purposes is a tile cutter. Buy a good-quality one, as a substandard cutter will not produce clean edges and will increase the number of tiles that you break while cutting. This is wasteful of materials and time, and will result in greater expense in the long run.

● **Buying wisely** Do not be deterred by the initial expense of a few key tiling items: they may prove themselves to be worth it in the long run, especially as your technique improves.

● **Renting instead of buying** Consider renting expensive pieces of equipment such as tile-cutting machines, which you will use only occasionally.

Power drill

Tile file

Score-and-snap pliers

Tile scorer

Tile saw

Nippers

Sponge

Tile spacers

Tile cutter

Caulk tube and gun

Pointing trowel

Felt-tip pen

Tape measure

Filling knife

Notched spreader

Grout spreader

Goggles

Level

Tile gauge

MAKING SURFACES READY

It is essential that tiles make good contact with a wall by means of a consistent and even spread of adhesive. Walls do not need to be perfectly smooth as long as the surface is sealed, is as flat as possible, and has no unstable areas that may cause tiles to bulge or fall away.

PREPARING A WALL

● **Filling** Fill major holes with all-purpose filler. Before it dries, trim rough areas with a filling knife so that no pieces protrude. These patches will not be smooth, but are quite adequate for tiles. You do not need to sand the walls.

● **Removing old coverings** Do not tile over paper, however firmly attached it may appear to be. The adhesive and weight of the new tiles will almost certainly pull it away.

● **Sealing** Stabilize dusty walls or new plaster with a PVA solution (five parts water to one PVA) before tiling.

DEALING WITH OBSTACLES

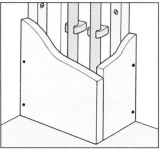

Boxing in
Create a neat, flat surface around obstacles such as pipes by boxing them in. Construct a simple wooden or plywood framework that is sturdy enough not to bow when it is pasted and tiled.

TILING OVER TILES

Old tiles make an excellent base for new as long as they are securely stuck to the wall.

● **Replacing damaged tiles** Remove cracked tiles, then fill the areas with one-coat plaster. This will be more economical than filler, especially if you need to remove several tiles.

● **Avoiding joints** Make sure that new tiles join in different places from those beneath.

● **Providing a key** Wash down old tiles with TSP, allow to dry, then sand with fine-grade sandpaper to provide a key for the new layer of tiles.

MEASURING

Accuracy when measuring is important so that overcalculations, which can prove expensive, and inconvenient undercalculations are avoided. You must first decide how much of a room to tile. Small variations at a later stage will make a large difference in requirements.

MAKING ALLOWANCES

● **Allowing for pictures** Picture tiles are usually more expensive than plain tiles, so you should calculate exactly how many you need, rather than working out the size of the area.

● **Tiling borders** Measure the total length of border tiles required rather than their area. Remember, however, to deduct the border area when you are calculating the area of the main body of tiles.

● **Using tiles of different sizes** If you wish to incorporate a complicated design in your tiled area, including tiles of different sizes for example, ask a tile retailer to work out your precise requirements. Supply a drawing of the tile design and the measurements of the area to be tiled.

MAKING A TILE GAUGE

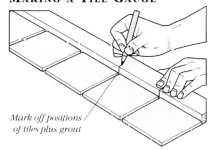

Mark off positions of tiles plus grout

Using a batten

Mark off tile-width measurements along a batten, either using sample tiles or based on tile sizes. Allow ⅛ in (2.5 mm) for grout between each tile. Use the gauge to calculate quantities of tiles and work out where cuts and joins will be.

CALCULATING QUANTITIES

Never estimate even the smallest part of a tiling area. Measure each section separately and accurately, then add the figures up to give the total area.

● **Measuring appropriately** Most retailers sell tiles in square yards (square meters), so work out coverage with this in mind.

● **Allowing for cuts and breaks** Add ten percent to the figure you have calculated to allow for wastage from cutting and the occasional breakage. Increase this percentage for awkward-shaped rooms that have many corners and cuts, and reduce it slightly for rooms that have broad expanses of wall surface.

PLANNING A TILING STRATEGY

Tiles are rigid and inflexible, so it is not possible to disguise mistakes like you can with wallpaper. You must, therefore, calculate exactly where rows of tiles will be, plan awkward areas carefully, and determine where cuts will fall.

ORDERING WORK

Tiling different sections in the correct order speeds up the job and produces the best finish. Take a little extra time to decide how you are going to tackle a particular area and to ensure that all equipment and materials are close at hand, clean, and ready for use.

STARTING OUT

● **Mixing tiles** When tiling a large area, mix different boxes of tiles in case there are color variations between batches. You will not notice them when the tiles are on the wall.
● **Starting at the bottom** Tile from the base of an area up.
● **Using natural levels** If bathtubs, sinks, or baseboards provide a natural base line within your tiling plan, use them as a starting point.
● **Accounting for corners** Make sure that corners look as if whole tiles are wrapped around them. Two small strips or two large scraps meeting at a corner join look unattractive. If you cannot plan so that whole tiles meet in a corner, two half-tiles look best.

TILING A WALL SECTION BY SECTION

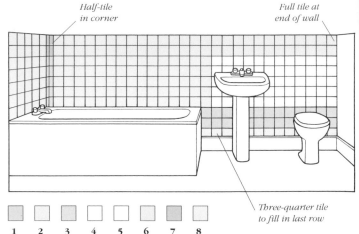

Half-tile in corner

Full tile at end of wall

Three-quarter tile to fill in last row

1 2 3 4 5 6 7 8

Dividing up a tiling area into sections
Lay tiles according to a plan (1–8). Do the easiest parts first, leaving cuts and other fine work until last. Plan so that whole tiles follow existing lines, such as the rim of a bathtub. Avoid using slivers of tiles, and check constantly that tiles are level.

USING A TILE GAUGE

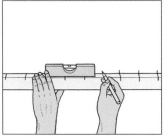

Measuring an area
Use a pencil and a tile gauge to mark all along the wall where the tiles should be placed. Make sure that the tile gauge remains horizontal by resting a small level on its upper edge.

FOLLOWING GUIDELINES

● **Using nonsquare tiles** You will need a second tile gauge for rectangular or nonsquare tiles in order to produce accurate vertical guidelines.
● **Limiting height** Tile tall walls in 1-yd (1-m) sections at a time; otherwise, the weight of the top layers can cause lower layers to bulge or pull away.
● **Checking tiles are flush** Use a tile gauge to see if tiles are flush. Run the flat edge across the tiled surface: it will knock against protruding tiles and show space in front of those that need building out.

MAKING A LEVEL BASE

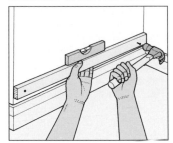

Attaching a batten
If there is no level base, carefully tack a batten to the wall, making sure that it is level, to create a base for tiling. When you have finished, remove the batten and fill in the area with cut tiles.

IMPROVING TECHNIQUES

Once you have a tiling strategy, the technique itself comes down to the mechanical process of applying adhesive and sticking tiles to a wall. Technical refinements should address methods of cutting and applying adhesive.

CUTTING AND ATTACHING TILES

You will produce a flat and even tiled finish if you apply adhesive correctly and if you take the right precautions to keep tiles level, both horizontally and vertically. Tiles cannot bend or stretch, so when you cut them make the incisions as precise as you possibly can.

APPLYING ADHESIVE

Using a notched spreader
Use a professional spreader to apply adhesive to a wall. Work in areas of up to 1 sq yd (1 m²), and make sure that the adhesive has a uniform, ridged appearance before applying any tiles.

LEVELING TILED WALLS

Reducing adhesive
On uneven walls, vary the depth of adhesive for an even finish. Before the adhesive dries, level out protruding tiles using a wide-bladed scraper. Remove some of the adhesive and replace the tile.

TRADITIONAL TIP

Spacing tiles
Matchsticks are ideal for maintaining the spaces between tiles while you grout. They can be used again and again – unlike plastic tile spacers, which cannot be removed once grout is dry.

TILING AROUND PLASTIC BATHTUBS

Plastic fixtures are prone to movement because they are flexible, so take extra care to ensure a good tiled finish.

● **Supporting** Provide extra support beneath a plastic tub to stop downward movement cracking the grout around the bottom row of tiles.
● **Filling** Fill a plastic tub with water before you start tiling around it so that it will be in the correct position and shape.
● **Sealing** Run silicone beading around the top of a plastic tub before tiling to make a barrier against water seepage.

PREEMPTING PROBLEMS

● **Using thin tiles** Spacers are too deep to be left in place between thin tiles and may show through the grout. Use them at right angles to the joins, and remove before grouting.
● **Making allowances** When measuring tiles for cutting, allow ⅛ in (2.5 mm) for grout.
● **Tiling with marble** Marble tiles should give the appearance of a solid sheet, though grout is required for waterproofing. Use strips of cardboard as spacers.
● **Reducing cleanup** Keep a damp sponge and a dry cloth handy so that you can keep tiles and hands clean at all times while you work.

CUTTING QUICKLY

Grip lever firmly

Tile cutter

Tile

Mounting a tile cutter
Using a tile cutter is the easiest way of making neat, accurate cuts. Mount the cutter on a workbench or clamp it to a tabletop to hold it firm and at the correct working height.

TILING AWKWARD AREAS

As with all decorating techniques, some areas are more difficult to tile than others. Corners, as you might expect, can present a challenge if you want them to look as neat as possible, and you may well need to cut intricate shapes to tile successfully around obstacles.

OVERCOMING OBSTACLES

● **Using nippers** To cut away awkward pieces of tile, use nippers. These resemble a pair of pliers and enable you to chip off small sections of tile between the sharp-edged jaws.
● **Dealing with pipes** Remove any pipe brackets so that tiles can be slipped directly behind. Reposition brackets after tiling by drilling new holes in the tiles (see p. 250). Take care not to overtighten the screws, which might crack the tiles.
● **Tiling recesses** To provide support once downward-facing tiles have been attached along the top surface of a recessed window, cut three pieces of batten – one the width of the recess and two the height of it. Rest the two uprights on the windowsill, supporting the horizontal flush to the top tiles until the adhesive has dried.

TILING AROUND CURVED OBSTACLES

● **Measuring curves** Mold a pipe cleaner or piece of wire to the curve's shape, then draw along it on the tile to be cut.

● **Choosing a blade** Select a tungsten carbide blade to make a precise cut and thus create the most accurate curve.

CUTTING CURVES USING A TEMPLATE

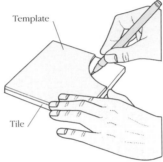

Template

Tile

Tile saw

1 Make a cardboard template of a curve – allowing for grout – and lay it on top of the tile. Trace around the edge with a nonpermanent felt-tip pen, so that the ink guideline can be wiped off the tile later.

2 Use a specialized tile saw to cut around the shape of the curve accurately. Place the tile on a workbench, hold it very firmly, and cut – using a normal sawing action – along the guideline you have marked.

TILING EXTERNAL & INTERNAL CORNERS

Hiding edges
Attach a plastic corner strip to an external corner to conceal and protect tile edges. Mount the strip onto the corner with tile adhesive. Using whole tiles, tile away from the strip on each wall, aligning the tiles vertically with it.

Making a neat edge
When tiling an internal corner, place tiles alternately on each wall to ensure an even corner join and to keep the tiles level and in position. Leave gaps for grout in between the corner tiles, using spacers in the usual way.

DEALING WITH SOCKETS AND SWITCHES

Tiling around sockets and switches offers no particular problems as long as you follow basic guidelines.

● **Turning off power** Always turn off the electricity supply before you begin work.
● **Loosening screws** Loosen electrical socket or switch screws so that tile edges can be inserted behind the socket plate. Do not retighten the screws until after grouting.
● **Adjusting screw length** If using thick tiles, it may be necessary to replace existing socket screws with longer ones so that the socket plate can be screwed firmly back on to the electrical housing.

TILING CREATIVELY

Tiling is a flexible option when it comes to making decorative decisions. You can create a variety of designs and tile arrangements using different shapes and sizes of tile to lend an individualistic and personal look to any room.

CHOOSING TILES OF DIFFERENT SIZES

The most obvious alternative to traditional tiling methods is to use different-sized tiles to achieve various effects. Application methods are similar to standard tiling techniques. Minor refinements, however, can speed up the tiling process as well as improve the finish.

USING LARGE TILES
● **Choosing surfaces** Large tiles look most impressive on large wall surfaces rather than in small, detailed places. Too many half-tiles and joins detract from the overall look.

● **Using marble tiles** Use marble tiles only on flat wall surfaces, since undulations will highlight grouted joins and spoil the "sheet" finish.

● **Cutting marble tiles** Cut marble tiles with a tile-cutting machine for greater accuracy. Ask your tile retailer to miter external corner joins, or rent a tabletop-mounted tile saw.

APPLYING MOSAICS

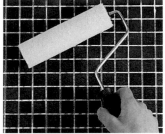

Bedding in
Use a short-pile roller to bed sheets of mosaic tiles into tile adhesive. This will ensure that you apply even pressure all over the area, so that the tiles stick firmly and lie flush to the wall.

USING SMALL TILES
● **Positioning tiles** Mosaic tiles within a sheet may drift out of position if the backing is defective. While the adhesive is still wet, reposition the tiles using the edge of a scraper, then support them with spacers.

● **Cutting tiles out** If the sheet backing will not allow you to reposition easily, cut the tile out of the sheet with a craft knife. Apply adhesive to the back and put it back in place, using spacers to keep it level.

● **Finishing edges** Cut up some of the mosaic sheets and use to edge other tiled areas.

DESIGNING LAYOUTS

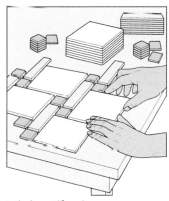

Mixing tile sizes
Lay out your tile design "dry" on a tabletop, then take the tiles directly from the table to the wall. By doing this, you will be able to see what the pattern looks like and make any adjustments before the tiles are stuck down.

MAKING YOUR OWN MOSAIC

As well as standard square mosaic tiles, you can use smaller and irregularly shaped tiles to create mosaics that are less uniform. Incorporate small pieces of broken tile to build up either simple patterns or more complicated images.

● **Making mosaic tiles** Use tile nippers to break up old and leftover tiles into small irregular pieces approximately $\frac{3}{4}$–$1\frac{1}{2}$ sq in (2–4 cm²) in area.

● **Producing a design** A design can be drawn on a wall using a method similar to that used for painting murals (see p. 216). Carefully fill in the shapes that make up the image with small pieces of tile instead of paint to create your own mosaic.

Creating a bold design
You can combine irregular-shaped fragments of tile with custom-made, square mosaic tiles to stunning effect. Framing the area with uniform but vivid bands of color adds drama.

INSERTING TILES AND BORDERS

Picture tiles, inset tiles, and border tiles can provide the finishing touches on a tiled surface. They add interest to a plain tile design, or – in the case of borders – frame the whole tiled area or a panel. The choice of tiles is huge, so finding some suitable ones should be easy.

USING BORDER TILES

● **Ordering work** Always finish the main body of tiling before applying border tiles.
● **Applying tiles** Because most border tiles are by nature very narrow, spread the adhesive on the back of the tile and then position it on the wall, rather than applying adhesive to the wall before mounting the tile.
● **Dealing with corners** Mitering corners is difficult with a standard tile cutter, so flush-join the tiles or calculate where miter cuts will be. Ask your supplier to cut them.
● **Tiling up to wallpaper** If you are papering a wall above a tiled area, insert the extreme edge of the paper beneath the tile edges. Complete the tiling as far as the border, then apply the paper to just below where the upper edge of the border tiles will be. Once the papering is complete, attach the border tiles in position.

INSERTING CHAIR RAILS

● **Using wood** Vary the texture of a tiled surface by inserting a wooden molding in the form of a chair rail. Paint it to match or complement the surrounding tiled area.

Using tiles
Create the effect of a chair rail within a tiled wall using flat tiles that provide a contrasting band of color or pattern. Alternatively, insert precisely cut half-tiles in another color or pattern to produce the same effect.

VARYING BORDERS

● **Offsetting joins** Many border tiles are a different width from the main tiles. Offset the joins when possible, so that they occur near the mid-point of the main tile width.

Deepening a border
Create a deep border by using two rows of border tiles, one beneath the other. Place relief border tiles along the top, for example, with decorated border tiles below to create a more interesting decorative effect.

PLANNING TILED IMAGES

Drawing a plan
Using squared paper, draw an accurate plan to scale of the whole area to be tiled, including any picture tiles. Follow the plan carefully as you tile. This will help to ensure that picture tiles are positioned accurately.

INSERTING PICTURE TILES

● **Changing existing tiles** Rejuvenate an old tiled surface by removing some tiles and inserting picture tiles. Remove tiles by means of the technique used for replacing broken or cracked tiles (see p. 251).
● **Creating panels** Use picture tiles to make up separate tiled panels on suitable flat areas of wall, making a decorative feature that is not necessarily part of a larger tiled area.
● **Making a border** Create a deep border using picture tiles instead of border tiles. Use the opportunity to introduce a theme. A border of fruits and vegetables, for example, will be suitable for a kitchen.

MONEY-SAVING TIP

Adding new tiles to old
Attach a new tiled border above old bathroom tiles to spruce the room up without completely retiling. Clean up the old tiles thoroughly, then regrout if necessary.

TILING WORK SURFACES

Most wall tiles, as their name suggests, are applied to flat, vertical surfaces. However, horizontal surfaces are often just as suitable for tiling, and some can benefit greatly. The most common application is to cover work surfaces with tiles, such as in kitchens and utility rooms.

TILING HORIZONTALLY

● **Supporting weight** Tiles are relatively heavy, so if a work surface is lightweight, you may need to give it some additional support. The best way of doing this is to build up the top of the work surface with a sheet of plywood to spread the extra weight.

● **Making surfaces ready** Many work surfaces are not suitable for direct tiling. To prepare such surfaces, cut out and fit a thin piece of plywood or MDF as a base on which you can then mount the tiles.

● **Neatening edges** Always use whole tiles along the front edge of a work surface, and work backward to a cut join if necessary at the wall.

ADJUSTING GROUT

● **Finishing flush** Apply grout so that it is absolutely flush with the tiles. This will make it easier to clean the tiled surface and reduce the risk of dirt lodging in grout crevices.

● **Cleaning grout** Use a commercial grout cleaner from time to time to help keep the grouted areas of a tiled work surface as clean as possible.

● **Grouting hygienically** The most hygienic way of grouting tiles is with an epoxy-based grout. This forms a longer-lasting surface that is far more resistant to bacterial growth than traditional grout. Epoxy-based grout is difficult to apply, however, so you may need to hire a professional.

EDGING WORK SURFACES

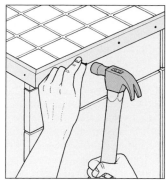

Attaching battens
Attach hardwood battens along work-surface edges to produce a neat finish. Paint or varnish as required. Make sure that the batten tops are flush with the tiles, otherwise cleaning the work surface will be difficult.

USING SPECIALLY MADE TILES

Besides their most obvious function of providing a tough washable surface, tiles have other practical uses around the home. Many types have been specially modified in design for a particular purpose, but ordinary tiles can also be put to a variety of uses.

SUPPORTING HEAVY TILES

Attaching soap dishes
Because of its weight, a soap-dish tile needs support to stay in place while the adhesive dries. Strap masking tape over it and the adjacent tiles for support. Remove the tape once the adhesive has dried.

MODIFYING WORKTOPS

Making a chopping board
Cut a hole and insert a tile in a worktop to create a permanent chopping board. A large marble tile is ideal, since it is tough and easily cleaned. Seal around the edges of the tile with a bead of clear silicone after inserting it.

IMPROVING EFFICIENCY

● **Waterproofing showers** Tiles in a shower area will be heavily bombarded by water and so require extra waterproofing. Use a specialized, commercial waterproofing grout, and seal all corners within the shower area with clear silicone after you have grouted to provide an extra waterproof barrier.

● **Tiling sills** Bathrooms are especially prone to high levels of condensation. Water runoff onto a sill can quickly degrade the surface if the sill is merely painted. It is a good idea, therefore, to tile all the sills in a bathroom to give them extra protection and increase their lifespan.

DECORATING PLAIN TILES

Completely retiling a room can be costly, so it is always worth considering whether or not the existing tiles can be renovated using other decorative methods. Similarly, you can buy inexpensive, plain tiles, and then enhance them using one or more painting techniques.

PAINTING TILES

● **Repairing grout** Rake out any old, loose grout from joints using a scraper, and fill the gaps with all-purpose filler.

● **Preparing surfaces** Prepare an old tiled surface by cleaning down thoroughly with TSP and rinsing with clean water. Allow to dry thoroughly, then apply a commercial tile primer.

● **Applying paint** After you have carried out the correct preparation, you can use either commercial tile paints or normal acrylic or oil-based paints. Protect the tiles with a coat of ceramic varnish once you have finished painting.

● **Painting selectively** There is no need to paint all the tiles on a wall. Simply painting in a border or stenciling images on a few tiles can revive the look of a "tired" tiled surface.

HAND-PAINTING TILES

Using ceramic paints, you can paint your own designs onto tiles as long as they have been correctly prepared. Depending on the extent of your artistic capabilities, you can transfer an image to a tile and color it in (as below) or paint it freehand.

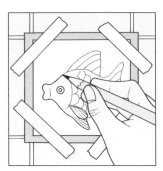 

1 Use masking tape to stick an image over a tile, placing carbon paper between the image and the tile. Draw around the picture outline, pressing hard enough for the carbon to transfer the image to the tile.

2 Paint in the image, taking care not to apply too much paint and risk drips and runs. Add as much detail as you wish. Allow one color to dry before applying any others, thus preventing them from running.

PAINTING TILES IN LOW-WEAR AREAS

If you do not use the correct materials, painted tiles will not wear well, since moisture and regular cleaning will damage the finish. In areas of low wear, however, painted surfaces will survive better, so you can substitute other materials.

● **Creating paint effects** Use an oil-based semigloss as a base coat for paint effects on tiles. Sponging and ragging are very effective. Finish off with a protective coat of varnish.

● **Using transfers** Commercial tile transfers will brighten up and change the appearance of even the plainest tiled area.

● **Creating mosaics** Paint old tiles different colors, and break them up into pieces for a mosaic.

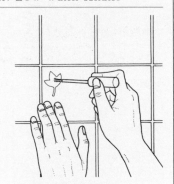

Using car paints
Car touch-up paints are ideal materials to use for painting small motifs or patterns on to a few tiles to brighten them up. You may not need to find a brush, since this is sometimes an integral part of the container.

PROTECTING IMAGES

Applying varnish
Protect stenciled images (see p. 215) on tiles with ceramic varnish. There is no need to varnish the whole tile. Use the stencil to ensure that the varnish is applied to the image only.

FINISHING

TILES REQUIRE CARE AFTER APPLICATION to ensure that they look good and wear well for as long as possible. As well as tidying them decoratively, you must finish tiles so that they serve their practical purpose efficiently.

WATERPROOFING TILES

Tiles are of little practical use unless they are completely waterproofed, providing an easily cleaned surface that is totally impermeable to water. Joins and tile edges are the areas most prone to water penetration and seepage, and therefore require the most attention.

GROUTING SUCCESSFULLY

● **Selecting grout** Choose powdered grout that you mix with water, since this is more durable than dual-purpose adhesive or other grouts.

● **Making neat lines** Run a grout shaper or the edge of your finger down the joints once excess grout has been removed but before it dries.

● **Grouting marble tiles** Ensure that grout is flush with the tile surface to give the illusion of a flat expanse of marble.

● **Producing a sheen** Wipe the tiles first with a damp sponge to remove excess grout. When dry, polish with a lint-free cloth. Polish several times.

APPLYING GROUT

Using a grout spreader
Distribute grout with a spreader, which will not scratch a glazed surface and will push the grout firmly into every gap. Keep passing over the joints until the grout is completely compacted.

CHOOSING COLOR

Matching grout
Grout is available in several different colors, so you can pick one to suit other decoration. Alternatively, mix white powdered grout with powdered pigments until you create the right color.

SEALING WITH SILICONE

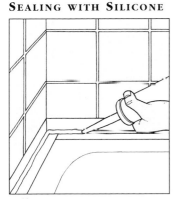

Filling a groove
Mask along a tile and the adjacent surface to make a straight-edged channel. Squeeze silicone into position from its tube. Smooth with a wetted finger, and remove the tape before the sealant dries.

USING PLASTIC STRIPS

● **Overlapping edges** Create a good seal by inserting custom-made plastic strips before you tile, so that the bottom edge of the bottom layer of tiles overlaps the top of the strip.

● **Double-sealing** Apply a bead of silicone behind a plastic strip as a double seal.

● **Dealing with corners** To create an effective water barrier at the same time as a mitered join, miter only one plastic strip in a corner and lay it on top of the adjacent strip, which should run all the way into the corner flush to the tiles.

● **Attaching strips** Fix a strip to tiles and adjacent surfaces with waterproof, double-sided tape.

BRIGHT IDEA

Using decorative moldings
Wooden moldings may be used as a seal along tile edges as long as the wood has been primed and painted with an oil-based paint. Mount the molding in position using silicone sealant.

ATTACHING FIXTURES

Tiling is not complete until any fixtures have been attached to the tiled surface. Tiled surfaces cannot be touched up easily in a similar manner to painted or wallpapered surfaces, so make sure that fixtures are placed in the correct position at the first attempt.

DRILLING WISELY
● **Keeping to the middle** Try to position attachments so that you drill holes in tiles away from the edges. Drilling near edges may cause cracking.
● **Making watertight** When putting a screw into a hole in a tile, apply a small bead of silicone to the point of the screw. This will prevent any water from seeping into the hole and behind the tile.
● **Protecting eyes** Use goggles when drilling to protect your eyes from flying tile splinters.
● **Finding alternatives** If an attachment will bear little weight, use self-adhesive pads to mount it in place.

DRILLING HOLES

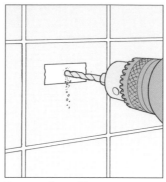

Preventing slippage
Place masking tape over the point at which a fixture will be attached, and drill through the tape into the wall. The tape will prevent the drill from slipping.

POSITIONING FIXTURES

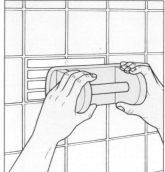

Using double-sided tape
Temporarily attach a fixture to the wall using double-sided tape. This will enable you to judge whether to make adjustments prior to mounting the fixing.

CLEANING UP

As with all decorating tasks, no tiling job is complete until the necessary cleaning up operation has been done. The finished tile surfaces should be wiped down well, and all equipment should be thoroughly washed and dried, then stored away carefully and safely.

REMOVING DRIED GROUT
● **Using scourers** To remove very small pieces of dried grout from a newly tiled surface, rub gently with a dampened, nonabrasive kitchen scourer.

Using a window scraper
Remove dried grout with a window scraper, running the sharp edge of the blade smoothly over the tiles. To prevent scratching the glazed surface, lubricate the scraper with dish detergent.

NEATENING GROUT
● **Touching up grout** It may take a day or so for grout to dry completely, and during this time air bubbles may form in the grouted joints (especially beneath the lower edges of tiles). Pierce any bubbles, then fill the holes with small beads of grout applied with one finger.
● **Cleaning tubs and sinks** To remove spots of dry grout from tubs or sinks, fill them with hot water and allow the grout to soak. Drain the water away, then wipe off the grout with a nonabrasive pad.
● **Cleaning carpet** If any tile adhesive or grout falls on to a carpet during tiling, allow it to dry before removing with a stiff-bristled brush.

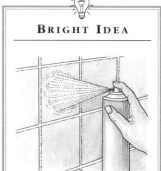

MAINTAINING TILES

Tiles have a long decorative life that tends to end because color preferences and design trends change rather than because of the deterioration of the tiles themselves. Sometimes, however, a little regular maintenance and a few repairs are needed to keep tiles looking pristine.

REPLACING AN ISOLATED DAMAGED TILE

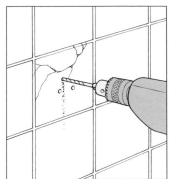

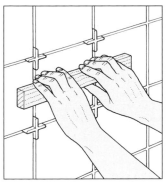

1 First, loosen the tile's adhesion to the wall. Do this by drilling several holes in the tile, thus breaking up the surface. Remember to wear goggles to protect your eyes.

2 With a hammer and chisel, chip out fragments of tile, taking care not to crack adjacent tiles. Keep the goggles on; you may also wish to wear gloves to protect your hands.

3 Spread adhesive on the back of a new tile, and stick it in position. Use spacers to hold it there and a batten to make sure that it is flush with adjacent tiles. Grout and polish.

DEALING WITH CRACKS
● **Using paint** Mix a small amount of an artist's paint (which matches the tile color) with grout to make a paste. Smooth it into small, hairline cracks to fill them. Remove excess, then allow to dry.

KEEPING GROUT WHITE
● **Cleaning grout** Treat dirty grout with a commercial grout cleaner or a mild solution of household bleach. Do a test patch to ensure that the tiles will not discolor. Work in with a toothbrush, then rinse off.

REPLACING GROUT
● **Starting over** Grout is prone to discoloration from dirt or simply through aging. Clear out old grout with a grout raker or the edge of a scraper, then regrout the whole tiled area as you would normally.

USING LEFTOVER TILES

Always keep some leftover tiles for replacement purposes. Trying to find a matching tile after a number of years is difficult. Even shades of white vary if different makes of tile are placed side by side. There are many ways of using up the rest of your leftover tiles.

● **Adding to the tiling plan** You can always add an additional row to an area that you have already tiled – for example, to increase the size of a tiled backsplash. It is usually worth reconsidering the extent of the original tiling design.

● **Tiling sills** Areas of heavy wear, such as windowsills, benefit from tiling. Use leftovers from another project for this. You will create a more hardwearing, easily wiped, as well as attractive, surface.
● **Making kitchen equipment** Attach a picture tile to a wooden block to make a cheese board. A large marble tile can be used as a chopping board. Attach rubber feet to prevent it from slipping.
● **Using broken tiles** Broken tiles are useful for making mosaic tiles (see p. 245). Alternatively, shape the fragments with tile nippers, then attach them to the rim of plant pots for extra decoration.

Cut down firmly into cork tile

Making a pot stand
Place a leftover picture tile squarely in the corner of a cork floor tile. Cut around the other two edges with a craft knife. Glue tile to cork with PVA.

DECORATING WOODWORK

QUICK REFERENCE
Preparing to Paint, p. 254
Painting Specific Areas, p. 256
Enhancing Wood, p. 258
Creating Paint Effects, p. 259
Painting Furniture, p. 263
Finishing, p. 266

IF THE WALLS ARE THE BACKDROP for all the decorative features of a room, then the woodwork is the frame upon which the whole look of the room hangs. It is up to you how prominent you make that framework, which offers you great scope for experimentation. Decorating woodwork is not confined to permanent fixtures: painting furniture adds a further decorative dimension.

SELECTING MATERIALS

There is great diversity in the types of finish available for wood. They vary considerably in terms of color and sheen as well as their level of opacity and translucency. Choosing the right finish depends on the type of wood and how it fits in with other decorated surfaces.

PAINT TYPES AND WOOD FINISHES

TYPE	FINISH	USES	COVERAGE
Gloss/ Quick-drying (QD) gloss	Gloss is oil-based with a high-gloss finish. It is extremely durable. QD gloss is water-based with a less shiny finish than standard gloss.	You can apply gloss to all woods. Use an oil-based primer on resinous woods. QD is suitable for all woods except resinous ones and is ideal for retouching.	680 sq ft/gal (17 m²/l) QD: 620 sq ft/gal (15 m²/l)
Semigloss/ Quick-drying (QD) semigloss	Durable semigloss is oil-based with a midsheen finish. Water-based QD semigloss has a similar finish, but is not as durable.	Semigloss is ideal on poor surfaces. QD is suitable for most woods except highly resinous ones. Its quick-drying properties make it ideal for busy areas.	650 sq ft/gal (16 m²/l) QD: 620 sq ft/gal (15 m²/l)
Varnish/ Quick-drying (QD) varnish	Varnish is oil-based with a matte to high-gloss finish. It is extremely durable. Water-based QD varnish has a matte to gloss finish and is durable.	Varnish is suitable for all woods. Smooth-planed surfaces produce the best finish. QD varnish is suitable for all woods and ideal for large-scale areas.	620 sq ft/gal (15 m²/l) QD: 420 sq ft/gal (10 m²/l)
Woodstain/ Quick-drying (QD) woodstain	Woodstain is oil-based with a low- to high-sheen, translucent finish and is durable. Water-based QD woodstain also has a translucent finish.	Woodstain can be applied to all woods (must be stripped) and is good for mixtures of wood. QD is suitable for all woods and allows several coats in a day.	910 sq ft/gal (22 m²/l) QD: 840 sq ft/gal (20 m²/l)
Linseed oil	Solvent-based, midsheen, nourishing finish.	Ideal for hardwoods and low-wear areas.	440 sq ft/gal (12 m²/l)
Wax	Solvent- or water-based finish that requires polishing.	Suitable for all woods. Can be applied over stains and dyes.	680 sq ft/gal (17 m²/l)

BASIC PAINTING EQUIPMENT

Equipment for painting wood is little different from that for painting walls, necessitating just a few additional items.

● **Choosing brushes** Painting woodwork involves more detailed and smaller-scale work than painting walls, so you will need a larger range of small brushes. Pure bristle brushes give the highest-quality finish but are more expensive than their synthetic counterparts. They are, however, easier to use.

● **Selecting sandpaper** Buy several grades of sandpapers. A good-quality, fine-grade paper is essential for the smoothest possible finish.

Angle-head paintbrush

Lint-free cloth

½-in (12.5-mm) paintbrush

2-in (50-mm) paintbrush

Varnish brush

Sandpaper

Hot-air gun

Dropcloth

Small roller and tray

CALCULATING QUANTITIES

Measuring solid surfaces such as doors and baseboards is realtively simple. With other items, a method of measuring may not be obvious. Use the table opposite to calculate how much paint you need for surfaces of average porosity.

● **Windows** To calculate the surface area of the frame of a picture window, measure the frame's width and perimeter. Casement windows have many rails, so measure the area of the whole window, including the glass.

● **Coverage** Paints and natural-wood finishes vary in their coverage. Consider this carefully when calculating the number of coats required.

● **Preparatory coats** Do not forget that bare wood needs priming, and most paints need an undercoat before painting.

WOOD TYPES COMMONLY FOUND AROUND THE HOME

Many types of wood are found around the average home. They are categorized according to suitability of finish.

● **Natural woods** You will find that planed wood is used generally for intricate areas such as moldings and baseboards. Rough-sawn wood is used for construction and is unlikely to require decorating. The exception to this may be houses in which beams are exposed.

● **Manufactured woods** You may prefer to use "manufactured" woods, whose appearance differs greatly from natural grain. Produced in large sheets, the versatility of these materials means that they can be used for structural purposes, such as floors, as well as for making doors, panels, and other items. Some are impregnated with fire-retardant substances that may affect paint application.

Softwood
Natural wood, usually pale in color. Used for all internal joinery. Takes most paints and natural wood finishes.

Hardwood
Natural wood, higher quality than softwood. Used for internal joinery. Best suited to natural wood finishes.

Plywood
Sheets made of layers of veneer. Takes all paints, but natural wood finishes may give patchy coverage.

Medium-density fiberboard (MDF)
Sheets of compressed wood fibers. Often used for cupboards and door panels. Takes all paints.

Hardboard
Smooth, high-density board made of compressed wood fibers. Thinner than MDF; used for floors. Takes most paints.

Chipboard
Sheets of compressed wood particles. Often used as a flooring material. Takes certain paints – follow suppliers' guidelines.

PREPARING TO PAINT

DEFECTS IN WOODWORK tend to be enhanced rather than disguised by paint, so it is important to prepare the wood as well as possible before you paint it. Then make sure that you apply the paint using the appropriate techniques.

STRIPPING AND SANDING

You will need to judge how much preparation work is required and, more importantly, whether or not to remove old paint. Multiple layers are best stripped, but a previously sound painted surface can very often be redecorated after a thorough sanding and washing down.

ORDER OF WORK

Use this checklist when planning your work. It may be varied slightly according to the paint system and manufacturers' guidelines.

● Mask adjacent surfaces.
● Strip old paint.
● Seal knots.
● Prime bare wood.
● Fill cracks and holes.
● Sand surfaces.
● Vacuum.
● Wipe down surfaces.
● Paint undercoat.
● Lightly sand.
● Wipe down.
● Paint top coat.

HEAT STRIPPING

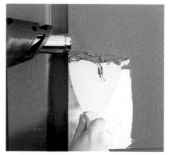

Using a hot-air gun
Scrape off paint as it bubbles with a broad-bladed stripping knife. Do not apply heat for long in one place, since the wood may scorch. Use the scraper to protect the previously stripped area.

STRIPPING SAFELY
● **Protecting yourself** Always wear a mask to reduce the risk of inhaling harmful fumes given off by the paint or a chemical stripper. In addition, you may like to protect your hands from injury or irritation by wearing gloves.
● **Reducing fire risks** Never leave a hot-air gun unattended while it is switched on.
● **Checking for lead** When stripping very old layers of paint, check that they do not contain lead, which is toxic if it gets into the body. Most home-supply stores sell lead tester kits for this purpose.

USING CHEMICALS
● **Applying stripper** Wear a pair of gloves and use an old brush to apply stripper. Use a dabbing rather than a brushing motion. Do not brush the stripper in too much since this will reduce its concentration over that area.
● **Stripping outside** Stripping can be a messy business, so if possible remove doors and strip them outdoors. Lay them horizontally on horses so that a thick coat of stripper can be applied without running off.
● **Neutralizing stripper** Once old paint has been removed, neutralize the chemicals in the stripper by washing down the wood with white vinegar. Then rinse with clean water.

SANDING MOLDINGS

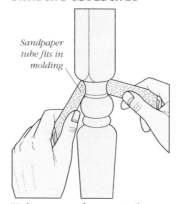

Sandpaper tube fits in molding

Using a sandpaper tube
To make sanding intricate areas such as banister moldings easier, roll up some sandpaper into a tube. Adjust the diameter of the tube so that it matches the rounded profile of the molding.

TRADITIONAL TIP

Wiping down
Before painting a horizontal surface, wipe it with a lint-free cloth dampened with turpentine. This will pick up dust and smooth the finish ready for painting.

FILLING

Most woodwork cannot be simply sanded then painted. Usually scratches and small holes will need some filling prior to painting. There are a variety of fillers available for this: some are all-purpose, while others, such as fine surface filler, serve a specific purpose.

FOLLOWING GUIDELINES
● **Removing dust** Once an area has been filled and sanded, remove any filler dust by wiping with a damp cloth.
● **Saving time** Keep a jar of ready-mixed filler handy for filling small holes that you may have missed the first time.
● **Smoothing surfaces** Use a fine surface filler on ornate moldings. When sanded, this will provide the smoothest possible surface for paint.
● **Molding filler** Smooth filler into position when repairing small holes and cracks by shaping it with a damp artist's brush. Smoothing the filler carefully will reduce the need for sanding once it has dried.

DEALING WITH BIG GAPS

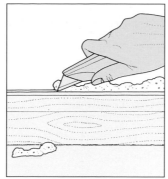

Filling and trimming
Use an aerosol foam filler to fill a large hole, such as a wide crack behind a baseboard. Traditional fillers will not hold in place as well. Trim any excess filler with a craft knife.

USING FLEXIBLE FILLER
● **Raking out** Remove flaky paint and other pieces of debris from cracked joints by running the edge of a scraper firmly down the joint. Dust well before applying the filler.
● **Smoothing** Tubed flexible filler cannot be sanded, so smooth it before it dries. Once the filler is in position, use a clean, damp sponge to smooth it over. To give the best finish, run down the joint with a wet finger.
● **Preventing cracking** Hairline cracks may appear in water-based paint applied over flexible filler. Avoid these by priming the filler with oil-based undercoat before painting.

PRIMING AND PAINTING

In order to produce the best finish, consider carefully any preparatory coats and the top coats that will be required. These will differ depending on whether you have chosen water- or oil-based materials. Also think about the techniques suitable for painting wooden surfaces.

APPLYING FIRST COATS
● **Sealing knots** Apply water-based knotter when using water-based paint. It will be more compatible with acrylic paints and will seal knots without showing through subsequent coats of paint.
● **Coating natural wood** When applying a natural wood coating, do not knot or prime. Most natural wood coatings will automatically be sealed when you apply the first coat.
● **Breaking in brushes** Always use new brushes for priming rather than painting, since they will probably molt bristles the first time they are used. This means they will be in a better condition for applying subsequent coats.

APPLYING TOP COATS TO FLAT SURFACES

1 First, paint a number of vertical strips about 12 in (30 cm) in length. Reload the brush with paint for each strip. Without reloading, spread the paint across the panel surface using horizontal strokes.

2 Without reloading, lightly brush the area vertically to lay off the paint and produce an even coverage. Use this technique for painting both undercoats and top coats on most flat surface areas.

PAINTING SPECIFIC AREAS

Your painting technique will always need to be adapted to suit different areas and surfaces. Most adaptations will be concerned with the order in which an area is painted and with obtaining the best finish quickly and efficiently.

PAINTING DOORS

Doors make up the largest proportion of wooden surfaces in most homes, and it is therefore important that they are painted in the right way. Door designs vary, but most common ones fall into two categories – paneled or flat – in terms of technical painting requirements.

PAINTING DOORS TO REFLECT ROOM COLORS

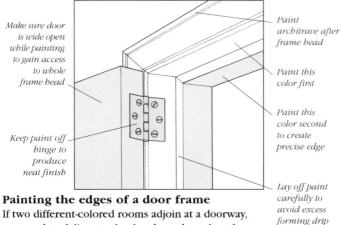

Make sure door is wide open while painting to gain access to whole frame head

Paint architrave after frame head

Paint this color first

Paint this color second to create precise edge

Keep paint off hinge to produce neat finish

Lay off paint carefully to avoid excess forming drip marks along frame edge

Painting the edges of a door frame
If two different-colored rooms adjoin at a doorway, you need to delineate clearly where the color of one room ends and the color of the other room begins. Following convention, paint certain edges within a door frame one color or the other in order to indicate which room they belong to decoratively.

DEFINING EDGES

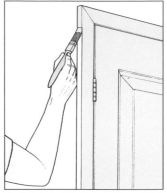

Resting your elbow
Facilitate the painting of straight lines between architrave and wall by resting your elbow against the wall. As you move the paintbrush down, your hand will be less likely to wobble.

PAINTING CUPBOARDS

Consider these points when painting cupboards to save time and increase efficiency.

● **Removing door furniture** Remove handles and door latches to make painting easier and prevent them from being splashed with paint.
● **Painting drawers** Paint the fronts of drawers but not the sides and runners, since this will hinder drawer motion.
● **Painting inside** Paint a pale color inside a cupboard to increase light reflection when the door is open. You will then see the contents more easily.

COVERING DOORS EFFICIENTLY

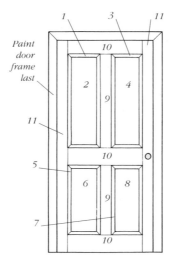

Paint door frame last

● **Opening and closing** Save time by removing door furniture before painting. It is difficult to move a door with no handle, so wedge it open with folded cardboard while painting, and use a screwdriver as a handle.

Working in order
Paint the panels of a door in a logical sequence (1–11). Starting at the top, and working from left to right, paint in narrow, horizontal sections. Use a small brush to paint moldings and for cutting in. Paint a flat door in 2.5-sq-ft (0.25-m^2) sections from top to bottom and left to right.

PAINTING WINDOWS

You may be concerned that painting around panes of glass is both difficult and time-consuming. This does not have to be the case, however, if you paint windows in a systematic way and extend your repertoire of painting techniques slightly to aid the process further.

PLANNING THE PAINTING OF WINDOWS

● **Starting early** Paint windows early in the day so that they can stay open to dry for as long as possible. Wedge them open with cardboard to prevent them from slamming shut.

● **Cleaning glass** Remove splashes of undercoat with a window scraper and polish the glass with a commercial household cleaner before top-coating the woodwork.

Paint precise lines between wood and wall

Working logically
Work from the top of a window frame downward, and from areas nearest the glass outward (1-6). Follow this system to ensure that you do not miss any part of the frame. It is easy to miss areas if the new paint color is similar to the old.

SHIELDING GLASS

Using a window guard
Cut the base out of a plastic food container, leaving part of one side as a handle. Hold the guard to the glass–frame junction, then paint without overspill on to the glass. Clean the guard regularly.

PAINTING OTHER AREAS

Not all the surfaces around a home fit into simple categories: some will require more diverse techniques. Metal surfaces, for example, might require specific preparation before you decorate them, and certain parts of the house, such as high-wear areas, need special attention.

DEALING WITH METAL

● **Removing rust** Patches of rust on metal should be sanded back – to the bare metal if necessary. Prime and paint the bare surface immediately to prevent moist air from getting at it and triggering the rusting process once again.
● **Choosing primers** You might find a vast array of different metals and alloys around your home. Make sure that you use a primer that suits each metal's individual properties.
● **Painting radiators** Always paint radiators when they are cold. Applying paint to a warm or hot surface will cause it to dry too quickly. The paint will therefore be difficult to brush out, resulting in a patchy finish.

NEGOTIATING PIPES

● **Painting large pipes** Use a radiator roller to cover large pipes quickly and evenly. Protect nearby areas from overspray. Cut in with a brush.

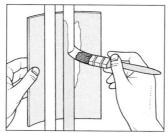

Shielding a wall
To make it easier to paint pipes that are against a wall, hold a piece of cardboard behind them to protect the wall from a buildup of paint splashes. Move it up or down as you progress.

PAINTING STAIRWAYS

When painting woodwork on a stairway, consider the specific requirements of this part of the building. A good finish is especially important if the stairs are in constant use.

● **Protecting handrails** Give handrails an extra top coat, since these are the areas that receive the most wear.
● **Painting edges** Before laying a new carpet, cut in carefully on each step so that the painted area extends well beyond the carpet edge.
● **Filling cracks** Staircases are prone to slight movement, so use flexible filler in gaps and joints to prevent paintwork from cracking. This will produce a longer-lasting finish.

ENHANCING WOOD

YOU MAY DECIDE THAT KEEPING WOODEN SURFACES LOOKING NATURAL is a preferable option to painting or decorating them. There is a large range of finishes at your disposal, and many of them are easy to use as well as being durable.

SELECTING WOOD FINISHES

Natural wood finishes can transform a lifeless wooden object into a vibrant decorative feature. Choose a finish according to the type of wood and the color and durability required. Water-based finishes are easy to apply; oil-based products are more durable.

Oil
Suitable for dark hardwoods, since it is a subtle, highlighting finish. Buff to create a sheen.

Wax
Most natural finish; enhances grain and texture. Buff for sheen. Needs frequent recoating.

Varnish
Most durable: use alone or as tough top coat on other finishes. Sheen varies from matte to gloss.

Wood dye
Colors wood to whatever shade required. Colors can be mixed. Finish with clear varnish.

Stain
Largest color range and great depth of finish, which varies according to the number of coats.

USING WOOD FINISHES

Natural wood finishes will enable you to match solid wooden fixtures in a room with pieces of furniture or to make several different types of wood match each other. You can even make pine surfaces resemble oak or transform fir so that it looks like mahogany.

TAKING CARE
● **Protecting yourself** Many wood finishes are runny, and spattering is unavoidable. Wear goggles, especially when coating at eye level.
● **Decanting** Always decant natural wood finishes into a metal paint kettle. The surfaces of plastic containers might be damaged by these products.

SAFETY

Dispose of oily rags in a metal container with a lid. Oil is highly combustible, and there is a danger that rags might combust spontaneously.

IMPROVING FINISH
● **Using a sponge** Apply wood dye with a household sponge, thus eliminating the possibility of unsightly brush marks.
● **Buffing easily** Attach a clean duster to the pad of an electric sander, then use it to buff a waxed or oiled surface.
● **Smoothing varnished coats** Use wire wool to rub down varnish after each coat. Remove residue with a lint-free cloth dampened with turpentine.
● **Staining evenly** Never stop halfway through staining a surface; otherwise, an overlap mark will gradually become visible as subsequent coats of stain are applied.

GREEN TIP

Crush fruit with metal spoon

Using natural dyes
Liquefy fruits or vegetables with a little hot water, then strain to extract their natural dyes. Apply several coats, and seal with a coat of varnish.

CREATING PAINT EFFECTS

A S WELL AS HAVING A CONSIDERABLE DECORATIVE IMPACT, paint effects can be fun to do and they allow you to experiment with different paint finishes. Adapt the various effects so that you can stamp your individuality upon your home.

ADDITIONAL PAINTING EQUIPMENT

Much of the equipment used for creating paint effects on walls can also be used for woodwork. Many tools are multipurpose.

● **Including brushes** Include a variety of sizes of brush in your toolkit to cater for different surface areas and finishes.
● **Meeting specific requirements** A tool such as a rocker will enable you to produce a highly individual wood effect.

Small brush

2-in (50-mm) paintbrush

Softener

Varnish brush

Wire brush

Comb

Rocker

Burnishing tool

Lint-free cloth

Steel wool

Jam jar

MIMICKING NATURAL WOOD

The invention of a graining tool, or rocker, has revolutionized the creation of realistic wood effects using a glaze (see p. 211). The choice of colors is virtually unlimited, so you can select natural, authentic wood tones or base your effects on bolder, brighter colors.

GRAINING WOOD

● **Choosing base colors** Create a solid feel by using a light base color beneath a dark top coat. For greater depth and translucency, use a light top coat over a darker base.
● **Cleaning a rocker** Remove excess glaze from the tooling part of a rocker at regular intervals to prevent smudging.
● **Creating knots** Improve the texture of a wood finish by creating a few knots here and there. Do this by rolling the rocker tool backward and forward gently as you draw it across the glazed surface.

GRAINING KITCHEN CUPBOARD DOORS

1 Take a cupboard door off, and lay it flat. Apply a base coat such as semigloss and allow it to dry. Apply a glaze evenly over the door using a 2-in (50-mm) brush.

2 While the glaze is wet, pull a rocker across the surface in vertical strokes to create a "grain." Do not stop midway, since glaze dries quickly and joins will show.

COLORING WOOD

The simplest way of coloring wood is to colorwash it, using a technique similar to the one applied to walls (see p. 211). Liming wax offers an alternative and provides greater texture and depth. As well as coloring the wood, both of these methods highlight the natural grain.

RAISING WOOD GRAIN

Using a wire brush
Stroke a wooden surface with a wire brush to open up the fiber that make up the grain. This will allow the surface to absorb more liming wax. Brush the wood gently; otherwise, you might make indentations in the surface.

APPLYING LIMING WAX
● **Covering totally** To ensure that liming wax gets into all the nooks and grooves in a wooden surface, use a circular brushing motion when you apply the wax. Use a fairly stiff-bristled brush, which will force the wax into these gaps.
● **Removing excess** Once you have applied liming wax, rub a clear wax over a wooden surface using a lint-free cloth. This will clean away any excess liming wax as well as provide a protective coating.
● **Buffing** Once a wax coating has dried, give the wooden surface a final buffing using a soft-bristled brush. A clean shoe-polishing brush is the ideal tool for this purpose.

COLORWASHING

Apply diluted paint or glaze to bare wood for a colored, grain-enhancing finish.

● **Making a wash** For a simple wash, dilute ordinary flat latex with water until it has a milklike consistency.
● **Rubbing back** Before a wash dries, rub the surface with a rag to remove excess paint and expose the grain, which will be highlighted.
● **Rough-sawn washing** Apply undiluted latex to rough-textured wood, allow to dry, then sand carefully with an electric sander. This will remove paint from the peaks but not the troughs, creating a colorwashed effect.

DRAGGING

Dragging is considered to be one of the more traditional paint effects, giving a wooden surface a textured look that tends to "lift" the finish, creating a realistic impression of depth. The technique is relatively simple, yet it can transform a flat wooden surface.

CREATING THE EFFECT
● **Varying texture** Vary texture by adjusting the angle at which you drag a brush across a glazed surface. Having the bristles at a steep angle to the wood produces a fine texture, whereas a shallow angle makes strokes coarser.
● **Using other tools** It is not essential to use a dragging brush, so experiment with other tools to vary the effect.
● **Dividing areas** Treat different sections of a door or different lengths of molding, for example, as separate entities. It is important to drag continuously in the direction of the grain and to end strokes at junctions, joints, or natural divides.

DRAGGING A GLAZE

Using a brush
Apply an even coat of glaze, then draw a brush slowly across the glazed surface at a constant speed and with the bristles parallel to the grain. Do not stop until you have dragged the whole extent. Mask adjacent areas if necessary.

IMPROVISING TOOLS

Use sharp scissors to cut through rubber

Adapting a window scraper
Produce a dragged effect using a large car window scraper. Cut out sections of the tough rubber blade, making a jagged edge. Use the scraper in the same way as a brush. Because of its size, it will be suitable for large areas.

CREATING A METALLIC FINISH

Traditional painting materials can be used to create the impression of a metallic surface. There are products now available, however, that actually contain the metal that they are emulating. These materials produce a highly realistic metallic finish on a wooden surface.

CREATING VERDIGRIS

● **Selecting a surface** If you want to create the impression of verdigris, choose a wooden surface that includes patterned moldings or other intricately shaped details. This will enable the surface to hold the colors more easily, so that a good range of color shading can be obtained across the area.

● **Choosing a subject** Consider creating a verdigris effect on an area or item that could well be made of metal, so that the deception is believable.

● **Building up color** Use at least three shades of green as you build up a verdigris effect, the first verging on pale blue.

● **Sponging on** Apply layers of color with a natural sponge, allowing one coat almost to dry before you apply another. Soften the sponged effect with a crumpled rag. This will expose the base coat in some places, adding authenticity.

HIGHLIGHTING IN GOLD

"Gilding" molding
Tape together a gold outliner pen and two blocks of wood, one of which slots around the molding. The blocks will steady the pen and help you draw a straight, "gilded" line equidistant from the edge all the way around.

ESTABLISHING COLOR

● **Painting a base color** To increase the realism of a verdigris effect, choose a bronze- or copper-colored paint for the base color.

Dust powder by lightly tapping surface with bag

"Weathering" verdigris
Secure white, powdered filler within a muslin square. Before the last top coat dries, dust it with filler. The surface will then resemble weathered copper.

FAKING METALS

● **Leading** Apply a base coat of iron-oxide paint, then highlight the surface edges with black and dark gray spray-paints. Spray a fine mist rather than covering the edges totally.

● **Choosing a hammered finish** Use a commercial paint intended to give a textured, hammered effect on exterior metalwork to create a similar finish on interior woodwork.

● **Enameling** Enamel paints mimic real metal effectively. Apply them to moldings or doors to add detail.

● **Using car paints** Many cars have a metallic finish. Use a touch-up spray-paint in an appropriate color to create metal effects on inside surfaces. Wear a mask when spraying.

USING METALLIC PAINT

Some commercial metallic paints produce a highly authentic finish. They do not require any special preparation, and – with a certain amount of specialized finishing – achieve very impressive results.

1 Metal paint can be applied directly to bare wood. A primer is advisable but not essential. Apply two coats of metal paint to create a totally opaque finish. Allow to dry overnight before proceeding.

2 Once the paint is dry, rub over the entire surface with a burnishing tool. Burnish in all directions over the surface, then buff with steel wool. This takes time, but the quality of the effect warrants the effort.

MARBLING

There are many ways of producing a fake marble finish, largely because of the fact that the surface of natural marble varies greatly, depending on the type. Your main aim should be to reproduce the cloudy integration of different colors that is common to all marbles.

MARBLING PANELS USING A RAG

Apply glaze with soft brush

Flick rag onto wet glaze all over panel

1 Having let a base coat dry, randomly cover each panel with two colors of glaze. Apply the second color before the first is dry; it does not matter if the colors run, since this will add to the effect.

2 Holding a damp, lint-free rag by one corner, flick it onto the glazed surface, thus mixing the colors. Work diagonally over each panel. Remove excess glaze from panel edges with a dry cloth.

INCREASING REALISM

● **Veining** Apply slightly diluted burnt umber with a fine-tipped artist's brush to suggest the veins characteristic of marble. Use a photograph or piece of marble as a guide. Drag the brush lightly in the same direction each time.
● **Softening** Soften a surface before the glaze dries. If you do not have a softening brush, gently use a soft dusting brush to blur the hard edges of "veins" or the base colors.
● **Protecting** Apply several protective coats of varnish to the finished product. A satin or semigloss varnish will create the most realistic finish.

COMBING

Combing is similar to dragging or graining, except that it offers greater diversity. You do not need to apply a combed pattern in the same direction as the wood grain. You will find that the creation of extravagant patterns is a very satisfying part of the combing technique.

COMBING EFFECTIVELY

● **Preparing surfaces** Combed designs look most effective when glaze lines are smooth. Prepare surfaces well so that they are perfectly level and free from depressions and lumps that would interfere with the comb's movement.
● **Choosing tools** Although you can buy specifically designed combing tools to create this effect, experiment with a notched grout spreader or traditional hair combs to introduce variety to the finish.
● **Creating combed designs** Choose from a number of designs created by combing. Basketweave designs, circles, or combinations of patterns, and images such as scrolls and lettering all look very effective.

CREATING PATTERNS ON A PANELED DOOR

1 Decorate a paneled door in sections. Glaze and comb the horizontal rails first, then the vertical rails. The combing tool will make the rails look grained, in contrast with the door panels.

2 Now apply glaze to the panels. Keep the combed pattern symmetrical by maintaining a constant hand motion. After each combing movement, remove excess glaze from the comb's teeth.

PAINTING FURNITURE

MANY OF THE PAINT EFFECTS used on woodwork may also be applied to furniture. Some, however, are especially suitable for furniture, mainly because they require great attention to detail and are labor intensive.

PREPARING SURFACES

Many pieces of furniture are smaller scale than other wooden surfaces, and their surfaces may include fine details and curves. You may, therefore, need to spend more time preparing the surfaces thoroughly. However, the surface area will not be as extensive.

MAKING FURNITURE READY TO PAINT

Choose and prepare furniture carefully before painting it.

● **Choosing nonwooden items** Prepare and prime wicker or metal surfaces before painting.
● **Masking vulnerable items** With semiupholstered items of furniture, mask the edges between wood and fabric.
● **Testing laminates** Do a test patch on laminated items. Many will not accept paint.

FILLING HOLES

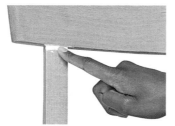

Ensuring smoothness
Use a commercial fine-surface filler for repairs, and apply with the end of one finger. Once sanded, this will produce a smoother finish than all-purpose filler.

PREPARING WOOD

● **Getting professional help** Hand-stripping old painted furniture can be difficult and time consuming, so take items to professional stripping firms where they can be dipped. The expense will be worth it.
● **Sanding** Use only fine-grade paper to sand furniture. Heavy sanding can easily distort furniture profiles and moldings.
● **Preparing detailed surfaces** Apply several base coats to curved and detailed furniture surfaces before creating effects.

GILDING

As well as being very expensive, authentic gilding or water-gilding is a highly skilled craft that requires several years of practice. Modern substitutes can reduce gilding costs dramatically and, if you apply an oil-based size, do not require special application skills.

APPLYING GILDING TO A FRAME

Size tinted with burnt umber

Apply size with paintbrush

Use small brush to push metal into crevices

Backing

1 Base-coat a frame and let it dry. Apply gold size evenly all over. Tint the size with a little burnt umber so that you can see which areas have been covered. Allow the surface to dry until it is tacky.

2 Gently position the sheets of gilt, metal-side down. Fit them around the molding with a soft brush. Remove the backing, leaving the metal. When the size is dry, dust away excess flakes of metal.

MONEY-SAVING TIP

Using enamel paint
Produce a gilded effect inexpensively using gold enamel paint. Apply it very sparingly with a brush to the edges of chair moldings.

AGING

There are many different ways of making a piece of furniture look old. These techniques are known collectively as distressing, and they involve the use of various decorative materials aimed at creating a look that occurs naturally only after years of continuous wear and tear.

AGING EFFECTIVELY

● **Using latex** Use water-based paints, especially flat latexes, which are much easier to distress than their oil-based equivalents. Their duller finish will give a more realistic impression of age.

● **Knocking around** Any piece of furniture with a history will have received the odd knock here and there. Randomly tap a screwdriver or chisel end over a wooden surface to create a well-worn effect.

● **Paying attention to edges** Make sure that you distress the edges of the object well, since this is where the most wear would have occurred.

● **Making details consistent** Exchange new handles on cupboards and cabinets for old ones. Dent metal door knobs with a hammer, and sand around the edges to imitate years of handling.

TIME-SAVING TIP

Using a hairdryer
A hairdryer will speed up the drying time of paint, allowing you to apply the next coat sooner. It is particularly useful when using crackle varnish, since the heat will also increase the size of the cracks.

DISTRESSING WOODEN DOOR PANELS

● **Masking areas to be aged** Mask areas that are likely to have been worn with scraps of masking tape. Remove the tape once you have painted.

1 Use petroleum jelly to mask the areas that you wish to distress on a base-coated surface that has dried. Use just enough to resist the paint before painting the top coat.

ANTIQUING WOOD

● **Using wax** Brush liquid wax onto a painted or distressed surface, then buff with steel wool. The wax will produce what appears to be a dirt-ingrained finish. Use an old toothbrush to reach into intricate areas such as corners.

● **Applying wood dye** Use a soft cloth to apply wood dye (medium or dark oak). It has a similar effect to wax but is more suitable on semigloss, which is oil-based, than water-based paints. Use sparingly.

● **Crackling successfully** To maximize the effectiveness of crackle varnish, ensure that the period of time between applying base-coat varnish and top-coat varnish is constant across the entire surface area.

● Sanding Use sandpaper

● **Sanding** Use sandpaper to complete a distressed finish. Use flat sandpaper rather than a block so that you can judge how much pressure to apply.

2 Remove the paint-covered petroleum jelly using sandpaper. Sand the surface again to take the wood back to its natural finish, which will add authenticity to the effect.

HIGHLIGHTING CRACKS

Using artist's paint
To accentuate a crackle-varnish finish, rub in a darker artist's color (such as burnt umber) to make the cracks more obvious. This is essential if you want to produce a good, delicately cracked (*craquelure*) finish.

APPLYING DÉCOUPAGE

Create the impression of a detailed, hand-painted surface without using any paint by applying the simple method of découpage. This involves cutting out appropriate images from a variety of sources – such as magazines – and attaching them to an object or piece of furniture.

DÉCOUPAGING SMALL CUPBOARDS

PVA

Acrylic varnish

1 Cut out the images of your choice, then stick them down using PVA glue. Brush more PVA over the images to hold them. The thinner the paper used, the greater the impression of painted images.

2 Once the adhesive has dried, apply acrylic varnish to seal and protect the images. The more varnish you apply, the greater the hand-painted feel. Crackle varnish will emphasize this even more.

TRADITIONAL TIP

Sealing with egg tempera
Separate and break the yolk of an egg. Add a teaspoonful of distilled water and the same amount of linseed oil, then mix. Apply with a brush. Once dry, buff with a cotton ball.

CREATING ADVANCED EFFECTS

To produce advanced effects on furniture, you can employ the same basic techniques as you would to create other paint effects. However, you will need to pay more attention to detail and authenticity to mimic natural substances such as marble or tortoiseshell.

FAKING OTHER SURFACES
● **Hand-painting designs** Stencil images onto furniture. Create a hand-painted finish by going over the designs with an artist's brush, varying the detail and color just enough to give it a freehand feel.
● **Graining accurately** Have an example of the wood you are imitating in front of you. This will make it easier to color-match and copy the subtle grain variations of the wood.
● **Using découpage** Create the effect of tortoiseshell or marble by finding examples in books or magazines (that are out of copyright) and using a photocopier to enlarge them to the size you want. Apply using découpage techniques.

PERFECTING THE ART OF PRETENSE
● **Paying attention to detail** *Trompe l'oeil* effects do not have to be complicated and difficult to execute. You can create just as much impact with small details as large images.

● **Extending *trompe l'oeil*** Do not limit your use of *trompe l'oeil* effects to walls. With a little imagination, you can apply deceptive images to pieces of furniture, too.

Being practical
Paint a clever *trompe l'oeil* tablecloth on a garden table, and you will never again need to cover it before you lay the table. This simple yet striking image serves a very useful purpose, but at the same time it does not require a high level of artistic skill.

FINISHING

WHEN FINISHING WOODWORK DECORATION, make sure that all necessary retouching is carried out. When the work is complete, clean equipment, then store it carefully. Finally, maintain painted surfaces to prolong their life.

CORRECTING MISTAKES

Expect to do a certain amount of mistake-rectifying before you store your equipment. Even experienced decorators sometimes need to retouch or even repaint some areas. Take time to make improvements and thus ensure that the finish is as good as possible.

REMOVING FLAWS
● **Drips** Shave off drips with a window scraper, then sand so that the whole area is flat. Undercoat and top-coat.
● **Brush marks** A few brush marks are inevitable. Those that appear grooved should be corrected. Sand the whole area, first with rough paper, then smooth. Wipe and recoat.
● **Patchy finishes** Patches or shaded areas indicate either poor coverage or inadequate mixing of paint. In either case, remix top-coat paint properly, and apply another coat.

DEALING WITH BLEEDING

Removing resin
Improperly prepared knots may suffer from resinous bleeding, spoiling a top coat of paint. Use a hot-air gun to bubble out all the resin. Remove the resin with a scraper. Prime and recoat.

SMOOTHING SURFACES
● **Grit and dust** Dirt can get into brushes and from them onto painted surfaces. If this occurs, sand lightly and recoat.
● **Orange-peel effect** Wrinkles are caused by oil-based paint being applied over paint that has not dried or that dries too quickly, for example in direct sunlight. Strip and repaint.
● **Insect invasions** Insects are attracted to paint and stick to a tacky surface. Allow paint to dry, then wipe away insects with a dry cloth. Sand lightly, and recoat if necessary.

CLEANING UP

Clean up thoroughly after completing a job, first to ensure that the work looks its best, and second to make sure that tools and equipment are kept in good working order. Oil-based paints are commonly used on wood, and these especially need to be cleaned up well.

REMOVING DRY PAINT

Gently force comb through encrusted bristles

Combing a paintbrush
Use a grooming comb or a metal household comb to break up caked-on paint. The bristles can then be cleaned more easily and will remain flexible in the future.

CLEANING PROPERLY
● **Cleaning hands** Use a commercial hand cleaner rather than solvent-based products, which may irritate the skin.
● **Cleaning according to type** Use turpentine for cleaning up oil-based paints and plain water for acrylic paints. Read the instructions on specialist commercial products carefully, since they may require thinners or other products.
● **Dealing with stubborn paint** Suspend a brush in solvent overnight to loosen paint. Do not let the bottom of the bristles touch the base of the container.

GREEN TIP

Reusing turpentine
Remove paint sediment from turpentine by sieving the solvent into another jar. This will prevent sediment getting into brushes as you clean them.

STORING MATERIALS

Not all the materials that you buy for a decorating job will be totally used up, so you will need to store leftovers. All pieces of equipment must be cleaned thoroughly before being stored so that they are kept in good working order until you need them again.

DEALING WITH PAINT

● **Decanting water-based paints** Transfer leftover water-based paints into small jars to save space during storage. Use them to tint glazes for paint effects, or as samples when you are trying to decide upon a new color scheme in the future.

● **Combining oil-based paints** Pour leftover oil-based paints into one can, then mix them together for storage. Use the mixture on surfaces where color is not important, such as the inside of exterior metal guttering to prevent corrosion.

● **Keeping tubes together** Store tubes of artist's color together in a clean paint can so that you do not lose them.

PROTECTING BRISTLES

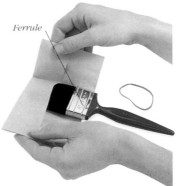

Ferrule

Maintaining shape
Wrap the bristle end of a clean brush in brown paper. Secure with a rubber band around the ferrule to protect and maintain bristle shape during storage.

STORING SMALL BRUSHES

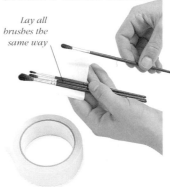

Lay all brushes the same way

Taping brushes together
Small brushes can easily be lost. Bind them together with masking tape, thus making several small objects into one large one, which will be more difficult to lose.

MAINTAINING WOODWORK

Like other decorated surfaces, woodwork needs a certain amount of care to maintain it in the best possible condition. Following a few simple guidelines will make a finish long-lasting. A little effort from time to time will prevent a lot more effort in the long term.

REVIVING SURFACES

● **Maintaining coats** Apply the occasional coat of varnish to appropriate wooden surfaces to revive and protect the finish.

● **Retouching marks** Paint can become affected by natural light only a few months after decorating, with the result that its color changes slightly from the original shade. When retouching a mark on a wall, make sure that you paint a wider area. If you need to retouch a door panel, cover the whole panel so that no color differences become visible across the surface.

● **Cleaning surfaces** Clean most wood finishes simply with a damp sponge and mild household detergent.

REDECORATING WINDOW FRAMES

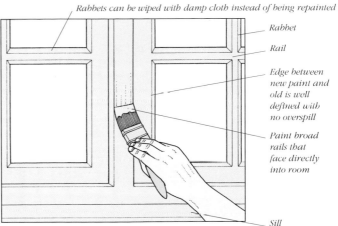

Rabbets can be wiped with damp cloth instead of being repainted

Rabbet

Rail

Edge between new paint and old is well defined with no overspill

Paint broad rails that face directly into room

Sill

Repainting selectively
Repaint only the rails and sills of a window frame rather than the entire frame. Rails are the most visible areas, and sills need regular maintenance. Avoid fiddly rabbets, thus speeding up the job. Use the same color paint as the original finish.

Covering Floors

Quick Reference

Selecting Floor Types, p. 269

Preparing Floors, p. 271

Wooden Floors, p. 273

Carpeting Floors, p. 276

Utility Flooring, p. 278

Hard-tile Flooring, p. 280

Painting Floors, p. 282

Finishing, p. 284

FLOORING IS WITHOUT DOUBT the most practical aspect of home decoration, and it clearly has a dual-purpose function. Practical considerations and decorative choices are both equally important. Make sure that flooring options are not an afterthought once you have completed all the other decoration in a room. Such a large surface area contributes significantly to the total decorative look, and it deserves careful thought at the same time as you choose other decorative materials.

Basic Flooring Equipment

Much of the equipment needed for flooring is already a part of most household tool kits.

● **Renting specialized tools** Rent specialized equipment if you need it. It is usually expensive, and you are unlikely to use it enough to justify buying it.
● **Checking rented equipment** Make sure that equipment is working and has all necessary operating instructions and safety recommendations.
● **Planning tool use** Plan work so that you rent equipment only when you need it. Do not rent an item on day one if you will not require it until day three.

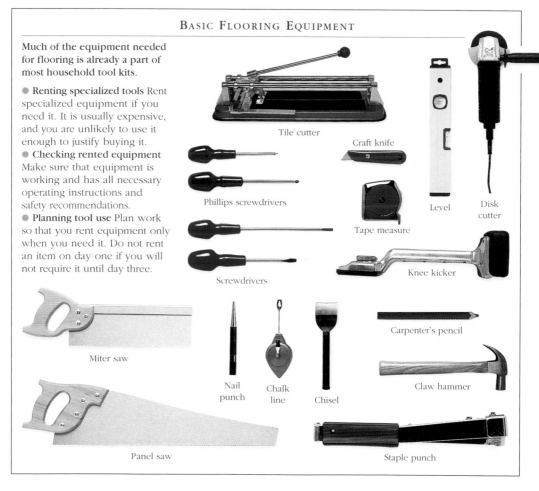

Tile cutter

Craft knife

Phillips screwdrivers

Tape measure

Level

Disk cutter

Knee kicker

Screwdrivers

Miter saw

Nail punch

Chalk line

Chisel

Carpenter's pencil

Claw hammer

Panel saw

Staple punch

SELECTING FLOOR TYPES

DECORATIVE FEATURES are highly influential when it comes to choosing flooring, but practicality also must be considered, as does the ease with which a floor can be laid. Take your time when weighing options before making choices.

COMMON FLOOR TYPES

Floor types are many and various, but most of them fall into four main categories.

● **Wooden flooring** These range from basic planking to veneers. Block floors are another option.
● **Carpets** These include good-quality burlap-backed as well as less expensive foam-backed varieties. Naturally occurring fibers such as seagrass and jute also fall into this category.
● **Utility flooring** Sheet flooring, such as vinyl and linoleum, is hardwearing and washable. Carpet and vinyl tiles are more decorative yet still practical.
● **Ceramic tiles** These make the most hardwearing floors and offer a huge decorative choice.

Ceramic floor tile

Vinyl floor tile

Vinyl sheet flooring

Parquet flooring strip

Floorboard

Parquet flooring panel

Seagrass

Carpet

Carpet tile

CONSIDERING OPTIONS

All purely decorative considerations aside, the economics of buying and laying flooring deserve serious consideration. A major factor is how long you expect a floor to last. Flooring is not permanent, but neither is it easily removed, and it represents a significant financial investment.

BUDGETING
● **Considering your stay** Many floor coverings are difficult to remove once laid so will need to be left behind when you move. Bear this in mind when deciding how much to spend on flooring.
● **Including the preparation** Consider the preparation that might be required prior to laying a floor. It may prove costly to lay flooring if the subfloor requires a great deal of work. Old floorboards, for example, would need a lot of preparation to make them ready for laying ceramic tiles.

REFLECTING ON STYLE
● **Planning an entire room** Remember to include flooring when color-scheming and styling a room. Obtain floor swatches as well as paint and paper samples. Budgeting will be far easier if you consider flooring when you plan the rest of your decorating.
● **Determining period** When choosing flooring, consider its pattern and style in terms of the historical period of your house, if appropriate, as well as the decoration in other rooms. Being accurate may require some research.

MEASURING
Working out floor surface area is relatively simple: just multiply together the relevant dimensions. Bear in mind a few other considerations, depending on the flooring.

● **Wooden floors** Allow ten percent extra for wastage arising from cutting.
● **Carpets** These are sold in rolls. Work out the direction in which it will be unrolled to minimize wastage.
● **Tiles** Allow extra tiles for any cutting that will be required at joins and edges.

CONSIDERING PRACTICALITIES

The suitablility of a flooring for a particular room is determined by the function of that room, how much flooring is required, and your preference. Any floor covering is clearly better suited to some areas than others, depending on its comfort, appearance, and durability.

SELECTING SUITABLE FLOORING FOR EACH INDIVIDUAL ROOM

Carpet is most suitable for a bedroom, providing comfort and a soft surface to walk on

Flooring need not be as durable on a landing as in a hallway, since there is less traffic and some of it may be barefoot

Vinyl tiles are excellent for tolerating water splashes in a bathroom

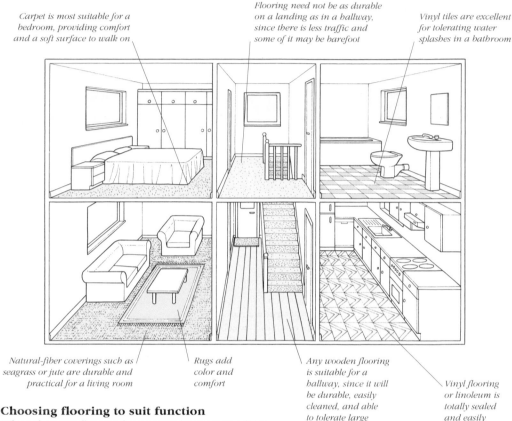

Natural-fiber coverings such as seagrass or jute are durable and practical for a living room

Rugs add color and comfort

Any wooden flooring is suitable for a hallway, since it will be durable, easily cleaned, and able to tolerate large amounts of traffic

Vinyl flooring or linoleum is totally sealed and easily wiped clean of kitchen spills and grease spots

Choosing flooring to suit function
When choosing flooring for a particular room in a home, it is essential to bear in mind how much the area will be used and whether, for example, people using the room will be wearing outdoor shoes or going barefoot. There are many options to choose from for each room in the home.

CONSIDERING OCCUPANTS
● **Children** Luxury carpeting can easily be spoiled by the activities of children. Consider laying inexpensive carpet or other types of flooring while children are young.
● **Pets** Hard flooring may be advisable in rooms to which animals have access. Young cats and dogs can spoil carpet and natural-fiber flooring.

CHOOSING MATERIALS
● **Establishing fiber content** Make sure that no one is allergic to the constituent materials of a floor covering. You cannot afford to discover this after you have laid it.
● **Going for quality** Choose as good a quality of flooring as you can afford. The better the quality, the longer the flooring will last without looking worn.

DISGUISING PROBLEMS
● **Protecting corridors** The flooring in areas leading into adjoining rooms usually wears most quickly. Lay durable flooring, or protect these areas by also laying rugs or carpets.
● **Adjusting to lifestyle** In busy households, choose a patterned or flecked carpet to disguise wear. Stains and dirt will also be camouflaged.

PREPARING FLOORS

BEFORE NEW FLOORING CAN BE LAID, an existing floor may require renovation so that it is in a good enough condition to accept a new covering. As with all decorating, sound preparation is most likely to produce the best finished product.

REPAIRING FLOORBOARDS

Floorboards deteriorate over time and may need repairing in order to bring them up to a satisfactory standard. Sometimes this will require total board replacement, but most of the problems resulting from normal wear and tear can be solved with far less drastic action.

PATCHING PROBLEM AREAS

● **Replacing sections** Remove an area of defective boards using a miter saw. Cut through the boards at the nearest joist to either side. Saw board edges at a 45-degree angle to make the replacement section slightly less obvious.
● **Patching tongue and groove** To remove a damaged section of tongue and groove, saw down each length of board, as well as at each end, in order to cut through the interlocking device. Use a hacksaw to cut through any hidden nails.
● **Concealing marks** To hide a badly pitted or grooved board, lift it out and turn it over so that the underside faces up.

LIFTING FLOORBOARDS

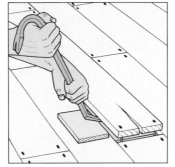

Using a crowbar
Use a crowbar to remove a floorboard quickly. Loosen any slightly protruding nails with the curled end of the crowbar. Then pivot it on a block of wood – to avoid damaging adjacent boards – as you lever out the board.

FILLING GAPS

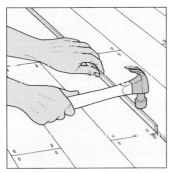

Using a sliver of wood
Where a gap has opened up between floorboards, gently drive in a thin, wedge-shaped sliver of wood with a hammer. Plane the wood down until it is flush with the floorboards.

MAKING MINOR REPAIRS
● **Fixing warped boards** Use screws rather than nails to hold down bulging boards, since the thread of a screw will pull a board down and prevent it from bouncing up (which happens with nails). Remember to countersink the screws to keep a level surface.
● **Filling minor cracks** Fill small cracks with all-purpose filler. If the floor will be exposed, mix in a little wood dye with the filler to match the color of the floorboards.
● **Silencing creaks** Sprinkle talcum powder in the gaps between creaking boards. This should lessen the noise.

BRIGHT IDEA

Matching existing color
Use a good board from an inconspicuous area, such as under a rug, to replace a damaged or discolored board that is visible. Put a new one under the rug instead.

PREPARING SUBFLOORS

If a floor – whether it consists of a concrete base or is floorboarded – is to be covered, the surface will need the appropriate preparation depending on the type of floor covering to be applied. As a general rule, boards will require covering and concrete will need leveling.

MAKING A START
● **Removing lumps** Lumps of concrete can sometimes be difficult to see. To locate them, slide a batten across the floor flush to the surface. Protrusions will impede the batten's progress. Remove them with a hammer and chisel.
● **Filling gaps** Fill small holes with exterior filler or a general cement mix. To correct an undulating floor, use a mix of self-leveling compound.
● **Soaking hardboard** Brush water over hardboard lengths, then leave them in the room in which they are to be used for 48 hours. This allows them to acclimatize to the room, preventing edge expansion or contraction once they are laid.
● **Arranging hardboard** Lay lengths of hardboard in a brick-bond pattern so that seams are continuous in one direction only. Make sure, too, that the seams do not coincide with floorboard joints below.

REDUCING DUST
● **Sealing concrete** Concrete floors are always dusty, so before laying carpets seal the floor with a solution of five parts water to one part PVA. Apply easily with a large pasting brush or a soft broom.

STRENGTHENING BOARDS
● **Inserting a nog** Having removed a damaged board, insert a nog, or small block of wood, between the floor joists as a support before fitting a new board. Make sure that the nog is flush with the joist tops.

REMOVING OLD FLOOR COVERINGS

It is best to remove all traces of an existing floor covering before you prepare for a new one.

● **Carpet** Discard old carpets but keep the tacking strips, since they can be reused. Padding may also be used again.
● **Vinyl flooring** Depending on how much adhesive was used to lay it, vinyl will usually lift fairly easily. A hot-air gun will soften vinyl and speed up its removal. Take care when using a hot-air gun (see p. 254).
● **Ceramic tiles** As long as they are level, ceramic tiles make a good base for a new floor and should be left undisturbed.

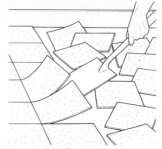

Removing floor tiles
Floor tiles or linoleum or can become brittle with age, and the strong adhesive used to attach them makes their removal difficult. Slide a shovel beneath them, then break sections away.

CUTTING TO FIT AND ATTACHING A HARDBOARD SUBFLOOR

1 If part of a hardboard sheet is required, cut it to fit in position. Place it rough-side up, butting up to a baseboard. Mark with a pencil the points on each edge where it reaches the sheets that have been laid.

2 Join the two marks using a straightedge, then cut along the line with a craft knife, using a steel ruler to keep the cut straight. Score deeply into the board, then bend it along the line. It should break cleanly.

3 Lay the hardboard in place smooth side up. Staple it down using a staple gun, which is inexpensive to rent and quick to use. This laying method ensures that only perimeter edges are not factory-finished.

LAYING WOODEN FLOORS

WOOD DEMONSTRATES GREAT VERSATILITY when used for flooring. It makes an excellent subfloor on which to lay other floor coverings, and it can be laid in a number of different ways to produce an attractive finish in its own right.

RENOVATING OLD FLOORS

Laying a new wooden floor can sometimes be avoided by renovating an existing one and giving it a decorative finish. There are obvious financial advantages to this approach: the raw material is already there, and a relatively simple process is all that is required to finish it.

MAKING DECISIONS

● **Considering amount of use** If a floor needs a lot of repair or board replacement (see p. 270), decide whether or not the renovation is worthwhile. This will depend on how much you use the room.

● **Covering a floor** If you are covering a floor with rugs so that only a small part is visible, the wooden surface will not be a prominent feature and need not be highly finished.

● **Assessing the job** When planning floor renovation, assess the work required to finish it. A rustic, distressed look will take far less work than a highly polished finish.

USING STRIPPER

● **Considering floor size** Use chemical stripper on a small floor or when only a small proportion of a floor requires stripping. Chemical stripper is not economical when it is used for large areas.

● **Masking** Use at least 2-in (5-cm) masking tape along the lower edge of baseboard to prevent stripping solution from reaching its painted surface.

● **Putting on and taking off** Dab on stripper with an old paintbrush in 3-sq-ft (0.25-m²) areas. Once it reacts, scrape away paint or varnish with a broad bladed scraper. Use a wire brush on uneven floors.

BRIGHT IDEA

Masking a door
If a large floor area requires sanding, mask around the door's edges to prevent dust from escaping. Open windows to allow dust to drift outside.

USING AN INDUSTRIAL FLOOR SANDER

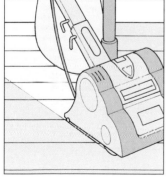

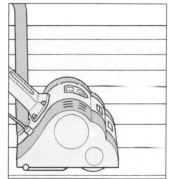

1 Start the sander in a slightly tilted back position, lower it to the surface, and proceed diagonally across the wood grain to smooth any rough areas. Use medium-grade sandpaper during this stage.

2 Change to a finer grade of paper, then sand with the grain this time. The number of times you have to do this will depend on the condition of the boards. Three or four times is usually sufficient.

SANDING EFFICIENTLY

● **Protecting yourself** Always wear goggles and a mask to protect yourself from flying particles and dust inhalation.

● **Removing protrusions** Use a hammer and nail punch to drive in protruding nails; otherwise, the sandpaper will tear, and there is a risk that you will damage the sander.

● **Dealing with edges** Most industrial sanders will not reach right to the edge of a floor, so use a hand-held electric sander to finish.

● **Reaching corners** Wrap some sandpaper around the end of a screwdriver to get right into corners. This will create a neat, squared finish.

LAYING NEW FLOORS

There are several ways of laying a new wooden floor. This is because there are several different construction systems that can be adapted to go over most existing subfloors. Follow the manufacturer's specific instructions when dealing with commercial products.

PREPARING TO LAY

● **Checking levels** Ensure that all joists are level by laying a long strip of wood across them. Check that the underside of the strip is touching the top of the joists all along its length. Any gaps should be filled with slivers of wood.

● **Ensuring dryness** Make sure that a new concrete base is completely dry before you lay a wooden floor; otherwise, moisture from the subfloor will cause the wood to buckle. Check newly laid bases with a moisture detector.

● **Acclimatizing wood** Store wooden flooring in the room in which it is to be laid for at least 48 hours before it is used. This will allow it to expand or contract slightly as it adjusts to the room temperature.

DESIGNING A LAYOUT

You have several options when it comes to designing the layout of a planked or tongue-and-groove floor. Much will depend on your woodworking skills.

● **Parallel** This is the most straightforward design and requires a minimal amount of technical know-how.
● **Diagonal** This design requires good planning and accurate woodwork, especially if you are laying directly on top of joists.
● **Concentric** A concentric, square or rectangular design requires an appropriately shaped room and a solid wooden or floating subfloor. If planks are to run in two directions, as in this design, a joisted subfloor will not have enough surface area in which to secure nails.

Parallel layout

Diagonal layout

Concentric layout

TONGUE-AND-GROOVING

● **Avoiding adjacent joins**
Stagger ends of boards so that cut ends of adjacent planks do not coincide. Nail ends down, or use secret nailing (see p. 235).

Butting up
Make sure that lengths of tongue and groove are butted up tightly. To protect a board that is being fitted from damage, use a small scrap of board as a driving tool against which to hammer.

DEALING WITH EDGES

● **Hiding gaps** Cover gaps between baseboards and floor with strips of molding of either a quadrant (convex) or a scotia (concave) variety.

Attaching molding
Attach molding to a baseboard rather than to the floor to allow for floor movement, which might pull the molding away. Use oval-headed nails, which need minimal filling once driven in.

CONSIDERING OPTIONS

● **Using padding** You can lay some floors onto foam padding rather than wooden joists or frames. Called "floating" floors, these have no real attachments and rely on jointing mechanisms to ensure stability. Mount baseboards after laying the floor, to cover the gap left around the floor's edge to allow for expansion.
● **Using clips** Hide floor fixtures by using metal clips, which will hold floorboards together without being visible. Insert the clips beneath and along the floorboard joins.
● **Buying prefinished flooring** You may choose a floor that requires no finishing once it is laid. It will be more expensive and require care when laying, but you will save a lot of time and money in the long term.

LAYING PARQUET FLOORS

Traditionally, wood-block floors were made up of rectangular wooden blocks laid tightly butted up against each other in a variety of patterns. Parquet floors are now made in strips or panels of rectangles, which are less costly to produce but create the same effect.

PREPARING FLOORS

● **Choosing a subfloor** Parquet requires a very flat surface. Concrete bases are ideal, while hardboard and chipboard are suitable as long as you make sure that there is no flexibility in movement as you walk across them.

● **Starting in the middle** Find the center of a room using a chalkline (see p. 279), thus dividing the floor into four. Complete one section before moving to the next.

● **Cleaning surfaces** Vacuum the floor and wash it with a mop before starting to lay blocks or panels. This will remove dust and grit particles that might prevent the floor from being laid level.

ALLOWING FOR MOVEMENT

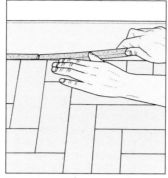

Coping with expansion
Leave a $3/8$-in (1-cm) gap around the perimeter of a wood-block or panel floor to allow for expansion caused by changing humidity. Fill in with cork strips to prevent edges from buckling or lifting, and to improve the finish.

FITTING PANELS

● **Applying adhesive** Flooring adhesive tends to be very viscous. Apply it with a grout spreader and work in areas no larger than 1 sq yd (1 m²).

● **Tapping into place** Parquet will require "bedding in." Tap each panel down by gently hammering a block of wood placed on top of it. This will avoid damaging the panel surface and will apply a more even pressure across it.

● **Dealing with obstacles** Parquet consists of equally sized wooden "fingers." Before you lay a floor, split a couple into sections ranging from groups of three to single fingers. You will thus have a choice for trimming around obstacles.

SEALING FLOORS

Most wooden floors need to have some sort of finish before they are used to protect them from wear and tear. The choice of products varies from traditional waxes, requiring regular maintenance, to hardwearing varnishes, which provide the toughest finish of all.

VARNISHING EVENLY

Keeping to edges
Apply a colored finish to a planked floor one floorboard at a time; otherwise, overlapping brush strokes will produce different levels of color intensity and a patchy finish.

COVERING EFFICIENTLY

● **Sealing with varnish** Thin the first coat of varnish slightly. It will then act as a primer, soaking in well and sealing the wooden surface.

● **Using quick-drying varnishes** Use acrylic or water based varnishes, since more than one coat can be applied in a day. This means that you will be able to get the floor back in use as quickly as possible.

● **Protecting high-wear areas** Apply extra coats of varnish to door entrances and natural "corridors" within a room. Use a clear varnish; otherwise, there will be too great a buildup of color in those areas that are receiving extra coats.

MONEY-SAVING TIP

Polishing waxed floors
To buff a waxed surface, attach a soft cloth to the end of a broom. (After the first application of wax to a newly laid floor, you might like to rent a polisher for buffing.)

CARPETING FLOORS

Laying carpet is a job that is often left to professional carpet layers, but there is no reason why you cannot do it as long as you follow the manufacturer's instructions. Carpet materials vary and, consequently, so do laying techniques.

LAYING BURLAP-BACKED CARPET

Burlap-backed carpet is among the best in terms of quality. The strong burlap backing always provides excellent durability. The type of pile, fiber, and weave can vary from one kind of burlap-backed carpet to another, but laying techniques remain more or less constant.

SECURING CURVED EDGES

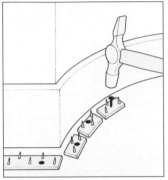

Using tacking strips
Tacking strips are straight and rigid, so saw them into 2-in (5-cm) sections to round a curved area such as a bay window. Attach them to the floor close to the baseboard in the usual way.

LEARNING THE BASICS

● **Using padding** Always use good-quality padding below burlap-backed carpet. Felt or rubber varieties are suitable and provide extra comfort as well as increasing the life of the carpet. Do not lay padding over the tacking strips.
● **Cutting roughly** Roll out a carpet, and cut it roughly to size. Allow an additional 6 in (15 cm) around the perimeter for final trimming.
● **Joining carpet** Not all rooms are regularly shaped, and you may need to join carpet rolls before laying them. Obtain professional help with this. Most suppliers will join lengths so that seams are invisible.

TRADITIONAL TIP

Tacking carpet
When laying carpet in position, a less expensive alternative to using tacking strips is to nail down carpet edges with tacks. Fold the edges of the carpet over, then nail through the folds.

LAYING FOAM-BACKED CARPET

Foam-backed carpet is usually less expensive and easier to lay than burlap-backed carpet.

● **Preparing** Padding is not usually required, but cover the floor with newspaper before laying the carpet to reduce dust and abrasion between carpet backing and floor.
● **Laying** Foam-backed carpet is relatively lightweight, so attach it to the floor with double-sided carpet tape.
● **Joining** Use single-sided tape to join lengths of carpet from below, ensuring that the pile goes in the same direction.

TRIMMING CARPET

Using a craft knife
Trim burlap-backed carpet tightly up to the baseboard using a craft knife. Keep the cut straight, although imperfections will be hidden when you stretch the carpet over the tacking strips.

LAYING CARPET

Using a chisel
Having stretched and smoothed out the carpet to the tacking strips with a knee kicker, use a chisel to push the carpet firmly over and behind the tacking strips at the baseboard–floor junction.

LAYING NATURAL-FIBER FLOORING

Natural-fiber flooring such as sisal is both decorative and hardwearing. The types of fiber used vary, but this causes only subtle variations in the pattern, texture, and comfort that they offer. Laying techniques differ only slightly from the methods used to lay carpet.

CARING FOR FLOORING

● **Acclimatizing** Allow a natural floor covering to acclimatize in the room in which it is to be laid for at least 24 hours before laying. It will need to adjust to the room's humidity.

● **Prolonging life** Check first in the manufacturer's guidelines, but a natural floor covering such as rush can usually benefit from occasional light watering. A household plant sprayer is ideal for this purpose.

● **Using padding** Attach padding beneath natural-fiber flooring using commercial adhesive. This will have the effect of smoothing an uneven subfloor as well as providing extra comfort underfoot. Use padding only with natural floor coverings that do not already have a latex backing.

USING DECORATIVE RUGS

Rugs, in a wide variety of designs, are traditional floor-decorating accessories. They can be used to complement other floor coverings or to enhance a plain floor by adding a splash of color. Small decorative rugs are particularly useful for both adding color and providing extra comfort when they are laid upon natural-fiber floor coverings.

● **Choosing rugs** The choice includes bold ethnic rugs such as kilims and durries – usually cotton or wool; modern, synthetic, mass-produced rugs; and sophisticated traditional weaves, often from Central Asia or China. You can decide to buy an inexpensive rug, or look upon a high-quality rug as an investment and pay much more.

Creating a splash of color
Rugs that incorporate many different colors in their design are often easy to fit into a color scheme. Splashes of color that blend or contrast with a room's color scheme both enhance the decorative appeal of the rug itself and provide a decorative focal point within the room.

LAYING FLOORING ON STAIRS

Laying flooring on stairs presents the problem of working vertically as well as horizontally. More trimming is necessary as a result, so there is more waste. You will also need to allow more time for laying flooring on stairs.

● **Using natural-fiber flooring** If you want to cover stairs with materials such as seagrass or jute, follow manufacturers' guidelines carefully. The rigidity and therefore the ability of these materials to fit stair profiles varies, making the use of different laying methods necessary.

● **Laying burlap-backed carpet** Attach an appropriate length of tacking strip to the bottom of each riser and at the back of each tread to make sure that the carpet is secured as firmly as possible on each stair.

● **Laying foam-backed carpet** Staple along the back of each tread in order to attach foam-backed carpet to stairs. This will prevent it from slipping.

● **Starting at the top** When laying stair carpet, place the first length firmly on the landing before continuing downstairs.

● **Placing stair rods** Fit a stair rod at the tread–riser junction to reduce the possibility of the carpet slipping. The rods can be painted to match the color of the carpet before you fit them to make them less conspicuous.

● **Reversing carpet** Before a stair carpet begins to wear in places – and if the dimensions of the treads and risers are the same – take up the carpet and reverse it top to bottom to extend its life. The treads will become risers and vice versa.

Finishing at the bottom
Trim the end of a length of stair carpet so that it folds under the lip of the bottom tread. Cut a jagged edge, allowing the carpet to mold around the curved edge. Secure with tacks or a staple gun. Fit a final piece of carpet over the jagged edge.

LAYING UTILITY FLOORING

SOME AREAS OF THE HOME demand flooring that is both easy to clean and very durable. Once thought of purely in practical terms, most utility flooring is now cushioned for comfort, and a large range of designs give it scope decoratively.

SHEET FLOORING

There are three catgories of sheet flooring: vinyl, linoleum, and rubber. Vinyl is very versatile, being available in a range of thicknesses and other properties. Rubber and linoleum are less common alternatives but are in demand for specific properties and characteristic finishes.

LAYING SHEET FLOORING

● **Preparing a subfloor** Clean a subfloor thoroughly – whether it is concrete or plywood – to make sure that there are no traces of dirt or grit, or lumps of any kind. Imperfections such as these can push into the back of the flooring, causing a weak spot that will eventually wear through.

● **Choosing adhesive** Flooring adhesives vary considerably. Make sure that you have the correct one for your flooring.

● **Applying adhesive** Apply adhesive around the edges of a room and along any joins. Do not waste adhesive, and therefore money, by covering the whole floor with it.

MAKING AN ACCURATE TEMPLATE FOR CUTTING

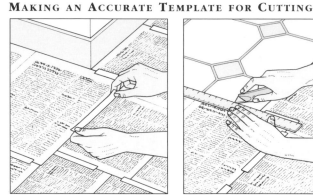

1 Cover the subfloor with sheets of newspaper, fitting them exactly around the edges of any obstacles. Tape all the pieces together, creating a large template that is the exact size and shape of the floor.

2 Tape the paper template securely to the flooring. Work in a large-enough space to be able to lay the template completely flat. Cut the flooring around the template so that it will fit the floor.

BRIGHT IDEA

Designing linoleum
Some manufacturers will make linoleum flooring to your requirements. You can design your own pattern, picking up a detail in a wallpaper, for example.

NEATENING EDGES

● **Cutting precisely** Push the edge of the sheet flooring into the floor–baseboard junction with a broad-bladed scraper. Cut precisely along the crease guideline with a sharp craft knife. Disguise imperfections along edges with molding.

● **Reducing cutting** Remove kicker boards in kitchens and bath panels in bathrooms, then lay flooring underneath these fixtures. Replace the boards or panels to give a precise edge.

● **Waterproofing** Run a thin bead of clear silicone around flooring and baseboard edges to make the surface completely waterproof and easy to clean.

JOINING SHEETS

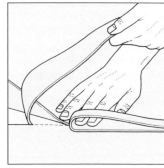

Making a butt join
Join two sheets of flooring as you would wallpaper. Overlap the edges and, using a steel-ruler guideline, cut through both sheets. Remove excess pieces and stick down the edges of the vinyl.

SOFT-TILE FLOORING

Many of the recommendations and methods applicable to sheet flooring also apply to soft-tile flooring, since tiles are made from the same materials. Other types of soft-tile flooring include cork and carpet tiles, and the same rules apply to their application and laying.

PLANNING THE JOB
● **Protecting a floor** Do not walk on a newly tiled surface for at least 24 hours while the adhesive dries. Tile in two halves, so that one part can be used while the other dries.

APPLYING ADHESIVE
● **Spreading evenly** Apply tile adhesive using a notched spreader. Cover about four tiles at once – a convenient working area – so that the adhesive does not dry too quickly.

FLATTENING TILES
● **Rolling down** Tiles will usually flatten and stick down easily. To ensure an absolutely flat surface, gently roll over the tiles with a rolling pin just after they have been laid.

FINDING THE CENTER

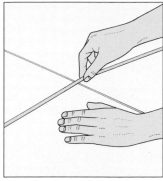

CUTTING TILES TO FIT AROUND A CORNER

Snapping a guideline
To locate the center of a room, snap a chalk line (see p. 214) between the midpoints of opposite walls. Use the chalk lines as guides for laying the first row of tiles in each quadrant.

1 Lay the tile to be cut exactly on top of the nearest whole tile to the corner. Lay another tile on top of this but with its edge butting right up to the baseboard. Draw a line along its edge on the tile to be cut.

2 Without rotating the tile to be cut, move both tiles around the corner to the nearest whole tile, then repeat the process. The lines you have drawn will show where to cut the tile to fit the corner.

TILING CLEVERLY
● **Cleaning off adhesive** Adhesive often gets onto tile surfaces. Keep turpentine and a cloth handy so that you can remove it immediately. Some manufacturers may suggest alternative solvents for this.
● **Making templates** Cut some pieces of paper exactly to tile size before you begin. Use them to make templates of awkward areas such as those around the bases of door moldings.
● **Negotiating pipes** Fitting a template around a pipe is not easy. Mark the pipe's position on a tile, then use a pipe scrap to create an accurate impression on the tile itself.

LAYING CARPET TILES

Carpet tiles are a practical, all-purpose flooring. They are more comfortable than vinyl tiles and easier to clean than carpet itself. Stained tiles can be replaced.

● **Sticking carpet tiles** Lay carpet tiles in the same way as soft tiles, except that there is no need to attach them, apart from around thresholds, where double-sided tape can be used.
● **Butting up** Cut some plywood to the size of a tile. Stick a strip of wood to the center of one side as a handle. Attach four or five cut lengths of tacking strip to the other side. Use this to pick up and butt up tiles tightly.

Place shape in cutout

Creating footprints
Cut left and right foot shapes out of different-colored floor tiles from the main color. Cut the exact same shape out of a few of the main-color tiles and fill in with the cut-out "feet." Position the tiles so that the footprints lead across the room.

LAYING HARD-TILE FLOORING

Floor tiles are usually larger and more substantial than wall tiles because they are load bearing and need to be more robust. There is a large variety of hard tiles from which to choose to complement other decoration in a room.

DESIGNS AND TECHNIQUES

Laying floor tiles is similar to attaching wall tiles, and many of the same principles and techniques apply. Mistakes in laying floors can prove expensive to rectify, so always make sure that you plan the job very carefully before you start work, and follow the instructions.

LAYING QUARRY TILES

● **Planning a layout** When working out exactly where floor tiles are to be positioned, use a tile gauge (see p. 242).

● **Starting out** In rooms with straight and true walls, use the baseboards as guidelines. This should reduce the amount of cutting necessary on at least two walls. If the walls are not true, start tiling from battened edges. Leave a gap between battens and walls so that infill tiles used to finish off the floor will be at least half-sized.

● **Using mortar** Always lay quarry tiles in a thick bed of mortar, rather than applying ceramic tile adhesive.

DESIGNING LAYOUTS

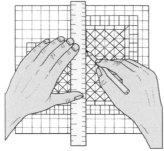

Planning a design
For an intricately patterned floor, make a plan to scale of where each tile will be positioned. This is especially important when you are intending to use marble inset tiles, to ensure that each one is laid in exactly the right place.

SPACING FLOOR TILES

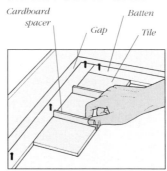

Cardboard spacer · *Gap* · *Batten* · *Tile*

Maintaining gaps
Floor tiles rarely have spacing mechanisms built into their design, so wedge pieces of thick cardboard between the tiles to keep them apart. Remove these improvised tile spacers once the mortar has started to set.

KEEPING TILES LEVEL

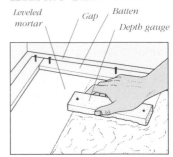

Leveled mortar · *Gap* · *Batten* · *Depth gauge*

Using a depth gauge
Hammer a nail through each end of a short length of batten so that the nails protrude by $\frac{1}{2}$ in (1 cm). Run this tool over the mortar, with the nails reaching through to the floor, so the mortar will be consistently $\frac{1}{2}$ in (1 cm) thick.

TILING BASEBOARDS

● **Cleaning easily** Attach a line of quarry tiles along the base of a wall as a substitute for a baseboard. You will then be able to clean easily, with no gap between floor and wall.

SAFETY

If you rent a disk cutter to speed up floor-tiling, follow these safety precautions.

● **Following instructions** Always read manufacturers' guidelines about operating disk cutters safely.

● **Protecting yourself** Wear a dust mask and goggles to protect the eyes from splinters.

TIME-SAVING TIP

Making a template
Most floor coverings need a few fussy cuts. Make templates around all obstacles, and let your local supplier make all your floor-tile cuts for you.

CERAMIC TILES

Much of the methodology for laying hard floor tiles can also be applied to ceramic floor tiles. However, with ceramic tiles you will have a little more flexibility when it comes to laying techniques. Since they are less heavy-duty, ceramic tiles are easier to work with.

MAKING ADJUSTMENTS

● **Dealing with doors** Remove doors that open onto a tiled floor surface before laying the tiles. Shave the same amount off the bottom of the door as the depth of a tile plus a little extra to allow for adhesive.

● **Finishing off the threshold** Cut a strip of hardwood doorstop the same width as the door to create an excellent threshold strip that is both decorative and provides a good barrier against which to tile.

● **Keeping level** Check that tiles are level from time to time by running a level or batten over the surface of newly laid tiles. Make any necessary adjustments while the adhesive is still wet, since mistakes will be difficult to rectify once it has dried.

● **Using inserts** To give a tiled area an opulent feel without spending a lot of money, buy a few high-quality, patterned tiles, and design a panel to insert in an appropriate place to lift the floor's appearance.

MAKING MOSAIC PANELS

● **Using an MDF base** When creating a mosaic panel as an insert feature to enhance a plain floor, attach the mosiac tiles to a piece of MDF cut to measure. The MDF will provide a rigid, sturdy base.

CUTTING SMALL PIECES

● **Using a nipper** As with wall tiles, when you need to cut intricate shapes – or if you want to cut up pieces of tile for insertion in a mosaic – use a nipper to give you greater accuracy (see p. 244).

INLAYING MOSAICS WITHIN TILED FLOORS

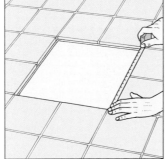

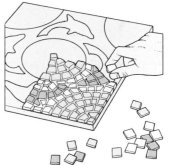

1 Leave a hole the size of the area required by the mosaic design within the floor layout. Cut a piece of MDF to fit the hole, making sure that it is of the correct thickness so that, once tiled and inlaid, the mosaic will be level with the surrounding tiled surface.

2 Draw the design you want on the MDF, and fill in with mosaic tiles. Make sure that you use floor adhesive to mount them in place, as this is the strongest method. Once complete, fit the mosaic into its hole. Use floor adhesive to attach the base in position.

CREATING A RUSTIC LOOK

As well as tiles that are custom- or factory-made, there are other alternatives that you can use for decorative hard flooring. These include a variety of more natural-looking materials. The particular characteristics of these products mean that you should consider practical requirements carefully.

● **Flagstones** These are extremely heavy-duty and can be found in regular or irregular shapes. Their surfaces tend to be uneven, so it is essential that you bed them in with plenty of mortar.

● **Bricks** These are best laid on their sides, especially if you want to create a herringbone pattern. Bricks should be bedded in mortar and butted up tightly together. Once laid, cover with several coats of varnish or commercial floor sealer to seal the surface.

● **Slate** Make sure that the subfloor is perfectly level before using slate tiles. Lay them onto adhesive, taking great care to prevent it from getting on the upper surfaces of the tiles, since it may stain them permanently.

Moving a heavy slab
Move a heavy stone slab using a simple yet effective method. Maneuver the slab onto two poles, then push the slab along as if it were on wheels. Bring each pole to the front as it is left behind as the slab progresses.

PAINTING FLOORS

CONCRETE BASES AND WOODEN SUBFLOORS can be painted rather than covered with flooring. Commercial floor paints should be used in high-wear areas, but other paints are acceptable on less well-used floors, as long as you varnish them well.

CREATING WOOD EFFECTS

One of the advantages of creating a wood effect is that it is far less expensive than laying a wooden floor. Using color cleverly, you can imitate natural wood convincingly. Alternatively, if you choose to use vivid colors, you can create an altogether surreal finish.

PREPARING TO PAINT

● **Checking** Read manufacturers' guidelines before painting sheet flooring (hardboard and chipboard). Some sheets are impregnated with fire-retardant chemicals that render them unsuitable for painting.
● **Filling** Fill imperfections on the surface of sheet flooring with all-purpose filler, which can be sanded back to a smooth finish. Fill small gaps between sheets with flexible filler, so that the cracks will not reopen when walked on.
● **Painting** Use a roller rather than a brush to paint a floor quickly. Attach an extension pole to the roller so that you can paint standing up.

PAINTING A FAUX RUG

Wooden surfaces can offer an ideal opportunity for *trompe l'oeil* effects, and a faux rug can be particularly eye-catching. The edges of floorboards provide ready-made guidelines for painting bands of color.

● **Planning a design** Work out a complete design for the faux rug before you start painting. Decide where on the floor you want the "rug" to be, then measure out an area guideline.
● **Painting narrow stripes** Use a mini roller for painting any narrow colored stripes.
● **Increasing realism** Add fine detail freehand to increase the realism, or "cheat" with stencils.

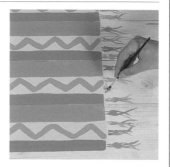

Adding the tassels
Use an artist's brush to finish a faux rug by painting tassels at each end. In reality, rug tassels are often pale in color or off-white, but vibrant colors show up better against wood.

CREATING THE IMPRESSION OF PAINTED FLOORBOARDS

1 Base-coat the floor, then draw pencil guidelines to represent the floorboard edges. Use an old plank or floorboard as a template, which will automatically give you "boards" of the right size.

2 Mix up a glaze (see p. 211). Using the plank as a straight-edge, apply a coat of glaze to each "floorboard." Draw a rocker through the glaze. Create knots by agitating the rocker backward and forward.

3 Once the glaze is dry, go over the pencil guidelines with a dark felt-tip pen. This will outline each "floorboard." Finally, cover the whole floor with two or three protective coats of acrylic matte varnish.

CREATING TILE EFFECTS

As in the case of wood effects, painting faux tiles rather than covering a floor with the real thing will greatly reduce your decorating expenditure. Tile effects are ideally suited to concrete bases: extra realism is provided by the noise created by walking on the surface.

CREATING "HARD TILES"

● **Ensuring dryness** Make sure that a floor has totally dried out before you paint it. A new concrete base should not be painted for several months.

● **Sealing a floor** Dilute commercial floor paints slightly for the first coat in order to prime and seal a floor surface. If you use alternative types of paint, make sure that you coat the floor with a commercial sealer before you start.

● **Choosing a base color** Choose a light color for the first coat. This will not only provide a realistic grout color but will also make a good foundation for the subsequent tile colors that you choose.

● **Applying effects** Marbling and sponging are two paint-effect techniques that are particularly useful. Use either or both to imitate various types of hard floor tile.

CREATING THE IMPRESSION OF TERRACOTTA TILES

● **"Tiling" freehand** Painting a tile effect need not be an exact science. To avoid the need for pencil guidelines, use a square object to produce the tiles by means of block printing.

1 Use a roller tray as a paint reservoir. Load a sponge with paint, removing excess. Place the sponge firmly on the floor, then apply pressure to print a well-defined tile shape. Leave gaps to represent grout.

● **Using a sponge** Make a block for creating "tiles" from a household sponge. Most are rectangular, so cut one down to tile size. Use the trimmed pieces for filling in detail.

2 After producing 10–20 "tiles," apply more paint to each one with a small piece of sponge to increase opacity. This buildup of depth will help to make the tiles look textured and more realistic.

FAKING CHECKERED VINYL TILES

1 Apply a base coat to a floor and let it dry. Measure out and draw a checkered pattern with a pencil. Cover alternate squares with pieces of newspaper. Spray black paint over the exposed squares.

2 Once the black paint has dried, peel away the newspaper masks to reveal a checkered, fake vinyl-tiled floor. As with all paint effects applied to floors, finish with a protective coat of varnish.

BRIGHT IDEA

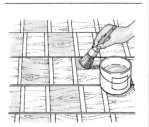

Checkering wood
Create a checkered effect on floorboards with wood stain. Use floorboard edges and masking tape to define the squares. Brush wood stain on alternate squares, which will highlight the wood grain and increase the contrast.

FINISHING

LAYING MANY TYPES OF FLOORING is quite a costly business and one you do not want to repeat very often. Make sure that the job is done well so that you reap the maximum benefit from the new floor and that it lasts as long as possible.

PROTECTING AND MAINTAINING FLOORS

A new floor covering will last a long time if it is well looked after. There are many varieties of flooring and a number of different ways of protecting and maintaining them, all of which are aimed at increasing the life of a floor and keeping it looking as good as possible.

CARING FOR CARPET
● **Cleaning** Vacuum carpets at least once a week, and have them professionally cleaned once a year to keep them in good condition and make them longer-lasting.
● **Protecting** In main walking thoroughfares, lay rugs on top of carpets to reduce heavy wear on the carpets. Rearrange the positions of the rugs from time to time so that they wear more evenly and last longer.
● **Using mats** Place a mat on the floor just inside each external door. Scraps of natural-fiber floor coverings make excellent mats, being both functional and decorative.

TRADITIONAL TIP

Making a sealer
Seal porous tiles with a wax made by warming four parts boiled linseed oil with one part beeswax until they are well mixed. Allow to cool, then apply to the tiles and buff.

DISTRIBUTING WEIGHT

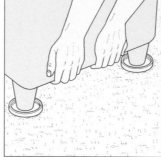

Using lids as coasters
Paint jam-jar lids to match the color of a carpet. Lift heavy items of furniture, then place the lids under the feet. The larger the lid, the greater the weight distribution and the less wear on the carpet.

MAINTAINING TILES
● **Cleaning vinyl** Always remove dirt and grit with a vacuum cleaner before mopping a vinyl floor. Otherwise, the mop may push bits of grit around the floor and scratch the surface of the vinyl.
● **Washing hard tiles** Mop a hard-tile floor with warm water regularly. Buff the floor occasionally with a commercial polish designed specifically for hard-tile floors; standard polishes will make it slippery.
● **Replacing carpet tiles** Simply lift out and replace worn or badly stained carpet tiles. This is an advantage of not having secured them in position with adhesive.

PROTECTING WOOD
● **Varnishing** Recoat well-used areas of a wooden floor at least once a year to maintain the floor's protective layer.
● **Waxing** Wax a wooden floor occasionally in order to maintain its durability properties as well as helping to build up a good depth of color and improve the appearance of the floor.
● **Padding rugs** Use a rug to protect a wooden floor, and insert a piece of nonslip padding beneath it. This will have the effect of slowing down the wear of the rug by preventing it from rubbing on the hard wooden surface.

REMOVING STAINS FROM CARPET

Accidental spills and the marking of carpets will happen from time to time. Most stains can be removed with care, fast action, and sometimes a little ingenuity.

● **Speed** Act quickly, since the success of stain removal depends upon the swift removal of the spill.
● **Action** Dab and blot stains rather than rubbing them.
● **Dampening** Do not use too much water, since this might damage the carpet backing.
● **Prevention** Treat carpets with commercial stain guard, following makers' instructions.

USING LEFTOVERS

Scraps and leftovers from a flooring project can be put to a variety of practical uses in a number of areas of the home. However, always retain some of the spare pieces of flooring for repairing damage or as swatches to aid decision-making about future decorating projects.

USING CARPET SCRAPS

● **Caring for pets** Carpet makes an excellent lining for pet beds and baskets. Simply cut and fit as required.

● **Using in cars** Car trunks receive a great amount of wear and tear. Line the base of a car trunk with carpet to protect the bodywork from damage and to make it much easier to clean. The piece of carpet can either be lifted out of the trunk to be cleaned or vacuumed *in situ*.

● **Lining paths** Gravel paths are notoriously difficult to keep free of weeds. Line a path with pieces of old carpet or padding scraps cut to size before laying gravel. This will greatly impede the growth of weeds or other stray plants.

● **Covering compost** Lay carpet over the top of a compost pile to keep heat in and therefore accelerate the natural processes of decomposition.

MAKING STAMPS FOR FLOOR EFFECTS

1 Cut cork into pieces the length of the strips of a parquet floor panel. Apply PVA along the edge of each cork piece, then attach to the panel. Stick a block of wood to the back of the panel as a handle.

2 Base-coat the floor and allow to dry. Load the stamp from a paint tray using a short-haired mohair roller. Position the stamp, then apply pressure to transfer the paint well. Reload after each impression.

USING VINYL

● **Cushioning movement** Cut up sheet vinyl or tiles and lay beneath a washing machine. Vinyl will provide a sturdy base but cushion the vibrations.

USING HARD TILES

● **Absorbing heat** Quarry tiles are thick and sturdy and make excellent pan rests. Use them to protect a worktop from hot pans removed from the fire.

USING UP CORK TILES

Cork is a versatile material, and leftovers can be put to a number of uses in the home.

● **Making coasters** Place an upturned drinking glass on a cork tile and draw around the rim. Cut out the shape to make a coaster.

● **Caring for cats** Stick a few cork tiles onto a block of wood for your cat to use as a scratcher instead of scratching the furniture.

● **Making pads** Cut pieces of cork tile to fit the bottoms of heavy ornaments. Stick them in position to protect the surface of furniture and prevent the ornaments from slipping.

Making a memo board
Attach some plywood to the back of a picture frame. Use PVA to stick cork tiles to the front surface of the plywood until the frame is filled. Remove excess PVA with a damp cloth. Hang the frame in the usual way and use it as a memo board.

PROTECTING DOORS

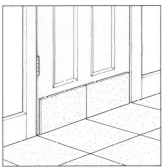

Making a kicker
The base of a door can easily be damaged by children and pets. Reduce this wear and tear by making a kicker board out of spare carpet tiles. Use spray adhesive to attach the tiles along the bottom edge of the door.

WINDOW TREATMENTS

QUICK REFERENCE

Selecting Materials, p. 288

Choosing Curtains, p. 289

Choosing Blinds, p. 292

Adding Trimmings, p. 294

Decorating Glass, p. 296

WINDOW TREATMENTS *are an important part of the decorative appeal of most rooms in the home. The options range from extravagant curtains and valances to plain blinds or shutters. These are all traditional ways of decorating windows, but with a little creativity you can break loose from convention and introduce your own innovative ideas.*

LOOKING AT WINDOWS

Before choosing any window treatment, look at the style and shape of a particular window and consider all decorative options. Take into account the practical functions that treatments will serve, such as increasing privacy, keeping out the cold or heat, or blocking light.

COMMON WINDOW TYPES

Window types and sizes vary considerably. Adapt your window treatments accordingly.

● **Sash** These are often tall and narrow. "Widen" them with curtains and a half-drawn blind.
● **French** Draw curtains back from the frame to ensure easy opening and closing.
● **Picture** These are simple in design. Choose from all types of window treatment.
● **Bay** Consider carefully the hanging system required for these multi-faceted windows.
● **Casement** These vary greatly in size and design. Assess each one individually.

Sash window

French windows

Picture window

Bay window

Casement window

SETTING A STYLE

Choosing window treatments can give you a wonderful opportunity to release your own artistic flair. Whether you drape lavish swaths of expensive fabric or adopt a more minimalist approach, the decorative style of a room can often be set by the window treatment alone.

CONSIDERING OPTIONS

Before choosing fabrics and styles of window treatments, think about these purely practical considerations.

● **Function** Choose simple, inexpensive hanging systems whenever you can, especially if your window treatments are purely decorative. You may need to invest in more costly hanging systems if you decide to hang curtains made of heavyweight material for warmth, for example.
● **Budget** Very full drapes usually result in great expense, so make sure that you work out what your budgetary restrictions are before you make choices.
● **Theme** If you decide to try to follow a regional or period theme, research appropriate materials, designs, and colors in order to create a complete, authentic look.

KEEPING FABRICS PLAIN
● **Color scheming simply** Use plain materials to make color scheming easier. Window treatments will thus play a complementary decorative role.

Dressing up plain fabric
Although a fabric may be plain in color, drape it effectively with an unusual tieback. Use windowsills as display areas for interesting collections of objects.

MAKING A STATEMENT
● **Drawing attention** If you want a window treatment to be a focal point, choose bold or contrasting colors and patterns to draw the eye.

Enhancing embellishments
Emphasize a flouncy window dressing by offsetting it against understated walls. Paint walls off-white or an extremely pale, complementary color.

TREATING A WINDOW IN DIFFERENT WAYS

Disguising window shape
Curtains hung outside a recess will disguise the shape of a window, especially if tied back from a closed position. Use a shaped valance to disguise the squareness of a window.

Emphasizing window shape
Hang a blind inside a window recess to emphasize the shape of the window. A patterned blind will draw attention to clear lines and square angles and help to make the window a feature.

SETTING THE SCENE
● **Having fun** Choose an appropriate fabric and use it for curtains, bedcovers, and cushions to produce a sense of fun in a child's room.
● **Aiding relaxation** Indulge yourself in swaths of curtain material in restful colors for a den that is used for calm recreation and relaxation.
● **Improving light** Use pale-colored treatments at windows that receive little or no direct sunlight. These will encourage the greatest amount of light reflection into the room.
● **Increasing privacy** In private areas of the home, such as a bedroom, cover the windows completely to help to create a secure, restful mood.

SELECTING MATERIALS

SELECTING THE RIGHT MATERIALS when dressing windows is as important as in any other decorating job. All tasks at this stage of your project will be easiest if you use the equipment and materials that are specifically designed for the job.

BASIC WINDOW-DRESSING EQUIPMENT

You may need to amalgamate several collections of tools and other items for dressing windows.

● **Toolkits** Include a basic sewing kit for making and altering furnishings, as well as general household tools for attaching treatments in place.
● **Hanging equipment** Choose a simple, relatively inexpensive hanging system – a track and gliders, or a lightweight rod – for light- to medium-weight curtains. Use a stronger, more complicated systems for hanging heavyweight fabrics.

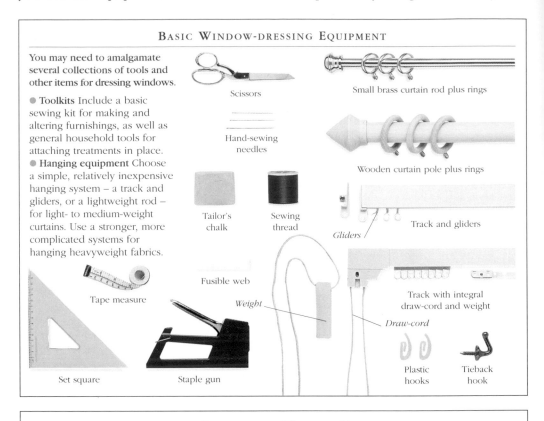

Scissors

Small brass curtain rod plus rings

Hand-sewing needles

Wooden curtain pole plus rings

Tailor's chalk

Sewing thread

Gliders

Track and gliders

Fusible web

Tape measure

Weight

Draw-cord

Track with integral draw-cord and weight

Set square

Staple gun

Plastic hooks

Tieback hook

CHOOSING FABRICS FOR WINDOW TREATMENTS

Most fabrics can be used for curtains or blinds. Make your choices based on practical as well as aesthetic factors.

● **Color, pattern, and fiber** Let colors and patterns, or the weave of fabric such as damask, guide your choice, but bear in mind practical factors also.
● **Weight** Choose heavy fabric such as brocade for sumptuous drapes. Sheer silk or fine fabrics such as lace, cotton, or calico will be more light and airy.
● **Function** If using thin curtain fabric, consider lining to block light or interlining for warmth.

Brocade

Cotton

Calico

Damask

Lace

Silk

CHOOSING CURTAINS

Y OU DO NOT NEED TO BE an expert at sewing to make curtains. Not all curtains need to be lined or hemmed. It is possible to adapt many curtaining techniques to suit your level of ability and still achieve the look you would like.

CONSIDERING OPTIONS

Curtains offer a lot of scope when it comes to covering windows. They come in many different materials, styles, and designs. You can make them, buy them ready-made, or adapt existing ones. Consider your preferences as well as practical requirements before you decide.

PLANNING CURTAINS

● **Lining** You do not need to line curtains, but if you do so it will improve the hang and provide the room with extra warmth. To avoid sewing lining in, attach it to curtain material using fusible web.

● **Avoiding obstacles** Pipes, radiators, and other obstacles or restrictions may prevent curtains from falling nicely. Take these into account when determining the style and the length of your curtains.

● **Selecting hanging systems** Choose a hanging system before you measure up for curtains, since the drop will clearly affect your calculations.

CHOOSING CURTAIN LENGTH

Curtain falls to floor

Curtain hangs to apron length, midway between sill and floor

Curtain hangs just above sill

Deciding length
While you are choosing a style and material for your curtains, consider the ideal length. This will be determined by a number of factors, not least of which are the shape and size of the window, the position of the window on the wall, and practical purposes that curtains serve such as keeping a room warm or cool or blocking light out of it.

CALCULATING FABRIC REQUIREMENTS

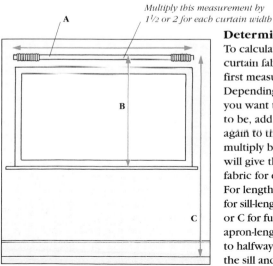

A

Multiply this measurement by 1½ or 2 for each curtain width

B

C

Determining size
To calculate the curtain fabric required, first measure width A. Depending on how full you want the curtains to be, add half as much again to this figure, or multiply by two. This will give the width of fabric for each curtain. For length, measure B for sill-length curtains or C for full-length. For apron-length, measure to halfway between the sill and floor.

MEASURING

Measure as accurately as possible to reduce the risk of making expensive mistakes.

● **Checking figures** The old adage about measuring twice and cutting once is wise advice. Always check your figures, because mistakes are easily made when taking a number of measurements.
● **Being precise** Not all floors, windows, and ceilings are absolutely "square," so take at least three width and length measurements.
● **Allowing for pattern repeats** As with wallpaper, centralize large patterns for balance.

CURTAINING CREATIVELY

Window treatments, and curtains particularly, offer a good opportunity to break with tradition and create your own designs and decorative themes. You can, of course, make or buy new curtains, but there are many ways of adapting and revamping existing curtains.

REDUCING COSTS

● **Reviving old curtains** Give old curtains a new lease on life simply by attaching some new braid or trim to their hems.

● **Cutting down curtains** To give a room a fresh new look, make some café curtains by cutting down an old pair of curtains from a different room in your home.

● **Using old for new** To save time and money, use old curtains as a lining around which to fit new fabric. Enclose the old in the new, then simply secure around the edges with fusible web.

● **Buying seconds** There is quite a market in secondhand curtains. Consider buying secondhand to reduce your expenses significantly. You may, however, need to make size adjustments for the curtains to fit your windows.

IMPROVING HEMS

● **Weighting** Make lightweight curtains hang better by placing coins or other weights inside hem corners, or gluing decorative beads along the outside edges of the hems.

Roll up fringed trim from one end

Making a tassel

Make a tassel by carefully rolling up some excess trim or braid and securing it with fabric glue. Insert a length of cord and use as a tieback, or hang several tassels from a curtain rail to dress it up.

USING OTHER MATERIALS

Consider how a curtain will hang when you are planning to use alternative materials, and keep headings simple.

● **Blankets** Use blankets as heavyweight "curtains" in very cold rooms. The insulating properties of blankets make them ideal.

● **Burlap** Sew burlap bags into a patchwork to create a rustic but very natural-looking window dressing.

● **Rugs** If you have a window with a poor view, use a decorative rug as a window treatment and distracting device. Use a rug's looped fringe to hang the rug from a substantial curtain pole.

USING APPLIQUÉ

Attaching shapes

Brighten up a plain material by cutting themed shapes out of a differently colored fabric. Attach the shapes to the curtain using fabric glue. Use a non-fraying fabric such as felt for the shapes to avoid finishing edges.

DECORATING SHEERS

Tracing outlines

Use sheer curtain fabric like a piece of tracing paper. Draw directly onto the material using a colorfast outliner pen. Leaves are an easy subject to draw around. Fix the outliner ink by ironing the back of the fabric.

HANGING CURTAINS

There are two main methods of hanging curtains: using poles or using tracks. Most types are straightforward to mount in place. You can, however, adapt either of these basic systems in order to add a touch of originality or to suit a particular decorative or color scheme.

USING POLES

● **Selecting materials** Choose a wooden pole for a fresh, lightweight appearance, or a sturdier-looking metal pole for a more solid, heavy look.

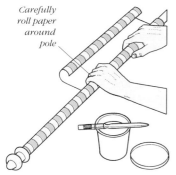

Carefully roll paper around pole

Covering poles

Cover a pole with wallpaper to match the walls. Attach the paper with PVA, let it dry, then apply several coats of matte varnish to protect the paper and facilitate curtain pulling.

MEASURING & MOUNTING

● **Adjusting width** Adjust the length of a curtain pole depending on whether the curtains will be gathered back beyond the edge of the window, or whether they will hang partly in front of the window and therefore require a shorter length of pole.

● **Allowing for finials** Do not forget to allow for finial attachments at each end when calculating a pole's length.

● **Making poles level** You will require only two brackets – one at each end – to mount a curtain pole in position above a narrow window. It will be easy to ensure that the brackets are level using a level. It is more difficult to align three brackets. Mount the central bracket first, and use this to take a level to where the other two need to be positioned.

ALTERNATIVE TO USING POLES

You can choose from a variety of alternative materials as substitutes for curtain poles. Alternatively, use your imagination and substitute a less obvious but still suitable item instead of a pole.

● **Driftwood** Use a slender length of driftwood to make a pole suitable for draping either curtains or swags.
● **Copper pipes** These make ideal curtain poles. You can bend them to fit around corners, so use them in bay and dormer windows.
● **Bamboo stakes** Use stakes as an inexpensive means of hanging lightweight, sheer curtain fabrics.
● **Pole supports** Use ornate shelf brackets to support any kind of pole, as well as providing a decorative finish.

ALTERNATIVES TO USING HEADING TAPE

With a little imagination you can substitute all sorts of items for standard heading tape when hanging curtains. Make holes in fabric with a punch-and-rivet set to facilitate the threading of ties.

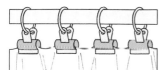

Bulldog clips
Hang bulldog clips from curtain rings. Paint them if you wish.

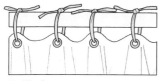

Raffia loops
Tie lengths of raffia or string around a pole for a rustic feel.

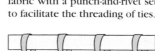

Bow-tie ribbons
Cut ribbons to the same length to ensure consistent loop size.

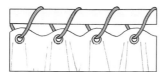

Strip of leather
Thread on, keeping a constant drop from pole to curtain.

USING TRACKS

● **Looking and learning** If you are concerned that you might not be able to assemble and mount a curtain track, have a look at a similar working system, either in your local supplier's showroom or in someone's home. You will then know what the track should look like once assembled.
● **Painting to match** Consider painting curtain tracks, which are usually supplied white, so that they blend in with wall colors or curtain materials. Semigloss gives the best paint finish on plastic surfaces.
● **Lubricating tracks** In order to maintain a curtain track in good running order, lubricate it occasionally with a few drops of dish detergent.

CHOOSING BLINDS

Blinds are the main alternative to curtains and can be made from a variety of different fabrics. Try to balance decorative and functional requirements, and assess to what extent a blind will need to block light or provide privacy.

STYLES OF BLIND

Blinds vary in shape and size as much as any other kind of window treatment and may be left plain or decorated extravagantly, depending on your own preferences and practical requirements. These factors affect both the material you choose for your blind and the hanging mechanism you will need.

Roller
Roller blinds are the most functional and require least material.

Gathered
Gathered blinds use more fabric and suit an opulent atmosphere.

Roman
Roman blinds consist of subtle, gently folded layers of material.

Venetian
Venetian or slatted blinds can be plastic, metal, or wooden.

MEASURING

Techniques for measuring for blinds depend upon whether you prefer a flat blind or one that consists of folds of fabric. The surface area will be determined by whether the blind will hang inside or outside a window recess as well as by the size of the window itself.

MEASURING FOR BLINDS IN RECESSED WINDOWS

● **Fitting attachments** Decide on the position of a blind, and fit the pole or track before you take the measurements for material. Your calculations will then be more accurate.

● **Overestimating** Err on the side of generosity when calculating amounts of material. It is better to need to trim than start afresh because you do not have enough material.

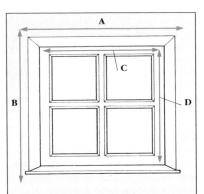

Measuring a recess
For a roller blind outside a recess, measure the width (A), including a 1¼-in (3-cm) overlap onto the walls, and the length (B) to below the sill. Add 2 in (5 cm), for attaching the fabric to a dowel. For a blind inside a recess, allow for brackets in the width measurement (C). Calculate length (D) to above the sill.

GATHERED BLINDS

● **Calculating width** Tape the end of a long length of string to one corner at the top of a window frame. Take the string along the frame to the other corner, forming a number of scallop shapes. Measure the length of string to give you the width of the blind including ruched folds. Add an extra 8 in (20 cm) for side turnings.

● **Measuring length** Add 12 in (30 cm) to the basic height measurement to allow for the depth of the scalloped edge when the blind is down.

● **Counting scallops** Bear in mind that an odd number of scallops creates a more balanced look than an even number.

MAKING AND FITTING BLINDS

Plain roller blinds work by means of a fairly simple mechanism, making them the easiest type of blind both to make and to fit. Most blinds are adapted from this system, although there are alternative types of blind that can be constructed to provide a more individual look.

CHOOSING FABRICS
● **Assessing suitability** For flouncy blinds with gathers, choose lightweight materials such as moiré or soft cotton, which will ruche well. Heavier fabrics will not gather well.

REVIVING BLINDS
● **Spraying** Paint old Venetian blinds to give them a new lease of life. Wash them thoroughly, allow to dry, then spray with an aerosol paint.
● **Stenciling** Transform a plain blind by stenciling it with fabric paints. Make your own stencil, picking out a design from fabrics or other decorations within the room.
● **Dyeing** If a blind remains in good condition but has become discolored by light, for example, use a cold-water dye to transform the look of it completely. Choose a color to match or tone in with other decorations within the room.

SQUARING CORNERS
● **Making angles** To ensure the smooth running of a roller blind, cut precise, 90-degree angled corners. Use a large set square and tailor's chalk to draw accurate guidelines.

ATTACHING MATERIAL

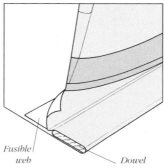

Fusible web *Dowel*

Avoiding stitching
To make a casing for a wooden dowel at the bottom of a blind without sewing, iron in some fusible web. Secure the material firmly to the roller at the top of the blind using a staple gun.

FINISHING EDGES
● **Preventing fraying** Use a stiffened fabric for roller blinds. This can be cut to an exact size and will not fray. Stabilize lightweight fabric edges with zigzag stitch.

ATTACHING SIMPLY

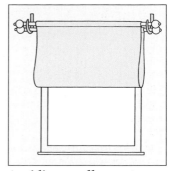

Avoiding a roller system
A mechanical roller system is not essential to pull a blind. Attach a dowel at each end of a blind and a hook in the wall at each end at the top. Rest the lower dowel over the hooks to let light in.

IMPROVISING YOUR OWN SHUTTER BLINDS

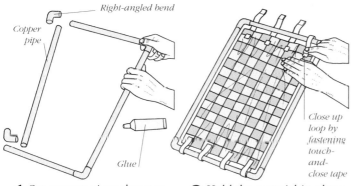

Right-angled bend

Copper pipe

Glue

Close up loop by fastening touch-and-close tape

1 Cut copper pipes down to the required size using a hacksaw. Use right-angled bends to fit the pipes together to make a frame. Use metal bonding adhesive to make sure that the joints are secure.

2 Hold the material in place in the center of the frame using a tabbed heading. Secure the tabs with touch-and-close tape. This is ideal since the material can be removed easily and cleaned as required.

3 Use standard pipe brackets as hinges. Attach two brackets on each side of the frame, which will hold the shutters secure but also allow enough movement for them to be opened and closed.

ADDING TRIMMINGS

Many of the trimmings for window treatments are purely decorative and are used as accessories to a color scheme or style. Other trimmings, however, are dual-purpose and perform a function within a window-dressing system.

CORNICES

Cornices form a decorative finish to hide the running systems of curtains and create a finished-looking window treatment. They tend to be used for grand curtain treatments, but lighter-weight, less elaborate versions can look effective in a simpler decorative plan.

USING CORNICES

● **Papering cornices** Decorate plain wooden cornices simply by painting or wallpapering them. Use the same paper as that covering the walls, which will make the job easier and less costly than using fabric.

● **Increasing impact** Add a decorative molding along the top of a cornice, or use it as a shelf for displaying ornaments to increase its visual impact.

● **Creating effects** Use a cornice to alter the apparent shape of a window. Position it higher than the top of the window treatment, for example, to make the window look taller than it actually is.

ATTACHING FABRIC CORNICES

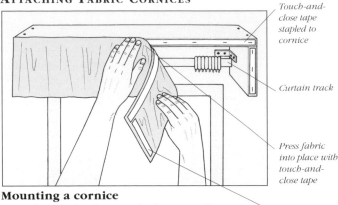

Touch-and-close tape stapled to cornice

Curtain track

Press fabric into place with touch-and-close tape

Touch-and-close tape fixed to fabric

Mounting a cornice
Once the wooden framework of a cornice has been assembled and mounted in place, attach its fabric front. Ideally, make this piece with a flexible frame so that it is easy to fit in place. It can be held there using touch-and-close tape.

SHAPING CORNICES

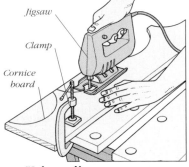

Jigsaw

Clamp

Cornice board

Using a jigsaw
Add to the decorative appeal of a wooden cornice by scalloping the lower edge. Mark out the curved design on the cornice board, clamp the cornice onto a workbench, and use a jigsaw carefully to cut the shapes.

VALANCES

A valance serves a similar purpose to a cornice, but it is constructed from fabric rather than a solid material. Despite being less substantial, a valance can contribute to the decorative impact of a window treatment.

● **Saving money** Make a valance rather than a cornice if you are working within a tight budget. The fabric needed to make a valance will cost less than for a more substantial alternative.

● **Using ceilings** In a room with a low ceiling, you can hang a valance directly from the ceiling above a window without a rail. Attach hooked screws directly to the valance's heading tape.

Hanging a valance alone
A valance is highly decorative and can be hung by itself – without curtains – as a finish in its own right. Mount it in position using a valance rail so that the fabric will hang with a good shape and be seen to the best effect.

SWAGS AND TAILS

Swags and tails can either accompany a cornice or be used alone as a decorative window treatment. These decorative items take the cornice and valance idea a stage further. Their function is purely decorative, but they can be used imaginatively to great effect.

MAKING SIMPLE SWAGS

Using door knockers
Creat a simple swag effect by mounting an ornate door knocker above each top corner of a window. Drape material around the window through the rings so that it hangs in a flowing style.

BEING INVENTIVE
● **Using alternative materials** Since swags are usually simply draped, experiment with different kinds of material. Try long silk scarves, saris, or other lightweight fabrics to create all sorts of voluminous and shapely draped effects.
● **Draping in position** For an informal hanging system, simply drape your material around a pole or other curtain-hanging mechanism. Make a few stitches in appropriate places to maintain the hold.
● **Attaching to cornices** When attaching swags and tails to a cornice, use a staple gun. This will allow you to create neat pleats easily as you secure the fabric which will improve the way the fabric falls.

BRIGHT IDEA

Using leftovers
Leftover pieces of material need never go to waste. You can use even the smallest slivers of material left over from making trimmings to add a coordinating or contrasting frilled edging around a plain cushion.

TIEBACKS

The traditional function of a tieback is to hold a window treatment back to one side of a window (or door) in order to allow light in. Tiebacks can, however, also have a decorative role as integral parts of the window treatment or even as decorations in their own right.

USING TIEBACKS
● **Using contrasting fabric** In a formal curtain arrangement that includes a cornice, for example, use a different fabric for the tiebacks and cornice to add definition to the curtains.
● **Tying easily** Choose ribbons or cords for the simplest of material tiebacks. Hold them secure by looping them over hooks screwed into the wall.
● **Positioning tiebacks** In the case of tall windows, tiebacks are best positioned about one-third of the way up the wall. Experiment with string before you finalize the position. This will also enable you to judge the length of the tieback.

USING ALTERNATIVE MATERIALS IN TIEBACKS

Being creative with leaves
Entwine wired artificial leaves together to create an unusual and attractive tieback resembling a wreath. Spray the leaves using aerosol paints to coordinate them with the color scheme.

Using a door knob
A door knob makes an ideal tieback as long as curtain material is not too heavy and does not fall over it. If it does, attach a block of wood to the back of the knob to make it more substantial.

DECORATING GLASS

WINDOW TREATMENTS are not the only way of decorating windows: you can decorate the glass itself. The design of stained-glass windows ranges from gothic to modern, so you will have a wealth of tradition on which to draw.

BASIC EQUIPMENT AND MATERIALS

Glass decoration requires specialized materials in order to achieve the desired finish.

● **Buying materials** You can buy all the tools and materials that you require for adding effects to glass from most good art suppliers. They should also be able to give you advice.

● **Choosing paints** You can use oil-based paints for applying simple painted designs to glass surfaces. However, these are translucent and will not be as effective as glass paints, which are designed and manufactured specifically for the job.

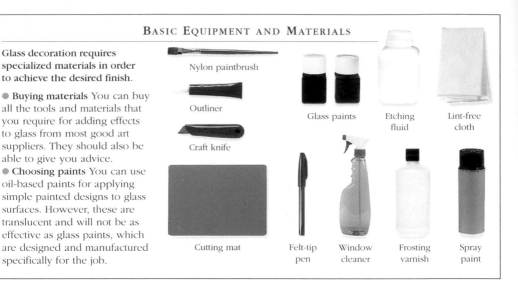

Nylon paintbrush

Outliner

Glass paints

Etching fluid

Lint-free cloth

Craft knife

Cutting mat

Felt-tip pen

Window cleaner

Frosting varnish

Spray paint

ETCHING WINDOWS

Etched windows are traditionally used in bathrooms, cloakrooms, and entrance halls in order to provide privacy as well as decoration. Etched glass can look effective in any window, but it is particularly useful if the window is very plain or overlooks an undesirable area.

USING FROSTING VARNISH
● **Cleaning windows** Before varnishing, clean a window with household cleaner so that the glass surface is free of grime and other impurities.
● **Applying varnish** Apply frosting varnish using the basic stenciling method (see p. 215). Mount a stencil in position on the window with a light covering of spray-on adhesive, and then apply the varnish to the outlined design.
● **Changing designs** Most frosting varnishes are acrylic, so you can easily modify or completely change a design simply by cleaning away the varnish using an abrasive cleaner and a window scraper.

ETCHING QUICKLY

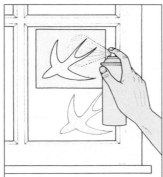

Using spray-on "snow"
With a stencil in place on a window, use spray-on festive snow for an etched effect. Two or three light coats are better than one thick one. Remove excess snow with fine sandpaper.

GREEN TIP

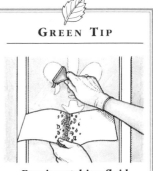

Reusing etching fluid
Commercial etching fluids can be used on any glass surface. Most can be reused, since once the fluid has dried the residue can be scraped away and returned to the container to be used again.

REPRODUCING STAINED-GLASS EFFECTS

Modern decorating materials make it relatively easy to reproduce the effect of stained glass on your windows without needing to use colored glass or lead. You can use commercial paints on plain glass to achieve a very authentic-looking stained-glass effect.

CREATING DESIGNS

● **Seeking inspiration** Having chosen a window to decorate, you must then select a design. Stained glass is traditionally associated with ornate settings and religious themes, while single motifs or original patterns on plain glass windows are a more modern option.

● **Tracing designs** Mount a design to the outside of a window using a low-tack adhesive. Draw the design on cardboard that is rigid enough to remain in place against the surface of the glass, making tracing much easier.

● **Finishing** Once it is dry, clean your stained glass using a soft cloth and mild household window cleaner.

IMITATING STAINED GLASS ON A WINDOW

1 Attach a design to the outside of a window. Apply the appropriate color to each area on the inside. Do not overload the brush, since paint will run easily. Work from the top down to avoid smudging.

2 Once the colors are dry, add the leaded effect using a tube of silver outliner. Keep a steady movement to avoid unevenness. Remove the design from the outside of the window when you have finished.

REPRODUCING LEADED-LIGHT EFFECTS

Leaded lights share a similar tradition to that of stained glass, although the technique for reproducing them is quite different. A leaded-light effect is ideal for large, plain windows that lack interesting features or for recreating a period look in line with a decorative style.

CREATING LEADED LIGHTS ON YOUR WINDOWS

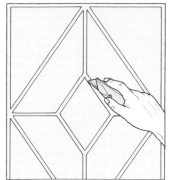

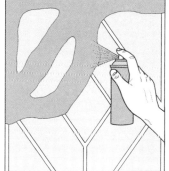

1 Draw the leaded-light design on clear sticky-backed plastic, and attach it to the inside of the window. Cut around the "panes" of glass, leaving them stuck to the glass but peeling away the rest.

2 With a commercial metallic aerosol paint, apply three or four thin coats to the entire area. Metallic paint is ideal since it adds texture and depth to the leaded areas as well as providing a realistic color.

3 When the paint is dry, remove the "panes" of sticky-backed plastic between the "leaded" strips to reveal the glass. Remove any excess drips or runs of paint using a standard window scraper.

FINISHING TOUCHES

QUICK REFERENCE

Lighting, p. 299

Shelving, p. 302

Wall Decorations, p. 304

Soft Furnishings, p. 306

Final Details, p. 309

THE MAJORITY OF DECORATIVE PLANS *are incomplete without a few final flourishes to complement and enhance the finish. Lighting, wall decorations, shelving, and soft furnishings can all be used for this purpose. Many such items have a mainly ornamental function, allowing you to indulge personal taste and add individuality to your decorative style.*

CONSIDERING OPTIONS

It is up to you how much you accessorize, but you will need to take certain factors into account when making any decisions. You can usually achieve a desired effect in a number of ways, and which one you should choose may depend on the function of a particular room.

DISPLAYING ITEMS
● **Adding interest** Create an inviting atmosphere in areas of the home used for recreation by hanging wall decorations and by displaying ornaments and other interesting items.

TAKING TIME
● **Building up a style** Do not rush to add the finishing touches to a room. Once the main decorating has been completed, you can introduce further additions over time.

USING UNDERSTATEMENT
● **Choosing carefully** In a minimalist decorative plan, keep the accessories to a minimum also. Finishing touches will be conspicuous, so select them very carefully.

SAFETY

When carrying out any of the tasks outlined in this chapter, be sure to take appropriate safety precautions.

● **Electricity** Do not allow anyone other than a fully trained, qualified electrician to carry out electrical work.
● **Pipes and wires** These are usually visible but may run behind a wall surface. Check for pipes and wires before hanging pictures and mirrors.
● **Fire hazards** Choose fire-retardant materials, or have their surfaces treated.
● **Harmful substances** Some products contain harmful substances that must not touch the skin or be inhaled. Follow manufacturers' guidelines.

USING LOTS OF ITEMS

Providing variety
A clutter of ornaments and other items can be used to create a comfortable, homely feel. Leave space to move, and do not use too many colors. Here, warm, natural woods balance cool blues.

MINIMIZING EXTRAS

Creating harmony
In a bedroom, keep ornaments and other items to a minimum, and harmonize colors for a restful feeling. Here, for example, matching covers and cushions, create a harmonious atmosphere.

LIGHTING

LIGHTING DOES FAR MORE THAN JUST PRODUCE LIGHT. It is one of the most influential tools for creating mood and atmosphere in a room, and there is an extensive range of options to choose from to achieve effects you like.

LIGHTING TYPES

Although styles of lighting vary considerably, there are only a few categories – based largely on function – into which the majority of lighting systems fall. Within these groups, designers have excelled in producing lighting to suit all tastes, and lighting styles and fashions contribute greatly to the overall decorative look of a room.

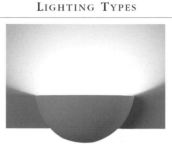
Opaque bowl

Pendant with shade

Tungsten reflector

Wooden base with paper shade

Desk light with clamp

Brass standard lamp with paper shade

ENERGY-EFFICIENT TYPES OF LIGHTBULB

Energy-efficient lightbulbs produce an attractive light and last up to five times longer than conventional bulbs.

● **Fluorescent** Substitute these for standard domestic bulbs.
● **Tungsten-halogen** These are low-voltage with specially built fixtures. Choose them for powerful yet unobtrusive lighting, such as in a kitchen.

2-D miniature fluorescent bulb

Bayonet cap fixture

Screw fixture

Fluorescent bulbs

Tungsten-halogen bulbs

Miniature, low-voltage reflector

Standard voltage reflector

FIXED LIGHTING

Most rooms have some fixed lighting, which is usually operated by switches located close to a door or entrance. In spite of this relatively limited setup, there are numerous ways in which fixed lighting can be adapted in order to achieve more interesting light effects.

CHOOSING LIGHTS

● **Changing pendant lights** Consider changing a pendant light fixture to sunken or track-mounted spotlights. These can totally change a room's mood.

● **Lighting alcoves** Fixed lighting is ideal for showing off room features and displays. Bringing in new electrical cables might necessitate redecoration, so consider battery-powered lighting, especially for occasional use.

● **Diffusing light** Paint and suspend a metal colander from the base of a lampshade. It will channel the light into many shafts, creating shadows and a varied intensity of light.

MAKING A STRIP-LIGHT DIFFUSER

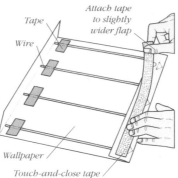

Tape
Attach tape to slightly wider flap
Wire
Wallpaper
Touch-and-close tape

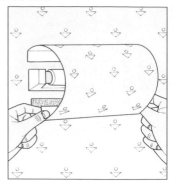

1 Cut some wallpaper to size, and strengthen it by taping lengths of wire across it. Fold the long edges of wallpaper to form two flaps, and attach touch-and-close tape to them.

2 Attach lengths of touch-and-close tape above and below the light. Gently bend the wired wallpaper to form a half-cylinder. Position it around the light and fasten the tape.

DIRECTIONAL LIGHTING

Directing light can significantly enhance the decorative style in a room or highlight specific features and thereby create a localized area of special interest. Directional lighting is also useful when you are reading or for work purposes, and therefore serves a dual function.

FOCUSING LIGHT

Creating a specific effect
Use uplighters to draw the eye upward, increasing the "height" of a room. Ensure that the ceiling is very well decorated, however, since concentrated light will highlight imperfections.

CONSIDERING USAGE

Mixing style and function
Choose bedside lighting that is atmospheric but also allows you to read adequately. An extending base on this wall light enables you to direct light and fits well in a modern decorative style.

ADAPTING LIGHTING

● **Using dimmers** Vary the intensity of directional light by using dimmer switches. These can be installed relatively inexpensively and will enable you to increase or decrease the amount of light in a room by a simple turn of the switch.

● **Hiding lights** Blend lights into their surroundings to create a harmonious and relaxed effect. For example, paint opaque bowl wall lights to match the wall color.

● **Using spotlights** These provide the most adaptable form of directional lighting since you can point them in any direction. Change the emphasis of lighting within a room by occasionally altering the direction of spotlights.

LAMPSHADES

Once you have chosen your light fixtures, consider how lampshades will affect the kind of light produced and the coordination of lighting with other decorative features. You can buy a shade as part of a lighting system or make or adapt your own for a personal note.

CONTRASTING SHADES

Cut-out shape enhances plain lampshade

Using different colors
As in all aspects of decor, the color of a lamp and its shade will affect the atmosphere and style of a room. Use strongly contrasting colors to make a localized decorative statement.

ENHANCING SHADES

Introducing shapes
Add interest to plain lamps and shades by adapting their designs. For example, cut simple patterns or shapes into a lampshade, perhaps linking to other designs and motifs within the room.

USING LAMPSHADES
● **Directing light** Line a lampshade with dark paper to channel light through the bottom and top openings and therefore create concentrated, directional shafts of light.
● **Varying color** Alter the effect of a lampshade by using a colored lightbulb. This will have a dramatic effect if you are using a pale lampshade and allow you to experiment with color and a dark shade.
● **Keeping clean** To ensure that a lampshade looks at its best, always keep it clean. Either vacuum it using the appropriate attachment, or wrap sticky tape around your hand (sticky-side out) and brush over the surface of the shade to pick up dust and dirt.

DECORATING SHADES
● **Attaching stickers** Stick shaped, fluorescent stickers onto a plain lampshade. Once they have absorbed light while the lamp is on, they will continue to shine after it has been turned off. This is a particularly good idea in a child's bedroom.
● **Stenciling designs** Coordinate lampshades with the rest of the decoration in a room by stenciling the same design on a shade as there is on a border, for example.
● **Using a wallpaper border** Cut down a wallpaper border to make a mini-border, then attach it around the edges of color-coordinating shades.
● **Adding trimmings** Use contrasting or matching braid, tassels, or other appropriate trimmings to enhance the lower edge of a plain shade.

THREADING A SHADE WITH DECORATIVE STRANDS
● **Making holes** A hole punch intended for paper will not cut lampshade material adequately, so use a leather punch to make however many holes you need.

● **Choosing threads** Once you have made the holes, change the ribbon or thread occasionally to reflect festive or other special occasions.

Punch holes around edge

1 Use a pencil to make a series of equidistant marks around the upper and lower edges of a lampshade. Make holes at these marks using a leather punch, holding the shade firmly as you do so.

2 Pass some ribbon through the holes, making a criss-cross pattern over the surface of the lampshade. Create any number of your own designs using the same method and a variety of alternative materials.

SHELVING

S HELVING IS ESSENTIALLY FUNCTIONAL, and its size and sturdiness will depend on load-bearing requirements. But it can also serve as a design accessory that, within the constraints of practicality, you can decorate as you like.

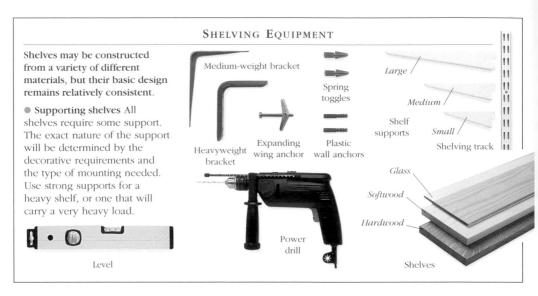

SHELVING EQUIPMENT

Shelves may be constructed from a variety of different materials, but their basic design remains relatively consistent.

● **Supporting shelves** All shelves require some support. The exact nature of the support will be determined by the decorative requirements and the type of mounting needed. Use strong supports for a heavy shelf, or one that will carry a very heavy load.

Medium-weight bracket

Spring toggles

Large

Medium

Shelf supports

Small

Shelving track

Heavyweight bracket

Expanding wing anchor

Plastic wall anchors

Glass

Softwood

Hardwood

Power drill

Level

Shelves

MOUNTING SHELVES

A side from certain types of freestanding unit, a shelf will always need firm wall hardware to hold it in position. Be sure to use hardware that is appropriate for the type of wall, since particular designs of screw are intended for specific types of construction materials.

BRIGHT IDEA

Searching for obstructions
Before attaching any shelf hardware into a wall, use a small metal detector to ensure that there are no wires or pipes beneath the surface. Such metal detectors are relatively inexpensive to buy.

USING WALL ANCHORS

● **Limiting drilling** When drilling holes, measure the length of the wall anchor against the drill bit. Place sticky tape around the bit at this point so that you can see when you have drilled the correct distance into the wall.

● **Inserting anchors** If it is necessary, use the handle end of a hammer to drive anchors into a wall. Using the striking face can damage them.

● **Rectifying overdrilling** If a hole is too large or a wall surface crumbles so that the hole widens, fill the hole with commercial filling adhesive and then insert the anchor. Let it dry before inserting the screw.

KEEPING SHELVES LEVEL

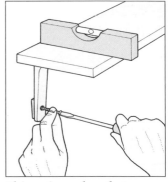

Shimming a bracket
If a shelf slopes forward due to the unevenness of the wall, shim its brackets with pieces of cardboard. Place a level on top of the shelf to help you judge how much cardboard to use.

DECORATING SHELVES

Shelves can be treated like any other item in a room in that they may be decorated in order to blend, complement, or contrast with their surroundings. When deciding how to decorate them, consider to what extent they will be obscured by items placed on them.

COVERING SHELVES

● **Allowing drying time** After painting shelves, let at least 72 hours pass before putting anything on them. This lets the paint dry completely, preventing denting or scraping when you place ornaments.

● **Adding trimmings** Decorate edges of shelves with material trim or a row of upholstery pins for a textured finish.

● **Using plastic** To produce a durable yet decorative surface, cover the tops of shelves with patterned sticky-backed plastic. This is ideal for kitchen shelves, which require regular cleaning. Alternatively, apply wallpaper to shelves and finish with several coats of varnish.

ADDING DECORATIVE MOLDINGS

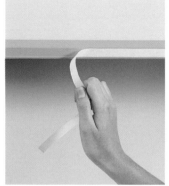

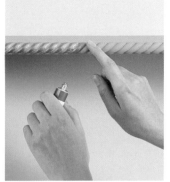

1 Attach double-sided tape along the front edge of the shelf. Cut a piece of molding to the required length and stick it to the shelf edge. The tape eliminates the need for nails, so no filling is required.

2 Apply gilding cream along the molding's surface. For the best effect, highlight parts of the molding rather than covering it totally with cream. Vary the extent to which the base color shows through.

IMPROVISING SHELVES

Adaptation and variation are the keys to the creation of individual decorative effects. Shelving provides an excellent opportunity to develop your innovative ideas. Its simple construction, requiring limited technical skills, means you can design and build from scratch.

USING ALTERNATIVES

Screw chrome rail into its socket

Supporting with rails
Improvise vertical supports between shelves with chrome towel rails. While not designed for this purpose, they provide adequate support and create a very modern, alternative look.

SERVING PRACTICALITIES

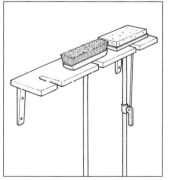

Storing equipment
Many household objects are awkwardly shaped and difficult to store. Adapt a plain shelf by cutting out holes along its front edge from which to hang brooms and mops, for example.

BEING INVENTIVE

● **Creating freestanding shelves** Shelves need not be secured to a wall as long as they are sturdy, not too tall, and do not carry heavy loads. Improvise shelving using large terracotta plant pots as supports for lengths of natural wood.

● **"Solidifying" shelves** Make open shelving look more solid by painting the back wall the same color as the shelves.

● **Hanging from the ceiling** Create unusual shelving for light loads by suspending it from the ceiling instead of using wall brackets. If you use chains with hook-and-eye hardware, secure them firmly into supporting beams.

WALL DECORATIONS

Pictures and other wall decorations make a statement about your taste, while the manner in which they are displayed contributes to a room's decorative atmosphere. The wide choice available allows a huge variety of effects.

BASIC HANGING EQUIPMENT

A limited amount of equipment is required for picture hanging, since it is a relatively simple job to carry out. However, using the correct equipment is essential to make sure that pictures are hung safely and securely.

● **Keeping pictures on the wall** Prevent picture fastenings or fixtures from failing by using the appropriate hooks and thread for each picture. Many hooks are sold with guidelines as to the weight they can bear.

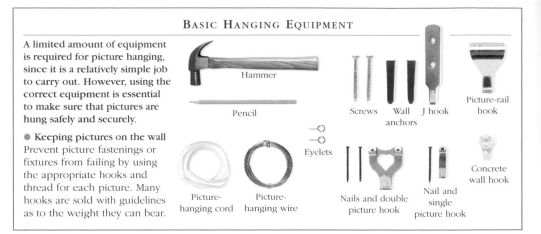

Hammer

Pencil

Screws

Wall anchors

J hook

Picture-rail hook

Eyelets

Picture-hanging cord

Picture-hanging wire

Nails and double picture hook

Nail and single picture hook

Concrete wall hook

CHOOSING HANGING SYSTEMS

Any wall-hanging system needs to be appropriate for the size of a picture and its weight, which is determined by its mount and frame. Once you have worked this out, you can decide whether the hanging system itself is to be a decorative feature or purely functional.

HANGING INVENTIVELY
● **Using picture rails** Picture rails are ideal for hanging pictures – especially heavy ones – by means of chains, picture wire, or heavyweight cord. For aesthetic effect, consider painting chains so that they match the color of the walls, or coordinate decorative cords with the soft furnishings in the room.
● **Deceiving the eye** Paint a cord between vertically aligned pictures or items such as plates to produce the *trompe l'oeil* effect of them hanging from each other.
● **Avoiding holes** Attach very small, lightweight pictures to a wall using self-adhesive pads rather than a hanging system. This will eliminate the need to make holes in the wall.

ATTACHING WIRE

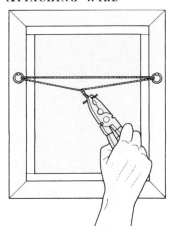

Twisting with pliers
Wire is the most secure means of hanging pictures. Thread wire through an eyelet on each side of a frame. Twist the ends of the wire together using pliers to form a secure and taut fastening.

HANGING ORNATELY

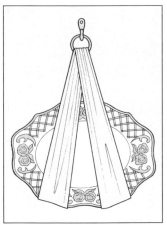

Using ribbon
When displaying plates or other decorative items, make a feature of the hanging system. Wrap wide ribbon around a plate and through a ring. Secure by sewing the ribbon behind the plate.

HANGING WALL DECORATIONS

Positioning wall decorations is important for creating the desired effect in a room. If you do it well, you will not only maintain an overall decorative balance but also ensure that each piece is fully appreciated, fulfilling its role as a finishing touch and a feature in its own right.

ENHANCING PICTURES

● **Lighting** Increase the impact of the pictures within a room by illuminating them with picture lights. Alternatively, use directional spotlights to serve the same purpose.

● **Moving pictures around** Give a room a fresh look by switching the positions of existing pictures or introducing one or two different ones.

● **Choosing frames** The frame plays an important role in showing off a picture. If you feel you have made a wrong choice of frame, you can modify it relatively easily by painting the molding.

● **Cleaning frames** Frames collect dust and dirt like any other surface. Use an old shaving brush to remove dust and debris from even the most intricate molding, thereby maintaining the frame in the best possible condition.

DETERMINING POSITION

● **Choosing height** Position pictures for viewing from the eye level of an average-height person. Needing to look up or down distorts perspective.

INSERTING HOOKS

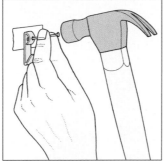

Taping over the spot
Apply a piece of masking tape to a wall where a picture hook is to be placed. This will prevent the hook from slipping and reduce the chance of plaster crumbling and the hook being dislodged.

MARKING POSITION

● **Using a finger** Rub chalk on one finger. Position a picture on the wall, then mark the point at which it will hang with the chalked finger.

TRADITIONAL TIP

Sanding a hammer
The striking face of a hammer needs cleaning occasionally to prevent it from slipping off nailheads. Sand the face with fine-grade sandpaper until it is shiny and clean.

USING POSTERS

Although posters are an inexpensive option, they can be used in such a way as to have great decorative impact.

● **Ironing** Use a cool iron to smooth a poster flat before hanging it. Nothing looks worse than a poster that is curling at the edges.

● **Mounting** Attach a poster to a wall using wallpaper adhesive. For the greatest visual impact, place several posters together on one wall, and then apply a coat of matte varnish over the whole surface for a flat finish.

● **Aging** Age posters or prints by rubbing a damp tea bag over the surface of the paper.

HANGING MIRRORS EFFECTIVELY

Mirrors require similar hardware as pictures, except those that sit flush against a wall. Use special corner angles, mirror pads, or mirror screws in such instances. Take time to consider a mirror's position, as it can dramatically affect the appearance of a room.

● **Hanging large mirrors** Most large mirrors have mounting brackets as an integral part of the frame. Drill rather than nail them, and ensure that the size of screws used will be sufficient to take the weight of the mirror.

● **Tightening screws** Take care not to overtighten mirror screws, cracking the mirror. Insert a thin piece of cardboard behind each screw as a tightening gauge.

Increasing space
Dramatically increase the impression of space in a room by carefully positioning a mirror, especially a large one. Center it on a wall or in an alcove to distribute its effect evenly over as much of the room as possible.

SOFT FURNISHINGS

Soft furnishings are an integral part of a decorative plan, contributing to color coordination and style. Complicated upholstering or covering is best left to experts, but in some areas limited skills can achieve effective results.

BASIC EQUIPMENT

A collection of tools necessary for working on soft furnishings is inexpensive to put together. Even the cost of a stapler has come down in price, and there is a good range of high-quality pieces to choose from.

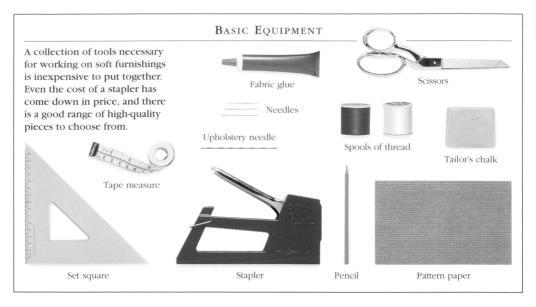

Fabric glue

Needles

Upholstery needle

Scissors

Spools of thread

Tailor's chalk

Tape measure

Set square

Stapler

Pencil

Pattern paper

CHOOSING FABRICS

Whereas assembling a toolkit is relatively inexpensive, fabrics can send your costs soaring. However, it is up to you to choose how extravagant to be, although in some cases fabric selection will be dictated by the type of finish you require and the look you aim for.

CONSIDERING FABRICS

● **Checking safety** Make sure that material is fire retardant. If it is not, you may need to buy a commercial spray and treat the material yourself.

● **Choosing colors** It can be difficult to choose fabric when you are not in the room in which it will be used. Paint some of the wall color on a piece of paper and take it to the store with you, or take fabric swatches home to view them in the appropriate light conditions and surroundings.

● **Assessing costs** Buy the best fabric that you can afford, since better-quality material is more hardwearing.

COMMON TYPES OF FURNISHING FABRIC

Medium to heavyweight fabrics are the most suitable for making furnishings. They are durable, but you may find that their bulk makes them more difficult to work with than lighter fabrics.

Velvet

Heavyweight cotton

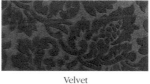

Chenille

Wool mix

USING CUSHIONS AND COVERS

Changing upholstery covers, introducing new cushions, and tying in soft furnishings with the rest of a room's decor can add the perfect finish to a room. How lavish these additions are depends on your preference and sewing ability. Simple ideas can often be very effective.

MAKING CUSHIONS

● **Buying secondhand** Buy secondhand curtains and use them to make cushion covers. This is an ideal way of saving money when making more luxurious cushion covers, since plush secondhand material will cost a fraction of the price of the equivalent new fabric.

● **Scenting cushions** Add one or two sprigs of lavender to the stuffing of a cushion to keep it smelling fresh.

● **Cushioning floors** Join two rag rugs together to make a large floor cushion that will be both decorative and practical. Use two different rug designs for a more interesting effect.

● **Making bean bags** Always make an inner lining for a bean bag so that the filling is enclosed in a separate bag, allowing for its easy removal when you want to wash the cover. As an inexpensive alternative filling, use loose-fill loft insulation material.

MEASURING A CHAIR FOR LOOSE COVERS

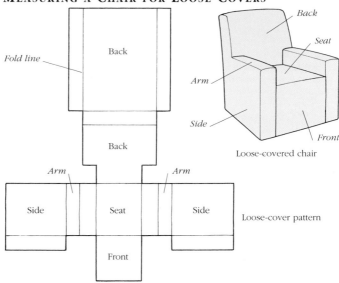

Loose-covered chair

Loose-cover pattern

Making a loose-cover paper pattern

The covering on a chair can be divided into a number of different sections, depending on the specific design of a chair. Measure the size of each section, and add them all together to give the total area of the chair cover so that you can calculate material quantities. Make a lifesize version of the cover layout from pattern paper, and use it as a pattern for cutting out the fabric. Remember to make allowances for seams and hems.

CREATING HEADRESTS

Adapting a cushion

Make a metal headboard more comfortable by attaching a customized cushion to the frame. Sew tabs to the cushion and use touch-and-close tape or press snaps to attach them.

IMPROVING CHAIRS

● **Creating comfort** You may want to make your kitchen chairs more comfortable, especially if the kitchen is the main dining area. Make simple cushions that will provide padding for hard seats.

● **Reviving chairs** Revive an old chair by covering it with a new throw. Alternatively, use a sheet or lightweight rug.

● **Covering arms** Chair arms receive more wear than other parts. Help to keep them in good condition longer by making covers from the same or different material. You can also add a pocket to house a television remote control.

BRIGHT IDEA

Painting snaps
Paint upholstery snaps with spray paint so that they coordinate with furnishings. Place the studs in an old sponge while applying paint, and avoid handling until dry.

FINISHINGS

Finishing the material accessories in your decorative plan is very much a case of knowing how much or how little to use, which is a matter of personal taste. Whether you choose to keep things simple or aim for an extravagant finish, trimmings should enhance a furnishing.

IDEAS FOR TRIMMINGS

There are numerous items – conventional or less so – that can be attached to the soft furnishings in a newly decorated room to add a final finishing touch of creativity.

- Braids.
- Piping and bindings.
- Ribbons.
- Raffia.
- Cord.
- Lace.
- Leather.
- Fabric scraps.
- Tassels.
- Fringes.
- Beads.
- Sequins.
- Buttons.
- Bows.
- Chains.
- Clasps and buckles.

FINISHING CUSHIONS

- **Stenciling** You need not confine stencils to walls and woodwork – apply them to cushions or the seats of chairs. This is a good way of tying in painted wall decorations with soft furnishings. It is also a particularly appropriate technique for imitating tapestry on a chair cover. Make sure that you use fabric paints rather than standard acrylics.
- **Edging cushions** Attach trimmings such as braid or piping (using fabric glue) along the edges of cushions, using a variety of colors and shapes for different effects. Add dark-colored piping to define and highlight the edges of a cushion, or – to soften them – shape the edges into scallops or attach a looped fringe.

BRIGHT IDEA

Hiding stapled edges
Staples can be unsightly, so you should disguise them. Attach a length of trim or braid over a line of staples using fabric glue. Press the braid firmly into place so that it maintains its position while the glue dries.

COVERING HEADBOARDS

Covering a headboard is an ideal way to finish bedroom trimmings. It makes a hard headboard more comfortable to lean against and can coordinate the bed with other decorations in the room. A fabric-covered headboard may be used to link a bedspread with other furnishings and window treatments.

Drill hole at intersection of lines

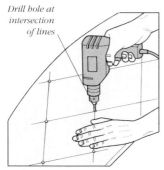

1 Cut a sheet of MDF to size (wear a dust mask and ensure good ventilation). Draw criss crossing pencil lines about 6 in (15 cm) apart on one side of the MDF. Drill small holes through where they intersect.

Thread cotton through hole

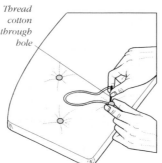

2 Cut wadding and fabric to size and fit over the MDF, folding enough fabric around the back to staple securely. Attach a length of cotton to a button. Locate the holes and thread the cotton through with a needle.

Turn nail to tighten thread

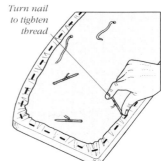

3 Secure the thread around a nail on the back of the MDF. Rotate the nail to adjust the button over the hole at the right tension. Repeat at each drill hole until you have the number of buttons you want.

FINAL DETAILS

T HE PLACING OF OBJECTS in a newly decorated room offers a great opportunity for experimentation. Arranging and displaying ornaments with individual flair will complete the decorative look that you planned to in the beginning.

ORNAMENTS

O rnaments of all kinds play an important part in our lives, either because they remind us of a special occasion or are part of a collection of similar items, or simply because we like them. Whatever the reason, ornaments can have a powerful decorative impact.

CHANGING CONTAINERS

Place soaps in glass jar

Decanting toiletries
Pour shampoo or bubble bath into glass containers, and arrange soaps in a matching jar to turn them into colorful decorative items. Select colors that fit in with the room's color scheme.

PLACING ORNAMENTS

● **Protecting surfaces** Attach pieces of sticky-backed felt that have been cut to size to the bases of ornaments – especially heavy ones. This will protect the surface on which they are standing from being scratched as they are moved during cleaning.
● **Arranging items** Ornaments are intended to be seen and should therefore be displayed to maximum effect. Place taller items at the back of a surface so that all items can be seen.
● **Grouping collections** Space objects that form part of a collection carefully, in order to show off each individual item as well as the whole group.

SECURING SMALL ITEMS

Attach small piece of tape to base

Using double-sided tape
Lightweight or small ornaments are easily knocked over. Fix them in position by attaching double-sided tape to their bases. Always ensure that the surface on which they stand will not be marked.

BEING PRACTICAL

Adding a finger plate
Screw an ornamental finger plate onto a door for a decorative edge that will protect the door from dirty hands. Finger plates are available in metal, plastic, or decorated ceramic finishes.

DISPLAYING NATURAL MATERIALS

The possibilities are endless for using natural items purely for show or for practical purposes.

● **Seashells** Glue seashells around the rim of a plant pot for a maritime theme. Paint the pot to suit a color scheme.
● **Dried flowers** Display dried flowers as they are, or highlight them with gold spray-paint.
● **Pressed flowers** Preserve a bouquet of flowers by pressing it. Use the flowers to create découpage effects on ceramics or on pieces of furniture.
● **Feathers** Use feathers in collage displays beneath glass table tops or in simple frames.

Making a soap dish
Cover the base of a ceramic or glass bowl with an assortment of colored pebbles to make an attractive display, and place a bar of soap on top. Any water will drain through the pebbles to collect at the bottom of the bowl.

TABLEWARE

Table accessories, whether they form part of a permanent display or are used only occasionally, can contribute effectively to a room's decorative style. They also give you the opportunity to use your imagination and bring a touch of originality to your home.

CHANGING USAGE

Press plant gently into cup

Using items as ornaments
Put cups or mugs to novel use by converting them into miniature herb gardens. Extend the idea to other containers for displaying plants. Coordinate them to fit in with the decorative theme.

DECORATING CERAMIC KITCHEN JUGS

Masking tape

1 Create bands around a ceramic jug using masking tape. Remove excess from the sponge before applying acrylic ceramic paint over the whole jug. This will avoid a gummy finish and give depth of color.

2 Once the paint has dried, remove the tape. This technique can be used to create a variety of designs. To make the jug dishwasher safe, bake in an oven for 40 minutes at 300°F (150°C).

DECORATIVE CONTAINERS

Storage systems often let a decorative plan down. Even general storage items can be made more attractive by means of a simple decorative overhaul. Boxes and other containers may be hidden away from view, but they too can be transformed into something attractive.

ADAPTING BOXES

● **Painting shoe boxes** Paint shoe boxes to create storage boxes for photographs, letters, or other paperwork. Use latex paint for a wipeable, hardwearing finish. Choose a different color for each category of item so that you can identify the contents by the exterior color of the box.
● **Decorating boxes** Use trimmings to decorate storage boxes. Upholstery snaps will give a sturdy look, while glass beads or buttons are colorful.
● **Using packaging** Remove the cardboard divider from a packing box, cut it to size, paint it with latex, and insert it in a drawer to create compartments for storing socks or other small items of clothing.

TIDYING BATHROOMS

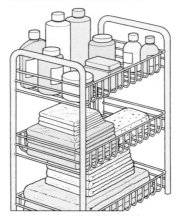

Using a vegetable rack
Most bathrooms are littered with all sorts of bottles and containers. Neaten the room up using a metal vegetable rack, which will save space and make it easier to find a particular item.

USING CONTAINERS

● **Storing toys** Hang a simple hammock of a suitable size in a child's bedroom and use it as a quick and easy solution to the problem of storing toys.
● **Doubling up** Create a double-sided storage shelf by attaching jar lids – using either a strong adhesive or screws – to the underside of a shelf. When you have filled them with small items, screw the containers onto their lids so that they hang below the shelf.
● **Using hanging baskets** Turn a hanging basket into a novel type of storage unit rather than using it simply as a plant holder. Hang the basket in a kitchen and use it for storing vegetables or small boxes or jars of dried herbs and spices.

ROOM DETAILS

Some finishing touches are particularly suited to certain rooms in the home. They tend to add yet another dimension to a completed decorative plan, but they can also be used to draw together various aspects of a style or simply update and renew an existing look.

CURTAINING OFF CORNERS OF ROOMS

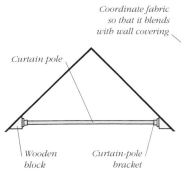

Coordinate fabric so that it blends with wall covering

Curtain pole

Wooden block

Curtain-pole bracket

1 Cut a small block of wood diagonally into two pieces. Screw one to each wall just above head height, and about 3¼ ft (1 m) from the corner. Secure a curtain-pole mount to each block, then attach a pole.

2 Paint the blocks to match the wall color. Hang a curtain from the pole, using a fabric that blends with the wall decoration. Attach several coat hooks to a rail inside this corner "cupboard" if required.

RENOVATING UNITS

● **Renewing a bath surface** Rather than re-enameling a bathtub or replacing it altogether, paint it with a commercial coating. Follow manufacturers' guidelines on the preparation of surfaces to ensure the best possible finish.

● **Finishing kitchen cupboards** The look of a kitchen can be transformed by changing or painting drawer and cupboard handles. Go a stage further by renewing kitchen unit fronts, saving money by retaining the original framework if it is in good condition.

● **Revitalizing equipment** Give old white refrigerators and freezers new life by coating them with colored paints. Check manufacturers' instructions to ensure that the surface is suitable. You can also apply paint effects.

USING FABRICS CLEVERLY

Clever use of fabrics will give visual cohesion as well as maximize space and money.

● **Saving money** Buy a new bedspread or throw to match a color scheme, rather than replacing all the bed linen.
● **Making a canopy** Attach a curtain pole to the ceiling above a headboard and another one to the ceiling above the foot of the bed. Drape material between the poles to create a canopy.
● **Screening** Cover a screen with material to match other fabrics in a room, then use it as a movable partition to conceal unattractive features or create a secluded corner.

REINFORCING THEMES WITH ACCESSORIES

Grouping bathroom items with ornaments
Position bathroom accessories simply but effectively to emphasize a theme – in this case a maritime theme in an assortment of blues. The starfish shapes and fish motifs contribute to the theme, while the ceramic fish also provide splashes of contrasting color.

COOKING

CHOOSING EQUIPMENT

•

SELECTING STAPLES

•

BUYING FRESH FOOD

•

PREPARING FOOD

•

CHOOSING COOKING METHODS

•

ENTERTAINING GUESTS

KITCHEN EQUIPMENT

QUICK REFERENCE

Kitchen
Improvements, p. 315

Cooking Appliances, p. 318

Cold Storage, p. 321

Pots and Pans, p. 324

Bakeware, p. 326

Utensils, p. 327

Small Appliances, p. 332

A GOOD COOK CAN PRODUCE MEALS with limited equipment, but a well-organized, fully equipped kitchen will improve your efficiency and reduce the time you spend cooking. The kitchen is the most difficult room in the house to plan, so you should take time to consider your requirements. Shop around and see what is available before making decisions about equipment, whether you are choosing major appliances or small utensils.

ORGANIZING A KITCHEN

The number of cabinets and appliances in a kitchen will be dictated largely by space. The quality and layout of your kitchen, both of which affect efficiency, are under your control. If you are planning to design a kitchen from scratch, get the advice of a professional.

PLANNING A KITCHEN

● **Working on paper** When you start to plan your kitchen, draw the walls and doors to scale on graph paper. Make cardboard cutouts, to scale, of all kitchen appliances to be used, and experiment with their positions. Draw up several plans before making decisions or spending money.

● **Determining a basic shape** Depending on the space available, plan your kitchen in a U-shape, L-shape, or galley shape. These are the best layouts for moving around efficiently while you work.

● **Keeping surfaces level** Try to plan an unbroken run of counters, built over and between kitchen appliances, to make efficient use of space and to facilitate cleaning.

● **Anticipating traffic flow** Plan a kitchen so that people passing through do not cross the work area, especially that between the sink and stove.

PLANNING FOR AN EASY WORK FLOW

● **Minimizing walking** Keep the total distance between the sink, storage area, and stove to no more than approximately 23 ft (7 m) in order to minimize the amount of walking around you will do while cooking.

● **Placing work surfaces** Link areas between appliances with counters so that there will be a work surface wherever you need it. This will allow you to prepare and cook food near the appropriate appliances.

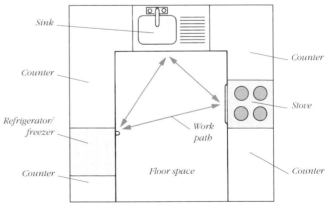

Sink

Counter

Counter

Refrigerator/
freezer

Work
path

Stove

Counter

Counter

Floor space

Creating a work triangle

If you are planning the design of a kitchen from scratch, try to arrange the positions of appliances so that you create a work path linking the refrigerator, sink, and stove. This will facilitate an easy flow of work that minimizes inefficient activity in the kitchen.

KITCHEN IMPROVEMENTS

I F YOU ARE PLANNING TO UPDATE OR IMPROVE an existing kitchen, there are many inexpensive adjustments to consider. Change the style of the kitchen by replacing cabinet doors, or improve existing doors with a new paint finish.

WORK SURFACES

Counters should be installed at a height that is comfortable to work at. A recommended, standard working height may not be suitable for you. Choose a hard-wearing material that is heat resistant, does not scratch, chip, or stain easily, and is easy to maintain and keep clean.

CREATING SURFACES

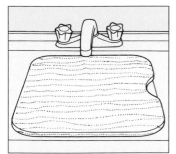

Covering a sink
To create a work surface that you can use if space becomes tight, cut a piece of wood to fit neatly over a sink. When the sink is not in use, put the wood in place.

MAKING PAN RESTS

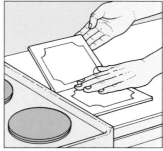

Using tiles
Make sure that there is always a stable, heatproof surface on which to place hot pans by keeping two sturdy kitchen tiles on the counter next to the stove.

LIGHTING WORK SURFACES

● **Using spotlights** Choose flexible spotlights so that you can direct the lighting. Recess them into the ceiling, or place on top of wall cabinets.
● **Avoiding glare** Eliminate glare by positioning diffusers over low-level lights.
● **Reducing heat** Reduce the heat generated in a kitchen by installing fluorescent lights.
● **Locating switches** For flexibility, install separate switches for each area, such as a counter or an eating area.

PLANNING AHEAD

● **Positioning counters** Make sure that there is a surface near the entrance on which to place shopping or garden produce when you enter the kitchen.
● **Adding insets** Consider having a marble or wooden inset put into a counter for chopping and pastry making. This should extend the whole depth of the counter to avoid creating dirt traps, and the front edge should match that of the counter.
● **Avoiding dirt traps** Avoid seams in countertops, since they may trap dirt and become a health risk. Seal unavoidable seams with kitchen sealant.
● **Preventing dripping** Look for a counter with a ridged front edge to prevent spilled liquids from dripping over the edge.

USING DEAD SPACE

● **Storing in corners** Make use of counter space in corners for storing small appliances, such as food processors.

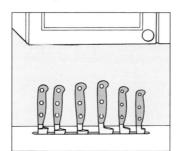

Installing a knife slot
Store sharp knives in a slot cut into the rear part of the counter behind a drawer. Check carefully before cutting the slot to make sure that the knives will not block the drawer.

SAVING SPACE

● **Folding items away** In a small kitchen, install a hinged counter or a table that will fold away while not in use.

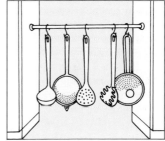

Using a rack
To help keep work surfaces clear, hang regularly used, small utensils from a rack between two wall cabinets, within easy reach of the area where you will need them.

CABINETS AND SHELVES

There is a wide range of kitchen cabinets to choose from today, and they are available in many different styles. Since cabinets last for years, do not be influenced by the latest fashion. If your budget is tight, use plain white cabinets, which are inexpensive and practical.

KEEPING CABINETS CLEAN

Using plastic coving
To prevent dust and dirt from collecting beneath a floor-mounted cabinet, put coving along the edge of the plinth. Lay flexible flooring, such as vinyl, to cover the coving, and tuck it into the corner where the cabinet meets the plinth.

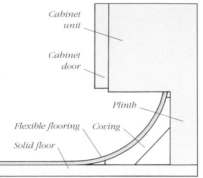

Cabinet unit

Cabinet door

Plinth

Flexible flooring *Coving*

Solid floor

● **Sealing wood** To protect natural wooden cabinets with a hard-wearing, water-repellent finish, coat with polyurethane. Seal hardwood cabinets with oil where appropriate, and reapply the seal frequently.

● **Cleaning interiors** Choose cabinets lined with laminated coatings and drawers lined with heavy-duty plastic, so that you will easily be able to wipe up spills and the sticky residues left by food containers.

CHOOSING & POSITIONING CABINETS

● **Positioning cabinets** If possible, attach a cabinet to a shaded, outside wall if it is to be used for storing food, since this will be cooler than an internal wall. Try to be aware of the temperature inside a cabinet – the cooler the better for food storage.
● **Checking stability** Ask a builder to check that a wall is structurally sound enough to take the weight of cabinets before installing wall units. You may find that a partition wall is unable to support the weight.
● **Making a partition** Divide kitchen and dining areas in the same room by installing a peninsula. This will provide extra storage space while permitting easy access from one area to another.
● **Selecting cabinet doors** Consider installing cabinets that have sliding doors, or doors that slide up and over.

● **Making a wine rack** To adapt a floor cabinet for storing bottles of wine, first remove any existing shelves. Then make an X-shaped shelf for the bottles using two pieces of plywood slotted together to fit the cabinet from corner to corner.

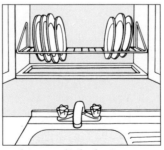

Making a dish drainer
Remove the bottom of a wall-mounted cabinet above the sink, and put a dish rack inside. Wet dishes can then drain into the sink, and you can close the doors to hide it away.

PLANNING STORAGE

● **Adjusting shelves** Choose cabinets with adjustable shelves or racks on runners, so that the heights can be adjusted to suit your needs.
● **Using corner space** Install a corner unit with revolving shelves to make use of an otherwise inaccessible corner.
● **Disposing of waste** Put a flip-top garbage pail in a cabinet beneath the sink or in the area where most of the food is prepared, so that trash can be disposed of easily.
● **Using wall space** Use the space beneath wall cabinets to hang a paper-towel holder or utensil rack. This will help to keep work surfaces clear.

KEEPING SHELVES CLEAN

● **Covering with a blind** Fit a fireproof roller blind over shelves built into a recess so that dust and grease do not settle on the shelves' contents.
● **Using open shelves** Dust settles easily on open shelves, so use them for items that are used and washed daily.

SAFETY

● **Choosing cabinets** Select units with rounded corners and recessed handles. Sharp corners and protruding knobs are likely to cause injury.
● **Placing wall cabinets** Avoid placing cabinets on a wall above a stove; reaching over a hot burner to gain access to a cabinet is dangerous.
● **Siting for height** Position wall cabinets so that the top shelves are easily accessible without necessitating a climb onto a chair or stepladder.

SPACE-SAVING DEVICES

Many home kitchens are quite small, with limited storage space, so creative use of space is essential for the efficient organization of a kitchen. Make use of corners by inserting corner shelves, and hang small items from racks on the wall if you run out of cabinet space.

SAVING CABINET SPACE

Hanging a rack
Suspend a wooden or metal rack from the kitchen ceiling, and hang pots and pans using butchers' hooks. Do not hang the rack too low, and check the length of chain needed to bring the pots and pans to an accessible height.

FILLING EMPTY SPACES

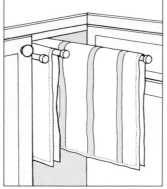

Filling gaps
Position a pull-out towel rack in a gap between two cabinets or appliances to keep dish towels tidy and accessible. Alternatively, use gaps between units for storing cookie sheets and trays, freeing cabinet space for other items.

BRIGHT IDEA

Using window space
If your kitchen window has an unattractive view, or no view at all, put safety glass shelves across the window. Use them for storing attractive glass jars and bottles, plants, or pots of fresh herbs.

COOKBOOKS AND RECIPES

Most cooks have a collection of favorite cookbooks, and inevitably these books become well worn. Buy a cookbook stand, or use the tips below to protect your books while cooking. Also make sure that you keep your favorite recipe clippings in good condition.

PROTECTING & STORING COOKBOOKS

● **Using a plastic bag** To protect the pages of a cookbook, slip the opened book inside a clear plastic bag to prevent it from being splashed during food preparation.
● **Keeping books dry** Attach a narrow wooden shelf with a rim to the wall above a work surface, and use it as a book rest. It will help keep books out of the way of food splashes.
● **Storing books** Place a bookshelf on top of a chest of drawers to create a kitchen dresser in which you can keep your cookbooks, display attractive pieces of china, and store kitchen equipment.

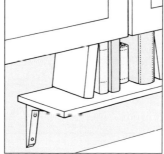

Adding an extra shelf
Hang a narrow shelf between a counter and a wall cabinet to create storage space for cookbooks. This will give you quick access to them, and save space on the counter.

KEEPING CLIPPINGS

● **Color-coding recipes** Store different categories of recipe clippings in differently colored photograph albums with peel-back plastic pages. Use blue for fish dishes, for example.
● **Using a scrapbook** Paste recipe cuttings into a scrapbook so that you can write notes next to them if necessary
● **Making clever clippings** Store favorite, frequently used recipe clippings in a decorative way by pasting them onto a board or tray to make a collage. Paint over or spray with waterproof varnish so that any splashes of food or grease can be wiped off.

COOKING APPLIANCES

STOVES REQUIRE MAJOR FINANCIAL INVESTMENT and should therefore be chosen for long-term use. Everyone has different requirements when selecting a stove, and there is a huge variety from which to choose.

CHOOSING A STOVE

When choosing an oven or a stovetop, consider your cooking needs, bearing in mind the advantages and availability of different fuels, and any space limitations in the kitchen. Look for a design that is attractive and practical, with few dirt traps so that cleaning will be easy.

CHOOSING AN OVEN

When buying an oven, decide which features will be most useful, bearing in mind your lifestyle. Below are some features to consider first.

● **Capacity** Choose a large or a double oven to give you flexibility, especially if you cook for a lot of people.
● **Cleaning facilities** Choose an oven that is self-cleaning, or that has stay-clean features.
● **Timer** Consider a timer to control cooking for you while you are busy.
● **Convection** To encourage even cooking and reduce cooking times, choose a fan-assisted convection oven that circulates heat evenly.

SELECTING BURNER SURFACE & FUEL TYPE

● **Choosing burners** Select burners that will be easy to clean. Consider ceramic burners, which also use electricity efficiently. When not in use, the cool surface can be used as a work surface for rolling out pastry or dough.

● **Combining fuels** If you are able to combine fuels, consider two gas burners and two electric rings. The mix combines the safety advantages of electricity with the easy heat adjustment of gas burners, and is useful in a power failure.

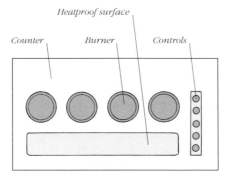

Heatproof surface

Counter   *Burner*   *Controls*

Placing burners
If you are planning a new kitchen, consider setting burners in a line, rather than a square formation, and set them well back from the front edge. Install a heatproof surface for resting hot saucepans in front of the burners.

CONSIDERING DETAILS

● **Catalytic liners** Reduce oven cleaning by choosing an oven with a catalytic oven lining that carbonizes food spills. Alternatively, select a pyrolytic oven, which has a high-temperature, self-cleaning cycle.
● **Built-in ovens** Choose a built-in oven, which is usually mounted at waist height, for convenient positioning.
● **Eye-level grills** Choose an oven with the grill positioned at eye level if you want to check food frequently during cooking. The grill pan should have a support and stops to prevent it from being pulled out too far.

USING OVEN DOORS

Resting a hot dish
Choose an oven with a strong door that pulls down rather than opening sideways. The door will provide a useful surface for hot casseroles or cookie sheets as they come out of the oven.

CONSIDERING SAFETY

● **Choosing warning lights** Pick a stove with controls that light up and warn you when the burners are hot, even if they are not glowing.
● **Checking safety** Make sure that, if a gas stovetop has a lid for covering burners when not in use, the stovetop has a cutoff switch, and the lid is made of heatproof glass.
● **Avoiding accidents** If you have young children, install a stove guard to deter them from touching hot pots and pans. Turn saucepan handles inward to prevent children from pulling them down.

USING A STOVE

Whatever type of cooking you do most often, it is a good idea to be aware of your oven's rate of energy consumption, and to check regularly that it is running efficiently. Refer to the manufacturer's handbook for tips on how to make good use of special functions.

CHECKING TEMPERATURE

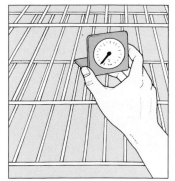

Using a thermometer
Check the accuracy of your oven regularly by placing an oven thermometer in the center of the middle shelf. Heat the oven to 350°F (180°C), then compare with the thermometer reading.

COOKING EFFICIENTLY

● **Saving energy** Turn solid-element burners off a few minutes before you finish cooking. The food will continue to cook on the residual heat.
● **Preheating the oven** Allow at least 10 minutes for an oven to preheat. Arrange the oven shelves before turning on the oven to avoid losing heat or burning yourself.
● **Setting a timer** Avoid opening the oven door, which lowers the oven temperature, to check if food is done. Use a timer to monitor cooking times.
● **Avoiding scratches** Prevent damage to ceramic burners by lifting pans off rather than sliding them across.

SAVING FUEL

Cooking a complete meal
Use fuel economically by cooking a complete meal in the oven at the same time. Place dishes that need the highest temperatures at the top of the oven, and other dishes on the lower shelves.

CLEANING A STOVE

Wipe up cooking spills on a burner or inside an oven immediately after they have occurred. Once they harden or burn onto the surface, you will have to use a commercial cleaner to remove them. Switch off the power before cleaning an electric oven or burner.

CLEANING EFFICIENTLY

● **Reducing cleaning** Stand pies and casseroles on a cookie sheet in an oven to catch spills.
● **Wiping a ceramic surface** Wipe up fruit juice, sugar, and acidic food spills on ceramic burners immediately, since they may cause etching or pitting on the surface.
● **Cleaning shelves** Wash oven racks in the dishwasher, remove them before the drying cycle, and wipe over with a cloth. Alternatively, place them on an old towel in the tub, and soak in a solution of ammonia and hot water to loosen food deposits.
● **Saving energy** Start a self-cleaning cycle when the oven is still warm to save energy.

REMOVING BURNED FOOD

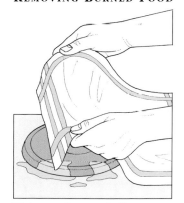

Using a damp cloth
If food burns onto a burner surround, turn the heat off, let cool, and cover with a cloth wrung out in a solution of water and dishwashing liquid. Let stand for two hours, then wipe clean.

MONEY-SAVING TIP

Cleaning chrome trim
To clean rust from chrome trim, rub it with a piece of aluminum foil wrapped around your finger, shiny side out. Buff up with a cloth dipped in rubbing alcohol.

USING A MICROWAVE

Cooking in a microwave is quick, easy, and economical. However many people you cook for, a microwave can be an invaluable addition to the kitchen, saving time and energy. If you have never used a microwave before, you will need to adapt your cooking methods.

CHOOSING A MICROWAVE

Many microwaves have useful features that you should consider before buying.

- **Power** Most full-power ovens use 650–750 watts. The higher the wattage, the shorter the cooking times.
- **Controls** Digital controls will give more accurate timings than dial controls.
- **Turntables** Ensure that the oven has a turntable. If it does not, the food will have to be turned manually.
- **Browning option** This will add a rich, golden color and crispness to food.
- **Cleaning** Look for self-cleaning interior panels on combination ovens.
- **Compact models** If kitchen space is limited, choose an under-cabinet model.

LEARNING BASIC SKILLS

- **Adapting recipes** To adapt a conventional recipe for the microwave, reduce the cooking time by about two thirds.
- **Adjusting cooking times** When doubling recipe amounts for the microwave, increase the cooking time by one quarter to one third. When halving recipe amounts, reduce the cooking time by approximately one third.
- **Checking temperature** Use a microwave thermometer to check that food is thoroughly cooked. Frozen dinners should reach 158°F (70°C).
- **Adding color** To enhance the color of food cooked in a microwave, top savory dishes with toasted nuts or a sprinkling of paprika, and top sweet dishes with toasted nuts, brown sugar, or ground spices.

INCREASING CAPACITY

- **Stacking plates** Use plate-stacking rings to cook two portions of food at once, and increase the cooking time by 1½ minutes. Move the plates around halfway through.

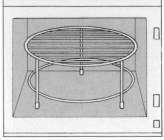

Using shelves
Buy shelves and trivets, both of which are available as microwave accessories, so that you can cook more than one item at a time. Alternatively, choose a microwave with a shelf.

MICROWAVING SAFELY

Follow a few basic guidelines to ensure that you use a microwave safely, choose suitable containers, and cook food thoroughly. Used correctly, a microwave is a versatile appliance, cooking and reheating food in a fraction of the time that it would take in a conventional oven.

COOKING THOROUGHLY

Place narrowest part of food inward

Arranging food
For safety, make sure food is cooked thoroughly. Distribute it evenly in a dish, and cook wedge-shaped items, such as pears or fish fillets, with the narrow ends pointing to the center of the dish.

CHOOSING DISHES

Checking heat resistance
To ensure that a dish will not overheat, place it in a microwave with a cup of cold water on High for two minutes. The water should heat up and warm the cup, while the dish should remain cold.

SAFETY

- **Following instructions** Read the manufacturer's handbook, and follow cooking instructions on packaged foods.
- **Avoiding metal** Do not use metal dishes, dishes that have metal decoration, or kitchen foil in a microwave.
- **Supervising cooking** Always avoid letting foods cook unattended, since some high-sugar foods may catch fire.
- **Cooking and reheating** Make sure that microwaved food is thoroughly and evenly cooked before serving.

COLD STORAGE

REFRIGERATORS AND FREEZERS ARE INVALUABLE ITEMS of equipment in the kitchen. Both of these appliances ensure that we have a wide choice of safe, fresh food at any time of the year, and they can help us create a varied, healthy diet.

CHOOSING APPLIANCES

When you are selecting a refrigerator or a freezer, consider carefully the needs of your household. Decide on the capacity that you require, taking into account the space available and the foods you store most often, such as garden produce or convenience foods.

ADDING STORAGE

Using baskets
Add extra storage baskets to a chest freezer. They will make it much easier to find and organize the contents of the freezer. Extra storage baskets can usually be ordered from the manufacturer.

BUYING A FREEZER
● **Assessing capacity** Allow 2 cu ft (57 liters) of freezer space for each person in your household, together with an extra 2 cu ft (57 liters) if you do a lot of entertaining.
● **Fitting the space** If space is tight, choose an upright freezer, which will take up less floor space than a chest freezer.
● **Positioning a freezer** Check that there is enough space to open the freezer door or lid. The door of an upright freezer may need to open through an angle of more than 90° so that the drawers can be pulled out.

KEEPING TRACK

Using drawer markers
If you choose an upright freezer, look for a model that has contents cards on the front of the drawers. These will help you keep track of items stored. List the foods in each drawer on the attached card.

BUYING A REFRIGERATOR
● **Assessing capacity** Make sure that your refrigerator is large enough for your needs. Allow 8 cu ft (228 liters) for the first two people in the household, then another 1 cu ft (28 liters) for each additional person.
● **Reducing workload** For easy maintenance, it is best to choose a frost-free refrigerator-freezer, since these do not need to be defrosted.
● **Selecting shelves** Make sure that refrigerator shelves are adjustable in order to accomodate large items.

LOOKING FOR FEATURES
● **Checking temperature** When choosing a freezer, look for one with a built-in temperature indicator on the outside. This will allow you to check that the appliance is running efficiently without opening the door.
● **Moving easily** If your house has solid floors, choose a refrigerator or freezer with casters, since they will make the appliance reasonably easy to move. Casters may damage soft flooring such as vinyl.
● **Lighting the interior** Check whether a freezer has an interior light, which is especially useful in a chest freezer. If not, keep a battery-operated clip-on light handy so that you can see the contents easily.

INSTALLING APPLIANCES

● **Adjusting height** Make sure that a refrigerator or freezer is stable. Use a level to check whether the appliance is level, and adjust the legs or casters accordingly.
● **Moving easily** To move an appliance without casters, slip an old piece of carpet under the foot to help it slide.
● **Avoiding dampness** To allow the air to circulate all around a freezer that is stored in a garage, raise the appliance 2 in (5 cm) off the ground by placing it on blocks.

Using Appliances Effectively

To maintain food stored in a refrigerator or freezer in the best condition, you must keep these appliances running efficiently. Regulating the temperature is important, since too high a temperature will cause food to deteriorate, and too low will cause energy to be wasted.

PREVENTING DEPOSITS

● **Wiping bases** When packing items into a refrigerator or a freezer, keep a clean, damp cloth handy to wipe the bases of messy containers. This will prevent food spills from transferring onto the shelves.

Lining with foil
Prevent ice-cube trays or frozen-foods spills from sticking to the base of a freezer or freezer compartment by lining with a layer of foil. Replace the foil regularly with a clean piece.

REDUCING FUEL USAGE

● **Positioning** Place freezers and refrigerators in a cool site away from direct sunlight and appliances that generate heat.

Filling spaces
If possible, keep your freezer full, since it is not energy-efficient to run it half empty. Fill large spaces with loaves of bread, or use crumpled newsprint to prevent air from circulating.

FREEZING EFFICIENTLY

● **Cooling foods** Cool foods completely before storing in a refrigerator or freezer. To cool hot food quickly, sit the base of the container in a sink half-filled with cold water.
● **Limiting amounts** To avoid raising the temperature of a freezer, freeze no more than one-tenth of the appliance's capacity of food at one time.

STORING SUCCESSFULLY

● **Arranging foods** When placing foods in a refrigerator, leave some space around each item so that air can circulate and chill the food evenly.
● **Avoiding "freezer burn"** Always wrap foods tightly before freezing to exclude air. This will prevent moisture from being drawn out of the foods, which results in loss of nutrients and dehydration.

CHECKING TEMPERATURES

For safe and efficient running of refrigerators and freezers, check the internal temperature regularly with a thermometer.

● **Refrigerators** Run a refrigerator at 40°F (5°C) or below. The coolest section of the refrigerator should be 34°F (1°C). To check the temperature, place a thermometer in the center of the top shelf, and leave overnight. In summer, adjust the refrigerator's thermostat.
● **Freezers** Keep a freezer at 0°F (−18°C) or below. Check the temperature by placing a thermometer on the top shelf or the upper edge of the top basket, and leave overnight.

PREVENTING PROBLEMS

● **Labeling switches** To ensure that a freezer is not turned off by mistake, place tape over the switch, or label the plug clearly with the word "freezer."
● **Avoiding stale smells** To prevent an unpleasant odor from developing while a refrigerator or freezer is in storage, clean and dry it thoroughly, then prop the door open with a block of wood and secure it in place with strips of masking tape.
● **Moving house** Before moving a refrigerator or freezer, turn it off 24 hours in advance. Clean thoroughly, remove loose parts, and secure the door. Always keep a refrigerator or freezer in an upright position during transportation.

MONEY-SAVING TIP

Checking a door seal
Make sure that the door seals on a refrigerator, freezer compartment, or freezer are working efficiently by closing the door on a piece of paper. If the paper can be pulled out easily, the seal is worn and should be replaced.

CLEANING REFRIGERATORS AND FREEZERS

Regular cleaning of refrigerators and freezers will help keep them as safe environments in which to store food. In addition to cleaning the insides, maintain the outer surfaces, since these are subject to daily wear and tear, and sometimes the damaging effects of steam.

PROTECTING SURFACES
● **Preventing rust** If a freezer or refrigerator is prone to condensation on the outside, protect the outer surface by rubbing it with silicone polish applied with a soft cloth.
● **Using glycerin** After defrosting a freezer, wipe the interior with glycerin. Next time you defrost it, the ice will be easier to remove, eliminating the need for scraping.
● **Cleaning doors** If someone uses permanent markers on the refrigerator door, remove marks by rubbing with lighter fluid applied with a soft cloth (test or ask manufacurer first). Wash with detergent, rinse, and dry.

RETOUCHING SCRATCHES

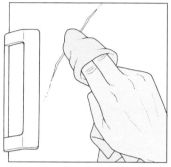

Using enamel paint
Cover a scratch on a refrigerator or freezer door with enamel paint. First, clean with detergent and wipe dry with a clean cloth. Test the color on an unseen area, and retouch with a fine brush.

CLEANING INTERIORS
● **Wiping spills** Always wipe up spills in the refrigerator as soon as they occur to avoid contamination or odors.
● **Removing odors** Remove lingering smells from the interior of a refrigerator or freezer by wiping with a cloth rinsed in a solution of 1 tbsp (15 ml) baking soda to 1 quart (1 liter) warm water.
● **Unpacking foods** Remove all foods from a refrigerator or freezer before cleaning or defrosting. Pack ice cream into a cooler, and stack chilled or frozen foods tightly together, covering them with a blanket for insulation.

DEFROSTING FREEZERS

The most convenient time to defrost a freezer is when stocks of food are at their lowest, for instance, after holiday seasons during which supplies are depleted, or in early summer before you stock up with garden produce. Remember to turn off and unplug the freezer before defrosting.

DEALING WITH A BREAKDOWN

If your freezer breaks down, or if there is an unexpected power outage, follow these simple emergency rules:

● **Check the electrics** Make sure that the wiring, plug, or fuse is not at fault before calling in a repair person.
● **Keep doors closed** Avoid opening the freezer. If it is full, the contents should stay frozen for at least 12 hours.
● **Save food** If the problem is long-term, ask neighbors or friends if they have spare freezer space you can use.
● **Use thawed food** Cook or use up thawed food quickly. Never refreeze food, since this can cause food poisoning.

DEFROSTING EFFICIENTLY
● **Lining with foil** Line the shelves of a freezer with foil when defrosting. Make a hole in the center of each layer to enable you to funnel water into a bowl underneath.
● **Lining with a towel** Before scraping ice from the sides of a freezer, lay a towel in the bottom to collect ice.
● **Cleaning up** If you have a wet-dry vacuum cleaner, use it to suck up ice debris and water during defrosting.
● **Drying thoroughly** Before switching the freezer back on after defrosting, wipe around the inside with a baking-soda solution, and dry thoroughly with paper towels. Let run for one hour after switching on before replacing contents.

SAVING TIME
● **Adding hot water** To defrost a freezer quickly, place bowls of hot water inside. Scrape off the ice as soon as it loosens.

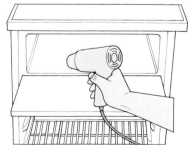

Using a hair dryer
If time is short, blow warm air from a small hair dryer over the ice in a freezer, moving the dryer to avoid overheating one area. Make sure your hands are dry, and keep the dryer moisture-free.

POTS AND PANS

WHEN YOU SET OUT TO BUY POTS AND PANS, you will find a wide range of styles and materials from which to choose. Prolong their durability by buying the best quality you can afford, protecting their linings, and cleaning them carefully.

CHOOSING POTS AND PANS

Your choice of pots and pans will affect the success of your cooking. The material they are made of should be suitable for the type of stove you have and the kind of cooking you do. Select good-quality pots and pans, and they will give you reliable service for many years.

POT AND PAN MATERIALS

Choose cast iron pots and pans for gas, electric, or solid-element burners, but make sure that they have enamel bases for ceramic or halogen burners. Steel or aluminum can be used on gas or electric burners, but if you have a ceramic, halogen, or solid burner, choose copper-based steel or heavy-based aluminum pots and pans. Glass can be used on electric, gas, ceramic, or halogen burners. Copper and earthenware perform best on electric or gas burners.

Cast iron

Stainless steel

Heatproof glass

Vitreous enameled steel

Earthenware

Copper lined with stainless steel

Aluminum

BUYING POTS & PANS

● **Cast iron** Buy the heaviest gauge of cast iron for the best results. Choose pots and pans with two handles, so that they will be easy to pick up when full. Look for wooden handles, which will remain cool.

● **Copper** Choose copper pots and pans lined with stainless steel. Although expensive, they are more durable than those that are lined with tin.

● **Heatproof glass** Buy heatproof-glass pots and pans for versatility, since they can be used to cook, freeze, reheat, microwave, and serve food.

IMPROVISING SPECIALTY PANS

Foil will hold asparagus in position

Steaming vegetables

To steam vegetables without a steamer, use a metal sieve and a wide saucepan. Place the sieve just inside the rim, above boiling water. Add the food, and cover.

Cooking asparagus

To make an asparagus steamer, use a deep saucepan and insert a ring of foil. The foil will ensure that the asparagus tips stay above water while they are cooking.

PROTECTING POTS AND PANS

Routine care of pots and pans will ensure that you get the best performance out of them. Whichever materials pots and pans are made of, their surfaces must be protected from damage, which can cause food to stick. Use nonmetal tools during cooking to minimize wear and tear.

PREPARING NEW POTS

● **Copper** Immerse new copper pans in boiling water, and let soak until cold to remove the lacquer coating.
● **Cast iron** To prevent sticking and protect the surface, season cast iron before use. Brush with vegetable oil. Pour in a little more oil, and place on a low burner for one hour. Cool, and wipe with a paper towel.
● **Enamel** Brush the inner surface of the enamel with oil, then place in a cool oven for one hour. Let cool 12 hours, and wipe clean.

PROTECTING COATINGS

Paper towel protects lining

Caring for nonstick pans
To prevent nonstick linings from becoming damaged by bumps and scratches, place paper towels between pans when stacking them together for storage.

CARING FOR CAST IRON

Preventing rusting
To prevent rusting during storage, dry uncoated cast iron pans well after washing. Rub all surfaces with a paper towel dipped in a little vegetable oil.

CLEANING POTS AND PANS

There are a few basic rules worth following when cleaning pots and pans. They will help maintain their performance during cooking. Techniques for cleaning different materials vary, so it is always advisable to read manufacturers' instructions before cleaning new pots and pans.

REMOVING STAINS

● **Bleaching enamel** To clean a badly stained enameled pan, fill it with a weak solution of about 2 tsp (10 ml) bleach to 2½ cups (600 ml) water. Let soak for a maximum of two hours to avoid damaging the surface of the enamel.

Brightening aluminum
To remove dark stains from an aluminum pot or pan, fill it with water, add the juice of one lemon, and simmer gently until the aluminum brightens.

CLEANING COPPER

● **Using half a lemon** To brighten up and remove stains from tarnished pots and pans made of copper, dip a cut half of lemon into table salt, then rub it gently over the stained copper surface. Rinse and dry thoroughly before use.

Using a vinegar paste
Make a thick paste from roughly equal parts of vinegar and flour. Dip a soft cloth into the paste, and rub it over the copper until clean. Rinse in hot water, and dry.

PREVENTING PROBLEMS

● **Protecting surfaces** Soak pots and pans in hot, soapy water to remove stuck-on foods. Soak pans coated with sugary substances in cold water.
● **Soaking earthenware** To prevent an earthenware pot from absorbing fat, fill it with boiling water, and let stand one hour before use. The pot will absorb water during soaking, keeping out fat and helping to create steam during cooking.
● **Cleaning handles** Wash wooden pan handles quickly in warm water, since soaking may cause them to crack.
● **Caring for steel** Make sure you wash stainless steel soon after cooking salty food, since salt causes surface pitting.
● **Drying pans** Always dry aluminum or polished steel pans immediately to prevent watermarks from forming.

BAKEWARE

A GOOD BASIC SELECTION OF BAKEWARE will be useful in any kitchen. Your choice of items will depend on the type of cooking you do. If you bake regularly, it is a good idea to collect a wide selection of pans in different shapes and sizes.

CHOOSING BAKEWARE

Bakeware is usually of a light or medium weight so that it can conduct heat quickly and efficiently. Traditional, uncoated pans are best for baking light sponge cakes, since they produce golden brown crusts. Nonstick surfaces tend to produce cakes with slightly dark, thick crusts.

BAKING EQUIPMENT

The equipment illustrated below makes up a useful collection of bakeware that would be suitable for most people's needs. Springform pans with removable bases allow for the easy removal of molded foods and facilitate cleaning, especially in the case of deep cake pans and flan pans. Include in your collection some cookie sheets that have a rim for baking mixtures that tend to spread, and some that have a rim on three sides only to allow you to slide off delicate items such as pastry easily. Whatever you bake, a large cooling rack is essential for cooling baked items after cooking.

Springform pan

Bundt pan

Large, loose-based flan pan

Individual flan pan

Deep cake tin

Cake pans

Loaf pan

Muffin tin

Jelly-roll pan

Ovenproof dish

Microwave-proof dish

Cookie sheet

Cooling rack

UTENSILS

EACH COOK WILL CHOOSE a unique range of utensils for the kitchen. However, many utensils can fulfil several functions, and a few well-made, good-quality tools are all that you need. Special gadgets are useful, but can be expensive.

CHOOSING KNIVES

The advice to buy the best equipment you can afford applies most especially to the purchase of kitchen knives. A good-quality set will save you time and energy, and should last a lifetime. Start with a selection for everyday cooking, which you can add to in the future.

SELECTING MATERIALS

● **Choosing blades** Make sure that the metal is of good quality. High-carbon stainless steel is expensive, but it is the most practical for cutting all kinds of food. It sharpens easily and does not discolor.

● **Choosing knife handles** Look for wooden knife handles that are sealed with heat-resistant plastic. These handles are hard-wearing and easy to clean.

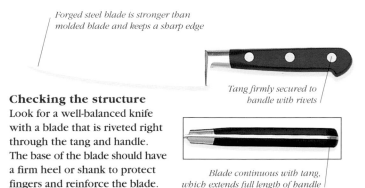

Forged steel blade is stronger than molded blade and keeps a sharp edge

Tang firmly secured to handle with rivets

Checking the structure

Look for a well-balanced knife with a blade that is riveted right through the tang and handle. The base of the blade should have a firm heel or shank to protect fingers and reinforce the blade.

Blade continuous with tang, which extends full length of handle

BASIC KITCHEN KNIVES

Follow some basic guidelines when selecting a range of good-quality kitchen knives.

● **Checking balance** Always pick up a knife to feel how well balanced it is. Rest the junction of the handle and blade on the edge of your hand. The handle should fall back gently if the balance is right.

● **Choosing a wide blade** Choose a heavy cook's knife with a wide blade, so that you can use it for crushing garlic as well as slicing other ingredients.

● **Buying heavy knives** When choosing knives for chopping, choose the heaviest that you can handle comfortably, since the heavier the blade, the less force you will need to apply.

● **Following instructions** Always read the manufacturer's instructions to see whether or not knives are suitable for washing in a dishwasher.

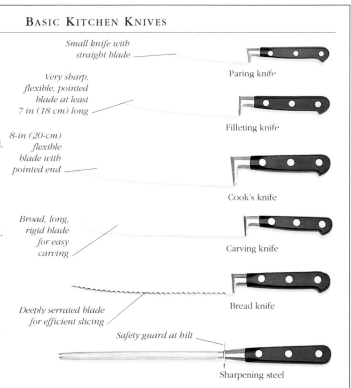

Small knife with straight blade — Paring knife

Very sharp, flexible, pointed blade at least 7 in (18 cm) long — Filleting knife

8-in (20-cm) flexible blade with pointed end — Cook's knife

Broad, long, rigid blade for easy carving — Carving knife

Bread knife

Deeply serrated blade for efficient slicing

Safety guard at hilt — Sharpening steel

CARING FOR KNIVES

After you have selected the best knives you can afford, it makes sense to store them safely and keep them in good condition. The safest way to store knives is to keep them in a knife block or on a magnetic rack. These will help prevent accidents and protect the blades.

PROTECTING POINTS

Hold cork firmly on counter and insert knife point carefully

Using corks

If you do not have a knife block or magnetic rack, **prevent the fine points of sharp knives from becoming damaged in a cutlery drawer by placing a wine cork securely on each knife tip.**

PROTECTING BLADES

● **Choosing a cutting board** Use a polypropylene or a wooden cutting board, since these do not blunt blades.
● **Restricting use** Keep good kitchen knives exclusively for preparing food. Do not use them to cut string or paper.
● **Washing knives** Wash carbon steel knives by hand immediately after use to avoid staining them. Remove any stubborn stains by rubbing the blade with a wet cork dipped in scouring powder.
● **Storing knives** Protect knife blades by using plastic paper binders, which are available from office supply stores. Slide a blade into a holder, and push it in as far as it will go.

SHARPENING KNIVES

It takes only a little time and trouble to sharpen knives. If you get into the habit of sharpening them every time you use them, they will perform well for years. If necessary, have your knives sharpened professionally every two or three years if the blades lose their edge.

USING SHARPENERS

● **Soaking in oil** Soak a whetstone in vegetable oil for smooth sharpening.
● **Sharpening regularly** Try to sharpen kitchen knives every time you use them so that they will be maintained in peak condition. Put them once through an electric or manual sharpener, or stroke them three or four times with a steel prior to use.
● **Protecting serrations** Take knives that have serrated edges to a professional knife sharpener, or do not sharpen them at all, since their serrations can be damaged easily during sharpening if extreme care is not taken.

USING ALTERNATIVE METHODS OF SHARPENING

Hold upside-down mug firmly by handle

Hammer in small tacks to secure paper to wood

Using a mug

If you do not have a steel or a special knife sharpener, use the base of an unglazed earthenware mug. Run the blade across it away from your hand and at a slight angle. Repeat several times.

Using fine sandpaper

To make a sharpening block, wrap a piece of wood in fine sandpaper, turn the edges underneath, and secure with tacks. Firmly run knives across the surface of the paper to sharpen the blades.

CHOOSING USEFUL TOOLS

K itchenware stores are packed with a huge array of useful gadgets for tackling all kinds of kitchen jobs. Many tools are designed specifically with one task in mind, but some of them are very versatile and can be invaluable tools that may be used for a variety of purposes.

CHOOSING THE BASICS

● **Peeling vegetables** Use a swivel-bladed peeler for peeling vegetables, since it will peel much more thinly than a knife. This tool can also be used for shaving curls of fresh Parmesan cheese, and for making decorative curls from fresh coconut.

● **Lifting delicate foods** Buy a fish server for lifting foods without breaking them. Use two servers together for moving large, delicate quiches or cakes onto serving plates. Slide them underneath the item from opposite sides.

● **Removing zest** Use a zester to remove the zest without the pith from citrus fruits.

● **Whisking foods** Choose a balloon whisk – a good all-purpose whisk – for a variety of tasks, from making meringue to smoothing lumpy sauce.

CHOPPING TOMATOES

Using kitchen scissors

Save money by buying cans of whole rather than chopped tomatoes for cooking. Then chop the whole tomatoes in the opened can using a pair of sharp kitchen scissors.

USING TOOLS FOR A VARIETY OF PURPOSES

● **Using a canelle knife** Decorate tall tumblers for serving cool summer drinks with long strips of cucumber peel that have been cut lengthwise from a cucumber with a canelle knife.

Banding new potatoes

Run a canelle knife quickly around the middle of new potatoes before cooking them whole in their skins. This will prevent the skins from splitting and improve their appearance.

FINDING ALTERNATIVES

● **Squeezing juice** If you do not have a citrus squeezer, place a halved lemon or lime over the prongs of a fork, and twist to extract the juice.

● **Making a funnel** To fill jars without spills, make a funnel by improvising with an empty plastic dishwashing liquid bottle. Remove the lid, and cut the top part off the bottle at the shoulder. Wash it thoroughly, and dry before use.

● **Cracking nuts** To crack nuts easily without a nutcracker, use a pair of pliers instead.

● **Removing corks** To uncork a bottle of wine without a corkscrew, screw a large metal hook into the cork, place a wooden spoon handle through the hook, and pull the cork out.

● **Using a melon baller** Instead of using a large ice-cream scoop for serving sorbet, use a melon baller to make tiny scoops. Pile these up in serving dishes for an unusual and attractive presentation.

Cleaning an artichoke

Use a melon baller to scrape out the hairy choke from inside a cooked globe artichoke. Pull out the inner leaves to expose the choke, then scrape it out with the edge of the baller.

BRIGHT IDEA

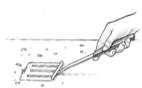

Cleaning a work surface

Use the edge of a fish server to scrape up pastry or dough that has stuck to a work surface during rolling out. Push the fish server firmly along the surface so that its edge dislodges any stubborn leftovers. Wipe over the entire area with a damp cloth to remove any remaining flour or pastry crumbs.

USING OTHER UTENSILS

A number of other utensils are useful in the kitchen, and a carefully selected assortment of items will help you tackle most everyday tasks confidently and efficiently. As with other kitchen equipment, buy the best you can afford, since the best-quality tools will last the longest.

USING SIEVES

Use wooden spoon to press fruit

Puréeing acidic fruits
When pressing acidic foods such as raspberries to make a purée or remove seeds, use a flexible nylon sieve. Metal sieves may react with the acid and can discolor a purée.

MOLDING DOUGH
● **Measuring thickness** To roll out dough to a precise depth, use pieces of wood or rulers of the required thickness. Place one on either side of the dough, and roll the pin along the wood and over the dough, using the wood as a guide.
● **Molding shortbread** To shape shortbread without the aid of an expensive wooden mold, press the dough into a fluted metal flan pan placed on a cookie sheet.

USING MIXING BOWLS
● **Cooking in heatproof bowls** Choose heatproof mixing bowls so that they can be used for cooking food in a microwave or for stirring mixtures over a pan of boiling water if necessary.
● **Preventing slipping** To stop a bowl from slipping on a counter while stirring, place it on a dampened cloth.

MARKING UTENSILS

Paint tip of spoon handle

Color-coding spoons
To avoid transferring flavors, mark wooden spoon handles with colored enamel paints so that they can be identified easily. Keep one spoon for stirring onions, one for fruit, and so on.

USING PASTRY BRUSHES
● **Buying colored brushes** Look in kitchenware stores for pastry brushes with colored bristles to use for different foods. For example, choose a red-bristled brush for meat.

Position brush in lid so that bristles are just touching base of jar

Making an oil jar
Make sure you always have a brush handy for greasing baking pans by attaching a pastry brush through a hole in the lid of a screw-top jar. Keep a shallow depth of oil inside the jar.

USING METAL EQUIPMENT
● **Lining molds** Line metal molds with plastic wrap before filling with acidic foods, such as fruit-based gelatin molds. This will prevent a reaction between the acid and the metal, which could affect the taste and appearance of the food.
● **Choosing colanders** When buying a colander, remember that a metal one will be more versatile than a plastic one. It can be placed over a pan as an improvised steamer.
● **Heating cups** When measuring sticky foods in metal cups, warm the cup first by rinsing in boiling water; the food will slide off easily.

HANDLING MEAT
● **Using tongs** When turning meat during cooking, use food tongs to lift and then turn it. Piercing with a knife or fork will result in a loss of juices.
● **Basting roasts** Use a syringe-type, bulb-shaped baster to baste roasts during cooking. This will save you from having to lift a heavy pan from the oven to baste the meat.

Hold hot skewer with thick pot holder

Branding foods
To create a decorative, branded effect on grilled poultry, meat, or fish, heat a metal skewer until red hot in a gas flame or on an electric burner, then press it onto the food to mark it.

MAINTAINING UTENSILS

If you maintain kitchen utensils well, they will give many years of service. Items made from modern materials such as plastic are easily maintained, but wooden utensils need to be of good quality, cleaned carefully, and checked regularly for cracks to remain efficient and safe.

SOLVING PROBLEMS

● **Releasing stuck pans** If pans or bowls become stuck inside each other, fill the inner pan with iced water to make it contract, and dip the outer one in hot water to expand it. Pull apart to separate.

● **Removing verdigris** Soak copper utensils for 2–3 hours in a solution of washing soda in warm water. Rub with a soft cloth, rinse, and dry well.

● **Removing tannin** Clean a teapot by filling it with boiling water and adding a handful of household borax. Let stand overnight, and wash well before use. Clean chrome-plated teapots with a cloth dipped in vinegar and salt.

REMOVING ODORS

Rubbing with lemon
After using a cutting board for preparing strong-smelling foods such as fish or onions, wash it, then rub the surface with a cut half of lemon. Use a lemon in the same way to remove strong smells from your hands.

CLEANING PRESSES

Bristles clean inside holes

Using a toothbrush
If a garlic press becomes clogged with pulp after use, clean out the holes using a toothbrush. For the best results, clean the garlic press immediately after you have used it, rather than letting the garlic residue dry out.

FINDING ALTERNATIVES

Although a very well-equipped kitchen may be the ideal, it is possible to manage with surprisingly few utensils. If you do certain kinds of cooking only occasionally, improvise with a range of basic items rather than investing in specialized equipment that will be used rarely.

ROLLING PASTRY

● **Dredging flour** To flour a countertop if you do not have a shaker, sprinkle flour through a sifter or fine sieve.

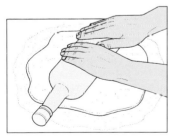

Rolling pastry
Use a straight-sided bottle to roll out pastry if you do not have a rolling pin. To keep the pastry cool and easy to handle, fill an empty bottle with water, and chill before using in this way.

MAKING FUNNELS

Using a piping bag
To fill a narrow-necked jar or bottle without a funnel, use a piping bag. Place the narrow end of the bag into the neck, then pour in the food or liquid carefully to avoid spills.

INVENTING SUBSTITUTES

● **Making a cookie sheet** Turn a large roasting pan upside down to make an extra cookie sheet. Alternatively, use a double thickness of foil, and turn it up at the edges to make a rim.

● **Creating a counter space** If you need a temporary extra work surface in the kitchen, place a cutting board over an open kitchen drawer. Use it only for lightweight jobs such as chopping or slicing.

● **Improvising lids** Make a tight-fitting lid for a large casserole or pan by placing a cookie sheet over the top of it. Alternatively, fit a piece of crumpled foil inside the top of the pan, and press it against the sides to enclose the steam.

SMALL APPLIANCES

Today there is a wide choice of electrical kitchen appliances that you can use to save time and energy when performing everyday kitchen tasks. Decide which appliances will benefit you most according to the kind of cooking you do.

USING SMALL APPLIANCES

Make maximum use of each appliance by reading the manual before you start to use it. This will tell you which tasks the appliance will tackle and how to get the best performance out of it. Keep regularly used items, such as toasters, close at hand on or near a counter.

SELECTING APPLIANCES
● **Checking ease of cleaning**
Before buying, check that small appliances can be dismantled for cleaning, and whether or not parts are dishwasher-proof.
● **Storing cords** When selecting an appliance for countertop use, such as a toaster, mixer, or food processor, look for a model that stores the cord inside the appliance, or one that has a self-retracting cord.
● **Preventing slipping** For safety, buy small appliances that have nonskid feet.
● **Buying a small bowl** If you need to purée small amounts of food for a baby, consider a food processor made for the task, or buy a smaller bowl to fit your large processor.

USING BLENDERS

Dish towel protects hand from steam

Covering the lid
When puréeing hot foods in a blender, let them cool for a few minutes before blending. While blending, hold the lid in place with a folded dish towel in case the steam pushes it off.

USING PROCESSORS

Using an extra bowl
If you use a food processor often for a variety of tasks, it is worth buying an extra bowl and blades so that you can prepare different foods in rapid succession. Spares are available from most suppliers.

SAFETY

● **Disconnecting power supply**
Before doing any cleaning, oiling, or maintenance of an electrical appliance, always switch it off first, and unplug it from the electricity supply.
● **Drying hands** Always dry your hands before touching switches or plugging in and unplugging appliances to prevent electrocution.
● **Washing blades** Always wash sharp food-processor or blender blades carefully with a brush. Keep your fingers out of the way of the blade edges. Do not leave blades to soak.

MAINTAINING MIXERS

Use pointed dropper to insert oil into holes

Oiling a mixer
If the beaters of your mixer become stiff and difficult to remove, place a drop of light household oil into each of the holes into which the beaters fit. Insert the beaters, and switch on.

PROCESSING EFFICIENTLY
● **Creating a pulse-switch effect**
If your food processor does not have an automatic pulse switch, alternately press the High and Off switches to achieve the same effect.
● **Preventing "walking"** If your food processor "walks" around on the counter while in use, or if it is noisy, place it on a rubberized or soft plastic mat.
● **Warming working parts**
Before mixing or kneading bread dough in a food processor, warm the bowl and blade by rinsing them in hot water before use. This will help the yeast rise.

CARING FOR SMALL APPLIANCES

Good-quality electrical appliances are built to withstand reasonable domestic use but will benefit from regular care and maintenance. Keep electrical appliances away from burners to prevent heat damage, and check cords regularly for wear, which could make them dangerous.

PREVENTING WEAR
● **Selecting speed** Use the correct speed on a food processor to avoid straining the motor. Check the manual to find the appropriate setting for the job to be done.
● **Changing speed** If a mixer or food processor motor strains during mixing, switch it onto High, or mix small quantities in separate batches. If a recipe recommends processing in batches, do so.
● **Correcting faults** If a blender or food processor stops, switch it off, and check that nothing is jamming the blade. Let it rest for a few seconds before turning it on again.

EASING SEALED LIDS

Spray oil inside lid

Using spray oil
Occasionally spray the inside edge of a food-processor lid with spray-on vegetable oil to ease the lid's fit within the rim of the bowl. Avoid spraying the bowl, since this may affect some foods.

STORING APPLIANCES
● **Hanging beaters** Rather than storing mixer beaters in a drawer, hang them on a small hook. This will help prevent them from becoming damaged and make them easy to find.
● **Storing blades** Store sharp appliance blades in a special rack or box instead of leaving them in a drawer with other utensils. Alternatively, cut slots in a piece of styrofoam from the appliance packaging. Keep blades in slots.
● **Covering appliances** Use a plastic cover to protect a food processor and keep it clean if the appliance is usually stored on a crowded counter.

CLEANING SMALL APPLIANCES

Kitchen appliances that are in everyday use will benefit from regular cleaning. Read the manufacturer's instruction booklet for special instructions before doing this. Always unplug electrical items before you clean them, and do not immerse electrical parts in water.

REMOVING DEBRIS
● **Using tongs** Keep wooden food tongs or two chopsticks near a toaster to remove foods that have become stuck inside.

Direct air spray into each compartment

Blowing out crumbs
Use a compressed air spray to expel crumbs through the bottom of a toaster. These sprays are available from photographic equipment suppliers. Unplug the toaster before cleaning.

REMOVING DEPOSITS
● **Clearing greasy deposits** If your garbage disposal unit becomes clogged with greasy food, drop a handful of ice cubes into it, then switch on for a few seconds. The ice will set the fat so that it can be ground up and disposed of.
● **Clearing clogged filters** Remove mineral deposits from a blocked coffee maker by filling the tank with equal parts distilled vinegar and water. Switch on and brew once, then brew again with clear water before use.
● **Using detergents** To clean a blender container after use, half-fill it with a solution of dishwashing liquid and warm water. Run it for a few seconds to remove food deposits.

PURIFYING GRINDERS

Using bread
If you have used a coffee grinder or mill for grinding spices, remove all traces of spice odor and flavor that may taint coffee by grinding a few pieces of bread before it is used again.

333

PREPARED INGREDIENTS

QUICK REFERENCE

Dry Storage, p. 335

Pantry
Staples, p. 337

Sugars and Sweet
Flavorings, p. 342

Herbs, Spices,
and Seasonings, p. 344

Convenience Foods, p. 347

*G*ATHERING TOGETHER A RELIABLE, *varied supply of prepared ingredients is essential to the smooth running of any kitchen. With such a stock, you will have the ingredients on hand to rustle up some tasty meals in minutes, without having to shop specifically for them. A versatile collection of staples and standbys is the key. Include a selection of good convenience foods in your supplies. Used with fresh foods, they have a valuable place in the kitchen.*

PANTRIES

It is important to remember when choosing where to store dry foods that they need cool, dry, and preferably dark conditions. The best place for them is in a cabinet or hutch in the coolest part of the kitchen. Alternatively, store dry foods in a basement larder.

ORGANIZING CABINETS

Large containers, cake pans, and boxes of UHT milk (for emergencies)

Narrow shelf makes it easy to see what is stored

Canisters and packs of dry ingredients such as flour, sugar, and dried fruits

Tall bottles behind smaller ones

Heavy items in regular use, pickles, preserves, and small herb and spice jars

PLANNING STORAGE

● **Siting cabinets** When choosing cabinets for food storage, bear in mind that they should be cool and dry. A cold outside wall is better than an internal one – ideally it should be at a temperature of about 50°F (10°C).

● **Choosing shelves** Where possible, store foods on narrow shelves, so that you can see and reach items easily. An ideal width for a shelf is about 5 in (13 cm).

● **Lining shelves** Before filling cabinets with food, line the shelves with a wipe-clean surface such as plastic laminate, spongeable shelf-lining paper, or aluminum foil.

Arranging ingredients

Ideally, you should aim to store large, lightweight foods such as cereals on the top shelves. Heavy bottles and cans are easy to remove if stored on lower shelves. Small spice jars should be located at the front of a shelf.

DRY STORAGE

THE WARM AND OFTEN STEAMY CONDITIONS of many kitchens are not ideal for storing dry ingredients. Careful storage and the appropriate choice of containers can help keep moisture and heat from damaging stored foods.

STORAGE CONTAINERS

Take a look at the storage facilities already available in your kitchen before buying expensive extra shelving or elaborate storage containers. Economical, space-saving ideas and recycled containers, such as coffee cans, can provide efficient food storage at little cost.

MAKING MAXIMUM USE OF CABINET SPACE

● **Stacking containers** When you are choosing containers for storage where space is limited, make sure that they stack easily. Containers can then be arranged in two layers to make the fullest use of the space between shelves.

Stuff tube with plastic bags for tidy storage

Storing plastic bags
To store plastic grocery bags for reuse, make a fabric tube about 8 x 20 in (20 x 50 cm), gather the ends, and secure them with elastic. Hang the tube from a hook inside a broom closet door.

Creating hanging space
To keep small packs of herbs, spices, and nuts organized, and to save on shelf space, use a clear plastic shoe organizer. Hang it from a hook inside a food pantry door for easy access.

Hanging racks
Keep frequently used small items and condiments on racks hung inside cabinet doors to save on shelf space. Put the items on butcher's hooks and in clip-on baskets attached to the racks.

INVENTING SHELF SPACE

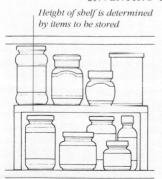

Height of shelf is determined by items to be stored

Making an extra shelf
Make maximum use of deep shelving by adding an extra shelf for storing small items between two existing shelves. A simple, wipe-clean wooden shelf built with two sides about 6 in (17 cm) high will be the most useful. Improvise with a quick, temporary version by resting a narrow length of wood on cans placed at either end of a shelf. Use the extra space for storing small cans and jars.

REUSING CONTAINERS

● **Recycling screw-top jars** Store dry goods in containers such as thoroughly washed coffee cans, which are airtight.
● **Making an airtight seal** To make sure that storage jars are airtight, wrap a strip of masking tape around the lids.
● **Coping without containers** If you do not have any airtight storage containers, place a whole package of a dry ingredient such as flour into a zip-top plastic bag.

CLEANING AND LABELING CONTAINERS

To make the best use of dry ingredients, it is important to store them correctly. Make a note of use-by dates, and always finish the contents of a container before refilling it so that you do not mix old and new ingredients. Wash and dry containers regularly to prevent odors.

CLEANING CONTAINERS

● **Removing odors** To rid a container of lingering odors, fill it with hot water, and add 1 tbsp (15 ml) baking soda. Let stand overnight, then rinse and dry before use.

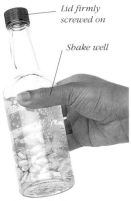

Lid firmly screwed on

Shake well

Loosening debris
Fill a dirty bottle or jar with warm water and a few drops of detergent. Add a ½-in (1-cm) layer of dried beans or rice, then shake to loosen the debris.

LABELING CONTAINERS

● **Using package labels** When transferring food from a package into a storage jar, cut out the name and cooking instructions on the package, and tape them to the jar.

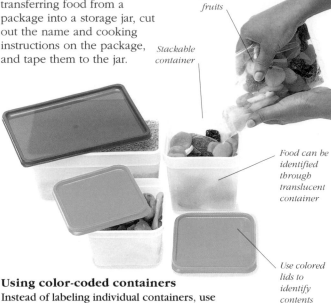

Dried fruits

Stackable container

Food can be identified through translucent container

Use colored lids to identify contents

Using color-coded containers
Instead of labeling individual containers, use color-coded plastic containers to store different types of ingredients. For example, use blue for beans and green for dried fruits, so that you can identify ingredients at a glance.

OPENING TIGHTLY SEALED JARS AND BOTTLES

Food jars and bottles are often difficult to open when food becomes stuck between the jar or bottle and the lid. To loosen, use a firm grip, tap the lid upside down on a flat surface, or try one of the methods below.

● **Loosening metal lids** Hold a metal lid under hot water to expand the metal. If the jar or bottle has been chilled, start with lukewarm water, and increase the heat gradually to prevent the glass from cracking.
● **Preventing sticky lids** Before resealing a jar or bottle with sticky food, wipe the rim and lid with a paper towel that has been dampened with hot water.

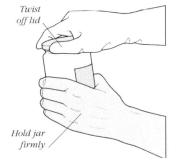

Twist off lid

Hold jar firmly

Loosening a tightly sealed jar
If a jar or bottle lid is difficult to twist open with a normal grip, wear a rubber glove to give you a firm hold on the lid. Or grip with a rubber band, a piece of sandpaper, or a damp cloth.

Lid protected with soft cloth

Apply gentle pressure

Using pliers
To loosen a tight lid on a bottle or jar with a narrow neck, use pliers or a nutcracker, but do not exert too much pressure. Place a cloth over plastic lids to prevent them from being damaged.

PANTRY STAPLES

N O KITCHEN IS COMPLETE without basic staple ingredients such as pasta, rice, flours, sugars, oils, and flavorings. These items provide the basis for almost every type of cooking, and combine well with fresh ingredients.

DRIED PASTA

T here are more than one hundred different pasta shapes. Most of them are versatile and are suitable for serving with a wide variety of dishes, but many shapes were designed with a particular sauce or type of food in mind. Dried pasta keeps well in a pantry or cabinet.

CHOOSING AND USING PASTA

BASIC SHAPES	EXAMPLES	COOKING SUGGESTIONS
LONG, ROUND PASTA Capelli d'angelo Spaghetti	Long, round pasta is available in many thicknesses and includes types such as spaghetti, long macaroni, and buccatini (a thick, hollow spaghetti). Vermicelli (little worms), capellini (fine hair), and capelli d'angelo (angel hair) are very fine pastas that are traditionally dried and packed in curls that resemble birds' nests.	● Use olive-oil-based sauces such as pesto to keep the strands slippery and separate. ● Use rich tomato, cheese, and meat sauces with spaghetti or buccatini. These are firm pastas that will not be weighed down by the sauce. ● Choose light tomato, butter, or cream sauces for serving with vermicelli-type pastas to keep the delicate strands intact.
LONG, FLAT PASTA Tagliatelle Lasagne	Lasagne is a broad, flat pasta, and may be smooth, ridged, or wavy-edged; lasagnette is a narrow type of lasagne. Tagliatelle and pappardelle are wide, flat pastas; tagliarini, linguine (little tongues), and trenette are narrower versions. Fettuccine, traditionally made with egg, is narrower and thicker than tagliatelle.	● Use no-boil lasagne in baked lasagne recipes to shorten preparation time. You may need to increase the liquid content of the recipe; consult the package directions. ● Choose thick, ribbon pastas for egg-based carbonara sauces, since the large surface area helps cook the sauce quickly. ● Toss cooked tagliatelle in a sauce or oil immediately after draining to separate the strands.
SHORT, SHAPED PASTA Penne Farfalle Fusilli	There is a seemingly endless choice of short pasta shapes, the most popular being penne (pens or quills), farfalle (butterflies or bows), fusilli and fusilli bucatti (spirals or springs), conchiglie (shells), orichiette (ears), lumache (snails), and ditali (fingers of glove or thimbles). Pastina is a general term for tiny pasta shapes such as farfallini, lumachine, stelline, and ditalini.	● Use penne, fusilli, lumache, and conchiglie with chunky tomato or meat sauces, or with ragù, which will penetrate into the pasta hollows. ● Make a pasta pie from leftover cooked short pasta. Layer with a savory sauce, top with cheese, and bake. ● To make a soup more substantial, sprinkle in a handful of any type of pastina near the end of cooking.

STORING AND USING PASTA

Pasta is available fresh or dried in a variety of shapes, and all types are an excellent source of fiber and carbohydrate. Dried pasta stores well and is a useful standby ingredient for everyday meals and last-minute entertaining. Whole-grain pasta is a healthy option.

STORING PASTA

● **Keeping long pasta** Keep several types of long pasta in one container, but tie each type into a bundle with raffia to avoid mixing them.

USING LEFTOVER PASTA

● **Using up pasta** If just a small amount of pasta is left in the package, cook all the pasta, and use the leftovers in salads, soups, and omelet fillings.

SERVING PASTA SHAPES

● **Encouraging children** Make meals more fun for children by using alphabet or animal shapes, or other pasta shapes in a variety of everyday meals.

Move dryer in circular motion to dry thoroughly

Add farfalle to fusilli

HEALTHY TIP

Using whole-grain pasta
Choose whole-grain pasta for high-fiber, healthy pasta dishes. If you find that whole-grain pasta is too heavy to eat on its own, mix it half-and-half with refined pasta that is the same shape.

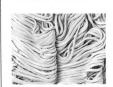

Drying a spaghetti tin
Always wash a spaghetti tin or jar with a mild detergent before refilling it. Dry with a cloth, and use a hair dryer to finish drying the inside thoroughly. Then fill with a fresh supply of pasta.

Making a pasta mix
Keep leftover pasta shapes that have similar cooking times together in an airtight container. Farfalle, fusilli, and conchiglie can be mixed together and used in everyday pasta dishes.

TYPES OF ORIENTAL NOODLE

Rice noodles
Rice noodles, made from rice, are available in different thicknesses and shapes. They are usually dried and should be soaked in warm water for 15 minutes before cooking. Use in soups and stir-fries.

Cellophane noodles
Also called bean-thread or pea starch noodles, these are made from mung beans. They are fine and white and are available dried in neat bundles. Soak for five minutes before adding to soups or braised dishes.

Wheat and egg noodles
These noodles are usually made from wheat or buckwheat flour and egg. Choose flat noodles for use in soups and rounded noodles for stir-fries, or cook them on their own and serve as a side dish with vegetables.

USING NOODLES

● **Bulking out salads** Keep some fine-thread Chinese or Japanese noodles in your pantry. Soak in hot water for 5–10 minutes, then drain and toss into salads to make them more substantial.

● **Frying noodles** If you are frying cellophane noodles, there is no need to soak them first. Just add the noodles straight from the package to hot oil, and fry until crisp.

● **Substituting in special diets** Many types of noodle, such as rice and cellophane noodles, are suitable for people on a wheat-free diet. Substitute these noodles in recipes that specify wheat pasta.

CHOOSING AND USING GRAINS

Grains are one of the world's most nutritious staple foods. They are a good source of protein and carbohydrate, and contain valuable minerals. Whole grains are high in fiber. Keep a variety of whole and refined grains in your pantry to use in different dishes.

STORING GRAINS

● **Storing white rice** Keep white rice in an airtight container stored in a cool, dark place. Whole, polished rice will store well for about one year if kept at room temperature. Ground rice will keep for up to six months.

● **Storing whole grains** Store whole grains for a maximum of six months before use. After this time, the oil content of unrefined grain turns rancid from exposure to heat, light, and moisture.

● **Mixing grains** Brown rice and wild rice can be stored and cooked together. They require similar cooking times, and they look interesting when mixed together in risotto- and pilaf-style dishes.

MEASURING & STORING RICE

Pour rice into measured container

Use lid as measuring tool

Marking quantities
Store rice in a clear, straight-sided container that is marked off in ½ cup (125 g) measures. Use the measure as a guide to pour out the correct amount of rice. Cook white rice with twice its volume of water – 1 cup (250 ml) water for every ½ cup (125 g) rice.

Measuring a portion
Containers such as coffee jars can be used to store rice or other types of grain. Choose a container with a lid that holds approximately ¼ cup (55 g) of rice, and which will therefore enable you to measure out rice portions quickly for cooking.

COMMON TYPES OF GRAIN

Grains form the basis of many main-course dishes, and can be served as a nutritious side dish. Check the instructions on the packet before cooking.

● **Long-grain rice** This may be brown or white, and it has a slim, long grain.
● **Short-grain rice** Short-grain rice is soft when cooked. It is ideal for rice pudding.
● **Basmati rice** This is a very flavorful, long-grain rice.
● **Glutinous rice** Used mainly in Chinese dishes, this round-grain rice has a sticky texture.
● **Arborio rice** This medium-grain rice absorbs more liquid than other types of rice.
● **Wild rice** This grain is the seed of a wild aquatic grass.
● **Cracked wheat** A processed wheat, this is also called bulgur.
● **Couscous** This is a processed grain made from semolina.

White long-grain rice

Brown long-grain rice

Short-grain rice

Basmati rice

Glutinous rice

Arborio rice

Wild rice

Cracked wheat

Couscous

FLOURS AND OTHER GRAINS

As long as your pantry is clean, dry, and cool, storing flours and other grain products should not be a problem. Products that are bought in paper packaging will keep best if they are transferred to clean, dry, airtight containers as soon as they are opened.

MAKING A SHAKER

Using a screw-top jar
To make a homemade flour shaker, make several holes in the metal lid of a screw-top jar by hammering a nail through it while resting it on a wooden board. Fill the jar with flour.

STORING FLOUR

● **Keeping fresh** Store all-purpose white flour in a cool, dry place for up to six months; store self-rising flour for up to three months. Whole-wheat and other flours have a higher fat content; buy small amounts and use within two months.
● **Storing in a cool place** If the temperature is above 75°F (24°C), or if humidity is high, wrap flour in a heavy plastic bag and refrigerate to prevent infestation and mold.
● **Using chilled flours** If flour has been stored in a cool place, bring it to room temperature before baking to avoid a heavy texture in the finished products.

FLOUR SUBSTITUTES

Each type of flour has different properties. Sometimes one type can be substituted for another.

● **Making self-rising flour** Sift 1½ tsp (7.5 ml) baking powder and ½ tsp (2.5 ml) salt with 1 cup (225 g) all-purpose flour. Use as store-bought self-rising flour.
● **Adding texture** Grind oats in a food processor, and use the resulting flour to replace up to one third of the white flour in bread recipes to provide texture and flavor.
● **Using cornstarch** If using cornstarch instead of white flour as a thickening agent, use half the amount given in the recipe.

DRIED FRUITS AND NUTS

Both dried fruits and nuts are useful for adding texture, flavor, and nutritive value to sweet and savory dishes. Keep a good selection on hand, but use them up or replace them regularly, since dried fruits can overdry and harden, and nuts quickly become rancid.

BUYING & STORING

● **Tasting before buying** If possible, taste nuts before you buy them to make sure that they are not rancid.
● **Buying nuts in their shells** Buy unshelled nuts, which keep twice as long as shelled nuts, as long as they are fresh when you buy them.
● **Choosing for freshness** Avoid shelled nuts that are shriveled or discolored. If they are in plastic bags, break one nut through the wrapping: if it is fresh it will snap apart rather than bend.
● **Storing at low temperature** Pack large quantities of fresh nuts in sealed bags, and store in the freezer for up to eight months. They will keep in the refrigerator for half that time.

STORING IN ALCOHOL

Cover fruits with brandy

Soaking fruits in brandy
Fill a canning jar with dried fruits such as prunes, apricots, bananas, and figs, and add brandy or a liqueur to cover. Use the plump, tasty fruits for making luxurious desserts.

ADDING VARIETY

Put flaked nuts in airtight container

Using a food processor
Make sliced hazelnuts in a food processor to use as an alternative to sliced almonds. Use whole, unskinned hazelnuts; the fine slicing blade of the processor will slice them finely.

LEGUMES

Legumes, including beans, peas, and lentils, are an excellent source of proteins, minerals, and carbohydrates. They can be used whole in salads, puréed in soups, or ground for dips. Legumes are inexpensive and store well, but buy in small quantities, since they toughen with age.

STORING UNCOOKED LEGUMES

● **Using glass jars** Store packages of legumes in airtight jars, and make a note of soaking and cooking times and purchase dates on the lids.

● **Rotating stock** Use up any old stock of legumes before adding newly bought ones to a jar. Cooking times may vary between old and new.

STORING COOKED BEANS

● **Refrigerating** If covered, cooked beans will store well in a refrigerator for several days. Alternatively, they can be frozen for up to three months.

Cannellini beans can be mixed with red kidney beans

Lay whole chilies on top of legumes

Making a bean mix
Make up your own colorful mixture of dried beans, and store in a jar ready to add to soups and casseroles. Combine types of beans with the same cooking time.

Deterring insects
To protect legumes from insect damage during storage, put a few dried chilies in the storage jars with them. Replace the lids tightly, and store as usual.

TRADITIONAL TIP

Checking beans
Put dried beans in a bowl of cold water, and discard any that float to the surface, since this is an indication of insect or mold damage.

VARIETIES OF LENTIL

Lentils are richer in protein than any other legumes except soybeans. Most do not need soaking before cooking.

● **Brown lentils** These are the most common type, flattish in shape, and green or brown in color. Brown lentils retain their shape well when cooked.
● **Split orange or red lentils** These quick-cooking lentils are useful for thickening curries or casseroles.
● **Puy lentils** Greenish gray in color, these are considered to have the best flavor. They complement smoked meats.
● **Yellow lentils** Also known as yellow dal, these lentils are often served as a side dish in Indian cooking.

CHECKING & CLEANING
● **Inspecting carefully** Before storage, check legumes and their packaging for signs of insect infestation. Discard any that are shriveled, discolored, or otherwise damaged.

Sift lentils with fingertips

Sifting out dirt
Spread legumes onto a shallow tray before use, and sift through them lightly to pick out any traces of dirt. Watch for damaged ones at the same time.

USING LEGUMES
● **Cooking dried peas** If you are short of time, use split dried peas rather than whole ones: split peas do not need to be soaked before cooking.
● **Combining proteins** Mix beans or lentils with cereals such as rice or pasta. These combinations provide a more nutritionally complete meal, so they are particularly useful foods in vegetarian diets.
● **Saving time** Cook a larger batch of beans than you need, and freeze half for later use to save time and fuel costs.
● **Pie weights** Save old and stale beans to use as pie weights when you make a pie shell. Store the beans in a separate jar and label clearly, since they will not be edible.

SUGARS AND SWEET FLAVORINGS

Sugars and sweet flavorings play a very important role in our enjoyment of food. Their appearance, texture, taste, and versatility can be utilized in many ways to enhance cakes and pastries, fruit desserts, and even savory dishes.

SUGARS

There is little difference in the calorie counts of white and brown sugars, but the flavors are very different. Some of the darkest sugars add a particularly rich flavor and color to both sweet and savory dishes, and they are often specified in recipes for desserts and cakes.

SOFTENING & STORING BROWN SUGAR

Softening in a microwave
To soften brown sugar, place in a microwave-proof dish and add a wedge of apple. Cover tightly, and microwave on High for 30 seconds. Remove apple and stir.

Storing brown sugar
Keep brown sugar moist by storing in an airtight container with one or two wedges of apple. Alternatively, use a whole citrus fruit, or a piece of fresh bread.

TRADITIONAL TIP

Making vanilla sugar
Bury two vanilla beans in a jar of sugar, and let stand at least one week. Stir occasionally. Use this vanilla-flavored sugar in sweet dishes.

FLAVORED SUGAR

Pare citrus zest thinly to remove long strip

Adding a citrus flavor
To add subtle flavor to sweet dishes, desserts, cakes, and cookies, flavor the sugar used. To impart a citrus flavor to sugar, pare long, thin strips of zest from an orange, lemon, or lime. Bury the strips of zest in a container of sugar, and store for at least three days before using.

● **Making scented sugar** Add two sprigs of fresh lavender or rosemary to a container of sugar, and shake well. Let stand 24 hours, then shake again, before leaving for one week. Use to sweeten milk-based puddings and fresh fruit desserts.

STORING & USING
● **Preventing lumps** To keep packages of brown sugar from absorbing moisture and forming lumps during storage, place them in a thick plastic bag in a cool, dry place.
● **Making superfine sugar** If you run out of superfine sugar, make your own from granulated sugar. Place it in a food processor with a metal blade, and process for a few seconds for a fine consistency.
● **Keeping a thermos fresh** Add a sugar cube or a teaspoonful of white sugar to a dry, empty thermos bottle before storing it away. This will prevent stale smells from developing inside.

HONEY, SYRUPS, JAMS, AND JELLIES

Like most natural products, honey is affected by light and heat and does not respond well to wide fluctuations in temperature. Processed syrups, jams, and jellies are more stable, but they will also deteriorate if exposed to air and heat. Once opened, keep them in a refrigerator.

RESTORING HONEY

Reliquefying in hot water
If clear honey becomes crystallized during storage, reliquefy it by standing the jar in a bowl of hot water for five minutes. Then rotate the jar a couple of times until the honey becomes clear and liquid.

MEASURING HONEY
● **Using a heated spoon** To measure amounts of set honey and syrups easily, use a metal spoon that has been dipped in hot water. Honey and syrup will not stick to a heated spoon.

USING SUBSTITUTES
● **Using blended honey** Choose blended types of honey for cooking, since these have a robust flavor. The delicate flavors of more expensive flower honeys are destroyed by heat during cooking.
● **Substituting syrup** Honey and corn syrup contain 20 percent water, so reduce the liquid content of recipes when using instead of sugar.

JAMS AND JELLIES

Making an apricot glaze
Gently warm some apricot jam with a squeeze of lemon juice, then push through a sieve. Store in a screw-top jar in the refrigerator for a ready-made sweet glaze.

● **Keeping preserves fresh**
Buy preserves that have a minimum of 60 percent sugar content, which prevents mold.

CHOCOLATE

Chocolate is available in several different forms. In general, the better the quality of the chocolate, the better the flavor will be, since inexpensive chocolate contains fewer cocoa solids and more sugar. Chocolate is damaged by moisture and heat, so store it carefully.

FREEZING CHOCOLATE

Press firmly against grater

Fine curls

Storing grated chocolate
Grate chilled chocolate on a food grater to make fine curls. Store in a plastic bag in the freezer so that you can remove just the amount you need for cooking or decorating.

STORING CHOCOLATE
● **Cooling to keep fresh** Wrap chocolate tightly and store at a low temperature, ideally around 60°F (15°C).
● **Preventing bloom** Seal in flavor and keep out moisture by storing chocolate wrapped in baking parchment, then overwrapped with foil.
● **Storing chocolate chips** Keep chocolate chips in a storage jar, ready to put into doughs and batters. They are low in cocoa solids, so they are less sensitive to temperature changes than other chocolate.
● **Preventing lumpy cocoa** Cocoa absorbs moisture easily, so store it in a container with a tight lid. Remove any lumps by sifting before using.

BRIGHT IDEA

Enriching meat dishes
Use chocolate to enrich the flavor of spicy meat or game casseroles. Add 1 oz (25 g) of dark chocolate for every four portions of chili con carne, for example, during cooking to enhance its flavor.

HERBS, SPICES, AND SEASONINGS

I̲T IS WELL WORTH WHILE HAVING A GOOD SELECTION of dried herbs and spices on hand to add flavor to all kinds of everyday dishes. Bear in mind that many dried herbs have a limited shelf life and should be used within six months.

═══ DRIED HERBS ═══

M̲ost herbs store successfully in dried form, and there is a wide range of commercially dried herbs to choose from. Freeze-dried herbs retain their color and are therefore visually more attractive than traditionally dried herbs, but they are usually a little more expensive.

BUYING DRIED HERBS

● **Choosing jars** When buying herbs packed in jars, choose jars that have a good, airtight seal. Herbs retain their flavor best if stored in either screw-top or flip-top jars, both of which are more securely airtight than jars with corks.

● **Buying whole-leaf herbs** If possible, choose whole-leaf dried herbs such as rosemary or bay. Dried herbs that have been crushed or ground are likely to lose their flavor much more quickly than those whose leaves are left whole.

STORING HERB JARS FOR EASY ACCESS

Place jars on their sides so that contents are clearly visible

Using drawer space
Herbs and spices are best stored in a dark place such as a cool kitchen drawer. Keep small jars flat and tidy; the herbs and spices will be easy to select since you can see the contents or labels of each jar at a glance.

DRYING & STORING HERBS

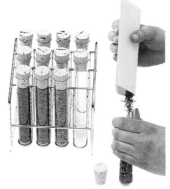

1 When drying herbs such as sage, thyme, or parsley, keep the leaves on the stems until completely dry. Rub the stems gently between your fingertips, crumbling the leaves into a small bowl. Discard stems, or use to flavor stocks.

2 Put some of the crumbled leaves into small containers such as test tubes, using a piece of paper to funnel the herbs in gently. Keep the containers in a rack ready to use in cooking. Store any remaining herbs for future use.

STORING DRIED HERBS

● **Keeping light out** Store dried herbs in airtight glass containers, and keep them in as dark a place as possible.

● **Extending storage life** To prolong the lives of dried herbs, wrap them tightly in plastic bags. Keep the herbs in the refrigerator for three months, or freeze for up to six months.

● **Noting storage times** Write the purchase dates of dried herbs on pieces of masking tape, and stick these on the bases of the containers. Alternatively, use a felt-tip pen to write the dates on the jars.

● **Arranging alphabetically** If you have a large selection of herb containers, arrange them in alphabetical order so that you can find the herbs you need quickly and easily.

SPICES

Spices, like herbs, need careful storage away from light and heat, both of which shorten their shelf lives. Spices keep their flavor best when stored whole, so it is best to grind them as you need them, or to store ground spices in small amounts and use them within a short time.

USEFUL SPICES

Ground nutmeg

Keep a selection of basic spices in your cabinet.

- **Black peppercorns** Crush coarsely for spiced coatings.
- **Nutmeg** Always grate fresh nutmeg since the ground spice loses flavor quickly.
- **Cinnamon** Keep cinnamon sticks and the ground spice for versatility in your cooking.
- **Coriander and cumin** These are useful ground spices to add to many ethnic dishes.

PREPARING SPICE MIXES

- **Making cinnamon sugar** Mix 1 cup (225 g) superfine sugar with 1½ tbsp (25 ml) cinnamon. Store in a shaker, and sprinkle on warm buttered toast.

Making pie spice

Make your own favorite mixture of spices, such as sweet mixed spice for harvest-time baking. Grind together whole cinnamon, nutmeg, and cloves, or allspice; add a pinch of ginger. Store the mixture in a small, screw-top jar.

CHOOSING WHOLE SPICES

- **Selecting seeds** Check that whole seeds such as caraway or coriander have a uniform shape and consistent color, with no stem or chaff content.
- **Checking cardamom** Buy whole cardamom pods that are pale green, plump, and unblemished. The seeds inside should be black or brown, and slightly sticky.
- **Buying cinnamon** Choose slim cinnamon sticks with an even, pale, soft brown color.
- **Choosing cloves** Look for whole cloves that are large, plump, and oily, with a warm, reddish brown color.
- **Testing beans for freshness** Bend vanilla beans: they should be supple and resilient.

GRINDING WHOLE SPICES

Put whole spices into grinder

Using a coffee grinder

Grind your own whole spices in an electric coffee grinder to make a spice blend in seconds. Use a pastry brush or paper towel to clean the grinder thoroughly immediately after use, removing any lingering spice flavors.

USING MUSTARDS

- **Mustard powder** Add a little mustard powder, which acts as a preservative, to mayonnaise and other dressings to prolong their shelf lives, and to add a sharp flavor to the dressings.

Making mustard

Crush white and black mustard seeds together, and mix to a paste with wine vinegar. Add honey and flavorings such as chilies to taste. Keep in a screw-top jar.

KEEPING FLAVORS

- **Using spices quickly** Ground spices lose their flavor and aroma quickly, so buy only a small quantity at a time, and make sure that you use it up within six months.
- **Choosing chilies** Choose red chilies, which are simply ripened green chilies, rather than green chilies if you want a sweeter flavor. Select yellow caribe chilies for a sweet, mild flavor; green jalapeño chilies, which are the most common type, for average heat; and orange habanero chilies for a hot and distinctive fruity flavor. Experiment with other varieties to find your favorites.
- **Toasting whole spices** To get the most intense flavor from spices, toast them whole in a heavy, dry frying pan. Shake the pan over fairly high heat for a minute or two, and use immediately.

OILS, VINEGARS, AND SEASONINGS

Oils are fats that are in liquid form at room temperature. Exposure to light and air can cause them to deteriorate, so keep them in airtight containers in a cool place along with vinegars, salt, and seasonings, all of which require similar storage conditions for long life.

FLAVORING OILS & VINEGARS

White wine vinegar with fresh herbs

Extra-virgin olive oil with orange zest and coriander seeds

Cider vinegar with honey, lemon, and mint

Olive oil with garlic and lime wedges

White wine vinegar with skewered ginger and garlic

Red wine vinegar with cumin, cinnamon, and cloves

Creating unique flavors

Flavored oils and vinegars are easy to make at home. Immerse clean, fresh herbs, spices, fruits, or edible flowers in oil or vinegar in sterilized screw-top bottles. Refrigerate for about two weeks before filtering and using.

INFUSING FLAVORS

● **Bruising ingredients** Lightly bruise fresh herbs before steeping in vinegar to help release their flavor. Cloves of garlic and shallots also benefit from being lightly crushed.

● **Infusing quickly** To infuse flavors into vinegar quickly, heat the vinegar gently until almost boiling. Pour it onto your chosen flavoring, cool, then seal in bottles.

● **Flavoring with fruits** Use fresh raspberries, strawberries, blackberries, blueberries, or slices of lemon or orange to make delicately flavored fruit vinegars, which can be used to add mellow flavors to savory dishes and drinks.

● **Storing fruit vinegars** To keep fruit vinegars for longer than about one week, strain and then discard the fruits before transferring the vinegar into clean bottles.

USING OILS

● **Nut oils** Oils that are made from nuts, such as walnut or hazelnut, have rich, intense flavors, making them ideal for use in salads or flavoring savory dishes. Once opened, store them in the refrigerator, since they deteriorate quickly.
● **Olive oil** Save the best-quality extra-virgin olive oil for lightly cooked dishes and salads, since too much heat will destroy the fine flavor and aroma of the oil.
● **Healthy oils** Use oils labeled monounsaturated, such as olive oil, or polyunsaturated, such as sunflower oil, for a healthy diet. These do not increase blood cholesterol levels, unlike saturated animal fats.

STORING OILS

Storing bottles of oil

To help keep cabinet shelves clean, stand bottles of oil on a tray that can easily be wiped clean. Use a tray that has deep sides to reduce the risk of the bottles being knocked over.

TRADITIONAL TIP

Storing free-running salt

To make sure salt stays dry, and therefore runs freely from the salt shaker, add a few grains of rice to the shaker. Replace the rice every few months – not every time you refill the shaker.

CONVENIENCE FOODS

MOST PEOPLE RELY ON CONVENIENCE FOODS from time to time, usually when they are unable to shop for and cook fresh ingredients. Fast food need not necessarily mean junk food, and there is a vast range to choose from.

STOCKING AND USING CONVENIENCE FOODS		
TYPES OF FOOD	EXAMPLES OF FOOD	GENERAL USES
CANNED, SAVORY FOODS	Keep a supply of whole and chopped plum tomatoes and beans; vegetables such as corn, asparagus, and artichoke hearts; tuna; cooked ham; sauces; condensed and ready-to-heat soups; peanut and other nut butters.	● Add chopped tomatoes to casseroles and pizza toppings. ● Fold whipped egg whites into condensed soup for an easy soufflé.
CANNED, SWEET FOODS	Store canned fruits such as pineapple and pear rings and chunks and peach halves or slices; exotic fruits such as litchis and guavas; fruit pie fillings; applesauce; and fruit cocktail.	● Layer fruits and rice pudding in tall glasses. Stir puréed fruits or jam into plain yogurt for quick ambrosia. ● Use ready-made fruit pie fillings as quick cheesecake toppings.
DRY FOODS AND PACKAGED MIXES	Stock sauce and gravy mixes; dried vegetables; instant mashed potatoes, pasta and rice mixes; instant desserts; dried milk and gelatin powder; bread, pastry, batter, and cake mixes.	● Enrich instant mashed potatoes with single cream and mixed dried herbs. ● Transform a simple cake mix by sprinkling with brandy, then filling with cream and canned fruits.
BOTTLED FOODS AND PRESERVES	Keep jams and jellies; fruits in brandy; ready-made meals such as chili or baked beans; pesto; olives; sun-dried tomatoes; and antipasto.	● Spread pesto on Italian bread; toast to make bruscetta. ● Add ricotta or feta cheese to sun-dried tomatoes for an easy appetizer.
PREPARED FOODS	Stock up with partly baked breads and pastries; prepared ready-to-serve meals and pasta dishes; milk, cream, and whipped desserts.	● Use partly baked breads and pastries to create a homemade effect. ● Make a dessert by filling a ready-made pastry shell with canned fruits.
REFRIGERATED FOODS	Chill prepared meals; fresh pasta; soups; sweet and savory sauces; fruit salad; prepared mixed salads and dressings; fresh pastry; pâtés; and dips.	● Add chopped herbs and crunchy croutons to prepared soups. ● Prepare salads in advance and chill while you prepare the rest of the meal.
FROZEN, SAVORY FOODS	Freeze vegetables and stir-fry mixes; French fries; cooked rice; pizza bases; prepared fish and shellfish; meat and poultry; pastry, pies, and quiches.	● Fill an omelet with a stir-fry mix. ● Use prerolled pastry sheets or sheets of phyllo dough to make a quick base for a flan or tart.
FROZEN, SWEET FOODS	Freeze prepared fruits, especially raspberries and seasonal soft-fruit mixes; melon balls; ices, sorbets, and iced desserts; cakes; and fruit juices.	● Make summer desserts in winter with frozen soft fruits. ● Purée frozen fruits with confectioners' sugar to make a sauce.

FRESH INGREDIENTS

QUICK REFERENCE
Vegetables, Fruits, and Herbs, p. 350
Dairy Foods, p. 354
Meat and Poultry, p. 356
Fish and Shellfish, p. 358
Baked Goods, p. 360

IF YOU ARE ABLE TO SHOP FOR FOOD on a daily basis, keeping perishable ingredients fresh is not a problem. For most people, though, this is not a practical option, and they have to buy large amounts of fresh foods less frequently. Good planning, sensible shopping, and careful storage will ensure that perishable foods remain fresh, flavorful, and safe.

SHOPPING

Food shopping must begin in the kitchen if it is to be successful. Making a detailed list of everything you need can be an ongoing task, and every member of the household can help. Plan several days' menus in advance, and use them as a basis for fresh-food shopping.

BUYING WISELY
● **Making the most of bargains** Watch for seasonal best buys, and plan your menus around foods that are in season.
● **Avoiding waste** You should buy only what you can store. Bulk buying is usually a false economy if you cannot use the food while it is fresh.

MAKING LISTS
● **Listing in order** Organize items on your shopping list into groups and, if possible, arrange the groups so that they follow the layout of the supermarket. This will make shopping quick and easy, and you will be less likely to miss items that are on the list.

USING REMINDERS
● **Noting dates** Note use-by dates on perishable foods, and keep these in mind when planning meals and shopping in advance. It may be possible to freeze certain items for a few days to extend their shelf lives, but check the package labels for refrigeration details.

MONEY-SAVING TIP

Collecting coupons
Clip cents-off coupons together with a large paper clip, and attach it to a kitchen bulletin board. The coupons will be easy to find when you are ready to go shopping.

Keeping a list handy
Keep a current shopping list attached to the refrigerator door with a magnet. Each time an item of food is used up, add it to the list as a reminder to replace your stock of ingredients.

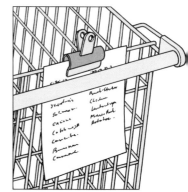

Clipping to a cart
When you go shopping, take a large clip or a clothes pin with you to attach your shopping list to the cart so that the list does not get lost. It will also help you to read the list at a glance.

PACKING

The priority on any food shopping trip is to keep the food cool and fresh until you get home. If possible, shop for perishable items last, and avoid leaving them in a warm car. Invest in cooler bags with ice packs if you cannot get food into a refrigerator quickly.

PACKING SHOPPING TO KEEP IT COOL

Keep foods cool with ice cubes

Using a cooler bag
If the weather is warm, pack perishable food into an insulated cooler bag. Put a tightly closed jar filled with ice cubes or several ice packs inside the bag.

Lining a shopping basket
Make your own improvised cooler bag by insulating an ordinary shopping bag or basket with a layer or two of crumpled newspaper or bubble wrap.

MAKING PACKING EASY
● **Starting with heavy items** When packing at the check-out, always begin by placing heavy items at the bottoms of bags or boxes. Lighter, more delicate items should be placed on top to avoid damage.
● **Keeping a spare bag** Always keep a string bag or folded shopping bag on hand, ready for any unexpected shopping.
● **Keeping foods separate** Pack chilled and frozen foods separately from your other shopping and, if you are traveling by car, load frozen foods last. You can then unload them first, and freeze them immediately.

STORING

Storing food safely is largely a matter of common sense. It is worth following some simple guidelines to avoid health risks. Check use-by dates when buying food, and adhere to them; always keep highly perishable foods cold; and keep raw and cooked foods separate.

STORING FOOD SAFELY
● **Finding the coldest zone** To identify the coldest zone of a refrigerator, check the manufacturer's handbook, since the location varies according to make and type. Frost-free refrigerators have an even temperature throughout.
● **Keeping opened canned foods** Empty the contents of an opened can of food into a bowl, cover, and refrigerate.
● **Avoiding contamination** Always store raw meats and foods to be defrosted beneath any cooked foods to prevent drips from raw foods from contaminating cooked foods.
● **Removing packaging** Leave foods wrapped unless their packaging recommends that you do otherwise.

ORGANIZING A REFRIGERATOR	
AREA	**FOODS TO BE STORED**
Cool zone: middle to lower shelves beneath freezer compartment	Milk, yogurt, fruit juices, hard cheeses, eggs, butter, margarine, low-fat spreads, and cooking fats.
Cold zone: shelf below freezer compartment, or bottom shelf of storage refrigerator	Precooked chilled foods, cooked meats, soft cheeses, prepared salads, home-prepared dishes and leftovers; raw meats and fish (a meat drawer is ideal).
Salad drawers or bins	Vegetables and fruits suitable for low-temperature storage, and salad items such as unwashed lettuce, whole tomatoes, radishes, cucumbers, and celery.
Refrigerator door and compartments	Milk, soft drinks, fruit juices, opened bottles and jars of sauces, preserves, and salad dressings.

VEGETABLES, FRUITS, AND HERBS

FOR A HEALTHY, WELL-BALANCED DIET, it is essential to include a wide range of vegetables and fruits that are rich in vitamins, minerals, and fiber. Fresh or dried herbs help add color and a distinctive flavor to every meal.

CHOOSING VEGETABLES

Each vegetable has particular indicators of quality, but in general crispness and a bright color are very good signs to look for. Choose vegetables in season for the best value. Out-of-season produce adds variety and interest to meals, but may cost more than locally grown vegetables.

CHECKING VEGETABLES FOR QUALITY & FRESHNESS

Press center gently

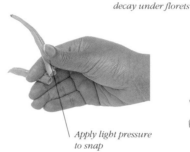

Apply light pressure to snap

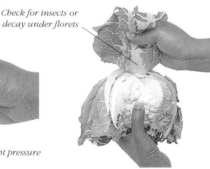

Check for insects or decay under florets

Checking a cabbage
Before buying a cabbage, check that the heart is firm by pressing the center with your thumb. Avoid those that have soft or discolored outer leaves, and brown or damaged patches.

Snapping a bean
To make sure that green beans are fresh, hold a bean between your forefinger and thumb, and bend it gently. If it is fresh, the bean will snap in two – not bend – under light pressure.

Checking a cauliflower
Always pull back the outer leaves of a cauliflower, and look carefully between the florets to ensure that there are no insects or signs of decay. The florets should be firm and white.

SHOPPING WISELY
● **Selecting shape and size** When buying vegetables such as Brussels sprouts, choose those of a uniform size and shape so that they cook evenly.
● **Testing avocados** Test an avocado by cupping it lightly in your hand and squeezing very gently. If it gives slightly, it is ready to eat. Pressing with fingertips will cause bruising.
● **Buying garlic** Buy plump garlic with tightly packed cloves and dry skin. Avoid any bulbs with soft, shriveled cloves or green shoots.
● **Selecting chilies** Choose chili peppers according to your taste. In general, the smaller the chili, the hotter it will be.

SALAD AND FRUIT VEGETABLES

Ripening tomatoes
If you need to speed up the ripening of green tomatoes, place them in a paper bag with an apple or a ripe, red tomato. Place the bag in a warm, dark place, and leave it there for a couple of days until the tomatoes ripen and turn red.

● **Lettuces** Choose lettuces that are firm and crisp, with bright, undamaged leaves. Avoid any that have discolored or yellow outer leaves.
● **Peppers** Red, yellow, and orange peppers have a sweeter flavor than green peppers and are more suitable for salads.
● **Cucumbers** Select cucumbers that are large, straight, and firm with fresh, shiny skin.
● **Other vegetables** Some vegetables, such as zucchini, cauliflower, and mushrooms, that are usually served cooked, make delicious salad ingredients. Use them raw or cooked to add extra texture to salads.

STORING VEGETABLES

Most vegetables have a limited storage time. Green vegetables should ideally be used within two days, but some root vegetables can be stored for several weeks in a cool, dark, airy place. All vegetables lose nutrients as soon as they are cut, so prepare them just before use.

STORING GARLIC

Garlic should be completely covered with oil

Storing in oil
To store garlic, peel a whole head of garlic, place the cloves in a jar, cover with olive oil, and refrigerate. The oil will preserve the garlic, and the garlic will flavor the oil, making it delicious for salad dressings. Refrigerate the flavored oil for up to two weeks.

REVIVING CELERY

Add drops of lemon juice

Iced water

Maintaining crispness
Revive wilted celery sticks by placing them in a bowl of iced water for at least one hour. Add a squeeze of fresh lemon juice to improve the flavor. To revive a whole head of celery, cut a thin slice from the root end, and stand the head in iced water.

BRIGHT IDEA

Making a garlic pot
Keep garlic fresh by allowing air to circulate around it. Instead of buying a specially made garlic pot, use an upturned terra-cotta pot that has a drainage hole in its base. Place the garlic on a small saucer, and cover with the terra-cotta pot.

COLD STORAGE

Most vegetables can be stored in a cool, dark, well-ventilated place. Vegetables that perish quickly should be stored in the refrigerator. However, low refrigeration temperatures can bring about changes to the flavor and texture of some vegetables, such as potatoes.

● **Mushrooms** Store fresh mushrooms in a paper bag at the bottom of the refrigerator.
● **Cabbage and celery** Keep cabbage and celery in the salad drawer of the refrigerator in order to retain flavor and texture.
● **Tomatoes** Avoid storing tomatoes in the refrigerator; low temperatures change their texture and can spoil the ripening process.

STORING ONIONS

● **Saving pieces of onion** Leave the skin, and try to retain the root end on the piece of onion that you wish to keep. Wrap in plastic wrap, and store in a refrigerator for up to three days.

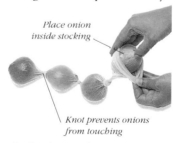

Place onion inside stocking

Knot prevents onions from touching

Stringing onions
Onions and garlic are best stored hung up in strings. Put the onions or garlic bulbs in a nylon stocking. Tie a knot between each onion or garlic bulb, then hang in a dry place.

KEEPING CHILIES

● **Freezing in freshness** Chilies freeze very successfully and can be used straight from the freezer, without thawing first. Freeze fresh, whole chilies in a freezer bag.

Thread through top of chili, not stem

Making a garland
String fresh chilies in a garland to dry and store. Using strong cotton or nylon thread and a clean needle, string them, knot the thread ends together, then hang the chilies to air-dry.

SHOPPING FOR FRUITS

Methods of testing ripeness vary from one fruit to another, but plumpness, firmness, and a good fragrance are usually good, general indicators of freshness in most types of fruit. Farm stands and greenmarkets offer the freshest produce, and often feature unusual items.

ENSURING FRESHNESS

● **Grapes** Before buying grapes, shake the bunch gently. The grapes should stay on the stem. If a few fall off, the branch is not fresh.
● **Citrus fruits** Citrus fruits such as lemons, oranges, and grapefruits should feel heavy for their size if they are juicy.
● **Banana skins** The skins of bananas become slightly flecked with brown when ripe. Slightly green, underripe bananas will ripen at room temperature in a few days.
● **Berries** These should be plump, not shriveled or moldy, with good color. If the hulls are still attached, the berries were picked when underripe, and they will be flavorless.

CHECKING FRUITS FOR QUALITY & RIPENESS

Gently press with both thumbs

Pull leaf out from top of pineapple

Checking a melon
To determine whether or not a melon is ripe, hold it firmly in both hands. Lightly press the area immediately around the tip of the melon, at the opposite end from the stem end; the surface should give slightly. A ripe melon will also have a pleasantly sweet scent.

Checking a pineapple
To check whether a whole pineapple is ripe and ready to eat, pull gently at a leaf at the top of the pineapple. If the leaf pulls out easily, the fruit is ripe. Like melons, pineapples have a sweet scent when ripe. Soft, dark patches indicate bruising.

STORING FRUITS

Most fruits should be consumed quickly, when they are at their best and most nutritious. If it is necessary to store fruits, the correct conditions will help preserve their flavors and vitamin content. Remove tight packaging unless the label states otherwise.

COLD STORAGE

Wrapping fruits
To store citrus or hard fruits for longer than one week, wipe each fruit dry, and wrap in newspaper. Pack in a plastic bag or a box, and store in a cool, dry place.

● **Storing long-term** Store pears for up to six months at 30°F (–0.5°C). Store in single layers to avoid bruising.

STORING BERRIES

Preventing damage
To store soft berries, invert the container onto a cookie sheet lined with paper towels. Arrange berries in a single layer. Discard any damaged or moldy berries, and cover lightly with more paper towels before chilling.

KEEPING FRUITS

● **Storing grapes** Wrap bunches of grapes loosely in newsprint, and keep them in the dark. For a tasty treat, freeze whole grapes and snack on them straight from the freezer.
● **Getting the most juice** Citrus fruits such as oranges, lemons, and limes will yield the most juice if they are stored at room temperature. If they have been stored in a refrigerator, warm each one in the microwave on High for about five seconds.
● **Freezing bananas** Freeze whole bananas in their skins, wrapped in plastic wrap, for up to six months. Eat them while slightly frozen, or mash them and use in baking or drinks.

MAINTAINING A SUPPLY OF HERBS

Herbs make such a wonderful difference in even the simplest everyday dishes that it is worthwhile ensuring that you always have a supply of both fresh and dried versions. Even in winter, you can have a choice of fragrant leaves for both cooking and garnishing.

HARVESTING HERBS

● **Using potted herbs** Herbs in pots bought from a farm stand often have a limited life, but if you use just a few top shoots at a time, they will thrive longer.

● **Managing growth** Allow herbs to become established before harvesting them regularly, and pick evenly to keep them in good shape.

● **Growing herbs closeby** Grow your herbs on a kitchen window ledge or by the kitchen door so that they are always within easy reach, even when it is dark or raining.

● **Letting herbs flower** Allow a few herbs, such as borage, rosemary, or chives, to flower, and use as a pretty garnish.

CHOOSING & GROWING HERBS

Oregano has a spicy aroma and enhances tomatoes and meats

Chives have a mild onion flavor

Sage is strongly flavored and is used in stuffings

Tender flat-leaved parsley can be served whole in salads

Trailing silver thyme is pretty

Golden lemon thyme complements fish and chicken well

Growing herbs for cooking

Grow a variety of herbs together on your kitchen window ledge. Herbs that will grow well together for culinary use are parsley (the Italian flat-leaved variety is best), chives, thyme, oregano, and sage.

STORING HERBS

Once herbs are cut, they have a short life, and their aroma and flavor soon diminish. With careful storage, however, herbs can be kept fresh for several days. Tender-leaved herbs such as basil, chervil, and coriander wilt quickly, so they should be used up as soon as possible.

PREPARING DELICATE HERBS FOR STORAGE

Cut stems diagonally

Be careful not to crush herbs with bag

1 Before storing delicate herbs, cut the ends off the stems with a sharp knife. Place the herbs in a tall glass of cold water covering at least 1 in (2.5 cm) of the stems. Add a pinch of sugar to the water.

2 Place a plastic bag loosely over the herbs and glass, and secure the bag with a rubber band. Store in a cool place or in the refrigerator. Change the water and trim the stems every one or two days.

REVIVING HERBS

Use plant mister

Reviving limp herbs
To refresh fresh sprigs of delicate herbs that have wilted, place them on paper towels and moisten them with a fine mist of water. Chill briefly in the refrigerator before use.

DAIRY FOODS

Dairy products are highly nutritious foods, but they are often high in fat and should therefore be used in moderate quantities. The refrigerator is the best place for storage, although many dairy products also freeze well.

EGGS

Eggs are an excellent source of both protein and vitamins. They are an extremely versatile food and can be boiled, fried, poached, or used to thicken, emulsify, coat, bind, or glaze. Eggs are sensitive to temperature changes and should be warmed to room temperature before use.

MARKING BOILED EGGS

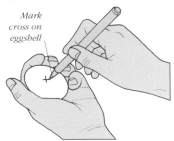

Mark cross on eggshell

Using a pen
Use a food-coloring pen to mark a cross on hard-cooked eggs. The cross will distinguish them from uncooked eggs if stored together.

TESTING EGGS

Salt water

Checking for freshness
Dissolve 2 tbsp (30 ml) salt in 2 cups (500 ml) water. Place the eggs in the water. If an egg sinks, it is fresh; if it floats, it is stale.

BUYING & STORING

● **Checking for cracks** When buying eggs, move each egg gently in the carton to check that none are damaged.
● **Keeping freshness** Store eggs in a carton in the refrigerator to prevent them from losing moisture and absorbing odors through their shells from strongly flavored foods nearby. Avoid poor caddies.
● **Storing correctly** Always store eggs with the pointed end down, to center the yolk and keep the eggs fresh.

CREAM

There are several types of cream, each of which has different properties, depending on the butterfat content. The butterfat content also determines the cream's richness, flavor, and whipping characteristics. The more fat a cream contains, the less likely it is to curdle.

STORING CREAM

Pour cream into ice-cube tray

Freezing in an ice tray
Open-freeze heavy cream in an ice-cube tray, then put the cubes into freezer bags, and store in the freezer. The cubes can be added directly to hot soups, sauces, or casseroles.

USING CREAM

● **Heavy cream** Choose heavy cream when you need softly whipped cream for folding into mousse-type desserts, or for piping. Light cream will not hold the air as well and will lose its fluffiness quickly.
● **Low-fat alternative** Mix a few tablespoonfuls of plain yogurt or whipped cottage cheese into whipped heavy cream to lighten creamy desserts or cake fillings.
● **Crème fraîche** Use crème fraîche as a substitute for light or sour cream in hot sauces, since it can be heated to boiling without curdling.

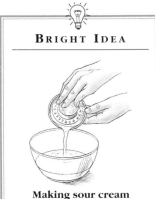

BRIGHT IDEA

Making sour cream
To make sour cream, add 1 tsp (5 ml) lemon juice to ⅔ cup (150 ml) light cream. Stir, and let stand until thickened.

CHEESE

Cheese is a high-protein food and has many culinary uses. It can be used to add flavor to fillings and sauces, and forms the basis of some desserts. Most cheese is eaten uncooked in salads and sandwiches, or as part of a buffet. All cheese is best served at room temperature.

STORING SOFT CHEESE

● **Freezing cheese** Freeze cheese only if it contains more than 45 percent fat, since cheese with a lower fat content will separate.

Wrapping in grape leaves
Wrap pieces of soft cheese such as brie in blanched, fresh grape leaves, or in brine-packed leaves that have been rinsed. This will keep the cheese fresh for 3–4 days if stored in the refrigerator.

KEEPING FETA CHEESE

Add sprigs of herbs for flavor

Preserving in oil
Store cubes of feta cheese in a jar. Add sprigs of herbs, garlic cloves, or chilies for flavor. Fill the jar with good-quality olive oil and refrigerate. Use the oil for salad dressings.

TRADITIONAL TIP

Keeping cheese moist
To keep hard cheeses such as mature cheddar or Parmesan moist during storage, wrap in a clean piece of muslin or cotton cloth that has been dampened with beer. Place in an airtight container, and store in the refrigerator for 1–2 weeks.

BUTTER

Butter is a natural product that is made from cream. It can be salted or unsalted and is a valuable fat for use in baking, since it adds body and richness. Butter can be used for light sautéeing or, if mixed with herbs or other ingredients, as a flavoring.

STORING BUTTER

● **Keeping odors out** Always wrap butter well or store it in a closed container, since it easily picks up tastes from strongly flavored foods.
● **Storing at low temperature** Keep unsalted butter in the freezer for up to six months. Freeze salted butter for only three months, since changes in flavor can occur at very low temperatures.
● **Clarifying butter** To store butter for several weeks, heat it gently until frothing but not browned. Strain through cheesecloth to remove salt and moisture, then refrigerate.

PREPARING & STORING HERB-FLAVORED BUTTER

Blending with herbs
Make flavored butter by stirring chopped fresh herbs or garlic into softened butter. Use a fork to work the herbs in thoroughly. Serve with grilled meats and fish.

Cutting out shapes
To make shaped butter pats, roll out the butter on a sheet of waxed paper. Use a small cookie cutter to cut out shapes. Store in a container in the refrigerator.

MEAT AND POULTRY

M EAT OF ALL KINDS IS A GOOD SOURCE OF PROTEIN, B vitamins, and iron. Fat, which is present in varying degrees, is necessary for flavor and tenderness, but you should avoid eating high-fat cuts of meat too often.

BUYING

T he most important rule to follow when you are buying fresh meat is to buy it from a reputable supplier. You must be able to rely on the butcher or grocery store to have hung and stored the meat properly, and perhaps to advise you correctly about cuts of meat and cooking.

SELECTING MEAT
● **Checking the color** Beef should be dark red with a slightly brownish tinge and a light marbling of fat. In the case of lamb, the darker the color, the older the animal.
● **Choosing the right cut** In general, the front part of an animal produces the toughest cuts of meat, suitable for slow cooking. Tender cuts come from the middle, which has the least-used muscles.
● **Buying quality cuts** Tough cuts may be inexpensive, but they take longer to cook, raising energy costs.

MONEY-SAVING TIP

Skinning chicken pieces
Chicken skin is high in fat, so it should be avoided in low-fat diets. If you need skinless chicken pieces, buy them with the skins on, and remove the skin yourself. Pull off the skin using your fingertips.

SERVING QUANTITIES PER PERSON	
CUTS OF MEAT OR POULTRY	QUANTITIES
Steaks without bone, such as beef, lamb, or pork fillet, lean beef sirloin, or pork loin.	4½–6 oz (125–175 g)
Steaks on the bone, such as T-bone steaks or leg-of-lamb steaks.	6–8 oz (175–225 g)
Lamb chops or cutlets on the bone, or boneless lamb chops.	2 small or 1 large
Pork chops with bone.	1 large
Cuts with a high proportion of bone, such as pork spare ribs, beef shanks, or oxtail.	14 oz–1 lb 2 oz (400–500 g)
Lean casserole meats, such as diced lamb shoulder, or stir-fry meats such as pork fillet.	4½–5½ oz (125–150 g)
Roasts on the bone, such as beef rib, leg or shoulder of lamb, or pork loin.	8–11 oz (225–300 g)
Roasts without bone, such as beef rib, rolled leg of lamb, or pork loin.	4½–6 oz (125–175 g)
Chicken pieces on the bone, such as drumsticks, thighs, wings, or quarters.	2 pieces or 1 quarter
Whole roast chicken or turkey on the bone.	12 oz (350 g) oven-ready
Whole roast duck or goose on the bone.	2 lb 4 oz (1 kg) oven-ready
Organ meats, such as liver, kidneys, or hearts.	3½–4½ oz (100–125 g)

STORING

The correct storage of meat and poultry is vitally important, since they can deteriorate quickly, especially if kept at warm temperatures. Refrigerate meat and poultry as soon as possible after buying. In warm weather, pack them in a cooler bag to transport them home.

FREEZING MEAT

Fold sheet of waxed paper around each chop

Separating meat pieces
When freezing hamburgers, chops, or steaks, which tend to stick together when frozen, separate them with pieces of waxed paper or freezer wrap. You will then be able to remove the quantity needed without thawing the whole batch.

FREEZING POULTRY

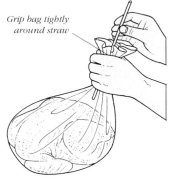

Grip bag tightly around straw

Expelling air
To remove excess air when packing whole poultry ready for freezing, place the bird in a plastic freezer bag, and gather up the opening, leaving a gap of about ¼ in (5 mm). Insert a straw through the gap, and suck out as much air as possible.

SAFETY

● **Keeping raw meats cold** Always put fresh meat and poultry into the refrigerator as soon as you arrive home. Store in covered containers so that the meat cannot drip onto other foods.
● **Preventing contamination** Keep different types of meat separate during storage. Always wash your hands and utensils after handling each type of raw meat and before preparing other types of meat or food.
● **Using thawed foods** Always use any thawed meat or poultry quickly, and do not be tempted to refreeze it, since this will increase the risk of food poisoning when the meat is eaten.

THAWING MEAT AND POULTRY

Immerse bird fully in water

Immersing in water
To speed up the thawing of a whole turkey or chicken, leave it in its freezer-proof wrapping, immerse it in a large basin of cold water, and place in the refrigerator. Change the water at frequent intervals until the poultry is completely thawed.

● **Allowing time** Allow plenty of time for meat and poultry to thaw. In a refrigerator, thawing may take several hours, or even two or three days in the case of large roasts or whole birds.

● **Preventing drips** Place meat or poultry on a large plate if thawing in a refrigerator. Lay paper towels underneath the meat or poultry to absorb the juices and prevent them from dripping onto other foods.
● **Thawing in the refrigerator** You may need to remove refrigerator shelves to fit a large bird into a small refrigerator. Leave the bird in its wrapping, but puncture the seal. Always use a drip tray.
● **Checking for ice** To ensure that whole poultry is completely thawed, feel inside the cavity, and check whether the legs and thigh joints move easily.
● **Using a skewer** To make sure that a large roast is completely thawed, push a skewer through the thickest part of the meat. You should be able to feel with the skewer if there is any ice remaining.

REFRIGERATING MEATS

● **Storing raw meat** Raw meat and poultry should ideally be stored on the bottom shelf of a refrigerator in a pan. This will ensure that their juices do not drip onto other foods.
● **Arranging meats** Keep fresh, ready-to-eat foods on the top shelf, and cooked meats on the middle shelf above raw meats.
● **Removing wrappings** If you purchase meat that is wrapped in paper, discard the paper and transfer the meat to a covered dish before storing it in the refrigerator. However, if meat is packed in a sealed tray, you can keep it safely in the tray for storage.
● **Using plastic wrap** Place meat or poultry in a deep dish for storing, and cover the dish tightly with plastic wrap. Make sure that the plastic wrap does not touch the food's surface.

FISH AND SHELLFISH

THE MOST IMPORTANT THING TO REMEMBER about using fish and shellfish is that they must be totally fresh. They deteriorate quickly, so to enjoy them at their best, buy only what you need, store it with care, and use it as soon as possible.

FISH

Fish is a very important part of a healthy diet. There are so many varieties from which to choose, suitable for all cooking methods, that you will find one that is appropriate for any occasion. If you prefer not to have to bone fish, ask the supplier to fillet it for you.

CHECKING FOR SIGNS OF FRESHNESS

Eyes are clear and bright, not sunken or dull

Scales are intact and shiny

Gills are bright red in color

Moist, shiny skin is not slimy and has no abrasions

Looking closely for freshness
Look for clear, bright eyes and moist, shiny skin. The gills, if present, should be bright red, and the scales should be difficult to remove. When pressed with a fingertip, the flesh should spring back easily. The fish should smell fresh and clean.

CHOOSING FISH

● **Round, white fish** Large round fish, such as cod, are usually sold cut into steaks, cutlets, or fillets, with or without the skin.
● **Flat fish** Large flat fish, such as halibut or turbot, are sold whole or in fillets or steaks. Small fish such as flounder are sold whole or in fillets.
● **Oily fish** These include salmon, herring, mackerel, trout, and sardines, and are sold whole or in fillets. Oily fish are an important source of omega-3 fatty acids, said to help prevent heart disease.

REFRESHING FISH

Immerse fillet completely in iced water

"Crimping" a fillet
If a fish fillet becomes slightly limp on the way home from shopping, revive it in the way that anglers do, by "crimping" it. Add 1 tbsp (15 ml) sea salt to 4 cups (1 liter) iced water in a bowl. Soak the fish in the icy salt water for about 15 minutes.

REFRIGERATING FISH

Pack ice cubes closely around sides of fish to chill it quickly

Packing with ice
Speed up the chilling of fresh fish in the refrigerator by placing ice cubes or crushed ice around it. Alternatively, fill two plastic bags with ice and seal, then place the fish between them. Make sure that you remove the bags before the ice has melted.

FREEZING FISH

● **Glazing** To keep fish fillets moist in the freezer, first open-freeze the fish until solid, then dip briefly into iced water. A thin covering of ice will form over the fish. Whole fish can be dipped twice in order to produce a thicker ice layer. Then wrap the fish and freeze.
● **Labeling** Always clearly label fish packs before freezing with the date they were frozen. White fish has a storage life of 12 months; oily fish, six months. Cooked fish dishes keep for just three months in the freezer.
● **Refreezing** Check with the supplier that fish has not been previously frozen. It is not advisable to refreeze fish.

SHELLFISH

It is especially important with shellfish to make sure that you buy them from a reputable supplier. Avoid any that may be contaminated or not fresh, since they could cause serious illness. As in the case of fish, shellfish should not be kept for long before preparing and cooking.

BUYING SHELLFISH

● **Mussels and clams** When buying live mussels or clams, choose those with tightly closed shells. Avoid any that will not close if tapped, and those with broken shells, since they may be dead and could therefore cause food poisoning if eaten.
● **Mussels** When buying mussels, avoid those covered with sand, since large amounts will be difficult to remove.
● **Scallops** Buy scallops that are a creamy ivory; coral, if attached, should be bright orange. If they are too white, they may have been soaked in water to increase weight.
● **Lobster** When buying a lobster, choose one that is between 1 and 2 lb (0.5 and 1 kg) in weight. Small lobsters may have too little flesh inside, while very large ones can be coarse, chewy, and dry.

BUYING CRAB

● **Choosing** If you like the white meat from the claws, buy a male crab. For the rich pink coral from inside the body shell, choose a female.

Hold crab by front claws, and shake gently

Checking the weight
When buying a cooked whole crab, hold it firmly by the claws, and shake it gently. The crab should feel heavy for its size. If it feels light or rattles, it is of poor quality and has water inside.

REFRIGERATING PRAWNS

● **Rinsing** Before storing fresh, raw shrimp in the refrigerator, rinse in cold water and drain well. Use within two days.

TRADITIONAL TIP

Cleaning mussels
To clean mussels or clams, place them in cold water with a handful of raw oatmeal or cornmeal. Let stand for two hours. Mussels and clams will expel dirt as they feed.

STORING OYSTERS

Place curved side of shells downward in deep tray

Cover with clean dish towel dampened with cold water

Preventing loss of juices
Store live oysters curved side down to prevent loss of juices. Arrange in an open tray, cover with a damp cloth, and store in the bottom of the refrigerator. Use as quickly as possible, within 24 hours of purchase.

STORING LIVE SHELLFISH

Keep flow of cold water constant

Keeping crayfish alive
If you buy live crayfish, lobsters, or crabs, keep them alive until you are ready to cook them. Place the crayfish in as large and deep a bowl as possible in the sink, and keep the cold-water tap running continuously into it.

OCTOPUS & SQUID

● **Checking the weight** Avoid buying octopus that is more than 2 lb (1 kg) in weight, since it is likely to be tough.
● **Choosing for freshness** Choose octopus or squid with a good color, a slippery appearance, and a fresh, salty smell. Avoid any with broken outer skins or those lying in puddles of ink.
● **Saving the ink** If you can, buy squid that has not already been cleaned and still has its ink sac, and clean it at home. Use the ink to add flavor and color to a sauce.
● **Cleaning** Clean octopus or squid before storing them. Put in the refrigerator in a bowl covered with plastic wrap.

BAKED GOODS

WHETHER YOU BAKE BREAD AND CAKES YOURSELF or buy them ready-made, smart storage will enable you to keep baked goods fresh and appetizing for as long as possible. Bread and most cakes can also be frozen successfully.

BREAD

You may not always be able to buy fresh bread every day, but it is possible to keep bread fresh for several days if you follow a few commonsense rules. Good air circulation is necessary to prevent bread from becoming stale or moldy in storage, or from drying out.

REVIVING STALE LOAVES OF BREAD

Adding garlic butter
Cut a stale French loaf in thick slices almost to the base, then spread garlic butter between the slices. Wrap in foil, and bake in a hot oven for 8-10 minutes.

Steaming in a pan
Place a slightly stale loaf of bread in a colander over a pan holding a small amount of boiling water. Cover with the pan lid until the bread is warmed by the steam.

PREVENTING STALENESS
● **Adding fat** For moist, home-baked bread that will keep well, add 1 tbsp (15 g) fat to every 4 cups (500 g) flour.
● **Cooling bread** Always cool freshly baked bread before storing because condensation would encourage mold.
● **Allowing air circulation** Stand a bread crock on a triangular wooden pot stand or brick to increase air circulation.
● **Scalding a bread crock** If you always store bread in an earthenware bread crock or metal bread box, scald the crock or box regularly with boiling water to kill any mold spores, then dry thoroughly.

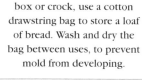
FREEZING BREAD
● **Separating slices** Before freezing sliced bread, place waxed paper between the slices so that you can remove them without having to thaw the whole loaf.
● **Keeping crust** Freeze crusty bread such as French baguettes for no longer than 7–10 days. If it is frozen longer, the crust will begin to flake off.
● **Freezing dough** Freeze unrisen bread dough for up to one month and thaw for about six hours at room temperature, let rise, and bake.
● **Thawing** Thaw bread loaves and rolls in a warm oven, and they will be crisp and fragrant, like freshly baked bread.

STORING BREAD

Bowl must be big enough to cover loaf completely

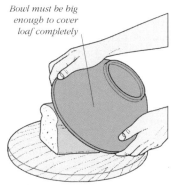

Making a bread crock
If you have nowhere to store a loaf of bread, place the loaf on a wooden bread board, and cover with an upturned earthenware bowl. Alternatively, wrap the loaf in a clean, dry dish towel.

BREAD CRUMBS

Bread crumbs are a valuable pantry ingredient, whether in their fresh form or dried for longer storage. Keep both white and whole-wheat bread crumbs for use in stuffings, coatings, or toppings. Bread crumbs add texture and interest to both sweet and savory dishes.

PREPARING BREAD CRUMBS FOR STORAGE

Bag keeps crumbs tidily in one place

Mix in herbs for savory bread crumbs

Making dry bread crumbs
Dry leftover bread to make into bread crumbs. Arrange slices on a baking sheet, and bake at 300°F (150°C) or until completely dry and lightly browned. Place in a plastic bag and crush with a rolling pin.

Seasoning bread crumbs
Add seasonings to fresh or dried bread crumbs to coat fish and chicken, or to use as toppings for baked and grilled dishes. Stir in crumbled dried herbs, finely grated Parmesan cheese, spices, salt, and pepper to taste.

MAKING & STORING

● **Using a food processor** To make fine fresh or dried bread crumbs quickly, drop pieces or slices of fresh bread or toast into the moving blade of a food processor.

● **Making small amounts** If you only need a small amount of bread crumbs, use a clean coffee grinder to grind small pieces of toast into crumbs.

● **Freezing crumbs** Keep freshly made bread crumbs in a plastic freezer bag in the freezer for up to six months.

● **Storing in a jar** Use a screw-top jar to store dried bread crumbs for about a month. The crumbs must be completely dry before storing.

CAKES AND MUFFINS

Most people enjoy eating cakes, whether their choice is a simple cupcake or a luxurious layer cake. The very many different kinds of cake present a range of storage problems. The longest-keeping cakes are rich fruit cakes and sponge cakes made with honey. Most cakes freeze well.

STORING & USING CAKES

● **Slicing in half** Improve the storage life of a large fruit cake by cutting it in half across the middle, taking slices from the inside of the cake, then sliding the two halves back together. Store in an airtight container.

● **Placing on lid** Store an iced cake on the lid of a cookie tin with the inverted tin over it. You can then slice and remove pieces without risking damage.

● **Making trifle** Crumble leftover stale sponge cake in a dish, sprinkle with liqueur, and top with fruit and whipped cream to make a quick, triflelike dessert.

● **Topping desserts** Make dry cake into crumbs, and sprinkle over desserts and ices.

FREEZING CAKES

Wrap sides of each slice in one piece of paper

Storing cake slices
When freezing a large cake, cut it into slices before freezing, and interleave each slice with a piece of waxed paper. Reassemble the cake, and freeze as usual. You can then remove as many slices as you need without thawing the whole cake first.

REFRESHING MUFFINS

Moistening muffins
If muffins or cupcakes have become a little dry in storage, refresh them by brushing with milk and placing them in a warm oven for 6–8 minutes, or until warmed thoroughly. If they are very dry, dip them in milk before placing them in the oven.

PREPARING INGREDIENTS

QUICK REFERENCE
Vegetables, p. 363
Fruits and Nuts, p. 366
Herbs and Spices, p. 370
Dairy Foods, p. 372
Meat and Poultry, p. 374
Fish and Shellfish, p. 376

ONCE YOU HAVE PLANNED a menu and shopped carefully, you will need to begin preparing the ingredients. All good cooks will agree that sound skills in basic preparation methods are very important, whatever the type of food you are cooking, and whatever the occasion. Learn the correct way to prepare ingredients and you will save time and effort in the kitchen.

PREPARATION BASICS

The use of good-quality utensils is important even for basic food preparation – not only for the sake of efficiency, but also to make the task more pleasant. A sharp knife, for example, will make chopping and slicing quick and safe. As your skills improve, try new techniques.

CUTTING UP FOODS

Slicing safely
When slicing vegetables, use your knuckles to guide the knife and prevent it from cutting too close to your fingertips. Keep fingertips tucked in, and slice downward and forward.

CHOPPING EFFECTIVELY
● **Chopping finely** To chop food finely, use your knife like a pivot. Hold the tip down, and use a rocking action to chop.
● **Dicing foods** First, square one end of the vegetable or fruit. Cut into slices, stack, and cut lengthwise into sticks. Cut crosswise for diced pieces.

SLICING THINLY

Cutting julienne strips
To produce extra-thin julienne strips of vegetables, use a vegetable peeler to slice very fine ribbons. Then stack these together, and slice lengthwise as thinly as possible.

PREPARING STRIPS
● **Trimming vegetables** Before cutting julienne strips from vegetables such as carrots or cucumber, trim the vegetables into neat, rectangular blocks.
● **Cutting cabbage** To slice cabbage into thin strips, roll each leaf firmly like a jelly roll. Slice with a sharp knife.

DICING FRUITS

Lemon juice

Preventing discoloration
Sprinkle your cutting board with lemon juice before you dice apples or pears, then squeeze lemon juice on the cut fruits. This will keep the fruit from browning during preparation.

USING DICED FRUITS
● **Preventing sticking** If the blade of your knife becomes sticky while dicing sugary ingredients, dip it from time to time into a deep cup of very hot water placed nearby.
● **Using color** Consider adding diced fruits to a salad for a colorful "confetti" effect.

VEGETABLES

WHEN PREPARING VEGETABLES FOR COOKING BY ANY METHOD, it is important to retain their color, flavor, and nutrients. Prepare vegetables just before you need them, since they deteriorate quickly once they are peeled or cut.

GREEN VEGETABLES

Green vegetables, especially those that have delicate leaves, such as spinach, lose vitamins quickly once cut. If possible, tear the leaves rather than cutting or slicing them; otherwise, use a very sharp knife to ensure that the leaves are damaged as little as possible.

TRIMMING SPINACH

Removing stalks
To remove the stalks from large spinach leaves without cutting, fold each leaf vertically, grasp both sides with one hand, and pull the stalk sharply away from the leaf with the other hand.

TRIMMING BROCCOLI

Using broccoli stalks
To make use of thick broccoli stalks instead of discarding them, trim and slice them horizontally into ¼-in (5-mm) thick slices. Cook them for the same period of time as the tender florets.

PREPARING LEAVES
● **Cleaning leaves** To remove insects and dirt from green-leaved vegetables, wash leaves in a large bowl of cold, salted water before using.
● **Shredding leaves** Stack and tightly roll leaves of spinach, lettuce, or cabbage, and slice into coarse shreds to prepare for sautéeing or frying.
● **Using outer leaves** Save the tough outer leaves of a green cabbage for stuffing with a savory filling. To make the leaves flexible, blanch them in boiling water for one minute, then drain.

BULB VEGETABLES

Bulb vegetables include different varieties of onion, garlic, and leek, all of which are an invaluable source of flavor in savory dishes. They are also natural antibiotics. Onions and garlic seem to help lower blood cholesterol levels and therefore protect against heart disease.

AVOIDING ONION TEARS

● **Leaving roots intact** Leave the root end intact when slicing or dicing an onion. This will prevent the release of the strong juices and fumes that cause eyes to water.
● **Using vinegar** Sprinkle a little distilled white vinegar onto the cutting board. This will counteract the effects of the onion juices.
● **Burning a candle** Light a candle nearby when preparing onions to burn off the sulfuric fumes.

CRUSHING GARLIC

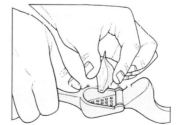

Using a garlic press
When using a garlic press, leave the peel on the garlic clove. The soft garlic flesh will still be pushed through the mesh, and the garlic press will be easy to clean out after using.

CLEANING LEEKS

Washing out dirt
To make sure you remove all the dirt between the leaves of a leek, slit it lengthwise, almost to the root end. Hold the leek under running water, fanning out the leaves to wash them thoroughly.

ROOT VEGETABLES

This category includes root vegetables such as carrots and turnips, as well as foods that are really tubers, the swollen roots of plants such as potatoes or yams. Root vegetables are good sources of vitamins and fiber, especially if the skins are not removed prior to cooking.

ADDING INTEREST
● **Keeping the tops** Trim all but ¾ in (2 cm) of the leafy tops from baby carrots and turnips, then cook and serve whole.

Making carrot flowers
Run a canelle knife or a fork crosswise down the length of a peeled carrot to make grooves. Then slice the carrot crosswise, producing flower shapes.

PREPARING ROOTS
● **Beets** Leave the roots and tops of whole beets untrimmed before boiling them, to prevent juices and color from leaking out.
● **Potatoes** To make crisp fries, rinse sliced potatoes in cold water to remove excess starch. Dry them thoroughly on paper towels before frying.
● **Jerusalem artichokes** To avoid annoying peeling, boil Jerusalem artichokes whole in their skins. The skins will rub off easily after cooking.
● **Young vegetables** Peel young root vegetables thinly or scrub them, because the peel is high in fiber and the flesh just under it is high in nutrients.

BRIGHT IDEA

Making hasselbacks
For really crisp, golden roast potatoes, make "hasselbacks." Peel the potatoes, then cut thin slices downward, not quite all the way through. Brush with oil, sprinkle with salt, and bake in a hot oven for 30–40 minutes until crisp and well browned.

SALAD VEGETABLES

Most salads need little preparation apart from the careful cleaning and trimming of all the ingredients to ensure that as many nutrients as possible are retained. To prevent loss of crispness, flavor, and vitamins, avoid preparing salad vegetables too far in advance.

PREPARING LEAVES
● **Tearing lettuce leaves** Always tear lettuce leaves, rather than cutting them with a knife, to make bite-sized pieces.
● **Removing the core** To take out the tough core from an iceberg lettuce, bang the lettuce firmly – core downward – on a countertop. Turn it over, and you should be able to twist and remove the core easily.
● **Drying the leaves** If you do not have a salad spinner, dry washed leaves by rolling them loosely in a clean dish towel. Hold both ends firmly, and shake the towel gently.
● **Refreshing a lettuce** To revive a limp head of lettuce, trim the stem and dip it into iced water for a few minutes.

STRINGING CELERY

Pull peeler blade down ridged outer edge of stem

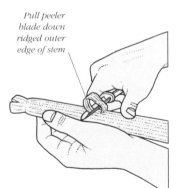

Using a vegetable peeler
To remove the tough strings quickly from the outer sticks of celery, separate all the celery ribs, and lightly stroke a swivel-bladed vegetable peeler down the length of each one.

PREPARING CUCUMBER

Drag edge of melon baller down cucumber

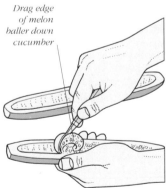

Removing seeds
Use a melon baller to scoop out the seeds from a cucumber before dicing or slicing. Cut the cucumber in half lengthwise, and scrape the melon baller down the middle to remove the seeds.

FRUIT VEGETABLES

These include sun-ripened vegetables such as eggplants, sweet peppers, tomatoes, and avocados. With their bright colors and fresh, rich flavors, fruit vegetables play an important role in ensuring that our everyday diet is not only varied, but also appetizing and nutritious.

CUTTING EGGPLANTS

● **Scoring** Cut a diamond pattern in the flesh of eggplant halves before grilling or baking, to ensure even cooking throughout.

Removing bitter juices
To reduce the bitterness of an eggplant, lay slices in a colander, and sprinkle with salt. Drain for 30 minutes, rinse, and dry. This also reduces oil absorption.

PEELING

● **Blanching** To peel tomatoes, place them in a pan of boiling water. Remove after one minute and place in cold water. The skins will peel off easily.

Grilling peppers
To skin whole peppers, place on foil, and grill until the skins blacken, turning often. Wrap the foil over so that steam will loosen the skins, then remove them.

TIMESAVING TIP

Insert spoon at wide end

Peeling a ripe avocado
Instead of trying to peel a ripe avocado with a knife, cut the avocado in half, and scoop out the flesh from each half in one piece using a large metal spoon. Keep the spoon close to the peel.

OTHER VEGETABLES

All kinds of vegetables, from all over the world, can be found in supermarkets today. Many do not fit into traditional categories, and some are, strictly speaking, not vegetables at all. Mushrooms are edible fungi, but they can be prepared in ways similar to many vegetables.

CLEANING & TRIMMING

● **Corn on the cob** Use a clean nylon hairbrush to remove the silk threads from corncobs without damaging the kernels.
● **Okra** When trimming the stalks from okra, ensure that you do not pierce the central parts and so release the sticky juices from the insides.
● **Chilies** If you need to reduce the strength of chilies for a milder flavor, scrape out the seeds and membranes inside. Wash your hands well or wear rubber gloves while preparing chilies, since they can irritate eyes or skin.
● **Zucchinis** If you are grating a zucchini for a salad, stir-fry, or stuffing, leave the stem on to give you a grip as you work.

PURÉEING SQUASH

Fibrous strings catch around blades

Removing fibers
To make a really smooth purée of cooked squash, whip with an electric mixer. The blades will pick up any fibrous strings during the process, so that you can remove them easily.

MUSHROOMS

Cultivated mushrooms should not be peeled or washed, since this reduces their flavor and vitamin content.

● **Cleaning** Wipe mushrooms gently with damp paper towels to remove dirt.
● **Keeping color** To ensure that cultivated mushrooms stay white during cooking, sprinkle with lemon juice.
● **Retaining vitamins** When marinating raw mushrooms, cover tightly with plastic wrap to prevent contact with the air and loss of vitamins.
● **Refreshing** To plump up dried mushrooms before use, immerse in boiling water for one minute. Dry before use.

FRUITS AND NUTS

Fruits and nuts require a range of preparation skills so that they can be presented at their best. Whether you are cooking fruits or serving them raw, whenever possible retain the skins and juices, since these contain nutrients.

CITRUS FRUITS

Citrus fruits are very versatile and are used in both sweet and savory dishes. Make use of every part of these fruits, including their zest or peels, juice, and flesh, which can be sliced or cut into segments. Always wash wax-coated fruits before removing the zest or cooking whole.

JUICING CITRUS FRUITS
● **Warming fruits** If citrus fruits have been stored in the refrigerator, they will yield the most juice if allowed to come to room temperature first.
● **Using a microwave** Pierce the skins of the fruits and heat for 10 seconds on High to increase the juice yield.
● **Squeezing easily** To make a citrus fruit easy to squeeze, first roll it under the palm of your hand on a counter.
● **Zesting and juicing** If you need both juice and zest from a citrus fruit, remove the zest before squeezing the fruit.

GARNISHING WITH FRUITS
● **Decorating slices** Before slicing citrus fruits for garnish, score grooves in the peel with a canelle knife or a fork; this gives the slices rippled edges.

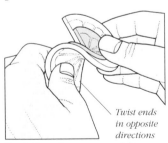

Twist ends in opposite directions

Twisting lemon and lime
Cut thin slices of lemon and lime. Place a lime slice on top of a lemon slice, and cut a slit halfway across the two. Twist the slices into a spiral, making an unusual fruit garnish.

CUTTING LEMON WEDGES

Removing pith
When making lemon wedges for garnishing, slice off the strip of pith running down the ridge of each wedge so that juice squeezes easily, without squirting.

PEELING & ZESTING
● **Removing pith** To peel an orange cleanly, immerse the whole fruit in boiling water for four minutes. Drain and cool, and the pith will come away with the zest.
● **Using a peeler** Pare citrus fruit rind with a vegetable peeler rather than a knife to avoid peeling the pith as well.
● **Saving zest** If you are squeezing fruit for juice but do not need the zest at the same time, remove it anyway, and freeze for later use.
● **Reusing skins** After squeezing citrus fruit halves, scrape the remaining flesh from inside the skins. Freeze the empty skins, and use as serving bowls for fruit salad, compote, or sorbet.

REMOVING SEGMENTS

Cut over bowl

Catching juice
Hold peeled citrus fruits such as oranges or grapefruit over a bowl when removing segments to catch excess juice. Add this juice to fruit salads or drinks.

USING LEFTOVER PEEL

Keep peel in canning jar, covered with alcohol

Flavoring vodka
Place strips of thinly pared orange, lemon, or lime zest in a canning jar, and pour vodka over to cover. Mature in a refrigerator for 6–8 months. Add the vodka to drinks, or stir a tablespoonful into desserts such as fruit salad, ice cream, or chocolate mousse.

FRUITS WITH PITS

Fruits with pits, such as peaches, apricots, and plums, usually need little preparation other than removing the pits. Occasionally, it is necessary to remove the skins to achieve a smooth texture. Fruits that have thick skins, such as mangoes, always need to be peeled.

PITTING & PEELING

● **Twisting fruits apart** Find the natural indentation in peaches or nectarines, and cut around each fruit along this line through to the pit. Then twist the two halves apart.
● **Pitting plums** Cut around the "waist" of a firm plum, across the indentation, then twist the two halves apart.
● **Blanching and peeling** Remove skins easily from plums or peaches by plunging them into boiling water for one minute, then into ice-cold water until they are cool. Drain, and peel off the skins.

PITTING & CUBING A MANGO

1 Remove a thick slice from both sides of the fruit, cutting as close to the pit as possible. Peel the skin and flesh around the pit with a sharp knife, and cube the flesh.

2 Score each thick slice into squares, cutting down to the skin but not through it. Push the skin out into a convex curve so that the cubes can be removed easily.

SOFT FRUITS

Luscious soft fruits are best served very simply, so preparation is usually minimal. The only essential task is to pick over the fruit thoroughly to remove damaged parts, hulls, and stems, as well as dirt. Always handle soft, ripe berries gently to prevent them from bruising.

PREPARING SOFT FRUITS

● **Washing berries** If delicate berry fruits need to be washed, place them in a colander and rinse under running water, shaking the colander gently. Place on a paper towel to dry.
● **Preparing gooseberries** Use scissors to snip off the tops and bottoms of gooseberries before cooking or serving.
● **Enhancing flavor** Add a squeeze of lemon juice to berry fruits such as blueberries or strawberries to bring out the flavor. For a special occasion, sprinkle the fruits lightly with rum or brandy.
● **Using overripe fruits** If soft fruits are slightly overripe and not looking their best, mash them lightly with a fork. Serve spooned over vanilla ice cream, or stir into plain yogurt to make a quick dessert.

HULLING SOFT FRUITS

● **Removing stems** To hull red- or blackcurrants easily, pull each stem gently through the prongs of a fork, and carefully push off the fruit.

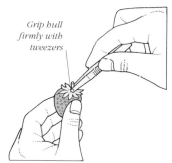

Grip hull firmly with tweezers

Hulling a strawberry
Use flat-ended tweezers to grasp and remove the leafy hull from a fresh strawberry without damaging the fruit. This method will also prevent the juice from staining your fingers.

USING FROZEN FRUITS

● **Keeping shape** To make sure frozen strawberries stay in good shape when thawing, put them into a serving dish while frozen, thaw slowly in the refrigerator, and serve while still slightly chilled.
● **Decorating from frozen** Decorate desserts with soft fruits such as raspberries or blackberries straight from the freezer. Let them thaw in place for about 30 minutes.
● **Quick-thawing fruits** To thaw frozen fruit quickly without using a microwave, place the fruits in a container in a dish of warm water for 30 minutes.
● **Making sorbet** Whip up an instant sorbet by puréeing frozen raspberries in a food processor with confectioners' sugar to taste. Spoon into chilled glasses, and serve.

OTHER FRESH FRUITS

This section includes many exotic tropical fruits, some of which may need different methods of preparation than those required for familiar, home-grown fruits. Many tropical fruits are in fact best served simply to show off their vibrant colors and delicate, scented flesh.

PREPARING KIWI FRUIT

Cut large slice off top, then scoop out flesh

Removing flesh
Instead of peeling kiwi fruit, cut a slice from the top, and scoop out the flesh with a teaspoon as you would with a soft-boiled egg. For packed lunches or picnics, slice off the top, and wrap the whole fruit in plastic.

CORING PEARS
● **Coring a pear half** Cut a pear in half before removing the core, rather than coring it whole. This makes it easy to see the core, and will ensure that no flesh is wasted.

Scoop core out carefully from base of whole pear

Using a melon baller
If you plan to cook and serve pears whole, remove the cores from the underside of each fruit by scooping out with a small melon baller or the pointed tip of a vegetable peeler. This way, the pears will keep their shape.

SERVING FRUITS SIMPLY
● **Strawberries** Bring out the delicious flavor of fresh strawberries by tossing them together with fresh, juicy segments of pink grapefruit.
● **Figs** To serve figs whole, cut a deep cross about two-thirds of the way through the fruit from the stem end. Squeeze the fruits gently to open them out ready to eat.
● **Papaya** Present papaya simply, like an avocado, as an appetizer. Cut the papaya in half or in quarters, and scoop out the seeds with a teaspoon. Serve with a slice of lime. Alternatively, serve slices of papaya sprinkled with lime juice as an appetizer or dessert.

PREPARING MELON
● **Leveling the base** Before serving a melon half or slice, cut a thin slice from the base of the fruit so that it sits firmly on the serving plate, making the cutting steady and easy.

Conserving juice
When scooping out melon seeds, hold the melon above a sieve placed over a bowl so that none of the juice is wasted. Spoon the melon juice over the melon to serve. Alternatively, add it to fruit salads or drinks.

BRIGHT IDEA

Coring pineapple rings
Remove the hard central core, and trim the edges of fresh pineapple slices with metal cookie cutters. Use a small round cutter to stamp out the central core, and a larger one to trim the skin and remove "eyes" from the slice.

TRIMMING & PEELING
● **Star fruit** To remove the brown, damaged edges that can spoil the appearance of a ripe star fruit, run a vegetable peeler quickly down the point of each ridge before slicing and serving the fruit.
● **Pomegranate** Make slits in the skin of a pomegranate, dividing it into segments. Peel each segment back, and remove with the pith.
● **Dates** If dates have become dull in color, or if sugar has crystallized on the surfaces, rinse them quickly under hot water. Then dry the dates thoroughly before serving.
● **Tamarillos** Always peel tamarillos thinly before serving, since the peel has an unpleasant, bitter taste.
● **Kiwi fruit** If the skin of a kiwi fruit is difficult to peel, plunge the fruit into boiling water for about 30 seconds, then try peeling it again.

DRIED FRUITS

Dried fruits are a concentrated source of nutrients, with apricots and peaches in particular being rich in iron and vitamin A. Many are ready to eat, but some need soaking, which provides an opportunity to add flavor by using fruit juice, tea, brandy, or wine.

PREPARING FRUITS
● **Chilling fruits** Chop dried fruits easily by freezing them for one hour before use.
● **Making a breakfast compote** Place dried fruit in a thermos, and top off with boiling water. Cap, let stand overnight, and serve warm for breakfast.
● **Saving time** To speed up soaking, put fruits in a bowl and cover with water. Cover the bowl, and microwave on High for 90 seconds. Let stand five minutes before use.
● **Using a food processor** Chop dried fruit with a little granulated sugar so that the fruits do not stick to the blades.

SOAKING FRUITS

Plumping up with tea
To plump up dried fruit for adding to cakes or quick breads, soak in tea instead of water. Choose a tea with a distinctive flavor, such as Earl Grey.

CHOPPING FRUITS

Preventing sticking
To chop sticky dried fruits, such as apricots, without the fruits sticking to the blades, cut with kitchen scissors or a sharp knife dipped frequently in hot water.

NUTS

Nuts are a versatile, highly nutritious food, useful in both sweet and savory dishes. Use fresh, whole nuts, with or without shells, and take the time to crack, chop, blanch, or grind them before adding to a dish, since their flavor is far better than ready-prepared nuts.

USING HAZELNUTS
● **Grinding** Grind whole, fresh hazelnuts in a food processor, and use them as a lower-fat alternative to ground almonds.

Removing skins
To remove the fine skins from hazelnuts easily, toast them lightly under a hot broiler until they are pale golden, then pour onto a clean dish towel. Fold the towel over the nuts, and rub them firmly. The skins will fall off.

USING FRESH COCONUT
● **Extracting milk** Pierce two of the eyes at one end of a fresh coconut with a skewer, and pour out the milk.

Continue tapping by crack

Opening the shell
Crack a whole, fresh coconut by tapping around the widest part with a small hammer to find the nut's natural fault line. Once a crack appears in the shell, continue turning and tapping the coconut to make a clean break.

SHELLING & BLANCHING
● **Cracking brazil nuts** To make brazil-nut shells easy to crack, place the nuts in the freezer for about six hours, or bake them for 15 minutes at 400°F (200°C). Let them cool before cracking.
● **Preventing breakage** To keep nut kernels whole and undamaged, press the middle of each shell gently with a nutcracker, turning the nut so that it cracks evenly.
● **Slitting chestnut skins** Before roasting or toasting whole chestnuts, cut a cross in each skin with a sharp knife to prevent them from exploding.
● **Microwave blanching** To blanch almonds, place them in boiling water, and microwave on High for two minutes. Drain, and peel off the skins.

HERBS AND SPICES

HERBS AND SPICES WILL CONTRIBUTE A WONDERFUL VARIETY OF FLAVORS to your cooking. Always add herbs and spices to a dish in small amounts, tasting the food after each addition, until you achieve the flavor you desire.

FRESH HERBS

Treat all herbs gently during preparation, since they contain volatile oils that can easily be lost. Soft-leaved herbs, such as basil, coriander, and chervil, are particularly delicate. Most herbs are best added toward the end of cooking to preserve their flavor and color.

MAXIMIZING FLAVOR

- **Washing herbs** Shake herbs quickly under cold running water. Dry on paper towels.
- **Using stems** After using the leaves of fresh herbs such as parsley or dill, chop the stems finely and use to flavor stocks, sauces, and stews.
- **Flavoring with sage** To add a rich, intense flavor to chicken or pork roasts, tuck whole sage leaves just under the skin of the chicken or into small slits cut into the fat of the pork before roasting.
- **Replacing chives** Scallion tops are similar in flavor and color to chives. Chop them and use as a substitute when chives are not available.

CHOPPING PARSLEY

Scissors cut herbs finely without mess

Using kitchen scissors
To chop parsley easily and quickly, remove the stems, wash and dry the sprigs, and place in a large cup. Use a pair of kitchen scissors to snip the parsley inside the cup.

PREPARING MINT

Releasing flavor
To obtain the maximum flavor from fresh mint leaves, bruise them first to release their volatile oils. Place them in a small bowl, and pound gently with the end of a rolling pin. Use immediately.

MAKING A BOUQUET GARNI

Orange zest

- **Mixing flavors** Combine sprigs of rosemary, parsley, and thyme with a bay leaf and a stick of celery to flavor red-meat dishes and rich bean dishes.
- **Flavoring fish** Add delicate herbs such as parsley, chervil, or dill to a bouquet garni for dishes including white fish.
- **Adding tarragon** For a scented flavor in chicken or pork dishes with white-wine or cream sauces, add a sprig of tarragon to the bouquet-garni mix.
- **Using horseradish** Add a bruised root of horseradish to a bouquet garni to flavor stocks or sauces for beef dishes.

Adding citrus flavor
Introduce a delicate citrus flavor to a bouquet garni by adding a thinly pared strip of orange, lemon, or lime zest to the mixed herbs. Use to flavor soups, sauces, or casseroles.

PREPARING BASIL

Use fingertips to tear gently

Tearing leaves
To avoid losing the flavor and color too quickly from delicate-leaved herbs such as basil, tear the leaves with your fingers instead of chopping them with a knife. Add to savory dishes at the end of the cooking period.

DRIED HERBS

Dried herbs are a convenient substitute if fresh herbs are not available. However, they have a much more concentrated flavor than fresh herbs, so you will need to reduce quantities. As a general rule, use about half the amount of dried herbs that you would of fresh.

USING DRIED HERBS

● **Thyme** To remove the leaves of dried thyme from their woody stems, place the sprigs on a clean paper towel, fold over, and rub the herbs vigorously. If using a small amount, rub the herb stems between your fingertips.

● **Bay leaves** Soak dried bay leaves in water for a few minutes before threading onto skewers between cubes of meat, chicken, or fish. The leaves will add flavor to the meat without burning.

● **Stalks** Scatter the stripped, dry stalks of thyme or rosemary onto the coals of a barbecue to give a smoky, herb flavor to the food that is being cooked.

PREPARING ROSEMARY

Stripping leaves
To strip the leaves quickly from the woody stems of rosemary, hold the tip of each sprig in one hand, and strip the leaves off with a finger and thumb, pushing against the direction of growth.

BRIGHT IDEA

Using a tea infuser
If you want to enhance the flavor of a dish without leaving bits of herb behind, put the herbs into a tea infuser, and stir them into the dish at the end of cooking.

SPICES

Most spices can be added directly to dishes during cooking. However, it is well worth spending a little time to crush, bruise, or roast them first to bring out as much flavor as possible. Once ground or bruised, spices should be used immediately to prevent loss of flavor.

USING VANILLA SEEDS

Use tip of knife to scrape seeds from inside opened pod

Removing seeds
To obtain a really strong flavor from a vanilla bean, use the tiny, oily seeds rather than infusing the whole pod. To extract the seeds, cut the pod lengthwise using a sharp knife. Then add the seeds directly to sweet dishes.

BRUISING GINGER

Use pan to crush ginger

Using a heavy pan
Bruise a whole piece of peeled, fresh ginger by placing it on a cutting board and hitting it with the flat base of a heavy pan. If bruised ginger is added to preserves or hot drinks, its flavor will be infused quickly.

CRUSHING & GRINDING

● **Avoiding mess** Crush whole spices by placing them in a small plastic bag and hitting them several times with a rolling pin or a meat mallet.

● **Mixing spices** Mix together 75 percent black or white peppercorns and 25 percent whole allspice. Keep in a peppermill ready to grind onto grilled meats or fish. You could also mix black, white, pink, and green peppercorns to spice up plain chicken.

● **Making chili powder** Roast four dried, red chilies at 400°F (200°C) for 10 minutes. Remove the stems and seeds, then use a mortar and pestle to grind the chilies into a ready-to-use powder.

DAIRY FOODS

THERE IS AN INCREASING CHOICE AMONG DAIRY PRODUCTS, and many of the new items offer a wide range of flavors and low-fat alternatives for good health. Some low-fat products are not stable if cooked, so heat them gently.

EGGS

Versatile and nutritious, eggs are the basis of countless sweet and savory dishes. Whole eggs are used for a range of cooked dishes, whites are used for adding volume and binding, and yolks are used for glazing and enriching. Extra yolks or whites can be stored.

SEPARATING EGGS

Using the eggshell
Crack the shell gently on the edge of a bowl, and carefully pull the two halves apart. Let the white run into the bowl, and pour the yolk several times from one half of the shell to the other.

MAKING MERINGUE

● **Whipping egg whites** Whip egg whites in a copper bowl if you have one; it will produce the greatest volume.
● **Using at room temperature** Remove egg whites from the refrigerator about an hour before needed; they whip best at room temperature.
● **Keeping whites** Egg whites whipped with sugar will keep their shape for several hours; plain whipped whites must be used directly after whipping.
● **Saving overwhipped whites** To rescue overbeaten egg whites, beat another white separately until frothy, then stir it into the mixture. Whip again to regain the bulk.

USING WHOLE EGGS

● **Glazing** To make a golden brown glaze for pastry, bread, or muffins, beat an egg with a pinch of salt, and brush over the food before baking.
● **Extending an egg glaze** Make eggs go further for glazing by beating 1 tbsp (15 ml) oil with each whole egg.
● **Making omelets** When mixing, beat in 1 tbsp (15 ml) of water to every two eggs for lighter results. Alternatively, separate the white and whip until stiff, then fold into the yolks for a soufflé omelet.
● **Scrambling eggs** Beat in a little milk with the eggs to make creamy scrambled eggs.

USING EGG WHITES

Wipe bowl with cut lemon

Removing traces of grease
Before whipping egg whites, make sure that your bowl is free of grease by wiping it with the cut surface of a fresh lemon. Alternatively, wipe with a paper towel moistened with vinegar.

REMOVING YOLK TRACES

Use edge of shell to pick up traces of yolk

Using a half shell
If you get even a trace of yolk in the white after separating an egg, remove it before whipping the white. The best way to do this is by scooping out the yolk with the edge of a halved eggshell.

USING SPARE YOLKS

● **Chilling egg yolks** Place left-over egg yolks in a small cup. Cover with cold water, and refrigerate for up to two days.
● **Freezing egg yolks** Beat spare yolks with either a pinch of salt for use in savory dishes, or a pinch of sugar for use in sweet dishes, then label and freeze for up to six months.
● **Enriching dishes** Spare egg yolks are useful for enriching many dishes. For invalids, add an extra yolk when making omelets, pancake batters, and custards to add nutrition.
● **Improving texture** Beat an egg yolk into a hot chocolate sauce or savory cream sauce for a smooth, glossy texture.

BUTTER AND CHEESE

Butter and cheese are rich sources of fat, so are best used in moderation, but both can bring richness and flavor to many dishes. Margarine can be substituted for butter where flavor is not critical, but low-fat spreads are most suitable for spreading, not cooking.

PREPARING BUTTER

● **Softening** Use a microwave to soften butter that has been refrigerated. Put the butter in a microwave-safe dish and cook on Defrost for about 30 seconds for each stick (100 g).

● **Clarifying** To make a really clear glaze for pâtés or vegetables, clarify butter by melting it with an equal quantity of water. Let set, then lift off the cleared butter, leaving the salts and other solids in the water.

● **Making perfect butter curls** Use firm, chilled butter, and dip the butter curler into warm water. Drop the curls into a bowl of iced water, and store in the refrigerator.

SHAVING HARD CHEESES

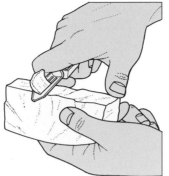

Using a peeler
Shave thin curls of Parmesan, pecorino, or other hard cheeses straight from the block with a vegetable peeler. Scatter the curls of cheese over hot pasta dishes, salads, or bruschetta.

MAKING LIGHT PASTRY

Grating butter
To make light shortcrust pastry without cutting in the butter, chill butter until hard, and grate it into the flour using a medium grater. Mix evenly with a fork before adding water to bind.

CREAM AND YOGURT

These foods enrich all kinds of sweet and savory dishes, and the lighter substitutes for cream make it possible to use dairy produce in almost any diet. Lower-fat forms of cream must be stabilized with cornstarch before cooking, so that they can be heated without curdling.

WHIPPING CREAM

● **Checking fat content** To maximize volume when whipping, use cream with a fat content of about 40 percent.

● **Increasing volume** Before whipping, chill the whisk and bowl as well as the cream.

● **Adding sugar** Whip 1 tsp (5 ml) confectioners' sugar into each ¾ cup (150 ml) of cream for a fluffy result that will hold its shape well.

● **Adding flavor** To produce an even texture, always add flavorings such as brandy to cream before whipping.

● **Whisking by hand** Use a balloon or spiral hand whisk, which will allow you to feel texture changes and to avoid overwhipping the cream.

USING EFFECTIVELY

● **Lightening a topping** Mix half plain yogurt with half whipped cream for a light, flavorful dessert topping.

● **Stabilizing** To keep plain yogurt from curdling in hot dishes, mix 1 tsp (5 ml) cornstarch into every ¾ cup (150 ml) yogurt before heating. Alternatively, add after cooking, without boiling.

● **Making crème fraîche** Mix together equal quantities of sour cream and heavy cream. Cover, and let the mixture stand at room temperature for two hours or until it thickens.

● **Whipped cream accents** Freeze dollops of whipped cream on a baking sheet, then use to top off Irish coffee.

BRIGHT IDEA

Making yogurt at home
Heat 2¼ cups (600 ml) pasteurized milk to 110°F (43°C). Stir in 1 tbsp (15 ml) plain yogurt and ⅓ cup (50 g) powdered skim milk. Pour into a thermos and let stand for seven hours, then chill in a bowl until thickened.

MEAT AND POULTRY

CAREFUL PREPARATION OF MEAT AND POULTRY is essential to the success of all types of cooking. The skillful use of different cutting methods, marinades, and coatings can make even the most inexpensive cut look and taste delicious.

MAKING GENERAL PREPARATIONS

There are many ways of preparing meat and poultry to enhance their appearance, flavor, and tenderness. For healthy cooking, trim off excess fat and skin, keeping some fat for flavor and moisture. Retain bones and trimmings to make stock, and freeze for future use.

CUTTING MEAT

● **Slicing for tenderness** Slice meat across, not with, the grain for a tender result.

● **Dicing evenly** When dicing meat for casseroles or curries, make the cubes the same size so that they cook evenly.

● **Trimming kidneys** Use kitchen scissors instead of a knife to cut out and remove the tough cores from kidneys.

● **Cutting stir-fry strips** Freeze meat for 30 minutes before slicing for a stir-fry. This will make it easy to cut thinly.

● **Snipping edges** To prevent the edges of grilled or fried steaks, chops, or bacon from curling, make slits in the fat at ½-in (1-cm) intervals.

COATING CHICKEN

Seasoned flour in plastic bag

Shaking in a bag
To coat chicken pieces in seasoned flour or spices quickly and cleanly, place the coating mixture in a plastic bag, and add the poultry. Shake the bag until the contents are evenly coated. Remove the pieces and cook.

TENDERIZING MEAT

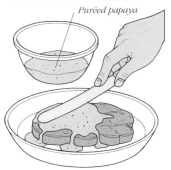

Puréed papaya

Marinating in papaya
To tenderize a tough cut of meat, purée fresh papaya and spread it over the surface of the meat. Alternatively, pour papaya or pineapple juice over the meat, cover, and refrigerate for three hours. Dry meat before cooking.

PREPARING DUCK

Scoring skin
To prepare duck breast for grilling or frying, score the skin deeply in a diamond pattern. This will help the meat cook evenly, keep its shape, and release excess fat during cooking.

PREPARING OFFAL

● **Soaking liver** For a milder flavor, soak strong-tasting liver, such as pig's liver, in milk for one hour prior to cooking.

● **Tenderizing liver** To make liver tender, pour tomato juice over it, and let soak three hours before cooking.

● **Cleaning hearts** Wash hearts thoroughly, then soak in lightly salted water for one hour to clean out any blood deposits.

● **Blanching sweetbreads** To keep sweetbreads firm, first blanch them for 20 minutes in salted, boiling water with the juice of half a lemon. Then drain, and press between two plates before cooking.

TIMESAVING TIP

Snipping bacon
To "chop" bacon quickly and easily, use a pair of kitchen scissors. Cut raw bacon slices straight into a pan. Snip cooked bacon over salads.

BONING

Most of the basic preparation of meat cuts is done before you buy them, but it is worth learning a few simple skills to get the best out of meat and poultry. Boning and trussing meat at home saves money, since prepared cuts are the most expensive.

PREPARING LAMB JOINTS
● **Protecting bones** Cover the bone ends of a rack of lamb with foil to prevent them from burning during cooking.

Use sharp knife to loosen bone

Loosening bone
For an easy-carving shoulder of lamb, loosen the blade bone from the flesh, but leave it in place. When roasted, the meat will shrink back, and the bone can then be pulled out easily.

TRUSSING POULTRY
● **Tying drumsticks** To truss a whole bird, tie only the drumsticks together, and the bird will keep its shape.

Using dental floss
To truss or sew meat or poultry unobtrusively, use some unwaxed dental floss. It is strong enough to hold the shape neatly and firmly, without spoiling the appearance of the dish.

SPLITTING FOR GRILLING
● **Pressing flat** To ensure that poultry lies as flat as possible when opened out for cooking, press firmly on the breastbone with the heel of your hand.

Using skewers
To hold a split Cornish hen in shape for cooking, push metal skewers through the thickest parts of the meat. They will allow the heat to penetrate and ensure thorough cooking.

USING CUT-UP POULTRY
● **Soaking duck pieces** Soak joints of wild duck in cold water for about an hour to remove any excess blood. Dry thoroughly on paper towels.
● **Cutting up whole birds** Buy a whole chicken, and cut it up yourself, since this is less expensive than buying precut pieces. Use the trimmings to make a stock for future use.
● **Adding flavors** Remove the skin from poultry pieces and slash the thickest parts of the flesh before coating in spices or marinades. This will allow the flavors to penetrate fully.
● **Using coatings** Use herb-flavored, packaged stuffing mix as a quick coating for chicken. Dip each piece in egg, and then into the stuffing mix before baking or frying.

FISH AND SHELLFISH

M OST OF THE PREPARATION OF FISH can be done before it reaches the kitchen. It is worth finding a supplier who will prepare the fish just as you want it. A few basic skills will help you get the most from this nutritious food.

FISH

F resh fish needs little preparation, and if it is bought already filleted or skinned it can be considered a ready-to-cook convenience food. Frozen fish can usually be used as a substitute for fresh fish. If possible, cook straight from frozen to retain all the juices and flavor.

SCALING FISH
● **Rinsing under water** Hold fish under cold water while removing scales, washing them away as you scrape.

Use sharp edge of scallop shell

Using a scallop shell
Remove all the scales from a whole fish with the edge of a scallop shell, scraping firmly down the length of the fish from the tail end toward the head.

REMOVING BONES
● **Boning cooked fish** When flaking fish, check for small bones after cooking, when they can be removed easily.

Using tweezers
Use tweezers to pluck out stray bones left in fish fillets after filleting. Press gently with your fingertips to feel for the small bones under the surface.

FILLETING FISH
● **Filleting flat fish** Fillet flat fish without gutting it: there is no danger of the gut being pierced and contaminating the flesh.

Boning mackerel
To bone mackerel, slit open the belly, and place the fish skin side up. Press firmly with your thumbs down the backbone. Turn over, and lift out the bones.

CLEANING & SKINNING
● **Preventing mess** To scale a whole fish cleanly, place it in a large heavy plastic bag, and scrape off the scales inside it.
● **Using salt** Dip fingertips into salt before skinning fish to give a better grip. Also, rub salt inside the belly cavity to remove any residues, then rinse well before cooking.
● **Skinning frozen fish** Pull the skin from frozen fillets while still frozen. Use paper towels to help you grip the skin.
● **Removing fishy smells** Rub the cut surface of a lemon over hands, knife, and cutting board after preparing fish to counteract fishy odors.

PREPARING A WHOLE FISH

Trimming the tail
If you are preparing a whole fish, such as salmon or trout, to serve with its tail on, trim the thin edges of the tail with scissors to make a V shape. This will prevent the tail from curling up in the heat during cooking.

● **Trimming the fins** Use kitchen scissors to snip the fins off a whole fish before cooking.
● **Cleaning through the gills** To preserve the shape of fish that is to be served whole, remove the stomach contents of the fish through the gill flaps instead of slitting open the belly.
● **Removing the gills** If a fish is to be cooked and served with the head intact, snip out the gills with scissors first, since they can impart a bitter taste.
● **Removing the head** To remove the head from a whole fish, cut following the natural curve behind the gills.

SHELLFISH

Much of the fresh shellfish we eat is sold in the shell and is often live, so preparation must be done at home. Live shellfish, such as oysters, mussels, and clams, are best prepared just before you serve them to ensure maximum freshness and safety, as well as the best results.

CLEANING & SERVING

● **Debearding mussels** Remove beards from mussels just before cooking, since they die once the beards are removed.

● **Using crushed ice** Prepare a serving platter with crushed ice before opening oysters, so that the shells can be firmly nestled in and the juices remain in the shells.

● **Chilling shellfish** Put clams or oysters, unopened, in the freezer for 10 minutes before serving; they will open easily.

● **Serving in shells** When buying shelled scallops, ask for the curved shells so that you can use them as serving dishes. Scrub and boil to clean.

CRACKING CRAB CLAWS

Tap claw gently but firmly with hammer

Using a hammer
To crack a crab claw without shattering it, cup it in the palm of your hand, and tap with a small hammer until the shell cracks. Alternatively, crack the claw on a folded dish towel on a board.

OPENING OYSTERS

● **Using the oven** Place oysters in one layer on a cookie sheet, and put in a hot oven for 3–4 minutes until they open.

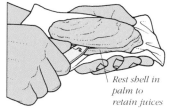

Rest shell in palm to retain juices

Using a can opener
Open oyster shells with the pointed tip of a can opener. Grasp each shell firmly in a cloth, holding the flat side upward, then insert the opener into the hinge and push down firmly.

CRUSTACEANS

Fresh shrimp, lobsters, and other crustaceans are usually sold in the shell, and a few simple skills are needed to prepare them. Do not be deterred by this preparation, which is speedy and worthwhile. The flavor of fresh crustaceans is better than peeled, frozen, or canned products.

DEVEINING SHRIMP

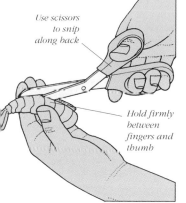

Use scissors to snip along back

Hold firmly between fingers and thumb

Using scissors
To devein large shrimp before cooking, cut along the back of each shell. It is easy to see the dark vein running down the back. Lift out the vein carefully, or scrape it out with a knife.

DEALING WITH SHELLS

● **Peeling easily** To peel cooked shrimp, grasp the head between finger and thumb, and twist to remove. Pull the legs to one side; as they break away, part of the shell should lift off. You will be able to peel it all off.

● **Cutting shells** Use kitchen scissors or poultry shears to cut lobster shells in half easily.

● **Wiping edges** After cutting lobster or crayfish shells in half for serving, wipe around the edges of the cut shells with a clean, damp cloth to remove small fragments.

● **Serving in shells** To serve lobster attractively in the shell, lift out the tail flesh from each half and replace it, rounded side up, in the opposite half.

USING SHELLS

Use shells to add color and flavor to stocks, sauces, and other accompaniments.

● **Making fish stock** After boiling lobster and scooping out the meat, return the shell pieces to the cooking liquid, and add a glass of white wine, a few onion slices, and a bouquet garni. Simmer for 20 minutes, then strain.

● **Making a fish sauce** Grind lobster shells in a food processor until smooth. Cook in a little butter, then add white wine and cream to make a rich sauce for white fish.

● **Making shrimp butter** Purée equal amounts of shrimp shells and butter with a little lemon juice in a food processor.

COOKING METHODS

QUICK REFERENCE

Vegetables, p. 379; Salads, p. 382

Fruits, p. 384; Eggs, p. 386

Meat and Poultry, p. 388

Fish and Shellfish, p. 394

Soups, Stocks, and Sauces, p. 398

Grains, Pasta, and Legumes, p. 400

Desserts, p. 402; Baking, p. 406

Preserving, p. 414

Freezing, p. 418

Drinks, p. 420

THE MAIN REASON for cooking food is to make it palatable and easily digestible. Different cooking methods have varying effects on foods, and it is important that you choose a suitable cooking method for each type of food. Rapid boiling, for instance, helps retain the color and texture of fresh vegetables, but tough cuts of meat need slow simmering to make them tender. Cooking methods may be combined, as in braising, in which quick frying and slow stewing brown and tenderize meat.

HEALTHY COOKING

The way in which food is cooked plays an important role in determining the food's nutritional contribution to our diet. Whenever possible, choose low-fat cooking methods, or cook with oils that are low in saturated fat, and use methods of cooking that retain nutrients.

STIR-FRYING
● **Adding in stages** When stir-frying mixtures of vegetables, place each vegetable in the pan separately to maintain the heat. Add the slowest-cooking first and the fastest-cooking last.

BOILING
● **Reusing cooking liquids** Refrigerate liquids that have been used for boiling food, since these contain flavor and nutrients. Add to gravies, sauces, soups, or stocks.

STEAMING
● **Cutting same-sized pieces** To ensure that pieces of food cook evenly and within the same period of time when steaming, cut them all to approximately the same size.

Stir constantly to seal food

Wrap paper securely around food

Sealing food quickly
Use less oil or fat for stir-frying than you would normally use for shallow frying, so that the surface of the food seals quickly. Add just enough oil to the pan to coat the food lightly.

Conserving nutrients
To preserve the vitamins when boiling vegetables, bring the water to a rolling boil before adding the vegetables to the pan. Bring back to the boil quickly, and keep the heat high until done.

Making a bundle
Retain the nutritious juices from steamed foods by wrapping food in bundles of baking parchment or aluminum foil before placing in a steamer. Pour the juices over the food to serve, or add to a sauce.

VEGETABLES

Most vegetables retain their color, texture, and flavor best if they are cooked quickly and lightly. Many different cooking methods can be used. Vegetables taste best if served as soon as possible after they have been cooked.

POTATOES

Potatoes are very versatile and respond well to most cooking methods. To a great extent the variety of potato determines which cooking method you use. For instance, grainy-textured potatoes are good for baking, roasting, and mashing, while waxy types are best boiled.

ENSURING SUCCESS

- **Baked potatoes** To speed up the cooking of baked potatoes, push metal skewers through their centers to conduct the heat. Alternatively, parboil the potatoes for 15 minutes before baking.
- **Mashed potatoes** Add a little hot milk (not cold) to mashed potatoes to give them a really fluffy texture. Warm the milk in a microwave for speed.
- **Boiled potatoes** Prevent old potatoes from blackening by adding a squeeze of lemon juice or a teaspoonful of vinegar to the cooking liquid.

CRISPING POTATOES

Roughing up the surfaces
For crisp roast potatoes, cut the potatoes into chunks, parboil, and drain. Shake the covered pan to roughen the surfaces of the potatoes, then roast as usual.

KEEPING POTATOES HOT

Preventing soggy potatoes
Use a clean dish towel to cover mashed potatoes and keep them hot before serving. The towel will absorb excess moisture, keeping them fluffy and dry.

GREEN VEGETABLES

Most green vegetables are rich in vitamin C, and they should be cooked quickly in the minimum of liquid to retain this very important nutrient. If you boil greens, keep the cooking water and add to gravies or soups. Alternatively, use water-free methods such as stir-frying.

COOKING CABBAGE

Steaming wedges
Instead of shredding cabbage, cut it into slim, portion-sized wedges and steam the wedges until just tender. The wedges will retain more nutrients than shredded cabbage and look decorative.

COOKING ASPARAGUS

Add water to create steam

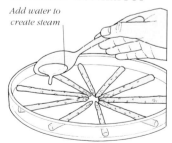

Using a microwave
Arrange asparagus spears in a wide, shallow dish with their pointed tips to the center. Add 3 tbsp (45 ml) water, cover, and cook on High for about 12–14 minutes per pound (500 g).

IMPROVING GREENS

- **Cabbage** Braise cabbage in a little stock instead of water. Shred finely, and cook with just enough stock to moisten, shaking the pan often.
- **Spinach** To remove excess moisture from cooked spinach, put spinach into a colander, and press with a potato masher, or press between two plates.
- **Napa cabbage** Shred the coarse outer leaves of Napa cabbage, and stir-fry. Save the tender leaves for salads.
- **Brussels sprouts** Cut crosses through the stems of Brussels sprouts for even cooking.

ENHANCING FLAVOR

Most vegetables are best cooked lightly to retain their flavor, color, and texture. By experimenting with different cooking methods and adding ingredients such as herbs, it is possible to add interest to, and enhance the flavor of, even the most ordinary vegetable.

USING ONIONS

● **Frying onions** To obtain a sweet, caramelized flavor, fry onions slowly in butter with a pinch of salt until they are a rich, golden-brown color.

Add juice to other ingredients

USING FRUIT JUICES

● **Sprinkling lemon juice** Fresh lemon juice will pep up the flavor of most vegetables. Use it instead of adding salt for people on low-salt diets.

Pour in orange juice to moisten carrots

ADDING SPICES

● **Spicing leeks** Add a spicy pungency to leeks by gently sautéeing them until soft in a little butter with a pinch of ground coriander and cumin.

Sprinkle with freshly grated nutmeg

Adding onion juice

To add the flavor of onion to savory dishes without including sliced or diced onion pieces, squeeze half an onion on a lemon squeezer to extract the juice. Add the liquid to the dish.

Flavoring carrots

Add a rich, sweet flavor to plain carrots by cooking in orange juice instead of water. Braise small, whole, new carrots until tender with just the juice of an orange and a pat of butter.

Using nutmeg

Sprinkle freshly grated nutmeg over cooked spinach, parsnips, or potatoes just before serving. The heat of the vegetables will bring out the full, warm, spicy aroma and flavor of the spice.

MAXIMIZING FLAVOR

● **Brussels sprouts** Instead of boiling Brussels sprouts, shred them finely, and stir-fry lightly in a little olive oil to retain flavor and crispness.
● **Beets** Wrap beets in foil, and bake instead of boiling to preserve flavor and color. Trim the tops of the beets, and wrap in buttered foil. Bake in a moderate oven for 1–2 hours.
● **Peas and snow peas** Add a sprig of fresh mint when boiling peas or snow peas.
● **Tomatoes** Add a pinch of sugar to cooked tomatoes and homemade tomato sauce.

USING LEFTOVERS

● **Grilling with cheese** Arrange vegetables in one layer in a heat dish. Cover with thin slices of Gruyère, and grill.
● **Making potato pancakes** Mix mashed potatoes with grated onion, then shallow-fry in cakes until golden.
● **Making fritters** Dip broccoli or cauliflower florets in batter. Then deep-fry in hot oil until they are a golden color.
● **Tossing salads** Dice cooked, mixed vegetables, and toss with mayonnaise and lemon juice. Serve cold as a salad.
● **Making soup** Purée cooked vegetables with leftover gravy, stock, or milk to taste.

TIMESAVING TIP

Making vegetable bundles
Wrap prepared vegetables in buttered foil, and cook in the oven in a roasting pan with roast meat for the final 30–40 minutes of cooking time. Add sprigs of fresh herbs to the bundles, and season with salt and pepper. Seal the bundles firmly to keep in the flavors.

ADDING VARIETY

Vegetables are versatile ingredients that will contribute significantly to a healthy diet, but if they are always cooked in the same way they lose their appeal. Be creative by combining vegetables with other ingredients in unusual ways and using different cooking methods.

VARYING PRESENTATION

Draw peeler along length of vegetable

Making vegetable ribbons

To serve carrots and zucchini in an unusual way, and to cook them quickly, slice them into thin ribbons by using a vegetable peeler instead of a knife. Steam or stir-fry the ribbons for 2–3 minutes or until they are tender.

COOKING CREATIVELY

● **Making "confetti"** Use the coarse shredder blade of a food processor to shred evenly vegetables such as carrots, peppers, zucchini, or celery root. Cook together in a quick "confetti" stir-fry.
● **Adding bacon** Transform cooked green beans into a dinner-party dish by tossing with crushed garlic, golden-fried crumbled bacon, and a chopped tomato.
● **Puréeing eggplants** Serve eggplants as a purée. Bake them whole in their skins for about 45 minutes in a moderate oven, or until tender. Scoop out the flesh, mash with a fork, and add salt, pepper, and olive oil to taste.

ADDING TEXTURE

Sunflower seeds

Sprinkling with seeds

To add an interesting texture to plain, cooked vegetables and increase their nutritive value, sprinkle with a few lightly toasted sunflower, pumpkin, or sesame seeds, or add chopped nuts just before cooking.

CORRECTING MISTAKES

If you have overcooked vegetables, there is no need to discard them, since they can usually be revived easily, or presented in a different way in order to disguise the mistake. You may even find that the end result is better than what you had originally intended.

PURÉEING VEGETABLES

Add heavy or light cream to taste

Mixing with cream

Rescue boiled carrots, spinach, or peas that have overcooked by serving them as a rich, creamy purée. Put the vegetables in a food processor, and purée until just smooth. Add a few tablespoonfuls of cream to taste.

REVIVING MASH

Rescuing soggy potatoes

If potatoes intended for mashing are overcooked or if they have collapsed, whip an egg white until stiff, and fold it carefully into the mashed potatoes. Pile the mixture into a dish, and bake in a hot oven until golden.

RESCUING DISASTERS

● **Counteracting salt** Rescue oversalted vegetables by pouring boiling water over them. If they are still too salty, stir them gently in a few tablespoonfuls of cream.
● **Reducing toughness** If mushrooms have become tough and dried out, add a few tablespoonfuls of red wine. Let the mushrooms soak for 10 minutes, then bring to a boil. Stir in a little cream.
● **Making soufflés** Mash overcooked cauliflower or broccoli, and mix in a can of condensed soup and three egg yolks. Fold in three whipped whites. Bake in ramekins in a hot oven for 20 minutes.

SALADS

SALADS FORM AN ESSENTIAL PART OF OUR DIET, whether they are simple side dishes or substantial main courses. Fresh, nutritious ingredients, served raw or lightly cooked, make a colorful, attractive dish to stimulate the appetite.

USING BASIC INGREDIENTS

Be creative with salad ingredients, and use fresh flavors, colors, and textures to the fullest. Use a variety of greens to make the most of a simple salad, or create interesting main courses by combining lots of salad ingredients. Match ingredients with dressings to your taste.

DRAINING SALADS

Using a saucer
Place an upside-down saucer in the bottom of a salad bowl before adding the salad. Excess water and dressing will gather underneath the saucer, keeping the salad leaves crisp.

PRESENTING LEAVES
● **Using whole leaves** Use crisp, whole lettuce leaves, such as romaine or iceberg, as natural serving dishes.
● **Cutting wedges** To produce interesting shapes and texture in a green salad, thinly slice an iceberg lettuce into wedges.
● **Lifting out a core** To remove the central core from an iceberg lettuce while keeping the leaves whole, slam the lettuce firmly, stem end down, onto a countertop. The core should then be loose enough to be lifted out by hand.
● **Removing bitterness** To avoid a bitter flavor in chicory, cut out the core at the stem end.

SPROUTING BEANS

Soaking beans in a jar
Sprout mung beans or other whole beans for use in salads. Put them in a large jar and soak overnight. Drain, cover the jar with cheesecloth, and rinse twice a day until the beans sprout.

IMPROVING INGREDIENTS
● **Cucumber** Before adding a sliced cucumber to salad, sprinkle the pieces with salt, and let drain for about 20 minutes to remove excess moisture. Rinse and dry.
● **Onions** To prevent the strong flavor of onions from dominating a salad, let the cut onion soak in cold water for one hour before use.
● **Tomatoes** Add interest to a tomato salad by mixing beefsteak, sun-dried, and cherry tomatoes. Sprinkle with olive oil as a dressing.
● **Celery** Keep leftover celery fresh for reuse by trimming and standing in chilled water.

MAKING RICE TIMBALES

Turn out compacted rice carefully

Shaping rice
Toss cooked rice in a dressing, then pack firmly into coffee or tea cups, or into a small bundt pan. Invert the cups onto a serving dish, and unmold for attractively shaped rice salads.

FLAVORING WARM SALADS

● **Adding vinegar** Sprinkle warm salad ingredients with a few drops of an aged vinegar, such as balsamic or sherry vinegar. The warmth of the salad will bring out the full flavor of the vinegar.
● **Using sesame oil** Give a Far Eastern flavor to a warm salad by adding a teaspoon of sesame oil to the dressing.
● **Cooking shallots** Simmer finely chopped shallots slowly in a few tablespoonfuls of red wine vinegar until soft. Toss them into a potato or bean salad for a warm, rich flavor.

ADDING VARIETY

Combine common and unusual ingredients to make imaginative and appetizing salads. Mix crunchy ingredients, such as croutons and seeds, with soft textures, such as fresh and dried fruits. Contrast sharp flavors with mild ones, and use herbs to add a distinctive flavor.

ENHANCING SALADS

- **Adding anchovies** Stir a few finely chopped canned anchovies into a potato salad.
- **Using herbs** Scatter generous amounts of fresh, chopped herbs, such as parsley, chervil, or chives, into a plain green salad, or add arugula for a peppery bite.
- **Adding texture** To add a crunchy texture to a simple salad, stir in a handful of toasted sunflower or sesame seeds, flaked almonds, or even salted peanuts just before serving the salad.
- **Shaving Parmesan** Scatter curled shavings of Parmesan cheese onto a plain salad.

MAKING MIXED SALADS

Layering ingredients
Pour a dressing into a straight-sided bowl, and place layers of colorful mixed salad vegetables into it. Turn the filled bowl over onto a serving dish for a dressed salad.

ADDING GARNISHES

Use cutter to stamp shapes from bread

Making croutons
To add a crunchy garnish to a simple salad, use croutons. Cut shapes from sliced bread with a small cutter. Gently fry the shapes in oil until golden, toss with parsley, and add to salad.

MAKING DRESSINGS

A well-balanced, freshly made dressing can add a subtle or a distinctive flavor to a salad. Classic recipes, such as vinaigrette, are a good starting point, but imaginative dressings can be created using flavored vinegars and oils, fruit juices, herbs, spices, seeds, and zests.

COMBINING INGREDIENTS

- **Dressing warm ingredients** Dress rice or pasta salads while they are still slightly warm so that they absorb the flavors of the dressing.
- **Adding nut oils** Enhance salad dressings by using nut oils, such as walnut or hazelnut, for a rich flavor.
- **Lowering fat** Use plain yogurt or milk, instead of oil, as a basis for a low-fat dressing.
- **Sweetening dressings** If you find vinegar-based dressings too sharp, substitute apple or orange juice for the vinegar, or add a teaspoonful of honey.
- **Adding cheese** Use ripe Stilton or Roquefort for a blue-cheese dressing. Mash cheese with a fork, and stir into light cream or mayonnaise.

MAKING VINAIGRETTE

Using a screwtop jar
To make vinaigrette quickly, pour vinegar, or lemon juice, and oil into a straight-sided, screw-top jar. Use three parts oil to one part vinegar, or four or five parts oil to one part lemon juice. Shake the jar to mix the ingredients.

BRIGHT IDEA

Using a mustard jar
When a mustard jar is almost empty, leave the last scrapings in the jar, and use it to make a salad dressing. Measure the other ingredients into the jar, and shake well. The remaining mustard will flavor the dressing.

FRUITS

SOME FRUITS – EVEN SOFT SUMMER FRUITS – tend to be more palatable cooked than uncooked, but most require only light cooking to bring out their full flavor. Gentle poaching, grilling, or baking will maintain flavor, color, and shape.

BAKING FRUITS

Fruits can be baked just as they are, as in the case of baked apples, or wrapped in pastry bundles to cook gently and retain the flavor. Always prepare fruits just before baking, since most of them soon start to brown and lose vitamins when they are exposed to the air.

ADDING FLAVOR
● **Sprinkling spice** Mix ½ cup (60 g) dark brown sugar with 1 tsp (5 ml) ground cinnamon, and sprinkle over fruit for a sweet and spicy glaze.
● **Adding chocolate** Bake bananas until their skins turn black, then slit down one side and spoon in melted chocolate. Eat this delicious dessert right from the skins.
● **Baking peaches** To bring out the flavor of slightly underripe peaches, bake them in their skins, whole or in halves, in a hot oven for approximately 20 minutes. Slip off the skins of the fruits before serving.

BAKING WHOLE APPLES

Score lines vertically from top to bottom

Scoring skins
Use a canelle knife or an ordinary knife to score the skins of whole, cored apples before baking, so that the fruits cook without splitting. Sprinkle lemon juice on the apple to prevent browning.

BAKING WHOLE ORANGES

Gather foil, then twist to secure

Wrapping in foil
Remove the peel and pith from oranges, and slice into rings. Reassemble on foil squares, and add a pat of butter and a dash of liqueur. Wrap in foil and bake in a hot oven for 10 minutes.

QUICK APPLE FILLINGS

To bake apples with a tasty filling, remove the cores but leave them unpeeled. Pack the hollowed centers with a filling before baking.

● **Using almond paste** Chop almond paste and dried apricots, and pack into the centers of cored apples. Sprinkle with lemon juice.
● **Crumbling cookies** Lightly crush macaroons or gingersnaps, and mix them with chopped almonds or walnuts. Spoon into apples.
● **Stuffing with nuts and dates** Make a stuffing for apples from chopped dates and walnuts. Spoon maple syrup on top before baking.

MAKING PIE FILLINGS

Mix cornstarch thoroughly with fruits

Thickening juices
To thicken juices in fruit pie fillings, toss the prepared fruits in a little cornstarch. If sugar is to be added, mix it with the cornstarch before adding to the fruits to distribute it evenly.

WRAPPING FRUITS
● **Wrapping pears in pastry** Cut long, thin strips of puff or shortcrust pastry, and spiral around peeled pears, leaving the stems exposed. Brush with milk, and bake in a hot oven until the pastry is golden.
● **Topping apples** Bake whole apples until almost tender, peel off the skins from the top halves, spread stiff meringue over the peeled parts, then bake in a hot oven until the meringue is golden.
● **Making phyllo bundles** Halve and pit plums or apricots, then put a blanched almond in each cavity. Put halves back together, and wrap in phyllo dough. Brush with oil, and bake in a moderate oven until golden.

POACHING FRUITS

Fruits can be poached by cooking gently in syrup until they are just tender. Cook over low heat to retain flavor and prevent the fruits from falling apart. To make a purée, poach fruits until soft, and beat with a wooden spoon or prepare in a food processor until smooth.

ENHANCING FLAVORS
● **Counteracting acidity** Reduce the acidity of rhubarb and improve its flavor by poaching it in orange juice or sprinkling it with ginger.
● **Using lemonade** Poach apple slices in leftover lemonade and white wine.
● **Adding tea** Use a scented tea such as Earl Grey for poaching dried fruits to make an exotic fruit compote. Add a few cardamom pods or star anise for a rich, spicy flavor.
● **Oven-poaching fruits** Allow the flavor of fruits to develop to their full intensity by poaching them in a tightly lidded dish in a cool oven for approximately one hour.

POACHING APRICOTS

Add enough liquid to moisten apricots

Using a microwave
Pour water or fruit liqueur and lemon juice over the apricots. Cover. Then cook on High 4–5 minutes, turning halfway through. Slip off the skins, and serve apricots in the juices.

SERVING POACHED PEARS

Slice up to, but not through, stem end

Slicing into a fan
Poach whole pears, peeled but with stems on, in wine or sugar syrup until tender. Drain and cut into very thin slices, almost through to the stem end. Press lightly to fan out the slices.

GRILLING AND BARBECUING FRUITS

Grilling fruits is an excellent way of bringing out their sweet, ripe flavors – and almost any fruits can be cooked using this method. The dying heat from a barbecue after cooking the main course is ideal for grilling fruits brushed with spicy glazes or wrapped in foil bundles.

GRILLING PEACH HALVES
● **Adding lemon juice** Sprinkle fresh peach halves with lemon juice before grilling to prevent the flesh from browning.

Adding a topping
Top fresh or canned peach halves with a spoonful of ricotta or mascarpone cheese, sprinkle with a sweet spice such as cinnamon, allspice, or anise, and grill until the cheese bubbles.

BARBECUING PINEAPPLE
● **Glazing** Brush pineapple pieces with a mixture of equal amounts of melted butter, rum, and brown sugar. Then grill.

Skewering wedges
Cut a pineapple lengthwise into quarters, remove the core, and cut between the skin and the flesh, leaving the flesh in position. Slice the flesh, secure with skewers, and barbecue.

GRILLING FRUITS
● **Using skewers** Thread strawberries onto bamboo skewers, brush with melted butter, and sprinkle with confectioners' sugar. Then grill.
● **Marinating fruits** Soak peach or apricot halves in brandy for 30 minutes before grilling.
● **Making exotic kebabs** Mix chunks of exotic fruits such as mangoes, kiwi fruits, guavas, and kumquats on skewers, brush with butter, then grill.
● **Using rum butter** Use leftover rum or brandy butter as a glaze for grilled fruits.
● **Serving with sweet toasts** Grill slices of fruit with slices of buttered brioche or raisin bread, and serve together, sprinkled with cinnamon.

EGGS

GGS ARE A VERSATILE COOKING INGREDIENT that can be used to thicken, aerate, enrich, bind, coat, or glaze sweet and savory foods. They can be enjoyed as a complete food in themselves, whether fried, boiled, poached, or baked.

FRYING EGGS

ried eggs need not be unhealthy, especially if you choose a light, unsaturated oil for frying. If your frying pan is of good quality or has a nonstick surface, you will need only a minimal amount of oil. To remove excess fat, drain eggs on a paper towel before serving.

COOKING OMELETS

Carefully fold one-third of omelet over filling

Enclosing a filling
To make a filled omelet, fold over one side to the middle using a spatula. Tip the frying pan, and slide the omelet down, then flip the other side over neatly to enclose the filling.

SHAPING FRIED EGGS

Pour egg into cutter

Using cookie cutters
Heat shaped cutters in a frying pan with oil. Pour an egg into each cutter, holding the cutter if necessary with a spatula, and fry. Run a knife around the inside of the cutter to remove the egg.

HEALTHY TIP

Reducing fat
To "fry" an egg without fat, place a heatproof plate over a pan of boiling water. When the plate is very hot, break an egg onto it. The egg should set in about eight minutes.

PREVENTING EGGS FROM STICKING

● **Using a clean pan** Start with a clean pan when frying eggs. If the pan has been used to cook other foods, such as bacon, the eggs may stick.

● **Choosing oil** Use a good-quality, light oil for frying eggs, such as sunflower or corn oil. Heat the oil, and cook the eggs over moderate heat.

SCRAMBLING EGGS

● **Lightening** For scrambled eggs that are light and fluffy, beat in a little carbonated water just before cooking.
● **Enriching** Add a dash of dry sherry to the beaten egg mixture before cooking to give a rich flavor to scrambled eggs.
● **Extending** To make scrambled eggs go further, add 1 tbsp (15 ml) fresh whole-wheat or white bread crumbs to each egg.

● **Adding extras** Stir finely sliced strips of smoked salmon or smoked ham into scrambled eggs as they cook. Alternatively, add finely chopped chervil or chives for a fresh, herby flavor.
● **Making sandwich fillings** If you are short of time to hard-cook eggs for sandwich fillings, scramble the eggs instead, then cool, and mix with mayonnaise and seasoning to taste.

USING A MICROWAVE

● **Frying on a browning dish** Preheat a browning dish according to the manufacturer's instructions, and lightly brush the surface with oil. Break an egg onto the browning dish; the heat will brown the base of the egg. Prick the yolk with a toothpick to prevent it from bursting, and cover with a paper towel. Cook on High for about one minute.

● **Allowing standing time** When cooking scrambled eggs in a microwave, remove them just before they set. Stir, and let stand for one minute. The eggs will finish cooking in the residual heat and have an even, creamy consistency.

BOILING AND POACHING EGGS

Boiling and poaching are quick and simple methods of cooking eggs, requiring no extra fat. With careful timing, it is easy to cook eggs to perfection. Eggs should be at room temperature prior to boiling to avoid cracking, so remove them from the refrigerator 30 minutes before cooking.

PREVENTING PROBLEMS
● **Preventing black rings** To prevent dark rings from forming around the yolks of hard-cooked eggs, drain them as soon as they are cooked. Crack the shells, and run under cold water to cool quickly.
● **Adding vinegar** If eggshells crack during boiling, add a tablespoonful of vinegar to the water to set the white.

POACHING EGGS
● **Using fresh eggs** Use very fresh eggs for poaching so that the whites will cling to the yolks. Keep the water at a low simmer during cooking for a smooth, soft-textured result.

BOILING EGGS

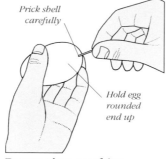

Prick shell carefully

Hold egg rounded end up

Preventing cracking
Before boiling eggs, prick the rounded end with a pin to allow the expanding air to escape during cooking and thus reduce the risk of cracking. Lower into cold water, and bring to a boil.

MARBLING BOILED EGGS

Using tea bags
Boil eggs for two minutes, remove each one, and tap with a spoon to crack the shell. Return to the pan with six tea bags, simmer for one minute, then cool. Remove shells, and eggs will be marbled.

BAKING EGGS

Eggs can be baked simply in ramekins with nothing more than salt and pepper, or used in more elaborate baked dishes such as soufflés and custards. A moderate oven temperature, which will prevent egg whites from becoming tough, is best for most baked egg recipes.

MAKING SOUFFLÉS

Cut just inside edge

Creating a "top-hat" effect
When making a hot soufflé, use a sharp knife to cut the mixture around the edge just inside the dish before cooking. This will encourage the mixture to rise evenly, creating a "top-hat" effect when the soufflé is cooked.

BAKING IN POTATOES

Sprinkle cheese on top of egg

Scooping out the flesh
Bake a large potato until tender, and cut a slice from the top. Scoop out the flesh from the center, and break an egg into it. Season with salt and pepper, cover with cheese, and continue baking until the egg is set.

PREPARING SOUFFLÉS
● **Preparing ahead** To prepare a hot soufflé in advance, make the mixture, and spoon it into a dish ready for baking. Cover with plastic wrap, and chill for two hours before baking.
● **Ensuring even rising** To dislodge any large air pockets in a soufflé mixture, give the dish a sharp tap on a counter before putting it into the oven.
● **Adding bread crumbs** For a good rise and a crisp, golden crust, sprinkle a greased soufflé dish with fine bread crumbs before adding the mixture.
● **Making soufflé tomatoes** For an unusual appetizer, slice the tops from large tomatoes, and scoop out the centers. Fill each with cheese soufflé mixture. Bake in a hot oven until risen.

MEAT AND POULTRY

WHEN CHOOSING A COOKING METHOD FOR MEAT OR POULTRY, consider the cut you have chosen. If you use the appropriate cooking method, it is possible to make even the toughest cuts of meat and poultry tender and succulent.

FLAVORING MEAT AND POULTRY

Even for everyday meals, it is worth making the most of meat dishes by adding extra flavor with coatings, glazes, or tasty stuffings. In many cases, an accompaniment that adds flavor, such as stuffing or a sauce served with roast meat, helps make the meat go further.

USING COATINGS

● **Sprinkling with spices** Brush poultry skin with oil, and sprinkle with curry spices to give a rich, spicy, crisp skin.
● **Making a glaze** Mix equal quantities of Worcestershire sauce and tomato paste to make a spicy glaze. Brush the mixture over beef, lamb steaks, chops, or chicken pieces before grilling.
● **Coating with crumbs** Toss fresh bread crumbs in olive oil. Add plenty of chopped fresh herbs, and cover the meat skin with the mixture for the last 30 minutes of roasting.

FLAVORING HAM

● **Studding with cloves** To give a spicy flavor and an attractive finish to roast ham, score the fat surface, and press a clove into each cut.

Glazing with mustard
For a quick, delicious glaze for roast ham or pork, mix equal amounts of powdered mustard and brown sugar. Sprinkle the mixture over the fat surface for the final 30 minutes of cooking.

FLAVORING CHICKEN

Adding lemon slices
To add flavor and keep a whole chicken moist during roasting, gently lift the breast skin, and tuck slices of lemon or orange underneath. Brush with oil, season, and place in a hot oven. Use unwaxed lemons if possible.

FLAVORING PORK

● **Adding herbs** Before tying up a roast of boned pork for cooking, tuck a handful of fresh sage leaves inside it for a rich flavor. Roast as usual.

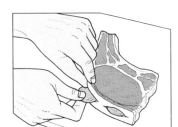

Stuffing a pork chop
To add a special taste to a plain pork chop, cut small slits along the fat edge, and open them out to make pockets. Tuck dried apricots or prunes inside, then grill, fry, or bake the chop.

ADDING STUFFING

● **Using mango** To give an exotic flavor to a whole turkey or chicken, and to moisten the flesh, tuck pieces of diced mango into the neck end. The fruit will cook to a purée, sweetening the poultry juices.
● **Flavoring packaged stuffing** Mix a few chopped nuts, some dried fruits, or grated Parmesan cheese into packaged stuffing to add flavor.
● **Serving separately** Press extra stuffing into oiled ramekins, bake for the last 20–25 minutes of roasting, and serve with the meat.

FLAVORING RED MEAT

● **Adding garlic** To flavor lamb, cut deep slits in the surface with a knife, and tuck a sliver of garlic into each slit. This will infuse a subtle flavor to the meat as it cooks.
● **Marinating meat** Immerse lamb or beef steaks in a marinade of olive oil, garlic, red or white wine, and herbs. Keep in the refrigerator for 2–3 days, then grill lightly.
● **Spreading with juniper** For a rich flavor, crush juniper berries to a paste with a little red wine. Spread over the surface of venison steaks or roasts before cooking.
● **Drawing out flavor** Season meat with salt just before cooking, since salt draws out the juices from meat.

STEWING MEAT AND POULTRY

Stewing is a slow, gentle cooking method, usually in a covered pan, and with cooking liquids partially covering the food. This method is especially suitable for tough cuts of meat, such as beef shanks (*osso buco*), which can become tender and juicy after long cooking in a stew.

THICKENING STEWS

It is best to thicken at the end of cooking, since thickened stews tend to stick and burn during cooking. If a stew contains too much liquid, reduce or thicken it by one of the following methods.

● **Reducing liquid** Reduce liquid by boiling it rapidly without a lid until the correct consistency is reached.
● **Using cornstarch** Blend some cornstarch with enough stock, water, or wine to make a thin paste, then stir it into the hot juices. Bring to a boil, and stir for two minutes.
● **Adding bread crumbs** To thicken stews and casseroles quickly, stir in a few spoonfuls of fresh, white bread crumbs.

ENHANCING STEWS

● **Replacing water** Use wine, tea, or beer in stews instead of water. These liquids will help tenderize tough meat.
● **Adding beets** Add a slice or two of beets to meat stews and casseroles to deepen the color of the sauce to a rich, golden brown.
● **Using herbs** Add tender herbs such as parsley or basil to stews and casseroles at the end of the cooking period, so they do not disintegrate during the long cooking.
● **Adjusting saltiness** To save a too-salty stew, peel a potato, and cut it into chunks. Add it to the pan, simmer until soft, then remove. Alternatively, dilute the stew with cream or a can of unsalted tomatoes.

TRADITIONAL TIP

Cooking lamb in coffee
Instead of using stock or water for a lamb stew or casserole, try the traditional method of adding black coffee. Coffee complements lamb surprisingly well, and makes the meat juices rich, flavorful, and dark.

BRAISING MEAT AND POULTRY

Braising is a slow, gentle method of cooking that often uses a bed of vegetables and little or no added liquid. Braising is suitable for tough, mature, or dry cuts of meat and poultry. Pot roasting is a similar method by which whole pieces are braised with a little liquid.

USING VEGETABLES

Place meat on top of vegetables

Increasing flavor
Braise meat on a bed of vegetables such as onions, celery, leeks, turnips, or carrots, which may be precooked if preferred. Brown the meat first to hold in juices before adding to the vegetables.

RETAINING JUICES

Cut paper to size of pot

Covering with paper
Press a buttered circle of baking parchment onto the meat before covering the pot with a lid. This will concentrate the cooking juices and help to prevent the food from steaming.

PREPARING MEAT

● **Browning meat** When browning meat prior to braising, fry a few pieces at a time, so that they cook quickly and the juices are sealed in.
● **Marinating game** Marinate mature game birds in red wine before braising to ensure tenderness and richness. Braise on a bed of celery or lentils.
● **Adding paprika** Sprinkle a little paprika over meat for simple braising to add color to the finished dish.
● **Using pork rind** Place a roast for pot roasting on a piece of pork rind, which will add flavor and prevent the meat from sticking to the pan.

GRILLING AND BARBECUING

Both grilling and barbecuing are quick, simple, and healthy methods of cooking that are suitable for most meat, fish, vegetables, and fruits. In each case, seal in the juices by cooking initially at a high heat. Then lower the heat to ensure that the food cooks thoroughly.

MAKING A HINGED WIRE RACK FOR BARBECUING

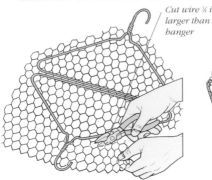

Cut wire ¾ in (2 cm) larger than hanger

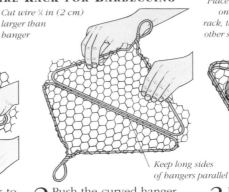

Keep long sides of hangers parallel

Place food on one side of rack, then fold other side over

1 Make a hinged wire rack to turn delicate foods on a barbecue. Lay two wire coat hangers over a square piece of flexible, lightweight chicken wire. Trim the wire to shape.

2 Push the curved hanger handles firmly inward to form round handles. Fold the edges of the wire over the outer edges of the hangers, tucking in any sharp points.

3 Fold the hangers together at the join. Use the rack for cooking both sides of delicate foods, such as fish and hamburgers, which tend to collapse if turned with tongs.

USING BAMBOO SKEWERS

● **Preventing burning** To grill or barbecue foods on bamboo skewers, first soak the skewers in water for about 20 minutes. This will prevent them from burning during cooking.

GRILLING SUCCESSFULLY

● **Using foil** Line the grill pan with a layer of foil, shiny side up, to reflect heat back onto food while it cooks. This will also make it easy to clean the pan after cooking.
● **Preheating a grill** Always preheat a grill for at least five minutes before cooking.
● **Absorbing fat** When grilling fatty meat, place a few pieces of stale bread in the bottom of the grill pan to absorb fat spills.
● **Turning meat** Use tongs, instead of a fork, for turning meat to prevent the loss of juices due to piercing.
● **Grilling low-fat foods** Brush low-fat foods, such as chicken, with oil to keep them moist.

ADDING WOOD CHIPS

● **Soaking** To extend the lives of hickory or oak wood chips, soak them in water for a few minutes. Then scatter the wood chips onto the coals to add aroma to the barbecue.

TURNING FRANKFURTERS

Thread frankfurters from end to end

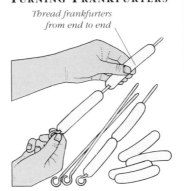

Using skewers

Thread frankfurters or sausages onto flat metal skewers to make it easy to turn them on a barbecue or grill. The skewers also conduct heat, which helps reduce the cooking time.

PREVENTING STICKING

● **Oiling a grill** Brush a barbecue grill with oil to prevent foods from sticking to it. Heat the grill to a high temperature before you place any food on it for cooking.

SAFETY

● **Placing a barbecue** Position a barbecue on a sheltered, level surface, away from trees and buildings.
● **Supervising children** Keep children away from the fire.
● **Controlling fire** Keep a bucket of sand and a water hose on hand in case of fire.
● **Using special tools** Use long-handled barbecue tools for turning and basting foods.
● **Keeping food cool** Keep perishable foods covered and place them in the refrigerator until just before cooking.
● **Ensuring thorough cooking** Make sure that all meat, especially pork, sausages, and poultry, is well cooked.

FRYING AND SAUTÉEING

Frying and sautéeing are quick methods of cooking that seal in food juices effectively. Control the heat carefully to cook foods evenly and prevent overheating. Delicate foods, such as fish fillets, may need to be coated before frying to give them a little extra protection from the heat.

CHECKING TEMPERATURE

Testing with bread
If you do not have a thermometer to check oil temperature, drop a piece of bread into the oil. When the bread browns, usually in about a minute, the oil is hot enough to add food for frying.

REUSING OIL

Paper towel retains food debris

Straining impurities
Before reusing oil left over from frying, filter out any food debris left in it. Line a sieve with an absorbent paper towel, hold the sieve over a bowl, and then pour the oil through it.

HEALTHY TIP

Brush pan with oil to prevent sticking

Using a ridged frying pan
To "dry" fry fatty foods such as bacon or sausages, use a heavy frying pan with a ridged base. The ridges hold the food above its own fatty juices, which can be poured off when cooking is finished.

COATING & BROWNING FRIED FOODS

● **Drying food** Dry food thoroughly by patting it with a paper towel before dipping it into batter for frying. This will help the batter cling to the food, coating it evenly.

● **Mixing butter and oil** To obtain a golden color when shallow-frying, use a mixture of half butter and half oil. The butter browns easily, and the oil prevents it from burning.

PREVENTING PROBLEMS

● **Controlling odors** Wear a shower cap when frying if you want to prevent smells from getting into your hair. After you have finished frying, remove the pan from the heat and cover. Let cool.

● **Avoiding spattering** Always dry food thoroughly to remove surface moisture before adding it to hot oil. If the oil starts to spatter, cover the pan with an upside-down metal colander or a wire-mesh pan guard.

USING A WOK EFFECTIVELY

Clip-on draining rack

Deep-frying in a wok
Use a wok for deep-frying foods, since the shape will allow you to use less oil than with conventional frying methods. If the wok has a curved base, use a wok stand to steady it.

● **Testing heat** To test whether a wok is hot enough before adding oil, hold the palm of your hand a few inches above the surface of the bottom of the pan until you feel the heat rising from it. Alternatively, wait until a wisp of smoke rises from the bottom of the empty wok.
● **Shaking the wok** When stir-frying food in a wok, keep shaking the pan and stirring the food constantly over a high heat. This will ensure that the food cooks evenly and quickly using minimal fat.
● **Using chopsticks** Use long wooden chopsticks to turn food cooked in a wok; they will stay cool to the touch.

SAFETY

● **Paying attention** Always stay near a pan of fried food while it is cooking.
● **Controlling temperature** Check the temperature of oil with a thermometer, and keep it just below smoking point.
● **Preventing fire** If fat catches fire, turn off the heat, and cover the pan. Do not use water to put out the fire.

ROASTING POULTRY

Poultry needs to be cooked thoroughly to kill all harmful bacteria. Chicken is ready when the juices run clear, not pink, when the flesh is pierced through the thickest part. Duck and squab are suitable for serving slightly less well cooked, with just a touch of pink in the flesh.

ROASTING SUCCESSFULLY
● **Using the cavity** Tuck a bunch of herbs, a lemon, or a whole onion inside the cavity of a chicken or turkey before roasting. The flavor will penetrate the meat, and will make tasty juices for gravy.
● **Resting poultry** Allow poultry to rest for about 20 minutes after roasting. This will make it easy to carve. Turn off the oven and leave the bird inside, or remove and cover with foil.
● **Using roasting bags** Cook poultry in a roasting bag to eliminate the need for basting. If you want to crisp up the skin, open the bag for the final 20 minutes of cooking.
● **Using a microwave** If you "roast" poultry in a microwave that does not have a browning option, sprinkle the bird with paprika to add color.

COVERING WITH BACON
● **Using bacon slices** Keep the breast of birds such as turkey, pheasant, or squab moist and tender by laying strips of bacon over the breast area.

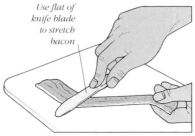

Use flat of knife blade to stretch bacon

Maintaining shape
To retain the shape of small birds such as squab, wrap bacon slices around them. Stretch each slice first by pressing firmly along its length with a round-bladed knife to elongate it. Then wrap slices around the bird.

ROASTING TURKEY
● **Maintaining moisture** Roast a turkey breast-down for the first hour of cooking to keep it moist. Then turn the turkey over to finish cooking.

Place turkey on celery

Laying on a bed of celery
Before placing turkey in a roasting pan, cover the base of the pan with celery sticks, which act like a roasting rack. The vegetables will add flavor to the meat juices for a delicious gravy.

ROASTING DUCK
● **Crisping skin** For crisp duck skin, prick the skin all over with a fork, sprinkle with salt, and roast on a rack to lift the bird above the fatty juices.

Protecting wings
To prevent the wing ends of a duck from overcooking before the rest of the bird has finished cooking, wrap them in foil before roasting. Remove the foil for the final 30 minutes of cooking to allow the wings to brown.

ROASTING CHICKEN
● **Browning skin** To boost the golden-brown color of a roast chicken, add a pinch of ground turmeric to the oil or butter that you use for basting.

Flavoring with wine
Pour about ⅔ cup (150 ml) red or dry white wine into a large, clean, empty food can. Sit a chicken on the can, then stand in a roasting pan. The wine will flavor meat juices that collect in the can.

TRADITIONAL TIP

Wrapping in cheesecloth
Instead of covering a large chicken or turkey with foil for roasting, dip a double layer of cheesecloth into melted butter or oil, and lay it over the bird's skin. The cheesecloth will allow the skin to brown and become crisp during cooking without trapping steam.

ROASTING MEAT

For a successful meat roast, it is important to place it in a hot oven at the start of cooking to seal in the tasty juices. Reduce the heat once the meat starts to brown. Remove chilled meat from the refrigerator 20 minutes before roasting, so that it comes to room temperature.

ROASTING FATTY MEAT

Rub powder into surface

Using dry mustard
When roasting a cut of beef or pork with a high fat content, cover the surface with dry mustard powder. This will counteract the fattiness and add flavor to the gravy.

CHECKING TEMPERATURE

Insert thermometer away from bone

Using a thermometer
Insert a meat thermometer into the thickest part of the meat, avoiding the bone. Bone conducts heat more quickly than flesh, so it may give a false reading. Leave the thermometer in during cooking.

PREPARATION BASICS

- **Choosing meat** The best cuts of beef, veal, or lamb will be labeled "Prime;" the best pork is "US No. 1." Prime meat may be difficult to find in grocery stores; fortunately the next grade of meat, "Choice," is also good.
- **Noting weights** Always take note of the weight and the cut of meat before discarding the label.
- **Trimming meat** Cut away excess fat from meat before roasting. Prime and Choice meat should still have sufficient marbling to keep the roast moist.

PREPARING ACCOMPANIMENTS

Roast meat and poultry are often associated with standard accompaniments – roast pork is usually accompanied by apple sauce, for example. There are no set rules, however, and trimmings can be varied to suit your taste, and to add extra color and texture to dishes.

SAVING TIME
- **Thickening gravy** To thicken the consistency of gravy quickly, whip in 1–2 tbsp (15–30 ml) instant potato buds.
- **Lowering fat content** A fat separator is a timesaving tool if you make roasts regularly. After roasting meat or poultry, pour pan juices into the separator, and pour off the rich, lower-fat juices. Discard the remaining fat, and use only the juices when making gravy.
- **Microwaving cranberries** Cook 2 cups (250 g) cranberries in 1 cup (225 ml) water on High until the water and juices are boiling. Continue to cook on High for a further five minutes, until the berries begin to burst. Sweeten with sugar to your liking.

IMPROVING GRAVY

Skim surface with paper towel

Skimming off fat
To remove a layer of fat from meat or poultry gravy, drag an absorbent paper towel lightly across the surface of the liquid. Repeat, if necessary, to remove any traces of fat that are left before serving the gravy.

ADDING EXTRAS
- **Flavoring gravy** Stir a generous dash of brandy or port into plain gravy to pep up the flavor for serving with a special roast. Boil for two minutes before serving.
- **Making stuffing balls** When stuffing a roast of meat or poultry, make more stuffing than you need. Roll the extra into balls, and place in the juices around the roast for the last 20 minutes of cooking. Alternatively, put extra stuffing in a separate pan, add pan juices, then bake with the roast for the last 20 minutes.
- **Glazing a roast** Just before serving, brush the surface of a roast with warmed apricot or cranberry jelly to give it an attractive, sweet-tasting glaze.

FISH AND SHELLFISH

FISH COOKS SIMPLY AND QUICKLY, and in its many forms it can be cooked by most methods. Whole fish cooked on the bone has the best flavor. Filleted fish is versatile enough to be fried, poached, grilled, or even barbecued.

ADDING FLAVOR

Most types of fresh fish need little flavor enhancement, but it is a good idea to use different accents to stimulate appetite and add variety. With a squeeze of lemon and a sprinkling of herbs, or with unusual marinades or glazes, fish can take on new dimensions.

FLAVORING OIL

Sliced ginger

Ginger

Adding fresh ginger
Before shallow-frying or stir-frying fish, add a few thin slices of fresh ginger to the oil for extra flavor. Stir over medium heat for 3–4 minutes, then remove, and cook the fish.

MARINATING RAW FISH
● **Choosing a marinade** Use an oil-based marinade for white fish to moisten and add flavor. Use an acidic marinade, based on citrus juice or vinegar, for oily fish to offset its richness.
● **Using yogurt** Spread a yogurt-based marinade, such as a tandoori mixture, over fish that is to be grilled. This will seal in the juices and produce a spicy low-fat crust.
● **"Cooking" in a marinade** Cut about 1 lb 2 oz (500 g) fresh, white fish into thin strips, and add the juice of four limes or lemons. Chop and stir in an onion, a chili, and a clove of garlic. Chill for 3–4 hours. The marinade will "cook" the fish, and it will be ready to eat cold.

FLAVORING FISH

Dribble marinade over warm fish

Seasoning with marinade
Slash the flesh of small, whole fish at intervals before you grill or fry them. Flavor with a marinade of white wine and herbs or spices after cooking. Let stand until cold before serving.

FLAVORING OILY FISH
● **Using mustard** Spread herring or mackerel fillets with a thin layer of mustard. Then roll the fish in raw oatmeal or rolled oats before frying.

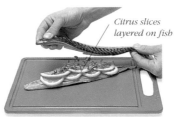

Citrus slices layered on fish

Sandwiching fillets
Add flavor to fillets of mackerel or herring by sandwiching the fillets together with lemon, lime, or orange slices and thyme sprigs. Bake in the oven, or tie firmly with string and grill.

USING COATINGS
● **Mixing with herbs** Instead of coating white fish fillets in plain bread crumbs, stir in a few crumbled dried herbs, curry spices, or crushed, dried chilies.
● **Using coconut** Dip pieces of monkfish or other white, firm fish in lightly beaten egg. Then toss the pieces in grated fresh coconut before frying. This will give the fish an unusual, nut-flavored covering.
● **Adding sesame** For extra flavor, add 1 tsp (5 ml) sesame oil to the egg you use for coating fish. Stir sesame seeds into bread crumbs to add flavor and texture to a coating.

FLAVORING WITH HERBS
● **Adding herbs** Tuck sprigs of fresh herbs into the cavity of a whole fish before cooking, so that the flavor of the herbs penetrates the flesh of the fish.

Baking with fennel
Bake whole fish such as sea bass on a bed of sliced fennel stalks, which will add a subtle flavor. Arrange the fennel in an even layer in a buttered ovenproof dish, then lay the fish over it.

GRILLING AND BARBECUING

Most whole fish, particularly oily fish, cook well on a barbecue or grill and need little more than an occasional brushing with oil to prevent them from drying out or sticking. Delicate fish fillets and steaks need careful basting and turning, or wrap them in foil.

GRILLING SUCCESSFULLY

● **Making kebabs** When making fish kebabs, add other quick-cooking ingredients, such as mushrooms or cherry tomatoes, which will cook in the same amount of time as the fish.

● **Slashing flesh** When cooking a whole fish or thick fillets, slash the thickest parts of the flesh to help the heat penetrate evenly, and speed up grilling.

● **Turning fish** Place a layer of oiled foil over the grill rack so that the fish will turn easily without sticking. Alternatively, grill fish steaks on a preheated cookie sheet, so that there is no need to turn them.

● **Preventing sticking** Preheat the grill rack to a high heat before cooking to seal in juices and prevent sticking.

GRILLING FISH FILLETS

● **Positioning fish** To prevent damage to the flesh, brush fish skin and grill rack with oil, and place fish skin side down.

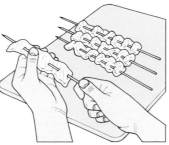

Using skewers
Thread small fish fillets onto wooden skewers for easy turning on a barbecue, and to prevent the fish from breaking up. Soak the skewers in water before use to keep them from burning.

GRILLING SHELLFISH

● **Keeping moist** Wrap shelled mussels or scallops in slices of bacon to keep them moist. Grill after threading onto skewers.

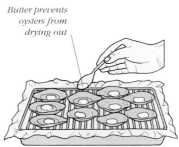

Butter prevents oysters from drying out

Grilling fresh oysters
Place fresh oysters in the deep halves of their shells on a grill pan. Top each with a spoonful of herb butter, and scatter with bread crumbs. Cook on a hot grill pan or under a broiler until bubbling.

ROASTING AND BAKING

Roasting fish at a high temperature seals in flavors and produces tender, moist flesh. Baking in foil or baking parchment bundles prevents the fish from drying out and allows it to cook in its own juices, which can be added to a sauce or poured over the fish before serving.

COOKING FISH IN BUNDLES

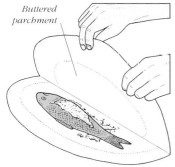

Buttered parchment

Follow shape, tucking in ends with fingertips

1 Bake small, whole fish or fish fillets in bundles. Cut a heart-shaped piece of waxed baking parchment to enclose the fish. Butter the center, and place the fish on one side. Add any flavorings.

2 Fold the other side of the paper over the fish, and tuck and fold along the edge, starting from the rounded end. Finish at the pointed end with a double fold to secure the bundle. Bake on a cookie sheet.

PRESERVING FLAVOR

● **Wrapping in foil** When baking a whole fish such as salmon, wrap it loosely in foil so that the fish stews in its own juices, keeping it moist.

● **Making crispy skin** Baste the skin of sea bass or trout with butter, and season. Roast the fish at a high temperature – about 450°F (230°C).

● **Baking in salt** Place a whole fish on a layer of rock salt. Completely cover it with salt to seal in the juices, then sprinkle with water. Bake at 400°F (200°C) until the salt is hard and dry, then break it with a hammer, discard the salt and skin, and serve.

FRYING

F rying is traditionally a popular method of cooking fish, and need not greatly increase the fat content of your diet. If you heat the oil before adding the fish, an outer crust will form instantly and hardly any fat will be absorbed, leaving the flesh tender and moist.

WORKING WITH OIL

● **Choosing oil** Use good-quality, clean oil for frying fish, since delicate fish flavors can be destroyed by strongly flavored or tainted oil. Lightly flavored oils, such as corn or sunflower, are ideal.
● **Heating the oil** For a crisp coating, make sure that the oil is hot enough before frying fish. For deep frying, the temperature of the oil should be 375°F (190°C).
● **Frying from frozen** To deep-fry fish from frozen, heat the oil to approximately 350°F (180°C), which will allow the inside of the fish to cook before the coating browns.

FRYING SHELLFISH

● **Leaving tails** When peeling shrimp for frying, remove the heads, legs, and skins, but leave the tails on. Use the tail to hold a shrimp when dipping it into the coating mixture.

FRYING JUMBO SHRIMP

Roll shrimp in seasoned cornstarch

Coating in cornstarch
Prepare jumbo shrimp for frying by dusting gently with seasoned cornstarch, then dipping in lightly beaten egg white. The cooked shrimp will have a light, crisp coating and remain juicy inside.

MAKING BATTER

Adding beer
To make a light, crisp batter for coating fish, substitute beer for the liquid, or add a tablespoonful of brandy. Alternatively, lighten the batter by folding a beaten egg white into the mixture just before coating and frying the fish.

ADDING EXTRA FLAVOR

● **Combining oils** When shallow-frying fish fillets, add a subtle, Asian flavor by mixing 1 tbsp (15 ml) sesame oil with a lightly flavored oil, such as sunflower, before cooking.

COATING & WRAPPING

● **Mussels** Dip mussels in a light batter and deep-fry in hot oil for about 30 seconds.
● **Fish fillets** When coating delicate fish fillets, dip first in flour, then in beaten egg. Coat evenly with fine bread crumbs to seal in flavor and prevent the fish from breaking up.
● **Whole fish** To coat small, whole fish, such as whitebait or sardines, in seasoned flour, place the flour and fish in a plastic bag, then shake well to coat evenly.
● **Peeled shrimp** For a light, crisp, golden coating, wrap peeled shrimp in thin strips of phyllo dough, enclosing all but the tail, before frying.

PREPARING SQUID

Diamond pattern will look attractive after cooking

Scoring flesh
Before frying the pouch flesh of squid, score its smooth surface lightly with a sharp knife, making a diamond pattern. This method of scoring the flesh will help the heat penetrate the flesh evenly during cooking.

PREVENTING SPITTING

● **Using a colander** If fish begins to spatter during frying, overturn a colander on top of the pan. This will prevent the grease from escaping, but let steam out.

STIR-FRYING

● **Choosing seafood** Choose a firm-textured, meaty piece of seafood, such as monkfish or squid, for stir-frying; softer-textured seafood breaks up.
● **Using delicate fish** To stir-fry delicate fish, such as cod, coat the pieces in cornstarch before cooking. Shake the pan instead of stirring it to keep the fish pieces whole.
● **Cooking small batches** To keep the heat high enough to seal in the juices, stir-fry a small quantity of fish at a time.
● **Keeping pieces separate** Toss pieces of squid in a little sesame oil before stir-frying to help keep them separate.

POACHING FISH

Poaching is a classic method of cooking fish and also one of the most healthy, since the fish is cooked in liquid with no fat added. Poaching is most suitable for cooking whole fish, such as salmon, and delicate white fish fillets, which require gentle, even cooking.

POACHING PERFECTLY

● **Handling fish gently** To poach a delicate fish, place it in warm liquid that just covers it. Slowly bring the liquid up to barely simmering.

● **Serving fish cold** To cook a whole fish or fish fillets to be served cold, bring the liquid up to simmering and steam gently for one minute. Turn off the heat, and allow the residual heat to cook the fish.

● **Using stock** Give your guests slotted spoons to poach fish at the table in a flavorful stock. Mongolian- or Chinese-style steamers or a fondue set can be used to cook the fish. Serve the stock as a soup.

COOKING LARGE WHOLE FISH

Fitting in a large pan
If you do not have a special pot in which to cook a large, whole fish, accommodate the fish in a large saucepan by curling it gently to fit inside the pan, with its backbone facing upward. Serve on a round platter.

Using a dishwasher
Double-wrap a salmon or any other large fish in foil. Seal thoroughly. Place it on the upper rack of an empty dishwasher. Run a wash cycle at 150°F (65°C), without prewash or dry. Remove, and cool in the foil.

STEAMING FISH

Steaming is a healthy method of cooking, suitable for fish fillets or thin steaks. The main rule is that the fish should not touch the water. You do not need a steamer, but if you steam fish often, it is useful to have a steaming compartment that fits over a saucepan.

COMBINING FOODS

Cooking over potatoes
When steaming fish, make economical use of energy by placing the fish in a steamer over a pot of boiling potatoes. Cover and simmer for 10–15 minutes, depending on thickness.

STEAMING SUCCESSFULLY

● **Steaming large fish** To steam a large, whole fish that will not fit into a steamer, pour a shallow depth of water into a deep roasting pan. Place the fish, covered tightly with foil, on a rack in the pan above the water level, and simmer on the stovetop for five minutes per 1 lb (450 g) weight.

● **Using individual baskets** Use Chinese-style steamer baskets, which stack easily, to steam and then to serve individual portions of fish.

● **Topping off liquid** Always keep a kettle of water close to boiling point while you are steaming foods, so that when topping off the liquid in the steamer, the added water will not lower the temperature.

SOUPS, STOCKS, AND SAUCES

Making your own soups, stocks, and sauces is rewarding, since you can make nutritious and inexpensive dishes that are far superior to anything you could buy, using simple, fresh ingredients and a few basic cooking skills.

MAKING SOUPS AND STOCKS

The basis of a good homemade soup is a flavorful stock. Bouillon cubes save time, but it is relatively easy and inexpensive to make your own stock using leftover vegetables or the bones from a roast. There is an infinite variety of soups that you can create in your kitchen.

MAKING SOUPS

● **Sweating vegetables** Before adding stock, cook vegetables first by "sweating" in a tightly covered pan with a little butter. Add a few tablespoonfuls of wine or dry sherry for extra flavor. Cook over low heat for one hour, shaking now and then to prevent sticking.

● **Using lettuce leaves** Instead of discarding the large, tough outer leaves of lettuce, shred them like cabbage, and cook in a stock. Purée when soft, and stir in a little cream.

● **Using leftovers** Make a quick vichyssoise with cooked potatoes. Fry an onion or a leek until soft, then purée it with the potato and vegetable stock. Add cream to taste.

PURÉEING VEGETABLES

Press vegetables through sieve

Using a ladle
To purée cooked vegetables by hand for adding to soups, put them into a large sieve over a bowl, and squash them with a ladle. This is quicker than using a wooden spoon for pressing, and requires less effort.

THICKENING SOUPS

Stir in a small amount at a time

Using a beurre manié
To thicken a soup quickly and easily, mix together equal amounts of butter and all-purpose flour to a thick paste. Drop small spoonfuls of the mixture into the hot soup, and stir over the heat until sufficiently thickened.

ADDING VARIETY

● **Using spices** Stir mild curry powder into carrot or parsnip soup to add a warm flavor.

● **Adding texture** Before puréeing vegetables for a soup, set aside a ladleful of the cooked, chopped vegetables to add texture to the soup.

● **Crumbling cheese** Liven up creamed or canned soups by stirring in some crumbled blue cheese before serving.

● **Making pistou** Crush three garlic cloves with 2 tbsp (30 ml) pine nuts, a handful of basil, and 2 tbsp (30 ml) olive oil. Stir the mixture into vegetable soups to taste.

USING STOCKS

Ice cubes

Fat

Stock

Removing fat
To remove fat from the surface of stock effectively, add a few ice cubes. When the fat has set around the ice, lift it off.

● **Cooking on low heat** To make a really rich, clear stock, simmer it slowly over very low heat. Boiling a stock tends to give a cloudy appearance.

● **Reducing stock** To store cooked stock, reduce it first by boiling it in an uncovered pan until it is very thick and syrupy. The stock will then set when cooled, and this will keep longer than a liquid.

● **Using leftovers** Add leftover vegetables, trimmings, or peelings to stock for flavor. Do not use potatoes, since they will make the stock cloudy.

MAKING EGG-BASED SAUCES

S auces incorporating eggs are made either by creating a thick emulsion, as in mayonnaise or hollandaise, or by gentle cooking, as in the case of custard or cream sauce. Egg-based sauces take longer to make than many other sauces, but their rich, creamy textures are unmatched.

CORRECTING FAULTS

● **Adding ice** If you overheat hollandaise sauce, and it is just starting to curdle, stir in an ice cube to cool it quickly.

● **Rewhisking hollandaise** To smooth a curdled hollandaise sauce, add it drop by drop to a spoonful of vinegar in a clean bowl, whipping hard until the sauce rethickens.

● **Using egg yolk** If mayonnaise separates, beat a fresh egg yolk in a clean bowl, and whip in the mayonnaise drop by drop until the mixture thickens.

● **Adding cornstarch** If a custard sauce begins to curdle, plunge the base of the pan into cold water, then push the sauce through a sieve. Whip a teaspoonful of cornstarch into the sauce, and reheat gently without boiling until thickened.

MAKING MAYONNAISE

● **Reducing fat** For a white, low-fat mayonnaise, use whole eggs instead of just the yolks, or mix the mayonnaise with plain yogurt in equal parts.

Add leaves to color mayonnaise

Using a blender
Put all the mayonnaise ingredients except the oil into a blender. Run the machine, and add the oil in a thin stream until the sauce thickens. Then add any extra ingredients, such as watercress.

MAKING HOLLANDAISE

● **Using a microwave** Heat 7 tbsp (100 g) butter in a large cup on High, and whip in two egg yolks and flavorings. Cook on Medium for one minute.

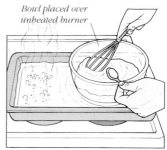
Bowl placed over unheated burner

Avoiding curdling
To make hollandaise sauce without a double boiler, prepare it in a bowl placed in a roasting pan containing simmering water. Make sure that the bowl is not directly above the heat source.

MAKING OTHER SAUCES

T here are numerous different types of sauce in addition to custard and the emulsions produced by traditional sauce-making methods. Flour-thickened mixtures are useful, and sauces made from simple purées, salsas, and cream reductions provide interesting alternatives.

MAKING SALSAS

Salsas are an essential part of Mexican cuisine, adding powerful flavors and rich colors to simple meals.

● **Saving time** Place chilies, garlic, onions, tomatoes, and seeded peppers in a food processor. Pulse until finely chopped for a *salsa cruda*.

● **Mixing fruits** Combine finely chopped fresh mango, pawpaw, and chilies to serve with grilled fish or chicken.

● **Creating mild flavors** To reduce the strong flavors of raw garlic and onions, simmer for 5–8 minutes before use.

WORKING WITH SAUCES

● **Adding cornstarch** To thicken a smooth sauce, blend 1 tsp (5 ml) cornstarch into 2 tsp (10 ml) cold water, add to the sauce, and stir over moderate heat until thickened.

● **Correcting lumpy sauces** If a sauce or gravy has become lumpy, pour it into a food processor, and process until smooth. Alternatively, press the sauce through a sieve.

● **Making purées** Use smooth purées of vegetables such as peppers for colorful, simple, low-fat sauces. Grill the peppers to remove the skins, then purée in a processor.

TRADITIONAL TIP

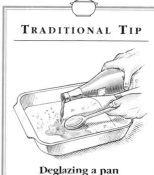

Deglazing a pan
Add wine, stock, or cream to the concentrated juices or sediment left in a roasting pan after cooking meat or poultry. Bring to a boil, and stir well.

GRAINS, PASTA, AND LEGUMES

THE WIDE VARIETY OF GRAINS, PASTA, AND LEGUMES now available from all over the world presents many choices for healthy meals that are easy to prepare. They form the basis of substantial main dishes and delicious side dishes.

GRAINS

Grains are usually boiled or steamed, either on their own or combined with a variety of other ingredients in dishes such as pilafs or risottos. Whole grains take longer to cook than processed white grains, but most varieties of grain will cook within about 30 minutes.

REMOVING STARCH

Rinsing basmati rice
Basmati rice needs to be rinsed thoroughly to keep the grains separate. Place it in a bowl of cold water, and swirl the rice around by hand. Drain, and repeat until the water is clear.

TRADITIONAL TIP

Making a stomach settler
As a cure for an upset stomach, boil white rice without having rinsed it first, then strain off the starchy cooking liquid. Allow the liquid to cool, then give it to the patient to drink.

COOLING COOKED RICE

Using a wooden spoon
To cool cooked rice quickly for use in salads, drain through a sieve and place over a bowl. Prod the rice at intervals with a wooden spoon handle to release the steam and heat.

COOKING PERFECT RICE
● **Presoaking rice** Reduce the cooking time of rice and other grains by soaking them first in cold water for 30 minutes.
● **Cooking on a low heat** When cooking glutinous rice, use a large pan, and simmer on the lowest heat possible. Keep the lid on during cooking, and let stand for 10 minutes after draining.
● **Using a microwave** Place 1 cup (250 g) white rice in a large bowl with 2 cups (450 ml) boiling water. Cook on High for nine minutes. Cook brown rice for about 15–20 minutes.
● **Forking rice** Fluff up cooked rice by separating the grains with a fork before serving.

STEAMING COUSCOUS

Lining a colander
If you do not have a couscous steamer, line a metal sieve with a piece of cheesecloth, and place it over a pan of boiling water. Pour the couscous into the sieve and cover. Steam until tender.

ADDING VARIETY
● **Cooking in stock** Add extra flavor to plain boiled grains by cooking them in a rich meat, chicken, or vegetable stock rather than water.
● **Coloring rice** If you do not have saffron for tinting rice and risottos, stir in a pinch of turmeric after cooking.
● **Using coconut milk** Simmer long-grain rice in coconut milk to accompany Asian dishes. Use about 1½ cups (400 ml) coconut milk to ¾ cup (200 g) rice, and cook until the liquid is absorbed.
● **Using pesto** Replace the butter or olive oil in cooked polenta with a roughly equal quantity of pesto sauce.

PASTA

There are only a few simple rules to follow when cooking fresh or dried pasta. Cook it lightly, in plenty of rapidly boiling water, until it is *al dente* – which translates literally as "to the tooth." This means the pasta is tender to the bite, but still offers a slight resistance in the center.

COOKING LONG PASTA

Feed pasta in as it softens

Feeding into a pan
To fit long spaghetti into a small pan of boiling water, hold it in a bunch, and put one end into the water. As the ends of the pieces soften, bend the pasta slightly, and push in the rest gradually.

COOKING STUFFED PASTA

Skimmer will not split pasta

Using a skimmer
To lift cooked, filled pasta such as ravioli out of water without damaging or bursting it, use a flat, metal skimmer or a flat, slotted, draining spoon. Toss in oil or sauce to prevent sticking.

COLORING PASTA

To add color and flavor when making pasta dough, mix in additional ingredients.

● **Tomato** Add 2 tsp (10 ml) tomato paste per egg to the beaten eggs, and stir well.
● **Spinach** Thaw ¼ cup (50 g) frozen, chopped spinach per egg. Squeeze well before adding to the beaten eggs.
● **Saffron** For rich, golden pasta, add a pinch of ground saffron to the flour.
● **Beets** Stir 1 tbsp (15 ml) cooked, puréed beet per egg to the pasta dough.

LEGUMES

Peas, beans, and lentils are a valuable source of protein and are versatile enough to be used in all kinds of dishes, including casseroles, pâtés, dals, and salads. Dried beans take some time to cook, but the cooking is simple, and they are less expensive than canned varieties.

COOKING TIMES

Most legumes need to be soaked in cold water for at least 4–8 hours. Alternatively, soak in boiling water for about one hour. The following cooking times are a rough guide only; recommended times may vary from one type to another, so check carefully.

● Split lentils: 15–20 minutes.
● Whole lentils, aduki beans, mung beans, split peas: 25–30 minutes.
● Black-eyed peas, Great Northern beans, lima beans, peas: 45 minutes.
● Black beans, white kidney beans, red kidney beans: about one hour.
● Pinto beans, chickpeas: 1¼ hours.
● Butter beans, fava beans: 1½ hours.

COOKING BEANS
● **Seasoning** Season beans toward the end of their cooking time, since salt can prevent them from softening.
● **Cooling** If you are cooking beans to serve cold, cool them in their cooking water rather than drying in a colander. This stops their skins from splitting.
● **Pressure cooking** If you are using a pressure cooker, cook beans on High for a third of their normal cooking time.

DIGESTIVE AID

Boil dried, soaked beans vigorously for 10 minutes, then drain and start again with fresh water. This process reduces the "gassiness" associated with eating beans. Simmer gently until the beans are tender.

PREPARING SNACKS
● **Making a dip** Mash cooked, drained butter beans well with a fork. Add crushed garlic, chili paste, and olive oil to make a rich, spicy dip. Serve with vegetable sticks.

Flour seasoned with ground pepper

Making chickpea nibbles
Mix cooked or drained canned chickpeas with seasoned whole-wheat flour and crushed garlic. Fry in a little butter and oil over high heat until crisp and golden. Serve with cocktails.

DESSERTS

A HOT OR COLD DESSERT rounds off a meal nicely. Whatever level of skill you possess, and however much time you have to prepare, it is always possible to make a delicious dessert that will bring the meal to a satisfying end.

BAKING PIES AND TARTS

There is no more memorable way of enjoying an abundance of ripe fruits in season than by baking them in a golden, homemade pastry case. Alternatively, dairy products or many pantry ingredients can be used to produce a quick, convenient filling for a delicious dessert.

PREPARING FILLINGS
● **Dicing cheese** Add tiny cubes of a tangy, mature cheese to complement a sweet apple filling in a pie.
● **Creating a quick filling** Make a festive dessert by mixing fresh seedless grapes with a few spoonfuls of store-bought mincemeat. Spoon into a pastry shell, and bake until hot. Serve with whipped cream.
● **Glazing fruits** To glaze and sweeten fresh fruits for a colorful tart or pie filling, warm a few spoonfuls of seedless raspberry jelly with a squeeze of lemon or orange juice in a pan. Brush the glaze over the fruits.

MAKING TOPPINGS

Pinch phyllo into ruffles

Using phyllo dough
Instead of laying sheets of pastry or phyllo flat on top of a fruit filling, crumple them slightly for a "chiffon" effect. Brush with butter, bake as usual, and sprinkle with confectioners' sugar.

ADDING EXTRA FLAVOR

Distribute coconut evenly

Sprinkling coconut
To add extra flavor to a fruit tart or pie, sprinkle a layer of dried coconut over the base before adding the filling. This will also help prevent the base from becoming soggy.

FRUIT TART TOPPINGS

● **Marshmallows** Arrange marshmallows to cover the fruits. Grill until golden.
● **Marzipan** Cut marzipan into dice, and scatter over the tart. Bake or grill until golden.
● **Almond crumble** Mix equal amounts of ground almonds, brown or raw sugar, and flaked almonds. Sprinkle the mixture over the fruits before baking to form a golden crust.
● **Meringue** Whip one egg white until stiff, then whip in ¼ cup (55 g) superfine sugar. Pipe a meringue lattice over the fruits, and bake for a delicious, decorative topping.

ADDING VARIETY
● **Baking upside-down tarts** Use a cake pan to make an upside-down fruit tart. Butter and sugar the base, add the fruits, and top with rolled-out pastry. Bake and invert.
● **Making sweet pizza** Roll out puff pastry or bread dough, and top with slices of fruits such as apples, pears, or plums. Sprinkle with brown sugar and spices, dot with butter, and bake in a hot oven until bubbling and golden.
● **Latticing phyllo strips** Cut phyllo dough into long strips with scissors to make a quick lattice for a pie or tart. Use two sheets together, brushed with butter, for the best effect.

MONEY-SAVING TIP

Making use of stale bread
Spread slices of stale bread with butter and marmalade or jam, and layer in an ovenproof dish. Add two eggs beaten in 1¼ cups (300 ml) milk. Bake in a moderate oven.

MAKING OTHER HOT DESSERTS

Hot desserts are warming and satisfying, and they can be very versatile. Whip up lemon pancakes for an informal occasion, or try flambéed crêpes suzettes for a dinner party. Add variety to puddings by stirring in dried fruits, spices, an extract such as vanilla, or citrus-fruit zest.

USING BATTER

● **Adding cocoa** To make delicious chocolate-flavored pancakes, replace 2 tsp (10 ml) of the quantity of flour used in the recipe with cocoa powder.
● **Baking easy tarts** To make a quick and easy fruit dessert, pour waffle batter over sugared fruit slices in a heated, greased cake pan. Bake in a hot oven until golden.
● **Making a light batter** For a crisp, light fritter batter, separate the eggs, and mix the yolks with the flour. Whip the egg whites until stiff, and fold into the mixture. Use the batter to coat sliced apple, pineapple, or banana.
● **Deep-frying pancakes** Place a spoonful of fruit in the centers of cooked pancakes. Fold the pancakes into squares, dip in batter and deep-fry until golden. Dust with sugar, and serve with fruit sauce.

FINISHING SOUFFLÉS

Caramelizing the top
Give a hot, sweet soufflé a golden, caramelized finish on top by sprinkling with confectioners' sugar at the end of cooking. Sprinkle quickly, and bake for 4–5 minutes to brown.

USING WAFFLE BATTER

Making beignets
Use waffle batter for making beignets as an alternative to waffles. Carefully drop spoonfuls of the batter into hot oil, and fry until puffy and golden. Serve the beignets topped with maple syrup or vanilla sugar.

UNUSUAL DESSERTS
● **Making Baked Alaska** Lightly brown crumpled phyllo dough under the broiler. Use to top scoops of ice cream, and cover with warm chocolate sauce.

USING A MICROWAVE
● **Baking apples** Peel and core apples, then fill with a pat of butter and brown sugar. Bake, covered, in the microwave until soft. Brown under the broiler if desired.
● **Cooking puddings** Use a very large, deep container to cook milk-based puddings in a microwave, since the milk will rise up the sides.
● **Setting meringue** Cook a meringue topping on a dessert in a microwave to save time. Scatter toasted nuts over the surface if it is too pale.
● **Melting chocolate** To melt chocolate in the microwave, break it up and heat for 1–2 minutes per ounce (25 g). Remove and stir until smooth.

FLAVORING MILK

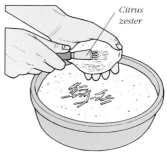

Citrus zester

Adding lemon zest
To lift the flavor of a plain pudding such as rice or bread, use a citrus zester to grate a few strips of lemon zest over the pudding, and stir to mix in evenly before cooking. Orange zest can also be used.

● **Flaming cherries** When flaming Cherries Jubilee, be sure to use cherry-flavored liqueur as the alcohol. It will intensify the flavor of the fruit.

QUICK DESSERTS
● **Filling croissants** Cut open warmed croissants, and fill with hot stewed plums, then scatter with flaked almonds.
● **Pan-frying bananas** Peel and thickly slice some bananas, and sauté in a little butter and brown sugar for two minutes. Sprinkle with orange juice and a dash of rum.
● **Grilling soft fruits** Sprinkle kirsch over frozen, mixed fruits in an ovenproof dish. Top with mascarpone cheese and brown sugar, and broil until hot and bubbling.
● **Making fruit compotes** Warm a mixture of canned fruits, their juices, grated lemon zest, and cinnamon in a pan. Serve with whipped cream.

COLD DESSERTS

There are several types of cold dessert, from fresh, light fruit salads and mousses to rich, creamy egg custards, cheesecakes, and filled meringues. They all have the advantage that they can be made in advance, leaving you free to prepare and serve other courses.

PREVENTING PROBLEMS

● **Preventing skin** Lay a piece of waxed paper over puddings and custards as they cool, to prevent a skin from forming on the surface.

● **Slicing meringue** Prevent a soft meringue dessert from sticking when being sliced, either by buttering the knife blade first, or by dipping the knife into boiling water.

● **Adding sparkle** Pep up the flavor of an oversweetened or plain fruit salad by adding a splash of sparkling wine just before the dessert is served.

● **Making crème caramel** Rinse the dish being used in hot water before pouring very hot caramel into it. This will help prevent the dish from cracking.

FINISHING CRÈME BRÛLÉE

Spray water evenly over surface of sugar topping

Caramelizing sugar
For a perfect, golden caramel topping on crème brûlée, sprinkle the set custard with a thick layer of superfine sugar, and spray with a fine water mister. Caramelize under a hot broiler.

MAKING PAVLOVAS

Shape meringue on plate

Preventing breakage
Spoon the meringue mixture for a pavlova onto a ceramic, ovenproof pizza plate so that it can be baked and served in the same dish. You will thus avoid cracking it while transferring it.

GELATIN-SET DESSERTS

Gelatin is the most common setting agent used in cooking. It is available in powdered form and should be thoroughly dissolved in hot water before use. Agar-agar, a vegetarian setting agent made from seaweed, is used in much the same way.

USING GELATIN

● **Dissolving gelatin** Always add gelatin to hot liquid to dissolve. Do not add the liquid to the gelatin.

● **Preparing fruits** Cook fresh pineapple or kiwi fruit before using in gelatin-set desserts; this destroys the enzyme that keeps gelatin from setting.

● **Eating outdoors** If serving a dessert outdoors in warm weather, slightly increase the amount of gelatin used. Add an extra 1 tsp (5 ml) gelatin for every envelopeful.

● **Turning out set desserts** Wet a mold for a thin gelatin mixture such as jelly to make turning out easy. Lightly oil a mold for a thick mixture.

DECORATING MOLDS

Gelatin holds fruit in place when set

Layering with fruits
Set fruits in a gelatin mold by swirling a little unset gelatin into the mold. Arrange the fruits around the base or sides. Chill, to set. Continue layering the fruit until the mold is full.

SERVING SET DESSERTS

● **Retaining flavor** Remove a gelatin-set mixture from the refrigerator 15 minutes before serving, since overchilling will reduce the flavor of a dessert.

● **Using water** Before unmolding a gelatin mold onto a serving plate, rinse the plate in cold water. Unmold, and slide into position.

● **Unmolding** To unmold set mixtures, dip the mold briefly in hot water. Put a plate over the mold, flip it over, and shake to dislodge the dessert.

● **Serving frozen** A cold soufflé that has not set can be served frozen. Put it in the freezer until firm, remove the paper collar, and serve.

CHOCOLATE DESSERTS

W hen using chocolate in either hot or cold desserts, buy the best you can afford. The better the quality, the more chocolatey tasting your dessert will be. Use cocoa to add a chocolate flavor to cooked mixtures, but remember to include some sugar to taste.

SHAPING CURLS

Cool marble board

Using a zester
Make decorative chocolate curls using a citrus zester. Spread melted chocolate evenly over a cool surface, and let stand until just set. Pull the zester across the surface to remove small curls.

MAKING EDIBLE LEAVES

Paint chocolate over leaf with small, soft brush

Imprinting leaves
Select clean, unblemished rose leaves or other nonpoisonous leaves. Brush melted chocolate evenly over each leaf. Let set, then very gently peel off the leaf to reveal its imprint.

USING CHOCOLATE

● **Melting chocolate** To melt chocolate without a double boiler, use a heatproof bowl over hot, not boiling, water.
● **Making curls** Add store-bought chocolate couveture to melted chocolate to make it pliable when shaping curls.
● **Adding gloss** Add a rich gloss to a chocolate sauce or a chocolate topping by stirring in two pats of unsalted butter.
● **Substituting cocoa** If you run out of baking chocolate, use 3 tbsp (45 ml) of cocoa and 1 tbsp (15 ml) of butter for every 1 oz (25 g) needed.
● **Replacing alcohol** Replace the alcohol in a chocolate dessert with the same amount of black coffee, if preferred.

ICE CREAMS AND SORBETS

I ce creams are based on simple mixtures and can be produced easily with or without an ice cream maker. Ice cream mixtures based on heavy cream and egg custards are very successful made by hand, but sorbets and frozen yogurt benefit from machine churning.

MAKING ICES

● **Flavoring ices** Slightly over-flavor or oversweeten sorbet and ice cream mixtures, since freezing masks flavors.
● **Using gelatin** To make a firm, scoopable sorbet, add a little dissolved gelatin to the mixture before freezing.
● **Sweetening with honey** For a soft texture, use honey rather than sugar to sweeten ices.
● **Making ices by hand** Whisk handmade ices at frequent intervals while freezing to break up ice crystals and produce a smooth texture.
● **Maturing ices** Mature the flavor of ices in the freezer for 24 hours. Soften at room temperature before serving.

USING AN IMPROVISED BOMBE MOLD

Fill center with soft-fruit sorbet

Hot towel loosens bombe from basin

1 To make an ice cream bombe without a mold, set a freezer-proof bowl in a basin of ice. Pack the base and sides of the bowl with firm but slightly softened ice cream. Fill the center, and freeze.

2 To turn out the bombe, wrap the bowl briefly in a dish towel that has been wrung out in hot water. Run a knife around the inside edge of the bowl, then invert the bombe onto a serving plate.

BAKING

H OME BAKING IS ONE OF THE MOST REWARDING cooking skills. While you are learning basic techniques, follow recipes and measure ingredients carefully. Once you have gained confidence, you can adapt recipes to your own taste.

MAKING CAKES

T here are four basic techniques used in making cakes: melting, creaming, cutting in, and beating. Whichever method you use, preheat the oven and prepare the pans first, since you are most likely to get a good rise if the cake is baked as soon as possible after mixing.

LINING TINS
● **Cutting spares** If you often use a particular pan for baking, cut several thicknesses of waxed paper at a time, and keep the spares for future use.
● **Protecting the edges** Line a cake pan for a fruit cake with a double layer of waxed paper to protect the edge of the cake from excessive heat.
● **Greasing pans** Use oil to grease a cake pan; it is easier to brush on than butter and is less likely to burn or stick.
● **Adding paper** Place a small square cut from nonstick paper in the base of a greased and floured pan to ease removal.

MAKING RING PANS

Dried beans

Using a food can
Make a ring pan by placing a tall food can, weighed down with pie weights, in the center of a round cake pan. The beans will stop the can from moving when the batter is poured around it.

MAKING HEART SHAPES

Combining two cakes
Bake a round and a square cake, with the diameter of the circle and the sides of the square the same length. Cut the circle in half, and place one half on each of two adjacent sides of the square.

REMOVING FROM PANS
● **Allowing standing time** Leave a sponge cake in the pan for 2–3 minutes to let it contract and firm up before removing it from the pan. Let a fruit cake cool completely.
● **Loosening sides** Run a knife around the inside of the pan to loosen the sides of a cake.
● **Using a can** To remove a cake from a loose-bottomed pan, rest the base on a tall can, and push the sides down.
● **Inverting pans** Prevent a cake from drying out by inverting it onto a cooling rack and placing the pan over it.
● **Using an oven rack** Use an oven shelf as a cooling rack. Raise it above the counter by placing it on a springform ring.

HEALTHY TIP

Dusting with bran
Grease a cake pan as usual, then, instead of flour, sprinkle a little wheat or oat bran inside it to add fiber as well as flavor to the cake. Turn the pan to coat the base and sides evenly.

TESTING DONENESS
● **Pressing the top** Apply light pressure to the top of a sponge cake with your fingertips. The top should feel firm and should spring back into shape without leaving an indentation.
● **Checking the edges** Look closely at the edges of a cake. They will have shrunk away slightly from the sides of the pan if the cake has cooked thoroughly.
● **Listening closely** Listen to a cake. A sizzling noise means that it is still cooking.
● **Using a skewer** Test a cake by inserting a metal or bamboo skewer into its middle. The skewer will be clean if the cake is cooked.

ADDING FLAVORINGS AND FILLINGS

A simple sponge or a plain fruit cake can be transformed through the imaginative use of fillings and flavorings. Try enhancing a basic sponge cake with scented leaves or extracts, or create a lavish showpiece in minutes by adding a dash of liqueur and a rich frosting.

ADDING FLAVOR

Place lemon-scented geranium leaf in center of pan

Using a geranium leaf
Before adding sponge cake batter to a pan for baking, place a lemon-scented geranium leaf in the bottom of the pan. As the cake cooks, the leaf's delicate scent will permeate it.

SANDWICHING CAKES

Filling will hold layers together

Spreading a filling
Before sandwiching two halves of a sponge cake together, spread a filling, such as frosting, onto both halves. Press them gently together so that they will remain in position when the cake is cut.

HEALTHY TIP

Making a low-fat filling
For a low-fat filling, mix together 7 oz (200 g) reduced-fat cream cheese made from skim milk with 2 tbsp (30 ml) honey, then flavor with finely grated citrus zest. Use as a filling or topping for a sponge or carrot cake as an alternative to a rich cream-cheese frosting.

DISGUISING MISTAKES

Even the most experienced cook can make a mistake when baking. However, most problems can be rectified. If a cake appears burned, for example, it is often only the outer crust that is affected. Remove the crust with a knife, and disguise the top with frosting.

RESCUING SPONGE
● **Correcting curdling** If a sponge cake mixture begins to separate during mixing, add 1 tbsp (15 ml) flour, then beat the mixture thoroughly.
● **Mending cracks** To repair a cake that has cracked while being removed from the pan, brush the pieces with warmed apricot jam. Reassemble the cake in the pan to cool.
● **Concealing cracks** To hide cracks in a roulade or jelly roll, pipe cream over them. Sprinkle with confectioners' sugar, cocoa, or grated chocolate.
● **Moistening sponge** Sprinkle a dry sponge cake with fresh orange or other fruit juice.

USING SUNKEN CAKES

Cut out center from cooled cake

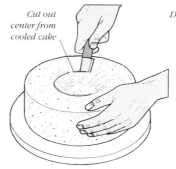

Cutting out the center
If a round fruit or sponge cake has an undercooked, sunken center, make it into a ring cake by cutting the center out neatly with a sharp knife. Cover the ring with frosting.

MOISTENING DRY CAKES

Dribble liqueur slowly to soak in evenly

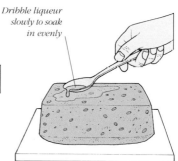

Adding liqueur
To moisten overcooked or dried-out fruit cake, turn the cake upside down, and pierce it with a skewer several times. Spoon brandy, whisky, or rum over the surface and let stand for 24 hours.

DECORATING CAKES

You do not need special skills to decorate cakes impressively. The simplest, most basic techniques are often the most effective, so there is no need to spend hours in the kitchen. Cool, dry conditions are best for sugar and icings, so avoid working in steamy kitchens.

APPLYING TOPPINGS

● **Pouring icing** To ice a sponge cake quickly, place it on a wire rack over a cookie sheet and pour glaze or melted chocolate over the surface in one movement, smoothing around the sides with a knife. Let set.

● **Softening almond paste** If almond paste dries out and is hard to roll, warm it in a microwave on Medium for 30 seconds. Knead the paste until it is soft enough to roll.

● **Using fondant** Roll out ready-made fondant icing on a surface lightly dusted with sifted cornstarch instead of confectioners' sugar. Cornstarch will be easier to brush off the cake than confectioners' sugar.

● **Smoothing fondant** To smooth the sides of a cake iced with fondant, roll a straight-sided jar around them. Dust the jar first with cornstarch to prevent it from sticking.

DECORATING WITH SUGAR

● **Using a doily** To decorate a plain cake, place a paper doily on top and sprinkle the cake with confectioners' sugar. Lift the doily off to reveal a lace pattern.

Shake confectioners' sugar through sieve

Using stencils
Cut out paper shapes, and arrange these stencils on top of the cake you wish to decorate. Sprinkle the cake with confectioners' sugar, then remove the shapes to reveal the stenciled design.

USING FLOWERS

● **Washing flowers** Wash delicate edible flowers with a fine water mist before using. Shake off excess water, and dry on an absorbent paper towel.

Brush gently with egg white

Coating edible flowers
Decorate edible flowers with a thin coating of sugar. First, brush egg white onto the petals with a soft paintbrush. Sprinkle the petals lightly with superfine sugar, and let dry for 24 hours.

COLORING ICING

Drip coloring into icing

Using a skewer
Control the addition of small amounts of liquid food coloring to icing by using a skewer or a toothpick. Dip it into the bottle, and use it like a dropper to drip the coloring into the icing.

FILLING PIPING BAGS

Working with a cup
To fill a piping bag without mess, fit the bag with a nozzle, place in a measuring cup, and turn the top of the bag over the top of the cup. The bag is held open while icing is spooned in.

MAKING A PIPING BAG

If you do not have a piping bag to ice a cake, improvise with one of the following:

● **Using a plastic bag** For plain icing, snip a corner off a strong plastic bag without a seam, and insert a nozzle.

● **Making a paper cone** Cut an 8-in (20-cm) square of waxed paper, and fold it diagonally to make a triangle. Lift a bottom corner, and curl it around to meet the tip of the triangle at the front. Then curl the other corner around the back to meet the tip. Snip the point off the cone, and pipe through the hole.

BAKING SMALL CAKES AND COOKIES

Baking small cakes and cookies is enjoyable as well as practical: techniques are simple, and cooking times are short. Make them to eat yourself or to give away to friends. Cupcakes and muffins should be eaten as fresh as possible, but cookies can often be stored for several days.

COOKING MUFFINS

Baking in a microwave
Use straight-sided cups to bake muffins in a microwave, rather than a microwave muffin tin. Brush the cups with oil before adding the mixture. Bake the muffins in small batches.

USING A MICROWAVE
● **Using a flan dish** Use a round porcelain flan dish to cook bar cookies in the microwave. Allow to cool, then cut into wedges.
● **Adding color** To add color to microwaved cookies and cakes, brush them with honey and scatter with toasted nuts.

MAKING SMALL CAKES
● **Using a piping bag** When making a large batch of cupcakes, spoon the cake batter into a piping bag fitted with a large, plain nozzle. Pipe the mixture into cupcake liners, and bake.
● **Topping with sugar** Create a crunchy topping for plain sponge cakes by sprinkling them lightly with brown sugar before baking.
● **Creating a surprise** Include a surprise in plain cakes by pressing a small square of chocolate into the center of the uncooked mixture.

MAKING COOKIES

Press rim firmly into dough

Cutting out circles
Use the rim of an upside-down wine glass to cut rounds from rolled-out cookie dough if you do not have a cookie cutter. Dip the rim into flour before using it to cut out sticky mixtures.

PREPARING AHEAD
● **Storing cookie dough** Roll up firm cookie dough and wrap it in foil. Store in the refrigerator for several weeks, baking batches as you need to.
● **Improving flavor** Store gingersnaps in a tin for several days to improve their flavor. Refresh in a hot oven to serve.

SHAPING DELICATE COOKIES AFTER BAKING
● **Using a jar** Use a fish server to lift almond tuiles onto the sides of clean jelly jars as they come out of the oven. This will allow them to cool quickly and will result in them setting in a curved shape.
● **Rolling on a wooden spoon** Shape cooked brandy-snap mixture into rolls around the handle of a wooden spoon while the mixture is still warm. Gently slide the roll off the handle, and cool on a rack. If the mixture sets before it has been shaped, return it to the oven for 30 seconds.

MAKING BISCUITS
● **Helping biscuits to rise** To help biscuits rise and soften the gluten in the flour, use buttermilk or sour cream instead of milk, and equal quantities of baking soda and cream of tartar instead of baking powder.
● **Rolling biscuit wedges** Instead of cutting out round biscuits, roll the dough into one smooth circle, and cut into wedges with a sharp knife. Bake, then pull apart to serve.
● **Adding savory flavor** To give plain biscuit dough a savory flavor, sift 1 tsp (5 ml) of celery salt with the flour, or stir in some herbs.

SHAPING STICKY DOUGH
● **Wetting hands** To prevent cookie dough from sticking to your hands, wet them in cold water before handling it.
● **Chilling dough** If cookie dough is too sticky to handle, wrap it in plastic wrap, and chill for 30 minutes. If it is still sticky, work in some flour.

Mold mixture over top of orange

Shaping over an orange
To shape delicate cookies or mold brandy-snap mixture into baskets, arrange each portion of cookie mixture gently over an orange as soon as it comes out of the oven. Let them set.

MAKING BASIC BREADS

Baking your own bread is easy, satisfying, and takes surprisingly little time. Use a food processor to take the hard work out of kneading, and reduce rising times by using fast-action yeast. Alternatively, let dough rise overnight in the refrigerator so that it is ready to bake the next day.

USING YEAST

● **Substituting dried yeast** When substituting dried yeast for fresh in a recipe, use 2 tsp (10 ml) dried yeast for ½ oz (15 g) fresh yeast.

● **Using fast-action yeast** Add fast-action yeast directly to a dry flour mix, not to liquid, or its action will be delayed.

● **Freezing dough** If you are making dough that is to be frozen before baking, increase the quantity of yeast by about one third, since freezing will kill some of the yeast.

● **Adding potato water** Save the water from boiled potatoes to add to bread mixes. It will feed the yeast, giving a good rise, and add to the flavor.

BAKING LARGE LOAVES

● **Testing for doneness** To make sure that a large loaf is cooked properly, turn it out of the pan, and tap the bottom with your knuckles. If it sounds hollow, the bread is thoroughly cooked. If not, return it to the oven for a few minutes to finish cooking.

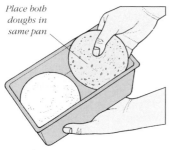

Place both doughs in same pan

Combining doughs

If some members of your family like whole-wheat bread and others prefer white bread, bake the two kinds of dough end to end in a large loaf pan. Then you can slice the loaf from either end.

HELPING DOUGH RISE

Make bowl airtight with plastic wrap

Covering with plastic wrap

To encourage dough to rise, place it in a bowl, and cover with plastic wrap that has been brushed with oil. The dampness and warmth created inside the bowl will speed up the rising.

CREATING CRUSTS

● **Baking crusty loaves** For a really crisp crust all over a loaf, take it out of the pan when it is cooked. Then return it to the oven, placing it directly on the shelf, for five minutes more to make sure the crust is crisp all over. Cool the loaf on a wire rack before storing.

Making soft crusts

For soft crusts on bread rolls or loaves, dust the tops with flour before baking, and cover with a clean dish towel when cooling. Also, add milk to the dough mix instead of using just water.

BRIGHT IDEA

Baking in a flowerpot
Bake bread in a new, lightly oiled terra-cotta flowerpot for an unusually shaped loaf. Terra-cotta gives bread a crisp, golden crust. Preheat the pot first for 30 minutes in the oven at 375°F (190°C).

RISING DOUGHS

● **Adding ascorbic acid** When using fresh yeast, speed up rising times by adding a 25-mg tablet of ascorbic acid for every 8 cups (1 kg) flour.

● **Warming flour** To help dough rise on a cold day, warm the flour first in an ovenproof bowl in the oven at 225°F (110°C). Alternatively, put the flour in a microwave on High for 10 seconds.

● **Using a microwave** Place dough in an oiled bowl, brush with oil, and cover with waxed paper. Stand the bowl in a shallow dish of hot water, and microwave on Low for four minutes. Let stand for about 20 minutes. Repeat the process until the dough is doubled.

● **Testing the rise** To test whether dough has risen enough, press it lightly with a floured finger. The dough should spring back without leaving an indentation.

ENHANCING FLAVOR

Even the most basic breads are transformed by adding extra flavors to the dough. Stir herbs or spices into the dry flour mix to ensure even distribution, or knead in chunky additions, such as olives, just before shaping. Brush tops of loaves or rolls with glaze for last-minute flavor.

ADDING EXTRAS

● **Chopping ingredients** Knead a few chopped olives, herbs, walnuts, or sun-dried tomatoes into plain bread dough for a Mediterranean flavor.

● **Mixing flours** Reduce the strong flavor of buckwheat flour by mixing it half and half with rice flour.

● **Adding spicy glaze** Brush the tops of loaves with a mixture of oil and curry paste or pesto sauce before baking for a spicy, golden crust.

● **Glazing with herbs** For a crisp, savory crust on bread, dissolve 2 tsp (10 ml) salt in 2 tbsp (30 ml) warm water, and brush over the tops of rolls. Sprinkle with herbs and bake.

MAKING SAVORY BREADS

Adding celery salt
Give plain bread a subtle, savory flavor by substituting celery salt or garlic salt for table salt. If the salt crystals are large, dissolve them first in the liquid that will be used to mix the dough.

MAKING SWEET GLAZES

Using honey
Brush bread loaves or rolls with warmed honey as soon as they are removed from the oven for a glossy, sweet glaze. Alternatively, brush with corn or maple syrup for the same effect.

SHAPING AND DECORATING DOUGH

Bread dough can be shaped before baking, whether in a loaf pan or on a cookie sheet. Traditional shapes such as braids or twists can be adapted for large loaves or small rolls. If you are short on time, decorate dough by scoring a lattice pattern on the surface with a sharp blade.

DECORATING LOAVES

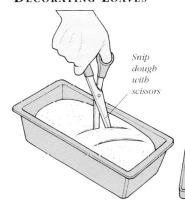

Snip dough with scissors

Snipping with scissors
To decorate a plain loaf quickly, use scissors to cut slashes across the top of the dough before rising or baking. The cuts will open out when the dough rises, making a patterned top.

MAKING ROUND LOAVES

● **Shaping a cottage loaf** Top a ball of dough with a smaller ball. Poke a hole through the center with your finger to secure them.

Cutting a cross
Cut a deep cross in a plain, round loaf before proving, using a floured, sharp knife. The cuts will open out to form an attractive crown shape when the loaf of bread is baked.

CREATING VARIETY

● **Using seeds** Scatter sesame or poppy seeds over soft rolls after glazing to make an attractive and tasty topping.

● **Marbling dough** Make two batches of dough; one whole-wheat, one plain. Pull off small pieces, then knead together before shaping to give the dough a marbled effect.

● **Sprinkling pans** After greasing loaf pans, sprinkle lightly with cracked wheat or rolled oats before adding bread dough to give the crust a nutty texture.

● **Baking rolls in clusters** Instead of baking rolls separately, pack them closely together in a pan or place on a cookie sheet. Serve them to be pulled apart as required.

WORKING WITH PASTRY

Pastry forms the basis of many kinds of dish, whether they are hot or cold, savory or sweet. Whatever type of pastry you are making, the same rules will apply. Always keep your tools, work surface, and hands cool. Try to handle the pastry lightly and as little as possible.

MAKING SHORTCRUST

● **Cooling hands** If your hands are warm, hold your wrists under cold water for a few minutes before handling pastry.
● **Enriching pastry** To make a rich, light-textured pastry, add an egg yolk with the water.
● **Letting pastry rest** Cover shortcrust pastry with plastic wrap, and place it in the refrigerator for 30 minutes before rolling out to prevent it from shrinking when baked.
● **Making quick pastry** To mix a quick dough, sift 1 cup (100 g) flour and a pinch of salt into a bowl. Stir in 2½ tbsp (40 ml) oil, 1 tbsp (15 ml) iced water, and a squeeze of lemon juice. Mix to a dough with a fork.

HELPING PASTRY RISE

● **Using water** Before using a cookie sheet for baking choux, flaky, or puff pastry dough, sprinkle it lightly with water instead of greasing it. The water will evaporate in the heat of the oven, and the steam will help the pastry rise.

AVOIDING SOGGY PASTRY

● **Using a cookie sheet** Bake a pie on a cookie sheet, the heat of which will help cook the pastry base. Preheat the cookie sheet in the oven while the oven heats up.
● **Using metal tins** Use a metal pie tin for baking a pie or tart. Metal will conduct heat to the pastry quickly.
● **Sealing with egg white** Brush the base of a pie shell with egg white to seal it and prevent leakage before adding a liquid filling.

USING TRIMMINGS

Grate pastry straight from freezer

Making a pastry topping
Coarsely grate frozen pastry over fruits as a topping, then bake until golden. Wrap leftover pastry trimmings in a freezer bag, and freeze so that they can be used in the future for this purpose.

USING FROZEN PASTRY

● **Preparing** Make and shape puff pastry ready for use. Freeze it until needed, then thaw before baking.
● **Thawing** Thaw frozen pastry by placing it in a microwave on Defrost; 7 oz (200 g) of pastry will need 2½–3 minutes.

PREVENTING PROBLEMS

● **Ensuring an even rise** Brush only the top surface of puff or flaky pastry when glazing with beaten egg or milk, avoiding any cut or fluted edges. The pastry will then rise evenly.
● **Avoiding leakage** When adding a filling with beaten eggs to a ready-made pie shell, heat the case in the oven first, so that the filling starts to set as soon as it touches the pastry.
● **Preventing overbrowning** When baking a fruit pie, allow the pastry to brown and rise first, then reduce the oven temperature to finish cooking.

HEALTHY TIP

Adding fiber
Instead of using all-purpose flour to roll out pastry dough, sprinkle the countertop with rolled oats, wheat germ, or bran. Roll out as usual for a finished pastry that has added texture and contains beneficial dietary fiber.

MAKING SWEET PASTRY

● **Adding sugar and egg** Mix a sweet shortcrust pastry for fruit pies by adding ¼ cup (50 g) of sugar and one egg yolk to every 1 cup (100 g) of flour. Bake at a lower temperature (about 375°F/190°C) than ordinary shortcrust pastry.

Adding ingredients
To add flavor and texture to shortcrust or puff pastry, stir finely chopped nuts such as walnuts or ground almonds into the flour. Alternatively, add spices or finely chopped herbs.

SHAPING PASTRY DECORATIVELY

There is a variety of ways in which you can use pastry as a decorative trim. Shortcrust pastry is the most versatile, since it holds its shape during cooking. Cut leftover pastry into decorative shapes, and bake them separately to keep on hand for use as a quick garnish.

MAKING LATTICE TOPS
● **Using trimmings** Cut rolled-out pastry trimmings into long, thin strips. Arrange them over a pie filling to form a lattice.

Space slits evenly

Cutting slits
To make an easy lattice top for a pie, roll out a circle of pastry to fit the top of the pie, then cut short slits parallel to each other. Stretch the pastry gently to open the slits and create a lattice top.

DECORATING EDGES
● **Cutting shapes** Roll out pastry trimmings, and cut into small leaves, hearts, or flowers. Overlap around the edges of a pie or tart before baking.
● **Making a braid** Roll spare pastry into long, thin strips, and braid these together. Arrange them around dampened pastry edges, and tuck in the seams.
● **Marking with a fork** To seal the edges of a double-crust pie quickly and easily, flatten the edges together with the floured prongs of a fork.
● **Pinching edges** Seal the edges of a double-crust pie by pressing them between your finger and thumb at an angle. This will create a rope effect.

BRIGHT IDEA

Using a pastry label
Use pastry trimmings to cut out a shaped, edible label to decorate a pie and indicate its contents. Alternatively, cut out letters from the pastry to spell out the name of the pie's contents. Brush with beaten egg before sticking on.

USING PHYLLO DOUGH

Phyllo is a delicate pastry that needs gentle handling. Nevertheless, it is easy to use for pies, tartlets, and filled pastries. Work quickly, and cover sheets you are not using to prevent them from drying out, since phyllo dough will become difficult to handle if it dries out.

WORKING WITH PHYLLO
● **Brushing with oil** Use olive or nut oil to brush phyllo before baking savory pastries. Use butter or a light-flavored oil for baking sweet pastries.
● **Brushing with egg** For those on a low-fat diet, brush phyllo lightly with egg white instead of oil. This will give the pastry a crisp texture when baked.
● **Baking in a microwave** Brush filled phyllo bundles with butter, and cook in a browning dish in a microwave on High until the pastry is crisp. Turn the bundles over halfway through the cooking period.
● **Making spring rolls** Use phyllo to make spring rolls. Seal with egg white, and deep-fry in hot oil for 2–3 minutes.

STORING PHYLLO
● **Storing for later** Wrap unused phyllo dough from a package in plastic wrap and refrigerate. Use the pastry within 3–4 days.

Keep pastry moist with damp towel

Preventing drying
Work with one sheet of phyllo at a time, and keep the rest moist by covering with a lightly dampened dish towel. To keep phyllo dough for long periods, cover it with plastic wrap first.

USING LEFTOVER PHYLLO
● **Using damaged sheets** Use up dried out or broken sheets of phyllo by inserting them between whole sheets.

Cup pastry in hand to shape

Making "moneybags"
To use up small pieces of phyllo dough, brush with oil, stack together, and place a spoonful of fruit in the center. Gather up the sides, pinch together firmly, leaving a ruffled edge, and bake.

PRESERVING

I N THE PAST, PRESERVING WAS AN ESSENTIAL PART of a cook's calendar to ensure that pantries were well stocked all year round. This is no longer necessary, but preserving is a skill worth having and has rewarding end results.

PREPARING TO PRESERVE

The basic principle of preserving is to take food at the peak of freshness and maintain its nutritive value at that stage. Little special equipment is necessary, but it is worthwhile to spend some time preparing equipment for use to ensure that your preserves are a success.

USING EQUIPMENT
● **Choosing pan material** For making acidic preserves such as chutneys and pickles, use a stainless steel pot, since aluminum or copper may react with the acid.
● **Choosing the right-sized pot** Use a large pot for making jam to allow room for expansion. The pan should be half full when all the sugar is added.
● **Warming a thermometer** To prevent a thermometer from cracking, warm it in hot water before placing in hot preserves.
● **Hooking a spoon** To prevent a wooden spoon from sliding into a pan, attach a wooden clothespin to the handle at right angles to it. Hook the pin over the side of the pan.

WEIGHING INGREDIENTS

Using bathroom scales
To weigh a large amount of ingredients easily, use bathroom scales. First, note the weight of the pot. Then weigh the ingredients in the pot, and deduct the weight of the pot.

PREVENTING SCUM

Applying glycerin
Brush the inner sides of a pot with glycerin before making jams and jellies. This will prevent scum from forming on the surface of the preserves during cooking.

PREPARING JARS

Jars placed upright

Preventing cracking
To prevent jars from cracking when filled with hot preserves, first wash them thoroughly. Stand them on a cookie sheet covered with newsprint, and place in a warm oven for 10 minutes.

STERILIZING LIDS

Plunging into boiling water
Sterilize the metal lids of the canning jars by placing them in boiling water for six minutes. Remove the lids with food tongs to protect your hands, and drain on absorbent paper towels.

CONSIDERING OPTIONS
● **Using a microwave** If you want to cook jams, jellies, or chutneys in a microwave, plan to make only a small amount at a time. To allow for expansion of the ingredients during cooking, use a heatproof bowl that is three times larger in volume than the quantity of preserve you are making in each batch.
● **Pressure cooking** Reduce the cooking times recommended in recipes for jams and jellies by making them in a pressure cooker. You will also need to use only about half the liquid specified in the recipe.

MAKING JAMS AND JELLIES

A successful jam or jelly is characterized by a firm, clear set, a bright color, and a good fruit flavor. Use fresh, undamaged produce, ideally mixing ripe with unripe fruits. Pectin is the setting agent found naturally in fruits, and unripe fruits contain the highest pectin levels.

STRAINING JELLIES

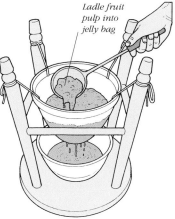

Ladle fruit pulp into jelly bag

Using a stool
To use a jelly bag to strain jelly, turn a small stool upside down, place a bowl on its base in the center, and tie the jelly bag to the legs of the stool. Fill with fruit pulp, and let drain.

PREVENTING PROBLEMS

● **Preventing mildew** Pick fruits for preserves when conditions are dry, since moisture on the fruits may cause mildew.
● **Using sugar** Cook fruits for jam until tender before adding sugar, which may toughen the skins. Always warm sugar first so that it will dissolve quickly and help give a clear set.
● **Removing scum** Skim jams and jellies to remove scum for a clear set. The last traces can be removed with a paper towel.
● **Distributing fruits** If jam or marmalade contains pieces of fruits or peel, let cool slightly before pouring into jars. This will prevent the pieces from rising to the surface.
● **Covering jam** Place jam jar covers on immediately after canning to discourage bacteria.

SELECTING FRUITS

Some fruits have a tendency to set much better than others.

● **Good** Apples, blackberries, cranberries, concord grapes, crabapples.
● **Average** Raspberries, plums, apricots, grapefruit, oranges, sour cherries.
● **Poor** Pears, sweet cherries, strawberries, rhubarb, peaches.
● **Good combination** Apples and raspberries, cranberries and peaches.

CANNING FRUITS

Successful canning is dependent on efficient sterilization. Modern canning jars extend the lives of preserves, and are available with screwband closures for a good seal. Preserves make delightful presents, particularly if they are decorated with ribbons and pretty gift tags.

PACKING JARS

Arranging slices
Make jars of canned fruits look attractive by arranging slices of fruits such as orange, star fruit, or kiwi fruit against the sides before filling. Pack firmly, avoiding gaps, since fruits rise when cooked.

PREVENTING SPLITTING

Prick skin with toothpick

Pricking fruits
To prevent fruit skins from bursting, prick whole fruits such as cherries, apricots, and plums before packing them into bottles. This will also aid the absorption of syrup by the fruits.

DEALING WITH LIDS

● **Testing the seal** To make sure that the seal on a canning jar is good after bottling, remove the screw cover, and lift the jar by its lid. If the lid stays in place, the seal is good.
● **Loosening bands** Once canning fruits have completely cooled, and the jar is properly sealed, slightly loosen the bands on screw-on closures so that they do not become stuck.
● **Releasing a lid** To loosen a lid that is firmly stuck on a jar with a screwband closure, stand the jar in hot water for a few minutes, then lever off the lid carefully with a knife.

415

MAKING CHUTNEYS AND PICKLES

Preserving fruits and vegetables in sugar and vinegar is a traditional cooking method that improves their flavors during storage. A good chutney is smooth in texture and mellow in flavor. This result is achieved through lengthy, slow cooking and maturation in the jar.

USING SPICES
● **Substituting whole spices** If you wish to substitute whole spices for ground when following a chutney recipe, you should double the quantity.

Strike spices with rolling pin

Bruising spices
If you are using whole spices such as cloves or cinnamon to flavor chutneys or pickles, bruise them lightly to release their flavors. Wrap them in cheesecloth, then add to the other ingredients.

USING SALT
● **Choosing the right salt** Buy rock salt for pickling or dry salting, since table salt contains additives that change the flavor and color of ingredients.

Sprinkle salt over vegetables

Retaining crispness
Make sure vegetables stay crisp by using dry salt instead of brine for salting before pickling. Sprinkle vegetables with salt, and let stand overnight to draw out the juices. Rinse and dry before use.

TRADITIONAL TIP

Testing a brine solution
To check whether a brine solution is concentrated enough for salting foods before pickling, lower a fresh egg into the solution. If the egg floats, the concentration of salt is about right. Make sure that you add about ¼ cup (50 g) salt for every 2 cups (500 ml) water.

PRESERVING LEMONS

Salting lemon quarters
Cut six lemons into quarters, not quite cutting them through at one end. Rub salt into the cut surfaces, and pack the lemons into a canning jar. Add the juice of one lemon and 1 tbsp (15 ml) salt. Top off the jar with boiling water, and seal. Refrigerate 2–3 weeks before using the lemons and the liquid in casseroles, soups, and salad dressings.

COOKING CHUTNEYS
● **Reducing liquid** To make sure that a chutney thickens to a good consistency, always cook it uncovered so that the excess liquid evaporates.

Testing before canning
To check whether a chutney is cooked and ready for canning, pull a wooden spoon through it, across the base of the pan. If it parts easily and there is no running liquid, it is cooked.

ADJUSTING RECIPES
● **Enriching color** Use brown sugar to give a rich color to chutneys with a short cooking time. Use white sugar to darken chutneys only if the recipe has a prolonged cooking time.
● **Lightening color** For a pale color and mild flavor, use white vinegar in chutneys, pickles, and relishes. Also, add the sugar only after the basic ingredients have reduced.
● **Reducing sugar** If you want to reduce the amount of sugar used in a chutney recipe, then add dried fruits such as dates or golden raisins instead.
● **Keeping onions soft** Soften onions before pickling by cooking them in a little water for a few minutes before adding vinegar, which has a slightly hardening effect on them.

DRYING FOODS

Drying is a traditional preserving method originating from the observed effects of the sun and wind on fish, fruits, and vegetables. These natural preserving processes can be imitated in the kitchen to dry particular foods by controlling temperature and ventilation.

DRYING HERBS

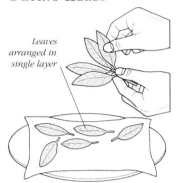

Leaves arranged in single layer

Using a microwave
Arrange fresh herb leaves on absorbent paper towels, and place in a microwave with a glass of water. Cook on High for about 30 seconds, and repeat until the leaves have dried thoroughly.

VARYING METHODS
● **Hanging bundles** Tie bundles of mixed fresh summer herbs such as parsley, mint, sage, and thyme. Before hanging them up to dry for the winter, cover with cheesecloth to keep them free from dust.
● **Stringing spices** Thread cotton string through fresh chilies so that they can be hung up for drying.
● **Drying in an oven** To dry mushrooms, first remove the stalks, since these tend to toughen. Thread the mushrooms onto bamboo skewers, and arrange on the shelf racks of an oven on the coolest setting until the mushrooms are crisp and dry. Store in a dry place.

PREVENTING PROBLEMS
● **Avoiding browning** To stop apples from browning during drying, soak in salted water for a few minutes. Use 1 tsp (5 ml) salt to 2 cups (500 ml) water.

Place slices on paper towels

Lining racks
When drying fruits or slices of fruit for decorative purposes, lay sheets of cheesecloth or paper towels between the fruits and the drying rack to prevent the ridges from leaving marks on the fruits.

CURING AND SMOKING FOODS

Curing is a method of preserving food by immersing it in dry salt or a salt solution. Curing is now done mainly to add flavor. Many meats are cured before smoking, both to ensure good preservation and to add flavor. Most fish can be preserved simply by smoking

PREPARING FOODS
● **Cheese** Remove any rind or wax from hard cheeses such as Cheddar or Emmental before home smoking. Cut the cheese into 1-in (2.5-cm) thick chunks, and smoke at 60°F (16°C) for 2–4 hours.
● **Nuts** Blanch whole nuts such as almonds or hazelnuts, then spread them in a single layer across a fine wire mesh screen before smoking.
● **Poultry** When smoking a whole bird such as a chicken or turkey, cover the breast with bacon strips or pork fat to prevent overdrying.
● **Meat and fish** Instead of salt-curing meat and fish, soak in a marinade for several hours to add a salty flavor.

STORING IN WOOD ASH
● **Keeping cured meat** Wrap salt-cured meat in cheesecloth, and roll in wood ash to deter insects. Hang in a cool place.

REMOVING SALT
● **Soaking** Remove excess salt from food that has been cured for longer than one week by soaking in cold, fresh water.

MAKING YOUR OWN GRAVLAX

Lay fresh dill on fish

1 Lay a fillet of salmon skin side down in a wide dish, and rub with oil. Cover with a layer of salt and sugar, then top with chopped dill and crushed peppercorns.

2 Cover with another fillet of salmon, skin side up. Wrap with plastic wrap, and place in the refrigerator for 12 hours, turning the fish over halfway through. Serve thinly sliced.

FREEZING

SUCCESSFUL FREEZING MAINTAINS FOODS at peak freshness, with the minimum loss of vitamins, color, or texture. Freezing converts water within the cells that make up food to ice, a process that must be done quickly to prevent damage to the cells.

PREPARING TO FREEZE

Most foods require only simple preparation before freezing. It is essential to blanch vegetables, since this will destroy the enzymes that cause deterioration and preserve color, flavor, texture, and nutrients. Secure packing is vital for all foods to keep them airtight.

PREFORMING LIQUIDS

Top of freezer bag turned over open carton

Using a cardboard pack
Preform liquid in a freezer bag for easy storage in the freezer. Put the bag upright in an empty, straight-sided cardboard container. Pour the liquid in and freeze. Lift out the bag, and seal the top.

PREFORMING CASSEROLES

Use enough foil to cover casserole completely

Making a foil lining
Line a casserole dish with foil, and freeze a casserole in it. Lift out of the dish, and overwrap for storing in the freezer. To cook the casserole, unwrap, and return to the dish to defrost and cook.

BLANCHING TIMES

The following blanching times are for medium pieces of common vegetables.

- Asparagus: 2–4 minutes.
- Brussels sprouts, broccoli: 3–4 minutes.
- Cabbage (shredded), red or green: 1½ minutes.
- Carrots: 3–5 minutes.
- Cauliflower, celery, peppers: 3 minutes.
- Corn: 4–8 minutes.
- Eggplants: 4 minutes.
- Green beans: 2–3 minutes.
- Onions, parsnips, spinach: 2 minutes.
- Peas: 1–2 minutes.
- Snow peas: 2–3 minutes.
- Turnips: 2½ minutes.
- Zucchini: 1 minute.

USING FRESH PRODUCE
- **Cooling quickly** Plunge foods into iced water after blanching. Drain well before freezing.
- **Retaining color** Dip cut fruits such as apples into lemon juice or ascorbic acid before freezing to retain color and supplement vitamin content.
- **Using excess fruits** If you have a glut of fresh fruits, stew with sugar, and freeze in pie tins lined with aluminum foil. When the fruits are firm, remove from the dishes, and overwrap before storing. Use frozen packs as ready-made pie fillings in the future.

OPEN-FREEZING FOODS

Keeping pieces separate
To keep delicate fruits or vegetable pieces separate while frozen, open-freeze them on cookie sheets until firm, then pack them into containers or freezer bags for storing.

PREVENTING PROBLEMS
- **Open-freezing cakes** Freeze frosted or decorated cakes until solid before wrapping so that the tops are not squashed.
- **Preventing damage** Protect the top of a pie or delicate dessert by putting an upturned foil pie tin over it. Secure the pie tin to the dish with tape.
- **Avoiding drying** If food does not fill a container, pack the space with crumpled paper to stop the food from drying out.
- **Omitting garlic** Leave garlic out of food to be frozen – it can taste musty when frozen. Add garlic to food after thawing.

STORING AND LABELING

Keep your freezer well organized, and rotate foods as you would in a pantry so that you use foods within their recommended storage times. Reuse suitable food containers for freezing, but always make sure that they are thoroughly clean before filling them.

PACKAGING FOOD

● **Repacking meats** When freezing prepacked meats, always remove the packaging, and rewrap. Cut off the label, then tape it onto the new packaging to save relabeling.
● **Using lids** To pack home-made burgers easily so that they do not stick together, and for easy removal, save plastic coffee can lids, and place each burger on a lid for stacking.
● **Recycling containers** Collect plastic containers with snap-on lids for use in the freezer. Some plastics become brittle at low temperatures, so if you are not sure, line containers with freezer bags.

STORING COOKED FRUITS

Mold paper so it presses down on fruits

Using crumpled paper
When freezing food with liquids such as fruits in syrup, prevent the pieces of food from rising above the surface of the liquid by pressing a sheet of crumpled waxed paper over the food.

LABELING CONTAINERS

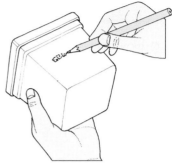

Marking a container
For easy labeling of foods in plastic containers, write the details on the container with a wax-based pencil. This will write easily on plastic and the writing will not rub off in the freezer.

PREPARING FREEZER STANDBYS

A freezer offers a wonderful opportunity for keeping timesaving supplies handy. Freeze containers of garnishes and decorations for use when time is short before a dinner party. Freeze leftovers for those days when you need a meal with the minimum amount of preparation.

SAVING TIME

● **Making extra meals** Freeze ready-cooked meals on foil plates. Arrange the food on the plates, ensuring that meats are covered with gravy or sauce, then cover with plastic wrap or foil, seal, and freeze.
● **Making butter balls** Prepare butter balls or curls in advance for entertaining, drop into iced water, then drain and pack into boxes to freeze. Remove and thaw at room temperature about an hour before use.
● **Slicing citrus fruits** Freeze slices of lemon or lime in plastic bags. Add the frozen slices to cocktails.
● **Scooping in advance** Before a dinner party, scoop ice cream or sorbet onto paper-lined trays. Refreeze, ready to serve.

FREEZING CHOCOLATE

● **Protecting with paper** When freezing delicate chocolate shapes, protect the shapes by placing sheets of absorbent paper towels between the layers that are to be stacked.

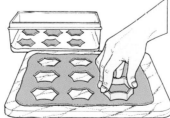

Using a cookie cutter
Spread melted chocolate onto a cold surface, let set, and use a small cookie cutter to cut into shapes. Layer in a box with waxed paper. Use from frozen to decorate cakes and desserts.

STORING USEFUL BASICS

● **Keeping milk** Freeze spare cartons of milk. Thaw in the refrigerator for two days or at room temperature for six hours.
● **Freezing leftovers** Store leftovers in portion sizes, so that you can take out exactly the number you need.
● **Freezing tomatoes** Freeze whole tomatoes in plastic bags. They can be added directly to casseroles or soups.
● **Keeping spare pastry** Roll out pastry trimmings, and cut into shapes such as leaves or hearts. Freeze in containers, and use straight from the freezer to decorate pies before baking.
● **Using ice trays** Make extra sauce or gravy, and freeze in ice-cube trays, then thaw just the amount you need.

DRINKS

THE MAIN ADVANTAGE OF CREATING both hot and cold drinks at home is that you can concoct special flavors and blends. The possibilities are endless, from nonalcoholic, flavored fruit drinks to highly spiced, mulled party punches.

FRUIT AND VEGETABLE JUICES

Fruit and vegetable juices are hard to beat for nutrients and fresh flavor. If you enjoy fresh juices, an electric juicer is a worthwhile investment. Otherwise, keep a variety of ready-made juices on hand to mix and match flavors and create refreshing drinks at any time of day.

ENHANCING FLAVORS

Add flower water to plain juice

MAKING SWIZZLE STICKS

Stir juice with spring onion to impart flavor

CHILLING DRINKS

Add frozen grapes

Adding flower water
Make the flavor of a plain fruit juice more interesting by adding a few drops of orange flower water or rosewater. Stir the juice thoroughly before serving.

Using scallions
Use scallions as edible swizzle sticks. Trim root ends and the tops of the leaves – leaving some green for color – just before serving to release flavor.

Adding frozen fruits
Instead of using ice to chill juices, freeze fresh fruits such as grapes or lemon slices. Add these to drinks just before serving to chill and decorate.

PRESSING JUICES
● **Pressing apples** If you are making apple juice in an electric juicer, add a handful of red fruits such as strawberries or raspberries to give the juice a rosy glow and add flavor.
● **Using pulp** Instead of discarding the high-fiber pulp that is left behind after pressing juice, use it in your cooking to add flavor. Add carrot or celery pulp to soups or bread, and include apple or peach pulp in fruit cake recipes.
● **Maintaining color** Add a squeeze of fresh lemon juice when pressing apples or pears to keep their color and prevent them from turning brown.

ADDING INTEREST
● **Using garlic** To pep up the flavor of vegetable juice, rub a cut clove of garlic around the inside of a glass or pitcher before adding the juice, or add a pinch of garlic or celery salt.
● **Chopping herbs** Improve the flavor and color of plain vegetable juices by adding chopped fresh herbs. Try basil, parsley, or lovage in tomato juice, and use tarragon or coriander in carrot juice.
● **Adding fruit and fizz** To make a refreshing summer drink, add chunks of fresh fruits to fresh fruit juice, half-fill tall tumblers, and top off the juice with soda or sparkling mineral water.

HEALTHY TIP

Making nut-milk shakes
For a nutritious, milk-free shake, place a handful of blanched almonds or cashews in a blender with a few strawberries or a banana. Add water to cover, and purée.

SPICED DRINKS

Mulled wines and spice-infused drinks are suitable for many occasions, whether as festive party punches or soothing bedtime drinks. Spices such as ginger, cinnamon, and cloves give a depth of flavor to even the simplest hot punch, with or without the addition of alcohol.

VARYING FLAVORS
● **Using star anise** Add pieces of whole star anise to mulled wine for a rich, spicy flavor.
● **Flavoring coffee** Make an invigorating winter coffee blend by adding ground spices to ground coffee, or grinding whole spices such as allspice, ginger, nutmeg, or cinnamon with fresh coffee beans.
● **Mixing juices** Combine equal quantities of cranberry juice and ginger ale, and mull the mixture gently with cloves or cinnamon to make a delicious nonalcoholic punch.
● **Using savory spice** Sprinkle a few toasted cumin seeds on top of the yogurt-based drinks that often accompany curries.

USING FRUITS

Studding with cloves
To add a spicy flavor and decorate a hot party punch, press whole cloves into the skins of several apples, then float the fruits in the punch while heating and serving the beverage.

SPICING HOT CHOCOLATE

Stir with cinnamon stick

Using a cinnamon stick
Add a mild hint of spice to hot chocolate or cocoa by adding a cinnamon stick. Alternatively, add a pinch of ground cinnamon to the chocolate or cocoa powder during preparation.

TEAS AND TISANES

Tea is an ancient drink that, depending on the particular choice of ingredients added, can be served as a soothing healer or as a refreshing, stimulating reviver. Most teas are usually served hot, but iced tea can be a very welcome cooler on a hot summer's day.

USING HERBS
● **Adding mint** To use fresh mint in iced tea, place a few sprigs in a large pitcher, bruise them with a wooden spoon, then add tea. Pour into glasses, and garnish with mint sprigs.
● **Soothing headaches** Try sipping rosemary tisane to relieve a tension headache. Put a few fresh rosemary sprigs in a pot, pour over boiling water, and infuse for 4–5 minutes.
● **Using alternatives** If herbal teas are not to your taste, try infusing herbs with ordinary black tea, adding sugar to taste.
● **Flavoring green tea** Plunge mint sprigs into freshly made, boiling hot Chinese green tea for a refreshing green tea in the Moroccan style.

ENHANCING FLAVOR

Spoon herbs into pot with tea

Using everyday teas
Bring an interesting flavor to a pot of ordinary leaf tea by adding a few dried herbs, such as dried camomile flowers, while the tea is brewing. Serve plain, or with lemon and sugar if preferred.

USING FRUITS & FLOWERS
● **Adding zest** To make a delicate, fruit-scented tea, add a thinly pared strip of citrus zest to a pot of Indian tea.
● **Making flower teas** Mix a few dried, scented rose petals or jasmine flowers with dry tea leaves, so that the delicate scent mingles with the tea.
● **Creating an exotic flavor** Make a fruit-scented tea by pressing a little juice from a freshly cut mango into tea.
● **Making tea punch** Combine iced tea with chilled fruit juice for a thirst-quenching summer drink. Pineapple or apple juice complements black tea.
● **Adding vanilla** Add a vanilla bean to the tea caddy to infuse a rich flavor during storage.

ENTERTAINING

QUICK REFERENCE
Table Settings and Decorations, p. 424
Cocktail Parties, p. 430
Buffets, p. 432
Dinner Parties, p. 434
Party Management, p. 438
Children's Parties, p. 440
Barbecues, p. 442
Picnics, p. 444
Impromptu Entertaining, p. 446

THROWING A SUCCESSFUL PARTY can be satisfying as well as enjoyable. There are no guaranteed methods to ensure success, but whether the occasion is formal or informal, large or small, good organization and careful advance planning will certainly help. You need to select an appropriate menu, invite a good mixture of guests, and create a pleasant atmosphere in which they feel comfortable. At the end of the party, you will be able to wave good-bye to happy guests with a great feeling of satisfaction and the knowledge that they – and you – thoroughly enjoyed the occasion.

PLANNING A TIMETABLE

When you are cooking for a large number of guests, it is worth planning the occasion well in advance to save yourself time and effort closer to the day. Prepare detailed checklists and timetables, taking all tasks into consideration. This will make the occasion easier to tackle.

PLANNING IN ADVANCE		
COUNTDOWN	PLANNING	ACTION NEEDED
4 WEEKS OR MORE BEFORE	Choose site, theme of occasion, and menu; draw up guest list.	Reserve party room; send invitations; arrange rental or loan of equipment.
2–3 WEEKS BEFORE	Make shopping lists; plan cooking schedule; list other jobs.	Order flowers, alcohol, and soft drinks; cook dishes that will freeze.
1 WEEK BEFORE	Monitor guest acceptances and regrets; decide on seating plans.	Order food; write name and menu cards; wash table linen; clean silver.
3 DAYS BEFORE	Check china and cutlery; finalize numbers of guests and equipment.	Cook food to be reheated or served cold; wash china/glasses.
1 DAY BEFORE	Update cooking schedule; check list of other tasks to be done.	Buy food for last-minute preparation; prepare vegetables/salads; set tables.
PARTY MORNING	Make list of jobs to be done by helpers and hired staff.	Buy fresh bread; arrange flowers and bar; set tables; prepare hot food.
1 HOUR BEFORE	Check tasks as they are completed; allow time for relaxation.	Finish off hot food in oven; put out canapés and cocktail snacks.

PLANNING MENUS

The dishes you choose in a party menu must depend not just on personal taste, but on the season, the occasion, and on limitations such as time and budget. Try to appeal to the eye as well as the appetite, keeping the menu simple, and choose tried-and-true recipes.

SELECTING RECIPES
● **Choosing a main course**
Unless you wish to use a particular appetizer or dessert, plan the main course first, then choose an appetizer and dessert to complement it.
● **Keeping courses simple**
Help yourself by choosing a simple, cold appetizer that can be prepared in advance.

BALANCING MENUS
● **Varying courses** Create an overall balance of color, texture, and flavor in the menu. Avoid choosing courses that are similar, for example, all egg- or cheese-based.
● **Offsetting rich dishes**
Balance a rich or spicy main course with a plain appetizer and a light, refreshing dessert.

PREVENTING PROBLEMS
● **Planning alternatives** In case you are unable to get hold of a particular ingredient, have an alternative dish in mind.
● **Checking diets** Check in advance whether guests have special dietary requirements.
● **Limiting courses** Unless you have extra help, keep to three courses to minimize work.

ESTIMATING QUANTITIES

It is a strange fact that the more people you cater for, the less food you need to allow per head, especially for buffets. If you are catering for 100 people, allow full quantities for about 85. Appetites vary from person to person, but allow half portions for children or elderly guests.

ASSESSING FOOD QUANTITIES			
BUFFET FOODS	10 PORTIONS	20 PORTIONS	40 PORTIONS
Soups, hot or cold	½ gallon (1.75 liters)	1 gallon (4 liters)	2 gallons (8 liters)
Cold, sliced meats off the bone	2 lb (900 g)	3 lb 14 oz (1.75 kg)	7 lb 11 oz (3.5 kg)
Boneless meat for casseroles, etc.	2 lb 3 oz (1 kg)	5 lb (2.25 kg)	10 lb (4.5 kg)
Roast meat on the bone, hot or cold	3 lb 14 oz (1.75 kg)	6 lb 10 oz (3 kg)	14 lb 5 oz (6.5 kg)
Cheese for a cheeseboard	12 oz (350 g)	2 lb (900 g)	2 lb 12 oz (1.25 kg)
Crackers for cheese	1 lb 1 oz (500 g)	1 lb 10 oz (750 g)	2 lb 3 oz (1 kg)
Fish, filleted (in cooked dishes)	2 lb 12 oz (1.25 kg)	5 lb (2.25 kg)	10 lb (4.5 kg)
Poultry on the bone (oven-ready weight)	7 lb 11 oz (3.5 kg)	15 lb 7 oz (7 kg)	2 x 7 lb 11 oz (2 x 3.5 kg)
Rice or pasta (uncooked weight)	1 lb 1 oz (500 g)	1 lb 9 oz (700 g)	2 lb 12 oz (1.25 kg)
Vegetables (uncooked weight)	3 lb 5 oz (1.5 kg)	6 lb 10 oz (3 kg)	12 lb 2 oz (5.5 kg)
Fresh fruits or fruit salad	3 lb 5 oz (1.5 kg)	6 lb 1 oz (2.75 kg)	12 lb 2 oz (5.5 kg)
Ice cream	½ gallon (1.75 liters)	¾ gallon (2.5 liters)	1¼ gallons (5 liters)

TABLE SETTINGS AND DECORATIONS

An ATTRACTIVE TABLE SETTING ENHANCES A MEAL, whether it is a formal dinner or an informal party. Use your imagination or look in books and magazines for inspiration to create an attractive table setting suitable for the occasion.

PREPARING TABLECLOTHS

In addition to serving a decorative purpose, a tablecloth protects the surface of the table. White linen or cotton damask tablecloths are conventionally used for formal occasions, but you may prefer to choose a cloth to match the setting or to follow the theme of the occasion.

PROTECTING TABLES

Plastic protects table

WEIGHTING CLOTHS

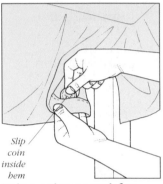

Slip coin inside hem

PREVENTING FLAPPING

Knot loosely to prevent corner from lifting

Covering with plastic
Prevent spills from damaging a polished table top by placing a layer of plastic wrap or oilcloth over it before laying the main tablecloth. Alternatively, use a plastic tablecloth.

Using coins as weights
Weight a tabletoth to be used outdoors by removing a few stitches around the hem and slipping coins or curtain weights inside. Alternatively, you can tack weights onto the cloth.

Tying knots
Knot the corners of a cloth when eating outdoors to prevent them from flapping. Place the cloth over one of a contrasting shade or slip bouquets of dried flowers into each knot for decoration.

FINDING ALTERNATIVES

● **Using sheets** If you need extra tablecloths for a large party, improvise with sheets or lengths of cheesecloth.
● **Using several cloths** If you have only small tablecloths, use a plain sheet as an undercloth, and lay several small, pretty tablecloths diagonally on top to cover a large table.
● **Using a blanket** If you do not have an undercloth, use a thick blanket underneath a tablecloth to prevent the top of the table from being marked.
● **Substituting rugs** For a party with an Arabian or Oriental theme, lay brightly colored kilims or rugs over large tables.

DECORATING PLAIN TABLECLOTHS

Making herb bouquets
Make small bouquets of fresh herbs, such as rosemary or thyme, to attach to a plain tablecloth. Tie the bouquets with ribbon, and pin them to the cloth in each corner.

● **Decorating with stencils** Use stencils and fabric paints to decorate a plain cloth. Stencil a border around each place setting.
● **Spray painting** Brighten up plain fabric or paper cloths with spray paints in colorful, abstract designs for children's parties.
● **Scattering petals** Scatter rose petals or other edible flowers over a cloth for a romantic touch.
● **Adding sparkle** At a festive event, sprinkle gold or silver stars over the tablecloth.
● **Using wallpaper borders** Decorate the edges of a plain cloth with a pretty wallpaper border, securing it around the edges with double-sided tape.

SETTING TABLES

The same basic principles apply to setting any table, whether for an informal or a formal meal, although the menu dictates which cutlery is used. To avoid overcrowding the table at the start of a meal, additional cutlery can be brought to the table with the appropriate courses.

LAYING A TABLE FOR DINNER

Large goblet for red wine

Dessert spoon laid above fork

Water glass

Small wine glass for white wine

Butter knife

Plate set for first course

Napkin placed on side plate

Forks to left of plate in order of use

Knives and spoon to right of plate, knife blades toward plate

Laying a setting
However many courses there are, lay the cutlery in the order it will be used, working from the outside inward. To save space, you can place both the dessert spoon and fork at the top of the setting. Arrange glasses at the top right-hand corner, with the main wine glass placed above the tip of the main knife.

CHOOSING GLASSWARE

If you have taken care with your choice of drinks, you will want to choose glassware equally carefully to complement the drinks and the table setting. When calculating how many glasses you need for entertaining on a large scale, allow an additional 10 percent for breakage.

CHOOSING WINE GLASSES

Choosing the right shape
To enjoy the bouquet of either white or red wine, serve it in glasses that are narrower at the rim than in the body. This shape enhances a wine's bouquet.

USING GLASSWARE

● **Removing labels** To remove sticky labels from new glasses, rub with lighter fluid.
● **Removing water marks** If glasses are dulled by water marks, restore their sparkle by soaking in water with a little vinegar. Rinse thoroughly in cold water, drain, and dry.
● **Washing crystal** Wash fine lead crystal glasses by hand in warm water and detergent. Rinse in clear water, and dry while warm. Washing lead crystal in a dishwasher will dull the surface of the glasses.
● **Serving champagne** Serve champagne in slender flutes, which show off the bubbles and color of the wine.

CHOOSING PITCHERS

Sturdy handle allows good grip when pouring

Fruit and ice remain in pitcher to flavor and cool

Pouring fruit punch
Serve fruit punches and iced drinks from a glass pitcher that has a pinched pouring lip or a filter to prevent fruit slices or ice cubes from falling into the glass.

CHOOSING TABLEWARE

The careful selection of tableware is essential to the visual success of a dinner party and to show off the food at its best. Choose simple yet striking colors and shapes when deciding which china, cutlery, and linen to use. Arrange them so that they do not detract from the food.

MIXING & MATCHING TABLEWARE

Contrasting side plate
Underplate contrasts with dinner plate
Patterned napkin

Mixing colors
If you do not have enough matching tableware for all your guests, then mix and match what you have, combining colors and styles to dramatic effect. Layer contrasting colors on top of one another.

USING LARGE PLATTERS

Arranging ingredients
If you do not have a plate that fits the size of a quiche or tart exactly, choose a large platter. Place the quiche in the center, and fill the space around it with a mixed salad or pretty garnish.

FINDING SERVING ALTERNATIVES

● **Using disposable platters** Buy large, disposable foil platters for buffet foods. To make them look decorative, line with lettuce leaves before arranging the food on top.

● **Using wicker containers** For an unusual presentation, serve bread and canapés in wicker containers. Line baskets with napkins for bread, and trays with lettuce leaves for canapés.

MAKING CENTERPIECES

Even on an informal occasion, a colorful centerpiece of flowers or fruits will bring an extra-special touch to the table. Make sure that the size and shape of a centerpiece allows your guests to see one another across the dining table. Stabilize vases with stones or marbles.

USING FRUITS

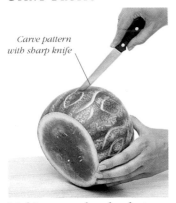

Carve pattern with sharp knife

Making a melon basket
Make a dessert centerpiece for serving fruit salad by making a melon basket. Cut a slice from the melon, and scoop out the flesh. Carve the melon skin to decorate, then fill with fruit salad.

ARRANGING FRUITY, FLORAL DISPLAYS

Apple wedge
Fruit holds stem in place
Citrus slice adds color and prevents other fruits from browning

Using fruits
Arrange flowers for a buffet-table centerpiece in a glass dish packed with pieces of fresh fruit. The fruits feed the flowers, keeping them fresh.

DECORATING PLACE SETTINGS

Whatever the occasion – whether formal or informal – imaginative place settings will help make guests feel welcome and break the ice as they sit down to eat. Always keep decorations simple and fresh, and use edible flowers if they will be in contact with the food.

CREATING AN INDIVIDUAL DISPLAY

Decorate underplate with flowers before serving food

Using flowers
To give a place setting a fresh, seasonal touch, arrange edible flowers or fresh herbs around a dinner plate on a wide underplate. Spray the flowers gently with water to keep them fresh for as long as possible.

GIVING EDIBLE FAVORS

Gathered edges of net form pretty frill

Tying net bundles
Make edible favors for guests to take home as mementos. Place Jordan almonds and chocolates on small circles of fine nylon net. Then gather up the net, and tie each bundle with ribbon.

DECORATING PLATES & PLACEMATS

● **Stenciling underplates**
Decorate large underplates by stenciling around their rims. Using nontoxic paints, spray holly leaves, hearts, stars, or a band of gold or silver color.

● **Decorating placemats** For a themed adults' or children's party, cut out paper shapes of hearts or cartoon characters to decorate plain placemats. Secure in place with glue.

SETTING THE SCENE

● **Making a pastry garland** For a romantic occasion, shape shortcrust pastry or cookie dough into small hearts. Pierce a hole in each with a skewer, and bake. Thread the hearts together with ribbon to make a garland around each plate.

● **Decorating chairs** To trim chairs for a wedding, use wired florist's ribbon to fashion extravagant bows, and attach one to the back of each guest's chair. Alternatively, tie on small bouquets of fresh flowers to match the bride's bouquet.

● **Adding roses** Place a single red rose across each place setting as a romantic gift for each guest at a wedding or anniversary celebration.

● **Lighting candles** Just before the guests are seated, place a red apple with a long taper candle stuck in it at each setting. Lower the lights when all the candles are lit.

USING FRUITS & SPICES

● **Making spice bundles**
Gather together small bundles of warm, winter spices such as cinnamon sticks and ginger with a few bay leaves. Tie together with ribbons as festive gifts for your guests.

Use toothpick to make holes in skin

Decorating citrus fruits
Make spice-scented pomanders as gifts to decorate each table setting. Stud small oranges or limes with cloves, then tie a patterned ribbon around each, and finish with a decorative bow.

USING FINGER FOODS

● **Making edible treats** For a summer party, thread two or three fresh strawberries onto wooden skewers with a mint leaf between the fruits. Place a skewer on each plate for a predinner appetizer.

Tuck herb sprigs between bread sticks

Decorating with herbs
Decorate a country-style table setting by tying each napkin loosely around two or three bread sticks. Add a few sprigs of fresh rosemary or bay leaves for a delicate scent.

MAKING MENU CARDS

Menu cards are most commonly used for formal dinners, but there is no reason why they cannot be used for any occasion. Follow the same theme that was used on the invitations. Guests may like to keep the menu cards as a fun memento of a special occasion.

COVERING MENUS

Tying with cord
To make a handwritten menu look more formal, place it on top of a large piece of colored cardboard. Put the cardboard and menu together with decorative cord, and finish with a bow.

DECORATING CARDS

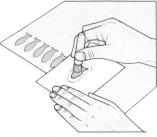

Using a stencil
Stencil a border onto a menu card using a food motif that reflects the menu. Cut a stencil from thin cardboard in the shape of your choice, then use a stiff brush to apply paint evenly.

DESIGNING INFORMALLY
- **Using marker pens** For festive occasions or special anniversaries, use silver or gold marker pens to write out menus and decorate the edges of simple menu cards.
- **Writing on plates** For an informal party, buy plain paper plates, and write menus on them with colored felt-tip pens. If you have children, they can decorate the menus. (Do not eat off the plates.)
- **Making a collage** Make plain menu cards look festive by cutting up old greetings cards and gluing on images.

DESIGNING PLACE CARDS

Name cards and seating plans can serve a useful purpose even on small, informal occasions. A successful seating plan will place guests so that they enjoy one another's company, avoid confusion as guests sit down at the start of a meal, and help shy guests break the ice.

CREATING MARKERS
- **Using fruits** Spray fruits such as apples, pears, or lemons with gold paint, let dry, then attach gold name tags for festive settings.
- **Baking gingerbread men** Make and bake gingerbread men, and tuck them into small envelopes, each labeled with a guest's name.
- **Piping icing** Cut cookie dough into decorative shapes, bake and cool them, then pipe a guest's name and a decorative motif onto each cookie with colored icing.
- **Painting eggs** For a spring party, paint eggs with guests' names incorporated into the design. Place in pretty egg cups, one at each setting.
- **Saving time** Buy gift tags to use as festive name cards if you are short of time.

USING THEMES
- **Making masks** For a themed costume party, buy plain party masks, and decorate them yourself in a way that reflects the theme. Individualize the masks by incorporating a guest's name into each design.

MODELING FIGURES
- **Using dough** Mix water and flour to make a paste, shape into figures, and bake in a low oven for two hours until dry. Inscribe a guest's name on each figure, decorate it with acrylic paint, and then varnish.

MAKING A POP-UP PLACE CARD

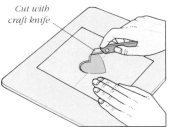

Cut with craft knife

1 Draw a shape in the center of a sheet of thin cardboard, and color if desired. Mark a fine line to indicate where the fold will be. Cut carefully around the shape above the fold line.

2 Fold the card along the marked line. The upper part of the shape will extend above the fold. Inscribe the guest's name on it, and then position the card on the table.

FOLDING NAPKINS

Folded table napkins can enhance a table setting on a special occasion, and knowledge of a few simple folds is all that you require. The best fabrics to use for folding are starched linen and cotton, which hold their shape well. Even paper napkins can be folded successfully.

FOLDING SIMPLE NAPKIN FANS

Pleat evenly

Tie pleats together with ribbon

Hold center pleats of napkin

1 To make a simple napkin fan, first starch and iron a fabric napkin, or use a good-quality paper napkin. Starting from one side, fold the napkin into evenly spaced accordion pleats all the way across.

2 Continue until the whole napkin is pleated, and press the pleats firmly in place. Fold the pleated napkin in half. Tie a small, decorative ribbon bow around the base of the pleats, above the folded end.

3 Place the napkin on a dinner plate, hold the two center pleats together, and open out the pleats to either side to form a fan shape. A napkin fan can also be placed upright in a wine glass.

CREATING NAPKIN RINGS

Napkin rings add a finishing touch to rolled or folded napkins, and there are many ways of creating decorative devices to hold napkins prettily as part of a table setting. Keep them simple, so that they enhance rather than detract from the food and the other table decorations.

FOLLOWING THEMES

● **Creating lavish effects** Buy opulent curtain braids and tassels to wrap around napkins for a sophisticated celebration.
● **Weaving raffia** For a rustic, harvest, or country theme, weave strips of raffia or straw into napkin rings. Tuck dried flowers into the ring.
● **Using ribbons** Tie simple colored ribbons around napkins to follow a color scheme, or buy special, festive ribbons to suit the occasion.
● **Celebrating anniversaries** Wind strings of imitation pearls or other costume jewelry around table napkins for an anniversary celebration.
● **Threading shells** Make a marine-themed napkin ring by threading small shells onto fine wire, then twisting the ends together to make a ring.

USING FRESH HERBS

● **Attaching herb sprigs** To bring a pleasant scent to the dinner table and decorate simple, rolled napkins, tuck sprigs of herbs or herb flowers into plain napkin rings.

Tying with chives
Tie freshly cut chive fronds around a plain, rolled napkin. Cut the chives so that they are as long as possible. The longer the fronds, the easier it will be to tie them. Trim the ends to neaten.

USING FOOD AND FLOWERS

● **Making garlands** Make garland napkin rings to match bridal flowers. Bend a piece of florist's wire into a ring, and bind it with ribbon. Cut sprays of flowers such as mimosa or freesia, and bind them around each ring with fine wire.
● **Using leaves** Select flat-shaped leaves from plants such as iris, and tie around a simply folded napkin in a loose knot.
● **Threading candies** Thread colorful licorice candies onto heavy thread, and tie to make edible napkin rings.
● **Baking bread rings** Instead of bread rolls, shape dough into rings, glaze with egg, and sprinkle with poppy or sesame seeds. Bake until golden, and slip one onto each napkin before serving.

COCKTAIL PARTIES

COCKTAIL PARTIES CAN BE FORMAL OR INFORMAL, offering a simple glass of sherry or a choice of cocktails, depending on the particular occasion. If you are inviting more than 20 guests, consider hiring a bartender to serve drinks.

MAKING AND SERVING CANAPÉS

Food is essential at any cocktail party, but there is no need to spend hours preparing elaborate dishes. Simple canapés or dips are all that is needed. Offer your guests a choice of finger foods and other tidbits that can be eaten with one hand, in one or two bites.

SKEWERING CANAPÉS

Thread small pieces onto toothpick

Making tricolor sticks
Thread cubes of feta cheese onto toothpicks or wooden skewers between squares of raw green and red peppers to make tricolor sticks. If you prefer, cook the peppers under the broiler.

SERVING CANAPÉS WITH STYLE

Using a mirror
Arrange bite-sized finger foods on a mirror tile instead of a plate for an unusual presentation at a formal cocktail party. Leave space between the canapés to achieve the best effect.

Use pastry brush to glaze

Making a dough platter
Roll out shortcrust pastry or bread dough in a round shape. Edge with shaped leftover dough, place on a cookie sheet, glaze with lightly beaten egg, and bake until golden. Use to serve canapés.

QUICK AND EASY CANAPÉS

● **Piped celery** Pipe soft, herb-flavored cream cheese into the hollows of celery sticks.
● **Paté-filled mushrooms** Remove the stalks from small cup mushrooms, and pipe paté into the hollows left by the stalks.
● **Blue-cheese grapes** Mix equal amounts of blue cheese and butter. Cut large black or green grapes in half, and sandwich back together with the mix.
● **Mini-biscuits** Make mini-sized savory biscuits, and bake until golden. Cool, and top with cream cheese and an olive.
● **Chicken-liver toasts** Sauté chicken livers quickly in a little butter and sherry. Cut into bite-sized pieces, and spoon onto small, French-bread toasts.

● **Nachos bites** Spoon a little spicy guacamole or hummus onto tortilla chips, and sprinkle with paprika to garnish.
● **Bacon twists** Twist thin slices of smoked bacon with strips of puff pastry. Bake at 400°F (200°C) for about 15 minutes, or until the pastry is firm and golden brown.
● **Salami cones** Wrap thin slices of salami carefully around melon sticks, and secure each one by piercing with a toothpick.
● **Almond olives** Stuff pitted olives with whole, salted, or smoked almonds.
● **Ham with kiwis** Wrap thinly sliced smoked ham around wedges of peeled kiwi fruit, and secure each with a toothpick.

PREVENTING PROBLEMS

● **Preventing soggy pastry** To serve vol-au-vents and other pastries with moist fillings, bake the pastry cases in advance, but add the fillings only one hour before serving.
● **Making bite-sized foods** Make canapés small enough to be easily held in the hand and to be eaten in one mouthful to prevent mess.
● **Serving in stages** Serve hot and cold canapés in small batches over a period of about an hour, instead of serving them all at the same time.
● **Clearing space** Make space so that guests can put down their drinks and not juggle food and drinks. Clear away empty glasses and food debris.

MAKING CRUDITÉS AND DIPS

Crudités and dips make excellent food for serving at informal cocktail parties, since they are simple to make and can be prepared in advance. Serve plenty of crudités and savory chips for dipping, and make the dippers small enough to be eaten in one mouthful.

PREPARING & PRESENTING CRUDITÉS

Deep serving dish allows ice to melt without spilling

Colorful mixture of vegetables for dipping

Making an ice ring
Keep vegetables fresh by serving them in an ice ring. Fill a large ring mold with water and freeze. Unmold onto a deep serving dish, and arrange vegetables in the center. Garnish around the ice ring to finish.

SIMPLE DIPS

● **Tuna** Drain a can of tuna, and mash with plain yogurt. Add chopped dill to taste.
● **Deviled sauce** Mix tomato ketchup with a small amount of Worcestershire sauce.
● **Pesto** Stir pesto sauce into light sour cream.
● **Blue cheese** Mash equal amounts of blue cheese and soft cream cheese, softening with a little milk if necessary.
● **Avocado** Mash avocado with a little mayonnaise, and add lemon juice to taste.

MAKING AND SERVING DRINKS

Offer drinks to guests as they arrive. Make sure that there is a good selection of soft drinks as well as alcoholic drinks. If you are serving only one or two different drinks, pour them out in advance, and place them on trays to serve. Mix cocktails in pitchers for easy serving.

CHILLING & SERVING
● **Chilling bottles** If you are short of refrigerator space for chilling bottles, fill the tub with ice, and store the bottles in it until you need them.
● **Freezing fruit juice** To prevent drinks from being watered down by plain ice cubes, freeze fruit juice into cubes as an alternative.
● **Rinsing glasses** Rinse all traces of detergent from glasses before pouring champagne, since detergent destroys the bubbles.
● **Serving soft drinks** Always include fresh fruit juices and mineral waters among soft drinks for nondrinkers.
● **Making punch** Serve a mixed punch at a large party. This is particularly suitable for large numbers, and can be less expensive than serving a wide selection of wines and spirits.

PREPARING & PRESENTING DRINKS

Strawberry stirrer adds flavor

Fizz created by dissolved, brandy-soaked sugar cube

Cucumber garnish

Rim frosted with food coloring and superfine sugar

Twist of peel adds flavor

Napkin placed under iced drink absorbs moisture

Adding finishing touches
It is worth taking care to serve drinks well, and some of the most effective ideas are quick and simple to achieve. If you want to add a garnish to a cocktail, make sure that you choose a large enough glass so that the drink will not overflow.

BUFFETS

Preparing a self-service, buffet-style meal is the easiest way to cater for a large number of people, since it allows you to provide for a range of different tastes, ages, and appetites, as long as you organize the food well in advance.

ARRANGING A BUFFET TABLE

For an appealing buffet, try to add variety to the appearance of dishes by varying their shapes and heights. Select food, tableware, utensils, and accessories such as napkins so that colors, textures, and shapes complement or contrast with one another in an imaginative way.

PLANNING THE LAYOUT OF A BUFFET TABLE

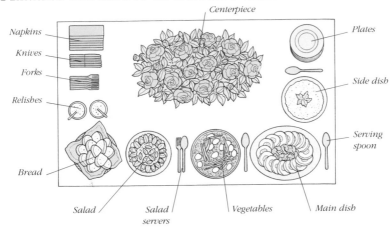

Napkins
Knives
Forks
Relishes
Bread
Centerpiece
Plates
Side dish
Serving spoon
Salad
Salad servers
Vegetables
Main dish

Arranging dishes
When arranging the dishes on a buffet table, start with the plates, then side dishes, followed by the main dish, and finally vegetables and salads, with serving utensils alongside. Breads, any relishes, cutlery, and napkins are usually positioned at the end of the selection. Place decorations in the middle of the table.

ORGANIZING BUFFETS
● **Positioning a buffet table** Leave room behind a buffet table so that you have easy access for replacing dishes.
● **Taping wires** If you place the buffet table in the center of a room, make sure that all electrical wires are taped down safely to the floor.
● **Grouping chairs** Make sure that there are enough chairs, and position them together in groups of three or more so that guests can sit and chat.
● **Setting drinks aside** Place drinks, glasses, and cups on a separate table to avoid congestion at the buffet table.
● **Leaving space on the table** Leave space between dishes on the buffet table so that guests can put down glasses or plates when serving themselves.

KEEPING FOODS COLD
● **Making a cold plate** Fill a dish with water, and freeze. Put it in a plastic bag, then place a plate on top to keep food cold.

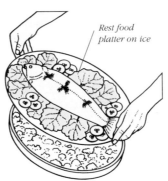

Rest food platter on ice

Using crushed ice
Remove chilled foods from the refrigerator just before serving. To keep food cold on the table, fill a wide dish with crushed ice, and nestle a serving dish into it.

CALCULATING QUANTITIES

Use this checklist to figure quantities for buffet foods. Use the guide on p. 118 to calculate main- and side-dish quantities.

● **Bread** A large, thinly sliced loaf has 18–20 slices. One baguette serves 10 people.
● **Butter** 2 tbsp (25 g) butter will cover seven slices of bread.
● **Green salad** A large iceberg lettuce will serve 10 people, a romaine will serve eight, and a Boston, four.
● **Celebration cake** A 5-lb (2.25-kg) sheet cake can be cut into about 50 slices.
● **Wine** A small (70-cl) bottle fills six glasses; a large (1-liter) bottle, nine.
● **Ice** 20 lb (10 kg) ice cools two cases (24 bottles) of wine.

PRESENTING FOOD

Take care with the presentation of food for a buffet table in order to show off the food at its very best. If you are feeding a large number of guests, replenish serving dishes and clear away empty plates frequently so that the table always looks attractive for your guests.

USING LARGE PLATTERS

● **Stacking sandwiches** Cut sandwiches into quarters, and place them with the points upward to show the fillings.

Fill center with grated carrot

Arranging a salad
Instead of tossing salad in a bowl, arrange ingredients in a colorful pattern on a large, wide platter. Spoon dressing, if desired, over the salad before serving.

DISPLAYING FRUITS

Making a fruit pyramid
Cut the flesh from a large pineapple, leaving the central core and leaves. Attach to a cake stand. Build up seasonal fruits around the core into a pyramid.

Making a cake stand
If you do not have a cake stand for a buffet table, use a large plate or platter. Stand it on an upside-down sugar bowl or soufflé dish. Make sure that the plate is centered. Secure the two firmly with removable putty.

SERVING DRINKS

If guests are to help themselves to drinks at a buffet party, punch is ideal, since it is easy to serve. Offering a punch is also a good way to make alcohol go further. Warm hot punches over low heat if you wish to prevent the alcohol from boiling off, and serve in heatproof cups.

SERVING COLD DRINKS

● **Making a punch bowl** You can use any large, glass bowl as a punch bowl. Decorate the edges with frosted sugar or fruit slices, and drape edible flowers around the sides. Tie ribbon to the ladle handle to serve.
● **Keeping punch chilled** To keep a fruit punch cold, and to serve it in an unusual way, cut the top off a large, round watermelon. Scoop out the flesh, and freeze the shell for 2-3 hours. Add the punch, and serve from the shell.
● **Flavoring ice cubes** To chill and flavor fruit cups, freeze strawberries, maraschino cherries, or mint into ice cubes.

SERVING COCKTAILS

Replace lid when straw is in place

Using melon shells
For an unusual way of serving a fruit cocktail, cut a slice from the top of a small melon and scoop out the flesh. Before filling, cut a hole in one side of the lid for a straw to fit through.

SERVING HOT PUNCHES

● **Mulling wine** To keep mulled wine or a hot punch warm, make the drink in an electric slow-cooking crockpot placed on the buffet table.
● **Floating apples** For a festive winter punch, float a few sweet apples and spices in a hot wine or ale punch. The apples will poach gently, and after an hour or so will make a delicious dessert.
● **Doubling up cups** If you are serving hot punch in disposable paper or plastic cups, test the cups first to check that they are heatproof. Double up cups to make them comfortable to hold.

DINNER PARTIES

ADINNER PARTY IS AN EXCUSE to show off cooking skills that you may not necessarily use in everyday cooking. Plan carefully, and prepare as much as possible in advance so that you are able to enjoy time with your guests.

PRESENTING FOOD

Good presentation of food needs only basic decorating skills and simple but effective garnishes. Elaborate presentation of food can be reserved for formal occasions, but always make sure that the way in which the food appears enhances rather than overshadows your cooking.

MOLDING VEGETABLES

Using a pastry cutter
To serve cut vegetables, place a round pastry cutter on each plate, and spoon in the cooked vegetables, packing them firmly. Lift off the cutter, leaving the vegetables molded to shape.

ARRANGING FOOD

● **Adding height** Pile stir-fried dishes high in the center of a plate so that the helping looks attractive and generous.
● **Fanning slices** To arrange sliced food decoratively, such as an avocado or a chicken breast, slice the food, and lift it whole onto a plate with a spatula. Then fan out the slices evenly.
● **Tieing bundles** Use a chive "ribbon," or thin strips of green leek blanched for 30 seconds, to tie vegetable sticks or baby vegetables together in small bundles.

SHAPING CHOCOLATE

Making chocolate baskets
Spread melted chocolate evenly over 7-in (18-cm) circles of waxed paper to within 1 in (2.5cm) of the edges. Mold over upside-down cups, let set, and peel off the paper. Use for serving desserts.

SERVING CREAMS AND SAUCES

Connect drops of cream with toothpick

Feathering cream
Flood a plate with chocolate sauce or fruit purée, then carefully spoon drops of heavy cream onto it at regular intervals. Draw the tip of a toothpick through each drop to make a chain of feathered heart shapes.

Spoon sauce carefully to create pattern

Designing a pattern
Serve two sauces of similar consistency but contrasting colors together to create an impact. Create a simple but effective pattern by swirling one around the other, for example, on each side of a plate.

● **Making shapes** Spoon a little sauce into a small piping bag, and pipe the outline of the shape you want on a plate. Carefully spoon the rest of the sauce to fill in the shape.
● **Setting purées** Dissolve 1 tsp (5 ml) gelatin in every 1 cup (250 ml) hot fruit purée, then pour the purée while still hot onto a serving plate. Chill the purée until set, then arrange the dessert however you wish.
● **Creating a marbled effect** Marble dark and white chocolate sauces by stirring them together very lightly immediately before serving.
● **Enhancing gravy** Sprinkle fine strips of citrus zest, such as lemon or lime, into plain gravy to accompany grilled meat.

ADDING FINISHING TOUCHES

Garnishes add an attractive finishing touch to a dish, particularly if you are cooking for a special occasion. Remember, however, that it is the dish that is important: garnishes should complement, not compete with, the ingredients. Prepare elaborate garnishes in advance.

ENHANCING GARNISHES
● **Shaping with a canelle knife** Before slicing a cucumber as a garnish, run a canelle knife or the prongs of a fork down its sides at intervals. The slices will then have a fluted edge.
● **Dipping in parsley** Add color to lemon or tomato wedges by dipping their edges into finely chopped parsley after cutting. Alternatively, dip the edges of tomatoes into finely grated Parmesan cheese.
● **Deep-frying parsley** To prevent parsley sprigs from becoming limp, deep-fry them first in hot oil until they are bright green and crisp. Drain on a piece of paper towel.

GARNISHING WITH FRUITS
● **Preparing strawberry fans** To decorate summer desserts, leave the leafy tops on fresh strawberries, and use a sharp knife to cut thin slices through the fruits, leaving the slices attached at the stem end. Hold each stem, and lightly press the slices into a fan shape.

Use sharp knife for accurate cutting

Cutting apple leaves
Cut a series of long, V-shaped notches in the side of an apple, each notch slightly bigger than the one before. Remove the pieces from the apple, and push each piece along on top of the one below to form a leaf shape.

PREPARING VEGETABLE GARNISHES

Slice horizontally to produce hearts

Making carrot hearts
For a romantic dinner garnish, shape a peeled carrot by cutting a groove down one side. Cut the opposite side to a point, so that cross-sections form heart shapes. Slice for individual hearts.

Cut leaves into thin ribbons

Making scallion tassels
Trim scallions, and cut short lengths from the leaf ends. Cut slits lengthwise, extending halfway along each piece from the leaf end. Place in iced water until the sliced leaf ends curl.

GARNISHING QUICKLY
● **Using trimmed leaves** Keep the central leaves from a head of celery, and scatter them over savory dishes to add color.
● **Scattering nuts** Keep toasted, flaked almonds in a jar for scattering over hot and cold savory or sweet dishes as an instant garnish.
● **Sprinkling sugar** As a quick, effective topping for hot or cold desserts, shake sifted confectioners' sugar lightly over the surface of the dish.
● **Using zest** Make a last-minute garnish for savory and sweet dishes by using a zester to grate fine strips of zest from citrus fruits. Scatter the zest over the food before serving.
● **Grating coconut** Use a vegetable peeler to grate curls of fresh coconut over main courses or desserts. Remove the flesh from the shell, but retain the brown skin. Grate across the skin and the flesh to keep the skin on the curls.

SAVING TIME
● **Preparing ahead** When entertaining, make garnishes such as lemon twists, scallion tassels, and tomato wedges in advance. Place on a plate, and add to the food at a later stage. Cover them with plastic wrap, and they will stay fresh for up to four hours.

EDIBLE FLOWERS

The following flowers are edible, and are therefore good for decorative purposes. The large flowers of some vegetables, such as zucchini, and the flowers of some herbs are also edible. If you cannot identify a flower, do not eat it.

Apple blossom	Lavender
Borage	Marigold
Calendula	Nasturtium
Clover	Orange
Dandelion	Pansy
Daylily	Primrose
Elderflower	Rose
Geranium	Violet

SERVING WINE

Alcoholic drinks stimulate the appetite and enhance the flavor of food, so they can add to the enjoyment of any meal, however simple the food or the setting. If you are unsure about choosing wines, consult a good wine merchant, who will let you taste a selection before you buy.

MATCHING WINE WITH FOOD

There are no strict rules about which wine to serve with which dish, but the following guidelines are useful.

- **Order of drinking** White wine is generally preferred before red, young before mature, and dry before sweet.
- **Appetizers or canapés** Serve crisp white wines, sparkling wines, or dry sherry.
- **Fish dishes** Serve dry white wines such as Muscadet, or young, light reds.
- **Pasta and cheese dishes** Serve robust wines such as Bardolino (red).
- **Creamy dishes** Choose slightly acidic wines such as Sauvignon Blanc (white).

PREPARING WINE

- **Chilling wines** To chill white wines, refrigerate for a maximum of two hours, or bury the bottles in crushed ice for 30 minutes before serving.
- **Accelerating chilling** Put wine in the freezer to cool quickly, leaving only for about five minutes. Set a timer so that you remember to remove it.
- **Loosening wires** To save time, loosen the wires of champagne corks while the bottles are chilling so that the corks are ready to pop.
- **Warming red wines** Pour red wine into a slightly warm decanter to warm quickly, instead of heating the wine directly. Uncork young red wine about an hour before serving to develop the flavor.

TRADITIONAL TIP

Decanting wine
Decant bottle-aged wine or port to remove sediment. To do this easily, insert an unbleached coffee filter into the neck of a glass pitcher, and pour the wine gently into it.

SERVING NONALCOHOLIC DRINKS

Whatever the occasion, offer your guests a selection of nonalcoholic drinks. Always have mineral water available for both drinkers and nondrinkers, as well as fruit juices and cordials. Some people may prefer wine "lookalikes" such as grape juice or alcohol-free wines.

ADDING FLAVOR

- **Stimulating the appetite** Add a thin slice of fresh lemon or lime to each glass of mineral water to sharpen the appetite.
- **Accompanying spicy food** Serve a refreshing, lassi-style yogurt drink with spicy food, such as an Indian curry, instead of wine or beer. Place 1 cup (250 ml) plain yogurt in a blender with 2 cups (500 ml) water, ½ tsp (2.5 ml) salt, and a sprig of fresh mint. Blend until smooth, then serve in tall, chilled glasses.
- **Adding celery sticks** Use a small, trimmed piece of celery as a swizzle stick for stirring tomato or vegetable juice.

MAKING MILK SHAKES

Shake until frothy before pouring

Using a screw-top jar
If you do not have a blender with which to make a milk shake, mix fruit purée and ice cream with milk in a large screw-top jar and shake. Alternatively, beat the mixture with a balloon whisk.

ALCOHOL-FREE COCKTAILS

- **Cranberry spritzer** Stir equal parts cranberry juice, white grape juice, and sparkling mineral water.
- **Raspberry mint fizz** Pour ¼ cup (50 ml) raspberry syrup into a tall glass. Add a handful of crushed mint leaves and ice. Top off with soda water.
- **Shirley Temple** Shake several dashes of grenadine into a glass. Top off with lemon-lime soda for a bubbly froth. Finish with a maraschino cherry.
- **Peppermint cream** Shake peppermint cordial with cream and a little crushed ice.

CATERING FOR SPECIAL OCCASIONS

A wedding, birthday, or other celebration is an excuse to prepare elaborate food, but clever presentation and original use of color can also contribute to a memorable meal. Use your imagination to carry the theme of an event through to the table decorations and the food.

MAKING UNUSUAL CAKES

EXTENDING COLOR THEMES TO FOOD

Duck with orange

Tomato and pepper salad

Selecting golden food
For a golden-themed celebration, serve yellow and orange foods such as carrots, yellow peppers, saffron rice, and fruits such as oranges and peaches.

Peach served with brandy snaps

Creating different shapes
For a celebration cake, fill small cream puffs with whipped cream or pastry cream, then pile into a pyramid shape. Tuck roses or mint leaves in the gaps, and sprinkle with confectioners' sugar.

USING FLOWERS
● **Making a cake stand** Instead of using a formal silver cake stand for a wedding or a christening cake, choose a firm wooden box that is slightly larger than the base of the cake, and cover it with a lace cloth. Pin on silk or fresh flowers and ribbons to decorate.
● **Flavoring with flowers** Add a few drops of orange flower water or rosewater to whipped fresh cream, and stir gently. Spoon into pretty bowls, and scatter with fresh orange blossom or rose petals. Serve with desserts instead of plain whipped cream.
● **Floating candles** To make an unusual evening table decoration, half fill a large, wide glass bowl with water. Float small candles and lavish fresh blooms, such as camellias, on the water.

● **Creating a tricolor dinner** Mix red, green, and white foods to carry an Italian theme through the meal. For example, use red and green peppers, or tomatoes and basil, with white cheeses.

CREATING MOLDED ICE DECORATIONS
● **Making ice sculptures** Use an elaborate gelatin mold to freeze an ice sculpture for a celebration buffet table. Unmold and use as a centerpiece for crudités or fresh fruits.

MOLDING A DECORATIVE ICE BOWL

Tape bowls to ensure evenly shaped ice

Use knife point to push flowers into position

● **Using dark foods** For an elegant dinner, create a stunning, almost black theme by using black plates and dark foods such as beets, purple basil, wild rice, black grapes, and blackberries.

● **Using boiled water** When making ice sculptures and bowls, first boil the water. This will result in clearer ice than if unboiled water is used. Cool completely before freezing.

1 Make an ice bowl in which to serve ices. Place a small, freezer-proof bowl inside a larger bowl, and tape the bowls in position. Fill the space in between with water.

2 Push some edible flowers into the water, and freeze. Fill the small bowl with warm water, and lift out. Dip the outer bowl in warm water, and unmold.

PARTY MANAGEMENT

THERE IS NO MYSTERY TO THROWING the perfect party, but careful planning in advance is the best insurance you can have against disasters. Once a party is organized, allow yourself some time to relax before your guests arrive.

OFFERING HOSPITALITY

Whatever the occasion, the most important thing to remember is that the guests come first. Give some thought to creating a warm atmosphere that will make guests comfortable as soon as they arrive, and spend time with them instead of disappearing into the kitchen.

PROVIDING FINGER BOWLS

Add lemon slices to refresh hands

Napkins for wiping hands

Placing finger bowls
If you are serving foods that are to be eaten with the fingers, such as crudités or shellfish, provide each guest with a finger bowl if they are sitting down to eat, or spread finger bowls liberally around the room for a buffet.

- **Scenting water** Add a few drops of orange flower water, rosewater, or lemon juice to the water, or scatter rose petals or jasmine flowers to leave a pleasant scent on the fingers.

- **Warming water** If you are serving sticky or fatty foods, such as spare ribs, warm the water to hand-hot for finger bowls, and put them out just before you serve the food.

WELCOMING GUESTS
- **Creating atmosphere**
Depending on the occasion, tie a garland of fresh flowers, a lantern, or a bunch of balloons on a mailbox or a door to set the scene as guests approach the house.
- **Adjusting lighting** Before your guests arrive for a party, dim the house lights or light some candles around the rooms. Make sure that the light is soft but not too low, so that guests can see their food as well as one another.
- **Checking bathrooms** Check bathrooms to make sure that they are clean, with soaps and towels put out for guests to use. Leave lights on if the switches are difficult to locate.

PLAN OF ACTION

Remember these points before and during a party.

- **Checking insurance** Check with an insurance broker in case you need special insurance for a large event.
- **Preparing ahead** Do as much as possible in advance to make sure that you are free to welcome guests.
- **Circulating among guests** Introduce guests to each other, and "rescue" anyone who is left on their own.
- **Drinking alcohol** Do not encourage guests to drink large quantities of alcohol.

CREATING A FRAGRANT ATMOSPHERE

Place ingredients in small bowls

Making potpourri
Instead of making a heavily flower-scented potpourri, make a food-based mixture. Combine bay leaves, thinly pared or dried citrus zest, cinnamon sticks, rosemary sprigs, juniper or allspice berries, and star anise. Sprinkle with vanilla or almond extract.

- **Reviving potpourri** Freshen up potpourri that has lost its scent by spreading it onto a cookie sheet and sprinkling it with water or scented oil. Place in a hot oven for five minutes to draw out the fragrances.

- **Positioning bowls** Place bowls of potpourri in the warmest areas of the room, such as on a mantelpiece, on a shelf above a table lamp, or around candles. The warmth will enhance the fragrances.

COPING WITH EMERGENCIES

However carefully you plan and prepare for entertaining, it is a good idea to be well prepared for emergencies. Whether someone experiences a medical problem or there is simply a spill, remain calm so that you can deal with the situation quickly and effectively.

CLEANING SPILLS

● **Preventing permanent stains** If red wine is spilled onto a carpet, splash it with soda water. Pat with paper towels to soak up the excess liquid, and treat with carpet shampoo.

Removing candle wax
If candle wax drips onto a tablecloth, rub it with an ice cube, and chip off the wax. Cover with paper towels, and press with a warm iron. Dab with rubbing alcohol to remove any residue before washing.

PREVENTING PROBLEMS

● **Informing neighbors** If you are throwing a party, let the neighbors know, or invite them over, so that noise will not be a source of irritation.
● **Spot-cleaning** Have on hand a bottle of spot-cleaner or dry-cleaning fluid, ready for dealing with minor spills.
● **Noting useful numbers** At a children's party, make sure that you have each parent's telephone number, and keep the number of the nearest hospital by the telephone.
● **Avoiding spoiled food** If cooking food such as a soufflé, the timing of which is critical, ensure that it will not be ready before it is due to be eaten.
● **Checking allergies** Be aware of any special dietary needs of guests, and ask parents if their children have food allergies.

COPING WITH DRINKERS

● **Preventing drunk driving** If a guest has drunk too much to drive, insist that a sober guest drive them home, or call for a taxi. Alternatively, suggest they stay overnight.

SAFETY

If someone is choking, follow this first-aid technique:

1 Remove food or false teeth from the mouth. Encourage the victim to cough.

2 If coughing fails and the person is making a high-pitched, wheezing sound, stand behind them, and put your clenched fist – thumb inward – underneath the breastbone. Hold the fist with the other hand, and pull firmly upward and inward up to four times.

CLEANING UP

Cleaning up after a party need not spoil the fun. If you work in a sensible, organized manner, the task will be simple and quick. A dishwasher will help, but if you do not have one enlist as many people as possible to help with the washing, drying, and putting away.

WORKING ORDER

Work in a logical order so that cleanup runs smoothly.

● **Clearing** Load glasses, cutlery, plates, ashtrays, and other items onto trays and carry them to the kitchen.
● **Removing food waste** Remove food debris from plates and serving dishes.
● **Soaking utensils** Soak plates, glasses, and cutlery in a sink full of soapy water.
● **Washing dishes** Wash in the sink, or load the dishwasher.
● **Putting away** Rinse, drain, dry, and put items away.

DRYING GLASSWARE

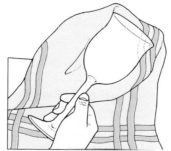

Avoiding damage
Cup the bowl of a stemmed glass in a dish towel when drying it, rotating the glass gently without twisting. Alternatively, rinse in clear water, and drain on a towel.

SAVING TIME & EFFORT

● **Heating water** Make sure that there is plenty of hot water for dishwashing.
● **Clearing the sink** Check that the sink or dishwasher is empty before starting to clean up.
● **Soaking cutlery** Prepare buckets of hot, soapy water, and drop cutlery into them to soak as you clean up.
● **Stocking up** Check that you have plenty of garbage bags, clean rags, detergent, and paper towels on hand.
● **Emptying ash** Empty the contents of ashtrays into an old cookie tin for safe disposal.

CHILDREN'S PARTIES

GOOD PLANNING IS THE SECRET OF SUCCESS for children's parties and will make them fun for you as well as for the young guests. Organize food, space, and activities well in advance, and enlist help from other parents on party day.

PREPARING FUN FOOD

Children's party food should be colorful, fun, and good to eat. Keep it simple and healthy, easy to hold in the hand and to eat in small mouthfuls. Encourage the children to eat more than just sweet foods by making savories in fun shapes and colors to tempt picky eaters.

MAKING NOVELTY CAKES

● **Using a jelly roll** Cover a ready-made jelly roll with colored, ready-to-use fondant icing that is longer than the roll. Pinch the icing at each end so that it resembles a giant piece of candy. Decorate.
● **Cutting blocks** For a young child's party, make individual cakes by cutting a sponge cake into large cubes and covering with fondant. Pipe a child's initial on each piece, and pile up the cakes like toy blocks.
● **Making a clock** Pipe a clock on a birthday cake, with the "time" showing the child's age.

FEEDING TODDLERS

● **Making traffic lights** Set green, yellow, and red gelatin in clear tumblers. Let each layer set before adding the next.

Pipe melted chocolate for face and tail

Creating meringue mice
Make oval meringues, and bake in a cool oven for 1½ hours. Stick halved chocolate buttons gently into the meringue for ears, and pipe other details such as eyes.

DECORATING BISCUITS

Baking window cookies
Roll out firm cookie dough, and cut into shapes, then remove centers with a small cutter. Fill the holes with crushed, clear, hard candies. Bake as usual.

SERVING HOT FOODS

● **Saving time** To make quick, individual pizzas, top English muffins or plain rolls with savory toppings. Grill.

Frankfurters resting against mashed-potato pyramid

Making a tepee
Mold mashed potatoes into a pointed heap on a plate. Pile frankfurters or sausages around the outside of the potatoes to form a decorative tepee shape.

USING FRUIT NOVELTIES

Fill with ice cream

Carving orange lanterns
Sculpt oranges to look like Halloween lanterns. Slice off the tops, scoop out the flesh, and carve faces into the skins. Fill, and replace the tops to serve.

FEEDING TEENAGERS

● **Choosing a theme** Try a Tex-Mex theme for a teenage party. Serve food such as tacos with fillings, salsas, chili con carne, and guacamole.
● **Making mini-kebabs** Thread chunks of salami, cheese, cherry tomatoes, and button mushrooms onto bamboo skewers to serve with dips.
● **Filling pita breads** Serve burgers in sandwich-sized pita breads. They will be easier and less messy to hold than in burger buns.
● **Making iced bananas** Push ice-pop sticks into peeled bananas, and freeze for 30 minutes. Dip in melted chocolate, and roll quickly in dried coconut. Serve while still slightly frozen.

MAKING PARTY DRINKS

Inventing children's drinks for parties can be fun, and you can be especially creative with the trimmings. Wherever possible, try to use healthy, nutritious ingredients, such as fresh fruit juices instead of highly sweetened soda, and use fresh fruits for decoration or in ice cubes.

DECORATING DRINKS

● **Adding ice cream** Put scoops of ice cream into fruit juice just before serving. Half-fill glasses with the drink, add ice cream, and serve.
● **Making lollipops** Freeze fruit juice on lollipop sticks to make drinks on sticks.
● **Decorating milk shakes** Sprinkle fruity milk shakes with grated chocolate or rainbow sprinkles.
● **Freezing juices** Fill separate ice cube trays with apple, cranberry, and orange juices, and freeze overnight. Put mixed cubes into tall glasses, top off with lemonade, and decorate with fresh fruits.

DECORATING GLASSES

Use brightly colored stickers

Using stick-on shapes
Instead of buying decorated party glasses, attach stick-on shapes to the outside of plain tumblers or plastic cups. Remove all the stickers before washing.

ADDING EXTRAS

Making "magic" drinks
Delight children with this special effect. Freeze chocolate chips for 30 minutes, then add a handful to glasses of lemon-lime soda. The chips will bounce up and down.

USING FOOD FOR PARTY GAMES

Incorporate fun foods into party games. Plan energetic games, preferably outdoors, before the children eat. Hunting for edible treasure is popular. Use novelty foods for this or for quiet activities after the meal. If the weather is bad, try egg decorating with food markers.

MAKING EDIBLE GAMES

● **Icing domino cookies** Pipe dots of white icing or cream cheese onto rectangular chocolate cookies or graham crackers to make dominoes. Let the children play with the dominoes and then eat them when the game is over.

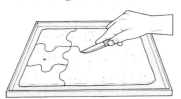

Baking a cookie jigsaw
Roll out plain, firm cookie dough. Cut jigsaw shapes in it. Bake and cool, then decorate with colored icing or food colors. Let the children fit the shapes together before they eat the cookies.

ENTERTAINING TODDLERS

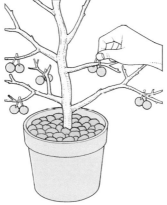

Making fruit trees
Encourage small children to eat fruit by making a "tree" for the table. Fill a plant pot with stones, and insert a small branch into it. Hang cherries, or tie other fruits to the branches, for children to pick.

PLAYING OUTDOORS

● **Apple bobbing** Float some apples in a large bowl or bucket of water. Ask each to try to bite an apple without using hands. The first child to do so wins the game.
● **Egg-and-spoon racing** Hold a race with each child carrying a hard-cooked egg in a spoon. The winner is the first to finish without dropping the egg.
● **Passing the orange** Form two teams. Put an orange under the chin of each team leader. The winning team is the first to pass the orange along the team line without using hands.
● **Playing tic tac toe** Bake bread dough into large Os and Xs. Mark a grid on an old sheet, and lay it down. Let the children place the shapes.

BARBECUES

N O MATTER HOW BASIC THE EQUIPMENT AND HOW SIMPLE THE FOOD, barbecues are often more fun and the food better-tasting than meals cooked indoors. They can even free you from the kitchen, and fresh air will sharpen appetites.

SETTING UP BARBECUES

There are many well-designed, sophisticated barbecues on the market today that are very easy to light, control, and clean. It is not essential, however, to spend a lot of money on barbecue equipment. You can improvise very successfully using only basic equipment.

BUILDING A SIMPLE BARBECUE

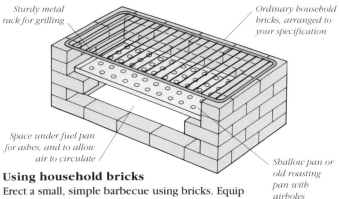

Sturdy metal rack for grilling

Ordinary household bricks, arranged to your specification

Space under fuel pan for ashes, and to allow air to circulate

Shallow pan or old roasting pan with airholes

Using household bricks
Erect a small, simple barbecue using bricks. Equip it with a metal grill rack and a pan in which to place the fuel. If the barbecue is to be permanent, then line the inside with fireproof bricks.

PREPARING FIRES
● **Using foil** Line the base of a barbecue with foil before adding fuel to reflect heat and to make cleaning easy.
● **Lighting fuel** If you find charcoal briquettes difficult to light, buy a bag of easy-light charcoal. It is clean and safe to use, since you need not handle the charcoal. Just place the specially designed bag of fuel in position, and light it.
● **Burning wood** Choose hardwoods from a sustainable source. Woods such as apple, oak, or cherry will burn slowly without crackling or smoking.

PREPARING TO COOK
● **Adding flavor** Instead of buying expensive bags of hickory or oak chips for a flavored, smoky taste, scatter sprigs or twigs of rosemary, thyme, or fennel over the fire just before cooking. Soak the sprigs in water first to make them last longer.
● **Greasing racks** Keep trimmed meat fat for rubbing over a barbecue rack before placing food on it to prevent food from sticking. Alternatively, brush the rack with oil.
● **Heating up** Wait for the flames to die down before starting to cook. Charcoal takes at least 25–30 minutes to heat up, and gas barbecues take 10 minutes. Coals should be ash gray in color.

PREVENTING PROBLEMS
● **Avoiding flare-ups** To prevent a fire from flaring up, do not add too much oil to marinades, and trim excess fat from meat.
● **Controlling a fire** Keep a bucket of sand and a garden hose nearby in case a fire flares up out of control.

SAFETY

● **Site** Choose a firm, level surface away from buildings and out of the wind.
● **Children and pets** Keep them away from the fire.
● **Protection** Use long-handled tools and insulated gloves.
● **Fire control** Let the fire heat naturally. Never use lighter fluid.
● **First aid** Keep a first-aid kit handy in case of accidents.

MONEY-SAVING TIP

Using a cookie tin
To make a small, impromptu picnic barbecue, punch holes around the sides of an old cookie tin. Fill the tin with briquettes, and place a metal grill rack or a piece of chicken wire on top to hold the food for grilling.

CHAR-GRILLING FOODS

Cooking foods on an open grill directly over charcoal will give them a unique, smoky flavor, and using robust marinades, herbs, and spices will give additional impact. Plan the order of char-grilling carefully so that foods receive the precise amount of cooking that they need.

COOKING EVENLY
● **Precooking foods** Make sure that meat and poultry are well cooked by precooking in the microwave. Transfer them immediately to the barbecue.
● **Parboiling potatoes** Parboil new potatoes for five minutes, then thread them onto metal skewers. Brush with oil, and grill for 8–10 minutes.
● **Using heat zones** Use the cooler, outer edges around the grill to avoid overcooking food that needs gentle heat, such as vegetables or fruits.
● **Controlling heat** If your barbecue has no heat control, raise and lower the grill rack to control the heat. Sear meats such as steaks about 1½–2 in (4–5 cm) above the coals, then raise the rack to finish cooking on a lower heat.

ADDING FLAVOR
● **Spicing vegetables** Toss vegetables such as corn on the cob in butter or oil, and sprinkle with Cajun or curry spice.

Spread pesto with pastry brush

Glazing food with pesto
Brush low-fat food such as turkey or chicken breasts with pesto to add flavor and to keep the flesh moist during cooking. Pesto will also impart a rich Mediterranean flavor to the dish.

WRAPPING FOODS

Some foods benefit from a little protection to prevent them from drying out or breaking up in the fierce heat of a barbecue. To seal in juices and keep foods moist, use natural wrappings such as grape leaves, corn husks, or banana leaves, or wrap foods in foil, and cook gently.

USING GRAPE LEAVES

Overlap grape leaves, enclosing food completely

Wrapping fish
Use grape leaves to wrap delicate foods such as fish to prevent them from drying out or breaking up during cooking. If you are using fresh grape leaves, blanch first for one minute to soften.

USING CORN HUSKS

Wrapping chicken
Retain unwanted husks from corn on the cob, and use them to wrap chicken breasts stuffed with dried apricots. Use several layers of husk to keep the chicken moist during cooking.

TRYING NEW IDEAS
● **Using bacon** Slice large sausages lengthwise, and spread with mustard. Wrap in bacon slices, secure with toothpicks, and cook.
● **Making calzone** Use pizza dough to enclose pizza-style toppings. Fold the dough in half, then pinch the edges together to seal them. Brush with oil before grilling.
● **Making fruit bundles** Wrap fruits in foil with a dash of liqueur and a pat of butter.
● **Cooking in skins** Grill whole bananas, turning occasionally, for 6–8 minutes. Slit the skins, and serve with maple syrup.

PICNICS

PICNICKING IS IN MANY RESPECTS THE IDEAL WAY to enjoy good food and company. It enables you to eat in a favorite scenic spot or at an outdoor event. Whatever the occasion, keep picnics simple for maximum fun and minimum fuss.

MAKING PICNIC FOOD

The type of picnic you are planning will determine your selection of food. For a walking trip, food will need to be packed into a small space, and must be eaten without utensils. If you are traveling by car, you can pack more sophisticated foods and equipment.

MAKING SANDWICHES

● **Freezing in advance** Make sandwiches for a picnic in advance, and freeze them. Fillings containing hard-cooked eggs, mayonnaise, or salad are not suitable for freezing.

● **Making crab bites** For bite-sized sandwiches, stamp out shapes from bread using a cookie cutter. Pipe with cream cheese from a tube, and wrap around crab sticks. Secure the bites with toothpicks, and pack into boxes.

● **Mixing breads** Add interest to sandwiches by using whole-wheat and white bread together with a filling between.

ADDING VARIETY

Damp towel prevents bread from cracking

Rolling pinwheels
Cut the crusts from thinly sliced bread, and spread with butter. Place on a dampened dish towel, spread with filling, and roll up inside the towel. Then slice to create pinwheel shapes.

USING WHOLE LOAVES

Wrap tightly in foil

Filling a baguette
Instead of packing individual, filled rolls for a picnic, split a long baguette lengthwise. Brush the surface with olive oil, add a savory filling, and wrap. Slice into portions at the picnic site.

TRANSPORTING DESSERTS

Dip sliced fruit into purée

Serving a fruit dip
Purée fresh fruits, such as strawberries or mangoes, with honey to taste. Pour into a small plastic container, and transport to the picnic site inside a larger container together with sliced fruits for dipping into the purée.

CHOOSING EASY FOODS

● **Serving crudités** Pack a basket of simple, fresh crudités with a tub of a favorite dip and an ice pack for easy eating without plates. Choose vegetables that require little preparation, such as whole baby carrots, baby corn, radishes, mushrooms, and cooked new potatoes.

● **Packing individual portions** Take individual quiches or pies instead of a large one, so that they can be eaten easily without utensils, and there will be no need to slice into portions.

● **Wrapping potatoes** For cold-weather picnics, wrap baked potatoes in foil. Pack in several layers of newsprint or in an insulated bag.

BRIGHT IDEA

Stacking desserts
Make individual mousses or crème brûlées in small ramekins, then stack them together with a piece of cardboard between each one. Wrap the stack in plastic wrap for transporting.

CHOOSING EQUIPMENT

There is no need to buy lots of special equipment for picnics, but an insulated cooler bag with ice packs is essential for keeping food cold and fresh, especially in summer. Disposable plates and glasses are lighter and safer to carry than china and glass.

SELECTING CONTAINERS

● **Packing foods** Use square food containers where possible, since they are easier to stack than round ones and therefore take up less space. Round plastic containers often have good seals, so use these for transporting liquids.

● **Choosing a thermos** Use a wide-necked food thermos to keep foods such as fruit salad cold. They can also be used to keep casseroles or soups hot.

● **Using boxes** If you do not have a picnic basket, use a large cardboard box instead. It will hold more and will be easier to pack than a traditional picnic basket.

USING CAMPING STOVES

Tray provides level base

Making a firm base
If you take a small portable camping stove on a picnic, make sure that you use it safely. Before lighting, place it on a metal tray on a level piece of ground, well away from plants and trees.

PICNIC CHECKLIST

Check that you have packed the following useful items:

● Salt and pepper.
● Paper napkins or towels.
● Corkscrew.
● Sharp knife for cutting bread and other foods.
● Plastic or paper plates, glasses, and cutlery.
● Serving spoons.
● Drinking water.
● Blanket or tablecloth.
● Large umbrella.
● Dampened disposable cloth in a plastic bag.
● Insect repellent.
● First-aid kit.
● Garbage bag.

PACKING FOOD

Packing food for a picnic is largely a matter of common sense. With a little careful planning, your food will arrive at the intended picnic site cool, undamaged, and ready to eat. A general rule is to pack heavy or unsquashable items first, and to put more delicate items on top of them.

TRANSPORTING SALADS

● **Leaving space** Pack salads loosely into rigid containers to prevent crushing and to allow the ingredients to breathe.

Packing a dressing
To keep the crispness of a green salad, toss it with the dressing at the picnic site. Transport the dressing in a screw-top jar packed in the same container as the salad.

PACKING SMALL ITEMS

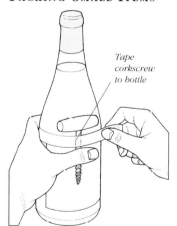

Tape corkscrew to bottle

Packing a corkscrew
To ensure that you remember to take a corkscrew, and to make it easy to find at the picnic site, tape a corkscrew to a bottle of wine using masking tape.

PREVENTING PROBLEMS

● **Using tissue paper** Place tarts with delicate edges in rigid boxes, and surround them with crumpled tissue paper for protection during transportation.

● **Wrapping glasses and china** Carefully wrap drinking glasses or china plates that you are taking on a picnic in bubble wrap to prevent damage.

● **Packing bottled drinks** Lie bottles on their side in ice in a covered cooler to keep them cool and avoid breakage.

● **Packing foods in order** As much as possible, pack foods in the order they will be needed, with desserts at the bottom.

● **Avoiding spills** Allow carbonated drinks to stand after the journey so that they do not squirt when opened.

IMPROMPTU ENTERTAINING

T HE MOST ENJOYABLE MEALS are often the ones that have not been planned – for example, when guests arrive unexpectedly. You will be able to cope with these occasions easily if you keep certain items on hand and use them creatively.

PREPARING STANDBY FOODS

A lways keep your kitchen pantry well stocked, so that if you have to entertain on short notice you will be prepared. Everyday foods can quickly be transformed into impressive dishes with a little imagination. Keep a stock of luxury foods to add last-minute special touches.

STORING IN THE FREEZER
● **Making individual portions** When freezing main dishes or desserts to keep as standbys, freeze in one-portion packs so that you can remove only as many servings as you need.
● **Freezing stuffings** Make rich fruit or herb stuffings for meat and poultry, and store them in the freezer to use on special occasions in the future.
● **Making bruscetta** Slice ciabatta bread, and reassemble for freezing. When guests arrive, spread the frozen slices with pesto sauce, sprinkle with grated cheese, and bake until golden. Serve with salad.

FREEZING CREAM

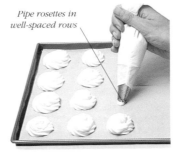

Pipe rosettes in well-spaced rows

Piping rosettes
Store whipped-cream rosettes in the freezer, ready for last-minute decorations. Pipe onto a cookie sheet lined with waxed paper. Freeze until solid, then pack in rigid boxes to store.

FREEZING PANCAKES

Interleaving with paper
When you cook pancakes, make more than you need, and freeze those you do not use. Interleave with waxed paper, overwrap, and freeze. You will be able to remove as many as you need.

USING BASIC STORES
● **Serving snacks** Keep jars of olives, nuts, and savory nibbles on hand to serve with drinks while you are preparing a meal for unexpected guests.
● **Making antipasto** Combine canned or bottled ingredients such as artichoke hearts, sun-dried tomatoes, cannellini beans, sardines, and pimentos to make a quick antipasto. Serve with crusty bread.
● **Creating rice dishes** Mix leftover long-grain rice with a variety of foods such as flaked salmon, tuna, or shreds of chicken and vegetables such as peas or corn. Heat all the ingredients gently before serving as a main course, or serve cold as a speedy salad.

PANTRY DESSERTS

Stuffing pancakes
Thaw frozen pancakes in the microwave, fold into quarters, and fill with canned fruits. Heat until bubbling, and serve with whipped cream or ice cream.

● **Baked peach snowballs** Fill the hollows of canned peach halves with crumbled macaroons or graham crackers, cover the peaches completely with meringue, and bake until the "snowballs" are golden.

● **Apple surprise** Mix together applesauce and vanilla pudding or yogurt. Spoon the mixture into serving dishes, and top with toasted nuts.
● **Raspberry rice** Stir frozen raspberries into store-bought rice pudding, and spoon into dessert glasses to serve.
● **Pears in port** Drain canned pear halves, and arrange the fruits in a shallow dish. Pour over enough port to cover, and chill before serving.
● **Fried pineapple rings** Drain canned pineapple rings, and sauté them gently in butter until they are golden in color. Sprinkle with brown sugar and a little brandy. Serve hot with whipped cream or ice cream.

COOKING FOR EXTRA GUESTS

If you find yourself with an extra mouth to feed, and it is too late to go shopping, think quickly and add extras to what you are already cooking. Bulk out casseroles with canned or frozen vegetables, offer bread with each course, and serve fresh fruits as well as a dessert.

ADDING TOPPINGS

● **Topping with cheese** To extend a vegetable dish, cover with a cheese sauce and flaked almonds, then grill.

Shaping a dough topping
Roll out biscuit dough, and cut into shapes with a cookie cutter. Arrange the dough shapes over a casserole filling, and bake in a hot oven for 12–15 minutes.

INCREASING QUANTITIES

● **Adding stock** Increase the volume of a soup by adding a flavorful stock or a glass of dry white wine. Heat until boiling, and then stir in cream or milk to taste before serving.
● **Adding beans** To bulk out cooked rice, stir in a can of drained kidney beans or chick peas and a few chopped herbs.
● **Stirring in oats** Add a handful of oatmeal and a can of chopped tomatoes to extend a bolognese sauce.
● **Serving an appetizer** To make a quick and easy appetizer to accompany a main meal, serve a tomato and onion salad with crusty bread.
● **Serving accompaniments** Serve stuffing or complementary sauces to extend roast meats.

DOUBLING UP DESSERTS

Alternate pudding and whipped cream

Layering with cream
If you have made a pudding or mousse that is not sufficient, increase the number of portions by layering the fruit with whipped cream in tall glasses.

ENHANCING BASIC DISHES

If you are faced with making an everyday family meal into something more exciting for visitors, create a sense of occasion by combining ingredients in unusual ways. Pep up casseroles with crispy, herbed croutons, or spoon desserts into pretty glasses instead of plain bowls.

SERVING SOUPS

Combining colors
Make canned soups special by lightly swirling two contrasting colors together. Cream soups work best, and good partners are tomato with asparagus or celery with green pea.

EMBELLISHING DESSERTS

Finish with cookies for crunchy topping

Layering ingredients
Sprinkle canned fruit with sherry or brandy, and serve with a store-bought dessert such as lemon mousse. Alternate layers of each with crumbled cookies, and spoon into attractive glasses.

BRIGHT IDEA

Flavoring UHT cream
Mask the distinctive flavor of UHT milk or cream by whipping in a few drops of vanilla extract or rosewater before adding it to a dessert.

GARDENING

TRANSFORMING GARDENS

•

STOCKING GARDENS

•

PROTECTING PLANTS

•

CREATING GARDEN FEATURES

•

PROPAGATION

•

GARDEN MAINTENANCE

RESTORING LANDSCAPES

QUICK REFERENCE
Transforming Lawns, p. 452
Restoring Borders, p. 456
Renovating Patios, p. 459
Paths and Steps, p. 464
Transforming Walls, p. 466
Constructing Screens, p. 469
Height & Perspective, p. 475

R*ENOVATING OR CHANGING A LANDSCAPE* does not need to be hard work. Planning, the right equipment, some basic gardening knowledge, and enthusiasm are all you need to transform your landscape. Begin with improvements that will not take too much time or money. These changes will help make you feel positive about the landscape and will inspire and encourage you to tackle it in more fundamental ways.

GARDEN PROBLEMS AND SOLUTIONS

GARDEN PROBLEMS	SIMPLE SOLUTIONS
LAWN The shape is boring or simply does not appeal to you; the edges are damaged and shabby-looking; the lawn is full of uneven areas, moss, weeds, and brown patches; there is too much of it.	Alter the shape; neaten lawn edges or remake them from scratch; level out humps and hollows; control moss and weeds; reseed bare areas; plant a specimen tree; make an island bed; make a path; create an ornamental divider.
FLOWER BEDS AND BORDERS Beds and borders are fine overall, but some plants are overwhelmed by others; some plants are in poor condition; there are gaps in a border.	Divide overcrowded plants, removing some entirely; add climbers to leggy shrubs; use annuals, perennials, and bulbs to fill gaps; grow climbers or groundcovers to cover bare slopes.
TREES Trees are overgrown and out of shape; they are blocking light for shrubs, and other plants, and the house; low branches restrict access around trees.	Create a bed using plants that enjoy woodland conditions; plant spring bulbs and water and feed them to counteract competition; crown-lift or crown-reduce the trees to increase light levels.
PATIO The area is untidy and covered with moss, algae, and weeds; the slabs are broken and cracked; you do not like the shape; it is stark and uninviting.	Remove debris; control moss, algae, and weeds; replace or remove broken slabs; add plants; alter the shape; use pots, baskets, and other containers; create a barbecue or water feature.
PATHS AND STEPS They are too angular and harsh, and do not fit in with the garden; they are slippery; they have loose slabs; weeds are growing in the cracks; they are deteriorating; they look untidy.	Plant up with edging to soften harsh lines and to make them look more attractive; remove algae and moss; repair loose or damaged areas; remove weeds and prevent their reappearance; liven them up with plants in containers.
WALLS They serve a purpose but are damaged, discolored, and ugly; they do not provide any benefit to the garden; they are uninteresting.	Clean, whitewash, or paint; plant and train fruit trees; plant climbers or thin out existing climbers; clean up the old trellis, or erect a new one; paint a mural; add a mirror; add a seat to make a bower.

A TRANSFORMED LANDSCAPE

A landscape that has been neglected over a long period of time can be a depressing sight. Restoring it may seem a daunting task, but you will be amazed at the transformation you can make in just one year. Start by clearing away any debris and cutting the grass.

IDEAS FOR RENOVATING AND RESTORING A LANDSCAPE

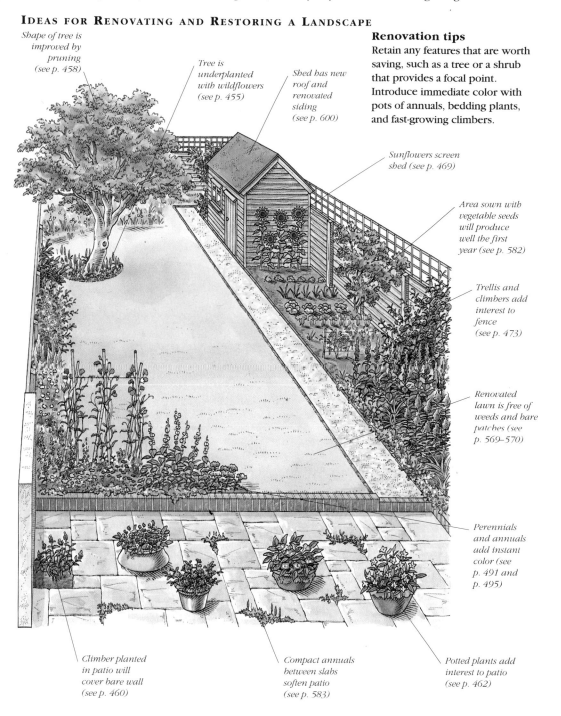

Shape of tree is improved by pruning (see p. 458)

Tree is underplanted with wildflowers (see p. 455)

Shed has new roof and renovated siding (see p. 600)

Renovation tips
Retain any features that are worth saving, such as a tree or a shrub that provides a focal point. Introduce immediate color with pots of annuals, bedding plants, and fast-growing climbers.

Sunflowers screen shed (see p. 469)

Area sown with vegetable seeds will produce well the first year (see p. 582)

Trellis and climbers add interest to fence (see p. 473)

Renovated lawn is free of weeds and bare patches (see p. 569–570)

Perennials and annuals add instant color (see p. 491 and p. 495)

Climber planted in patio will cover bare wall (see p. 460)

Compact annuals between slabs soften patio (see p. 583)

Potted plants add interest to patio (see p. 462)

TRANSFORMING LAWNS

A LAWN OFTEN FORMS one of the central parts of a landscape and, in many cases, takes up the largest portion of the area. If the lawn is unkempt or uninspiring, it can make the rest of the landscape look uninviting.

RESHAPING LAWNS

The shape of a lawn is fundamental to the look of a landscape. It may impart a degree of formality, or it may have a casual, relaxed effect. Changing a lawn's shape need not be difficult and does not necessarily involve buying more sod or grass seed.

CURVED LAWNS
● **Marking off** Use string and pegs (see p. 565) to mark regular curves. For complicated curves, use a flexible hose.

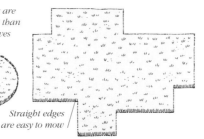
Wide curves are easier to cut than narrow curves

Straight edges are easy to mow

STRAIGHT LAWNS
● **Marking off** Pull string tightly between pegs driven into the lawn. Cut along the edge of a board (see p. 568).

PLANNING SHAPES
● **Viewing the effect** After marking off the proposed new shape of a lawn, view the design from several different places before starting to make the changes. If possible, check to see what the new shape looks like when viewed from an upstairs window.

PLANTING FOR EFFECT
● **A formal look** Plant neatly clipped shrubs in beds and borders to increase the formal appearance of a straight-edged lawn.
● **An informal look** Allow herbaceous plants with rounded shapes to hang over the edges of a curved lawn.

Using curves
Combine a curved lawn with informal plantings to give your landscape a casual look. Keep in mind that curves are harder to mow than straight edges.

Using straight edges
Use straight edges and right angles to create a formal, elegant look. To retain the effect, keep the lawn edges neat and well maintained (see p. 568).

MAKING AND SHAPING ISLAND BEDS
● **Adapting to conditions** Turn any areas where grass does not grow well – perhaps because the ground is too dry, too wet, or too shaded – into an island bed. Use plants that are suited to the prevailing conditions (see p. 484).
● **Alternative planting** Instead of planting herbaceous and annual flowers or shrubs in an island bed, try filling it with some attractive vegetables and fruits. Rhubarb, chard, runner beans, lettuce, radicchio, and strawberries – or a selection of herbs – will all look good, and will provide fresh produce for several months.

● **Scale** Create an island bed to break up a lawn. Make sure that the scale of the bed is in proportion to the lawn size.

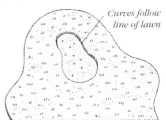
Curves follow line of lawn

Following lawn shapes
To create a coordinated and balanced look in a garden, make a curved island bed in a curved lawn, and make a straight-edged bed in a formal lawn.

TRADITIONAL TIP

Creating a focal point
Transform an expanse of green by planting a specimen tree. Choose one that will grow to a suitable size; a large tree looks confined in a small setting, and a tiny tree is lost in a large area.

BREAKING UP LAWNS

Another way to alter an existing lawn is to divide it up. This can be done, both by altering the structure of the lawn itself and by using plants, paths, or stepping-stones. Dividing a lawn into sections can often make a narrow garden look wider.

DIVIDING LAWNS
● **Different uses** If a lawn is large enough, consider dividing it into two distinct areas – perhaps one for children to play on, and one for adults to relax on.

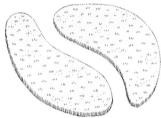

Shaping lawn areas
To create continuity between divided areas of lawn, be sure shapes complement each other. Also make sure the edges are easy to mow, and that any dividing borders are in proportion to the grassy areas.

USING PATHS
● **Ideal width** Make sure that a new path crossing a lawn is unobstructed and that it is wide enough for at least one person to walk along easily.
● **Curved path** If laying a path across a curved lawn, make sure that the path follows the shape of the existing curves.
● **Direction of path** Try to design a path so that it leads either to a particular object, such as a shed or greenhouse, or to a different section of the landscape. A path that obviously leads nowhere can look odd and out of place.
● **Fruit edging** Plant stepover apples, trained to grow to roughly 18–24 in (45–60 cm) above ground level, to create interesting edges on a straight path that crosses a lawn.

USING HEDGES

Creating landscape rooms
Use hedges to divide a large lawn into a series of different "rooms." Each area can have its own distinctive character. Divisions can add interest to a landscape, and also make it seem longer or larger. Screens made up of shrubs planted at intervals, and arranged informally or trained over supports, can be used to create the same effect (see p. 469).

MAKING STEPPING-STONE PATHS

If your planned path is not going to be subjected to heavy use, paving slabs – laid either in a line to make a symmetrical path or informally as a stepping-stone path – can look attractive. If the soil is compacted, the slabs can be laid on sand rather than crushed stone.

LAYING A STEPPING-STONE PATH

1 Mark off the position of the slabs by cutting around them, and remove enough soil to sink each slab just beneath the level of the grass. Allow for at least ½ in (1 cm) of sand or hardcore for bedding in.

2 Note the depth required, and repeat for each slab along the path. Thoroughly compact the soil, add the sand or hardcore, and bed each slab firmly in. Check the level, and adjust the slabs, if necessary.

POSITIONING SLABS
● **Arranging slabs** Experiment with different positions for a series of slabs before cutting and removing turf. Check to be sure the slabs are spaced conveniently for walking.
● **Tools** Use a half-moon edger for cutting turf and a spade or trowel to remove soil.
● **Depth of slabs** Make sure that paving slabs are sunk sufficiently deep into turf that they present no obstruction to a lawnmower.
● **Secondary path** Use stepping stones to provide access from the main pathway to a play area, garden seat, or arbor.

LEVELING LAWNS

If the look of a landscape is informal, a few small hollows or humps in a lawn may not matter much. If, however, hollows and humps are numerous or obvious, you will need to level them out. Small hollows can be filled with a sandy top-dressing.

LEVELING A HOLLOW OR HUMP IN A LAWN

1 Using a half-moon edger, cut a deep cross through the center of the uneven area. Cut right through the soil and beyond the problem area. Carefully peel back the sections of turf, and fold them back.

2 Turn over the soil lightly with a hand fork. To fill a hollow, add sandy topsoil a little at a time. To remove a hump underneath the turf, remove as much soil as necessary. Firm the soil.

3 Carefully lower the turf back into position. Firm gently, and make sure that the area is completely level. Firm again, and sprinkle top-dressing into any gaps. Water the area thoroughly.

ESTABLISHING CAUSES OF HOLLOWS AND HUMPS

● **Poor drainage** Hollows can be caused by poor drainage, which may be indicated by the presence of moss. Make sure that the soil used to fill the hollow contains plenty of coarse sand. Use a sandy top-dressing mixture.

● **Hidden causes** Check to see if uneven areas are caused by any underlying debris or buried tree roots. If necessary, dig out the cause of the problem, then even out the area using topsoil or a sandy top-dressing mixture.

● **Burrowing moles** Severe hollows in a lawn can be caused by the collapse of mole tunnels, which must be excavated and filled in. To prevent further damage, keep moles from coming back into your yard (see p. 553).

PLANNING REPAIRS

● **Best time** If possible, level out uneven areas in autumn or spring, when turf will re-establish quickly. Water the lawn frequently and thoroughly to encourage rapid rooting.

PROTECTING REPAIRS

● **Regular use** If children use a lawn regularly, consider fencing off repaired areas with stakes and string until the turf is re-established.

BRIGHT IDEA

Making turf resilient
For areas of lawn that develop hollows due to heavy use, add finely chopped car tires to the top-dressing. The rubber will make the turf more resistant to damage from regular pounding.

LEVELING WITH TOP-DRESSING

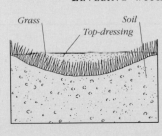

Grass   Soil
Top-dressing

Slight hollows in a lawn can be filled with a sandy top-dressing; the grass will grow through and then root in the top-dressing. Use this method only for shallow hollows, since excessive quantities of top-dressing may smother the grass and prevent growth.

ENHANCING TREES IN LAWNS

A tree planted in a lawn can provide a natural central feature for a landscape, especially if it has an attractive and interesting shape. A tree that offers particular seasonal interest – perhaps spring blossoms or striking color in autumn – can also form a stunning focal point.

PROVIDING SEATING

Adding a seat
Put a large, old tree to good use by placing a bench or seat around or under it. Make sure that there is enough room for the tree trunk to expand without being constricted by the bench.

CARING FOR TREES

● **Trees in lawns** Leave a circle about three or four times the diameter of each tree's root ball free of grass. This makes feeding easy and minimizes competition from the grass.
● **Soil level** If making a flower bed under a tree, do not raise the soil level more than about 2–3 in (5–8 cm). If the bed is any deeper than this, the tree roots may be suffocated.

PLANTING GROUNDCOVER

● **Bulbs under trees** Bulbs form decorative groundcover under trees. Choose bulbs that flower mainly in spring, when the tree will not create much shade.

FEEDING TREES

● **When planting** Give a new tree a good start. Mix plenty of bulky organic matter, with added fertilizer, into as large a planting hole as possible.
● **Stimulating growth** Foliar feed a newly planted tree throughout its first and second growing season. This will help to speed up the tree's establishment by stimulating root growth.
● **Feeding area** When feeding an established tree, lift squares of turf around the outermost spread of the branches, and fork fertilizer into the soil. Replace the turf, and water well.

CREATING WILDFLOWER AREAS

Grass growing directly beneath a tree rarely thrives. Although it is occasionally possible to cultivate a fairly green area if you choose a suitable grass seed mixture or sod, it may be easier to plant flowers instead. Choose plants that are tolerant of shade and dry soil.

PLANTING WILDFLOWERS UNDER TREES

Flowers will attract pollinating insects

Self-seeding foxgloves quickly establish in shade of tree

Choosing appropriate plants
Choose any plants that grow naturally in the conditions found under trees. Because suitable plants all enjoy the same habitat, they will look natural together. Groundcover plants, such as periwinkle, keep the weeds down and are easy to maintain.

Small groundcover plants at edges keep weeds down

SELECTING PLANTS

● **Correct choice** Choose from the following plants, all of which will grow well under a tree: *Anemone* x *hybrida*, *Anemone nemorosa*, *Bergenia* spp., *Brunnera macrophylla*, *Convallaria mujalis*, *Cyclamen*, *Galanthus nivalis*, *Geranium macrorrhizum*, *Hyacinthoides non-scripta*, *Iris foetidissima*, *Lamium* spp., *Liriope muscari*, *Tiarella cordifolia*, *Viola*.

MAINTAINING PLANTS

● **Watering** Although plants that grow under a tree do not require much water, you will need to water them regularly during dry periods, when little rain penetrates the canopy.

RESTORING BORDERS

A BADLY PLANTED BORDER, or one that has become too crowded, can spoil the look of a landscape. However, if the basic design is good, it may be possible to transform a border with some careful thinning or additional planting.

THINNING OUT BORDERS

It is very easy to overplant a border. Planted at the correct spacing, a border invariably looks sparse until the plants have grown and matured. When they have, you may need to remove a number of entire plants, or simply divide existing plants.

DEALING WITH AN OVERCROWDED BORDER

Rapidly growing, vigorous shrub *Plant too large for space* *Perennial clump*

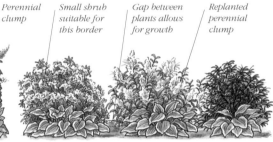

Small shrub suitable for this border *Gap between plants allows for growth* *Replanted perennial clump*

Border before thinning
Rapidly growing shrubs create competition and shade, and should be removed to allow more space for other plants to grow and develop properly. Herbaceous perennial clumps become crowded and need to be divided every two or three years.

Border after thinning
Divide crowded herbaceous perennial clumps (see p. 500). Keep some sections for the border, and use others to fill gaps elsewhere in the landscape. Move some shrubs (see p. 499) to another site, and prune back others as required.

USING CLEMATIS

Reviving a shrub
Instead of digging up a straggly, leggy shrub, plant a clematis close by, and allow it to scramble through the shrub. This will soon cover any sparseness and will also provide color.

IMPROVING BORDERS
● **Starting again** If a border is beyond repair, move the plants into a spare patch of ground. Redesign the area, and replant.
● **Improving the soil** If you start over, take the opportunity to revitalize the soil. Incorporate compost and well-rotted manure, and use a general fertilizer (see p. 524). If the soil is heavy and sticky, dig in coarse sand to improve the drainage (see p. 482).
● **Digging in winter** Do not do extensive work on a border with heavy soil during during a wet winter; this could damage plants. Wait until spring.
● **Mulching** Cover any bare areas between plants with a 2–3 in (5–7 cm) deep layer of mulch to retain moisture and suppress weeds (see p. 530).

MOVING AND PLANTING
● **Recycling** Move shrubs from a mixed border to other areas of the landscape in late autumn, when the roots are dormant (see p. 498–499).
● **Dividing perennials** Use only the vigorous sections of divided perennials. If you have any spare clumps, you can plant them in containers and in other areas of the garden.
● **Planting distance** When planting, always check a plant's potential height and spread (see p. 491), and group plants together accordingly. This can save a lot of time and effort later.
● **Roots** Always check the roots of any plant you are moving. If they are tangled, soak the root ball for a few hours before loosening them.

FILLING GAPS IN BORDERS

If a mixed or herbaceous border is planted correctly, it will take a few years for it to reach its full potential. The planting will look sparse for the first few years; fill temporary gaps with bulbs, annuals, and potted plants until the border plants are well established.

SPRING COLOR

Planting bulbs

Use bulbs to fill gaps in a newly planted or thinned out border. Spring-flowering bulbs, such as *Narcissi*, are useful because they look their best when shrubs and herbaceous plants are bare.

SUMMER COLOR

Planting perennials

Use herbaceous perennials and a few annuals in spaces between young shrubs in a border to give an immediate, full look. As the shrubs mature, remove the plants as necessary.

SOWING ANNUALS

● **Planting times** Try sowing some traditionally spring-sown annuals in autumn instead. This can often result in a long, sustained flowering period.

USING CONTAINERS

● **Planting pots** Bring temporary color to a border with containerized plants. Bury the pots in the soil up to their rims, or stand them in the border, making sure that the bases are hidden by the foliage of nearby plants.
● **Autumn color** Use pots of autumn crocus and *Colchicum* to brighten up borders in late summer or autumn.

COVERING SLOPES

Sloping areas often help to add interest to a garden, and can provide useful and unusual opportunities for planting. If your landscape varies, use this to your advantage. However, dealing with slopes requires careful planning and planting to avoid soil erosion and slippage.

DEALING WITH SLOPES

● **Terraces** One way of dealing with a steep slope is to terrace it. Build a series of retaining walls to support the soil.

Planting up a slope

If access to plants on a slope is difficult, choose plants that do not need much maintenance. You may need to use groundcover plants initially to help keep the soil in place (see p. 484).

STABILIZING SOIL

● **Retaining walls** Make sure that any wood you use to make retaining walls has been pressure-treated, and that it is sturdy enough to bear the weight of the soil.
● **Netting** Keep soil on a steep slope in place with netting (see p. 484). This is best left in place, although you can cut it away when plants are established, if you prefer.
● **Adding mulch** Use a layer of mulch to disguise netting. The mulch will also help to keep the soil in place.

CHOOSING PLANTS

● **Wet soil** Consider planting moisture-loving plants at the bottom of a slope, where it is usually damp (see p. 484).

TIME-SAVING TIP

Hiding rubble
Instead of disposing of an unwanted pile of rubble, plant a climber to hide it. Many climbers, including roses and clematis, grow well horizontally. If the pile includes concrete, do not use acid-loving plants.

CREATING A WOODLAND GARDEN

Rather than struggling to radically alter a landscape that is planted with trees, it may be more sensible to work with the trees and develop a woodland-style garden. If you have trees growing in a border, underplant them with suitable, dry shade-loving plants.

DEVELOPING A WOODLAND GARDEN

Tree trunk adds to woodland atmosphere

Foxgloves self-seed to produce more plants each year

Thick undergrowth provides shelter for wildlife

Looking natural

For a natural, woodland look, select plants that multiply by self-seeding. Include bulbs in your planting design, too. Choose plants with small, simple flowers and plain leaves.

PLANNING SHADY BEDS

● **Shrubs** Underplant large trees with shade-tolerant shrubs. Take care not to damage the trees' roots as you dig.
● **Groundcovers** Choose herbaceous plants that thrive in shade. Some make useful groundcovers for what would otherwise be bare ground.
● **Gradual shade** Soil at the edge of a tree canopy receives more light than that closer to the trunk, so choose your plants accordingly.

THINNING TREES

A large, mature tree in a landscape is something very special. If a tree causes problems by creating excessive shade, or if its branches are encroaching too far toward a building, it may be possible to remedy the problem without having to spoil the tree.

PRUNING TREES

● **Professional help** Always hire a professional arborist to perform any tree surgery. This type of work can be dangerous and the outcome disastrous, if it is done by somebody who has not been properly trained.
● **Height and spread** If a tree has outgrown its site, and its lower branches are casting shade, it may be possible to have it "crown-reduced," or to have both the height and the spread reduced. If this is done properly, the tree will retain its natural shape after pruning but will be significantly smaller.

THE EFFECTS OF CROWN-LIFTING A TREE

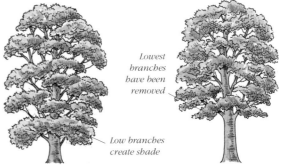

Lowest branches have been removed

Low branches create shade

An unpruned tree

This large tree may cause problems, especially if lower branches are shading a large area, and access beneath or around the tree is restricted.

A crown-lifted tree

This tree has been crown-lifted. The lower branches only have been removed, which will improve access and allow more light into the garden.

RENOVATING PATIOS

A NEGLECTED PATIO can look very dull. Common patio problems include weed infestation and loose, cracked slabs, which may be covered with slippery moss and algae. Even subtle alterations can have a surprising impact.

CLEARING AND CLEANING PATIOS

Before deciding how you want to change a patio, you should remove any debris that has accumulated, as well as stains and algal deposits. You will also need to eliminate weeds. This initial, basic work will go a long way toward improving the look of the patio.

CLEANING AND REPAIRING PATIOS

● **Debris** Place any organic debris in a compost pile for future use in the garden.

● **Drips** If you have an external faucet on a patio wall, make sure it is not dripping constantly. The algal growths that cause slippery, green patches are often caused by drips or leaks.

● **Green slime** Clean unsightly and dangerous slippery slabs with a stiff brush and soapy water, or use a commercial algae and moss killer.

● **Weeds** Always check the label before using a weedkiller, and perform a test on a small piece of slab in an obscure corner. Old or porous stone or concrete slabs may be stained by certain products. If in doubt, hand weed the area.

● **Repairs** If possible, repair or replace cracked slabs (see p. 607). If you cannot buy matching replacements, swap damaged slabs in prominent places with perfect ones from less obvious areas.

REMOVING WEEDS

Using weedkillers
Weeds may appear between patio slabs, or in cracks in broken slabs. Use a watering can with a special attachment to apply liquid weedkiller (see p. 537).

SOFTENING PATIOS

An established patio that is very angular can look harsh and uninviting. Slabs on a new patio that have not yet mellowed as a result of weathering can have a similar effect on the area as a whole. A few plants, and a variety of materials, can make all the difference.

COVERING A WALL

Planting in a patio
Bring color and shape to a bare patio wall by removing a nearby slab and planting a climber or wall shrub. Attach a support to the wall, and tie in young stems.

CHOOSING MATERIALS

Mixing and matching
Try combining different materials for a soft, interesting effect. Bricks, paving stones, and gravel – or bricks and cobblestones – look good together.

ADDING INTEREST

● **Containers** Use pots, barrels, and other containers to brighten up and soften a patio, particularly one that has no plants growing in it.

● **Focal point** Add a small statue or a water feature (see p. 573). Bubbling or cascading water, or a striking statue, will draw the eye away from plain, stark areas of a patio.

● **Wall shrubs** Choose shrubs that benefit from the protection of a wall. Wall shrubs will quickly add color and interest, and are generally more suitable for small patios than wide-spreading climbers.

PLANTING IN PATIOS

Broken slabs or sections of a patio can be removed with a spade or trowel, enabling you to plant directly in the soil beneath.

Undamaged paving may also benefit from selective planting, introducing new colors, shapes, and textures to liven up a bare patio.

PLANTING BETWEEN PATIO SLABS

● **Removing mortar** Use a chisel or a screwdriver to scrape out any debris, moss, or old mortar that remains between paving slabs.

● **Forking soil** Remove any crushed stone with a spade, and then lightly turn over the soil beneath with a hand fork to loosen it.

● **Adding scent** Try to include some plants with fragrant flowers or scented foliage. Choose plants that grow well in a confined space.

1 Insert the blade of a spade or trowel in a gap between paving slabs. Work the blade so that it digs in lower than the base of a slab, ease it beneath, and lever out the slab. Dig out any crushed stone or sand.

2 Loosen the soil around the edges of the hole, then remove it. Add plenty of good garden soil, along with compost or well-rotted manure and some general fertilizer. Mix together well.

3 Plant shrubs or perennials following as you would normally (see p. 487). Make sure they are at the correct depth, and loosen the roots, if necessary. Add a few bulbs if you wish, and water well.

CARING FOR PLANTS

Patio plants need special attention. Many patios are in sunny locations, which means that temperatures can be high during the summer. In addition, patio paving quickly depletes the area of moisture and nutrients.

● **Watering** To keep patio plants fresh, water them regularly and thoroughly. Add mulch to help retain moisture around the plants' roots.

● **Feeding** Feed patio plants throughout the growing season with a weak liquid fertilizer. Alternatively, apply a balanced granular fertilizer once a year (see p. 526).

● **Pruning** Occasional pruning may be necessary to keep a plant's growth in check once it is established.

TRANSFORMING A PATIO

● **Improving soil** Never skimp on soil preparation before planting in a patio. Any soil beneath a patio will probably contain very few nutrients or beneficial microorganisms (see p. 482). The soil may also be badly compacted.

● **Winter interest** Include a few evergreen plants with variegated leaves for added interest during winter.

● **Unsuitable plants** Do not choose plants that are invasive, or any that may create unwanted shade. Avoid plants with vigorous root systems, since the roots may start to push up the patio over time. Avoid using thorny plants, or those that are prone to aphid infestations, in places where people gather.

BRIGHT IDEA

Aging a patio
If you want to give your new patio a weathered look, paint the paving slabs with yogurt or liquid manure. This will encourage the growth of moss and algae on the surface of the slabs.

USING RAISED BEDS

Break up the monotony of a large patio area with a permanent raised bed. This can be planted with climbers and trailing plants to introduce both height and color. By selecting the appropriate soil, you will be able to grow plants that would not thrive in your garden soil.

MAKING RAISED BEDS ON PATIOS

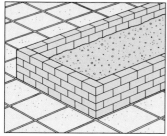

Using bricks
If you are building a raised bed out of bricks, make sure that they are frostproof. Choose bricks that match any others that are nearby so that the bed blends in well with its surroundings.

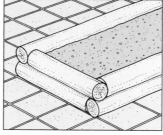

Using logs
Logs that have been pressure-treated with clear wood preservative make a long-lasting, rustic-style raised bed. Use rustproof galvanized nails to nail the logs together.

MAKING AND PLANTING
● **Using concrete** Make an inexpensive raised bed with concrete blocks. If you want to grow acid-loving plants, line the sides of the bed with rubber or heavy-duty plastic. Alternatively, paint the interior with several coats of sealant.
● **Drainage** Always make drainage holes at the bottom of a raised bed, and line the sides to prevent soil from spilling onto the patio.
● **Choosing plants** To disguise hard edges, select a number of plants that will trail down the sides of a raised bed.

ENHANCING SUNKEN PATIOS

Create planting areas around a sunken patio by building retaining walls and planting on top of them. Use materials that are the same as existing materials in that part of the landscape. Make sure that there is easy access between the sunken patio and the rest of the garden.

PLANTING AREAS AROUND SUNKEN PATIOS
● **Grass or flowers** Use a small, raised bed behind a retaining wall for planting annuals and perennials, or for laying out a grassy area.

● **Color** Use trailing plants to mask patio edges. Choose evergreens for interest all year around, and select other plants to provide seasonal color.

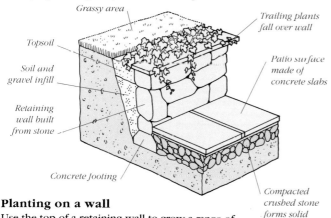

Grassy area

Topsoil

Soil and gravel infill

Retaining wall built from stone

Concrete footing

Trailing plants fall over wall

Patio surface made of concrete slabs

Compacted crushed stone forms solid bed for slabs

Planting on a wall
Use the top of a retaining wall to grow a range of plants, but first make sure that there is a fair amount of topsoil on top of the infill behind the wall. For best results, choose shallow-rooted plants.

TRADITIONAL TIP

Providing drainage
Retaining brick walls do not allow excess water from the soil to drain away. Prevent waterlogging by creating "weep holes" in the lowest layer of bricks. To do this, leave a few joints without mortar. Be sure to keep weep holes clear of debris.

CREATING TEMPORARY PLANTINGS

Containers of every size or shape – whether made from plastic, terracotta, stone, or lead – can be used to transform a patio instantly.

Containers can be moved around each new season and planted up to provide color, interest, and fragrance (see p. 510–511).

PLANTING A TALL CONTAINER

Make good use of unsightly rubble to stabilize container

1 Stabilize a tall container by placing rubble or large stones at the bottom. This is important when a container will be used on a patio, where it is likely to be knocked over if not weighed down.

2 To conserve soil mix, find a separate plastic pot that fits snugly into the top of the container. Fill it with soil mix, and plant it up (see p. 506). The pot can be removed easily for replanting when necessary.

USING CONTAINERS

● **Maintenance** Most shrubs and some small, slow-growing climbers can be grown in containers on a patio. To keep them in good condition, water and feed them regularly (see p. 509). You may also need to prune the plants frequently.

● **Moving containers** As soon as the plants in a container are past their prime, move the container to an inconspicuous or hidden part of the patio. Place another container that is full of flowering plants in the same place.

● **Introducing water** Use a large, watertight half barrel to make a water feature that you can place in a corner of the patio (see p. 574).

USING BROKEN AND EMPTY POTS

There is no need to throw away broken containers. You can put them to good use by planting them up and using them on a patio

or in the garden. If you plant them up correctly and use the right kinds of plants, cracks and missing chunks can be hidden.

CONCEALING DAMAGE

● **Positioning pots** Hide scratches, a missing piece, or a crack on a large pot by placing a smaller container of plants in front of it.

● **Trailing plants** Use trailing annuals such as *Lobelia erinus* or perennials such as *Aubrieta* to conceal any broken or chipped edges on pots. After planting up, apply a foliar feed (see p. 526) to encourage the plants to grow quickly.

USING EMPTY POTS

● **Decorated pots** Try grouping glazed, painted, or stenciled pots (see p. 519) together for an effective display of empty pots.

USING A BROKEN POT

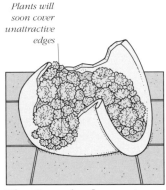

Plants will soon cover unattractive edges

Planting a broken pot
Lay a broken pot on its side, and plant it up with *Sempervivum*. These plants grow well in sparse, dry conditions and will soon grow over any broken edges.

GROUPING EMPTY POTS

Empty pot

Displaying empty pots
Use empty pots – either by themselves, or grouped with planted-up containers – to create an original display. Change the arrangement from time to time.

BUILDING A BARBECUE

A patio can be an ideal place for a barbecue. Although you can buy a barbecue from a store or garden center, building your own is a simple and cheap alternative. It also allows you to incorporate features that many barbecues do not have, such as a good-sized worktop.

CONSIDERING BARBECUE FEATURES

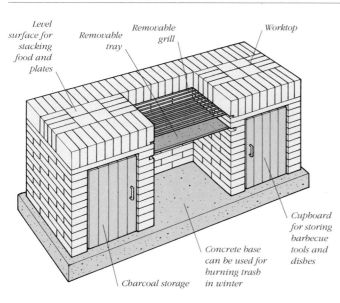

Level surface for stacking food and plates

Removable tray

Removable grill

Worktop

Cupboard for storing barbecue tools and dishes

Concrete base can be used for burning trash in winter

Charcoal storage

Constructing and siting a barbecue
A sturdily constructed barbecue is useful on any patio. Choose the right spot and the right materials so that it blends in with its surroundings.

DESIGNING A BARBECUE
● **Grill racks** Build your barbecue to fit standard-sized metal grill racks so that they can be replaced easily, if necessary.
● **Access** Locate a barbecue so that there is easy access to the house and to any seating area. Do not site it in the middle of a patio, where children may play.
● **Support** If you are not sure how well a patio was laid, build the barbecue on a concrete plinth to ensure that it will not sink into the patio.
● **Size** Always build a barbecue a little larger than you think you need it to be. A large barbecue will allow you to hold outdoor parties.
● **Built-in incineration** If your local ordinances permit outdoor burning, consider using your barbecue as an incinerator for trash and excess leaves. Put the grill rack in front to keep trash contained.

LOCATING A BARBECUE
● **Reducing smells** Do not build a barbecue close to the house; smoke and cooking smells may filter in.
● **Avoiding trees** Do not build a barbecue directly under a tree, which may be scorched if the heat becomes too intense. Also, trees may attract insects, which could also be attracted to your food.
● **Considering others** To avoid bothering your neighbors with smoke and noise, build the barbecue away from dividing walls or fences.
● **Seasonal use** Do not site a barbecue in a central location, since it will be used only for a small portion of the year.

ADDING LIGHTING
● **Electricity supply** Install an electricity supply from the house to a weatherproof, sealable socket on the patio. This will enable you to install lighting for a barbecue.
● **Safety** To avoid potential dangers, bury an electricity cable underground. If this is not possible, run the cable along an outside wall – do not string it along a fence or hedge.

MAINTENANCE

To keep a barbecue hygienic and in good condition, you need to clean it thoroughly after each use. Clean up ashes and any spilled fat, and throw away any debris that may attract vermin.

● **Removing fat** Scrub off fat deposits with a stiff brush and a strong solution of dishwashing liquid.
● **Caring for metal** As soon as the barbecue season is over, clean the racks and tools thoroughly. When dry, rub them with a rag soaked in cooking oil. Store them in a dry place to minimize rusting. Scrub well before reusing.

TRANSFORMING PATHS AND STEPS

Well-CONSTRUCTED PATHS AND STEPS should be maintained, since rebuilding them can be time-consuming. If they are unsightly, there are a number of ways to alter their appearance that do not require you to start from scratch.

SOFTENING EDGES

The severe edges and straight lines of some paths and steps can look out of place among the gentle, natural shapes of a garden. These structures may benefit from a fresh design or inspiring planting, transforming them into useful and attractive landscape features.

PERFUMING A PATH

Planting a lavender hedge
To add fragrance and shape to a garden path, plant a low hedge of lavender along its edge. If brushed against or crushed slightly, the foliage will perfume the air. Plant in a dry, sunny site.

SUITABLE PLANTS FOR EDGING

Arenaria spp. (most),
Armeria maritima,
Aubrieta deltoidea and cvs.,
Aurinia spp.,
Campanula poscharskyana,
Dianthus deltoides,
Draba spp.,
Erinus alpinus,
Helianthemum spp.,
Iberis sempervirens,
Phlox (dwarf spp.),
Portulaca grandiflora,
Salvia officinalis,
Saxifraga (including
'Hi Ace' and 'Penélope'),
Sempervivum montanum,
Thymus spp. and cvs.
including *T.* x *citriodorus*
T. 'Anderson's Gold',
Viola odorata.

PLANTING ALONG A PATH

Creating gentle shapes
Make a gentle, rippling path by planting bushy, sprawling plants in adjacent borders. Consider sinking terracotta pots at the edge of the path to break up straight lines further.

MAINTAINING EDGES

● **Repairing edges** Damaged paving can be dangerous, particularly if located in the center of a path or steps. Repair promptly (see p. 606).
● **Raising edges** Build a raised edge along a gravel path to prevent gravel from spreading onto a lawn and damaging a lawn mower. It will also keep soil from borders from spilling onto a path.
● **Planting edges** Path edges may become damaged with use. Remove the broken brick or slab, scoop out the soil beneath, add a new layer of compost, and plant a bushy, trailing evergreen in the space. The plant will spread and conceal the area below.

HIDING EDGES

● **Featuring stones** Conceal damage or alter the outline of a path by using large, rounded, or colored stones to create an attractive edging.
● **Planting seasonally** Plantings along a path's edge need not be permanent. Replace seasonal bedding at least twice a year to ensure constant color and to prevent plants from becoming too invasive.
● **Adding color** Lighten a dark, gloomy path or steps by filling the surrounding borders with evergreens that offer cream, yellow, and brightly variegated foliage year-round.

TRADITIONAL TIP

Laying brick edges
Make an inexpensive, striking edging to a path with bricks. Dig a small trench along both sides of the path. Place each brick in its trench on its side, so that it rests on the point of one corner and leans on the neighboring brick. Pack soil tightly around the bricks.

MAINTAINING GRAVEL PATHS

Gravel paths are inexpensive and easy to lay, and do not require special equipment to maintain. However, they can be difficult to walk on and are prone to invasion by weeds. Also, because of their loose surface, they are not suitable for a pronounced slope.

LAYING A NEW PATH

Laying a plastic base
Compact the soil, then create a raised edge with a strip of treated wood. Lay a plastic sheet over the soil to prevent weeds from appearing. Spread gravel over the plastic with the back of a rake.

RENOVATING A PATH

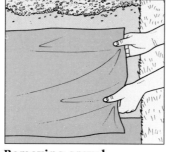

Removing gravel
Renovate an old path by laying sheets of plastic beneath the gravel: Work in sections along the path's length, raking the gravel away. Then position the plastic sheets so that their edges overlap.

WORKING WITH GRAVEL
● **Selecting gravel** If children are likely to use a path, be sure you use a smooth gravel that consists of well-rounded stones, such as pea gravel.
● **Creating drainage** Plastic underlay may prevent a path from draining properly, leading to waterlogging in wet weather. If this is a problem, replace the plastic with a layer of landscape fabric that acts as a barrier against weeds, but allows water to drain to the soil beneath.
● **Raking** Rake gravel regularly to level the surface of a path and redistribute the stones.

BRIGHTENING CONCRETE STEPS

Concrete forms a tough and resilient surface, making it a popular material for constructing steps. However, its bare, angular shape can look harsh and unattractive, and it rarely fits in well with surrounding garden features. Lighten this effect with clever planting.

IMPROVING STEPS
● **Featuring alpines** If steps are wide, sink a few pots of cushion-forming alpines into piles of gravel at intervals along the length of the steps. Planting in the pots ensures that growth is restricted and makes it easy to remove the plants.
● **Stacking terracotta** Break up a long, wide flight of steps by stacking planted-up, weathered terracotta pots in groups along the edge of the steps.
● **Creating form** Add an air of formality to the base of steps with two carefully chosen container plants placed on either side of the step. Spiral or cone-shaped box plants and standard bay or rose trees planted in Versailles tubs or large, terracotta pots, will make a striking, memorable display.

PLANTING FOR EASE
● **Using small pots** If steps are used infrequently, or if they are deep, add color with a number of small pots that are portable and easy to move.

Planting containers
Place seasonal bedding plants – such as bulbs, annuals, and tender perennials – on steps. Replace these at intervals for year-round interest. Alternatives are clipped shrubs and herbs.

PLANTING FOR EFFECT
● **Softening steps** Plant around steps to permanently soften their outline. Make sure that you choose plants that will not become too invasive.

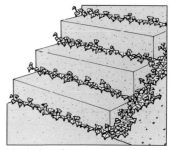

Training ivy
Plant small-leaved ivy in the soil adjacent to steps. Train the ivy along pieces of garden wire attached to the risers. Trim the ivy regularly to keep it from growing over the steps.

TRANSFORMING WALLS

WITH A LITTLE IMAGINATION, a wall can be transformed from a functional boundary marker into an exciting, vertical growing space, literally adding a new dimension to a garden. Train climbers and fruit trees for best results.

COVERING WALLS

The height and shape of the wall, as well as the choice of building material, affect how the structure fits in with its surroundings. If an old wall is unsightly, fruit trees, small flowering trees, or flowering shrubs can be trained to make an attractive, productive covering.

FAN-TRAINING A FRUIT TREE AGAINST A WALL

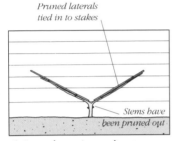

Pruned laterals tied in to stakes

New side shoots tied to stakes and attached to wires

New side shoots are tied in

Stems have been pruned out

1 In early spring, select two laterals on a young fruit tree that are 12 in (30 cm) above ground level to form the main arms. Prune each one to 15 in (38 cm) and tie to a stake at a 40-degree angle. Prune the leader to just above the laterals.

2 The following year, in early spring, prune arms by one third to an outward-facing bud. In early summer, tie new side-shoots to stakes. Prune out any stems that develop below the two main arms or that point down or away from the wall.

3 In early summer, thin out excess stems to leave them 4–6 in (10–15 cm) apart. During summer, tie the sideshoots, and pinch out any that overlap the main framework of arms. Prune fruiting shoots back to a new shoot at the base of the tree.

CREATING WALL SPACE

Designing a wall
Be adventurous when planning a wall. Consider incorporating a porthole or a gate that is large enough to walk through. This will introduce light to new areas of the garden and could encompass distant views.

IMPROVING WALLS

● **Stains** Discolored bricks make a wall look unsightly. Scrub the surface (see p. 604) before deciding if any further action is necessary.

● **Tending climbers** Thin out and prune back climbers. If they are not responding to care, replace them.

● **Screening a wall** Cover a wall with more than one climber. Choose plants with different flowering times – evergreen and deciduous – to ensure that the wall is screened for as long as possible throughout the year.

● **Fruit trees** If a wall is in a shady site but you would like to fan-train a fruit tree, plant a sour cherry tree.

BRIGHT IDEA

Creating a new shape
To make a new climber that has put on uniform growth look more established and natural, trim it back unevenly to create an irregular, informal outline.

USING TRELLISES

Attaching trellises to a wall can be the answer to a variety of problems in a garden. Trellises provide privacy from neighbors, conceal eyesores, disguise damaged or discolored surfaces, and increase the potential planting space in a garden.

ATTACHING TRELLISES

● **Material** If using a trellis in a garden, choose a wooden frame. It will look good, is long-lasting, and can support more weight than most plastic or plastic-coated frames.

● **Supports** Use pressure-treated lumber to support a trellis. After cutting, paint the surface with wood preservative safe for plants.

● **Hardware** Use galvanized nails, screws, and other hardware to prevent rust.

● **Paint** Before attaching a trellis to a painted wall, apply a fresh coat of paint to the surface, and make any necessary repairs.

PROVIDING EASY ACCESS TO A WALL

1 To provide easy access to a wall for maintenance, attach narrow strips of wood to the trellis and the wall. Attach hooks to both ends of the wall strips, and eyes to the ends of the trellis strips.

2 To secure the trellis base to the wall, attach hinges to the bottom of the trellis. Alternatively, attach a pair of hooks and eyes to the lower wooden strips to make the removal of the trellis easy.

PLANTING UP A TRELLIS

Main shoots tied to trellis

Stable container of enough depth

Supporting a climber

Use a triangular trellis to support a climber growing in a container. Before planting, place the trellis in the pot, then pack soil firmly around its base. Tie the top of the trellis to a wall, if necessary.

DESIGNING WITH TRELLIS

● **Adding color** Brighten up a standard, unpainted wooden trellis by painting it with a coat of colored wood preservative. Alternatively, mix together latex paint and clear wood preservative to create a unique color.

● **Selecting color** When painting a trellis, select a color that either complements or dramatically contrasts with the garden furniture and nearby plants and structures.

● **Choosing shape** Be adventurous when selecting new trellises; they are available in many different shapes and sizes. Alter the line of the top of a wall or screen with a concave or convex trellis, or use alternating square- and diamond-shaped pieces to bring variety to a garden.

● **Dividing trellis** Add an air of formality to a garden by using ornamental trellis posts.

COVERING A NEW TRELLIS

● **Annuals** Plant up a new, bare trellis with annual climbers the first year. These will provide a good covering while the permanent planting becomes established. Just one season's growth of sweet peas and morning glories will have the desired effect.

Using a temporary display

Screen a new trellis with a selection of containers filled with climbers, trailers, and tender perennials. These can be used elsewhere once any permanent planting has covered the trellis.

DESIGNING WITH SPECIAL EFFECTS

An ugly wall can be transformed by training climbers and fruit trees on it. Other clever devices can be used to make an area look different. Use colored paint, mirrors, and decoratively shaped trellises to create changes in a garden, both real and imaginary.

BRIGHTENING WALLS

● **Whitewash** If a garden is dark and gloomy, paint fences and walls with whitewash to lighten up the area.

● **Murals** Add another dimension to a garden by painting a mural on a flat, vertical surface. To add to the illusion, place a real pot by a painted one, and match the colors of the plant with those in the mural.

● **Mediterranean style** Put sunny walls and fences to use by planting climbers that require the protection and warmth they provide. Add terracotta pots of geraniums, pelargoniums, and nasturtiums to create a Mediterranean feel.

ADDING DEPTH

Attaching a decorative trellis
Add a sense of depth to a garden by attaching a trellis with a false perspective to a wall or other flat, vertical surface. Plant up the trellis with a sprawling climber, and position shrubs around it to add to the illusion of reality.

REFLECTING SPACE

Using a mirror
Attach a mirror to a wall or fence to increase light in a garden and give the impression of size and space. Be sure its position offers an attractive reflection. Cover mirror edges with wood, or plant with evergreen climbers.

USING ARCHES

An arch is often erected in the middle of a garden to link one area to another. It may also be placed randomly, acting mainly as a support for climbers. Attach an arch to a wall and create an arbor, to bring instant shade, seclusion, and privacy to a garden.

POSITIONING AN ARCH

Creating an arbor
Place a metal or wooden arch against a wall, and train climbers up it to make an attractive garden feature. Convert it into an arbor or secluded seating area by placing a bench inside.

WORKING WITH AN ARCH

● **Outside room** Convert part of a garden into an outside room by including seating space in a sheltered arbor. Consider adding a small table if space permits.

● **Selection** Choose an arbor carefully if it is to be located in a central site all year round. A wooden arch can look good by itself, and need not be covered with climbers. Treat regularly with wood preservative (see p. 602).

● **Position** Situate an arbor according to the amount of sun desired for the intended use of the garden – perhaps in the morning to eat a leisurely summer breakfast, or to enjoy the last of the evening sun.

TRANSFORMING AN ARCH

● **Fragrance** When planning an arbor, include scented climbers in your summer planting design. If you are likely to use the area only in the evening, be sure to select plants that remain fragrant during the evening.

● **Illusion** Place a mirror on the wall behind an arch to add a feeling of spaciousness.

● **Hiding place** Link two arches together to create a miniature hideaway or summer play area for children.

● **Using evergreens** If an arbor is to be used in early spring, late autumn, or winter, make sure that it has a covering of attractive evergreens as well as seasonal climbers.

CONSTRUCTING SCREENS

A BEAUTIFUL GARDEN can be spoiled by an ugly view or the intrusion of other houses. Necessary but unattractive items, such as trash cans, clotheslines, and sheds, can have the same effect. With planning, these can be screened from view.

CONCEALING UNSIGHTLY FEATURES

Take a careful and objective look at your landscape from a variety of positions, including inside the house, on the patio, and at the back door. Make a list of all the objects you would like to conceal or obscure; this can be achieved in a number of different ways.

DECORATING A DIVIDER

Covering a screen
Plant up both sides of a trellis or fence to make the most of the growing area and to create an effective and attractive screen.

CARING FOR PLANTS
● **Positioning** Stagger plantings along the two sides of a dividing screen to reduce possible interference between the root systems. This will also help to reduce competition for water and nutrients.
● **Maintenance** Feed the soil at the base of a densely planted screen, and make sure that it is always moist. Mulch regularly to provide the best possible soil conditions for plant growth.
● **Growth** Keep plant growth in check to ensure that a dividing screen does not become too wide and encroach upon adjacent areas.

SUITABLE PLANTS

Berberis darwinii,
B. thunbergii,
Corylus avellana,
Cotoneaster franchetii,
Cotoneaster lacteus,
Crataegus monogyna,
Euonymus japonica,
Forsythia x intermedia,
Fuchsia magellanica,
Garrya elliptica,
Ilex aquifolium,
Pittosporum tenuifolium,
Potentilla fruticosa,
Prunus spinosa, Pyracantha,
Rosa 'Nevada',
Rosa 'Roseraie de l'Hay',
Rosa rugosa,
Viburnum opulus
'Compactum'.

MONEY-SAVING TIP

Growing an annual screen
Plant a cheerful annual screen using sunflowers. Grow scarlet runner beans up the stems to add density and provide a source of fresh vegetables.

HIDING A TREE STUMP

Planting a climber
Always try to remove a tree stump, since it may encourage diseases such as root rot. If this is impossible, treat the stump with a commercial solution. After a few months, plant a climber to cover the stump with flowers and foliage.

CREATING A SCREEN
● **Appearance** Use sections of a trellis to make a screen around garbage cans and other unsightly objects (see p. 470). Make sure that the enclosed area is large enough for easy access once climbers have reached to their full size.
● **Scent** When screening potentially strong-smelling items, such as compost piles, wormeries, and liquid-manure containers, plant a selection of scented climbers to act as natural air fresheners.
● **Bamboo** To create a striking screen of foliage, plant clumps of bamboo. Their densely packed stems make them an ideal screen.

CONCEALING SERVICE AREAS

No matter how large a landscape is, you will probably want to fill every spare corner of it with plants. However, there will inevitably be items that take up valuable gardening space and are potential eyesores. Use temporary and permanent screens to conceal these objects.

POSITIONING AND PLANTING UP SCREENS

● **Using trellis** If you are using trellises to hide unsightly items, make sure they are strong enough to support climbers. To add strength, construct a frame around the structure using wooden strips.

● **Using evergreens** A trellis can be used on its own, but it is most effective and attractive if plants are climbing over it. Include evergreens in your planting design to ensure year-round concealment.

Partitioning
Use trellis panels and a trellis door to partition off a large, unsightly area in a garden. Plant up the trellis lightly so that the screen and the area beyond merge in with the rest of the landscape.

SELECTING A DISGUISE

● **Metal covers** Use containers to conceal metal service covers. Make sure they are lightweight so that they can be moved quickly in an emergency. If you would like to feature a heavy container, make it easy to move by fixing wheels to its base, or stand it on a wheeled platform.
● **Pipes** Group several different pots together to hide a cistern or septic tank pipes.
● **Large eyesores** Obtrusive oil tanks and gas cylinders are often situated close to houses. Use trellises, wattle hurdles, or fence panels as screens, and plant with climbers.

CONCEALING GARBAGE CANS

Most buildings have at least one garbage can. Both these and large, unsightly, wheeled plastic bins can be easily hidden. When using screens, avoid the temptation to conceal garbage cans and bins completely, since access must be unrestricted.

MAKING SCREENS
● **Small screen** To make a simple and effective screen, to hide a single garbage can from view, attach a trellis panel at right angles to an existing fence or wall.
● **Large screen** Use a trellis, willow panels, or fence panels to make an open-ended partition behind which garbage cans can be stored. Be sure the area is densely planted in the summer, to keep the sun off the garbage.
● **Scented screen** Plant up a garbage area with fragrant flowers. Mix strongly scented roses, honeysuckle, and jasmine with other climbers, and complete the colorful and perfumed effect with an annual sowing of sweet peas.

DESIGNING WITH BRICKS

Building for permanence
Construct a permanent garbage screen out of bricks, leaving holes for ventilation. Allow for access, but keep the top low to prevent animals from removing lids. Build a trough above, and plant up with trailing foliage.

USING A CONTAINER

Using temporary color
To create an attractive, temporary display, use a large, planted-up container to partially hide a garbage can. Slip a section of a trellis panel between the container and the garbage can for additional concealment.

USING HEDGES AS SCREENS

In some cases, a natural, living screen or divider is more appropriate for a particular area than a constructed one. A hedge makes an attractive and long-lasting screen. However, for a hedge to look good, it must be planted, maintained, and clipped correctly.

CONCEALING THE SPARSE BASES OF HEDGES

● **Using a trellis** If the base of a hedge becomes sparse and leggy, construct a low trellis to hide the area. This can then be used as a support for climbers.

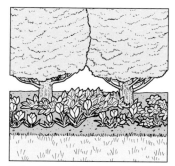

Positioning a screen
Position a fence so that it screens only the bare base of a hedge. When digging holes for the support posts, make sure that you avoid the roots of the hedge.

● **Partial screen** If you do not want to completely conceal the area beneath a hedge, partially obscure it with a selection of herbaceous plants.

Selecting plants
If the soil beneath a hedge is dry, plant drought-tolerant plants and bulbs. Water and feed regularly to be sure that the plants and hedge do not compete for nutrients.

CARING FOR HEDGES

● **Maintaining** Feed and water hedges regularly, since they are constantly clipped and grow rapidly, using up large amounts of energy.
● **Trimming** To ensure that the top of a hedge is cut flat and level, keep shear blades parallel to the line of the hedge.
● **Roadside hedges** Before winter, place plastic screens around hedges that are planted along a road. This should prevent the roots from absorbing de-icing salt and also keep the foliage from being scorched.
● **Climbers** Erect a system of straining wires between posts along the length of a sparse hedge. Train twining climbers along them to create a curtain of color and foliage.

PROMOTING GROWTH

To promote even and sustained growth in a formal or informal hedge, it is important to trim it carefully on a regular basis.

● **Deciduous hedges** To create an attractive, dense deciduous hedge, trim it twice annually with shears or an electric hedge trimmer. (Be sure to keep the cord out of the way as you trim.)
● **Coniferous hedges** Treat conifers with care. When pruning in the first years, remove only the lateral branches until a hedge reaches its desired height. Do not cut back hard, since the inner brown foliage may be revealed. Because there is little replacement growth from these stems, it will be difficult to hide the damage.

TRIMMING HEDGES

● **Nests** Avoid trimming a hedge when birds are nesting. Wait until the fledgings have left the nest. The hedge will not suffer, and you will help to preserve the next generation of garden birds.
● **Shaping** Formal hedges look messy if cut unevenly or at the wrong angle. Use a taut piece of string tied between two upright posts to make sure that a hedge is level, and use a template to shape the top.
● **Clippings** Put clippings to good use by incorporating them in a compost pile. Do not do this if you know a hedge is diseased.
● **Shocking information** Never trim a hedge with electric shears in rainy weather: you could receive a severe shock.

MONEY-SAVING TIP

Restoring a hawthorn
To rejuvenate a hawthorn hedge that has become sparse and leggy at the base, bend a number of pliable stems downward. Hold these in the soil using small metal pegs. In time, these stems will root and fill out the base of the hedge.

SCREENING SHEDS

A shed is a practical – and often essential – addition to a landscape, offering a work area and storage space for tools, bulbs, seeds, and other items. However, even if it is in good condition, a shed is a potential eyesore and can detract from the overall effect of a garden.

CREATING A SCREEN USING A TRELLIS

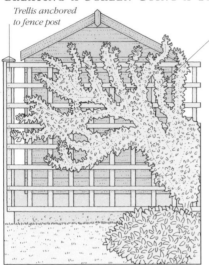

Trellis anchored to fence post

Climber trained to cover trellis

Building a screen
Erect a trellis to create an effective screen for a functional shed. Use fence posts to support the structure and to keep it away from the sides of the shed, allowing easy access for maintenance. When planting, choose a climber that will not outgrow the trellis.

MAKING SCREENS
● **Using chicken wire** Create a freestanding, column-shaped screen by rolling up a length of galvanized chicken wire. Train climbers over and through it.
● **Using natural materials** Use willow panels or hazel-wattle hurdles to make a functional and attractive screen. Although expensive, these are well suited to an informal or cottage-style garden.

PREVENTING WOOD ROT
● **Protecting screens** Be sure that the base of a wooden screen is raised 2–3 in (5–7.5 cm) above the soil to prevent wood rot.

ENHANCING SHEDS

Screening a shed can be impractical if access is limited. In such a situation, consider highlighting the shed rather than hiding it. With careful planting and grouped selections of decorative containers, an old shed can become an attractive, integral part of a landscape.

MAINTAINING SHEDS
● **Reroofing** Prolong the life of an old shed and improve its appearance by reroofing with new felt and fixtures and hardware (see p. 600).
● **Renovating** Scrub off algae and other debris from the surface, and allow the shed to dry thoroughly before applying a coat of wood preservative. Consider using a colored preservative or adding paint to camouflage discolored areas and to create a brand new look.
● **Cleaning** Check for wood decay, and treat and refill the wood, if necessary (see p. 602). At the same time, wipe the glazing with a commercial cleaning agent to remove the buildup of debris.

PLANTING FOR COLOR

Adding containers
Decorate a shed with hanging baskets and windowboxes packed full of annual flowers and trailing foliage. Strategically placed terracotta pots and other containers will help to hide damaged and discolored areas.

TRAINING CLIMBERS

Creating shapes
To create a striking effect, grow a climber up and over the roof of a shed. Since this method may encourage deterioration of the wood, it is best reserved for old sheds that have a limited function and life expectancy.

BLOCKING UNSIGHTLY VIEWS

Even when every effort is made to design, create, and maintain an attractive garden, the surrounding environment often presents an unsightly view. This effect can be countered by hiding and blocking unattractive objects with natural and constructed screens.

PLANNING A SECLUDED GARDEN

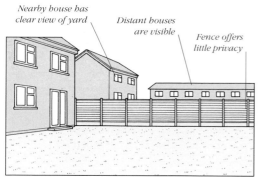

Nearby house has clear view of yard

Distant houses are visible

Fence offers little privacy

Assessing the surrounding area
Neighboring buildings sometimes overlook a house and have a clear view into the yard. These buildings may also be prominently visible from the yard, even with a high, wooden fence. Privacy and a sense of seclusion are important in a built-up area.

ADDING HEIGHT AND SHAPE

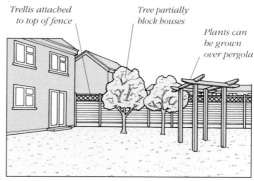

Trellis attached to top of fence

Tree partially block houses

Plants can be grown over pergola

Adding permanent structures
Trees give shape to a landscape and conceal unsightly views. A pergola and a trellis attached to the top of a fence bring shelter and seclusion to a yard. These permanent structures can be planted up for additional shape and color.

ADDING TRELLIS EXTENSIONS

Raising the height of a wall or fence is an inexpensive and relatively easy way to conceal unsightly views and ensure privacy. Trellis sections can be attached to the top of a wooden fence or brick wall, then planted up with annual and evergreen climbers.

PERMANENT EXTENSION

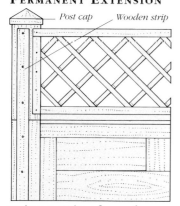

Post cap *Wooden strip*

Using a strip of wood
To extend a fence using wood, remove the post cap, and nail the fence and an extension post together with a narrow strip of wood. Using galvanized nails, attach the trellis section to the post, and replace the cap.

REMOVABLE EXTENSION

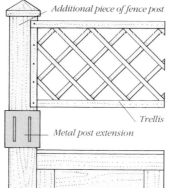

Additional piece of fence post

Trellis

Metal post extension

Using a metal fixture
Metal post extensions allow easy replacement of trellis panels. Remove the post cap, and slide the extension onto the post. Insert the additional piece of fence post, attach the trellis, and refit the cap.

WORKING WITH TRELLIS
- **Changing outlines** Alter the outline of a fence or wall by attaching concave or convex trellis sections to the top.
- **Limiting shade** Before extending the height of a fence or wall, assess how much light will be lost. Limit the amount of shade by attaching trellis sections, and planting a few small-leaved climbers. Avoid creating a wall of foliage.
- **Protecting wood** Once the trellis is in place, treat the fence with a coat of wood preservative to help blend the new wood with the old.
- **Planting** To conceal the joints connecting a fence and trellis, plant fast-growing climbers along with the permanent plantings.

PLANTING TREES

An established tree brings a sense of stability and permanence to a landscape. Its height can create shade and privacy, and its shape can significantly alter the overall look. When planting a tree, carefully choose a spot where it is least likely to cause damage.

USING TREES FOR SHADE AND PRIVACY

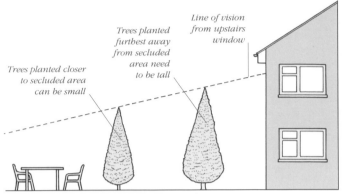

Trees planted furthest away from secluded area need to be tall

Line of vision from upstairs window

Trees planted closer to secluded area can be small

Planning the positions of trees for privacy
Carefully consider the position, shape, and overall design of your landscape before planting trees. Take into account the direction and path of the sun, and decide whether you want to divide one section of the landscape from another, create a secluded and shaded seating area, or conceal part of the landscape from the house. Conversely, you may want to screen certain rooms in the house, such as bedrooms or bathrooms, from general view.

SELECTING TREES
● **Seasonal use** Plant deciduous trees in an area that is used only in the summer. These will provide screening from late spring to autumn.
● **Size** Use small trees and shrubs to create a natural screen that partially blocks nearby objects from view.
● **Roots** Check the growth habit of a tree before purchasing it, particularly if your garden soil is clay-based. In certain conditions, tree roots can cause major damage to structural foundations.
● **Suckers** Some trees look good, but produce suckers. If you cannot spare the time required to remove suckers, avoid planting *Prunus* spp. and cvs., lilacs, and sumac.

USING PERGOLAS

A pergola adds height and diversity to a garden and can provide an attractive area for vertical planting. At the same time, it creates a decorative division that can also serve as a screen to conceal functional areas, damaged surfaces, and unsightly features.

CREATING COLOR

Planting climbers
Heavily plant a pergola with foliage and flowers. The climbers may take several years to become fully established but if they are given adequate attention and care, the wait will be worh it.

FEATURING PERGOLAS
● **Purchasing** When buying a pergola, make sure that its construction is strong enough to support the climbers in your planting design.
● **Constructing** Use pressure-treated wood for a pergola. The appearance of the completed structure can be altered with a coat of non-toxic, colored wood preservative, as long as it will not damage plants.
● **Renovating** When replanting an old pergola, take the opportunity to replace timber that is broken or rotten, and consider painting the repaired structure a different color.

SUITABLE PLANTS

Akebia quinata,
Berberidopsis corallina,
Campsis grandiflora,
C. radicans,
Celastrus,
Clematis spp. and cvs.,
Hedera,
Humulus lupulus 'Aureus',
Jasminum officinale,
Laburnum,
Lardizabala biternata,
Lonicera x *americana,*
L. x *brownii,*
Passiflora caerulea,
Rosa spp. and rambling and climbing cvs.,
Tropaeolum speciosum,
Vitis coignetiae,
Wisteria.

ADDING HEIGHT AND PERSPECTIVE

THERE ARE MANY DIFFERENT FACTORS to be considered when planning a landscape. Introducing height adds a new dimension to the landscape while adjusting the perspective can make a landscape appear narrow and long or wide and short.

INTRODUCING HEIGHT WITH ARCHES

Trees and large shrubs can be used to add height and shape to a landscape. Other permanent features, such as arches, pergolas, and decorative posts, can also be arranged to create points of interest. In a small landscape, just one feature can alter the overall look.

SELECTING AN ARCH STYLE

Horizontal beams provide support for climbers

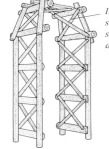

Diagonal struts strengthen arch

Pointed arch
Construct a pointed, rustic arch from unplaned wood. Use galvanized nails or screws to fix the wood pieces to each other.

"Cottage-style" arch
Diagonal struts of unplaned wood add strength and support to an arch. Its "cottage-style" look is suitable for an informal garden.

PLANNING ARCHES
● **Height** When building an arch, make sure that it is tall enough for a person to walk through comfortably. Also, consider the types of flower that you are intending to plant; if they are pendulous, take this into consideration, and make the arch even taller.
● **Width** If a garden arch is to be walked through, make sure it is wide enough to allow two people to pass through side by side.
● **Planting** Use cross beams to increase the strength of an arch, making it suitable for supporting heavy climbers.

PLANTING A WALKWAY

Training climbers
Create an attractive walkway by training lightweight climbers over a series of wooden or plastic arches. Consider planting annuals or ornamental, runner, or edible pole beans.

CREATING NEW ARCHES
● **Building** To prolong the life of an archway, assemble with pressure-treated wood. Stabilize an upright arch post by setting it in concrete, or else use galvanized metal supports (see p. 603).
● **Transformation** Transform a new arch with fast-growing annuals such as *Eccremocarpus scaber, Ipomoea, Rhodochiton atrosanguineum,* and *Thunbergia alata.*
● **Planting beans** To make an "edible" arch, plant scarlet runner or pole beans with different flower colors.
● **Planting roses** When buying a rose for an arch, select a rambler; this has more flexible stems than a climbing rose.

TRADITIONAL TIP

Dividing an area
Use a trellis arch to divide an area into two distinct sections. Plant a screen of evergreen shrubs on either side.

USING PLANT SUPPORTS

Most climbing plants need to be trained on supports, such as tree trunks, bamboo-stake wigwams, and obelisks. Whether these supports occur naturally or are added to a landscape their height and shape can be used to create high points and enhance existing features.

USING A WIGWAM

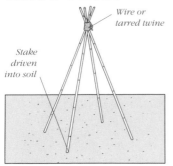

Wire or tarred twine

Stake driven into soil

Creating a pillar of color
Bamboo-cane wigwams are used traditionally to support pole beans. Plant up a wigwam with annual climbers to bring pillars of striking color to a border.

USING AN OBELISK

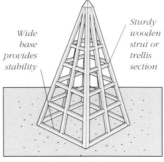

Wide base provides stability

Sturdy wooden strut or trellis section

Supporting climbers
An obelisk looks good by itself and can be left outside through the winter. Use it to support climbers and create a permanent, attractive display.

MAINTAINING WOOD
● **Preserving** Treat a wooden structure regularly with a coat of wood preservative. Use pressure-treated wood and galvanized hardware for repairs to further extend its life.
● **Painting** Enhance a plant's appearance and help make its support attractive in winter by applying a brightly colored paint to the support.

CREATING SHAPES
● **Planting** Use a dense climber with attractive foliage, such as a variegated ivy, to create a solid, three-dimensional shape or screen.

PLANTING CLIMBERS

Evergreen and annual climbers can be used both to emphasize the height of an object and to conceal or alter the appearance of an eyesore. Some climbing plants need support in the form of a trellis or wires, while others can grow over an object without support.

COVERING A TREE

Transforming a dead tree
Try to remove a dead or dying tree, which may pose a hazard. If this is not possible, cut away the branches, leaving only the trunk standing. Grow a climber or two over the tree, adding wire supports, if necesssary.

CHOOSING SUPPORTS
● **Temporary** Form an arch from chicken wire, and use it to support lightweight, annual climbers for a colorful, temporary summer display.
● **Long-term** Use a sturdy wire frame to train climbers or to create unusual topiary shapes. Although not an instant or even quick effect, the frame will form a stylish, permanent plant support.
● **Using hose pipe** To support a lightweight plant, make a small arch using two wooden pegs and a piece of an old garden hose. Place a peg in one end of the pipe, and push it in so that only a third of the peg remains visible. Repeat with the second peg. Drive one end into the ground, form an arch with the hose, and secure the other end.

GREEN TIP

Transforming a post
If an old metal post or clothesline is embedded in concrete and cannot be removed easily, use it as a vertical support for a climber. The density of the climber's growth will hide the post.

DECEIVING THE EYE WITH DESIGN

When designing a garden, consider the effect you wish to create, and decide whether you would like to alter the shape and the perspective of the garden.

● **Divisions** To make a long garden seem wider and shorter, partially divide it up with trellis sections. Alternatively, use shrubs and other bushy plants to create a natural divider.

● **Rooms** Divide a garden into a series of different "rooms," each with a different theme or style. A garden will seem to be larger than it really is if it is not possible to see all areas from one spot.

● **Hedges** To alter the perspective in a short garden bordered by a hedge, cut the top of the hedge slightly lower along the back or far end of the garden. This will give the illusion that the hedge is farther away than it actually is.

● **Secret places** Create alcoves and arbors around walls or fences to increase the sense of hidden and unexplored areas.

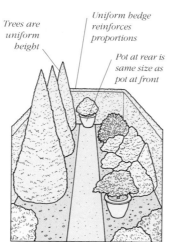

Trees are uniform height

Uniform hedge reinforces proportions

Pot at rear is same size as pot at front

Planting for a natural view
Retain the natural perspective of a garden by considered repetition of heights and shapes. Lay a parallel-sided path, and flank it with trees of equal height. Place a planted-up container near the house, and place another at the end of the garden.

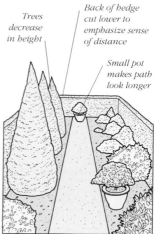

Trees decrease in height

Back of hedge cut lower to emphasize sense of distance

Small pot makes path look longer

Exaggerating distance
To exaggerate the natural perspective of a garden, lay a tapering path, and plant it up with trees that are progressively shorter toward the back of the garden. Place a pot in the background the same style as – but smaller than – a pot in the foreground.

USING PLANTS TO SUGGEST SIZE

The design of a garden can create illusions, and the apparent size of an area can be altered at little cost with careful planting. When purchasing a plant, make sure that you consider its color and shape, since these characteristics can increase or decrease the sense of space.

INCREASING LENGTH

Working with color
To increase the apparent length of a border, position brightly colored flowers and foliage in the foreground, and frame these against darker colors. Plant pale colors at the back of a garden.

CREATING SPACE

Featuring foliage shapes
To suggest space in a small garden, place plants with large, flamboyant foliage and bold outlines at the front of a border. Where possible, vary the colors for additional emphasis.

CHOOSING PLANTS

● **Pastels** Choose pale or pastel colors for the back of a border to create a sense of distance.

● **Grays** To make a border seem larger, include a variety of plants with gray foliage.

● **Hot colors** Make a garden seem shorter by planting fiery, hot-colored flowers. This will bring these plants to the foreground.

● **Glossy foliage** Brighten a dull corner with glossy foliage that reflects the light, such as that of *Ajuga, Fatsia,* and *Mahonia.*

● **Strategic planting** Scatter distinctive plants through a border to draw it together and make the area appear smaller.

PLANTS & PLANTING

QUICK REFERENCE

Planting Preparation, p. 480

Choosing Plants, p. 485

Planting Know-How, p. 487

Planting Shrubs, p. 488

Planting Perennials, p. 490

Planting Annuals, p. 494

Planting Bulbs, p. 496

Moving Plants, p. 498

IF A PLANT IS TO SUCCEED, you need to do your homework before planting it. Is the plant suited to the type and texture of soil present in the site you have chosen for it? Will it receive the right amount of sun or shade? Is the plant the right size for the site, or will it grow too large? Will it look good alongside its new neighbors, or would its size, shape, and flower color be more suitable elsewhere? When you know you have the right plant, invest time and care in preparing the soil.

SOIL CONDITIONERS

Digging and turning the soil will improve its texture to some extent, but to improve the texture, nutrient content, drainage, or moisture retention considerably, you need to incorporate suitable materials before you begin to plant.

● **Soil texture** Use coarse sand and gravel to loosen the soil and improve its texture. Always use horticultural sand and gravel, since builder's materials sometimes contain contaminants that are harmful.

● **Soil pH** Lime and peat can be used to alter a soil's acidity or alkalinity. Lime will raise soil pH and help to break up a heavy or compacted soil. Peat or a peat alternative lowers soil pH and improves moisture retention, which makes it especially useful for light soils.

● **Soil improvers** Cocoa fiber, organic matter, composted bark, and leaf mold all improve moisture retention, texture, and drainage. Manure improves soil texture and fertility because of its nitrogen content. Always use well-rotted manure (see p. 489).

Peat   Cocoa fiber   Organic matter

Leaf mold   Manure   Composted bark

Lime   Coarse sand   Gravel

BASIC EQUIPMENT

Before you buy any tools, test them for size and weight, and make sure they are comfortable to handle. Stainless steel tools will not rust, but are more expensive than other tools.

● **Cultivation** A hand fork and trowel are excellent for planting, weeding around, or moving small plants. Use a Dutch hoe for weeding between young and established plants and vegetable rows, and for marking off rows for planting. A garden fork and spade are essential for digging and turning over the soil. Use a garden rake to collect debris, to break up the soil surface, and to rake the soil level before sowing seed.

● **Pruning** Use pruners for most pruning jobs. A sharp knife is good for light pruning tasks and is useful for cutting string. Wear gloves to protect your hands.

● **Watering can** Choose a watering can that is large enough to carry a useful amount of water, but not so large that it is too heavy when full of water.

Watering can

Pruners

Hand fork

Trowel

Sharp knife

Gardening gloves

Garden fork

Spade

Dutch hoe

Garden rake

PLANTING PREPARATION

Good preparation saves you time and effort later, so find out about your garden before planting up beds and borders. Plants that are planted under optimal conditions perform well and are equipped to resist attack from pests and diseases.

DETERMINING THE TEXTURE OF SOIL

You can find out a lot about your soil simply by feeling it. Its texture affects the amount of work you need to do on it, as well as the types of plants you can grow successfully. The ideal soil is loam, which is a mixture of the two extreme soil types – sand and clay.

CHECKING SOIL
● **Local research** To get a general idea of your soil type and the plants you will be able to grow most successfully, find out what is growing in your neighbors' gardens. Make a note of the plants that are doing well and those that are struggling.
● **Soil compaction** Check for localized areas of compaction, such as a path in a lawn, or an area next to a barbecue or under a child's swing. These compacted areas need to be prepared by spiking (see p. 571) or digging over.

CLAY SOIL

Clay soil feels smooth and sticky

Sticky and smooth
Clay soil is made up of tiny particles, making it heavy, sticky, and moisture-retentive. Although clay soils are often difficult to work, they are usually fertile.

SANDY SOIL

Sandy soil feels dry and gritty

Dry and loose
Sandy soil can dry out rapidly and does not retain nutrients well. It usually needs more maintenance than clay soil, but is easy to work initially.

TESTING THE pH OF SOIL

The acidity or alkalinity of your soil (the soil pH) is one of the factors that most influences the plants you can grow. Some plants will suffer, and may even die, if grown in an unsuitable soil. Use a testing kit to find out which kind of soil you have, and grow plants suited to the pH.

COLOR TESTING KIT

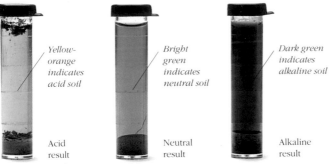

Yellow-orange indicates acid soil

Bright green indicates neutral soil

Dark green indicates alkaline soil

Acid result

Neutral result

Alkaline result

Using a color testing kit
Take a small sample of garden soil, and mix it with the chemical solution in the kit. Allow the mixture to stabilize. Match the resulting color against the pH chart in the kit.

ADJUSTING SOIL pH
● **Alkalinity** Increase the alkalinity of your soil by applying lime at the recommended rate. Mushroom compost, which usually contains a lot of lime, can have a similar effect.
● **Acidity** Making soil more acidic is difficult. Add ammonium sulfate or sulfur.
● **Treatments** Try to change the acidity of your soil before you start planting. Recheck the pH. frequently to see how much it has changed.

CHOOSING THE RIGHT PLANTS

Putting the right plant in the right place is essential to your success as a gardener. When deciding on a design, consider your soil texture and pH, as well as the site's exposure (see p. 484). Use the chart below to help you to decide which plant to put where.

SOIL TEXTURE	SUITABLE PLANTS	
CLAY SOIL A clay soil is able to retain moisture and nutrients efficiently. However, during very dry weather it may crack, while during wet periods it can become waterlogged. The erratic moisture levels can harm plants.	*Acer* spp., *Aucuba, Bergenia,* *Campanula* spp., *Celastrus scandens,* *Clematis, Cornus* spp., *Cotoneaster,* *Euonymus fortunei,* *Forsythia,* hardy herbaceous geraniums,	*Helleborus* spp., *Hosta* spp., *Kerria,* *Laburnum, Lathyrus,* *Lonicera* spp., *Malus* spp., *Philadelphus,* *Prunus* spp., roses, *Rudbeckia,* *Sedum* spp., *Syringa,* *Viburnum, Vitis* *coignetiae, Wisteria.* *Syringa*
SANDY SOIL A sandy soil is light and drains quickly. It is prone to drying out and generally does not remain as fertile as a clay soil. A sandy soil is much easier to dig. However, because it does not retain nutrients well, plants may need extra attention, especially during dry weather.	*Abutilon* (some), *Achillea* spp., *Artemisia,* *Ceanothus,* *Cercis siliquastrum,* *Cistus,* *Cotinus,* *Cytisus,* *Elaeagnus,* *Jasminum*	(hardy types), *Kerria,* *Laburnum,* *Lavandula,* *Mahonia,* *Perovskia,* *Rosmarinus,* *Sorbus,* *Verbascum,* *Wisteria.* *Verbascum*

SOIL pH	SUITABLE PLANTS	
ALKALINE SOIL The types of plants you can grow in alkaline soil are limited, largely because of the effect that the high soil pH has on nutrient availability. Unsuitable plants often show deficiencies in iron and manganese, resulting in a distinct yellowing between the veins on the new leaves.	*Acanthus,* *Acer* (some), *Achillea, Aesculus,* *Alcea, Alchemilla,* *Allium, Alyssum,* *Anemone, Aquilegia,* *Arabis, Artemisia,* *Aubrieta, Bergenia,* *Campanula,* *Caryopteris,* *Ceanothus,*	*Ceratostigma,* *Chaenomeles,* *Clematis, Crataegus,* *Crocosmia, Fuchsia,* *Gypsophila, Kerria,* *Lavatera arborea,* *Lonicera, Matthiola,* *Pyracantha, Silene,* *Syringa, Tulipa,* *Verbascum,* *Viburnum, Weigela.* *Tulipa*
ACID SOIL An acid soil may have a sandy, clay, or loam (a mixture of sand and clay) content. Most plants are able to survive in a typically acid soil, while some plants will not flourish in any other kind of soil.	*Arctostaphylos,* *Berberidopsis* *corallina, Calluna,* *Camellia, Daboecia,* *Enkianthus,* *Eucryphia,* *Fothergilla,* *Gaultheria,* *Hamamelis,* *Kalmia,*	*Lapageria rosea,* *Lithodora,* *Magnolia* spp. (some), *Nomocharis,* *Nyssa, Pernettya,* *Philesia magellanica,* *Phyllodoce,* *Rhododendron,* *Trillium,* *Vaccinium.* *Rhododendron*

IMPROVING SOIL

Before planting your garden, take the time to work on the soil. Both its texture and its fertility can be improved considerably, and this is easy to do before the beds are full of plants. Exactly what you need to do depends on the kind of soil you have.

ADDING ORGANIC MATTER TO SOIL

- **Adding life** Bring your soil to life by adding organic matter (see p. 478), which contains a whole host of micro-organisms that help to keep garden soil in good condition.

- **Different types** Each type of organic matter has slightly different properties. These may alter the moisture retention, pH, aeration, and nutrient levels of the soil (see p. 480).

Saving time
Instead of digging in organic matter, spread it evenly over the soil in autumn. Winter temperatures help to break it down, enabling worms and other organisms to incorporate it into the soil for you.

MAKING LEAF MOLD

Collect fallen leaves, and pack them loosely into a large, black plastic bag. Make a few holes in the bag. Loosely fold over the top and secure with a brick. The leaves should be thoroughly decomposed after 6 to 12 months, when the leaf mold will be ready to use.

WORKING THE SOIL

- **Using frost** Dig heavy clay soils in late autumn. Frost will help to improve the soil's texture by breaking the soil down into small pieces.
- **Wet weather** Try to avoid digging heavy soil when it is very wet, since this causes compaction of the soil. Reduce soil compaction by standing on a board to spread your weight (see p. 582) across a large area.
- **Even surface** After the soil is dug or turned, the surface may be rough and lumpy. To produce a fine tilth before planting or sowing, dig or turn the soil over again, breaking up any lumps of soil on the surface with a rake.
- **Organic matter** You can compost virtually any organic garden waste to make organic matter. Leaves, grass clippings, shredder by-products, prunings, and annual weeds can all be used (see opposite).

CLAY SOIL

- **Improving drainage** Always use a fork for a clay soil. A spade may seal the edges of the holes as it is driven in, making it even harder for water to drain through.

Opening up clay soil
Incorporate horticultural gravel into a clay soil to a depth of at least 12 in (30 cm). This helps to improve drainage, but does not affect nutrient levels. Do not use builder's gravel (see p. 478) which may contain contaminants.

STONY SOIL

- **Root crops** Remove as many large stones as possible before planting, especially if you intend to grow root crops. Their shape and development can be spoiled by stones.

Enriching stony soil
Fork in leaf mold or compost to enrich a dry, stony soil. Choose a dry day to do this work, if possible. Start at one end of the bed and work backward so that you do not step on the soil you have just turned over.

MAKING COMPOST

Making your own compost is an easy, quick, and environmentally friendly way to dispose of organic garden and kitchen waste. It also provides you with a very inexpensive, high-quality material that will greatly improve the quality of your garden soil.

COMPOST INGREDIENTS

Almost any organic kitchen or garden waste can be composted, but avoid diseased material or perennial weeds. Natural-fiber pillows, carpets, and knitted items can be composted, as can old, shredded newspapers. Avoid meat and strong-smelling waste, since these attract vermin. Turn the compost once a week.

Grass
Grass clippings should be used sparingly.

Clippings
Pruning clippings are made from chopped twigs.

Weeds
Mix annual weeds with drier materials.

Waste
Kitchen waste, such as peelings, can be used.

Knitted items
Cut up natural-fiber items and add to compost pile.

Carpets
Old carpet should be cut up into small squares.

Feather pillows
Old feather pillows are a useful ingredient.

Newspapers
Newspaper should be shredded or cut into strips.

GOOD COMPOST

- **Layering** Add material to the pile in thin layers; never use very much of any one ingredient at once. Try to intersperse moist, leafy material with drier ingredients such as shredded twigs.
- **Nitrogen** Green material has a high nitrogen content, which helps to speed up the composting process. Avoid using too much moist greenery, since it can turn into strong-smelling slime rather than good, well-rotted compost.
- **Hot weather** Add water to the compost pile during very hot, dry weather, or if you are using lots of dry material. Moisture encourages the materials to break down.
- **Cold weather** Keep the compost pile well insulated during cool weather so that the rotting process does not slow down too much.

MAKING YOUR OWN CONTAINER

- **Barrel bin** Use a plastic barrel to make a compost bin. Cut off the top and bottom, drill 1-in (2.5-cm) holes around the sides, and use one end as a lid.
- **Recycled wood** Make a compost container from sturdy corner posts and old floor boards nailed together with galvanized nails.

Chicken wire is attached with galvanized nails

Old carpet used as lid

Old tool handles make effective stakes

Simple container
Make a low-cost compost or leaf mold container using galvanized chicken wire held in place with wooden stakes driven firmly into the ground. Use a piece of old carpet to form a warm, insulating lid.

EASY ACCESS

Removable panel
Choose a compost container that has a removable front panel. This allows easy access to the compost so you can turn it regularly or remove some of it for use in the garden. Always make sure that the compost is well rotted before using it.

EXPOSURE

The exposure of a garden is the direction it faces, and this determines how much sun or shade various areas in the garden will receive. Other factors to consider include the soil type, as well as any overhanging trees, high walls, slopes, or nearby buildings.

ASSESSING A GARDEN

● **Careful planning** Study your garden before planting. Notice where shade falls throughout the day, and remember that evergreens cast shade all year. Determine whether shady areas are moist (at the bottom of a slope) or dry (at the top), and choose appropriate plants.

● **Sunny walls** Soil at the base of a sunny wall is particularly prone to being hot and dry. Improve the soil's ability to retain moisture (see p. 478), and choose drought-resistant plants (see p. 529).

DEALING WITH A SLOPING FLOWER BED

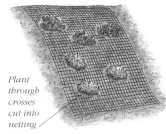

Plant through crosses cut into netting

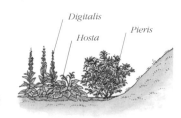

Digitalis

Hosta

Pieris

Planting through netting
Groundcover plants stabilize the soil on a slope. On a steep slope, plant through plastic netting secured with pegs. This will retain the soil in place.

Choosing the right plants
Choose plants that prefer a moist site for the base of a slope, since water will run off the slope down to the bottom. *Digitalis*, *Hosta*, and *Pieris* are all suitable.

PLANTS FOR DIFFERENT EXPOSURES

EXPOSURE	SUITABLE PLANTS		
SUNNY AND DRY Many plants are well suited to a fairly dry, sunny site. However, even these plants will need plenty of water in their first year to encourage healthy, sturdy growth and to help them become fully established.	*Achillea* spp., *Arabis* spp., *Aster* spp. and cvs., *Aubrieta*, *Campsis radicans*, *Cistus*, *Cytisus* spp., *Eryngium*, *Fremontodendron*, *Genista* spp.,	*Hypericum* spp., *Iberis* spp., *Phlomis* spp., *Rosmarinus*, *Santolina*, *Sedum* spp., *Senecio* spp., *Tamarix*, *Vitis coignetiae*, *Weigela*, *Yucca gloriosa*.	 *Aster novae-angliae*
DRY SHADE Dry shade is common in areas with light soil, and beneath trees and hedges. Walls or fences can shelter an area so that it receives little or no rain. A brick wall will absorb moisture from the soil. Fortunately, a number of plants will tolerate dry shade.	*Alchemilla mollis*, *Anemone nemorosa*, *Aucuba*, *Cyclamen* spp., *Daphne laureola*, *Epimedium* spp., *Euonymus* spp., *Hyacinthoides non-scripta*, *Hypericum* x *inodorum* and cvs.,	*Ilex aquifolium* and cvs., *Iris foetidissima*, *Lonicera japonica* 'Halliana', *Mahonia* spp., *Pulmonaria* spp. and cvs., *Ranunculus* spp. and cvs., *Ruscus aculeatus*, *Vinca* spp.	 *Ilex aquifolium*
MOIST SHADE This occurs in gardens that have a naturally moisture-retentive soil. It can also occur at the base of a shaded slope or in areas that are overshadowed by trees. Many plants will not flower well in shade, so foliage is an important consideration.	*Anemone blanda*, *Aucuba*, *Camellia japonica* and cvs., *Convallaria majalis*, *Digitalis*, *Eranthis*, *Erythronium*, *Fritillaria* (most), *Galanthus nivalis*, *Helleborus* spp.,	*Hosta* spp. and cvs., *Lonicera* spp., *Paeonia suffruticosa*, *Pieris* spp. and cvs., *Primula* spp. (most), *Rhododendron* spp. and cvs., *Skimmia japonica*, *Vinca* spp.	 *Primula vulgaris*

CHOOSING PLANTS

SELECTING THE BEST POSSIBLE PLANTS is one of the surest ways of increasing your chances of success. Whether you buy your plants from a local store or from a reliable garden center or nursery, always make sure they are in good condition.

USING A PLANT LABEL

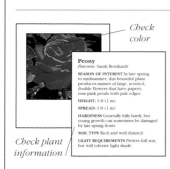

Check color

Peony
Paeonia 'Sarah Bernhardt'
SEASON OF INTEREST In late spring to midsummer, this beautiful plant produces masses of large, scented, double flowers that have papery, rose-pink petals with pale edges.
HEIGHT: 3 ft (1 m)
SPREAD: 3 ft (1 m)
HARDINESS Generally fully hardy, but young growth can sometimes be damaged by late spring frosts.
SOIL TYPE Rich and well drained.
LIGHT REQUIREMENTS Prefers full sun, but will tolerate light shade.

Check plant information

● **Season of interest** Find out when the flowering period is, and whether the flowers are fragrant.
● **Potential size** Use the label to check what the plant's potential height and spread will be.
● **Hardiness** Check to see if the plant is fully hardy. If it is not, it will need protection from harsh winds and low temperatures throughout the winter months.

POISONOUS PLANTS

● **Plant safety** The plant label should indicate whether skin reactions or poisoning are a potential problem. This information is especially important if children play in or near the garden.

CHOOSING PLANTS FOR YOUR GARDEN SOIL

BEFORE buying a plant, be sure that it is suitable for the spot you have in mind. Knowing the range of different growing conditions in your garden will help you decide what to buy. You should also consider what the plant will look like with its neighbors.

BUYING GOOD PLANTS
● **When to buy** Avoid buying plants during or just after an extremely cold spell. Even the root balls of hardy plants may freeze if unprotected, and this can prove fatal. Delay buying until spring, when a plant's state of health is apparent from the foliage.
● **Clean soil mix** Select plants with soil mix that is free of weeds, algae, moss, or liverworts. These all indicate that the plant may have been in its pot too long.
● **Damaged plants** Avoid wilting plants and those with blotched leaves. If plants have been underfed, or have suffered from drought or waterlogged conditions, they may be permanently damaged.
● **Fragrance** Try to choose some plants specifically for their scented blooms.

CHOOSING FOR A SPECIFIC SITE
● **Narrow bed** Choosing plants suitable for a narrow bed can be tricky. If the bed is adjacent to a wall or fence, choose plants that can tolerate dry shade. If the bed is next to a path, avoid plants with thorns or prickly leaves.
● **Island bed** If the bed is wide, choose tall plants that require little maintenance for central areas where access is difficult. If the bed is in a lawn, choose plants that will not flop over the grass.

Corner bed
This type of bed often needs plants that can thrive in a relatively dry soil. Choose tall plants for the back and small, trailing plants for the edges.

● **Easy border** Choose shrubs that require little pruning, and combine these with perennials that need no winter protection. Avoid plants that must be supported, and try to buy drought-resistant plants (see p. 529). Bulbs are useful, but plant only hardy ones that do not need to be lifted and stored during the winter.

Tall plants at back of bed

Small, trailing plants at edges

STORING PLANTS

Always try to transfer plants into the ground as soon as possible after purchasing them. If extremes of cold or wet make the soil totally unsuitable at the time, or if you cannot plant everything in one day, you may need to store plants. Do this for as short a time as possible.

STORING PLANTS OUTDOORS

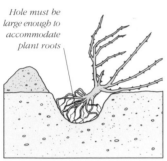

Hole must be large enough to accommodate plant roots

Heeling in
Heel in bare-root shrubs and trees to keep the roots moist and in good condition. Place the plant at an angle in a hole in the ground. This reduces the effect of wind on the stems, which can rock the roots.

Planting in a pot
Sink a container-grown plant into the ground while it is still in its pot. This will help to protect the plant's roots from extremes of temperature. It will also help keep the soil mix from drying out.

BRIGHT IDEA

Short-term storage
Put evergreen shrubs and conifers in a sheltered spot, where they will be protected from the sun, wind, and freezing temperatures.

CARING FOR STORED PLANTS

● **Protecting roots** The roots of a stored plant are very susceptible to damage. Extremes of temperature can kill roots. Protect the root ball by insulating it with soil, burlap, or plastic bubblewrap.
● **Preventing growth** Never feed a plant while it is being stored. This could stimulate growth at a time when the plant needs a resting period.

● **Moist roots** Keep roots moist, but do not overwater them. Roots that are confined to a sunken pot or to a temporary planting hole are easier to overwater than those that are in open ground.
● **Dormant plants** Plants that are dormant adapt to storage conditions much more successfully than plants that are still actively growing.

STORING PLANTS INDOORS

● **Sheds and garages** Do not allow temperatures to rise high enough to encourage growth. This will make it difficult for a stored plant to become established once it is planted outside.
● **Rodents** Keep mice away; they will eat plants in storage.

STORING BULBS

● **Dry conditions** Place bulbs on dry sand or newspaper in a tray, and make sure they are not touching each other. Label each tray with the date and the type of each bulb.
● **Circulating air** A cool, but frost-free shed, greenhouse, or garage is ideal for storing bulbs. Air circulation helps to prevent diseases, but avoid exposing the bulbs to drafts.

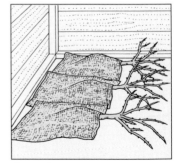

Covering roots
Store bare-root plants temporarily in an unheated garage or shed. Cover the roots loosely with plastic or moist burlap to prevent them from drying out.

PLANTING KNOW-HOW

Provided you choose well and follow the correct planting technique, your plants should have a healthy and promising start. Follow up with good care to ensure that your plants stay vigorous and healthy (see p. 520).

KEEPING A PLANT MOIST

Do not risk putting a potbound plant in the ground without first improving its condition. Gently loosen any circling roots, and use pruners to prune back damaged or very tangled roots. After planting, water your plants regularly until they are well established (see p. 532).

BEFORE PLANTING

● **Planting hole** Prepare a planting hole before you take a plant out of its container.

● **Tangled roots** If tangled roots are difficult to loosen, first soak the root ball in a bucket of water for several hours, or even overnight. Soaking the roots makes it easier to move them, and limits the damage you cause in the process.

● **Soil conditions** Whenever possible, choose suitable weather conditions for planting. Do not plant when the soil is excessively dry, waterlogged, or frozen.

WEED CONTROL

Removing weeds
Remove any weeds from a pot. This limits their spread and prevents them from competing with the plant for water.

DIRECT WATERING

Positioning a pipe
Place a section of drainpipe or wide-bore hose in a planting hole. This will allow you to direct water straight to a plant's roots.

BASIC PLANTING TECHNIQUE

Whatever you are planting, treat it with the care it deserves, and it will respond positively. One of the most common mistakes is to plant too deeply. Always make sure that the top of the planting hole is level with the top of the soil mix.

CORRECT PLANTING PROCEDURE

Soak plants thoroughly

Leave stem area clear

1 Dig a planting hole about twice the size of the plant's root ball. Water the hole well to ensure that it is thoroughly moist, and make sure the soil drains freely (see p. 482).

2 Place plants waiting to be planted in a bowl of water. Position each plant at the correct depth in its hole, then backfill the hole with a mixture of compost, fertilizer, and soil.

3 Firm the soil, and water the plant thoroughly to settle the soil around the roots. Lay 2–3 in (5–7 cm) of mulch all around the root area, leaving the stem area clear.

PLANTING SHRUBS

Shrubs form the permanent structure of the garden. Choosing the best specimens and making sure they get a good start is very important, and well worth your investment of time, money, and care in the long run.

CHOOSING SHRUBS

You can buy shrubs container-grown, containerized, balled-and-burlapped, or bare-root. If you buy them when not in leaf, examine the roots and the general shape. Each plant should have a healthy, well-developed root system and evenly distributed stems.

CONTAINER-GROWN SHRUBS

Foliage should not be yellow or withered

Shrub should have healthy, well-spaced top-growth

Stems should be free of damage, pests, and diseases

Roots should be firm and white or pale brown

Checking roots
Remove the pot carefully to check the root system. If the soil mix falls away as you remove the pot, the root system is poorly developed. If there is a mass of tangled roots, the shrub is potbound.

CONTAINERIZED SHRUBS

Soil mix falls away when pot is removed

Roots have been cut before potting

Slow to establish
Containerized shrubs are shrubs that have been lifted and potted up just before sale. They may be slow to establish.

BALLED-AND-BURLAPPED SHRUBS

● **Good value** Balled-and-burlapped shrubs may be less expensive than container-grown shrubs, and often grow better than bare-root specimens.
● **Squeeze the soil** Gently squeeze the soil to be sure it is moist and firmly packed.

TIPS ON CHOOSING
● **Good buy** Small, young shrubs are usually easy to establish. In general, they grow more rapidly and more successfully than larger, more expensive specimens.
● **Unnecessary pruning** Avoid plants that have been strangely or unnecessarily pruned. This is often a sign that the plants have been damaged or that they have suffered from dieback.
● **Careful inspection** It is a waste of your time and money to buy a plant that has an inadequate root system. Do not hesitate to remove the pot to check the condition of the roots, if necessary.

BARE-ROOT SHRUBS

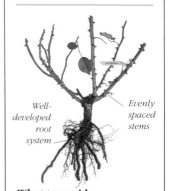

Well-developed root system

Evenly spaced stems

What to avoid
Avoid shrubs with withered buds, too much leaf growth, or shriveled, damaged, or crossing stems. Keep the shrub moist after planting.

WHEN AND HOW TO PLANT A SHRUB

Always try to plant shrubs during autumn or spring so they have time to become established before the dry summer weather arrives. Container-grown shrubs can be planted all year round, but even these shrubs often perform best after autumn or spring planting.

BEFORE PLANTING

- **Loosening roots** Soak the roots in tap water before planting. This helps to ensure that they are really moist, which makes it easier to loosen them when tangled.
- **Dry site** If planting in a dry spot, make a slight depression in the soil around the shrub. This ensures that water runs toward the plant rather than off the soil surface.
- **Heavy soil** If planting in a heavy soil, do not put moisture-retentive organic matter in the planting hole. This may act like a sump and draw water from the wet soil, making a dangerously wet area around the roots.

PLANTING TECHNIQUES

- **Replant sickness** Never use the same, or a closely related, plant to replace one that you have removed. If planted in the same spot, the new shrub may suffer replant sickness and fail to thrive.
- **Correct depth** Make sure that all the roots are covered, but that the stem base is no deeper than it was before.

PLANTING A BARE-ROOT ROSE

Graft union

Checking depth
Place a stake across the planting hole, and hold the rose in the center of the hole with its roots well spread. The graft union should be a maximum of 1 in (2.5 cm) below the stake.

- **Planting hole** Make sure the planting hole is at least twice the size of the root ball, and prepare it well with organic matter and fertilizer.
- **Underplanting** Underplant new shrubs with small bulbs for seasonal interest, or choose bulbs to coordinate with the form and color of the shrub's foliage or flowers.

Soil must be moist before applying mulch

Cover mulch with soil to prevent rapid evaporation and to disguise it

Mulching
Use newspaper as a low-cost, efficient mulch. Make sure the soil is moist, then lay very wet newspaper on the soil surface around the shrub. Spread soil over the newspaper to disguise it.

Pruning out dead wood
Use sharp pruners to prune out any dead, diseased, damaged, crossing, or straggly stems. Cut back to a healthy, outward-facing bud. Make sure that the remaining stems form an even shape.

USING MANURE

- **Root damage** To avoid damaging the roots, always mix fertilizer and well-rotted manure into the planting mix. This prevents direct contact of "hot" materials with the roots.

GREEN TIP

Planting roses
Add roughly chopped banana skins when planting roses. This improves the texture and moisture retention of the soil, and also adds potassium to it.

PLANTING PERENNIALS

Although perennials are available throughout the year, it is best to buy them in autumn or spring, when they will become established rapidly once planted. If your soil is heavy and wet, delay buying and planting perennials until spring.

CHOOSING A PERENNIAL

Small perennial plants are generally a better value than large specimens, though larger plants are useful for providing more immediate results. You will be getting very good value for your money if you choose large plants that are ready to be divided (see p. 500).

HEALTHY CONTAINER-GROWN PERENNIALS

Top-growth is green and healthy

Crown has sturdy new shoots

No weed growth visible on soil mix surface

Strong roots with no signs of dieback

Checking a crown
When choosing a perennial plant, look for signs of new growth at the crown. If the plant is dormant, be sure the crown is firm and undamaged.

TIPS ON CHOOSING

● **Wilting plants** Before buying plants, be sure the surface of the soil mix is neither too wet nor too dry. Never buy wilted perennials; if they have been allowed to dry out once, they have probably been without water before and suffered considerably.
● **Moss-free** Choose plants that do not have any surface growth of algae, moss, weeds, or liverworts. This is a sign that they have been in their pots too long.
● **Cracked containers** Check to make sure the container is intact. If it is cracked, the roots may be damaged.

ROOTS IN MESH

Some perennials have a mesh bag around their roots. The roots should be able to grow out of the mesh and become established in the soil. However, if the plant is not vigorous, this may not happen, in which case the roots will remain restricted.

Mesh may be visible at surface of soil near base of stem

Cutting mesh
Before planting, carefully cut through the mesh in several places with sharp scissors, a knife, or pruners, taking care not to cut through the plant's roots. This will make it easier for the roots to grow out into the surrounding soil.

MONEY-SAVING TIP

Making new plants
Take cuttings from tender perennials in late summer to ensure that you have plenty of plants the following year (see p. 593).

WHEN AND HOW TO PLANT A PERENNIAL

Perennials can be planted at any time of the year, except during extreme weather conditions. They should grow rapidly, and usually perform well within their first year. Use the chart below as a guide to the ideal planting distances for perennials.

REMOVING A PLANT

Slide your fingers between stems

Tapping a pot
Turn the pot upside down, and firmly tap the bottom with your hand or the handle of a trowel. The plant should slip out of the pot quickly and easily, with the root ball still intact.

REDUCING STRESS

Use pruners to remove large leaves and flowers

Preventing moisture loss
To reduce stress on the plant during dry or hot weather, prune off flowers and large leaves before planting. Cover the plant with a "tent" of netting supported by sticks.

GREEN TIP

Adding ferns
Incorporate a handful of coarsely chopped ferns into a planting hole to improve the texture of the soil. Do not use ferns with lime-loving plants, since they are slightly acidic.

PLANTING DISTANCES FOR PERENNIALS

PLANT	DISTANCE	HEIGHT
Acanthus mollis	24 in (60 cm)	36 in (90 cm)
Ajuga reptans	12–18 in (30–45 cm)	4–12 in (10–30 cm)
Alchemilla mollis	15 in (40 cm)	12–18 in (30–45 cm)
Anaphalis spp.	12–18 in (30–45 cm)	12–24 in (30–60 cm)
Aruncus sylvester	12–18 in (30–45 cm)	4–6 ft (120–180 cm)
Coreopsis grandiflora	18 in (45 cm)	12–18 in (30–45 cm)
Dicentra spectabilis	18 in (45 cm)	12–30 in (30–75 cm)
Doronicum spp.	12 in (30 cm)	24 in (60 cm)
Geranium endressii	18 in (45 cm)	12–18 in (30–45 cm)
Geum chiloense	12–18 in (30–45 cm)	18–24 in (45–60 cm)
Gypsophila elegans	12 in (30 cm)	24 in (60 cm)
Gypsophila paniculata	24–36 in (60–90 cm)	3 ft (90 cm)
Helenium autumnale	12–18 in (30–45 cm)	4–6 ft (120–180 cm)
Heuchera sanguinea	18 in (45 cm)	12–18 in (30–45 cm)
Liatris spicata	18 in (45 cm)	2–3 ft (60–90 cm)
Lupinus	24 in (60 cm)	36 in (90 cm)
Lychnis coronaria	9–12 in (22–30 cm)	18–24 in (45–60 cm)
Lysimachia punctata	18 in (45 cm)	2–3 ft (60–90 cm)
Monarda didyma	15 in (37.5 cm)	2–3 ft (60–90 cm)
Penstemon barbatus	24 in (60 cm)	36 in (90 cm)
Potentilla cvs.	12–18 in (30–45 cm)	12–24 in (30–60 cm)
Pulmonaria saccharata	12 in (30 cm)	12 in (30 cm)
Rudbeckia fulgida	18 in (45 cm)	12–36 in (30–90 cm)
Tiarella cordifolia	12 in (30 cm)	6–14 in (15–35 cm)
Verbascum	18–24 in (45–60 cm)	3–5 ft (90–150 cm)
Veronica spicata	12–24 in (30–60 cm)	6–18 in (15–45 cm)

PLANTING DISTANCES
● **Width and height** Check the potential height and spread of plants before planting. Refer to plant labels, and use the chart on the left as a guide. Remember, different cultivars can vary considerably.
● **Filling in gaps** A newly planted herbaceous border can look very sparse. If necessary, use bulbs and temporary seasonal bedding to fill in any gaps (see p. 457).

FOLIAGE AND FLOWERS
● **Winter appearance** Consider the season of interest of each perennial, and its appearance in winter. Most perennials die back in winter, but some retain many of their leaves.
● **Grouping plants** For a stunning display, try planting several of each type of plant together, rather than dotting individual plants throughout the whole border.

SUPPORTING A CLIMBER

Covering walls and fences with perennial climbers gives a new dimension to a garden. Some climbers are self-clinging and need no support, but most need a trellis or wires to keep them in place. Before planting, make sure the support is both stable and strong.

NETTING AND STAPLES

● **Light support** Use plastic or wire netting to support lightweight or annual climbers. Bird netting or plastic fruit-tree netting is ideal.

Using netting
Galvanized stock netting is suitable for lightweight, permanent climbers. Use rustproof galvanized U-shaped staples to hold the netting slightly away from the fence.

TRELLIS ON WALLS

● **Wooden support** A trellis makes a good support for light- or medium-weight climbers, and can be cut to size.

Attaching the trellis
Attach the trellis to narrow strips of wood with hinges on the lower section (see p. 467). You can then swing the trellis down to repair or maintain the wall behind without damaging the trellis.

WIRE AND EYE SCREWS

● **Strong support** Galvanized wire makes a good supporting structure for vigorous climbers. A system of horizontal wires works best for heavy climbers.

Using wire
Use eye screws to hold heavy-duty wire in place on a fence or wall. Screw in an eye screw, wind one end of the wire around its head, pull the wire tight, then secure it to another eye screw.

LOOSE FITTINGS

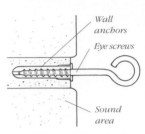

Wall anchors
Eye screws
Sound area

● **Repairing supports** If a few eye screws, nails, or staples are loose, drill a new hole in a nearby area, and reattach the hardware. Always try to repair plant supports with the plant in place.
● **Broken wire** If one of the supporting wires breaks, it is probably a good idea to replace all of them, since other wires may break soon after the first one.

BASIC EQUIPMENT

Always buy good-quality fittings; they are durable and save a lot of time, money, and frustration in the long run. Do not skimp on the number you use; too few may cause the support to fail.

Soft twine for tying plants

Eye screws for holding wires

Flat eye screws

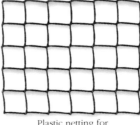

Plastic netting for lightweight support

Staples

Galvanized wire

PLANTING A ROSE

Most roses are bought bare-root in late autumn or winter and should be treated like any other bare-root plant (see p. 489). A much smaller selection of container-grown roses is available throughout the year; treat these like container-grown shrubs (see p. 488).

PROVIDING SUPPORT

Soft twine

Tying new stems
Container-grown roses may have some leafy stems. Tie these to supporting wires with soft twine or use commercial ties to ensure that the stems are not damaged by the support.

CLIMBERS ON WALLS
● **Flaky walls** Avoid planting self-clinging climbers against a wall that has a flaky surface or loose mortar. These plants are likely to make the problem worse and may cause extensive damage to the wall.

CLIMBER COVER
● **Temporary cover** Newly planted climbers may take a few years to grow to a useful size. Create a temporary covering with rapid-growing annual climbers such as *Ipomoea purpurea* or *Lathyrus*. You may end up liking them so much that you decide to keep them – even when the permanent climbers are larger.
● **Leggy climbers** Many climbers become rather sparse at the base as they get older. If they do not respond to feeding or other maintenance (see p. 526 and p. 542), plant decorative shrubs at the base to hide the straggly stems.

CONSERVING MOISTURE

Using mulch
After planting, water the rose well. Apply a 2–3 in (5–7.5 cm) layer of mulch over the moist soil. Keep the mulch away from the base of the support and the rose stem, since it can rot both.

DISTANCE FROM WALL
● **Avoiding the rainshadow** Dig the planting hole for a wall-trained climber 12–18 in (30–45 cm) away from the wall or fence so that the plant's roots are not in an area of ground sheltered from the rain.

Stake provides temporary support for young stems

Planting at an angle
Plant a climber at an angle to encourage it to grow toward the support. Use a stake as a temporary support for young, fragile stems. Train a few of the larger stems into position on the lower end of the support.

COMPANION PLANTING

Deterring pests
Try planting marigolds around the base of your roses. Although not scientifically proven, this technique is worth trying and may deter several rose pests, such as nematodes.

PLANTING CLEMATIS

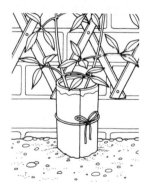

● **Protecting the base** Plant clematis several inches deeper than it was in its container. Place strong cardboard or plastic around the base of the plant to protect it from slugs and snails. Secure with twine.
● **Extra precaution** Smear grease around the top of the cardboard or plastic. Slugs and snails will not be able to climb over this, so they will not reach any young stems and cause them damage.

PLANTING ANNUALS

Annual bedding plants bring color and shape to a garden, and are relatively easy to grow from seed. If you lack time, space, or equipment, choose from the many plants available through local or mail-order companies.

CHOOSING ANNUALS

Most annuals are grown for the colorful displays they provide during the summer months. They are available from midspring. Some, such as *Viola* x *wittrockiana* and *Bellis,* are grown as annuals for winter color and are best bought in late summer or autumn.

IDENTIFYING HEALTHY ANNUALS

Good-quality plants in center of tray

Sturdy growth

Compact, green foliage

QUALITY AND COLOR
● **Quality** Be sure you are buying a full and healthy tray of annuals. Do not purchase poor-quality plants.
● **Color and type** You can brighten up your garden at minimal expense by buying annuals in bulk. For best results, limit the number of colors you use to two or three.

Buying plants
Choose plants that are strong and sturdy, with no signs of diseases, pests, or nutrient deficiencies. Avoid old plants, which rarely transplant satisfactorily and have less flowering potential.

MAIL-ORDER BUYING
● **Saving time** Save both time and windowsill or greenhouse space by ordering annuals from mail-order companies. Annuals are available at various growth stages, from seedlings to plantlets, and they should arrive with protective packaging and full planting instructions.

FRAGRANT ANNUALS
● **Providing scent** Most annuals are only slightly scented. Plant one of the exceptions, *Matthiola bicornis,* for a strong scent in the evening. Try training *Lathyrus odoratus* among other border plants, or use the dwarf forms in pots.

BUYING SEEDS
● **Catalogs** Most garden centers stock a good selection of seeds. However, it is worth looking through the catalogs produced by major seed suppliers, which usually offer a wide range of choices.
● **Early ordering** Whether you buy your seeds from garden centers or catalogs, make sure you do your seed shopping early. New kinds are available starting in winter, and the most popular varieties are likely to sell out quickly.
● **Damaging heat** Garden centers can become very hot during the summer. Avoid buying seeds at this time, since extreme temperatures can damage seeds.

SEEDLING PLUGS

Many annuals are available as seedling "plugs," each with its own plug of soil mix. When planted, the well-developed root system suffers little damage and grows rapidly, helping to ensure growth of stems, leaves, and flowers.

ESTABLISHING ANNUALS

The lifespan of an annual is no more than a year. In order for these plants to look their best during the short time they are in flower, they must be well planted. A moist soil, a good supply of nutrients, and regular deadheading are the keys to success.

REMOVING ANNUALS

Hold firmly, and push bottom with thumb

Root ball

Releasing root balls
Water trays well before removing the plants. Release the root balls by pushing up from the bottom of the tray and easing the plants out. Plant on cool days or when the area is shady. Early evening is best, since the plants can settle before the midday heat.

FEEDING ANNUALS

Apply foliar feed if leaves turn yellow

Applying foliar feed
Shortly after planting, spray the leaves with a foliar feed. This stimulates the roots to grow and speeds their establishment. Apply another foliar feed if the plant leaves begin to turn yellow; this is an indication of nutrient deficiency.

BRIGHT IDEA

Tying stakes
When constructing a wigwam support for a climber, use a rubber band to hold the stakes in place temporarily. This allows you to keep both hands free so you can tie the stakes in position easily.

CONSIDERING HEIGHT AND COLOR

The charm of an annual flower bed often depends on an irregular planting plan, with one color flowing into another. Vary the plant heights, introducing as many levels as you can, and – unless you have a very large flower bed – stick wtih two or three colors.

PLANTING ANNUALS IN A FLOWER BED

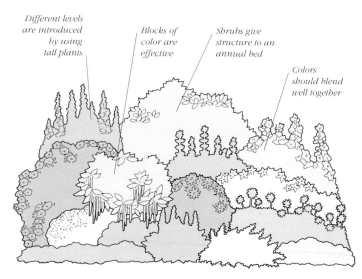

Different levels are introduced by using tall plants

Blocks of color are effective

Shrubs give structure to an annual bed

Colors should blend well together

SELECTING COLORS
● **Blocks of color** Group bold blocks of annuals in a limited range of colors together to show this kind of planting off to best advantage.
● **Combinations** Soft pinks and mauves, rich blues toned with pinks, and warm yellows, reds, and oranges are all good color combinations.

Foliage and texture
A variety of textures and shapes make an eye-catching display. Use different plants and foliage to add texture to your design. Annual foliage plants can also be used to provide contrasting or harmonizing colors.

PLANTING BULBS

A LTHOUGH MOST BULBS are fairly inexpensive, those that are fully hardy can provide a regular display of flowers for many years. All they need are an adequate supply of food and water, and a little maintenance (see p. 497 and p. 596).

CHOOSING BULBS

Always try to choose bulbs that show no signs of new root development. However, if they have started into growth, make sure the growth tips are firm and healthy. If you choose double-nosed bulbs, remember that the smaller of the two may not flower for a year or two.

HEALTHY BULB

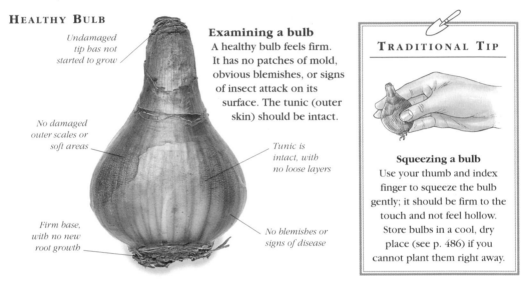

Undamaged tip has not started to grow

Examining a bulb
A healthy bulb feels firm. It has no patches of mold, obvious blemishes, or signs of insect attack on its surface. The tunic (outer skin) should be intact.

No damaged outer scales or soft areas

Tunic is intact, with no loose layers

Firm base, with no new root growth

No blemishes or signs of disease

TRADITIONAL TIP

Squeezing a bulb
Use your thumb and index finger to squeeze the bulb gently; it should be firm to the touch and not feel hollow. Store bulbs in a cool, dry place (see p. 486) if you cannot plant them right away.

PLANTING BULBS IN A BASKET

Flowering bulbs look good until the flowers and foliage start to fade. Removing the foliage too soon prevents the bulbs from performing properly the next year. Plant bulbs in a basket, then lift the basket and put it in an inconspicuous place while the leaves die down.

BULBS IN CONTAINERS
● **Recycle containers** You can use many suitable household containers for planting bulbs. A pond basket is also ideal.
● **Extra holes** Good drainage is essential. If the container does not have many holes, make extra holes in the bottom.
● **Tender bulbs** Basket planting is an easy way of dealing with tender bulbs. When temperatures fall, lift the basket and put it in a cool, but frost- and mouse-proof shed or garage for the winter.

PREPARING AND PLANTING A BASKET OF BULBS

Place bulbs at random

1 Fill the bottom third or quarter of the basket with garden soil. Plant the bulbs as you would normally (see p. 497), and fill the basket to the top with soil.

2 Dig a hole slightly deeper than the basket, and lower the basket into it. Backfill the hole with soil, then water. Hide the plant label in the basket so that it stays with the bulbs.

PLANTING BULBS IN BEDS

Most bulbs need sun, but a few prefer shade, so be sure to select the right bulbs for the spot you have in mind. Choose small bulbs for the front of beds and for planting next to paths or a lawn. Their small size does not cause problems with other plants' foliage.

WET SOIL

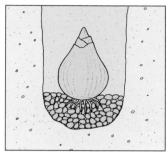

Improving drainage
Most bulbs prefer a well-drained site. To improve drainage if planting in a heavy soil, put a 1-in (2.5-cm) deep layer of coarse grit in the bottom of each planting trench or individual planting hole.

GROUPING BULBS
● **Odd numbers** Bulbs look best planted in groups of odd numbers. Most will start to multiply after a few years, creating a miniature drift.
● **Set patterns** As a general rule, avoid set patterns and straight lines. However, some bulbs, such as gladioli, look fine in a formal planting.

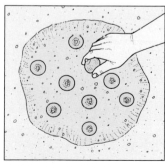

Saving time
Plant several bulbs in one large hole to save time and effort. Bulbs planted in this way look less formal than those that have been planted individually.

DRY SOIL

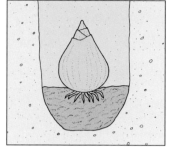

Retaining moisture
Bulbs may not flower properly in very dry soil, and they may even die. To improve the soil's moisture retention, place a 1.5-in (3.5-cm) deep layer of moist compost in the bottom of each planting hole or trench.

BULB MAINTENANCE
● **Regular watering** Adequate moisture throughout the year is essential if flower buds are to form properly. Be sure to water bulbs regularly during dry spells in summer.
● **Unsuitable conditions** Do not risk planting bulbs if weather conditions are not suitable and the ground is very wet or frozen. Store the bulbs (see p. 486) until conditions improve, or plant them loosely in boxes filled with compost their first year.
● **Tulip fire** To avoid this fungal disease, wait until late autumn to plant tulip bulbs.
● **Pot bulbs** Plant hardy pot bulbs in the garden when they have finished flowering. These bulbs are often crammed together, so make sure you divide the clump into individual bulbs.
● **Bulb boost** Apply a foliar feed to dying foliage (see p. 596).

PLANTING DEPTHS

Checking depth
Always check the instructions on the packet; most bulbs are planted at a depth of three to five times their height. If winter temperatures are very cold or summers are very dry, plant the bulbs slightly deeper.

LILY BULBS

● **Drainage** Use a 1-in (2.5-cm) layer of gravel in the planting hole when planting lilies. This will encourage any excess water to drain away.
● **Planting on their sides** Lily bulbs are notoriously prone to rotting in damp weather conditions. If water gathers around the scales, the bulbs die off rapidly. If you plant each lily bulb on its side, water is less likely to remain around the crown, and the chance of rotting is reduced.

MOVING PLANTS

D ON'T BE AFRAID TO MOVE a plant that is not thriving because it is in the wrong place. It probably has a better chance of survival if it is moved than if it is left in its original site. Spring and autumn are the best seasons for transplanting.

CHOOSING PLANTS TO TRANSPLANT

T he most important factor in transplanting is to avoid damage and disturbance to plant roots as much as possible. Small, young plants are invariably easier to transplant than older, more established ones. Use the tables below to help you decide which plants to transplant.

EASY TO MOVE	RISKY TO MOVE	DIFFICULT TO MOVE
Most herbaceous perennials and shrubs that have not been planted in open ground for more than two or three years can be moved easily and successfully. Good aftercare is essential, however.	Old, well-established plants are generally harder to move than young plants because they have wide-spreading roots. Specimens only three or four years old have a reasonable chance of success, but moving them is risky.	Generally speaking, plants of Mediterranean origin have a very fine and wide-spreading root system, and do not transplant successfully. The following plants are best left where they are, if possible.
Azaleas Bamboos *Camellia* *Gaultheria* Heathers *Kalmia* *Pieris* *Rhododendron* *Vaccinium*	*Buddleia,* *Chaenomeles* Peonies* *Rosa* spp. and cvs. Most conifers All climbing plants (unless they are very young, with little root development) *To increase your chances of transplanting peonies successfully, try undercutting them (see p. 59).	*Cistus* spp. *Cytisus* *Eucalyptus* *Lavandula* *Magnolia* spp. *Mahonia* spp. Poppies Rosemary

TRANSPLANTING CHECKLIST

● **Time of year** Move plants in autumn or early spring, never when they are growing actively and growth is soft.
● **Time of day** Whenever possible, move plants late in the day, when temperatures have dropped. This reduces the possibility of moisture loss.
● **Weak plants** Avoid transplanting a plant that is already showing signs of distress. Try to improve its growing conditions before moving it.
● **Insurance** In case of failure, take several cuttings from the plant before moving it.

● **Stems** Tie back foliage and stems before transplanting. The process is much easier if you do not have to contend with floppy branches. This also reduces the risk of damage to the plant.
● **Spreading roots** The roots of shrubs and trees usually extend past the outermost spread of the branches. Try to move as much of the root system as possible, even if this means persuading several friends to help.
● **Watering** Water the ground thoroughly before starting work. If possible, do this for several days before transplanting.

● **Soil level** Position a transplanted plant so that the soil level in its new planting hole is the same as the soil level in its original position.
● **Water loss** After transplanting, consider using an anti-transpirant spray to reduce water loss from the leaves. This is especially effective on large leaves.
● **Pruning** If possible, prune back the foliage to reduce stress from moisture loss.
● **Mulch** After transplanting, water, mulch with a deep layer of organic material, and protect the plant from sun and wind.

TRANSPLANTING A SMALL SHRUB

Small shrubs are usually fairly straightforward to move. Their root balls are compact and are easy to lift with minimal disturbance. If the plants have wide-spreading roots, they are more difficult to move. Keep shrubs well watered and mulched after they have been replanted.

IDEAL CONDITIONS
● **Check the ground** Do not attempt to transplant a shrub if the ground is either waterlogged or frozen.

PREPARATION
● **New position** Prepare a new planting hole before lifting the shrub. Transfer the plant as quickly as possible.

CONSERVING MOISTURE
● **Moisture loss** If a delay between lifting and planting is unavoidable, wrap the root ball in plastic or damp burlap.

TYING AND DIGGING UP A SMALL SHRUB

Use string or raffia to tie branches

Tie lower branches to aid digging

Ease roots out of the ground

Support top-growth when moving plant

1 Loosely tie up the branches. This makes the shrub easier to dig, and reduces the risk of stems being broken.

2 Dig a circle around the root ball. Angle the spade at about 45 degrees so that you can dig out the lowermost roots.

3 Lift the plant onto a sheet of plastic to transport it. Steady the top-growth to minimize root damage.

TRANSPLANTING A LARGE SHRUB OR TREE

Moving a large shrub or tree is risky, but it is often worth the effort and may be the only chance you have of saving a particularly valuable specimen. If you are able to plan a few months ahead, a two-step process called "undercutting" is the most reliable method.

UNWANTED SHRUBS
● **Making a screen** If digging up specimens you no longer need, group them together to screen a shed or compost pile.

PLANT CARE
● **Evergreens** Spray the foliage of evergreens every day for two weeks after transplanting.
● **Securing** If a shrub seems loose in its new location, drive three stakes into the ground around the planting hole. Secure the shrub's main stem to each stake with plastic rope. To protect the shrub's bark, thread the rope through a piece of old garden hose.

UNDERCUTTING A LARGE SHRUB

Branches are tied together

Dig trench outside root ball

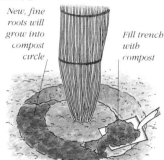

New, fine roots will grow into compost circle

Fill trench with compost

1 Tie all the branches together firmly with twine or garden wire. The autumn before you want to move the shrub, dig a circular trench around the outer edge of the root ball.

2 Fill in with compost, and water thoroughly. Keep this area moist at all times. Next autumn, dig around the outer edge of the circle and lift the plant with its new roots.

TRANSPLANTING PERENNIALS

Although most perennials are easier to transplant than trees or shrubs, it still pays to transplant them with care, and at a time when they are least likely to resent disturbance – in autumn or spring. When lifting a plant, check to see if the clump also needs dividing.

MOVING AND DIVIDING A WELL-ESTABLISHED PERENNIAL PLANT

Use thumbs to split plant

1 Choose as cool a day as possible, and try to wait until early evening. Use a garden fork to dig up a well-established clump. To minimize damage, dig deeply and lift as much of the root system as you can.

2 Divide the plant (see below). Make sure that each section has its own piece of the root system. Discard sections that are weak or badly damaged. The center of the clump often contains the older, less vigorous parts of the plant.

3 Replant divided sections immediately. Considerable moisture can be lost through the leaves. To minimize this, trim off any old, damaged, or very large leaves, but make sure you do not cut into the crown of the plant.

MOVING PERENNIALS

● **Ideal conditions** Autumn and spring are the traditional times for moving and dividing perennials. However, if your soil is particularly heavy and wet, reserve this job for the spring. If subjected to very wet soil, newly transplanted perennials are likely to suffer over the winter.

● **Summer transplanting** If a plant has to be moved or divided in the summer, choose as cool a day as possible. Water the plant thoroughly beforehand. Move it late in the day, preferably just before dark, so that it has time to recover before being subjected to midday temperatures.

● **Division points** Take a close look at the clump; you should be able to see where to separate it. Using your fingers, you can feel where the natural division points are. Divide the plant at these points.

DIVIDING METHODS

The most appropriate way to divide a perennial plant depends on the type of plant it is. Small, fibrous-rooted perennials can be divided by using two hand forks back-to-back. You may need to use a spade for tough, fleshy-rooted plants.

Be sure each section has at least one visible bud

Dividing with forks
Drive a garden fork into the clump. Then drive a second fork in so that the two are back-to-back. Ease the forks up and down before pulling them apart gently and slowly. Repeat this method to divide the plant up into a number of pieces.

Dividing with a spade
Cut through the center of the mass of roots with a spade to divide them into sections. Some roots and buds will be damaged in the process, but this is unavoidable. Use a sharp knife to neaten the cut surfaces before replanting.

CARING FOR A NEWLY PLANTED PLANT

All too often, newly planted plants are abandoned to the elements. The care and attention provided up to this point are soon wasted if not followed by good care. Anything that is newly planted, or recently replanted or divided, needs special attention.

SHADING A PLANT

Shading on sunny side only

Erecting a shelter
A new plant does not have a well-established root system, so it is unable to replace lost moisture easily. Provide temporary shading using netting stapled around bamboo stakes.

STAKING A PLANT

Making a twig support
Twigs make unobtrusive supports for tall, multistemmed plants. Drive them into the ground early in the year, before the plant has made much growth. Tie them together with soft twine.

TYING A PLANT

Tie string loosely

Tying a tall plant
Tall flower spikes or stems often require support, especially in exposed places. Attach them to stakes using string tied loosely in a figure eight, plant ties, or strips cut from old panty hose.

RETAINING MOISTURE
● **Mulching** Regular and thorough watering is essential. Mulch to reduce moisture loss from the soil surface and competition from weeds.

Leave stem area clear

Mulching with carpet
Old carpet makes an excellent mulch. Cut a square or circle of carpet slightly larger than the root system. Cut a slit in it, then position the carpet around the plant. Disguise the carpet with a thin covering of mulching material, such as bark chips or soil.

THE FIRST YEAR
● **Critical period** Lavish attention on a transplanted or new plant during its first year. During this period, a new plant is more prone to problems and less able to cope under adverse conditions than at any other time in its life.

WATERING AND FEEDING
● **Organic matter** Improve the moisture retention of light soil by incorporating bulky organic matter before replanting (see p. 478).
● **Small areas** Polymer granules may help to improve moisture retention in a small area. These absorb a large quantity of water and slowly release it as conditions become drier.
● **Fertilizers** Regular feeding of newly planted plants is essential. Never let granular fertilizers or manure touch the plants directly, or the leaves may be scorched (see p. 489).

DEADHEADING

● **Rhododendrons** At regular intervals, remove faded flower clusters cleanly, but carefully to limit damage to surrounding buds and new growth. Remove any dry, dead, or diseased buds at the same time.
● **Long stems** When deadheading plants that have long stems, cut each stem back to the next growth point or set of leaves.
● **Reducing stress** After planting, minimize the stress to plants by removing any faded flowers, as well as several of the new buds.

CONTAINER GARDENING

QUICK REFERENCE
Container Know-How, p. 504
Planting Containers, p. 506
Pots and Barrels, p. 510
Windowboxes, p. 513
Hanging Baskets, p. 515
Recycling Containers, p. 518

*C*ONTAINER GARDENING *is understandably popular. Not only does it give you the freedom to create and control your planting environment, it also makes it possible for each plant to have the most suitable growing medium, as well as the best position for healthy growth. Containers can be used for long-term plantings in permanent locations, or moved around depending on the season.*

TYPES OF CONTAINERS

Containers are available in several materials: plastic, terracotta, cast stone, and wood. Weight is an important factor, especially if the container is for a balcony or roof. Size is another consideration; small pots dry out quickly, but large ones are harder to move around.

Plastic windowbox with built-in drip tray

● **Plastic containers** These are relatively inexpensive and very easy to maintain. They are lightweight and weather-resistant. Plastic is available in a range of colors that can be coordinated with buildings, garden furniture, and plants.

● **Terracotta and cast stone** For year-round use, choose frost-resistant containers. Cast stone pots are generally heavier and more expensive than other containers. They may not be suitable for acid-loving plants.

● **Wooden containers** These need regular maintenance and are heavy, but they provide good insulation for plant roots in cold weather.

● **Hanging baskets** These are available in a range of sizes and are best suited to seasonal plantings. Carefully planted, they look equally good from all angles. They can be used on all kinds of vertical surfaces.

Terracotta pot

Plastic-coated wire hanging basket

Cast stone urn

Wooden half barrel

EQUIPMENT

The items shown here are useful for planting up, maintaining, and decorating containers.

● **Planting up** All you need are a few key items: a good-quality trowel for filling and emptying containers, and for planting; a watering can for watering the plants before and after planting; pot feet or bricks to help prevent drainage holes from becoming blocked; and a layer of broken pots or broken-up styrofoam to provide good drainage (if the pot has no drainage holes).

● **Maintaining** A hand fork is good for weeding the surface of established containers. You will need sharp pruners and scissors for trimming and deadheading plants.

● **Decorating** Use a paintbrush to paint your containers with oil-based, matte, or latex paint, or a water-based preservative, depending on the material.

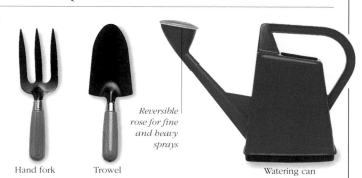

Hand fork

Trowel

Reversible rose for fine and heavy sprays

Watering can

Pruners

Scissors

Paintbrush

Broken flower pots

Windowbox feet

Pot feet

Broken-up styrofoam plant trays

Bricks

PLANTING MATERIALS

It is essential to choose the correct growing medium for your plants and their containers.

● **Soil mixes** Peat-based mixes are suitable for short-term use. Soil-based mixes are useful for stabilizing pots, but only when weight is not a factor.

● **Granules** Slow-release fertilizers gradually release nutrients according to soil temperature. Water-retaining granules release water when the soil mix dries out.

Peat-based mix

Soil-based mix

Peat-substitute mix

Slow-release fertilizer granules

Water retaining granules

CONTAINER KNOW-HOW

W HATEVER TYPE OF CONTAINER you choose, the preparation, planting up, and maintenance are basically the same. All containers require adequate drainage, suitable soil mix, and an appropriate selection of plants.

MAKING THE MOST OF A CONTAINER

B y choosing plants carefully, you can create a display that will last throughout the year. Shrubs, perennials, and bulbs can be left undisturbed to come up year after year. You can complete the planting with seasonal plants around the edges of your container.

SOIL MIX AND PLANTS
● **Soil mix** Use a peat-based, or peat-substitute, soil mix for large containers. It is lighter than soil-based mixes.
● **Permanent plants** Permanent container plants need regular feeding and watering. You should also repot them if their roots become crowded.

Seasonal planting
The larger the container, the more you can plant in it, especially if bulbs are planted at different depths. Put a shrub or perennial in the center of the container, where it has more room to spread its roots, and add seasonal bedding plants around the edges.

Permanent plant in center of pot

Trailing plants are planted around edges of pot

Small bulbs are planted toward top of pot about three times as deep as their height

Large bulbs are planted toward bottom of pot about three times as deep as their height

DRAINAGE FOR CONTAINERS

A dequate drainage is just as important to healthy container plants as adequate watering. If the container has no drainage holes, add a layer of broken pots or broken-up styrofoam before planting. If the container has holes, keep them completely clear.

CHECKING HOLES

Use a high-speed drill to create holes

Making drainage holes
Check to be sure the drainage holes in your container have been drilled properly. If they have not, use a drill to do this yourself.

TEABAGS

Drainage layer
Try using a layer or two of used teabags instead of broken flower pots. Teabags are readily available and are easy to recycle.

DRAINAGE FEET

Keeping holes clear
Prevent drainage holes from becoming blocked with garden debris by placing your container on bricks or pot feet.

SEASONAL PLANTING

All too often containers are full of plants during the summer, but empty the rest of the year. Use this chart to help you choose plants that will thrive in all seasons, and that can be either part of a permanent display or planted during the appropriate season.

SEASON	SUITABLE PLANTS	
SPRING Brighten up walls, patios, and gardens with a cheerful spring container or two. The warmth from your house may cause spring flowers in hanging baskets and windowboxes to bloom even earlier than similar plants in open ground.	*Azalea*, **Bellis** ('Pompette Mixed'), *Chiondoxa*, crocus, *Erica*, variegated *Hedera helix* cvs.*, hyacinths, dwarf irises, *Muscari azureum*, dwarf narcissus ('Hawera', 'Tête-à-Tête', 'Peeping Tom', 'February	Gold', 'February Silver'), *Primula, Scilla siberica* and cvs., dwarf tulips including *Tulipa kaufmanniana, Vinca minor* 'Variegata', *Viola* x *wittrockiana*, wallflowers. * = Trailing  *Tulipa*
SUMMER There is almost no limit to the range of plants that are suitable for planting up in summer containers. New species and cultivars are available every year, so the variety is unbeatable. There are so many different colors to choose from that you can design your container almost any way you want.	*Anisodontea capensis, Argyranthemum frutescens* and cvs., *Brachycome, Cineraria* x *hybrida, Convolvulus sabaticus* cvs.*, *Dianthus chinensis, Fuchsia* (some*), *Helichrysum petiolare, Heliotropium*,	*Impatiens, Lobelia erinus* (some*), *Nicotiana alata* cvs., *Osteospermum, Pelargonium, Petunia* x *hybrida, Portulaca grandiflora, Thunbergia alata*, *Tropaeolum, Verbena* x *hybrida, Viola*. * = Trailing  *Helichrysum petiolare*
AUTUMN Some summer plants will still be going strong in early autumn, but all the plants listed here can be used either on their own or combined with large plants that have good autumn color.	*Ajuga reptans* cvs., *Callistephus chinensis, Chrysanthemum koreanum, Chrysanthemum morifolium, Chrysanthemum rubellum, Cyclamen cilicium*, dahlias (bedding cvs.), *Euonymus fortunei*	cvs., *Gazania, Hedera* cvs.*, *Lamium maculatum* cvs., *Lobelia siphilitica, Oxalis floribunda, Sedum spectabile*. * = Trailing  *Cyclamen*
WINTER Although the choice is more limited for winter than for other seasons, it is still possible to create splashes of color with what is available. You can enjoy fragrance, too, by including some winter-scented shrubs such as *Daphne odora, Lonicera fragrantissima*, and *Hamamelis*.	*Buxus*, conifers, *Cotoneaster, Cyclamen* cvs., *Eranthis hyemalis, Erica carnea* cvs , *Euonymus fortunei* cvs., *Euonymus japonica, Galanthus nivalis, Hedera helix* cvs.*, *Helleborus, Ilex, Iris unguicularis*,	*Laurus, Mahonia* cvs., *Ophiopogon planiscapus, Phormium* cvs., *Pieris, Senecio maritima, Solanum capsicastrum, Vinca minor, Vinca major* cvs., *Viola* x *wittrockiana* cvs. * = Trailing  *Daphne*

PLANTING UP CONTAINERS

IT IS SURPRISING HOW MANY bedding plants you can squeeze into a container. Generally, the more you use, the better the end result. For best results, buy good-quality plants, and keep the container well fed and watered.

CONTAINER SUCCESS

Use a combination of upright, trailing, and bulky plants to create a full effect. For a more dramatic look, try a single larger plant, such as a shrub or small tree. After planting, leave the container in a sheltered spot for a few days before putting it in its final location.

PREPARING AND PLANTING UP A CONTAINER

Soak container with water

Use an upside-down plastic flower pot

Experiment with arrangements before planting

Soaking a container
Terracotta and stone absorb water. To keep the soil mix from drying out, water both container and plants well before planting.

Saving soil mix
Deep pots are not necessary for shallow-rooted plants. Put an upside-down pot inside your container to save soil mix.

Positioning a pot
If a plant is prone to drying out, place a plastic pot near it, and water into the pot. The water will go directly to the plant's roots.

BASIC PLANTING METHOD

Once you have chosen a suitable soil mix and container for the types and number of plants you want to use, the basic planting method used for all containers is the same. Remember to bury the plant labels in the soil mix next to the plants so that you have a record of your successes and failures.

Mix well before planting

Loosen compacted root ball with your fingers

Firm soil mix between plants

1 Make maintenance easier by mixing slow-release fertilizer and water-retaining granules with the soil mix before you plant up your container.

2 Start in the center and work outward, planting your largest plant first. Make sure the plants are level, and gently loosen any compacted root balls.

3 Use your fingers to firm the soil mix between plants, leaving no spaces. Water well, and leave the plants in a sheltered spot for a few days.

MAKING AN HERB GARDEN

A container allows you to have a miniature herb garden full of the herbs you use the most in a convenient place. It also makes it possible for you to move the herbs around so that they receive the summer sun and the winter protection they need in order to thrive.

HERB CONTAINERS

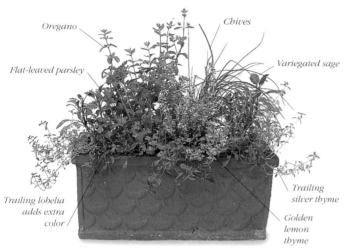

Oregano

Chives

Flat-leaved parsley

Variegated sage

Trailing lobelia adds extra color

Trailing silver thyme

Golden lemon thyme

Decorative planting
Herbs in containers look attractive and smell delicious. Use variegated or colored varieties for added interest.

CARING FOR HERBS
● **Tender herbs** Plant tender herbs in their own small pots within the container so that you can replace them easily if they become damaged.
● **Pesticides** Avoid pesticides whenever possible. If you have no choice, use only those that are suitable for edible crops. Check for pests and diseases regularly, and deal with them immediately.
● **Large herbs** Herbs such as rosemary and bay need to be planted in their own containers, since they can grow much larger than other herbs.

MAINTAINING HERBS

STORING HERBS

Add chopped herbs to water in ice cubes

Clip regularly
To prevent small plants from being crowded out, clip vigorous herbs with sharp scissors to remove straggly growth.

Freezing to preserve
Store herb clippings in ice cubes or entire trays for use in winter when herbs are scarce. Thaw them before using.

BRIGHT IDEA

Controlling mint
Mint is an invasive herb that can quickly crowd out other less vigorous plants in the same container. Restrict its root growth by planting it in its pot when it is still small.

SUITABLE HERBS

Most herbs are suitable for containers, provided they have a well-drained soil mix and plenty of sun. Small herbs, such as chives, basil, marjoram, oregano, parsley, and sage, are particularly well suited to container cultivation. Larger herbs, such as bay and rosemary, need regular trimming. Tender herbs, such as cilantro and basil, are fairly easy to grow in a container, but must be brought indoors before frost in colder climates. Generally, it's best to just resow them annually to ensure a new crop of vigorous plants.

Rosemary

COMBINING FRUITS AND VEGETABLES

Pots, windowboxes, and even hanging baskets can all be used for growing vegetables and fruits, provided you feed and water them well. You do not need to restrict a container to just fruits or vegetables – some fruits and vegetables can be combined.

FRUIT AND VEGETABLE COMBINATIONS

Early cropping lettuces are most suited for growing with strawberries

Plant strawberries around edges of container

Looking good
Strawberries and lettuce grow well together in a container. For visual impact, plant red and frilly-leafed lettuce with the strawberries.

IDEAL FRUITS
Strawberries grow well in containers, and most other fruits can be grown successfully in containers as long as they are maintained. Choose apples, pears, plums, nectarines, or other tree fruit on a dwarfing rootstock.

IDEAL VEGETABLES
Green beans, tomatoes, zucchini, radishes, beets, eggplant, peppers, carrots, lettuce, and scallions can all be grown in containers.   Peppers

MONEY-SAVING TIP

Homemade grow bags
Save money by making your own grow bags from plastic trash bags filled with inexpensive soil mix. Water before inserting the plants. These work especially well for crops that prefer their own container.

CONTAINER CROPS
● **Attracting pollinators** Create a mixed container with scarlet runner beans and sweet peas trained up the same support. The sweet peas will help to attract pollinating insects. The container must be large and deep, and will need regular and thorough watering.
● **Intercropping** Grow quick-maturing crops, such as lettuce or radishes, between slower crops that are more demanding later in the season.
● **Water loss** Avoid windy sites for your fruit and vegetable containers, since wind causes rapid evaporation. Make sure that rainfall is not blocked by any overhanging trees or nearby walls and roofs.
● **Mulching** Mulch containers with a 2-in (5-cm) deep layer of cocoa bean shells, gravel, stones, or similar material to conserve moisture.

STRAWBERRY JARS
● **Jar size** Choose large jars; they are much easier to maintain than small ones.

Position pipe in center of jar

Watering strawberry jars
Make some small holes in a length of hose, and put it in the jar before planting. Water through the hose to make sure that all the strawberry plants get their share of water.

MAINTAINING YOUR PLANTS

Maintenance for container-grown plants is far more intensive than that for plants grown in the open ground. Because container plants do not have access to the garden soil, they are completely dependent on you for all their food and water requirements.

PLANT MAINTENANCE

● **Feeding** Start fertilizing six to eight weeks after planting, and continue for as long as the plants are still growing. Choose a high-phosphorus fertilizer to encourage flowering. For immediate results, use a foliar feed.

● **Pests and diseases** Deal with pests and diseases promptly. The close proximity of plants in a container can cause a minor infestation to rapidly become a serious outbreak.

● **Pruning** Large plants may need regular pruning so they don't outgrow their containers. It's also a good idea to repot plants occasionally into slightly larger containers.

TRIMMING PLANTS

● **Controlling growth** Some plants tend to take over the whole container. Trim vigorous plants regularly to keep them in check.

Encouraging bushy growth
Use sharp scissors to prune any straggly stems; this will encourage bushy growth. Cut any flower heads off trailing plants to encourage the growth of new foliage.

RENEWING SOIL MIX

Use trowel to remove soil mix

Maintaining fertility
Top-dress permanent plantings in spring to maintain soil fertility. Carefully scrape away the top layer of soil mix, making sure you do not damage any plant roots, and replace it with new mix or well-rotted manure.

REMOVING LEAVES

● **Falling leaves** Remove leaves from overhanging trees and other plants promptly, since they encourage rotting and may exclude air.

Pinch out with thumb and fingers

Keeping plants healthy
Remove diseased leaves – or even entire plants – regularly to prevent the problem from spreading further. Always cut plants back to perfectly healthy, sound growth.

DEADHEADING

Encouraging flowers
Pinch out – or use pruners to cut off – faded flower heads or any that are beginning to form seedpods. This will stimulate the plant to produce more flowers of a larger size, and over a longer period of time.

GREEN TIP

Saving water
Keep water and liquid fertilizer from being wasted by putting pots or other containers directly underneath your hanging baskets. Any overflow from the baskets will then drip into the containers below.

POTS AND BARRELS

THERE IS AN EVER-INCREASING range of pots and barrels available, from the very basic and cheap to the extremely elaborate and expensive. Some can hold only one small plant, while others are suitable for a good-size shrub or tree.

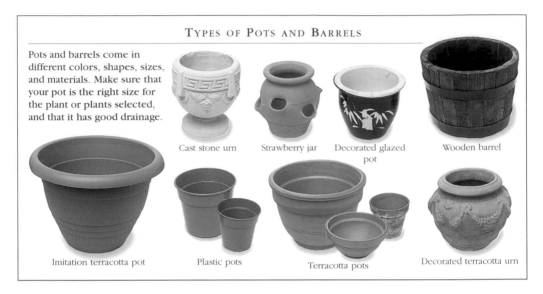

TYPES OF POTS AND BARRELS

Pots and barrels come in different colors, shapes, sizes, and materials. Make sure that your pot is the right size for the plant or plants selected, and that it has good drainage.

Cast stone urn

Strawberry jar

Decorated glazed pot

Wooden barrel

Imitation terracotta pot

Plastic pots

Terracotta pots

Decorated terracotta urn

USING POTS AND BARRELS

An unattractive container can be hidden by clever planting, but always try to use pots, barrels, and windowboxes that complement their surroundings for a pleasing, coordinated look. These containers should also be the right size and style for the plants you choose.

SINGLE SPECIMEN

Creating a focal point
Make an eye-catching focal point in your garden by planting a single specimen in a large container. For year-round interest, choose an evergreen or shrub that has colorful leaves or berries in autumn.

GROUPING POTS

Softening hard edges
Group pots together to hide ugly, hard edges or to liven up a boring part of your garden. Plant tender plants in small pots so that they can be easily moved to a sheltered area for protection during the winter months.

BRIGHT IDEA

Plastic insulation
In milder areas, before planting up, line the sides of a pot with bubblewrap to prevent the root balls from freezing over winter.

DISPLAYING POTS AND BARRELS

Pots and barrels are normally used to soften and brighten up paved areas, but they can also add a whole new dimension to established gardens. You can move your pots wherever they are needed in order to create different focal points throughout the season.

IN THE GARDEN

● **A friendly garden** Brighten up a new garden, or one that you are renovating, with temporary pots and barrels. They will make the garden a friendlier place to work in.

● **Rotating pots** Make a flower bed full of color and interest throughout the year by introducing pots and barrels that are packed with flowers. As soon as these displays are past their prime, replace the pots with others that are in full flower.

● **Hiding eyesores** Use a carefully positioned, colorful pot or barrel to hide an eyesore in your garden (see p. 470), or to protect a damaged area of lawn edging (see p. 570).

POSITIONING POTS AND BARRELS

Stacking pots
Create a living statue of plants by stacking several pots on top of each other. This arrangement forms a dramatic garden ornament and looks especially striking if you restrict yourself to a limited range of colors.

Filling gaps
Rather than overplanting a new border, use pots to fill gaps temporarily until the border plants have matured. Using pots also allows you to experiment with many different plant and color combinations.

BALCONIES AND ROOFS

Gardening above ground level usually means gardening in pots and barrels. This need not be too restricting, though, since a wide range of plants can be grown in suitable pots, allowing you to fill even the bleakest balcony or roof with color and fragrance.

MAKING A WINDBREAK

Protecting tender plants
Create a windbreak on a balcony or roof by growing climbers or wall shrubs up a trellis. Besides providing shelter for less hardy plants, it looks very attractive, especially if painted to match the overall color scheme.

LIGHTWEIGHT POTS

Use broken-up plant trays

Lessening the load
To keep weight to a minimum, use lightweight plastic pots and pieces of broken-up styrofoam instead of broken pots or stones. If you are planting shallow-rooted plants, you can fill up to a third of the pot with styrofoam.

STRENGTH AND SAFETY

● **Suitability of area** Always check the suitability and load-bearing capacity of a balcony or roof before using it to create a garden. Use lightweight soil mix and pots to be safe.

● **Container size** If space is limited and weight is restricted, use a few large containers rather than many small ones. Large containers support just as many plants, but they do not dry out as quickly.

FRESHENING THE AIR

● **Fragrant plants** Include fragrant plants in your selection so that you can enjoy their scent from inside or outside the house.

511

ALPINE TROUGHS

Make your own trough with hypertufa – a mixture of cement, sand, and peat. Use two boxes as the mold – one inside the other – and place the inner box on small wooden blocks to allow the base to form. When these are removed, they will form drainage holes.

MAKING A HYPERTUFA TROUGH

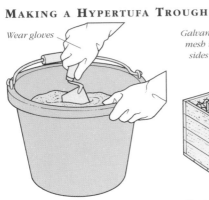

Wear gloves

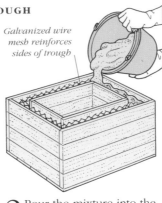

Galvanized wire mesh reinforces sides of trough

MAKING ROCKS

1 Mix 1 part cement, 1 part coarse sand, and 1–2 parts peat, or peat substitute, in a large plastic bucket. Using a sturdy tool, stir in water until the mixture thickens.

2 Pour the mixture into the space between the boxes, which should be about 2 in (5 cm) wide. Cover the top with plastic, and allow the mixture to set for one week.

Hypertufa rocks
Dig a small, unevenly shaped hole in the ground. Fill it with hypertufa, and allow it to set. The hypertufa will form a realistic-looking rock for your trough.

PLANTING AN ALPINE TROUGH

Choose mound-forming plants, since these are less invasive than the sprawling types. For continuous seasonal interest, visit your local garden center or nursery throughout the year to see what is in bloom. The trough will need replanting when the available nutrients in the soil have been depleted.

● **Drainage** Place the trough on bricks. Place fine, galvanized mesh over the drainage holes, and add broken pots, keeping the holes clear. Cover the bottom with a layer of coarse grit.

Take care not to damage roots

Protecting roots
Wrap the delicate roots of small alpines in moist tissue paper before planting them in a crevice. This minimizes root damage and helps the plants become established.

Slow-growing plants will not deplete soil nutrients too quickly

Place trailing plants near edges

In hot weather, soak hypertufa regularly

Plant rosette-forming succulents

Mulch with a layer of gravel

Trough maintenance
A well-planted trough will look good throughout the year and be easy to maintain. Plant trailing plants around the edges, and mulch with a layer of gravel to prevent the leaves from rotting under wet conditions.

WINDOWBOXES

PLANTED UP CAREFULLY, windowboxes can look stunning from both inside and outside the house. Use a selection of upright, trailing, and gap-filling plants, and include some fragrant plants to enjoy when the windows are open.

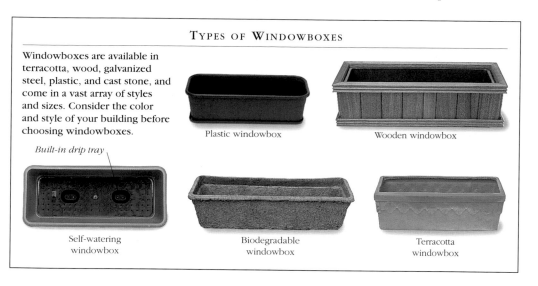

TYPES OF WINDOWBOXES

Windowboxes are available in terracotta, wood, galvanized steel, plastic, and cast stone, and come in a vast array of styles and sizes. Consider the color and style of your building before choosing windowboxes.

Plastic windowbox

Wooden windowbox

Built-in drip tray

Self-watering windowbox

Biodegradable windowbox

Terracotta windowbox

PLANNING A WINDOWBOX

Unless you have a sturdy window ledge to support the box, it is best to use a lightweight peat or peat-substitute soil mix.

Before finalizing your planting plan, make sure you can open your window and that you can reach the box to maintain it

SHAPES AND COLORS
● **Foliage** Use foliage plants to add shapes and colors to your planting throughout the year. These form a framework to which you can add flowering plants at different times during the year.

CHOOSING PLANTS
● **Tender plants** Include a few tender plants in your planting. They will thrive better in the shelter of a wall than if planted in open ground.
● **Tall plants** Avoid using very tall plants unless the box is in a sheltered location. Tall plants may make the windowbox top-heavy and therefore unstable. Look for compact forms of your chosen plants.

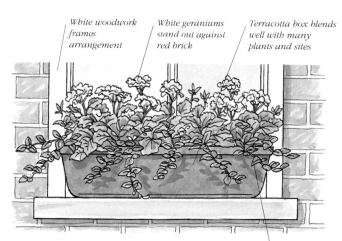

White woodwork frames arrangement

White geraniums stand out against red brick

Terracotta box blends well with many plants and sites

Trailing silver foliage blends well with geraniums

Blending and matching colors
Consider the background color of your building when selecting your plants and choosing or decorating your windowbox. Also, make sure your box is a suitable size for the window ledge.

USING A WINDOWBOX

Windowboxes can be invaluable when it comes to brightening up gray, uninspiring buildings. They can also be used successfully in many other places. The bleakest of surroundings can be brought to life by an imaginatively planted windowbox.

DISPLAYING A WINDOWBOX

Attaching to railings
You need a sturdy windowbox with a strong base for hanging on railings, since there is little, if any, support from below. Use strong metal hooks or brackets to attach the windowbox to the horizontal top rail. You will also need a lightweight soil mix.

Tumbling down walls
Used like an elongated planter on top of a wall, a windowbox like this should include trailing plants to tumble down the wall. Make sure it is firmly attached with brackets or galvanized screws, and that your neighbor has agreed to the idea.

WINDOWBOX SITES
● **Balconies** Windowboxes that are attached to a balcony railing, or are placed on a balcony floor so that the plants can cascade through the railings, do not use up too much precious floor space.
● **Culinary box** A sunny window ledge is the ideal place for a windowbox planted up with herbs. Small cherry tomatoes also grow well in a windowbox.
● **High up** If you live in a high-rise building, choose only low-growing plants for your windowboxes, and plant them firmly to protect them from the wind. Be sure to stake any fragile plants.

MAINTAINING A WINDOWBOX

Wooden windowboxes may need to be treated with a water-based preservative every few years. Painted boxes may require stripping and repainting. It is not just the box that needs attention; the hardware may also need to be repaired or replaced.

PRESERVING WOOD

Apply at least one coat

Applying preservative
Be sure that the surface of the wood is clean and dry before applying paint or preservative. Remove the windowbox from its position so that you can paint the bottom and sides as well as the front.

PAINTING A WINDOWBOX
● **Renovating a box** Brighten up a dull windowbox by painting the visible surfaces. Use an oil-based (gloss) paint or a water-based wood preservative for wooden windowboxes, and a latex paint for discolored, shabby plastic boxes. Be sure that the painted surface is dry before adding plants.

INSURANCE COVERAGE
● **Damage** Make sure your insurance policy covers windowboxes, as well as any damage they might do to people or property if they fall. If you do not own the building you live in, make sure you are allowed to use windowboxes.

SECURING BOXES

● **Supported box** Screw galvanized L-shaped brackets into wall anchors in the wall. Screw a bracket to each side of the windowbox.
● **Hanging box** If the box hangs below the window, support it with brackets attached to the wall and base.

HANGING BASKETS

ONE OF THE MOST popular types of containers, hanging baskets can be used very effectively in the smallest areas. Choose as large a basket as possible, as well as a good-quality liner, to ensure that the plants do not dry out quickly.

TYPES OF BASKETS

Hanging baskets are available in many different styles and sizes, so you can choose exactly what you want. A good-quality basket will last a long time and look attractive for many years.

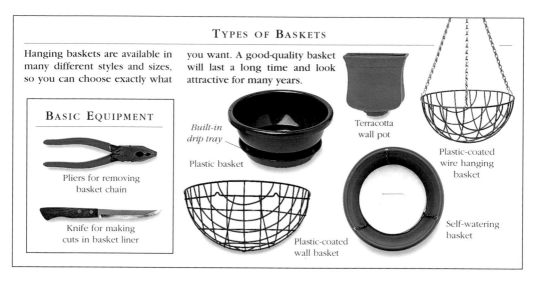

BASIC EQUIPMENT

Pliers for removing basket chain

Knife for making cuts in basket liner

Built-in drip tray

Plastic basket

Terracotta wall pot

Plastic-coated wire hanging basket

Self-watering basket

Plastic-coated wall basket

PLANTING UP A HANGING BASKET

For a really full effect, pack as many plants as you can into your basket, and plant up the sides as much as possible to hide the liner (see p. 516). With trailing plants such as lobelia, alternate one trailing and one upright plant to prevent the basket from looking straggly.

PLANTING TRAILING PLANTS

Wrap from leafy end

Cover roots with wide end of cone

1 Wrap any trailing plants in small pieces of plastic shaped into narrow cones. This protects the root balls when they are pulled through the sides of the basket.

Ease plant through slit

2 Use a sharp knife to cut a slit in the lining, then ease the plant through. Remove the plastic immediately. Always plant up in the shade to minimize stress on the plants.

BRIGHT IDEA

Disguising chains
Hide ugly basket chains by training trailing plants to cover them. Wind the stems around the chain gently, or tie them loosely with garden string or plastic ties.

HANGING BASKET LININGS

TRADITIONAL LININGS
● **Felt and foam** These liners are not too expensive, and are unobtrusive if green.
● **Coconut fiber** These bulky liners provide winter insulation.
● **Recycled wool** Woolen liners are backed with plastic.
● **Sphagnum moss** This is a popular lining material, but is not always environmentally acceptable.
● **Cardboard** These liners are designed to fit the basket, but are difficult to fit properly.

ALTERNATIVE LININGS
● **Newspaper** Cut several sheets of newspaper into circles to use as a liner. However, it is not very attractive.
● **Old sweaters** Recycle a wool sweater by cutting it up and using it as a liner. Although not very attractive, it is efficient.
● **Blanket weed** Try using a dense layer of blanket weed as a moss substitute.

Felt liner   Foam liner   Coconut fiber liner

Premarked holes for trailing plants

Recycled wool liner   Sphagnum moss   Cardboard liner

Newspaper   Old sweater   Blanket weed

USING HANGING BASKETS

Most hanging baskets are suspended from brackets attached to buildings. However, they lend themselves to far more exciting uses. A porch, sunroom, conservatory, and garage are all suitable sites for hanging baskets, as are arches, pergolas, and garden walls.

DISPLAYING A HANGING BASKET

Baskets for arches
Brighten up a wooden arch or pergola with a few hanging baskets. Choose shade-tolerant plants such as impatiens, begonias, and fuchsias if the arch is well established and covered with dense foliage.

Baskets for walls
Half-baskets are especially well suited to garden walls, and the protection from the wall may prolong their growing season. Winter baskets attached directly to a building wall benefit from the extra warmth.

COLORFUL BALL
● **Hanging ball** Create a sphere of color using two baskets planted up with bushy plants through the sides only. When the plants have settled tie the baskets together – flat surface to flat surface – to form a ball.

WINTER PROTECTION
● **Extra warmth** Winter baskets benefit from a very dense liner to protect their roots from freezing. Use an attractive, but thin liner that is lined with a cheaper, less attractive liner for additional insulation. A piece of wool from an old sweater or a few sheets of newspaper are both suitable.

HANGING A BASKET

Hang your planted basket where you can still reach it. If it is too high, it may be difficult to maintain. Before you hang the basket, be sure the bracket is firmly in place, and rotate the basket so that its most attractive sides are showing.

PULLEY SYSTEM

Lower basket for watering and feeding

Lowering a basket
To make watering a high basket easy, buy a special bracket and basket hanger that incorporates a pulley system so that you can lower and raise the basket.

SUCCESS WITH BASKETS
● **Checking brackets** Use wall anchors and galvanized screws to attach a bracket to a wall. Make sure the bracket is long enough to hold the basket away from the wall.
● **Suitable site** In sunny gardens, avoid siting baskets on the sunniest walls. Plants benefit from some shade.
● **Saving plants** If you run out of plants, leave one side of your basket more sparsely planted than the others, then hang the basket in a corner so that the sparsely planted side is hidden.
● **Keeping a record** Photograph any baskets you are particularly pleased with so that you have a permanent record of your successes.

PRESSURE SPRAYER

Make sure bracket will take weight of watered basket

Direct spray close to plant roots

Pumping water
Use a long tube attached to a spray-pump container to water and feed hanging baskets that are too high to reach easily.

MAINTAINING A HANGING BASKET

Of all containers, hanging baskets are the most difficult to keep looking good. Because they are often located in windy, sunny areas, they need watering at least once a day in summer. Once a basket has dried out, it can be difficult to revive the plants.

CONSERVING MOISTURE

Remove chain before planting up

Making a water reservoir
When planting up, place an old saucer or an aluminum pie pan in the bottom of the basket before adding the soil mix. This will act as a water reservoir.

REWETTING SOIL MIX

Add only a couple of drops of dishwashing liquid

Using a wetting agent
If the soil mix becomes so dry that water runs off, add a couple of drops of mild dishwashing liquid to the water so that it can penetrate the surface.

EMERGENCY ACTION

Rescuing a dry basket
Lower a very dry basket into a bowl of water, and leave until the soil mix looks moist. Remove the basket, then leave it in the shade until the plants perk up.

RECYCLING CONTAINERS

WITH A LITTLE IMAGINATION, you can transform something quite unexpected into an attractive planter. If you use household items creatively, you can have plenty of pots at a fraction of the cost of traditional containers.

CONTAINER IDEAS

Almost any remotely suitable item can be used as a plant container. To be usable, it must be large enough to hold sufficient soil mix for proper root growth and to prevent it from drying out rapidly. Good drainage is also essential.

USING AN ALTERNATIVE CONTAINER

Disguise sides of colander with trailing plants

Tall plant is supported by stake

● **Catering containers** Catering food containers can often be obtained inexpensively. Made from plastic or metal, they are not very attractive, but – if carefully planted with plenty of trailing plants – the sides of the containers can be completely hidden.

● **Car tires** For a container that you can make as deep or as shallow as you like, try stacking a few old car or tractor tires on top of each other.

● **Old bathtub** Use an old bathtub as a planter. The depth of the soil allows you to grow large plants successfully.

Holey basket
A colander comes complete with drainage holes. All you need to do is attach a set of basket chains. You can also use a large sieve, as long as it is lined first.

Ornamental pot
An old ceramic pot can make an ornamental pot that is suitable for seasonal displays of annuals. Be sure to create a drainage hole in the bottom.

BRIGHT IDEA

Keeping insects out
Put a piece of open-mesh fabric or fine-gauge wire mesh under a bottomless container to keep pests out.

MAKING DRAINAGE HOLES

Proper drainage is absolutely essential. Without it, water will accumulate and kill the plant roots. Use any suitable, safe method to make drainage holes, and always wear goggles.

Use a high-speed steel drill bit

Metal container
Use a drill bit to make several drainage holes in the bottom of a metal container.

Push point through carefully

Plastic container
A metal awl should pierce plastic. You may need to heat the tool first to penetrate thick surfaces.

DECORATING A CONTAINER

Ugly, shabby, or dull containers can be transformed instantly with a coat of paint or wood stain. New terracotta, hypertufa, or stone can be artificially aged, too. Well-weathered containers look softer than new ones, and fit in better with their surroundings.

USING WOOD STAIN
● **Colors** Subdued colors are usually best, because they do not detract from the beauty and style of the plants.

Try using an old wooden crate as a windowbox

Staining wood
Change the look of a wooden container by painting it with a wood preservative or stain. Stains come in a wide range of colors.

PAINTING CONTAINERS
● **Matching** Try linking your containers with your garden furniture by painting them in matching colors.

Paint the rim in a contrasting color

Painting terracotta
Create a subtle, but effective look by painting just the rim or raised pattern of a container, leaving the rest its original color.

WEATHERING EFFECTS

Apply yogurt with paintbrush

Green surfaces
Yogurt encourages surface growth of algae and mosses, which make stone, concrete, and terracotta containers appear older. A liquid-manure solution creates a similar effect. Rubbing with fresh parsley gives immediate results, but requires more time.

REPAIRING A CONTAINER

It is sometimes possible to repair a cracked, chipped, or slightly broken container. However, you should repair any cracks as soon as they appear. A neglected crack can fill with water, which expands as it freezes during the winter, causing even more damage.

SEALING SHALLOW CRACKS IN POTS

Apply mixture with putty knife

Apply sealant with paintbrush

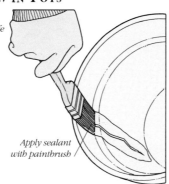

Outside cracks
Shallow cracks may develop if a pot is knocked over or as a result of a heavy frost. Apply a mixture of white glue and sand to fill cracks in concrete or cast stone containers.

Inside cracks
Cracks on the inside can be repaired simply by applying a sealant with a paintbrush. This rather obvious kind of repair cannot be seen from the outside of the pot.

CONTAINER CARE
● **Frost resistant pots** Always make sure your containers are frost-resistant. A pot that is not frost-tolerant may be reduced rapidly to a crumbling mass.
● **Damaged pots** Use damaged or repaired pots for temporary, seasonal plantings of annuals or herbaceous plants. These plants exert little, if any, pressure on the sides of containers.
● **Barrel-shaped pots** Never put a potentially large plant in a barrel-shaped pot; it will be impossible to remove without breaking the pot.
● **Repotting** Woody plants may outgrow a small container. Repot them regularly to prevent pots from shattering.

PLANT CARE

QUICK REFERENCE

Protecting Plants, p. 522

Feeding Plants, p. 524

Watering Plants, p. 529

Weeding, p. 534

Pruning Plants, p. 540

O NCE YOU HAVE CHOSEN *and planted the ideal plants for your garden, you must continue to look after them according to their needs. Regular maintenance and aftercare, especially during the first year, are vital to their long-term success. Plants that are well cared for will perform well, look attractive, and resist attack from pests and diseases.*

AVOIDING PROBLEMS

Most problems in the garden can be avoided, or at least their impact kept to a minimum, by good aftercare. A plant should thrive if it is kept well watered, fed, and pruned. Some tasks, such as feeding, watering, and mulching, should be carried out as required throughout the year. Others, such as pruning and deadheading, may need to be done at specific times. Even problems with pests and diseases can be kept to a minimum if plants are well cared for; a vigorous, healthy plant is, in most cases, well equipped to fight off a problem and to compensate for any damage that does occur.

LEAVES

Protect young foliage from late frost; once it is damaged, dieback may occur. Check foliage for pests and diseases, and take prompt action to deal with problems (see p. 548). Apply a foliar feed during the growing period to stimulate growth.

FLOWERS

Flower buds may require adequate sunlight and warmth to form. A regular supply of moisture to plants is necessary for the continuing development of healthy buds. Use a high-phosphorus fertilizer (see p. 526) to encourage flowering.

ROOTS

Keep roots well fed and watered. Avoid drought and waterlogged conditions, since both can prevent roots from taking up nutrients in the soil. Do not restrict roots by poor planting, planting in a cramped position, or planting in compacted soil.

STEMS

Check plant stems for diseases and pests; prune out, if necessary, or apply other control measures. Prune to encourage flowering and to maintain an open structure. This will allow air to circulate, making the plant less prone to attack from diseases.

FRUITS

To ensure good size and quality, supply adequate moisture to plants during fruit development. Regular watering prevents fruits from cracking and developing disorders. Feed with a high-phosphorus fertilizer (see p. 525) to encourage fruiting.

BASIC EQUIPMENT

Caring for your garden with good-quality tools will help you perform tasks efficiently and will prove cost-effective. The tools you need will depend on the size and type of your garden.

● **Comfort** Make sure your tools, pruners, hand forks, and hand trowels are comfortable to hold and easy to grip. A molded plastic handle is comfortable, even in cold weather, and is easy to clean.

● **Weight** You may prefer to use lightweight tools. Many tools traditionally made of metal are available in plastic, including wheelbarrows and watering cans.

● **Length** It is important to use spades, forks, hoes, and rakes with the correct shaft length.

● **Tread** Choose a spade with lined or checkered tread at the top of the blade. This will relieve pressure on your instep and improve your grip.

● **Reach** Choose a hose that reaches all parts of the garden.

● **Small areas** Use a hand sprayer to apply pesticides to plants in a small area.

● **Protection** Protect your hands with gardening gloves.

Tread

Spade

Garden fork

Watering can

Dutch hoe

Garden rake

Hose-end attachment

Pruners

Wheelbarrow

Hand sprayer

Hand fork

Trowel

Gardening gloves

Hose

PROTECTING PLANTS

W EATHER CONDITIONS VARY not only from season to season, but also from day to day. Many plants are able to withstand changing temperatures, but some will need special care and attention during extreme weather conditions.

PROTECTING FROM FROST

F rost is potentially very damaging. Its arrival may be unexpected, and it often follows or precedes fairly mild weather, when plants are particularly vulnerable. Early-winter frosts, and the late frosts that occur once plants have started growing again in spring, are the most damaging.

PROVIDING INSULATION

Protecting plant and pot
Protect the root ball of a container plant – and the pot itself – by wrapping the container in burlap, newspaper, or bubblewrap. Tie in place.

COVERING OVERNIGHT
● **Row covers** Drape plants with horticultural fleece or film, or old net curtains, to protect flower buds and soft, new growth. Remove as soon as frost is no longer a danger.

Using newspaper
For simple and inexpensive overnight frost protection, cover vulnerable plants with a layer or two of newspaper held in place with bricks or large stones.

PROTECTING ROSES

Mounding soil
Mound up soil around rose stems during very cold weather. Remove the soil when the weather warms up. If the soil is heavy or wet, use compost.

FIGHTING FROST
● **Insulation** Protect the crowns of herbaceous plants and shrubs by surrounding them loosely with chicken wire. Anchor the wire to the ground, and pack it with dry leaves, hay, or straw.
● **Air circulation** Make sure that air can circulate around insulated plants. Stagnant air allows moisture to accumulate, which can lead to rotting.
● **Fertilizers** Soft growth is prone to frost damage, so do not use high-nitrogen fertilizers late in the season (see p. 524–525). Feed with potash to encourage strong growth.

PROTECTING FROM SNOW

A covering of snow on hedges, shrubs, and trees is potentially damaging, since snow will weigh down stems. The greatest danger is from snow that has partly thawed and then frozen again.

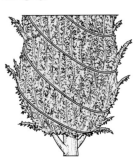

Protecting trees
Protect trees that have dense branch structures, such as conifers, by tying the branches together with galvanized wire.

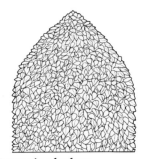

Protecting hedges
Clip hedges so that their upper surfaces slope. This will prevent snow from settling on them and causing them to lose their shape.

PROTECTING FROM HEAT

Excessive heat can be damaging to plants at all stages of growth. High temperatures can cause too much moisture loss, scorching, poor nutrient uptake, and wilting. Temperatures that fluctuate are potentially more damaging than those that are consistently too high.

PREVENTING WILTING
● **Vulnerability** Protect young plants, as well as any that have been transplanted recently. These are particularly prone to damage from wilting.

KEEPING TEMPERATURES DOWN IN A GREENHOUSE

Paving slabs absorb heat during daytime   *Water away from plants*

Damping down Reduce greenhouse temperatures in very hot weather by wetting the floor with water several times a day. This will increase the humidity and lower the overall temperature. Avoid splashing the plants, since this may cause scorching.

Using a flower pot
Protect a small, vulnerable plant with a temporary sun shield such as a flower pot. Position the pot early in the day, before temperatures start to rise. Choose as large a pot as possible so that air can circulate inside it.

CONTROLLING PESTS
● **Maintaining humidity** Spider mites thrive in hot, dry environments. Damp a greenhouse down regularly to maintain high humidity and deter these pests (see above).

KEEPING AIR FRESH
● **Ventilation** Be sure that there is good ventilation in a greenhouse. Install blinds or use paint-on shading to reduce high temperatures and the scorching effect of bright light.

PROTECTING FROM WIND AND POLLUTION

Within any garden, plants need to be protected from a wide range of potential problems. Some, such as strong winds, occur naturally. Others, such as pollution, result from industry and automobiles. Take steps to minimize the effects of some of these problems.

PREVENTING DAMAGE
● **Exposed areas** Permeable windbreaks are suitable for large, exposed areas. Erect them around the affected area, and secure them with stakes.
● **Wind tunnels** Wind rushes through gaps between buildings. When siting a new shed or greenhouse, do not create a wind tunnel by putting it too close to another building.
● **Suitable plants** Choose plants that suit the conditions. Plants with small, thick, or waxy leaves are more resistant to wind than those with thin, delicate, or large leaves.

MAKING A WINDBREAK

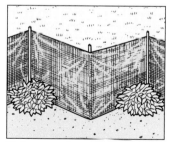

Using netting
Young plants are especially prone to damage from strong winds. Protect susceptible plants with a temporary windbreak made from netting or burlap secured with stakes.

BUILDING A BARRIER

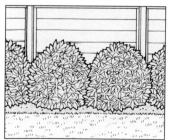

Using a hedge
A garden near a busy road is exposed to high pollution levels. Help keep excessive lead out by erecting a barrier of panel fencing. Plant with a pollution-tolerant hedge such as privet.

FEEDING PLANTS

To perform properly, plants almost always need additional feeding. In any garden, but especially one in which plants are packed together, use either a complete fertilizer or specific nutrients. For more details, consult the chart.

BASIC FERTILIZERS

Some fertilizers contain a range of nutrients. Others provide a selection of nutrients tailored to specific plants, deficiencies, or growing conditions.

● **Compost** Usually formed from a combination of garden and kitchen waste, compost is a good source of nitrogen.
● **Manure** This is a good source of nitrogen and trace elements.
● **Mushroom compost** Use this to improve soil texture. It also contains a range of nutrients.
● **Liquid seaweed extract** Apply this to soil, or use it as a foliar feed. It contains nitrogen, potassium, and phosphate.
● **Bone meal** This is a good source of phosphate.
● **Fish, blood, and bone meal** Use this as a general fertilizer. It contains phosphorus, nitrogen, and potassium.
● **Amonium sulfate** This contains concentrated nitrogen.
● **Potassium sulfate** A good source of potassium, this fertilizer is readily available.
● **Wood ashes** These contain a small amount of potassium.

Compost

Manure

Mushroom compost

Liquid seaweed extract

Bone meal

Fish, blood, and bone meal

Ammonium sulfate

Potassium sulfate

Wood ashes

SAFETY

● **Protecting skin and lungs** Always wear gloves when using fertilizer, and do not breathe in vapor or dust. Read the instructions, and use the recommended amount.
● **Storage** Store fertilizers in a cool, dry, and preferably dark place. Make sure that all containers are tightly closed and that they are out of the reach of children and animals.

USING FERTILIZERS

● **When to use** Correct timing of application is essential. Feeding late in the season may promote soft growth, which will be vulnerable to early frost. Late feeding may also cause bud failure on ornamental shrubs such as camellias.
● **Avoiding scorching** Keep all fertilizers – except for foliar feeds – off leaves, flowers, and stems (see p. 526).

● **Appropriate choice** Choose a fertilizer that is formulated for the specific needs of the plants you are feeding, and for the time of year you are planning to apply the fertilizer.
● **Watering in fertilizers** Always keep a separate watering can specifically for applying liquid and foliar feeds. Never use this can for watering or for applying chemical pesticides to plants.

FORMS OF FERTILIZER

The type of fertilizer you choose depends on the requirements of your plants and on how often you apply it.

- **Granular fertilizers** These usually contain balanced amounts of major nutrients.
- **Slow-release fertilizers** Nutrients contained in these are released into soil in response to temperature changes.
- **Liquid and soluble fertilizers** These are diluted with water. Most are applied to roots, but some can be applied to the leaves as a foliar feed (see p. 526).
- **Sticks and tablets** Push these fertilizers into soil or soil mix after planting has taken place.

Granular fertilizer

Slow-release pellets

Liquid fertilizer

Fertilizer sticks

Fertilizer tablets

Soluble, all-purpose fertilizer

SELECTING THE RIGHT FERTILIZER

NUTRIENT	PLANTS MOST IN NEED	SOILS MOST IN NEED	SIGNS OF DEFICIENCY
NITROGEN	All plants, but especially those grown for their foliage.	Most soils following heavy cropping, but especially poor soils.	Pale leaves and generally unhealthy-looking growth.
PHOSPHATE	All plants; especially useful for root development and for newly planted plants and bulbs.	Most soils following heavy cropping, but especially sandy or poor soils.	Poor root development and establishment, which is indicated by stunted growth.
POTASSIUM	All plants, especially those grown for their flowers or fruit; use to harden plants before a harsh winter.	All soils, especially those that have had lots of high-nitrogen fertilizer or manure incorporated.	Poor flowering, poor fruiting; plants may also be prone to frost or general winter damage.
MAGNESIUM	All plants, since this is a major component of chlorophyll.	Sandy, acid, wet soils, or those with a high potassium content.	Yellow or brown patches around edges and between leaf veins.
IRON	All plants, especially those intolerant of alkaline soils, e.g. *Rhododendron.*	All soils, but especially those with a high pH caused by chalk, limestone, and lime.	Yellowing between leaf veins, especially on younger growth.
OTHER NUTRIENTS	Various minor nutrients and trace elements are needed in small amounts by plants.	Most light soils, and any soil that has been used heavily.	Poor general growth; symptoms may indicate a deficiency of a particular nutrient.

APPLYING FERTILIZERS

Fertilizers can be applied using one of many different methods, depending largely on the type or formulation of the fertilizer you use. Choose the type best suited to the size of your garden, the results you wish to achieve, and the amount of time you have available.

DILUTING FERTILIZERS
● **Quick absorption** Use a liquid fertilizer for quick results. This type is usually applied with a watering can.
● **Large areas** If you are fertilizing a large area, use a hose-end applicator that dilutes the fertilizer.

Watering fertilizer in
Apply liquid fertilizer directly to roots by getting as close to the base of the plant as possible. Any liquid that is not absorbed by the soil is wasted, or may even feed nearby weeds.

APPLYING FOLIAR FEED

Spraying leaves
Apply foliar feed with a hose-end applicator, or use a fine-rosed watering can. Most of the fertilizer will be absorbed by the leaves; any excess will be absorbed by the plant roots.

SCATTERING FERTILIZER
● **Saving time** Scatter fertilizer granules over the entire soil surface to benefit the greatest area of soil and to minimize the risk of overfeeding.
● **Individual feeding** Apply fertilizer granules around the bases of individual plants.

Forking in fertilizer
Take great care not to damage plant roots when forking granules into the soil around the base of a plant. Water the granules in well afterward unless heavy rain is forecast.

TIMING FOLIAR FEEDS
● **When to apply** Dusk is the best time to apply a foliar feed. Never use a foliar feed in bright sunlight, or leaves and petals may be scorched.
● **Late application** Foliar feeds can be used relatively late in the growing season because they will not continue to promote plant growth during the cold winter months.

PHOSPHORUS FERTILIZERS
● **High flower yield** Encourage flowers by applying a high-phosphorus fertilizer – the type used on tomato plants This is most beneficial to bedding plants (see p. 527).

USING FERTILIZER
● **Watering in** Always water fertilizer in thoroughly. Plants can absorb nutrients only if they are dissolved in liquid.
● **Adjusting soil pH** If your soil has a high pH, or if you are growing acid-loving plants, choose a fertilizer formulated especially for this kind of soil or these plants (see p. 525).
● **Applying lime** Do not apply lime at the same time as manure. Lime reacts with the nitrogen in the manure, releasing nitrogen in the form of ammonia. This can cause damage to plants and is a waste of nitrogen.
● **Avoiding scorch** Do not let concentrated fertilizer come into direct contact with leaves, flowers, or young stems, or they may be scorched.
● **Drastic action** Combine a quick-acting foliar feed with a long-lasting general fertilizer applied at the roots for a plant in urgent need of feeding.

MIXING FERTILIZER

Avoiding scorching
When planting, mix the fertilizer with soil or compost before backfilling the hole. This makes the fertilizer available to all parts of the root system, and minimizes the risk of scorching.

TIMING THE APPLICATION OF FERTILIZERS

Fertilize during a period of active plant growth, but not when it could promote new growth too late in the season. The precise timing of applications depends on the type of fertilizer you are using as well as on the individual requirements of the plant.

FEEDING SEEDLINGS
● **Seedling boost** If your seedlings look unhealthy, it is possible that the nutrients in the soil mix have been depleted. Unless you are able to transplant the seedlings immediately, apply a combined foliar and root feed.

Be careful not to drench seedlings when applying fertilizer

Applying fertilizer
Use a small watering can or plant mister to apply a liquid fertilizer to seedlings that are waiting to be pricked out. Make sure that you dilute the fertilizer to half its normal strength.

FEEDING A SHRUB
Keep feed away from stem

Boosting a pruned shrub
Encourage new growth in an extensively pruned shrub by applying a complete fertilizer. Sprinkle the fertilizer around the base of the shrub, and fork it in without damaging the roots.

FEEDING BULBS
● **Promoting flowering** The flowering capacity of bulbs can be improved by applying a foliar feed to the leaves. This especially benefits naturalized bulbs, and bulbs that have been growing in the same place for some time.

Feeding after flowering
Once flowering is over, apply a foliar feed every 10–14 days. Continue doing this until the foliage starts to turn yellow and die back. Do not tie or cut down any leaves for at least six weeks.

FEEDING A LAWN
● **Dry weather** If your lawn needs feeding during a hot, dry summer, and it is not possible to water in a granular fertilizer, use liquid fertilizer on the lawn instead. Inadequate feeding often encourages disease.
● **Application** To feed a lawn, weigh the correct amount of fertilizer, and divide it in half. Apply the first half in one direction, up and down the lawn, apply the second half across, at right angles to this.
● **Yellow grass** If the grass begins to turn yellow and is generally lacking in vigor, apply a nitrogen-rich fertilizer.

REGULATING FEEDINGS
● **Dry weather** Do not feed plants if they are suffering from lack of water. They will not be able to absorb the fertilizer properly and may be damaged in the process.
● **Overfeeding** Late in the season, avoid using more high-nitrogen fertilizer than plants require. This could promote soft growth, which is particularly prone to frost damage (see p. 522).
● **Encouraging flowers** To increase the flower yield, apply a dressing of potassium sulfate to a flower bed in autumn and in early spring.
● **Vegetables** Leafy plants that are in the ground for a long time, such as cabbage, may need an extra feeding of nitrogen before harvest.
● **Liquid seaweed** Feed tomatoes, eggplant, and zucchini with liquid seaweed every two weeks during the growing season.

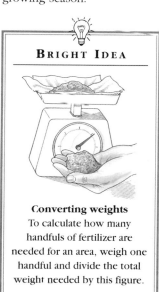

BRIGHT IDEA

Converting weights
To calculate how many handfuls of fertilizer are needed for an area, weigh one handful and divide the total weight needed by this figure.

USING NATURAL FERTILIZERS

Some gardeners may prefer to use fertilizers of a natural origin; others use only chemical fertilizers. The best results are usually achieved by using a combination of both for different purposes. Whichever type you select, there are plenty of fertilizers from which to choose.

UTILIZING NITROGEN

Cut plants close to ground level

Nourishing the soil
Peas and beans have bacteria in their roots that allow them to convert nitrogen into a usable form. Cut the plants down to ground level after harvesting, and leave the roots to break down and nourish the soil.

ADDING NUTRIENTS

● **Peas and beans** Always include these and other legumes in a crop rotation (see p. 549). They will help to increase nitrogen levels in the soil – even if their roots are not left in the ground at the end of the season.

● **Compost** Start a compost pile immediately if you do not already have one (see p. 483). Compost contains many natural plant nutrients and helps to improve and condition the soil.

● **Wood ashes** Collect wood ash from a cold bonfire after burning plant material, and use it as a fertilizer. Wood ashes contain useful nutrients, particularly potassium sulfate.

GREEN TIP

Using eggshells
Add a layer of crushed eggshells to the bottom of a planting hole to provide calcium and to improve drainage. Use for all plants, except those that prefer an acid soil, because eggshells are alkaline.

MAKING YOUR OWN FERTILIZER

Make your own totally organic liquid fertilizer from plants such as stinging nettles (or comfrey). The process is very simple and, provided that you have somewhere to store a quantity of fertilizer, is a cheap and satisfying way of providing your plants with good-quality, effective nutrients.

Pour water over nettles in bowl

Use wooden spoon to stir nettles

Strain liquid into plastic bucket

Leftover nettles can be used on compost pile

Plastic wrap

1 Collect freshly picked stinging nettles, and press them into a large bowl or bucket. Start with as many nettles as you can, since they decrease in volume once they start to rot down. Add water, allowing roughly 18 pints (10 liters) of water to about 2 lbs (1 kg) of nettles.

2 Mix the stinging nettles and water thoroughly, making sure that all the nettles are covered with water. Cover with plastic wrap or a tight-fitting lid. Stir several times with a wooden spoon over a period of several weeks. Always replace the plastic wrap or lid.

3 In a few weeks, after the mixture has rotted down, strain it into a bucket. Before using the liquid fertilizer, dilute it with water about ten times. The remaining solid matter can be incorporated into a compost pile for future use.

WATERING PLANTS

A REGULAR SUPPLY OF WATER IS ESSENTIAL for your plants. Without it, plants suffer moisture stress and may wilt and die. Established shrubs and trees can last without water longer than plants with shallow roots, such as annuals.

KEEPING A GARDEN WATERED

Water is often in short supply, particularly during long dry spells in summer, and is a precious resource we should try not to waste.

The watering technique you use – that is, how, when, and where the water is applied – is important if you are to avoid wasting water.

WATERING CORRECTLY

Directing water
To be sure water is able to penetrate right down to the roots, position the hose or watering can spout at the base of the plant, and water gently.

WATERING INCORRECTLY

Watering too strongly
Never direct a strong stream of water at the base of a plant. This washes away the soil from the roots and prevents the water from seeping down into the soil.

ASSESSING CONDITIONS
● **When not to water** Avoid watering during the heat of the day. Watering in bright light can cause scorching, especially on flowers, buds, and petals. The resulting humidity may also encourage fungal diseases such as powdery mildew, scab, and botrytis, to develop.
● **Watering twice** Water the surface of very dry soil lightly to prevent water from running off the surface. Water again once the initial water has been absorbed into the soil.
● **Pot watering** To water a large plant, sink a pot with a drainage hole into the nearby soil, and fill with water.

PLANT-WATERING CHECKLIST

There are some situations in which soil is particularly prone to drying out. Use drought-resistant plants for these areas. Some plants and planting situations always need plenty of water.

SITUATIONS THAT ARE DROUGHT-PRONE
● Free-draining, light, sandy soil.
● Some alkaline soils.
● Soil adjacent to walls (the walls absorb soil moisture).
● Plants growing against a house wall (rain falling onto the soil is restricted by overhanging roofs and gutters).
● Plants on steep slopes, especially if they face the sun.
● Plants in windy areas.

PLANTS THAT ARE RESISTANT TO DROUGHT
● Silver foliaged plants such as *Helichrysum* and *Stachys lanata*.
● Shrubs such as *Abelia* x *grandiflora*, *Azara*, *Ceanothus*, *Cistus*, *Cotinus coggygria*, *Genista*, *Hibiscus syriacus*, *Olearia*, *Potentilla fruticosa*, *Senecio*, and *Weigela*.
● Perennials such as *Alyssum*, *Armeria*, *Aubrieta*, *Coreopsis verticillata*, *Crassula*, *Dianthus*, *Oenothera*, *Phlox douglasii*, *Sempervivum*, and *Thymus*.

PLANTS THAT NEED PLENTY OF WATER
● Newly planted trees, shrubs, climbers, and perennials.

● Seedlings and transplants.
● Young trees, shrubs, and perennials.
● Leafy vegetables, which may flower and seed early if deprived of water.
● Peas, beans and other legumes, as well as sweet corn – particularly during and just after the flowering period.
● Fruiting crops such as eggplant, zucchini, and tomato – particularly during and just after flowering, and when fruiting.
● Tree, bush, and cane fruit, from flowering until harvest.
● Shrubs such as *Camellia* and *Rhododendron*, the buds of which form at the end of the summer and flower in spring.

CONSERVING AND SAVING WATER

Water may be in short supply at any time of the year. However, a long, hot summer is most likely to put plants at risk, and this is just the time when restrictions on garden watering are often in force. It therefore makes good sense to conserve water in any way you can.

IMPROVING MOISTURE RETENTION IN SOIL

● **Organic matter** Improve the water retention of soil by incorporating plenty of organic matter (see p. 482). This is especially important for sandy or light soils that drain very quickly.

● **Mulch** Apply a layer of mulch to the soil to retain moisture. An organic mulch should be applied in a 2–3 in (5–7.5 cm) deep layer. Keep the stem area free of organic mulch, since it can cause rotting.

Digging in compost
In all but the heaviest of soils, dig compost into the soil before creating a bed. When planting, incorporate compost into each planting hole and the soil used to backfill them.

Using plastic
Black plastic is a useful and inexpensive moisture-retaining material. Once it is in place, cover it with a layer of garden soil or a traditional and attractive mulching material.

USING CONTAINERS

● **Water-retaining granules** These are especially useful for plants in containers. You can either mix them with the soil mix and water thoroughly, or mix them with water and allow them to swell thoroughly before incorporating them into the soil mix (see p. 506).

● **Positioning** Containers are usually displayed in the sunniest part of the garden, since this is where most plants flower best. During very hot weather, move them to an area that is sometimes in shade.

● **Avoiding waste** Check outdoor containers daily during very hot weather; they may need watering once or even twice a day.

● **Self-watering** Use planters that are designed to supply water on demand. They are particularly suitable for use on balconies and verandahs.

CONTROLLING WEEDS

Use hand fork to remove weeds

Removing competition
Pull weeds from around plants regularly. Weeds grow rapidly and absorb a surprising amount of water from the soil in the process. As you weed, try to minimize disturbance to the soil.

WEEDING IN DROUGHT

● **Cutting weeds** In extremely dry conditions, cut off weeds at soil level instead of pulling them. This method reduces disturbance to the soil and prevents further moisture loss from the soil.

● **Wilting weeds** In very hot weather, leave uprooted or decapitated annual weeds on the soil surface to die, forming a "mini-mulch" layer.

MULCHING A LAWN

● **Using grass clippings** During drought conditions, do not rake up or collect grass clippings. Leave them as a mulch on the surface of the lawn after mowing.

TRADITIONAL TIP

Making a windbreak
Wind, especially from the sea, has a drying effect on plants and soil. Create a windbreak of trees and shrubs to protect an exposed garden.

COLLECTING AND RECYCLING WATER

Inside any house, a huge quantity of water is used every day. Much of it could be recycled for use in a garden with little effort. Not all water is suitable, however, so it is important to be selective. Use containers to collect and store as much water for recycling as you can.

COLLECTING WATER FOR GARDEN USE

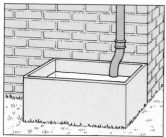

Using a container
Position any clean, watertight container under a downpipe to collect and store water for a garden. Make sure that you will be able to lift it when it is full. If it is too heavy, siphon off the water with a section of hosepipe.

Diverting water
The downpipe that carries water from a bathroom sink or tub is an excellent source of water throughout the year. To collect the water, attach a section of pipe to divert it from the downpipe into a suitable container.

USING RECYCLED WATER
● **Safe water** Use water from the bathtub (it must not contain very much bubble bath) and the bathroom sink for recycling. Suction pumps are available to drain bathwater through a hose to the garden.
● **Unsafe water** Do not use excess water from a washing machine or from a dishwasher. Some of the chemicals contained in detergents could be damaging to plants and soil in the long run. The water from water-softening units can also be very damaging to garden plants because it contains salts.

USING A WATER BARREL

A water barrel is ideal for collecting and storing rain and suitable waste water. If possible, install several water barrels in different places. Position them to collect rainwater from a greenhouse, shed, or other outbuilding, and from gutters on a house and garage.

RAISING ON BRICKS

Adjusting height
If the faucet on your water barrel is difficult to operate because it is too close to the ground, raise the barrel by placing it on several bricks. The extra height will also make it easier to fill a watering can.

MAINTAINING HYGIENE
● **Preventing algae** Clean water barrels regularly to prevent a buildup of algae and debris. Scrub the interior with a stiff brush and soapy water, and rinse thoroughly. Use a long-handled broom to reach inside.
● **Keeping water clean** Add some crystals of potassium permanganate to the water at regular intervals. These help to keep the water "sweet," and have no adverse effect on young or established plants.

USING THE WATER
● **Preventing disease** Use water collected from gutters on open ground only. It may contain harmful organisms that cause fungal diseases in seedlings, young plants, or plants in containers.

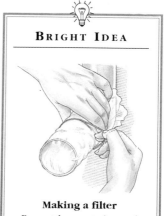

BRIGHT IDEA

Making a filter
Prevent leaves, twigs, and other debris from entering a water barrel by using a filter. Put a piece of old panty hose over the end of the downspout, and secure with a rubber band. Clean regularly, especially after heavy rain.

WATERING BEDS AND BORDERS

Successful flowering and fruiting, as well as healthy vegetable growth and development, are dependent on a regular and adequate supply of water. Applying the right amount of water at the right time and in the right way, while wasting as little as possible, is important.

WATERING EFFICIENTLY
● **Frequency** Water plants thoroughly from time to time rather than applying too little water too often.

Making a basin
To make sure that water goes down to the roots instead of lying on top of the soil, scoop out soil from around the base of the plant. Fill the hollow with water and let it soak in slowly.

SAVING WATER
● **Dry areas** Select drought-resistant plants, such as those from Mediterranean countries (see p. 529), for dry sun.
● **Grouping plants** Keep plants that need a lot of water together so that when watering, you will not waste water on nearby plants that do not need as much.
● **Directing a hose** Always point the end of the hose beneath the foliage when watering beds and borders. This will prevent water from being wasted, and will reduce the risk of leaf scorch.
● **Positioning plants** Do not put plants that prefer shade in a sunny spot. They will wilt very quickly, and large amounts of water will be needed to revive them.

BRIGHT IDEA

Protecting plants
A hose pipe may drag over flower beds and squash the plants as you pull it from place to place in the yard. To prevent this, drive short wooden posts into the corners of each bed, or at intervals along the edges.

WATERING VEGETABLES IN BEDS AND BORDERS
● **Cloches** The soil inside a cloche dries out faster than the open ground; use a leaky hose to water in a cloche.

● **When to water** Water vegetables regularly, preferably in the evening. If crops are wilting, water immediately.

● **Helping pollination** Apply plenty of water to the roots of runner beans at flowering time to encourage pollination.

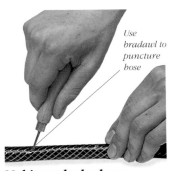

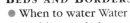
Use bradawl to puncture hose

Making a leaky hose
Take a length of hose – preferably one that is already leaky, and make small holes along it. Tightly tie up or block one end. Lay the hose along a row of plants, attach the open end to a tap, and turn the faucet on very gently.

Making trenches
Use a hoe to make shallow trenches between rows of vegetables. Be sure to leave plenty of room for normal root development. Water into the trench, thus allowing the water to seep down to the roots.

Watering long rows
To water long, inaccessible rows, first make small holes along a length of plastic guttering. Lay this between two rows, and pour water into one end. The water will run along the guttering so that each plant receives water.

WATERING LAWNS

During a dry summer, the grass in a lawn turns brown and growth slows down. An established lawn generally resists drought well. If there are no water restrictions in force, water your lawn as soon as you notice that the grass does not spring back after it is walked on.

IMPROVING DRAINAGE

Spiking a dry lawn
Before watering a dry lawn, use a garden fork to spike the soil. Drive the prongs in to make drainage channels. This will encourage the water to penetrate the soil, rather than run off the surface.

LOOKING AFTER A LAWN
● **Watering** After watering, the soil should be moist to a depth of 4–6 in (10–15 cm). Dig a small hole to see if the soil is damp to the required depth. If it is, note how long it took to water.
● **Feeding** Never use a granular fertilizer on a lawn during drought conditions, since grass needs thorough watering both before and after the fertilizer is applied. Use a specially formulated liquid lawn fertilizer instead.
● **Dry weather** Allow grass to grow slightly longer than usual in very dry weather. Moisture is retained in the blades, and excessive cutting will deplete a lawn's store of moisture.

WATERING GREENHOUSE PLANTS

However well a greenhouse is shaded, the plants inside will be more vulnerable to heat or drought stress than those growing outside. Plants in pots will be in particular need of attention. Always choose a greenhouse that has adequate vents, windows, and doors.

USING CAPILLARY MATTING

Matting soaks up water

Plant is above the water so that it can draw water as needed

Constant watering
To ensure that plants are well watered, place them on one end of a piece of capillary matting. Submerge the other end in a water trough or other reservoir of water.

WATERING EFFICIENTLY WITH CAPILLARY MATTING
● **Rapid action** Wet capillary matting before using it. This allows the capillary action of the fibers to work more rapidly and efficiently.
● **Wick** To help a plant in a large pot absorb water, insert a small matting wick through a drainage hole to protrude onto the matting below.

WATERING A GROW BAG

Bottle tied to plant support with string

Using a plastic bottle
Cut off the bottom from a plastic bottle, take the cap off, and insert this end into the soil mix in the grow bag. Water through the bottle so that the water does not run straight off the top of the soil mix.

WEEDING

A S WEEDS GROW, THEY COMPETE WITH PLANTS for water, light, and nutrients. Weeds are invasive and set seed quickly if you do not act promptly. The first, and most important, step in eradicating weeds is to identify them (see p. 535).

BASIC EQUIPMENT

Weeds can be controlled using a variety of different methods and equipment. A combination of cultivation and chemical methods is usually effective.

● **Suppressing weeds** Use a 1–2-in (2.5–5-cm) layer of gravel or grass clippings to prevent weeds from growing. Black plastic, though less attractive, has the same effect.

● **Choosing a hoe** Use a Dutch hoe to cut through weeds without damaging plant roots. An eye hoe is good for chopping weeds in half. Use an onion hoe for weeding between onions and other closely grown plants.

● **Crevices and lawns** For narrow crevices in a hard surface, use a pavement weeder. Use a dandelion weeder or an old kitchen knife for removing weeds such as dandelions, docks, and daisies from lawns.

● **Applying weedkiller** Prevent spray from drifting onto nearby plants by using a dribble bar attached to a watering can. This also makes it possible to apply weedkiller accurately.

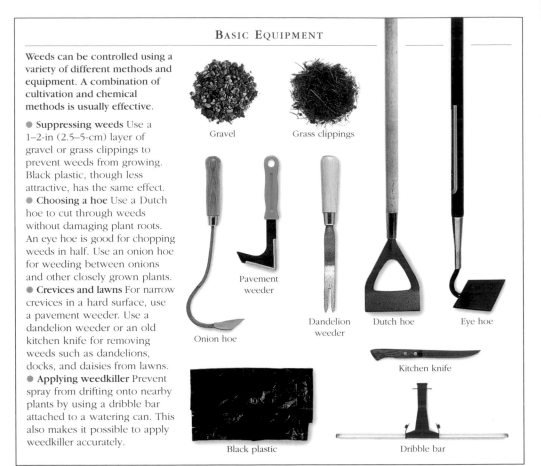

Gravel

Grass clippings

Pavement weeder

Onion hoe

Dandelion weeder

Dutch hoe

Eye hoe

Kitchen knife

Black plastic

Dribble bar

USING WEEDKILLERS SAFELY

● **Protection** Wear protective clothing such as rubber gloves and old clothes when mixing and applying weedkillers.

● **Mouth and skin** Never eat, drink, or smoke while mixing or applying chemicals. Wash you hands thoroughly after use.

● **Dilution** Dilute soluble weedkillers according to the manufacturer's instructions on the label.

● **Correct use** Always use each product only for the purpose recommended on the label.

● **Amount** Apply weedkiller at the rate stated on the label.

● **Wind** Never use weedkillers in windy weather, when spray can blow onto nearby plants.

● **Storage** Keep weedkillers safely out of reach of children and animals, preferably locked away in a cupboard or in a garden shed.

● **Containers** Store weedkillers in their original containers. Make sure they are clearly labelled.

● **Watering cans** Do not use the same watering can for watering and applying liquid weedkillers. Keep one watering can and dribble bar, or sprayer, solely for applying weedkiller.

● **Disposal** Always dispose of leftover diluted weedlkiller. Never store and reuse it.

COMMON WEEDS

ANNUAL	HOW TO TREAT	PERENNIAL	HOW TO TREAT
HAIRY BITTER CRESS	This is a common annual weed that develops quickly. It often grows on the soil mix of potted plants; check new purchases before planting. Hoe regularly before it sets seed. Hand weed, or cover with mulch.	HORSETAIL	Underground stems of horsetail can penetrate 10 ft (3 m) below the soil surface, so digging out is rarely successful in the long run. Use repeated spot treatments with glyphosate or other systemic weedkillers.
ANNUAL MEADOW GRASS	Usually found in lawns, this may also appear in poorly maintained borders. It can be prevented by good lawn cultivation, including regular mowing, appropriate feeding, watering, and aeration.	BINDWEED	Bindweed regenerates from sections of underground stems or roots, which can be spread by digging and caught up in new plants. Repeated digging out is necessary. Apply glyphosate to leaves.
ANNUAL NETTLE	Annual nettle grows in beds, borders, and vacant spaces between plants. Hand weed, or spot treat it with a suitable weedkiller such as glyphosate or similar product.	QUACK GRASS	Quack grass is common in beds, borders, vacant ground, and lawns. It spreads by creeping roots. Try forking it out from light soils, or smother it with plastic. Treat with glyphosate, and mow the lawn regularly.
GROUNDSEL	This annual is found in borders, beds, and vacant spaces between plants. Hoe or hand weed regularly before the weeds can set seed. Cover affected ground with a deep mulch.	DOCK	Dock grows in lawns, beds, and paths. It regenerates from small root sections and spreads by seed. For docks in lawns, use a weedkiller containing 2,4-D or MCPA. On vacant ground, use a glyphosate weedkiller.
COMMON CHICKWEED	Common chickweed grows in borders, beds, and vacant spaces between plants. Hoe or hand weed regularly before weeds set seed. Cover with a deep mulch.	PERENNIAL NETTLE	This regenerates from a creeping root system and spreads by seed. Eradicate before mid summer, when plants set seed. In light soils, dig it out. Use glyphosate spray in uncultivated areas.

PREVENTING WEEDS

Try to prevent weeds from invading your garden whenever possible. Once weeds are established and have started to set seed, they can be extremely difficult to eradicate. Depriving weeds of light is one of the best natural ways of suppressing weed growth, and it is easy to do.

DEPRIVING WEEDS OF LIGHT TO INHIBIT GROWTH

● **Weeds in crops** Use black plastic as an inexpensive way of inhibiting the growth of weeds in a vegetable plot.

● **Uncultivated ground** Cover the ground with black plastic or old carpet to suppress perennial weeds.

● **Mulch** Before applying a weed-suppressing mulch, make sure the ground is moist, and apply a fertilizer.

Using groundcover
Plant dense-growing plants close together to suppress weed growth attractively. Use a suitable mulch until the plants become sufficiently established to do the job on their own.

Using matting
Fruit bushes and many other plants cannot be planted very close together. If regular hoeing is impossible, deprive weeds of light by placing polypropylene matting around the plants.

Using grass clippings
Use a mulch of fresh grass clippings around plants. Do not use composted grass, since it may form an impenetrable barrier through which water and air cannot pass.

USING GRAVEL

● **Gravel mulch** Use a 2-in (5-cm) layer of coarse gravel around ornamental plants to suppress weed growth.

Preventing weeds and rot
Gravel is a particularly suitable mulch for alpines. It keeps weeds at bay and prevents rotting caused by moisture build up around the crowns of the plants.

STOPPING THE SPREAD

● **Before mulching** Remove all annual and perennial weeds from the soil before putting down weed-suppressing mulch or matting. Weed seeds in the soil will still germinate once the mulch is in place, but these seedlings will be far easier to deal with than large, well-established weeds.

● **New plants** Before planting new purchases, remove any seedlings that are growing on the surface of the soil mix.

● **Weed regeneration** Never compost noxious weeds, since many of them can regenerate from underground roots or stems, even if they have been chopped up. Do not incorporate weeds that have set seed into a compost pile; some seeds may survive the composting process.

BRIGHT IDEA

Plastic lines one side of trench

Trench needs to be 30 cm (12 in) deep

Making a weed barrier
Prevent the creeping roots of weeds in a neighbor's garden from finding their way under a fence. Dig a 12-in (30-cm) deep trench, line one side with heavy-duty plastic, then replace the soil.

USING CHEMICAL WEEDKILLERS

Used with care, chemical weedkillers are a useful and labor-saving way of dealing with weeds. They offer a means of eradicating weeds when cultivation methods are not feasible. You can combine chemicals with other control methods, or use just the chemicals.

TYPES OF CHEMICAL WEEDKILLER

Weedkillers are available in several forms, including powders, gels, liquids, and ready-to-use formulations, such as sprays.

WARNING!
Wear rubber gloves and old clothes when mixing and applying weedkillers. Always follow the instructions carefully.

Soluble powder   Gel   Liquid   Spray

WEEDING IN BORDERS

Using paint-on gel
Paint a gel-formulation weedkiller on to weeds that are growing where hand weeding or spraying would be difficult without damaging nearby plants.

WEEDING IN PATHS

Using a liquid
Use a liquid weedkiller on surfaces such as paths, patios, and driveways. A dribble bar is an efficient, low-cost way of applying a liquid weedkiller.

BRIGHT IDEA

Using a shield
Protect garden plants with a sheet of cardboard when applying a weedkiller. Cover plants with cardboard boxes or plastic trash bags.

APPLYING WEEDKILLERS
● **Effective timing** Apply weedkillers when weeds are growing actively; this is usually when they are most effective.
● **Dry weather** Check the weather forecast before using weedkillers. Rain can ruin the effect of many weedkillers.
● **Nettles** When treating nettles, apply the weedkiller just before the foliage starts to die back at the end of the growing season.

AIDING ABSORPTION OF WEEDKILLERS

Some weeds absorb weedkillers more easily than others. Increase the effect of weedkiller on stubborn weeds such as goutweed and docks by crushing their foliage before application; the chemicals are more easily absorbed by bruised leaves. Use your foot or the back of a rake, but take care not to sever the foliage completely.

WEEDING BY HAND

Many weeds can be dealt with successfully using just a few hand tools. Like many other gardening jobs, the key to success when weeding by hand is timing and frequency. Remove weeds before they set seed and before they begin to compete with garden plants.

KILLING ANNUAL WEEDS

Hoeing around plants
Use a Dutch hoe to control annual weeds. During dry, sunny weather, hoe in the morning or middle of the day, and do not gather the weeds, but leave them lying on the soil; they will soon shrivel under the sun.

KNEELING PAD

● **Knee protection** Knees can become very uncomfortable during prolonged spells of hand weeding. Buy a kneeling pad from your garden center.

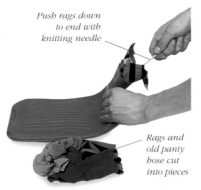

Push rags down to end with knitting needle

Rags and old panty hose cut into pieces

Making your own pad
Stuff an old hot-water bottle with rags and panty hose to make an inexpensive kneeling pad. Do not stuff the hot water bottle so full that it becomes rigid. Use just enough stuffing to create a cushion effect.

PREVENTING THE SPREAD OF WEEDS

● **When to weed** Start weeding in early spring to prevent the development and spread of weeds. Weeds can grow during mild winters and relatively warm spells, so watch for out-of-season growth, and remove it.
● **Flowering weeds** Always remove flowering weeds before they have set seed, preferably before they flower.
● **Large areas** If tackling a large expanse of weeds, start by cutting off all the flower heads and seedheads rather than removing entire weeds in a small area. This will prevent most of the seeds from escaping into the soil.

WEEDING A LAWN

● **Hand weeding** If you have a small lawn or one with only a few weeds, you will not need to use chemical weedkillers; hand weed instead.

Removing a dandelion
Use an old kitchen knife to remove a dandelion. Keep the blade as vertical as possible, and cut downward in a circle all around the weed. Rock the knife back and forth, then pull out the weed with its roots intact.

● **Pulling weed roots** Many noxious weeds can regenerate from tiny portions of roots or underground stems left in the ground. Always pull as much of the root out of the ground as possible.
● **Weed disposal** Do not put weeds that have set seed in the compost pile. Place them directly into a plastic bag for disposal elsewhere.

> **WARNING!**
> Cover the tops of stakes with upside-down flower pots or yogurt containers to protect your eyes while bending down to weed in the garden.

LOOKING AFTER A LAWN

● **Control by mowing** Regular mowing at the correct height will kill many lawn weeds. Rosette-forming weeds, such as daisies, and those that form creeping stems, such as speedwell and buttercups, will escape the blades most easily. These will require more drastic action (see p. 569).
● **Blade height** Never mow a lawn with the blades set very low. This weakens the grass considerably, making it vulnerable to invasion by unwanted weeds and moss.
● **Weeding and feeding** Apply a lawn weedkiller shortly after – or at the same time – you apply a lawn fertilizer. The fertilizer increases the rate at which the weeds absorb the chemicals that kill them. Fertilizer also stimulates the grass to grow over any bare areas left in the lawn after the weeds have died.

CLEARING NEGLECTED SITES

Without regular maintenance, a garden can quickly turn into a jungle of unwelcome weeds, particularly during the summer months. Tackle an uncultivated area by combining cultivation and chemical techniques. For heavy weed infestations, use a weedkiller.

FORKING OUT WEEDS

Removing woody weeds
Fork out large, woody weeds such as brambles. Remove the top–growth, and dig out as many of the roots as possible. Treat any subsequent growth with a brushwood killer, or dig out the remaining pieces of root.

SUPPRESSING WEEDS

Using black plastic
To protect a cleared area from new weed growth, cover it with heavy-duty black plastic. Make slits in the soil, and push the edges of the plastic into them. You may also need a few bricks if the site is exposed.

USING WEEDKILLERS

● **Contact weedkillers** Consider using a total weedkiller on a site that needs to be cleared of weeds. Use one that contains glyphosate, which will kill most weeds. It is deactivated upon contact with the soil, so you can replant the area as soon as the weeds are dead.
● **Second application** Heavily weed-infested sites will need more than one application of weedkiller. Wait until there is a good covering of foliage before reapplying.

IMPROVING THE LOOK

● **Covering up** Disguise black plastic with a layer of bark chips or garden soil.

DEALING WITH PERSISTENT WEEDS

Weeds with roots that break off into pieces underground, such as oxalis, or those with deep, creeping roots, such as bindweed, are particularly difficult to eradicate from a garden. If left unattended, however, these weeds will take over a garden in no time flat.

REMOVING BINDWEED

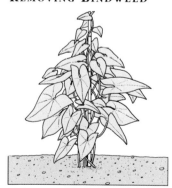

Using a stake
The twining nature of bindweed makes it difficult to treat without putting garden plants at risk. Train bindweed stems up a stake. You will then be able to apply weedkiller to the weed without damaging other garden plants.

WEEDING EFFECTIVELY

● **Disposing of roots** Never leave pieces of weed roots lying on the ground, or they may reroot. Gather them up, and either put them in the garbage, or add them to your compost pile.
● **Systemic weedkillers** For persistent weeds or for those with deep roots, choose a systemic weedkiller, which is carried from the leaves right through the plants to the roots.
● **Correct dose** Never attempt to apply a weedkiller in a more concentrated form than that recommended by the manufacturer. This may scorch the foliage, limiting the amount of weedkiller that the weed is able to absorb.

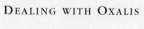
DEALING WITH OXALIS

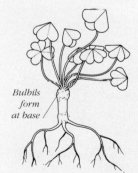

Bulbils form at base

Every oxalis has tiny bulbils around its base, each of which can form a new plant. These bulbils drop off and disperse in summer. Always dig out oxalis in spring before the bulbils spread the weed.

PRUNING PLANTS

PRUNING SERVES MANY PURPOSES. It can keep a plant's size in check, encourage flowering or fruiting, remove or deter pest and disease problems, or help to improve the overall appearance of a plant by changing its shape.

BASIC EQUIPMENT

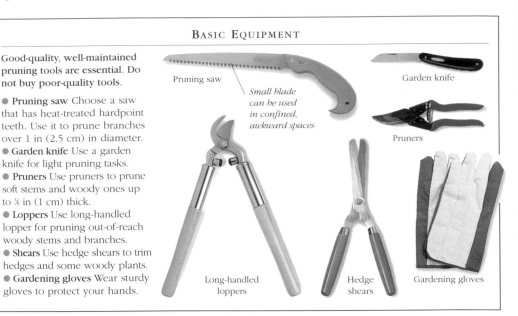

Good-quality, well-maintained pruning tools are essential. Do not buy poor-quality tools.

● **Pruning saw** Choose a saw that has heat-treated hardpoint teeth. Use it to prune branches over 1 in (2.5 cm) in diameter.
● **Garden knife** Use a garden knife for light pruning tasks.
● **Pruners** Use pruners to prune soft stems and woody ones up to ⅜ in (1 cm) thick.
● **Loppers** Use long-handled lopper for pruning out-of-reach woody stems and branches.
● **Shears** Use hedge shears to trim hedges and some woody plants.
● **Gardening gloves** Wear sturdy gloves to protect your hands.

Pruning saw

Small blade can be used in confined, awkward spaces

Garden knife

Pruners

Long-handled loppers

Hedge shears

Gardening gloves

DEADHEADING AND DISBUDDING

Deadheading is the most basic pruning job of all. Regularly remove faded flowers to encourage new flowers throughout summer and possibly into autumn. Disbudding is the removal of small flower buds around the main bud so that it can develop without competition.

DEADHEADING PLANTS
● **Using hands** Deadhead soft-stemmed plants by hand. Using pruners is inefficient and time-consuming, and does not allow proper access to small flower heads.
● **Preventing disease** Remove faded flowers as soon as possible to prevent them from becoming colonized by pathogens such as *Botrytis cinerea* (see p. 546).
● **Geraniums** To encourage a second flush of flowers on herbaceous geraniums, use shears to cut back about one-quarter to one-third of the top-growth when flowering is over.

DEADHEADING ROSES

Encouraging new flowers
Use sharp pruners to remove rose blooms as soon as they start to fade. Cut back the stem to a strong shoot or to an outward-facing bud lower on the stem.

DISBUDDING DAHLIAS

Use forefinger and thumb to remove buds

Removing competition
Disbud dahlias by pinching out surplus buds with your forefinger and thumb. This will allow the remaining bud to develop into a full-sized flower.

PRUNING ROSES

Roses need regular pruning in order to produce lots of good-sized flowers year after year. A rose that is not pruned will soon lose its shape, and its flowering capacity will be diminished. Old, faded flowers and buds will also be vulnerable to attack from diseases.

LOOKING AFTER ROSES

● **Inspecting stems** Always examine rose stems carefully. Blackspot disease (see p. 561) may overwinter on the stems.
● **Avoiding disease** Prune out diseased stems. Prune cracked or injured stems, since they are vulnerable to infection.
● **Neglected roses** Sudden, excessive pruning can sometimes cause dieback and may prove fatal. Over a period of time, gradually prune any roses that have been left unpruned
● **Protecting hands** Always wear a pair of sturdy gardening gloves to protect your hands from rose thorns. It is impossible to prune properly without them.

PRUNING POOR GROWTH

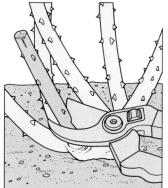

Cutting out weak growth
Use sharp pruners to prune out any diseased, damaged, dead, or weak, spindly stems. Make a diagonal cut just above an outward-facing, vigorous bud toward the base of the stem.

PRUNING STEMS

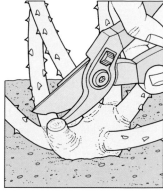

Improving air circulation
Crossing stems crowd a plant and encourage diseases such as blackspot, rust, and powdery mildew. Prune any crossing, overcrowded stems back to a sturdy, outward-facing bud.

CUTTING AT THE CORRECT ANGLE

Plants vary in their pruning requirements, and some require no routine pruning at all. Regardless of the plant, however, there are some pruning techniques that always apply. One of the most important of these is making the pruning cut at the correct angle.

ALTERNATE SHOOTS

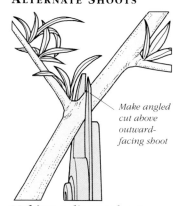

Make angled cut above outward-facing shoot

Making a diagonal cut
Use a diagonal cut to prune stems with alternate shoots or buds. This will prevent any shoots or buds from being damaged by the pruners.

OPPOSITE SHOOTS

Making a straight cut
Use a straight cut to prune stems with opposite shoots or buds. Always use sharp pruners to make a precise, swift, and clean cutting movement.

CUTTING AND SEALING

● **Where to cut** Never cut too close to a bud, since this may damage it and cause it to produce a weak shoot.
Do not prune too far away from a bud, since this leaves a "snag" of stem, which dies back and may also cause more of the stem to deteriorate.
● **Sealing wounds** Apply shellac to large pruning wounds on trees that are prone to fresh-wound diseases such as canker.

CARING FOR TOOLS

● **Blades** Keep pruners sharp. Blunt blades may crush a stem, leaving it vulnerable to infection from disease.

RENOVATING CLIMBERS

Most climbers produce vigorous growth. Sometimes this may be just what you need, but if a climber outgrows its location, it will need cutting back. Some climbers require pruning to encourage them to flower. Other, established climbers need thinning from time to time.

REMOVING OLD WOOD

Cutting back old stems
Old stems that become woody rarely flower properly. Prune old, unproductive stems back to ground level with long-handled loppers, pruners, or a saw, depending on their thickness.

PRUNING HONEYSUCKLE

Removing congestion
Many honeysuckles grow rapidly, and become dense and too heavy or extensive for their supports. Prune them by cutting away dead and damaged stems from beneath the new growth.

PRUNING CLIMBERS

● **Preserving foliage** When pruning a climber try to minimize damage to the foliage. This will prevent the plant from looking too stark after it has been pruned.

● **Checking supports** When pruning, take the opportunity to check the condition of walls, pointing, trellises, and other structures or supports. They may be in need of renovation or repair (see p. 492).

● **Looking after birds** Climbers make perfect nesting sites for a variety of birds. To keep disturbance to a minimum, try to delay major pruning work until after any fledglings have flown the nest.

PRUNING HEDGES

A well-pruned, properly maintained hedge looks attractive and can provide a functional divider or boundary within or around a garden. Proper pruning should be carried out from the very beginning if you want to keep your hedge in the best possible shape.

BRIGHT IDEA

Adding color
Brighten up a straggly or thin hedge by growing a flowering vine through it. Besides helping to mask a hedge's condition, the flowers can provide both color and scent.

SHAPING CONIFERS

Hedge cut into wedge shape

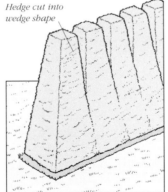

Maintaining shape
Leyland cypress and other hedging conifers need regular clipping to look good. Once a hedge has reached the desired height, cut it back into a wedge shape at least once a year.

REJUVENATING HEDGES

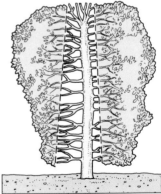

Alternating sides
Avoid cutting back all shoots severely in one season. In the first year, cut one side back hard to encourage new shoots. The next year, trim the new shoots lightly, and cut back the other side hard.

PRUNING SHRUBS

Many shrubs need regular, annual pruning in order to stimulate the production of stems that bear flower buds, and to keep them a manageable shape and size. If you are in doubt about your shrub's flowering habit, consult a book on pruning.

PRUNING DEAD WOOD

Spotting dead wood
Dead wood can be removed at any time of the year, but it is easier to spot and prune out the dead wood when the shrub is in leaf. Use sharp pruners to cut stems back into perfectly sound, healthy wood.

PRUNING OLD WOOD

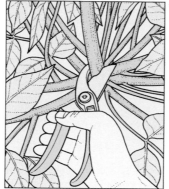

Cutting out old wood
Remove up to one-fifth of a shrub's old wood, cutting back to within 2–3 in (5–8 cm) of ground level. To maintain a well-balanced, even shape, remove the stems evenly over the entire plant.

PRUNING WEAK GROWTH

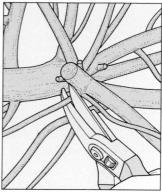

Promoting healthy growth
Prune out spindly and crossing stems. Prune back to a vigorous, outward-facing bud so that similar shoots are not encouraged. Removing unwanted stems ensures that all the nutrients go directly into the healthy growth.

WHEN TO PRUNE SHRUBS

As a general rule, if a shrub flowers after midsummer, it should be pruned in early spring. If it flowers earlier in the year, pruning should be done immediately after flowering.

EXAMPLES OF SHRUBS THAT NEED PRUNING IN SPRING
Abutilon (some),
Buddleia davidii,
Caryopteris,
Ceanothus,
Ceratostigma,
Cotinus,
Forsythia,
Fuchsia (hardy types),
Hibiscus syriacus,
Hydrangea,
Lavatera (shrubby forms),
Prunus triloba,
Spiraea douglasii,
Spiraea japonica,
Tamarix.

EXAMPLES OF SHRUBS THAT NEED PRUNING IN SUMMER
Buddleia alternifolia,
Chaenomeles,
Cotoneaster,
Deutzia,
Forsythia,
Magnolia soulangiana,
Magnolia stellata,
Philadelphus,
Syringa,
Weigela.

Fuchsia

TRADITIONAL TIP

Encouraging berries
To ensure that a *Pyracantha* is covered with berries in autumn, prune it in stages. Prune some stems in early spring, then leave them the rest of the year; the flowers they produce will turn into berries. Cut back some of the other stems immediately after flowering.

PESTS & DISEASES

QUICK REFERENCE

Preventing Problems, p. 548

Controlling Animals, p. 553

Using Pest Controls, p. 555

Specific Problems, p. 558

EVERY GARDENER *encounters different garden pests and diseases, some of which can have a devastating effect. As long as you can identify them and take the appropriate action immediately, many pests and diseases need not cause too much harm or devastation to your garden plants.*

IDENTIFYING PESTS AND DISEASES

Some pests and diseases are potentially very harmful. Others may cause serious problems only if a plant is badly stressed or already under attack from something else. Use the following chart to identify the major problems and to learn how to deal with them effectively.

PESTS/DISEASE	SYMPTOMS	CONTROLS
SLUGS AND SNAILS  Slug  Snail	Both these pests feed mainly at night and after rain. Smooth-edged holes appear on foliage, stems, and petals. Both pests may tunnel into corms, bulbs, and tubers, making large holes. Silvery slime trails are often found nearby.	Use nematodes to control slugs (see p. 555). Cultivate soil to expose eggs, and remove debris. Reduce the use of organic mulches. Lure slugs to inverted citrus peels, collect the peels, and discard.
CATERPILLARS 	Many garden plants are attacked by caterpillars, the larvae of butterflies and moths. Leaves, soft stems, and occasionally flowers develop holes as they are eaten. Some caterpillars spin a fine web around the leaves.	Pick off the caterpillars. Prune out damaged stems and heavily webbed areas. Spray with the biological control *Bacillus thuringiensis* or with a suitable pesticide.
GREENHOUSE WHITEFLIES 	Greenhouse whiteflies are most common in greenhouses but may also be found outside in hot weather. Leaves are discolored and distorted, and may be covered with sticky excreta, which attracts black sooty mold growth.	Introduce the parasitic wasp *Encarsia formosa* (see p. 555) into greenhouses and conservatories. Alternatively, spray with insecticidal soaps, or other insecticides.
WEEVILS 	Adult beetles cause notching around leaf edges. The white grubs attack many plants, particularly those in containers. They eat and tunnel into roots, tubers, and corms.	In midspring or early autumn, biological control drenches of nematodes (*Steinernema* and *Heterorhabditis* spp.) to warm, moist soil. Gather and destroy adult beetles and grubs.

544

Pests/Disease	Symptoms	Controls
RUST	Various fungi are responsible for rust infections. They are most severe in damp or moist weather and on soft, lush growth. Orange, yellow, or brown spots appear on leaves, mostly on the lower surface. The upper surface may have yellow blotches.	Remove infected leaves promptly. Improve air circulation around the plants. To decrease humidity, avoid wetting the foliage. Spray with a suitable fungicide.
LEAF SPOT	Various bacteria and fungi cause leaf spots. If this is caused by bacteria, spots may be irregular with a yellow edge. Fungal spots have concentric rings and an area of tiny fungal fruiting bodies. Black, brown, or gray spots may cover the leaves.	Most leaf spots do not cause serious problems and may develop only on plants that are in poor condition. Remove badly infected leaves, and improve the plant's growing conditions. Spray with a suitable fungicide for fungal leaf spots.
POWDERY MILDEW	These mildews cause a white, powdery layer of fungal growth to appear – usually in distinct patches or spots, which then coalesce. A few mildews are pale brown and felty. Leaves, stems, and flowers may be attacked, and may wither and die.	Powdery mildew thrives in humid air. Prune to improve air circulation, and keep plants well watered and mulched. Avoid wetting leaves. Spray with a suitable fungicide.
EARWIGS	Many plants are attacked by these pests, particularly dahlias, chrysanthemums, clematis, peaches, and certain annuals. Young leaves and petals are eaten, especially during the summer. In extreme cases, a plant can be severely damaged.	Make traps with rolled-up corrugated cardboard or flower pots stuffed with straw (see p. 550); gather and destroy the pests. Alternatively, spray at dusk with an insecticide.
TOADSTOOLS	Toadstools are usually seen in lawns in the autumn, especially during mild, damp spells. Toadstools are usually short lived and rarely survive the first frosts. They may form "fairy rings," which cause grass to become discolored.	If the grass is unharmed, simply brush off the toadstools as soon as they appear, preferably before their caps open (see p. 561). If they reappear, they may be growing on buried organic debris, such as old tree roots; dig these out.
SPIDER MITES	Several species of spider mite occur on garden and greenhouse plants. A common and troublesome species is the two-spotted, or greenhouse, spider mite. In severe cases, leaves may turn brown and die. Fine webbing may appear on affected plants.	Control spider mites with predatory mites (see p. 555). Allow adequate ventilation, and damp down frequently (see p. 523). Spray with an insecticidal soap or miticide.

PESTS/DISEASE	SYMPTOMS	CONTROLS
BOTRYTIS	Many plants are susceptible to this fungus. Fuzzy, gray patches develop on infected areas. Plant tissue becomes discolored and deteriorates, and there may be extensive dieback. White or yellow circles appear on tomato skins.	Clear out all plant debris. Remove and destroy infected tissue promptly. Avoid injury to plants, and improve air circulation around them by pruning. If necessary, spray with a suitable fungicide.
APHIDS	Aphids feed by sucking sap and may cause plant parts to become discolored and distorted. Their sticky excreta may encourage the growth of black sooty mold. Aphids can be many colors; some are covered with white, waxy wool.	Natural or introduced predators and parasites may help to reduce numbers (see p. 550). Spray with a strong stream of water from a hose to dislodge them, or with an insecticidal soap, or insecticide.
VIRUSES	Many viruses have a wide and diverse host range. Symptoms can vary. Stunting, poor growth, leaf yellowing (usually as flecks, ring-spots, streaks, or mosaic patterns), distortion, and flower-color changes are the most common symptoms.	Viruses are spread by handling or other mechanical injuries, and by pests such as aphids, thrips, and nematodes. Some are seedborne. Avoid damaging plants, and disinfect pruning tools frequently. Control virus-carrying pests, and remove infected plants promptly.
CLUBROOT	Clubroot affects many brassicas, including broccoli, brussels sprouts, cabbage, radishes, and rutabagas, as well as some ornamentals. Symptoms include distorted and swollen roots, and poorly developed, often discolored, stunted foliage.	Improve soil drainage and add lime to discourage the slime mold responsible for clubroot. Raise plants in individual pots, and plant out when they have a strong root system (see p. 560). If possible, choose resistant cultivars.
FOOT AND ROOT ROT	Bedding plants, seedlings, beans, cucumbers, tomatoes, and peas are particularly susceptible. Soil- or waterborne fungi cause discoloration of stem bases, which shrink inward. Plants grow poorly and ultimately wilt, wither, and die.	Observe strict hygiene: use sterilized commercial soil mix, clean trays and pots, and tap water. Do not overwater or crowd plants. Water seeds and seedlings with a copper-based fungicide. Remove affected plants immediately.
SCAB	These are most common on apples, pears, and Pyracantha. Gray or black, scabby patches develop on affected plants. Leaves and fruit are commonly affected, but stems may be attacked, too. Leaf puckering and fruit distortion often occur.	Avoid overhead watering. Rake up and dispose of affected leaves, and prune out infected shoots. Keep the center of plants open by pruning carefully. Spray with a suitable fungicide.

PESTS/DISEASE	SYMPTOMS	CONTROLS
CODLING MOTHS	Apples and pears may be attacked by the larvae of codling moths. Holes, often surrounded by brown, powder-like droppings, appear on ripe fruit. The codling moth larvae feed in the core of the fruit, tunneling out when mature.	Hang pheromone traps in trees from late spring to midsummer to catch male moths (see p. 559); this will reduce the number of codling moth eggs that will be fertilized by the males. Spray with a suitable pesticide.
CABBAGE ROOT FLIES	Many brassicas, including cabbage, rutabagas, cauliflower, and brussels sprouts, may be attacked by this pest. Seedlings die, and plants may wilt and become discolored. Larvae measuring up to ½ in (9 mm) long tunnel into the roots of crops.	Place collars of carpet padding, roofing felt, or cardboard around the base of each plant when it is transplanted (see p. 559). Alternatively, dust transplanted brassicas and seed rows with a suitable soil insecticide.
CARROT RUST FLIES	Carrots are the most common host to this pest, but other plants may also be attacked, including celery and parsley. Carrot rust fly larvae tunnel into roots, causing rust-brown lesions on roots and plants. Plants may develop discolored foliage.	Erect a plastic barrier around crops to keep out female flies (see p. 559), or protect a whole crop with a row cover. Avoid handling crops, since the smell of the leaves may attract adult flies. Treat seed rows with a suitable insecticide.
FLEA BEETLES	Seedlings of brassicas, leafy vegetables, radishes, stocks, nasturtiums, and wallflowers are particularly vulnerable. The tiny beetles feed on leaves, making numerous holes on the upper surfaces. Hot, dry summers encourage this pest.	Flea beetles overwinter in plant debris, so clean up debris thoroughly to avoid damage. Use sticky traps (see p. 558). Warm soil before sowing seeds, and water regularly to encourage rapid, strong growth. Use a suitable insecticide.
WIREWORMS	Many plants may be attacked, particularly potatoes and other root crops. Perennials, annuals, seedlings, and bulbous plants may also be damaged. Young plants may wilt, wither, and die as wireworms tunnel into their roots.	Recently cultivated soil, or an area recently converted from grass, is most likely to harbor these pests. Bury carrot and potato pieces as bait (see p. 560). Lift root crops as early as possible. Apply a suitable insecticide to infested soil.
PEACH LEAF CURL	Peaches, nectarines, and ornamental and edible almonds may be attacked by this fungus. Affected leaves pucker and become blistered and swollen, then turn red or purple; as spore layers develop on the surfaces, the leaves turn white.	Erect a plastic shelter over susceptible trees to prevent the air- or waterborne spores from landing (see p. 561). Pick off affected leaves. Spray with a copper fungicide in midwinter, and again two weeks later. Spray again when the leaves fall.

PREVENTING PROBLEMS

M OST PEST AND DISEASE PROBLEMS can be avoided to a large extent with careful planting, good hygiene, the use of disease-resistant plant cultivars, and good cultivation practices. If problems do occur, immediate action is vital.

ESTABLISHING HEALTHY GARDENS

S trong, healthy plants, are generally less prone to disease and are better able to compensate for damage done by pests or diseases than weak plants. Encouraging natural predators into a garden will also help to keep the pest population under control.

MAKING A GOOD START

● **Positioning plants** Always choose the best site and location for your plants. Plants grown in a spot that suits them and that is properly maintained are unlikely to suffer serious or significant damage if attacked by pests or disease-causing organisms.

● **Spacing plants** Space plants correctly when planting. Crowded plants are prone to disease because of poor air circulation. The buildup of muggy conditions encourages a variety of diseases. Fungal spores and pests can also spread easily if plants are positioned close together.

TRADITIONAL TIP

Using plastic containers
Use plastic trays and pots for young plants, because they are much easier to clean properly than those made of terracotta or wood. Wooden trays and clay pots are porous, so are likely to harbor pests.

INSPECTING PLANTS

Removing pests
Pick off pests or diseased leaves regularly. Prompt action should prevent a problem from spreading to healthy parts of a plant. Dispose of pests and diseased leaves carefully.

USING GREENHOUSES

● **Watering** Water seeds, seedlings, young plants, and container plants with tap water. Water taken from barrels often harbors soil or water-borne pathogens that attack and damage these plants.

● **Stakes** Always check that the ends of stakes are completely clean. They can contain soil that harbors fungal spores or pests.

● **Rubbish** Always clear away deteriorating or dead plant material and debris that is lying around the greenhouse; it may be infected.

● **Ventilation** Always provide good ventilation in a greenhouse or cold frame.

CULTIVATING PLANTS

● **Encouraging growth** Always use the correct amount of water and fertilizer (see p. 526) to encourage sturdy, vigorous growth. Certain nutrients, such as potassium, toughen plant growth slightly and improve a plant's resistance to attack by many pathogens.

● **Pruning plants** Pruning is a useful way of limiting certain pests and diseases. Create an open-centered crown or branch structure to reduce humidity and the onset of various diseases. Some pest and disease infestations can be eradicated simply by removing infected stems.

STERILIZING CONTAINERS

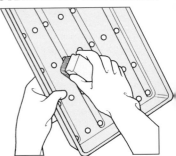

Scrubbing trays and pots
Healthy growth must be encouraged from the beginning. Before sowing seeds, use a stiff scrub brush and very hot water to clean plastic seed trays and pots. As an extra precaution, add a little kitchen disinfectant, soap, or detergent.

PRACTICING CROP ROTATION

By rotating crops around a number of plots, you can prevent the buildup of many serious pests and pathogens. This traditional method of crop cultivation encourages healthy plants and high yields with relatively little effort. Leave one plot free for permanent crops.

USING MANURE
● **Quality soil** Whenever possible, treat vegetable plots with well-rotted manure. This results in a water- and nutrient-retentive soil that will give your crops the best possible start.

USING LIME
● **Brassicas** It is a good idea to lime the soil if you are growing brassicas, but take care if the next crop is to include potatoes: lime will encourage scab potato.

ROTATING BORDERS
● **Bedding plants** Although rotation is used mainly for vegetable crops, try rotating bedding plants in flower borders from year to year. It can have a beneficial effect.

THREE-YEAR CROP-ROTATION PLAN

Regardless of the size of your plot, you can use a system based on this three-year plan. Divide the area, and your crops, into four groups. Each year, prepare the soil as indicated, and move three of the groups to another plot, ensuring a two-year gap before these crops return to their original sites.

Plot A
Plant cauliflower, brussels sprouts, turnips, rutabagas, cabbage, radishes, kale, Chinese cabbage, broccoli, and other brassicas. Before planting, turn over the soil, and apply lime to raise the soil pH to 6.5–7.0. Incorporate blood, fish, and bone meal or another general fertilizer. Additional feeding during the growing period is beneficial.

Plot B
Plant peas, green beans, runner beans, spinach, lettuce, broad beans, Swiss chard, globe artichokes, and chicory. Two to three weeks before sowing takes place, turn over the soil, and apply blood, fish, and bone meal or another general fertilizer. Maintain a regular watering program to ensure a good set of leguminous crops such as peas and beans.

Plot C
Plant potatoes, carrots, onions, tomatoes, leeks, parsnips, beets, shallots, squash, salsify, celery, scorzonera, eggplant, and Florence fennel. Before planting, double dig the plot, and incorporate well-rotted manure into both levels of ground, adding a small amount of blood, fish, and bone meal or another general fertilizer. Some crops may need additional feeding.

Plot D
Keep a plot free for permanent crops that do not fit in the rotation plan. Leave space for some tender or half-hardy herbs. Plant rosemary, chives, parsley, mint, basil, globe artichokes, Jerusalem artichokes, rhubarb, and asparagus. In a small garden, grow some permanent crops in the flower border, ensuring adequate soil fertility for the crop.

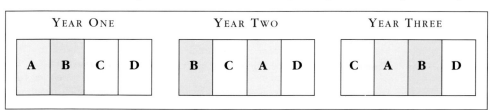

YEAR ONE				YEAR TWO				YEAR THREE			
A	B	C	D	B	C	A	D	C	A	B	D

ENCOURAGING USEFUL WILDLIFE

All too often, any small creature that walks, flies, or crawls in a garden is squashed, just in case it could damage the plants. The vast majority of insects, however, are completely harmless to plants. Many are actually beneficial and should be encouraged and protected.

BENEFICIAL GARDEN CREATURES

Many insects – in either their adult or their juvenile stage, or sometimes both – are active predators. They help to reduce the number of plant pests by eating them. In some cases, this may mean pesticides are unnecessary.

Centipede
Centipedes feed on many different soil pests. Do not confuse them with harmful millipedes.

Ladybug
Both the adult beetles and their larvae feed on pests, aphids in particular.

Lacewing
Lacewings lay their eggs on leaves. When they hatch, the larvae eat vast quantities of aphids.

Garden spider
Spiders feed on a range of insects, including many pests, which they ensnare or catch.

Hoverfly
Hoverflies and their larvae, which look like caterpillars, feed on aphids. The flies also pollinate flowers.

ENCOURAGING ALLIES

● **Garden allies** There are many beneficial garden creatures. These include assassin bugs, frogs, toads, snakes, bees, earthworms, ground beetles, praying mantises, many birds, parasitic wasps and ants.

● **Providing shelter** Although you should aim to have a clean, tidy garden to prevent as many pest and disease outbreaks as possible, try to leave a few dead leaves and stems as shelter for beneficial garden creatures.

● **Using chemicals** Use chemical sprays (see p. 557) only if they are absolutely necessary. Select the spray carefully, and choose one that is as specific as possible in order to reduce the risk to harmless insects.

ATTRACTING BIRDS

Some birds can cause damage to gardens, but this can be kept to a minimum by using nets or other barriers (see p. 553). Many birds are useful predators of garden pests, such as slugs, caterpillars, and aphids, and should be actively attracted into the garden.

FEEDING BIRDS

● **Providing food** Hang suitable food directly from tree branches. Nuts and fat will help to keep many bird species alive during a cold winter. Do not feed them with spicy or salty food.

● **Providing water** Always make sure that garden birds have a source of water so that they can drink and bathe throughout the year. Replace water regularly in winter so that it does not freeze.

● **Lurking cats** Make sure you place bird food and water out of the reach of lurking cats.

SUPPLYING FEEDERS

Using a bird feeder
Erect a bird feeder so that you can supply suitable food in a safe place. Use it to hang suet, peanut feeders and halved coconuts.

TENDING CLIMBERS

Protecting birds
Climbers are ideal nesting sites. Remember this when cutting back climbers, and try to avoid pruning during the nesting season.

CREATING A WILDLIFE POND

A pond never fails to add interest to a garden, but if constructed to encourage and attract wildlife it can be a special feature all year long. Birds, toads, frogs, and a wide range of other small animals and beneficial insects will visit to feed and drink.

ATTRACTING WILDLIFE TO A POND

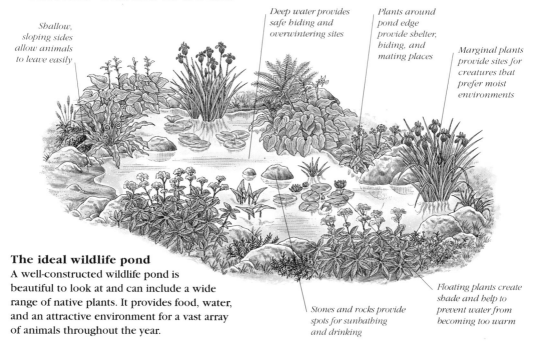

Shallow, sloping sides allow animals to leave easily

Deep water provides safe hiding and overwintering sites

Plants around pond edge provide shelter, hiding, and mating places

Marginal plants provide sites for creatures that prefer moist environments

Floating plants create shade and help to prevent water from becoming too warm

Stones and rocks provide spots for sunbathing and drinking

The ideal wildlife pond
A well-constructed wildlife pond is beautiful to look at and can include a wide range of native plants. It provides food, water, and an attractive environment for a vast array of animals throughout the year.

PLANTING TO ATTRACT INSECTS

Insects not only add interest to a garden, but many species also help to keep down pest populations and pollinate flowers. Any garden will attract some insects, but – to make sure you encourage the ones you want – provide as varied a collection of plant life as possible.

ATTRACTING INSECTS

Growing varieties
Grow a wide range of plants to create food sources for insects. *Helianthus, Nicotiana, Stachys, Gazania,* and fennel – and others with open, daisylike blooms – are particularly useful.

PLANTING FOR INSECTS
● **Single flowers** Always try to include some single-flowered varieties in your planting. These plants are far more attractive to bees and other pollinating insects than double-flowered plants.
● **Weeds** Include a rough area to accommodate a few weeds. These provide a useful source of insects early in the year, which will attract many predatory insects. Cut back the weeds in midspring so that the predators move on to other plants, where they will help to control pests.

SUITABLE PLANTS

Include as wide a variety of plants as possible in your garden. Daisylike flowers are particularly accessible and attractive to insects.

Alyssum, Anchusa azurea, Anemone x hybrida, Arabis, Campanula, Erigeron, Eryngium spp., *Geranium* spp., *Geum* spp., *Gypsophila paniculata, Liatris spicata, Papaver* spp., *Polemonium caeruleum, Rudbeckia, Salvia x superba, Scabiosa* spp., *Veronica longifolia.*

GROWING COMPANION PLANTS

Companion planting involves growing a combination of plants that benefit one or more of the plants in the particular area. Not all gardeners believe in companion planting, and attempts to prove its success are often inconclusive. It is, however, worth a try.

GROWING CROPS

● **Onions and carrots** Plant a combination of onions and carrots to minimize attacks by both onion flies and carrot rust flies. For best results, plant four rows of onions for every row of carrots.

● **Cabbage and beans** To reduce the number of cabbage aphids and cabbage root flies, plant one row of a compact form of cabbage with one row of dwarf beans.

● **Marigolds and cabbage** Try planting French marigolds between rows of cabbage plants. The marigolds may help to deter attacks from cabbage whiteflies.

● **Mixing crops** Avoid planting a large area with a single crop. This acts like an advertising sign, and it will attract plenty of hungry pests.

PLANTING PEPPERS

● **Peppers** These plants are prone to aphids. Grow them with basil, which seems to grow well with peppers, and okra. All these plants need warmth and shelter.

Deterring fungi
Try planting *Capsicum* peppers among plants that are prone to *Fusarium* foot or root rots or wilts. The secretion from the peppers' roots is believed to deter attack from these fungi.

PROTECTING POTATOES

● **Companion plants** *Tagetes* (marigolds), *Lamium,* savory, and nasturtiums may all help to protect potatoes from pests. Peas are also thought to be beneficial when grown with potatoes.

● **Nematodes** Try growing French marigolds in soil that is infested with nematodes which attack potatoes in particular. The secretion from the marigold roots is said to kill these destructive pests.

GROWING ZUCCHINI

● **Mutual benefit** Try growing zucchini with peas, beans, and corn. The legumes turn the nitrogen in the soil into a usable form, the zucchini shades the soil, and the corn provides support.

HELPING ROSES

● **Roses** To prevent roses from being attacked by aphids, try planting them with alliums and catmint. Parsley, thyme, and *Limnanthes douglasii* may also be beneficial to roses.

Combining plants
There is some evidence that foxgloves, rhododendrons, and azaleas thrive when grown together. Foxgloves help to keep the shrubs healthy and seem to grow particularly well themselves.

DISGUISING CROPS

● **Visibility** Large areas of a crop are easily visible to pests. Grow small areas, and disguise the crop by interplanting with unrelated vegetables.

Hiding vegetables
Grow ornamental plants and vegetables together. This makes the crop less obvious to those pests that see their host plants instead of smelling them.

CONTROLLING ANIMALS

Many animals are likely to come into a garden, including birds and other wildlife, as well as domestic animals such as cats and dogs. These are often harmless but may need to be deterred if they cause any damage.

CONTROLLING BIRDS

Most birds are welcomed by gardeners, but some, such as finches, eat fruit tree buds and the buds of ornamental shrubs and trees during late autumn and winter. Others, such as blackbirds and thrushes, eat ripening fruits, while starlings may pull up seedlings.

PROTECTING SQUASH

Using panty hose
Use an old pair of panty hose to protect ripening squash from birds and other pests. Pull a leg section over each squash, and tie at each end.

MAKING A SNAKE

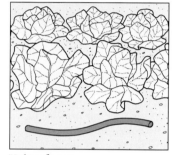

Using hose
Use an old hose to deter large pests such as birds and cats. Lay it in a bed, and bend the hose in a couple of places so that it resembles a snake.

DETERRING BIRDS

● **Humming tape** Keep birds away from crops by using thin strips of commercial buzzing or humming tape stretched between posts. As the wind blows, the vibrating tape produces a sound that deters many birds. The tape from the inside of a broken music cassette is a useful alternative.
● **Netting** Drape netting over crops, but check regularly to ensure that no birds or other animals are trapped in it.
● **Fake cats** Make cutout cats, using marbles for eyes. Hang these in vegetable plots.

CONTROLLING MOLES

Moles create unsightly mounds of loose soil in flower beds and on lawns. Their underground activity loosens the soil. This can cause plants to suffer from drought stress, because their roots can absorb water only from firm soil.

USING SMELLS

● **Smoke** Consider using commercial mole smokes that are placed inside, or at the entrance to, a mole tunnel. Although these are often effective, the mole may return once the smoke has dispersed.
● **Strong smells** Put household items such as strong-smelling scents, mothballs, and orange peels inside a mole tunnel.
● **Plant smells** Try planting caper spurge, (*Euphorbia lathyrus*) the smell of which seems to be intensely disliked by moles.

MAKING VIBRATIONS

Planting bottles
Dig several holes, and push an empty bottle into each one. As the wind blows across the top of each bottle, it will produce a noise that drives away moles.

CREATING SOUNDS

● **Windmills** Push plastic toy windmills into the ground at regular intervals. The noise they make as they spin in the wind can often deter any nearby moles.
● **Using ultrasound** Try using electronic devices that emit ultrasonic waves. These seem to work in some cases.

USING PROFESSIONALS

● **Last resort** If all else fails, employ the services of a reputable exterminator to deal with the problem for you.

CONTROLLING RABBITS AND MICE

Both rabbits and mice can cause considerable damage in gardens and greenhouses. Rabbits particularly enjoy vegetables, fruit, and tender young shoot growth, while mice are particularly fond of fruit, vegetables, and seeds – especially when other food is in short supply.

PROTECTING CROPS AND TREES FROM RABBITS

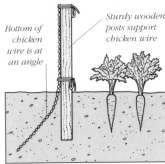

Bottom of chicken wire is at an angle

Sturdy wooden posts support chicken wire

Making a rabbit fence

Make a rabbit-proof barrier with galvanized chicken wire that is at least 3 ft (90 cm) high. Bury about 1 ft (30 cm) below the soil. Angle the bottom 6 in (15 cm) outward so that rabbits cannot tunnel underneath it.

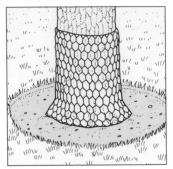

Making a tree guard

Rabbits may gnaw at tree bark, particularly on young trees. To prevent this, wrap a collar of chicken wire around a trunk. Check the wire at least once a year to make sure that it is not restricting trunk expansion.

CURBING MICE

- **Conventional traps** Use mousetraps in greenhouses, plastic tunnels, and cloches if mice are a serious problem. This is also the most effective way of controlling mice that are raiding seeds stored inside a shed or garage.
- **Humane traps** These trap mice, but do not kill them, which means that you can dispose of the mice humanely. If released several miles from your garden, they are unlikely to trouble you again.
- **Feline solution** If you do not mind dead mice being brought into the house from time to time, a cat may help to control this pest.

CONTROLLING CATS AND DOGS

Domestic animals can prove to be some of the worst pests in the garden. If at all possible, try to deter them from going into the garden in the first place. If this fails, there are a number of solutions to some of the problems that cats and dogs can cause.

DETERRING CATS

Lay bottle on ground among plants

Positioning bottles

Cats seem to strongly dislike the reflections from clear plastic bottles half-filled with water. To keep cats away from areas that they use as a litter box, place these bottles among plants. This can look unsightly but may force cats to look for another litter area.

USING OTHER METHODS

- **Moist soil** Keep soil moist to deter cats. Water regularly, and use a moisture-retentive mulch whenever possible.
- **Chicken wire** Buried chicken wire may prevent a cat from digging up soil where seeds have been recently sown. Lay the wire on the ground surface, and cover it lightly with soil.
- **Buried prickles** Buried prickly stems, such as holly, are often enough to deter a cat as soon as it begins to scratch up the soil.
- **Electronic devices** Use these to deter cats and dogs; they emit a high-frequency sound that humans cannot hear, but cats and dogs dislike it.

BRIGHT IDEA

Keeping dogs out

Stop a neighbor's dog from crawling under or through a fence into your garden by planting a prickly hedge. Shrubs such as *Pyracantha* work well. Plant them so that they will grow to form an impenetrable barrier.

USING PEST CONTROLS

W HENEVER GARDEN PESTS ARE A PROBLEM, there is usually a cultural or chemical remedy. In many cases, it is a combination of the two methods that proves to be the most effective solution in the long run.

BIOLOGICAL CONTROLS

T he use of biological controls has become increasingly popular over recent years, and the range of predators and parasites available to gardeners has increased dramatically. Many biological controls are most effective when used in a greenhouse or conservatory.

IN THE GARDEN

● **Helping out** Try to remove some pests by hand to help predators or parasites. Be sure to leave enough pests so that the population of the biological control agent can build up sufficiently.

● **Chemicals** Before using chemicals to control pests, check that they will not harm any biological control agents.

● **Caterpillars** Use a biological control for caterpillars. Mix *Bacillus thuringiensis* with water, and spray it on caterpillar-infested plants. Eating the sprayed foliage poisons the pests.

CONTROLLING SLUGS AND VINE WEEVILS

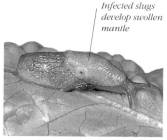

Infected slugs develop swollen mantle

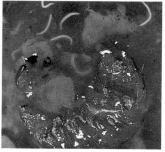

Infecting slugs
Use a nematode parasite to control slugs. Infected slugs develop a swollen mantle, stop feeding, and die within a few days. The soil must be moist and warm for this to work.

Eliminating vine weevils
Control vine weevil grubs with nematodes, tiny, white worms that kill and then feed on the remains of the grub's body. This method is most effective on plants grown in containers.

GREENHOUSE CONTROLS

Biological controls are generally most successful in the controlled environment of a greenhouse or conservatory. Make sure that you introduce enough predators or parasites to deal with the pests.

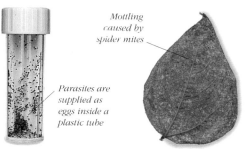

Mottling caused by spider mites

Parasites are supplied as eggs inside a plastic tube

Controlling whiteflies
Use the wasp *Encarsia formosa,* which parasitizes young whiteflies. A wasp develops inside the whitefly, then kills it.

Controlling spider mite
The predatory mite *Phytoseiulus persimilis* moves rapidly and eats all stages of the spider mite, including the eggs.

IN THE GREENHOUSE

● **Suitable pests** Try using biological controls for aphids, slugs, vine weevils, thrips, caterpillars, mealybugs, and scale insects.

● **Temperature** Always make sure that the temperature in a greenhouse is suitable before introducing biological controls.

● **Timing** Introduce biological controls when pests are present, but do not wait until the infestation is too heavy; the biological controls may not be able to multiply rapidly enough to keep up.

● **Ventilation** Ventilate a greenhouse when necessary. Predators and parasites will not escape – they usually stay where the pest population is.

ORGANIC CONTROLS

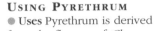

Organic controls are derived mostly from plants. Although they can be effective, the range of problems they control is limited, and none are systemic (carried to the roots). Many organic remedies are not selective and kill a variety of insects, including beneficial ones.

USING DERRIS
● **Uses** Derris is derived from *Derris* and *Lonchocarpus* roots. It controls flea beetles, thrips, caterpillars, raspberry beetles, sawflies, and spider mites.

Applying powder
For effective control, apply derris powder regularly and thoroughly, following the manufacturer's instructions. Derris is not selective, so target only the pests you wish to control.

USING PYRETHRUM
● **Uses** Pyrethrum is derived from the flowers of *Chrysanthemum cinerariifolium*. Use it to treat caterpillars, whiteflies, ants, and aphids.

Spraying liquid
Pyrethrum is a nonselective but quick-acting pesticide, so aim at target pests only. Spray leaves on both surfaces to ensure that most of the pests are killed. Pyrethrum is harmless to mammals.

APPLYING CONTROLS
● **Nonpersistent controls** Many organic treatments remain active for no more than a day, so you may therefore need to apply them more frequently than their chemical counterparts.
● **Spraying** Always use a good-quality sprayer to apply a control, and be sure to wash it out thoroughly between applications. Never keep leftover solution for future use.
● **Protecting bees** Never allow spray to drift onto open flowers, especially blossoms, or you may harm visiting bees.
● **Harvesting crops** It is usually safe to eat most crop plants fairly soon after an organic control has been applied, but always check the product label carefully for preparation details.

GREEN TIP

Making a barrier
To lay their eggs, vine weevils must crawl or climb to their destination, since they cannot fly. To prevent weevils from laying eggs in soil mix, apply a circle of nonsetting glue around pots. Remove any debris that accumulates on the glue.

USING OTHER ORGANIC CONTROLS

There are several different types of organic treatment available to gardeners, but availability may change, since, like chemical controls, they are constantly subject to legislation. Because some organic treatments are not selective, find out all you can about each one to determine which products are suitable for your purposes.

● **Insecticidal soaps** Use these for effective control of aphids, spider mites, thrips, leafhoppers, scale insects, mealybugs, and whiteflies. Insecticidal soaps are made from fatty acids produced by animal or plant sources. The soaps are not selective in their action, however, and last only approximately one day.

● **Copper-based sprays** Copper-based fungicides are suitable for use on edible crops. They control a range of plant diseases, including potato blights, celery leaf spot, apple canker, bacterial canker, and leaf spots on fruits.
● **Sulfur** Use sulfur to control diseases such as storage rots and powdery mildew on ornamental plants and fruits.

SAFETY TIPS
● **Storage** Keep all organic concentrates out of reach of children and pets.
● **Checking the label** Read the manufacturer's instructions, and follow them very carefully.
● **When to use** Spray on a calm day, in the evening.

CHEMICAL CONTROLS

There are many different chemicals available to gardeners for use against a large number of pests and diseases on a wide range of plants. Provided that they are used safely, carefully, and never indiscriminately, chemical controls are a useful aid to trouble-free gardening.

USING CHEMICAL CONTROLS SAFELY

● **Combining methods** Use chemicals only if they are absolutely necessary. Whenever possible, combine chemical controls with cultivation methods.
● **Accurate choice** Choose the chemical that is most appropriate for a particular problem, and follow the instructions carefully. Not all products are suitable for every type of plant.
● **Checking the label** Always observe the stated precautions and restrictions.
● **Protecting hands** Always use gloves when handling or mixing chemical concentrates.

● **Avoiding contamination** Never eat, drink, or smoke when working with pesticides. Always wash your hands thoroughly after using them.
● **Using chemicals safely** Avoid contact with the skin, and wash off any splashes immediately. Do not inhale any dusts or sprays.
● **Treated areas** Keep children and animals away from the area being treated. Most chemicals are considered safe once the foliage in the treated area is dry.
● **Conditions for use** Do not spray or treat with pesticides on windy, gusty, or very hot days.

● **Bee protection** If possible, spray at dusk to minimize risk to pollinating insects, such as bees.
● **Containers** After use, always thoroughly wash out containers used to apply chemicals.
● **Labelling items clearly** Always label every piece of equipment used for applying pesticides. Never pour chemicals into other containers.
● **Storage** Store pesticides in their original containers, and make sure they are tightly closed. Keep all pesticides in a safe place well out of the reach of animals and children.

AVOIDING DAMAGE

● **Following instructions** All pesticides carry detailed instructions. Always apply the product at the precise rate and frequency stated. If used incorrectly, pesticides can damage both the plant and the environment.

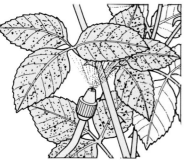

Covering a plant
Many pests and diseases, such as rose rust, lurk on the undersides of leaves. To ensure efficient coverage and control of the pest or pathogen, use a curved nozzle so that you can spray the undersides of the leaves as well as the upper surfaces.

APPLYING CHEMICALS

● **Suitability** If you are uncertain about whether a particular chemical will cause an adverse reaction in a plant, test it first on a small area before treating the whole plant.
● **Size of spray** Choose a fine-droplet spray for controlling insects, since they are most likely to be killed by small droplets. Large droplets are more suitable for weed control.
● **Ready-mixed chemicals** If you have only a minor problem or a small garden, buy ready-to-use commercial pesticides and fungicides in a spray bottle.
● **Minimizing stress** Do not apply chemicals to young plants or plants under stress; these can be easily damaged.
● **Shiny leaves** If you need to treat a plant that has shiny leaves, choose a product that contains a wetting agent. Without this, the chemicals will not adhere to the leaf surfaces and will not be effective.

DISCARDING CHEMICALS

● **Leftover solution** Always dispose of old left-over chemicals. Apply any excess to a suitable plant, or dispose of it properly. Never pour unwanted chemicals down the toilet or sink, or into bodies of water.

RESISTANCE TO CHEMICALS

More and more pests and pathogens are becoming resistant to chemicals – spider mite and greenhouse whitefly, for example. Some thrips and aphids are also now resistant to common pesticides.

● **Changing products** Reduce the likelihood of resistance by using pesticides only when really necessary, and by changing the product from time to time. Some fungi are resistant to specific fungicides. Choose an alternative product.

Controlling Specific Problems

Although pests and diseases can be controlled by currently available pesticides, some are often most easily kept at bay by cultivation or organic methods. You can use these as an alternative to, or in conjunction with, pesticides.

Slugs, Snails, and Earwigs

Slugs and snails can strip plants of their leaves. They feed mostly at night and in wet weather, attacking seedlings, annuals, shrubs, herbaceous perennials, climbers, bulbs, vegetables, and fruits. Earwigs are particularly fond of chrysanthemum, dahlia, and clematis leaves and petals.

SLUGS AND SNAILS

Making a barrier
Slugs and snails dislike crawling over rough surfaces. Use this to your advantage: Create a barrier around susceptible plants with coarsely crushed eggshells.

EARWIGS

Creating a hiding place
Make a shelter in which earwigs will collect by using rolled-up, corrugated cardboard. Tie a roll onto a stake near earwig-prone plants. Crush the earwigs.

METHODS OF CONTROL
● **Snail search** Hunt for slugs and snails after rain, and with a flashlight at night. Collect and dispose of the pests.
● **Beer traps** Pour a little beer into a small container, and sink it so that the edge protrudes just above the soil. Slugs and snails will drink the beer, fall in, and drown – but, unfortunately, so will other species that are not pests.
● **Flower pot traps** Trap earwigs by placing an inverted flower pot filled with hay on a stake near susceptible plants.

Flea Beetles

Although small, these black, metallic blue, or striped jumping beetles are capable of causing a lot of damage, since they can make hundreds of small holes in plant leaves. Young plants are particularly prone to attack and are likely to be seriously damaged or killed.

METHODS OF CONTROL
● **Sticky card** Try using a yellow card coated with non-setting glue for catching flea beetles. These and other flying or jumping pests are attracted by the color yellow and will fly or jump onto the card.
● **Clearing debris** Flea beetle grubs may cause slight damage by nibbling on roots of seedlings. Clear away plant debris to remove the grubs' usual overwintering sites.
● **Using chemicals** If an infestation is severe, dust the soil surface, as well as plant leaves, with an insecticide.

TRAPPING FLEA BEETLES ON INFECTED PLANTS

1 Coat the surface of a piece of board measuring about 6 x 3 in (15 x 7.5 cm) with heavy grease or nonsetting glue. Take care not to disturb the foliage of infected plants.

2 Run the sticky side of the board over the plants, about 1–2 in (2.5–5 cm) above them. Many of the flea beetles will jump or fly up and stick to the grease or glue.

CABBAGE ROOT FLIES AND CODLING MOTHS

These pests are not related to one another, but the damage that both cause can be limited by anticipating and interrupting their reproductive cycles, and by setting traps. Cabbage root flies devastate brassica crops, while codling moths lay their eggs on apples.

CABBAGE ROOT FLIES

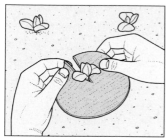

Surrounding stems
To prevent female cabbage root flies from laying eggs close to host plants, cut out circles of carpet padding, felt, or cardboard. Make slits in the circles, and place the circles around the base of young brassica plants.

CODLING MOTHS

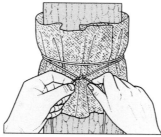

Wrapping a trunk
Scrape off loose bark on an apple-tree trunk in midsummer, and wrap a small area of each trunk in burlap. As the moth caterpillars crawl up the trunk to pupate, they will hide in the burlap; remove and discard it.

METHODS OF CONTROL

● **Moth traps** In late spring, try hanging pheromone traps in apple trees. These triangular, plastic boxes contain sticky paper, and in the middle of each is a capsule containing pheromone, which a female moth excretes to attract a mate. The male moths are attracted by the smell and become trapped on the sticky paper. The female's eggs remain unfertilized.
● **Last resort** If all else fails, protect transplanted cabbages and seedlings with a suitable contact insecticide, or start over again and replant.

CARROT RUST FLIES AND POLLEN BEETLES

Carrot rust flies can kill young carrots and other susceptible crops, including parsley, celery, and parsnips. Although pollen beetles do not cause much direct damage, they are present in large numbers on flowers and can be very irritating when cut flowers are brought indoors.

CARROT RUST FLIES

● **Resistant plants** Select relatively resistant carrot cultivars to grow. Contact a local vegetable expert for specific cultivars.

Obstructing flies
Protect young carrot plants by making a plastic barrier 24 in (60 cm) high. The carrot rust fly is a low-flying pest and will not be able to reach the crop.

METHODS OF CONTROL

● **Timing** To avoid much of the damage caused by carrot rust flies, sow carrots after late spring, or harvest the crop before midsummer.
● **Killing larvae** When sowing carrot seed, treat the row with a soil insecticide to kill off any fly larvae in the soil that have not yet hatched.
● **Avoiding smells** Avoid bruising the carrot crop, or excessive thinning, since the smell of carrots attracts carrot rust flies. Use pelleted carrot seed, which is easier to sow thinly and reduces or eliminates the need for thinning the crop.
● **Row cover** Lay row covers over carrot crops. Make sure that there are no gaps through which the flies can enter.

BRIGHT IDEA

Removing pollen beetles
Shake any cut flowers infested with pollen beetles, and leave them overnight in a dark shed or garage with a single light source. Most of the beetles will fly toward the light, leaving the flowers beetle-free.

WIREWORMS

Wireworms are the larvae of click beetles. Although they are common, especially in recently cultivated soil, wireworms are mainly a vegetable pest. They bore into potato tubers and other root crops, and sometimes attack perennials, annuals, and bulbs as well.

METHODS OF CONTROL

● **Exposing pests** If you are developing a new garden or plot that was previously grass, turn the soil over regularly. This will expose both the eggs and hatched wireworms to predators.

● **Planting wheat** In the first year or two of cultivating new ground, try growing a row of wheat between crops. The wireworms will be attracted to the wheat, which you can then dig up and discard.

● **Chemical control** As a last resort, use insecticide as an effective wireworm control.

MAKING WIREWORM TRAPS

1 Make wireworm traps by cutting unwanted potatoes and carrots into chunks. Spear each piece with a wooden skewer, which will act as a marker for each trap.

2 Bury the chunks among crops to entice the wireworms away from the vegetables. When the traps are infested, remove them, and dispose of the wireworms.

CLUBROOT

Clubroot is a vegetable grower's nightmare. The fungus attacks several members of the cabbage family. It can also infect stocks and wallflowers. The symptoms of this disease are distortion and swelling of the roots, and affected plants fail to develop properly, if at all.

AVOIDING CLUBROOT INFECTION

● **Growing from seed** Raise your plants from seed. Clubroot is often introduced into gardens via soil adhering to roots of infested plants.

● **Strong roots** Help your plants to resist attack by establishing strong roots before planting out. This can work for kale, cabbage, and brussels sprouts.

1 Check seed catalogs, and choose disease-resistant cultivars whenever possible. Sow the seed in a tray. When the seedlings are about 1½ in (4 cm) tall, transfer each one to a pot that is at least 2 in (5 cm) in diameter.

2 Water the pots regularly, and grow the plants for about six weeks, until the roots fill the pot. Plant them in open ground, and water well. The plants should be strong and healthy enough to cope with any club root.

METHODS OF CONTROL

● **Adding lime** The slime mold responsible for clubroot thrives in heavy, acidic soils. Improve drainage and add lime to decrease the mold's chances of thriving.

● **Limiting spread** Do not move soil from areas infected with clubroot to other areas. Clean all tools and boots thoroughly after use.

● **Regular weeding** Keep the vegetable plot free of weeds, which can harbor infection.

● **Checking roots** Inspect the roots of all vulnerable plants very carefully before planting out. Discard any vegetables with roots that appear to be swollen or distorted.

● **Disposing of plants** Do not compost infected plants. Dispose of them, with the household trash.

PEACH LEAF CURL AND BLACKSPOT

Peach leaf curl is caused by a fungus that attacks ornamental and edible nectarines, peaches, and almonds. An unrelated fungus causes rose blackspot, and affects only roses. These leaf infections cause leaves to fall early from a plant, progressively weakening it.

PEACH LEAF CURL

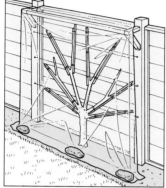

Making a shelter
The fungal spores of peach leaf curl are carried in rain and on air currents. Protect plants by erecting an open-sided shelter with narrow strips of wood and clear plastic. Put in place by late winter, and remove in midspring.

BLACKSPOT

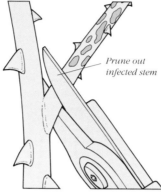

Prune out infected stem

Removing infected stems
Blackspot fungus is able to overwinter on fallen leaves and rose stems. When pruning in early spring, cut out any stems bearing the tiny, purple-black lesions that are typical of this disfiguring fungal disease.

METHODS OF CONTROL
● **Using fungicide** Spray trees infected by peach leaf curl with a copper-based fungicide such as Bordeaux mixture; apply in midwinter and again two weeks later. This mixture will kill the majority of the overwintering spores and will protect the new leaves as they open in spring.
● **Early treatment** Straight after pruning roses in spring, spray the whole of each plant with a suitable fungicide.
● **Fallen leaves** Rake up and dispose of fallen leaves infected with black spot; the fungus may overwinter on them. Do not add them to the compost pile or leave them lying around the garden. Discarding them is the safest option.

LAWN PROBLEMS

A lawn may occasionally suffer from unsightly brown or yellow patches, which can be caused by drought, fungal diseases, or pests. Sometimes a lawn is disfigured by heaps of fine soil – molehills. Dealing with moles can be difficult, but there are remedies (see p. 553).

CONTROLLING PROBLEMS
● **Lawn maintenance** Follow a regular schedule of lawn maintenance (see p. 568–569). A well-fed and properly watered lawn – which is also aerated, spiked, and scarified – will be less vulnerable to pests, diseases, and weeds.
● **Late feeding** Do not feed a lawn with a high-nitrogen fertilizer very late in the year, since this will encourage the development of *Fusarium* patch (snow mold).
● **Nitrogen deficiency** Feed a lawn throughout the season to avoid nitrogen deficiency, which can lead to the onset of red thread disease.

REMOVING TOADSTOOLS

Sweeping toadstools
Most lawn toadstools are short-lived and have little detrimental effect. Use a stiff broom to break the fungi before the caps open to release their spores. Collect and dispose of the fungi.

ANIMAL URINE

Large brown patches on a lawn may be caused by dog, fox, or cat urine. Prompt action can alleviate the problem considerably. If you catch an animal in the act, wash down the area immediately with plenty of water. This will noticeably reduce the scorching effect on the grass. If you reseed an area, make sure you remove all the urine-soaked soil first; otherwise, the grass seed will not germinate. Prevent animals from urinating on small areas of lawn by using plastic netting.

LAWNS

QUICK REFERENCE

Creating a Lawn, p. 564

Planting in a Lawn, p. 566

Lawn Maintenance, p. 568

Lawn Problems, p. 570

A GREEN, GRASSY CARPET *can be the perfect setting and foil for the colors of an ornamental garden. If a lawn is seeded or sodded properly, maintaining it will not be difficult. Regular mowing and watering are required in the summer, but other routine tasks need to be done only occasionally.*

SELECTING THE RIGHT SURFACE

Choosing the right type of lawn is essential to its future success. Standard lawn grass mixtures (see below) are not always ideal in certain situations. There are grasses to meet all kinds of needs, so take the time to research the various possibilities, and choose carefully.

LAWN ALTERNATIVES
● **Moist areas** *Cotula squalida* has soft, fernlike, bronzy green foliage and forms a closely knit carpet. It prefers a moist site and light shade, although it will tolerate direct sun. Moneywort (*Lysimachia nummularia*) also thrives in moist areas.
● **Sunny banks** *Acaena novae-zelandiae* is a semievergreen subshrub that forms a dense, 1–2 in (2.5–5 cm) carpet of soft, feathery foliage. It is especially useful where mowing is difficult. *Dichondra repens* is another good choice, as are many junipers and *Sedum.*

CREATING A NONGRASS LAWN

Chamomile lawn
Chamomile makes a good alternative to grass, but it requires weeding by hand. The fine leaves are strongly aromatic when crushed underfoot. Chamomile grows best in an open, sunny site.

Thyme lawn
Thyme has tiny, dark green, aromatic foliage and produces purple-pink flowers in summer. It is best suited to a well-drained, sunny site and works well on uneven or stony ground.

CHOOSING A SEED TYPE

Use a standard seed mixture for most situations, except those mentioned below. You can buy mixtures that grow rapidly or that do not need much mowing because they grow slowly.

● **Family lawns** Mixtures with a high proportion of rye grasses are best for play areas.

● **Shady sites** Choose a special shady lawn seed mixture for growing under trees, or if your yard is not very sunny.
● **Fine lawns** To create a formal, high-quality lawn with even color and texture, choose a special seed mixture that contains a high proportion of fine-leaved bent and fescue grasses.

THE PROPOSED SITE
● **Measuring** Always measure the area to be sown before buying grass seed, and remember to subtract areas such as island beds and paths.
● **Eradicating weeds** Eliminate perennial weeds that have deep taproots or underground rhizomes before sowing seed. Spray the weeds with a suitable weedkiller (see p. 564).

LAWN EQUIPMENT

The equipment you need to maintain your lawn depends on both its size and your budget. Most of the necessary items are readily available.

● **Cutting and trimming** Lawn mowers are essential items for cutting. The most common are rotary and reel types. A rotary mower is always powered, and performs well on long, uneven grass. A reel mower may be manual or powered, and gives a neat cut on a good-quality lawn. A half-moon edger is useful for neatening edges and for cutting and shaping sod. Long-handled edging shears allow you to neaten the edges of an established lawn quickly and easily, and without danger of straining your back.

● **Maintenance** A garden fork can be used to prepare the ground before a lawn is seeded or sodded. A fork also comes in handy for aerating small, compacted areas in autumn. A spring-tined rake is useful for raking up leaves and small twigs. It is also ideal for removing moss once it has been killed, and for raking an established lawn to remove dead grass, leaves, small twigs, and other debris.

● **Sowing seed** Small items such as stakes, string, and plastic are useful for helping to shape your lawn.

● **Watering** Unless you have a tiny yard, a garden hose is essential. An oscillating sprinkler, which delivers water evenly over a rectangular area, or a rotating sprinkler, which covers a circular area, makes watering your lawn an almost effortless task.

Rotating sprinkler

Oscillating sprinkler

Garden hose

Spring-tined rake

Long-handled edging shears

Half-moon edger

Garden fork

Stake

Plastic

String

Powered reel lawn mower

Powered rotary lawn mower

WARNING!

To be safe, install a circuit breaker if you are using electrical tools in the yard. Do not use electric mowers on wet grass.

CREATING A LAWN

WHETHER YOU DECIDE TO SEED A LAWN or lay sod, creating a lawn does not take too long. It is the preparation that consumes the most time and is the most important factor contributing to the ultimate success of your lawn.

SEEDING A LAWN

Sowing seed may not produce the instant results that you can achieve with sod, but it is much more economical. Unless you have access to a wide range of sod types, sowing seed also allows you the greatest choice. Select the most appropriate seed mixture for your yard.

STRAIGHT EDGES

Using a plastic sheet
Lay down a piece of heavy-duty plastic, and use the edge to make a straight line. Sow the grass seed over the area. The ground under the plastic sheet will remain unseeded.

SMOOTH CURVES

Using stakes and string
Mark a curve using two stakes and some string. Tie the string to one stake, and drive this into the ground. Tie another stake to the free end of the string, pull it taut, and draw a curve into the soil.

SOWING GRASS SEED
● **Before sowing** Thorough preparation is essential. Remove all large stones and other debris. Then apply a complete or balanced fertilizer to the whole area to encourage strong, healthy growth.
● **Using a mask** Grass seed can be very dusty. To avoid breathing this dust, wear a dust mask when sowing the seed.
● **Where to start** Start sowing at the far end of the designated area so that you do not need to walk on the newly sown seed.
● **Raking** After sowing, lightly rake a thin layer of soil over the seed. This improves germination and helps to protect the seed from birds.

BRIGHT IDEA

Keeping birds off
To protect a small, newly sown area from birds, push stakes into the ground, and put flower pots on top of them. Drape lightweight fruit netting over these, and weigh the edges down with stones.

AVOIDING PROBLEMS
● **Weeds** Kill off all old grass and weeds before you start to sow any seed. Choose a non-selective weedkiller such as glyphosate. This is inactivated upon contact with the soil, so once the weeds are dead, you can start to work safely.
● **Sowing thinly** Sowing grass seed very sparsely adds work in the long run. Thin grass is readily invaded by weedy grasses, broadleaved weeds, and moss.
● **Sowing densely** This can lead to problems, since the poor air circulation caused by dense sowing encourages a variety of fungal diseases.

SEED DISTRIBUTION

To help you distribute grass seed evenly, use a plastic flower pot with several holes in the bottom as a shaker. Once you know how much area a pot full of grass seed covers, this method will help you sow at a consistent rate.

LAYING SOD

Making a lawn from sod can be one of the most instantly gratifying garden jobs. Once you have prepared the site, the next step is easy, and the results are immediate. Always buy good-quality sod from a reputable supplier; cheap sod may be infested with weeds, pests, and diseases.

STORING SOD

● **Rolls** Sod is often delivered in rolls. Order it for delivery on the day you need it; sod should not be left rolled up for more than a day or two.

Unrolling sod

If you cannot use the sod right away, you must unroll it. If you do not, the grass will deteriorate rapidly. Once the sod is unrolled, water it, and keep it moist until you are ready to lay it.

GOOD LAYING PRACTICE

● **Best time** Sod can be laid most of the year, but late summer, early autumn, or early spring are the best times. Avoid very wet, dry, or cold weather.

Staggering rows

Lay the first row alongside a straight edge. To lay the next row, kneel on a board to protect the sod. Stagger the seams to give an even finish, and brush top-dressing into any gaps.

TRADITIONAL TIP

Boxing sod

If you are using sod lifted from another area of your yard, it may be uneven. To trim these pieces so they are the same depth, place each piece upside down in a box of the correct depth, then scrape off excess soil with any suitable sharp implement. Re-lay the sod as soon as possible.

SHAPING SOD

The edges of a newly laid lawn are formed by the ends of the sod pieces, which will need to be shaped. It is easier to do this after laying the sod than beforehand. The same technique can be used for reshaping the lawn once it is established.

DEALING WITH EDGES

● **Sharp spade** Use a sharp spade to shape sod if you do not have a half-moon edger.
● **Straight edge** Use two pegs and some string to mark off a straight edge. Drive the pegs into the ground, then mark off the line by stretching the string taut between the two pegs. Cut just inside the line.
● **Watering** Do not water a new lawn until you have finished shaping the edges. Watering before cutting will make it hard to make a sharp cut, and will increase the amount of damage done as you stand on the sod.

MARKING AND CUTTING A CURVE

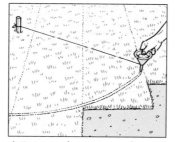

1 Drive a short piece of wood into the ground, and tie a piece of string to it. Pull the string tight, then attach a funnel to the string. Fill the funnel with sand, and use the funnel to mark off an accurate and even curve on the sod.

2 When you have finished marking the curve on the sod, use a half-moon edger to cut alongside it. To make a sharp, accurate cut, stand directly above the edger and cut into the sod with a straight, downward motion.

PLANTING IN A LAWN

A N EXPANSE OF PURE GREEN is ideal in some situations, but you may decide to break up and enliven the area. Whether you choose to plant bulbs, shrubs, or trees, or to introduce an island bed (see p. 452), the effect can be dramatic.

PLANTING BULBS

Many bulbs are suitable for growing in lawns, especially those that flower in the spring. Once they are established, most bulbs naturalize well and multiply each year. Planting bulbs in a lawn is easier if you cut the grass as short as possible beforehand.

PLANTING SMALL BULBS

Cutting turf
Make a cut in the turf, and peel back the flaps. Turn the soil over lightly, and add fertilizer. Set the bulbs in place, replace the turf, then tamp it down by hand or with the back of a rake.

PLANTING LARGE BULBS

Scattering bulbs
To create a random, informal display, scatter bulbs over the planting area. While planting the bulbs, make sure they are not touching one another to prevent the spread of diseases.

BULBS IN GRASS

● **Choosing** Choose bulbs with relatively small foliage. Dwarf cultivars of *Narcissus* work well. Small foliage is especially important if you are planting in an area you need to mow.
● **Preparation** Before planting bulbs, cut the grass short to make the job easier.
● **Planting hole** When using a bulb planter, make sure that the base of the bulb is firmly in contact with the soil.
● **Feeding** Feed naturalized bulbs once a year to ensure that they continue to grow and flower well (see p. 527).

NATURALIZING BULBS

Drifts of naturalized bulbs in a lawn can look stunning, but try to keep the extent of a drift in proportion to the size of the lawn. If you are planting a small area, it may be best to use dwarf bulb varieties. Always consider what the drift will look like once flowering is over.

CARING FOR BULBS IN GRASS

● **Soil** Make sure that the soil is not too dry for the type of bulb you choose. The soil underneath trees and large shrubs is often very dry.
● **Flowering** When bulbs become overcrowded, they may flower poorly. Prevent this by dividing and replanting clumps regularly (see p. 596).
● **Foliage** Leave *Narcissus* foliage intact for at least six weeks after flowering; if it is tied up or cut back any sooner, flowering will be affected the following year.

● **Feeding** If bulbs in grass need feeding, use a high-phosphorus fertilizer to encourage flowering (see p. 525). Do not use a nitrogen-rich fertilizer; if you do, the grass will grow at the expense of the growth of the bulbs.

SHAPING DRIFTS

● **Drifts** Plant bulbs in naturally shaped, uneven drifts with irregular edges. If planting more than one area, make each one a slightly different shape and size.

SUITABLE BULBS

● **Economical choice** Daffodils and other narcissi are often naturalized. Purchased in large quantities, they are reasonably priced and can produce a great show over a number of years.
● **Snowdrops (***Galanthus***)** These naturalize well and quickly increase in number.
● ***Crocus*** Select a complete mixture of colors, or restrict your choice to just one or two. Choose crocuses that reach the same height.

PLANTING A WILDFLOWER MEADOW

W hen surrounded by grass, wildflowers can transform an uninteresting or unattractive patch of land into a flower-rich area that attracts insects and other wildlife into the yard. Choose fine grasses, such as bents and fescues, that will not overwhelm the other plants.

SOWING SEED

Add seed to sand in bucket

Sowing evenly
To ensure that the seeds are evenly distributed, mix grass seed, wildflower seed, and some fine sand together in a bucket before sowing. Do not fertilize the soil beforehand.

USING AN EXISTING SITE
● **Soil** Wildflowers thrive in poor soil. If your lawn is not growing well, consider turning it into a wildflower meadow.

Planting holes
Use a trowel or bulb planter to make holes in existing grass. Plant up with pot-grown wildflowers. For the most natural effect, plant several of a single type in each group.

BUYING SEED
● **Conservation** Buy wildflower seed from a reputable source. Seeds of wild origin may carry diseases or pests; make sure that you buy commercially cultivated wildflower seeds.

MAINTENANCE
● **Cutting a meadow** Never cut the grass until the flowers have set seed; otherwise, you may seriously limit the meadow's life span.
● **Infertile soil** Never feed a wildflower area, since these flowers thrive in soil that is poor and infertile. Feeding invariably causes excessive growth of grass and weeds at the expense of the wildflowers.

ADDING INTEREST

T ake a good look at your lawn before you decide how to make it more interesting. A tree could create a visual break, for example, but what effect would it have on the rest of your yard? If your grass is not thriving, it may be best to abandon the idea of a lawn altogether.

PLANTING A TREE

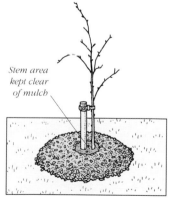

Stem area kept clear of mulch

Digging a hole
When planting a tree in a lawn, make the hole three or four times the diameter of the tree's root ball to minimize competition from grass. Lay a mulch 2–3 in (5–7 cm) deep around the tree.

LAWN ALTERNATIVES
● **Maintenance** Areas of lawn that are difficult to maintain are perfect for shrubs, bulbs, or single trees. A thriving planted area looks much better, and is easier to maintain, than grass that grows poorly.
● **Island bed** Break up a large expanse of grass by creating an island bed. Plant this up with herbaceous plants or shrubs and bulbs so that it looks good throughout the year.
● **Damp areas** Grass in very damp areas is quickly invaded by moss and other weeds. A site like this is ideal for planting up with moisture-loving plants, or for converting into a bog garden (see p. 573).

BRIGHT IDEA

Plants help to keep soil on slope in place

Planting a slope
The angle of a slope may make it extremely difficult to mow, especially if the slope is extensive. Instead of putting in grass, try planting the slope with groundcover plants and climbers.

LAWN MAINTENANCE

I F YOU WANT A LAWN TO BE PROUD OF, you need to do a certain amount of routine maintenance. The results you achieve are almost entirely dependent on the amount of time and effort you put into caring for your lawn.

MOWING A LAWN

R egular mowing is essential if a lawn is to look good. Mowing must be done to the correct height for the time of year. If left too long, a lawn will become yellow and uneven when cut; cutting too short can scalp a lawn. Both of these extremes encourage weak grass.

ESTABLISHING AND MAINTAINING A NEAT EDGE

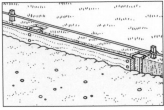

Buried edging
Use a narrow strip of lumber, corrugated metal, or plastic lawn edging to create a buried edge. Set it so that most of it is buried in the soil but the top is slightly higher than the grass roots.

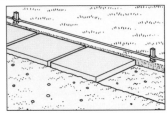

Mowing strip
A mowing strip made from bricks or narrow paving slabs prevents grass from spreading into adjacent flower beds. Instead of using edging shears, simply mow over the edges.

CUTTING GRASS
● **Dry weather** Avoid mowing in dry weather. If you do mow, raise the blades so that the grass is not cut very short.
● **Wet weather** Do not mow if the ground is very wet. This will encourage soil compaction, and the wet clippings may clog the mower.
● **Lawn edging** Always set edging lower than the grass. It must be level with, or only slightly higher than, the roots of the grass. If set too high, it could damage your mower.

TRIMMING EDGES

E ven if your lawn is growing well, it will still look untidy if the edges are left uncut, or if they are uneven. Once lawn edges start to collapse, it is better to recut them than to try to neaten them up. Even on neat lawns, it is worth doing this once or twice a year.

STRAIGHT EDGES

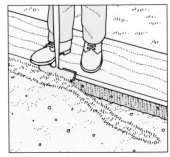

Using a board
Use a board to guide you when cutting a lawn edge with a half-moon edger. This will ensure that you make a straight edge and will prevent you from crushing the edge when you step on it.

SUITABLE TOOLS
● **Tools** Use edging shears to trim or cut lawn edges regularly. Once or twice a year, use a half-moon edger to neaten the edges. This tool cuts cleanly through soil and through any grass that has escaped into the borders.
● **Adjustable heads** Some lawn trimmers have an adjustable head that allows you to use them for edging as well as for cutting. Check for this feature before you buy.
● **Cutting technique** Cut down through the roots, and keep the edger in a vertical position. Compost any trimmings.

TRADITIONAL TIP

Frozen grass
Do not walk on frozen or frost-covered grass. This causes damage that makes the grass susceptible to diseases such as *Fusarium* patch.

FEEDING A LAWN

Your lawn will need feeding if it is to grow dense and lush. When grass is mowed regularly, it responds by growing more, which uses a lot of energy. There are different methods of feeding; choose the one that best suits your lawn and your budget.

APPLICATION RATES

Estimating quantity
Use four flower pots to mark off a test area measuring 1 sq yd (1 sq m). Weigh out the quantity of fertilizer recommended for this area, and apply it using another flower pot. Use this as a guide for feeding the rest of the lawn.

APPLYING FERTILIZERS
● **Selecting fertilizers** Choose the right fertilizer for the time of year. Some formulations are more suitable for spring application; others are more appropriate for autumn.
● **Late feeding** Avoid feeding late in the year, since this can promote new growth, which is vulnerable to winter damage and fungal attack.
● **Avoiding scorch** Use a liquid lawn fertilizer if the weather is very dry, or if a dry spell is forecast. This minimizes the likelihood of scorch.
● **Excess fertilizer** Avoid over-application or double-dosing the lawn; this can scorch grass.

BRIGHT IDEA

Feed the birds
If you have starlings feeding on grubs in your lawn, you should not need to apply insecticides, unless the grub infestation is particularly severe. The hungry birds will do the work for you.

WEEDING A LAWN

No matter how well you plant your lawn and subsequently maintain it, some weeds are bound to appear. For small areas, hand weeding may be the answer (see p. 538), but in most cases a chemical weedkiller is necessary to rid the lawn of weeds.

USING A DRIBBLE BAR
● **Special attachment** Apply a selective weedkiller using a dribble bar. Keep one watering can just for weedkillers.

Applying weedkiller
Use a dribble bar for accurate application with the lowest risk of contaminating plants. More than one application may be necessary for stubborn weeds.

IMPROVING DRAINAGE
● **Aeration** Prevent moss from growing on damp, compacted soil by aerating the lawn regularly (see p. 571).

Eliminating moss
Apply moss killer, and wait for the specified time before raking any dead moss out. If it is not dead, you will spread the spores and make the problem worse.

USING WEEDKILLER
● **When to apply** To avoid accidental contamination of garden plants, choose suitable weather and time of day for applying lawn weedkillers (see p. 534).
● **Saving time** Do two jobs at once by using a combined fertilizer and weedkiller.
● **Strength** Select a weedkiller with two or more active ingredients to increase the chances of killing all weeds.

WEEDKILLER SAFETY
● **Reading instructions** Most lawn weedkillers are safe for pets, wildlife, and humans. If applying a liquid weedkiller, allow time for the treated area to dry before use. Check the label for details (see p. 534).

LAWN PROBLEMS

THE WEAR AND TEAR ON A LAWN can be considerable, especially if the lawn is subjected to heavy use. Both the weather and the type of soil you have in your yard can affect the sorts of problems your lawn may develop.

REPAIRING A DAMAGED EDGE

Neat edges are just as important as the lawn itself. However well maintained a lawn is, the overall effect will be spoiled if the edges are left untrimmed or damaged. Edges that have been damaged in only one or two small areas can be repaired very easily.

LIFTING AND TURNING TURF

1 To repair a damaged edge, use a half-moon edger to cut an accurate square of turf around the damage (see right). Carefully lift the turf, and turn it around so that the damaged area faces the lawn.

2 Re-lay the turf, checking the level, and reseed the damaged area with suitable grass seed mixed with a little topsoil. Water well. Away from the edge, the damaged area will be able to recover quickly.

CUTTING TURF
● **Accuracy** Always cut a section of turf into an accurate, regular square or oblong shape so that it fits in place when rotated 180 degrees.

PROTECTING EDGES
● **Mowing strips** Consider installing a mowing strip or brick edge. Both of these will protect edges (see p. 568).
● **Using containers** Give frequently damaged areas alongside a path a rest by placing a stable container of flowers on the path by the damaged area.

REPAIRING A DAMAGED PATCH

Localized soil conditions or frequent heavy use by children may cause parts of an otherwise healthy, vigorous lawn to deteriorate. The resulting patches can spoil the appearance of the entire lawn. If ignored, the problem may become worse, so always take prompt action.

LAWN REPAIRS
● **Timing** The best time to do lawn repairs is when grass seed or sod is most likely to establish quickly and thoroughly. Spring and late summer or early autumn are generally the best times of year for this task.
● **Starting again** If damage to a lawn is extensive, or if it recurs frequently, this could suggest a fundamental problem. It may be best to replant the whole area, but be sure to prepare it thoroughly first.

REPLACING DAMAGED TURF

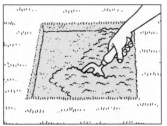

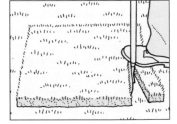

1 Use a half-moon edger to cut around the damaged area, and remove the turf with a spade. Lightly turn over the exposed soil, and incorporate a liquid or granular fertilizer. Firm the surface before resodding.

2 Try to use grass of the same type and quality as the original in order to achieve a good match. Place the new sod in the hole, and use a half-moon edger to cut it to size. Firm the sod in, and water.

HEAVY-USE AREAS

Some parts of a lawn are more likely than others to be subjected to heavy use – around a barbecue, a children's play area, or strips used as shortcuts, for instance. These areas will probably need more attention than other areas that get less use.

IMPROVING DRAINAGE
● **Annual maintenance** Poor drainage is often the cause of poor grass growth. Improve drainage by aerating and top-dressing once a year in autumn. This improves root growth and rain penetration.

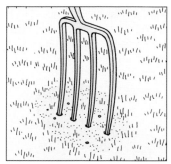

Spiking a lawn
Aerate compacted areas using a garden fork. Drive the fork into the lawn to a depth of at least 4 in (10 cm). Repeat this action every 6 in (15 cm) or so, easing the fork backward and forward each time to enlarge the holes.

LAWN MAINTENANCE
● **Top-dressing** After spiking a lawn (see left), use a brush to work a sandy top-dressing mixture into all the holes. Doing this will create long-lasting drainage channels.
● **Aerating large areas** If you need to aerate a large area, consider renting a power aerator machine. This tool will remove cores of soil every time it is driven into the turf, and is especially useful for aerating heavy soil.
● **Mowing height** Never cut grass very short in a heavily used area. A regular schedule of feeding, watering, and general maintenance (see p. 568–569) will encourage replacement grass to grow quickly, densely, and vigorously.
● **Making a path** An area that is subjected to heavy use may benefit from the installation of a path. Use stepping-stones to create a pathway (see below).

PLAY AREAS

To help protect the grass under a swing or other play equipment, secure sturdy netting to the ground with U-shaped staples. If this does not give enough protection, reseed the area with a specially formulated mixture of tough grasses (see p. 562), after incorporating ground-up tires in the soil (see p. 454). Or, change the surface completely: Use 2–3 in (5–7 cm) of finely chipped bark in areas that are prone to damage.

HOMEMADE PAVING

Making your own paving slabs allows you to design exactly the shape and size that you want, and for a fraction of the cost of manufactured slabs. If you want colored slabs, buy concrete dye to mix in with the cement mixture. To make an irregular surface on your slabs, lay a crisscross of small twigs in the bottom of the mold, and pour the mix carefully so that you do not dislodge them.

Use a flat wooden board

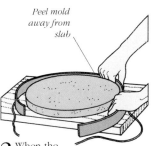

Peel mold away from slab

1 Use semirigid, smooth plastic or metal to form the sides of the paving slab mold. Allow for expansion during setting by tying the side pieces together with string or plastic tape.

2 Put the mold on a wooden base, and make sure that there are no gaps for the concrete mix to seep out. Carefully fill the mold with concrete. Wipe up any spillage with a damp cloth.

3 When the concrete has set properly (allow about 48 hours for this), remove the mold. Protect the slab from frost until the concrete is completely dry.

WATER FEATURES

QUICK REFERENCE

Introducing Water, p. 573

Water Plants, p. 575

Pond Maintenance, p. 577

Pond Repair, p. 579

*I*NTRODUCING WATER INTO A GARDEN *instantly adds life. The sight or sound of water helps to give a feeling of calm and relaxation, whatever the size or style of the garden. The water will soon attract all kinds of wildlife, too (see p. 551). If you do not have room for a pond, add a small water feature instead.*

BASIC EQUIPMENT

● **Creating ponds** To convert an old half barrel into a miniature pond, use a wire brush, scraper, paintbrush, and wood preservative. Wear rubber gloves to protect your hands. Heavy-duty plastic can be used to line a bog garden. Use a garden hose to fill a large pond.

● **Siting and maintaining plants** When positioning planted-up containers, soft twine is useful for lowering down the plants. Gravel can be used for weighing the plants down and keeping them in place. Lining a container with burlap trimmed with scissors helps to retain the soil around the plant's roots. You may need a sharp knife to trim water plants. An old colander is an effective piece of equipment for removing unwanted algae and other weeds from the surface of the pond.

● **Protecting your pond** Plastic netting is useful for catching fallen leaves, which can cause the buildup of toxic gases. A log will help to protect your pond from ice damage.

Wire brush

Paintbrush

Colander

Rubber gloves

Gravel

Scissors

Twine

Sharp knife

Wide gauge

Log

Narrow gauge

Garden hose

Plastic netting

Scraper

WARNING!

Always install electrical equipment properly; use a professional, if necessary. Be sure that it is inspected and serviced regularly.

Wood preservative

Burlap

Heavy-duty plastic

INTRODUCING WATER

BEFORE CHOOSING A WATER FEATURE, take the time to look at the variety of features offered in catalogs and at garden centers. Consider the style, shape, and size, and think about how the feature will fit in with the rest of your garden.

POND SAFETY

Always consider the potential danger of water in a garden used by children. If you feel a pond is unsuitable, there are many features you can buy or make yourself that do not require deep water. Existing features can be made safe by filling them with smooth pebbles.

MAKING WATER SAFE

● **Natural barrier** Block access to a pond by creating a miniature rock garden or a wide planting strip around it.
● **Pond covering** Place heavy-duty mesh across the surface to keep young children out.
● **Shallow end** Make a shallow end to a pond, and line it with large stones to help children climb out if they fall in.
● **Water pots** Using a selection of pots and a pump is the safest way of introducing water to a garden (see p. 574). However, do not allow water to accumulate to any depth.

RAISED POND

Creating a barrier
A raised pond is less dangerous than a pond at ground level. A child would have to climb in, rather than fall in, which is how accidents usually occur.

BUBBLE FOUNTAIN

Trickling water
A bubble fountain is an attractive and safe alternative to a pond. Water is pumped up through the center of an object, then trickles down over pebbles.

MAKING A BOG GARDEN

Some of the most interesting plants can be grown around the edges of a pond in boggy or marginal areas. You may even prefer to drain the central area of water and have a larger area purely for marginal plants. It is possible to make a bog garden even if you do not have a pond.

DIGGING AND PREPARING A SITE

1 Dig out the designated area, and line it with a sheet of heavy-duty plastic. Use a fork to make a few holes in the plastic to allow excess water to drain away.

2 Fill the hollow with garden soil, and firm gently. Water thoroughly, adding the water in stages so that it soaks right through. Leave overnight to settle before planting up.

PLANNING A BOG

● **Size** A large bog garden does not dry up as quickly as a very small one, so is easier to keep looking good.
● **Different depths** Slope the sides of a bog garden, or cut shelves into it to provide varying depths of soil. The wider the range of conditions, the more plants you will be able to grow successfully.
● **Attracting wildlife** Make a small depression in the bog garden, and line it with a tray or basin to make a mini-pool to provide water for wildlife.

USING CONTAINERS

Water in the garden does not have to be restricted to ponds or pools. Features such as freestanding ponds, bubble fountains, and spouts provide the sight and sound of running water, and all are suitable for small areas – or even a conservatory.

SUITABLE CONTAINERS
● **Durability** All water containers must be frostproof, since they are especially vulnerable to extensive damage from frost.
● **Avoiding toxins** Do not use containers that are coated with flaking paint, which could harm plants or fish.
● **Unique feature** Try a combination of pots piled on top of each other. Use a pond pump to circulate the water from one pot to another.

ELECTRICAL SAFETY
● **Cables** Make sure that any electrical cabling is buried underground in a conduit to protect it from damage.

TERRACOTTA POTS

Bubbling water
Used singly or in groups, pots make an attractive water feature. A bubbling spout of water coming from each one provides both movement and the relaxing sound of moving water. Pots such as these can be used in even the smallest garden.

SUITABLE PLANTS

Single dwarf waterlilies, such as *Nymphaea alba* 'Pygmaea', or water hyacinths (*Eichhornia crassipes*) work well in a small pond or in a container. Many normal water plants can be used, but because of their potential size, they will need to be divided and cut back regularly.

Nymphaea alba 'Pygmaea'

MAKING A BARREL POND

A half-barrel miniature pond is particularly suitable for a small or overcrowded garden. It is also portable, which allows you to take it with you if you move. In addition, you can move it out of a central spot into a secluded area when the plants begin to die back in winter.

PREPARING THE WOOD

Coat inside of barrel with sealant

Sealing the surface
Use a scraper and wire brush to scrape off all loose or rotted wood on the inside. Make sure that the wood is completely dry before applying plenty of sealant (see right) with a paintbrush. Allow this to dry thoroughly before applying a second coat.

BEFORE PLANTING UP
● **Sealant** Make sure that the sealant you use is not toxic to plants and animals.
● **Suitable weather** Do not attempt to apply sealant in frosty or extremely cold weather; the sealant may not work effectively.
● **Drying** Allow the sealant to dry thoroughly out of direct sunlight or frost. Wait to fill the barrel with water until the sealant is completely dry.
● **Metal bands** Treat any rust, and repaint the metal bands.
● **Allow to stand** Make sure that the barrel is watertight by allowing it to stand full of water for several hours. Discard this water, and refill before planting up.

SITING A HALF BARREL

Standing or burying
You can stand a barrel pond on almost any surface in the yard, such as a gravel area, or a paved patio or terrace. Alternatively, you can partially bury a barrel in soil in a suitable spot in the garden, or sink it to just beneath the level of its rim.

WATER PLANTS

I T IS PLANTS THAT BRING A POND TO LIFE, and the combination of plants and water that brings wildlife to a pond. There are plenty of water plants to choose from; hardy plants are easier to maintain than those requiring special attention.

PLANTING DEPTHS

D ifferent water plants have different needs and preferences. Of these needs, planting depth is the most important. If planted at an unsuitable depth, even a vigorous plant will fail to flourish. If you are building a pond, incorporate shelves to create different depths.

SITING WATER PLANTS

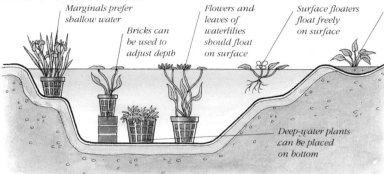

Marginals prefer shallow water

Bricks can be used to adjust depth

Flowers and leaves of waterlilies should float on surface

Surface floaters float freely on surface

Bog plants thrive in constantly wet, but not submerged, soil at edges of ponds

Deep-water plants can be placed on bottom

Correct depth
Make sure that you place plants at the correct depth for the species. Measure depth as the distance from the top of the soil in the pot to the surface of the water.

ADJUSTING DEPTH
● **Stacking bricks** Use bricks to place a plant at exactly the right depth. If necessary, you can remove some of the bricks as the plant grows.

SURFACE FLOATERS
● **Deterring algae** Use surface floaters to provide shade, which deters algae. Some surface floaters grow rapidly, so they may require thinning.

MARGINAL PLANTS
● **Wildlife shelter** Include marginal plants in your planting design. Not only do they look good, they also provide shelter for wildlife.

OXYGENATING PLANTS

Oxygenating plants are essential for a healthy pond. The oxygen released from their leaves helps to deter algae, especially during the summer. Some oxygenators need to be planted; others should be left to float on the surface.

● **Planting oxygenators** Some oxygenators are planted as bunches of unrooted cuttings. Prepare a small container (see p. 576), then insert several bunches together.
● **Keeping wet** Keep oxygenating plants moist until they are ready to plant. Even while being planted, they should not be exposed to the air any longer than absolutely necessary.

SUITABLE PLANTS
Callitriche spp., *Ceratophyllum demersum, Elodea canadensis; Fontinalis antipyretica, Hottonia palustris, Lagarosiphon major, Potamogeton crispus.*

Potamogeton crispus

TIME-SAVING TIP

Eliminating duckweed
New water plants often harbor tiny duckweed plants, which multiply rapidly. Save time and frustration by rinsing all new water plants.

PLANTING UP

Like any new planting, a newly planted pond takes time to become established, but it will soon take shape. For best results, choose plants for as many depths as possible, and include a few surface floaters. In addition, select plants with striking foliage.

BASKET LININGS
● **Burlap** Use basket linings to help keep soil around the roots of a plant without interfering with the flow of water. Burlap is traditionally used for this purpose, but coconut-fiber hanging basket liners also work well.

PLANTING CONDITIONS
● **Keeping moist** Water plants are easily damaged by dry conditions, so make every attempt to minimize this risk by keeping them in water until you are ready to plant up. Always plant in the shade, never in direct sunlight.

GRAVEL
● **Preventing disturbance** A 1-in (2.5-cm) thick layer of gravel on the soil surface helps to keep the soil and plant in place. It also prevents disturbance by fish or other pond creatures, and helps to weigh the pot down.

PLANTING A WATER PLANT IN A BASKET

Trim excess burlap

Position plant in center

Add gravel to just beneath rim of basket

1 Choose a basket large enough to hold the root system of the plant when the plant is fully grown. Line the basket with burlap, and fill it halfway with aquatic soil to hold the burlap in place.

2 Place the plant in the center of the basket. Add more soil as necessary, and firm gently. Top up the soil to within about 1 in (2.5 cm) of the basket rim. Water the plant gently; do not flood the basket.

3 Gently top-dress the soil with a layer of horticultural gravel or tiny stones. Take great care not to bury any small leaves as you do this, or to damage the vulnerable young shoots and stems.

SUITABLE MATERIALS
● **Soil** Use aquatic soil, not garden soil. Aquatic soil contains the correct amount of nutrients for healthy growth.
● **Gravel** Use horticultural or special aquatic gravel. Avoid builder's gravel, which may contain several contaminants.
● **Alternative containers** Try using plastic crates, which you can buy in most supermarkets at a fraction of the cost of special pond baskets.
● **Taking notes** Always keep a record of the water plants you use and where you plant them. This information will come in handy if you ever need to replace the plants.

ADDING HANDLES

Thread string through holes in basket

Lowering a water plant
Position a planted basket easily and safely by attaching string handles to opposite sides of the basket's rim. Allow enough string to lower the basket to the correct depth, whether this is on a shelf or in the middle of a large pond.

ANCHORING A PLANT

Young plants, especially those with small root systems, are easily dislodged. Use several large stones, or an extra-deep layer of gravel, to help anchor a plant and keep its roots beneath the soil. The extra weight also helps to keep the container in place.

POND MAINTENANCE

Although a pond or water feature requires a lot less maintenance than many other areas of a garden, it may deteriorate over time if left unattended. A little routine maintenance should keep everything in order.

REMOVING WEEDS

Weeds can build up in water very quickly, especially if a pond has not yet reached a good, natural balance. Unwelcome water weeds can be present in the soil of new plants (see p. 575), while other weeds may be introduced by visiting birds and other wildlife.

BLANKET WEED

Using a stick
Blanket weed is formed from a very dense, matlike growth of algae. Left to grow unchecked, this weed will soon clog the water. Use a stick to remove it, turning the stick slowly in one direction to gather up the weed in large quantities.

DEALING WITH WEEDS
● **Natural balance** A new pond invariably turns bright green with algae soon after it is planted up. However, do not be tempted to clear it out and refill with fresh water, since this usually makes it worse. Be patient; the situation should improve once a natural balance is established.
● **Seasonal growth** Algal blooms and duckweed infestations are usually seasonal; depending on the temperatures, most die down in autumn or winter. Keep a close eye out for any reappearance in spring, and remove them promptly.

DUCKWEED

Using a colander
Duckweed floats on the surface of the water and can be scooped off a small pond with a large sieve or colander. Use a slow skimming or scooping motion to gather it up. Remove as much of the weed as you possibly can; duckweed multiplies rapidly.

DISPOSAL OF DUCKWEED

Burying duckweed
Duckweed is a natural survivor and spreads very easily. Once you have removed it, never leave it lying around. Dispose of it safely by burying it in a deep hole, or by putting it in the compost pile or in a garbage can.

PREVENTING WEEDS
● **Surface floaters** Use surface floaters such as waterlilies. Algae thrives in the sun, and the large leaves of these plants help to provide shade.
● **Fish** Overstocking with fish can cause a sudden and dramatic increase in algal growth, due largely to the nitrogenous material in fish excreta. Combat this with oxygenating plants (see p. 575).

LARGE PONDS
● **Removing duckweed** Hold a board vertically, and pull it slowly across the surface of the water to collect the duckweed. Remove with a colander or sieve.

GREEN TIP

Using straw
To help keep a pond clear of unwanted algae, stuff a leg of panty hose with straw. Tie both ends securely, and attach a weight to the bundle before submerging it.

WINTER CARE

Autumn is the time of year when a water feature or a pond will need the most maintenance. While many plants die back over winter, it is essential that the remaining plants, water, and living creatures are protected from the effects of plummeting temperatures.

LOW TEMPERATURES
● **Feeding fish** Fish do not eat much in the winter, since their metabolism slows down. Do not allow fish food to accumulate in the water.
● **Plywood cover** If severe weather is forecast, cover a small pond or water feature with a piece of plywood. Make sure that the water plants are not deprived of light for too long, however.
● **Heating the water** If you have a pump, consider replacing it with a water heater during the late autumn and winter months. Be sure to put the heater in place before the really cold weather arrives.

PROTECTING PLANTS
● **Using buckets** Protect tender plants by removing them from the water and placing them in a bucket of water. Leave the bucket in a sheltered, frost-free location until spring.

BRIGHT IDEA

Melting ice
Fill a saucepan with hot water, and rest it on the ice. Hold it there until it melts a hole in the ice, so that any potentially toxic gases can escape.

DIVIDING AND TRIMMING
● **Container plants** Divide any crowded water plants in early autumn. Treat them like herbaceous perennials, discarding any weak or damaged sections before replanting the rest (see p. 500).

Trimming leaves
In late autumn, trim back deteriorating and trailing foliage on all water plants, including marginal plants. Be sure not to let any leaves fall into the water; gather them up, and add them to the compost pile.

DEALING WITH ICE
● **Removing ice** Never smash up any ice on a pond, since the vibrations this would cause could seriously harm any fish or other wildlife.
● **Creating air space** If water freezes over, melt a hole in the ice. Carefully bail out water to lower the level by 1 in (2.5 cm). If the water freezes over again, any toxic gases will accumulate in the gap between the ice and the water.
● **Open water** Install a small submersible electric pump in the area of the pond to be left open. This will keep ice from forming while the water is aerated by the pump, regardless of the ambient temperature.

FALLEN LEAVES
● **Toxic gases** Prevent leaves from falling into the water. If the water freezes over, leaves can cause the buildup of methane and other toxic gases that are harmful to fish and other pond wildlife.

Catching falling leaves
Use rigid plastic netting to prevent leaves from falling into the water. To make collecting many of leaves easier, lay a curtain over the netting. When the curtain is covered with leaves, remove it, and shake it out.

AVOIDING ICE DAMAGE

Floating a log
As water freezes and expands, it can cause substantial damage to a pond or water container. To prevent this, float a log or plastic ball on the water. The floating object will absorb some of the pressure, thus alleviating pressure on the pond or container.

POND REPAIR

However carefully you install your pond, it may start to leak at some stage, and repairs will be necessary to maintain the water level. The method you use will depend entirely on the material from which your pond is made.

EMPTYING A POND

You will need to drain your pond before making any repairs. Most ponds can be drained either with an electric pump or by siphoning off the water. Small ponds and individual water features can be emptied by bailing out the water with a bucket.

SMALL POND

Removing contents
You may have to remove some or all of the pond's contents before making any repairs. Put plants, fish, and any other aquatic life into plastic buckets. Handle everything as carefully and as gently as possible.

CONCRETE PONDS
● **New lining** If a concrete or rigid-lined pond is leaking badly, you will probably need to reline it. Empty the pond, then simply lay a rubber liner over the old shell. Refill the pond with water.
●**Tiny cracks** Clean and dry the surface thoroughly, then paint the whole area with a commercial pond sealant.
● **Large cracks** To prolong the effectiveness of a repair, undercut the crack (see p. 606) so that it is wider at the base than it is at the surface.
● **Ice** In very cold areas, you may need to empty a concrete pond entirely to prevent damage from freezing water.

LARGE POND

Making a temporary pond
Provide a home for the contents of a large pond by making a temporary pond. Dig a hole, and line it with heavy-duty plastic. Fill it with water from your pond, and gradually add the plants and any pond animals.

REPAIRING CONCRETE

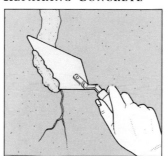

Filling a large crack
Concrete ponds are the most difficult to repair once they have sprung a leak. First, chisel out the crack with a chisel. Then fill it with waterproof cement, which should prevent further leakage. Follow this with a coat of pond sealant.

CHECKING PLANTS
● Unhealthy plants When removing plants from a pond, take the opportunity to dispose of any that show signs of disease or pest infestations.

TEMPORARY STORAGE
● **Providing shade** Be sure to store pond plants and creatures in the shade. Without the usual depth of water to protect them, they will be particularly susceptible to damage from high temperatures.
● **Providing protection** Place wire mesh over temporary containers to prevent cats and other animals from preying on any fish or frogs.

MENDING A POND LINER

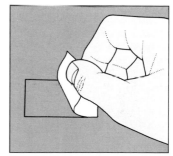

Patching a tear
Dry and clean the damaged area. Place double-sided adhesive sealing tape over the tear, and wait until it becomes sticky. Cut out a patch from a spare piece of liner, and press it firmly onto the adhesive, making sure that all edges are stuck down flat.

PROPAGATING PLANTS

QUICK REFERENCE

Seeds Outdoors, p. 582

Seeds Indoors, p. 584

Thinning Seedlings, p. 588

Layering Plants, p. 590

Taking Cuttings, p. 592

Dividing Plants, p. 595

PROPAGATING YOUR OWN PLANTS *is immensely satisfying and exciting. Growing plants from seed is the most common method of propagation, but it is not the only one. Other methods include layering, dividing, and taking cuttings. Whether you collect propagating material in your own garden or from a friend, you can quickly build up your collection of plants without having to spend a lot of money.*

EQUIPMENT FOR SOWING SEEDS OUTDOORS

You can achieve excellent results with minimal equipment by sowing seeds directly into the ground. This makes direct sowing extremely economical, even if you buy the seeds.

● **Surface preparation** The soil must be prepared properly before sowing. Use a rake to create a fine, level seedbed.
● **Warming the soil** Use black plastic or floating row covers to warm up the soil. Hold the plastic or row covers in place with bricks or large stones.
● **Marking** Use stakes and twine to mark off rows, which are particularly useful for sowing vegetable seeds.
A hand fork and trowel are useful for marking off straight lines for sowing annuals, and are also essential for moving or thinning seedlings and young plants. Use white sandbox or other fine sand in a plastic bottle to mark off areas when creating a mixed border of hardy annuals. Do not use builder's sand, which can harm the seedlings. Mark each area with a label.
● **Watering** Use a watering can to water seeds; the spray from a hose may be too strong.

Sand

Labels

Brick

Black plastic

Plastic bottle

Twine

Watering can

Trowel

Hand fork

Stakes

Rake

EQUIPMENT FOR SOWING SEEDS INDOORS

Although you need slightly more equipment for sowing seeds indoors than outdoors, much of it need not be specially purchased. A propagator, preferably one that is heated, is a useful item but not essential.

● **Sowing** Seed trays are available in either full or half sizes and are usually made from semirigid plastic. Invest in a selection of small plastic pots, and reuse any that come with plants you buy. Use a screen to remove the large lumps and partly decomposed twigs often found in soil mix. A light dusting of screened soil mix can also be used to cover fine seeds. A plant mister is useful for moistening the surface of soil mix with minimal disturbance to the seeds or seedlings.

● **Storing seed** Film canisters and envelopes make excellent containers for storing any seeds that you have collected, and for leftover seeds from any opened packets (see p. 587). Use paper towels and newspaper to dry seeds before storage.

● **Aftercare** Use plastic wrap to cover seed trays while the seeds germinate, to prevent the soil mix from drying out. Plastic wrap also protects the tiny seedlings from cold drafts, which can damage them.

● **Transplanting** A plastic dibber and fork are invaluable for transplanting seedlings.

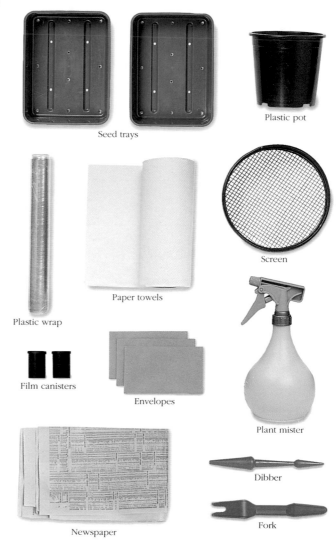

Seed trays

Plastic pot

Plastic wrap

Paper towels

Screen

Film canisters

Envelopes

Plant mister

Dibber

Newspaper

Fork

SEED-STARTING MIXES

Most seeds can be sown in any potting or seed-starting mix. The most important feature of these mixes is that they have an open texture and a suitable nutrient content. For healthy seedling growth, provide a relatively low level of nutrients; otherwise, the roots will be scorched and will die back.

Peat-free mix

Soil-based mix

All-purpose potting mix

Sowing Seeds Outdoors

Some seeds can be sown directly into the ground, without the need for trays, soil mix, or a propagator. This works particularly well for seedlings that resent root disturbance. Check each seed packet for individual seed requirements.

Sowing Vegetable Beds

Many vegetables can be raised successfully from seeds sown into the ground where they are to mature. To ensure success, prepare the soil by adding organic matter (see p. 478) and fertilizer (see p. 524) well before sowing. Keep all seeds and young plants well watered.

Straight Rows

Mark stake to indicate correct sowing depth

Making rows
Push a stake into the ground at each end of the proposed row. Tie string tightly between the two stakes to indicate the position of the row. Use another stake to mark a straight line along the string.

Good Soil Contact

Sowing seeds
Sprinkle seeds into a row, and cover them with soil by running the back of a rake down the middle of the row. Use the back of the rake to tamp down the soil gently so that the seeds are in close contact with the soil.

Early Sowings

Warming up the soil
Early sowings are possible if you warm up the soil first. A few days to a week before sowing, cover the prepared seedbed with a sheet of black plastic or floating row cover. Weigh down the edges with bricks or stones.

Soil Compaction

Reduce soil compaction when you sow seeds in a vegetable plot by standing on a board. If you do this whenever you work in the plot (use a brick and board bridge, if necessary), you will need to redig only every five years or so.

Successful Sowing

● **Seed stations** For most direct-sown vegetable seeds, sow two seeds at each station to allow for poor germination. Thin if more than one seed germinates in any one spot.
● **Intersowing** To save space, try sowing two different crops in a single row. Sow a slow-growing crop, such as parsnips or carrots, at well-spaced intervals, and a fast-growing crop, such as lettuce or radishes, in between.
● **Capturing heat** If you are using a floating row cover or black plastic, try to position it over the soil during the warmest part of the day.

Avoiding Disease

● **Soil condition** Sowing under cold, damp conditions may cause the seeds to rot. If the soil is very wet or frozen, delay sowing until conditions are more suitable.
● **Preventing disease** Water rows with a copper-based fungicide to reduce the risk of damping off (a fungal disease). Guard against slugs and snails (see p. 558).
● **Crop rotation** Rotate all vegetable crops to minimize the risk of disease. Some crops, such as beans and peas, are especially prone to foot- and root-rotting diseases that build up in the soil (see p. 546).

SOWING FLOWER BEDS

Propagating by seed produces a wealth of new plants with very little effort. A bright, colorful summer border is easy to achieve with direct sowing, and the only cost is that of a few packets of seeds. It is an ideal way to raise many annuals – and wildflowers, too.

MARKING OFF INDIVIDUAL AREAS FOR SOWING

1 Rake the soil level before marking individual areas to be sown. To mark off sowing areas, fill a plastic bottle with fine sand, and pour it out to mark off each separate area.

2 Rather than scattering the seeds, mark off straight rows for them within each area. You will then be able to distinguish between the seedlings and young weeds.

3 Cover the seeds with soil. Mark each area with a weather-resistant label. Push the labels firmly into the soil to prevent them from being dislodged by wind or animals.

SELF-SEEDING PLANTS

Shake plant over soil to scatter seeds

Scattering seed
Create new patches of flowers by lifting plants that have set seed. Shake the seedheads where you want new plants to grow.

SEEDS AND SEEDLINGS

● **Using colors** For an elegant effect, restrict yourself to a few colors when sowing a hardy annual border. Use a wider range of shades for an eye-catching display.
● **Good value** Save partially used seed packets from one year to the next (see p. 587).
● **Second choice** Transplant any seedlings you have thinned out from the main display into containers or into another patch of ground. They may be seconds, but most flowers will still look good if they are well watered and fed.

HARD-COATED SEEDS

● **Successful germination** Help seeds with hard coats to germinate by soaking them overnight in water. To encourage water absorption, file very hard seeds with a nail file before soaking them.

TIME-SAVING TIP

Keeping weeds down
Scatter the seeds of hardy annuals in the gaps and cracks between pavers to help prevent a patio from becoming overrun by unwelcome weeds.

SEEDS FOR DIRECT SOWING

Amaranthus caudatus,
Brachycome iberidifolia,
Calendula officinalis,
Centaurea cyanus,
Clarkia elegans, Consolida ajacis,
Convolvulus tricolor,
Dimorphotheca aurantiaca,
Echium lycopsis,
Eschscholzia californica,

Gilia lutea, Godetia grandiflora,
Gypsophila elegans,
Iberis umbellata, Linaria
maroccana, Lobularia
maritima, Lychnis viscaria,
Malcolmia maritima,
Nemophila menziesii,
Nigella damascena,
Papaver rhoeas, Reseda odorata.

SOWING SEEDS INDOORS

Sowing seeds in trays or pots, either in a greenhouse or on a windowsill, gives you control over the growth of the seedlings. The extra warmth is especially suitable for seeds that do not germinate reliably outdoors.

SOWING IN TRAYS

Trays are ideal containers for sowing seeds; they already have drainage holes and are the correct depth for the early development of seedlings. If you want to grow only a small number of any one type of seedling, choose trays that are divided into strips or cells.

SOWING SEEDS IN PLASTIC TRAYS

Place soil mix lumps on bottom of tray

1 Large lumps of soil mix inhibit seed germination. If you do not have a screen, remove large lumps from the soil mix by hand, and place them in the bottom of the tray.

Hold seed tray level

2 Use the bottom of an empty seed tray to level the soil mix. Holding the tray level, press it down firmly into the soil mix to create an ideal surface for sowing.

Cup your hand slightly

3 Dry your hands thoroughly, and place a small amount of seeds in the palm of one hand. Gently tap your palm with the other hand to distribute the seeds evenly.

TRADITIONAL TIP

Sowing fine seeds

Sowing fine seeds evenly can be difficult. To make it easier, fold a piece of cardboard or paper in half. Tip the seeds into the fold, and gently tap the cardboard with your finger to scatter the seeds over the soil mix.

SOWING SMALL SEEDS

Gently shake screen over seeds

Covering small seeds
Small seeds should not be covered with too much soil mix. To avoid dislodging the seeds when covering them, use a screen to shake a fine layer of soil mix over them.

SUCCESSFUL SOWING

● **Sticky hands** To stop seeds from sticking to your hands, sow seeds in a cool room, or run cold water over your wrist before you begin sowing.
● **Watering** Water the soil mix before you sow seeds, to prevent them from being washed into a heap.
● **Tiny seeds** Settle tiny seeds into the soil mix with a fine mist from a plant mister.
● **Light** If your seeds require light for germination, cover the tray with a sheet of glass or plastic wrap to prevent the soil mix from drying out.
● **Heat control** Too much or too little heat can hinder germination. Invest in a propagating thermometer.

SOWING IN POTS

Some seeds, particularly large ones, are best sown in individual pots, since they need room to develop. This also minimizes root disturbance when the seedlings are transplanted. Using separate pots is ideal if you are sowing only a small quantity of each seed.

PLANTING IN POTS

Seeds sown thinly in each pot

Filling gaps
Use thinly sown seedlings in pots as temporary gap fillers to provide spots of color in flower beds. You can plant out entire pots and then remove them once the beds fill out.

SOWING SWEET PEAS

Put one sweet pea seed into each tube

Avoiding root disturbance
Roll newspaper strips into 1½ in- (3 cm-) diameter tubes. Fill each one with soil mix, and moisten before sowing the seeds. Plant out each tube; the roots will grow through the newspaper.

SEEDLING CONTAINERS

Use empty household pots as seedling containers. Yogurt and dessert containers make good pots, and margarine tubs can be used as seed trays. Make sure that you clean all containers thoroughly, and remember to make drainage holes in the bottom.

LOOKING AFTER SEEDLINGS

The correct conditions and proper care are essential for growth once seeds have been sown. Always consult each seed packet for details on temperature and light requirements. When the seeds have germinated, the seedlings usually require a lower temperature.

CARING FOR SEEDLINGS
● **Using fungicide** Prevent fungal diseases from developing by drenching the soil mix with a copper-based fungicide before sowing seeds. Repeat once the seedlings have emerged.
● **Best conditions** Provide plenty of natural light, increase air circulation, and lower the temperature.
● **Sun scorch** Do not put developing seedlings in direct sunlight, since this may cause too great a rise in temperature.
● **Reflecting light** If light levels are low, place trays or pots of seedlings on aluminum foil. Put foil behind the seedlings, too, to ensure that they receive plenty of reflected light.

USING PLASTIC WRAP
● **Versatility** Cover seedlings with a sheet of plastic wrap to conserve moisture, keep out drafts, and keep the temperature constant.

Remove plastic wrap gently

Preventing condensation
Remove the plastic wrap from time to time to prevent the buildup of condensation. Allow any water droplets to run back into the tray or pot before replacing the plastic.

PROVIDING LIGHT
● **Lighting** Light is essential for the development of sturdy seedlings. Seedlings that do not receive enough light soon become pale and leggy.

Turn pots and trays regularly

Turning toward the light
Seedlings grown by a window or exposed to a one-sided light source will grow toward the light. Prevent them from becoming lopsided and bent by turning the container regularly.

IDEAL GERMINATION CONDITIONS

Some seeds are capable of germinating under almost any conditions, but most have fairly specific requirements. Temperature is a major factor. Check the recommended temperature for sowing, and make sure that you provide it throughout the germination period.

PROVIDING HEAT IN A GREENHOUSE

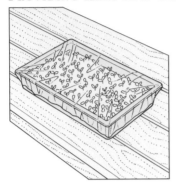

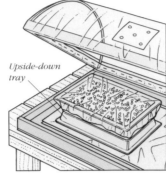

Upside-down tray

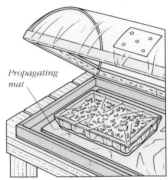

Propagating mat

Greenhouse bench
Seeds and seedlings that do not require much heat can be placed in a frame or on a greenhouse bench. Cover them with plastic wrap to help reduce temperature fluctuations and exposure to damaging drafts.

Indirect heat
Some seeds and seedlings can be damaged by high temperatures, but still require extra warmth. Place them on an upside-down tray in a propagator so that they are not in direct contact with the heated propagating mat.

Direct heat
Seeds that require high temperatures for germination can be placed directly on a heated propagating mat in a propagator. This makes it possible for them to benefit from the highest temperatures.

PROPAGATORS

● **Condensation** Wipe the inner surface of the lid regularly to remove condensation, which can reduce the amount of light reaching the seedlings if it is allowed to build up.
● **Algae** Wiping the lid of the propagator will also prevent the buildup of algae, which not only looks unsightly, but also prevents light from reaching the seedlings.

USING A PROPAGATOR
● **Uneven heat** The heating element in the propagator may supply heat unevenly. Find the warmest and coolest areas, and use them for the appropriate plants.
● **Water supply** Always keep the capillary matting at the bottom of a propagator moist. This ensures a constant supply of water for the seedlings.
● **Cleaning** After each use, clean out the propagator thoroughly to limit the risk of disease buildup. Take care not to wet the electrical apparatus.
● **Safety** If you are worried about the safety of your propagator, have it checked by a qualified electrician.
● **Bottle propagator** To make a basic propagator, cut off the bottom of a clear plastic bottle, remove the screw top, and place the top half of the bottle over a pot of seedlings.

MONEY-SAVING TIP

Ready-made propagator
Use the warmth of a linen closet to propagate seeds that do not need light. Check the temperature on each shelf with a thermometer to determine the best place for each tray. Cover the trays with plastic wrap, and check them daily. Remove each tray as soon as the first seedlings emerge.

COLLECTING AND STORING SEEDS

Collecting seeds from your own plants is great fun and can be a very inexpensive and exciting way to fill your beds and borders with color. Swap your seeds with friends and neighbors, too. Remember that home-saved seeds may not grow true to type.

CATCHING SEEDS
● **Paper bag** Most garden plants reliably set seed. Tie a paper bag loosely around ripe seedheads to catch the seeds as they are released.

COLLECTING SEEDS FROM VEGETABLES AND FRUITS
● **Plant variations** Many vegetable varieties will not produce plants identical to the parent plant, so be prepared for variations.

● **Diseases** Some viral diseases are seed-borne. Minimize the risk of producing unhealthy plants by collecting only from healthy-looking plants.

On a dry day, shake seeds onto folded paper

Remove seeds from fleshy fruits with thumb

Leave seeds to dry on paper towel

Collecting seedheads
Cut ripe seedheads off plants, and shake them to release the seeds inside. Store these in an envelope or paper bag. Mark each one clearly with the plant name and date of collection.

Scooping out seeds
Choose ripe, healthy-looking vegetables or fruits. Cut each one in half, and carefully scoop out the seeds. Examine them carefully, and discard any that do not look perfect.

Drying seeds
Dry home-saved seeds by spreading them out on a clean paper towel. Put this into a clean, dry seed tray, and allow the seeds to dry thoroughly. Store them in a cool, dry place.

STORING SEEDS
● **Suitable containers** Seeds are best stored in an airtight container. They must be completely free of moist plant material; otherwise, they may rot or start to germinate.

STORING PODS
● **Seed pods** Seeds in pods should not be stored in airtight conditions. To dry naturally, the pods require air circulation. Once the seeds are ripe, they can be removed.

Use folded paper to pour out seeds

Pods spaced out to allow good air circulation

Excluding light
Black film canisters are good for storing seeds. Be sure that the seeds are thoroughly clean and dry before putting them in the canisters, and remember to label each canister clearly.

Drying seed pods
Store pods on newspaper in a seed tray until they are quite dry. Do not apply artificial heat. When the pods are completely dry, carefully remove the seeds, and store them in paper bags.

CYCLAMEN SEEDS
Ripe seed capsule

● **Seed capsules** Collect seeds from hardy cyclamen as soon as the capsules begin to split open. Tie a paper bag loosely around the capsules to ensure that no seeds are lost.
● **Soaking seeds** To improve germination, remove the seeds from each capsule and soak them overnight. Sow them as soon as possible.

THINNING SEEDLINGS

ONCE SEEDLINGS HAVE EMERGED, they usually require thinning or transplanting. Although this is quite a delicate job, it gives you the chance to select the best seedlings, which you can then provide with a fresh supply of nutrients.

THINNING IN OPEN GROUND

Seedlings raised in open ground are usually thinned as soon as they are large enough to handle. A few seeds – mainly vegetables – are sown thinly and then transplanted. Thinning is best done twice, providing two chances to choose the most vigorous seedlings.

THINNING SEEDLINGS

Weak seedlings
Carefully remove any weak or diseased seedlings. Be careful not to disturb the roots of the remaining seedlings.

TRANSPLANTING PLANTS

Moisture loss
Use a hand fork to lift young plants. Immediately put them into a plastic bag to reduce moisture loss from the leaves.

MOVING SEEDLINGS
● **Before lifting** To reduce root damage, water the soil thoroughly before lifting plants for transplanting.
● **Cool temperatures** Thin or transplant seedlings and young plants during the coolest part of the day – preferably at dusk. This reduces both moisture loss and stress on the plants. The plants will also have sufficient time to recover before temperatures rise again.
● **Watering** To settle the soil around the roots, water well after thinning or transplanting.

THINNING IN POTS AND TRAYS

Seedlings raised indoors will need thinning or transplanting, too. The controlled conditions make the timing less critical, but you should still minimize stress to the seedlings by working out of direct sunlight. Water the seedlings well, both before and after transplanting them.

TRANSPLANTING AND WATERING SEEDLINGS

Remove seedling with widger

1 Ease the roots of the seedling out of the soil mix, then support it by gently holding it by the seed leaves. Do not hold the seedling by the stem or the true leaves.

2 Make a hole with a dibber, and carefully lower a seedling into the hole. Press the soil mix firmly around the seedling so the roots are in close contact with the mix.

Water is absorbed by soil

3 To prevent the soil mix from being washed away from the base of the seedlings, water them by placing the pot in water until the soil surface appears moist.

CARING FOR YOUNG PLANTS

Seedlings and young plants need special care and attention. Their stems and foliage are relatively soft, which makes them especially vulnerable. Young plants need to be weaned gradually so that they have time to adjust to their new conditions in the garden.

MAINTAINING PLANTS

● **Avoiding extremes** Young plants can suffer in extreme conditions. Do not subject them to very bright sunlight or very dark conditions. Avoid extremes in temperature, too.

● **Watering** A regular and adequate water supply is essential, since young root systems are easily damaged by erratic moisture levels.

● **Disease** Reduce the risk of fungal diseases by watering with a copper-based fungicide after transplanting or thinning.

● **Scorching** Soft foliage is easily scorched, especially if it is exposed to sunlight when wet. Keep moisture off the leaf surfaces, particularly in bright light and when temperatures are low.

PROTECTING YOUNG PLANTS FROM DAMAGE

● **Plant care** Protect plants from pests and diseases (see p. 544) and adverse weather conditions (see p. 522–523).

Making a mini-cloche
Put half a clear plastic bottle over seedlings or young plants to make a mini-cloche. Harden off the plants gradually by making holes in the bottle.

● **Pest barriers** Prevent pests from ever reaching young plants with a strategically placed barrier. Some barriers can also insulate large areas of plants from the cold.

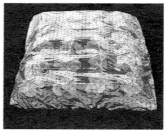

Floating row covers
Perforated plastic and fabric covers allow light and air to penetrate. They also protect against cold and pests. Weigh down or tuck in the edges.

MAKING A PLASTIC TUNNEL

Plastic tunnels are usually used to protect low-growing plants from extreme weather conditions (see p. 522-523). Make a tunnel to cover a small area of your vegetable patch. For each supporting hoop, you need 6.5 ft (2 m) of ½ in (12 mm) diameter flexible pipe and two 18 in (45 cm) lengths of dowel to fit inside the pipe. You will also need clear plastic, narrow strips of wood, and

1 Mark off the tunnel base with narrow strips of wood. Push a piece of dowel into each end of the pipe. Make hoops by pushing the dowels into the ground just inside the strips.

2 Place the hoops about 5 ft (1.5 m) apart along the length of the strips, and cover them with plastic. Wrap the plastic edges under the strips; hold down with thumbtacks.

3 Secure the plastic at the ends of the tunnel with bricks or large stones. Seal the tunnel for maximum warmth, and open it up to provide ventilation when the weather gets warm.

LAYERING PLANTS

Propagating plants by layering is not difficult. Plant stems are encouraged to produce roots, usually by bending them down to ground level and covering them with soil. Making a cut in the stems helps to stimulate the rooting process.

BASIC EQUIPMENT

Layering does not require much equipment. Some plants self-layer, needing little more than a covering of soil where the stem touches the soil.

● **Rooting hormone** Hormone rooting powder stimulates the natural rooting process. Treating the cut stem area produces the best results. A good-quality soil mix or rooting medium also encourages rapid rooting. This can be used in a sunken plastic pot, or it can be incorporated into the soil around the plant you are layering.

● **Other items** Stakes, twine, a sharp knife, and some metal pegs are useful for many types of layering techniques.

Soil mix

Hormone rooting powder

Plastic pots

Sharp knife

Twine

Metal pegs

Stake

SUITABLE PLANTS FOR LAYERING

Many commonly grown trees, shrubs, and climbers are propagated by layering. Those described as self-layering will root unaided when in contact with garden soil. Pot them up when they are well rooted.

Actinidia, Akebia, Andromeda, Aucuba, Carpenteria, Cassiope, Celastrus (S), *Chaenomeles, Chionanthus, Cissus, Corylopsis, Ercilla, Erica, Fothergilla, Hedera* (S), *Humulus, Hydrangea petiolaris* (S), *Kalmia, Laurus, Lonicera, Magnolia, Mandevilla, Osmanthus, Parthenocissus* (S), *Passiflora* (most), *Periploca* (S), *Pileostegia,*

Rhododendron, Rosa, Rubus, Scindapsus, Skimmia, Stachyurus, Strongylodon, Syringa, Trachelospermum (S), *Vaccinium corymbosum, Vitis amurensis, Vitis coignetiae, Wisteria.*

(S) – plants that are self-layering

Magnolia

BRIGHT IDEA

Foliar feeding
Invigorate a developing young plant by spraying the leaves with a foliar feed of water-soluble fertilizer. This method of feeding also helps to stimulate root growth, ensuring a well-developed and strong root system.

LAYERING TECHNIQUES

There are a number of layering techniques, all suited to different plants and to different purposes. Simple layering, as shown below using a clematis, is the most straightforward method. Propagating clematis in this way is best suited to the large-flowered hybrids.

CUTTING, ROOTING, AND SECURING A CLEMATIS

1 Sometime between autumn and spring, choose a vigorous, flexible stem that you can bend down to the ground. Make a diagonal cut on the lower side of the stem, preferably just below a node joint. Cut about halfway into the stem to form a "tongue."

2 Sink a pot of moist soil mix beneath the plant, close to the stem you are layering. Dip the cut stem, into hormone rooting powder, and shake off any excess. Hold the cut open with a piece of wood to ensure the powder gets right inside it.

3 Bury the cut area into the pot of soil mix. Hold it in place with a metal peg or a small piece of wire. Water the cut area well, and continue to water over the next few months. After six months, check for roots by pulling gently on the end of the stem.

IMPROVING THE SOIL
● **Soil condition** If rooting directly into the soil, improve the soil's texture and fertility by incorporating compost. If the soil is heavy, dig in some sand as well; good drainage is essential for healthy roots.

Use twine to tie shoot to stake

Avoiding moisture loss
Mound moist soil mix over the pegged area to prevent the soil from drying out and to encourage root development. Tie the shoot carefully to a stake to minimize any disturbance to the developing roots from wind.

STEMS AND SHOOTS
● **Healthy stems** Always choose healthy, flexible stems for layering. These are easy to bend down and most likely to produce good-quality plants.
● **Shoots** Prune the plant hard in the appropriate season to encourage shoots for layering.

OTHER METHODS
● **Serpentine layering** This method is suitable for climbing plants such as *Clematis, Celastrus, Campsis,* and *Schisandra.* Make a cut in a long, young stem close to each node. Peg the stem down with the buds exposed, to produce several plants along one stem.
● **Air layering** Shrubs such as *Hamamelis, Kalmia, Magnolia,* and *Rhododendron* respond well to air layering. Make a cut in the stem, and wrap it in moist sphagnum moss tied into position with plastic. New roots will grow into the moss.

MONEY-SAVING TIP

Mound layering
Instead of buying new heather plants, revitalize old, straggly heathers by mound layering. To do this, place a mound of rooting medium in the center of the plant, and firm it around the shoots. Moisten the medium. New roots will form in the rooting medium in about six months.

TAKING CUTTINGS

TAKING CUTTINGS IS AN ECONOMICAL WAY of increasing your stock. Remember, though, that cuttings have to survive until new roots have grown, so they need the best possible conditions and care throughout the rooting process.

BASIC EQUIPMENT

You probably already own most of what you need to raise cuttings. These items are all you need to produce plants from those in your garden, and from friends and neighbors, too.

● **Tools** Use a sharp knife or pruners to take cuttings.
● **Rooting mediums** A good-quality soil mix or rooting medium is suitable for rooting many cuttings. Some will root in garden soil, but this is not suitable for cuttings raised in pots. Hormone rooting powder helps to stimulate root formation. Choose a brand that contains a fungicide to deter fungal attack.
● **Identification tags** Labels are essential, since cuttings can look remarkably similar until they start to develop.
● **Containers** Plastic and terracotta pots are both suitable. Glass jars and yogurt pots can also be used (see p. 585).
● **Other items** Chicken wire (for securing softwood cuttings), rubber bands (for creating a mini-cloche), and plastic bags are also useful items.

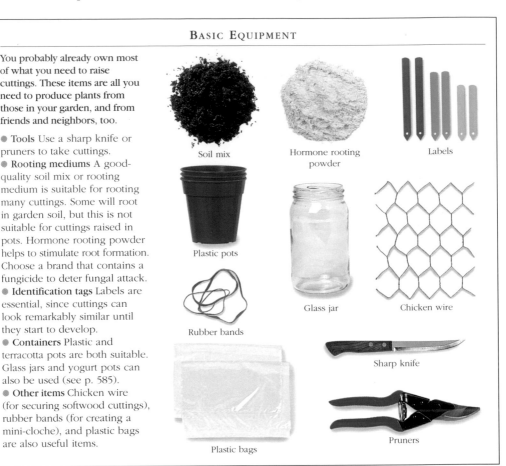

Soil mix

Hormone rooting powder

Labels

Plastic pots

Glass jar

Chicken wire

Rubber bands

Plastic bags

Sharp knife

Pruners

SUITABLE PLANTS FOR CUTTINGS

SOFTWOOD CUTTINGS
Abelia, Abutilon, Betula, Bignonia, Caryopteris, Catalpa, Ceratostigma, Clematis, Cotinus coggygria, Enkianthus, Eucryphia lucida, Forsythia, Fuchsia, Hydrangea, Koelreuteria paniculata, Kolkwitzia, Liquidambar styraciflua, Lonicera, Metasequoia glyptostroboides, Parthenocissus, Perovskia,

Philadelphus, Potentilla, Prunus, Solanum, Tropaeolum, Ulmus, Wisteria.

SEMIRIPE CUTTINGS
Abutilon, Andromeda, Aucuba*, Berberis*, Camellia, Carpenteria*, Caryopteris, Ceanothus*, Chamaecyparis*, Clematis, Cotoneaster x cupressocyparis*, Cupressus*, Cytisus*, Daphne, Deutzia, Elaeagnus*, Enkianthus,

Eucryphia lucida, Fallopia, Garrya*, Ilex, Juniperus*, Lavandula, Ligustrum lucidum, Magnolia grandiflora*, Mahonia, Olearia*, Parthenocissus, Philadelphus, Photinia*, Pieris*, Prunus lusitanica, Rhododendron*, Skimmia*, Solanum, Thuja*, Tsuga*, Viburnum, Weigela.

* = take cutting with a heel

SOFTWOOD CUTTINGS

Take softwood cuttings in spring, when the new shoot growth should root readily. Softwood cuttings require extreme care; although they root easily, they can also wilt and deteriorate quickly. Choose the strongest, healthiest, nonflowering sideshoots.

TAKING A CUTTING

Removing lower leaves
Choose a shoot with three to five pairs of leaves. Use a sharp knife to take a 3–5 in (7–12 cm) cutting, making a straight cut just below a leaf node. Pinch off the lowest pair of leaves.

STANDING IN WATER

Place several cuttings in jar

Securing cuttings
To hold cuttings in place, bend a piece of chicken wire over a jar of water, and secure it with a rubber band. Softwood cuttings can also be rooted successfully in a rooting medium.

COLLECTING CUTTINGS

Preventing moisture loss
Young shoots lose moisture rapidly. To avoid this, leave cuttings in a plastic bag until you are ready to prepare them.

SEMIRIPE CUTTINGS

Take semiripe cuttings from stems of the current year's growth during mid- to late summer or in early autumn. Some cuttings, particularly evergreens, root best if taken with a "heel" of old wood at the base. Always choose a healthy-looking, vigorous shoot.

TIPS FOR SUCCESS

● **Woody stem base** Choose cuttings where the stem base is slightly woody but the tip is still soft. If in doubt, take several batches of cuttings at two-week intervals.
● **Cutting leaves** Reduce moisture loss from large-leaved shrub cuttings by cutting the leaves in half before inserting the cuttings in soil mix.
● **Rooting** Apply hormone rooting powder to stimulate growth of new roots and to deter fungal infections. Shake off any excess; too much can damage the cutting base.
● **Labeling** Put pots of cuttings into a propagator or a cold frame. Label them with date and plant name.

SEVERAL CUTTINGS

Slice away strip of bark 1–1½ in (2.5–4 cm) in length

Making a heel
Trim a healthy stem into several cuttings, each about 4–6 in (10–15 cm) long. Sever each one just below a node. Remove sideshoots and the lowest pair of leaves. Stimulate root formation by removing a sliver of bark from one side of the base.

USING A PLASTIC BAG

Secure bag with rubber band

Making a mini-cloche
If you do not have a propagator, use a clear plastic bag as a mini-cloche instead. This will retain both moisture and warmth. Before removing the bag completely, harden off the cuttings gradually by cutting the corners of the bag.

HARDWOOD CUTTINGS

Hardwood cuttings are taken from fully ripened or hardened stem growth that is produced during the current season. Suitable stems can be selected from midautumn to ear winter. Wait until the leaves have fallen befor taking cuttings from deciduous plants.

TAKING CUTTINGS

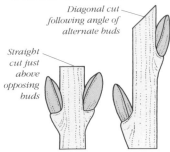

Diagonal cut following angle of alternate buds

Straight cut just above opposing buds

Different cuts
Take cuttings large enough to trim to about 6 in (15 cm). Cut off any soft wood at the tip of each cutting. Make a straight cut above opposing buds and a diagonal cut above alternate buds.

PLANTING CUTTINGS

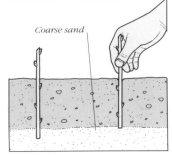

Coarse sand

Sandy trench
Insert cuttings 5-6 in (12-15 cm) deep into a well-prepared bed or trench with a 1-2 in (2.5-5 cm) layer of coarse sand at the bottom. Plant the cuttings against the side of the trench.

ADDITIONAL TIPS
● **Suitable shrubs** *Forsythia, Salix, Spiraea, Tamarix,* and *Philadelphus* root easily from hardwood cuttings.
● **Soft fruits** Many soft fruits can be increased with hardwood cuttings. For gooseberries and red currants, prepare cuttings that are at least 15 in (81 cm) long. Remove the lower buds, leaving only the top three or four. Leave all the buds on black currant cuttings.
● **Roses** Take rose cuttings from shoots that have flowered.
● **Saving space** If you need to root only a few cuttings, insert them at the back of a border.

ROOT CUTTINGS

Root cuttings should be taken when the plant is dormant. Lift a young plant, and tease the root system apart to expose the roots, then loosen the surrounding soil. Alternatively, cut out part of the root system of larger plants, leaving the rest of the roots in the ground.

SUCCESSFUL CUTTINGS
● **Suitable plants** *Acanthus, Aesculus parviflora, Anemone* x *hybrida, Aralia, Campanula, Clerodendrum, Echinops, Erodium, Gypsophila, Papaver orientale, Phlox, Primula denticulata, Pulsatilla vulgaris, Rhus, Trollius,* and *Verbascum.*
● **Watering** Water cuttings after inserting. This may prove sufficient until the cuttings have rooted; excess moisture may lead to rotting.
● **Nematodes** Avoid attack by nematodes by taking root cuttings; the pests do not enter the roots.
● **Keeping moist** Keep root cuttings in a plastic bag until you prepare them for insertion. This will prevent them from drying out quickly.

MAKING AND INSERTING ROOT CUTTINGS
● **Minimum size** Choose roots from a healthy plant. The roots should be at least ¼ in (5 mm) in diameter and close to the base of the stem.

Cutting technique
Cut off any lateral roots. Make a straight cut at the end where the root has been removed from the plant. Make a diagonal cut at the other end. Repeat this process along the length of the root.

● **Ideal length** The ideal length of the roots depends on the plant. After trimming, each root cutting should be 2–6 in (5–15 cm) long.

Space cuttings about 2 in (5 cm) apart

Inserting in soil mix
Firm soil mix into a tray, and insert the cuttings with the diagonal cut facing downward. Add soil mix so that the tips of the cuttings are just showing. Cover with ⅛ in (3 mm) of sand.

DIVISION

MANY HERBACEOUS PLANTS respond well to division, especially those that produce lots of basal shoots and those with a wide-spreading root system. The best time for dividing most plants is between late autumn and early spring.

BASIC EQUIPMENT

The few items of equipment shown here are all you need to divide plants successfully.

● **Cutting tools** A sharp knife is essential to ensure neat cuts and divisions. A smoothly cut surface is an important factor in preventing attacks by organisms that cause disease.
● **Forks** A garden fork is useful for dividing perennials. (You may need two for dividing large clumps.) A hand fork is useful for dividing small perennials.
● **Other items** Fine gravel can be used to improve soil texture and drainage. Wire pegs are useful for securing runners.

Sharp knife

Metal pegs

Fine gravel    Garden fork

Hand fork

SUITABLE PLANTS

Achillea, Anemone hupehensis, Arum, Aster, Astilbe, Astrantia, Bergenia, Campanula, Centaurea dealbata, Coreopsis verticillata, Crambe cordifolia, Doronicum, Epilobium, Geranium, Helianthus, Helleborus orientalis, Hemerocallis, Heuchera, Hosta, Liatris, Lobelia cardinalis, Lychnis, Nepeta, Oenothera, Paeonia, Phormium, Polemonium, Pulmonaria, Rheum, Rudbeckia, Sedum spectabile, Sidalcea, Solidago, Thalictrum, Trollius, Veronica.

DIVIDING RHIZOMES

Division of plants provides the opportunity to rejuvenate old clumps of rhizomes and bulbs, and to create new clumps at the same time. Tough plants may require two large forks back-to-back to divide them, but many can be divided by hand or with a knife.

LIFTING, TRIMMING, AND PLANTING IRIS RHIZOMES

Cut out and discard old rhizomes

1 Use a large fork to lift the clump. To reduce the risk of root damage, drive the fork into the ground at an angle and well away from the rhizomes. Shake off excess soil, and split up the clump.

2 Detach any new, healthy rhizomes from the clump, and trim their ends with a sharp knife. Dust the cut surfaces with a sulfur-based fungicide. Discard old or diseased rhizomes.

3 Make a diagonal cut on each leaf to about 6 in (15 cm) to minimize root disturbance from wind rock. Replant, leaving just the tops above soil level. Be sure the foliage is upright.

CARING FOR BULBS

Bulbs require some attention if they are to perform well over a long period. Clumps become overcrowded after a few years and need to be divided. It is best to lift clumps during dormancy, and to replant the bulbs in irregular groups immediately after division.

BULB MAINTENANCE

● **Marking clumps** When clumps begin to flower unreliably, it is a sign that they need to be divided. Mark these clumps with a stake when the foliage starts to die back so that they can be identified easily when dormant.

● **Foliar feeding** Bulbs that need dividing are often considerably undersized. Help to boost their growth by giving them a foliar feed immediately after replanting. Continue to feed regularly during the growing season.

● **Offset bulbs** Do not discard offset bulbs. Plant them in a separate site or nursery bed until they are fully grown.

DIVIDING OVERCROWDED BULBS

Lifting a clump
Lift a clump using a hand fork. A garden fork may be necessary for big or deep clumps. Try to avoid piercing any bulbs, and discard any that are damaged. Prepare a fresh planting hole, and incorporate fertilizer into it.

Remove offsets from parent bulb, along with loose outer layers of bulb tunic

Removing offsets
Carefully remove offsets from the parent bulbs; discard bulbs that appear unhealthy. Replant bulbs that are full-size or nearly full-size immediately, at the correct depth (see p. 497), and in a suitable site for the bulb type.

SCALING BULBS

Bulb scaling is a method of propagation for any bulbs with scales. It is most frequently used for lilies and *Fritillaria*, and it is carried out in late summer or early autumn. Look for scales with bulbils (miniature bulbs), which form at the base of the scales.

PROPAGATING WITH LILY SCALES AND BULBILS

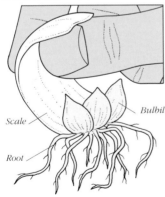

Bulbil

Scale

Root

1 Remove any soil and damaged or diseased scales from around the bulb. Gently pull off any healthy scales that have bulbils at the bases. Be careful not to separate the scales from the bulbils.

Shake scales in sulfur to deter fungal infections

2 Shake the scales in a bag containing sulfur. Remove the scales, and tap gently. Put them in a bag of peat and perlite. Seal, and keep in the dark at 70°F (21°C) for three months.

3 Plant the scales in individual pots of sandy potting mix. The tops of the scales should be just beneath the surface of the mix. Keep in a cold greenhouse or well-shaded cold frame.

DIVIDING PLANTS

Most plants will reproduce readily in their natural habitat, and propagation often takes advantage of this process. Propagation by division produces sizable plants very quickly. Correct timing and proper aftercare of new plants are the key to guaranteed success.

DIVISION SUCCESS

● **Timing** Choose the time of day carefully for this task. Divisions are likely to fail if they become dehydrated. Try to divide plants during the coolest part of the day – if possible, early in the evening.
● **Cool spot** Replant any divisions as soon as possible to minimize moisture loss. Keep the new plants in a cool spot out of direct sunlight.
● **Healthy material** Use only healthy stock as propagating material. When dividing plants, take the opportunity to discard weak or old sections.
● **Weeds** Before replanting divisions, remove any weeds that are growing among the crown and roots.

USING RUNNERS

Dividing strawberry plants
Strawberry plants produce runners that make propagation very easy. Space the runners out around the plant, and peg them down. When they are rooted and showing signs of strong growth, sever the runners from the plants, and replant.

USING OFFSETS

Dividing *Sempervivum*
These plants produce many small plants in clusters. Carefully remove these from the parent plant. Some may have already grown small root systems, but even those that have not will readily root when potted up in sandy potting mix.

DIVIDING RASPBERRY PLANTS

Raspberry canes naturally form suckers. If these are healthy and disease-free, they can be used to replace old stock or to add to the existing crop. In late autumn, you can lift any suckers that have developed around vigorous, healthy plants.

1 Select suckers from a well-established plant. Use a fork to lift suckers, taking care not to damage the roots. Sever each sucker with pruners or a sharp knife. Be sure that each sucker has a good root system.

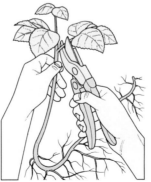

2 Remove the remaining leaves, and replant the rooted suckers in a well-prepared site. Choose a new site to limit the risk of soil-borne pests and diseases. Water the suckers well.

DIVIDING PERENNIALS

● **Clumps** Perennials respond particularly well to propagation by division. Once a clump has become well established, there are few herbaceous plants that will not benefit from this propagation method.
● **Timing** Division is usually carried out while the plant is dormant in autumn or early spring. Spring division is usually most successful in heavy soils (see p. 500).

GENERAL MAINTENANCE

QUICK REFERENCE

Wooden Structures, p. 600

Concrete and Brick, p. 604

Garden Furniture, p. 609

Garden Tools, p. 610

Greenhouses, p. 612

PLANTS ARE NOT THE ONLY FEATURES *in a garden that benefit from care and* attention. Tools, structures, and buildings should be kept in good condition. The materials from which they are made determine the type and frequency of maintenance required. Use the chart below to assess the pros and cons of each material.

GARDEN MATERIALS

MATERIAL	PROS	CONS
HARDWOODS Hardwoods – such as beech, mahogany, and teak – are used in the construction of most garden structures and furniture.	Hardwoods are strong and long-lasting, and are not easily damaged. They retain their finish with relatively little maintenance, and are not prone to rotting.	Hardwoods are available mainly from specialized suppliers, and items made from them can be costly. Be sure the wood comes from a sustainable source.
SOFTWOODS Softwoods – such as cedar, fir, pine, and spruce – are used principally to make garden furniture, arches, pergolas, gates, and fences. They can be stained or painted.	Production of softwoods is widespread and, as a result, they are cheaper and easier to obtain than hardwoods, and come in a wide variety of sizes. Their light density and weight make them easy to work with.	Softwoods have a shorter lifespan and are more prone to damage than hardwoods. Regular treatment with a preservative is essential if these woods are to last, particularly if kept outside over winter.
PLASTIC Injection-molded plastic is a popular construction material for garden furniture, as well as for windowboxes, pots, and other plant containers.	Plastic does not rot, warp, or corrode; it is not affected by cold or damp weather; and it requires little maintenance. One of a gardener's less expensive options, it is also lightweight.	The colors in which plastic is available can seem too bright and artificial for a small or traditional garden. The color of some plastics will fade after prolonged exposure to the sun.
CAST IRON Cast iron was used in the last century to make garden furniture and ornaments.	Cast iron is very heavy, making it ideal for containers in which stability is required. It is easy to paint with a brush or spray gun.	Cast iron must be painted regularly to prevent rust. Its weight makes it difficult to move, and it may break on impact.
ALUMINUM This alloy is used for structures such as frames and greenhouses.	Aluminum can be painted with enamel for consistent color. It is lightweight and easy to move.	Weathered aluminum surfaces can become covered with a white and powdery corrosion.
STEEL Steel is used for items such as children's play equipment.	Steel is strong and sturdy, and is not easily damaged, so it requires minimal maintenance.	Paint on galvanized steel surfaces may chip and peel off over time.

BASIC EQUIPMENT

Maintaining garden features may require a range of tools. Consider the nature of the particular task before deciding whether to purchase or hire expensive equipment.

● **Removing deposits** Use a stiff wire brush for demanding cleaning jobs, such as removing rust, paint, algae, and other deposits from hard surfaces.
● **Cleaning surfaces** Use a stiff bristle brush to clean surfaces that may be stained or rusty.
● **Painting** Select paintbrushes in a range of sizes to apply wood treatments and stains, paints, and other liquids.
● **Filling small areas** Remove rotten wood or crumbling mortar with a chisel, then fill the hole with wood filler or putty. Apply these with a putty knife for a smooth finish.
● **Filling large areas** Fill in and smooth large areas of concrete or mortar with a trowel.
● **Replacing nails** Remove old nails with a claw hammer. Replace with galvanized nails.
● **Hammering** Pound fence posts and paving stones into place using a club hammer.
● **Handling** Wear sturdy gloves when moving rough or sharp materials and objects.

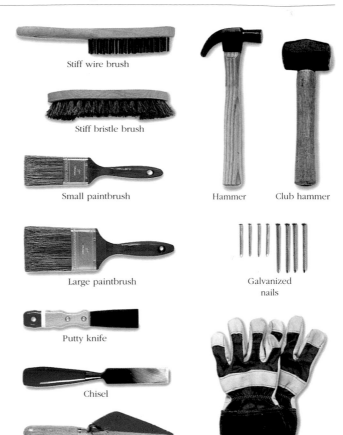

Stiff wire brush

Stiff bristle brush

Small paintbrush

Hammer   Club hammer

Large paintbrush

Galvanized nails

Putty knife

Chisel

Bricklayer's trowel

Sturdy gloves

ADHESIVES, PRESERVATIVES, AND SEALANTS

Liquid treatments can often be customized to your needs by mixing with paints and other materials.

● **Protection** Apply wood preservative regularly to extend the life of a wooden structure.
● **Color** Select a wood filler that matches the wood in color.
● **Strength** PVA is a sealant and bonding agent. It can be mixed with other materials in order to strengthen them.
● **Repairs** Sealants are available for repairing particular features or structures, including roofs and ponds.

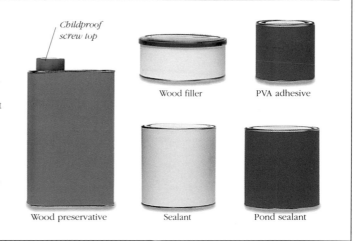

Childproof screw top

Wood filler

PVA adhesive

Wood preservative

Sealant

Pond sealant

WOODEN STRUCTURES

WOOD COMPLEMENTS ALMOST ANY GARDEN. Soft- and hardwoods are available in a range of colors, weights, sizes, and prices. They can be stained, treated, or painted to alter their color and blend in with their environment.

REPAIRING SHEDS

A shed can last for many years. It should not need a great deal of maintenance, but routine jobs, such as treating the wood and painting it occasionally, will extend a shed's life considerably. Repairing or replacing the roof and replacing glass may also be necessary.

REPAIRING ROOFS

● **Reroofing** Do this in warm weather, when felt is unlikely to crack. If you must climb onto the roof, kneel on a board to spread your weight.
● **Roofing felt** Select a thick grade of roofing felt. Make sure that it is sufficiently flexible for easy handling.
● **Old nails** Remove old nails from the roof with a claw hammer before replacing felt. If any break, hammer them in before securing the new felt with rustproof, galvanized nails.
● **Wood** Strip off the roofing felt, and make sure the wood underneath is sound.

REPLACING DAMAGED ROOFING FELT

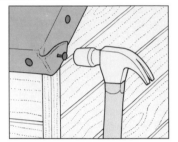

Eliminating air pockets
Place the first sheet of felt so that it extends over the eaves by about 1 in (2.5 cm) and the ends overlap the fascia boards by about 1 in (2.5 cm). Press down with a strip of wood to smooth out air pockets in the felt.

Securing a corner
Where the eaves and fascia boards meet, tuck the felt into a triangle, and fold it toward the fascia board, securing it in place with galvanized nails. Tuck the corner in to ensure that it does not collect rainwater.

REPAIRING WOOD SIDING

Wood siding has a tendency to splinter, crack, and rot. If a small area is affected, it is a relatively simple process to replace the wood. Once it has been replaced, be sure to protect it from moisture by filling gaps with putty, then treating the wood with wood preservative.

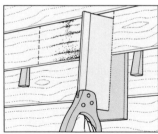

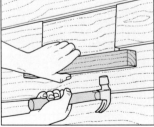

1 Lift the siding with a crowbar, and drive wedges under the damaged area. Insert a thin piece of wood to protect the wood below, then cut out the damaged area with a saw.

2 Measure and cut a replacement section, then hammer it in, protecting the new board from the hammer with a block of wood. Nail the board in with galvanized nails.

USING WOOD
● **Cut ends** Treat freshly cut ends before using the wood.
● **Drying** After treating wood, allow it to dry before use.
● **Damaged boards** If more than one area of a board is damaged, replace the whole board.
● **Siding** Use pressure-treated wood to extend the life of siding. This wood resists insects and fungi, and is ideal for damp locations.
● **Wood putty** For filling gaps, select wood putty that matches the color of the wood.

MAINTAINING GUTTERS

It is essential that gutters and downspouts on greenhouses, conservatories, and sheds are kept in good condition. Pipes are liable to become blocked and may leak or overflow, causing serious damage to the structure, which will take time and money to repair.

PREVENTING PROBLEMS

● **Rust** Scrape off rust as soon as it appears, and apply an antirust solution. Allow this to dry before painting the area with oil-based paint.

● **Plastic gutters** Replacing a damaged section of plastic guttering is more effective in the long run than repairing it. However, minor damage can be repaired with a sealant or PVA. Waterproof tape is also useful for short periods.

● **Chicken wire** If inspecting or repairing gutters, take the opportunity to attach narrow-gauge chicken wire along the length of the gutters to prevent them from becoming blocked with debris.

REPAIRING PLASTIC AND METAL GUTTERS

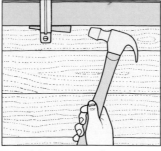

Repairing a sagging gutter
Loose or sagging plastic gutters will not drain properly, and this may cause their contents to overflow. As a temporary measure, hammer in a wooden wedge between each bracket and the gutter to hold each section in place until you can replace it.

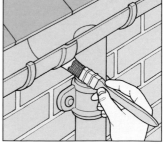

Sealing a crack
If metal gutters crack and develop leaks, scrape off any rust, then paint the affected area with a sealing compound. Protect from rain until the sealant has dried. If the gutter is damaged at several points, replace the entire section.

INSULATING AND SECURING SHEDS

To serve its purpose effectively, a shed must be dry and watertight. It should also be a safe, secure, and comfortable place in which to work and store tools and equipment. With a little effort, an unwelcoming, damp shed can be transformed into a warm, dry workplace.

INSTALLING INSULATION

Using polystyrene
Nail polystyrene panels between the supporting struts of the roof and walls on the inside of a shed. Use short nails to avoid damaging the outer surface of the siding or the roofing felt. Cover the polystyrene with a layer of hardboard.

MAINTAINING SHEDS

● **Wood preservative** If the wood on your shed needs to be treated with preservative, do this in the summer months. In warm weather, the shed door and windows can be left open to diffuse any noxious fumes.

● **Curtains** Hang a curtain over a shed door for added insulation against drafts.

● **Drafts** Install foam strips around the door and window frames to keep out drafts.

● **Heating** If working in a shed during cold and wet winter months, use a kerosene heater to keep it warm and dry. Be sure the heater is well maintained and operated so that it does not pose a fire or health hazard.

LOCKING SHEDS

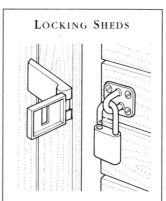

Many locks on sheds are easily broken. Install a strong locking bar with screws drilled through the back of the door. Fasten with a good-quality padlock. Block out windows with blinds if the shed is used for storing valuable tools.

PREVENTING WOOD FROM ROTTING

Garden structures and furniture are continually exposed to the adverse effects of the weather. Seasonal changes and damp conditions encourage rotting. If wood comes in contact with soil or any other moist material, the damage can be extensive.

PRESERVING WOOD

Wear gloves to protect hands

Cleaning and applying
Prevent the wood from rotting by applying a coat of suitable wood preservative. Clean off all loose material and debris, and be sure that it is thoroughly dry before applying the preservative.

DISCOURAGING ROT

● **Using preservative** Place the legs of wooden furniture in saucers of wood preservative for several hours to ensure that the solution is absorbed.

● **Positioning furniture** Place garden furniture on a flat, even surface that does not collect rainwater. Avoid putting wooden furniture on grass.

● **Treating corners** Wood is likely to rot in the corners of structures. Prevent this by regularly treating these areas with wood preservative.

● **Removing debris** The accumulation of debris on or around wood encourages decay. Remove fallen leaves and encroaching undergrowth.

FUNGAL ROT

Fungal rot – dry and wet – is not difficult to identify but, apart from treatable patches of wet rot, should be dealt with by a professional.

● **Dry rot** The first signs of dry rot are white, fibrous growths that become dusty red. Wood surfaces split into cubes and are covered by gray mold; if probed with a knife, the wood will crumble. Plaster bulges and cracks.

● **Wet rot** This affects only areas where moisture has penetrated. It produces narrow, brown strips of fungus, and causes wood to crack, and paint to flake.

TREATING ROTTED WOOD

It is best to prevent wood from rotting, but occasional treatment of damaged areas will still be necessary. Before making any repairs, make sure that the wood is as dry as possible; bring wooden furniture under cover for a few weeks before repairing it.

REMOVING DAMAGED WOOD AND FILLING HOLES

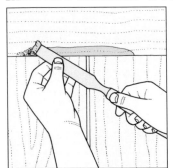

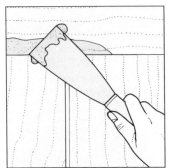

DRYING WOOD

1 Remove damaged wood with a chisel or sturdy kitchen knife. Cut back to the sound wood, removing any discolored or decayed areas. If in doubt, keep cutting; just be sure you do not diminish the overall strength of the structure.

2 If possible, select a wood filler that dries to the same color as the structure being repaired. Fill the hole with the filler, firmly pressing it in to expel any air bubbles. To deter moisture accumulation, angle the surface. When this is dry, apply a preservative.

Treating a small area
Frequently, a small patch of wood on a large structure needs to be repaired. Instead of waiting for the entire structure to dry out naturally, try drying the damaged area quickly with a hair dryer.

MAINTAINING FENCES

Fences must remain outside regardless of the weather. The location of some sections may expose them permanently to cold and damp conditions. Dense planting of climbers and shrubs also encourages the buildup of moist air. Ultimately, deterioration is inevitable.

REPAIRING FENCES

● **Crushed stone** Drive crushed stone firmly into place using the base of a concrete spur or a spare wooden post.
● **Concrete** If you have only a few posts to replace and little time to spare, use a quick-setting concrete mix.
● **Winter protection** In cold and wet weather, create a screen to protect fence posts from frost and to prevent water from accumulating on the surface of any concrete.
● **Decayed wood** Do not repair a fence post that shows signs of deterioration; its strength as a support has probably been reduced, and the whole post should always be replaced.
● **Corrosion** Check metal bolts and nails for corrosion, which may reduce their strength.
● **Treatment** Regularly treat fences with wood preservative.

REPLACING A SECTION

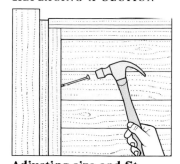

Adjusting size and fit
Fence sections are available in standard sizes, making their replacement relatively easy. However, if a new section is too thin, insert a board or a small strip of pressure-treated wood between the fence post and the edge of the section. Nail the section in position with galvanized nails.

REPOSITIONING AND MENDING POSTS

● **Loose foundations** Repair a loose post promptly to avoid damage to the fence. Avoid disturbing nearby plants.

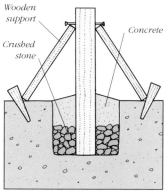

Restoring a wooden post
Dig a hole 8 x 8 in (20 x 20 cm) around the post. Reposition the post, using a level, if necessary, and hold it in place with wooden supports. Pour crushed stone around the base, force it down, then set in concrete.

PROTECTING AND MAINTAINING FENCES

● **Avoiding damp** Fit a concrete or timber board along the base of a fence to protect it from rising damp. Try to keep gravel and soil away from the board.
● **Matching color** A new section may appear out of place on an old, weathered fence. After replacing a section, treat the entire fence with a colored wood preservative to give it a uniform look.
● **Wide sections** Plane the edges of a new section if it is a little too wide to fit into the frame of a fence.
● **Plants** To keep damage to nearby plants to a minimum, repair and maintain fences in the autumn or winter.

● **Concrete** Rotted wood can make a fence unstable. Replace the base with concrete, which is impervious to moisture.

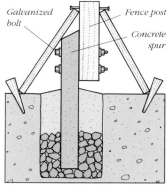

Replacing a section
Replace a post section with a concrete spur and, if necessary, a new post. Attach the post to the spur above the soil with galvanized bolts. Hold with temporary supports, and pack with crushed stone and concrete.

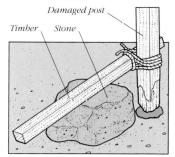

Removing a post
If a damaged post is difficult to remove, lever it out with a length of sturdy timber and a large stone or pile of bricks. Tie the timber firmly to the damaged post, balancing it over the stone. Push down repeatedly on the timber with your foot until the post is free.

CONCRETE AND BRICKWORK

STONE, CONCRETE, AND BRICKS ARE RESILIENT, long-lasting materials. However, some weather conditions, such as cold or heavy frost, may cause these normally sturdy substances to chip and break, making maintenance and repairs necessary.

PREPARING CONCRETE AND MORTAR

MIXING CEMENT
● **Small amounts** Mix the components together by hand if you need only a small amount of concrete. This saves on preparation time and money, enabling you to measure the required quantities of sand and stone accurately.
● **Large amounts** If a large amount of concrete is needed, it is worth renting a cement mixer, which will make the process relatively quick and simple.

MAKING CONCRETE
● **Mixing** Measure out the sand and stone according to the instructions on the packet. Mix the components together on a flat surface, smooth the top of the mixture, make a depression in the center, and pour in the cement. Combine, and add water, if necessary.
● **Consistency** Slap the surface of the mixture with the back of a trowel. If water trickles out, add more sand and stone.

MAKING MORTAR
● **Ready-mixed mortar** Although this is expensive, ready-mixed mortar is more time- and cost-effective for small jobs than buying separate components.
● **Preparation** Dampen the surface of a mixing board, and pour the mortar powder onto it. Flatten the top of the dry mixture, and make a depression in the center. Add water slowly, mixing thoroughly to produce a moist, even consistency.

MAINTAINING WALLS

The external and dividing walls of a garden, as well as those on which sheds and greenhouses are built, should serve a purpose and look attractive. A weathered wall can look good, but an excessive buildup of algae and other deposits can spoil its appearance.

REMOVING DEPOSITS
● **Efflorescence** A white, salty deposit, called efflorescence, may appear on the surface of new bricks. Remove these deposits to prevent ugly marks.

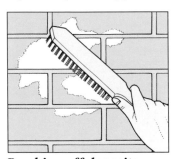

Brushing off deposits
Scrub with a dry wire brush to remove efflorescence. Repeat this process several times. Do not wash deposits off with water, because extra moisture will make the problem worse.

DEALING WITH DEPOSITS
● **Prevention** Use sealants and treatments on brickwork to keep walls dry and prevent deposits from collecting.
● **Gutters** Check gutters for debris to ensure that they do not overflow and encourage the buildup of algae on walls.
● **Cleaning agents** When removing deposits with a brush, be sure not to use cleaning agents or soaps that can encourage efflorescence.
● **Recurring deposits** If algal deposits recur, remove with a commercial algicidal product.
● **Pressure washing** Walls that are difficult to clean should be pressure-washed. Do this in warm weather, when water will evaporate rapidly, and make sure nearby doors and windows are shut firmly.

BRIGHT IDEA

Restoring bricks
Renovate discolored, stained, or marked brickwork using an old brick of a matching color. Keep the old brick wet (place a bucket of water nearby), and rub the brick vigorously over the damaged areas.

REPAIRING BRICKWORK

Over time, the mortar in a brick wall may crack, allowing moisture to penetrate through to the interior walls of a structure. Extremes of weather can cause the mortar to become loose, crumble, and begin to fall away. Accurate and immediate repair is essential.

WEATHERPROOFING

● **Loose mortar** Remove all loose mortar from a wall to a depth of 1 in (2.5 cm) before attempting to replace with fresh mortar.

● **Power drill** Remove large amounts of loose mortar with a power drill. Protective goggles are essential.

● **Depth** If in doubt, chip away between the bricks until all loose mortar has been removed, but make sure that you do not damage the surrounding brickwork.

● **Adding adhesive** Increase the strength of the new mortar by adding some PVA. This will also increase the bonding ability of the mixture.

● **Cleaning** Remove all excess mortar from the brickwork immediately. Use a wet brush or stiff cloth.

CHOOSING A FINISH

● **Matching mortars** Try to match the finish of new mortar with that of the old. This will help to disguise repairs made to the brickwork.

REPOINTING BRICKS

● **Preparation** Chip away any loose mortar with a screwdriver or a slim chisel and a club hammer. Wear goggles to protect your eyes.

Soaking brickwork
Use a soft brush to wipe away sandy deposits after removing loose mortar. Wipe the affected area with a sponge soaked in water before repointing. This will help the new mortar adhere better to the bricks.

ANGLING MORTAR

● **Trowel** To achieve angled pointing, use a trowel to project the mortar over the top of a brick and recess into the base of the brick above.

APPLYING MORTAR

● **Equipment** Repoint a wall using a good-quality bricklayer's trowel. Be sure it is small enough to maneuver and it gives a smooth finish.

Renovating brickwork
Begin by replacing the mortar in the vertical joints. When a section is completed, move on to the horizontal joints. Wet the wall again if it starts to dry out. Press the mortar in firmly, and trim away excess mortar.

TIME-SAVING TIP

Harmonizing colors
The color of new mortar may change considerably when it dries. To avoid color clashes on a wall, mix a small quantity of the new mortar and allow it to dry, then scoop it onto a trowel, and compare it with the old.

Using a garden hose
Use a piece of an old garden hose to create an even, concave surface after applying the mortar to the brickwork. Bend the hose into a slight curve to make it easy to handle.

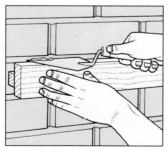

Catching excess
Nail a block of wood to each end of a board, then hold it level with the edge of the mortar. Drag a trowel across the board, in line with the bricks. Excess mortar will fall onto the wood.

REPAIRING CRACKS IN CONCRETE

Concrete paths and steps may develop cracks and even break up, particularly if they have been subjected to heavy use. Cold, wet, and frosty weather, foot traffic, heavy wheelbarrows, and other factors will eventually take their toll on these essential garden features.

MAINTAINING CONCRETE

● **Hairline cracks** Do not immediately fill a thin crack. Wait for a month or two to be sure it does not increase in size before making necessary repairs.

● **Foundation** Large cracks can be caused by a weakness in the foundation on which a step or path is laid. Remove the area, and lay it again on a new, strong foundation.

● **Drying** Cover a repaired area with a plastic sheet to protect the concrete filler from rain. Allow it to dry gradually.

● **Insulating** If freezing weather conditions are forecast, cover a newly filled surface with newspaper, cloth, or other insulating material.

PREPARING AND FILLING CRACKS IN CONCRETE

● **Enlarging areas** Repair any crack or hole that is more than ½ in (1.5 cm) in depth. Enlarge the area to ensure that the filler is packed firmly.

● **Preparation** Remove debris that may have accumulated in the affected area, since it will prevent the filler from adhering to the concrete.

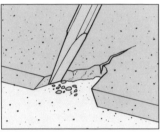

1 Use a chisel to chip away material in the affected area. To ensure that the filler will be held firmly in place, angle the chisel to make the hole larger at the base than at the surface.

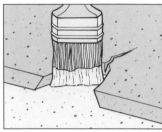

2 Brush away any debris, then apply some PVA to the sides of the crack or hole. Plug the hole with concrete filler, making it level with the surrounding area.

REPAIRING CONCRETE EDGES

The edges of a concrete path or steps are subject to potentially damaging wear and tear. Air pockets beneath the surface, formed when the concrete is first laid, can cause the material to decay and crumble. For this reason, edges require frequent maintenance.

REPAIRING EDGES

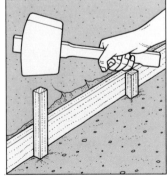

Using wooden edging
Hammer blocks of wood into the ground with a mallet to create a temporary wooden edge. Make sure that the top of the wood is level with the concrete. Fill the space with fresh cement.

MAINTAINING EDGES

● **Loose material** Remove any loose or crumbling material from around a broken edge, leaving a stable rim. If in doubt, remove more material than is necessary.

● **Crushed stone** If any of the base stone is exposed during repairs, pack it down firmly with a wooden post or concrete spur. Pack a new layer of crushed stone into any weak areas.

● **Protective covering** If small children or pets are likely to use a freshly repaired area, cover the new edge with a sheet of plastic and a layer of chicken wire until the concrete has dried.

SAFETY MEASURES

It is essential that eyes, skin, and lungs are fully covered and protected when making any repairs to concrete or stone paths, steps, or walls.

● **Goggles** Wear goggles when working with concrete and stone; small fragments of debris can injure the eyes. Be sure they are clean so that you can see clearly.

● **Gloves** Wear rubber gloves to protect your hands from the caustic effects of cement.

● **Face mask** Cement dust is harmful to the lungs. To prevent lung damage wear a face mask when mixing the components together.

REPLACING PAVING SLABS

Patio paving slabs can be exposed to a great deal of stress, especially during periods of warm weather. Eventually, they will need to be repaired as cracks appear or mortar crumbles. However, the repairs should not be extensive or costly if they are done promptly.

INSTALLING SLABS

● **Individual slabs** Replace any slabs that have shattered or cracked. Use the opportunity to make sure that the crushed stone below is firm and level.

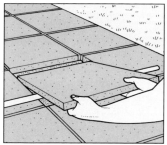

Easing into position
To prevent the surrounding slabs from being damaged, lay a broom handle or piece of pipe across the gap to be filled. Use this as a support to ease the new paving stone into place.

WORKING WITH SLABS

● **Safety** The edges of paving slabs can be very sharp, particularly if cut using a chisel. Wear goggles when cutting, and use thick gloves when handling sharp slabs.
● **Cutting surface** Place a slab on a solid, flat surface to ensure an accurate cut.
● **Level surface** When a new slab is in place, use a level to make sure that the surface is completely level before replacing the mortar.
● **Uneven slabs** To realign an uneven slab, place a block of wood on the surface to prevent damage to the slab, and lightly strike it with a club hammer until level.
● **Cleaning** When the mortar is dry, wash the entire paved surface with a commercial cleaning agent.

FILLING JOINTS

● **Positioning** Before filling in a joint with mortar, allow the replacement paving stone to settle on the crushed stone for a minimum of two days.

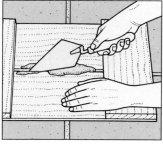

Using a wooden jigger
Fill the joints using a wooden jigger. Align the narrow central opening to the joint, and push the mortar through. Used correctly, a jigger prevents excess mortar from spilling onto the slabs.

PLACING AND CLEANING

● **Spacing** If existing slabs are separated by mortar, use a wooden spacer of the same width as the mortar to position a new slab. Remove the spacer when laying mortar in the joint.
● **Cleaning** Clean up excess mortar with water and a stiff brush or broom as promptly as possible. Mortar sets quickly and can be difficult to remove once it is dry.
● **Planting up** If a paving slab is badly damaged and you are unable to find a suitable replacement, consider removing the damaged slab and replacing it with plants (see p. 460).
● **Stains** Paving slabs can be marked by oil, rust, and moss. Use a commercial cleaning agent to remove the stains.

CUTTING A PAVING SLAB

Paving slabs are available in a wide range of sizes. However, the shape of a patio or terrace may require a slab to be cut to size. Rent an angle grinder if you have a number of slabs to alter.

Work along score mark

Chisel

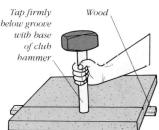

Tap firmly below groove with base of club hammer

Wood

1 Score both sides of the slab with a chisel. Work along the line with a club hammer and chisel to make a groove ⅛ in (3 mm) deep. If the slab has to fit tightly, cut it to size, less ¼ in (6 mm) all around to allow for uneven edges.

2 Rest the paving slab on a firm surface. Place a section of wood under the groove. Tap the surface of the slab with the base of a club hammer, to one side of the score mark. Repeat until the slab breaks. Protect your eyes from flying debris.

REPAIRING BRICK PATHS

Individual bricks are not easily broken in a path or patio, but occasionally one will crack or shatter. A damaged brick should be replaced as soon as possible. Once the brick is cracked, moisture may penetrate and freeze in cold weather, making the problem worse.

DESIGNING WITH BRICKS

● **Color** Try to match the color of a new brick with its surroundings. Although it will stand out when new, the brick will weather with age.

● **Used bricks** Buy second-hand bricks for an instant weathered effect. Make sure that the bricks are frostproof before you purchase them.

● **Combinations** If you cannot locate new bricks that match the old, use the originals to replace broken sections, and place the new bricks in less conspicuous spots.

● **Contrast** Place different bricks among the originals to create contrast between the old and new bricks, and raise some above the others to form a pattern.

REPLACING BRICKS

● **Removing** Chip away any surrounding mortar, then use a bricklayer's trowel to pry out the broken brick, taking care not to damage adjacent paving.

Inserting a new brick
Place a piece of wood on top of the new brick to avoid damaging the surface, then tamp with a club hammer. Fill in any gaps between the bricks with sand.

BRIGHT IDEA

Storing bricks
If bricks become damp, they will not adhere to mortar. Store them in a dry place, or cover with a heavy plastic. Stack bricks on a board that has been placed on a level, firm surface. To prevent the pile from collapsing, place the bricks in a pyramid shape so that the outer layer leans inward.

RECONSTRUCTING CONCRETE STEPS

If the main body of a set of steps begins to fall down, the entire set should be replaced because the steps may be unsafe and collapse without warning. However, it is normally the fronts of the steps, and occasionally the sides, that are most likely to incur damage.

MAINTAINING AND RESTORING CONCRETE STEPS

● **Preparation** Remove the damaged area. Brush off all dust and other loose material, then apply white glue to the newly prepared surface.

● **Concrete** To form a good replacement edge, be sure to use a dry mixture of concrete made up of one part cement to five parts ballast.

● **Prevention** Avoid further damage to a set of steps by occasionally varying your path, especially if carrying a heavy load or pushing a heavy wheelbarrow. Simple measures, such as steering the wheel away from the center of a step, will help.

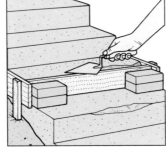

Using a wooden form
A new step edge must be straight. Hold boards in place with bricks and stakes hammered into the ground. Firmly pack the concrete mixture into this form, and smooth over with a trowel.

COMPLETING REPAIRS

● **Form** Check that boards used to make a form are not warped or marked with knots.

● **Setting** Leave the supporting boards in place for a minimum of four weeks after carrying out a repair. This gives the concrete time to set completely.

● **Protecting** To protect newly repaired areas on concrete steps from rain or frost, cover them with a plastic sheet.

● **Aging** Dust the surface of wet concrete with sifted sand to give the edge an aged look. When the concrete is set, brush off any excess sand.

GARDEN FURNITURE

I F LEFT OUTSIDE THROUGHOUT THE YEAR, garden furniture will rapidly start to show signs of aging. If possible, shelter these items in wet or windy weather. Or, cover bulky furniture with plastic to avoid using valuable storage space.

MAINTAINING FURNITURE

The kind of maintenance your garden furniture requires depends upon the material from which the item is made, and how it has been treated in the past. The appearance of old garden furniture can be greatly improved or altered with a coat of paint or a stain.

CARING FOR WOOD
● **Softwood** To prolong the life of softwood, be sure to apply a coat of wood preservative every year.
● **Hardwood** Treat hardwood with an annual application of teak oil. Although hardwood has a long life expectancy and is not prone to rotting, it will benefit from treatment.
● **Preparation** Before treating or painting wood, rub the surface down to remove any loose material, and allow the wood to dry thoroughly.

PAINTING AND STAINING WOODEN FURNITURE
● **Color** Wooden furniture can be painted or stained using a colored wood preservative, or a coat of paint followed by a coat of wood preservative.

Pour paint into measured quantity of preservative

Creating a color
Create your own color by mixing latex paint with clear wood preservative. Line a container with foil, pour in the two components, and stir thoroughly.

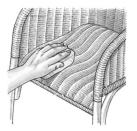
CARING FOR PLASTIC
● **Cleaning** Wash down plastic garden furniture regularly to keep it clean and comfortable, and to minimize any scratching on the surface.
● **Painting** Restore a stained or discolored item using paint made for plastic furniture. Ask for advice at a hardware store or paint store.

LOOKING AFTER METAL
● **Light metal** If purchasing furniture made of light metal, ensure that it is strong and stable. Dents in metal are difficult to remove successfully.
● **Weatherproofing** If a metal item is to remain in the garden throughout the winter, protect all the exposed surfaces with an application of heavy oil. Wipe off the residue before using the furniture again.

OILING FURNITURE

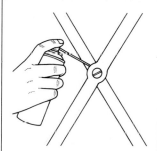

● **Dealing with rust** Choose an aerosol product that inhibits rust. If it has an extension tube, it can also be used as a lubricant for springs, hinges, and rivets. Wipe off the oil before use.
● **Using paint** If rust does appear, rub it off with a wire brush. Treat the area with antirust paint, and allow it to dry before painting with the color of your choice.

GARDEN TOOLS

Garden tools are valuable pieces of equipment, and are well worth keeping in good condition by maintaining them on a regular basis. Regular care will ensure that your tools continue to perform efficiently.

MAINTAINING TOOLS

Routine maintenance needs to be done only once a year if tools are handled with care, cleaned, and oiled if necessary, and repaired promptly and correctly. Regular care ensures that damage and deterioration of valuable equipment are kept to a minimum.

CLEANING A FORK

Scrape away lumps of soil

Making digging easier
When working in soil that is heavy and sticky, periodically remove soil from the tines of a fork. At the same time, remove any stones that are jammed between the tines that may cause the metal to bend.

REMOVING SOIL

● **Dried soil** An old, but sturdy kitchen knife makes an excellent tool for manually removing lumps of soil that have dried on garden tools.
● **Clay soil** To remove stubborn lumps of clay from a fork or spade, push the tool into a compost pile or a bucket of fine, oily gravel. Much of the adhering clay will come off and mix with the compost or gravel.
● **Tires** Clean the tires of a wheelbarrow regularly. A heavy coating of mud may conceal sharp stones that could cause punctures when the wheelbarrow is used again.

LOOKING AFTER BLADES

Thoroughly wipe blades with oil

Oiling blades
Cutting blades must be clean and dry before oiling. Put plenty of oil on a clean rag, and use this to wipe over the blades and other metal parts. This should be done at least several times a year, and preferably after each use.

LOOKING AFTER WOOD

● **Drying** Before putting tools away, stand them upright to dry, preferably in the sun. If the tools are still damp, store them vertically to prevent water from accumulating and rotting the wood.
● **Removing splinters** To remove scratches or splintered areas on wooden handles, rub down the whole handle with fine-grade sandpaper, following the grain of the wood.
● **Applying oil** When storing equipment for a long period of time, rub linseed oil on the handles or shafts of wooden tools. Allow the oil to penetrate, and remove any excess with a dry rag.

COVERING UNCOMFORTABLE TOOL HANDLES

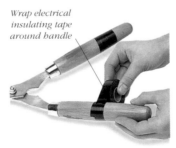

Wrap electrical insulating tape around handle

Taping around wood
Wrap a layer of insulating tape around wooden tool handles that have become rough or splintered. Make sure that the wood is completely dry so that the tape can adhere properly. The tape should last for several months and can be easily replaced.

Foam pipe insulation

Making a foam handle
Small sections of foam, such as pipe-insulating material, can form a soft covering for an uncomfortable handle. Hold the foam in place with insulating tape at each end. Make sure that the foam is not too bulky for a comfortable grip.

PREPARING TOOLS FOR STORAGE

During much of the winter, many tools will be required only occasionally, unless digging and soil preparation need to be done during this time. Before putting equipment away in an appropriate place, ensure that it is clean, dry, and ready to be stored for a long period.

CHECKING EQUIPMENT

● **Dried debris** Rub dried garden debris off metal blades using a clean cloth soaked in denatured alcohol.

● **Fuel tanks** Very cold weather alters the consistency of gas. Insulate gas-powered equipment with an old blanket before storage.

● **Cords** Check the cords of electrically driven equipment for signs of wear and tear. Replace cords if necessary.

● **Clean blades** To keep blades and tines in good condition, scrub them with a wire brush and warm water. Allow to dry, then file the cutting edges if they have deteriorated.

PREVENTING RUST

Oily sand

Cleaning and oiling
Mix with a bucketful of sharp sand. To clean and oil large tools before storage, plunge them into the sand several times. Use oily sand to clean nonelectrical equipment, such as forks, spades, and other tools with metal heads.

SHARPENING BLADES

Maintaining cutting tools
Cutting tools, such as pruners and shears, need regular sharpening if they are to continue to cut well. Run the blades regularly through a sharpener, or take the equipment to a professional for servicing.

STORING TOOLS

When the gardening season comes to an end, tools should be placed in a suitable place for storage. Before storing the tools, be sure that the area is dry to avoid problems such as rust, wood rot, and frost damage. If in doubt, check the condition of the tools regularly.

HANGING TOOLS

● **Hand tools** Store hand tools off the ground to help keep them dry and to reduce the possibility of knocking them over or hitting them.

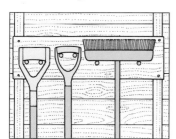

Constructing a tool rack
Make a tool rack by laying the tools to be stored flat on a piece of wood. The tools will be hung on galvanized nails, so mark their positions with a pencil. Remove the tools, and hammer in nails.

STORING CORRECTLY

● **Plastic wrap** Never wrap tools tightly in plastic since condensation may build up and encourage rotting and rust.

● **Hooks** Heavy tools can be suspended above the ground on sturdy hooks, such as those used for storing bicycles.

● **Soil** Never store tools directly on soil. Hang them or stand them on a board wrapped in plastic.

● **Shed** Before using a shed as a storage area for tools, make sure it is dry and in good condition.

● **Power tools** Keep electrically powered garden tools in a dry place. If the storage area is excessively damp, consider storing this equipment in the house.

TRADITIONAL TIP

Maintaining a lawn mower
To ensure that a lawn mower works efficiently at the beginning of a new gardening season, have the machine professionally serviced before putting it into storage, and be sure to place it on a level, wooden base when it is not in use.

GREENHOUSES

CONSTRUCTING AND FILLING A NEW GREENHOUSE can be an exciting experience. However, greenhouses also represent a considerable financial investment, making appropriate and thorough maintenance essential.

CLEANING GREENHOUSES

The type of maintenance needed to keep a greenhouse in pristine condition varies according to its construction. However, there are tasks that are common to all types that should be carried out annually in autumn in order to prolong their effectiveness.

CARING FOR PLANTS
● **Providing light** Clean both sides of the glass to remove debris. This is essential if plants are to benefit from natural light during dark winter months.
● **Protecting plants** If using a commercial cleaner, remove all plants from the area, or cover them with plastic.

WARNING!

Before cleaning a greenhouse with water, it is essential that the electricity supply is turned off and that all sockets are covered securely.

MONEY-SAVING TIP

Keeping drainpipes clear
Wedge a plastic scouring pad or a ball of galvanized wire netting into the opening of a drainpipe. This will act as a filter and prevent falling leaves and other debris from clogging up the pipe or entering a water barrel.

CLEANING A ROOF

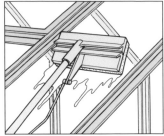

Reaching the roof
Use a long-handled floor mop to clean the upper sections of the roof on the inside and outside of a greenhouse. If the glass is very dirty, add dishwashing liquid or detergent to the water.

PROTECTING METAL
● **Fittings** Although aluminum frames should not rust, treat any other hardware of metal fittings to prevent corrosion.

Preventing rust
To avoid stiffness and rust, apply a thin film of light oil or a layer of antirust paint regularly to metal hardware. Replace corroded hinges and screws with galvanized ones.

REMOVING PESTS

Scrubbing T-bars
Pests may lurk in the T-bars of aluminum greenhouses and remain there unless removed. Use a stream of water and a scrub brush to clean out these areas. If pests persist, rub with steel wool.

MAINTAINING INTERIORS
● **Contents** Sort through the contents of your greenhouse every year, and throw away anything that is not needed.
● **Plants** When cleaning a greenhouse interior, use the opportunity to remove dead flowerheads and leaves.
● **Surfaces** Clean flooring using garden disinfectant. Rinse with clean water. Paint or spray on diluted disinfectant to clean shelves and other surfaces.
● **Drafts** Check vents and doors for drafts, and replace insulation tape if necessary.
● **Insulation** To reduce heat loss during winter, install strips of bubble plastic along the bottom panels of a greenhouse, and put sheets of plastic on the floor.

REPLACING GLASS

Clean, undamaged glass is essential for a productive greenhouse. Cracked panes will make it impossible to maintain temperatures accurately and can be dangerous. Most metal frames use a system of clips to secure the glass panes; putty is necessary for wooden frames.

REPLACING GLASS
● **Positioning** Replace broken glass in wooden frames only if you feel confident handling and positioning glass. If in doubt, call a professional.

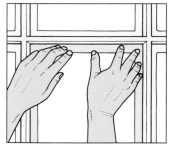

Installing replacement glass
Chisel away any old putty, and replace with a fresh layer. Press the edges, not the middle, of the pane to make contact with the putty. Hold in place with a second application of putty.

WORKING WITH GLASS
● **Damaged glass** Do not wait to replace a pane of glass that is broken. Once a pane is damaged, the whole pane may fall out, with dangerous consequences.
● **Selecting panes** Use special greenhouse glass to replace any panes that are broken or damaged.
● **Clips** To replace glass held in place with clips, unhook the clips and remove the pane, then slide in the new glass and fasten the clips.
● **Cleaning** Remove dirty marks from a new pane of glass with a cloth soaked in denatured alcohol.
● **Trees** If you cannot prune a tree that regularly damages a roof, replace the roof glass with a high-impact polymer.

USING PUTTY

● **Storing** Roll unused putty into balls and store in jars of water. Label the storage jars carefully, and keep out of the reach of children.
● **Positioning** Apply putty at an angle to ensure that rain and condensation do not collect on a wooden frame, which may lead to wet rot.

MAINTAINING FRAMES AND GLASS

Greenhouse frames are available in a variety of materials, which will determine the type of maintenance required. All glass needs regular cleaning, since debris and algae reduces the penetration of light. Dirt inside may also provide a hiding place for pests.

TREATING FRAMES
● **Aluminum** Do not remove the gray patina that forms on aluminum. It will protect a frame against damp weather.
● **Steel** Although steel greenhouse frames are strong, they are also prone to rust. Treat them regularly with a coat of antirust paint. Replace the paint promptly if the surface is scratched.
● **Wood** Hardwood frames need little maintenance. Treat softwood frames with wood preservative every two years (see p. 602). Use a plant-friendly solution, or remove plants until the solution is dry.

REMOVING DEPOSITS

Cleaning between panes
To remove all deposits from overlapping panes of glass, slide a plastic plant label or a piece of thin, flexible plastic in between the panes. Wash off the loose debris with a clean, damp cloth.

CLEANING GLASS
● **Timing** Avoid cleaning glass on hot days; loosened dirt may dry in the heat.
● **Cleaners** Use a commercial garden disinfectant or cleaner on persistently dirty areas or those harboring pests. Be sure to remove plants from the area beforehand.
● **Ventilation** After cleaning interior glass, ventilate the greenhouse thoroughly to reduce moisture in the air.
● **Leaves** If the roof is often covered with leaves, drape lightweight garden netting over the affected area. Empty the netting regularly.

SPRING TASKS

AREA OF THE GARDEN	EARLY SPRING
THE ORNAMENTAL GARDEN Once weather conditions improve and plants begin to grow, there is a great deal to do. There are many seeds that can be sown now, especially those that are sown directly into open ground. Some transplanting and dividing is also possible. The mild conditions of spring stimulate the germination and growth of weeds, as well as the development of many pests and diseases. Prompt action is therefore essential in order to prevent serious problems from developing later in the year. Snowdrops	● Turn the soil over, remove weeds, and fertilize the soil before sowing annuals. Those that can be sown now include *Adonis aestivalis, Brachycome, Centaurea cyanus, Clarkia elegans, Convolvulus tricolor,* and *Eschscholzia californica.* ● Plant out hardy bulbs that have grown inside over winter. Feed and water them well. ● Lift, divide, and replant crowded clumps of snowdrops as soon as the flowers have faded. ● Lift, divide, and replant established or oversized herbaceous plants, discarding any weak sections. ● Plant summer-flowering bulbs and perennials if the ground is not frozen or waterlogged. ● Prune hybrid bush roses, cutting out any frost-damaged, dead, or crossing stems.
THE VEGETABLE GARDEN Warm weather encourages the growth of many vegetables. Toward the end of spring, many tender vegetables can be planted outside, provided that the frosts are over. Pests and weeds may multiply rapidly, so keep a close watch on all crops. Broccoli	● Sow broad beans, cauliflower, brussels sprouts, carrots, onions, radishes, spinach, and parsnips. Make a second sowing of early peas. ● Dig well-rotted manure into celery trenches. ● Plant early potatoes and onion sets. ● Apply a balanced fertilizer to lettuce that will be harvested in early or late spring. ● Prepare runner-bean trenches by digging in compost or well-rotted manure.
THE FRUIT GARDEN Although the first garden-grown fruit does not ripen until toward the end of spring, there is still a lot of watering and feeding to be done to ensure that fruiting trees, bushes, and canes all perform well. Strawberries 	● Prune back the stems of newly planted and two-year-old gooseberries by about one-half. ● Plant currant bushes and raspberry canes, and water in thoroughly. Cut the canes down to 12 in (30 cm) above the ground. ● Spray gooseberries and black currants for gooseberry mildew. ● Protect strawberry plants with cloches. ● Spray apples and pears prone to scab infection.
THE GREENHOUSE As the days become warm, windows and doors will need to be left open on sunny days. They should, however, still be closed up at night. The overall atmosphere should be reasonably dry. Thoroughly clean all of the glass, both inside and out, to let in the maximum amount of light.	● Begin sowing herbs. ● Take cuttings of bedding plants such as fuchsias, heliotropes, marguerites, and pelargoniums. ● Sow seeds of *Anemone coronaria, Antirrhinum majus, Aster novi-belgii, Dianthus chinensis, Lobelia erinus, Petunia, Salvia, Tropaeolum peregrinum,* and *Verbena.*
THE LAWN Having spent most of the winter virtually dormant, the lawn grass will suddenly start to grow. Any damage incurred during the winter must be tended to before summer arrives. Now is the time to begin regular lawn maintenance.	● Rake the lawn clear of twigs, leaves, and other debris that may be clogging the surface. ● To prevent scalping, cut the lawn with the lawnmower blades set reasonably high. ● Neaten lawn edges with edging shears. ● Brush off worm castings regularly.

MIDSPRING	LATE SPRING
• Continue to direct-sow annuals such as *Linaria, Mesembryanthemum,* annual *Rudbeckia,* sunflowers, *Tagetes,* and Virginian stocks. • Prune shrubs grown for their decorative winter stems, such as willows and dogwoods. Prune *Forsythia* as soon as it has finished flowering. • Plant out *Antirrhinum* and *Penstemon* raised from autumn cuttings or sowings. Make sure to harden them off gradually first. • Take root cuttings of *Delphinium, Lupinus,* and herbaceous *Phlox.* • Apply a high-phosphorus fertilizer around the base of summer-flowering shrubs, including roses. • Layer shrubs and climbers such as *Carpenteria, Fothergilla, Kalmia, Lonicera,* and *Syringa.*	• Stake young, herbaceous perennials. • Harden off bedding plants in preparation for planting them in open ground. • Plant young perennials grown from seed into a nursery bed where they can grow until autumn. • Begin to thin out seedlings of any annuals sown directly into the ground. • Tie new, vigorous rambler-rose growth gently, but securely to supports. • Sow seeds of *Achillea* spp., *Alcea rosea, Aquilegia vulgaris, Delphinium elatum, Erigeron speciosus,* and *Lychnis chalcedonica.* • Plant up hanging baskets, barrels, and other containers. Leave them in a greenhouse or cold frame until all danger of frost has passed.
• Thin out overcrowded vegetable seedlings. • Harden off young plants from winter sowings of cauliflower, leeks, onions, lettuce, peas, and broad beans before planting out. • Prepare and plant new asparagus beds. • Support peas with sticks or netting. • Sow broccoli, leeks, kohlrabi, and cauliflower for planting out in early summer. • Sow cabbage in fertile soil.	• Thin seedlings from root crops and onions. • Direct-sow runner beans, squash, pumpkins, cucumbers, sweet corn, peas, endive, green beans, leaf lettuce, Chinese cabbage, and chicory. • Transplant brussels sprouts and leeks; water in. • Form a little mound of soil over young potato shoots to protect them from frost. • Sow cucumbers in mounds enriched with plenty of well-rotted manure and compost.
• Feed summer-fruiting plants with potassium sulfate to promote good flowering and fruit. • Control weeds around bush and cane fruit. • Check for pests and diseases. Use sprays at dusk to avoid harming pollinating insects. • Thin heavy-cropping nectarines and peaches when the fruit is ½ in(1–1.5 cm) in diameter. • Feed blackberry and hybrid berry plants with ammonium sulfate or other high-nitrogen fertilizer.	• Mulch raspberries and other cane fruit. • Carefully remove runners from strawberries. Place mats or straw beneath stems with developing fruit to keep them off the ground. • Control slugs and snails in strawberry beds before they start to attack the fruit. • Tie new raspberry canes to supports. • Keep all fruit well watered, especially those on light soils, and those that are trained against a wall.
• Plant greenhouse tomato plants in large pots, or plant them in grow bags. • Start to harden off bedding plants. • Introduce biological controls to keep down pests such as greenhouse whiteflies and spider mites. • Pot established begonias, chrysanthemums, *Cyclamen,* and gloxinias as necessary.	• Apply a high-phosphorus liquid fertilizer to any tomato plants with setting fruit. • Protect greenhouse plants from heat with greenhouse shading or special shading paint. • Water seedlings with a copper-based fungicide. • Check for powdery mildew, gray mold, aphids, and other problems. Take immediate action.
• Apply a spring fertilizer to stimulate growth. • Remove weeds such as dandelions. • Thoroughly prepare the ground to be seeded or sodded. Fertilize it with a complete fertilizer. Sow grass seed unless the soil is still very wet. • Protect new seed from birds, and water regularly.	• Control lawn weeds. Remove by hand, or use an appropriate weedkiller. • Level off uneven areas of the lawn. • Repair or replace worn-out or bare areas of turf. • Use a half-moon edger to neaten any ragged squashed, or damaged lawn edges.

SUMMER TASKS

AREA OF THE GARDEN	EARLY SUMMER
THE ORNAMENTAL GARDEN Warm weather continues to encourage all plants to grow rapidly, although this growth may slow down considerably if it becomes very hot and dry. Regular watering and feeding are essential to ensure that the garden stays colorful and thrives throughout the summer. Many plants will need to be tied to supports, and prompt action must be taken with any outbreaks of pests and diseases.  Lilac	● Continue to plant out annual bedding and to fill baskets and other containers. Hang up and display any baskets that have been kept in the greenhouse. ● Prune back *Arabis, Aubrieta,* and perennial candytuft as soon as they have finished flowering. ● Divide crowded clumps of primroses, and water irises as soon as flowering is over. ● Remove flowerheads from lilacs and late-flowering camellias as soon as the flowers fade. ● Remove suckers from roses. Be sure to cut them off close to the rootstock. ● Water all ornamental plants regularly to prevent developing buds from dropping off. ● Sow biennials and perennials, including *Aubrietia, Coreopsis,* delphiniums, and wallflowers.
THE VEGETABLE GARDEN There is a great deal to do in the vegetable garden in summer. In order for vegetables to grow as they should, they need a constant supply of water and careful feeding. Weeds compete for water and nutrients, so weed control, although time-consuming, is vital for a healthy crop.  Asparagus	● Make successive sowings of lettuce, turnips, runner beans, green beans, endive, radishes, and kohlrabi. Sow Chinese cabbage. ● Pinch out the tips on broad beans to encourage good pod set and to deter attack from aphids. ● Stop picking asparagus so that the plants do not exhaust themselves. ● Plant outdoor tomatoes, and tie them gently, but firmly, to stakes to secure them.
THE FRUIT GARDEN Summer is when you can begin to enjoy the fruit from many of your trees, bushes, and canes. The plants themselves need relatively little maintenance, except for regular watering, some feeding, and possible spraying against pests and diseases.  Peaches	● Spray raspberries against raspberry beetles. Apply the first spray as soon as the first fruit turns pink. ● Hang codling-moth traps on apple trees. ● Spray against apple scab, mildew, and aphids. ● Tie new canes of blackberries and hybrid berries to a system of support wires, allowing a maximum of eight canes per plant. ● Summer-prune gooseberries by cutting back sideshoots to five leaves.
THE GREENHOUSE Prevent high temperatures in the greenhouse from damaging plants. Open doors, vents, and windows, and damp down regularly to increase the humidity.	● Water and feed tomatoes, cucumbers, and peppers, never letting the soil dry out. ● Attach slings or nets to melons as they swell. ● Continue to remove sideshoots from tomatoes.
THE LAWN Lawn grass grows strongly throughout the summer, so regular mowing is one of the most frequent tasks. Wear and tear is often at its height, too; the lawn is heavily used for parties, sunbathing, barbecues, and playing. The amount of mowing and watering required will be greatly influenced by the weather, and this may vary considerably from year to year.	● Mow as often as necessary, taking care not to cut too short, especially in hot, dry weather. ● Control broadleaved weeds by handweeding or by using suitable commercial weedkillers. ● Water regularly with a sprinkler, but first check to see if there are any local watering restrictions. ● If necessary, apply a nitrogen-rich liquid fertilizer to the lawn to make it greener and to encourage the grass to grow rapidly.

MIDSUMMER	LATE SUMMER
● Feed roses and other flowering plants in open ground and in containers with a high-phosphorus fertilizer to encourage flowering. ● Deadhead faded flowers to promote the formation of new buds and encourage growth. ● Trim hedges regularly to avoid having to cut them back too much at any one time. ● Weed carefully between plants in borders and beneath trees, shrubs, and climbers. ● Layer border carnations and propagate pinks by taking 3-in (7.5-cm) long cuttings. ● Transplant Canterbury bells, sweet Williams, and wallflowers into a nursery bed. Water in well. ● Take semiripe cuttings of many shrubs, including *Deutzia* and *Weigela*.	● Plant *Amaryllis belladonna*, autumn crocus, *Colchicum, Fritillaria imperialis, Lilium candidum,* and *Sternbergia* bulbs. ● Continue to deadhead all flowering plants, unless you intend to save seed. ● Control earwigs and powdery mildew on dahlias and chrysanthemums. ● Prune rambler roses once flowering is over. ● Spray roses against fungal attack such as powdery mildew, rust, and blackspot. ● Water all plants regularly, giving priority to relatively new plants and those that are particularly intolerant of drought. ● Move layered border carnations to their permanent locations.
● Spray outdoor tomatoes and potatoes with a fungicide to protect them from blight. ● Mound soil around celery stems, and tie together. ● Harvest herbs for use in the winter, preferably before they begin to flower. ● Start to make successive sowings of spring cabbage. Sow turnips and rutabagas. ● Harvest runner and green beans as soon as they are ready. Freeze while they are still tender.	● Ripen onions by lifting them gently and leaving them in place for a couple of weeks. ● Sow onions (for an early crop next year), plus spinach, radishes, beets, and chard. ● Continue to water crops regularly, especially those that bolt or fail if allowed to dry out. ● Weed regularly between rows of crops. ● Use a commercial spray on all crops, particularly cabbages, to prevent attacks by caterpillars.
● Prune fan-trained cherries and plums to prevent excessive growth toward the wall or fence. ● Remove and dispose of any apples and pears showing signs of pest infestation. ● Water apple trees regularly and thoroughly to decrease the risk of bitter pit developing. Spray developing fruit with calcium nitrate. ● Erect netting around developing fruit to protect them from being attacked by birds.	● Control woolly aphids on apple trees. ● Prune summer-fruiting raspberries. As soon as they have finished fruiting, cut all the raspberry canes that have just fruited back to ground level, and tie new canes to supports. ● Remove old leaves and runners from strawberries once they have finished fruiting. ● Start to prune apples, and continue to prune cherries, plums, apricots, nectarines, and peaches.
● Continue to water tomato plants frequently to prevent the development of blossom-end rot. ● Remove excessive leaf growth from tomatoes. ● Add extra shading to the glass if necessary.	● Take cuttings of ivy-leaved and zonal pelargoniums, and pot them up. ● Take semiripe cuttings of *Berberis, Camellia, Ceanothus, Cotoneaster, Daphne,* and *Mahonia*.
● Protect areas that are frequently used by children, or move swings and other play equipment around to spread the wear and tear. ● Continue to water regularly, if possible. Water in the early evening to minimize waste. ● Control any ants that may be in the lawn. ● Drench any areas of lawn that have been urinated on by pets and wildlife. ● Leave grass clippings on the lawn in dry weather.	● Apply a lawn fertilizer with relatively high phosphate and potassium levels to encourage the development of strong roots. ● Trim back herbaceous plants that have grown excessively and flopped over the lawn edges. ● Continue to water regularly and thoroughly during hot, dry weather. Always water well after applying any kind of fertilizer. ● Continue to mow the lawn regularly.

AUTUMN TASKS

AREA OF THE GARDEN	EARLY AUTUMN
THE ORNAMENTAL GARDEN Summer borders have now begun to deteriorate. You will need to neaten the plants for the winter, weed, and in some cases divide and replant crowded clumps. Damp weather often encourages an outbreak of diseases, so you may need to control these, too. Remove fallen leaves, since they may harbor diseases and overwhelm small plants. Autumn is a good time to plan next year's planting. *Schizostylis* 	● Plant daffodils, hyacinths, crocuses, scillas, iris, and most lilies for a spring display. ● Remove the remains of summer-flowering annuals, and prepare the soil thoroughly for winter-flowering bedding plants. ● In light, well-drained soils, direct-sow hardy annuals, including *Alyssum, Calendula,* candytuft, *Clarkia, Nigella,* and poppies. ● Lift and store gladiolus corms. ● Place nets over ponds to prevent the water from becoming polluted by falling leaves. ● Continue to prune rambler roses. ● Make sure that autumn-flowering herbaceous plants are properly staked. ● Rake autumn leaves regularly.
THE VEGETABLE GARDEN Some vegetables will be used immediately, while others can be harvested carefully and stored. There is also a considerable amount of clean up to do in preparation for new crops. Remove all diseased debris and dispose of it well away from the vegetable garden. *Squash* 	● Harvest carrots, potatoes, and beets, preferably when the soil is not wet. ● Plant spring cabbage. ● Lift parsley seedlings from around the parent plant, and plant them in containers or directly into a cold frame or cold greenhouse border. ● Harvest and store the bulk of the squash crop. ● Pick outdoor tomatoes, and ripen them in a warm spot indoors, away from the frost.
THE FRUIT GARDEN Most fruit trees yield the majority of their fruit during autumn. Late varieties of some bush and cane fruit are productive now, too. Many apples, and some pears, can be stored for use later in the year. *Grapes* 	● Plant peaches and nectarines, preferably in a sheltered spot, and trained against a sunny wall. ● Begin planting blackberries and hybrid berries. ● Prune raspberry canes that fruited in the summer back to soil level. Carefully tie new canes to the support system. ● Rake up and dispose of fallen leaves from scab-infected apple and pear trees, and from any rust-infected plum trees.
THE GREENHOUSE Before cold weather arrives, move tender plants into the greenhouse for protection over winter. Reduce ventilation and humidity levels.	● Take off all shading from greenhouse glass. ● Pot up bulbs for winter displays. ● Sow lettuce, radish, and carrot varieties for subsequent growing under cloches.
THE LAWN The lawn can now begin to recover from the heavy use it may have sustained over the summer months, as well as from any damaging dry periods when adequate watering may not have been possible. As autumn approaches, grass growth slows down, allowing much essential maintenance work to be done. Work carried out now will benefit the lawn throughout the coming year.	● Rake fallen leaves off the grass as soon as possible, especially if the weather is wet. ● Reseed any worn patches in the lawn. ● Prepare areas ready to be sodded or seeded. ● Aerate the lawn to encourage good drainage and to stimulate root growth. Use a garden fork for small areas or a powered aerator for large areas. ● Apply an insecticide drench if Japanese beetle grubs are present in the lawn.

MIDAUTUMN	LATE AUTUMN
● Pick and dry attractive seedheads for use in dried-flower arrangements. ● Protect alpines, which are intolerant of wet conditions, with a pane of glass. ● Cut back chrysanthemums to about 6 in (15 cm) above ground level, lift, and store in boxes. ● To prolong the flowering period of *Schizostylis,* pot up garden-grown plants, and overwinter them in a greenhouse or cold frame. ● Plant winter and spring bedding plants such as *Bellis,* forget-me-nots, *Polyanthus,* pansies, and wallflowers. Plant lily-of-the-valley. ● Remove dead and dying herbaceous plants, leaving enough foliage behind to protect the crowns from severe winter weather.	● If necessary, transplant trees and shrubs while the soil is still warm and moist, but not too wet. ● Prune deciduous hedges, and carry out any necessary major cutting back. ● Protect half-hardy bulbs such as *Agapanthus.* ● Plant tulip bulbs, preferably in a sunny, sheltered border, or in containers. ● Plant spring-flowering plants for added color to fill any gaps between shrubs next spring. ● Continue to remove the last of the weeds, taking care not to spread seeds. ● To ensure good bud formation for plenty of spring flowers, provide all plants with enough water during dry spells. ● Remove fallen leaves from gutters.
● Harvest onions and cauliflower. ● Remove leaves showing signs of infection from lettuce and brassicas. ● Harvest chicory as the foliage dies back, and store in a cool shed in boxes of sand. ● For a winter crop of spinach, put cloches over late spinach sowings to protect them from frost. ● Cut back foliage of asparagus crowns planted in midspring. Mound soil over crowns.	● Sow broad beans in a sheltered spot to obtain a very early crop without the aid of a greenhouse. ● Harvest and store parsnip, horseradish, and Jerusalem artichoke crops. ● Pick brussels sprouts when the buttons firm up. ● Harvest leeks, trimming off roots and carefully disposing of any outer, rust-infested foliage. ● Dig over vacant areas thoroughly, and allow the soil to be broken down by winter frosts.
● Plant black currants, red and white currants, and raspberry canes from now until early spring, provided that the soil is not too cold or too wet. ● Take hardwood cuttings from grapevines, black currants, and gooseberries. Root them in sandy soil in a sheltered spot. ● Remove all weeds from between strawberry plants, water well, and apply a mulch. ● Continue to rake up and dispose of fallen leaves.	● Cut canes of blackberry and hybrid berries that fruited this year back to soil level, and tie newly formed canes to supports. ● Plant gooseberries, apples, and pears, provided that the soil is not too wet or too cold. ● Prune back newly planted apple trees immediately after planting. Reduce all sideshoots by about one-half, and cut back maiden trees to approximately 20 in (50 cm) above soil level.
● Pick the last of the tomatoes. Remove and dispose of all the plant remains. ● Bring in the last of the chrysanthemums for protection during the winter months.	● Water overwintering plants occasionally so that they do not dry out completely. ● Lift crowns of lily-of-the-valley, and pot them up for an early, indoor, scented display.
● Seed new lawns, or lay sod. ● Scarify the lawn using a spring-tined rake, or a power rake for very large areas. This removes any dead matter and debris from the surface. ● Continue to rake up autumn leaves regularly. Use them to make leaf mold. ● Use a commercial moss killer for moss-infested lawns. To prevent the spread of moss spores, wait until the moss is completely dead before raking it out.	● Plant *Narcissus* and any other suitable bulbs in drifts or clumps in lawns. ● Repair any humps and hollows created by excessive summer wear and tear. ● Continue to trim back herbaceous plants that have flopped over the lawn edges. ● Clean up the lawn mower, and do any necessary repairs before storing it for the winter. ● Repair broken and crushed lawn edges.

WINTER TASKS

AREA OF THE GARDEN	EARLY WINTER
THE ORNAMENTAL GARDEN Frosts, freezing conditions, and snow may make it difficult, if not inadvisable, to do much work outside during a good part of the winter season. It is, however, possible to create a winter garden that has plenty of visual interest as well as fragrance. Temporary color can be introduced in the form of winter-flowering bedding plants as well as a few winter-flowering bulbs. Combine these with a selection of shrubs grown for their winter bark, flowers, and berries (such as *Skimmia*), or for their evergreen foliage.  *Skimmia*	● Protect crowns of herbaceous plants from frost damage with straw or dry leaves. ● Protect root balls of container-grown plants by wrapping the containers in burlap or newspaper. ● Continue to clear vacant beds and borders. ● Where necessary, firm soil that has been lifted around shrub roots by frost. ● In a windy garden, prune back some of the top-growth on roses to minimize windrock. ● If soil in flower beds is very wet, try to avoid walking on it, which could compact it. Stand on a board so that your weight is spread over a large area. ● Sow alpine and tree seeds that benefit from exposure to frost, and leave them outside. ● Begin winter-pruning trees and shrubs. ● Browse through seed catalogs, and decide what to buy. Place orders to seed companies early so that you are not disappointed.
THE VEGETABLE GARDEN A carefully planned vegetable garden will continue to yield some fresh crops throughout the winter. Protect crops with row covers and cloches for best results.  Cauliflower	● Continue to harvest trench celery. Check for slug damage, and take appropriate action. ● Continue to harvest leek, turnip, rutabagas, kohlrabi, and parsnip crops. ● Bend the leaves of cauliflower over the curds to protect them from frost damage. ● Plant chicory roots in pots, and place them in a dark spot at about 45°F (7°C). Harvest young shoots as they appear.
THE FRUIT GARDEN Winter weather provides a relatively quiet period in the fruit garden, since fruit trees and bushes are now fully dormant. Check fruit in storage, and remove any showing signs of deterioration or disease.  Stored apples	● Prune red and white currants from now until late winter. After pruning, apply a mulch of well-rotted manure or compost. ● Prune apples and pears. Check branches, stems, and trunks for signs of fungal canker. Prune out and treat affected areas as necessary. ● Make sure that any stakes and ties around fruit bushes and trees are held firmly in place. ● Apply dormant oil or similar to help control overwintering pests and diseases.
THE GREENHOUSE Use a greenhouse to make early sowings of many vegetables and flowers. Check the thermometer regularly, and adjust the heating as necessary.	● Sow the seeds of herbaceous perennials such as anemones, *Canna*, columbines, *Dianthus*, hollyhocks, and poppies. ● Prune grapevines grown under glass.
THE LAWN The lawn needs little attention during the winter. Unless any urgent action is required, it is best to avoid working on the lawn much until spring.	● Continue to rake up any fallen leaves that have blown onto the lawn. ● Use a brush with stiff bristles to scatter any worm castings that have appeared on the lawn.

MIDWINTER	LATE WINTER
● Slugs may cause damage during mild spells, so control them before they attack any plant crowns that are left in the ground. ● Prevent the sides of ponds from being cracked by pressure from freezing water. Float a ball, empty plastic bottle, or log on the surface. ● Brush heavy snow off branches to prevent the weight from snapping them. ● Protect winter-flowering hellebores from being splashed with mud by covering them with cloches. ● Carefully fork over the surface soil in flower beds containing spring-flowering bulbs to break up compaction and to deter the growth of algae, moss, and weeds. ● Dig the soil in preparation for planting dahlias when all danger of frost has passed. ● Make sure that garden birds have a regular supply of food and water during the cold weather. ● Plant trees and shrubs on dry, warm days.	● Sow a selection of herbaceous perennials to incorporate into your flower borders in the spring. ● Once winter-flowering heathers have finished flowering, trim them back lightly. Do not cut into woody growth – just trim off old flowering stems. ● Plant *Tigridia* bulbs outside in a sheltered, warm spot. Also plant *Crocosmia*. ● Check dahlias in storage, and remove any that are showing signs of rotting. ● Prune winter-flowering jasmine as soon as the last of the flowers have finished. ● Prune and train stems of ornamental climbers such as *Vitis coignetiae*. ● Start to prune *Cornus* (dogwoods), that have brightly colored winter stems. ● Plant gladioli, anemones, lilies, *Ranunculus,* and hedges in mild areas. ● Feed established flower beds and borders with well-rotted manure.
● Continue to harvest winter cabbage, brussels sprouts, parsnips, and leeks. ● Spray brussels sprouts and other winter brassicas for whitefly. ● Harvest Jerusalem artichokes. Make sure that you lift every piece of tuber. Store tubers in a paper bag in a cool, well-ventilated shed or garage. ● Plant early potatoes in pots in a greenhouse or a cold frame to produce a very early crop.	● Choose a sheltered spot with moist soil, to make the first sowing of carrots. ● Sow early peas in a sheltered spot. ● Sow onions and scallions. ● Continue to harvest winter brassicas, leeks, celery, and root crops. ● Continue to spray against brassica whitefly. ● In mild areas shallots may be planted. ● Thin lettuce sown in midsummer.
● Spray peaches, nectarines, and almonds with a copper-based fungicide to prevent attacks of peach-leaf curl. Cover fan-trained trees with an open-sided plastic shelter. ● Start forcing rhubarb. Cover the crowns with a deep layer of leaves or leaf mold, then cover with a pot. ● Apply a mulch of well-rotted manure or compost around the bases of gooseberries. ● Complete the last pruning of apples and pears.	● Apply a second spray of copper-based fungicide to trees susceptible to peach-leaf curl about 14 days after the first application. ● Sprinkle sulphate of potash around the root-feeding area of apples, pears, and plums to encourage good fruiting later in the year. ● Prune autumn-fruiting raspberries. Cut back to ground level the canes that fruited last autumn. ● Prune back canes of raspberries planted last year to about 12 in (30 cm) above ground level.
● Start to sow seeds of *Antirrhinum,* begonias, pelargoniums, salvias, verbenas, and at 65°F (18°C). ● Take cuttings from perpetual-flowering carnations; root in sandy soil mix at 50°F (10°C).	● Water trays of seedlings with a copper-based fungicide to prevent damping off. ● Ventilate as much as possible to prevent the buildup of diseases in the damp atmosphere.
● Have your lawnmower serviced and repaired if you have not already done so. ● Make sure that all lawn tools are properly cleaned, oiled, and stored for the winter.	● Try to keep off the grass if it is frozen, since damage will encourage the onset of diseases. ● Lift loose or sunken stepping-stones in the lawn. Level them, and re-lay.

USEFUL INFORMATION

T HERE ARE A NUMBER OF DIFFERENT MEASUREMENT SYSTEMS *in use around the world. The conversion charts on the following pages show some of the most common shoe and clothing sizes, the standard body measurements for clothing, as well as metric and imperial systems for converting length, weight, and other measurements.*

SHOE AND CLOTHING SIZES

S hoe and clothing sizes vary between makes, so use the following conversions as a rough guide to adult sizes. Manufacturers may classify children's sizes by age or height, but children may not fit these categories, so always carry a child's measurements (see opposite).

SHOE SIZES

FOOT LENGTH	UK	EUROPE	US (MEN)	US (WOMEN)
24.2 cm	3½	36	4	5
24.6 cm	4	36	4½	5½
25.0 cm	4½	37	5	6
25.4 cm	5	38	5½	6½
25.8 cm	5½	38	6	7
26.2 cm	6	39	6½	7½
26.7 cm	6½	40	7	8
27.1 cm	7	40	7½	8½
27.5 cm	7½	41	8	9
27.9 cm	8	42	8½	9½
28.4 cm	8½	42	9	10
28.8 cm	9	43	9½	10½
29.2 cm	9½	43	10	11
29.6 cm	10	44	10½	11½
30.1 cm	10½	45	11	12
30.5 cm	11	45	11½	12½
30.9 cm	11½	46	12	13
31.3 cm	12	47	12½	13½

SHIRT COLLAR SIZES

EUROPE	UK/US
36 cm	14 in
37 cm	14½ in
38 cm	15 in
40 cm	15½ in
41 cm	16 in
42 cm	16½ in
43 cm	17 in
44 cm	17½ in

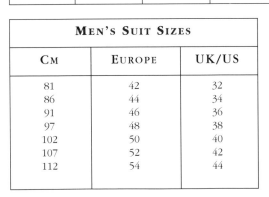

MEN'S SUIT SIZES

CM	EUROPE	UK/US
81	42	32
86	44	34
91	46	36
97	48	38
102	50	40
107	52	42
112	54	44

WOMEN'S CLOTHING SIZES

UK	EUROPE	US
10	38	8
12	40	10
14	42	12
16	44	14
18	47	16
20	50	18
22	52	20

TAKING BODY MEASUREMENTS FOR CLOTHING

Keep accurate measurements for yourself and other family members, and use them as reference when buying or making clothes. When taking a person's measurements, be sure that he or she is standing straight. When you go shopping to buy clothes, carry the measurements with you. Revise children's measurements frequently, and always have their shoe sizes tested by professional fitters.

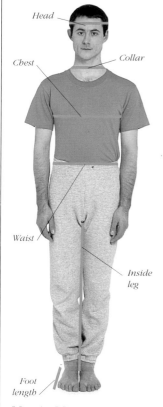

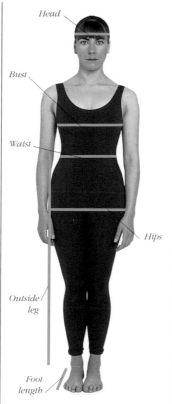

MAN'S MEASUREMENTS

● **Head** Measure horizontally around the head, level with the middle of the forehead.
● **Collar** Measure around the fullest part of the neck.
● **Chest** Measure around the fullest part of the chest, keeping the tape measure straight across the back.
● **Waist** Tie a piece of string around the waist, and let it settle into the natural waistline. Measure around this marker with a tape measure.
● **Inside leg** Measure vertically down the inside of the leg, from the crotch to the ankle bone.
● **Foot length** Measure along the sole of the foot, from the big toe to the heel.

WOMAN'S MEASUREMENTS

● **Head** Measure horizontally around the head, level with the middle of the forehead.
● **Bust** Measure around the fullest part of the chest, keeping the tape measure straight across the back.
● **Waist** Tie a piece of string around the waist, and let it settle into the natural waistline. Measure around this with a tape measure.
● **Hips** Measure around the fullest part of the hips and buttocks, keeping the tape measure straight.
● **Outside leg** Tie string around the waist to find the natural waistline. Measure the outside leg from the string to the ankle bone.
● **Foot length** Measure along the sole of the foot, from the big toe to the heel.

CHILD'S MEASUREMENTS

● **Height** Stand the child against a wall. Mark the wall by the top of the child's head, and measure from this mark to the floor.
● **Head** Measure horizontally around the head, level with the middle of the forehead.
● **Chest** Measure the fullest part of the chest, keeping the tape measure straight across the back.
● **Waist** Measure around the waist, keeping the tape measure level with the navel.
● **Outside leg** Use string to mark the natural waistline. Measure the outside leg from the string to the ankle bone.
● **Foot length** Measure along the sole of the foot, from the big toe to the heel.

WEIGHTS AND MEASURES

The charts below give conversions for metric and imperial measures. The central columns show the number of units to be converted. For example, to convert 7 miles to kilometers, let 7 stand for miles, then find the number beside 7 in the kilometers column (11.27). To multiply by 10, move the decimal point one place right. For numbers not shown, add the chart figures together. For example, to convert 14 inches to centimeters, add the figures for 10 inches and for 4 inches: 25.40 + 10.16 = 35.56. Use these charts to help make quick conversions.

MILES AND KILOMETERS

MILES	NUMBER	KM
0.62	1	1.61
1.24	2	3.22
1.86	3	4.83
2.49	4	6.44
3.11	5	8.05
3.73	6	9.66
4.35	7	11.27
4.97	8	12.88
5.59	9	14.48
6.21	10	16.09
12.43	20	32.19
18.64	30	48.28
24.86	40	64.37
31.07	50	80.47
62.14	100	160.93
155.34	250	402.34
310.69	500	804.67
621.37	1,000	1,609.34

INCHES AND CENTIMETERS

IN	NUMBER	CM
⅛	0.25	0.64
¼	0.5	1.27
5⁄16	0.75	1.91
⅜	1	2.54
¾	2	5.08
1¼	3	7.62
1½	4	10.16
2	5	12.70
2⅜	6	15.24
2¾	7	17.78
3⅛	8	20.32
3½	9	22.86
4	10	25.40
8	20	50.80
12	30	76.20
16	40	101.60
19½	50	127.00
39⅜	100	254.00

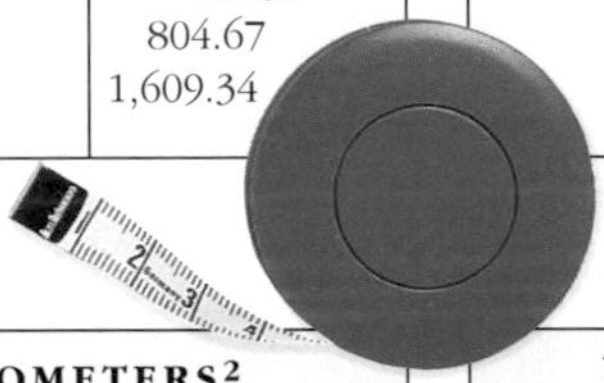

MILES^2 AND KILOMETERS^2

MILES^2	NUMBER	KM^2
0.39	1	2.59
0.77	2	5.18
1.16	3	7.77
1.54	4	10.36
1.93	5	12.95
2.32	6	15.54
2.70	7	18.13
3.09	8	20.72
3.48	9	23.31
3.86	10	25.90
7.72	20	51.80
11.58	30	77.70
15.44	40	103.60
19.31	50	129.50
38.61	100	259.00
96.53	250	647.50
193.05	500	1,294.99
386.10	1,000	2,589.99

INCHES^2 AND CENTIMETERS^2

IN^2	NUMBER	CM^2
0.04	0.25	1.61
0.08	0.5	3.23
0.12	0.75	4.84
0.16	1	6.45
0.31	2	12.90
0.47	3	19.36
0.62	4	25.81
0.78	5	32.26
0.93	6	38.71
1.09	7	45.16
1.24	8	51.61
1.40	9	58.06
1.55	10	64.52
3.10	20	129.03
4.65	30	193.55
6.20	40	258.06
7.75	50	322.58
15.50	100	645.16

INCHES³ AND CENTIMETERS³

IN³	NUMBER	CM³
0.06	1	16.39
0.12	2	32.77
0.18	3	49.16
0.24	4	65.55
0.31	5	81.94
0.37	6	98.32
0.43	7	114.71
0.49	8	131.10
0.55	9	147.48
0.61	10	163.87
3.05	50	819.35
6.10	100	1,638.71
61.02	1,000	16,387.06

GALLONS AND LITERS

GALLONS	NUMBER	LITERS
0.22	1	4.55
0.44	2	9.09
0.66	3	13.64
0.88	4	18.18
1.10	5	22.73
1.32	6	27.28
1.54	7	31.82
1.76	8	36.37
1.98	9	40.91
2.20	10	45.46
11.00	50	227.30
22.00	100	454.60
220.00	1,000	4,546.00

POUNDS AND KILOGRAMS

LB	NUMBER	KG
2.21	1	0.45
4.41	2	0.91
6.61	3	1.36
8.82	4	1.81
11.02	5	2.27
13.23	6	2.72
15.43	7	3.18
17.64	8	3.63
19.84	9	4.08
22.05	10	4.54
110.23	50	22.68
220.46	100	45.36
2204.62	1,000	453.59

FLUID OUNCES AND MILLILITERS

FL OZ	NUMBER	ML
—	1	30
1/16	2	57
—	3	85
1/8	4	114
—	5	142
3/16	6	170
—	7	199
1/4	8	227
—	9	256
5/16	10	284
1	30	852
1½	50	1,420
3⅛	100	2,840

OUNCES AND GRAMS

OUNCES	NUMBER	GRAMS
—	1	28.35
1/16	2	56.70
—	3	85.05
1/8	4	113.40
3/16	5	141.75
—	6	170.10
1/4	7	198.45
—	8	226.80
5/16	9	255.15
3/8	10	283.50
½	15	425.24
3/4	20	566.99
1	30	850.49
2	50	1,417.48
4	100	2,834.95

°FAHRENHEIT AND °CENTIGRADE

°F	NUMBER	°C
14	−10	−23.3
23	−5	−20.6
32	0	−17.8
41	5	−15.0
50	10	−12.2
59	15	−9.4
68	20	−6.7
86	30	−1.1
104	40	4.4
122	50	10.0
140	60	15.6
158	70	21.1
176	80	26.7
194	90	32.2
212	100	37.8

COOKING MEASUREMENTS

SUCCESSFUL COOKING OFTEN DEPENDS UPON ACCURATE MEASUREMENT. If you lack the experience to guess amounts accurately, make sure that you have sets of measuring cups and standard measuring spoons, and a good oven.

EASY MEASURING

Many recipes give measurements in both metric and imperial units. Use whichever system you prefer, but do not mix the two, since they are not interchangeable. Teaspoons and tablespoons are always treated as level measurements and should not be heaped.

PROPORTIONAL MEASURES
● **Relative sizes** You can make many recipes (but not those for baking) without using measuring cups. Use a small coffee cup and assume it holds 1 cup (225 ml). Use the same cup for all the measurements in a recipe; correct proportions usually produce good results.

CONTAINER USES
● **Using food containers** Items such as yogurt containers and tomato cans can help you get precise measurements without using measuring cups. A yogurt container, for example, will range from 5 oz (150 ml) to 1 cup (225 ml). Mark the size on the container.

MEASURING FATS
● **Measuring with cups** Hard fats such as butter or lard are easier to measure in cups by using the displacement method. To measure ¼ cup butter, fill a measuring cup with ¾ cup water, then add butter until the water reaches the 1 cup mark.

APPROXIMATE IMPERIAL/METRIC EQUIVALENTS					
WEIGHT		VOLUME		LENGTH	
IMPERIAL	METRIC	IMPERIAL	METRIC	IMPERIAL	METRIC
½ oz	15 g	¼ tsp	1.25 ml	⅛ in	3 mm
1 oz	25 g	½ tsp	2.5 ml	¼ in	5 mm
1¾ oz	50 g	1 tsp	5 ml	½ in	1 cm
2¾ oz	75 g	2 tsp	10 ml	¾ in	2 cm
3½ oz	100 g	1 tbsp/3 tsp	15 ml	1 in	2.5 cm
4½ oz	125 g	2 tbsp/1 fl oz	30 ml	1¼ in	3 cm
5½ oz	150 g	3 tbsp	45 ml	1½ in	4 cm
6 oz	175 g	2 fl oz/¼ cup	50 ml	2 in	5 cm
7 oz	200 g	3½ fl oz	100 ml	2½ in	6 cm
8 oz	225 g	4 fl oz/½ cup	125 ml	2¾ in	7 cm
10½ oz	300 g	7 fl oz	200 ml	3¼ in	8 cm
11½ oz	325 g	8 fl oz/1 cup	225 ml	3½ in	9 cm
12 oz	350 g	9 fl oz	250 ml	4 in	10 cm
14 oz	400 g	10 fl oz	300 ml	4½ in	12 cm
15 oz	425 g	14 fl oz	400 ml	5 in	13 cm
1 lb	450 g	16 fl oz/2 cups	450 ml	5½ in	14 cm
1 lb 2 oz	500 g	18 fl oz	500 ml	6 in	15 cm
1 lb 10 oz	750 g	21 fl oz	600 ml	6¼ in	16 cm
2 lb 4 oz	1 kg	24 fl oz/3 cups	675 ml	6½ in	17 cm
2 lb 12 oz	1.25 kg	25 fl oz	700 ml	7 in	18 cm
3 lb 5 oz	1.5 kg	4 cups	900 ml	7½ in	19 cm
4 lb 8 oz	2 kg	4½ cups	1 liter	8 in	20 cm
5 lb	2.25 kg	6¾ cups	1.5 liters	8½ in	22 cm
5 lb 8 oz	2.5 kg	9 cups	2 liters	9 in	23 cm
6 lb	2.7 kg	11 cups	2.5 liters	10 in	25 cm
6 lb 8 oz	3 kg	13 cups	3 liters	12 in	30 cm

TEMPERATURE CONVERSIONS

Most recipes specify a cooking temperature to ensure the best results. Ovens vary according to type, fuel used, and fluctuations in power, so you may need to make adjustments if a dish is cooking more quickly or slowly than the suggested cooking time in the recipe.

OVEN TEMPERATURE CONVERSIONS			
DESCRIPTION	°F	°C	USES
COOL	225°F 250°F	110°C 120°C	Warming
WARM	275°F 300°F	140°C 150°C	Slow cooking
MODERATE	325°F 350°F	170°C 180°C	Baked goods
FAIRLY HOT	375°F 400°F	190°C 200°C	Baked goods Meats/Poultry
HOT	425°F 450°F	220°C 230°C	Meats/Poultry
VERY HOT	475°F	240°C	Meats/Poultry

MAXIMIZING OVEN USE
● **Baking dishes together** To bake several dishes that each require different temperatures together, adjust cooking times instead. With the oven on a moderate setting, cook dishes requiring a higher temperature for longer, and those needing a lower temperature for less.

CONVECTION OVENS
● **Adjusting times** Reduce cooking times in a fan-assisted oven by 5–10 minutes per hour, or reduce the oven temperature by 20–50°F (10–20°C), since a fan-assisted oven will cook food faster than a conventional oven. Check the manufacturer's handbook for specific timings.

ROASTING TEMPERATURES

Use these roasting times as a rough guide only, since they will vary according to the cut of meat. Meat on the bone will cook more quickly, since bone conducts heat. Beef, lamb, and duck may be served rare, but other meat must be cooked until the juices run clear.

ROASTING TEMPERATURES AND TIMES					
MEAT TYPE		°F	°C	BASE TIME	ADDITIONAL TIME
BEEF	rare	400°F	200°C	20 minutes	20 minutes per 1 lb (500 g)
	medium	400°F	200°C	20 minutes	25 minutes per 1 lb (500 g)
	well done	400°F	200°C	20 minutes	30 minutes per 1 lb (500 g)
LAMB		350°F	180°C	30 minutes	30 minutes per 1 lb (500 g)
PORK		350°F	180°C	35 minutes	35 minutes per 1 lb (500 g)
CHICKEN		350°F	180°C	25 minutes	25 minutes per 1 lb (500 g)
TURKEY		375°F	190°C	20 minutes	20 minutes per 1 lb (500 g)
DUCK		375°F	190°C	30 minutes	30 minutes per 1 lb (500 g)
GOOSE		350°F	190°C	30 minutes	30 minutes per 1 lb (500 g)

NUTRITION

A HEALTHY DIET IS IMPORTANT TO EVERYONE, young or old, and not only helps prevent heart disease, tooth decay, and obesity, but protects against some serious illnesses. Achieving a balanced diet is easy and can be enjoyable.

BALANCING YOUR DIET

The nutritional value of any diet depends upon a good balance of all the essential nutrients. The best way to achieve this is to eat a variety of foods from all the different food groups. Try to eat at least one balanced meal every day, and limit unhealthy snacks.

INCREASING FIBER
● **Serving whole-grain bread** Switch from white to whole-grain bread, and use less filling and more bread in sandwiches.
● **Varying salads** Mix beans, rice, or pasta into green salads.
● **Eating healthy snacks** Serve whole-grain toast with peanut butter instead of sweet cookies.

REDUCING SUGAR
● **Cutting down gradually** If you add sugar to drinks, reduce the amount gradually, and you will not notice the difference.
● **Buying fruits** Keep fruits handy to replace sugary snacks.
● **Adding mineral water** Dilute fruit juices with mineral water to reduce natural sugar intake.

REDUCING FAT
● **Using substitutes** Consider using ground turkey in recipes instead of ground beef or lamb, since it is much lower in fat.
● **Spreading butter thinly** If you like butter on bread, soften it first for a few seconds in the microwave so that it will be easy to spread thinly.

RECOMMENDED DAILY INTAKE OF ESSENTIAL FOODS

Choosing food for a balanced diet
To achieve a balanced diet, you should eat the right amounts of the foods that provide protein, vitamins, carbohydrate, fiber, and minerals every day. This pyramid shows the number of servings of each type of food you should eat, and lists a selection of sample servings.

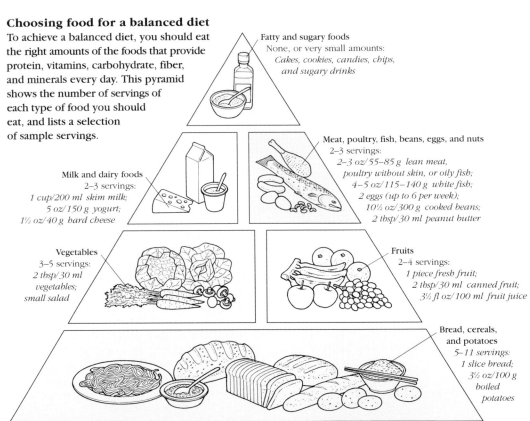

Fatty and sugary foods
None, or very small amounts:
Cakes, cookies, candies, chips, and sugary drinks

Meat, poultry, fish, beans, eggs, and nuts
2–3 servings:
*2–3 oz/55–85 g lean meat, poultry without skin, or oily fish;
4–5 oz/115–140 g white fish;
2 eggs (up to 6 per week);
10½ oz/300 g cooked beans;
2 tbsp/30 ml peanut butter*

Milk and dairy foods
2–3 servings:
*1 cup/200 ml skim milk;
5 oz/150 g yogurt;
1½ oz/40 g hard cheese*

Vegetables
3–5 servings:
*2 tbsp/30 ml vegetables;
small salad*

Fruits
2–4 servings:
*1 piece fresh fruit;
2 tbsp/30 ml canned fruit;
3½ fl oz/100 ml fruit juice*

Bread, cereals, and potatoes
5–11 servings:
*1 slice bread;
3½ oz/100 g boiled potatoes*

EATING THE RIGHT NUTRIENTS

A well-balanced diet should include all the vitamins and minerals listed below. Many of them cannot be stored in the body, so they need to be included in your diet on a daily basis. Specific dietary requirements vary from person to person, but use this chart as a guide.

IMPORTANT VITAMINS AND MINERALS		
NUTRIENT	GOOD SOURCES	FUNCTIONS IN THE BODY
VITAMIN A	Milk and dairy foods, oily fish and fish-liver oils, liver, butter, margarine, spinach, carrots, dried apricots and yellow fruits, nuts and seeds.	Aids vision in dim light; essential for growth of healthy skin and normal development of tissues, especially those that secrete mucus.
B-GROUP VITAMINS	Fortified breakfast cereals, meat, organ meats, fish, cheese, bread, eggs, whole cereals.	Encourage release of energy for growth; repair and maintain nervous system; aid muscle and heart function; encourage healthy skin and hair.
VITAMIN C	Citrus fruits and juice, lightly cooked green vegetables such as Brussels sprouts and cabbage, potatoes, most fresh fruits.	Maintains healthy skin, gums, teeth, and blood vessels; essential for iron absorption. Heavy smoking and drinking increase the need for vitamin C.
VITAMIN D	Fortified milk, oily fish, margarine, eggs, fortified breakfast cereals.	Controls calcium and phosphorus levels in blood; develops strong bones.
VITAMIN E	Vegetable oils, whole-grain cereals, butter, eggs, animal fats, green vegetables, nuts.	Helps body cells function properly; protects essential fats against oxidization.
IRON	Meat, especially liver and kidneys, bread, flour and other cereals, vegetables.	Vital component of red blood cells, which carry oxygen from lungs to cells.
CALCIUM	Milk, cheese, bread and flour, green vegetables, canned sardines and salmon.	Develops strong bones and teeth; aids muscle development and blood clotting.
PHOSPHORUS	Milk and milk products, bread and other cereals, meat and meat products.	Develops healthy bones and teeth; is essential for release of energy.
MAGNESIUM	Milk, bread and other cereal products, potatoes and other vegetables.	Essential constituent of all cells; is necessary for utilization of energy.
SODIUM	Salt, bread, most processed foods.	Essential for maintaining water balance and for muscle and nerve activity.
POTASSIUM	Vegetables, meat and milk, fruits and fruit juices.	Works with sodium in the functioning of muscles and nerve cells.
ZINC	Meat and meat products, milk, bread and other cereal products, oysters, sardines.	Needed for development of reproductive organs, healthy teeth, immune system.
TRACE ELEMENTS	*Copper* meat/vegetables; *iodine* seafood/milk; *fluorine* water/seafood; *selenium* meat/fish/cereals; *chromium* widely distributed.	All known to be essential. Research is ongoing to discover specific roles and consequences of dietary deficiencies.

USEFUL TERMS

T HIS GLOSSARY OF USEFUL TERMS EXPLAINS THE MEANING of terms used in connection with tasks and projects in and around the home. The terms describe tools and equipment, materials, methods and techniques, and many others.

● **Acetone** A colorless liquid used as a solvent.

● **Acid soil** A soil containing little or no lime and with a pH of less than 7.0.

● **Acrylic** A term describing decorating materials, such as paint, that are water based.

● **Address** To place a length of pasted wallpaper on a wall ready for maneuvering into a precise position and attaching.

● **Aerate** To introduce more air within the structure of soil.

● **Aging** In decorating, the application of one of a number of techniques to create the impression of wear and tear on a wooden, painted, or plaster surface over a period of time.

● **Air-layering** A method of plant propagation whereby a stem is cut and wrapped in damp moss and plastic in order to encourage rooting.

● **Al dente** An Italian term describing cooked pasta that is just firm to the bite.

● **Alkaline soil** A soil that is rich in lime or chalk and has a pH of more than 7.0.

● **Alpines** A term used generally to describe small plants that are suitable for growing in rock gardens.

● **Ambrosia** Sweetened fruit purée mixed with yogurt or whipped cream to make a light, refreshing dessert.

● **Annual** A plant that is sown, grown, sets seed, and dies within one year.

● **Antipasti** An Italian term for hot or cold hors d'oeuvres.

● **Antiquing** The application of one of a number of decorating techniques in order to create the impression of the changes to a wooden, painted, or metal surface over time.

● **Aphids** A type of small insect, occurring on a wide range of plants, that feeds by sucking plant sap.

● **Arbor** A leafy, shady area of garden created by the presence of trees and/or the training of shrubs or climbing plants over a trellis or other structure.

● **Architrave** The molded edging of a door, window, archway, or wall panel that forms the boundary between that feature and a wall.

● **Au gratin** A French term describing a dish topped with a sauce, sprinkled with bread crumbs or cheese, and grilled or baked until golden.

● **Axil** The angle between a plant stem and the upper surface of each lateral growth.

● **Bagging** A paint-effect technique whereby a crumpled plastic bag is dabbed on a glaze or emulsion to create a pattern.

● **Bain marie** A French term describing a pan or dish half-filled with hot water in which a container of food is cooked. The water is kept heated to just below boiling point.

● **Baize** A coarse, woollen material often used to make covers or linings.

● **Baking empty** Partly baking a pastry shell for a tart or flan. The pastry is weighed down, with pie weights for example, to prevent it from rising and from remaining uncooked beneath a moist filling.

● **Barding** Tying bacon or pork fat over meat or poultry before roasting to keep it moist and eliminate the need for basting.

● **Basting** Brushing or spooning liquid fat or juices over meat or poultry during roasting to prevent it from drying out.

● **Batten** A length of wood that is rectangular in section and of narrow dimensions, used for a variety of purposes.

● **Bay window** A window that forms a recess in a room, often with three sections looking out in different directions.

● **Bead** To spread paint using a small paintbrush into corner junctions, such as where walls meet ceilings, to create a precise edge between the two.

● **Beading** A thin, wooden, decorative molding used as an ornamental edging.

● **Bedding plants** Plants, usually annuals, grown to provide a temporary but impressive display.

● **Beignet** A French term describing a sweet fritter lightened with whipped egg whites and often flavored with ground almonds.

● **Beurre manié** A French term for a paste that is made by kneading together equal parts of butter and flour. The paste is then used as a thickener for both sauces and stews.

● **Biennial** A plant that is sown and produces leaves in the first year, then flowers, sets seed, and dies in the next.

● **Biological control** A method of controlling the numbers of a pest by introducing one of its predators or parasites.

● **Blacking** Any of a number of substances that are applied to metal or other surfaces in order to blacken the finish.

● **Blanching** Plunging foods into boiling water for a short time to reduce strong flavors, whiten, preserve color, destroy bacteria, or parboil.

● **Bleed** The seepage of unwanted substances, such as resin from wood, through the surface of a painted finish.

● **Blocking** A technique of applying a design to a wall, floor, or other area using a cut-out, shaped object whose surface is dipped in paint and then applied to that area.

● **Bolster chisel** A heavyweight, broad-bladed chisel mainly intended for masonry work, but useful for laying burlap-backed carpet over tack strips.

● **Borax** A white, crystalline salt used for laundry purposes since it cuts grease, loosens dirt, and retards the growth of mold and bacteria.

● **Bouquet garni** A French term describing a small bunch of herbs, tied together or wrapped in cheesecloth, that is added to stews or casseroles for flavor.

● **Braising** Baking or stewing meat, poultry, or vegetables in a small amount of liquid in a covered pot.

● **Brick bond** A design taken from bricklaying and applied to the laying of tiles, whereby rows of tiles are arranged so that no vertical joins align with those of the previous row.

● **Brine** A salt and water solution in which food is immersed for preserving.

● **Brocade** A luxurious, heavyweight, silk fabric with a raised design woven into it.

● **Brûlée** A French term describing a dish that has been sprinkled with sugar and grilled until a caramelized crust has formed on top.

● **Bulb** A swollen underground plant stem, formed from a modified bud, which acts as a food store during the plant's resting period.

● **Bulbil** A small bulb or bulb-like growth in a leaf axil or on a flower stalk.

● **Burlap** A coarse, plain fabric made from jute fiber.

● **Café curtain** A curtain that covers only the lower half of a window and hangs from a wire or slim curtain pole suspended across the center of the frame.

● **Canapés** A French term describing small, bite-sized appetizers.

● **Caramel** A dark, sweet substance made by heating sugar or sugar syrup.

● **Casement window** A window that has vertically hinged sections and sometimes also includes horizontally hinged and/or fixed sections.

● **Casserole** A covered baking dish used for cooking stews in the oven; the name of dishes cooked by this method.

● **Chair rail** A molding attached along a wall, roughly at waist height, which separates upper and lower areas.

● **Chalk line** A length of string, coated in chalk dust, used to produce accurately positioned, straight guidelines for many decorating tasks. The chalk line may alternatively be housed in a special vessel that contains a chalk reservoir.

● **Char-grilling** Cooking food, unwrapped, on an open grill directly over charcoal to allow the unique, smoky flavor of the fuel to penetrate the food.

● **Chase in** To cut a groove in a wall to take a cable or pipe.

● **Chenille** A thick, velvetlike fabric used for soft furnishings.

● **Chipboard** A manufactured building board made from compressed wooden particles, used mainly for subfloors.

● **Clarifying** Removing the impurities from butter or stock by heating the liquid, then skimming or straining it.

● **Cloche** A small structure made from glass or plastic in a metal or plastic frame and used to protect plants from unsuitable weather.

● **Coir** A coconut-husk fiber used for natural-fiber flooring.

● **Colorwashing** A traditional paint technique whereby paint is diluted and used to create a semitransparent rather than an opaque finish on a surface.

● **Combing** A paint-effect technique whereby a decorator's comb is dragged across a glaze in order to produce a series of lines.

● **Compost** Organic material resulting from the breakdown of organic matter collected from the garden and kitchen for use on the garden.

● **Compote** A mixture of fruits cooked in a syrup. The mixture is usually served warm.

● **Corm** A swollen plant stem-base that is found underground and stores food. It differs from a bulb in that its structure is not layered. Small corms on the parent produce new plants.

● **Cornice** A wooden or fabric-covered hard edging that conceals the hanging system of a window treatment.

● **Coulis** A French term for a pourable, liquid purée used as a sauce. Usually made of fruit.

● **Countersink** To insert a screw into a wooden surface so that its head does not protrude above that surface. This is achieved by means of a specially designed drill bit.

● **Coving** A decorative plaster or polystyrene molding used at a wall-ceiling junction.

● **Crackle glaze** A particular type of glaze used to achieve a craquelure effect.

● **Craquelure** A term describing a paint effect used to age a surface with the appearance of a network of fine cracks, and created by the application of varnish to a painted surface.

● **Creaming** Beating together fat and sugar. Used as the basis of some cake mixtures.

● **Crêpe** A large, thin, French-style pancake with either a sweet or savory filling.

● **Crockpot** An electric pot that simmers food very slowly over a long period.

● **Croutons** A French term describing small pieces of fried or toasted bread used for garnishing soups or salads. A croute is toasted bread on which food is served; en croute describes baked food wrapped in pastry, while a croustade is a fried bread or pastry case in which hot, savory mixtures are served.

● **Crown** The junction of roots and stems in a herbaceous plant, from which point new growth develops; the upper branch system of a tree.

● **Crown lift** To remove the lower branches of a tree, to prevent them from casting shade for example, thus creating the impression of having raised the tree's branch system.

● **Crudités** Raw vegetables cut into sticks to be dipped into a sauce as an appetizer or an hors d'oeuvre.

● **Crushed stone** Material, such as broken fragments of bricks and stones, used as a foundation on top of which paving stones are laid or buildings constructed.

● **Crystallize** To form into crystals. This occurs in sugar- or honey-based syrups. The term also describes the coating of fruits or flowers with sugar.

● **Cultivar** Short for cultivated variety, describing a plant variety that has been produced by cultivation as opposed to occurring naturally.

● **Curdling** The separation of a food, usually as a result of the overheating of or the addition of an acid substance to milk- or egg-based sauces.

● **Cut in** To paint the edge of a wall or ceiling to complete the coverage of the surface.

● **Damask** A silk or linen fabric with a design woven into it.

● **Damp down** To wet the floor and other horizontal surfaces of a greenhouse in order to increase humidity and decrease temperature during hot weather.

● **Deadhead** To remove faded flowers in order to improve a plant's appearance, prevent the production of seeds, and improve subsequent flowering.

● **Decanting** Pouring a liquid such as wine or vinegar from its bottle into a clean container, leaving behind the sediment.

● **Deciduous** Describing a plant that loses all its leaves at one time of year, either in autumn or winter.

● **Découpage** A term describing a technique used to decorate a surface by attaching cut-out paper images to give the impression of painted items.

● **Deglazing** Diluting sediment or concentrated juices left in a pan after cooking meat by stirring in a liquid such as water, stock, or wine.

● **Denatured alcohol** An alcohol, usually ethanol, to which various compounds are added and which is used as a solvent.

● **Dieback** The death of shoots on a plant as a result of damage, by frost for example, or disease.

● **Distressing** One of a number of techniques of deliberately eroding a wooden or painted surface so that it appears worn.

● **Dowel** A short length of wood, round in section, used for a variety of purposes in decorating and soft furnishings.

● **Dragging** A paint-effect technique whereby a brush is dragged across a glaze to create a series of very fine lines.

● **Dredging** Sprinkling lightly and evenly with flour or sugar. A dredger has holes pierced in the lid for even sprinkling.

● **Drift** An extensive but natural-looking area of the garden devoted to one plant, especially bulbs; when spraying a chemical control, the spread of the product beyond the intended area.

● **Dusting** Sprinkling food lightly with flour, sugar, or spices for a light coating.

● **Egg tempera** A traditional eggyolk-based mixture used as a protective coating for paintwork and paint effects, or mixed with color to produce a finish in its own right.

● **Emulsion** A mixture of two normally insoluble liquids. Droplets of oil, for instance, are emulsified in vinegar in a vinaigrette dressing.

● **Evergreen** Describing a plant that retains leaves throughout the year.

● **Fan-train** To shape a tree so that the branches grow straight and radiate outward from the top of a central trunk.

● **Faux** A term used when creating paint effects to describe a surface that is very realistically painted to imitate another material, such as wood, ceramic tiles, or marble.

● **Ferrule** The metal strip around the central area of a paintbrush that houses the base of the bristles.

● **Foliar** Describing something relating to or resembling the leaves of a plant.

● **Flambé** A French term describing a dish that is sprinkled with alcohol and set alight. The alcohol burns off, but its flavor remains.

● **Flameproof** Describes equipment resistant to direct heat and oven heat, which can be used on a burner, under a grill, and in an oven.

● **Flat** A broad surface of a window rail or frame.

● **Fleur-de-lys** A term describing a traditional motif resembling a lily or iris flower.

● **Flexible filler** A filling compound that is able to absorb minor movements in wood or plaster surfaces and is therefore able to maintain a continuous, smooth, and unbroken paint finish.

● **Floppy disk** A flexible, magnetic disk that stores information and can be used to store data for a computer.

● **Flush** A term describing two adjacent surfaces that join without any unevenness, or where a surface is repaired to create a totally level finish.

● **Folding** Incorporating a light mixture into a heavier one – such as whipped egg whites into a cake mixture – by cutting and mixing lightly with a spoon to keep as much air in the mixture as possible.

● **Frame head** The broadest area running around the inside of a wooden door frame that acts as a base for the doorstop.

● **Freezer burn** Dried out and discolored patches on food, caused by a long period of exposure to air in the freezer, resulting in dehydration.

● **French polish** A varnish for furniture made from shellac, a resin, dissolved in alcohol.

● **French windows** A casement window or pair of windows that extend to floor level and commonly open outward onto a garden or other outside area.

● **Frosting** A fluffy icing used to cover cakes; a coating of sugar around the rim of a glass.

● **Fusible web** A meshlike tape that is used to join two fabric surfaces together but avoids the need for stitching. The fusing process is activated by the heat from an iron.

● **Gathered blind** A highly decorative window treatment with a scalloped lower edge. The blind is drawn up to maintain this shaped edge and to create the effect of folds of tumbling material.

● **Gilding** A technique of producing a gold surface by the application of either gold leaf or gold paint.

● **Gingham** A fabric with a checked pattern usually created by the weaving of different-colored yarns.

● **Glaze** An oil- or water-based medium (made by adding a tint to transparent glaze), used for creating paint effects and broken color finishes.

● **Glazing** Brushing the surface of a food with a liquid such as beaten egg, milk, or honey to moisten the food or give the surface a glossy appearance.

● **Gloss** A hardwearing, high-sheen paint, mainly used as a top coat on woodwork.

● **Gold leaf** A very thin sheet of rolled or hammered gold that is used for gilding.

● **Graft union** The point on a tree, shrub, rose, or woody climber at which the top growth was grafted on to the rootstock.

● **Graining** A paint-effect technique for creating a realistic, natural wood effect.

● **Groundcover** Plants, especially low-growing, spreading ones, that are planted in order to provide an attractive blanket over the soil and stifle weeds.

● **Grout** A fine plaster or mortar for filling in between tiles to create a flush surface.

● **Hacksaw** A fine-toothed saw used for cutting through metal.

● **Hardboard** A thin manufactured building board made from compressed wooden particles and used mainly for covering subfloors.

● **Hard disk/Hard drive** A rigid, magnetizable disk on which a computer's data is stored.

● **Harden off** The gradual acclimatization of a plant previously raised in a protected environment so that it can withstand more extreme or a greater range of temperature and humidity.

● **Hardware** The pieces of equipment that make up a computer system, such as the main processing unit.

● **Hardwood** A wood of higher quality than softwood, used for interior joinery. Good for natural wood finishes.

● **Hardy** Describing plants that can survive the prevailing climate and soil conditions in a given area.

● **Herbaceous** Describing a plant with soft, not woody, top-growth, and which usually dies back in winter.

● **Hue** A variety or degree of a color. Different hues of a particular color are often used in the same decorative plan.

● **Hulling** Removing the leafy parts from soft fruits such as strawberries or blackberries.

● **Hybrid** A plant produced by the cross-breeding of two genetically different plant species or two different cultivars within a species.

● **Hydrogen peroxide** A colorless liquid used as a bleaching agent.

● **Infusing** Extracting the flavors of spices or herbs by soaking them in liquid heated in a covered pan.

● **Inlay** To insert a section within a flat surface by filling a hole with a differently colored material or alternative material, such as wood or tiles, for decorative purposes.

● **Inset tile** A tile of a different design or color from the surrounding body of tiles.

● **Interlining** An additional layer of muslin or another lightweight material placed next to a fabric to increase its insulatory or fire-retardant properties and, in the case of curtains, to provide extra bulk to improve the hang.

● **Joist** A large wooden supporting beam used to make a framework on which a floor is constructed.

Julienne strips Vegetable pieces that have been cut very finely into matchstick slices.

Jute A plant whose fiber is used for natural-fiber flooring.

Kneading Working a dough firmly by pressing, stretching, and folding it with the hands.

Knee kicker A gripping and stretching device that can be used to lay most carpets.

Lateral A side shoot off a stem or branch off a trunk.

Latex A water-based paint applied mainly to large surfaces such as walls and ceilings.

Layering A method of plant propagation whereby the stem of a plant is cut and buried in soil mix or soil in order to encourage it to root while it is still attached to the parent plant.

Lay off To brush an unloaded paintbrush across a wet painted surface to disperse the brushmarks in order to create as smooth a finish as possible. Laying off can also be done with a paint roller.

Liaison A thickening agent, such as flour, egg yolk, cream, or beurre manié, which is used for thickening or binding sauces and soups.

Liming A technique for staining wood a whitish color using liming wax.

Linoleum A floor covering made from a mixture including linseed oil and resins, mounted on a burlap backing.

Load-bearing Describing the capacity of a structure or item to carry weight.

Low-tack A term usually describing a variety of masking tape that creates just enough adhesion to stick to a surface without damaging that surface when it is removed.

Macerating Softening food by soaking in a liquid or syrup.

Make good To prepare a surface ready for decorating.

Mallet A large hammer with a heavy head, commonly used for masonry purposes.

Marbling A paint-effect technique produced in one of a number of ways to create the impression of a marble surface.

Marginal A plant that grows in the very wet, boggy areas surrounding a pond or other water feature.

Marinating Soaking food in a seasoned liquid – often a blend of oil, wine, and vinegar – to add flavor or to tenderize it.

Mask To cover an area – with paper, cardboard, or masking tape – to prevent it from being covered by paint or other decorating material.

Matte A term describing a dull finish, commonly associated with latex and some natural wood finishes.

Medium-density fiberboard (MDF) A manufactured building board of varying thickness composed of compressed wooden fibers and used for a variety of interior joinery work as well as building tasks.

Miter saw A fine-toothed saw that is short in length and is used for joinery purposes.

Miter To join two pieces of material – for example, tiles or baseboard – at a corner by cutting each at 45 degrees so that they meet neatly.

Mocha A combination of coffee and chocolate.

Mousse A lightly set mixture, which may be sweet or savory, that is usually based on whipped eggs or egg whites.

Mulch Materials, such as grass clippings, compost, peat, straw, or manure, that are spread over soil to reduce temperature fluctuations, and to prevent water evaporation and the proliferation of weeds.

Mural A large painting or painted decoration on a wall.

Muslin A finely woven cotton fabric.

Nail punch A small metal rod which, when placed vertically over a nail, can be hammered to drive in the nail head below surface level.

Natural-fiber flooring A floor covering made from plant fiber, such as jute, seagrass, coir, or sisal.

Nippers A hand tool, resembling pliers with sharp teeth, that is used to cut small portions off the edges of ceramic tiles in order to cut them to size or shape them.

Node The point on the stem of a plant at which leaves or leaf buds appear.

Nog A small block of wood that is attached to joists to lend extra support for floorboards.

Notched spreader A tiling tool with a castellated edge used to spread adhesive over a wall prior to attaching tiles.

Offsets New bulbs or plants produced by runners that grow from the base of the parent plant.

Organic Describing a substance that is of plant or animal origin and therefore contains carbon; a method of gardening that avoids the use of any nonorganic products.

Ovenproof Describes equipment resistant to oven heat only, not direct heat.

Overspray A fine spray or splatters of paint that have unintentionally been splashed over the wrong surface.

Paint effect The use of paint and other materials to create a pattern, texture, or illusion. A glaze is often the most suitable material, but paint can be used as an alternative.

Paint system A method of paint application, using a specific type of paint, required to achieve a particular finish.

Parboiling Partly cooking food in water or stock.

Paring Peeling or trimming a food, usually vegetables.

● **Parquet flooring** A flooring traditionally made up of small wooden blocks, commonly arranged in a herringbone or other geometrical pattern. Modern alternatives consist of wooden panels that reproduce the same effect.

● **Pattern repeat** The measurement from where a pattern begins to where it finishes on wallpaper or fabric.

● **Peaks** The mounds created in a mixture, such as egg white, that has been whipped to stiffness. Peaks are "soft" if they curl over or "stiff" if they stay upright.

● **Pectin** A substance that is found naturally in fruits and vegetables, and is essential for setting jams and jellies. Artificially produced pectin can be bought from stores.

● **Perennial** A plant, usually herbaceous, that lives for more than two years.

● **Pergola** A framework consisting of panels and posts that forms a broad arch or covered walkway and can be draped with a variety of climbing plants.

● **Petits fours** French-style, bite-sized treats and cakes served with coffee.

● **Picture rail** A molding that runs along a wall a short distance from the ceiling, over which are hooked devices from which to hang framed wall decorations.

● **Picture window** A window consisting of a single, large pane or sheet of glass.

● **Pilaf/pilau** A spiced, savory rice dish, usually including meat, poultry, or fish.

● **Piquant** A French term meaning pleasantly sharp, pungent, or sour in flavor.

● **Pith** The white, fleshy part of citrus rind that lies just beneath the colored zest.

● **Plywood** A manufactured building board constructed from a number of layers of wood

veneer stuck together in such a way that the grain of one layer runs at right angles to that of the previous layer. Also known as ply or plyboard.

● **Polyvinyl adhesive (PVA)** A multipurpose adhesive that, when concentrated, acts as a strong glue, but when diluted acts as a stabilizing solution for applying to powdery surfaces.

● **Pressure-treated** Describing the application of a treatment to a material, such as wood, under pressure in order to increase the effectiveness of the treatment and hence the durability of the material.

● **pH** A measure of acidity or alkalinity. A pH of less than 7.0 indicates acidity; one of more than 7.0, alkalinity.

● **Primary color** One of three colors – red, blue, and yellow. They are mixed in a variety of ratios to make other colors.

● **Primer** A paint used to seal and stabilize a surface before further coats are applied.

● **Propagator** A covered box, sometimes with a heat source, used for germinating seeds or rooting plant cuttings.

● **Proving** Letting dough or a yeast mixture rise.

● **Punch-and-rivet set** A hole-making gadget, used on paper or fabric, which leaves a small hole with a rivet finishing.

● **Purée** A French term describing food that has been mashed, liquidized, or strained until completely smooth.

● **Rag rolling** A paint-effect technique that is similar to ragging except that the rag is made into a sausagelike length and rolled down a glaze or paint to produce a directional pattern.

● **Ragging** A paint-effect technique whereby a crumpled rag is used to create a pattern, either by applying it to a glazed or painted surface, or dipping the rag into a glaze or paint, then applying it to a surface.

● **Rail** A horizontal or vertical strut that makes up a paneled door or window frame.

● **Ramekin** A small, straight-sided ovenproof dish.

● **Rebate** An area of a window rail bordering a pane of glass.

● **Reducing** Thickening a liquid mixture, such as a soup or sauce, by boiling uncovered to evaporate excess liquid.

● **Refreshing** Pouring cold water over freshly cooked vegetables to retain color and prevent further cooking; reviving limp salad ingredients by standing in cold water.

● **Rendering** Melting down solid fat to make drippings.

● **Repeat size** The actual dimension of a pattern repeat.

● **Rhizome** A swollen plant stem that grows horizontally underground and is an organ of food storage. It produces roots and shoots.

● **Rising** The expansion of dough or a yeast mixture as a result of the action of the yeast.

● **Rocker** A paint-effect tool used to create the impression of wood grain.

● **Roman blind** A flat window treatment with a number of horizontal struts that gather the material into a folded concertina as the blind is raised.

● **Rootball** The spherical mass formed by the root system of a plant and including soil. Some plants, such as trees and shrubs, are grown in open ground, lifted, and wrapped in burlap or a similar material, rather than placed in a container, prior to sale; these are described as balled-and-burlapped.

● **Rootstock** An underground stem such as a rhizome; the root system of a plant on to which the top-growth of another plant is grafted for propagation purposes.

● **Roux** A French term describing a mixture of equal amounts of fat and flour, which are cooked together as a basis for thickening sauces.

● **Rub back** To remove the top coat of a surface to expose what is underneath.

● **Sand back** To use sandpaper to level and smooth a surface.

● **Sash window** A window made up of two main parts that slide past each other vertically on sash cords.

● **Sautéeing** A French term describing the continual tossing of food in shallow fat so that it browns evenly.

● **Scalding** Plunging fruits or vegetables into boiling water to facilitate the peeling of skins; heating a liquid to just below boiling point.

● **Scale** An encrustation, such as the mineral deposit left on faucets and appliances in hard-water areas.

● **Scale down/up** To transfer the outline of a pattern or image from a source on to a flat surface where it will be reproduced by adjusting its size accordingly.

● **Scorched** Describing the leaves, and occasionally the petals, of plants that have dried out, either totally or in part, and have become discolored as a result of one of many factors, including sunlight that is too strong.

● **Seagrass** A durable fiber used for natural-fiber flooring.

● **Secondary color** A color made by mixing equal amounts of two primary colors.

● **Self-leveling compound** A compound poured over an uneven floor to produce a level surface.

● **Semigloss** An oil- or water-based, midsheen paint suitable for walls and ceilings.

● **Shade** In everyday usage, a variety or degree of a color; in scientific terminology, a color mixed with black.

● **Sheen** The degree to which a particular finish shines.

● **Sheet flooring** A term used to describe a variety of utility flooring that is laid in large continuous sheets, such as linoleum, vinyl, or rubber.

● **Sisal** An agave fiber used for natural-fiber flooring.

● **Size** To prepare a plaster surface with size (diluted wallpaper paste or a PVA solution) to stabilize the surface and ease the maneuvering of wallpaper once it is on the wall.

● **Skimming** Removing the surface layer of impurities, scum, or fat from liquids such as stocks and jams while cooking. This is usually done with a flat, slotted spoon.

● **Soaking time** The period for which wallpaper is left after pasting before hanging, to allow paste to soak in and prevent the formation of bubbles.

● **Soft growth** New growth on a plant that has not hardened or become woody.

● **Software** The application programs that are used with a particular computer for specific purposes.

● **Softwood** A natural wood that is pale in color and used for interior joinery.

● **Soil conditioners** A variety of materials, such as cocoa fiber, soil mix, and lime, that are added to soil to improve its texture, acidity or alkalinity, and fertility prior to planting.

● **Soil mix** A growing medium, the constituents of which vary according to the plants for which it is intended.

● **Solvent** The chemical base of certain decorating materials. The term solvent also refers specifically to oil-based paints. Also, a substance, usually liquid, that dissolves another substance and is therefore used for cleaning purposes.

● **Sponging** A paint-effect technique whereby a natural sponge is used to create an impression in a glaze or paint, or is used to apply a glaze or paint to a wall.

● **Stamping** A technique of applying a design to a wall, floor, or other area using a hand-held block, whose surface bears a design and is dipped in paint and then applied.

● **Stenciling** A decorative technique whereby paint is applied in the cut-out areas of a cardboard or acetate template to create a design on a surface.

● **Stippling** A paint-effect technique whereby the extreme tips of bristles are dipped into a wet glaze to create a velvety texture.

● **Stripper** A solution used to remove old layers of paint from a surface.

● **Subfloor** The surface beneath flooring, usually of concrete or floorboards, and sometimes covered with hardboard.

● **Swags and tails** Fabric curtain accessories added to a basic window treatment.

● **Sweating** Cooking food, usually vegetables, very gently in melted fat to release juices for flavor, but without allowing the food to brown.

● **Syrup** A concentrated solution of sugar and water.

● **Tang** The prong of a knife blade embedded in the handle.

● **Template** A design made of paper, cardboard, or acetate that acts as a guide in cutting out a shape from fabric or other materials, or in painting a design on a surface.

● **Tender** Describing a plant that is damaged or dies in cold weather.

● **Terrine** An earthenware or china dish used for baking or steaming pâtés and meat loaves; the name given to food that is cooked in this way.

● **Tertiary color** A color made by mixing a primary color with a secondary one.

● **Tieback** A material or other device that holds a curtain to one side of a window frame.

● **Tile gauge** A length of wood, calibrated with tile-width measurements and used to mark off the positions that tiles will occupy on a wall.

● **Tint** To adjust the color of a paint or glaze. Alternatively, in everyday usage, a variety or degree of a color; in scientific terminology, a color mixed with white.

● **Tone** A variety or degree of a color, particularly in terms of its depth or brilliance.

● **Tongue and groove** A system of interlocking wooden boards that are joined to produce a panelled surface.

● **Top-dressing** The spreading of fertilizer, soil mix, or fresh soil arouond a plant or over a lawn; the removal of the top few inches of soil in a container and the replacement of it with compost.

● **Topsoil** The upper layer of soil.

● **Trompe l'oeil** A term meaning "trick of the eye" and, in decorating, describing a painted image that gives the impression of a real object.

● **Trussing** Tying or skewering meat or poultry into a neat shape before cooking.

● **TSP (trisodium phospahte)** An alkaline compound used for cleaning or stripping paint off surfaces.

● **Tuber** A swollen plant stem or root, usually underground, that stores food. A stem tuber produces new growth from the attached stem; a root tuber produces new plants from buds.

● **Tuiles** A French term for thin, sweet cookies shaped to resemble curved tiles.

● **Turpentine** A colorless liquid obtained from conifers such as pine and fir and used as a solvent.

● **Underplant** To plant smaller or lower plants in between taller ones for groundcover or infilling purposes.

● **Valance** A decorative fabric edging that conceals the hanging system of a window treatment rather like a cornice.

● **Varnish** A resinous solution that seals and protects surfaces.

● **Varnishing brush** A long-haired paintbrush used to create a dragged paint effect.

● **Venetian blind** A window treatment consisting of a number of slats of wood, plastic, or other material, the angle of which can be adjusted to control the amount of light passing through.

● **Verdigris** A greenish coating on copper, bronze, or brass that forms naturally with age as a result of corrosion. Its appearance is copied as a decorative effect on metal or wooden surfaces.

● **Vintage** Wine from a particular year's harvest.

● **Vinyl** A soft flooring – in sheets or tiles – that is flexible and cushioned.

● **Washing soda** Sodium carbonate, a colorless crystalline compound that is manufactured for a variety of cleaning purposes and as a water softener.

● **Wood paneling** A wooden wall covering consisting of panels constructed in a variety of different finishes.

● **Wood-block flooring** A type of wooden sheet flooring consisting of small blocks.

● **Woodstain** A natural wood finish that colors and protects a bare wooden surface.

● **Zest** The outer, colored part of citrus peel, which contains strong flavor in its oils.

● **Zigzag stitch** In sewing, a machine stitch that takes the form of a zigzag sawtooth and is used for neatening edges.

INDEX

A

accessories, 298, 311
  adding, 201, 298
  caring for, 111, 130–131
  choosing, 196, 222
  grouping, 33
accidents, preventing:
  with children, 38–39
  with filing cabinets, 161
acid soils, 480, 481
acrylic bathtubs, 68
address, changing, 146, 147
adhesives:
  cleaning off, 279
  for laying flooring, 275,
    278, 279
  for tiling, 63
  general purpose, 114
  removing marks, 95
  using, 124
aerating lawns:
  before watering, 533
  large areas, 571
  to prevent moss, 569
aerosol paints,
  for stenciling, 215
aging:
  furniture, 264
  posters and prints, 305
ailments, treating, 184–187
air conditioners, 140
airing:
  bedding, 57, 104
  clothes, 104
  homemade rack, 107
alabaster, cleaning, 125
alarms, installing, 42
  see also burglar alarms
alarm systems, 144
alcoves, lighting, 300
algae:
  in ponds, 575, 577
  in propagators, 586
  in water barrels, 531
  on patios, 459
  on sheds, 472
  on walls, 604
alkaline soils, 480, 481
almond paste, 384, 408

almonds:
  blanching, 369
  garnishing with, 435
  in crumble, 402
  stuffing olives with, 430
alpines, 465, 512, 536
aluminum, 158,
  pans, cleaning, 333
  greenhouse frames, 613
aluminum foil:
  on ironing board, 108
  reusing, 74
ammonium sulfate, 524
anaphylactic shock, treating,
  180
anchovies, 383
animal bites, treating, 179
animals:
  controlling, 553–554
  urine on lawns, 561
annuals:
  autumn-sowing, 457
  choosing, 494
  climbers, 467, 493
  establishing, 495
  filling border gaps, 457
  instant color, 451
  planting, 494–495
  screens, 469
answering machines, 128
anti-transpirant sprays, 498
antipasti, 446
antique furniture:
  cleaning, 66
  polish for, 115
antiquing, 264, 312
ants, deterring, 470
aphids, 546
appendicitis, symptoms, 186
appetizers, 447
  serving wines with, 436
apples:
  as edging plants, 453
  bobbing for, 441
  fillings for baked apples, 384
  floating in punch, 433
  garnishing with, 435
  methods of cooking, 384,
    385
  pressing, 420

  preventing browning, 362,
    417
  using as candle holders,
    427
appliances, 318–323, 332–333
  buying for special needs, 42
  keeping manuals, 146
  moving, 146, 150
appliquéing curtains, 290
appointments:
  confirming business, 163
  making medical, 43
apricots, 369, 384, 385
arborists, 458
arbors, 468, 477
arches, 468
  chicken-wire, 476
  constructing, 475
  hanging baskets, 516
  homemade, 476
  styles, 475
  walkways, 475
archways, papering, 230
arm injuries, treating, 181
aromatherapy, practicing, 35
artichokes, 329
arugula, 383
asparagus, 324, 379
assaults, coping with, 46
audio equipment:
  moving, 147, 151
  protecting, 20
autumn tasks, 618–619
avocados, 350, 365

B

babies:
  equipment for, 36
  feeding, 37
  planning time with, 37
baby monitors, using, 37, 38
baby-sitters:
  briefing, 40
  finding, 40
bacon:
  flavoring with, 381, 392
  glazing with mustard,
    388
  preparing, 374
  using in canapés, 430, 443

bagging, 210, 312
  painting walls, 213
  texturing ceilings, 209
baguettes, filled, 444
baked foods, 360–361
baked potatoes, 379
  baking eggs in, 387
  wrapping for picnics, 444
bakeware, 326
baking, 98, 102
  blind, 341
  eggs, 387
  fish, 395
  fruits, 384
  in microwave, 413
baking pans, 326
  sprinkling, 411
  unsticking, 331
  see also cake pans
baking sheets, 331
balconies, 511
  windowboxes, 514
bananas:
  cooking, 384, 443
  freezing, 352
  pan-frying, 403
  ripening, 352
bandages, in first-aid kit, 170
banks:
  checking statements, 169
  depositing documents, 161, 169
  keeping records, 168, 169
baptisms, organizing, 49
barbecues, 463
barbecuing, 390, 442–443
  fish, 395, 443
  fruits, 385
  scenting coals, 371, 390
bark, composted, 478
barrel ponds:
  making, 572, 574
  on patios, 462
barrels, 502, 510–511
  see also containers
    (garden)
baseboards:
  attaching moldings, 274
  cleaning, 63
  cutting in, 207
  masking, 273
  tiling, 280
basil, 370
baskets, planting:
  bulbs, 496
  ponds, 572, 576

bathing:
  babies, 37
  drawing up a bathlist, 157
bath plugs, removing, 69
bathrooms 14,
  accessories, 311
  children using, 38
  cleaning, 57, 68–69
  repairs, 133–136
  storage, 18, 31
bathtub rings, 68
bathtubs:
  blocked drains, 135
  cleaning, 68, 157
  hanging shelves by, 18
  installing handles above, 42
  laying flooring beneath, 278
  removing grout from, 250
  renewing surface, 311
  rust marks, 98
  tiling around, 243
battens:
  as a tiling base, 242
  attaching wall hangings, 234
  building panel frames, 235
  edging work surfaces, 245
  making a tile gauge, 241
batter:
  coating food with, 391
  for hot desserts, 403
  making, 396
  spicing, 393
bay leaves, 344, 371
bay windows, 286
beading:
  painting technique, 207
  silicone, 243, 278
beans:
  checking before buying, 350
  companion plants, 552
  cooking, 401
  dried, 341, 401
  flavoring, 381
  source of nitrogen, 523
bedding:
  airing, 57, 104
  buying for special needs, 41
  laundering, 105
  storing, 30
bedding plants:
  edging paths, 464
  rotating, 549
bed linen:
  laundering, 105
  moth proofing, 112
  storing, 112, 127

bedrooms, 14, 192, 298
  lighting, 300
  planning, 19
  saving space, 19
beds:
  buying, 19
  providing extra, 19
  storing under, 26
  using table in, 19
  see also flowerbeds
bedside lights, positioning, 19
bedside tables, creating, 19
beef, marinating, 388
beer traps, 558
bees, 556, 557
beeswax polish, 66
  recipe for, 115
beets:
  baking, 380
  coloring pasta with, 401
  in stews, 389
  preparing, 364
belts:
  drying, 106
  storing, 111
bicycles:
  maintaining, 51
  preventing theft, 51
  storing, 27
bills, dividing, 157
bindweed, 535, 539
biological detergents:
  laundering, 100
  stain removal, 79
biological pest controls, 555
bird feeders, 550
birds, 550
  buying and keeping
    as pets, 53
  controlling, 553, 564
blackberries, 352
blackcurrants, 367
blacking, applying, 65
blades, protecting, 25, 31
blanching:
  almonds, 369
  sweetbreads, 374
  vegetables, 418
blankets:
  electric, 127
  moth proofing, 112
  storing, 30
blanket weed, 516, 577
bleach, 55
  laundering, 100, 102
  stain removal, 79

bleeding, 176
blenders, 73, 332, 333
blinds, 292–293
  cleaning and care, 27
  emphasizing window shape, 287
  fitting, 293
  improvising shutter blinds, 293
  measuring, 292
  reviving, 293
blisters, treating, 183
blocking,
  painting technique, 216
bog gardens, 573
boiling, 514
  eggs, 523
  potatoes, 515
bone, ornamental, 119, 125
bone injuries, 181
bonemeal, 524
boning, 375, 376
book cases, moving, 150
bookkeeping, 169
books:
  caring for, 129
  dusting, 156
  packing, 151
  storing, 29, 159
bookshelves, preventing
  mildew on, 29
boots:
  care, 113
borders (decorative):
  stenciling, 215
  using border tiles, 241, 246
  see also wallpaper borders
borders (garden), 456–457
  clearing, 456
  filling gaps, 491, 511
  improving soil, 456
  mulching, 456
  plants, 485
  renovating, 450
  suggesting size, 477
  thinning, 456
  watering, 532
botrytis, 546
bottles:
  baby's, sterilizing, 37
  chilling, 431
  opening, 41
  releasing lids from, 336
  storing, 25
  transporting, 44
  using as mini cloches, 589

using as propagators, 586
using to repel animals, 553, 554
bottling fruits, 415
bouquet garni, 370
boxes:
  fitting wheels on, 152
  preparing for moving, 168
  storing files in, 168
  using as steps, 38
  wooden, 117
boxing in pipes, 241
braising, 389
brambles, 539
bran, 406, 108
brass, cleaning and
  care, 121
brassicas, 413
brazil nuts, 369
bread, 432
  decorating, 411
  dough, 410, 411
  for sandwiches, 444
  freezing, 360
  keeping fresh, 360
  kneading in a food
    processor, 332
  methods of cooking, 410, 411
  novelty, 441
  part-baked, 347
  reviving stale bread, 360
  savory, 411
  thawing, 360
bread bins, cleaning, 73
breadcrumbs, 361
  as a coating, 388, 396
  for thickening stews, 389
bricks:
  edging paths, 464
  laying flooring, 281
  repairing paths, 608
  sealing, 209
  storing, 608
brick surfaces:
  cleaning, 65, 75
  removing soot stains, 98
  sealing, 63
brickwork:
  raised beds, 461
  removing, 605
  repointing, 605
  retaining walls, 461
  weatherproofing, 605
broccoli, 363, 381
bronze, cleaning and care, 121

brooms:
  cleaning and storing, 56
  improvising tools, 58, 63
brown sugar, 342
bruises, treating, 181
brushes:
  hairbrushes, 35
  household, 16
brush marks, removing, 218, 266
Brussels sprouts, 350
  cooking, 379
  shredding, 363, 380
bubble wrap, 148
  making kneeling board, 42
  using for insulation, 510, 12
  using for relaxation, 35
  wrapping items, 30, 149
buckets, 57
buckwheat flour, 411
budgeting, 198
  buying secondhand, 290, 307
  choosing flooring, 269
  choosing tiles, 238
  choosing window
    treatments, 287, 294
  for weddings, 48
  in a shared home, 157
buffets, 432, 433
bulbs:
  choosing, 496
  dividing, 596
  feeding, 527
  filling borders, 457
  in borders, 479
  in lawns, 566
  maintaining, 497
  naturalizing, 566
  planting, 496–497
  scaling, 596
  storing, 480, 496
  underplanting with, 93
buns, freshening, 361
burgers, 419, 440
burglaries:
  coping with, 46
  preventing, 144–145
burlap wall coverings, 62
burn marks:
  on brick surfaces, 65, 75
  on flooring, 60, 97
  on polished wood, 97, 116
burns, treating, 177
business cards,
  filing, 169

butter, 373, 432
  clarifying, 355, 373
  flavoring, 355
  frying in, 391
  pats, 355
  shaping, 373, 419
  softening, 373
  storing, 355
buttons, 110

C

cabbage, 350, 351
  braising, 379
  serving in wedges, 379
  shredding, 362
  stuffing, 363
cabbage root fly, 54, 559
cabinets, 22, 316–317, 334
  choosing and siting, 316
  decorating, 259, 265
  keeping clean, 316
  laying flooring beneath,
    278
  packing, 150
  painting, 256
  replacing fronts, 311
  sharing space in, 157
  using in kitchens, 17, 22
cakes, 347, 361, 406, 409
  celebration, 432, 437
  decorating, 408
  freezing, 361, 418
  novelty, 440
  storing, 361
cake pans, 326, 406
cake stand, 433, 437
calculating quantities:
  flooring, 269
  glazes, 211
  loose covers, 307
  paint, 203
  tiles, 241
  wallpaper, 223
  window treatments, 289,
    292
  woodwork finishes, 253
cameras,
  cleaning and care, 128
camp beds, keeping, 19
canapés, 430
candles:
  caring for, 129
  for emergencies, 138
candlesticks:
  pewter, cleaning, 120
  silver, cleaning, 119

candle wax:
  on fabric and carpet, 95
  on wood floors, 60
cane furniture, 609
  cleaning, 66
  fixing sagging seats, 117
canned foods, 43, 45
canopy, making a, 131
canvas shoes:
  cleaning, 113
  removing grass stains, 88
capillary matting, 533, 586
cardiopulmonary resuscitation
  (CPR), 175
caregivers:
  finding for children, 40
  finding for pets, 52
care symbols, 100
  drying, 106
  ironing, 108
  washing, 103
carpet beetles,
  eradicating, 61
carpets:
  calculating quantities, 269
  caring for, 284
  choosing, 197, 269
  cleaning, 61, 78, 250
  insulating, 15
  laying, 276–277
  removing, 272
  removing dents from, 20
  removing paint from, 219
  removing stains from, 284
  scraps, 285
  stain removal, 77–99
  using as a mulch, 501
  using as wall hangings, 234
  using to suppress weeds,
    536
carpet shampoo, 61
  for stain removal, 77
carpet tiles:
  laying, 279
  replacing, 284
carrot rust fly, 547, 119
carrots:
  flavoring, 380
  garnishing with, 364, 435
  slicing into ribbons, 381
  trimming baby carrots, 364
cars, 50
  checking, 50
  insuring drivers, 86
  keeping data for, 168
  loading, 153

loading roof rack, 151
  maintaining, 50
  protecting children in, 39
  securing against assault,
    46
  servicing, 147
car seats, using in car, 39
carts, using in offices, 159
casement windows, 286,
  painting, 253
cash:
  avoiding theft, 46
  moving, 147
  storing, 161
casserole dishes, 124
casseroles, freezing, 418
cast iron, 598
cast-iron pans:
  cleaning, 333
  seasoning, 380
catering quantities, 423, 432
caterpillars, 544
  biological controls, 555
cats, 553, 554
  caring for, 52
  moving, 154
cauliflower, 350, 381
ceilings:
  choosing colors, 192, 194
  cleaning, 62–65, 205
  hanging items from, 16, 26
  painting, 207
  papering, 223, 225
  preparing, 225
  reaching, 205, 207, 225
  stripping, 224
  suspending shelves from,
    303
  testing, 225
  texturing, 209
celebrations, planning, 49
celery:
  garnishing with, 435
  reviving, 351
  roasting turkey on, 392
  storing, 351, 382
  stringing, 364
  using in canapés, 430
cement, mixing, 604
centerpieces, 426
centipedes, 550
ceramic tiles:
  cleaning, 63, 75
  fire surround, 65
  flooring, 59
  repairs, 60

cereals, 340
chains:
  cleaning, 121
  untangling, 130, 131
chair rails, 234, 235
  using tiles, 246
  using wallpaper borders, 233
chairs:
  covering, 307
  improving, 307
  stenciling seats, 308
chalk line, 214, 279
chamois leather, 56
champagne:
  glasses, 425, 431
  opening, 436
chandeliers, cleaning, 123
char-grilling, 443
checks, painting, 214, 283
cheese, 373
  adding to soup, 398
  dressing, 79
  sauce, 447
  shaving hard cheese, 373
  smoking, 417
  storing, 355
  using in canapés, 430
  with fruits, 385, 402
chemicals:
  burns, 177
  fumes, 55
  poisoning, 178
chest compressions, 175
chestnuts, 369
chicken:
  barbecuing, 579
  cutting up, 511
  flavoring with herbs, 506
  preparing, 511
  roasting, 524, 528
  skinning, 492
chicken wire:
  arches, 476
  cat deterrents, 554
  compost containers, 483
  frost protection, 522
  in guttering, 601
  screens, 472
  tree guards, 554
chick peas, 401
chickweed, 535
chicory, 518
childcare, 40
  and moving, 146

children, 36–40
  choking, 184
  keeping safe, 55, 38–39, 465
  moving, 154
  planning celebrations for, 49
  play areas, 453, 468
  sharing a bedroom, 23
  taking to the doctor, 43
  visiting in the hospital, 44
children's parties, 440, 441
  decorations for, 424, 427
chilies, 481, 486
  drying, 417
  reducing strength of, 365
  storing, 351
chili powder, 371
chilled foods, 483, 485
chimney fires, 139, 172
china:
  care and repair, 124
  organizing, 16
  packing, 149, 150
  washing, 72
chipboard, 253
  filling and painting, 282
chips, 364
chives, 370, 429
chocolate:
  adding to meat dishes, 343
  desserts, 384, 405
  freezing, 343, 419
  in plain cakes, 409
  making chips, 343, 441
  making curls, 405
  pancakes, 403
  preventing bloom, 343
  storing, 343
  using, 405
choking, treating, 182
chopping, 362
chopping boards, 15, 328
  cleaning, 73
  removing smells from, 331
  sealing splits, 117
chops, 357, 374, 388
chrome:
  caring for, 120
  taps, cleaning, 69
chutney, 414, 416
cigarette burns, 97
cigarette smoke, 61
cinnamon, 345
circuit breakers, 563

cisterns, overflowing, 136
citrus fruits:
  buying, 352
  decorating, 427
  for flavouring sugar, 342
  freezing slices, 419
  garnishing with, 366
  juicing, 329, 366
  preparing, 366
  removing segments, 366
  storing, 352
  using skins, 366
citrus peel:
  moth proofing, 112
  scenting, 65
clams, 359, 377
clay soil, 480
  improving, 478, 482
  planting bulbs, 4497
  planting shrubs, 489
  removing from tools, 610
  suitable plants, 481
  working, 456, 482
cleaners, household, 55
cleaning, 54–75
  dividing tasks, 157
  methods and routine, 57
  office items, 160
  safety aspects, 55
  surfaces, 75
  when moving, 148, 155
cleaning equipment:
  bathroom, 68
  care and storage, 16, 56
  kit, 54
  kitchen, 70
climbing plants:
  adding height, 476
  annuals, 467, 475
  container-grown, 462, 467
  leggy, 493
  layering, 590, 591
  nests in, 542, 550
  on fences, 451
  on hedges, 471, 542
  on patio walls 474
  on rubble, 457
  on sheds, 472
  on shrubs, 456
  on tree stumps, 469, 470
  on trellis, 467
  on walls, 466, 493
  planting, 493
  pruning, 466, 542
  supports, 476, 492,
  temporary cover, 493

cloches:
  mini, 589, 593
  watering, 532
clothes:
  assembling for babies, 36
  buying, 33
  choosing basics, 33
  choosing for toddlers, 37
  color coordinating, 33
  dressing for medical
    appointments, 43
  embellishing, 33
  laundering and care, 100–109
  mildew, removing, 96
  minor repairs, 110
  ordering for weddings,
    48, 49
  organizing for next day, 33
  packing for a move, 150
  stain removal, 78–98
  storage, 111–112
cloves, 345, 388
  moth deterrent, 112
  oil of, 187
clubroot, 546, 560
coal fires, 65
coat hangers:
  color-coding, 23
  labeling, 33
  securing items on, 150
coatings:
  for fish, 394, 396
  for meat and poultry, 388
  using batter, 391
  using seasoned flour, 374
  using stuffing mix, 375
coats:
  altering sleeves, 33
  attaching reflective
    shapes to, 39
  dry cleaning, 104
  hanging, 21, 33
cockroaches, eradicating, 74
cocktails:
  alcohol-free, 436
  garnishes for, 431
cocoa, 343, 421
  as chocolate substitute, 405
cocoa fiber, 478
coconut:
  coating fish with, 394
  cooking rice in coconut
    milk, 400
  making curls, 435
  preparing, 369
  using in fruit pies, 402

codling moths, 547, 559
coffee:
  flavoring, 421
  stewing lamb in, 389
  using in place of alcohol,
    405
coffee machines, 333
  cleaning, 73
  grinders, 345
colanders, 330, 518, 577
  steaming couscous in,
    400
  using to prevent
    spitting, 391, 396
cold compresses, 181
cold plate, 432
colds, treating, 185
collarbone, broken, 175
collars:
  dirty, 105
  ironing, 108
collections, 198
  displaying, 287, 309
color charts, 196
color-coding, 330, 336
  coat hangers, 23
  files, 168
  room contents, 152, 156
  taps, 41
color coordinating, 195,
    222
  borders, 233
colored fabrics:
  colorfast test, 104
  machine washing, 103
  preventing fading, 102, 106
coloring glazes, 211
  tiles, 239
color runs, in laundry:
  preventing, 103
  removing, 90
colors:
  adjacent, 190, 191
  blending, 195
  choosing, 190–197
  complementary, 190, 191
  contrasting, 191, 121
  cool, 190, 193
  in the garden, 495, 513, 583
  mixing, 215
  primary, 190
  secondary, 190
  tertiary, 190
  warm, 190, 193
color scheming, 190, 195
  window treatments, 287

color-themed parties, 437
colorwashing, 211, 260
color wheel, 190
combing, 262
combs, cleaning, 267
communication, 166–167
compact discs:
  cleaning, 128
  racks, making, 27
complaints, in writing, 166
compost, 524, 528
  containers for, 483
  making, 471, 483
  weeds in, 536
compote, 369, 403
computers:
  caring for, 128
  filing on, 168
  keeping clean, 160
  packing, 149, 151
  protecting, 161
  straightening disks for, 168
concrete:
  cracks, repairing, 579, 606
  damaged edges, 606
  mixing, 604
  ponds, repairing, 579
  raised beds, 461
  repairs, 606, 608
  steps, repairing, 608
  surfaces, 58, 75
condensation:
  papering window recesses,
    230
  reducing, 68, 143
  tiling sills, 245
conifers:
  hedges, trimming, 471, 542
  snow protection, 522
  storing, 486
containers (household), 335
  cleaning and labeling, 336
  for picnic food, 445
  making for hanging files, 168
  reusing, 335, 555
  saving for a move, 149
containers (plants), 502–519
  climber supports, 467
  damaged, 462, 519
  decorating, 251, 309, 310,
    519
  decorative uses, 465, 472
  drainage, 504
  empty, displaying, 462
  equipment, 503
  filling border gaps, 457, 511

for cuttings, 592
for herbs, 507
frost protection, 510, 522
fruit and vegetables, 508
growing media, 503, 504
hygiene, 548
maintaining, 509
mending, 519
on patios, 459, 462
pests, 509, 518
planting, 506
planting designs, 504
plants, division, 578
plunged pots, 457, 486
pot bulbs, planting out, 497
recycling, 518–519, 585
saving soil mix, 506
screening with, 470, 511
self-watering, 530
stabilizing, 462
using tableware, 310
types, 502
water features, 573, 574
water retention, 530
wheeled, 470
convection ovens, 318, 626
convenience foods, 43
conversion tables, 622, 624–625, 626–627
cook books, storing, 317
cookies, 428, 440, 441
storing, 409
cooking methods, 378–421
cooler bags, 349
cooling:
fevers, 185
houses, 140–141
cooling racks, 406
copper, cleaning and care, 121
pans, 73, 121
cords, 574, 611
checking, 161
choosing for safety, 38
repairs to, 137
straightening, 21
coriander, 345
cork flooring:
burn marks, treating, 60
cleaning, 59
laying tiles, 279
using up tiles, 285

corks:
removing without a corkscrew, 329
using to protect knife points, 328
corners:
beading, 207
laying soft-tile flooring, 279
painting, 207, 209
painting effects, 212, 213
papering around, 231, 233
repairing, 204
sanding floors, 273
tiling, 242, 244, 246
using plastic tile strips, 249
cornices, 294
attaching swags to, 295
fabric, attaching, 294
wooden, shaping, 294
cornstarch, 340, 373
thickening fruit juices with, 304
thickening sauces with, 399
thickening stews with, 389
correspondence:
including in work log, 165
organizing, 166
corridors:
choosing colors, 193
planning, 21
protecting flooring, 270
costume jewelry, 130, 131
coughs, soothing, 185
couscous, 400
coving:
attaching, 204, 235
repairing, 235
crab, 359
bites, 444
cracking claws, 377
crackle glaze, 388
cracks, 218
in concrete, 579, 606
in pots, 519
craft knives:
marking blades, 228
recycling blades, 237
cranberries, 393, 436
craquelure, 264
crayfish, 359, 377
cream, 354, 373
feathering, 434
flavoring, 373, 437
floating on coffee or soup, 373

freezing rosettes, 446
longlife, 447
low-fat substitutes, 354, 373
sour, 354
storing, 354
using, 354
whipping, 69
credit cards:
canceling, 468
destroying, 169
photocopying, 161
recording data from, 169
crème fraîche, 354, 373
crevices, weeding, 534
crises, 46–47
crockery, see china
croissants, filled, 403
crop rotation, 549
peas and beans, 528
vegetables, 582
croutons, 383
crown-lifting, 458
crown-reducing, 458
crudités, 431, 444
crustaceans, 377
crystal:
glasses, 72, 122
vases, 123
cucumber, 364, 382, 435
cuffs:
dirty, 105
reshaping, 104
cup hooks:
hanging necklaces on, 27
putting in cabinets, 17
curing, 113
curtain poles, 288, 291
hanging rugs from, 234
curtain tracks, 288, 291
curtains, 288–290
appliquéing, 290
choosing, 288, 289
drawing, 141, 145
hanging, 155, 291
hooks, 67
improvising, 156
laundering, 64
lengthening, 127
lining, 289
reviving, 290
rings and rods, 127
using alternative materials, 290–291
weighting, 127, 290
window cleaning, 64

curves:
cutting tiles, 64
in lawns, 452, 565, 564
in paths, 453
cushions:
edging, 308
making, 307
making frills for, 295
trimming, 308
using in bed, 19
cutlery, 425
silver, 119
washing, 72
cuts and scrapes, 176
cutting in, 207
using textured paints, 209
cuttings, 498, 592–594
equipment, 592
hardwood, 594
perennials, 490
roots, 594
semiripe, 593
softwood, 593
suitable plants, 592, 594

D
dairy foods, 254, 255
in balanced diet, 146
preparing, 372, 373
damping off, 582
data:
preserving, 168
protecting, 161, 169
storing, 169
dates, 368, 384
deadheading, 540
container plants, 509
when replanting, 501
death, coping with, 47
decanters, cleaning, 123
deciduous plants, 471, 474
decorating, 180–311,
see also under individual
topics
découpage:
decorating furniture, 265
using leftover wallpaper,
237
using pressed flowers, 309
deep breathing, 35
deep-frying, 391
deglazing, 399
delegating, 165
dental records, including in
family health log, 45
deodorants, for shoes, 113

descaling, 73
designing gardens, 475–477
desk lamps, using, 162
desk organizers, making, 160
desks, using in offices, 158,
159
tidying drawers, 160
desserts:
chocolate, 405
cold, 404
decorating with fruits, 367
embellishing, 447
from pantry, 446
gelatin-set, 404
hot, 403
methods of cooking, 402,
405
picnic, 444
pies and tarts, 402
quick, 403
using convenience foods
in, 347
dessert toppings:
cake-crumb, 361
for fruit tart, 402
pastry, 412
detergent, 55
laundering, 100
quantities, 103
dicing, 362, 374
digging, 482
dimmers, 300
dining areas, planning, 14, 20
dining chairs, stacking, 20
dining tables, making, 16
dinner parties, 434, 436
dips, 431
avocado, 431
butter-bean, 401
fruit, 444
pesto, 431
tuna, 431
disbudding, 540
diseases in plants, 544–561
container plants, 509
deadheading, 540
fungal, 529
hedges, 471
powdery mildew, 545
preventing, 548–552
recycled water, 91
roses, 541
seedlings, 589
seeds, 582, 587
vegetables, 582
wounds in plants, 541

dishwashers, 72
overflowing, 136
silver items, 119
dishwashing brushes, 70
dishwashing liquid, 55, 70
distressing, 264
dividing gardens:
arches, 475
garden rooms, 453, 477
lawns, 453
long garden, 477
screens, 469
division of plants:
perennials, 456, 500
suitable plants, 595
water plants, 578
dock, 535
doctors:
obtaining death certificates
from, 47
visiting, 43
documents, 167
arranging for weddings, 49
carrying during a move, 147
depositing in banks, 161,
169
laying out information in,
167
organizing for deceased, 47
protecting, 161
storing copies of, 169
dogs:
caring for, 52
controlling, 554
moving, 154
door frames:
painting, 256
papering around, 230
threshold strip,
making, 281
door furniture:
distressing, 264
finger plates, adding, 309
removing for painting, 256
doors:
adjusting height, 281
cabinet, utilizing, 17
cleaning, 63
defining edges, 256
glass, 171
installing door stop, 38
installing shelves over, 26
locking, 38
masking edges, 273
painting, 256
painting effects, 262, 264

paneling with wallpaper, 237
security, 144–145
sticking, 142
wardrobe, utilizing, 23
double glazing, 15, 140
temporary, 141
dough:
biscuit dough topping, 447
bread, 410, 411
flavoring, 411
freezing, 360
molding, 330
platter made from, 430
rolling out, 330
sticky cookie, 409
shaping and decorating, 411
using to make place cards, 428
drafts:
blocking out, 15
preventing, 141
dragging, 260
drainage:
alpine troughs, 512
containers, 504, 518
gravel paths, 465
lawns, 454, 571
raised beds, 461
retaining walls, 461
soil, 456, 482
when planting bulbs, 497
drainholes, cleaning, 68
drainpipes, 612
and security, 144
drains:
covering, 39
unblocking, 135
drawers, 25
clothes storage, 111
greasing runners, 117
lining, 25, 237
making dividers, 25
making safety stops, 25
painting, 256
standing in wardrobe, 19
using as work surfaces, 17
waxing runners, 25
wrapping for a move, 150
dress rails, using, 21
dressing-tables, lighting, 19
dressings, 283
adding mustard powder, 345
transporting, 445

dried fruits:
preparing, 369
soaking in brandy, 340
storing, 340
drilling:
inserting wall anchors, 302
tiles, 250
drink cabinets, creating, 20
drinks, 420, 421
buying for weddings, 48, 49
children's, 441
for a buffet, 433
nonalcoholic, 436
party, 430, 431
wine, 436
drip-dry clothes, 106, 109
drip guard, 207
drips, removing, 218, 266
driveways, cleaning, 136
dropcloths:
securing, 204
storing, 219
drought:
feeding plants, 527
lawns, 533
situations prone to, 529
weeding, 530
drought-resistant plants, 529, 532
drowning, rescue from, 173
drug poisoning, treating, 178
dry areas, 529
planting bulbs, 497
planting shrubs, 489
suitable plants, 484
dry cleaning, 104
curtains, 105
duvets, 61
drying:
foods, 417
laundry, 101, 106–107
mattresses, 87
shoes, 113
dry rot, 602
dry shampoo, improvising, 34
duck:
preparing breasts, 374
roasting, 392
soaking wild, 375
duckweed, 575, 577
dust, 16, 21
duster, time-saving, 57

dusting:
keyboards, 160
lampshades, 148
mouse mats, 160
using old socks, 42
duvet covers, choosing, 41
duvets, 127
laundering, 105

E

earrings:
cleaning, 130
organizing, 28
silver, 119
ears:
earache, 187
foreign bodies, 183
injuries, 184
popping, 187
earwigs, 545, 558
ebony, caring for, 115
edging plants:
formal and informal, 452
paths, 464
stepover apples, 453
suitable plants, 464
edgings:
lawns, buried, 568
paths, 464
edible flowers, 408, 435
eggplant, 365, 381, 443
eggs, 354
buying and storing, 354
checking for freshness, 354
egg whites, 372
frying, 386
glazing with, 372
hard-boiled, 354, 387
in balanced diet, 628
in sauces, 399
marbling, 387
methods of cooking, 386, 387
preparing, 372
scrambling, 372, 386
separating, 372
using up yolks, 372
eggshells:
calcium source, 528
slug and snail barriers, 558
egg tempera, 265
electrical injuries:
rescuing a victim, 173
treating burns, 177

electric appliances, 332, 333, 572
circuit breakers, 563
cleaning, 72–73
on fire, 172
safety, 137, 138
storing tools, 611
electric blankets, 42, 127
electric fixtures:
cleaning, 64
painting around, 207
protecting surround of, 237
removing paint from, 218
tiling around, 244
wallpapering around, 232
electricity, 137–138
cords, 574
supply to patios, 463
electric outlets:
cleaning, 64
overloading, 138
safety 171
electrics:
siting in home office, 158
testing in new home, 155
using in bathrooms, 18
using in garages and sheds, 26
using in hobby rooms, 21
using time switches, 46
see also appliances
electronic deterrents, 553, 554
electronic equipment:
cleaning and care, 128
energy-saving tips, 139
embroidery:
ironing, 109
transfers, 99
emergency services, 171
enamel bathtubs, 68
enamel paint:
faking enamel, 261
gilding with, 263
energy efficiency, 139
entertaining, 422, 446, 447
equipment:
babies, 36
care and repair, 114, 118
child safety, 38
cleaning, 54–55, 219, 229, 537
decorating glass, 296
first-aid, 170
flooring, 268
home offices, 160

household maintenance, 133, 137
improvising, 211, 216
laundry, 100
kitchen, 318–333
maintaining bicycles, 51
moving home, 149
paint effects, 203, 211, 259
painting, 203, 208, 253
personal grooming, 34
picnic, 445
picture-hanging, 304
plumbing, 133
shelving, 302
soft furnishings, 306
special needs, 41
stenciling, 215
stain-removal, 32
storing, 219
tiling, 240
wallpapering, 221, 226, 237
window-treatment, 288
see also tools and equipment
etching glass, 296
evergreens:
as patio plants, 460
as screens, 470
for arbors, 468
storing, 486
transplanting, 499
everyday items, organizing, 31
exercising, 35, 162
hands, 41
eyeglasses, cleaning, 123
eyes:
relaxing, 162
foreign bodies in, 183

F

fabric protector, 81
fabrics, 199
choosing, 208, 293, 306
color scheming, 197, 287
dressing up, 287
laundering, 100–109
stain removal, 78–99
using leftovers, 295
wall coverings, 234, 237
fabric softener, 100, 107
face:
massaging, 35
refreshing, 34
relaxing, 162

family health log, 45
fan-trained fruit trees, 466
fats, 628
faucets:
cleaning, 69
dripping, 133, 136
external, 459
fixing leaks, 155
marking, 41
repairs, 133
shining, 120
faux effects, 217, 282, 283
faxes:
filing, 166
writing, 166
fax machines:
cleaning, 128
siting, 161
feeding plants, 524–528
annuals, 495
container plants, 509
late-season, 524, 527
naturalized bulbs, 566
patio plantings, 460
screening plants, 469
stored plants, 486
timing, 527
trees, 455
fences:
maintaining, 603
rabbit-proof, 554
renovating, 451
trellis extensions, 473
with hedges, 471
fennel, 394
fertilizers, 524
applying, 526
forms, 525
granular, 503, 525
liquid, 525, 526
making your own, 528
natural, using, 528
saving time, 526
using, 524
festive lights, packing, 30
fever, reducing, 185
fiber, 626
figs, 368
filing, 168
boxes, making, 168
business cards, 169
filing cabinets, 158
protecting, 161
filing trays, 159
filleting fish, 376

filling:
  concrete subfloors, 272
  corners, 204
  cracks, 218
  decorative coving, 235
  furniture, 263
  gaps between floorboards, 271
  grouting, 248
  stairs, 257
  walls, 204, 225, 241
  woodwork, 255
film:
  horticultural, 589
  storing, 28
finances, managing, 169
  in a shared home, 157
fire blankets, 132, 171
fire escapes,
  keeping clear, 21
fireguards, 171
fireplaces:
  cleaning, 21
  putting cabinets in, 22
fire precautions, 171
fire-retardant materials, 298, 306
fires, 172
  electrical, 137, 172
  house, 171, 172
  open, 139
  using guards, 38
first aid, 47
  kit, 170
fish (cooking):
  barbecuing, 395, 443
  blood and bonemeal, 524
  boning, 376
  bouquet garni for, 370
  choosing, 358
  cleaning, 376
  filleting, 376
  freezing, 358
  frozen, 376
  methods of cooking, 394, 397
  preparing, 376
  refreshing, 358
  removing smells, 331, 376
  scaling, 376
  serving wines with, 436
  skinning, 376
  whole, 376
fish (pets), 53
  transporting, 154
fish (ponds), 577, 578
fish stock, 377

flagstone flooring, 281
flea beetles, 547, 558
fleece, horticultural, 522, 559, 580, 582
floating floors, laying, 274
floorboards:
  joining, 274
  lifting, 271
  repairing, 271
  replacing, 271
  sanding, 273
  staining, 283
  turning, 271
flooring, 268–285
  choosing, 38, 42, 269–270
  cleaning, 58–59
  covering, 204, 224
  equipment, 268
  laying in bathroom, 18
  leftovers, using, 285
  maintaining, 284
  preparing floors, 269, 271–272, 275
  protecting, 270, 284
  removing, 272
  special treatments, 60
  types, 269
  utility, 278–279
  see also carpet; wooden floors
floor plans, 15, 146, 152
floor polish, 58, 59
floors:
  finding the center of, 275, 279
  insulating, 140, 142
  painting, 282–283
  protecting, 156
  repairing, 142
  testing, 155
  see also wooden floors
floor tiles, 269
  calculating quantities, 269
  inlaying mosaics, 281
  laying flooring over, 272
  laying hard tiles, 280–281
  laying soft tiles, 279
  maintaining, 284
  removing, 272
  sealing with wax, 284
floppy disks,
  arranging, 168, 169

flour:
  chilling, 340
  coating with, 374, 396
  for savory scones, 409
  storing, 340
  substituting, 340
flower beds:
  annuals in, 495
  containers in, 511, 585
  planting bulbs, 497
  renovating, 450
  seasonal diary, 614–621
  sloping, 484
  sowing, 583
  under trees, 455
  watering, 532
  weedkillers, 537
flower pots,
  see pots
flowers, 426, 427
  edible, 408, 435
  encouraging:
    bulbs, 527
    deadheading, 540
    with fertilizer, 520, 526
  making napkin rings with, 429
  ordering for a wedding, 49
flower teas, 421
flower water, 420
focal points, 459
  specimen plants, 452, 510
foil:
  cooking in, 395, 397
  making platters, 426
foliage plants, 520
  annuals, 495
  glossy, 477
  in windowboxes, 513
foliar feeds, 525, 526
  bulbs, 527, 596
  young plants, 590
fondant icing, 408
food:
  buying and storing, 334–361
  cooking 362–421
  ordering for weddings, 49
  organizing in a shared home, 157
  planning for family celebrations, 49
  planning for pets, 52
food processors, 332, 333
  cleaning, 73
foot rot, 546, 582
foreign bodies, removing, 183

formal-looking garden:
  beds and borders, 452
  hedging, 471
  lawn shapes, 452
  steps, 465
  trellis, 467
fountain pens,
  cleaning, 131
fragile objects:
  moving, 147
  packing, 149
  positioning, 31
frames, gilding, 263
  see also picture frames
frankfurters, 390
freezers, 321–323, 419
  cleaning, 71, 323
  defrosting, 71, 323
  emptying, 146
  saving energy, 139
  stocking, 44
freezing, 418, 419
  bananas, 352
  beans, 341
  bread, 360
  breadcrumbs, 361
  butter, 355, 419
  cakes, 361, 418
  cheese, 355
  chilies, 351
  chocolate, 343, 419
  citrus fruits, 366
  cream, 354
  dough, 360, 410
  egg yolks, 372
  fish, 358
  fruits, 418, 419
  herbs, 344
  meat and poultry, 357
  nuts, 340
  pastry, 412
  sandwiches, 444
  soufflé, 404
  stand-by foods, 419,
    446
French polish, 66
French windows, 286
frost:
  breaking down soil, 482
  damage to pots, 519,
    574
  lawns, 568
  protecting concrete, 606
  protecting plants, 522
  protecting ponds, 572
frosting, 407

frozen foods, 347, 349
  frying fish from frozen, 396
  labeling, 358, 419
  see also thawing
frozen pipes, 135
fruit cakes, 361, 406
fruit cocktail, serving, 433
fruit juice, 420
  making ice cubes from, 431
  moistening cake with, 407
fruit pies, 402, 412
fruit purée, 332, 385,
  setting, 434
fruits (cooking):
  barbecuing, 385, 443
  buying and storing, 352
  canning, 347, 415
  dicing, 362
  drying, 417
  freezing, 418, 419
  garnishing with, 435
  in drinks, 420
  in tea, 421
  making table decorations
    from, 426, 428
  methods of cooking,
    384–385
  preparing, 362, 366–369
  setting in jelly, 404
  using frozen fruits, 347,
    367
  using in jams and
    jellies, 415
  see also dried fruits
fruits (gardening), 520
  collecting seeds, 587
  cuttings, 594
  gardener's diary, 614–621
  in containers, 508
  in island beds, 452
fruit salad, 404
fruit tarts, 402
fruit trees, fan-trained, 466
fruit vinegars, 346
frying:
  eggs, 386
  fish and shellfish, 396
  meat, 391
fumes, chemical, 55
funerals, organizing, 47
fungal diseases in plants:
  overcrowding, 548
  seedlings, 589
  watering, 529
fungal rot, 602
fungal scab, 529, 546

fungicides, 556, 585
furnishing fabrics, 306
furniture:
  aging, 264
  cleaning, 66
  collecting, 198
  decorating, 263–265
  fire risk, 171
  gilding, 263
  mildew, 96
  moving, 60, 156
  packing, 150, 152
  positioning, 15
  preparing for painting, 263
  protecting, 204
  putting in new home, 146
  showing on floor plans, 15
  siting in home offices, 158
  stain removal, 80–98
  see also garden furniture;
    upholstery
furniture polish, 55, 66
  homemade, 115
furs, caring for, 111
fuses, faulty, 138
futons, using, 19

G

game, 389
garages:
  security, 144, 145
  storing in, 26
gardener's diary, 614–621
garden furniture,
  maintenance, 602, 609
garden maintenance,
  598 613
gardening, 448–621,
  see also under individual
    topics
gardens, 450–477, 562–579
  making safe, 39, 155
garlic:
  buying, 350
  crushing, 327
  flavoring with, 388, 420
  freezing food without, 418
  pressing, 363
  reducing flavor of, 399
  storing, 351
garlic bread, 360 443
garnishes, 366, 435
gas leaks, 139
gathered blinds, 292
gelatin, 404, 405
  desserts, 404, 440

gilding:
using gold pen, 261
gilt frames, restoring, 121
ginger, 371, 394
glass:
broken, 143
cleaning, 75, 122–123, 257, 296
chipped, 122
decorating, 296–297
effects, 296, 297
grease marks, 99
picture glass, 129
shielding, 257
glass doors, safety, 171
glasses, 122, 425
decorating, 441
drying, 439
packing, 149
rinsing, 431
storing, 30
transporting, 445
washing, 72, 122
glazing (coating), 210
applying, 212, 213
calculating quantities, 211
coloring, 211
dragging, 260
graining wood, 259
storing, 219
traditional, making, 211
glazing (food):
bread, 411
fruit tarts, 402
meat, 388, 393
pastry, 372
with apricot jam, 343
with mustard, 388
glazing (glass),
cleaning and replacing, 613
gloves, 111
for gardening, 521, 540
protecting hands during a move, 156
glycerin, 55, 77
gold, caring for, 121
gooseberries, 367
graining, 265
cupboard doors, 259
grains, 339, 400
granules:
fertilizer, 503, 525
water-retaining, 503, 530
grape leaves, 491, 443

grapes, 352
using in canapés, 430
grass clippings, 530, 534, 536
grasscloth, cleaning, 62
grass seeds, 562, 564
graters, cleaning, 73
grates, clearing, 65
gravel:
adding to soil, 478, 595
aquatic, 576
paths, 464, 465
suppressing weeds, 534, 536
gravlax, 417
gravy, 393
adding citrus zest to, 434
freezing, 419
removing lumps from, 399
gray mold, 529, 540
grease:
disposing of, 74
on fabric and carpets, 80–81
on glass, 75
on paper, 99, 129
on wall coverings, 62
on wood, 116
grease solvent, 77
greenhouses:
cleaning, 612
damping down, 523
gardener's diary, 614–621
heat protection, 523
maintaining, 612
pests, 523, 612
seeds and seedlings, 586
ventilation, 523, 555
watering, 533
grief, coping with, 47
grilling:
fish, 395
fruits, 385
meat, 390
grills, cleaning, 71
gripper rods:
attaching to stairs, 277
securing curved edges, 276
grit, 456
grooming, organizing, 34
groundcover:
slopes, 457, 484
suppressing weeds, 536
wildflower areas, 455
groundsel, 535

grout:
applying, 247, 249
choosing, 249
cleaning, 247, 251
dried, removing, 250
replacing, 251
sealing, 250
touching up, 250
grouting, 59, 63
grow bags, 508, 533
guests:
catering for extra, 447
inviting to wedding, 48, 49
gutters, 532, 601, 604

H

hair, paint in, 99
hairbrushes:
bone, 125
cleaning, 34
hair conditioner, making, 34
hair ribbons, 109
hairy bittercress, 535
hallways, planning, 21
ham:
flavoring, 388
glazing with mustard, 388
using in canapés, 430
hammered finish, 261
hand washing, 104
handbags:
caring for, 131
removing mildew, 96
handles, putting on walls, 42
hangers, adapting, 111
hanging baskets, 502, 515–517
disguising chains, 515
dry, rescuing, 517
hanging, 517
linings, 516
maintaining, 517
planting, 515
types, 515
using, 472, 516
watering, 509
hanging files, 158
making containers for, 168
hanging frames, 16
hanging pictures, 129
hanging systems:
for blinds, 292
for curtains, 287, 288, 289
for pictures, 304

hard drives, organizing, 168
hardboard, 253
    acclimatizing, 272
    filling, 282
    fitting subfloors, 272
    painting, 282
hardwood, 253, 598, 609
    cuttings, 594
hats, storing, 22, 111
hazelnuts, 340, 369
headboards:
    attaching cushions, 307
    covering, 308
    making, 19
health:
    making log, 45
    healthy plants, 548
hearts, cleaning, 374
heat:
    germination, 584
    protecting plants, 523
heaters, cleaning, 65
heating, 140–141
heat marks, 99, 116
hedges:
    care, 471
    clippings, 471
    diseases, 471
    dividing lawn, 453
    lavender, 464
    planting, 471
    pollution-tolerant, 523
    prickly, 554
    pruning, 542
    renovating, 542
    short gardens, 477
    snow protection, 522
    sparse, 471, 542
    trimming, 471
    underplanting, 471
heeling in, 486
help:
    having in bereavement, 47
    organizing for a move, 145
hems, ironing, 108
herbs, 350
    adding to coating, 394
    adding to stews, 389
    dried, 344, 371
    drying, 417
    flavoring butter with, 355
    flavoring fish with, 394
    flavoring vinegar with, 346
    freezing, 507
    fresh, 353, 370
    glazing bread with, 411

in green salad, 383
    in island beds, 452
    in vegetable juice, 420
    in windowboxes, 514
    making napkin rings, 429
    making table decorations
        from, 429
    preparing, 370, 371
    storing, 344, 353
herb teas, 421
herrings, 394
hiccups, cures for, 187
hinges, sticking, 142
hives, treating, 180
hobby rooms, planning, 21
hobs, 318
    cleaning, 71
hoeing, 538
hollandaise sauce, 399
home log book, making, 55
home maintenance, when
    inspecting a new home, 147
home offices, 158–162
    creating under stairs, 21
    equipping, 160
    making comfortable, 162
    planning, 158
    protecting equipment, 161
    setting up, 159
home:
    making safe, 38, 155
    sharing, 157
honey, 343
    cold cure, 185
    glazing bread with, 411
    sweetening ices with,
        405
hormone rooting powder, 590,
    592, 593
horseradish, 370
horsetails, 535
hoses, 521, 563
    hose-end applicators, 526
    leaky, mending, 532
    neatening, 29
    protecting plants, 532
    snake, 553
hospitals:
    staying in, 44, 45
    visiting patients, 44
hot chocolate, 421
household, running, 32–47
household cleaners, 55
household organizer, 32
household product stains,
    93–98

house plants:
    discouraging pets from
        damaging, 52
    keeping in home offices, 162
    packing for a move, 151
house rules, setting, 157
hoverfly, 550, 552
humidifiers, 61, 115
    cold treatment, 185
humidity, 141
    protecting books, 29
    protecting tools, 31
humming tape, 553
humus, see organic matter
hutches:
    moving, 154
    siting, 52
hydrogen peroxide, 77
hypertufa, 512
hypothermia, preventing, 173

I
ice, 432, 437, 578, 579
ice cream, 405
    adding to drinks, 441
    scooping, 329, 419
ice cubes:
    flavoring, 433
    making from fruit juice,
        431, 441
iced cakes, 361
ice pops, 441
ice ring, 431
icing, 408
icing cakes, 441
identification, keeping for
    computer, 161
illnesses, recording in family
    health log, 45
immunizations, recording in
    family health log, 45
incinerators, 463
information, arranging in
    documents, 167
injuries:
    dealing with, 47
    treating, 176–179
insecticidal soaps, 556, 172
insects:
    attracting, 455, 508
    beneficial, 550
    in ear, 183
    deterring, 61, 74
    stings from, 180
    suitable plants, 551
    using repellent, 65, 115

insetting tiles, 239, 246
insulation, 140, 142
  checking, 127, 155
  containers, 510, 522
  greenhouses, 612
  installing, 15
  plants, 522
  pipes, 140
  ponds, 578
  sheds, 601
insuring:
  against burglaries, 46
  audio equipment, 27
  cars, 40
  jewelry, 28
  keeping records, 169
  for moving, 146–147
intercropping, 508, 382
inventories,
  making, 146, 148
invoices, setting out, 167
ironing, 101, 108–109
ironing boards, 108
irons:
  cleaning and care, 108
  safety, 171
island beds, 252, 485, 567
ivory,
  cleaning and care, 125
ivy, 465, 476

J

jade, cleaning, 125, 130
jam making, 414, 415
jars:
  as storage containers, 79
  canning, 415
  cleaning, 336
  opening, 41
  recycling, 335
  releasing lids from, 336,
    415
  removing smells, 122
  screw-top, 340
  sterilizing, 414
  using a mustard jar, 79
jelly, 415, 416
Jerusalem artichokes, 364
jewelry:
  cleaning and care, 130–131
  gold jewelry, 121
  moving, 147
  packing, 149
  security, 145
  silver jewelry, 118–119
  storing, 23, 28

julienne strips, 362
juniper berries, 388
jute flooring, 277

K

kebabs:
  cheese, 430
  fish, 395
  fruit, 385
  mini, 440
  tofu, 443
kennels, leaving pets in, 154
keyboards, cleaning, 112
keys:
  and security, 145
  oiling locks with, 142
kidneys, 374
kitchen appliances, 318–323,
    332–333
  cleaning, 73
  energy-saving, 139
  problems, 136
kitchens:
  cleaning, 57, 70–74
  filling niches in, 26
  fires, 172
  improvements, 315
  organization, 314
  organizing in a new home,
    156
  planning, 14, 16–17
  safety, 165
  using cabinets, 17, 22
  waste, 74
kitchen utensils, 327–331,
  care, 117
  using for special needs, 42
kiwi fruit, 368, 404
kneeling pads, 538
knee protectors, making, 42
knives, 327–328, 362
  caring for, 76
  decorative handles, 75
  garden, 540, 595
  silver, 74–75
knots (wood):
  creating, 123
  dealing with bleeding, 266
  sealing, 255

L

labeling:
  as reminders, 41
  child's possessions, 37
  coat hangers, 33
  drawers, 25

files, 168
floppy disks, 168
linen cabinets, 22
medicine bottles, 43
for moving, 146, 152, 156
preprinting labels, 164
shelves, 24, 168
video tapes, 27
lace:
  laundering, 101, 104
  mildew on, 96
lacewing, 550
ladders, 208
  securing, 27
  security risk, 144
  using safely, 203, 230
ladybugs, 550
lamb:
  flavoring, 388
  marinating, 388
  preparing roasts, 375
  stewing in coffee, 389
laminates, painting, 263
lampshades, 301,
  cleaning, 127
  dusting, 148
laptop computers,
  protecting, 161
laundry, 100–111
  preparing for a move, 146,
    150
laundry aids, 100
  stain removal, 77, 79
laundry borax, 55, 100
  stain removal, 77, 79
laurels, 471
lavender:
  hedges, 464
  sachets, making, 112
lawnmower, 563
  maintenance, 611
  packing, 151
lawns, 562–571
  aerating, 533, 571
  breaking up, 453
  drainage, 454, 569
  feeding, 527, 569
  gardener's diary, 614–621
  heavy-use areas, 571
  island beds, 452, 567
  lawn care, 561
  laying stepping stones, 453
  leveling, 454
  maintaining, 561, 568–569
  marking out, 452
  moss, 454

mowing, 568
mulching, 530
nongrass, 562
paths in, 453
planting in, 566–567
problems, 527, 570–571
renovating, 450–455, 570
reshaping, 452
sod, laying, 565
sowing, 562, 564
top-dressing, 454, 571
trees in, 455, 567
trimming edges, 565, 568
watering, 533
weeding, 538, 569
yellowing, 527
lawyers:
  depositing data with, 169
  taking legal advice, 157
layering plants, 590–591
laying off, 206
laying out rooms,
  see room layouts
lead:
  caring for, 121
  testing paint for, 254
leaded lights, reproducing,
  297
leading, faking, 261
leafmold, 478, 482
leaf spots, 541, 545, 561
leather:
  care, 75
  mildew, 96
  stain removal, 99
  washability check, 126
  water marks on, 97
leather-bound books, 129
leather furniture:
  cleaning and care, 67, 126
  removing ink stains, 126
leather shoes, cleaning, 113
  stain removal, 80, 87
leaves:
  fallen, 561, 578, 613
  making from apples, 435
  making from chocolate,
  405
  making napkin rings, 429
leeks, 363, 380
leftovers, 380, 419
leg injuries, treating, 181
legs, padding fractures, 47
legumes, 341, 401
leisure time, scheduling, 162
lemonade, 385, 441

lemon juice:
  cooking vegetables, 380
  removing smells, 331,
  376
  removing stains, 55, 77
lemons:
  cutting wedges, 366
  flavoring with, 388, 403
  freezing slices, 419
  lemon and lime twists,
  366
  preserving, 416
lentils, 341, 401
letters:
  drafting, 166
  setting out, 166, 167
  storing, 168
  writing to complain,
  166
lettuce:
  buying, 350
  container-grown, 508
  cutting wedges, 382
  preparing, 364, 382
  refreshing, 304
  soup, 398
  using leaves as bowls,
  382
levels, storing, 237
lifestyles, 200–201
lifting, 153
light:
  depriving weeds of, 536
  diffusing, 300
  fence extensions, 473
  improving, 287
  seedlings, 585
lightbulbs, 138, 299, 301
  cleaning, 64
  scenting, 64
  using daylight bulbs,
  158
lighting, 138, 196, 299–301
  bedrooms, 19
  for painting, 206
  for special needs, 42
  home offices, 158, 162
  lighting pictures, 305
  in the kitchen, 315
  parties, 438
  safety, 171
  saving energy, 139
  security, 144–145
  using time switches, 46
light switches:
  cleaning, 64

lime:
  and manure, 526
  and soil pH, 342, 344
  crop rotation, 413
  preventing clubroot, 424
liming, 260
line drying, 106
linen closets, 112
  neatening, 22
lining paper, 220, 223, 226
linoleum, 269
  cleaning, 59
  cracks in, 60
  designing your own,
  278
  laying, 278
  paint stains, 60
  removing, 272
linseed oil, 610
  uses, 114
lint:
  on clothes, 111
  on upholstery, 67
lipsticks, using up, 34
liqueurs, 407
liquid fertilizers, 525, 526
  making your own, 528
liquid seaweed, 524
lists, making:
  for insurance, 27
  of tasks for a move, 147,
  148
  of wedding presents, 48,
  49
  of wedding tasks, 48
liver, 374
living areas, planning, 14, 20
  laying out, 15
lobster:
  buying, 359
  making stock from,
  377
  preparing, 377
locks, 142
  changing, 46
  preventing burglary, 46
  using on filing cabinet,
  161
loft insulation, 140
logs, making:
  for family health, 45
  for telephone calls, 157
  for work, 165
longlife foods, 447, 347
loose covers, cleaning, 126
  measuring for, 307

low-fat diet, 628
  alternative to cream
    frosting, 407
  cream substitutes, 373
  low-fat dressing, 383
  low-fat mayonnaise, 399
luggage labels, 145

M

machine washing, 103
mackerel, 376, 394
magazine racks, using, 20
magnesium, 525
mahogany, caring for, 115
mangoes, 367
  stuffing poultry with, 388
manure, 84
  and lime, 526
  crop rotation, 549
  planting shrubs, 489
marble:
  cleaning, 65, 75
  stain removal, 125
marble tiles, 243, 245
  cutting, 245
  grouting, 249
marbling:
  creating tile effects, 283
  decorating woodwork,
    262
  dough, 411
  eggs, 387
  sauces, 434
margarine, 373
marinating, 417,
  fish, 394
  fruits, 385
  game, 389
  meat, 374, 388
mashed potatoes, 347, 379
  making a hot-dog tepee
    with, 440
  reviving, 381
masking:
  distressing woodwork,
    264
  painting furniture, 263
  painting stripes, 214
  painting wall edges, 207
  sealing with silicone,
    249
  spray painting, 208
  stripping floors, 273
massaging face, 35
mats and matting,
  cleaning, 61

mattresses:
  drying, 87
  pressing clothes under, 109
  stain removal, 86
  using as spare beds, 19
mayonnaise, 345, 399
MDF, 253
meadow grass, 535
measurements, 622–627
measuring:
  blinds, 292
  wallpaper, 226, 231
  see also calculating
    quantities
meat, 356–357
  avoiding contamination,
    349, 357, 375
  buying, 356
  cutting, 374
  freezing, 419
  handling, 330
  methods of cooking,
    388–393
  preparing, 374–375
  refrigerating, 357
  roasting times, 626
  serving quantities, 356
  storing, 357
  tenderizing, 374
medical care, 43–45
  seeking after assaults, 46
medications:
  protecting labels, 43
  storing, 38
  taking to hospital, 44
medicine kit, keeping in the
  home, 43
meditation, practicing, 35
medium-density fiberboard,
  see MDF
meetings, planning, 163, 165
melons:
  checking for ripeness, 352
  making a melon basket, 426
  preparing, 368
  serving drinks in, 433
memo boards, making, 159
memory, aiding, 41
mending, see repairs
meningitis, symptoms, 185
menu planning, 423
meringue:
  making, 372
  microwaving, 403
  slicing, 404
  topping, 384, 402

mesh, roots in, 490
messages, taking, 166
metal polish, 55, 114
metallic finish,
  creating, 261
metallic paint, using, 261
metals, 598
  caring for, 118–121
    furniture, 66
  containers, 518
  covers, concealing, 470
  faking, 261
  furniture, 609
  painting, 257, 263
meters, having read, 144,
  145
mice, controlling, 486, 554
microwave ovens:
  cleaning, 71
  using, 139
  wall-mounting, 17
microwaving, 320
  almonds, 369
  apricots, 385
  asparagus, 379
  bread dough, 410
  butter, 373
  citrus fruits, 366
  desserts, 403
  dried fruits, 369
  eggs, 386
  herbs, 417
  hollandaise sauce, 399
  muffins, 409
  phyllo dough, 413
  poultry, 392
  preserves, 415
  rice, 400
mildew:
  preventing, 29
  removing, 96
    from books, 129
    from bread bins, 73
    from shower curtains,
      68, 96
milk:
  freezing, 419
  in low-fat dressing,
    383
milk shakes, 420, 436
  decorating, 441
mineral water, 436, 628
minerals, in diet, 629
mint, 370
  controlling, 507
mint tea, 421

mirrors:
cleaning, 64, 123
hairspray marks, 94
hanging, 305
siting in bedrooms, 23
wrapping for a move,
150
mitering, 235
borders, 233
tiles, 246, 249
mixed spice, 345
mixers, 332, 333
mixing bowls, grouping, 16
mobile telephones,
keeping, 161
moisture:
bases of slopes, 457
carpets, 61
cupboards, 112
lawns, 567
lining wallpaper, 236
prints, 129
when papering window
recess, 230
wooden floors, 60
moisturizers:
applying, 34
making, 34
moldings, decorative:
covering panel edges, 235
coving,
repairing and fixing, 235
edging floorings, 274, 278
edging shelves, 303
gilding, 261
filling, 255
painting edges, 207, 256
sanding, 254
sealing tile edges, 249
molds:
lining, 330
turning out, 404
using pastry cutter, 434
moles, 454, 553
mood, creating, 190, 192–195,
287
morale, boosting, 162
mortar:
for the garden, 604, 605
gauging depth, 280
laying quarry tiles, 280
simulating, 217
mosaic tiles:
applying, 245
making a floor panel, 281
making your own, 245, 251

moss:
in lawns, 454, 569
on patios, 459
moth proofing, 112
moths, deterring, 30
motorcycles:
checking, 50
positioning luggage, 50
mouse mats, cleaning, 160
mouth wounds, treating, 184
moving, 146–157
caring for children
and pets, 154
carrying essentials, 153
moving into a new home,
155
preparing for, 146–147
sorting and packing,
148–152
using floor plan, 15, 152
moving plants,
see transplanting
mowing, 538, 568, 570
mud, on shoes, 113
mugging, dealing with, 46
mulching, 530
borders, 456
containers, 508
disguising netting, 457
new plantings, 501
organic, 530
patio plantings, 460
planting roses, 493
screening plants, 469
transplanting, 498
using carpets, 501
using newspapers, 489
using plastic, 530
water-retaining, 530
weed-suppressing, 534,
536
murals:
painting, 216
using mosaic tiles, 245
muscle injuries,
treating, 181
mushroom compost, 524
mushrooms:
dried, 365, 417
preparing, 365
softening, 381
storing, 351
using in canapés, 430
music, listening to, 35, 162
musical instruments,
care, 117

mussels:
buying, 359
cleaning, 359
debearding, 377
frying, 396
grilling, 395
mustard:
flavoring fish with, 394
glazing with, 388
making, 345
roasting meat in, 393

N

nail polish:
keeping, 34
marking faucets with, 41
napkin rings, 429
silver, 75
napkins, 427, 429
natural-fiber flooring, 269
choosing, 270
cutting for door mats, 284
laying, 277
natural floor coverings, 61
necklaces,
storage and care, 28, 131
nectarines, 367
nematodes, 552, 594
nests, 471, 542
netting:
cat deterrents, 554
on greenhouse roof, 613
protecting crops, 553
protecting lawns, 571
protecting play areas, 571
protecting ponds, 572,
578
retaining soil, 457, 484
securing cuttings, 593
shading plants, 501
supporting climbers, 492
nettles, 535, 537
attracting insects, 551
fertilizer from, 528
newspapers:
basket liners, 516
carpet padding, 115
cleaning windows, 64, 156
composting, 483
frost protection, 522
mulch, 489
protecting floors, 156
shoe care, 113
newsprint stains, 99
sowing tubes, 585
wrapping fragile items, 149

nitrogen, 525, 528
nonstick pans, 325
noodles, 338
noses:
  bleeding, 184
  congested, 185
  foreign bodies in, 183
notice boards, making, 285
novelty foods, 440
nutmeg, 345, 380
nut oils, 346, 383
nutrients (cooking), 629
nutrients (garden), 525
nutrition, 628
nuts:
  adding to pastry, 412
  buying and storing, 340
  flaking, 340
  in milk shakes, 420
  preparing, 329, 369
  smoking, 417
  unshelled, 340

O

oak, caring for, 115
oats, 447
  creating texture with, 340,
    412
octopus, 359
odors:
  neutralizing for mice, 52
  removing,
    from bathrooms, 69
    from bottles and jars,
      122
    from hands, 72
    from pans, 73
    from plastic containers, 75
    from refrigerators, 71
  types of:
    cigarette smoke, 61
    food, 74
    urine, 87
offal, 374
office equipment,
  cleaning, 128
offices,
  see home offices
oil:
  brushing on phyllo dough,
    413
  flavoring, 346, 394
  frying eggs in, 386
  frying in, 396
  frying meat in, 391
  greasing pans with, 406

nut, 346, 383
  olive, 365
  sesame, 382
  storing, 346
  storing feta cheese in,
    355
  storing garlic in, 351
  types of, 346
  using for massage, 35
okra, 365
olive oil, 346
omelet:
  making, 372
  turning out, 386
  filling with stir-fry mix,
    347
onions:
  adding onion juice, 380
  avoiding tears, 363
  frying, 380
  pickling, 416
  reducing flavor of, 399
  removing smell of, 331
  soaking, 382
  storing, 351
oranges:
  baking whole, 384
  decorating with, 403
  flavoring with, 384
  peeling, 366
  removing segments from,
    366
organic matter, 478, 482
  transplanting, 501
  water retention, 530
organic pest controls, 556
ormolu, caring for, 121
ornaments, 459, 511
  adding, 201
  choosing, 195, 197
  displaying, 298, 309
  packing, 149, 150
  positioning, 31
  securing, 309
  washing, 156
ovens, 318–319
  cleaning, 71
  energy-saving, 139
  microwave, 320
oven temperatures, 626
oven thermometer, 319, 393
oxalis, 539
oysters:
  grilling, 395
  opening, 377
  storing, 359

P

packaged mixes, 347
packaging, 349
  freezer foods, 419
  meat, 357, 419
packaging materials, 148
packing:
  for a move, 146, 149–152
  for vacations, 112
  paint, 202, 252
  calculating quantities, 203
  choosing colors, 196, 197
  disposing of, 219
  glass paints, 296
  one-coat paints, 208
  preparing, 205
  storing, 219, 267
  tile paints, 248
  types, 202, 252
padding:
  carpeting over, 276
  for rugs, 284
  improvising, 15
  laying natural flooring, 277
  laying wooden floors, 274
paintbrushes, 208, 253
  battery-powered, 208
  breaking in, 255
  cleaning, 219, 266
  ferrule, 313
  for paint effects, 211, 259
  for stippling, 212
  making a stenciling brush,
    215
  selecting, 206, 207, 253
  storing, 219, 267
  washing, 206
paint cans:
  labeling, 219
  packing, 151
  recycling, 219
paint effects, 210
  bagging, 210, 212
  blocking, 216
  creating checks, 214, 283
  creating stripes, 214
  choosing, 210
  colorwashing, 211
  combing, 262
  decorating woodwork,
    259–262
  dragging, 260
  equipment, 203, 211, 259
  liming, 260
  painting murals, 216, 245

painting floors, 283
painting tiles, 248
painting walls, 202–217
printing, 216
ragging, 210, 213, 248
rag rolling, 210, 213
sponging, 210, 212
staining glass, 297
stamping, 216
stenciling, 215,
stippling, 210, 212
trompe l'oeil:
    on floors, 282,
    on furniture, 265
    on walls, 217, 304
painting:
    ceilings, 207
    cleaning up, 219, 266
    containers, 503, 519
    correcting mistakes, 218, 266
    cutting in, 207
    equipment, 203, 208, 253,
        599
    finishing off, 218–219,
        266–267
    floors, 282–283
    furniture, 263–265
    garden furniture, 609
    glass, 296–297
    kitchen equipment, 311
    metal, 257
    pipes, 257
    plant supports, 476
    retouching, 267
    shelves, 303
    storing materials, 219, 267
    texturing, 209
    tiles, 248
    trellis, 467
    Venetian blinds, 293
    walls, 202–219
    windowboxes, 514
    woodwork, 255–257
paint stripper, 254, 273
paintwork, cleaning, 63, 66
pancakes:
    deep-fried, 403
    freezing, 446
    stuffed, 446
panels:
    combing, 262
    distressing, 264
    faking, 235
    inserting in floor tiles, 281
    using tiles, 246
    see also wood paneling

pans, see pots and pans
pantry, 446
    choosing staples for,
        337–341
    organizing, 334
papaya, 368, 374
paper:
    grease marks, 99, 129
    recycling, 160
    removing from wood, 117
paper towels, 76
paprika, 389
parsley:
    chopped, 370, 435
    deep-frying, 435
parties, 438–439
    planning, 422–423
    playing games at, 441
partitions, trellis, 470
pasta, 337–338
    coloring pasta dough,
        401
    cooking, 401
    dried, 337–338
    serving wines with, 436
    shapes, 337, 338
    storing, 338
pasting, 227
    borders, 233
    stairwell lengths, 231
pastry, 412–413
    adding texture to, 412
    avoiding soggy pastry,
        412, 430
    decorating, 413, 419
    ready-rolled, 347
    rolling, 331
    shortcrust, 373, 412
pastry brushes, 330
patching:
    flooring, 60
    upholstery, 126
    wallpaper, 62
patent leather, cleaning, 113
paths, 464–465
    brick, repairing, 608
    direction of, 453
    edging plants, 453, 464
    edgings, 464
    gravel, maintaining, 465
    in lawns, 453, 571
    renovating, 450
    softening edges, 464
    stepping stones,
    laying, 453
    weedkillers, 537

patios, 459–463
    barbecues, 463
    cleaning, 459
    containers, 459, 462
    electricity supply, 463
    focal points, 459
    mixing materials, 459
    plant care, 460
    planting in, 460, 607
    raised beds, 461
    renovation,450–451,459–463
    replacing slabs, 459
    softening, 459
    sowing between slabs, 451,
        583
    suitable plants, 460
    sunken, 461
    wall plants, 459
    water features, 459, 462
    weathering, 460
    weeds, 459, 537
patterns:
    centralizing, 223, 229
    choosing, 222
    linking, 195
    matching, 236
    repeats, 223, 289
    rollering, 214
    stenciling, 215
    in textured finish, 209
paving:
    cutting slabs, 607
    homemade, 571
    laying stepping stones, 453
    path repairs, 464
    patio repairs, 459
    planting in, 460, 607
    replacing slabs, 459, 607
    sowing cracks, 451, 583
    stains, 459
    working with slabs, 607
peaches:
    methods of cooking, 384,
        385
    preparing, 367
    as standby dessert, 446
    topping with cheese, 385
peach leaf curl, 547, 561
pearls, caring for, 130
pears:
    coring, 368
    in pastry, 384
    poaching, 385
    in port, 446
    preventing discoloration,
        362

peas:
  dried, 341, 401
  flavoring with mint, 380
  nitrogen source, 528
peat, 478
peppercorns, 345, 371
peppers:
  buying, 350
  puréeing, 399
  skinning, 365
perennials:
  choosing, 490
  cuttings, 490
  dividing, 456, 500
  heights, 491
  in borders, 451, 457
  in containers, 490
  planting, 490–493
  planting distances, 491
  transplanting, 500
pergolas, 473, 474, 516
personal alarms, using, 42
personal care,
  organizing, 33–35
pesticides:
  chemical, 550, 555
  herb garden, 507
  organic, 556
pesto, 347, 443
  adding to polenta, 400
  dip, 431
pests, 544–561
  animals, 553–554
  biological controls, 555
  chemical controls, 557
  containers, 509, 518
  controlling, 555–561
  greenhouses, 612
  household, 61, 74
  organic controls, 556
  preventing, 548–552
  specific controls, 558–561
  types, 544–547
pets, 70,
  and choosing flooring,
    270
  keeping data on, 168
  moving with, 146,
    154
  planning care for, 52–53
  removing hairs, 67
  removing stains, 89
pewter,
  cleaning and care, 120
pH, 478, 480
pheromone traps, 559

phosphates, 525
  encouraging flowers,
    520, 526
photographs, sorting, 28
phyllo dough, 413
  as pie topping, 402
  latticing, 402
  making bundles from, 384,
    396
  making moneybags, 413
pianos:
  cleaning and care, 125
pickles, 416
picnics, 444–445
  taking equipment, 27
picture frames, choosing, 305
picture hooks:
  inserting, 305
  removing, 230
picture lights, 305
picture rails, 304
pictures, 198, 304–305
  cleaning and care, 129,
    305
  hanging, 304
  restoring gilt frames, 121
picture tiles, 239, 241, 246
picture windows, 286
pie charts, making, 164
pies:
  decorating, 413
  for picnics, 444
  freezing fruit fillings, 418
  fruit, 384, 402
  meat, 412
  sweet pastry for, 412
pillows, laundering, 105
pin boards, making, 159
pineapple:
  barbecuing, 385
  checking for ripeness, 352
  coring rings, 368
pipes:
  accessing, 235
  boxing in, 241
  concealing, 470
  hidden, avoiding, 298, 302
  painting, 257
  painting around, 207, 208
  papering around, 232
  frozen, 135
  repairs to, 134–135
  tiling around, 244, 279
piping, 409, 434
piping bags, 331,
  improvising, 408

pizza:
  quick, 440
  sweet, 402
  using dough to make
    calzone, 443
plan chests, storing in, 25
planners, using in offices, 159
planning:
  family celebrations, 49
  flooring, 269
  funerals, 47
  hiring tools, 268
  kitchens, 314
  moving home, 146–147
  parties, 422–423
  personal grooming, 34
  telephone use, 166
  tiling floors, 280
  tiling walls, 242, 246
  time with babies, 37
  wallpapering, 223
  weddings, 48–49
  work, 163
plant containers,
  see containers (plants)
planting:
  annuals, 494–495
  basic techniques, 487
  bulbs, 496–497
  cuttings, 594
  dividing, 595
  in alpine troughs, 512
  in containers, 506
  in hanging baskets, 515
  keeping plants moist, 487
  perennials, 490–493
  preparation, 480–484, 487
  roses, 489, 493
  shrubs, 488–489
  spacing, 456, 491, 548
  trees, 474, 567
  water plants, 575–576
plant labels, 485
plants:
  annuals, 494
  bulbs, 496
  caring for, 520–543
    new plantings, 501
    young plants, 589
  choosing, 485
  dealing with poisonous, 567
  perennials, 490
  shrubs, 488
  varieties:
    and exposure, 484
    and soil pH, 481

and soil texture, 481
for attracting insects, 551
for cuttings, 592
for direct sowing, 583
for division, 155
for dry conditions, 529
for edging, 464
for layering, 590
for oxygenating water, 575
for perennials, 491
for pergolas, 474
for seasonal containers, 505
for screening plants, 469
for transplanting, 498
shrubs, pruning times, 543
wildflowers, 455
plaster:
  coving, fixing, 235
  filling, 204
  sealing, 204, 209
plastic:
  carrot rust fly barrier, 559
  cleaning, 75
  containers, 502, 510
    hygiene, 548
    making drainage holes, 518
  furniture, 609
  garden, 598
  mulching, 530
  reusing, 74
  removing smells from, 75
  warming soil, 580, 582
  weed suppressor, 536, 539
plates:
  packing, 149
  stacking, 124
platinum, caring for, 121
play areas, 453, 468, 571
  surfacing, 39
playing cards, cleaning, 131
plugs, electric, 137
plumbing, 18, 133–134
plums, 367, 384
plungers, 135
plywood, 253
poaching:
  eggs, 387
  fish, 397
  fruits, 385
poisoning, treating, 178
poisonous plants, 485
police, contacting, 46

polish, 55
  build up, 63, 117
  reviving, 117
polishing:
  fireplaces, 65
  floors, 58, 59
  wood, 66, 115
pollution barrier, 523
polymer granules, 501
polypropylene matting, 536
polystyrene insulation, 601
polytunnel, making, 589
pomanders, 427
pomegranates, 368
ponds:
  barrels 462, 572, 574
  baskets, 572
  emptying, 579
  equipment, 572
  maintaining, 577–578
  planting, 575–576
  repairs, 579
  safety, 573
  wildlife, 551
pond weeds, 577
porcelain bathtubs, 68
porcelain sinks, 70
pork:
  flavoring with herbs, 370, 388
  rind, 389, 393
  stuffing pork chops, 388
portable cribs,
  using, 36, 37
possessions,
  protecting, 147
potassium, 524, 525
  applying, 527
  fighting frost, 522
  wood ash, 528
potassium sulfate, 524
potatoes:
  adding cooking water to bread dough, 410
  methods of cooking, 379
  new, 329, 443
  quick potato soup, 398
pot roasting, 389
pots (garden), 510–511
  decorative uses, 465
  flowerpot traps, 118
  grouping, 510
  lightweight, 511
  repairs, 519
  sowing in, 585
  sun protection, 523

types, 510
using, 510–511
water features, 573, 574
see also containers
pots and pans, 324–325
  energy-saving, 139
  making lids for, 331
  materials for, 324–325
  preserving, 414
  washing, 72, 73
poultry, 356–357
  char-grilling, 443
  coating, 374, 375
  freezing, 357
  methods of cooking, 388–393
  preparing, 374–375
  serving quantities, 356
  skinning, 375
  smoking, 416
  splitting, 375
  thawing, 357
  trussing, 375
powdery mildew, 529, 541
power cutages, 138
precious stones,
  cleaning, 130
preprinting:
  invoice forms, 167
  labels, 164
preserves, 343, 347
preserving, 414–417
pressure cooking:
  dried beans, 401
  preserves, 414
pressure washing, 604
priming:
  metal, 257
  plaster 205
  woodwork, 255
printing, 216
propagation, 580–597
  cuttings, 490, 592–594
  division, 500, 595–597
  from seeds, 580–589
  layering, 590–591
propagators, 581, 586
protective clothing:
  drilling tiles, 250
  painting ceilings, 207
  sanding floors, 273
  stripping woodwork, 254
  using a disk cutter, 280
  using a paint sprayer, 208
  using a steam stripper, 224
  using wood finishes, 258

pruning, 540–543
  climbers, 466, 542
  container-grown shrubs, 462
  container plants, 509
  cutting angle, 541
  fan-trained trees, 466
  hedges, 542
  patio plants, 460
  roses, 489, 541, 561
  shrubs, 543
  stem care, 520
  timing, 543
  tools, 478
  transplanting, 498
  trees, 458
punch, 421, 431
  serving, 425, 433
purée:
  piping, 434
  setting, 484
  using as sauce, 399
puréeing:
  eggplant, 381
  fruits, 330, 385
  squash, 365
  vegetables, 381, 398
putty repairs, 143

Q

quack grass, 535
quarry tiles:
  care, 59, 60
  laying, 280
  making a pan rest, 285

R

rabbits, controlling, 554
radiators:
  cleaning, 65
  hanging shelf over, 15
  painting, 257
  painting around, 207
  papering around, 232
  reducing visual impact of, 195
  reflecting heat, 141
radios, cleaning, 128
rag rolling, 210, 213
ragging, 210, 213
  tiles, 248
railings:
  attaching windowboxes, 514
  patios, 473
raised beds, 461

raspberries, 436, 446
receipts, filing, 169
recesses, storing in, 22, 23
recipes:
  making book holders for, 17
  putting inside cabinet doors, 17
  typing, 42
records, keeping, 168–169
recovery position, 174
recycling:
  containers, 518–519, 585
  fabric items, 110
  jars, 335
  paper, 160
  plastic pots and bags, 74, 156
  water, 531
redcurrants, 367
reference numbers,
  using on documents, 167
refrigerating:
  cooked beans, 341
  dried herbs, 344
  egg yolks, 372
  fish, 358
  fruits, 352
  meat and poultry, 357
  nuts, 340
  perishable foods, 348
  shrimp, 359
  vegetables, 351
refrigerators, 321–323, 349, 361
  cleaning, 71, 102, 323
  defrosting, 323
  painting, 311
relaxing, 35
  eyes, at work, 162
relief tiles, using, 239
removal firms,
  using, 146–148
renovation of gardens,
  450–451, 539
renting equipment, 224, 240, 268
repairing:
  cars, 50
  clothes, 30, 110
  house, 142–143
  household items, 114–131
  plumbing, 133–136
repetitive strain injury (RSI),
  avoiding, 162
repointing brickwork, 605

reptiles, keeping, 53
rescue breathing, 175
résumé, setting out
  information, 167
resuscitation, 174
retaining walls, 457, 461
rhizomes, dividing, 595
rhubarb, 385
rice:
  bulking out with beans, 447
  cooling, 400
  methods of cooking, 400
  molding, 382
  rinsing, 400
  standby dishes, 446
  storing, 339
ring marks,
  removing, 110
rings:
  cleaning and care, 130
  stuck, 131
roasting:
  fish, 395
  meat, 393
  potatoes, 379
  poultry, 392
roasting bags, 392
roasting times, 626
roasts:
  basting, 330
  increasing servings of, 447
rocking chairs, 60
rodents, caring for, 52
  moving with, 154
roller blinds, 292
  cleaning, 203
  fitting, 293
rollers, 208
  applying glazes, 212
  dampening, 206
  extending, 207, 282
  painting floors, 282
  painting stripes, 314
  painting walls, 206
  removing excess paint, 206
  removing trails, 218
  rollers, improvising, 123
rolling pins:
  cleaning, 73
rolls, baking, 411
Roman blinds, 292
roof gardens, 511
roof racks, loading, 151

roofs:
  greenhouse, 612, 613
  insulating, 15
  shed, repairs, 600
room layouts, planning, 14
  for bathrooms, 18
  for home offices, 158,
    159
  for kitchens, 16
  for living areas, 15
roommates, finding, 157
rooms:
  adapting, 42
  assessing, 155
  clearing, 152
  dividing, 24
  functions of, 192, 195,
    270
  increasing space, 194,
    305
  planning, 15–21
root crops, 482
root cuttings, 594
root rot, 546, 582
roots, 520
  alpines, 512
  choosing shrubs, 488
  clubroot fungus, 560
  congested, 487, 489
  in mesh, 490
  moving plants, 456, 498
  stored plants, 486
  trees, 454, 474
  weeds, 538, 539
rosemary:
  dried, 344
  preparing, 371
  scenting sugar with, 342
  tisane, 421
roses:
  climbers, 457
  companion plants, 493,
    552
  cuttings, 594
  deadheading, 540
  diseases, 541, 561
  frost protection, 522
  pests, 493
  planting, 489, 493
  pruning, 541, 561
  rambler, 475
  scented, 470
routines, setting up:
  for babies, 37
  for childcare, 40
RSI, see repetitive strain injury

rubber flooring, laying, 278
rubber gloves, 55, 76
rugs:
  cleaning, 61
  choosing, 277
  covering wooden floors,
    273
  faux, painting, 282
  floor cushions, making, 307
  hanging, 234
  packing, 151
  padding, 284
  protecting carpet, 284
  securing, 42, 171
  using as a throw, 307
  using at a window, 290
rush flooring, 277
rust:
  metal furniture, 66
  preventing, 219, 611, 612
  removing marks, 68, 98, 257
  treating, 601, 609
rust disease, 541, 545

S

safes, 161, 169
  making mini, 28
safety, 171, 203, 221
  avoiding pipes and wires,
    298, 302
  barbecuing, 390, 442
  choosing appliances, 318,
  choosing kitchen units, 316
  cleaning appliances, 332
  cleaning materials, 55
  concrete repairs, 606
  cooking beans, 401
  disposing of oily rags, 258
  electrical equipment, 128,
    572, 586
  electric cords, 574, 611
  electricity, 64, 137, 232,
    298
  fertilizers, 524
  fire-retardant materials, 298,
    306
  for children, 38–39
  frying, 391
  garden power tools, 563
  harmful substances, 298
  in the home, 38, 170–173
  irons, 108
  lighting, 138
  microwaving, 320
  pesticides, 556, 557
  ponds, 573

positioning kitchen units,
    316
  safety gates, using, 38
  stopping choking, 439
  using a disk cutter, 280
  using a spray gun, 208
  using a steam stripper, 224
  using knives, 328
  using ladders, 203, 270, 231
  weedkillers, 534, 569
  when driving, 50
safety deposit boxes,
  using, 169
saffron, 401
sage, 370, 388
salad bowls, cleaning, 117
salads, 382–383
  adding fruits, 362
  adding texture, 383
  arranging, 433
  calculating quantities of,
    432
  draining, 382
  enhancing, 383
  increasing fiber in, 628
  layering, 383
  preparing in advance,
    347
  preparing leaves, 364,
    382
  transporting, 445
  using herbs in, 383
  vegetables, 350, 380
  warm, 382, 383
salmon, 376, 416
salt:
  adjusting saltiness, 381,
    389
  baking fish in, 395
  for pickling, 416
  removing, 417
  seasoning meat with, 388
salt shakers, silver, 119
sand, 478, 580
sanding:
  distressing, 264
  floors, 273
  furniture, 254
  moldings, 254
  walls, 205, 206, 225
  woodwork, 254
sandpaper, 114, 253, 254
sandwiches, 433, 444
sandy soil, 478, 480, 481
sash windows, 286
saucepans, stacking, 16

sauces:
  adding egg yolk to, 372
  egg-based, 399
  freezing, 419
  serving, 434
  using shells for, 377
sausages, 390, 443
sautéeing meat, 391
savings, organizing, 169
scab, 546, 549
scalds, treating, 177
scale, removing:
  from faucets, 69
  from irons, 108
  from showers, 68, 69
  from sinks, 70
  from toilets, 69
scales, 330
scaling down/up, 36
scallions:
  as substitutes for chives, 370
  swizzle sticks, 420, 436
scallops:
  buying, 359
  grilling, 395
  serving in shells, 377
scarves, storing, 111
scrapes, 176
scented plants:
  annuals, 494
  for arbors, 468
  for balconies, 511
  for path edges, 464
  for patios, 460
  for screens, 469, 470
scheduling, 163, 146
scorch marks:
  on fabric and carpet, 97
  on wood, 116
scouring pads, using, 70
scrapes, 176
scratches:
  on baths, 68
  on watch glass, 123
  on wood, 60, 116
screens, 451, 469–473
  concealing garbage cans, 470
  concealing service area, 470
  concealing shed, 472
  constructing, 469
  dividing lawn, 453
  hedge, 471
  obscuring view, 473
  planting, 469
  suitable plants, 469
  transplanting shrubs, 499

seagrass flooring, 269
  covering stairs, 97
sealing:
  bath edges, 243
  concrete subfloors, 272
  découpage, 265
  dusty walls, 205, 225, 241
  grout, 250
  lining-paper edges, 226
  new plaster, 205
  subfloors, 275, 283
  waterproofing tiles, 247,
    249
seam roller, 229
seams:
  fabric, ironing, 108
seasonal foods, 348, 350
seasonal plants:
  arbors, 468
  borders, 457
  containers, 505
  patios, 460
seasonings, 346
seat covers, upholstery, 126
seating:
  providing in bathrooms, 18
  using in showers, 42
security, 132, 144–145
  ensuring personal, 46
  marking property, 51
  protecting data, 169
  protecting office items, 161
  sheds, 601
seedlings:
  feeding, 527
  looking after, 585, 589
  plugs, 494
  thinning, 588
  transplanting, 581, 583
seed pods, drying, 587
seeds, 381, 411
  buying, 494
  collecting, 587
  drying, 587
  germination, 583, 586
  hygiene, 548
  plant list, 583
  storing, 581, 587
seed trays, 581, 584
self-raising flour, 340
self-seeding plants, 583
self-watering planters, 530
sesame oil:
  frying fish in, 396
  in fish coatings, 394
  in salad dressing, 382

shading:
  containers, 530
  plants, 501
shallots, 382
shared home,
  organizing a, 157
sharpening blades, 611
sharp objects, storing, 25
sheds:
  enhancing, 472
  repairing, 451, 600–601
  reroofing, 472
  screening, 451, 472
  storing plants in, 486
sheet flooring, laying, 278
sheet music, keeping, 29
sheets:
  ironing, 109
  laundering, 105
  quick-drying, 106
  using as curtains, 290
  using as dropcloths, 204
  using as throws, 307
shellfish:
  buying and storing, 359
  methods of cooking,
    394–397
  preparing, 377
shells, 377
shelves, 24, 26, 302–303,
  316–317, 334–335
  above radiators, 65, 141
  adapting, 17
  building, 24
  decorating, 303
  equipment, 302
  faux, painting, 217
  installing above doors, 226
  installing above radiator,
    15
  installing above sink, 17
  installing in cabinets, 17
  installing in hallway, 21
  installing in home offices,
    159
  fixing, 302
  improvising, 303
  labeling, 24, 168
  marking the position of,
    230
  sharing, 157
  under-shelf storage, 310
  using cornices as, 294
  using glass, 26
  using space under, 159
  using to divide rooms, 24

shock:
   coping with, 47
   treating, 176
      anaphylactic shock, 180
shoe containers, 111
shoe polish, 113
shoes:
   cleaning and care, 113
   grass stains, 88
   grease stains, 80
   storing, 23
   tar stains, 95
   urine stains, 87
shopping:
   buying clothes, 33
   buying fruits, 352
   buying vegetables, 350
   packing, 349
   using lists, 348
shortcrust pastry, 373, 412
shoulder, dislocated, 181
shower curtains, 68, 96
shower heads, cleaning, 69
showers:
   cleaning, 68
   providing seating in, 42
   tiling, 245
shrimp:
   frying, 396
   preparing, 377
   refrigerating, 359
shrubs:
   choosing, 488
   cuttings, 594
   feeding, 527
   growing climbers on, 456
   in borders, 456
   in containers, 462
   layering, 590, 591
   moving, 456
   planting, 489
   pruning, 456, 543
   securing, 499
   transplanting, 499
   undercutting, 499
   underplanting, 499
   with hedge, 471
shutter blinds,
   improvising, 293
siding, repairs, 600
silicone, applying, 247, 249
silk, care, 101
   drying, 109
   hand washing, 104
silver, cleaning, 118–119
silverplate, cleaning, 119

sinks:
   blocked drain, 135
   cleaning, 68, 70
   outlets, 74
   storing under, 18
   using steps for children, 38
skin:
   care, 55
   foreign bodies in, 183
   paint removal, 99
   stains, 91
slate, cleaning, 75
slate floors, laying, 281
sleep, ensuring for baby, 37
sleeping bags, 27
   packing for moving, 150
slicing:
   cake for freezing, 361
   meat, 374
   vegetables, 362
slipcovers:
   cleaning, 67
   using, 126
slopes, 17, 44, 127
slugs, 544, 582
   biological controls, 555
   traps and barriers, 558
smells, see odors
smoke alarms, 171
smoking, 417
snacks, 446
snails, 544, 582
   traps and barriers, 558
snake bites, treating, 179
snow peas, 380
soaking clothes, 102
soap:
   attaching dishes, 67
   in face cloths, 105
   storing, 80, 112
   using leftover pieces, 69
soapflakes:
   laundering, 100
   ink stains, 79
socks:
   keeping in pairs, 103
   line drying, 106
   storing, 111
   using as dusters, 42
   white cotton, 102
sod:
   cutting, 565, 570
   laying, 565
   repairs, 570
sofa-beds, using, 19
soft drinks, 431, 436

soft fruits:
   freezing, 347
   grilling, 403
   hulling, 367
   mashing overripe fruits, 367
   preparing, 367
   storing, 352
soft furnishings, 67, 126–127,
   306–308
   choosing fabrics, 192, 197
   equipment, 306
   see also window treatments
soft toys, organizing, 19
softwood, 253, 598, 609
softwood cuttings, 592, 593
soil:
   aquatic, 576
   compaction, 480, 582
   conditioners, 478
   nutrient requirements,
      525
   patio plantings, 460
   pH, 478, 480
   preparation for layering,
      591
   preparation for planting,
      482
   preparation for sowing,
      580
   restoring borders, 456
   stabilizing, 457, 484
   texture, 480
   warming, 580, 582
   water retention, 530
soil mix:
   for containers, 503, 504
   for cuttings, 590, 592
   seed-potting mixes, 581
solvents, 114
soot marks, 65, 98
sore throats, soothing, 185
sorting washing, 103
soufflés, 387
   caramelizing sweet soufflé,
      403
   easy, 347
   freezing cold soufflé, 404
   vegetable, 381
soup, 398
   canned, 347
   increasing servings of, 447
   serving, 447
   storing condensed soup,
      347
   thickening, 398
   vegetable, 380, 398

sowing:
  annuals, 457
  equipment, 580–581
  indoors, 581, 584–585
  outdoors, 580, 582–583
  small seeds, 584
  suitable plants, 583
spaghetti, 401
spaghetti jars, 338
spare rooms, storing in, 23
speakers,
  making stands for, 20
special events,
  planning, 48–49
special needs,
  catering for, 41–42
spices, 345
  adding to drinks, 421
  on baked fruits, 384
  bruising, 416
  coating meat and poultry
    with, 388
  flavoring with, 380, 398
  grinding 333, 345
  preparing, 247
  toasting, 221
  whole, 221
spider mites, 523, 545, 555
spiders, 550
spin drying, 107
spinach:
  coloring pasta with, 401
  correcting mistakes, 407
  draining, 379
  trimming, 363
splinters, removing, 183
splitting poultry, 375
sponge cakes:
  crunchy topping for, 409
  fillings and flavorings for,
    407
  icing, 408
  testing for doneness, 406
  turning out, 406
sponge mop, storing, 56
sponges, 76
  slimy, 68
sponging:
  creating a verdigris effect,
    261
  dyeing wood, 258
  painting floors, 283
  painting tableware, 310
  painting tiles, 248
  painting walls, 210, 212
  stenciling, 215

sports equipment,
  storing, 212, 27, 30
spotlights, using, 300, 305
sprains, treating, 181
spring tasks, 614–615
squash, 365
squid, 359, 396
stacking pots, 71
stained glass,
  reproducing, 297
stainless steel:
  cleaning, 75, 120
  shining, 70, 120
stain removal, 76–99
  bathtubs and sinks, 68
  china, 72
  furnishings, 66
  laundry, 105
  marble, 125
  skin, 91
stain removers, 55, 77
stains:
  masking, 218, 225
  patio slabs, 459
  removing from carpet, 284
  removing from wallpaper,
    236
  walls, 466
stair rods, placing, 277
stairs:
  carrying children on, 38
  creaking, 143
  fitting extra banisters by, 42
  laying flooring, 277
  moving furniture up, 156
  painting, 257
  reversing worn carpet,
    277
stairwells, papering, 231
staking plants, 501
stamping:
  making stamps, 285
  stamping floors, 285
  stamping walls, 216
standby foods, 419, 446
staple foods, 337–341
starch, 100
  using, 107
star fruit, 368
stationery:
  buying for offices, 159,
    160
  organizing for weddings,
    49
steaks, 374, 388
steamers, 397

steaming, 374
  cabbage, 379
  couscous, 400
  fish, 397
  vegetables, 324
steam irons, cleaning, 108
steam stripper,
  using safely, 224
steel, 598, 613
steel wool, 114
  pads, 56, 70
stems, 520
  layering, 591
stenciling, 198
  blinds, 293
  cakes, 408
  cushions, 308
  hand-painting over,
    265
  lampshades, 301
  menu cards, 428
  tablecloths, 424
  tiles, 248
  walls, 215
  underplates, 427
stencils:
  storing, 219
  tracing and cutting, 215
stepladders, 203, 208
stepping stones,
  laying, 453
steps, 464–465
  brightening, 465
  concrete, repairs, 608
  formal look, 465
  marking edges, 42
  renovation, 450
sterilizing:
  baby bottles, 37
  jars and lids, 414
stews, 389
stippling:
  decorating walls, 210,
    212
  rag rolling over, 213
stir-frying:
  Chinese cabbage, 379
  fish, 396
  meat strips, 374
  vegetables, 347, 378
stock, 377, 398, 400
stomachache, treating, 186
stone surfaces:
  cleaning, 125
  removing soot marks, 98
  stone floors, 58

stone:
  containers, 502, 506
  faux, painting, 217
  moving slabs, 281
  repairs, 604–607
  sealing, 209
  stone-effect wall covering,
    234
stones, path edging, 264
stony soil, 482
storage:
  containers, decorating, 310
    see also containers
      (household)
  of equipment, 219, 237
storage spaces, cleaning, 156
storing, 22–31
  baked foods, 360–361
  books and papers, 29
  bulky items, 27
  chocolate, 343
  dairy foods, 354–355
  data, 169
  dried fruits and nuts, 340
  dry ingredients, 335
  fish and shellfish, 358–359
  flour, 340
  freezer basics, 115
  frequently used items, 31
  fresh foods, 349
  fruits, 352
  grains, 339
  herbs and spices, 344–345,
    353
  in bathrooms, 18
  in bedrooms, 19, 26
  in cupboards, 22
  in drawers, 25
  in garages and sheds, 26
  in hobby rooms, 21
  in home offices, 158
  in kitchens, 16–17
  in living rooms, 20
  in wardrobes, 23
  jewelry, 28
  legumes, 341
  long-term, 30
  meat and poultry, 357
  oils, 346
  on shelves, 24
  pasta, 338
  photographs and films, 28
  plants, 486
  rarely used objects, 30
  sugars, 342
  tools, 29, 31

vegetables, 351
video tapes and music, 27
  while moving, 146
stoves:
  choosing, 318
  cleaning, 71, 319
  economy, 139
  safety, 38, 171
  testing, 155
  using, 319
straightening up, 20
  in a shared home, 157
strangers:
  dealing with, 161, 166
  protecting children from,
    39
strawberries:
  garnishing with, 345
  hulling, 367
  thawing, 367
  threading on skewers,
    385, 427
strawberry jars, 510
  watering, 508
stress, relieving, 162
stretching shoes, 113
stringing onions and garlic,
  351
stripes:
  creating an impression
    of height, 222
  painting, 214
stripping:
  furniture, 263
  wallpaper, 224, 241
  wooden floors, 273
  woodwork, 254
strollers, choosing, 39
stuffing, 388
  coating chicken with, 375
  flavoring packaged stuffing,
    388
  freezing, 446
  making balls, 393
style, 198–201
  dressing windows, 287
subfloors:
  allowing to dry, 274, 283
  choosing, for woodblock
    floors, 275
  preparing, 272, 278
suckers, trees, 474
suede:
  erasing marks, 113
  grease marks, 80
  ink marks, 91

removing fluff, 111
stain removal, 87, 99
water marks, 97
sugar, 342
  caramelizing, 404
  in crunchy sponge
    topping, 409
  flavoring, 342, 345
  flavoring tomatoes with, 380
  reducing intake of, 146
  softening, 342
  storing, 342
  using in jam making, 415
suitcases:
  removing mildew, 96
  storing, 112
  storing in, 30
sulfur, 556
summer tasks, 616–617
sunflower screens, 451, 469
supports:
  climbers, 476, 542
  for height, 476
  roses, 493
  staking, 501
  tying in, 501
  windowboxes, 512
surfacing:
  bathroom, 18
  play area, 39
sweaters:
  drying, 106, 107
  storing, 112
  washing, 104
sweeping floors, 58, 59
  damping down dust, 60
sweetbreads, 374
swelling, treating, 181
switches, *see* electrical fittings
swizzle sticks, 420, 436
synthetic fabrics:
  stains, 79
  tumble drying, 109
syrup, 343

T

tablecloths, ironing, 109
table decorating, 424, 426, 436
tables:
  covering corners, 38
  dining, improvising, 20
  kitchen, 71
  laying in advance, 31
  packing, 150
  repairing wobbly tables, 117
  using in bedroom, 19

tableware, 310, 426
  silver, 119
  wood, 117
talcum powder:
  on stains, 80, 83
  squeaky floors, 142
tantrums,
  coping with, 37
tape recorder, using, 148
tapestry furniture,
  cleaning, 126
tarragon, 370
tarts:
  baking, 402
  toppings for, 402
tasks:
  organizing in a shared
    home, 157
  prioritizing, 165
  scheduling, 31, 163, 48
tea, 421
  marbling eggs in, 387
  soaking dried fruits in, 369,
    385
tea infuser, 371
teak, caring for, 66, 115
teakettles:
  choosing, 41, 332
  descaling, 333
  saving energy, 139
teapots, 331
  cleaning, 119, 124
teenagers,
  ensuring outdoor safety, 39
teeth:
  knocked out, 184
  temporary fillings, 187
  toothache, 187
telephones:
  cleaning, 128, 160
  emergency calls, 171
  keeping log, 157
  planning calls, 166
  positioning, 158
  protecting, 161
  staying on hold, 166
  using in emergencies,
    39
televisions:
  cleaning, 128
  saving energy, 139
temperatures:
  of air, 41, 162
  of baby, monitoring, 37
  oven, 627
  refrigerator/freezer, 322

templates:
  cutting curves, 244
  cutting sheet flooring,
    278
  laying floor tiles, 279,
    280
tenants, finding, 157
tension, relieving, 35
terraces, building, 457
terracotta pots, 502, 510
  on steps, 465
  painting, 519
  soaking, 506
terrarium, keeping, 53
tetanus, preventing, 179
texture, 195
  selecting fabrics, 234,
    237
textured paints, 202
  applying, 209
  plastering over, 225
thawing:
  bread, 360
  fruits, 367
  meat and poultry, 357
  pastry, 412
  using thawed foods, 357
theft, preventing, 46
themed parties:
  color themes, 437
  decorating tablemats
    for, 427
  for teenagers, 440
thermometers:
  microwave, 320
  oven, 319, 393
  preserving, 414
thermos flasks, 342, 445
thermostats, 140
throws, 307
ticks, 180
tiebacks, 287, 290, 295
ties:
  fabric-protector, 80
  ironing, 109
tights and panty hose:
  line drying, 106
  prolonging life of, 110
tile cutters, 240
  mounting, 243
tile gauge:
  making, 241
  using, 242, 280
tiles see ceramic tiles;
  floor tiles; quarry tiles;
    wall tiles

tiling:
  awkward areas, 244
  calculating quantities, 241
  designing layouts, 238–239,
    245
  equipment, 240
  inserting tiles and borders,
    246
  planning, 242
  preparing walls, 240–241
  tiling up to wallpaper, 236,
    246
  tiling walls, 238–246
  tiling work surfaces, 247
  waterproofing tiles, 247,
    249, 250
time, managing, 163–165
timer switches, 46, 145
toadstools, 545, 561
toddlers, caring for, 37
tofu, 443
toilet brush, 68
toilet cleaner, 68
toiletries:
  choosing essentials, 34
  renewing, 31
  storing, 18
toilets:
  cleaning, 69
  installing handles by, 42
  plumbing repairs, 136
  providing child steps, 38
  storing behind, 18
tomatoes:
  buying, 350
  canned, 329, 347
  coloring pasta with, 401
  flavoring with sugar, 380
  freezing, 419
  mixed tomato salad, 382
  ripening, 350
  skinning, 365
  soufflé, 387
  storing, 351
  sun-dried, 347
tongue-and-groove:
  laying floors, 274
  patching, 271
tool rack, 611
tools and equipment:
  adapting, 42
  container gardening, 503
  dividing plants, 595
  general maintenance, 599
  handles, covering, 610
  hanging, 26, 31

hanging baskets, 515
keeping for bicycles, 51
keeping for cars, 50
lawns, 563, 568
maintaining, 610–611
packing, 151
plant care, 521
planting, 479
propagating, 590, 592
pruning, 540
sowing seeds, 580–581
storing, 29, 611
water features, 572
weeding, 534
see also equipment
toothbrushes, 12, 70
top-dressing:
    containers, 509
    lawns, 454, 571
topiary, 476
towel racks, 17
    fixing inside closets, 23
towels, laundering, 105
toys:
    choosing for pets, 52
    keeping in bathrooms, 18
    keeping in living rooms, 20
    soft, storing, 19
trailing plants, 462, 515
train sets, covering, 21
transfers, decorating tiles, 248
transplanting, 498, 501
    perennials, 500
    seedlings, 581, 583
    shrubs, 499
transportation:
    arranging for weddings, 49
    ensuring safety, 39
    maintaining, 50–51
    see also vehicles
travel sickness, relieving:
    in car, 50
tree guards, 554
trees:
    and barbecues, 463
    feeding, 455
    in lawns, 452, 455
    obscuring unsightly views,
        473
    planting, 474, 567
    privacy, 474
    pruning, 451, 458
    renovating, 450, 451
    roots, 454, 474
    seating around, 455
    snow protection, 522

thinning, 458
transplanting, 499
underplanting, 451, 455
windbreaks, 530
trellises, 451, 467
    attaching, 467
    designing with, 467
    false perspective, 468
    fence extensions, 473
    in containers, 467
    on walls, 467, 492
    painting, 467
    planting up, 467
    screens, 469–470, 472
    strengthening, 470
trompe l'oeil, 217
    cords, 217, 304
    painting floors, 282–283
    stonework, 217
    tablecloth, 265
troughs, 512
trout, 376
trussing, 375
tumble drying, 107, 109
tumblers, unsticking, 122
turkey, 392
turmeric, 400
turpentine, 55, 77
    reusing, 266
typewriters, cleaning, 112

U

U-bends, unblocking, 135
umbrella holders,
    making, 21
undercutting, 499
underplanting,
    hedges, 471
    new shrubs, 489
    suitable plants, 455
    wildflower area, 451, 455
unpacking, 156
upholstery:
    cleaning, 67
    renovations, 126
    stain removal, 77–98
upholstery snaps:
    decorating boxes, 310
    painting, 307
uplighters, 300
urine, animal, 561
urns, 502, 510
use-by dates, 348, 349
utensils, 327–331
utility flooring, 269
    laying, 278

V

vacations:
    packing for, 112
    security, 145
vacuum cleaners, using, 16
vacuum cleaning, 54
    behind radiators, 65
    carpets, 61
    lampshades, 127
valances, 287, 294
valuables:
    hiding under clothes, 46
    packing, 149
    protecting, 28
    see also jewelry
vanilla pods:
    buying, 345
    extracting seeds from, 371
    flavoring with, 342, 421
    in vegetable juice, 420
varnish:
    crackle varnish, drying, 264
    enhancing wood, 252, 258
    frosting varnish,
        applying, 296
    maintaining wood, 267
    protecting painted tiles, 248
    protecting wallpaper, 237
    smoothing, 258
    wooden floors, 275, 284
vases:
    cleaning, 123, 124
    deep, 124
vegetable peelers, 329
vegetable racks:
    using as filing trays, 159
    using to store items in
        hobby rooms, 21
    using to store toys in
        bathrooms, 18
vegetables, 451
    blanching, 414
    boiling, 378
    braising with meat, 389
    bundles, 434
    char-grilling, 443
    choosing, 350
    collecting seeds, 587
    crop rotation, 549, 582
    feeding, 527
    for salads, 350
    freezing, 418
    gardener's diary, 614–621
    in containers, 508
    increasing servings of, 447

in island beds, 452
in julienne strips, 362
in soufflés, 381
making baby food with, 37
methods of cooking,
  379–381
molding, 434
preparing, 362–365
puréeing, 381, 398
slicing, 362, 381
soup, 380, 398
steaming, 324
stir-frying, 378, 381
storing, 351
sowing, 582
using leftovers, 380
using overcooked
  vegetables, 381
watering, 532
vehicles:
  loading, 153
  unloading, 156
  see also cars, motorcycles
Venetian blinds, 292
  cleaning, 67
  painting, 293
venison, 388
ventilation:
  rooms, 15, 21, 160
  greenhouses, 523,
    548, 555
verdigris effect:
  creating, 261
  removing, 121
video players and tapes, 128
  storing tapes, 27
vinegar, 55, 77
  air freshener, 61
  as salad dressing, 382
  cleaning pans, 325
  cleaning windows, 64
  cutting grease, 72
  flavoring, 346
  using for pickling, 416
vine weevils, 544
  biological controls, 555
  protecting containers,
    556
vinyl flooring, 269
  cleaning, 59, 284
  laying, 278
  removing, 272
  removing marks, 59, 60
  using leftovers, 285
vinyl surfaces, cleaning, 67
vinyl tiles, 269

vinyl wall coverings, 220
  cleaning, 62
  hanging, 228
viruses in plants, 546
visualization, practicing, 35
vitamins, 147
vomiting, 186

W

wall anchors, inserting, 302
wall coverings:
  cleaning, 62
  decorative moldings, 235
  wallhangings, 234
  wallpaper, 220–233
  wood paneling, 235
wall decorations, 298
  hanging, 304–305
wallhangings, attaching, 234
wall lights:
  papering around, 232
  protecting, 204
wall-mounting:
  microwaves, 17
  office equipment, 159
wallpaper, 220
  checking batch numbers,
    226
  choosing, 222
  cleaning, 62
  covering curtain poles,
    291
  maintaining, 237
  patching, 62
  prepasted, 227
  protecting, 237
  removing stains, 236
  stripping, 224
  using leftovers, 237
  see also wallpapering
wallpaper borders:
  attaching, 233
  decorating lampshades,
    301
wallpapering, 220–233
  anchoring edges, 227,
    229, 236
  centralizing patterns, 223,
    229
  cornices, 294
  correcting mistakes, 228,
    236
  equipment, 221, 237
  finishing, 236–237
  hanging, 228–232
  lining walls, 226

measuring and cutting, 226,
  231
pasting up, 227
planning, 223
preparing walls, 224–225
shelves, 303
wallpaper paste:
  hanging posters, 305
  keeping, 237
  mixing, 227
  removing excess, 229
walls, 466, 468
  avoiding pipes and wires,
    298, 302
  building, 466
  cleaning, 62–65, 466
  climbers, 466, 493
  covering, 451, 466
  fan-trained fruit trees, 466
  filling, 204, 225, 241
  hanging baskets, 516
  maintaining, 604
  mildew, 96
  painting, 202–219
  preparing, 204–205, 225
  rainshadow, 493
  renovating, 450, 451
  retaining, 457, 461
  sanding, 204, 225
  screening, 466
  special effects, 468
  sunny, 484
  sealing, 205, 225, 241
  tiling, 238–251
  trellis panels, 467, 492
  wall shrubs, 459
  windowboxes, 514
wall tiles, 239
  attaching fixtures to, 250
  choosing, 239, 245
  cutting, 243, 244, 245
  decorating, 248
  drilling, 250
  leftovers, using, 251
  maintaining, 251
  polishing, 249, 250
  replacing, 246, 251
  sprucing up, 246, 248
  tiling over, 241
  see also tiling
walnuts, 436
wardrobes and closets, 23
  arranging, 33
  moving, 150
  putting drawers in, 19
  storage, 111

washcloths, laundering, 34
washers, replacing, 133
washing clothes, 101–104
washing lines, 106
washing machines, 103
  overflowing, 136
  water-economy, 136
washing powder,
  see detergent
washing up, 72
  in shared home, 157
  silver cutlery, 119
  water-economy, 136
wastebaskets:
  installing in cabinet, 17
  siting, 316
waste-disposal units, 74
watches, caring for, 123
water:
  collecting and recycling,
    531
  conserving, 530
  for birds, 550
  tap water, 548
water barrels, 531, 548
water economy, 136
water features, 572–579
  on patios, 459, 462
watering, 529–533
  beds and borders, 532
  bulbs, 497
  direct, 487
  hanging baskets, 509, 517
  lawns, 563, 565
  new plantings, 501
  patio plantings, 460
  plant requirements, 529
  pot watering, 506, 529
  seedlings, 588, 589
  seeds, 580, 584
  strawberry jars, 508
  techniques, 529
  transplanting, 498
  underplantings, 455
  when feeding, 524, 526
water marks, removing:
  on hides and clothes, 97
  on wood, 116
water plants, 574
  oxygenating, 575
  planting, 575–576
waterproofing:
  tiles, 245, 249, 250
  utility flooring, 278
water system, checking, in
  a new home, 155

water tanks, 146
  insulating, 15
wax floor polish, 58, 59
weather conditions:
  mowing, 568
  planting, 487, 497
  protecting plants, 522–523
  sowing, 582
  using weedkillers, 537
  working soil, 482
weathering effects:
  containers, 519
  patios, 462
weatherproofing:
  brickwork, 605
  furniture, 609
weather stripping, 140
wedding anniversaries:
  choosing decorations
    for, 49
wedding decorations, 427
weddings, planning, 48–49
  countdown, 49
weed barriers, 536
weeding, 534–539
  hand-weeding, 538, 569
  lawns, 538, 569
  neglected sites, 539
  patios, 459
  sowing lawns, 562, 564
  vegetable plots, 560
  water features, 577
weedkillers:
  applying, 534, 537
  chemicals, 537
  contact, 539
  lawns, 569
  staining slabs, 459
  systemic, 539
weeds, 535
  persistent, 539
  preventing, 536, 577
wet rot, 602
wheelbarrows, 465
whisks, 329
whitefly, 544, 555
whitewashing walls, 468
wholegrain foods:
  bread, 146
  pasta, 338
  storing grains 339
wicker furniture, cleaning, 66
wicker, painting, 263
wildflower areas:
  meadows, 567
  underplantings, 451, 455

wildlife:
  beneficial, 550
  controlling, 553–554
  water features, 551, 573
wills, locating, 77
wilting, preventing, 523
windmills, 553
wind protection, 523
  windbreaks, 511, 523
wind tunnels, 523
windowboxes, 502, 513–514
  improvised, 519
  maintaining, 514
  planning, 513
  sites, 472, 514
  types, 513
  using, 514
window frames:
  painting, 253, 257
  rails, 267
  repainting, 267
window recesses:
  measuring for blinds, 292
  papering, 230
  tiling, 244
windows:
  altering apparent shape,
    287, 294
  cleaning, 64, 156
  installing glass shelves, 26
  papering around, 230
  repairs, 143
  security, 144, 145
  types, 286
  windowsills, tiling, 245, 251
window treatments, 286–295
  blinds, 292–293
  choosing fabrics, 288
  choosing hanging systems,
    287, 288
  cornices, 294
  curtains, 289–291
  equipment, 288
  swags and tails, 295
  tiebacks, 295
wine, 432
  chilling, 436
  dealing with spills, 436
  decanting, 436
  mulling, 421, 433
  roasting chicken in, 392
  serving, 436
wine glasses, 425
wine racks, improvising, 26
wine stains, 83
wine store, 316

winter tasks, 620–621
wires:
  hidden, avoiding, 298, 302
  picture-hanging, 304
wireworms, 547, 560
wiring, and safety, 137
woks, 267
wood:
  burn marks, 97
  caring for, 115–117
  cleaning, 75
  conditioning, 115
  hard and soft, 598
  preserving, 476, 514
  raised beds, 461
  removing marks, 116
  repairs, 600–603
  retaining walls, 457
  types of, 253
  untreated, 86, 99
  using, 600
wood ash, 524, 528
wood-block floors:
  laying, 275
wood dyes, 258
  antiquing wood, 264
wood effects:
  graining, 259
  painting floors, 282–283
wooden containers, 502, 510
wooden floors, 58–60
  calculating quantities, 269
  cleaning, 59
  designing a layout, 274
  laying, 274–275
  protecting, 284
  removing candle wax, 60
  removing ink stains, 60
  removing scratches, 60
  renovating, 273
  rising dampness, 60
  sanding, 273
  using prefinished flooring, 274
  varnishing, 275
  waxed, buffing, 275

wooden furniture, 602, 609
  care and repair, 115–117
  cleaning, 66
wooden objects,
  caring for, 117
wooden screens, 472
wooden structures, 600–603, 613
wooden tools, 610
wooden trellises, 267
wood finishes, 252
  enhancing woodwork, 258
  sealing floors, 275
wood paneling, 63
  covering walls, 235
wood preservative, 599, 602
  colored, 467, 472
  coloring, 609
  fences, 473, 603
  sheds, 472, 601
  windowboxes, 514
wood rot, preventing, 602
woodstains, 252, 258, 519, 609
woodwork:
  choosing colors, 192, 194
  cleaning, 267
  coloring, 260
  decorating, 252–267
  enhancing natural wood, 258
  filling, 255
  graining, 259, 265
  maintaining, 267
  masking, 207
  painting, 27, 379–381
  painting effects, 383–386
  preparing, 378–379
  priming, 379
  replacing, 204
  removing paint splashes, 38
  sanding, 254
  stripping, 254

wool:
  care, 101
  discolored, 102
  drying, 104
  ironing, 109
work:
  allocating time, 164
  communicating, 166–167
  keeping records, 168–169
  making pie charts, 164
  managing time, 163–165
  setting up a home office, 158–162
  structuring, 158–169
work log, 165
work surfaces:
  cleaning, 56, 70
  inserting a chopping board, 245
  organizing in home offices, 158, 159
  tiling, 245
  using in kitchens, 17
workshops:
  adding work surfaces, 26
  cleaning, 29
worktops, 314, 315
  creating, 315, 331

Y

yeast, 410
yoga, practicing, 35
yogurt, 373
  drinks, 436
  in low-fat dressing, 383
  marinade, 394
  stabilizing, 373

Z

zest, 366
  garnishing with, 435
  in bouquet garni, 370
  in tea, 421
zester, 329
zippers, common problems, 110
zucchini, 365, 381

ACKNOWLEDGMENTS

THE AUTHORS

Cassandra Kent is a writer and broadcaster. She worked for
many years for *Good Housekeeping* magazine and
has written more than 20 practical housekeeping books.

Julian Cassell and **Peter Parham** are professional decorators
with many years' experience running their own
successful decorating business. They have written
several books on home decorating.

Christine France was Deputy Cooking Editor at *Good
Housekeeping*, and later Cooking Editor at *Woman's Realm*,
before starting her own consulting firm in 1989.
She has written many books and is a regular
contributor to newspapers and magazines.

Pippa Greenwood is well known through her work on
television and radio and as a journalist. She is one of the hosts
of the BBC's *Gardeners' World* and is on the panel
of BBC Radio 4's *Gardeners' Question Time*. She contributes
regularly to newspapers and magazines.

PUBLISHER'S ACKNOWLEDGMENTS
Dorling Kindersley would like to thank the following:

EDITORIAL AND DESIGN
Austin Barlow, Helen Benfield, Chris Bernstein, Laaren Brown,
Lynne Brown, Josephine Bryan, Dr Sue Davidson,
Colette Connolly, Penelope Cream, Jackie Dollar,
Samantha Gray, Jill Hamilton, Adèle Hayward, Sasha Heseltine,
Darren Hill, Katie John, Jayne Jones, Will Lach, Emma Lawson,
Linda Martin, Krystyna Mayer, Lynn McGowan,
Chacasta Pritlove, Jo Richardson, Jan Richter,
Catherine Rubinstein, Debbie Scholes, Victoria Sorzano,
Mary Sutherland, Rachel Symons, and Ellen Woodward.

PRODUCTION AND DTP
Raúl López Cabello, Sarah Coltman, Silvia La Greca, and
Harvey De Roemar.

ILLUSTRATION
Kuo Kang Chen, Halli Marie Verrinder, John Woodcock.
Additional Illustration David Ashby, Karen Cochrane,
Geoff Denney, and Simone End.
Model Making Peter Griffiths.

PHOTOGRAPHY
Sarah Ashum, Andy Crawford, John Elliot, Steve Gorton,
Gary Ombler, and Steve Tanner.

Additional Photography Peter Anderson, Andreas Einsiedel, Glin Keates, Graham Kirk, Tim Ridley, Steve Shott, Jane Stockman, Harry Taylor, Matthew Ward, and Jerry Young. Photographic Assistance Mary Wadsworth and Lee Walsh. Hand Modeling Ade Bakare, Linda Birungy, Lisa Broomhead, Michelle Culham, Andy Faithful, Mun Fong, Carl Gough, Nicola Hampel, Toby Heran, Darren Hill, Duncan Horastead, Pepukai Makoni, Katie Martin, Charmen Menzies, Helen Oyo, Marlon Reddin, Victoria Sorzano, Nick Turpin, Mary Wadsworth, and Sara Watkins.

PICTURE CREDITS
Dorling Kindersley would like to thank the following for permission to reproduce their photographs:

Key: a above, b below, c center, f far, l left r right, t top.

Fired Earth: 239bc, 246c, 246cr, 277tr; Jake Fitzjohns: 194br; Chris Forsey: 197; Anna French Ltd.: 233cr; Robert Harding Syndication: Dominic Blackmore/Homes & Ideas © IPC Magazines: 199clb, 199br, Homes & Gardens © IPC Magazines: 222c; Homestyle and Fads (paint and wall coverings): 190bl, 190cla, 190cra, 192ca, 192cr, 195bl, 233c, 287tl, 287br, 287bl, 295bc, 303c; 303cla, 311br; Marks & Spencer: 292cfl; Gwenan Murphy: 195cr, 234bl; Colin Poole: 193bl, 298bc, 298br, /J. Brown 217bc, /M. Reeve 217br; Sanderson: 192bl, 193br; Sunway (Venetian blind collection): 292 cfr; Steve Tanner (for Perfect Home DMG Home Interest Magazines Ltd.): 192bc, Steve Tanner/Perfect Home DMG Home Interest Magazines Ltd: 287tl; Elizabeth Whiting & Associates: 200cl, 239br, 292cl, 292cr; Andreas von Einsiedel 222cr,/Eric Karson 194bl; Brian Harrison 200bl; Michael Dunn 200br, 201tr, 245br; Peter Wolosynski 201bl; Tom Leighton 201tl, 305br; Garden Picture Library: J. Baker 573c; A. Bedding 459bc; J. Bouchier 513tl; L. Burgess 511bl; T. Candler 511tc; B. Carter 453tr; J. Glover 457tc, 510bc; S. Harte 472br, 573cr; M. Howes 531bl; Lamontagne 510bl; J. Legate 556c; J. Miller 455tl; C. Perry 551bl; J. Wade 552br; S. Wooster 468cl; John Glover: 456bl, 477bc; Harpur Garden Library: 472bc, 474bl, 475bl, 477bl; design: Chris Grey-Wilson 464ca; design: Yong Man Kim 467br; design: Mrs. Wethered 468bl; design G. & F. Whiten 466bl; Holt Studios International Ltd.: N. Caitlin 544cla, 546clb, 547tl, 547cla, 547clb, 547cbl, 552c, 555c 555cr; Frank Lane Picture Agency: B. Borrell 545 br, 546cla; E. & A. Hosking 545clb; R. Wilmshurst 550br; Andrew Lawson Photography: 516 cb; Natural History Photographic Agency: S Dalton 550bc; Photos Horticultural: 544bcl, 545cl, 552cr, 556cl; Harry Smith Photographic Collection: 457tl, 457bl, 468tr, 476, 477bc, 511ltr, 514tc, 516bl, 544bl, 562c, 562cr.

Picture Research Mollie Gillard and Sarah Moule